Tariffs in the United States, 1828–1985

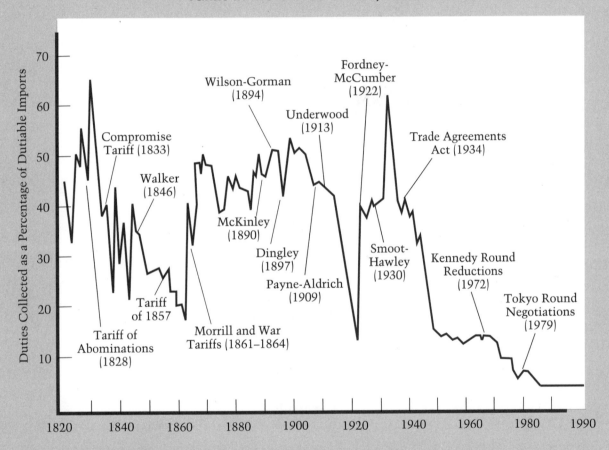

ECONOMICS

Ninth Edition

ECONOMICS

Richard G. Lipsey
Simon Fraser University

Peter O. Steiner
The University of Michigan

Douglas D. Purvis
Queen's University

Paul N. Courant
The University of Michigan

1817

HARPER & ROW, PUBLISHERS
New York, Grand Rapids, Philadelphia,
San Francisco, London, Singapore, Sydney,
Tokyo

Sponsoring Editor: John Greenman
Project Editor: Donna Conte
Art Direction: Kathie Vaccaro
Text Design: Graphics, Etcetera
Cover Coordinator: Mary Archondes
Production: Kewal K. Sharma

Economics, Ninth Edition

Library of Congress Cataloging-in-Publication Data

Lipsey, Richard G., 1928-
    Economics / Richard G. Lipsey, Peter O. Steiner, Douglas D.
Purvis. — 9th ed.
        p.   cm.
    ISBN 0-60-043908-4
    1. Economics.   I. Steiner, Peter Otto, 1922-   II. Purvis,
Douglas D. III. Title.
    HB171.5.L733   1990
    330—dc20   89-26783
                                                            CIP

90 91 92 93 9 8 7 6 5 4 3 2 1

Brief
CONTENTS

Detailed
CONTENTS

PREFACE

Economics is a living discipline. Through nine editions of *Economics,* our basic motivation has been to provide a text that reflects the tremendous changes in that discipline over the decades.

The first major theme of this book is to reflect the movement of economics toward becoming a science and exhibiting the key characteristic that marks any science: the systematic confrontation of theory with observation. Today most economists agree that their subject is more than a stage for parading pet theories and is not just a container for collecting masses of unrelated institutional and statistical material. Economists are expanding the frontiers of knowledge about the economic environment and are learning to understand and sometimes to control it, but new problems and new events are always challenging existing knowledge. Economists are therefore continually concerned with how theory, institutions, and facts relate to each other. Every theory is subject to empirical challenge.

A second major theme of this book concerns the relationship between economic theory and economic policy. Decades of systematic observations have provided an ever-growing understanding of how things relate to one another quantitatively. This knowledge has increased economists' ability to make sensible and relevant statements about public policy. True, there remain many areas where economists' knowledge is painfully sparse, as current debates about our international competitiveness and about the nature of an appropriate monetary policy remind us.

The third major feature of the book has to do with the way we view students. We have tried to be as honest with them as possible within the limits of an introductory textbook. No subject worth studying is always easy, and we do not approve of slipping particularly hard bits of analysis past students without letting them see what is happening and what has been assumed, nor do we approve of teaching them things that they will have to unlearn if they continue their study of economics (a practice sometimes justified on the grounds that it is important to get to

the big issues quickly). In short, we have tried to follow Albert Einstein's advice: *Make thngs as simple as possible, but not simpler.*

Effective criticism of existing ideas is the springboard to progress in science. We believe that introductory economics should introduce students to methods for testing, criticizing, and evaluating the present state of the subject. We do not believe that it is wrong to suggest to students the possibility of criticizing current economic theory. Students will always criticize and evaluate their course content, and their criticisms are more likely to be informed and relevant if they are given practice and instruction in how to challenge what they have been taught in an effective, constructive manner.

Major Revisions in This Edition

The revisions introduced in this ninth edition are the result of an extensive series of reviews and feedback from those who have used the previous edition of this book. There are a number of major additions, including several completely new chapters, but we have also strived very hard to improve the "teachability and readability" of the book. Every part of the book has been thoroughly reviewed with these two goals in mind.

Changes in Microeconomics

1. In Chapter 1 we report on the remarkable shift toward markets that has occurred worldwide and especially in the major socialist countries. A new box, "Will *Perestroika* Succeed?" highlights some of the problems that might be encountered as a result of a rapid shift toward reliance on markets, even when the shift is beneficial in the long run.

2. In Chapter 5 the distinction between long-run and short-run elasticity is stressed, both for demand

and supply elasticities, which follows the development in the eighth edition. In this edition we have extended that discussion to incorporate the distinction (due to the famous nineteenth century British economist Alfred Marshall) between short-run and long-run responses of markets to supply and demand shocks, stressing that prices can "overshoot" (i.e., adjust by more than is required for long-run equilibrium) in the short run.

3. Chapter 6 has been rewritten to emphasize *applyng* the tools that were developed in Chapters 4 and 5, rather than attempting complete coverage of the topics chosen for illustrative purposes. The chapter now begins with a wholly new section on the determination of exports and imports in competitive international markets. This is in line with our desire to emphasize wherever possible the increasingly important international linkages of the American economy.

4. The basic theory of demand has been completely restructured in this edition. The new structure has been chosen to give instructors maximum flexibility in covering the material. This has been achieved by putting the two major theories—indifference curves and marginal utility—in two appendixes to Chapter 7. The text of Chapter 7 does as much as can be done with demand theory by stressing the budget constraint and rational choice, without developing either marginal utility or indifference curves. Surprisingly, a lot can be done, but very few instructors would choose not to use one or the other of the appendixes. The old structure forced instructors to use marginal utility and left indifference curves optional. Thus, they covered either marginal utility or both marginal utility and indifference curves. Now readers can do one or the other, or both, or neither.

5. Chapter 8 is almost entirely new. It starts off with some material on *using* demand theory that was included in the eighth edition, and it then turns to an extended treatment of a new and currently fashionable topic—the economics of uncertainty. Boxes on "The Economics of Gambling" and "The Problem of 'Lemons' " (used cars) will appeal to students and can be read separately from the text itself.

6. The structure of Part 4 has been altered so that all of the positive analysis is done before a discussion of efficiency considerations is introduced. Chapter 14 on imperfect competition has been completely rewritten to improve its teachability and to increase its coverage of modern industrial organization theory.

Chapter 16 has been rewritten to discuss the "market for corporate control," emphasizing hostile takeovers, leveraged buyouts, and their effects on industrial organization.

7. The final two chapters of the micro section in the eighth edition have been completely reorganized and rewritten, and we have included a new chapter, Chapter 23, on environmental and social regulation.

Changes in Macroeconomics

This is now the fourth edition in which the macroeconomics material has relied mainly on the tools of aggregate demand and aggregate supply. Our emphasis in this revision has been on improving the teachability of this section. We have simplified the discussion in several places and have restructured the material in two chapters to provide flexibility to the instructor. The book now builds up much more systematically: The first seven macroeconomic chapters are a presentation of the model and some simple applications before the "elaboration" begins in Chapter 31. From a teaching viewpoint this is a major improvement.

Other specific macroeconomics changes include these:

1. The aggregate demand and aggregate supply curves are now introduced only as they are needed. Thus, the necessarily brief introduction of the two curves that previously occurred in the first macro chapter has been dropped. This not only simplifies the introduction to macroeconomics but also means that the whole macro development follows a much more even flow, with concepts introduced only as they become used.

2. Chapter 24 is now devoted solely to the introduction of the main macro variables, including a discussion of how some of these are measured by index numbers. Chapter 25 deals with national income accounting, while Chapter 26 covers the Keynesian expenditure-equals-income equilibrium for the goods market and the simple multiplier. Only then, in Chapter 27, are the aggregate demand *(AD)* and the short-run aggregate supply *(SRAS)* curves introduced, and macroeconomic equilibrium of the price level and national income determined.

3. Chapter 28 introduces long-run equilibrium by first showing the induced shifts in the *SRAS* curve when income diverges from its potential level. This leads to the derivation of the long-run aggregate supply *(LRAS)* curve. The distinction between the

two curves is then carefully examined. We feel that it is worth the effort required to establish this distinction, because, as economists, we are concerned about the many textbooks that carry out the bulk of their analysis with a single, stable AS curve. This simplifies teaching, but it risks serious confusion. The alert student, faced with a fixed AS curve and an AD curve that can be shifted by policy, will wonder why anyone would hesitate to pay the price of a once-and-for-all increase in the price level in order to obtain a permanent increase in output and employment. Who faced with such a trade-off, would hesitate to pay the price increase? To avoid such serious confusions, we introduce the shifting, short-run AS curve and the vertical, long-run AS curve at the outset.

4. Chapter 29 has been completely rewritten to better integrate it into the book and to redirect it toward its initial purpose—elucidating the role of fluctuations and cycles as motivation for studying economic policy. Chapter 30, "An Introduction to Fiscal Policy," also has been very thoroughly rewritten and shortened. Chapters 29 and 30 now appear essentially as applications of the aggregate demand and aggregate supply apparatus that the student has just mastered (or at least encountered). All extraneous material has been excised or moved to later parts of the book. For example, the detailed discussion of the debate on government budget deficits (which really requires understanding of the monetary issues in Chapters 31–33) now appears later in the book in a new chapter, Chapter 37.

5. Chapter 33, "Monetary Policy," has been revised thoroughly. There is now more focus on the external value of the U.S. dollar in the formulation and appraisal of monetary policy. A second (not unrelated) change is increased attention to the "globalization" of financial markets, including a box with that title.

6. Chapter 34, "Inflation," has been reworked and greatly simplified. The emphasis now is more on long-term inflation control and less on the issue of how to break an entrenched inflation, which was important at the time of writing the previous edition.

7. Chapter 36, "Economic Growth," has also received some revision. We now pay some notice to the new "endogenous growth" models that are currently attracting attention and also develop the modern theme that growth and cycles are really part of the same phenomenon and need to be studied in a common model.

8. In order to emphasize its continuing importance and to provide maximum flexibility for the instructor, the material on budget deficits and related political economy issues now appears in a self-contained chapter, Chapter 37. (The appendix to Chapter 36 provides a detailed discussion of the Ricardian equivalence hypothesis.) "Macroeconomic Controversies" now appears as Chapter 38; here we have added a lot of new material, including a treatment of real business cycle theory and of several aspects of the so-called New Keynesian economics.

9. Finally, the international material has been updated and revised to reflect current concerns. We have included a new chapter on the policy issues created by openness of the economy: the role of exchange rates and external balances, and their impact on policy choices and the consequences of such choices. The international section has been revised and expanded to reflect the growing importance of international economic issues in American policy formation. The treatments of dynamic comparative advantage, nontariff barriers to trade, including voluntary export restrictions, and the longer-term consequences of the overvaluation of the American dollar (which is only being rectified at the time of writing) are all new or greatly expanded.

Teaching Aids

Key ideas in macroeconomics and microeconomics. New to this edition are four full-color insert sections—two for microeconomics and two for macroeconomics—which repeat important conceptual diagrams from the text with abbreviated captions as a review device for students. Each of these diagrams is intended to be a memory-jogger that says to the student, "Do you remember and understand this concept? If not, return to the proper chapter and reread it in detail."

Tag lines and captions for figures and tables. The boldface tag line below or next to a figure or a table states briefly the central conclusion to be drawn from the illustration; the lightface caption gives information needed to reach that conclusion. Each title, tag line, and caption, along with the figure or table, forms a self-contained unit, useful for reviewing.

Boxes. The boxes contain examples or materials that are relevant extensions of the main text but need not be read as part of the text sequence. They are all optional. Some have further theoretical material. Others contain expansions and applications of points already covered in the text. The boxes give flexibility in expanding or contracting the coverage of specific chapters.

End-of-chapter material. Each chapter has a Summary, a list of Topics for Review, and Discussion Questions. The questions are designed for class discussion or for "quiz sections." Answers appear in the Instructor's Manual.

Appendixes. All of the appendixes are optional, and most contain material that is less central to a first-year course than is the text material. One exception to this, at least in the view of many instructors, is the use of appendixes in Chapter 7. These are designed for flexibility, rather than to suggest that the material is in some sense peripheral. The present structure allows the instructor to choose to cover either marginal utility or indifference curves, or both, or neither.

Mathematical notes. Mathematical notes are collected in a separate section at the end of the book. Since mathematical notation and derivation is not necessary to understand the principles of economics but is helpful in more advanced work, this segregation seems to be a sensible arrangement. Mathematical notes provide clues to the uses of mathematics for the increasing number of students who have some background in math, without loading the text with notes that are useless and a put off to other readers. Students with a mathematical background have often told us that they find the mathematical notes helpful.

Glossary. The glossary covers widely used definitions of economic terms. Words in the glossary that are technical terms are printed in boldface the first time that they occur in both the micro and the macro parts of the book. In addition, the glossary also includes, for ease of reference, some commonly used terms that are not printed in boldface in the text because they are not, strictly speaking, technical terms.

Endpapers. Inside the front cover on the left is a list of the most commonly used abbreviations in the text; on the right appears a figure that represents the relative importance of the national debt. Inside the back cover on the left is an illustration that represents the major forms of federal expenditure; on the right is a table of selected time series, useful data on the United States economy since 1929.

Supplements

Our book is accompanied by a workbook. *Study Guide and Problems,* by Fredric C. Menz, John H. Mutti, and Dascomb R. Forbush. The workbook can be used either in the classroom or by the students on their own. It offers additional study support for each text chapter, including chapter overviews, objectives, matching self-tests, exercises, review questions, additional problems, and a special case with related questions for each Part of the text. It is available in one- or two-volume editions.

An *Instructor's Manual,* prepared by us, includes an explanation of the approach used in each text chapter, along with a chapter overview, answers to all end-of-chapter questions, and additional teaching suggestions. Also provided are answers to all problems and cases in the student *Study Guide.*

Test Bank I, by Clark Ross, contains 2,500 updated multiple-choice questions, nearly one-third of which are completely new. *Test Bank II,* by Kevin O'Brien, Clark Ross, and Dereka Rushbrook, offers 2,000 completely new multiple-choice questions. Both test banks are free to adopters. The *Test Banks* are also available in a microcomputerized version, called *Harper Test,* which provides customized testing capabilities.

The Lipsey Disk 2: Key Concepts for Review, a computerized student review tool, provides 20 crucial multiple-choice questions for each chapter in the text. If an incorrect answer is given, the student is referred to specific text pages for further study. Free to adopters, it is available for use with IBM PCs and compatibles. *Lipsey MACROVIEW Simulation* is a new software package that gives students hands-on experience in dealing with macro problems and variables that have been inherited by the Bush administration. *Lipsey Micro Tutorial* is a new interactive software tutorial package that helps students review microeconomic concepts in 10 key areas. Both of these programs are available free to adopters for use with IBM PCs and compatibles.

For this edition, all illustrations in 15 key theory chapters are reproduced as two- or four-color transparency acetates. In addition, the remaining figures in the text are reproduced in the form of transparency masters. All of these are available free to adopters.

Using the Book

Needs of students differ: Some want material that goes beyond the average class level, but others have gaps in their backgrounds. To accommodate the former, we have included more material than we would assign to every student. Also, because there are many different kinds of first-year economics courses in colleges and universities, we have included more material than normally would be included in any single course.

Although instructors can best design their own courses, it may help if we indicate certain views of our own as to how this book *might* be adapted to different courses.

Sequence

The choice of whether to study macro first or micro first is partly a personal one that cannot be decided solely by objective criteria. We believe that in the 1990s there are good reasons for preferring the micro-macro order. The thrust over the last 25 years has been to examine the micro underpinnings of macro functions and to erect macroeconomics on a firmer base of micro behavioral relations. Virtually every current macro controversy turns on some micro underpinning. For "micro-firsters" this poses no problem. For "macro-firsters" it is often hard to explain what is at issue.

Changes occur, not only in economic theory, but also in the problems that excite students. Many of today's problems that students find most challenging—the plight of the cities, poverty, pollution—are microeconomic in character. The micro-macro order, moreover, reflects the historical evolution of the subject. A century of classical and neoclassical development of microeconomics preceded the Keynesian development of macroeconomics.

For those who prefer the macro-micro order, we have attempted to make reversibility easy. The overview chapter that ends Part 1 provides a base on which to build either the microeconomics of Part 2 or the macroeconomics of Part 7. Chapters 4 and 5 should be assigned after Chapter 3, even in macro-first courses. Where further microeconomic concepts are required—as in the macro investment chapter—we have added brief sections to make the treatment self-contained, while providing review material for those who have covered the microeconomic section.

One-Semester Courses

Many first courses in economics are only one semester (or equivalent) in length. Our book can be easily adapted to such courses. Suggestions for using this book in such courses are given on page xxvii.

Those Who Helped with This Edition

Several individuals provided reviews of the ninth edition micro chapters in various drafts: Ernest Ankrim, Pacific Lutheran University; Stephen A. Baker, Capital University; Trudy Cameron, University of California at Los Angeles; Kathleen A. Carroll, University of Maryland, Baltimore; David H. Dean, University of Richmond; Bruce Herrick, Washington and Lee University; Bruce E. Kaufman, Georgia State University; Dennis Koepke, University of Wisconsin—Whitewater; Jerome K. Laurent, University of Wisconsin—Whitewater; Thea M. Lee, University of Michigan; Richard McIntyre, University of Rhode Island; Robert C. Puth, University of New Hampshire; William Doyle Smith, University of Texas at El Paso; and Mira Wilkins, Florida International University.

Other instructors provided reviews of the ninth edition macro chapters: Willie J. Belton, Georgia Institute of Technology; George S. Bohler, Florida Community College—North Campus, Jacksonville; James L. Butkiewicz, University of Delaware; Conrad Caligaris, Northeastern University; David Denslow, University of Florida; Carl E. Enomoto, New Mexico State University; Ziad Keilany, University of Tennessee, Chattanooga; Luther D. Lawson, University of North Carolina—Wilmington; Richard McIntyre, University of Rhode Island; W. Douglas Morgan, University of California, Santa Barbara; James Nordyke, New Mexico State University;

Donald H. Silva, University of Wisconsin—Whitewater; and Habib A. Zuberi, Central Michigan University.

We are most grateful to all of these people for their helpful suggestions.

The new edition has benefited greatly from the research assistance of Carolyn Betts, Heather Latle, Patricia Casey-Purvis, David Scoones, Charlotte Mack, and Kevin O'Brien. Ellen McKay and Elaine Fitzpatrick handled with skill and patience our mountains of manuscript and innumerable revisions.

Weidenfeld and Nicholson generously gave permission to use material first prepared for the sixth and seventh editions of *An Introduction to Positive Economics* by R. G. Lipsey. With this edition, we are pleased to welcome Professor Paul N. Courant of the University of Michigan to our team of authors.

Richard G. Lipsey
Peter O. Steiner
Douglas D. Purvis
Paul N. Courant

ACKNOWLEDGMENTS

So many teachers, colleagues, students, and friends contributed to the original book and to its continuing revision that it is impossible for us to acknowledge our debt to all of them individually. Hundreds of users, both teachers and students, have written us with specific suggested improvements, and much of the credit for the fact that the book has become more teachable belongs to them. We are listing here the names of all those who reviewed the first through the seventh editions.

Robert M. Aduddell
Phillip Allman
Wells Allred
Richard Anderson
G. C. Archibald
Christine Augustyniak
Douglas A. L. Auld
Bixio Barenco
Peter S. Barth
Maurice C. Benewitz
Robert M. Bernado
Jeff Blais
Tom Bonsor
Charles Britton
Charles Brown
Owen M. Broyles
Trudy Cameron
James T. Campen
Kathleen Carroll
Ira C. Castles
Richard J. Cebula
Robert J. Cheney
Charles Chittle
Wallace Cohen
John R. Coleman
Cynthia Cross
Robert Crouch
Robert Dernberger
Charles Donahue, Jr.
Kenneth G. Elzinga
Frances Esposito
Patricia Euzent
Jerry Evensky
Francis Flanagan
Belton M. Fleischer

Dascomb R. Forbush
Dorothy F. Forbush
Virginia L. Galbraith
Louis C. Gasper
J. Fred Giertz
E. Kenneth Grant
Eric Gustafson
Malcom D. Gutter
Scott D. Hakala
Hiroaki Hayakawa
Stephen A. Hoenack
Emily Hoffman
John Isbister
Taka Ito
Janice Jacobson
William R. Johnson
Edward J. Kane
Allen C. Kelley
Kenneth J. Kopecky
Arthur Kruger
Michael Kupilik
Rodney H. Mabry
A. McKee
John Madden
James R. Marsden
Gerald M. Miller
Felipe Montt
Theodore J. Morgan
W. D. Morgan
Edward J. Mulholland
Edwin Nadel
Stephen Nord
Gerald T. O'Boyle
Kenji Okuda
Kent Olsen

Michael Perelman
Charlotte Phelps
George B. Pidot
Mark W. Plant
Joseph E. Pluta
Richard C. Porter
James Price
Joe Rabianski
Maury Rabinowitz
Stephen E. Reynolds
Randolph Rice
Richard Rosenberg
Louis Rossiter
Bernard Saffran
B. Sahni
Arnold W. Sametz
Terrance Sandalow
Joseph L. Sax
W. M. Scammell
Elliot Schlar
Harvey Schwartz
Nancy Schwartz
Stuart O. Schweitzer
Frank A. Scott, Jr.
Joseph J. Seneca

Donald Shoup
A. P. Simson
Murray Smith
Gordon R. Sparks
Frank Stafford
Dennis Starleaf
M. Stelcner
Courtenay Stone
Kenneth Strand
William J. Swift
Josephine K. Tan
David Terkla
John Throckmorton, Jr.
John M. Trapani, III
W. R. Trenton
Laura Tyson
Charles Vars
Gerald Visgilio
Robert F. Wallace
Stanislaw Wasowski
Pamela Weidler
C. R. Winegarden
Jeffrey Wolcowitz
William C. Wood

Suggested Outlines for a
ONE-SEMESTER COURSE

Core chapters for courses in either microeconomics or macroeconomics are in bold black numerals.
Additional core chapters for courses in microeconomics are in bold blue numerals.
Additional core chapters for courses in macroeconomics are in light blue numerals.

Chapters shown with an * are particularly appropriate for courses with a heavy policy orientation.

Note: A full-semester course can cover not more than 25 full chapters. The core consists of about 13 chapters. Selections from other chapters, as listed below in lightface black, can produce courses with various emphases.

TO THE STUDENT

A good course in economics will give you insight into how an economy functions and into some currently debated policy issues. Like all rewarding subjects, economics will not be mastered without effort. A book on economics must be worked at. It cannot be read like a novel.

Each of you must develop an individual technique for studying, but the following suggestions may prove helpful. It is usually a good idea to read a chapter quickly in order to get the general run of the argument. At this first reading, you may want to skip the boxes and any footnotes. Then, after reading the Topics for Review and the Discussion Questions, reread the chapter more slowly, making sure that you understand each step of the argument. With respect to the figures and tables, be sure you understand how the conclusions that are stated in the brief tag lines with each table or figure have been reached. You should be prepared to spend time on difficult sections; occasionally, you may spend an hour on only a few pages. Paper and a pencil are indispensable equipment in your reading. It is best to follow a difficult argument by building your own diagram while the argument unfolds rather than by relying on the finished diagram as it appears in the book. It is often helpful to invent numerical examples to illustrate general propositions. The end-of-chapter questions require you to apply what you have studied. We advise you to outline answers to some of the questions. In short, you should seek to understand economics, not to memorize it.

After you have read each part in detail, reread it quickly from beginning to end. It is often difficult to understand why certain things are done when they are viewed as isolated points, but when you reread a whole part, much that did not seem relevant or entirely comprehensible will fall into place in the analysis.

We call your attention to the glossary at the end of the book. Any time that you encounter a concept that seems vaguely familiar but is not clear to you, check the glossary. The chances are that it will be there and that its definition will remind you of what you once understood. If you are still in doubt, check the index entry to find where the concept is discussed more fully. Incidentally, the glossary, along with the captions that accompany figures and tables and the end-of-chapter summaries, may prove to be very helpful when you are reviewing for examinations.

The bracketed colored numbers in the text itself refer to a series of 49 mathematical notes that are found starting on page 945. For those of you who like mathematics or prefer mathematical argument to verbal or geometric exposition, these may prove useful. Others may ignore them.

We hope that you will find the book rewarding and stimulating. Students who used earlier editions made some of the most helpful suggestions for revision, and we hope that you will carry on the tradition. If you are moved to write to us, please do.

ECONOMICS

THE
NATURE
OF
ECONOMICS

Chapter 1

The Economic Problem

Many of the world's most pressing problems are economic. The dominant problem of the 1930s was the massive unemployment of workers and other resources that resulted from the Great Depression. The wartime economy of the 1940s solved that problem but created a new one: how to reallocate scarce resources quickly between military and civilian needs. The period from 1945 to 1955 was a time of worldwide economic growth as the major economies recovered from World War II. As the European nations tried to rebuild their war-shattered economies, a major concern was whether they could export enough to pay for all that they needed to import.

The period from 1955 to 1965 was a time of unparalleled growth in prosperity as the world experienced a period of expanding output and trade. Unemployment was a concern during some of this period, as was the inability of most economies to achieve *both* full employment and zero inflation. From 1965 to 1975 a slowdown in growth and rising inflation became matters for serious concern. The central problems of the late 1970s and early 1980s were the rising cost of energy—oil prices increased tenfold from 1974 to 1980—and the disturbing combination of rising unemployment and rising inflation, called *stagflation*.

In the United States, high unemployment was a major problem of the early 1980s, and persistent balance-of-trade deficits throughout the rest of the decade led to a concern about the threat to American jobs from foreign competition. Dramatic increases in agricultural subsidies in many advanced countries and the persistent debt crisis faced by a number of poorer countries created an uncertain international environment. Massive government deficits and the growth of the public debt cast a shadow of concern that will linger throughout the rest of the century.

Problems change over the decades, yet there are always problems. Of course, not all the world's problems are primarily economic. Political, biological, social, cultural, and philosophical issues often predominate. However, as the following examples suggest, no matter how "noneconomic" a particular problem may seem, it will almost always have a significant economic dimension.

1. The crises that lead to wars often have economic roots. Nations fight for oil and rice and land to live on, although the rhetoric of their leaders evokes God, Glory, and the Fatherland.
2. The current rate of world population growth is 2.1 persons per second, or about 65 million people a year. The economic

consequences of this are steady pressures on the available natural resources, especially arable land. Unless the human race can find ways to increase its food supply as fast as its population, increasing millions face starvation.

3. The "greenhouse effect" describes the gradual warming of the earth's climate due to a cumulative buildup of CO_2 in the atmosphere. Scientists predict that the melting of the polar ice cap and the further warming of desert regions will alter the earth's physical geography dramatically. Perhaps even more dramatic will be the economic consequences of resulting changes in consumption patterns and production possibilities.

Current Economic Problems

International Trade and Protection

The issue of free trade versus protectionism has been central to international policy discussions throughout this century. In the 1930s, following the Great Depression, country after country imposed tariffs and other restrictions on imports. At the time politicians thought they were creating jobs, but most economists believe that all they did was prolong the worldwide stagnation and reduce living standards. The next 40 years witnessed increased trade liberalization *and* unprecedented economic growth. During the serious worldwide recession in the early 1980s and in the ensuing years, pressures again mounted in the United States and elsewhere to restrict imports in an attempt to save jobs. Would such measures once again lead to a decline in world living standards?

Deficits and Debt

Almost everyone running for public office these days calls for a major reduction in government deficits, but large deficits persist and, as a result, the national debt continues to grow. Did these deficits contribute to the sustained recovery from the 1982 recession, or would that recovery have occurred anyway? The national debt in 1989 was over $2.5 trillion and growing at 7 percent per annum. Will the growth in the debt eventually cause inflation? Will it lead to a deterioration in living standards for Americans? Does

the growing debt threaten us with national bankruptcy? Since politicians apparently cannot balance the federal budget on their own, should they be compelled to do so by law?

In the 1980s our trade deficit, a measure of how much more we imported from foreigners than we exported to them, reached record levels. Did this deficit, and the massive foreign borrowing required to pay for the imports, represent a problem that needs correcting? Was it the result of a massive "consumption binge" by Americans? Was it related to the government budget deficit? Can the trade deficit be eliminated by protectionist measures that restrict imports? Should it be?

Unemployment and Inflation

In 1978 Congress enacted the Humphrey-Hawkins Full Employment and Balanced Growth Act, which officially established full employment and stable prices as twin goals of economic policy. Reasonable as this may sound, the fact is that we have seldom had both full employment *and* stable prices at the same time; indeed, often during the last decade we have had neither. At the start of 1989 unemployment stood at about 5.4 percent of the labor force, and prices were rising at an annual rate of about 4.5 percent.

Are zero unemployment and zero inflation reasonable long-run goals? What is an "acceptable" level of unemployment? Can we be sure that we will never again experience the trauma of the 1930s, when up to one-quarter of all those who sought work were unable to find it? What is an "acceptable" level of inflation? Why do prices in some countries rise 30 percent or 40 percent a year, while in others they rise at a rate of 3 percent or 4 percent? Why did inflation accelerate dramatically throughout most of the world in the early 1970s and again in the late 1970s? Why did it fall sharply in the early 1980s? Can a country control unemployment *and* inflation?

Government and the Individual

Poverty is a dominant problem in the world. It is still a major problem in the United States, even though the average American continues to be one of the richest individuals in the world. How can poverty survive in the midst of relative plenty? Who are the poor, and what makes them so? Can poverty ever be eliminated in the United States? Is a more equal distribution of income a desirable or attainable national goal? Do government policies improve or impair the lot of those who are poor?

Do we, as John Kenneth Galbraith once argued, allocate too little to government expenditure for such valuable things as health and education while we grow sated on frivolous, privately produced goods such as electric can openers? Or, as charged by Milton Friedman, do we instead invite the government to do badly many things that private groups could do well? Do we, as some "supply-side" economists charge, create *dis*incentives to work effort by imposing high tax rates in order to pay for all those governmental expenditures while providing a "welfare net" that saps people's initiative even as it protects them from economic hardship?

What Is Economics?

The discussion so far has presented only a handful of the important current issues on which economics can shed some light. One way to define *economics* is to say that it is the social science that deals with such problems. Another definition, perhaps better known, is Alfred Marshall's: "Economics is a study of mankind in the ordinary business of life." A more penetrating definition might be the following:

Economics is the study of the use of scarce resources to satisfy unlimited human wants.

Scarcity is inevitable and is central to economic problems. What are society's resources? Why is scarcity inevitable? What are the consequences of scarcity?

Resources and Commodities

A society's resources consist of natural gifts such as land, forests, and minerals; human resources, both mental and physical; and manufactured aids to production such as tools, machinery, and buildings. Economists call such resources **factors of production**[1] because they are used to produce those things that people desire. The things produced are

called **commodities,** which may be divided into goods and services. **Goods** are tangible (e.g., cars or shoes), and **services** are intangible (e.g., haircuts or education). Notice the implication of positive value contained in the terms goods *and* services. (Compare the terms *bads* and *disservices.*)

People use goods and services to satisfy many of their wants. The act of making them is called **production**, and the act of using them to satisfy wants is called **consumption**. Goods are valued for the services they provide. An automobile, for example, helps to satisfy its owner's desires for transportation, mobility, and possibly status.

Scarcity

For most of the world's 4 billion human beings, scarcity is real and ever present. In relation to desires (for more and better food, clothing, housing, schooling, entertainment, and so forth), existing resources are woefully inadequate; there are enough to produce only a small fraction of the goods and services that are wanted.

Is not the United States rich enough that scarcity is nearly banished? After all, we have been characterized as the affluent society. Whatever affluence may mean, it does not mean the end of the problem of scarcity. Most households that earn $80,000 a year (a princely amount by worldwide standards) have no trouble spending it on things that seem useful to them. Yet it would take more than twice the present output of the American economy to produce enough to allow all American households to consume that amount.

Choice

Because resources are scarce, all societies face the problem of deciding what to produce and how to divide the products among their members. Societies differ in who makes the choices and how they are made, but the need to choose is common to all. Just as scarcity implies the need for choice, so choice implies the existence of cost.

Opportunity Cost

A decision to have more of one thing requires a decision to have less of something else. It is this fact that makes the first decision costly. We look first at

---

[1] The definitions of the terms in boldface type can be found in the glossary at the end of the book.

a trivial example and then at one that vitally affects all of us; both examples involve precisely the same fundamental principles.

Consider the choice that must be made by a small boy who has 10 cents to spend and who is determined to spend it all on candy. For him there are only two kinds of candy in the world: gumdrops, which sell for 1 cent each, and chocolates, which sell for 2 cents. The boy would like to buy 10 gumdrops and 10 chocolates, but he knows (or will soon discover) that this is not possible: It is not an *attainable combination* given his scarce resources. There are, however, several attainable combinations: 8 gumdrops and 1 chocolate, 4 gumdrops and 3 chocolates, 2 gumdrops and 1 chocolate, and so on. Some of these combinations leave him with money unspent, and he is not interested in them. Only six combinations, as shown in Figure 1-1, are both attainable and use all his money.

After careful thought, the boy has almost decided

FIGURE 1-1   A Choice Between Gumdrops and Chocolates

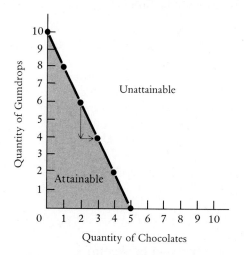

A limited amount of money forces a choice among alternatives. Six combinations of gumdrops and chocolates are attainable and use all of the boy's money. The downward-sloping line provides a boundary between attainable and unattainable combinations. The arrows show that the opportunity cost of 1 more chocolate is 2 gumdrops. In this example the opportunity cost is constant and therefore the boundary is a straight line.

to buy 6 gumdrops and 2 chocolates, but at the last moment he decides that he simply must have 3 chocolates. What will it cost him to get this extra chocolate? One answer is 2 gumdrops. As seen in the figure, this is the number of gumdrops he must give up to get the extra chocolate. Economists would describe the 2 gumdrops as the *opportunity cost* of the third chocolate.

Another answer is that the cost of the third chocolate is 2 cents. However, given the boy's budget and his intentions, this answer is less revealing than the first one. Where the real choice is between more of this and more of that, the cost of "this" is usefully looked at as what you cannot have of "that." The idea of opportunity cost is one of the central insights of economics.

The **opportunity cost** is the cost of using resources for a certain purpose, measured in terms of the benefit given up by not using them in an alternative way, that is, measured in terms of other commodities that could have been obtained instead.

Every time a choice must be made, opportunity costs are incurred.

Production Possibilities

Although the choice between gumdrops and chocolates is a minor consumption decision, the essential nature of the decision is the same whatever the choice being made is. Consider, for example, the important choice between military and civilian goods. It is not possible to produce an unlimited quantity of both military and civilian goods. If resources are fully employed and the government wishes to produce more arms, then less civilian goods can be produced. The opportunity cost of increased arms production is forgone production of civilian goods.

The choice is illustrated in Figure 1-2. Because resources are limited, some combinations—those that would require more than the total available supply of resources for their production—cannot be attained. The downward-sloping curve on the graph divides the combinations that can be attained from those that cannot. Points above and to the right of this curve cannot be attained because there are not enough resources; points below and to the left of the curve can be attained without using all of the available resources; and points on the curve can just be attained if all the available resources are used. The

FIGURE 1-2   A Production Possibility Boundary

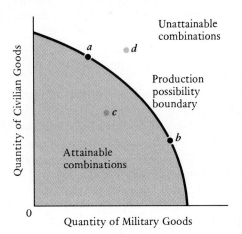

The downward-sloping boundary shows the combinations that are just attainable when all of the society's resources are efficiently employed. The quantity of military goods produced is measured along the horizontal axis; the quantity of civilian goods, along the vertical axis. Thus any point on the diagram indicates some amount of each kind of good produced. The production possibility boundary separates the attainable combinations of goods such as *a*, *b*, and *c* from unattainable combinations such as *d*. It slopes downward because resources are scarce: More of one good can be produced only if resources are freed by producing less of the other goods. Points *a* and *b* represent efficient use of society's resources. Point *c* represents either inefficient use of resources or failure to use all the available resources.

curve is called the **production possibility boundary.** It has a negative slope because, when all resources are being used, having more of one kind of goods requires having less of the other kind.

A production possibility boundary illustrates three concepts: scarcity, choice, and opportunity cost. Scarcity is indicated by the unattainable combinations above the boundary, choice by the need to choose among the alternative attainable points along the boundary, and opportunity cost by the downward slope of the boundary.

The shape of the production possibility boundary in Figure 1-2 implies that more and more civilian

goods must be given up to achieve equal successive increases in military goods. This shape, referred to as *concave* to the origin, indicates that the opportunity cost of either good grows larger and larger as we increase the amount of it that is produced. A slope that forms a straight line, as in Figure 1-1, indicates that the opportunity cost of one good in terms of the other stays constant, no matter how much of it is produced. As we shall see, there are reasons to believe that the case of rising opportunity cost applies to many important choices.[2]

Four Key Economic Problems

While modern economies are complex, many basic decisions that must be made by consumers and producers are not very different from those made in a primitive economy in which people work with few tools and barter with their neighbors. Nor do capitalist, socialist, and communist economies differ in their need to solve the same basic problems, although they do differ, of course, in how they solve them. Most problems studied by economists can be grouped under four main headings.

1. What Is Produced and How?

The allocation of scarce resources among alternative uses, called **resource allocation**, determines the quantities of various goods that are produced. Choosing to produce a particular combination of goods means choosing a particular allocation of resources among the industries or regions producing the goods because, for example, producing a lot of one good requires that a lot of resources be allocated to its production.

Further, because resources are scarce, it is desirable that they be used efficiently. Hence it matters which of the available methods of production is used to produce each of the goods that is to be produced.

2. What Is Consumed and by Whom?

What is the relation between the economy's production of commodities and the consumption enjoyed by its citizens? Economists want to understand what

---

[2] The importance of scarcity, choice, and opportunity cost has led some people to define economics as the study of the allocation of scarce resources among competing ends. The issues emphasized by this definition are important, but, as will be seen in the next section, there are also other important issues.

determines the distribution of a nation's total output among its population. Who gets a lot, who gets a little, and why? What role does international trade play in this?

Questions 1 and 2 fall within **microeconomics,** the study of the allocation of resources and the distribution of income as they are affected by the workings of the price system and the government policies.

3. How Much Unemployment and Inflation Exist?

When an economy is in a recession, unemployed workers would like to have jobs, the factories in which they could work are available, the managers and owners would like to be able to operate their factories, raw materials are available in abundance, and the goods that could be produced by these resources are needed by individuals in the community, but for some reason resources remain unemployed. This forces the economy within its production possibility boundary, at a point such as *c* in Figure 1-2.

The world's economies have often experienced bouts of prolonged and substantial changes in price levels. In recent decades the course of prices has almost always been upward. The 1970s was a period of accelerating inflation, not only in the United States but in most of the world. Inflation slowed in the early 1980s while unemployment soared. Were these two events related?

Why do governments worry that short-run reductions in either unemployment or inflation will be at the cost of increasing the other?

4. Is Productive Capacity Growing?

The capacity to produce commodities to satisfy human wants grows rapidly in some countries, slowly in others, and actually declines in still others. Growth in productive capacity can be represented by a pushing outward of the production possibility boundary, as shown in Figure 1-3. If an economy's capacity to produce goods and services is growing, combinations that are unattainable today will become attainable tomorrow. Growth makes it possible to have more of all goods.

Questions 3 and 4 fall within **macroeconomics,** the study of the determination of economic aggregates such as total output, total employment, the price level, and the rate of economic growth.

FIGURE 1-3   The Effect of Economic Growth on the Production Possibility Boundary

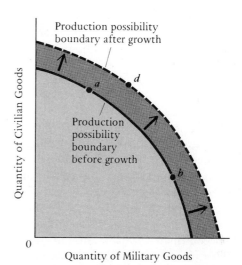

Economic growth shifts the boundary outward and makes it possible to produce more of all commodities. Before growth in productive capacity, points *a* and *b* were on the production possibility boundary and point *d* was an unattainable combination. After growth, as shown by the dark shaded band, point *d* and many other previously unattainable combinations are attainable.

Alternative Economic Systems

This book examines the four basic questions just outlined in the context of a market economy in which private firms and households interact in markets with some assistance (and interference) from the government. We study the market economy for several reasons. First, this is the kind of economy *we* live in. Second, it is the economic environment in which the serious study of economics was born and has grown.

Today, however, one-third of the world's population live in the Soviet Union and China, countries that in the past have rejected important elements of our kind of economic system. They have relied heavily on centrally planned actions to deal with the four basic questions. At least another third of the world's population live in countries whose economies have not yet developed to the point where they could accurately be described as either *market* or *planned* economies.

To the extent that economics deals with the ways in which people respond to incentives and mobilize scarce means to achieve given ends, the same economic principles are applicable under a variety of different institutional, political, and social arrangements.

All economies face scarcity, and all must decide how to allocate scarce resources and distribute goods and services; all may face problems of inflation, unemployment, and unsatisfactory rates of growth.

Because all economies face many common problems, economics can contribute valuable insights even when familiar institutions are modified or absent.

Differences Among Economies

It is common to speak of only two economic systems, capitalism (or, a market-oriented system) and socialism (or, a centrally planned system). But this is at best a simplification and at worst a confusion.

There are dozens of economic systems in existence today, not just two. Just as there are many differences among the United States, Canada, the United Kingdom, Germany, Sweden, Japan, and Brazil, so are there differences among the Soviet Union, China, Poland, Cuba, Czechoslovakia, and Yugoslavia. Countries are dissimilar in many respects, including who owns resources and who makes decisions. These two aspects are discussed in the next two sections.

Ownership of Resources

Who owns a nation's farms and factories, its coal mines and forests? Who owns its railways, its streams and golf courses? Who owns its houses and hotels?

One characteristic of capitalism is that the basic raw materials, the productive assets of the society, and the goods produced in the economy are predominantly privately owned. By this standard the United States is predominantly a capitalist economy. However, even in the United States public ownership extends beyond the usual basic services such as

schools and local transport systems to include other activities such as electric power utilities and housing projects.

In contrast, in a socialist society the productive assets are predominantly publicly owned. Although the Soviets officially designate their economy as socialist, there are three sectors—agriculture, retail trade, and housing—in which some private ownership exists. However, even though the USSR is not a pure socialist economy, public ownership is sufficiently widespread to place the USSR near one end of a spectrum and the United States near the other.

Other countries fall between them on the spectrum. Great Britain has six times in this century elected Labor governments that have been officially committed to socialism to the point of nationalizing key industries, including railroads, steel, coal, electricity, postal services, and telephones. However, the bulk of industries that produce goods and services for household consumption, and machinery and equipment for firms, have always remained privately owned. Furthermore, a major thrust for privatization, or the return of publicly owned firms to private ownership, has been underway since 1980.

Ownership patterns are generally mixed and variable rather than exclusive and unchanging. Figure 1-4 shows the division of investment between public and private sectors in 11 countries.

The Decision Process (Coordinating Principles)

A distinction is sometimes made between two kinds of systems: a *market system*, in which decisions are made in a decentralized way by the interaction of individuals in markets, and a *command system*, in which centralized decision makers decide what is to be done and issue appropriate commands to achieve the desired results.

Again, no country offers an example of either system working alone. But it is true that some economies, such as those of the United States, Canada, France, and Yugoslavia, rely much more heavily on market decisions than do others, such as the economies of East Germany, the Soviet Union, and Cuba. Yet even in the United States the command principle has some sway. Minimum wages, quotas on some agricultural outputs, and quotas on textile imports are obvious examples. More subtle examples are public expenditures and taxes that in effect transfer command of some resources from private individuals to public officials.

FIGURE 1-4 An Indicator of Differences in Ownership Patterns for Selected Countries

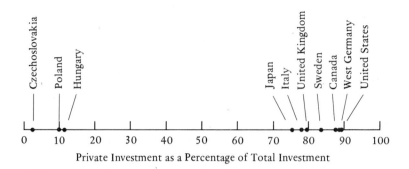

Private Investment as a Percentage of Total Investment

Actual economies never rely solely on private or public investment. These estimates are based on the percentage of gross fixed investment accounted for by the private sector. Such investment provides additions to the stock of productive capital. Private capital investment plays a role even in communist countries; public capital is a significant part of investment in all countries. (*Source*: World Book, *World Tables*.)

In the planned economies of the Soviet bloc, where targets, quotas, and directives are important aspects of the decision-making system, the command principle dominates, but the market principle also operates. For example, at the retail level people have considerable discretion in how they spend their income on a wide variety of goods.

A key plank in Marxian economic proposals was public ownership of the means of production. Yet modern experience suggests that economic behavior usually depends more on the decision pattern than on the ownership pattern. Thus, in the United Kingdom, when many key industries were publicly owned, their control was vested in semiautonomous boards over which Parliament exerted little control. By and large, the boards tried to make their enterprises profitable, and to the extent that they succeeded, their behavior was similar to that of profit-seeking, privately owned firms. In contrast, firms in Hitler's Germany were under a high degree of state control, even though they were privately owned. The behavior of these firms was very different from that of privately owned firms that are managed in order to earn profits for their owners.

Ends and Means

To many, the choice between a market and a planned economy implies a choice between ends and means. Suppose that citizens of a developing country with low living standards were asked to choose between a highly planned, socialist society that offers a good chance of a 4 percent growth rate and a market-oriented, democratic society that offers only a 2 percent growth rate. It is possible that in many such countries the citizens would choose the planned economy. To warn them that in so doing they may compromise their freedom may evoke the reply that the only freedom they perceive is the choice of being exploited by government officials or by powerful monopoly interests. To them, the ends are more important than the means.

Yet many people in Western industrialized societies value the means of the free market and democratic processes even more highly than they value the ends of high and rising living standards. Many Americans distrust the agglomeration of central power and the loss of democratic institutions that accompany a high degree of socialism. It is clear that markets are less personal than bureaucrats, and this makes them more acceptable to many people because they are less arbitrary and less subject to autocratic abuse.

How many Americans would decide to go over to Russian-style socialism, even if there were *proof* that it would produce higher material living standards than the free-market system? In the 1930s some people believed that Fascist dictatorships were more efficient than democracies. Mussolini, it was said, "made the Italian trains run on time." It is debatable that the belief was correct, but many people accepted it. Yet few Americans advocated that the United States become a Fascist dictatorship.

Recent history, however, supports the view—

BOX 1-1

Will *Perestroika* Succeed?

At the start of 1989, Mikhail Gorbachev was in the midst of attempting a major restructuring of the Soviet economy. Fast on the heels of *glasnost,* his dramatic initiative to reform and to open up Russian society and politics, Gorbachev unveiled *perestroika,* an equally dramatic shift in the Soviet economy away from state planning toward an increased role of markets.

Perestroika generated enormous interest in Western countries. Many observers expressed doubt as to whether the reforms could succeed, since the long period of centrally planned mismanagement had wreaked such havoc with the economy. As *The Economist* put it,

Much of the country's industry has yet to reach the technological and competitive standards achieved by capitalist economies in the 1950s. . . . After decades of being told that the state will provide, many ordinary Russians . . . expect it to go on doing just that. . . . When Mr. Gorbachev rattles on about the need for competition and a market, even a "socialist" one, he meets blank incomprehension. . . . The entrepreneurial sparks that glowed briefly at the start of the century have long since been snuffed out.

A key step in the reform, and one that is necessary if the reform is to succeed, is to let prices adjust freely in response to market pressures. However, when market forces and prices have been suppressed for so long, and when enormous amounts of purchasing power have been accumulated by citizens who have few goods available on which to spend their incomes, the *initial* reaction to freeing prices can be devastating. As *The Economist* said,

In a country where the price of a basic loaf has not changed in 30 years, putting up prices is dangerous. . . . free prices tomorrow would bring the sort of inflation that would make perestroika go pop. Yet, without freer prices pretty soon, both as a guide to what people want to buy and as an incentive to cut costs, perestroika will simply go phut.

Dramatic reactions to economic reform have caused governments to fall or to reverse course many times throughout history. Early in the 1980s reforms in Poland were halted when people rioted over rising food prices, and the world was shocked when riots over the same issue occurred in Venezuela in late 1988. In both cases the reforms were modest compared to what Mr. Gorbachev is attempting. The changes involved in perestroika are enormous, and the Russian people, like most people, can be expected to react negatively and defensively when their everyday lives are affected by such enormous change.

Often gradual reform has a better chance of success, but governments do not always have the time to pursue gradual policies; their leaders may get thrown out of office before the reforms have had their effect. Certainly, many observers think that a major issue governing the chances of success for glasnost are whether Mr. Gorbachev's political skills are powerful enough to allow him to remain in office long enough to see the reforms through to a point where the benefits become apparent to the Russian people.

long held by many Americans—that there is no need to choose. The dismal economic record of many planned economies over the past two decades and the recent increased role given to markets in many socialist countries suggest that market-oriented economies and democratic government produce better results than do alternative systems, in terms of both ends and means. There is still disagreement about the appropriate amount of government intervention in a decentralized market economy, but events of the last decade suggest a surprising amount of agreement that such an economy functions more efficiently than a highly centralized, planned economy. However, a cautionary note about the prospects for some of the recent market-oriented reforms is given in Box 1-1.

Alternative Systems: A Final Word

A wide variety of economic systems have been able to coexist. Three basic points are worth remembering:

1. **All countries have "mixed" economies.**
2. **Among countries the mixture differs in ways that are appreciable and significant.**
3. **Over time, the mixture changes.**

No economic system seems to do everything better than any major competing system; indeed, each has its strengths and weaknesses. To talk of "better" and "worse" in this context may itself be misleading. Although almost all systems today are moving toward more reliance on decentralized market forces, the differences among economic systems are still enormous.

Differences of opinion about the answer to the question of which system is best may simply reflect differences in emphasis on particular outcomes. Americans may view their economic system as being the reason for their high standard of living and may see in their well-stocked stores proof of the superiority of free-enterprise capitalism. Sweden's slum-free public housing, nationalized medicine, and high productivity in private industry lead many Swedes to regard their "mixed" economic system as more desirable than others.

The 1980s witnessed a noticeable worldwide shift toward the use of markets. Margaret Thatcher in the United Kingdom and Ronald Reagan here in the United States were modern politicians with the highest profiles who pushed policies that reduced the role of government in the economy and increased the role played by markets. Other Western countries, however, have also deregulated key industries, privatized large government enterprises, and initiated other pro-market reforms. The trend is also evident among planned economies. Major economic reforms in China in the 1980s saw considerable reliance on market signals and rewards, and Soviet Premier Gorbachev's commitment to *perestroika* introduced what may turn out to be revolutionary pro-market changes in the Russian economy. As noted in Box 1-1, the verdict of history will tell us whether this experience of the 1980s is just one more "blip" in the oscillations between capitalism and socialism or whether it is the harbinger of a long-run worldwide shift toward increased reliance on market forces to solve economic problems. In the meantime, however, the contemporary verdict of many governments is that their experiment with socialist planning has been a failure and that more reliance on market forces is a necessary condition for increasing their economic prosperity.

SUMMARY

1. Every generation faces important economic problems. A common feature of such problems is that they concern the use of limited resources to satisfy virtually unlimited human wants.
2. Scarcity is a fundamental problem faced by all economies. Not enough resources are available to produce all the goods and services that people would like to consume. Scarcity makes it necessary to choose. All societies must have a mechanism for choosing what commodities will be produced and in what quantities.
3. The concept of opportunity cost emphasizes the problem of scarcity and choice by measuring the cost of obtaining a unit of one commodity in terms of the number of units of other commodities that could have been obtained instead.
4. Four basic questions that must be answered in all economies are: What commodities are being produced and how? What commodities are being consumed and by whom? What are the unemployment and inflation rates, and are they related? Is productive capacity changing?
5. Not all economies resolve these questions in the same ways or equally satisfactorily. Economists study how these problems are addressed in

various societies and the consequences of using one method rather than another to provide solutions.

6. Economies can differ from one another in many ways, and such capsule classifications as "capitalism" and "socialism" represent simplifications of complex matters.

7. Among the important dimensions in which economies can differ from one another are (a) the pattern of ownership of goods and resources and (b) the decision process used, with a particularly important distinction between command and market coordinating principles.

8. All countries have mixed economies in that they exhibit a mixture of public and private ownership, and of market and command decision-making systems. The mixtures differ among countries and change over time; recently, a number of socialist, planned economies—including China and Russia—have introduced economic reforms that placed increased reliance on markets.

TOPICS FOR REVIEW

Scarcity and the need for choice
Choice and opportunity cost
Production possibility boundary
Resource allocation
Unemployed resources
Growth in productive capacity
Alternative economic systems
Public versus private ownership
Market versus command systems

DISCUSSION QUESTIONS

1. What does each of the following quotations tell you about the policy conflicts perceived by the person making the statement and about how he or she has resolved them?

   a. Russell Baker, commenting on the decision of Nantucket Island residents to approve a Holiday Inn to cater to oil drillers: "Economics compels us all to turn things into slums. Although it will be too bad, it will be absolutely justifiable. An economic necessity. Another step down the ladder to paradise."

   b. "Considering our limited energy resources and the growing demand for electricity, the United States really has no choice but to use all of its possible domestic energy sources, including nuclear energy. Despite possible environmental and safety hazards, nuclear power is a necessity."

   c. "As growth picks up, beware inflation picking up too. Politicians should resist the temptation to seek faster real growth by inflating nominal demand."

2. What is the difference between scarcity and poverty? If everyone in the world had enough to eat, could we say that food was no longer scarce?

3. Consider the right to free speech in political campaigns. Suppose that the Flat Earth Society, the Communist party, the Republican party, and the Democratic party all demand equal time on network television in a presidential election. What economic questions are involved? Can there be freedom of speech without free access to the scarce resources needed to make one's speech heard?

4. Evidence accumulates that the use of chemical fertilizers, which increases agricultural production greatly, causes damage to water quality. Show the choice involved between more food and cleaner water in using such fertilizers. Use a production possibility curve with agricultural output on the vertical axis and water quality on the horizontal axis. In what ways does this production possibility curve reflect scarcity, choice, and opportunity cost? How would an improved fertilizer that increased agricultural output without further worsening water quality affect the curve? Suppose a pollution-free fertilizer were developed; would this mean there would no longer be any opportunity cost in using it?

5. "What the world of economics needs is an end to ideology and *isms*. If there is a best system of economic organization, it will prove its superiority in its superior ability to solve economic problems." Do you agree with this statement? Would you expect that if the world survives for another 100 years, a single form of economic system would be found superior to all others? Why or why not?

6. Identify the coordinating principle suggested by each of the following.
    a. Taxes on tobacco and alcohol
    b. Production targets assigned to a Russian factory manager by the state planning agency
    c. Legislation establishing minimum wages to be paid
    d. State government directing its agencies to use local suppliers of goods and services
    e. Legislation prohibiting the sale and use of cocaine

7. Pick one of the major socialist countries that have recently introduced market-oriented reforms and discuss the "start-up" problems that the reforms encounter. Explain why you think these problems will or will not persist over the next few years.

8. Discuss the following quote of Professor Paul McCracken, a former chairman of the President's Council of Economic Advisers: "One of the mysteries of semantics is why the government-managed economies ever came to be called *planned,* and the market economies *unplanned.* It is the former that are in chronic chaos, in which buyers stand in line hoping to buy some toilet paper or soap. It is the latter that are in reasonable equilibrium—where if you want a cake of soap or a steak or a shirt or a car, you can go to the store and find that the item is magically there for you to buy. It is the liberal economies that reflect a highly sophisticated planning system, and the government-managed economies that are primitive and unplanned."

Chapter 2

Economics as a Social Science

Economics is generally regarded as a social science. What exactly does it mean to be scientific? Can economics ever hope to be "scientific" in its study of those aspects of human behavior with which it is concerned?

The Distinction Between Positive and Normative

The success of modern science rests partly on the ability of scientists to separate their views on *what does happen* from their views on *what they would like to happen.* For example, until the nineteenth century most people in the Western world believed that the earth was only a few thousand years old. About 200 years ago evidence that some existing rocks were millions or even billions of years old began to accumulate. Most people found this hard to accept: It forced them to rethink their religious beliefs. Many people wanted the evidence to be wrong; they wanted rocks to be only a few thousand years old. Nevertheless, the evidence accumulated until today most people accept the belief that the earth is neither thousands, nor millions, but 4 or 5 billion years old.

This advance in our knowledge came because the question "How old are observable rocks?" could be separated from the feelings of scientists (many of them devoutly religious) about the age they would have liked the rocks to be. Distinguishing what *is* true from what we would *like* to be true depends on recognizing the difference between positive and normative statements.

Positive statements concern what is, was, or will be. **Normative statements** concern what one believes ought to be. Positive statements, assertions, or theories may be simple or complex, but they are basically about matters of fact.

Disagreements over positive statements are appropriately handled by an appeal to the facts.

Normative statements, because they concern what ought to be, are inextricably bound up with philosophical, cultural, and religious systems. A normative statement is one that makes, or is based on, a *value judgment*—a judgment about what is good and what is bad.

Disagreements over normative statements cannot be handled merely by an appeal to facts.

Some related issues about disagreements among economists are discussed in Box 2-1.

BOX 2-1

Why Economists Disagree

If you listen to a discussion among economists on "Meet the Press" or "The MacNeil/Lehrer News Hour," or if you read about their debates in the daily press or weekly magazines, you will find economists constantly disagreeing among themselves. Why do economists disagree, and what should we make of this fact?

In a recent column in *Newsweek,* Charles Wolf, Jr., suggests four reasons for the disagreement among economists: (1) Different economists use different benchmarks (inflation is *down* compared with last year, but *up* compared with the 1950s); (2) Economists fail to make it clear to their listeners whether they are talking about short-term or long-term consequences (tax cuts will stimulate consumption in the short run and investment in the long run); (3) Economists often fail to acknowledge the full extent of their ignorance; (4) Different economists have different values, and these normative views play a large part in their public discussions.

There is surely some truth in each of these assessments, but there is also a fifth reason: the public's *demand for disagreement.* For example, suppose that all economists were in fact agreed on the proposition that unions are not a major cause of inflation. This view would be unpalatable to some individuals. Those who are hostile to unions, for instance, would like to blame inflation on them and would be looking for an intellectual champion. Fame and fortune would await the economist who espoused their cause, and a champion would soon be found.

Disagreement will always exist. It is also true that any disagreement that does exist will likely get exaggerated by the media. This is not necessarily intentional; it happens because of the nature of reporting. When the media cover an issue, they naturally wish to give both sides of it. Normally, the public will hear one or two economists on each side of a debate, regardless of whether the profession is divided right down the middle or is nearly unanimous in its support of one side. Thus, the public will not know that in one case a reporter could have chosen from dozens of economists to present each side, while in another case the reporter had to spend three days trying to locate someone willing to take a particular side because nearly all the economists contacted thought it was wrong. On many issues, the profession overwhelmingly supports one side. In their desire to show both sides of the case, however, the media present the public with the appearance of a profession equally split over all matters.

Thus, anyone seeking to discredit some particular economist's advice by showing that there is disagreement among economists will have no trouble finding evidence to support his or her case. But those who wish to know if there is a majority view or even a strong consensus will find one on a surprisingly large number of issues, such as the housing shortages caused by rent control laws and the unemployment caused by minimum wage laws. Of course, there are disagreements among economists on many issues, especially those that involve recent and incompletely understood events, and there will always be controversies at the frontiers of current research.

The Distinction Illustrated

The statement "It is impossible to break up atoms" is a positive statement that can quite definitely be (and of course has been) refuted by empirical observations, while the statement "Scientists ought not to break up atoms" is a normative statement that involves ethical judgments. The questions "What government policies will reduce unemployment?" and "What policies will prevent inflation?" are positive ones, while the question "Ought we to be more concerned about unemployment than about inflation?" is a normative one.

The Importance of the Distinction

If we think something ought to be done, we can deduce other things that, if we wish to be consistent, ought to be done, but we can deduce nothing about what is done (i.e., about what is true). Similarly, if we know that two things are true, we can deduce other things that must be true, but we can deduce nothing about what is desirable (i.e., about what *ought* to be).

It is logically impossible to deduce normative statements from only positive statements or positive statements from only normative ones.

Positive statements assert things about the world. If it is possible for a statement to be proved wrong by empirical evidence, we call it a *testable statement*. Many positive statements are testable, and disagreements over them are appropriately handled by an appeal to the facts.

In contrast to positive statements, normative statements are never testable. Disagreements over such normative statements as "It is wrong to steal" or "It is immoral to have sexual relations out of wedlock" cannot be settled by an appeal to empirical observations. Thus, for a rational consideration of normative questions, different techniques are needed from those used for a rational consideration of positive questions. Because of this, it is convenient to separate normative and positive inquiries. We do this not because we think the former are less important than the latter, but merely because they must be handled in different ways.

As an example of the importance of this distinction, consider the question "Has the payment of generous unemployment benefits increased the amount of unemployment?" This positive question can be turned into a testable hypothesis such as "The higher the benefits paid to the unemployed, the higher will be the total amount of unemployment." If we are not careful, however, our attitudes and value judgments may get in the way of our study of this hypothesis. Some people are opposed to the welfare state and believe in an individualist, self-help ethic. They may hope that the hypothesis is correct because its truth then could be used as an argument against welfare measures in general. Others feel that the welfare state is a good thing, reducing misery and contributing to human dignity. They may hope that the

hypothesis is wrong because they do not want any welfare measures to come under attack. In spite of different value judgments and social attitudes, however, evidence is accumulating on this particular hypothesis. As a result, we have more knowledge than we had 10 years ago of why and by how much unemployment benefits increase unemployment. This evidence could never have been accumulated or accepted if investigators had not been able to distinguish their feelings about how they wanted the answer to turn out from their assessment of evidence on how people actually behaved.

The distinction between positive and normative statements allows us to keep our views on how we would like the world to work separate from our views on how the world actually does work. We may be interested in both. It can only obscure the truth, however, if we let our views on what we would like to be bias our investigations of what actually is. It is for this reason that the separation of positive from normative statements is one of the foundation stones of science and that scientific inquiry, as it is normally understood, is usually confined to positive questions. Some important limitations on the distinction between positive and normative are discussed in Box 2-2.

Positive and Normative Statements in Economics

Economics, like other sciences, is concerned with questions, statements, and hypotheses that could conceivably be shown to be false by actual observations of the world. It is not necessary to show them to be either consistent or inconsistent with the facts tomorrow or the next day; it is only necessary to be able to imagine evidence that could show them to be false. Normative questions cannot be settled by a mere appeal to facts. Of course, this does not mean that they are unimportant. Such questions as "Should we subsidize higher education?" and "Should we send food to Afghanistan?" must still be decided somehow. In democracies, such questions are sometimes settled by voting.

Economists need not confine their discussions to positive, testable statements. Economists can usefully hold and discuss value judgments as long as they do not confuse such judgments with evaluations of testable statements.

Indeed, the pursuit of what appears to be a nor-

BOX 2-2

Limits on the Positive-Normative Distinction

While the distinction between positive and normative statements is useful, it has a number of limitations.

The classification is not exhaustive. The classifications *positive* and *normative* do not cover all statements that can be made. For example, there is an important class, called *analytic statements,* whose validity depends only on the rules of logic. Thus, the sentence "If all humans are immortal and if you are a human, then you are immortal" is a valid analytic statement. It tells us that *if* two things are true, *then* a third thing must be true. The validity of this statement is not dependent on whether or not its individual parts are in fact true. Indeed the sentence "All humans are immortal" is a positive statement that has been decisively refuted. Yet no amount of empirical evidence on the mortality of humans can upset the truth of the "if-then" sentence quoted above. Analytic statements—which proceed by logical analysis—play an important role in scientific work and form the basis for much of our ability to theorize.

Not all positive statements are testable. A positive statement asserts something about the universe. It may be empirically true or false in the sense that what it asserts may or may not be true of the universe. If it is true, it adds to our knowledge of what can and cannot happen. Many positive statements are refutable: If they are wrong this can be

ascertained (within a margin for error of observation) by checking them against data. For example, the positive statement that the earth is less than 5,000 years old was tested and refuted by a mass of evidence accumulated in the nineteenth century.

The statement "Extraterrestrials exist and frequently visit the earth in visible form" is also a positive statement. It asserts something about the universe, but we could never refute this statement with evidence because, no matter how hard we searched, believers could argue that we did not look in the right places or in the right way, or that E.T.s do not reveal themselves to nonbelievers, or any one of a host of other alibis. Thus, some positive statements are irrefutable.

The distinction is not unerringly applied. Because the positive-normative distinction helps the advancement of knowledge, it does not follow that all scientists automatically and unerringly apply it. Scientists are human beings. Many have strongly held values, and they may let their value judgments get in the way of their assessment of evidence. Nonetheless, the desire to separate what is from what we would like to be is a guiding light, an ideal, of science. The ability to do so, albeit imperfectly, is attested to by the acceptance, first by scientists and then by the general public, of many ideas that were initially extremely unpalatable—ideas such as the age of the earth and the theory of evolution.

mative statement will often turn up positive hypotheses on which the *ought* conclusion depends. For example, there are probably relatively few people who believe that government control of industry is in itself good or bad. Their advocacy or opposition will be based on beliefs that can be stated as positive rather than normative hypotheses; for example, "Government control reduces efficiency, changes the distribution of income, and leads to an increase of

state control in other spheres." A careful study of this subject would reveal enough positive economic questions to keep a research team of economists occupied for many years.

The Scientific Approach

An important aspect of the scientific approach consists of relating questions to evidence. When presented with a controversial issue, scientists will look for all relevant evidence. If they find that the issue is framed in terms that make it impossible to gather evidence for or against it, they will then usually try to recast the question so that it can be answered by an appeal to evidence.

In some fields scientists are able to generate observations that will provide evidence against which to test their hypotheses. Experimental sciences such as chemistry and some branches of psychology have an advantage because it is possible for them to produce relevant evidence through controlled laboratory experiments.

Other sciences such as astronomy and economics cannot do this. They must wait for natural events to produce observations that can be used as evidence in testing their theories. The evidence that then arises does not come from laboratory conditions under which everything is held constant except the forces being studied. Instead, it arises from situations in which many things are changing at the same time, and great care is therefore needed in drawing conclusions from what is observed.

The ease or difficulty with which one can collect evidence does not determine whether a subject is scientific or nonscientific.

Later in this chapter, we shall consider some of the problems that arise when analyzing evidence that is not generated under controlled laboratory conditions. For the moment, however, we shall consider some general problems that are more or less common to all sciences and are particularly important in the social sciences.

Is Human Behavior Predictable?

Social scientists seek to understand and to predict human behavior. A scientific prediction is based on discovering stable response patterns, but are such patterns possible with anything so complex as human beings? Sometimes this question is answered "no" on the basis of the following argument. While the natural sciences deal with inanimate matter that is subject to natural laws, the social sciences deal with human beings who have free will and cannot therefore be subject to such laws.

This view implies that inanimate matter will show stable response patterns, but human beings will not. For example—so goes this argument—if you

put a match to a piece of dry paper, the paper will burn, whereas if you subject human beings to torture, some will break down and do what you want them to do and others will not. Even more confusing, the same individual may react differently to torture at different times.

Does human behavior show sufficiently stable responses to factors influencing it to be predictable within an acceptable margin of error? This is a positive question that can be settled only by an appeal to evidence and not by a priori speculation. (**A priori** may be defined as that which is prior to actual experience.) The question itself might concern either the behavior of groups or that of isolated individuals.

Group Behavior Versus Individual Behavior

There are many situations in which group behavior can be predicted accurately without certain knowledge of individual behavior. The warmer the weather, for example, the more people visit the beach and the higher the sales of ice cream. It may be hard to say if or when one individual will buy an ice cream cone, but a stable response pattern from a large group of individuals can be seen. Although social scientists cannot predict which particular individuals will be killed in auto accidents during the next holiday weekend, they can come very close to knowing the total number who will die. The more objectively measurable data they have (for example, the state of the weather on the days in question and the trend in gasoline prices), the more closely they will be able to predict total deaths.

The well-known fact that pollsters usually do a good job of predicting elections on the basis of surveys provides evidence that human attitudes do not change capriciously. If group behavior were truly capricious, there would be no point in trying to predict anything on the basis of such surveys. The fact that 80 percent of the voters who were surveyed said they intended to vote for a certain candidate would give no information about the probable outcome of the election. Today's information would commonly be reversed tomorrow.

The difference between predicting individual and group behavior is illustrated by the fact that economists can predict with fair accuracy what households as a group will do when their take-home pay is increased. Some individuals may do surprising and unpredictable things, but the total response of all households to a permanent change in tax rates that will leave more money in their hands is predictable within quite a narrow margin of error. This stability in the response of households' spending to a change in their available income is the basis of economists' ability to predict successfully the outcome of major revisions in the tax laws.

This does not mean that people never change their minds or that future events can be foretold by a casual study of the past. The stability discussed here is a stable response to causal factors (e.g., next time it gets warm, ice cream sales will rise) and not merely inertia (e.g., ice cream sales will go on rising in the future because they have risen in the past).

The "Law" of Large Numbers

Successfully predicting the behavior of large groups of people is made possible by the statistical "law" of large numbers. Broadly speaking, this law asserts that random movements of many individual items tend to offset one another. The law is based on one of the most beautiful constants of behavior in the whole of science, natural and social, and yet it can be derived from the fact that human beings make errors! The law is based on the statistical relation called the *normal curve of error*.

What is implied by this law? Ask any one person to measure the length of a room, and it will be almost impossible to predict in advance what sort of error of measurement will be made. Dozens of things will affect the accuracy of the measurement, and, furthermore, the person may make one error today and quite a different one tomorrow. But ask a thousand people to measure the length of the same room, and we can predict within a small margin just how this *group* will make its errors. We can assert with confidence that more people will make small errors than will make large errors, that the larger the error, the fewer will be the number making it, that roughly the same number of people will overstate as will understate the distance, and that the larger the number of people making the measurement, the smaller the average of their errors will tend to be.

If a common cause should act on each member of the group, the average behavior of the group can be predicted even though any one member may act in a surprising fashion. If, for example, each of the thousand individuals is given a tape measure that understates "actual" distances, it can be predicted that, on the average, the group will understate the length of the room. It is, of course, quite possible

that one member who had in the past been consistently undermeasuring distance because of psychological depression will now overmeasure the distance because the state of his health has changed, but some other event may happen to another individual that will turn her from an overmeasurer into an undermeasurer. Individuals may act strangely for inexplicable reasons, but the group's behavior, when the inaccurate tape is substituted for the accurate one, will be predictable precisely because the odd things that one individual does will tend to cancel out the odd things that some other individual does.

Irregularities in individual behavior tend to cancel one another out, and the regularities tend to show up in repeated observations.

The Nature of Scientific Theories

When some regularity between two or more things is observed, we may ask why this should be so. A *theory* is an attempt to answer this question, and by providing an explanation for the regularity, it enables us to predict as yet unobserved events. For example, national income theory predicts that a reduction in tax rates will reduce the unemployment rate. The simple theory of market behavior predicts that, under specified conditions, a partial failure of the potato crop will cause an increase in the incomes of potato farmers.

Theories are used in explaining observed phenomena. A successful theory enables us to predict behavior.

Any explanation whatsoever of how given observations are linked together is a theoretical construction. Theories are used to impose order on our observations, to explain how what we see is linked together. Without theories there would be only a shapeless mass of meaningless observations.

The choice is not between theory and observation but between better or worse theories to explain observations.

Misunderstandings about the place of theories in scientific explanation give rise to many misconceptions. One of these is illustrated by the phrase "True in theory but not in practice." The next time you hear someone say this (or, indeed, the next time you say it yourself), you should immediately reply, "All right then, tell me what does happen in practice." Usually you will not be told mere facts, but you will be given an alternative theory—a different explanation of the facts. The speaker should have said, "The theory in question provides a poor explanation of the facts (that is, it is contradicted by some factual observations). I have a different theory that does a much better job."

A theory consists of (1) a set of definitions that clearly define the *variables* to be used, (2) a set of *assumptions* that outline the conditions under which the theory is to apply, (3) one or more *hypotheses* about the relationships among the variables, and (4) *predictions* that are deduced from the assumptions of the theory and can be tested against actual empirical observations. We consider these constituents in the following four sections.

Variables

A **variable** is a magnitude that can take on different possible values. Variables are the basic elements of theories, and each one needs to be carefully defined.

Price is an example of an important economic variable. The price of a commodity is the amount of money that must be given up to purchase one unit of that commodity. To define a price, we must first define the commodity to which it is attached. Such a commodity might be one dozen grade A large eggs. The price of such eggs sold in, say, supermarkets in Fargo, North Dakota, defines a variable. The particular values taken on by that variable might be $.98 on July 1, 1988, $1.02 on July 8, 1989, and $.99 on July 15, 1990.

There are many distinctions between kinds of variables; two of the most important are discussed below.

Endogenous and exogenous variables. An **endogenous variable** is a variable that is explained within a theory. An **exogenous variable** influences endogenous variables but is itself determined by factors outside the theory.

For example, consider the theory that the price of apples in Seattle, Washington, on a particular day is a function of several things, one of which is the weather in the Yakima Valley during the previous apple-growing season. We can safely assume that the state of the weather is not determined by economic

conditions. The price of apples in this case is an endogenous variable—something determined within the framework of the theory. The state of the weather in the Yakima Valley is an exogenous variable; changes in it influence prices because the changes affect the output of apples, but the state of the weather is not influenced by the prices.

Other words are sometimes used for the same distinction. One frequently used pair is *induced* for endogenous and *autonomous* for exogenous; another is *dependent* for endogenous and *independent* for exogenous.

Stock and flow variables. A flow variable has a time dimension; it is so much per unit of time. The quantity of grade A large eggs purchased in Fargo is a flow variable. No useful information is conveyed if we are told that the number purchased was 2,000 dozen eggs unless we are also told the period of time over which these purchases occurred. Two thousand dozen per hour would indicate an active market in eggs, while 2,000 dozen per month would indicate a sluggish market.

A stock variable has no time dimension; it is just so much. Thus, the number of eggs in the egg producer's coop warehouse—for example, 20,000 dozen eggs—is a stock variable. All those eggs are there at one time, and they remain there until something happens to change the stock held by the coop. The stock variable is just a number, not a rate of flow of so much per day or per month.

Economic theories use both flow variables and stock variables, and it takes a little practice to keep them straight. The amount of income earned is a flow; there is so much per year or per month or per hour. The amount of a household's expenditure is also a flow—so much spent per week or per month. The amount of money in a bank account or a miser's hoard (earned, perhaps, in the past but unspent) is a stock—just so many thousands of dollars. The key test is always whether a time dimension is required to give the variable meaning.

Assumptions

Assumptions are essential to theorizing. Students are often greatly concerned about the justification of assumptions, particularly if they seem unrealistic.

An example will illustrate some of the issues involved in this question of realism. Much of the theory that we are going to study in this book uses the assumption that the sole motive of all those who run firms is to make as much money as they possibly can, or, as economists put it, firms are assumed to be run so as to *maximize their profits*. The assumption of profit maximization allows economists to make predictions about the behavior of firms. They study the effects that alternatives open to firms would have on profits, and then they predict that the alternative selected will be the one that produces the most profits.

Profit maximization may seem like a rather crude assumption. Surely the managers of firms sometimes have philanthropic or political motives. Does this not discredit the assumption of profit maximization by showing it to be unrealistic?

To make successful predictions, however, the theory does not require that managers are solely and always motivated by the desire to maximize profits. All that is required is that profits are a sufficiently important consideration that a theory based on the assumption of profit maximization will produce predictions that are substantially correct.

This illustration shows that it is not always appropriate to criticize a theory because its assumptions seem unrealistic. All theory is an abstraction from reality. If it were not, it would merely duplicate the world and would add nothing to our understanding of it. A good theory abstracts in a useful way; a poor theory does not. If a theory has ignored some really important factors, then its predictions will be contradicted by the evidence—at least where the factor ignored exerts an important influence on the outcome.

Now, put this way, the statement becomes an empirical assertion. The only way to test it is to see if the predictions that follow from the theory do or do not fit the facts that the theory is trying to explain. If they do, then the theorist was correct in the assumption that the government could be ignored for the particular purposes at hand. In this case the criticism that the theory is unrealistic because there really is a government is completely beside the point.

Models

Economists often speak of using *economic models* when they are developing and testing theories. The term *model* conveys the idea that we are abstracting from reality, but the term also can cause some con-

fusion, since it is used in several different ways. Typically, a model refers to an explicit statement of the definitions, assumptions, and behavioral hypotheses being used. Sometimes it refers to a rather general statement of the theory under consideration; for example, one model of consumption is that household consumption expenditure is positively related to the household's disposable income. However, sometimes the term *model* refers to a more specific case of the general theory that arises when specific values are attached to the relationships; for example, one specific model of consumption is that when the typical household's disposable income rises by $1,000, its consumption expenditures will rise by $900.

Hypotheses

Relations among variables.   The critical step in theorizing is formulating hypotheses. A hypothesis is a statement about how two or more variables are related to each other. For example, it is a basic hypothesis of economics that the quantity produced of any commodity depends upon its own price in such a way that the higher is the price, the larger is the quantity produced. To illustrate, the higher the price of eggs, the larger the quantity of eggs that the farmers will produce. Stated in more formal terms, the hypothesis is that the two variables, price of eggs and quantity of eggs, are positively related to each other.[1]

Functional relations.   A **function,** or a *functional relation,* is a formal expression of a relationship between two or more variables.[2]

The particular hypothesis that the quantity of eggs produced is related to the price of eggs is an example of a functional relation in economics. In its most general form, it merely says that quantity produced is related to price. The more specific hypothesis is that as the price of eggs rises, the quantity produced also rises.

---

[1] When two variables are related in such a way that an increase in one is associated with an increase in the other, they are said to be *positively related*. When two variables are related in such a way that an increase in one is associated with a decrease in the other, they are said to be *negatively related*.

[2] The appendix to this chapter gives a more detailed discussion of functional relations and the use of graphs in economics.

In the case of many hypotheses of this kind, economists can be even more specific about the nature of the functional relation. On the basis of detailed factual studies, economists often have a pretty good idea of by how much quantity produced will change as a result of specified changes in price; that is, they can predict magnitude as well as direction.

Predictions

A theory's predictions are the propositions that can be deduced from that theory. An example of a prediction would be a deduction that *if* firms maximize their profits, and *if* certain other assumptions and hypotheses of the theory hold true, *then* a rise in the rate of corporate tax will cause a reduction in the amount of investment that firms make in new plant and equipment. The prediction is that the rise in the tax rate will be accompanied by a fall in investment. The reasons that lie behind the prediction are contained in the assumptions and hypotheses that constitute the theory in question.

It should be apparent from this discussion that a scientific prediction is not the same thing as a prophecy.

A scientific prediction is a conditional statement that takes the form: *If you do this, then* such and such will follow.

If hydrogen and oxygen are combined under specified conditions, *then* water will be the result. *If* the government cuts taxes, *then* the rate of unemployment will decrease. It is important to realize that this second prediction is very different from the statement: "I prophesy that in two years' time there will be a large reduction in unemployment, because I believe the government will decide to cut tax rates." The government's decision to cut tax rates in two years' time will be the outcome of many influences, both economic and political. If the economist's prophecy about unemployment turns out to be wrong because in two years' time the government does not cut tax rates, then all that has been learned is that the economist is not a good guesser about the behavior of the government. However, *if* the government does cut tax rates (in two years' time or at any other time) and *then* the rate of unemployment does not decrease, a conditional scientific prediction in economic theory has been contradicted.

Testing Theories

A theory is tested by confronting its predictions with evidence. It is necessary to discover if certain events are followed by the consequences predicted by the theory. For example, is an increase in the corporate tax rate followed by a decline in business investment? (Box 2-3 gives further discussion of what can be learned from testing theories.)

Generally, theories tend to be abandoned when they are no longer useful, and theories cease to be useful when they cannot predict the consequences of actions in which one is interested better than the next best alternative. When a theory consistently fails to predict better than the available alternatives, it is either modified or replaced. Figure 2-1 summarizes the discussion of theories and their testing.

Refutation or confirmation.   The scientific approach to any issue consists in setting up a theory that will explain it and then seeing if that theory can be refuted by evidence.

The alternative to this approach is to set up a theory and then look for confirming evidence. Such an approach is hazardous because the world is sufficiently complex that *some* confirming evidence can be found for any theory, no matter how unlikely the theory may be. For example, the advocates of conspiracy theories, such as the theory that President Kennedy's assassination was a plot involving many persons and at least two gunmen, can always find some confirming evidence. The scientific way to deal with such questions is to set up the simplest theory—in this case that the president was assassinated by Lee Harvey Oswald acting alone—and then see if the evidence can refute it.

An example of the unfruitful approach of seeking confirmation is frequently seen when a leader—be he an American president or a foreign dictator—is surrounded by yes-men who only provide evidence that confirms the leader's existing views. This approach is usually a road to disaster, because the leader's decisions become more and more out of touch with reality.

A wise leader adopts a scientific approach instinctively, constantly checking the realism of accepted views by encouraging subordinates to criticize them. This tests how far the leader's existing views correspond to all available evidence and encourages

BOX 2-3

Can Hypotheses Be Proved or Refuted?

Most hypotheses in economics are universal. They say that whenever certain specified conditions are fulfilled, cause X will always produce effect Y. Such universal hypotheses cannot be proved correct with certainty. No matter how many observations are collected that agree with the hypothesis, there is always some chance that a long series of untypical observations has been made or that there have been systematic errors of observation. After all, the mass of well-documented evidence accumulated several centuries ago on the existence of the power of witches is no longer accepted, even though it fully satisfied most contemporary observers. The existence of observational errors, even on a vast scale, has been shown to be possible, although (one fervently hopes) it is not very frequent. Observations that disagree with the theory may begin to accumulate, and after some time a theory that looked nearly certain may begin to look rather shaky.

By the same token, a universal hypothesis can never be proved false with certainty. Even when current observations consistently conflict with the theory, it is still possible that a large number of untypical cases has been selected or systematic errors of observation have been made. For instance,

evidence was once gathered "disproving" the theory that high income taxes tend to discourage work. More recent research suggests that economists may have been wrong to reject this theory. As a result of measurement errors and bad experimental design, the conflicting evidence may not have been as decisive as was once thought.

There is no absolute certainty in any knowledge. No doubt some of the things we now think are true will eventually turn out to be false, and some of the things we currently think are false will eventually turn out to be true. Yet while we can never be certain, we can assess the balance of evidence. Some hypotheses are so unlikely to be true, given current evidence, that for all practical purposes we may regard them as false. Other hypotheses are so unlikely to be false, given current evidence, that for all practical purposes we may regard them as true. This kind of practical decision must always be regarded as tentative. Every once in a while we will find that we have to change our mind: Something that looked right will begin to look doubtful, or something that looked wrong will begin to look possible.

---

amendment in the light of evidence that conflicts with the current views.

Measurement and Testing of Economic Relations

It is one thing for economists to theorize that two or more variables are related to each other; it is quite another for them to be able to say how these variables are related. Economists might generalize on the basis of a casual observation that when households receive more income, they are likely to buy more of most commodities. But precisely how much will the consumption of a particular commodity rise as house-

hold incomes rise? Are there exceptions to the rule that the purchase of a commodity rises as income rises? For estimating precise magnitudes and for testing general rules or hypotheses, common sense, intuition, and casual observation do not take us very far. More systematic statistical analysis is required.

Statistical analysis is used to test the hypothesis that two things are related and to estimate the numerical values of the function that describes the relation.

In practice, the same data can be used simultaneously to test whether a relationship exists and, when it does exist, to provide a measure of it.

We have seen that economics is a nonlaboratory

FIGURE 2-1   The Interaction of Deduction and Measurement in Theorizing

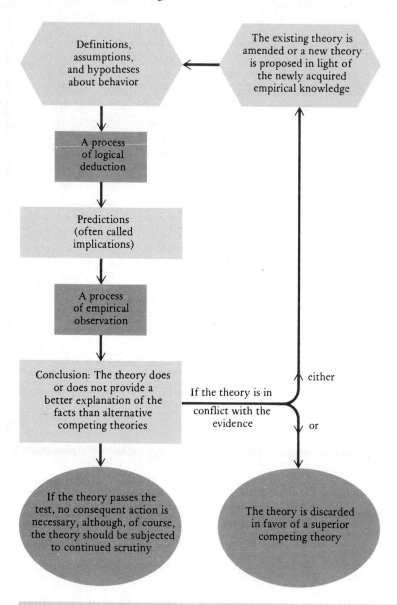

Definitions, assumptions, and hypotheses about behavior

↓

A process of logical deduction

↓

Predictions (often called implications)

↓

A process of empirical observation

↓

Conclusion: The theory does or does not provide a better explanation of the facts than alternative competing theories

↓

If the theory passes the test, no consequent action is necessary, although, of course, the theory should be subjected to continued scrutiny

The existing theory is amended or a new theory is proposed in light of the newly acquired empirical knowledge

If the theory is in conflict with the evidence

either

or

The theory is discarded in favor of a superior competing theory

Theory and observation are in continuous interaction. Starting (at the top left) with the assumptions of a theory and the definitions of relevant terms, the theorist deduces by logical analysis everything that is implied by the assumptions. These implications are the predictions of the theory. The theory is then tested by confronting its predictions with evidence. If the theory is in conflict with facts, it will usually be amended to make it consistent with those facts (thereby making it a better theory); in extreme cases it will be discarded, to be replaced by a superior alternative. The process then begins again: The new or amended theory is subjected first to logical analysis and then to empirical testing.

science. It is rarely possible to conduct controlled experiments with the economy. However, millions of uncontrolled experiments are going on every day. Households are deciding what to purchase given changing prices and incomes; firms are deciding what to produce and how to produce it; and the government is involved in the economy through its various taxes, subsidies, and controls. Because all these activities can be observed and recorded, a mass of data is continually produced by the economy.

The variables that interest economists, such as the volume of unemployment, the price of wheat, and the share of income going to wage earners, are generally influenced by many factors, all of which vary simultaneously. If economists are to test their theories about relations among variables in the economy, they must use statistical techniques designed for situations in which other things cannot be held constant.

An Example of Statistical Testing

To illustrate how data may be used to test theories even while other things are not held constant, we take the very simple and intuitively plausible hypothesis that the federal income taxes paid by American families increase as their incomes increase.

A Sample

To begin with, observations must be made of family income and tax payments. It is not practical to do so for all American families, so a small number (called a *sample*) is studied on the assumption that these households are typical of the entire group.

It is important that the sample be what is called a random sample. A **random sample** is chosen according to a rigidly defined set of conditions guaranteeing, among other things, that every member of the group from which we are selecting the sample has an equal chance of being selected. Choosing the sample in a random fashion has two important consequences.

First, it reduces the chance that the sample will be unrepresentative of the population from which it is selected. Second, and more important, it allows us to calculate just how likely it is that the sample will be unrepresentative by any specified amount. For example, if the average amount of income tax paid by the households in our sample is $2,000, then it is most likely that the average tax paid by all American households is in the vicinity of $2,000. But that is not necessarily so. The sample might be so unrepresentative that the actual figure for average tax paid by all American households is only $1,500, or it might be $2,750. If the sample is random, we are able to calculate the probability that the actual data for the whole population differs from the data in our sample by any stated amount.

The reason for the predictability of random samples is that such samples are chosen by chance, and chance events are predictable.

That chance events are predictable may sound surprising, but consider these questions. If you pick a card from a deck of ordinary playing cards, how likely is it that you will pick a heart? An ace? An ace of hearts? You play a game in which you pick a card and win if it is a heart and lose if it is anything else; a friend offers you $5 if you win against $1 if you lose. Who will make money if the game is played a large number of times? The same game is played again, but now you get $3 if you win and pay $1 if you lose. Who will make money over a large number of draws? If you can answer these questions (we will bet that most of you can), you must believe that chance events are in some sense predictable.

To test the hypothesis about taxes, we have chosen a random sample of 212 families from data collected by the Survey Research Center of the University of Michigan. For each family we record its income and the federal income tax it pays.

Graphical and Tabular Analysis

There are several ways in which the data may be used to evaluate the hypothesis.

Scatter diagram. One is the **scatter diagram**, which plots paired values of two variables.[3] Figure 2-2 is a scatter diagram that relates family income to federal income tax payments. The pattern of the dots suggests that there is a strong tendency for tax payments to be higher when family income is higher. It thus supports the hypothesis.

There is some scattering of the dots because the relationship is not "perfect"; in other words, there is some variation in tax payments that cannot be associated with variations in family income. These variations in tax payments occur mainly for two reasons. First, factors other than income influence tax payments, and some of these other factors will undoubtedly have varied among the families in the sample. Second, inevitably there will be some errors in measurement. For example, a family might have incorrectly reported its tax payments to the person who collected our data.

---

[3] The second half of the appendix to this chapter outlines the elements of graphs and the graphical analysis of economic data. If you find graphical analysis baffling, you might read this appendix now.

FIGURE 2-2   A Scatter Diagram Relating Taxes Paid to Family Income

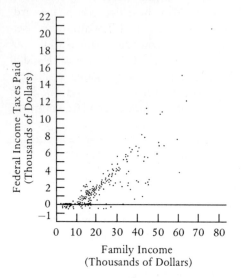

The scatter pattern shows a clear tendency for taxes paid to rise with family income. Family income is measured along the horizontal axis, and federal income taxes paid are measured along the vertical axis. Each dot represents a single family in the sample and is located on the graph according to the family's income and taxes paid. The dots fall mainly within a narrow, rising band, suggesting the existence of a systematic relationship between income and taxes paid, but they do not fall along a single line, which suggests that things other than family income affect taxes paid. The data are for 1979. (Negative amounts of tax liability arise because of such things as capital losses that may be carried forward.)

Cross-classification table. A cross-classification table provides another way to examine the hypothesis that tax payments vary directly with income. Table 2-1 cross-classifies families by their incomes and their average tax payments. At the loss of considerable detail, the table makes clear the general tendency for tax payments to rise as income rises.

Regression Analysis

While both the scatter diagram and the cross-classification table reflect the general relationship between federal income tax payments and family income, neither characterizes what the precise relationship is.

TABLE 2-1   Federal Tax Payments Cross-Classified by Family Income

Annual family income	Average income tax payment	Number of families
Less than $10,000	$ 70	38
$ 10,000–19,999	893	76
20,000–29,999	2,470	42
30,000–39,999	4,205	28
40,000–99,999	7,755	28
100,000 or more	—	None

Tax payments tend to increase as family income increases. The data on 212 families are grouped into the income classes shown in the first column. The average tax payment for families in each income group is calculated and listed in the second column. When we read down this second column, we find an unbroken rise in tax payments. This cross-classification reduces 212 individual observations to a mere 5. More (or less) detail could have been preserved by varying the size of the income classes used in the first column.

Regression analysis, a widely used technique, provides a quantitative measure of the systematic relationship between two or more variables and of how closely that relationship holds.[4] It employs a **regression equation** that represents the best estimate of the *average* relationship between the variables being tested. The equation can be used in this case to describe the tendency for higher family income to be associated with higher tax payments.[5]

A measure of how closely the relationship holds can be obtained by calculating the percentage of the variance in federal tax payments that can be accounted for by variations in household income.[6] This measure is called the **coefficient of determination** (r^2). For our sample $r^2 = 0.734$. This number tells us that in this case 73.4 percent of the variance in tax payments can be "explained" by associating it with variations in family incomes.

---

[4] The detailed discussion of techniques and conditions that must hold for the technique to be valid is left to courses in statistics and econometrics.

[5] The equation of a straight line fitted to the data shown in Figure 2-2 is $T = -1,924 + 0.19Y$, where T is taxes paid and Y is income in thousands of dollars per year. The equation shows that for every increase of $1,000 in family income, taxes paid tend to increase by $190.

[6] *Variance* is a precise statistical measure of the amount of variability (dispersion) in a set of data.

A *significance test* can be applied to determine the odds that the relation discovered in the sample does not exist for the whole population but has arisen by chance because the families selected happen not to be representative of the entire set of American families. It turns out that in this example there is less than one chance in a million that the rising pattern of dots shown in Figure 2-2 would have been observed if there were no positive association between income and tax payments for U.S. families. We conclude, with less than one chance in a million of being wrong, that the hypothesis that tax payments and family income are positively related is correct. Statistically, the relationship is said to be *significant*.

Extending the Analysis to Three Variables

The scatter diagram and the regression equation show that *all* the variations in income tax payments cannot be accounted for by observed variations in family income. If it could, all the dots would lie on a line, and r^2 would equal 1.0. Since they do not, some other factors must influence tax payments. Why might one family with an income of $12,000 pay 20 percent more in income taxes than another family with the same income?

One reason is difference in family size, for American tax laws provide exemptions based on the number of family members. (There will be other reasons too, such as differences in itemized deductions for medical expenses or charitable donations.) We anticipate that family size will be an important second reason. The survey also collected data on family size, which we now use.

There are now *three* observations for each of the 212 families: annual income, federal income tax payments, and family size. How should these data be handled? The scatter diagram technique is not available because the relationship among three sets of data cannot conveniently be shown on a two-dimensional graph.

The data may, however, be classified into groups once again. This time we are testing two variables that are thought to influence tax payments, and the data have to be cross-classified in a more complicated manner, as shown in Table 2-2.

The table can be used to hold one variable roughly constant while allowing another to vary. Reading across each row, we see that income is held constant within a specified range and family size is

TABLE 2-2 Federal Tax Payments Cross-Classified by Family Income and Family Size

Annual family income	Number of family members		
	3 or less	4 or 5	6 or more
$ 0–9,999	$ 175	$ 142	$ 26
10,000–19,999	1,028	995	507
20,000–29,999	2,950	2,491	935
30,000–39,999	5,349	3,802	2,372
40,000–99,999	9,459	8,624	4,193
100,000 or more	None in the sample		

Tax payments tend to vary positively with family income and negatively with family size. Each row in the table shows the effect of family size on tax payments for a given level of income. For example, reading across the second row, we see that families with incomes between $10,000 and $19,999 paid an average of $1,028 if the family had less than 4 members, $995 if the family had 4 or 5 members, and $507 if the family had 6 or more members. The declining numbers across each row show that for each income group tax payments tend to decline as family size increases. Each column in the table shows the effect of income on tax payments for a given family size. The increase in taxes paid as we move down each column shows that tax payments increase with family income.

varied; reading down each column, we see that size of family is held constant within a specified range and income is varied.

To estimate a numerical relation among family income, family size, and tax payments, *multiple regression analysis* is used.[7] This type of analysis allows estimation of both the separate and the joint effects on tax payments of variations in family size and variations in income by fitting to the data an equation that "best" describes them. It also permits the measurement of the proportion of the total variation in tax payments that can be explained by associating it with variations in both income and family size. Finally, it permits the use of significance tests to determine how likely it is that the relationships found in

[7] Details must be left to a course in statistics. The regression equation for our example is $T = -733 + 0.197Y - 344F$, where F is the number of family members. On average, an additional family member decreases taxes paid by $344. R^2, the coefficient of determination in multiple regression analysis, is 0.774. Comparison with the previous $r^2 = 0.734$ shows that adding family size to the analysis increased the percentage of variance explained from 73.4 percent to 77.4 percent.

the sample are the result of chance and thus do not reflect a similar relationship for all U.S. families. Chance plays a role, because by bad luck an unrepresentative sample of families might have been chosen.

The Decision to Reject or Accept

In general, a hypothesis can never be proven or refuted with absolute certainty, no matter how many observations are made. Those who are interested in pursuing this matter will find further discussion of it in Box 2-3.

Although we can never be certain about a hypothesis, we do have to make decisions. To do so it is necessary to accept some hypotheses (to act as if they were proven) and reject some hypotheses (to act as if they were refuted). Just as a jury can make two kinds of errors (finding an innocent person guilty or letting a guilty person go free), so can statistical decision makers make two kinds of errors. They can reject hypotheses that are true, and they can accept hypotheses that are false. Luckily, like a jury, they can also make correct decisions—and indeed they expect to do so most of the time.

Although the possibility of error cannot be eliminated in statistics, it can be controlled.

The method of control is to decide in advance how large a risk to take of accepting a hypothesis that is in fact false.[8] Conventionally in statistics this risk is often set at 5 percent or 1 percent. When the 5 percent cutoff point is used, we will accept the

hypothesis if the results that appear to establish it could have happened by chance no more than 1 time in 20. Using the 1 percent decision rule gives the hypothesis a more difficult test. A hypothesis is accepted only if the results that appear to establish it could have happened by chance no more than 1 time in 100.

Consider the hypothesis that a certain coin is "loaded," favoring heads over tails. The coin is flipped 100 times and comes up heads 53 times. This result is not inconsistent with the hypothesis because such an unbalanced result could happen by chance more than 22 percent of the time. Thus the hypothesis of a head-biased coin would not be accepted using either a 1 percent or a 5 percent cutoff. Had the experiment produced 65 heads and 35 tails, a result that would occur by chance less than 1 percent of the time, we would (given a 1 percent or a 5 percent cutoff) accept the hypothesis of a loaded coin.[9]

When action must be taken, some rule of thumb is necessary, but it is important to understand, first, that no one can ever be certain about being right in rejecting any hypothesis and, second, that there is nothing magical about arbitrary cutoff points. Some cutoff point must be used whenever decisions have to be made.

Finally, recall that the rejection of a hypothesis is seldom the end of inquiry. Decisions can be reversed should new evidence come to light. Often the result of a statistical test of a theory is to suggest a new hypothesis that "fits the facts" better than the old one. Indeed, in some cases just looking at a scatter diagram or making a regression analysis uncovers apparent relationships that no one anticipated and leads economists to formulate a new hypothesis.

[8] Return to the jury analogy: Our notion of a person's being innocent unless the jury is persuaded of guilt "beyond a reasonable doubt" rests on our wishing to take only a small risk of accepting the hypothesis of guilt if the person being tried is in fact innocent.

[9] The actual statistical testing process is more complex than this example suggests but must be left to a course in statistics.

SUMMARY

1. It is possible, and fruitful, to distinguish between positive and normative statements. Positive statements concern what is, was, or will be, while normative statements concern what ought to be. Disagreements over positive, testable statements are appropriately settled by an appeal to the facts. Disagreements over normative statements can never be settled in this way.
2. The success of scientific inquiry depends on separating positive questions about the way the world works from normative questions about how one would like the world to work, formulating positive questions precisely enough so that they can be settled by an appeal to evidence, and then finding means of gathering the necessary evidence.

3. Some people feel that although natural phenomena can be subject to scientific inquiry and "laws" of behavior, human phenomena cannot. The evidence, however, is otherwise. Social scientists have observed many stable human behavior patterns. These form the basis for successful predictions of how people will behave under certain conditions.

4. The fact that people sometimes act strangely, even capriciously, does not destroy the possibility of scientific study of group behavior. The odd and inexplicable things that one person does will tend to cancel out the odd and inexplicable things that another person does.

5. Theories are designed to give meaning and coherence to observed sequences of events. A theory consists of a set of definitions of the variables to be employed, a set of assumptions under which the theory is meant to apply, and a set of hypotheses about how things behave. Any theory has certain logical implications that must be true if the theory is true. These are the theory's predictions.

6. A theory provides predictions of the type "*if* one event occurs, *then* another event will also occur." An important method of testing theories is to confront their predictions with evidence. The progress of any science lies in finding better explanations of events than are now available. Thus, in any developing science, one must expect to discard present theories and replace them with demonstrably superior alternatives.

7. Theories are tested by checking their predictions against evidence. In some sciences these tests can be conducted under laboratory conditions where only one thing changes at a time. In other sciences testing must be done using the data produced by the world of ordinary events. Modern statistical analysis is designed to test hypotheses when many variables are changing at once.

8. Sample data are often used in testing economic theories. If the sample is random, the probability that the measured characteristics of the sample will be misleading (because of the unlucky choice of an unrepresentative sample) can be calculated.

9. Scatter diagrams or simple cross-classification tables are devices for discovering systematic relationships between two variables. Regression analysis permits more specific measurement of the relationship: what it is, how closely it holds, and whether or not it is "significant."

10. Hypotheses involving several variables require more sophisticated statistical techniques, such as the use of complex cross-classification tables and multiple regression analysis. These techniques attempt to identify the separate and joint effects of several variables on one another.

TOPICS FOR REVIEW

Positive and normative statements
Testable statements
The law of large numbers and the predictability of human behavior
Variables, assumptions, and predictions in theorizing
Functional relationships
Prediction versus prophecy
Measurement and testing
Scatter diagrams
Cross-classification tables
Rejection and acceptance of hypotheses

DISCUSSION QUESTIONS

1. A baby doesn't "know" of the theory of gravity, yet in walking and eating the child soon begins to use its principles. Distinguish between behavior and the explanation of behavior. Does a business executive or a farmer have to understand economic theory to behave in a pattern consistent with economic theory?

2. "If human behavior were completely capricious and unpredictable, life insurance could not be a profitable business." Explain. Can you think of any businesses that do *not* depend on predictable human behavior?

3. Write five statements about inflation. (It does not matter whether the statements are correct, but you should confine yourself to those you think might be correct.) Classify each statement as positive or normative. If your list contains only one type of statement, try to add a sixth statement of the other type.

4. Each of the following unrealistic assumptions is sometimes made. See if you can visualize situations in which each of them might be useful.
   a. The earth is flat.
   b. There are no differences between men and women.
   c. There is no tomorrow.
   d. People are wholly selfish.

5. "The following theory of wage determination proceeds on the assumption that labor unions do not exist." Of what use can such a theory be in the United States today?

6. What may at first appear to be untestable statements can often be reworded so that they can be tested by an appeal to evidence. How might you do that with respect to each of the following assertions?
   a. The American economic system is the best in the world.
   b. The provision of free medical care for more and more people will inevitably end in socialized medicine for all, and socialized medicine will destroy our standards of medical practice by destroying the doctor's incentive to do his or her job well.
   c. Robotics ought to be outlawed, because it will destroy the future of the working classes.
   d. Inflation is eroding the standard of living of the American worker and undermining the integrity of the family.

7. Since the data used in Figure 2-2 were collected, federal tax laws have changed, lowering the tax rates that apply to higher incomes. How would you expect this development to change a scatter diagram of income and tax payments? Would you expect it to change the regression results? Do these changes lead you to reject the conclusions of the analysis of the data given in the text?

8. There are hundreds of eyewitnesses to the existence of flying saucers and other UFOs. There are films and eyewitness accounts of Nessie, the Loch Ness monster. Are you persuaded of their existence? If not, what would it take to persuade you? If so, what would it take to make you change your mind?

9. Relate the role of the law of large numbers to the statistical idea that one can test hypotheses by using average relationships based on random samples.

10. A classic example of biased sampling was the attempt made by the *Literary Digest* in 1936 to predict the result of the presidential election. The magazine forecast a substantial Republican victory, and its subsequent demise has been attributed to this error. (Franklin D.

Roosevelt won every state but Maine and Vermont from Republican Alfred Landon, and the political platitude "As Maine goes, so goes the nation" was reworded to "As Maine goes, so goes Vermont.") The *Literary Digest* poll was based on a random sample of names in telephone directories. Can you spot a potential flaw in this sample? Remember that this happened in 1936. Would the same bias have existed if the survey had been made in 1988? By 1948 the selection of the sample was much more sophisticated, but the Roper polls predicted Dewey over Truman by such a substantial margin that polling was discontinued after September 30. Truman won the election. What was the nature of the sampling error this time?

Appendix to Chapter 2

Expressing and Graphing Relations Among Variables

The idea of relations among variables is one of the basic notions behind all science. Many such relations are found in economics.

Expressing Relations: Correspondences and Functions

When mathematicians want to say that there is a relation between two variables, let us call them X and Y, they say that there is a correspondence between them. When the relation is such that for every value of X there is one and only one value of Y, mathematicians say that Y is a function of X. In what follows we confine ourselves to the subclass of correspondences that are functions.

Consider two examples, one from a natural science and one from economics. The gravitational attraction of two bodies depends on their mass and on the distance separating them, attraction increasing with size and diminishing with distance; the amount of a commodity that people would like to buy depends on (among other things) the price of the commodity, purchases increasing as price falls. Thus, gravitational attraction is a function of the mass of the two bodies concerned and the distance between them, and the quantity of a product demanded is a function of the price of the product.

One of the virtues of mathematics is that it permits the concise expression of ideas that would otherwise require long, drawn-out verbal statements. There are two steps in giving compact symbolic expression to functional relations. First, each variable is given a symbol. Second, a symbol is designated to express the idea of one variable's dependence on another. Thus, if G equals gravitational attraction, M equals the mass of two bodies, and d equals the distance between the two bodies, we may write

$$G = f(M, d)$$

where f is read "is a function of" and means "is uniquely related to." The whole equation states a hypothesis and is read "gravitational attraction is a function of the mass of the two bodies concerned and the distance between them." The same hypothesis can be written as

$$G = G(M, d)$$

This is read in exactly the same way and means the same thing as the previous expression. Instead of using f to represent "a function of," the left-hand symbol, G, is repeated.[1]

The hypothesis about desired purchases and price can be written

$$q = f(p)$$

or

$$q = q(p)$$

where q stands for the quantity people wish to purchase of some commodity and p is the price of the commodity. The expression says that the quantity of some commodity that people desire to purchase is a function of its price. The alternative way of writing this merely uses a different letter to stand for the same functional relationship between p and q.

Functional Forms: Precise Relationships Among Variables

The expression $Y = Y(X)$ merely states that the variables Y and X are related; it says nothing about the form that this relationship takes. Usually the hypothesis to be expressed says more than that. Does Y increase as X increases? Does Y decrease as X

---

[1] Any convenient symbol may be used on the right-hand side before the parenthesis to mean "a function of." The repetition of the left-hand symbol may be convenient in reminding us of what is a function of what.

increases? Or is the relationship more complicated? Take a very simple example, where Y is the length of a board in feet, and X is the length of the same board in yards. Quite clearly, $Y = Y(X)$. Further, in this case the exact form of the function is known, for length in feet (Y) is exactly three times the length in yards (X), so we may write $Y = 3X$.

This relationship is a definitional one, for the length of something measured in feet is defined to be three times its length measured in yards. It is nonetheless useful to have a way of writing relationships that are definitionally true. The expression $Y = 3X$ specifies the exact form of the relationship between Y and X and provides a rule whereby, if we have the value of one, we can calculate the value of the other.

Now consider a second example. Let C stand for consumption expenditure, the total amount spent on purchasing goods and services by all American households during a year. Let Y_d stand for the total amount of income that these households had available to spend during the year. We might state the hypothesis that

$C = f(Y_d)$

and, even more specifically,

$C = 0.8Y_d$

The first expression gives the hypothesis that the total consumption expenditure of households depends on their income. The second expression says, more specifically, that total consumption expenditure is 80 percent of the total available for spending. The second equation expresses a specific hypothesis about the relationship between two observable magnitudes. There is no reason why it *must* be true; it may be consistent or inconsistent with the facts. This is a matter for testing. However, the equation is a concise statement of a particular hypothesis.

Thus, the general view that there is a functional relationship between Y and X is denoted by $Y = f(X)$, whereas any precise relationship is expressed by a particular equation such as $Y = 2X$, $Y = 4X^2$, or $Y = X + 2.0X^2 + 0.5X^3$.

If Y increases as X increases (e.g., $Y = 10 + 2X$), we say that Y is an *increasing function* of X or that Y and X *vary positively* with each other. If Y decreases as X increases (e.g., $Y = 10 - 2X$), we say that Y is a *decreasing function* of X or that Y and X *vary negatively* with each other. Y varying nega-

tively with X merely means that Y changes in the opposite direction from X.

Error Terms in Economic Hypotheses

Expressing hypotheses in the form of functions is misleading in one respect. When we say that the world behaves so that $Y = f(X)$, we do not expect that knowing X will tell us *exactly* what Y will be, only that it will tell us what Y will be *within some margin of error.*

This error in predicting Y from a knowledge of X arises for two distinct reasons. First, there may be other variables that also affect Y. When, for example, we say that the quantity of butter that people wish to purchase is a function of the price of butter, $q_b = f(p_b)$, we know that other factors will also influence this demand. A change in the price of margarine will certainly affect the demand for butter, even though the price of butter does not change. Thus we do not expect to find a perfect relationship between q_b and p_b that will allow us to predict q_b exactly from a knowledge of p_b.

Second, variables can never be measured exactly. Even if X is the only cause of Y, measurements will give various Ys corresponding to the same X. In the case of the demand for butter, errors of measurement might not be large. In other cases, errors can be substantial—as, for example, in the case of a relationship between the total consumption expenditure of all American households and their total income. The measurements of consumption and income may be subject to quite wide margins of error, and various values of consumption associated with the same measured value of income may be observed, not because consumption is varying independently of income but because the error of measurement is varying from period to period.

When we say Y is a function of X, we appear to say that Y is completely determined by X. Instead of the deterministic formulation

$Y = f(X)$

it would be more accurate to write

$Y = f(X, \epsilon)$

where ϵ, the Greek letter epsilon, represents an *error term.*[2] Such a term indicates that the observed value

[2] The relationship with the error term in it is frequently written $Y = f(X) + \epsilon$.

of Y will differ from the value predicted by the functional relationship between Y and X. Divergences will occur both because of observational errors and because of neglected variables. While economists always mean this, they usually do not say so.

The deterministic formulation is a simplification; an error term is really present in all assumed and observed functional relationships in economics.

Graphing Relationships Among Variables

The popular saying "The facts speak for themselves" is almost always wrong when there are many facts. Theories are needed to explain how facts are linked together, and summary measures are needed to assist in sorting out what it is that facts show in relation to theories. The simplest means of providing compact summaries of a large number of observations is the use of tables and graphs. Graphs play an important role in economics by representing geometrically both observed data and the correspondence among variables that are the subject of economic theory.

Because the surface of a piece of paper is two-dimensional, a graph may readily be used to represent pictorially any correspondence between two variables. Flip through this book and you will see dozens of examples. Figure 2A-1 shows generally how a coordinate graph can permit the representation of any two measurable variables.[3]

Representing Theories on Graphs

Figure 2A-2 shows a simple two-variable graph, which will be analyzed in detail in Chapter 4. For now it is sufficient to notice that the graph permits us to show the relationship between two variables, the *price* of carrots on the vertical axis and the *quantity* of carrots per month on the horizontal axis.[4] The downward-sloping curve, labeled D for a *demand curve,* shows the relationship between the price of carrots and the quantity of carrots buyers wish to purchase.

[3] Economics is often concerned only with the positive values of variables, and the graph is confined to the upper right-hand (or "positive") quadrant. Whenever a variable has a negative value, one or more of the other quadrants must be included.

[4] The choice of which variable to put on which axis is discussed in footnote 3 on page 84 and in math note [8].

FIGURE 2A-1   A Coordinate Graph

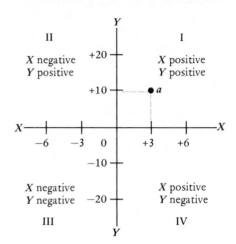

The axes divide the total space into four quadrants according to the signs of the variables. In the upper right-hand quadrant, both X and Y are greater than zero; this is usually called the *positive quadrant.* Point a has *coordinates* $Y = 10$ and $X = 3$ in the coordinate graph. These coordinates *define* point a.

Figure 2A-3 is very much like Figure 2A-2, with one difference. It generalizes from the specific example of carrots to an unspecified commodity and focuses on the slope of the demand curve rather than on specific numerical values. Note that the quantity labeled q_0 is associated with the price p_0, while the quantity q_1 is associated with the price p_1.

Straight Lines and Their Slopes

Figure 2A-4 illustrates a variety of straight lines. They differ according to their slopes. **Slope** is defined as the ratio of the vertical change to the corresponding horizontal change as one moves along a curve.

The symbol Δ is used to indicate a change in any variable. Thus ΔX means the change in X, and ΔY means the change in Y. The ratio $\Delta Y/\Delta X$ is the slope of a straight line. Where both increase or decrease together, the ratio is positive and the line slopes upward to the right, as in part (i) of Figure 2A-4. Where ΔY and ΔX have the opposite sign, that is, one increases while the other decreases, the ratio is negative

FIGURE 2A-2   The Relationship Between the Price of Carrots and the Quantity of Carrots That Purchasers Wish to Buy: A Numerical Illustration

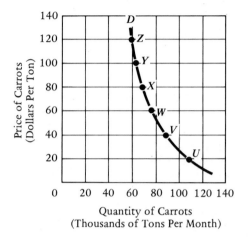

Quantity of Carrots
(Thousands of Tons Per Month)

A two-dimensional graph can show how two variables are related. The two variables, the price of carrots and the quantity that people wish to purchase, are shown by the downward-sloping curve labeled D. Particular points on the curve are labeled U through Z. For example, point Z shows that at a price of $120, the demand to purchase carrots is 60,000 tons per month.

FIGURE 2A-3   The Relationship Between the Price of a Commodity and the Quantity of the Commodity That Purchasers Wish to Buy

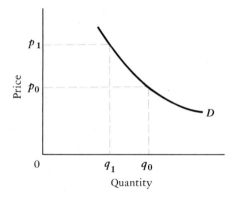

Graphs can illustrate general relationships between variables as well as between specific quantities. Here, in contrast to Figure 2A-2, price and quantity are shown as general variables. The demand curve illustrates a quantitatively unspecified *negative* relationship between price and quantity. For example, at the price p_0 the quantity that purchasers demand is q_0, while at the higher price of p_1 purchasers demand the lower quantity of q_1.

and the line slopes downward to the right, as in part (ii). Where ΔY does not change, the line is horizontal, as in part (iii), and the slope is zero. Where ΔX is zero, the line is vertical, as in part (iv), and the slope is often said to be infinite, although the ratio $\Delta Y/\Delta X$ is indeterminate. [1][5]

Slope is a quantitative measure, not merely a qualitative one. For example, in Figure 2A-5 two upward-sloping straight lines have different slopes. Line A has a slope of 2 ($\Delta Y/\Delta X = 2.0$); line B has a slope of 1/2 ($\Delta Y/\Delta X = 0.5$).

Curved Lines and Their Slopes

Figure 2A-6 shows four curved lines. The line in part (i) is plainly upward sloping and in part (ii) downward sloping. The other two change from one to the

other, as the labels indicate. Unlike straight lines, whose slope is the same at every point on the line, the slope of a curve changes. The slope of a curve must be measured at a particular point and is defined as the slope of a straight line that just touches (is tangent to) the straight line at that point. This is illustrated in Figure 2A-7. The slope at point A is measured by the slope of the tangent line a. The slope at point B is measured by the slope of the tangent line b.

Graphing Observations

A coordinate graph such as that shown in Figure 2A-1 can be used to diagram the observed values of two variables as well as the theoretical relationships between them. For example, curve D in Figure 2A-2 might have arisen as a freehand line drawn to generalize actual observations of the points labeled U, V, W, X, Y, Z. Although that graph was not constructed from actual observations, many graphs are.

[5] Notes giving mathematical demonstrations of the concepts presented in the text are designated by colored reference numbers. These notes can be found beginning on page 945.

FIGURE 2A-4   Four Straight Lines with Different Slopes

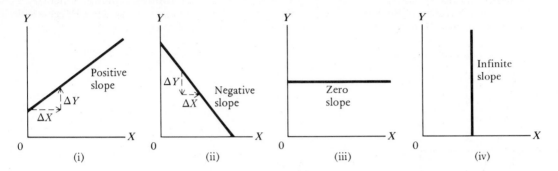

The slope of a straight line is constant but can vary from one line to another. The direction of slope of a straight line is characterized by the signs of the ratio $\Delta Y/\Delta X$. In (i) that ratio is positive because X and Y vary in the same direction; in (ii) the ratio is negative because X and Y vary in opposite directions; in (iii) it is zero because Y does not change as X increases; in (iv) it is infinite.

Two of the most important kinds are called *scatter diagrams* and *time-series graphs*.

Scatter Diagrams

Scatter diagrams provide a method of graphing any number of *paired* observations made on two variables. In Chapter 2 data for family income and taxes paid for a sample of 212 American families were studied. Figure 2-2 on page 26 shows these data on a scatter diagram. Income is measured on the horizontal axis and taxes paid on the vertical axis. Any point in the diagram represents a particular family's income combined with the tax payment of that family. Thus each family for which there are observations can be represented on the diagram by a dot, the coordinates of which indicate the family's income and the amount of taxes it paid in 1979.

The scatter diagram is useful because if there is a simple relationship between the two variables, it will be apparent to the eye once the data are plotted. Figure 2-2, for example, makes it apparent that more taxes tend to be paid as income rises. It also makes it apparent that the relationship between taxes and income is approximately linear. A rising straight line fits the data reasonably well between about $10,000 and $40,000 of income. Above $40,000 and below $10,000 the line does not fit the data as well, but since more than two-thirds of the families sampled have incomes in the $10,000 to $40,000 range, the

straight line provides a fairly good description of the basic relationship for middle-income families.

The diagram also gives some idea of the strength of the relationship. If income were the only deter-

FIGURE 2A-5   Two Straight Lines with Different Slopes

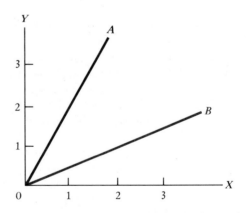

Slope is a quantitative measure. Both lines have positive slopes and thus are similar to Figure 2A-4 (i). However, curve A is steeper (i.e., has a greater slope) than curve B. For each 1-unit increase in X, the value of Y increases by 2 units along curve A, but by only 1/2 unit along curve B. The ratio $\Delta Y/\Delta X$ is 2 for curve A and 1/2 for curve B.

FIGURE 2A-6 Four Curved Lines

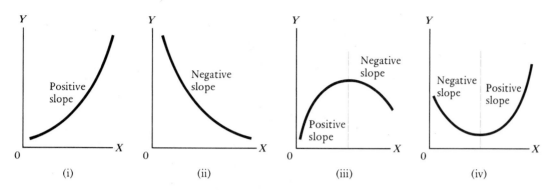

(i) (ii) (iii) (iv)

The slope of a curved line is not constant and may change direction. The slopes of the curves in (i) and (ii) change in size but not direction, whereas those in (iii) and (iv) change in both size and direction. Unlike that of a straight line, the slope of a curved line cannot be defined by a single number because it changes as the value of X changes.

minant of taxes paid, all the dots would cluster closely around a line or a smooth curve; as it is, the points are somewhat scattered, and particular in-

comes are often represented by several households, each with a different amount of taxes paid.

Time-Series Data

The data used in the example of Figure 2–2 are **cross-sectional data** (several different measurements or observations made at the same point in time) because the incomes and taxes paid of different households are compared over a single period of time—the year 1979. Scatter diagrams may also be drawn for a number of observations taken on two variables at successive periods of time.

For example, if one wanted to know whether there was any simple relationship between personal income and personal consumption in the United States between 1965 and 1988, data would be collected for the levels of personal income and expenditure per capita in each year from 1965 to 1988, as is done in Table 2A-1. This information could be plotted on a scatter diagram, with income on the X axis and consumption on the Y axis. The data are plotted in Figure 2A-8, and they do indeed suggest a systematic, almost linear relationship.

Figure 2A-8 is a scatter diagram of observations taken repeatedly over successive periods of time. Such data are called **time-series data,** and plotting them on a scatter diagram involves no new tech-

FIGURE 2A-7 Defining the Slope of a Curve

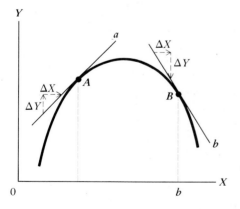

The slope of a curve at any point on the curve is defined by the slope of the straight line that is tangent to the curve at that point. The slope of the curve at point A is defined by the slope of the line a, which is tangent to the curve at point A. The slope of the curve at point B is defined by the slope of the tangent line b.

TABLE 2A-1   Income and Consumption in the United States, 1965–1988 (*1982 dollars*)

Year	Disposable personal income per capita	Personal consumption expenditures per capita
1965	$ 7,027	$6,362
1966	7,280	6,607
1967	7,513	6,730
1968	7,728	7,003
1969	7,891	7,185
1970	8,134	7,275
1971	8,322	7,409
1972	8,562	7,726
1973	9,042	7,972
1974	8,867	7,826
1975	8,944	7,926
1976	9,175	8,272
1977	9,381	8,551
1978	9,735	8,808
1979	9,829	8,904
1980	9,723	8,784
1981	9,773	8,798
1982	9,732	8,825
1983	9,952	9,148
1984	10,427	9,462
1985	10,504	9,682
1986	10,929	10,160
1987	11,012	10,334
1988	11,362	10,564

Source: Economic Report of the President, 1989.

Real disposable personal income per capita and real personal consumption expenditures both grew steadily from 1965 to 1988. The former grew from just over $7,000 to over $11,000, while the latter grew from $6,300 to over $10,500.

FIGURE 2A-8   A Scatter Diagram Relating Consumption and Disposable Income

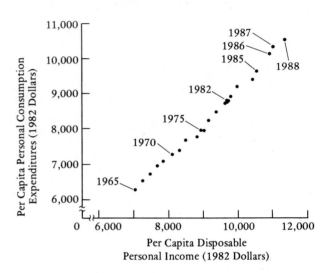

This scatter diagram shows paired values of two variables. The data of Table 2A-1 are plotted here. Each dot shows the values of per capita personal consumption expenditures and per capita disposable personal income for a given year. A close, positive, linear relationship between the two variables is established. Note that in this diagram the axes are shown with a break in them to indicate that not all the values of the variables between $6,000 and zero are given. Since no *observations* occurred in those ranges, it was unnecessary to provide space for them.

nique. When cross-sectional data are plotted, each point gives the values of two variables for a particular unit (say, a family); when time-series data are plotted, each point tells the values of two variables for a particular year.

Instead of studying the relationship between income and consumption suggested in the preceding paragraph, a study of the pattern of the changes in either one of these variables over time could be made. Figure 2A-9 shows this information for consumption. Time is one variable, and consumption expenditure is the other. However, time is a special variable; the order in which successive events happen is important. The year 1985 followed 1984; they were not two independent and unrelated years. In contrast,

two randomly selected households are independent and unrelated. For this reason it is customary to draw in the line segments connecting the successive points, as has been done in Figure 2A-9.

Such a figure is called a *time-series graph* or a *time series*. This kind of graph makes it easy to see if the variable being considered has varied in a systematic way over the years or if its behavior has been more or less erratic.

Ratio (Logarithmic) Scales

All the foregoing graphs use axes that plot numbers on a natural arithmetic scale, with distances between two values shown by the size of the numerical difference. If *proportionate* rather than *absolute* changes in variables are important, it is more revealing to use a ratio scale rather than a natural scale. On a **natural**

FIGURE 2A-9   A Time Series of Consumption Expenditures, 1965–1988

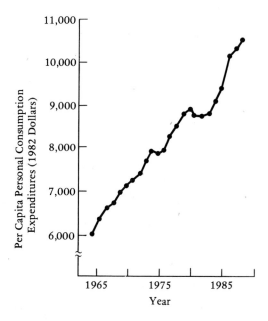

A time series plots values of a single variable in chronological order. This graph shows that, with only minor interruptions, consumption measured in 1982 dollars rose from 1965 to 1988. The data are given in the last column of Table 2A-1.

scale the distance between numbers is proportionate to the absolute difference between those numbers. Thus 200 is placed halfway between 100 and 300. On a **ratio scale** the distance between numbers is proportionate to the percentage difference between the two numbers (which can also be measured as the absolute difference between their logarithms). Equal

TABLE 2A-2   Two Series

Time period	Series A	Series B
0	$10	$ 10
1	18	20
2	26	40
3	34	80
4	42	160

Series A shows constant absolute growth ($8 per period) but declining percentage growth. Series B shows constant percentage growth (100 percent per period) but rising absolute growth.

FIGURE 2A-10   The Difference Between Natural and Ratio Scales

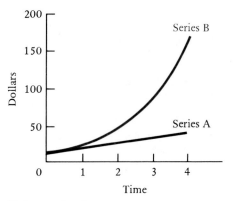

(i) A natural scale

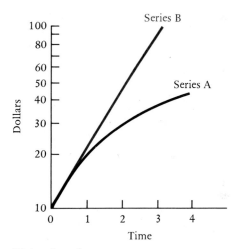

(ii) A ratio scale

On a natural scale equal distances represent equal amounts; on a ratio scale equal distances represent equal percentage changes. The two series in Table 2A-2 are plotted in each chart. Series A, which grows at a constant absolute amount, is shown by a straight line on a natural scale but by a curve of diminishing slope on a ratio scale because the same absolute growth represents a decreasing percentage growth. Series B, which grows at a rising absolute rate but a constant percentage rate, is shown by a curve of increasing slope on a natural scale but by a straight line on a ratio scale.

distances anywhere on a ratio scale represent equal percentage changes rather than equal absolute changes. On a ratio scale the distance between 100 and 200 is the same as the distance between 200 and

FIGURE 2A-11 A Contour Map of a Small Mountain

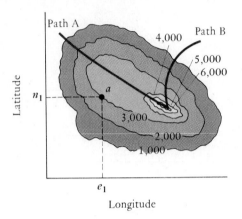

A contour map shows three variables in two-dimensional space. This familiar kind of three-variable graph shows latitude and longitude on the axes and altitude on the contour lines. The contour line labeled 1,000 connects all locations with an altitude of 1,000 feet, the contour line labeled 2,000 connects those with an altitude of 2,000 feet, and so forth. Point a, for example, has a latitude n_1, a longitude e_1, and an altitude of 3,000 feet. Where the lines are closely bunched, they represent a steep ascent; where they are far apart, a gradual one. Clearly, path A is a gentler climb from 3,000 to 4,000 feet on this mountain than path B.

400, between 1,000 and 2,000, and between any two numbers that stand in the ratio 1:2 to each other. For obvious reasons a ratio scale is also called a **logarithmic scale.**

Table 2A-2 shows two series, one growing at a constant absolute amount of 8 units per period and the other growing at a constant rate of 100 percent per period. In Figure 2A-10 the series are plotted first on a natural scale and then on a ratio scale. The natural scale makes it easy for the eye to judge absolute variations, and the logarithmic scale makes it easy for the eye to judge proportionate variations.[6]

[6] Graphs with a ratio scale on one axis and a natural scale on the other are frequently encountered in economics. In the cases just illustrated there is a ratio scale on the vertical axis and a natural scale on the horizontal (or time) axis. Such graphs are often called *semi-log* graphs. In scientific work, graphs with ratio scales on both axes are frequently encountered. Such graphs are often referred to as *double-log* graphs.

FIGURE 2A-12 Three Variables Shown in Two Dimensions

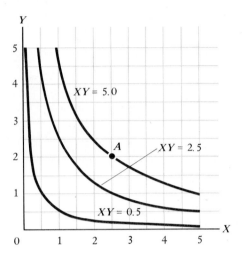

This chart illustrates examples of the three-variable function $XY = a$. The function $XY = a$ is called a *rectangular hyperbola*. The figure shows three members of the family. For example, point A represents $Y = 2.0$, $X = 2.5$, and $a = 5.0$.

Graphing Three Variables in Two Dimensions

Often we want to show graphically more than two dimensions. For example, a topographic map seeks to show latitude, longitude, and altitude on a two-dimensional page. This is done by using contour lines, as in Figure 2A-11. Now consider the function $XY = a$, where X, Y, and a are variables. Figure 2A-12 plots this function for three different values of a. The variables X and Y are represented on the two axes. The variable a is represented by the labels on the curves. Several examples of this procedure occur throughout the book (see, for example, the discussion of indifference curves in Appendix A to Chapter 7 and isoquants in the appendix to Chapter 11).

Chapter 3

An Overview of the Market Economy

The Evolution of Market Economies

Until about 10,000 years ago, homo sapiens were hunter-gatherers, providing for their wants and needs by using foods that were freely provided by nature. The neolithic agricultural revolution changed all that. People gradually abandoned their nomadic life of hunting and food gathering and settled down to tend crops and domesticated animals. Since that time all societies have faced the problem of choice under conditions of scarcity.

Surplus, Specialization, and Trade

Along with permanent settlement, the agricultural revolution brought surplus production. Farmers could produce substantially more than they needed for survival. The agricultural surplus allowed the creation of new occupations. Freed from having to grow their own food, new classes (such as artisans, soldiers, priests, and government officials) turned their talents to performing specialized services and producing goods other than food. They also produced more than they themselves needed, so they traded the excess to obtain whatever other goods they required.

The allocation of different jobs to different people is called **specialization of labor.** Specialization has proven to be extraordinarily efficient compared with self-sufficiency, for at least two reasons. First, individual talents and abilities differ, and specialization allows each person to do the job he or she can do relatively best, while leaving everything else to be done by others. Second, a person who concentrates on one activity becomes better at it than could a jack-of-all-trades.

The exchange of goods and services in early societies commonly took place by simple mutual agreement among neighbors. In the course of time, however, trading became centered in particular gathering places called markets. Today we use the term **market economy** to refer to a society in which people specialize in productive activities and meet most of their material wants through exchanges voluntarily agreed upon by the contracting parties.

Specialization must be accompanied by trade. People who produce only one thing must trade much of their production in order to obtain all the other things they require.

The earliest market economies depended on **barter,** the trading of goods directly for other goods. However, barter can be a costly process in terms of time spent searching out satisfactory exchanges. The evolution of money made trading easier. Money eliminates the inconvenience of barter by allowing the two sides of the barter transaction to be separated. If a farmer has wheat and wants a hammer, he does not have to search for an individual who has a hammer and wants wheat. He merely has to find someone who wants wheat. The farmer takes money in exchange, then finds another person who wishes to trade a hammer and swaps the money for the hammer.

By eliminating the need for barter, money greatly facilitates trade and specialization.

The Division of Labor

Market transactions in early economies mainly involved consumption goods. Producers specialized in making a commodity and then traded it for the other products they needed. Over the past several hundred years, many technical advances in methods of production have made it efficient to organize agriculture and industry on a large scale. These technical developments have made use of what is called the **division of labor,** which is a further step in the specialization of labor. This term refers to specialization within the production process of a particular commodity. The labor involved is divided into a series of repetitive tasks, and each individual does a single task that may be just one of hundreds of tasks necessary to produce the commodity. Today it is possible for an individual to work on a production line without knowing what commodity emerges at the end of that line!

To gain the advantages of the division of labor, it became necessary to organize production in large factories. With this development, urban workers lost their status as artisans and became members of the working class, wholly dependent on their ability to sell their labor to factory owners. The day of artisans who made and sold their own goods was over. Today's typical workers do not earn their incomes by selling commodities they personally have produced; rather, they sell their labor services to firms and receive money wages in return. They have increasingly become cogs in a machine they do not fully understand or control. Adam Smith, the eighteenth

century Scottish political economist, was the first to develop the idea of the division of labor, as discussed in Box 3-1.

Markets and Resource Allocation

The term *resource allocation* refers to the distribution of the available factors of production among the various uses to which they might be put. There are not enough resources to produce all the goods and services that could be consumed. It is therefore necessary to allocate the available resources among their various possible uses and in so doing to choose what to produce and what not to produce. In a market economy millions of consumers decide what commodities to buy and in what quantities; a vast number of firms produce these commodities and buy the factor services that are needed to make them; and millions of factor owners decide to whom they will sell these services. These individual decisions collectively determine the economy's allocation of resources.

In a market economy the allocation of resources is the outcome of countless independent decisions made by consumers and producers, all acting through the medium of markets.

Our main objective in this chapter is to provide an overview of this market mechanism.

The Decision Makers

Economics is about the behavior of people. Much that we observe in the world and that economists assume in their theories can be traced back to decisions made by individuals. There are millions of individuals in most economies. To make a systematic study of their behavior more manageable, we categorize them into three important groups: households, firms, and the government.[1] These groups are

[1] Although in basic economic theory we can get away with three sets of decision makers, it is worth noting that there are others. Probably the most important are such nonprofit organizations as private universities and hospitals, charities such as the American Cancer Society, and funding organizations such as the Ford Foundation. These bodies have an important influence on the allocation of the economy's resources.

BOX 3-1

The Division of Labor

Adam Smith begins *The Wealth of Nations* (1776) with a long study of the division of labor.

The greatest improvements in the productive powers of labour . . . have been the effects of the division of labour.

To take an example . . . the trade of the pinmaker; a workman not educated to this business (which the division of labour has rendered a distinct trade), nor acquainted with the use of the machinery employed in it could scarce, perhaps, with his utmost industry, make one pin in a day, and certainly could not make twenty. But in the way in which this business is now carried on . . . it is divided into a number of branches. . . . One man draws out the wire, another straightens it, a third cuts it, a fourth points it, a fifth grinds it at the top for receiving the head; to make the head requires two or three distinct operations; to put it on, is a peculiar business, to whiten the pins is another; it is even a trade by itself to put them into the paper; and the important business of making a pin is, in this manner, divided into about eighteen distinct operations, which, in some manufactories, are all performed by distinct hands, though in others the same man will sometimes perform two or three of them.

Smith observes that even in smallish factories, where the division of labor is exploited only in part, output is as high as 4,800 pins per person per day!

Later Smith discusses the general importance of the division of labor and the forces that limit its application.

Each animal is still obliged to support and defend itself, separately and independently, and derives no sort of advantage from that variety of talents with which nature has distinguished its fellows. Among men, on the contrary, the most dissimilar geniuses are of use to one another; the different produces of their respective talents, by the general disposition to truck, barter, and exchange, being brought, as it were, into a common stock, where every man may purchase whatever part of the produce of other men's talents he has occasion for.

As it is the power of exchanging that gives occasion to the division of labour, so the extent of this division must always be limited by the extent of that power, or, in other words, by the extent of the market. When the market is very small, no person can have any encouragement to dedicate himself entirely to one employment for want [i.e., lack] of the power to exchange all that surplus part of the produce of his own labour, which is over and above his own consumption, for such parts of the produce of other men's labour as he has occasion for.

Smith notes that there is no point in specializing to produce a large quantity of pins, or anything else, unless there are enough persons making other commodities to provide a market for all the pins that are produced. Thus, the larger the market, the greater the scope for the division of labor and the higher the resulting opportunities for efficient production.

---

economic theory's cast of characters, and the market is the stage on which their play is enacted.

Households

A **household** is defined as all the people who live under one roof and who make, or are subject to others making for them, joint financial decisions. The members of households are often referred to as consumers. Economic theory gives households a number of attributes.

First, economists assume that each household makes consistent decisions, as though it were composed of a single individual. Thus economists ignore many interesting problems of how the household reaches its decisions. Family conflicts and the moral and legal problems concerning parental control over minors are dealt with by other social sciences. These problems are avoided in economics by the assumption that the household is the basic decision-making atom of consumption behavior.

Second, economists assume that each household

is consistently attempting to achieve maximum *satisfaction* or *well-being* or *utility,* as the concept is variously called. The household tries to do this within the limitations of its available resources.

Third, economists assume that households are the principal owners of factors of production. They sell the services of these factors to firms and receive their incomes in return. It is assumed that in making these decisions on how much to sell and to whom to sell, each household seeks to maximize its utility.

Firms

A **firm** is defined as the unit that employs factors of production to produce commodities that it sells to other firms, to households, or to government. For obvious reasons a firm is often called a *producer.* Economic theory gives firms several attributes.

First, economists assume that each firm makes consistent decisions, as though it were composed of a single individual. Thus economics ignores the internal problems of how particular decisions are reached. In doing this, economists assume that the firm's internal organization is irrelevant to its decisions. This allows them to treat the firm as the atom of behavior on the production or supply side of commodity markets, just as the household is treated as the atom of behavior on the consumption or demand side.

Second, economists assume that most firms make their decisions with a single goal in mind: to make as much profit as possible. This goal of *profit maximization* is analogous to the household's goal of utility maximization.

Third, economists assume that in their role as producers, firms are the principal users of the services of factors of production. In markets where factor services are bought and sold, the roles of firms and households are thus reversed from what they are in commodity markets: In factor markets firms do the buying and households do the selling.

Government

The term **government** is used in economics in a broad sense to include all public officials, agencies, government bodies, and other organizations belonging to or under the direct control of federal, state, and local governments. For example, in the United States, the term *government* includes, among others, the president, the Federal Reserve System, city councils, commissions and regulatory bodies, legislative bodies, and police forces. It is not important to draw up a comprehensive list, but one should have in mind a general idea of the organizations that have legal and political power to exert control over individual decision makers and over markets.

It is *not* a basic assumption of economics that the government always acts in a consistent fashion. Three important reasons for this may be mentioned here. First, the mayor of Los Angeles, a Utah state legislator, and a United States senator from Maine represent different constituencies, and therefore they may express different and conflicting views and objectives.

Second, individual public servants, whether elected or appointed, have personal objectives (such as staying in office, achieving higher office, power, prestige, and personal aggrandizement) as well as public service objectives. Although the balance of importance given to the two types of objectives will vary among persons and among types of office, both will almost always have some importance. It would be a rare senator, for example, who would vote against a measure that slightly reduced the "public good" if this vote almost guaranteed defeat during the next election. ("After all," the senator could reason, "if I am defeated, I won't be around to vote against *really* bad measures.")

Third, the system of checks and balances is designed to set one part of the government against another, thereby producing the characteristic American division of authority and responsibility among branches of government. (Here American practice differs sharply from that of most of the rest of the English-speaking world, whose governments are based on the British parliamentary system that was not designed to produce pluralism.)

Decisions on interrelated issues of policy are made by many different bodies. Federal and state legislatures pass laws, the courts interpret laws, the governments decide which laws to enforce with vigor and which not to enforce, the Treasury and the Federal Reserve Board influence monetary conditions, and a host of other agencies and semiautonomous bodies determine actions with respect to different aspects of policy goals. Because of the multiplicity of decision makers, it would be truly amazing if fully consistent behavior resulted. Most Americans believe that there are advantages to this separation of responsibilities, but one of its consequences is that inconsistent decisions will be made.

Another problem arises from the fact that in a democracy legislators and political officials have as important goals their own and their leader's reelection. This means, for example, that any measure that imposes large costs and few obvious benefits over the short run is unlikely to find favor, no matter how large the long-term benefits are. There is a strong bias toward shortsightedness in an elective system. Although much of this bias stems from an inability to grasp long-run consequences or a selfish unwillingness to look beyond the present, some of it reflects genuine uncertainty about the future.

Markets and Economies

We have seen that households, firms, and the government are the main actors in the economic drama. Their action takes place in individual markets.

Markets

The word *market* originally designated a place where goods were traded. The Fulton fish market in New York is a modern example of markets in the everyday sense, and most cities have fruit and vegetable markets. Much early economic theory attempted to explain price behavior in just such markets. Why, for example, can you sometimes obtain great bargains at the end of the day and at other times get what you want only at prices that appear exorbitant in relation to prices quoted only a few hours before?

As theories of market behavior were developed, they were extended to cover commodities such as wheat. Wheat produced anywhere in the world can be purchased almost anywhere else in the world, and the price of a given grade of wheat tends to be nearly uniform the world over. When we talk about the wheat market, the concept of a market has been extended well beyond the idea of a single place to which the producer, the storekeeper, and the homemaker go to sell and buy.

Economists distinguish two broad types of markets: **product markets** (sometimes called *goods* markets), in which outputs of goods and services are sold, and **factor markets,** in which the services of factors of production are sold.

Economies

An **economy** can be rather loosely defined as a set of interrelated production and consumption activities. It may refer to these activities in a region of one country (for example, the economy of New England), in a country (the American economy), or in a group of countries (the economy of Western Europe). In any economy the allocation of resources is determined by the production, sales, and purchase decisions made by firms, households, and government.

As we saw in Chapter 1, a **free-market economy** is an economy in which the decisions of individual households and firms (as distinct from the government) exert the major influence over the allocation of resources.

The opposite of a free-market economy is a **command economy,** in which the major decisions about the allocation of resources are made by the government. In a command economy, firms produce only those goods that they are directed to produce, and often they must distribute them to households in a manner also determined by the government.

As we saw in Chapter 1, the terms *free-market* and *command economy* are often used to describe economies. In practice all economies are **mixed economies** in the sense that some decisions are made by firms, households, and the government acting through markets, and some decisions are made by the government using the command principle.

Sectors of an Economy

Parts of an economy are usually referred to as **sectors** of that economy. For example, the agricultural sector is the part of the economy that produces agricultural commodities.

Market and Nonmarket Sectors

Producers make commodities. Consumers use them. Commodities may pass from one group to the other in two ways: They may be sold by producers and bought by consumers through markets, or they may be given away.

When commodities are bought and sold, producers expect to cover their costs with the revenue they obtain from selling the product. We call this type of production *marketed production,* and we refer to this part of the economy's activity as belonging to the **market sector.**

When the product is given away, the costs of production must be covered from some source other than sales revenue. We call this *nonmarketed production,* and we refer to this part of the economy's activity as belonging to the **nonmarket sector.** In the case of private charities the money required to pay for factor services may be raised from the public by voluntary contributions. In the case of production by the government—which accounts for the bulk of nonmarketed production—the money is provided from government revenue, which in turn comes mainly from taxes.

Whenever a government enterprise *sells* its output, its production is in the market sector. Yet much state output is in the nonmarket sector by the very nature of the product provided. For example, one could hardly expect the criminal to pay the judge for providing the service of criminal justice. Other products are in the nonmarket sector because governments have decided that there are advantages to removing them from the market sector. This is the case, for example, with much of American education. Public policy places it in the nonmarket sector even though much of it could be provided by the market sector.

Private and Public Sectors

An alternative division of an economy's productive activity is between private and public sectors. The **private sector** refers to all production that is in private hands, and the **public sector** refers to all production that is in public hands. The distinction between the two sectors depends on the legal distinction of ownership. In the private sector the organization that does the producing is owned by households or other firms; in the public sector it is owned and operated by the government. The public sector includes all production of goods and services by the government plus all production by government-operated industries that is sold to consumers through markets.

The distinction between market and nonmarket sectors is economic; it depends on whether or not the producer earns revenue by selling output to users. The distinction between the private and the public sectors is legal; it depends on
whether the producing organizations are privately or publicly owned.

Microeconomics and Macroeconomics

As we saw in Chapter 1, there are two different but complementary ways of viewing the economy. The first, *microeconomics,* studies the detailed workings of individual markets and interrelations between markets. The second, *macroeconomics,* suppresses much of the detail and concentrates on the behavior of broad aggregates.[2]

An Overview of Microeconomics

Early economists observed the market economy with wonder. They saw that most commodities were made by a large number of independent producers, yet in approximately the quantities that people wanted to purchase them. Natural disasters aside, there were neither vast surpluses nor severe shortages of products. They also saw that in spite of the ever-changing geographical, industrial, and occupational patterns of demand for labor services, most laborers were able to sell their services to employers most of the time.

How does the market produce this order in the absence of conscious coordination? It is one thing to have the same good produced year in and year out when people's wants and incomes do not change; it is quite another thing to have production adjusting continually to changing wants, incomes, and techniques of production. Yet this adjustment is accomplished relatively smoothly by markets—albeit with occasional, and sometimes serious, interruptions.

A major discovery of eighteenth century economists was that the price system is a social control mechanism.

Adam Smith, in his classic *The Wealth of Nations,* published in 1776, spoke of the price system as "the invisible hand." It allows decision making to be decentralized under the control of millions of individual

[2] The prefixes *micro* and *macro* derive from the Greek words *mikros,* for small, and *makro,* for large.

producers and consumers but nonetheless to be co-ordinated. Two examples may help to illustrate how this coordination occurs.

A Change in Demand

For the first example, assume that households wish to purchase more of some commodity than previously. To see the market's reaction to such a change, imagine a situation in which farmers find it equally profitable to produce either of two crops, carrots or brussels sprouts, and so are willing to produce some of both commodities, thereby satisfying the demands of households who wish to consume both. Now imagine that consumers develop a greatly increased desire for brussels sprouts and a diminished desire for carrots. This change might have occurred because of the discovery of hitherto unsuspected nutritive or curative powers of brussels sprouts.

When consumers buy more brussels sprouts and fewer carrots, a shortage of brussels sprouts and a glut of carrots develop. To unload their surplus stocks of carrots, merchants reduce the price of carrots—in the belief that it is better to sell them at a reduced price than not to sell them at all. Sellers of brussels sprouts, however, find that they are unable to satisfy all their customers' demands for that product. Brussels sprouts have become more scarce, so merchants charge more for them. As the price rises, fewer people are willing and able to purchase brussels sprouts. Thus, making them more expensive limits the quantity demanded to the available supply.

Farmers see a rise in the price of brussels sprouts and a fall in the price of carrots. Brussels sprout production has become more profitable than in the past; the costs of producing brussels sprouts remain unchanged while their market price has risen. Similarly, carrot production is less profitable than in the past because costs are unchanged while the price has fallen. Attracted by high profits in brussels sprouts and deterred by low profits or potential losses in carrots, farmers expand the production of brussels sprouts and curtail the production of carrots. Thus the change in consumers' tastes, working through the price system, causes a reallocation of resources—land and labor—out of carrot production and into brussels sprout production.

As the production of carrots declines, the glut of carrots on the market diminishes and their price begins to rise. On the other hand, the expansion in brussels sprout production reduces the shortage and the price begins to fall. These price movements will continue until it no longer pays farmers to contract carrot production and to expand brussels sprout production. When all of the adjustments have occurred, the price of brussels sprouts is higher than it was originally but lower than it was when the shortage sent the price soaring before output could be adjusted; and the price of carrots is lower than it was originally but higher than when the initial glut sent the price tumbling before output could be adjusted.

The reaction of the market to a change in demand leads to a transfer of resources. Carrot producers reduce their production; they will therefore be laying off workers and generally demanding fewer factors of production. Brussels sprout producers expand production; they will therefore be hiring workers and generally increasing their demand for factors of production.

Labor can probably switch from carrot to brussels sprout production without much difficulty. Certain types of land, however, may be better suited for growing one crop than the other. When farmers increase their brussels sprout production, their demands for those factors especially suited to growing brussels sprouts also increase—and this creates a shortage of these resources and a consequent rise in their prices. Meanwhile, with carrot production falling, the demand for land and other factors of production especially suited to carrot growing is reduced. A surplus results, and the prices of these factors are forced down.

Thus factors particularly suited to brussels sprout production will earn more and will obtain a higher share of total national income than before. Factors particularly suited to carrot production, however, will earn less and will obtain a smaller share of the total national income than before.

Changes of this kind will be studied more fully later; the important thing to notice now is how a change in demand causes a reallocation of resources in the direction required to cater to the new, higher level of demand.

A Change in Supply

For a second example, consider a change originating with producers. Begin as before with a situation in which farmers find it equally profitable to produce either brussels sprouts or carrots and in which consumers are willing to buy, at prevailing prices, the quantities of these two commodities that are being produced. Now imagine that, at existing prices, farmers become more willing to produce brussels sprouts than in the past and less willing to produce carrots. This shift might be caused, for example, by a change in the costs of producing the two goods— a rise in carrot costs and a fall in brussels sprouts costs that would raise the profitability of brussels sprout production and lower that of carrot production.

What will happen now? For a short time, nothing at all will happen; the existing supply of brussels sprouts and carrots on the market is the result of decisions made by farmers at some time in the past. Farmers, however, now begin to plant fewer carrots and more brussels sprouts, and soon the quantities on the market begin to change. The quantity of brussels sprouts available for sale rises, and the quantity of carrots falls. A shortage of carrots and a glut of brussels sprouts results. The price of carrots consequently rises, and the price of brussels sprouts falls. This provides the incentive for two types of adjustments. First, households will buy fewer carrots and more brussels sprouts. Second, farmers will move back into carrot production and out of brussels sprouts.

This example began with a situation in which a shortage of carrots caused the price of carrots to rise. The rise in the price of carrots removed the shortage in two ways: It reduced the quantity of carrots demanded, and it increased the quantity offered for sale (in response to the rise in the profitability of carrot production). Remember that there was also a surplus of brussels sprouts that caused the price to fall. The fall in price removed the surplus in two ways: It encouraged consumers to buy more of this commodity, and it reduced the quantity of brussels sprouts produced and offered for sale (in response to a fall in the profitability of brussels sprout production).

These examples illustrate a general point:

The price system is a mechanism that coordinates individual, decentralized decisions.

The existence of such a control mechanism is beyond dispute. How well it works in comparison with alternative coordinating systems has been in serious dispute for over 100 years, although, as we noted at the end of Chapter 1, the world has recently experienced a dramatic shift toward increased reliance on market forces in many economies.

Microeconomics and Macroeconomics Compared

Microeconomics and macroeconomics differ in the questions each asks and in the level of aggregation each uses. Microeconomics deals with the determination of prices and quantities in individual markets and with the relationships among these markets. Thus it looks at the details of the market economy. It asks, for example, how much labor is employed in the fast food industry and why the amount is increasing. It asks about the determinants of the output of brussels sprouts, pocket calculators, automobiles, and Domino's pizzas. It asks, too, about the prices of these things—why some prices go up and others down. Economists interested in microeconomics analyze how prices and outputs respond to exogenous shocks caused by events in other markets or by government policy. They ask, for example, how a technical innovation, a government subsidy, or a drought will affect the price and output of beet sugar and the employment of farm workers.

In contrast, macroeconomics focuses on much broader aggregates. It looks at such things as the total number of people employed and unemployed, the average level of prices and how it changes over time, national output, and aggregate consumption. Macroeconomics asks what determines these aggregates and how they respond to changing conditions. Whereas microeconomics looks at demand and supply with regard to particular commodities, macroeconomics looks at aggregate demand and aggregate supply.

An Overview of Macroeconomics

We can group together all the buyers of the nation's output and call their total desired purchases **aggregate demand.** We can also group together all the producers of the nation's output and call their total desired sales **aggregate supply.** Determining the magnitude of these and explaining why they change are among the major problems of macroeconomics.

Major changes in aggregate demand are called

demand shocks, and major changes in aggregate supply are called *supply shocks.* Such shocks will cause important changes in the broad averages and aggregates that are the concern of macroeconomics, including total output, total employment, and average levels of prices and wages. Government actions sometimes are the cause of demand or supply shocks, while at other times they are reactions to such shocks and are used in an attempt to cushion or to change the effects of such shocks.

The Circular Flow of Income

One way to gain insight into aggregate demand and aggregate supply is to view the economy as a giant set of flows. A major part of aggregate demand arises from the purchases of consumption commodities by the nation's households. These purchases generate income for the firms that produce and sell commodities for consumption. A major part of aggregate supply arises from the production and sale of consumption goods by the nation's firms. This production generates income for all the factors that are employed in making these goods.

The large colored arrows in Figure 3-1 show the interaction between firms and households in two sets of markets—factor markets and product markets—through which their decisions are coordinated. Consider households first. The members of households want commodities to keep themselves fed, clothed, housed, entertained, healthy, and secure. They also want commodities to educate, edify, beautify, stupefy, and otherwise amuse themselves. Households have resources with which to attempt to satisfy these wants, but not all their wants can be satisfied with the resources available. Households are forced, therefore, to make choices as to which goods and services to buy in product markets that offer them myriad ways to spend their incomes.

Now consider firms. They must choose among the products they might produce and sell, among the ways of producing them, and among the various quantities (and qualities) they can supply. Firms must also buy factors of production. Payments by firms to factor owners provide the factor owners with incomes. The recipients of these incomes are households whose members want commodities to keep themselves fed, clothed, housed, and entertained.

We have now come full circle! The action of this drama involves firms and households interacting with one another.

Payments flow from households to firms through product markets and back to households again through factor markets.

If the economy consisted only of households and firms, if households spent all the income they received on buying goods and services produced by firms, and if firms distributed all their receipts to households either by purchasing factor services or by distributing profits to owners, then the circular flow would be simple indeed. Everything received by households would be passed on to firms, and everything received by firms would be passed back to households. The circular flow would be a completely closed system; aggregate demand and aggregate supply would consist only of consumption goods; and macroeconomics would involve little more than measuring the flows of production of and expenditure on consumption goods.

The circular flow is not, however, a completely closed system. First, households do not spend all their income. Some of their income is saved, and some goes to governments as taxes. Further, some household expenditures go to purchases of imports from foreign firms. These three *leakages* from the circular flow are shown by the light-gray arrows flowing out of the households in Figure 3-1. (Of course, firms may also save and pay taxes, but these leakages are omitted from the figure for simplicity.)

A second reason why the circular flow is not a closed system is that there are elements of aggregate demand that do not arise from household spending. One important component of aggregate demand stems from firms that borrow in order to purchase such investment goods as plant and equipment. A further major component of aggregate demand comes from governments—federal, state, and local. They add to total expenditure on the nation's output by spending on a whole range of goods and services, from national defense through the provision of justice to the building of roads and schools. A third component of aggregate demand arises from sales of exports to foreign purchasers. These three major additions to the circular flow of income are shown by the light-gray arrows flowing into the firms' sales receipts in Figure 3-1. (Of course, households may

FIGURE 3-1   The Circular Flow of Expenditures and Income

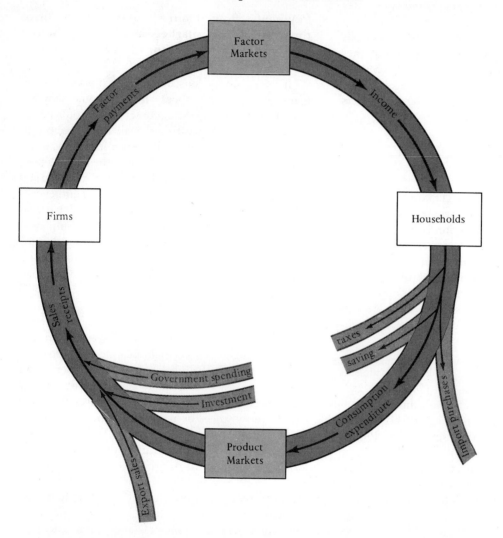

The interaction of firms and households in product and factor markets generates a circular flow of expenditure and income. Factor services are sold by households through factor markets to firms; this leads to a flow of income from firms to households, as shown in the top half of the figure. Commodities are sold by firms through product markets to households; this leads to a flow of receipts from households to firms, as shown in the bottom half of the figure. If these primary flows, shown by the dark-colored arrows, were the only flow, the circular flow would be a closed system.

However, the circular flow is not a closed system because there exist other flows that give rise to leakages and additions to the primary flows. Three leakages—household savings, household tax payments, and household expenditures on imports—are shown by the smaller, light-colored arrows flowing out of the households. Three additions—investment expenditures, government expenditures, and sales of exports—are shown by the smaller, light-colored arrows flowing into the firms' sales receipts.

also receive payments from government and may borrow from financial institutions to finance current consumption expenditure, but for simplicity these additions are omitted from the figure.)

When any one of these elements of aggregate demand changes, aggregate output and total income earned by households are likely to change as a result. Thus, studying the determinants of total consumption, investment, and government spending is crucial to understanding the causes of changes both in the nation's total output and in the employment generated by the production of that output.

The Next Step

Soon you will be going on to study micro- or macroeconomics. Whichever branch of the subject you study first, it is important to remember that microeconomics and macroeconomics are complementary, not competing, views of the economy. Both are needed for a full understanding of the functioning of a modern economy.

SUMMARY

1. This chapter provides an overview of the workings of the market economy. Modern economies are based on the specialization and division of labor, which necessitate the exchange of goods and services. Exchange takes place in markets and is facilitated by the use of money. Much of economics is devoted to a study of how markets work to coordinate millions of individual, decentralized decisions.

2. In economic theory three kinds of decision makers—households, firms, and government—interact in markets. Households are assumed to maximize their satisfaction and firms to maximize their profits. Government may have multiple objectives.

3. A free-market economy is one in which the allocation of resources is determined by the production, sales, and purchase decisions made by firms and households acting in response to such market signals as prices and profits.

4. Subdivisions of an economy are called sectors. Economies are commonly divided into market and nonmarket sectors and into public and private sectors. These divisions cut across each other; the first is based on the economic distinction of how costs are covered, and the second is based on a legal distinction of ownership.

5. A key difference between micro- and macroeconomics is in the level of aggregation to which attention is directed. Microeconomics looks at prices and quantities in individual markets and how they respond to various shocks that impinge on those markets. Macroeconomics looks at broader aggregates such as aggregate consumption, employment and unemployment, and rate of change of the price level.

6. The questions asked in micro- and macroeconomics differ, but they are complementary parts of economic theory. They study different aspects of a single economic system, and both are needed for an understanding of the whole.

7. Microeconomics deals with the determination of prices and quantities in individual markets and the relationships among those markets. It shows how the price system provides signals that reflect changes in demand and supply and to which producers and consumers react in an individual but nonetheless coordinated manner.

8. The microeconomic interactions between households and firms through markets may be illustrated in a circular flow diagram that traces money flows between households and firms. These flows are the starting point for studying the circular flows of aggregate income that are key elements of macroeconomics.

9. Household purchases of consumption goods generate income for firms whose payments to factors then flow back to the households as income. This circular flow is not a simple closed system, because not all income received by households is spent for the output of firms and some receipts of firms are not paid out to households. Also, some payments to firms do not result from the spending of households, and some payments to households do not result from the spending of firms. The flows of expenditure in the economy determine total output, total income, and total employment.

TOPICS FOR REVIEW

Specialization and division of labor
Economic decision makers
Markets and market economies
Market and nonmarket sectors
Private and public sectors
The price system as a social control mechanism
Relationship between microeconomics and macroeconomics

DISCUSSION QUESTIONS

1. Suggest some examples of specialization and division of labor among people you know.
2. There is a greater variety of specialists and specialty stores in large cities than in small towns having populations with the same average income. Explain this in economic terms.
3. Define the household of which you are a member. Consider your household's income last year. What proportion of it came from the sale of factor services? Identify other sources of income. Approximately what proportion of the expenditures by your household became income for firms?
4. "It is not from the benevolence of the butcher, the brewer, or the baker that we expect our dinner, but from their regard to their self-interest. We address ourselves, not to their humanity, but to their self-love, and never talk to them of our necessities, but of their advantages." Do you agree with this quotation from *The Wealth of Nations?* How are "their self-love" and "our dinner" related to the price system? What are assumed to be the motives of firms and of households?
5. Trace the effect of a sharp change in consumer demand away from red meat and toward poultry as a result of continuing reports that too much red meat in a diet is unhealthy.
6. Make a list of other decision makers in the economy today that do not fit into the categories of firm, household, and government. Are you sure that the concept of a firm will not stretch sufficiently to cover some of the items on your list?
7. Trace out some significant microeconomic and macroeconomic effects of a baby boom, such as occurred following World War II.
8. Which, if any, of the arrows in Figure 3-1 does each of the following affect in the first instance?
   a. Households increase their consumption expenditures by reducing saving.
   b. The government lowers income tax rates.
   c. In view of a recession, firms decide to postpone production of some new products.
   d. Consumers like the new model American cars and borrow money from the banking system to buy them in record numbers.

A GENERAL VIEW OF THE PRICE SYSTEM

Chapter 4

Demand, Supply, and Price

Some people believe that economics begins and ends with the "laws" of supply and demand. It is, of course, too much to hope for "economics in one lesson." (An unkind critic of a book with that title remarked that the author needed a second lesson.) Still, the so-called laws of supply and demand are an important part of our understanding of the market system.

As a first step, we need to understand what determines the demand for commodities and the supply of them. Then we can see how demand and supply together determine the prices of goods and services and the quantities that are bought and sold. Finally, we examine how the price system allows the economy to respond to the many changes that impinge on it. Demand and supply help us in understanding the price system's successes and its failures, as well as the consequences of such government intervention as price controls, minimum-wage laws, and sales taxes.

Demand

The American consumer spent about $3.2 trillion on goods and services in 1988. Table 4-1 shows the composition of this expenditure and how it has changed over 33 years. Economists ask many questions about the pattern of consumer expenditure: Why is it what it is at any moment of time? Why does it change in the way it does? Why did the fraction of total consumer expenditure for food decline from more than one-third in 1910 to less than one-fifth by 1988? Why did U.S. consumers allocate a negligible percentage of their total expenditure to automobiles in 1920, 4 percent in 1929, only 2 percent in 1932, and 7 percent in both 1972 and 1985? How have Americans reacted to the large changes in fuel prices that occurred in the late 1970s and early 1980s? Why do people who build houses in Norway and the American West rarely use brick, while it is commonly used in England and the eastern United States? Why have the maid and the washerwoman been replaced by the vacuum cleaner and the washing machine?

Quantity Demanded

The total amount of a commodity that all households wish to purchase in some time period is called the **quantity demanded** of that commodity.[1] It is important to notice three things about

[1] In this chapter we concentrate on the demand of *all* households for commodities. Of course, what all households do is only the sum of what each individual household does, and in Chapters 7 and 8 we shall study the behavior of individual households in greater detail.

TABLE 4-1	Composition of Personal Consumption Expenditures, 1955 and 1988 *(percentages)*		
	1955		**1988**
Motor vehicles and parts	7.0		6.5
Furniture and household equipment	6.4		4.9
Other	1.8		2.6
Total durable goods		15.2	14.0
Food	26.5		17.4
Clothing and shoes	9.1		5.9
Gasoline and oil	3.4		2.6
Other	9.5		7.2
Total nondurable goods		48.5	33.1
Housing and household operation	19.0		24.7
Other	17.3		28.2
Total services		36.3	52.9
Total all goods and services		100.0	100.0

Source: *Economic Report of the President, 1989.*

The declining relative importance of food, clothing, and durables and the rising importance of gasoline and oil and services of all kinds stand out.

this concept. First, quantity demanded is a *desired* quantity. It is how much households wish to purchase, given the price of the commodity, other prices, their incomes, tastes, and so on. This may be different from the amount that households actually succeed in purchasing. If sufficient quantities are not available, the amount households wish to purchase may exceed the amount they actually do purchase. To distinguish these two concepts, the term *quantity demanded* is used to refer to desired purchases, and a phrase such as *quantity actually bought* is used to refer to actual purchases.

Second, *desired* does not refer to idle dreams but to effective demands, that is, to the amounts people are willing to buy given the price they must pay for the commodity.

Third, quantity demanded refers to a continuous *flow* of purchases. It must therefore be expressed as so much per period of time: 1 million units per day, 7 million per week, or 365 million per year. For example, being told that the quantity of new television sets demanded (at current prices) in the United States is 500,000 means nothing unless you are also

told the period of time involved. Five hundred thousand television sets demanded per day would be an enormous rate of demand; 500,000 per year would be a very small rate. (The important distinction between stocks and flows was discussed on page 20.)

What Determines Quantity Demanded?

The amount of some commodity that all households wish to buy in a given time period is influenced by the following important variables:[2] **[2]**

Commodity's own price
Average household income
Prices of related commodities
Tastes
Distribution of income among households
Size of the population

We cannot understand the separate influence of each of the above variables if we try to consider what happens when everything changes at once. Instead, we consider the influence of the variables one at a time. To do this, we hold all but one of them constant. Then we let that one selected variable vary and study how it affects quantity demanded. We can do the same for each of the other variables in turn, and in this way we can come to understand the importance of each.[3] Once this is done, we can aggregate the separate influences of the variables to discover what would happen if several things changed at the same time—as they often do in practice.

Holding all other influencing variables constant is often described by the words "other things being equal" or by the equivalent Latin phrase, ***ceteris paribus.*** When economists speak of the influence of the price of wheat on the quantity of wheat demanded *ceteris paribus,* they refer to what a change in the price of wheat would do to the quantity demanded if all other factors that influence the demand for wheat did not change.

[2] Notes giving mathematical demonstrations of the concepts presented in the text are designated by colored reference numbers. These notes can be found beginning on page 945.

[3] A relationship in which many variables (in this case average income, population, tastes, and many prices) influence a single variable (in this case quantity demanded) is called a *multivariate* relationship. The technique of studying the effect of each of the influencing variables one at a time, while holding the others constant, is common in mathematics and there is a specific concept, the *partial derivative,* designed to do so.

Demand and Price

We are interested in developing a theory of how commodities get priced. To do this we need to study the relationship between the quantity demanded of each commodity and that commodity's own price. This requires that we hold all other influences constant and ask: How will the quantity of a commodity demanded vary as its own price varies?

A basic economic hypothesis is that the lower the price of a commodity, the larger the quantity that will be demanded, other things being equal.

Why might this be so? Commodities are used to satisfy desires and needs, and there is almost always more than one commodity that will satisfy any given desire or need. Such commodities compete with one another for the purchasers' attention. Hunger may be satisfied by meat or vegetables, a desire for green vegetables by broccoli or spinach. The need to keep warm at night may be satisfied by several woolen blankets or one electric blanket, or a sheet and a lot of oil burned in the furnace. The desire for a vacation may be satisfied by a trip to the seashore or to the mountains, the need to get there by different airlines, a bus, a car, a train. And so it goes. Name any general desire or need, and there will be at least two and often dozens of different commodities that will satisfy it.

Now consider what happens if we hold income, tastes, population, and the prices of all other commodities constant and vary only the price of one commodity. As that price goes up, the commodity becomes an increasingly expensive way to satisfy a want. Some households will stop buying it altogether; others will buy smaller amounts; still others may continue to buy the same quantity. Because many households will switch wholly or partially to other commodities to satisfy the same want, less will be bought of the commodity whose price has risen. As meat becomes more expensive, for example, households may switch to some extent to meat substitutes; they may also forego meat at some meals and eat less meat at others.

Alternatively, a fall in a commodity's price makes it a cheaper method of satisfying a want. Households will buy more of it. Consequently, they will buy less of similar commodities whose prices have not fallen and which as a result have become expensive *relative* to the commodity in question. When a bumper tomato harvest drives prices down, shoppers switch to tomatoes and cut their purchases of many other vegetables that now look relatively more expensive.

The Demand Schedule and the Demand Curve

A **demand schedule** is one way of showing the relationship between quantity demanded and the price of that commodity, other things being equal. It is a numerical tabulation showing the quantity that is demanded at selected prices.

Table 4-2 is a hypothetical demand schedule for carrots. It lists the quantity of carrots that would be demanded at various prices on the assumption that all other influences on quantity demanded are held constant. We note in particular that average household income is fixed at $20,000 because later we will wish to see what happens when income changes. The table gives the quantities demanded for six selected prices, but actually a separate quantity would be demanded at each possible price from one cent to several hundreds of dollars.

A second method of showing the relationship between quantity demanded and price is to draw a graph. The six price-quantity combinations shown in Table 4-2 are plotted on the graph shown in Figure 4-1. Price is plotted on the vertical axis, and quantity is plotted on the horizontal axis. The smooth curve drawn through these points is called a **demand**

TABLE 4-2   A Demand Schedule for Carrots

	Price per ton	Quantity demanded when income is $20,000 per year (thousands of tons per month)
U	$ 20	110.0
V	40	90.0
W	60	77.5
X	80	67.5
Y	100	62.5
Z	120	60.0

The table shows the quantity of carrots that would be demanded at various prices, *ceteris paribus*. For example, row *W* indicates that if the price of carrots were $60 per ton, consumers would desire to purchase 77,500 tons of carrots per month, given the values of the other variables that affect quantity demanded, including average household income.

FIGURE 4-1 A Demand Curve for Carrots

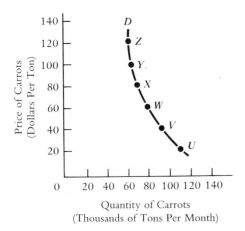

This demand curve relates quantity of carrots demanded to the price of carrots; its downward slope
indicates that quantity demanded increases as price
falls. The six points correspond to the price-quantity
combinations shown in Table 4-2. Each row in the table
defines a point on the demand curve. The smooth curve
drawn through all of the points and labeled D is the demand curve.

curve. It shows the quantity that purchasers would
like to buy at each price. The negative slope of the
curve indicates that the quantity demanded increases
as the price falls.

Each point on the demand curve indicates a single
price-quantity combination. The demand curve as a
whole shows more.

**The demand curve represents the relationship
between quantity demanded and price, other
things being equal.**

When economists speak of the conditions of demand in a particular market as being given or
known, they are referring not just to the particular
quantity being demanded at the moment (i.e., not
just to one point on the demand curve) but, instead,
to the entire demand curve—to the relationship between desired purchases and all the possible alternative prices of the commodity.

Thus, the term **demand** refers to the entire relationship between the quantity demanded of a commodity and the price of that commodity (as shown,

for example, by the demand schedule in Table 4-2
or the demand curve in Figure 4-1). In contrast, a
single point on a demand schedule or curve is the
quantity demanded at that point (for example, at point
W in Figure 4-1, 77,500 tons of carrots a month are
demanded at a price of $60 per ton).

Shifts in the Demand Curve

The demand schedule is constructed and the demand
curve is plotted on the assumption of *ceteris paribus,*
but what if other things change, as surely they must?
What if, for example, households find themselves
with more income? If they spend their extra income,
they will buy additional quantities of many commodities *even though their prices are unchanged.*

If households increase their purchases of any one
commodity whose price has not changed, the purchases cannot be represented on the original demand
curve. They must be represented on a new demand
curve, which is to the right of the old curve. Thus
the rise in household income shifts the demand curve
to the right, as shown in Figure 4-2. This illustrates
the operation of an important general rule.

**A demand curve is drawn on the assumption
that everything except the commodity's own
price is held constant. A change in any of the
variables previously held constant will shift the
demand curve to a new position.**

A demand curve can shift in many ways; two of
them are particularly important. In the first case,
more is bought at *each* price, and the demand curve
shifts rightward so that each price corresponds to a
higher quantity than it did before. In the second case,
less is bought at *each* price, and the demand curve
shifts leftward so that each price corresponds to a
lower quantity than it did before.

The influence of changes in variables other than
price may be studied by determining how changes
in each variable shift the demand curve. Any change
will shift the demand curve to the right if it increases
the amount that households wish to buy, other things
remaining equal, and to the left if it decreases the
amount that households wish to buy, other things
remaining equal. Note that changes in people's *expectations* about *future* values of variables such as income and prices can influence demand; however, for
simplicity we cast the discussion in terms of observed
actual changes in the current values of these variables.

FIGURE 4-2   Two Demand Curves for Carrots

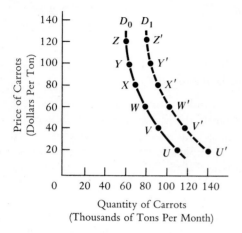

The rightward shift in the demand curve from D_0 to D_1 indicates an increase in the quantity demanded at each price. The lettered points correspond to those in Table 4-3. A rightward shift in the demand curve indicates an increase in demand in the sense that more is demanded at each price and that a higher price would be paid for each quantity.

TABLE 4-3   Two Alternative Demand Schedules for Carrots

Price per ton p	Quantity demanded when average household income is $20,000 per year (thousands of tons per month) D_0		Quantity demanded when average income is $24,000 per year (thousands of tons per month) D_1	
$ 20	110.0	U	140.0	U'
40	90.0	V	116.0	V'
60	77.5	W	100.8	W'
80	67.5	X	87.5	X'
100	62.5	Y	81.3	Y'
120	60.0	Z	78.0	Z'

An increase in average household income increases the quantity demanded at each price. When average income rises from $20,000 to $24,000 per year, quantity demanded at a price of $60 per ton rises from 77,500 tons per month to 100,800 tons per month. A similar rise occurs at every other price. Thus the demand schedule relating columns p and D_0 is replaced by one relating columns p and D_1. The graphical representations of these two functions are labeled D_0 and D_1 in Figure 4-2.

Average household income.   If households receive more income on average, they can be expected to purchase more of most commodities even though commodity prices remain the same.[4] Considering all households, we expect that no matter what price we pick, more of any commodity will be demanded than was previously demanded at that price. This shift is illustrated in Table 4-3 and Figure 4-2.

A rise in average household income shifts the demand curve for most commodities to the right. This indicates that more will be demanded at each price.

Other prices.   We saw that the downward slope of a commodity's demand curve occurs because the lower its price, the cheaper the commodity is relative to other commodities that can satisfy the same needs or desires. Those other commodities are called **substitutes.** Another way for the same change to come

about is for the price of the substitute commodity to rise. For example, carrots can become cheap relative to cabbage either because the price of carrots falls or because the price of cabbage rises. Either change will increase the amount of carrots that households are prepared to buy.

A rise in the price of a substitute for a commodity shifts the demand curve for the commodity to the right. More will be purchased at each price.

For example, a rise in the price of cabbage could cause the demand curve for carrots to shift to the right as in Figure 4-2.

Complements are commodities that tend to be used jointly with each other. Cars and gasoline are complements; so are golf clubs and golf balls, electric stoves and electricity, an airplane trip to Vail and lift tickets on the mountain. Since complements tend to be consumed together, a fall in the price of either one will increase the demand for both.

A fall in the price of a complementary commodity will shift a commodity's demand curve

---

[4] Such commodities are called *normal goods*. Commodities for which the amount purchased falls as income rises are called *inferior goods*. These concepts are defined and discussed in Chapter 5.

to the right. More will be purchased at each price.

For example, a fall in the price of airplane trips to Vail will lead to a rise in the demand for lift tickets at Vail even though their price is unchanged.

Tastes.   Tastes have a large effect on people's desired purchases. A change in tastes may be long lasting, such as the shift from fountain pens to ball-point pens or from slide rules to pocket calculators; or it may be a short-lived fad such as hula hoops or pet rocks. In either case, a change in tastes in favor of a commodity shifts the demand curve to the right. More will be bought at each price.

Distribution of income.   If a constant total of income is redistributed among the population, demands may change. If, for example, the government increases the deductions that may be taken for children on income tax returns and compensates by raising basic tax rates, income will be transferred from childless persons to households with large families. Demands for commodities more heavily bought by childless persons will decline, while demands for commodities more heavily bought by households with large families will increase.

A change in the distribution of income will shift the demand curves for commodities bought most by those households with increasing incomes to the right, and it will shift the demand curves for commodities bought most by those households with decreasing incomes to the left.

Population.   Population growth does not by itself create new demand. The additional people must have purchasing power before demand is changed. Extra people of working age who are employed, however, will earn new income. When this happens, the demands for all the commodities purchased by the new income earners will rise. Thus it is usually true that:

A rise in population will shift the demand curves for commodities to the right, indicating that more will be bought at each price.

The reasons that demand curves shift are summarized in Figure 4-3.

FIGURE 4-3   Shifts in the Demand Curve

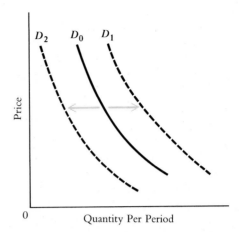

A rightward shift in the demand curve from D_0 to D_1 indicates an increase in demand; a leftward shift from D_0 to D_2 indicates a decrease in demand. An increase in demand means that more is demanded at each price. Such a rightward shift can be caused by a rise in income, a rise in the price of a substitute, a fall in the price of a complement, a change in tastes that favors the commodity, an increase in population, or a redistribution of income toward groups who favor the commodity.

A decrease in demand means that less is demanded at each price. Such a leftward shift can be caused by a fall in income, a fall in the price of a substitute, a rise in the price of a complement, a change in tastes that disfavors the commodity, a decrease in population, or a redistribution of income away from groups who favor the commodity.

Movements Along the Demand Curve Versus Shifts of the Whole Curve

Suppose you read in today's newspaper that a soaring price of carrots has been caused by a greatly increased demand for that commodity. Then tomorrow you read that the rising price of carrots is greatly reducing the typical household's purchases of carrots as shoppers switch to potatoes, yams, and peas. The two statements appear to contradict each other. The first associates a rising price with a rising demand; the second associates a rising price with a declining demand. Can both statements be true? The answer is yes because they refer to different things. The first describes a shift in the demand curve; the second describes a movement along a demand curve in response to a change in price.

Consider first the statement that the increase in the price of carrots has been caused by an increased demand for carrots. This statement refers to a shift in the demand curve for carrots. In this case the demand curve must have shifted to the right, indicating more carrots demanded *at each price*. This shift will, as we shall see later in this chapter, increase the price of carrots.

Now consider the statement that fewer carrots are being bought because carrots have become more expensive. This refers to a movement along a given demand curve and reflects a change between two specific quantities being bought—one before the price rose and one afterward.

So what lay behind the two stories might have been something like the following explanations.

1. A rise in the population is shifting the demand curve for carrots to the right as more carrots are demanded at each price. This in turn is raising the price of carrots (for reasons we will soon study in detail). This was the first newspaper story.
2. The rising price of carrots is causing each individual household to cut back on its purchase of carrots. This causes a movement upward to the left along any particular demand curve for carrots. This was the second newspaper story.

To prevent the type of confusion caused by our two newspaper stories, economists have developed a specialized vocabulary to distinguish shifts of curves from movements along curves.

We have seen that *demand* refers to the *whole* demand curve. Economists reserve the term **change in demand** to describe a shift in the whole demand curve, that is, a change in the amount that will be bought at *every* price.

An increase in demand means that the whole demand curve will shift to the right; a decrease in demand means that the whole demand curve will shift to the left.

Any point on a demand curve represents a specific amount being bought at a specified price. It represents, therefore, a particular quantity demanded. A movement along a demand curve is referred to as a **change in the quantity demanded.** [3]

A movement down a demand curve is called an increase (or a rise) in the quantity demanded; a movement up a demand curve is called a decrease (or a fall) in the quantity demanded.

To illustrate this terminology, look again at Table 4-3. When average income is \$20,000, an increase in price from \$60 to \$80 decreases the *quantity demanded* from 77.5 to 67.5 thousand tons per month. An increase in average income from \$20,000 to \$24,000 increases *demand* from D_0 to D_1.

Figure 4-4 shows the combined effect of a rise in demand, shown by a rightward shift in the whole demand curve, and a fall in the quantity demanded, shown by a movement upward to the left along a given demand curve in response to a change in price.

Supply

America's private sector produced goods and services worth nearly \$4 trillion in 1988. A broad classification of what was produced is given in Table 4-4. The percentages shown in Table 4-4 reflect some of the changes that have taken place over 33 years. Even more dramatic changes can be seen in more detailed data.

Economists have as many questions to ask about production and its changing composition as they do about consumption. For example, why have the country's manufacturing industries declined in relative importance? What is the significance of the rising importance of service industries?

At the more detailed level, economists want to know such things as why the aluminum industry grew faster than the steel industry; why the increase in output of the chemical industries was almost 60 times that of the primary metals industries, 3 times that of the apparel industry, and twice that of the motor vehicle industry in the 33 years since 1955. Why and how do firms and industries come into being, grow, and decline?

All of these questions and many others are aspects of a single question: *What determines the quantities of commodities that will be produced and offered for sale?*

Full discussion of these questions of supply will come later (in Part Four). For now it is enough to develop the basic relationship between the price of a commodity and the quantity that will be produced

FIGURE 4-4   Shifts of and Movements Along the Demand Curve

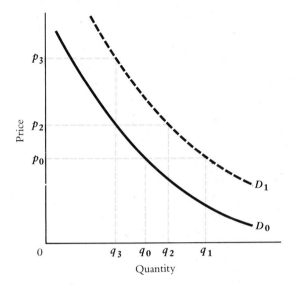

A rise in demand means that more will be bought at each price, but it does not mean that more will be bought under all circumstances. The demand curve is originally D_0 and price is p_0 at which q_0 is bought. Demand then increases to D_1, which implies that at the old price of p_0 there is a larger quantity demanded, q_1. Now assume the price rises above p_0. This causes quantity demanded to fall below q_1. *The shift in the demand curve means that more is bought at each price. A movement upward along the demand curve means that less will be bought in response to a rise in price.* The net effect of these two changes can be either an increase or a decrease in the quantity demanded. In this figure a rise in price to p_2 means that the quantity demanded, q_2, is still in excess of the original quantity q_0, while a rise in price to p_3 means that the final quantity, q_3, is below the original quantity q_0.

TABLE 4-4   Composition of National Product by Industry of Origin, 1955 and 1988 *(percentages)*

Industry group[a]	1955	1988
Manufacturing	29.8	18.6
Mining and construction	7.7	6.7
Agriculture, forestry, and fisheries	4.9	2.1
Transport and public utilities	9.0	9.0
Wholesale and retail trade	16.5	16.3
Finance, insurance, and real estate	12.4	17.1
Other services	8.6	17.5
Government and government enterprises	9.6	11.8
Other	1.5	0.9
	100.0	100.0

Source: Economic Report of the President, 1989.
[a] Excluding government and government enterprises.

Over a generation manufacturing, agriculture, forestry, and fisheries have all declined in relative importance, while services have become more important.

and offered for sale by firms, and to understand what forces lead to shifts in this relationship.

Quantity Supplied

The amount of a commodity that firms wish to sell in some time period is called the **quantity supplied** of that commodity. Note that this is the amount that firms are willing to offer for sale; it is not necessarily the amount they succeed in selling. The term *quantity actually sold* indicates what they succeed in selling.

Quantity supplied is a flow; it is so much per unit of time.

Although households may desire to purchase an amount that differs from what firms desire to sell, they cannot succeed in buying what someone else does not sell. A purchase and a sale are merely two sides of the same transaction. Looked at from the buyer's side, there is a purchase; looked at from the seller's side, there is a sale.

Since desired purchases do not have to equal desired sales, quantity demanded does not have to equal quantity supplied, but because no one can buy what someone does not sell, the quantity actually purchased must equal the quantity actually sold.

What Determines Quantity Supplied?

The amount of a commodity that firms will be willing to produce and offer for sale is influenced by the following important variables: [4]

Commodity's own price
Prices of inputs
Goals of firms
State of technology

The situation is the same here as it is on the demand side. The list of influencing variables is long, and we will not get far if we try to discover what happens when they all change at the same time. So, again, we use the convenient *ceteris paribus* technique to study the influence of the variables one at a time.

Supply and Price

Since we want to develop a theory of how commodities get priced, we study the relationship between the quantity supplied of each commodity and that commodity's own price. We start by holding all other influences constant and asking: How do we expect the quantity of a commodity supplied to vary with its own price?

A basic economic hypothesis is that, for many commodities, the higher the price of a commodity, the larger the quantity that will be supplied, other things being equal.

Why might this be so? It is because the profits that can be earned from producing a commodity are almost certain to increase if the price of that commodity rises while the costs of inputs used to produce it remain unchanged. This will make firms, which are in business to earn profits, wish to produce more of the commodity whose price has risen and less of other commodities.[5]

The Supply Schedule and the Supply Curve

The general relationship just discussed can be illustrated by a **supply schedule**, which shows the relationship between quantity supplied of a commodity and the price of the commodity, other things being equal. A supply schedule is analogous to a demand schedule; the former shows what producers would be willing to sell, while the latter shows what households would be willing to buy, at alternative prices of the commodity. Table 4-5 presents a hypothetical supply schedule for carrots.

A **supply curve,** the graphical representation of the supply schedule, is illustrated in Figure 4-5. While each point on the supply curve represents a

[5] Notice, however, the qualifying word *many* in the hypothesis stated above. It is used because, as we shall see in Part Four, there are exceptions to this rule. Although the rule states the usual case, a rise in price (*ceteris paribus*) is not always necessary to call forth an increase in quantity in the case of all commodities.

TABLE 4-5   A Supply Schedule for Carrots

	Price per ton	Quantity supplied (thousands of tons per month)
u	$ 20	5.0
v	40	46.0
w	60	77.5
x	80	100.0
y	100	115.0
z	120	122.5

The table shows the quantities that producers wish to sell at various prices, *ceteris paribus*.   For example, row *y* indicates that if the price were $100 per ton, producers would wish to sell 115,000 tons of carrots per month.

specific price-quantity combination, the whole curve shows more.

The supply curve represents the relationship between quantity supplied and price, other things being equal.

FIGURE 4-5   A Supply Curve for Carrots

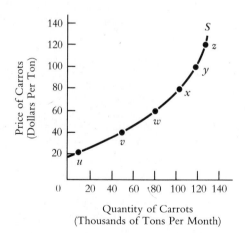

This supply curve relates quantity of carrots supplied to the price of carrots; its upward slope indicates that quantity supplied increases as price increases.   The six points correspond to the price-quantity combinations shown in Table 4-5. Each row in the table defines a point on the supply curve. The smooth curve drawn through all of the points and labeled *S* is the supply curve.

When economists speak of the conditions of supply as being given or known, they refer not just to the particular quantity being supplied at the moment, that is, not to just one point on the supply curve. Instead, they are referring to the entire supply curve, to the complete relationship between desired sales and all possible alternative prices of the commodity.

Supply refers to the entire relationship between the quantity supplied of a commodity and the price of that commodity, other things being equal. A single point on the supply curve refers to the *quantity supplied* at that price.

Shifts in the Supply Curve

A shift in the supply curve means that at each price a different quantity will be supplied than previously. An increase in the quantity supplied at each price is shown in Table 4-6 and is graphed in Figure 4-6. This change appears as a rightward shift in the supply curve. In contrast, a decrease in the quantity supplied at each price would appear as a leftward shift. A shift in the supply curve must be the result of a change in one of the factors that influence the quantity supplied

TABLE 4-6 Two Alternative Supply Schedules for Carrots

Price per ton p	Quantity supplied before cost-saving innovation (thousands of tons per month) S_0		Quantity supplied after innovation (thousands of tons per month) S_1	
$ 20	5.0	u	28.0	u'
40	46.0	v	76.0	v'
60	77.5	w	102.0	w'
80	100.0	x	120.0	x'
100	115.0	y	132.0	y'
120	122.5	z	140.0	z'

A cost-saving innovation increases the quantity supplied at each price. As a result of a cost-saving innovation, the quantity that is supplied at $100 per ton rises from 115,000 to 132,000 tons per month. A similar rise occurs at every price. Thus, the supply schedule relating p and S_0 is replaced by one relating p and S_1.

other than the commodity's own price. The major possible causes of such shifts are summarized in the caption of Figure 4-7 and are considered briefly below.

For supply, as for demand, there is an important general rule:

A change in any of the variables (other than the commodity's own price) that affects the amount of a commodity that firms are willing to produce and sell will shift the supply curve for that commodity.

Prices of inputs. All things that a firm uses to produce its outputs, such as materials, labor, and machines, are called the firm's *inputs*. Other things being equal, the higher the price of any input used to make a commodity, the less will be the profit from making that commodity. We expect, therefore, that the higher the price of any input used by a firm, the lower will be the amount that the firm will produce and offer for sale at any given price of the commodity.

A rise in the price of inputs shifts the supply curve to the left, indicating that less will be supplied at any given price; a fall in the cost of inputs shifts the supply curve to the right.

Goals of the firm. In elementary economic theory, the firm is assumed to have the single goal of profit

FIGURE 4-6 Two Supply Curves for Carrots

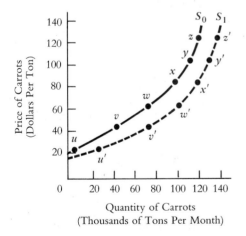

The rightward shift in the supply curve from S_0 to S_1 indicates an increase in the quantity supplied at each price. The lettered points correspond to those in Table 4-6. A rightward shift in the supply curve indicates an increase in supply such that more carrots are supplied at each price.

FIGURE 4-7   Shifts in the Supply Curve

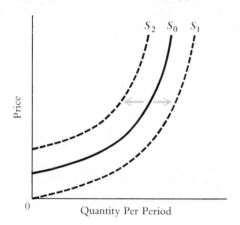

A shift in the supply curve from S_0 to S_1 indicates an increase in supply; a shift from S_0 to S_2 indicates a decrease in supply. An increase in supply means that more is supplied at each price. Such a rightward shift can be caused by certain changes in producers' goals, improvements in technology, or decreases in the costs of inputs that are important in producing the commodity.

A decrease in supply means that less is supplied at each price. Such a leftward shift can be caused by certain changes in producers' goals or increases in the costs of inputs that are important in producing the commodity.

maximization. A firm might, however, have other goals either in addition to or as substitutes for profit maximization. If the firm worries about risk, it will pursue safer lines of activity even though it promises lower probable profits. If the firm values size, it may produce and sell more than the profit-maximizing quantities. If it worries about its image in society, it may forsake highly profitable activities (such as the production of some chemical fertilizers) when there is major public disapproval. However, as long as the firm prefers more profits to less, it will respond to changes in the profitabilities of alternative lines of action, and supply curves will slope upward.

A change in the importance that a firm gives to other goals will shift the supply curve one way or the other, indicating a changed willingness to supply the quantity at any given price and hence a changed level of profitability.

Technology. At any time what is produced and how it is produced depend on what is known. Over time

knowledge changes; so do the quantities of individual commodities supplied. The enormous increase in production per worker that has been going on in industrial societies for about 200 years is largely due to improved methods of production. Yet the Industrial Revolution is more than a historical event; it is a present reality. Discoveries in chemistry have led to lower costs of production of well-established products, such as paints, and to a large variety of new products made of plastics and synthetic fibers. The invention of transistors and silicon chips has radically changed products such as computers, audiovisual equipment, and guidance-control systems, and the consequent development of compact computers is revolutionizing the production of countless other nonelectronic products.

Any technological change that decreases production costs will increase the profits that can be earned at any given price of the commodity. Since increased profitability leads to increased production, this change shifts the supply curve to the right, indicating an increased willingness to produce the commodity and offer it for sale at each possible price.

Movements Along the Supply Curve Versus Shifts of the Whole Curve

As with demand, it is important to distinguish movements along supply curves from shifts of the whole curve. Economists reserve the term **change in supply** to describe a shift of the whole supply curve. This means a change in the quantity supplied at each price of the commodity. A movement along the supply curve indicates a *change in the quantity supplied* in response to a change in the price of the commodity. Thus an increase in supply means that the whole supply curve has shifted to the right; an increase in the quantity supplied means a movement upward to the right along a given supply curve.

Determination of Price by Demand and Supply

So far demand and supply have been considered separately. The next question is this: How do the two forces interact to determine price in a competitive market? Table 4-7 brings together the demand and supply schedules from Tables 4-2 and 4-5. The quan-

TABLE 4-7 Demand and Supply Schedules for Carrots and Equilibrium Price

(1) Price per ton p	(2) Quantity demanded (thousands of tons per month) D	(3) Quantity supplied (thousands of tons per month) S	(4) Excess demand (+) or excess supply (−) (thousands of tons per month) D − S
$ 20	110.0	5.0	+105.0
40	90.0	46.0	+ 44.0
60	77.5	77.5	0.0
80	67.5	100.0	− 32.5
100	62.5	115.0	− 52.5
120	60.0	122.5	− 62.5

Equilibrium occurs where quantity demanded equals quantity supplied—where there is neither excess demand nor excess supply. These schedules are those of Tables 4-2 and 4-5. The equilibrium price is $60. For lower prices there is excess demand; for higher prices there is excess supply.

tities of carrots demanded and supplied at each price may now be compared.

There is only one price, $60 per ton, at which the quantity of carrots demanded equals the quantity supplied. At prices less than $60 per ton there is a shortage of carrots because the quantity demanded exceeds the quantity supplied. This is often called a situation of **excess demand.** At prices greater than $60 per ton there is a surplus of carrots because the quantity supplied exceeds the quantity demanded. This is called a situation of **excess supply.**

To discuss the determination of market price, suppose first that the price is $100 per ton. At this price 115,000 tons would be offered for sale, but only 62,500 tons would be demanded. There would be an excess supply of 52,500 tons per month. We assume that sellers will then cut their prices to get rid of this surplus and that purchasers, observing the stock of unsold carrots, will offer less for what they are prepared to buy.

Excess supply causes a downward pressure on price.

Next consider the price of $20 per ton. At this price there is excess demand. The 5,000 tons produced each month are snapped up quickly, and 105,000 tons of desired purchases cannot be made. Rivalry between would-be purchasers may lead them to offer more than the prevailing price in order to outbid other purchasers. Also, perceiving that they could have sold their available supplies many times

over, sellers may begin to ask a higher price for the quantities that they do have to sell.

Excess demand causes an upward pressure on price.

Finally, consider a price of $60. At this price producers wish to sell 77,500 tons per month, and purchasers wish to buy that quantity. There is neither a shortage nor a surplus of carrots. There are no unsatisfied buyers to bid the price up, nor are there unsatisfied sellers to force the price down. Once the price of $60 has been reached, therefore, there will be no tendency for it to change.

An equilibrium implies a state of rest, or balance, between opposing forces. The **equilibrium price** is the one toward which the actual market price will tend. It will persist once established, unless it is disturbed by some change in market conditions.

The price at which the quantity demanded equals the quantity supplied is called the equilibrium price.

Any other price is called a **disequilibrium price:** the price at which quantity demanded does not equal quantity supplied. The price will be changing. A market that exhibits either excess demand or excess supply is said to be in a state of **disequilibrium.**

A condition that must be fulfilled if equilibrium is to be obtained in some market is called an **equilibrium condition.** In a competitive market, the equality of quantity demanded and quantity supplied is an equilibrium condition. **[5]**

This same story is told in graphical terms in Figure 4-8. The quantities demanded and supplied at any price can be read off the two curves; the excess supply or excess demand is shown by the horizontal distance between the curves at each price. The figure makes it clear that the equilibrium price occurs where the demand and supply curves intersect. Below that price there will be excess demand and hence an upward pressure on the existing price. Above that price there will be an excess supply and hence a downward pressure on the existing price. These pressures are represented by the vertical arrows in the figure.

The Laws of Demand and Supply

Changes in any of the variables other than price that influence quantity demanded or supplied will cause a shift in the supply curve or the demand curve, or both. There are four possible shifts: (1) a rise in demand (a rightward shift in the demand curve), (2) a fall in demand (a leftward shift in the demand curve), (3) a rise in supply (a rightward shift in the supply curve), and (4) a fall in supply (a leftward shift in the supply curve).

Each of these shifts causes changes that are described by one of the four "laws" of demand and supply. Each of the laws summarizes what happens when an initial position of equilibrium is upset by some shift in either the demand or the supply curve and a new equilibrium position is then established. The sense in which it is correct to call these propositions "laws" is discussed in Box 4-1.

To discover the effects of each of the curve shifts that we wish to study, we use the method known as **comparative statics**, short for comparative static equilibrium analysis.[6] In this method we derive predictions by analyzing the effect of a change in some exogenous variable on the equilibrium position. We start from a position of equilibrium and then introduce the change to be studied. The new equilibrium position is determined and compared with the original one. The differences between the two positions of equilibrium must result from changes in the data that were introduced, because everything else has been held constant.

The four laws of demand and supply are derived in Figure 4-9, which generalizes our specific discussion about carrots. Previously, we had given the axes specific labels, but from here on we will simplify. Because it is intended to apply to any commodity, the horizontal axis is simply labeled *Quantity*. This should be understood to mean quantity per period in whatever units output is measured. *Price*, the vertical axis, should be understood to mean the price measured as dollars per unit of quantity for the same commodity. The four laws of demand and supply are:

1. **A rise in demand causes an increase in both the equilibrium price and the equilibrium quantity exchanged.**
2. **A fall in demand causes a decrease in both**

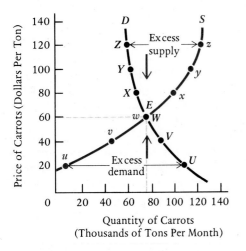

FIGURE 4-8   Determination of the Equilibrium Price of Carrots

The equilibrium price corresponds to the intersection of the demand and supply curves. Equilibrium is indicated by *E*, which is point *W* on the demand curve and point *w* on the supply curve. At a price of $60 quantity demanded equals quantity supplied. At prices above equilibrium there is excess supply and downward pressure on price. At prices below equilibrium there is excess demand and upward pressure on price. The pressures on price are represented by the vertical arrows.

---

[6] The term *statics* is used because we are not concerned about the actual path by which the market goes from the first equilibrium position to the second. Analysis of that path would be described as dynamic analysis.

BOX 4-1

Laws, Predictions, Hypotheses

In what sense can the four propositions developed for supply and demand be called "laws"? They are not like acts passed by Congress, interpreted by courts, and enforced by the police; they cannot be repealed if people do not like their effects. Nor are they like the laws of Moses, revealed to man by the voice of God. Are they natural laws similar to Newton's law of gravity? In labeling them *laws*, classical economists clearly had in mind Newton's laws as analogies.

The term *law* is used in science to describe a theory that has stood up to substantial testing. A law of this kind is not something that has been proven to be true for all times and all circumstances, nor is it regarded as immutable. As observations accumulate, laws may often be modified or the range of phenomena to which they apply may be restricted or redefined. Einstein's theory of relativity, as one example, forced such amendments and restrictions on Newton's laws.

The laws of supply and demand have stood up well to many empirical tests, but no one believes that they explain all market behavior. They are thus laws in the sense that they predict certain kinds of behavior in certain situations and the predicted behavior occurs sufficiently often to lead people to continue to have confidence in the predictions of the theory. They are not laws—any more than are the laws of natural science—that are beyond being challenged by present or future observations that may cast doubt on some of their predictions. Nor is it a heresy to question their applicability to any particular situation.

Laws, then, are hypotheses that have led to predictions that account for observed behavior. They are theories that, in some circumstances at least, have survived attempts to refute them and have proven useful. It is possible, in economics as in the natural sciences, to be impressed both with the "laws" we do have and with their limitations: to be impressed, that is, both with the power of what we know and with the magnitude of what we have yet to understand.

the equilibrium price and the equilibrium quantity exchanged.
3. **A rise in supply causes a decrease in the equilibrium price and an increase in the equilibrium quantity exchanged.**
4. **A fall in supply causes an increase in the equilibrium price and a decrease in the equilibrium quantity exchanged.**

In this chapter we have studied many forces that can cause demand or supply curves to shift. These were summarized in Figures 4-3 and 4-7. By combining this analysis with the four laws of demand and supply, we can link many real-world events that cause demand or supply curves to shift with changes in market prices and quantities.

The theory of the determination of price by de-

mand and supply is beautiful in its simplicity. Yet, as we shall see, it is powerful in its wide range of applications. The usefulness of this theory in interpreting what we see in the world around us is further discussed in Box 4-2.

Prices and Inflation

Up to now we have developed the theory of the prices of individual commodities under the assumption that all other prices remained constant. Does this mean that the theory is inapplicable to an inflationary world when almost all prices are rising? Fortunately the answer is no.

The price of a commodity usually refers to the amount of money that must be spent to acquire one unit of that commodity. This is called the **absolute**

FIGURE 4-9 The Four "Laws" of Demand and Supply

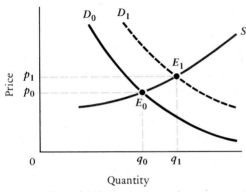

(i) The effect of shifts in the demand curve

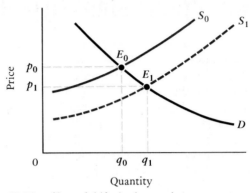

(ii) The effect of shifts in the supply curve

The effects on equilibrium price and quantity of shifts in either demand or supply are called the laws of demand and supply.

A rise in demand. In (i) assume that the original demand and supply curves are D_0 and S, which intersect to produce equilibrium at E_0, with a price of p_0 and a quantity of q_0. An increase in demand shifts the demand curve to D_1, taking the new equilibrium to E_1. Price rises to p_1 and quantity to q_1.

A fall in demand. In (i) assume that the original demand and supply curves are D_1 and S, which intersect to produce equilibrium at E_1, with a price of p_1 and a quantity of q_1. A decrease in demand shifts the demand curve to D_0, taking the new equilibrium to E_0. Price falls to p_0 and quantity falls to q_0.

A rise in supply. In (ii) assume that the original demand and supply curves are D and S_0, which intersect to produce an equilibrium at E_0, with a price of p_0 and a quantity of q_0. An increase in supply shifts the supply curve to S_1, taking the new equilibrium to E_1. Price falls to p_1 and quantity rises to q_1.

A fall in supply. In (ii) assume that the original demand and supply curves are D and S_1, which intersect to produce an equilibrium at E_1, with a price of p_1 and a quantity of q_1. A decrease in supply shifts the supply curve to S_0, taking the new equilibrium to E_0. Price rises to p_0, and quantity falls to q_0.

price, or *money price*. A **relative price** is the ratio of two absolute prices; it expresses the price of one good in terms of (i.e., *relative* to) another.

We have mentioned several times that what matters for demand and supply is the price of the commodity in question relative to the prices of other commodities; that is, what matters is the *relative price*.

In an inflationary world we are often interested in the price of a given commodity as it relates to the average price of all other commodities. If, during a period when the general price level rose by 40 percent, the price of oranges rose by 60 percent, then the price of oranges rose relative to the price level as a whole. Oranges became *relatively* expensive. However, if oranges had risen in price by only 30 percent when the general price level rose by 40 percent, then

the relative price of oranges would have fallen. Although the money price of oranges rose substantially, oranges became *relatively* cheap.

In Lewis Carroll's famous story *Through the Looking Glass*, Alice finds a country where you have to run in order to stay still. So it is with inflation. A commodity's price must rise as fast as the general level of prices rises just to keep its relative price constant.

It has been convenient in this chapter to analyze changes in particular prices in the context of a constant price level. The analysis is easily extended to an inflationary period by remembering that any force that raises the price of one commodity when other prices remain constant will, given general inflation, raise the price of that commodity faster than the price

BOX 4-2

Demand and Supply: What Really Happens

"The theory of supply and demand is neat enough," said the skeptic, "but tell me what really happens."

"What really happens," said the economist, "is that, first, demand curves slope downward; second, supply curves slope upward; third, prices rise in response to excess demand; and fourth, prices fall in response to excess supply."

"But that's theory," insisted the skeptic. "What about reality?"

"That is reality as well," said the economist.

"Show me," said the skeptic.

The economist produced the following passages from articles in the *New York Times*.

Increased demand for macadamia nuts causes price to rise above competing nuts. Major producer now plans to double the size of its orchards during the next five years.

*   *   *

OPEC countries once again fail to agree on output quotas. Output soars and prices plummet.

*   *   *

Last summer, Rhode Island officials reopened the northern third of Narragansett Bay, a 9,500-acre fishing ground that had been closed since 1978 because of pollution. Suddenly clam prices dropped, thanks to an underwater population explosion that had transformed the Narragansett area into a clam harvester's dream.

*   *   *

Increasing third world agricultural production threatens the stability of American agriculture. In the 1970s American farm prosperity was built on rising demand due to world prosperity and on falling output in Eastern Europe. Farm experts now worry that the propensity will prove fragile in the face of major increases in world output.

*   *   *

The effects of [the first year of] deregulation of the nation's airlines were spectacular: cuts in air fares of up to 70 percent in some cases, record passenger jam-ups at the airports, and a spectacular increase in the average load factor [the proportion of occupied seats on the average commercial flight].

The skeptic's response is not recorded, but you should be able to tell which clippings illustrate each of the economist's four statements about "what really happens."

---

level is rising. For example, a change in tastes in favor of carrots that would raise their price by 20 percent when other prices were constant, would raise their price by 32 percent if at the same time the general price level rises by 10 percent.[7] In each case the price of carrots rises 20 percent *relative to the average of all prices.*

[7] Let the price level be 100 in the first case and 110 in the second. Let the price of carrots be 120 in the first case and x in the second. To preserve the same relative price we need x such that $120/100 = x/110$, which makes $x = 132$.

In price theory, whenever we talk of a change in the price of one commodity, we mean a change relative to other prices.

If the price level is constant, this change requires only that the money price of the commodity in question should rise. If the price level is itself rising, this change requires that the money price of the commodity in question should rise faster than the price level.

SUMMARY

1. The amount of a commodity that households wish to purchase is called the *quantity demanded*. It is a flow expressed as so much per period of time. It is determined by the commodity's own price, average household income, the prices of related commodities, tastes,

the distribution of income among households, and the size of the population.

2. Quantity demanded is assumed to increase as the price of the commodity falls, *ceteris paribus*. The relationship between quantity demanded and price is represented graphically by a demand curve that shows how much will be demanded at each market price. A movement along a demand curve indicates a change in the quantity demanded in response to a change in the price of the commodity.

3. A shift in a demand curve represents a change in the quantity demanded at each price and is referred to as a *change in demand*. The demand curve shifts to the right (an increase in demand) if average income rises, if the price of a substitute rises, if the price of a complement falls, if population rises, or if there is a change in tastes in favor of the product. The opposite changes shift the demand curve to the left (a decrease in demand).

4. The amount of a commodity that firms wish to sell is called the *quantity supplied*. It is a flow expressed as so much per period of time. It depends on the commodity's own price, the costs of inputs, the goals of the firm, and the state of technology.

5. Quantity supplied is assumed to increase as the price of the commodity increases, *ceteris paribus*. The relationship between quantity supplied and price is represented graphically by a supply curve that shows how much will be supplied at each market price. A movement along a supply curve indicates a change in the quantity supplied in response to a change in price.

6. A shift in the supply curve indicates a change in the quantity supplied at each price and is referred to as a *change in supply*. The supply curve shifts to the right (an increase in supply) if the costs of producing the commodity fall or if, for any reason, producers become more willing to produce the commodity. The opposite changes shift the supply curve to the left (a decrease in supply).

7. The *equilibrium price* is the one at which the quantity demanded equals the quantity supplied. At any price below equilibrium there will be excess demand; at any price above equilibrium there will be excess supply. Graphically, equilibrium occurs where demand and supply curves intersect.

8. Price is assumed to rise when there is excess demand and to fall when there is excess supply. Thus, the actual market price will be pushed toward the equilibrium price, and when it is reached, there will be neither excess demand nor excess supply and the price will not change until either the supply curve or the demand curve shifts.

9. Using the method of *comparative statics,* the effects of a shift in either demand or supply can be determined. A rise in demand raises both equilibrium price and equilibrium quantity; a fall in demand lowers both. A rise in supply raises equilibrium quantity but lowers equilibrium price; a fall in supply lowers equilibrium quantity but raises equilibrium price. These are the so-called laws of demand and supply.

10. Price theory is most simply developed in the context of a constant price level. Price changes discussed in the theory are changes relative to the average level of all prices. The absolute price of a commodity is its price in terms of money; its relative price is its price in terms of another commodity. In an inflationary period a rise in the *relative price* of one commodity means that its absolute price rises by more

than the price level; a fall in its relative price means that its absolute price rises by less than the price level.

TOPICS FOR REVIEW

Quantity demanded and quantity exchanged
Demand schedule and demand curve
Quantity supplied and quantity exchanged
Supply schedule and supply curve
Movement along a curve and shift of a whole curve
Change in quantity demanded and change in demand
Change in quantity supplied and change in supply
Equilibrium, equilibrium price, and disequilibrium
Comparative statics
Laws of supply and demand
Relative price

DISCUSSION QUESTIONS

1. What shifts in demand or supply curves would produce the following results? (Assume that only one of the two curves has shifted.)
   a. The price of pocket calculators has fallen over the last few years, and the quantity exchanged has risen greatly.
   b. As the American standard of living rose over the past three decades, both the prices and the consumption of prime cuts of beef rose steadily.
   c. Rental prices of summer sublets in Ann Arbor, Michigan, are about 50 percent of the regular rental.
   d. Fashion changes cause the sale of jeans to decline.
   e. Potato blight causes spud prices to soar.
   f. "Gourmet food market grows as affluent shoppers indulge."
   g. Oil prices tumble as OPEC countries violate production quotas.
   h. Do the same for the examples given in Box 4-2.
2. Recently the Department of Agriculture predicted that this spring's excellent weather would result in larger crops of corn and wheat than farmers had expected. Its chief economist, however, warned consumers not to expect prices to decrease, since foreign demand for American crops was increasing. "The classic pattern of supply and demand won't work this time," the economist said. Discuss his observation.
3. Explain each of the following in terms of changes in supply and demand.
   a. Du Pont increased the price of synthetic fibers, although it acknowledged that demand was weak.
   b. The Edsel was a lemon when it was produced during 1958–1960 but is now a best-seller among cars of its vintage.
   c. The decision not to deploy the MX missile in western Utah signaled a collapse in land prices in that area.
   d. Some of the first $10 coins minted in Canada to commemorate the 1976 Olympics were imperfectly stamped. These flawed pieces are currently worth as much as $1,000.
4. Suppose that compact disk producers find that they are selling more disks at the same price than they did two years ago. Is this a shift of the demand curve or a movement along the curve? Suggest at least four reasons why this rise in sales at an unchanged price might occur.

5. What would be the effect on the equilibrium price and quantity of marijuana if its sale were legalized?

6. The relative price of personal computers has dropped drastically over time. Would you explain this falling price in terms of demand or supply changes? What factors are likely to have caused the demand or supply shifts (or both) that did occur?

7. Classify the effect of each of the following as (i) a decrease in the demand for fish, (ii) a decrease in the quantity of fish demanded, or (iii) other. Illustrate each diagrammatically.

   a. The government of Iceland bars fishermen of other nations from its waters.

   b. People buy less fish because of a rise in fish prices.

   c. The Roman Catholic Church relaxes its ban on eating meat on Fridays.

   d. The price of beef falls, and as a result households buy more beef and less fish.

   e. In the interests of training marine personnel for national defense, the U.S. government decides to subsidize the American fishing industry.

   f. It is discovered that eating fish is better for one's health than eating meat.

8. Predict the effect on the price of at least one commodity of each of the following:

   a. Winter snowfall is at a record high in Colorado, but drought continues in New England ski areas.

   b. A recession decreases employment in Detroit automobile factories.

   c. The French grape harvest is the smallest in 20 years.

   d. The state of New York cancels permission for citizens to cut firewood in state parks.

9. Are the following two observations inconsistent? (a) Rising demand for housing causes prices of new homes to soar; (b) families reduce purchases of housing as prices become prohibitive.

Chapter 5

Elasticity and Market Adjustment

The laws of demand and supply predict the direction of changes in price and quantity in response to various shifts in demand and supply, but often it is not enough to know merely whether price and quantity each rise or fall; it is also important to know by how much each changes.

When flood damage led to major destruction of the onion crop in the early 1980s, onion prices rose sharply. Not surprisingly, overall consumption of onions fell. The press reported that many consumers stopped using onions altogether and substituted onion salt, sauerkraut, cabbage, and other products. Other consumers still bought onions but in reduced quantities. Was the dollar value (price times quantity) higher or lower? The data above do not tell, but the answer is important. A government concerned with the effect of a bad crop on farm income will not be satisfied with being told that food prices will rise and quantities consumed will fall; it will need to know by approximately how much they will change if it is to assess the effects on farmers.

Measuring and describing the extent of the responsiveness of quantities to changes in prices and other variables is often essential if we are to understand the significance of these changes. This is what the concept of *elasticity* does.

Price Elasticity of Demand

Suppose there is an increase in a farm crop, that is, a rightward shift in the supply curve. The two parts of Figure 5-1 have the same initial equilibrium, and that equilibrium is disturbed by the same rightward shift in the supply curve. Because the demand curves are different in the two parts of the figure, the new equilibrium position is different, and hence the magnitude of the effects of the increase in supply on equilibrium price and quantity are different.

A shift in supply will have different quantitative effects depending on the shape of the demand curve.

The difference may be significant for government policy. Consider what would happen if the rightward shift of the supply curve shown in Figure 5-1 occurs because the government has persuaded farmers to produce more of a certain crop. (It might, for example, have paid a subsidy to farmers for producing that crop.)

FIGURE 5-1   The Effect of the Shape of the Demand Curve

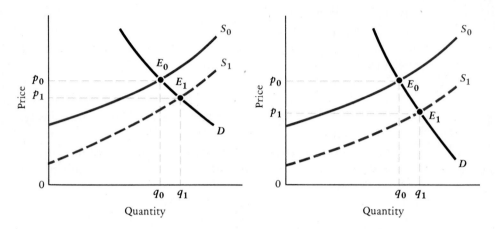

The flatter the demand curve, the less the change in price and the greater the change in quantity. The two parts of the figure show the same initial equilibrium and the same shift in the supply curve. In each part initial equilibrium is at price p_0 and output q_0, and the new equilibrium is at p_1 and q_1. In (i) the effect of the shift in supply from S_0 to S_1 is a slight fall in the price and a large increase in quantity. In (ii) the effect of the identical shift in the supply curve from S_0 to S_1 is a large fall in the price and a relatively small increase in quantity.

Part (i) of Figure 5-1 illustrates a case in which the quantity that consumers demand is very sensitive to price changes. The rise in production brings down the price, but because the quantity demanded is quite responsive, only a small change in price is necessary to restore equilibrium. The effect of the government's policy, therefore, is to achieve a large increase in the production and sales of this commodity and only a small decrease in price.

Part (ii) of Figure 5-1 shows a case in which the quantity demanded is quite unresponsive to price changes. As before, the increase in supply at the original price causes a surplus that brings the price down. However, this time the quantity demanded by consumers does not increase much in response to the fall in price. Thus the price continues to drop until, discouraged by lower and lower prices, farmers reduce the quantity supplied nearly to the level attained before they received the subsidy. The effect of the government's policy is to achieve a large decrease in the price of this commodity and only a small increase in the quantity produced and sold.

In both of the cases shown in Figure 5-1, it can be seen that the government's policy has exactly the

same effectiveness as far as the farmers' willingness to supply the commodity is concerned—the supply curve shifts are identical. The magnitude of the effects on the equilibrium price and quantity, however, are very different because of the different degrees to which the quantity demanded by consumers responds to price changes. If the purpose of the government's policy is to increase the quantity of this commodity produced and consumed, it will be a great success when the demand curve is similar to the one shown in (i) of Figure 5-1, but it will be a failure when the demand curve is similar to the one shown in (ii) of Figure 5-1. If, however, the purpose of the government's policy is to achieve a large reduction in the price of the commodity, the policy will be a failure when demand is as shown in (i), but it will be a great success when demand is as shown in (ii).

The Measurement of Price Elasticity

In Figure 5-1 a measure of demand responsiveness to a change in price could be obtained by comparing the slopes of the two demand curves. However, in general the slope of a demand curve is not a very good measure of demand responsiveness since it ignores the initial levels of quantity and price. A fall in price of, say, $1 will have far different implications if the initial price is only $2 than if the initial price is $2,000! Similarly, an increase in quantity of, say, 1 bushel means something quite different if the initial quantity is in tens of bushels than if it were 10,000 bushels.

To take account of the initial price and quantity, the responsiveness of demand is best calculated by comparing the *percentage* change in price to the *percentage* change in quantity. The comparison made using the slopes in Figure 5-1 works only because the two parts of the figure were constructed so that the quantity and price at the initial equilibrium were identical; hence, in the special case of that figure any differences in the changes in actual price and quantity correspond to similar differences in the percentage changes.[1]

Assume that we have the information shown in Table 5-1. Should we conclude that the demand for radios is not as responsive to price changes as the demand for beef? After all, price cuts of $.20 cause quite a large increase in the quantity of beef demanded but only a small increase in radios.

There are two problems here. First, a reduction in the price of $.20 will be a large price cut for a low-priced commodity and an insignificant price cut for a high-priced commodity. The price reductions listed in Table 5-1 represent different fractions of the total prices. It is usually more revealing to know the percentage change in the prices of the various commodities. Second, by an analogous argument, knowing the quantity by which demand changes is not very revealing unless the initial level of demand is also known. An increase of 7,500 pounds is quite a significant reaction to demand if the quantity formerly bought was 15,000 pounds, but it is insignif-

TABLE 5-1   Price Reductions and Corresponding Increases in Quantity Demanded

Commodity	Reduction in price	Increase in quantity demanded
Beef	$.20 per pound	7,500 pounds
Men's shirts	.20 per shirt	5,000 shirts
Radios	.20 per radio	100 radios

The data show, for each of the three commodities, the change in quantity demanded in response to the same absolute fall in price. The data are fairly uninformative about the responsiveness of demand to price because they do not tell us either the original price or the original quantity demanded.

icant if the quantity formerly bought was 10 million pounds.

Table 5-2 shows the original and the new levels of price and quantity. Changes in price and quantity expressed as percentages of the average prices and quantities are shown in the first two columns of Table 5-3.[2] The **price elasticity of demand,** the measure of responsiveness of quantity of a commodity demanded to a change in market price, is symbolized by the Greek letter eta, η. It is defined as

$$\eta = \frac{\text{percentage change in quantity demanded}}{\text{percentage change in price}}$$

This measure is frequently called the *elasticity of demand*, or simply *demand elasticity*. Since the variable causing the change in quantity demanded is the commodity's own price, the term *own* price elasticity of demand is also used. [6]

Interpreting Numerical Elasticities

Because demand curves slope downward, an *increase* in price is associated with a *decrease* in quantity de-

---

[1] It is also necessary that the two parts of Figure 5-1 be drawn on the same scale. Thus, for any given price change, the quantity changes more on the flatter curve than it does on the steeper one. It can be misleading to inspect a single curve and to conclude from its general appearance something about the degree of responsiveness of quantity demanded to price changes. You can make a curve appear as steep or as flat as you like by changing the scales. For example, a curve that looks steep when the horizontal scale is 1 inch = 100 units will look much flatter when it is drawn on a graph with the same vertical scale but when the horizontal scale is 1 inch = 1 unit.

[2] The use of averages is designed to avoid the ambiguity caused by the fact that, for example, the $.20 change in the price of beef is a different percentage of the original price, $1.70, than it is of the new price, $1.50 (11.8 percent versus 13.3 percent). We want the elasticity of demand between any two points A and B to be independent of whether we move from A to B or from B to A; as a result, using either original prices and quantities or new prices and quantities would be less satisfactory than using averages. In this illustration $.20 is unambiguously 12.5 percent of $1.60 and applies to a price increase from $1.50 to $1.70, as well as to the decrease discussed in the text. Further discussion is found in the appendix to this chapter.

TABLE 5-2   Price and Quantity Information Underlying Data of Table 5-1

Commodity	Unit	Original price	New price	Average price	Original quantity	New quantity	Average quantity
Beef	per pound	$ 1.70	$ 1.50	$ 1.60	116,250	123,750	120,000
Men's shirts	per shirt	8.10	7.90	8.00	197,500	202,500	200,000
Radios	per radio	40.10	39.90	40.00	9,950	10,050	10,000

These data provide the appropriate context of the data given in Table 5-1. The table relates the $.20 per unit price reduction of each commodity to the actual prices and quantities demanded.

manded, and vice versa. Since the percentage changes in price and quantity have opposite signs, demand elasticity is a negative number. (We shall follow the usual practice of ignoring the negative sign and speak of the measure as a positive number, as we have done in the illustrative calculations in Table 5-3.) Thus, the more responsive the quantity demanded (for example, radios relative to beef), the greater the elasticity of demand and the higher the measure (e.g., 2.0 compared to 0.5).

The numerical value of elasticity can vary from zero to infinity. Elasticity is zero when quantity demanded does not respond at all to a price change. As long as the percentage change in quantity is less than the percentage change in price, the elasticity of demand has a value of less than unity (i.e., less than 1). When the two percentage changes are equal to each other, elasticity is equal to unity. When the percentage change in quantity exceeds the percentage change in price, the value for the elasticity of demand is greater than unity.

When the percentage change in quantity is less than the percentage change in price (elasticity less than 1), there is said to be an **inelastic demand.** When the percentage change in quantity is greater than the percentage change in price (elasticity greater than 1), there is said to be an **elastic demand.** This

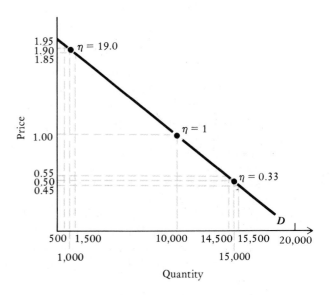

FIGURE 5-2   Elasticity Along a Straight-Line Demand Curve

Moving down a straight-line demand curve, elasticity falls continuously. On this straight line a reduction in price of $.10 always leads to the same increase (1,000 units) in quantity. Near the upper end of the curve, however, where price is $1.90 and quantity is 1,000 units, a reduction in price of $.10 (from $1.95 to $1.85) is just over a 5 percent price reduction, but the 1,000-unit increase in quantity is a 100 percent quantity increase. Here, elasticity (η) is 19. At the price of $.50 and quantity of 15,000 units, a price reduction of $.10 (from $.55 to $.45) leads to the same 1,000-unit increase in demand. The 20 percent price decrease combines with the 6.67 percent quantity increase to give an elasticity of 0.33.

TABLE 5-3   Calculation of Demand Elasticities

Commodity	(1) Percentage decrease in price	(2) Percentage increase in quantity	(3) Elasticity of demand (2) ÷ (1)
Beef	12.5	6.25	0.5
Men's shirts	2.5	2.50	1.0
Radios	0.5	1.00	2.0

Elasticity of demand is the percentage change in quantity divided by the percentage change in price. The percentage changes are based on average prices and quantities shown in Table 5-2. For example, the $.20 per pound decrease in the price of beef is 12.5 percent of $1.60. A $.20 change in the price of radios is only 0.5 percent of the average price per radio of $40.

FIGURE 5-3 Three Demand Curves

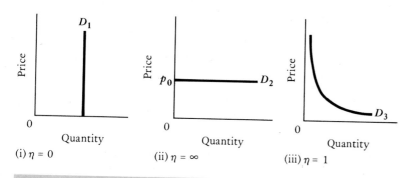

(i) $\eta = 0$ (ii) $\eta = \infty$ (iii) $\eta = 1$

Each of these demand curves has constant elasticity. D_1 has *zero elasticity*: The quantity demanded does not change at all when price changes. D_2 has *infinite elasticity at the price* p_0: A small price increase from p_0 decreases quantity demanded from an indefinitely large amount to zero. D_3 has *unit elasticity*: A given percentage increase in price brings an equal percentage decrease in quantity demanded at all points on the curve.

terminology is important, and you should become familiar with it. It is summarized in the first half of Box 5-1.

A demand curve need not, and usually does not, have the same elasticity over every part of the curve. Figure 5-2 shows that a negatively sloped, straight-line demand curve does not have a constant elasticity. A straight line has constant elasticity only when it is vertical or when it is horizontal. Figure 5-3 illustrates three special cases of demand curves with constant elasticities.

Price Elasticity and Changes in Total Expenditure

Assuming no taxes, the total amount spent by purchasers is also the total revenue received by the sellers. How does this revenue react when the price of a product is changed?

What happens to total revenue depends on the price elasticity of demand. If elasticity is less than unity, the percentage change in price exceeds the percentage change in quantity. The price change will then dominate, so that total revenue will change in the same direction as the price changes. If, however, elasticity exceeds unity, the percentage change in quantity exceeds the percentage change in price. The quantity change will then dominate, so that total revenue will change in the same direction as quantity changes (that is, in the opposite direction to the change in price).

The general relationship between elasticity and change in price can be summarized as follows:

1. **If demand is elastic, a fall in price increases total revenue and a rise in price reduces it.**
2. **If demand is inelastic, a fall in price reduces total revenue and a rise in price increases it.**
3. **If elasticity of demand is unity, a rise or a fall in price leaves total revenue unaffected. [7]**

Figure 5-4 illustrates the relationship between elasticity of demand and total expenditure; the straight-line demand curve from Figure 5-2 is reproduced in part (i), while the total expenditure (equal to the area under the demand curve) corresponding to each possible quantity demanded is shown in part (ii).

Consider two examples. When a bumper potato crop in the United States sent prices down 50 percent, quantity sold increased only 15 percent. Demand was clearly inelastic, and the result of the bumper crop was that potato farmers experienced a sharp *fall* in revenues. When, some years ago, Salt Lake City's transit authority cut its bus fares by 40 percent for the average journey, the volume of passenger traffic increased from 4.4 million to 14 million journeys within 2 years. Demand was clearly elastic, and revenues *rose* sharply as a result of the reduction in price.

Other examples can be constructed from Table 5-2. Calculations for what happens to total revenue when the prices of radios, men's shirts, and beef fall are shown in Table 5-4. In the case of beef, the demand is inelastic, and a cut in price lowers the sellers' revenue; in the case of radios, the demand is elastic, and a cut in price raises revenue. The bor-

BOX 5-1

Terminology of Elasticity

Term	Symbol	Numerical measure of elasticity	Verbal description
A. Price elasticity of demand (supply)	$\eta(\eta_S)$		
Perfectly or completely inelastic		Zero	Quantity demanded (supplied) does not change as price changes.
Inelastic		Greater than zero, less than one	Quantity demanded (supplied) changes by a smaller percentage than does price.
Unit elasticity		One	Quantity demanded (supplied) changes by exactly the same percentage as does price.
Elastic		Greater than one but finite	Quantity demanded (supplied) changes by a larger percentage than does price.
Perfectly, completely, or infinitely elastic		Infinity	Purchasers (sellers) are prepared to buy (sell) all they can at some price and none at all at an even slightly higher (lower) price.
B. Income elasticity of demand	η_Y		
Inferior good		Negative	Quantity demanded decreases as income increases.
Normal good		Positive	Quantity demanded increases as income increases:
Income-inelastic		Less than one	less than in proportion to income increase
Income-elastic		Greater than one	More than in proportion to income increase
C. Cross elasticity of demand	η_{xy}		
Substitute		Positive	Price increase of a substitute leads to an increase in quantity demanded of this good (and less of the substitute).
Complement		Negative	Price increase of a complement leads to a decrease in quantity demanded of this good (as well as less of the complement).

derline case is men's shirts; here, the elasticity is unity, and the cut in price leaves revenue unchanged.

What Determines Elasticity of Demand?

Table 5-5 shows some estimated price elasticities of demand. Evidently, elasticity can vary considerably.

The main determinant of elasticity is the availability of substitutes. Some commodities, such as margarine, cabbage, lamb, and Fords, have quite close substitutes—butter, other green vegetables, beef, and similar makes of cars. A change in the prices of these commodities, *the prices of the substitutes remaining constant,* can be expected to cause much substitution. A fall in price leads consumers to buy more of the

FIGURE 5-4   Elasticity of Demand and Total Expenditure

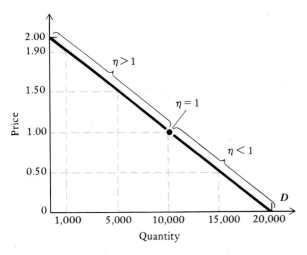

(i) Demand curve

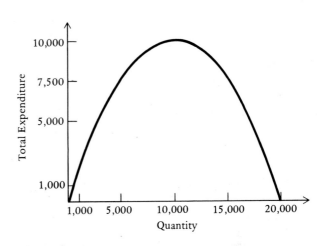

(ii) Total revenue

The change in total expenditure on a commodity in response to a change in price depends upon the elasticity of demand. The linear demand curve in part (i) reproduces Figure 5-2. Part (i) also shows three distinct ranges for the demand curve. Along the upper-left-hand range of the demand curve, elasticity is greater than 1. Along the lower-right-hand range, elasticity is less than 1. At the midpoint, elasticity is exactly equal to 1.

In part (ii), the total expenditure for each possible quantity demanded is plotted. For quantities demanded that are less than 10,000, elasticity of demand is greater than 1, and hence any increase in quantity demanded will be proportionately larger than the fall in price that caused it. In that range total expenditure is increasing. For quantities greater than 10,000, elasticity of demand is less than 1, and hence any increase in quantity demanded will be proportionately smaller than the fall in price that caused it. In that range total expenditure is falling. The maximum of total expenditure occurs at the midpoint where the elasticity of demand equals 1.

commodity and less of the substitutes, and a rise in price leads consumers to buy less of the commodity and more of the substitutes. More broadly defined commodities, such as all foods, all clothing, ciga-

rettes, and gasoline, have few, if any, satisfactory substitutes. A rise in their prices can be expected to cause a smaller fall in quantities demanded than would be the case if close substitutes were available.

TABLE 5-4   Changes in Total Revenue (Total Expenditure) for the Example of Table 5-2

Commodity	Price × quantity (original prices and quantities)	Price × quantity (new prices and quantities)	Change in revenue (expenditure)	Elasticity of demand from Table 5-3
Beef	$ 197,625	$ 185,625	− $12,000	0.5
Men's shirts	1,599,750	1,599,750	0	1.0
Radios	398,995	400,995	+ 2,000	2.0

Whether revenue increases or decreases in response to a price cut depends on whether demand is elastic or inelastic. The $197,625 figure is the product of the original price of beef ($1.70) and the original quantity (116,250 pounds); $185,625 is the product of the new price ($1.50) and quantity (123,750), and so on.

A commodity with close substitutes tends to have an elastic demand; a commodity with no close substitutes tends to have an inelastic demand.

Closeness of substitutes—and thus measured elasticity—depends upon both how the commodity is defined and the time period. This is explored in the following sections.

Definition of the Commodity

For food taken as a whole, demand is inelastic over a large price range. It does not follow, however, that any one food, such as white bread or beef, is a necessity in the same sense. Individual foods can have quite elastic demands, and they frequently do.

Durable goods provide a similar example. Durables as a whole are less elastic than individual kinds of durable goods. For example, when the price of television sets rises, many households may replace their lawnmower or their vacuum cleaner instead of buying that extra television set. Thus, while their purchases of television sets fall, their total purchases of durables do not.

Because most specific manufactured goods have close substitutes, studies show they tend to have price-elastic demand. Millinery, for example, has been estimated to have an elasticity of 3.0. In contrast, clothing in general tends to be inelastic.

Any one of a group of related products will tend to have an elastic demand, even though the demand for the group as a whole may be inelastic.

Long-Run and Short-Run Elasticity of Demand

Because it takes time to develop satisfactory substitutes, a demand that is inelastic in the short run may prove elastic when enough time has passed. For example, when the Tennessee Valley Authority (TVA) brought cheap electric power to the rural South in the 1930s, few households were wired for electricity. The initial measurements showed demand for electricity to be very inelastic. Some commentators even argued that it was foolish to invest so much money in bringing cheap electricity to the South because people did not buy it even at low prices. Gradually, however, households became electrified and purchased appliances, and new industries moved into the area to take advantage of the TVA's cheap electric

TABLE 5-5 Estimated Price Elasticities of Demand[a] *(selected commodities)*	
Demand significantly inelastic (less than 0.9)	
Potatoes	0.3
Sugar	0.3
Public transportation	0.4
All foods	0.4
Cigarettes	0.5
Gasoline	0.6
All clothing	0.6
Consumer durables	0.8
Demand of close to unit elasticity (between 0.9 and 1.1)	
Beef	
Beer	
Marijuana	
Demand significantly elastic (more than 1.1)	
Furniture	1.2
Electricity	1.3
Lamb and mutton (U.K.)	1.5
Automobiles	2.1
Millinery	3.0

[a] For the United States except where noted.

The wide range of price elasticities is illustrated by these selected measures. These elasticities, from various studies, are representative of literally hundreds of existing estimates. Explanations of some of the differences are discussed in the text.

power. As this occurred, measured elasticity steadily increased.

Petroleum provides a more recent example. When the first OPEC oil price shock occurred in the mid-1970s, the short-run demand for oil proved to be highly inelastic. Large price increases were met in the short run by very small reductions in quantity demanded. In this case the short run lasted for several years. Gradually, however, the high price of petroleum products led to such adjustments as the development of smaller, more fuel-efficient cars, economizing on heating oil by installing more efficient insulation, and replacement of fuel oil in many industrial processes with such other power sources as coal and hydroelectricity. The long-run elasticity of demand, relating the change in price to the change in quantity demanded after all adjustments were made, turned out to have an elasticity of well over 1, although the long-run adjustments took as much as a decade to work out.

The degree of response to a price change, and thus the measured price elasticity of demand, will tend to be greater the longer is the time span considered.

Because the elasticity of demand for a commodity changes over time as consumers adjust their habits and substitutes are developed, the demand curve also changes; hence, a distinction can be made between short-run and long-run demand curves. Every demand curve shows the response of consumer demand to a change in price. For such commodities as cornflakes and pillowcases, the full response occurs quickly and there is little reason to worry about longer-term effects, but other commodities are typically used in connection with highly durable appliances or machines. A change in price of, say, electricity and gasoline may not have its major effect until the stock of appliances and machines using these commodities has been adjusted. This adjustment may take a long time to occur.

For commodities whose substitutes are developed over a period of time, it is helpful to identify two kinds of demand curve. A *short-run demand curve* shows the response of quantity demanded to a change in price for a given structure of the durable goods that use the commodity and for the existing sets of substitute commodities. A different short-run demand curve will exist for each such structure.

The *long-run demand curve* shows the response of quantity demanded to a change in price after enough time has passed to assure that all adjustments to the changed price have occurred. The relationship between long-run and short-run demand curves is shown in Figure 5-5. The principal conclusion, already suggested in the above discussion of elasticity, is:

The long-run demand curve for a commodity will tend to be substantially more elastic than any of the short-run demand curves.

Market adjustment.   The distinction between long-run and short-run demand curves, and hence between long-run and short-run demand elasticity, has important implications for the market response to a shift in supply.

In the short run, when demand is relatively inelastic, a shift in supply leads to a sharp change in the equilibrium price but leads to only a small change in the equilibrium quantity exchanged. However, in the long run demand is more elastic than in the short

FIGURE 5-5   Short-Run and Long-Run Demand Curves

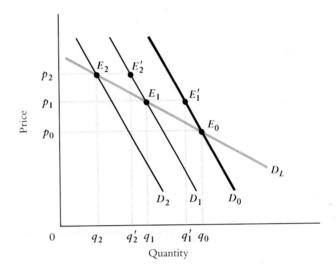

The long-run demand curve is more elastic than the short-run demand curve. D_L is a long-run demand curve. Suppose consumers are fully adjusted to price p_0. Equilibrium is then at E_0, with quantity demanded q_0. Now suppose price rises to p_1. In the short run consumers will react along the short-run demand curve D_0 and reduce consumption to q_1'. Once time has permitted the full range of adjustments to price p_1, however, a new equilibrium at E_1 will be reached with quantity q_1. At E_1 there is a new short-run demand curve D_1. A further rise in price to p_2 would lead first to a short-run equilibrium at E_2, but eventually to a new long-run equilibrium at E_2. The screened long-run demand curve is more elastic than the short-run curves.

run. This responsiveness of demand means that in the long run the shift in supply gives rise to a smaller change in the equilibrium price and a larger change in quantity.

Figure 5-6 shows the case of an increase in supply. In the short run the increase in supply leads to a movement down the relatively inelastic short-run demand curve; it thus gives rise to a large fall in price but to only a small increase in quantity. In the long run demand is more elastic, so that long-run equilibrium has price and quantity above those that prevailed in the short-run equilibrium.

The fact that price falls more in the short run than in the long run is referred to as *overshooting* of the price. This overshooting of price, and the under-shooting of quantity that is also evident in the figure, is a direct consequence of demand being less elastic in the short run than in the long run.

Other Demand Elasticities

Income Elasticity of Demand

One of the most important determinants of demand is the income of the potential customers. When the Food and Agricultural Organization (FAO) of the United Nations wants to estimate the future demand for some crop, it needs to know by how much world income will grow and how much of that additional income will be spent on the particular foodstuff. For example, as a nation gets richer, its consumption patterns change, with relatively more being spent on meat and relatively less being spent on staples such as rice and potatoes.

The responsiveness of demand to changes in income is termed **income elasticity of demand** and may be symbolized η_y.

$$\eta_y = \frac{\text{percentage change in quantity demanded}}{\text{percentage change in income}}$$

For most goods, increases in income lead to increases in demand, and income elasticity will be positive. These are called **normal goods.** Goods for which consumption decreases in response to a rise in income have negative income elasticities and are called **inferior goods.**

The income elasticity of normal goods may be greater than unity (elastic) or less than unity (inelastic), depending on whether the percentage change in the quantity demanded is greater or less than the percentage change in income that brought it about. It is also common to use the terms *income-elastic* and *income-inelastic* to refer to income elasticities of greater or less than unity. See Box 5-1 for further discussion of elasticity terminology.

The reaction of demand to changes in income is extremely important. We know that in most Western countries economic growth has caused the level of

FIGURE 5-6 Short-Run and Long-Run Equilibrium Following an Increase in Supply

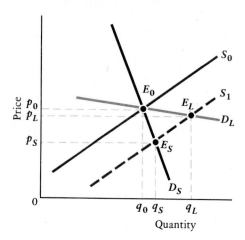

The magnitude of the changes in the equilibrium price and quantity following a shift in supply depends upon the time allowed for demand to adjust. In the short run the change in the price is greater and the change in quantity is less than in the long run. The initial equilibrium is at E_0, with price p_0 and quantity q_0. There is then an increase in supply so that the supply curve shifts from S_0 to S_1.

On impact the relevant demand curve is the short-run curve D_S, so that the new equilibrium immediately following the supply shock is E_S. Price falls sharply to p_S, and quantity rises only to q_S. In the long run, the demand curve is the more elastic one given by D_L, and equilibrium is at E_L. The long-run equilibrium price is p_L (greater than p_S), and quantity is q_L (greater than q_S).

The overshooting of the price is clear, since price initially falls from p_0 to p_S and rises back towards p_S, reaching p_L. Quantity, however, undershoots, since it rises first from q_0 to q_S, and then again from q_S to q_L.

While revenue at the new long-run equilibrium (given by the product $p_L q_L$) is thus clearly greater than that at the short-run equilibrium (given by the product $p_S q_S$), whether it is greater than or less than revenue at the initial equilibrium (given by the product $p_0 q_0$) depends upon the elasticity of the long-run demand curve.

income to double every 20 to 30 years over a sustained period of at least a century. This rise in income is shared to some extent by most citizens. As they find their incomes increasing, they increase their demands for most commodities, but the demands for some commodities such as food and basic clothing

100

will not increase much, while the demands for other commodities will increase rapidly. In developing countries, such as Ireland and Mexico, the demand for durable goods is increasing most rapidly as household incomes rise, while in the United States it is the demand for services that is rising most rapidly. The uneven impact of the growth of income on the demands for different commodities has important economic effects, which are studied at several different points in this book, beginning with the discussion of agriculture in Chapter 6.

What Determines Income Elasticity?

The variations in income elasticities shown in Table 5-6 suggest that the more basic or staple a commodity is, the lower is its income elasticity. Food as a whole has an income elasticity of 0.2; consumer durables, of 1.8. In the United States pork and such starchy roots as potatoes are inferior goods; their quantity consumed falls as income rises.

Does the distinction between luxuries and necessities explain differences in income elasticities? Table 5-6 suggests that it does. The case of meals

eaten away from home is one example. Such meals are almost always more expensive, calorie for calorie, than meals prepared at home. It would thus be expected that at lower ranges of income restaurant meals would be regarded as an expensive luxury, but the demand for them would expand substantially as households became richer. This is in fact what happens.

Does this mean that the market demand for the foodstuffs that appear on restaurant menus will also have high income elasticities? Generally, the answer is no. When a household eats out rather than prepares meals at home, the main change is not in what is eaten but in who prepares it. The additional expenditure on "food" goes mainly to pay cooks and waiters and to yield a return on the restaurateur's capital. Thus, when a household expands its expenditure on restaurant food by 2.4 percent in response to a 1 percent rise in its income, most of the extra expenditure on "food" goes to workers in service industries; little, if any, finds its way into the pockets of farmers. Here is a striking example of the general tendency for households to spend a rising proportion of their incomes on services and a lower proportion on foodstuffs as their incomes rise.

The more basic is an item in the consumption pattern of households, the lower is its income elasticity.

So far we have focused on differences in income elasticities among commodities. However, income elasticities for any one commodity also vary with the level of a household's income. When incomes are low, households may eat almost no meat and consume lots of starchy foods such as bread and potatoes; when incomes are higher, they may eat cheap cuts of meat and more green vegetables along with their bread and potatoes; when incomes are even higher, they are likely to eat more (and more expensive) meat, to substitute frozen for canned vegetables, and to eat a greater variety of foods.

What is true of individual households is also true of countries. Empirical studies show that for different countries at comparable stages of economic development, income elasticities are similiar. However, the countries of the world are at various stages of economic development and so have widely different

---

TABLE 5-6   Estimated Income Elasticities of Demand[a] (selected commodities)

Inferior goods (negative income elasticities)	
Whole milk	−0.5
Pig products	−0.2
Starchy roots	−0.2
Inelastic normal goods (0.0 to 1.0)	
Wine (France)	0.1
All food	0.2
Poultry	0.3
Cheese	0.4
Cigarettes	0.8
Elastic normal goods (greater than 1.0)	
Gasoline	1.1
Wine	1.4
Cream (U.K.)	1.7
Consumer durables	1.8
Poultry (Sri Lanka)	2.0
Restaurant meals (U.K.)	2.4

[a] For the United States except where noted.

Income elasticities vary widely across commodities and sometimes across countries. The basic source of food estimates by country is the FAO, but many individual studies have been made. Explanations of some of the differences are discussed in the text.

FIGURE 5-7   **Income-Consumption Curves of Different Commodities**

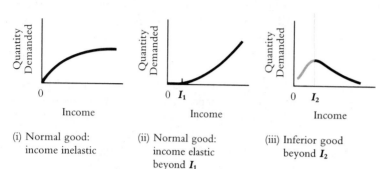

(i) Normal good: income inelastic

(ii) Normal good: income elastic beyond I_1

(iii) Inferior good beyond I_2

Different shapes of the curve relating quantity demanded to income correspond to different ranges of income elasticity. Normal goods have rising curves; inferior goods have falling curves. Many different patterns of income elasticity have been observed. The good in (i) is a typical normal good that is a necessity. It is purchased at all levels of income; even at high levels of income some fraction of extra income is spent on it, although this fraction steadily decreases. The good in (ii) is a luxury good that is income elastic beyond income I_1. The good in (iii) is a necessity at low incomes that becomes an inferior good for incomes beyond I_2.

income elasticities for the same products. Notice in Table 5-6 the different income elasticity of poultry in the United States, where it is a standard item of consumption, and in Sri Lanka, where it is a luxury.

Graphical Representation

Increases in income shift the demand curve for a normal good to the right and for an inferior good to the left. Figure 5-7 shows a different kind of graph, an **income-consumption curve.** The curve resembles an ordinary demand curve in one respect: It shows the relationship of quantity demanded to one variable, *ceteris paribus.* The variable, however, is not price but household income. (An increase in the price of the commodity, incomes remaining constant, would shift the curves shown in Figure 5-7 downward.)

The figure shows three different patterns of income elasticity. Goods that consumers regard as necessities will have high income elasticities at low levels of income but will show low income elasticities beyond some level. The obvious reason is that as incomes rise, it becomes possible for households to devote a smaller proportion of their income to meeting basic needs and a larger proportion to buying things they have always wanted but could not afford. Some of these necessities may even become inferior goods. So-called luxury goods will not tend to be purchased at low levels of income but will have high income elasticities once incomes rise enough to

permit households to sample the better things of life available to them.[3]

Cross Elasticity of Demand

The responsiveness of demand to changes in the price of another commodity is called **cross elasticity of demand.** It is often denoted η_{xy} and defined as[4]

$$\eta_{xy} = \frac{\text{percentage change in quantity demanded of one good } (X)}{\text{percentage change in price of another good } (Y)}$$

Cross elasticity can vary from minus infinity to plus infinity. Complementary commodities, such as cars and gasoline, have negative cross elasticities. A large rise in the price of gasoline will lead (as it did in the United States) to a decline in the demand for

[3] In Figure 5-7, in contrast to the ordinary demand curve, quantity demanded is on the vertical axis. This follows the usual practice of putting the variable to be explained (called the *dependent variable*) on the vertical axis and the explanatory variable (called the *independent variable*) on the horizontal axis. It is the ordinary demand curve that has the axes "backward." The explanation is buried in the history of economics, and dates to Alfred Marshall's *Principles of Economics* (1890), the classic that is one of the foundation stones of modern price theory. **[8]** For better or worse, Marshall's scheme is now used by everybody, although mathematicians never fail to wonder at this further example of the odd ways of economists.

[4] The change in price of good Y causes the *demand curve* for good X to shift. Holding the price of good X constant means that we can measure the shift in the demand curve in terms of the change in quantity demanded of good X at the given price of good X.

cars, as some people decided to do without a car and others decided not to buy a second (or third) car. Substitute commodities, such as cars and public transport, have positive cross elasticities. A large rise in the price of cars (relative to public transport) would lead to a rise in the demand for public transport as some people shifted from cars to public transport.

Measures of cross elasticity sometimes prove helpful in defining whether producers of similar products are in competition with each other. For example, glass bottles and tin cans have a high cross elasticity of demand. The producer of bottles is thus in competition with the producer of cans. If the bottle company raises its price, it will lose substantial sales to the can producer. Men's shoes and women's shoes have a low cross elasticity. A producer of men's shoes is not in close competition with a producer of women's shoes. If the former raises its price, it will not lose many sales to the latter. This kind of knowledge has been extremely important in antitrust cases in which the issue was whether a firm in one industry was or was not in active competition with firms in another industry. Indeed, many of the most interesting studies of cross elasticity have been made during antitrust inquiries to determine whether specific products are substitutes (see Chapter 15). Whether cellophane and Saran Wrap or aluminum cable and copper cable are or are not substitutes may determine questions of monopoly under the law. The positive or negative sign and the size of cross elasticities tell us whether or not goods are substitutes.

Elasticity of Supply

The concept of elasticity can be applied to supply as well as to demand. Just as elasticity of demand measures the response of quantity demanded to changes in any of the forces that influence it, so elasticity of supply measures the response of quantity supplied to changes in any of the forces that influence it. We will focus on the commodity's own price as a factor influencing supply.

Elasticity of supply measures the responsiveness of the quantity supplied to a change in the commodity's own price. It is denoted η_S and defined as

$$\eta_S = \frac{\text{percentage change in quantity supplied}}{\text{percentage change in price}}$$

This is also often called *supply elasticity.*

The supply curves considered in this chapter all have positive slopes: An increase in price causes an increase in quantity sold. Such supply curves all have positive elasticities.

There are important special cases. If the supply curve is vertical—the quantity supplied does not change as price changes—elasticity of supply is zero. This would be the case, for example, if suppliers produced a given quantity and dumped it on the market for whatever it would bring. A horizontal supply curve has an infinitely high elasticity of supply: A small drop in price would reduce the quantity producers are willing to supply from an indefinitely large amount to zero. Between these two extremes elasticity of supply will vary with the shape of the supply curve.[5]

Long-Run and Short-Run Elasticity of Supply

Supply elasticities are important for many problems in economics. Much of the treatment of demand elasticity carries over to supply elasticity. For example, the ease of substitution can vary in production as well as in consumption. If the price of a commodity rises, how much more can be produced profitably? This depends in part on whether it is easy to shift from the production of other commodities to the one whose price has risen. If agricultural land and labor can be readily shifted from one crop to another, the supply of any one crop will be more elastic than if they cannot.

As with demand, length of time for response is critical. It may be difficult to change quantities supplied in response to a price increase in a matter of weeks or months but easy to do so over a period of years. An obvious example concerns the planting cycle of crops. Also, new oil fields can be discovered, wells drilled, and pipelines built over a period of years but not in a few months. Thus elasticity of oil

---

[5] Steepness, which is related to absolute rather than percentage changes, is *not* always a reliable guide. For example, as is shown in the appendix to this chapter, *any* upward-sloping straight line passing through the origin has an elasticity of $+1.0$ over its entire range.

FIGURE 5-8   Short-Run and Long-Run Equilibrium Following a Shift in Demand

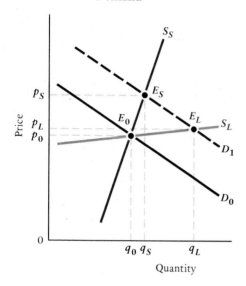

The magnitudes of the changes in the equilibrium price and quantity following a shift in demand depend upon the time frame of the analysis. In the short run the change in the price is greater and the change in quantity is less than in the long run. The initial equilibrium is at E_0, with price p_0 and quantity q_0. There is then an increase in demand so that the demand curve shifts from D_0 to D_1.

On impact the relevant supply curve is the short–run curve S_S, so that the new equilibrium immediately following the demand shock is E_S. Price rises sharply to p_S, and quantity rises only to q_S. In the long run the supply curve is the more elastic one given by S_L. In the long run equilibrium is at E_L; price is p_L (less than p_S), and quantity is q_L (greater than q_S).

The "overshooting" of the price discussed in the text is clear. As we can see also, quantity adjusts only partially on impact, so that the long-run change in quantity exceeds the short-run change.

While revenue at the new long-run equilibrium (given by the product $p_L q_L$) is thus clearly greater than that at the initial equilibrium (given by the product $p_0 q_0$), whether it is greater than or less than revenue at the short-run equilibrium (given by the product $p_S q_S$) depends on the elasticity of the demand curve.

supply is much greater over five years than over one year.

Market adjustment.   The distinction between long-run and short-run supply curves, and hence between long-run and short-run supply elasticity, has important implications for the market response to a shift in demand.

In the short run, when supply is relatively inelastic, a shift in demand leads to a sharp change in the equilibrium price but to only a small change in the equilibrium quantity exchanged. However, in the long run, when supply is more elastic than in the short run, the shift in demand leads to a smaller change in the equilibrium price and a larger change in quantity.

Figure 5-8 illustrates the case of an increase in demand. In the short run the increase in demand leads to a large increase in price but to only a small increase in quantity as supply rises along the inelastic short-run supply curve. In the long run supply is more elastic; as supply responds, price falls but quantity continues to grow as the market adjusts toward the new long-run equilibrium.

The overshooting of price, and the undershooting of quantity that is also evident in the figure, is analogous to that shown in Figure 5-6 in response to a shift in supply. Here it arises following a shift in demand and is a direct consequence of supply being less elastic in the short run than in the long run.

Supply Elasticity and Costs

Supply elasticity depends to a great extent on how costs behave as output is varied, an issue that will be treated at length in Part Three. If costs of production rise rapidly as output rises, then the stimulus to expand production in response to a rise in price will quickly be choked off by increases in costs. In this case supply will tend to be rather inelastic. If, however, costs rise only slowly as production increases, a rise in price that raises profits will elicit a large increase in quantity supplied before the rise in costs puts a halt to the expansion in output. In this case supply will tend to be rather elastic.

SUMMARY

1. *Price elasticity of demand* (also simply called *elasticity of demand*) is a measure of the extent to which the quantity demanded of a commodity responds to a change in its price. It is defined as the percentage change in quantity demanded divided by the percentage change in

price that brought it about. Elasticity is defined to be a positive number, and it can vary from zero to infinity.

2. When the numerical measure of elasticity is less than unity, demand is *inelastic*. This means that the percentage change in quantity demanded is less than the percentage change in price that brought it about. When the numerical measure exceeds unity, demand is *elastic*. This means that the percentage change in quantity demanded is greater than the percentage change in price that brought it about.

3. Elasticity and total revenue of sellers are related in the following way: If elasticity is less than unity, a fall in price lowers total revenue; if elasticity is greater than unity, a fall in price raises total revenue; and if elasticity is unity, total revenue does not change as price changes.

4. The main determinant of the price elasticity of demand is the availability of substitutes for the commodity. Any one of a group of close substitutes will tend to have an elastic demand even though the group as a whole may have a highly inelastic demand.

5. Elasticity of demand tends to be greater the longer the time over which adjustment occurs. Items that have few substitutes in the short run may develop ample substitutes when consumers and producers have time to adapt. Hence, a shift in supply will lead to a larger change in price and a smaller change in quantity in the short run than in the long run.

6. *Income elasticity of demand* is the percentage change in quantity demanded divided by the percentage change in income that brought it about. Luxuries tend to have higher income elasticities than necessities. The income elasticity of demand for a commodity will usually change as income varies. For example, a commodity that has a high income elasticity at a low income (because increases in income bring it within reach of the typical household) may have a low or negative income elasticity at higher incomes (because with further rises in incomes it can be replaced by a superior substitute).

7. *Cross elasticity of demand* is the percentage change in quantity demanded divided by the percentage change in the price of some other commodity that brought it about. It is used to define commodities that are substitutes for one another (positive cross elasticity) and commodities that complement one another (negative cross elasticity).

8. *Elasticity of supply* is an important concept in economics. It measures the ratio of the percentage change in the quantity supplied of a commodity to the percentage change in its price. It is the analogue on the supply side to the elasticity of demand.

9. Supply tends to be more elastic in the long run than in the short run, since there are more possibilities for substituting production techniques and uses of inputs. This means that a shift in demand will lead to a larger change in price and a smaller change in quantity in the short run than in the long run.

TOPICS FOR REVIEW

Elasticity of demand

Significance of elastic and inelastic demands

Difference between inelastic and perfectly inelastic and between elastic and infinitely elastic

Relationship between demand elasticity and total expenditure

Short-run and long-run demand curves

Income elasticity of demand

Income-elastic and income-inelastic demands
Normal goods and inferior goods
Cross elasticity of demand
Substitutes and complements
Elasticity of supply
Short-run and long-run supply curves

DISCUSSION QUESTIONS

1. From the following quotations, what (if anything) can you conclude about elasticity of demand?
   a. "Good weather resulted in record corn harvests and sent corn prices tumbling. For many corn farmers the result has been calamitous."
   b. "Ridership always went up when bus fares came down, but the increased patronage never was enough to prevent a decrease in overall revenue."
   c. "The 30 percent increase in postal rates has led us [The Narragansett Electric Co.] to have 60 percent of our bills hand delivered instead of mailed."
   d. "Coffee to me is an essential—you've gotta have it no matter what the price."
   e. "Soaring real estate prices does little to curb housing demand in Palo Alto."

2. What would you predict about the relative price elasticity of demand of (a) food, (b) meat, (c) beef, (d) chuck roast, (e) chuck roast sold at Safeway? What would you predict about their relative income elasticities?

3. "Avocados have a limited market, not greatly affected by price until the price falls to less than $.25 a pound. At that price they are much demanded by manufacturers of dog food." Interpret this statement in terms of price elasticity.

4. "Home computers were a leader in sales appeal through much of the 1980s. However, per capita sales are much lower in Puerto Rico than in the United States, lower in Mississippi and Arkansas than in Illinois and Texas. Manufacturers are puzzled by the big differences." Can you offer an explanation in terms of elasticity?

5. What elasticity measure or measures would be useful in answering the following questions?
   a. Will cheaper transport into the central city help keep downtown shopping centers profitable?
   b. Will raising the bulk-postage rate increase or decrease the postal deficit?
   c. Are producers of toothpaste and mouthwash in competition with each other?
   d. What effect will falling gasoline prices have on the sale of cars that use diesel fuel?

6. Interpret the following statements in terms of the relevant elasticity concept:
   a. "As fuel for tractors has gotten more expensive, many farmers have shifted from plowing their fields to no-till farming. No-till acreage increased from 30 million acres to 95 million acres in less than ten years."
   b. "Fertilizer makers brace for a dismal year as fertilizer prices soar."
   c. "When farmers are hurting, small towns feel the pain."

7. It has been observed recently that obesity is a more frequent medical problem for the relatively poor than for the middle-income classes. Can you use the theory of demand to shed light on this observation?

8. Suggest commodities that you think might have the following patterns of elasticity of demand.
    a. High income elasticity, high price elasticity
    b. High income elasticity, low price elasticity
    c. Low income elasticity, low price elasticity
    d. Low income elasticity, high price elasticity

9. In 1983 the new United States Football League was playing to half empty stadiums. The Michigan Panthers averaged 22,250 people at its regular season games. When the team made the playoffs, its owner, Alfred Taubman, *lowered* ticket prices by about 30 percent and drew a crowd of over 60,000 to the Silverdome, near Detroit. "This crowd gave us a hint," said the Panthers' general manager. "We will sit down and take that turnout into consideration. I think tickets for Panther games will be cheaper next season."

    What does this tell us about price elasticity of demand? Does the fact that Detroit was suffering from 25 percent unemployment at the time have any relevance in evaluating the experience?

10. When the New York City Opera was faced with a growing deficit, it cut its ticket prices by 20 percent, hoping to attract more customers. At the same time, the New York Transit Authority raised subway fares to reduce its growing deficit. Was one of these two opposite approaches to reducing a deficit necessarily wrong?

Elasticity: A Formal Analysis

The verbal definition of elasticity used in the text may be written symbolically in the following form:

$$\eta = \frac{\Delta q}{\Delta p} \times \frac{\text{average } p}{\text{average } q}$$

where the averages are over the arc of the demand curve being considered. This is called **arc elasticity,** and it measures the average responsiveness of quantity to price over an interval of the demand curve.

Most theoretical treatments use a different but related concept called **point elasticity.** This is the measure of responsiveness of quantity to price at a particular point on the demand curve. The precise definition of point elasticity uses the concept of a derivative, which is drawn from differential calculus.

In this appendix we first study arc elasticity, which may be regarded as an approximation to point elasticity. Then we study point elasticity.

Before proceeding, we should notice one further change. In the text to this chapter we reported our price elasticities as positive values, and thus implicitly multiplied all our calculations by −1. In theoretical work it is more convenient to retain the concept's natural sign. Thus normal demand curves will have negative signs, and statements about "more" or "less" elastic must be understood to refer to the absolute, not the algebraic, value of demand elasticity.

The following symbols will be used throughout.

$\eta \equiv$ elasticity of demand
$\eta_s \equiv$ elasticity of supply
$q \equiv$ the original quantity
$\Delta q \equiv$ the change in quantity
$p \equiv$ the original price
$\Delta p \equiv$ the change in price

Arc Elasticity as an Approximation to Point Elasticity

Point elasticity measures elasticity at some point (p,q). In the approximate definition, however, the responsiveness is measured over a small range starting from that point. For example, in Figure 5A-1 the elasticity at point 1 can be measured by the responsiveness of quantity demanded to a change in price that takes price and quantity from point 1 to point 2. The algebraic formula for this elasticity concept is

$$\eta = \frac{\Delta q}{\Delta p} \times \frac{p}{q} \qquad [1]$$

This is similar to the definition of arc elasticity used in the text except that since elasticity is being measured at a point, the p and q corresponding to that point are used (rather than the average p and q over an arc of the curve).

Equation 1 splits elasticity into two parts: $\Delta q/\Delta p$, the ratio of the change in quantity to the change in price, which is related to the *slope* of the demand curve, and p/q, which is related to the *point* on the curve at which the measurement is made.

Figure 5A-1 shows a straight-line demand curve. To measure the elasticity at point 1, take p and q at that point and then consider a price change, say, to point 2, and measure Δp and Δq as indicated. The slope of the straight line joining points 1 and 2 is $\Delta p/\Delta q$. The term in Equation 1 is $\Delta q/\Delta p$, which is the reciprocal of $\Delta p/\Delta q$. Therefore, the first term in the elasticity formula is the reciprocal of the slope of the straight line joining the two price-quantity positions under consideration.

Although point elasticity of demand refers to a point (p,q) on the demand curve, the first term in Equation 1 still refers to changes over an arc of the curve. This is the part of the formula that involves approximation, and, as we shall see, it has some unsatisfactory results. Nonetheless, some interesting theorems can be derived by using this formula as long as we confine ourselves to straight-line demand and supply curves.

1. The elasticity of a downward-sloping straight-line demand curve varies from zero at the quantity axis to infinity at the price axis. First notice that a straight line has a constant slope, so the ratio $\Delta p/\Delta q$ is the same

FIGURE 5A-1   A Straight-Line Demand Curve

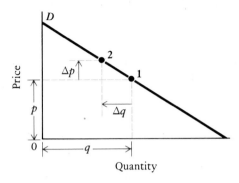

Because p/q varies with $\Delta q/\Delta p$ constant, the elasticity varies along this demand curve, being high at the left and low at the right.

FIGURE 5A-2   Two Parallel Straight-Line Demand Curves

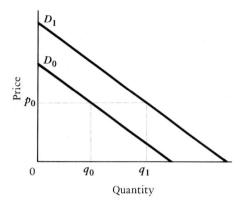

For any given price the quantities are different on these two parallel curves; thus the elasticities are different, being higher on D_0 than on D_1.

everywhere on the line. Therefore its reciprocal, $\Delta q/\Delta p$, must also be constant. The changes in η can now be inferred by inspecting the ratio p/q. Where the line cuts the quantity axis, price is zero, so the ratio p/q is zero; thus $\eta = 0$. Moving up the line, p rises and q falls, so the ratio p/q rises; thus elasticity rises. Approaching the top of the line, q approaches zero, so the ratio becomes very large. Thus elasticity increases without limit as the price axis is approached.

   2. *Where there are two straight-line demand curves of the same slope, the one farther from the origin is less elastic at each price than the one closer to the origin.* Figure 5A-2 shows two parallel straight-line demand curves. Compare the elasticities of the two curves at any price, say, p_0. Since the curves are parallel, the ratio $\Delta q/\Delta p$ is the same on both curves. Since elasticities at the same price are being compared on both curves, p is the same, and the only factor left to vary is q. On the curve farther from the origin, quantity is larger (i.e., $q_1 > q_0$) and hence p_0/q_1 is smaller than p_0/q_0; thus η is smaller.

   It follows from theorem 2 that parallel shifts of a straight-line demand curve lower elasticity (at each price) when the line shifts outward and raise elasticity when the line shifts inward.

   3. *The elasticities of two intersecting straight-line demand curves can be compared at the point of intersection merely by comparing slopes, the steeper curve being the* less elastic. In Figure 5A-3 there are two intersecting curves. At the point of intersection, p and q are common to both curves and hence the ratio p/q is the same. Therefore η varies only with $\Delta p/\Delta q$. On

FIGURE 5A-3   Two Intersecting Straight-Line Demand Curves

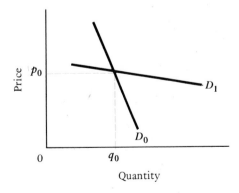

Elasticities are different at the point of intersection of these demand curves because the slopes are different, being higher on D_0 than on D_1. D_1 is more elastic at p_0.

the steeper curve, $\Delta q/\Delta p$ is smaller than on the flatter curve, so elasticity is lower.

4. *If the slope of a straight-line demand curve changes while the price intercept remains constant, elasticity at any given price is unchanged.* This is an interesting case for at least two reasons. First, when more customers having similar tastes to those already in the market enter the market, the demand curve pivots outward in this way. Second, when more firms enter a market that is shared proportionally among all firms, each firm's demand curve shifts inward in this way.

Consider in Figure 5A-4 the elasticities at point b on demand curve D_0 and at point c on demand curve D_1. We shall focus on the two triangles, abp_0 on D_0 and acp_0 on D_1, formed by the two straight-line demand curves emanating from point a and by the price p_0.

The price p_0 is the line segment $0p_0$. The quantities q_0 and q_1 are the line segments p_0b and p_0c, respectively. The slope of D_0 is $\Delta p/\Delta q = ap_0/p_0b$ and the slope of D_1 is $\Delta p/\Delta q = ap_0/p_0c$.

From Equation 1 we can represent the elasticities of D_0 and D_1 at the points b and c, respectively, as

$$\eta \text{ at point } b = \frac{p_0b}{ap_0} \times \frac{0p_0}{p_0b} = \frac{0p_0}{ap_0}$$

$$\eta \text{ at point } c = \frac{p_0c}{ap_0} \times \frac{0p_0}{p_0c} = \frac{0p_0}{ap_0}$$

The two are the same. The reason is that the distance corresponding to the quantity demanded at p_0 appears in both the numerator and the denominator and thus cancels out.

Put differently, if the straight-line demand curve D_0 is twice as steep as D_1, it has half the quantity demanded at p_0. Therefore in the expression

$$\eta = \frac{\Delta q}{q} \times \frac{p}{\Delta p}$$

the steeper slope (a smaller Δq for the same Δp) is exactly offset by the smaller quantity demanded (a smaller q for the same p).

5. *Any straight-line supply curve through the origin has an elasticity of 1.* Such a supply curve is shown in Figure 5A-5. Consider the two triangles with the sides p, q, and S curve, and the Δp, Δq, and the S curve. Clearly, these are similar triangles. Therefore, the ratios of their sides are equal; that is,

$$\frac{p}{q} = \frac{\Delta p}{\Delta q} \qquad\qquad [2]$$

FIGURE 5A-4   Two Straight-Line Demand Curves from the Same Price Intercept

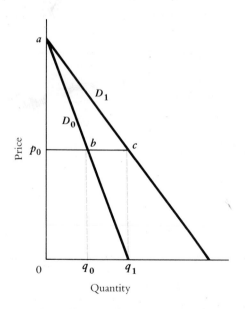

The elasticity is the same on D_0 and D_1 at any price p_0. This situation occurs because the steeper slope of D_0 is exactly offset by the smaller quantity demanded at any price.

FIGURE 5A-5   A Straight-Line Supply Curve Through the Origin

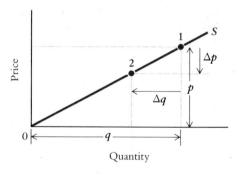

At every point on the curve, p/q equals $\Delta p/\Delta q$; thus elasticity equals unity at every point.

Elasticity of supply is defined as

$$\eta_s = \frac{\Delta q}{\Delta p} \times \frac{p}{q}$$

which, by substitution from Equation 2, gives

$$\eta_s = \frac{q}{p} \times \frac{p}{q} \equiv 1$$

6. *The elasticity measured from any point p,q, according to Equation 1, is dependent on the direction and magnitude of the change in price and quantity.* Except for a straight line (for which the slope does not change), the ratio $\Delta q/\Delta p$ will not be the same at different points on a curve. Figure 5A-6 shows a demand curve that is not a straight line. To measure the elasticity from point 1, the ratio $\Delta q/\Delta p$—and thus η—will vary according to the size and the direction of the price change.

Theorem 6 yields a result that is very inconvenient and is avoided by use of a different definition of point elasticity.

Point Elasticity According to the Precise Definition

To measure the elasticity at a point exactly, it is necessary to know the reaction of quantity to a change in price *at that point,* not over a range of the curve.

The reaction of quantity to price change at a point is called *dq/dp,* and this is defined to be the reciprocal of the slope of the straight line tangent to the demand curve at the point in question. In Figure 5A-7 the elasticity of demand at point 1 is the ratio *p/q* (as it has been in all previous measures), now multiplied by the ratio of $\Delta q/\Delta p$ measured along the straight line *T,* tangent to the curve at 1, that is, by *dq/dp.*

Thus, the exact definition of point elasticity is

$$\eta = \frac{dq}{dp} \times \frac{p}{q} \qquad [3]$$

The ratio *dq/dp,* as defined, is in fact the differential calculus concept of the *derivative* of quantity with respect to price.

This definition of point elasticity is the one nor-

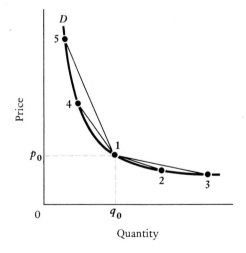

FIGURE 5A-6   Point Elasticity of Demand Measured by the Approximate Formula

When the approximation of $\eta = \frac{\Delta q}{\Delta p} \times \frac{p}{q}$ is used, **many elasticities are measured from point 1 because the slope of the chord between point 1 and every other point on the curve varies.**

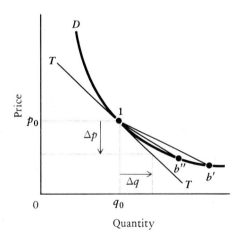

FIGURE 5A-7   Point Elasticity of Demand Measured by the Exact Formula

When the exact definition $\eta = \frac{dq}{dp} \times \frac{p}{q}$ is used, only **one elasticity is measured from point 1 because there is only one tangent to the demand curve at that point.**

mally used in economic theory. Equation 1 is mathematically only an approximation of this expression. It is obvious from Figure 5A-7 that arc elasticity will come closer to point elasticity the smaller the price change used to calculate the arc elasticity. The $\Delta q/\Delta p$ in Equation 1 is the reciprocal of the slope of the chord connecting the two points being compared.

As the chord becomes shorter, its slope gets closer to that of the tangent T. (Compare the chords connecting point 1 to b' and b'' in Figure 5A-7.) Thus, the error in using Equation 1 as an approximation of Equation 3 tends to diminish as the size of Δp diminishes.

Chapter 6

Supply and Demand in Action: Foreign Trade, Price Controls, and Agriculture

Now that you have mastered the theory of how prices are determined by supply and demand, you have a very powerful tool at your command. However, a full understanding of any theory only comes with practice. This chapter is designed to give you that practice by applying supply and demand to cases drawn from real-world experience. Although we hope that these illustrations are interesting in themselves, the most important reason for studying is to gain mastery of the theory so that you can use it yourself to understand other cases.

This chapter uses the method of comparative statics, first encountered on page 66. In this method, you will recall, we start from a position of market equilibrium and then introduce the event to be studied. The new equilibrium position is then determined and compared with the original one. For example, we might start with an equilibrium in the wheat market and then introduce a reduction in supply due to a failure of this year's crop. A comparison of the price and quantity in the new and the original equilibrium would show the effects of the crop failure.

Foreign Trade at Fixed World Prices

For our first example, we look to foreign trade, an area of concern that is becoming increasingly important to the American economy. About 6 percent of American national income is currently generated by selling American products in foreign markets—these are U.S. exports. About 8 percent of American national income is spent on purchasing foreign-produced commodities—these are U.S. imports.

The Determination of Imports and Exports

What determines whether a single country, such the United States, imports or exports some internationally traded commodity? If the United States produces none of the commodity at home—as with nickel, coffee, and bananas—any domestic consumption must be satisfied by imports. At the other extreme, if the United States is the only (or even the major) world producer, demand in the rest of the world must be met by exports from the United States. What of the many intermediate cases in which the United States is only one of many producers of an internationally traded commodity, as with beef, oil, and wheat? Will the United States be an exporter or an importer of such commodities, or will it just produce exactly enough to satisfy its domestic demand for the commodity?

The Law of One Price

Whether the United States imports or exports a commodity for which it is only one of many producers to a great extent will depend on the commodity's price.

The law of one price states that when an easily transported commodity is traded throughout the entire world, it will tend to have a single worldwide price, which economists refer to as the "world price."

Many basic commodities, such as copper wire, steel pipe, iron ore, and coal, fall within this category. The single price for each good is the price that equates the quantity demanded worldwide with the quantity supplied worldwide.

The single world price of an internationally traded commodity may be influenced greatly, or only slightly, by the demand and supply coming from any one country. The extent of one country's influence will depend on how important its demands and supplies are in relation to the worldwide totals.

A Country Facing Given World Prices

The simplest case for us to study arises when the country, which we will take to be the United States, accounts for only a small part of the total worldwide demand and supply. In this case the United States does not itself produce enough to influence the world price significantly. Furthermore, United States purchasers are too small a proportion of worldwide demand to affect the world price materially. U.S. producers and consumers thus face a world price that they cannot significantly influence by their own actions.

Notice that in this case the price that rules in the United States market must be the world price. The law of one price says that this must be so. What would happen if the U.S. domestic price diverged from the world price? If the U.S. domestic price were above the single world price, no buyers would buy from a U.S. source, since money could be saved by buying abroad. Conversely, if the U.S. price were

below the world price, no supplier would sell in the U.S. market, since more money could be made by selling abroad.

Now let us see what determines the pattern of U.S. foreign trade in such circumstances.

An Exported Commodity

To determine the pattern of U.S. foreign trade, we first show the U.S. domestic demand and supply curves for some commodity, say soybeans. The intersection of these two curves tells us what the price and quantity would be *if there were no foreign trade*. Now compare this "no-trade" price with the world price of that commodity.[1] If the world price is higher, then the actual price in the United States will exceed the "no-trade" price. There will be an excess of U.S. supply over U.S. demand, and the surplus production will be exported for sale abroad.

Countries export products whose world price exceeds the price that would rule domestically if there were no foreign trade.

This result is demonstrated in Figure 6-1.

An Imported Commodity

Now consider some other commodity, for example, oil. Once again, look first at the domestic demand and supply curves shown this time in Figure 6-2. The intersection of these curves determines the "no-trade" price that would rule if there were no international trade. The world price of oil is below the U.S. "no-trade" price, so that, at the price ruling in the United States, domestic demand is larger and domestic supply is smaller than if the "no-trade" price had ruled. The excess of domestic demand over domestic supply is met by imports.

Countries import products whose world price is less than the price that would rule domestically if there were no foreign trade.

---

[1] If the world price is stated in U.S. dollars (as it usually is, for example, with oil), we have no problem with putting it on the diagram showing domestic demand and supply curves. If the world price is stated in terms of some foreign currency, such as Japanese yen, then the price must be converted into dollars using the current exchange rate between the foreign currency and dollars.

FIGURE 6-1   The Determination of Exports

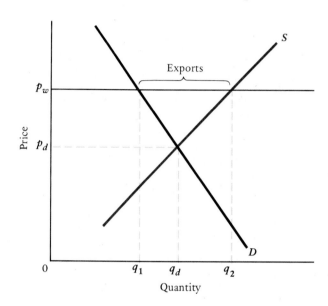

FIGURE 6-2   The Determination of Imports

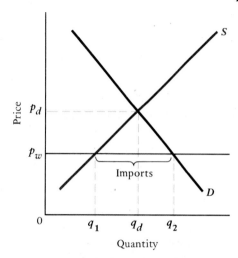

Exports occur whenever there is excess supply domestically at the world price. The domestic demand and supply curves are D and S, respectively. The domestic price in the absence of foreign trade is p_d, with q_d produced *and* consumed domestically. The world price of p_w is higher than p_d. At p_w, q_1 is demanded while q_2 is supplied domestically. The excess of the domestic supply over the domestic demand is exported.

Imports occur whenever there is excess demand domestically at the world price. The domestic demand and supply curves are D and S, respectively. The domestic price in the absence of foreign trade is p_d, with q_d produced *and* consumed domestically. The world price of p_w is less than p_d. At p_w, q_2 is demanded while q_1 is supplied domestically. The excess of domestic demand over domestic supply is satisfied through imports.

This result is demonstrated in Figure 6-2.

We have now developed the basic theory of how imports and exports are determined in competitive markets. Later in the book this theory will be used to study the effects on U.S. imports and exports of changes in the world price and changes in U.S. domestic demand or supply.

Government-Controlled Prices

Our next application concerns a number of important cases that arise when the government fixes the price at which a commodity must be sold on the domestic market. For simplicity, we consider a commodity that is not traded internationally.

For such a commodity, equilibrium occurs where the domestic demand and domestic supply curves intersect. Government price controls attempt to hold the market in some disequilibrium situation that could not be maintained in the absence of intervention. Some controls hold the market price below its equilibrium value. This creates a shortage, with quantity demanded exceeding quantity supplied at the controlled price. Other controls hold price above equilibrium. This creates a surplus, with quantity supplied exceeding quantity demanded at the controlled price.

Disequilibrium Prices

In competitive markets, price changes whenever quantity supplied does not equal quantity demanded. Price then moves toward its equilibrium value, at which point there are neither unsatisfied suppliers nor unsatisfied demanders.

When controls hold price at some disequilibrium

value, what determines the quantity actually traded on the market? The key to the answer is the fact that any voluntary market transaction requires both a willing buyer and a willing seller. This means that if quantity demanded is less than quantity supplied, demand will determine the amount actually exchanged, while the rest of the quantity supplied will remain in the hands of the unsuccessful sellers. On the other hand, if quantity demanded exceeds quantity supplied, supply will determine the amount actually exchanged, while the rest of the quantity demanded will represent desired purchases of unsuccessful buyers. This argument is spelled out in more detail in Figure 6-3, which establishes the general conclusion that

At any disequilibrium price, quantity exchanged is determined by *the lesser* of quantity demanded or quantity supplied.

FIGURE 6-3   The Determination of Quantity Exchanged in Disequilibrium

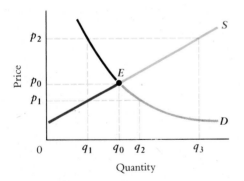

In disequilibrium, quantity exchanged is determined by *whichever is less* of quantity demanded or quantity supplied. At p_0 the market is in equilibrium, with quantity demanded equal to quantity supplied at q_0. For prices below p_0, the quantity exchanged will be determined by the supply curve. For example, the quantity q_1 will be exchanged at the disequilibrium price p_1 in spite of the excess demand of q_1q_2. For prices above p_0, the quantity exchanged will be determined by the demand curve. For example, the quantity q_1 will be exchanged at the disequilibrium price p_2 in spite of the excess supply of q_1q_3. Thus the darker portions of the S and D curves show the actual quantities exchanged at different prices.

Price Floors

The government sometimes establishes a minimum price, or **price floor**, for a good or a service. A price floor that is set at or below the equilibrium price has no effect, because equilibrium remains attainable. If, however, the price floor is set above the equilibrium, it will raise the price, in which case it is said to be *binding* or *effective*.

Price floors may be established by rules that make it illegal to sell the commodity below the prescribed price, as in the case of the minimum wage (examined in Chapter 19). Further, the government may establish a price floor by announcing that it will guarantee a certain price by buying any excess supply of the product that emerges at that price. Such guarantees are a feature of many agricultural support policies (examined later in this chapter).

The effects of binding price floors are illustrated in Figure 6-4, which establishes the following key result:

FIGURE 6-4   A Price Floor

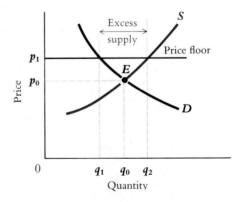

If a price floor is above the equilibrium price, quantity supplied will exceed quantity demanded. The free-market equilibrium is at E, with price p_0 and quantity q_0. The government now establishes an effective price floor at p_1. Quantity supplied exceeds quantity demanded by q_1q_2.

If the government does nothing else, this excess supply will either go to waste or accumulate in the sellers' inventories. If the government buys the excess supply, q_2 will be sold — q_1 being bought by ordinary purchasers and q_1q_2 by the government, which will have to store it or find some way of disposing of it.

Effective price floors lead to excess supply. Either an unsold surplus will exist or someone must enter the market and buy the excess supply.

The consequences of excess supply will, of course, differ from commodity to commodity. If the commodity is labor, subject to a minimum wage, excess supply translates into people without jobs. If the commodity is wheat, and more is produced than can be sold, the surplus wheat will accumulate in grain elevators or government warehouses. These consequences may or may not be "worth it" in terms of the other goals achieved. Whether they are worth it or not, these consequences are inevitable whenever a price floor is set above the market-clearing, equilibrium price.

Why might the government wish to incur these consequences? One reason is that those who actually succeed in selling their commodities at the price floor are better off than if they had to accept the lower equilibrium price. Workers and farmers are among those who have persuaded the government to establish price floors that enable them to sell their outputs at prices above free-market levels.

Price Ceilings

Governments sometimes fix the *maximum prices* at which certain goods and services may be sold. Price controls on oil, natural gas, and rental housing frequently have been imposed by various levels of government—federal, state, or local.

Although sometimes they are referred to as *fixed* or *frozen prices*, most price controls actually specify a **price ceiling,** which is the highest permissible price that producers may legally charge. If the price ceiling is set above the equilibrium price, it has no effect, since the equilibrium remains attainable. If, however, the price ceiling is set below the equilibrium price, the price ceiling lowers the price and is said to be *binding* or *effective*. The effects of price ceilings are shown in Figure 6-5, which establishes the following conclusion:

Effective price ceilings lead to excess demand, with the quantity exchanged being less than its equilibrium amount.

FIGURE 6-5   A Price Ceiling and Black-Market Pricing

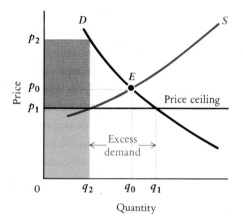

An effective price ceiling causes excess demand and invites a black market. Equilibrium price is at p_0. If a price ceiling is set at p_1, the quantity demanded will rise to q_1 and the quantity supplied will fall to q_2. Quantity actually exchanged will be q_2. Price may not rise legally to restore equilibrium.

If all the available supply of q_2 were sold on a black market, price to consumers would rise to p_2, with black marketeers earning receipts shown by the shaded areas. Since they buy at the ceiling price of p_1 and sell at the black-market price of p_2, their profits are represented by the dark shaded area.

Allocating a Commodity in Short Supply

The free market eliminates excess demand by allowing prices to rise, thereby allocating the available supply among would-be purchasers. Since this does not happen under price ceilings, some other method of allocation must be adopted. Experience shows what we can expect.

If stores sell their available supplies on a first-come, first-served basis, people will rush to those stores that are said to have stocks of the commodity. In most Eastern European and some African countries, where prices of essentials are subject to effective price ceilings, even the rumor that a shop is selling supplies of a scarce commodity can cause a local stampede. Buyers may wait hours to get into the store, only to find that supplies are exhausted before they can be served. This is why standing in lines is a way of life in many command economies.

In market economies first-come, first-served is often the basis for allocating tickets to rock concerts and sporting events when demand exceeds the supply of available seats.

Instead of selling their supplies on a first-come, first-served basis, storekeepers may decide to keep goods "under the counter" and sell only to customers of their own choosing. For example, in the United States in 1978 during a gasoline shortage, some gas station operators sold only to regular customers. When sellers decide to whom they will (and will not) sell scarce supplies, allocation is by **sellers' preferences**.

If the government dislikes this allocation system, there are at least two things it can do. First, it can pass laws requiring suppliers to sell on a first-come, first-served basis. To the extent that this legislation is effective, it leads to allocation according to the buyers' willingness to stand in line.

Second—and more drastic—the government can ration the commodity. To do so, it prints only enough ration coupons to match the available supply and then distributes the coupons to would-be purchasers, who need both money and coupons to buy the commodity. The coupons may be distributed equally among the population or on the basis of some criterion such as age, family status, or occupation.

Rationing substitutes the government's preferences for the sellers' preferences in allocating a commodity that is in excess demand because of an effective price ceiling.

Rationing was used in the United States and most other belligerent countries during both World War I and World War II.

Black Markets

Price ceilings, with or without rationing, usually give rise to black markets. A **black market** is any market in which goods are sold illegally at prices that violate a legal price control.

Many manufactured products are produced by only a few firms but are sold by many retailers. Thus, although it may be easy to police the few producers, it is often impossible to enforce the price at which the many retailers sell to the general public. If the government is able to control the price received by producers but not by retailers, production re-

mains at a level consistent with the price ceiling because the producers receive only the controlled price. At the retail level, however, the opportunity for a black market arises because purchasers are willing to pay more than the price ceiling for the limited amounts of the commodity that are available.

Effective price ceilings create the potential for a black market, because a profit can be made by buying at the controlled price and selling at the black-market price.

Figure 6-5 illustrates the extreme case in which all the available supply is sold on a black market.[2]

Does the existence of a black market mean that the goals sought by imposing price ceilings have been thwarted? The answer depends upon what the goals are. A government might be interested mainly in (1) restricting production (perhaps to release resources for war production); (2) keeping prices down; or (3) satisfying notions of equity in the consumption of a commodity that is temporarily in short supply. When price ceilings are accompanied by a black market, only the first objective is achieved. Black markets frustrate the second objective. Effective price ceilings on manufacturers plus an extensive black market at the retail level may produce the opposite of the third goal. There will be less to go around than if there were no controls, and the available quantities will tend to go to those with the most money or the least social conscience.

Rent Controls: A Case Study of Price Ceilings

Price ceilings are applied to the rental of houses and apartments for private occupancy in many parts of the United States. Rent controls have been used worldwide with similar consequences: severe housing shortages, private allocation systems, and black markets.

Rent controls have existed in New York, Lon-

[2] This case is extreme because there are law-abiding people in every society and because governments ordinarily have considerable power to enforce their price ceilings. Although *some* of a commodity subject to an effective price ceiling will be sold on the black market, it is unlikely that *all* of that commodity will be sold on the black market.

don, Paris, and many other large cities at least since World War II. In Sweden and in Britain, where rent controls on unfurnished apartments have existed for decades, shortages of rental accommodations are chronic. When British controls were extended to furnished apartments in 1973, the supply of such accommodations dried up, at least until loopholes were found in the law. When rent controls were initiated in Rome in 1978 and in Toronto in 1985, severe housing shortages developed. Such control-induced shortages led University of Chicago Professors George Stigler and Milton Friedman to point to the conflict between the "ceilings" created by controls and the "roofs" provided by housing.

Many of the rent controls instituted by American cities in the 1970s and early 1980s are still in force today. Economic theory is useful in understanding the current experience with rent controls and in predicting further consequences.

General Effects of Rent Controls

Each city that decides to control rents passes its own particular set of rent control laws: Some of these laws cover all rental accommodations, whereas others exempt new buildings; some allow full adjustments for inflation and maintenance costs, whereas others do not. For simplicity, we deal with a case in which one city's rent controls are effective in reducing the price of all rental accommodations below its free-market equilibrium. This allows us to use Figure 6-5 on page 99 to make the following predictions about the effects of rent controls, which are straightforward applications of our study of price ceilings.

1. There will be a housing shortage in the sense that quantity demanded will exceed quantity supplied.
2. The actual quantity of rental housing will be less than if free-market rents had been charged.
3. The shortage will lead to alternative allocation schemes. Landlords may allocate by sellers' preferences, or the government may intervene, often through security-of-tenure laws, which protect tenants from eviction and thereby give them priority over prospective new tenants.
4. Black markets will appear. For example, landlords may require large "entrance fees" from new tenants, which reflect the difference in value between the free-market and the controlled rents.

In the absence of security-of-tenure laws, landlords may force tenants out when their leases expire in order to extract a large entrance fee from new tenants.

Specific Effects of Rent Controls

Further effects of rent control arise because housing is a **durable good,** a good that yields its services gradually over an extended period of time. Once it has been built, an apartment can be used for decades and often centuries.

The Supply of Rental Accommodations

The supply of rental accommodations depends on the stock of rental housing available, which in any year is composed mainly of buildings put up in the past. The stock is augmented by conversions of housing from other uses and construction of new buildings; it is diminished by conversions to other uses and by demolition or abandonment.

All of these reactions take time, which suggests that we need to use the distinction between short- and long-run supply that was first introduced in Chapter 5.

Short-run supply. The short-run reaction to changes in rents tends to be quite limited. When rents rise, some conversions from other uses are possible, but it takes years to plan and to build new apartments. When rents fall, some conversions to condominiums and cooperatives may occur, and if rents fall so low that variable cost cannot be covered, buildings will be abandoned, as they were on a large scale in some boroughs of New York City. However, quite wide ranges of variations in rents will be met by quite small changes in the short-run supply of rental accommodations, making the short-run supply curve quite inelastic.

Long-run supply. If the expected return from investing in new apartments falls significantly below what can be earned on other comparable investments, funds will go elsewhere. New construction will be halted, and old buildings will be converted to other uses, or, where this is impossible, they will not be replaced when they wear out. If the return rises significantly above the return on comparable investments, there will be a flow of investment funds into the building of new apartments. It takes years to increase the quantity of housing through new construction; reducing the quantity through nonreplacement takes decades. When all such adjustments are allowed for, the long-run supply curve of rental accommodations (which refers to the quantity supplied after enough time has been allowed for all adjustments) is highly elastic under most market conditions.

The Demand for Rental Accommodations

Does the fact that housing is a basic necessity mean that the demand for rental accommodations is highly inelastic? Although some form of shelter is a necessity, rental accommodations have many close substitutes, and empirical estimates show substantial elasticity in the demand *for a square foot* of rental accommodations.

A rise in the price of rental accommodations will lead to the following types of changes: Some people will stop renting and will buy instead; some will move to smaller, lower-grade rental housing; some will move to other areas where rents are lower; some will stay longer with their parents; and others will find roommates. For example, in response to a dramatic increase during recent decades in the cost of housing—both purchased and rented—the sharing of apartments among middle-income persons is more common today than it was only a few decades ago; they share in larger numbers per apartment, and they remain sharing for more years of their lives.

For all of these reasons, the demand for rental accommodations is quite responsive to changes in its (relative) price.

Rent Control and a Growing Housing Shortage

Because the short-run supply of housing is inelastic, rent controls that hold rentals somewhat below their free-market levels cause only a moderate housing shortage in the short run. Indeed, most of the shortage comes from an expansion in quantity demanded rather than from a shrinking in quantity supplied. As time passes, however, fewer new apartments are built, more conversions take place, and older buildings are not replaced as they wear out. As a result, the quantity supplied shrinks steadily. Furthermore, it is not worthwhile for landlords to spend as much on repairs as under free-market conditions because rent controls lower the return on capital invested in

rental accommodations. Concern over the deteriorating quality of housing is a recurring theme when effective rent controls have been in place for some time.

Both the long- and the short-run effects of rent control are shown in Figure 6-6.

When Rent Controls May Work: Short-Term Shortages

Pressure for rent controls is strongest when prices are rising most rapidly. The case for controlling rising rentals is strongest when the shortages causing the increasing rents are temporary.

Sometimes there is a temporary influx of population into an area. Possibly an army camp is established in wartime, or a pipeline or a nuclear power complex is being built, and many workers are re-

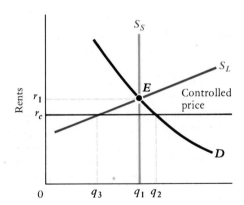

FIGURE 6-6   Effects of Rent Control in the Short and Long Run

Rent control causes housing shortages that worsen as time passes. The controlled rent of r_c forces rents below their free-market equilibrium value of r_1. The short-run supply of housing is shown by the inelastic curve S_S. Thus, quantity supplied remains at q_1 in the short run, and the housing shortage is q_1q_2. Over time, the quantity supplied shrinks, as shown by the long-run supply curve S_L. In long-run equilibrium there are only q_3 units of rental accommodations, far fewer than when controls were instituted. The housing shortage of q_3q_2, which occurs after supply has fully adjusted, is much larger than the initial shortage of q_1q_2.

quired, even though few will remain behind once the job is done. When the temporary population floods in, market rents will rise. New construction of apartments will not occur, however, because investors recognize that the rise in demand and the rise in rentals is temporary. In such a situation, rent controls may stop existing owners from making large profits and may result in few harmful supply effects, since a long-run supply response is not expected in any case. After the boom is over, demand will fall, and free-market equilibrium rents will return to the controlled level (which is also their original level). Rent controls may then be removed with little further effect.

Although under these circumstances the rent controls have no long-run adverse effect, they will have some disadvantages. At controlled rents there will be a severe housing shortage but no *price incentive* for existing tenants to economize on housing or for potential suppliers to find ways to provide extra short-run accommodations. If rents were allowed to rise on the free market, existing tenants would economize on the space they used, and some people would find it profitable to rent out some of their own rooms. Even though the supply of permanent apartments does not change, the supply of temporary accommodations (mobile homes, for example) can increase. Such reactions are encouraged by the signal of rising rents but are inhibited by rent controls.

There is also a risk that political pressure may build up to turn temporary controls into permanent controls. During World War II many American cities imposed rent controls because of temporary housing shortages. Most cities removed rent controls after the war to allow the housing supply to expand when factors of production were again available for construction. Some cities, among them New York, kept the rent controls, thus inhibiting the adjustments in supply that were needed to eliminate the shortages.

New York City exempted new construction from rent controls, thus ensuring an elastic supply of new buildings, but its rent controls were responsible for the rents of existing buildings being held further and further below their equilibrium values, with the result that the owners of many buildings could not even cover their current costs of operation. These buildings were then abandoned by their owners, creating desolate areas that still can be seen today in several of New York City's boroughs.

Other cities have used rent controls successfully to cope with temporary increases in demand for housing and then have eliminated them when normal conditions returned. During the construction of the Alaska pipeline, for example, the city of Anchorage used rent controls to hold rents down in the face of a massive increase in demand for housing. After the pipeline was completed, the demand subsided and rent controls were removed, leaving rents once more in equilibrium at their original levels.

When Rent Controls Fail: Long-Term Shortages

Long-Run Increases in Demand

Consider what happens when there is a long-term increase in the demand for rental accommodations. Examples occur in the Sunbelt states, where a rapidly increasing population is creating severe local housing shortages and forcing rents to increase. Such increases in rents give the signal that apartments are highly profitable investments. A consequent building boom will lead to increases in the quantity supplied, and it will continue as long as windfall profits can be enjoyed.

If rent controls are imposed in the face of such long-term increases in demand, they will prevent short-run windfalls, but they will also prevent the needed long-run construction boom from occurring. Thus, controls will convert a temporary shortage into a permanent one. There is also the danger, often realized in practice, that even when increases are granted in the controlled rents to allow for inflation and costs of repairs, they will not fully reflect the resulting rises in costs. When this happens, the discrepancy between the controlled and the equilibrium rents increases, and the housing shortage grows ever more acute as time passes.

Figure 6-7 shows rent controls used successfully to cope with a temporary increase in demand and used unsuccessfully in the face of a permanent increase.

Who Gains and Who Loses

Tenants in rent controlled accommodations are the principal gainers. As the gap between the controlled and the equilibrium rents grows, those who are lucky enough to be tenants gain more and more.

FIGURE 6-7   Rent Controls in Response to Increasing Demand

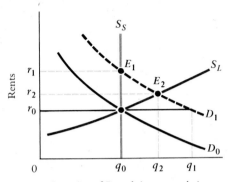

Quantity of Rental Accommodations

Rent controls prevent a temporary skyrocketing of rents when demand rises but also prevent the long-term supply adjustment where it is required.

Temporary demand fluctuations. The short-run supply curve S_S applies. In the free market a temporary rise in demand from D_0 to D_1 and then back to D_0 will change rents from r_0 to r_1 and then back to r_0. Rent control would hold rents at r_0 throughout; there would be a housing shortage of q_0q_1 due to excess demand, as long as demand was D_1, but rent control would not affect the quantity of housing available.

Permanent changes in demand. The long–run supply curve S_L applies. A permanent rise in demand from D_0 to D_1 will cause free-market rents to rise temporarily from r_0 to r_1 and then to fall to r_2 as the quantity of accommodations supplied grows from q_0 to q_2. Controlling the rent at r_0 produces a permanent housing shortage of q_0q_1.

If the beneficiaries of rent controls are existing tenants, the losers are the present generation of landlords and those would-be tenants of the future who do not succeed in finding rent controlled accommodations.

Landlords suffer, because they do not get the return that they had expected on their investments. In many cases, the return shrinks to zero. Some landlords are large companies, and others are rich individuals. Neither one of these groups attracts great public sympathy—even though the rental companies' stockholders are not all rich. Nonetheless, they learn from their experience and stop supplying further rental accommodations when the rent con-

trols reduce the return on their capital investment below what could be earned in other lines of activity. Many other landlords are people of modest means who have put their retirement savings into a small apartment or a house or two. They find that the value of their savings is greatly diminished, and often they find themselves in the ironic position of subsidizing tenants who are far better off than they are.

The other major class of people who suffer from rent controls are potential future tenants. The housing shortage hurts them because the rental housing they would require will not be there in the future. The elderly couples who fight to keep rent controls on the apartments that they occupy are behaving in their own best interest. If and when they succeed, they are making life more difficult for the next generation of aged couples, many of whom will not find housing of the same quality if rent controls are continued. The welfare family protected today will have a hard time finding housing if it moves or if its present apartment house is abandoned. Members of minority groups who are existing renters will gain, but those who follow in their footsteps a generation later will find that they are hurt by the steadily shrinking quantity and quality of available rental housing.

Alternative Responses to the Rising Costs of Housing

Most rent controls today are meant to protect lower-income tenants, not only against profiteering by landlords in the face of severe local shortages but also against the steadily rising cost of housing.

The free-market solution is to let rents rise sufficiently to cover the rising costs. If people decide they cannot afford the market price of apartments and will not rent them, then construction will cease. Given what we know about past consumer behavior, however, it is more likely that people will make agonizing choices, both to economize on housing and to spend a higher proportion of total income on it, which means consuming less housing and less of other things as well.

If governments do not wish to accept this free-market solution, what can be done? Three important alternatives are now considered.

Rent controls alone.   One alternative is to control rents below the cost of constructing new buildings, which will inevitably result in a housing shortage that grows as the stock of rental accommodations wears out and is not replaced. Rent controls transfer real income from landlords, and future generations of would-be tenants, to the present generation of tenants. This may appeal to present tenants (and to those who want their votes, money, and approval), but it is difficult to find it appealing in terms of a broader sense of social justice that can be applied to the whole society and over time.

Rent controls plus public housing. A second alternative is for government to fill the gap between total demand and private supply with subsidized public housing, financed at the taxpayers' expense (since *someone* must pay the full cost of providing housing).

Because rent controls hold rentals below the free-market return on capital, public housing supplied at controlled rents must be run at a loss. If the gap between the amount supplied from the private sector and the total amount demanded at the controlled price is large, the burden on the public purse strings may become unacceptable. Few cities in the United States, and few authorities elsewhere in the world, have been willing to pay the enormous costs of providing subsidized public housing to remove fully the shortage created by their own effective controls. Thus, the shortage continues, in spite of some efforts to construct public housing. The ones who gain are those who are lucky enough to obtain public housing; the ones who lose are the growing numbers of those who are not lucky enough to have rent controlled accommodations or accommodations in subsidized public housing. They are worse off than they would have been under free-market conditions.

Housing vouchers. A third alternative is for the government to subsidize the housing of citizens who are less well off by providing them with housing vouchers. These would be used to pay rent to a stated value and would be redeemable by landlords in cash paid by the government. Under this scheme taxpayers would be subsidizing the rentals of those who receive the vouchers.

The scheme has the advantage of targeting the expenditures toward those who are judged to be in need. Comprehensive rent controls seek to help the less well off by benefiting all tenants, many of whom are themselves well off. The voucher scheme allows the government to target only those whom it feels are really in need of help. The disadvantage, from

the political point of view, is that taxpayers must pay the difference between the free-market and the subsidized rents. With rent controls, the government forces landlords to pay this difference, at least as long as they remain landlords. Rent controls thus transfer income from landlords to tenants at no cost to the government.

The choice. The government's desire to do something, or at least to be seen as trying to do something, while not spending a lot of money doing it, may explain why the government usually selects the first alternative, makes only a small effort on the second, and does nothing on the third. Evidence from around the world suggests that relief from high rents is bought in the short run at the cost of a severe lack of housing in the long run.

The providing of rental accommodations has a definite resource cost. If rental housing is to be provided, the only question is who is to pay the cost. Under free-market conditions, tenants pay, which is why investors are willing to go on supplying the rental accommodations. Under rent controls, investors are forced to pay some of the cost, which is why they are no longer willing to supply the same quantity of accommodations—so a housing shortage ensues. If the government wishes to avoid a housing shortage while having rent controls, it must fill the gap with public housing. Its tenants then pay a portion of the cost of their housing, but, insofar as the housing is rented below the free-market rate, the taxpayers also pay a portion of this cost. The voucher scheme is cheaper, because in this scheme the taxpayers only pay the difference between the market rental and the subsidized rental and because the subsidy is paid only to those who are judged to be in need of it.

The costs of providing additional housing cannot be voted out of existence; these costs can be transferred only from one set of persons to another.

Agriculture and the Farm Problem

For nearly 80 years, U.S. policymakers have been challenged, and often frustrated, by what is called "the farm problem." Actually it consists of two quite distinct problems. First, there is a long-run tendency for farm incomes to fall below urban incomes, and, second, agricultural prices fluctuate from year to year, causing much variability in farm incomes.

Less than 3 percent of the American population live on farms, and even for this group less than 40 percent of their income comes from farm sources. Why then have farming and the farm problem loomed so large in American politics and economic policy?

The answer is partly historical. Farmers have not always been so few in number. In 1910 farmers constituted over 35 percent of the American population. More importantly, the declining importance of farmers in the population has not been matched by a comparable decline in their political influence. Farmers—and those who make their living supplying farmers—constitute the dominant political force in over 15 states. They elect one-third of the 100 U.S. senators. The farm bloc remains a potent political influence in Congress.

American farm problems matter, not only because of the importance of farmers in American life but also because American agriculture produces a significant proportion of the world's food supply. In recent years the United States has emerged as one of the world's largest exporters of food products. For example, the United States now provides two-thirds of all grain and soybeans exported in world trade. American agriculture is the regular supplier to hundreds of millions of people outside the United States and is the buffer against crop failure for more than 3 billion others.

To deal with the farm problem, governments have tried a variety of techniques including price supports, crop insurance, transportation and storage subsidies, and payments not to produce. Each of these "solutions," however, seems to create further problems, which are sometimes more serious than the original problem they were meant to solve.

Long-Term Trends

The first major problem that faces farm policy arises from long-term trends. In 1935 the disposable income of the average American farm family was less than one-third that of the average American urban family. By 1950 this ratio had risen to one-half, and the gap continued to narrow until it was briefly eliminated in the 1970s. During the 1980s, however, the gap opened again, until the disposable income of farm families in 1988 was less than *two-thirds that of urban families.*

Relatively low farm incomes have not been caused by low productivity or poor and depleted soils. American agriculture is, and has long been, one of the world's most innovative industries. New seeds and crops, new propagation methods, new mechanical cultivating methods, and computerization have led to rising production per worker and per acre. Farming is increasingly a vast, capital-intensive, corporate activity, with giant farms accounting for about one-half of all current U.S. farm output. Many modern American farmers have postgraduate degrees in business administration and spend more time in their offices analyzing computer printouts than in their fields tending to crops. In some ways, modern, large-scale farming resembles a factory assembly line more than it does the traditional family farm.

What has happened to American agriculture over this century can be understood in terms of changes in domestic supply, domestic demand, and foreign demand.

Surging Domestic Supply

Since 1900 the output per worker in American agriculture has increased tenfold, roughly twice as fast as manufacturing productivity has increased. In 1900 one farm worker could produce enough food to feed about 2½ people—the farm worker and 1½ nonfarm people. By 1990 the figure was over 60 persons—the farm worker and at least 60 nonfarm workers!

The rapid growth of farm productivity means that the supply curves of U.S. farm products have been shifting rapidly to the right.

Lagging Domestic Demand

The overall growth of output throughout the entire American economy has resulted in a rising trend for the real income of the average American family during the last 150 years. How have American households elected to consume their extra incomes? The relevant measure is, as we have seen, the income elasticity of demand. At the levels of income existing in the United States and in other advanced industrial nations, most foodstuffs have low income elasticities because most people are well fed. When these people receive their extra incomes, they tend to spend much of it on consumer durables, entertainment, travel, and dining out (rather than cooking at home). The enormous increase in the demand for fast foods and other restaurant meals—dining out was a rare luxury a scant 50 years ago—has caused an increase in the demand for the services provided by eating establishments but not for food itself. Thus:

As American incomes grow, the American demand for agricultural goods also grows but less rapidly.

Export Demand

Over the last two decades the export market has provided a large increase in demand for American farm produce. This has certainly helped to alleviate the overall impact of the farm problem. In the 1960s only about 14 percent of the agricultural output of the United States was sold abroad. During the 1970s, however, the value of agricultural exports increased by an average of over 20 percent *per year*, and by 1980 the percentage of U.S. agricultural output that was exported had doubled to 30 percent. This figure remained roughly constant throughout the 1980s.

These changes had a number of important causes. First, there were dramatic events related to the Communist countries. These included a series of crop failures in the USSR and normalization of trade with China. Second, there has been a steady rise in world demand. This has resulted from both the rapid growth of the world's population and the rising incomes in many developing countries. These countries are at a stage of development where income elasticities of demand for wheat, dairy products, and meat are relatively high; thus, their consumers spend a large fraction of the increases in their incomes on these commodities. Third, much of the growth in foreign demand was carefully cultivated by U.S. government agencies. The Foreign Agricultural Service sought new markets and provided both technical and financial assistance to other countries, teaching them how to buy and to process American agricultural output. Other agencies helped by providing agricultural exports as aid to less developed countries.

Unfortunately, the high export demand is not guaranteed to last. One reason for this is that the low value of the U.S. dollar on foreign-exchange markets that existed throughout the last half of the 1980s cannot be guaranteed to continue (although economists expect that its value will probably stay low compared to its value in the first half of the 1980s). Another reason is that the United States is only one among many sources of supply. Many of these other countries that are sources of supply operate farm policies that encourage output and subsidize foreign sales.

The importance of exports for American agriculture and everyone's anxiety about losing export markets is shown by the increasing concern of the U.S. government with the agricultural subsidies that are being paid to farmers in Europe, Japan, and several other countries. The U.S. government argues that these subsidies give an unfair foreign-trade advantage to farm products produced in these countries, keeping U.S. farm products out of many potential export markets.

Excess Supply

In spite of the growth in foreign demand for American farm produce, the overall demand has not been increasing as fast as the supply. The typical situation in an agricultrual market is, therefore, that both the demand and the supply curves are shifting to the right, but the demand curve is shifting more slowly than the supply curve. As a result,

There is a continuing tendency for an excess supply of American agricultural produce to develop at existing market prices.

This, in turn, tends to depress market prices. Because most agricultural produce tends to have price elasticities of demand significantly less than 1, the fall in price tends to depress agricultural incomes, other things being equal. The result is that there is less money available for farmers to pay as wages to agricultural workers and as incomes to themselves.

The Required Supply Response

Depressed prices, wages, and farm incomes signal the need for resources to move out of agriculture and into other rapidly growing sectors. However necessary they may be, incentives of this kind prove to be painful to those who live and work on farms, especially when resources move slowly in response to depressed incomes.

The magnitude of the required supply response

has been enormous. In 1929 there were 12.8 million people employed on farms. The output they produced in 1929 could be produced today by 1.5 million people! If resources had not been reallocated out of farming, there would have been vast increases in output, which hardly could have been sold within the United States or exported at any price, and/or high unemployment of farm resources. Fortunately, resources were reallocated: Actual employment on farms was under 3 million in 1988.

The movement out of farming has not, however, been as fast as required if the incomes of those remaining are to be maintained by market forces. Adjusting for increases in productivity and population, the number of people working on farms was at least 20 percent higher than was needed to meet domestic needs at prices that were constant in real terms.

Government Intervention

It is one thing for farmers' sons and daughters to move to the city; it is quite another for existing farmers to be displaced. Usually, they have grown up on the farm, they have been trained to be farmers, and all their experience is with rural life—indeed, farming is their way of life. Some people claim that leaving the farm is a much more dramatic upheaval than it is for an urban worker to move from a job in a declining industry to a job in an expanding industry, which even may be in the same city.

Because farmers attract the public's sympathy when they are in difficulty, governments tend to respond to their calls for help in overcoming the depressed conditions in agriculture that free markets often produce. Notice, however, that the problem of adjustment exists for any industry in which growth in demand is low while growth in productivity is high. Similar problems are beginning to affect many American manufacturing industries, although the political system has not been as responsive to their distress.

Through a variety of programs dating from 1929 to the present, the government has bought surplus farm products from farmers at "support prices" set above the free-market level. These schemes are discussed in detail in the next section. In the meantime, we can note the types of long-run problems that they create. The programs can, and often do, solve the surplus problem for individual farmers, but they do not solve it for the nation.

When the government buys the excess of market supply over market demand at the support price, its purchases accumulate as unsold stocks. Eventually, if agricultural surpluses persist, the stored crops have to be destroyed or disposed of at a fraction of the price that the government paid for them. If the crops are thrown on the market and allowed to depress the market price, then the original purpose in purchasing them—to stabilize prices and raise farm incomes—is defeated. If the crops are destroyed or allowed to rot, the efforts of a large quantity of the country's scarce factors of production (the land, labor, and capital that went into producing the stored goods) will have been completely wasted.

Destroying crops is a vexing moral problem when billions of the world's peoples do not have enough to eat. However, if the intention is not to have the stored crops depress the price, they must be kept off the market. One alternative, which is used to dispose of relatively small quantities of surplus crops, is to give them away to those who would not otherwise buy them.

When support schemes begin to produce ever larger surpluses, often the next step is to try to limit each farmer's production. Quotas may be assigned to individual farmers, and penalties may be imposed for exceeding the quotas, or bonuses may be paid for leaving the land idle and for plowing crops under. Such measures waste resources, because the actual output could be produced with fewer resources and the remaining resources could be used to produce other goods. Such measures only avoid the visible symbol of trouble—the accumulating surpluses.

Indeed, schemes that do try to solve the long-run supply problem without creating new markets or inducing resources to shift to other, more productive uses often prove to be self-defeating. The subsidized profits and stable market conditions produced by government intervention in agricultural markets provide a stimulus for research and development (R&D). (Agricultural R&D also is encouraged by federal and state government-financed research and agricultural assistance services.) The increased R&D helps to raise productivity in the farm sector and shift agricultural supply curves yet further to the right. The result is more rapid growth in the excess of quantity supplied over quantity demanded at the support prices.

Of course, R&D is useful. It is also scarce, and when it is allocated to sectors where its economic return is low or negative, it is wasted. It may yield a high *physical return* in terms of increased output, but if it increases the production of commodities already in excess supply, it adds little of *economic value*. If it is allocated instead to sectors where demand is rising faster than supply at existing prices, it would produce economic value by creating output that people are eager to buy.

The full benefit of increases in agricultural productivity, which permit the same farm output to be produced with fewer resources, will only be felt when the displaced factors of production find alternative uses where they can raise the output of valuable goods and services.

Short-Term Fluctuations

The second problem that farm policy has addressed is the short-term price volatility typical of many agricultural markets. Farm crops are subject to variations in output because of many factors completely beyond farmers' control. Pests, floods, and drought can reduce farm output drastically, while exceptionally favorable conditions can cause production to exceed expectations. By now you should not be surprised to hear that such unplanned fluctuations in supply cause fluctuations in farm prices and in farm incomes.

Here are two examples. In a recent year, good weather generated bumper fruit crops in California, where more than one-half of America's fruit—and almost the entire crop for canning—is grown. At prevailing prices, the state director of food and agriculture predicted that there would be 100,000 tons of unsold peaches, 50,000 tons of unsold pears, and large surpluses of apricots, cherries, and nectarines. California's canneries would take the surplus, but only at sharply reduced prices—prices that would mean lower incomes for fruit growers. While the fruit growers cursed bountiful nature, consumers stood to benefit.

When bad weather destroyed 80 percent of the U.S. soybean crop in a year when most other grains were also in short supply, a series of indirect but predictable repercussions occurred. One of them was the price that households had to pay for chicken bought in supermarkets. Soybeans are a primary ingredient of chicken feed for the mass-production broiler chicken industry. The decrease in supply of soybeans (a leftward shift of the supply curve) caused the price of soybeans to triple in two months. Chicken farmers found that the cost of soybeans was rising so fast that it was not worthwhile continuing to feed the baby chicks. Millions were killed, and many more millions were not allowed to hatch. This led to a decrease in the supply of chickens (a leftward shift in the supply curve) and a rise in the price of chicken to households.

Fluctuating Supply with Inelastic Demand

Figure 6-8 shows variations in farm output causing price fluctuations in the opposite direction to crop sizes. A bumper crop sends prices down; a small crop sends them up. The price fluctuation is larger when the demand curve is less elastic.

Because farm products typically have inelastic demands, unplanned fluctuations in production tend to cause relatively large fluctuations in price.

What are the effects on the receipts of farmers? In those few cases in which demands are elastic, increases in supply cause increases in farmers' receipts. In the more typical cases demands are inelastic.

Wherever demands are inelastic, good harvests will bring reductions in total farm receipts and bad harvests will bring increases in total farm receipts.

The conflict of interest between the farmer and the consumer is illustrated dramatically whenever a partial crop failure sends food prices soaring but raises farm incomes, and whenever a bumper crop that brings relief to consumers evokes a cry for help from the Farm Belt, where incomes are shrinking.

Fluctuating Demand with Inelastic Supply

So much for supply fluctuations. Agricultural markets are also subject—in common with all products—to demand fluctuations. As the tide of business activity flows and ebbs in what is called the business cycle, demand curves for all commodities shift first to the right and then to the left. The effects on prices and outputs depend on the elasticity of *supply*.

Industrial products typically have rather elastic supply curves, so shifts in demand cause fairly large changes in outputs but only small changes in prices.

When demand for manufactured goods falls, revenues fall, mainly because output falls.

FIGURE 6-8   The Effect on Price of Unplanned Variations in Output Depends on Elasticity of Demand

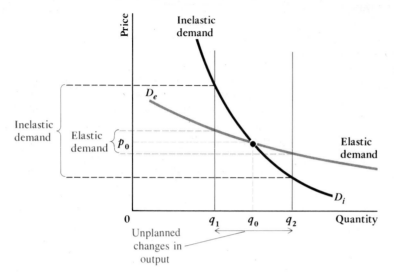

Unplanned fluctuations in output lead to larger fluctuations in price when the demand curve is inelastic than when it is elastic. Suppose that the expected price is p_0 and the planned output is q_0. The two curves D_i and D_e are *alternative* demand curves. If actual production always equaled planned production, the equilibrium price and quantity would be p_0 and q_0 with either demand curve. Unplanned variations in output, however, cause quantity to fluctuate year by year between q_1 (a bad harvest) and q_2 (a good harvest). When demand is inelastic (shown by the black curve), prices will show large fluctuations. When demand is elastic (shown by the gray curve), price fluctuations will be much smaller.

FIGURE 6-9   The Effect on Receipts of a Decrease in Demand

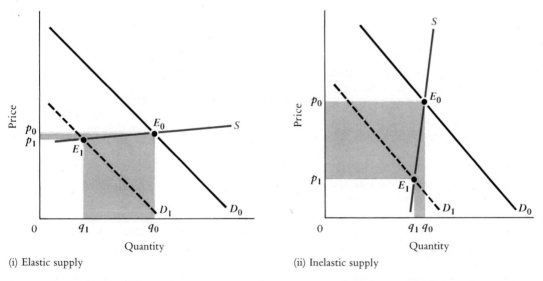

(i) Elastic supply

(ii) Inelastic supply

Both inelastic and elastic supply curves can lead to sharp decreases in receipts, but the effects on prices are very different in the two cases. In each part of the figure, when demand decreases from D_0 to D_1, price and quantity decrease to p_1 and q_1 and total receipts decline by the shaded area. In (i) the symptom is primarily the sharp decrease in quantity. Employment and total profits earned fall drastically, though wage rates and profit margins on what is produced may remain close to their former level. In (ii) the symptom is mainly the sharp decrease in price. Output and employment remain high, but the drastic fall in price will reduce or eliminate profits and result in a downward pressure on wages.

Agricultural commodities typically have inelastic supply curves because land, labor, and capital are not easily transferred to other uses when demand falls and are not easily brought in from other uses when demand rises. This means that shifts in demand cause fairly large changes in prices but relatively small changes in output. The fall in demand causes a fall in producers' incomes.

When demand for agricultural commodities falls, revenues fall, mainly because price falls.

The effects of demand fluctuations on prices and output of manufactured and agricultural goods are shown in Figure 6-9. Farmers often feel that if only prices for their products were stable, all their troubles would be over. As Figure 6-9 shows, however, this is not necessarily the case. Both agriculture and industry suffer when a recession reduces the demand for their products. Only the symptoms of their suffering are different: Farmers lose income because of low prices; industry loses income because of low sales.

Agricultural Stabilization in Theory

Governments throughout the world intervene in agricultural markets in an attempt to stabilize agricultural prices and incomes in the face of uncontrollable fluctuations in supply and cyclical fluctuations in demand. We consider several types of schemes that are frequently used to accomplish this stabilization.

To handle unplanned fluctuations we must be careful with our definition of the supply curve. We let the supply curve refer to *planned* production per year. Unplanned variations in crop yield then cause the actual supply to fluctuate around the planned level. In a free market this causes both prices and farmers' incomes to fluctuate widely from year to year.

The Ever Normal Granary

One method of preventing fluctuations in prices and gross receipts is for the government to permit individual farmers to form a producers' association that tries to stabilize—to keep "ever normal"—the supply *actually coming onto the market* in spite of variations in production.[3] The association does this by storing a

[3] Government permission is required because of antitrust laws, which are discussed in Chapter 15.

crop, say, grain, in years of above average production and selling it from its storage elevators in years of below average production.

Since one farmer's production is an insignificant part of total production, an individual farmer has no incentive to hold produce off the market in an effort to hold the price up in the face of a bumper crop. However, if all farmers get together and agree to do the same thing, then, collectively, they can have a major effect on price. The appropriate policy is shown in Figure 6-10.

Since revenues accrue to the producers when the goods are actually sold on the market, total revenues can be stabilized by keeping sales constant at the equilibrium output even though production varies. This can be accomplished by adding to or subtracting from inventories the excesses or shortages of production at the price that would be set on the free market if actual production were equal to planned production.

FIGURE 6-10   The Ever Normal Granary

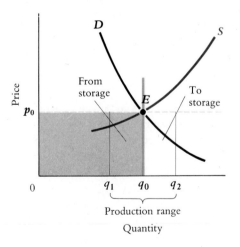

The ever normal granary scheme stabilizes the quantity sold by farmers even though actual production varies. The planned supply curve is S; p_0 and q_0 are the equilibrium price and quantity, respectively. Actual production varies between q_1 and q_2. When production is q_2, the producers' association sells q_0 and stores $q_0 q_2$. When production is q_1, it still sells q_0, supplementing the current production by selling $q_1 q_0$ from its stored crops. Producers' revenues are stabilized at $p_0 \times q_0$ (the shaded area) every year.

The fully successful ever normal granary stabilizes both prices and revenues of producers.

The costs of this scheme are those of providing storage and organizing and administering the program.

The most serious danger of this scheme is that the producers' association will try to stabilize too high a price. It is essential for the long-run success of this scheme that the stabilized price be at the intersection of the market demand and the supply curves (i.e., the equilibrium price in the absence of uncontrolled fluctuations in supply). If the price is stabilized at a higher level, the producers' association more often will be buying to absorb excess supplies than it will be selling to meet excess demand, and it will accumulate ever increasing stockpiles.

Government Stabilization of Farm Prices at Their Equilibrium Levels

Suppose the government, instead of the producers' association, enters the market, buying and thereby adding to its own stocks when there is a surplus, and selling and thereby reducing its own stocks when there is a shortage. If it had enough grain elevators and warehouses, and if its support price were set at a realistic level, the government could stabilize *prices* indefinitely. However, as Figure 6-11 illustrates, it would not succeed in stabilizing farmers' revenues, which would be high with bumper crops and low with small crops.

Government price supports at the equilibrium price would not stabilize revenues. They would, however, reverse the pattern of fluctuations in revenues.

In effect, the government policy imposes a demand curve that is perfectly elastic at the support price. This stabilizes price, but it does not stabilize receipts to producers.

Government Stabilization of Farm Incomes

What are some of the major characteristics of the government policy that will help to stabilize farmers' receipts? As has been seen, too much price stability causes receipts to vary directly with production, and too little price stability causes receipts to vary inversely with production. It appears that the government should aim at some intermediate degree of price

stability. The required policy is to allow prices to vary in inverse proportion to variations in production. Receipts will then be stabilized. The government needs to alter its own purchases and sales so as to allow a 10 percent rise in production to be met by a 10 percent fall in price, and a 10 percent fall in production by a 10 percent rise in price.

To stabilize farmers' receipts, the government must make the demand curve facing the farmers one of unit elasticity. It must buy in periods of high output and sell in periods of low output, but only enough to let prices change in inverse proportion to output.

Government Stabilization of Farm Prices Above Their Equilibrium Levels

We have seen that there are two distinct farm problems: short-term fluctuations in farm prices and long-term depression of farm incomes. Policies designed to alleviate one of these problems often fail because they are used also in an unsuccessful attempt to alleviate the other.

The most common type of conflict arises when a policy designed to provide some short-term *stability* to farm incomes is also used to raise farm incomes to a level comparable with urban incomes.

When this happens, the government continues to buy in periods of high output and to sell in periods of low output. On average, however, it buys much more than it sells, with the result that unsold surpluses accumulate (see Figure 6-4, on page 98). Taxpayers generally are paying farmers for producing goods that no one is willing to purchase—at least at prices that come near to covering costs.

Farm Policy in Action: Sixty Years of American Farm Policy

The final section of this chapter reviews the American experience of trying to help the large, often poor, and always politically influential farm population—an experience that amply illustrates the theory just developed. In particular, it shows the policy conflicts that arise in the attempt to alleviate the short-run instability of agricultural markets, to ensure a high average income for farmers, and to encourage the needed long-run reallocation of resources out of the agricultural sector. There is no doubt that a policy

FIGURE 6-11   Government Price Supports at the Equilibrium Price

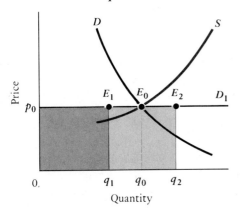

Government price supports at the equilibrium price stabilize prices (not quantities sold by farmers) and do not accumulate surpluses but cause revenues to vary directly with production. Actual production varies around the equilibrium level of q_0. When production is q_2, the government buys q_0q_2 and stores it. When production is q_1, the government sells q_1q_0 from storage. The quantity sold to the public is always q_0, and this stabilizes price at p_0. The government policy converts the demand curve facing farmers to D_1. If q_0 is average production, there is no trend toward the accumulation of storage crops.

Farmers' revenues vary from p_0q_1 (the darker shaded area) when production is q_1 to p_0q_2 (the entire shaded area) when production is q_2.

of allowing agricultural prices and outputs to be determined on free markets would avoid surplus production, but the human and political costs of this policy have been judged to be unacceptable. The challenge has been to respond to the real hardships of the farm population without intensifying the long-term problems. American farm policy has not always succeeded in doing so; the economic analysis in the previous sections helps us to understand why.

Before 1950

The first serious government intervention in agricultural markets occurred in 1929. The newly formed Federal Farm Board specified "support prices"—usually well above free-market equilibrium prices—and offered to buy anything that could not otherwise be sold at these prices. (A brief glossary of basic terms used in discussions about American farm policy is

given in Box 6-1.) It should surprise no one who understands the theory of demand and supply that the Board failed because its funds were soon exhausted due to a rapid accumulation of unsold stocks.

The Roosevelt administration (1933–1945), which was concerned with alleviating the hardship that the Great Depression brought to farmers, reestablished support prices and set them at "parity." Parity prices were meant to reestablish the relative prices between farm and manufactured goods that had existed 25 years earlier, before World War I. Since farm prices had fallen relative to the prices of manufactured goods in the intervening 25 years, this meant that farm prices would have to be raised well above their existing equilibrium levels.

In order to prevent the predictable buildup of surplus stocks, the government paid farmers not to produce crops, and imposed acreage restrictions and marketing quotas. However, support prices and guaranteed sales, as well as government loans for farm improvements, were powerful incentives. Both output per acre and per worker soared. As a result, total output rose in spite of all the restrictions, while federal costs of buying and storing the resulting surplus remained high.

The 1950s and the 1960s

In the 1950s the notion of parity with pre-World War I prices was finally dropped, and the base for parity was the average of the ruling prices during the previous 10 years. This modification allowed a slow decline in relative prices over time. Moreover, actual prices were allowed to fall at a specified fraction of parity prices before the full price support was given. The influence on resource reallocation was weakened, however, by additional measures that reduced the incentive to shift resources out of farming and encouraged research and development.

Efforts to restrict production were stepped up, and by 1970 the number of farms had been reduced to only one-half the number that had existed in 1950. Yet the average size of farms increased, making the acreage under cultivation in 1970 only about 9 percent less than the acreage that had existed 20 years earlier. Furthermore, productivity increases allowed output to increase by 30 percent between 1950 and 1970. As a result, the problem of excess supply was just as acute as it had been during the preceding decades.

BOX 6-1

The Vocabulary of American Farm Policy

Here is a lexicon of some of the basic terms used in discussions of farm policy.

Basic commodities   The six crops—corn, cotton, peanuts, rice, tobacco, and wheat—for which government price supports are legally mandated.

Support price   The price at which the government will buy farmers' output to assure farmers the income level they would get if market prices were at support price levels.

Parity price   The price for a bushel today that would be necessary to buy the same quantity of goods that the price of a bushel would buy in the 1910–1914 base period. At one time used as level of support price.

Target price   A fictional price set by the government as a benchmark for subsidizing farmers' income. Sometimes used as a basis for setting support prices (e.g., support price at 80 percent of target price).

Loan rate   The price at which the government will provide loans to farmers to enable them to store their crops for later sale. If market price falls below the loan rate, the farmers keep the loan and forfeit their grain, effectively selling their grain to the government and receiving what amounts to a government-guaranteed minimum price.

Deficiency payment   A direct income subsidy paid to the farmer equal to the difference between the target price and the higher of the market price or the loan rate, if the market price falls below the target price.

Acreage reduction program   A program under which farmers agree to cut their planted acreage to gain entry into other farm programs.

Soil bank   A form of acreage reduction program under which land is left fallow for a specified number of years to restore its quality.

Paid diversion   A program under which farmers agree to cut their planted acreage in exchange for cash from the government.

Payments-in-kind (PIK)   A payment to farmers of a specified quantity of a commodity in return for their agreement to cut their planted acreage of that commodity.

Guaranteed farm loans   Loans that are made by farm banks to eligible farmers and that are guaranteed by the government.

Farm bank   A bank with one-fourth or more of its loans for agricultural purposes.

The 1970s

As we mentioned earlier in this chapter, the 1970s saw a dramatic increase in the demand for American agricultural goods on world markets. Rising demand and good harvests led to sharp increases in farm incomes. Farmers borrowed heavily to mechanize their operations and to increase their outputs, while the outflow of resources from agriculture slowed to a snail's pace.

Direct price supports were replaced by a system that was still in use at the beginning of the 1990s. The key to this system was that loans were made to farmers whenever market prices fell below what

were called "loan rates"—prices designed to cover most, but not all, farm costs. The loans were secured by the crop that the farmers stored for themselves. If the price rose above the loan rate, farmers could sell the crop, using the proceeds to repay the loan. Only if the farmer defaulted on the interest payments did the government take over the crop.

Under the buoyant conditions of the 1970s, many observers asserted that the farm problem had been solved. By the last half of the 1970s, however, problems were once again apparent. Farmers had borrowed heavily to expand production, and, consequently, even the modest weakening of demand that occurred toward the end of the decade put many farmers into financial difficulties. They marched on Washington, demanding higher support prices to protect their investments, once again showing that they expected special treatment that producers in most other sectors could never hope to receive. A general economic recovery at the end of the decade provided temporary relief.

The 1980s

1980 saw the onset of a serious worldwide recession. Farmers, heavily in debt because of expansions during the 1970s, found themselves in a serious plight. Then in 1981 bumper crops and rapidly rising interest rates caught farmers in the twin bind of falling prices and rising costs. Although the Reagan administration had come to office committed to letting the market, rather than the federal government, regulate the agricultural sector, political realities dictated otherwise.

In expectation of a return to buoyant market conditions, the 1981 Farm Bill raised target prices and loan rates, indexing them to the rate of inflation. Export demand did not rise as much as was anticipated, due to rising production in other countries, the onset of a worldwide recession, and a rising value of the dollar that forced up the foreign price of U.S. farm products. As a result—to give one example—the U.S. share of the world wheat market plummeted from 48 percent during 1981–1982 to 25 percent during 1985–1986.

Farm prices remained depressed. For example, by 1984 the price of a bushel of wheat had fallen to $3.40, which was well below the target price of $4.45 and even below the loan rate of $3.65. Farmers preferred to produce and earn the loan rate rather than to cut production and earn nothing. As a result, massive surpluses began to build up in spite of programs to reduce the acreage under cultivation. With prices and export sales down, the number of defaults on loans and the number of farm bankruptcies rose.

Early in 1985 stories of the desperate conditions of American farmers began to appear in the press. Many farmers could not even raise the money needed for the spring planting.

The 1985 Farm Bill attempted to raise the American share of export markets by drastically reducing prices while maintaining income support for farmers.

This strategy relied on three elements: lowering loan rates and target prices, making deficiency payments, and offering export subsidies.

Loan rates and target prices were lowered in the farm bill itself, and power was given to the secretary of agriculture to lower them still further should market conditions weaken. As a result, U.S. prices became more competitive on world markets. Incomes were supported by deficiency payments, which were based on the difference between the target and the market prices. Under the Export Enhancement Program (EEP), government stocks were provided free to exporters to be used as bonuses to foreign customers. The EEP originally was intended only to recapture the markets that were lost to subsidized exports from the European Community (EC). Since late 1986, however, the program has been expanded to include sales to most markets.[4]

Due to rising demand and competitive pricing of U.S. exports in the late 1980s, the farm crisis abated somewhat. Accumulated food stocks were no longer so great, and farmers' debt burdens lightened. Due to lower prices, however, the rising quantity of sales of agricultural products was not matched by a rising value of sales.

The successes in maintaining sales through competitive pricing and incomes through deficiency payments, while holding down surplus stocks through a combination of high sales and crop restrictions, came at a high cost. The U.S. government's spending on agricultural policy measures totaled $55 billion in 1988 and showed no sign of falling, but the greatest cost was to the world's trading system. The United States and the European Community were engaged in a major subsidy war that covered most farm goods. As a result, prices were depressed, production was too high to be absorbed by market demand at existing prices, and markets were often rendered unstable. Less developed nations found it difficult to compete against heavily subsidized products from the EC and the United States, and this accentuated their own development problems.

The United States took some major international

---

[4] This organization, which was formed in 1958 by France, Germany, Italy, Holland, Belgium, and Luxembourg, now includes 12 countries. It was originally called the European Common Market, then the European Economic Community, and now just the European Community (EC).

BOX 6-2

Four General Lessons About Resource Allocation

We have examined examples of government intervention in markets that might have been left unregulated. Our discussion suggests four widely applicable lessons.

1. Costs May Be Shifted, but They Cannot Be Avoided

Production, whether in response to free-market signals or to government controls, uses resources; thus it involves costs to members of society. If it takes 5 percent of the nation's resources to provide housing at some stated average standard, those resources will not be available to produce other commodities. If resources are used to produce unwanted soybeans, those resources will not be available to produce other commodities. For society there is no such thing as free housing or free soybeans.

The average standard of living depends on the amount of resources available to the economy and the efficiency with which these resources are used. It follows that *costs are real* and are incurred no matter who provides the goods. Rent controls or subsidies to agriculture can change the share of the costs paid by particular individuals or groups, lowering the share for some and raising the share for others, but they cannot make the costs go away.

Different ways of *allocating* the costs may also affect the total amount of resources used and thus the amount of costs incurred. For example, controls that keep prices and profits of some commodity below free-market levels will lead to increased quantities demanded and decreased quantities supplied. Unless government steps in to provide additional supplies, fewer resources will be allocated to producing the commodity. If government chooses to supply all the demand at the controlled prices, more resources will be allocated to it, which means fewer resources will be devoted to other kinds of goods and services.

2. Free-Market Prices and Profits Encourage Economical Use of Resources

Prices and profits in a market economy provide signals to both demanders and suppliers. Prices that are high and rising (relative to other prices) provide an incentive to purchasers to economize on the commodity. They may choose to satisfy the want in question with substitutes whose prices have not risen so much (because they are less costly to provide) or to satisfy less of that want by shifting expenditure to the satisfaction of other wants.

On the supply side, rising prices tend to produce rising profits. High profits attract further resources into production. Short-term profits that bear no relation to current costs repeatedly occur in market economies. They cause resources to move into those industries with profits until profits fall to levels that can be earned elsewhere in the economy.

Falling prices and falling profits provide the opposite motivations. Purchasers are inclined to buy more; sellers are inclined to produce less and to move resources out of the industry and into more profitable undertakings.

---

initiatives whose expressed intention was to eliminate farm subsidization worldwide. However, political resistance was great. In the unlikely event that the U.S. government's efforts were to succeed, American farmers would have to make some dramatic readjustments in order to cope with the end of the many subsidization programs that have provided them with vast sums of money during the past decades.

Evaluating Farm Policy

American farm policy reflects the central dilemma when government intervenes in competitive markets

The price system responds to need for change in the allocation of resources, say, in response to an external event such as the loss of a source of a raw material or the outbreak of a war. Changing relative prices and profits signal the need for change to which consumers and producers respond.

3. Government Intervention Affects Resource Allocation

Governments intervene in the price system sometimes to satisfy generally agreed social goals and sometimes to help politically influential interest groups. Government intervention changes the allocation of resources that the price system would achieve.

Interventions have allocative consequences because they inhibit the free-market allocative mechanism. Some controls, such as rent controls, prevent prices from rising (in response, say, to an increase in demand with no change in supply). If the price is held down, the signal is not given to consumers to economize on a commodity that is in short supply. On the supply side, when prices and profits are prevented from rising, the profit signals that would attract new resources into the industry are never given. The shortage continues, and the movements of demand and supply that would resolve it are not set in motion.

Other controls, such as agricultural price supports, prevent prices from falling (in response, say, to an increase in supply with no increase in demand). This leads to excess supply, and the signal

is not given to producers to produce less or to buyers to increase their purchases. Surpluses continue, and the movements of demand and supply that would eliminate them are not set in motion.

4. Intervention Requires Alternative Allocative Mechanisms

Intervention typically requires alternative allocative mechanisms. During times of shortages, allocation will be by sellers' preferences, by first-come, first-served, or by some system of government rationing. During periods of surplus, there will be unsold supplies unless the government buys and stores the surpluses. Since long-run changes in demand and costs do not induce resource reallocations through private decisions, the government will have to step in. It will have to force resources out of industries in which prices are held too high, as it has tried to do in agriculture, and into industries in which prices are held too low, as it can do, for example, by providing public housing.

Intervention almost always has both benefits and costs. Economics cannot answer the question of whether a particular intervention with free markets is desirable, but it can clarify the issues by identifying benefits and costs and who will enjoy or bear them. In doing so it can identify the competing values involved. This matter will be discussed in detail in Chapter 22.

with the intention of protecting a portion of the population from economic hardship. By doing so it impedes the reallocation of resources that is required in a changing economy.

Box 6-2 provides some general lessons concerning resource allocation—lessons that apply to all parts of the economy, including the agricultural sector.

Most economists—and many politicians—believe that American farm policies have been unnecessarily expensive and wasteful and that they have impeded the long-run adjustments required by changing tastes and technology. Yet these policies were continued, even under the Reagan administration, which had promised to reverse them.

One reason for its continuation is that a radical reversal of traditional farm policy would entail exposing the current generation of farmers to harsh free-market forces, and farmers are still too politically influential to allow this to happen. Few people quarrel with the objective of protecting farmers from a long period of severe hardship, but many people hope for less expensive and less wasteful *means* than those relied upon in past decades. Let us review how these means have been wasteful.

Price parity.   Price parity, in effect, freezes relative prices. To freeze any one set of relative prices prevents the price system from allocating resources in response to changes in tastes and incomes on the demand side and to costs and availabilities on the supply side. Society progresses by substituting newer products and less costly production methods for older products and more expensive methods, not by keeping relative prices the same forever.

Support prices above market levels.   Support prices above market levels create surpluses that must be stored, given away, or destroyed. They also encourage more production than would otherwise occur if there were no support prices.

Loan guarantees to avoid bankruptcy.   When people know that the government will bail them out if they overinvest in some industry, they will tend to take excessive risks. If demand turns out to be unexpectedly strong, they will earn the profits; if it turns out to be unexpectedly weak, the government will pay the bill. Whereas those individuals who invest cannot lose, society as a whole is sure to lose when overinvestment in a particular industry wastes scarce capital.

Guaranteeing relative incomes by direct payments to farmers.   Changes in relative incomes signal the need for resources to move from one occupation to another. By freezing relative incomes, the government not only eliminates the incentive to use resources efficiently but also reduces incentives to owners and workers to move resources to more productive uses.

The Future

Is there a better way to make farming an occupation in which people can invest and work without being disadvantaged relative to other citizens and without needing large payments of funds raised from the nation's taxpayers? Most economists believe that a more efficient system would subsidize farm workers to change occupations and farm producers to change products rather than subsidize them to stay where they are not needed and to produce products that cannot be marketed profitably. Such subsidies would require significant outlays—as do the present schemes—but would allow the market to do the job of allocating resources to agriculture.

SUMMARY

1. The elementary theory of supply, demand, and price provides powerful tools for analyzing and understanding some real-world problems and policies. The chapter illustrates a few of them.
2. The volume and direction of international trade are determined by the relationship between the world prices of tradeable goods and the no-trade prices that would rule in the domestic market in the absence of international trade. The difference between the quantities demanded and the quantities supplied domestically at the world price of each good is exported when the world price exceeds the no-trade price and is imported when the world price is less than the no-trade price.
3. Effective price floors lead to excess supply. Either the potential seller is left with quantities that cannot be sold, or the government must step in and buy the surplus. Effective price ceilings lead to excess demand and provide a strong incentive for black marketeers to buy at the controlled price and sell at the higher free-market price.
4. Rent controls are a persistent and spreading form of price ceiling. The major consequence of effective rent controls is a shortage of rental accommodations that gets worse due to a decline in the quantity of rental housing.

5. Rent controls can be an effective response to temporary situations in which there is a ban on building or a transitory increase in demand. They usually fail when they are introduced as a response to a long-run increase in demand.

6. Average farm incomes in the United States have lagged behind urban incomes. The long-term problems of agriculture arise from a high rate of productivity growth on the supply side and a low income elasticity on the demand side. This means that, unless resources are constantly being transferred out of agriculture, quantity supplied increases faster than quantity demanded year after year.

7. Although the number of farmers has decreased, it has not done so nearly fast enough to keep domestic demand and supply in balance without incurring sharply falling prices. During the 1970s a sharp rise in demand for American farm products by foreign nations temporarily relieved the long-standing supply surplus and led to a burst of prosperity that showed signs of eliminating the income gap of farmers relative to the rest of the population.

8. Agricultural prices and incomes are depressed by chronic surpluses in agricultural markets. Government policies to protect farm incomes have included buying farmers' output at above free-market prices, limiting production and acreage through quotas, and paying farmers to leave crops unproduced. Such policies tend to inhibit the reallocation mechanism and thus to increase farm surpluses above what they would otherwise be and to lead to accumulating stocks.

9. Agricultural commodities are subject to wide fluctuations in market prices, which cause fluctuations in producers' incomes. This is because of year-to-year unplanned fluctuations in supplies combined with inelastic demands and because of cyclical fluctuations in demands combined with inelastic supplies. Where demand is inelastic, large crops tend to be associated with low total receipts for farmers, and small crops tend to be associated with high total receipts.

10. Fluctuations in farm income can be reduced by producers' associations that store unsold crops when output is high and sell from inventories when output is low or by appropriate government purchases and sales in the open market. To stabilize farm incomes, the government should not stabilize prices. Instead, it should buy and sell just enough to allow prices to vary in proportion to changes in quantity, thus making the elasticity of demand for the product unity.

11. The history of American farm policy illustrates dramatically these theoretical predictions, as well as the more general lessons that government intervention to prevent the working of the market mechanisms affects resource allocation and requires alternative allocative mechanisms. While farm policy has protected farmers from certain hardships, it has slowed the required outflow of resources that alone would solve the problem of chronic excess supply.

TOPICS FOR REVIEW

The dermination of imports and exports
Price floor and price ceiling
Allocation by sellers' preferences, rationing, and black market
The allocative function of profits
Short-run and long-run supply curves
Effects of high productivity growth and low income elasticity
Importance of export demand
Price supports at and above the level of free-market equilibrium
Price stabilization versus income stabilization

DISCUSSION QUESTIONS

1. Use the theory that you have learned in this chapter to interpret the following news stories from the past and the present.
   a. "Rising world price of soybeans increases U.S. exports."
   b. "New discoveries of oil in the North Sea during the 1970s turned Norway from an oil importer into an oil exporter."
   c. "American imports of Canadian natural gas soar as U.S. demand rises."
   d. "The failure of Soviet agricultural policy turned the USSR from a wheat exporter into a wheat importer."
   e. "British exports of automobiles to Europe rose when a local recession caused domestic purchases to slump."

2. "When a controlled item is vital to everyone, it is easier to start controlling the price than to stop controlling it. Such controls are popular with consumers, regardless of their harmful consequences." Explain why it may be inefficient to have such controls, why they may be popular, and why, if they are popular, the government might nevertheless choose to decontrol these prices.

3. Commenting on a shortage of natural gas, the columnist William Safire called it "the unnatural shortage of natural gas." He wrote: "Be angry at the real villains: the Washington-knows-best Congressmen, the self-anointed consumer 'protectors' and the regulatory bureaucracy. They thought they could protect the consumer by breaking the laws of supply and demand, and as a result have made a classic case against government intervention." From these remarks, what do you judge the policy to have been? How would you define a "shortage"? Is there a useful distinction between a "natural shortage" and an "unnatural shortage"?

4. Medical and hospital care in Britain is provided free to individuals by the National Health Service, with the costs paid by taxation. Some British doctors complain that patients want "too much" medical care; patients complain that they have to wait "too long" in doctors' offices for the care they get and months or years for needed operations. Use the theory of supply and demand to discuss these complaints. Would you expect a private (pay) medical market to grow up alongside the National Health Service? Can you reconcile your analysis with the fact that polls always show the National Health Service to be very popular with the population at large?

5. The Yarvard Law School, in Princetown, has 1,000 qualified applicants for 200 places in the first-year class. It is debating whether or not to institute a number of alternative admission criteria: (a) a lottery, (b) LSAT score, (c) recommendations from alumni, (d) place of residence of applicant. An economist on the faculty determined that if the tuition level is doubled, the excess demand will disappear. Argue for (or against) using the tuition rate to replace each of the other suggested criteria.

6. It is sometimes asserted that the rising costs of construction are putting housing out of the reach of ordinary citizens. Who bears the heaviest cost when rentals are kept down by (a) rent controls, (b) a subsidy to tenants equal to some fraction of their rent payments, and (c) low-cost public housing?

7. "This year the weather smiled on us, God smiled on us and we made a crop," says Don Marble, a grain and cotton farmer in South Plains, Texas. "But just as we made a crop, the economic situation changed." This quotation brings to mind the old saying, "If you

are a farmer, the weather is always bad." Discuss the sense in which this saying might be true.

8. The Kenya Meat Commission (KMC) decided that it was undemocratic to allow meat prices to be out of the reach of the ordinary citizen. It decided to freeze meat prices. Six months later, in a press interview, the managing commissioner of the KMC made the following statements.

   a. "Cattle are scarce in the country, but I do not know why."

   b. "People are eating too much beef, and unless they diversify their eating habits and eat other foodstuffs, the shortage of beef will continue."

   Can you explain to the commissioner why these things have happened?

9. Three million acres of American farmland are being converted each year to other uses (out of about 525 million acres available). The American Farmland Trust calls this "one of the most critical problems facing our country and the world today." It has appealed to the public for contributions on the ground that "steps need to be taken immediately to preserve the prime agricultural land on which the food you eat is now grown." Discuss whether this is a critical problem and, if it is, whether the free market can be expected to solve it.

10. Compare the following two headlines that appeared within days of each other. Do American consumers benefit or lose when bumper crops occur?

    a. "Bumper potato crop dashes farmers' hopes."

    b. "Record high corn crop leaves farmers smiling."

    Hint: Corn is a "basic commodity"; potatoes are not.

11. What do the following quotes tell you about the politics of farm policy?

    a. Farmer Peter de Gravelles, Jr., of Franklin, Louisiana, an ardent supporter of President Reagan's free enterprise philosophy: "I am not asking the government to guarantee me a profit for my sugar cane. I just wanted a safety net so that I would not go bankrupt in bad years like this one."

    b. "The whole Agriculture Committee is biased toward agricultural interests," said Representative George E. Brown, Jr., of California, a senior Democrat on the panel. "We're not evil or anything, just a little one-sided."

3

CONSUMPTION, PRODUCTION, AND COST

Chapter 7

Household Consumption Behavior

In Part 2 we saw that demand is an important part of the explanation of market prices and that the shapes of demand curves influence how markets behave. Why do market demand curves have the shapes they do? To address this question, we need to study the behavior of individual households, since that behavior underlies market demand curves.

We start by studying the choices that face every household that has money to spend and that desires to purchase certain commodities. Later in the chapter we develop theories of how households make their choices.

The Choices Households Face

To begin, we reduce the problem to its basics by considering a household that has a specific income that it can spend on just two commodities—food and clothing. (Simplifying the problem by considering only two commodities allows us to see the essential points more easily.) Suppose that the household has a money income of $360 per week and that the prices for food and clothing are $12 per unit for food and $6 per unit for clothing. For the purpose of our example, further suppose that the household does not save; its only choice is in deciding how much of its $360 to spend on food ($F$) and how much to spend on clothing (C).

The Budget Line

The household's alternatives are described by the solid line ab in Figure 7-1. That line, which is called a **budget line,** shows all the combinations of food and clothing that the household can buy. It indicates all the combinations of commodities available to the household if it spends a fixed amount of money, in this case all its income, at fixed prices of the commodities. (It is also sometimes called an *isocost line,* since all points on it represent bundles of goods with the same total cost.) The budget line has several important properties.

1. Points on the budget line indicate bundles of commodities that use up the household's entire income. (Try, for example, the point $20C$, $20F$.)
2. Points between the budget line and the origin indicate bundles of commodities that cost less than the household's income. (Try, for example, the point $20C$, $10F$.)

3. Points above the budget line indicate combinations of commodities that cost more than the household's income. (Try, for example, the point 30C, 40F.)

The budget line shows all combinations of commodities that are available to the household given its money income and the prices of the goods that it purchases.

Shifts in the Budget Line

Recall from Chapter 4 (see pages 67–69) that the *absolute,* or *money,* price of a commodity refers to the amount of money that must be spent to acquire one unit of the commodity. We contrasted this with the *relative* price of the commodity, which is the ratio of its absolute price to the absolute price of some other commodity or group of commodities.

We now encounter a similar distinction for income. A household's **money income** is its income measured in monetary units per period of time—so many dollars per week or per year. A household's **real income** is the *purchasing power* of its money income; it is the quantity of goods and services that can be purchased with that money income. The next few paragraphs show this important distinction in terms of the budget line.

Changes in Money Income

What happens to the budget line when money income changes? If the household's money income is halved from $360 to $180 per week, while money prices remain unchanged at $12 per unit for food and $6 per unit for clothing, the amount of goods that the household can buy will also be halved. This causes the budget line to shift inward toward the origin, as shown in Figure 7-2. All possible combinations that are now open to the household appear on budget line *cd*, which is closer to the origin than the original budget line *ab*.

If the household's money income *rises* to $540, while the money prices of food and clothing remain unchanged, it will be able to increase its purchases of both commodities. The budget line shifts outward, as shown by the line *ef* in Figure 7-2.

Variations in the household's money income, with money prices constant, shift the budget line parallel to itself. It shifts outward (away

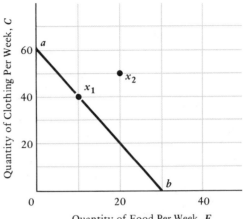

FIGURE 7-1   A Budget Line

The budget line shows the quantities of goods available to a household given its money income and the prices of goods it buys. Any point in this diagram indicates a combination (or bundle) of so much food and so much clothing. Point x_1, for example, indicates 40 units of clothing and 10 units of food per week.

With an income of $360 a week and prices of $12 per unit for food and $6 per unit for clothing, respectively, the household's budget line is *ab*. This line shows all combinations of F and C available to a household spending this income at these prices. The household could spend all of its money income on clothing and obtain 60 units of clothing and zero food each week. It could also go to the other extreme and purchase only food, buying 30 units of F and zero units of C. On the other hand, it could choose an intermediate position and consume some of both goods; for example, it could spend $120 to buy 10 units of F and $240 to buy 40 units of C (point x_1). Points above the budget line, such as x_2, are not available.

from the origin) when money income rises and inward (toward the origin) when money income falls.

Proportional Changes in All Money Prices

Now return to the initial situation, in which the household has a money income of $360 and faces prices of $12 per unit for food and $6 per unit for clothing. Let the money prices of food and clothing double to $24 per unit for food and $12 per unit for clothing, respectively. This halves the quantities of food and clothing that can be bought and so shifts

FIGURE 7-2 The Effect on the Budget Line of Changes in Money Income

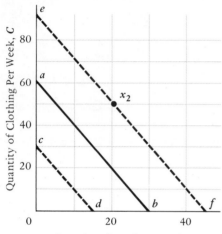

Changes in the household's money income shift the budget line outward when money income rises and inward when money income falls. The original budget line *ab* refers to a money income of $360 and prices of $12 per unit for *F* and $6 per unit for *C*. If the household's money income is halved from $360 to $180 per week, while prices remain unchanged, the amount of goods the household can buy will also be halved. This causes the budget line to shift inward (toward the origin) to *cd*. If the household spends all its money income on clothing, it will now get 30 units of clothing and zero units of food (point *c* in the figure). If it spends all its money income on food, it will get 15 units of food and zero units of clothing (point *d*).

If the household's money income rises to $540, while the prices of food and clothing remain unchanged, the budget line shifts outward to *ef*. If the household buys only clothing, it can have 90 units of clothing; if it buys only food, it can have 45 units of food. Point x_2, indicating 50 units of *C* and 20 of *F*, is now available, as shown by the fact that it lies on the new budget line *ef*.

Proportional changes in the money prices of all goods, if money income remains constant, shift the budget line parallel to itself. It shifts outward (away from the origin) when money prices fall and inward (toward the origin) when money prices rise.

Money Income and Real Income

Clearly, there can be exact offsetting changes in money prices and money incomes that leave the real choices available to the household unchanged. For example, if money income and money prices all rise by 10 percent, the position of the budget line is unchanged.

A proportional change in money income and in all money prices leaves the household neither better nor worse off in terms of its ability to purchase commodities.

The foregoing observations show the importance of the distinction between *money* income and *real* income.

If money prices remain constant, any change in money income will cause a corresponding change in real income. If the household's money income rises by 10 percent (say, from $10,000 to $11,000), the household is able to buy 10 percent more of all commodities—its purchasing power has also risen by 10 percent.

If money prices change, real and money incomes will not change in the same proportion; indeed, they can easily change in *opposite* directions. Consider a situation in which all money prices rise by 10 percent. If money income rises by any amount less than 10 percent, real income falls. If money income also rises by 10 percent, real income will be unchanged. Only if money income rises by more than 10 percent will real income also rise.

A household's ability to purchase goods and services is measured by its real income, not by its money income.

Changes in real income are shown graphically by shifts in the budget line. When the budget line in Figure 7-2 shifts away from the origin, real income rises; when the budget line shifts toward the origin, real income falls.

the budget line inward, parallel to itself. These money changes have exactly the same effect as when prices remain constant at $12 per unit for food and $6 per unit for clothing, but money income falls from $360 to $180. Similarly, a proportional reduction of both money prices causes the budget line to shift outward in exactly the same manner that an increase in money income does.

FIGURE 7-3   The Effect on the Budget Line of Changes in the Price of Food

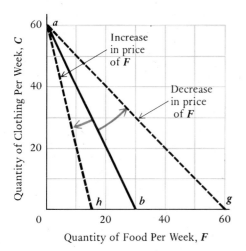

A change in the absolute price of one commodity changes relative prices and thus changes the slope of the budget line. The original budget line *ab* occurred with a money income of $360, with units of *C* priced at $6 and units of *F* at $12. A fall in the price of *F* to $6 doubles the quantity of *F* obtainable for any given quantity of *C* purchased and pivots the budget line outward to *ag*. A rise in the price of *F* to $24 reduces the quantity of *F* obtainable and pivots the budget line inward to *ah*.

Changes in Relative Prices

A *relative price* is the ratio of two absolute prices. The statement "The price of *F* is $12" refers to an absolute price; the statement "The price of *F* is twice the price of *C*" refers to a relative price.

A change in a relative price can be accomplished by changing both of the absolute prices in different proportions or by holding one absolute price constant and changing the other. The points we wish to make can be established by studying the case in which changes in relative prices are accomplished by holding one money price constant and changing the other.

Return, for example, to our illustration, in which a household with a money income of $360 faced prices of $12 per unit for food and $6 per unit for clothing. Now let the price of food fall to $6 per unit. This lowers the price of food *relative to the price*

of clothing and, as shown in Figure 7-3, changes the slope of the budget line.

The important conclusion is this:

A change in relative prices alters the slope of the budget line.

The significance of the slope of the budget line for food and clothing is that it reflects the opportunity cost of food in terms of clothing. This is because, as we have just seen, the slope of the budget line reflects the relative prices of the two commodities. In order to increase food consumption while maintaining expenditure constant, one must move along the budget line and therefore consume less clothing.

Return for the moment to the original situation, in which the price of food (p_F) is $12 per unit and the price of clothing (p_C) is $6 per unit. With income fixed, it is necessary to forego the purchase of two units of clothing to acquire one extra unit of food. The opportunity cost of a unit of food is thus two units of clothing. This opportunity cost can also be stated as p_F/p_C, which is the relative price of food in terms of clothing.

Notice that the relative price (in our example $p_F/p_C = 2$) is consistent with an infinite number of absolute prices. If $p_F = $40 and $p_C = $20, it still is necessary to sacrifice two units of clothing to acquire one unit of food. This shows that it is relative, not absolute, prices that determine opportunity cost.

The opportunity cost of food in terms of clothing is measured by the slope of the budget line and also by the relative price ratio, p_F/p_C. [9]

The Choices Households Make

The combination of commodities that the household chooses to purchase will depend both on what it can do and on what it wants to do. What it can do is shown by the budget line it faces, which we have just studied; what it wants to do is determined by its tastes. Given its budget line and its tastes, what will the household do?[1]

---

[1] In the two appendixes to this chapter we develop two theories of household choice. In the text we show how far we can get using the budget line alone plus the simple assumption that households are consistent in their decision making.

The key assumption about household behavior is that *households maximize what is variously called their satisfactions, their welfare, their well-being, or their utility*. In Appendix A this assumption is worded to show that households seek to maximize welfare by reaching the highest attainable indifference curve. In Appendix B you will find this assumption worded to show that households seek to maximize utility. However it is worded, and whatever theory is used to develop it, the important thing to remember is that it is assumed that households try to do as well for themselves as they can. Faced with a choice between two alternative consumption bundles, each household is assumed to choose the bundle that it prefers, which is the same thing as saying that the household makes its choices so as to maximize its satisfactions or its welfare. The popular but misguided criticism that this assumption is to be rejected because it is "unrealistic" is considered in Box 7-1.

Income and Substitution Effects

How does the household react to a change in the price of one good? (For purposes of illustration we consider a fall in price.) A fall in the price of one good affects the household in two ways. First, relative prices change, providing an incentive to buy *more* of the good in question because it is cheaper. Second, the household's real income increases, because it can buy more of all commodities (as can be seen, for example, by comparing budget lines *ab* and *ag* in Figure 7-3). This rise in real income provides an incentive to buy *different* amounts of all goods. (Recall from Chapter 5 that when its real income rises, the household buys more of all normal goods and less of all inferior goods.)

These two effects are illustrated in Table 7-1 and Figure 7-4, both of which continue the example used earlier in this chapter. The household initially has a money income of $360 and faces prices of food and clothing of $12 and $6 per unit, respectively. The data are shown in the table, and the budget line is shown in the figure. Given the household's tastes, it will prefer a combination of goods shown by some particular point on this budget line. For our purposes it does not matter which particular point is chosen, so we let it be the point shown by row 2 of Table 7-1, indicated by the point E_0 in part (i) of Figure 7-4.

The price of food then falls to $6 per unit, making it possible for the household to buy more of both commodities, which is why we say its real income has risen. The household chooses its preferred position on the new budget line, which we assume to be the one indicated in row 5 of Table 7-1 and by point E_1 in Figure 7-4. The shift in consumption is partly a response to the change in the *slope* of the budget line, reflecting the change in relative prices. It is also partly a response to an *outward* shift in the budget line, reflecting the increase in the household's real income due to the fall in one money price with money income and all other money prices remaining constant.

To isolate the effect of the change in relative price when the price of food falls, we can consider what would happen if we also reduced the household's money income to restore its original purchasing power. To do this, we reduce money income until the original bundle of food and clothing can just be bought at the new prices. When the household is faced with the new prices and with the reduced money income that just allows it to purchase its original bundle of goods, the effects of the change in relative prices when the purchasing power of income is held constant are isolated. The household's reaction is the **substitution effect,** which is the change in quantity demanded as a result of a change in relative prices, with the purchasing power of income being held constant.[2] As shown by row 9 of Table 7-1 and part (ii) of Figure 7-4, the household buys more food, whose relative price has fallen, and less clothing, whose relative price has risen.

Next, we restore the household's money income, which shifts the budget line outward, parallel to itself. Assuming that we are dealing with a normal good, the household will increase its consumption of food. (It will also increase its consumption of clothing.) The change in quantity demanded as a result of the household's reaction to this shift of its budget line is called the **income effect.** It is shown by the change between rows 9 and 13 in Table 7-1 and points E' and E_1 in part (iii) of Figure 7-4.

We have now broken down the reaction to a fall in the price of a commodity (food, in our example)

[2] This method of isolating the substitution effect is based on what is known as the *Slutsky equation*. An alternative way of holding "real income" constant is discussed in Appendix A to this chapter.

BOX 7-1

Does Demand Theory Require That Households Always Act Rationally?

The theory of household behavior uses the key assumption that households always act rationally in the maximization of their satisfaction. This assumption of rationality appears in slightly different form in various theories, but it always amounts to assuming that each household assesses any choices it faces and consistently chooses its preferred alternative.

It is tempting to dismiss demand theory with the objection that consumer rationality is an unrealistic assumption. After all, most of us know people who occasionally buy strawberries in spite of, even because of, a rise in their price and others who sometimes spend a week's pay on a binge or a frivolous purchase that they afterward regret.

To assess the significance of such observed "irrationalities," it is helpful to distinguish three possible uses of demand theory. The first is to study the aggregate behavior of all households—as illustrated, for example, by the market demand curve for gasoline or carrots. The second use is to make statements about an individual household's probable actions. The third is to make statements about what each household will certainly do.

The criticism that the assumption of rationality is not realistic applies primarily to the third use of demand theory. Observations of unusual or irrational behavior refute only the prediction that *all* households *always* behave as assumed by the theory. To predict the existence of a relatively stable, negatively sloped market demand curve (the first use) or to predict what an individual household will probably do (the second use), we do *not* require that *all* households behave as assumed by the theory all of the time. Consider two illustrations.

First, some households may always behave in a manner that is not assumed by the theory. House-

holds whose members have serious emotional disturbances are one obvious example. The inconsistent or erratic behavior of such households will not cause market demand curves to depart from their downward slope, provided these households account for a minority of total purchasers of any product. Their erratic behavior will be swamped by the normal behavior of the majority of households.

Second, an occasional spurt of impulse buying or of downright irrationality on the part of every household will not upset the downward slope of the market demand curve as long as these isolated inconsistencies do not occur at the same time and in the same way in all households. As long as such inconsistencies are unrelated across households, occurring now in one and now in another, their effects will be offset by the normal behavior of the majority of households.

The downward slope of the demand curve requires only that at any moment in time most households are behaving as predicted by the theory. This is compatible with inconsistent behavior on the part of some households all of the time and on the part of all households some of the time.

Long ago the great U.S. President Abraham Lincoln said, "You can fool some of the people all of the time and all of the people some of the time, but you cannot fool all of the people all of the time." The same thought holds true for irrational behavior: Most people may behave irrationally some of the time; some people behave irrationally all of the time; but all people will not behave irrationally all of the time. Lincoln's observation helps make clear why the assumption of rationality yields correct predictions about the slope of market demand curves.

TABLE 7-1   The Income and Substitution Effects: A Numerical Example

	Food	Clothing	Total
I. Initial position (price of food = $12 per unit)			
(1) Price	$ 12	$ 6	
(2) Quantity	15	30	
(3) Expenditure	$180	$180	$360
II. New position (price of food = $6 per unit)			
(4) Price	$ 6	$ 6	
(5) Quantity	25	35	
(6) Expenditure	$150	$210	$360
(7) Total effect:			
Line (5) − Line (2) = 10 additional units of food purchased			
III. Substitution effect: money income is reduced to $270 so that the initial bundle can still just be purchased at the new prices			
(8) Price	$ 6	$ 6	
(9) Quantity	21	24	
(10) Expenditure	$126	$144	$270
(11) Substitution effect:			
Line (9) − Line (2) = 6 additional units of food purchased			
IV. Income effect: money income is returned to $360			
(12) Price	$ 6	$ 6	
(13) Quantity	25	35	
(14) Expenditure	$150	$210	$360
(15) Income effect:			
Line (13) − Line (9) = 4 additional units of food purchased			
V. Total effect: change in food purchases in response to a change in the price of food			

Substitution effect (from line (11)):	6 units of food
Income effect (from line (15)):	4 units of food
Total effect (confirms line (7)):	10 units of food

The substitution effect measures the response to a change in relative prices when purchasing power of income is held constant; the income effect measures the response to a change in purchasing power when relative prices are held constant. In the initial position shown in panel I, a consumer with a money income of $360 faces prices of $12 per unit for food and $6 per unit for clothing, buying 15F and 30C. As shown in panel II, the money price of food then falls to $6 per unit. The consumer now buys 25F and 35C, so the demand for food rises by 10 units.

Panel III shows the substitution effect. Money income is reduced to $270, so the initial bundle of 15F and 30C can just be bought at the new prices of $6 each. In this example, the household now purchases 21F and 24C.

Panel IV shows the income effect. Money income is returned to its original level of $360. As a result, the consumption of F and C both rise. In this example, F rises to 25 and C to 35.

As shown in panel V, the total effect is the sum of the income and the substitution effects, so a fall in the price of F from $12 to $6 leads to an increase of 10 units in the quantity of F demanded, from 15 to 25 units per week.

into a substitution effect and an income effect. In our numerical example the substitution effect raises the consumption of food by 6 units, and the income effect raises it by 4 units, making the overall response to the fall in price of food an increase of 10 units. Of course, when the price of food falls, the household moves directly from its initial position to its final position, buying 10 more units of food. By breaking

FIGURE 7-4 The Income and Substitution Effects

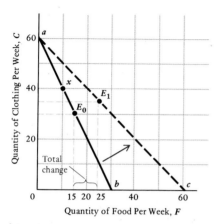

(i) A fall in the price of food

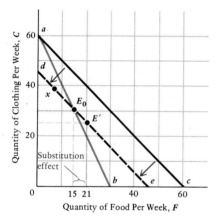

(ii) The substitution effect

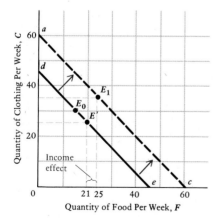

(iii) The income effect

The effect on household choice of a change in price can be broken into (1) a substitution effect measuring the response to a change in relative prices with purchasing power being held constant, and (2) an income effect measuring the response to the change in purchasing power caused by the price change.

(i) The initial budget line is ab, and the household's chosen position is E_0. E_0 corresponds to row 2 of Table 7-1, and at E_0 food consumption is 15 units. The price of food then falls, taking the budget line to ac and consumption to the bundle indicated by E_1. E_1 corresponds to row 5 of Table 7-1, and at E_1 food consumption is 25 units. Hence, the total change in the demand for food is 10 units.

(ii) The substitution effect is shown by reducing money income so that the original bundle can just be bought at the new prices. Graphically, this shifts the budget line to de, where it is parallel to ac but passes through E_0. The combined effect of the change in the price and the fall in income is that the budget line rotates through the initial consumption point E_0. The household chooses point E' on de, making the substitution effect the movement from E_0 to E'. This corresponds to row 9 of Table 7-1; the substitution effect on the demand for food is 6 units.

(iii) The income effect is measured by restoring money income to its original level. Graphically, this shifts the budget line from de to ac. The income effect is the change in consumption from E' to E_1. This corresponds to row 13 of Table 7-1; the income effect on the demand for food is 4 units.

The figure also shows why the substitution effect can never lead the household to buy less food when its price falls. Such an outcome would mean that the household had chosen a bundle such as x, which lies to the left of E_0 on the budget line de in part (ii). However, when the household had budget line ab, it could have chosen x (by not spending all its income). Instead it rejected x in favor of E_0. If the household is consistent, it will not choose now a previously rejected combination. Instead it will choose some position on de at, or to the right of, E_0; such points were not available to it when it chose E_0 on budget line ab. Any point on de to the right of E_0 indicates more consumption of food, the good whose price has fallen.

this movement into two parts, however, we are able to study the household's total change in quantities demanded in terms of a response to a change in relative prices and a response to a change in real income.

Notice that the size of the income effect depends on the amount of income spent on the good whose price changes and on the amount by which the price changes. In our simple example, where the household was spending one-half of its income on food, a 50 percent fall in the food price was equivalent (at the new prices) to a 25 percent increase in income. Now consider a different case. Assume that the price of petroleum falls by 20 percent. For a household that was spending only 5 percent of its income on gas and oil, this is equivalent (at the new prices) to only a 1 percent increase in purchasing power.

Derivation of a Demand Curve

The demand curve relates the quantity of a particular commodity demanded to the commodity's price. Figure 7-5 shows the derivation of the demand curve for food based on the example in Table 7-1. Part (i) reproduces part (i) of Figure 7-4; it shows the effect of a fall in the price of food on the budget line and on the consumption bundle chosen by the household. Each combination of a price of food and the corresponding quantity of food purchased is then plotted as a point in part (ii) of Figure 7-5. When joined together, such points give rise to the demand curve for food. As shown, the demand curve is negatively sloped.

The Slope of the Demand Curve

The negative slope of the demand curve shows that a fall in price leads to an increase in the quantity demanded. Earlier in this book we merely assumed this slope, but the analysis underlying Figure 7-4 allows us to explain it. As it is drawn in Figure 7-4, the substitution effect leads the household to buy more food, which is the commodity whose price has fallen.

We now ask a fundamental question. Could the substitution effect of a fall in the price of food have led the household to buy less food? Graphically, this would mean that the household would select some bundle that had less food and more clothing than its initial bundle. An example would be the bundle indicated by the point x on budget line de in part (ii)

of Figure 7-4. When the household was faced with its original budget line, ab, it could have gone to x (by not spending all of its income), but it chose not to do so, going to E_0 instead. So, as long as its preferences remain unchanged, the household will not now go to x.

This argument, which is laid out more fully in Box 7-2, leads us to an important conclusion:

The substitution effect can *never* lead a household to purchase less of a commodity whose price has fallen.

Now consider the second half of the household's adjustment to the fall in price, the income effect. A rise in income leads the household to buy more of all normal goods. This leads to the second conclusion:

The income effect leads the household to buy more of the commodity whose price has fallen, provided that it is a normal commodity.

Putting these two effects together gives the following conclusion:

Because of the combined operation of the substitution and the income effects, the demand curve for any normal commodity will be negatively sloped, indicating that a fall in price will lead to an increase in quantity demanded.

The Role of Tastes

Earlier we observed that what the household can do depends on its budget line, while what it does do depends on its tastes. Yet we appear to have studied the household's reactions to a change in price without saying much about the household's tastes. In fact, we did make use of a simple assumption about tastes. We assumed that households were consistent in the sense that if once they chose bundle of goods A over bundle B, they would not subsequently choose bundle B over bundle A. This is what allowed us to say that when the price of food fell and income was adjusted so that the original bundle could just be purchased, the household would never choose a new bundle containing less food because any such bundle could have been chosen in the initial situation. This assumption is laid out in more detail in Box 7-2 for

FIGURE 7-5   Derivation of the Demand Curve for Food

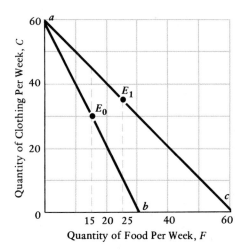

(i) The budget line and consumption bundles

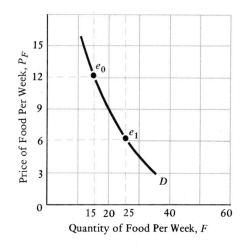

(ii) **The demand curve for food**

With a given money income, a change in the price of food causes the budget line to rotate and a new bundle of food and clothing to be purchased. This gives the information needed to derive the demand curve for food. (i) Part (i) reproduces part (i) of Figure 7-4. The household has an income of $360, and prices are initially $12 per unit of food and $6 per unit of clothing. The budget line is ab and the household consumes at point E_0, purchasing 15 units of food. When the price of food falls to $6 per unit, the budget line shifts to ac. The household consumes at point E_1, purchasing 25 units of food.

(ii) Part (ii) plots the quantity of food demanded against the price of food to yield the demand curve for food. Point e_0 corresponds to point E_0 in (i), where we saw that at a price of $12 per unit the household purchases 15 units of food. Point e_1 corresponds to point E_1 in (i); at the lower price of $6 per unit the household's demand for food rises to 25 units. Considering other prices would give rise to a series of points that, when joined, would yield the demand curve D.

those readers who would like to study it further. In Box 7-2 we also consider the possibility of the unusual case in which the demand curve for an inferior good could be positively sloped.

Can Demand Curves Ever Have Positive Slopes?

What the great English economist Alfred Marshall called the **law of demand** asserts that, other things being constant, the market price of a product and the quantity demanded in the market are negatively associated with each other, that is, the demand curves slope downward. Criticisms of the law have taken various forms, focusing on Giffen goods, conspicuous consumption goods, and goods whose demands

are perfectly inelastic. Let us consider each of these in turn.

Giffen Goods

Great interest was attached to the nineteenth century English economist Sir Robert Giffen's apparent refutation of the law of demand. He is alleged to have observed that when a rise in the price of imported wheat led to an increase in the price of bread, members of the British working class *increased* their consumption of bread. This meant that their demand curve for bread was positively sloped.

Theoretical reasoning shows that such an exception to the law of demand could occur. There are two requisites: (1) The good must be an inferior good, and (2) the good must take a large proportion

BOX 7-2

More About the Slope of Demand Curves

This box gives a more precise treatment of the discussion found in the text and then discusses the implications of the negative income effects that arise with inferior goods. The basic assumption about tastes that is used in this approach is called the *consistency assumption*. It states that if the household chose some bundle of goods that we call A over some other bundle that we call B in one situation, it would never choose B over A in some subsequent situation in which A and B are both available to it.

Normal Sloped Demand Curves

Let the initial budget line be ab and the chosen position be E_0. This means that the household has chosen the combination indicated by E_0 over all other attainable combinations. The rejected combinations are indicated by the points in the shaded triangle between ab and the origin. (Note that when it is faced with the budget line ab, the household can reach any point on ab by spending all of its income and can reach any point lying in the shaded area below ab by spending less than all its income.) If the household is consistent, it will never choose another bundle within that area when the bundle indicated by E_0 is also available.

   Now let the price of F fall, taking the budget line to ac. To isolate the substitution effect, we also reduce money income so that the budget line be-

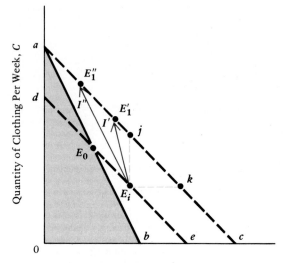

Quantity of Food Per Week, F

comes de. This new budget line is parallel to ac, indicating that the household faces the new relative price. The new budget line also passes through E_0, indicating that the household has only its original purchasing power.

   Consistency requires that the household cannot choose any point to the left of E_0 on the new budget line de, since those points lie within the shaded area that was rejected when E_0 was chosen on the budget line ab. The household either stays at E_0 or moves

of total household expenditure; that is, its income effect must be large. Bread was indeed a dietary staple of the British working classes during the nineteenth century. A rise in the price of bread would cause a large reduction in their real income. This could lead to increased consumption of bread as households cut out their few luxuries in order to be able to consume enough bread to keep alive. Though possible, such cases are all but unknown in the modern world. The reason is that in all but the poorest societies, typical households do not spend large proportions of their incomes on a single inferior good. (See Box 7-2 for further discussion of this.)

Conspicuous Consumption Goods

Thorstein Veblen in *The Theory of the Leisure Class* noted that some commodities were consumed not for their intrinsic qualities but because they carried a snob appeal. He suggested that the more expensive such a commodity became, the *greater* might be its ability to confer status on its purchaser.

   Consumers might buy diamonds, for example, not because they particularly like diamonds per se but because they wish to show off their wealth in an ostentatious but socially acceptable way. They are assumed to value diamonds precisely because dia-

to some point to the right of E_0—let us say it goes to E_i.

The foregoing argument shows that the substitution effect cannot be positive; when the price of food falls, the household cannot buy less food.

Now consider the income effect. Begin by drawing a vertical and a horizontal line from E_i to cut ac at j and k. Points on ac between j and k indicate an increase in the consumption of both commodities when the budget line goes from de to ac. This is what must happen if both goods are normal goods. This shows that the income effect of a fall in the price of food must lead to an increase in the demand for food, assuming only that it is a normal (noninferior) good.

So we know that if the price of some product falls, the substitution effect cannot lead to less of it being consumed if the good is normal, and the income effect leads to more of it being consumed. A fall in the price of any normal good must lead to an increase in its demand; that is, its demand curve has a negative slope.

Positively Sloped Demand Curves

Could the demand curve for F ever be positively sloped? This can happen only if F is an inferior good (a necessary condition). The figure illustrates two cases in which F is inferior. In the first case,

the movement of the budget line from de to ac takes the equilibrium position along the arrow I' to E_1'. In this case, the income effect leads to a fall in the demand for F, but the substitution effect is stronger than the income effect. Hence, the overall change in the quantity of F is an increase as the chosen position goes from E_0 to E_1'. In the second case, the negative income effect is stronger, and the equilibrium follows the path I'' from E_i to E_1''. In this case, the income effect of the inferior good outweighs the substitution effect, and the quantity of F demanded falls from that indicated by E_0 to that indicated by E_1'', as a result of a fall in the price of F.

We can now conclude the following:

1. **All normal goods have negatively sloped demand curves.**
2. **All inferior goods for which the substitution effect outweighs the income effect have negatively sloped demand curves.**
3. **A positively sloped demand curve requires an inferior good for which the income effect outweighs the substitution effect.**

monds are expensive. Thus, a fall in price might lead them to stop buying diamonds and to switch to a more satisfactory object of conspicuous consumption. They may behave in the same way with respect to luxury cars, buying them *because* they are expensive.

Households that behave in this way will have positively sloped *individual demand curves* for diamonds and cars. However, no one has ever observed a positively sloped *market demand curve* for such commodities. The reason for this is easy to discover. A consideration of the countless lower-income consumers who would be glad to buy diamonds or Cad-

illacs if these commodities were sufficiently inexpensive suggests that upward-sloping demand curves for a few individual wealthy households are much more likely than a positively sloped market demand curve for the same commodity.

Perfectly Inelastic Demand Curves

Even if demand curves never had positive slopes, the substantial insight provided by the law of demand would be diminished if there were important commodities for which changes in price had virtually no effect on quantity demanded.

It is surprising how often the assumption of a vertical demand curve is implicit. A common response of urban bus or subway systems to financial difficulties is to propose a percentage increase in fares equal to the percentage increase that they require in their revenues. Even professors are not immune to this type of response. At a meeting of the American Association of University Professors, a motion was introduced "to raise annual dues by 20 percent in order to raise revenues by 20 percent," in spite of the empirical evidence showing that a previous increase in dues had led (as theory would predict) to a significant drop in membership.

It was once widely argued that the demand for gasoline was almost perfectly inelastic on the grounds that people who had paid thousands of dollars for cars would not balk at paying a few cents extra for gasoline. The events of the past 15 years have proven how wrong this argument is: Higher gasoline prices in the 1970s led to production of smaller cars, to more car pools, to more economical driving speeds, and to less pleasure driving. Falling gasoline prices in the mid-1980s led to a reversal of these trends.

In summary, there is a mass of accumulated evidence confirming that most demand curves do in fact have a negative slope.

The hypothesis that demand curves are negatively sloped is strongly supported by the evidence.

Consumers' Surplus

Imagine yourself faced with an *either-or* choice concerning some particular commodity: You can have the amount you are now consuming or you can have none of it. Assume that you would be willing to pay as much as $100 per month for that amount rather than do without it. Further assume that you actually buy that amount of the commodity for $60 instead of $100. What a bargain! You have paid $40 less than the top figure you were willing to pay. Yet, this sort of bargain is not rare; it occurs every day in any economy in which prices do the rationing. Indeed, it is so common that the $40 "saved" in this example has been given a name: *consumers' surplus*. We will

define the term later; first let us look at how this surplus arises.

Consumers' surplus is a direct consequence of downward-sloping demand curves. To illustrate this connection, suppose that we have collected the information in Table 7-2 on the basis of an interview with Mrs. Swartz. Our first question to Mrs. Swartz is, "If you were getting no milk at all, how much would you be willing to pay for one glass per week?" With no hesitation she replies $3.00. We then ask, "If you had already consumed that one glass, how much would you pay for a second glass per week?" After a bit of thought she answers $1.50. Adding one glass per week with each question, we discover that she would be willing to pay $1.00 to get a third glass per week and $.80, $.60, $.50, $.40, $.30, $.25, and $.20 for successive glasses from the fourth to the tenth glass per week.

The sum of the values that she places on each glass of milk gives us the *total value* that she places

TABLE 7-2	Consumers' Surplus on Milk Consumption by One Consumer	
(1) Glasses of milk consumed per week	(2) Amount the consumer would pay to get this glass	(3) Consumers' surplus on each glass if milk costs $.30 per glass
First	$3.00	$2.70
Second	1.50	1.20
Third	1.00	.70
Fourth	.80	.50
Fifth	.60	.30
Sixth	.50	.20
Seventh	.40	.10
Eighth	.30	.00
Ninth	.25	—
Tenth	.20	—

Consumers' surplus on each unit consumed is the difference between the market price and the maximum price the consumer would pay to obtain that unit. The table shows the value that one consumer, Mrs. Swartz, puts on successive glasses of milk consumed each week. Her negatively sloped demand curve shows that she would be willing to pay progressively smaller amounts for each additional unit consumed. As long as she would be willing to pay more than the market price for any unit, she obtains a consumers' surplus on it when she buys it. The marginal unit is the one valued just at the market price and on which no consumers' surplus is earned.

on all 10 glasses. In this case, Mrs. Swartz values 10 glasses of milk per week at $8.55. This is the amount she would be willing to pay if faced with the either-or choice of 10 glasses or none. This is also the amount she would be willing to pay if she were offered the milk one glass at a time and if she were charged the maximum she was willing to pay for each.

However, Mrs. Swartz does not have to pay a different price for each glass of milk she consumes each week; she can buy all she wants at the prevailing market price. Suppose the price is $.30 per glass. She will buy eight glasses per week (one each weekday and two on Sunday) because she values the eighth glass just at the market price but all earlier glasses at higher amounts. She does not buy a ninth glass because she values it at less than the market price.

Because she values the first glass at $3.00 but gets it for $.30, she makes a "profit" of $2.70 on that glass. Between her $1.50 valuation of the second glass and what she has to pay for it, she clears a "profit" of $1.20. She clears a "profit" of $.70 on the third glass, and so on. These "profits" are called her consumer's surplus on each glass. They are shown in column 3 of Table 7-2; the total consumers' surplus is $5.70 per week.

In Table 7-2 we arrive at her consumers' surplus by summing her surpluses on each glass. We arrive at the same total by first summing what she would pay for all eight glasses, which is $8.10, and then by subtracting the $2.40 that she does pay.

The value placed by each household on its total consumption of some commodity can be estimated in at least two ways: The valuation that the household places on each successive unit may be summed, or the household may be asked how much it would pay to consume the amount in question if the alternative were to have none of that commodity.[3]

---

[3] This is only an approximation, but it is good enough for our purposes. More advanced theory shows that the calculations presented here overestimate consumers' surplus because they ignore the income effect. Although it is sometimes necessary to correct for this bias, no amount of refinement upsets the general result that we establish here: When consumers can buy all units they require at a single market price, they pay much less than they would be willing to pay if faced with the choice between having the quantity they consume and having none of it.

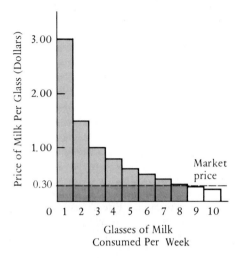

FIGURE 7-6   Consumers' Surplus for an Individual

Consumers' surplus is the sum of the extra valuations placed on each unit above the market price paid for each. This figure is based on the data in Table 7-2. Mrs. Swartz will pay the amounts shown in the dark shaded area for the eight glasses of milk she will consume per week when the market price is $.30 per glass. The total value she places on these eight glasses is the entire shaded area. Hence, her consumers' surplus is the light shaded area.

Although other households would put different numerical values into Table 7-2, the negative slope of the demand curve implies that the figures in column 2 would be declining for each household. Since a household will go on buying additional units until the value placed on the last unit equals the market price, it follows that there will be a consumers' surplus on every unit consumed except the last one.

In general, **consumers' surplus** is the difference between the total value that consumers place on all the units consumed of some commodity and the payment they must make to purchase that amount of the commodity.

The data in columns 1 and 2 of Table 7-2 give Mrs. Swartz's demand curve for milk. It is her demand curve because she will go on buying glasses of milk as long as she values each glass at least as much as the market price she must pay for it. When the market price is $3.00 per glass, she will buy only one

FIGURE 7-7   Consumers' Surplus for the Market

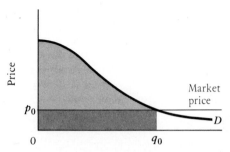

Quantity Consumed Per Period

Total consumers' surplus is the area under the demand curve and above the price line. The demand curve shows the amount consumers would pay for each unit of the commodity if they had to buy their units one at a time. The area under the demand curve shows the total valuation that consumers place on all units consumed. For example, the total value that consumers place on q_0 units is the entire shaded area under the demand curve up to q_0. At a market price of p_0 the amount paid for q_0 units is the dark shaded area. Hence, consumers' surplus is the light shaded area.

glass; when it is $1.50, she will buy two glasses; and so on. The total valuation is the area below her demand curve, and consumers' surplus is the part of the area that lies above the price line. This is shown in Figure 7-6.

Figure 7-7 shows that the same relationship holds

for the smooth market demand curve that indicates the total amount all consumers would buy at each price.[4]

Consumers' surplus is an extremely important and useful concept. Understanding it is the key to understanding the theory of demand. In the next chapter we shall see how it helps us to resolve some real-world events that on the surface seem paradoxical. In later chapters consumers' surplus will play a key role in our analysis of certain aspects of the performance of the market system.

A Preview

In this chapter we have presented the minimum amount of demand theory that is needed for the rest of this book. In the next chapter we shall present a number of applications. The two appendixes to this chapter present more formal theories of household tastes that lead to the prediction of negatively sloped demand curves. Some of you will skip both of these appendixes; others will read one or both. Whatever you do, remember that although abstract in its current presentation, modern demand theory grew up to handle a number of real and interesting problems. We shall see how the theory can be applied to real issues both in the next chapter and later in this book.

[4] Figure 7-6 is a bar chart because we only allowed Mrs. Swartz to vary her consumption in discrete units of one glass at a time. Had we allowed her to vary her consumption of milk one drop at a time, we could have traced out a continuous curve similar to the one shown in Figure 7-7.

SUMMARY

1. The budget line shows all combinations of commodities that are available to the household, given its money income and the prices of the goods it purchases.
2. The budget line is shifted parallel to itself by either a change in money income, with all money prices being held constant, or a proportionate change in all money prices, with money income being held constant.
3. Changes in relative prices change the slope of the budget line.
4. While the budget line describes what the household *can* purchase, what it does purchase depends on its tastes.
5. A change in one money price has an income effect and a substitution effect. The substitution effect is the reaction of the household to the change in relative prices, with purchasing power of income being held constant. It can be measured by allowing price to change and then by altering money income until the original bundle can just be purchased. In this situation, a consistent household would never

reduce its purchases of the commodity whose relative price has fallen. The income effect is then measured by a parallel shift of the budget line to restore its initial money income. The income effect of a fall in one money price will lead to an increase in the purchases of all normal commodities.

6. The combined effect of the income and the substitution effects ensure that the quantity demanded of any normal good will increase when its money price falls, other things being equal. This means that normal goods have negatively sloped demand curves.

7. Three conceivable exceptions to the law of negatively sloped demand curves are a Giffen good, which is an inferior good on which a household spends much of its income; conspicuous consumption goods, which are goods consumed *because* they are expensive; and goods with perfectly inelastic demands. Examples of any of these possible exceptions are rarely, if ever, observed.

8. Consumers' surplus arises because a household can purchase every unit of a commodity at a price equal to the value it places on the last unit purchased. The negative slope of demand curves implies that the value that households place on all other units purchased exceeds the value of the last unit purchased and hence that all but the last unit purchased yield a consumers' surplus.

9. It is important to distinguish between total and marginal values because choices concerning a bit more and a bit less cannot be predicted from a knowledge of total values.

10. The total value that consumers place on some quantity of a commodity consumed is given by the area under the demand curve up to that quantity. The market value is given by an area below the market price up to that quantity. Consumers' surplus is the difference between the two.

TOPICS FOR REVIEW

Causes of shifts in the budget line
Real income and money income
Absolute (or money) prices and relative prices
Income effect and substitution effect
The law of demand and its possible exceptions
Consumers' surplus

DISCUSSION QUESTIONS

1. Is a household relatively better off if its money income is decreased by 10 percent or if the prices of all the goods it buys are increased by 10 percent? Does it matter in answering this question whether the household spends all its income?

2. Look at Figure 7-4 and see what happened to the quantity of clothing demanded when the price of food fell. Could that change in the quantity of clothing consumed have been in the opposite direction from the one you determine? What would that have implied about the change in the quantity of food? Can you use Figure 7-4 to discover a relationship between the price elasticity of demand for food and the change in the quantity of clothing bought when the price of food changes?

3. A middle-aged business executive reports that he now drinks a lot more French wine than he used to when he first started working for the company, even though imported wine is now much more ex-

pensive than it used to be. Do you think he has a positively sloped demand curve for French wine?

4. The measured elasticity of demand for salt is quite low. Why do you think this is so? Does this low elasticity imply that if one firm were to monopolize the sales of salt in the whole country, it could go on raising its revenues indefinitely by continually increasing the price of salt?

5. From 1977 to 1987 the cost of purchasing a representative bundle of consumers' goods rose by just over 100 percent, as measured by the Consumer Price Index. What else would you need to know to find out what had happened to the average American's real income?

6. When the prices of fuel oil and gasoline rose drastically in the early 1980s, many Americans reported that they felt worse off. Did this feeling have anything to do with the income or the substitution effect, or both? What do you think the income and the substitution effects of these prices were?

7. Compare and contrast the consequences of the income effect of a drastic fall in food prices with the consequences of a rise in money incomes when money prices are constant.

8. In recent years, the cost of housing has increased dramatically in Boston and Los Angeles but only slightly in Denver and Houston. What income and substitution effects would you expect from these changes?

9. Consider a household that, on average, uses 1,500 kilowatt hours (kwh) of electricity per month, at a price of $.05 per kwh. Suppose that the local utility company, the only supplier of electricity, adopts a new policy whereby its customers will be billed $100 per month plus $.05 for each kwh in excess of 2,000 that it uses in any month. How will this affect the household's demand for electricity? How will this affect the consumers' surplus that it derives from consumption of electricity?

10. Professors Jeff Biddle and Daniel Hamermesch of Michigan State University have recently estimated that a 25 percent increase in wages will cause the average individual to reduce the time that they spend sleeping by about 1 percent. Interpret this in terms of the "substitution effect." Would you also expect to find an income effect on the amount of time that a person spends sleeping?

Appendix A to Chapter 7

Indifference Theory

The history of demand theory has seen two major breakthroughs. The first was the marginal utility theory, which assumed that the utility that people received from consuming commodities could be measured objectively. By distinguishing total and marginal values, this theory explained why what seemed like a paradox—necessary goods that cannot be dispensed with often have low market values, while luxury goods that could easily be dispensed with often have high market values—was not a paradox at all. (See a further discussion of this so-called paradox of value in Chapter 8.)

The second breakthrough came with indifference theory, which showed that demand theory could dispense with the dubious assumption of measurable utility on which marginal utility theory was based. All that was needed in this new theory was to assume that households could say which of two consumption bundles they preferred without having to say by how much they preferred it.

Appendix A develops the modern indifference theory, and Appendix B deals with marginal utility theory.

An Indifference Curve

Start with an imaginary household that currently has available to it some specific bundle of goods. Say that bundle is 18 units of clothing and 10 units of food. Now offer the household an alternative bundle, say, 13 units of clothing and 15 units of food. This alternative combination of goods has 5 fewer units of clothing and 5 more units of food than the first one. Whether the household prefers this bundle depends on the relative valuation that it places on 5 more units of food and 5 fewer units of clothing. If it values the extra food more than the foregone clothing, it will prefer the new bundle to the original one. If it values the food less than the clothing, it will prefer the original bundle. If the household values the extra food the same as it values the foregone clothing, it is said to be *indifferent between* the two bundles.

Assume that after much trial and error we have identified several bundles among which the household is indifferent. In other words, each bundle gives the household equal satisfaction. They are shown in Table 7A-1.

There will, of course, be combinations of the two commodities other than those enumerated in Table 7A-1 that will give the same level of satisfaction to the household. All of these combinations are shown in Figure 7A-1 by the smooth curve that passes through the points plotted from the table. This curve is an indifference curve. In general, an **indifference curve** shows all combinations of commodities that yield the same satisfaction to the household; the household is indifferent between the combinations indicated by any two points on one indifference curve.

Any points above the curve show combinations of food and clothing that the household would prefer to combinations indicated by points on the curve. Consider, for example, the combination of 20 units of food and 18 units of clothing, represented by point *g* in Figure 7A-1. Although it may not be obvious that this bundle must be preferred to bundle *a* (which has more clothing but less food), it is obvious that it will be preferred to bundle *c* because there is both less clothing and less food represented at *c* than at *g*. Inspection of the graph shows that *any* point above

TABLE 7A-1	Alternative Bundles Giving a Household Equal Satisfaction	
Bundle	Clothing	Food
a	30	5
b	18	10
c	13	15
d	10	20
e	8	25
f	7	30

These bundles all lie on a single indifference curve. Since all of these bundles of food and clothing give equal satisfaction, the household is "indifferent" among them.

FIGURE 7A-1 An Indifference Curve

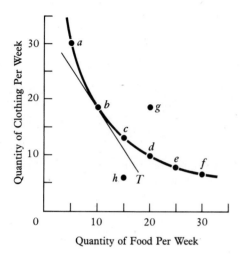

This indifference curve shows combinations of food and clothing that yield equal satisfaction and among which the household is indifferent. Points *a* to *f* are plotted from Table 7A-1. The smooth curve through them is an indifference curve; each combination on it gives equal satisfaction to the household. Point *g* above the line is a preferred combination to any point on the line; point *h* below the line is an inferior combination to any point on the line. The slope of the line *T* gives the marginal rate of substitution at point *b*. Moving down the curve from *b* to *f*, the slope flattens, showing that the more food and the less clothing the household has, the less willing it will be to sacrifice further clothing to get more food.

the curve will be obviously superior to *some* points on the curve in the sense that it will contain both more food and more clothing than those points on the curve. However, since all points on the curve are equal in the household's eyes, the point above the curve must be superior to *all* points on the curve. By a similar argument, points below and to the left of the curve represent bundles that are inferior to bundles represented by points on the curve.

The Hypothesis of Diminishing Marginal Rate of Substitution

How much clothing would the household be prepared to give up to get one more unit of food? The answer to this question measures what is called the marginal rate of substitution of clothing for food.

The **marginal rate of substitution (MRS)** is the amount of one commodity that a consumer would be prepared to give up in order to get one more unit of another commodity.

The first basic assumption of indifference theory is that the algebraic value of the *MRS* is always negative.

This means that to gain a positive change in its consumption of one commodity, the household is prepared to incur a negative change in its consumption of a second. The negative marginal rate of substitution is indicated in graphical representation by the downward slope of all indifference curves. (See, for example, the curve in Figure 7A-1.)

The second basic assumption of indifference theory is that the marginal rate of substitution between any two commodities depends on the amounts of the commodities currently being consumed by the household.

Consider a case in which the household has a lot of clothing and only a little food. Common sense suggests that the household might be willing to give up quite a bit of its plentiful clothing in order to get one unit more of scarce food. It suggests as well that the household with a little clothing and a lot of food would be willing to give up only a little of its scarce clothing in order to get one more unit of already plentiful food.

This example illustrates the hypothesis of diminishing marginal rate of substitution. The less of one commodity, *A*, and the more of a second commodity, *B*, the household has already, the smaller will be the amount of *A* that it will be willing to give up in order to get additional unit of *B*. The hypothesis says that the marginal rate of substitution changes systematically as the amounts of two commodities presently consumed vary. The graphical expression of this is that the slope of any indifference curve becomes flatter as the household moves downward and to the right along the curve. In Figure 7A-1 a movement downward to the right means that less clothing and more food is being consumed. The decreasing steepness of the curve means that the household is willing to sacrifice less and less clothing to get each additional unit of food. [10]

The hypothesis is illustrated in Table 7A-2, which is based on the example of food and clothing in Table

TABLE 7A-2	The Marginal Rate of Substitution Between Clothing and Food		
Movement	(1) Change in clothing	(2) Change in food	(3) Marginal rate of substitution (1) ÷ (2)
From *a* to *b*	− 12	5	− 2.4
From *b* to *c*	− 5	5	− 1.0
From *c* to *d*	− 3	5	− 0.6
From *d* to *e*	− 2	5	− 0.4
From *e* to *f*	− 1	5	− 0.2

The marginal rate of substitution of clothing for food declines as the quantity of food increases. This table is based on Table 7A-1. When the household moves from *a* to *b*, it gives up 12 units of clothing and gains 5 units of food; it remains at the same level of overall satisfaction. The household at point *a* was prepared to sacrifice 12 units of clothing for 5 units of food (i.e., 12/5 = 2.4 units of clothing per unit of food obtained). When the household moves from *b* to *c*, it sacrifices 5 units of clothing for 5 units of food (a rate of substitution of 1 unit of clothing for each unit of food).

7A-1. The last column of the table shows the rate at which the household is prepared to sacrifice units of clothing per unit of food obtained. At first the household will sacrifice 2.4 units of clothing to get 1 unit more of food, but as its consumption of clothing diminishes and that of food increases, the household becomes less and less willing to sacrifice further clothing for more food.[1]

The Indifference Map

So far we have constructed only a single indifference curve. However, starting at any other point in Figure 7A-1, such as *g*, there will be other combinations that will yield equal satisfaction to the household. If the points indicating all of these combinations are connected, they will form another indifference curve. This exercise can be repeated as many times as we

[1] Movements between widely separated points on the indifference curve have been examined. In terms of a small movement from any of the points on the curve, the rate at which the household will give up clothing to get food is shown by the slope of the tangent to the curve at that point. The slope of the line *T*, which is a tangent to the curve at point *b* in Figure 7A-1, may thus be thought of as the slope of the curve at that precise point. It tells us the rate at which the household will sacrifice clothing per unit of food obtained when it is currently consuming 18 units of clothing and 10 units of food (the coordinates of point *b*).

FIGURE 7A-2   An Indifference Map

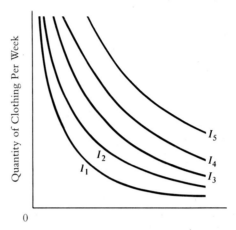

An indifference map consists of a set of indifference curves. All points on a particular curve indicate alternative combinations of food and clothing that give the household equal satisfaction. The further the curve is from the origin, the higher is the level of satisfaction it represents. For example, I_5 is a higher indifference curve than I_4, which means that all the points on I_5 yield a higher level of satisfaction than do the points on I_4.

wish, and as many indifference curves as we wish can be generated. The farther any indifference curve is from the origin, the higher will be the level of satisfaction given by any of the combinations of goods indicated by points on the curve.

A set of indifference curves is called an **indifference map,** an example of which is shown in Figure 7A-2. It specifies the household's tastes by showing its rate of substitution between the two commodities for every level of current consumption of these commodities. When economists say that a household's tastes are *given,* they do not mean that the household's current consumption pattern is given; rather, they mean that the household's entire indifference map is given.

The Equilibrium of the Household

Indifference maps describe the preferences of households. Budget lines describe the possibilities open to each household. To predict what households will

FIGURE 7A-3   The Equilibrium of a Household

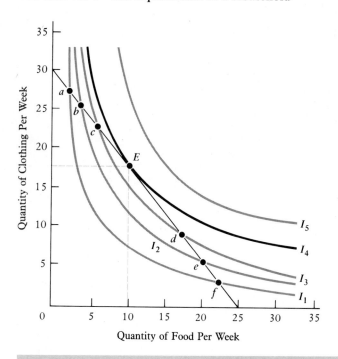

Equilibrium occurs at *E*, where an indifference curve is tangent to the budget line. The household has a money income of $750 per week and faces money prices of $25 per unit for clothing and $30 per unit for food. A combination of units of clothing and food indicated by point *a* is attainable, but by moving along the budget line, higher indifference curves can be reached. The same is true at *b* and at *c*. At *E*, however, where an indifference curve is tangent to the budget line, it is impossible to reach a higher curve by moving along the budget line. If the household did alter its consumption bundle by moving from *E* to *d*, for example, it would move to the lower indifference curve I_3 and thus to a lower level of satisfaction.

actually do, both sets of information must be put together. This is done in Figure 7A-3. The household's budget line is shown by the straight line, and the curves from the indifference map are also shown. Any point on the budget line is attainable, but which point will actually be chosen by the household?

Since the household wishes to maximize its satisfactions, it wishes to reach its highest attainable indifference curve. Inspection of Figure 7A-3 shows that if the household purchases any bundle on its budget line at a point cut by an indifference curve, a higher indifference curve can be reached. Only when the bundle purchased is such that the indifference curve is tangent to the budget line is it impossible for the household to alter its purchases and reach a higher curve.

The household's satisfaction is maximized at the point where an indifference curve is tangent to the budget line.

At such a tangency position the slope of the indifference curve (the household's marginal rate of substitution of the goods) is the same as the slope of the

budget line (the relative prices of the goods in the market).

The common sense found in this result is that if the household values goods differently than the market does, there is room for profitable exchange. The household can give up some of the good it values relatively less than the market does and take in return some of the good it values relatively more than the market does. When the household is prepared to swap goods at the same rate as they can be traded on the market, there is no further opportunity for it to raise its satisfaction by substituting one commodity for the other.

The household is presented with market prices that it cannot change. It adjusts to these prices by choosing a bundle of goods such that, at the margin, its own subjective evaluation of the goods conforms with the valuations given by market prices.

The Household's Reaction to a Change in Income

We have seen that a change in income leads to parallel shifts of the budget line—toward the origin when income falls and away from the origin when income rises. For each level of income there will be an equilibrium position at which an indifference curve is tangent to the relevant budget line. Each such equilibrium position means that the household is doing as well as it possibly can for that level of income. If we move the budget line through all possible levels of income, and if we join up all the points of equilibrium, we will trace out what is called an *income-consumption curve,* an example of which is shown in Figure 7A-4. This line shows how consumption bundles change as income changes, with relative prices being held constant.

The Household's Reaction to a Change in Price

We already know that a change in the relative price of the two goods changes the slope of the budget line. Given a price of clothing, for each possible price of food there is an equilibrium consumption position for the household. If we connect these positions, we will trace out a **price-consumption line,** as is shown in Figure 7A-5. Notice that as the relative price of food and clothing changes, the relative quantities of food and clothing purchased also change. In

FIGURE 7A-5   **The Price-Consumption Line**

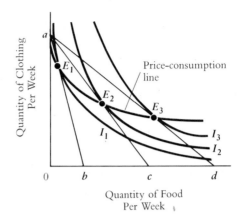

The price-consumption line shows how the household's purchases react to a change in one price with money income and other prices being held constant. Decreases in the price of food (with money income and the price of clothing being held constant) pivot the budget line from *ab* to *ac* to *ad*. The equilibrium position moves from E_1 to E_2 to E_3. By joining up all the points of equilibrium, a price–consumption line is traced out.

particular, as the price of food falls, the household buys more food.

Derivation of the Demand Curve

If food and clothing were the only two commodities purchased by households, we could derive a demand curve for food from the price-consumption line in Figure 7A-5. This line represents how the quantity of food demanded varies as the price of food changes, with the price of clothing remaining unchanged. This is what we did in Chapter 7 to explain the general idea. Now, however, we can be more precise. To use indifference theory in order to derive the type of demand curve introduced in Chapter 4, it is necessary to depart from the world of two commodities.

What happens to the household's demand for some commodity, say, gasoline, as the price of that commodity changes, *all other prices being held constant?* In part (i) of Figure 7A-6 a new type of indifference map is plotted in which gallons of gasoline per month are measured on the horizontal axis and the value of all other goods consumed per month is

FIGURE 7A-4   **The Income-Consumption Line**

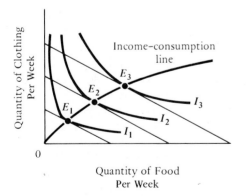

The income-consumption line shows how the household's purchases react to a change in money income with relative prices being held constant. Increases in money income shift the budget line out parallel to itself, moving the equilibrium from E_1 to E_2 to E_3. By joining up all the points of equilibrium, an income-consumption line is traced out.

FIGURE 7A-6   **Derivation of a Household's Demand Curve**

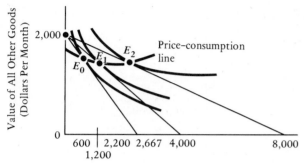

(i)

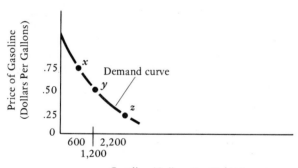

(ii)

Every point on the price-consumption line corresponds to both a price of the commodity and a quantity demanded; this is the information required for a demand curve. In part (i) the household has a money income of $2,000 and alternatively faces prices of $.75, $.50, and $.25 per gallon of gas, choosing positions E_0, E_1, and E_2 at each price. The information for gallons demanded at each price is then plotted in part (ii) to yield the household's demand curve. The three points x, y, and z in part (ii) correspond to the three equilibrium positions E_0, E_1, and E_2 in part (i).

plotted on the vertical axis. We have in effect used *everything but gasoline* as the second commodity. The indifference curves give the rate at which the household is prepared to substitute gasoline for money (which allows it to buy all other goods) at each level of consumption of gasoline and of all other goods.

To illustrate the derivation of demand curves, we

use the numerical example shown in Figure 7A-6. The household is assumed to have an after-tax money income of $2,000 per month. This money income is plotted on the vertical axis, showing that if the household consumes no gasoline, it can consume $2,000 worth of other goods each month. When gasoline costs $.75 per gallon, the household could buy a maximum of 2,667 gallons per month. This gives rise to the innermost budget line. Given its tastes, the household reaches equilibrium at point E_0, consuming 600 gallons of gasoline and $1,550 worth of other commodities.[2] Next, let the price of gasoline fall to $.50 per gallon. Now the maximum possible consumption of gasoline is 4,000 gallons per month, giving rise to the middle budget line in the figure. The household's equilibrium is, as always, at the point where the new budget line is tangent to an indifference curve. At this point, E_1, the household is consuming 1,200 gallons of gasoline per month and spending $1,400 on all other goods. Finally, let the price fall to $.25 per gallon. The household can now buy a maximum of 8,000 gallons per month, giving rise to the outermost of the three budget lines. The household reaches equilibrium by consuming 2,200 gallons of gasoline per month and by spending $1,450 on other commodities.

If we let the price vary over all possible amounts, we will trace out a complete price-consumption line, as shown in the figure. The points derived in the preceding paragraph are merely three points in this line.

We have now derived all that we need to plot the household's demand curve for gasoline, since we know how much the household will purchase at each price. To draw the curve we merely replot the data from part (i) for Figure 7A-6 onto a demand graph, as shown in part (ii) of Figure 7A-6.

Like part (i), part (ii) has quantity of gas on the horizontal axis. By placing the two graphs one under the other, we can directly transcribe the quantity determined on the upper graph to the lower one. We first do this for the 600 gallons consumed on the innermost budget line. We now note that the price of gasoline that gives rise to that budget line is $.75. Plotting 600 gallons against $.75 in part (ii) produces

---

[2] Our household must do a lot of traveling! If we chose more realistic figures for its consumption of gasoline, however, the various equilibrium positions would all be so close to the horizontal axis that the graph would be difficult to read.

FIGURE 7A-7   The Income Effect and the Substitution Effect in Indifference Theory

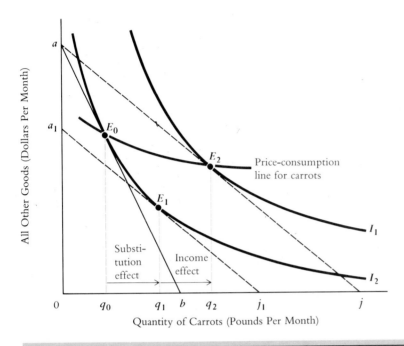

The substitution effect is defined by sliding the budget line around a fixed indifference curve; the income effect is defined by a parallel shift of the budget line. The original budget line is at ab, and a fall in the price of carrots takes it to aj. The original equilibrium is at E_0 with q_0 of carrots being consumed, and the final equilibrium is at E_2 with q_2 of carrots being consumed. To remove the income effect, imagine reducing the household's money income until it is just able to attain its original indifference curve. We do this by shifting the line aj to a parallel line nearer the origin that just touches the indifference curve that passes through E_0. The intermediate point E_1 divides the quantity change into a substitution effect q_0q_1 and an income effect q_1q_2. It can also be obtained by sliding the original budget line ab around the indifference curve until its slope reflects the new relative prices.

the point x, derived from point E_0 in part (i). This is one point on the household's demand curve. Next, we consider the middle budget line, which occurs when the price of gasoline is \$.50. We take the figure of 1,200 gallons from point E_1 in part (i) and transfer it to part (ii). We then plot this quantity against the price of \$.50 to get the point y on the demand curve. Doing the same thing for point E_2 yields the point z in part (ii): price \$.25, quantity 2,200 gallons.

Repeating the operation for all prices yields the demand curve in part (ii). Note that the two parts of Figure 7A-6 describe the same behavior. Both parts measure the quantity of gasoline on the horizontal axes; The only difference is that in part (i) the price of gasoline determines the slope of the budget line, while in part (ii) the price of gasoline is plotted explicitly on the vertical axis.

The Slope of the Demand Curve

The price-consumption line in part (i) of Figure 7A-6 indicates that as price decreases, quantity of

gasoline demanded increases, but one can draw the indifference curves in such a way that the response to a given decrease in price is for less to be consumed rather than more. This possibility gives rise to the positively sloped demand curve, referred to as a Giffen good, that was briefly discussed in Chapter 7. Let us see how the conditions leading to this case are analyzed using indifference curves.

Income and Substitution Effects

The key, as we saw in the text, is to distinguish between the income effect and the substitution effect of a change in price. In Chapter 7 we eliminated the income effect by changing money income *until the original bundle of goods could just be consumed*. This is the approach used in the famous Slutsky equation, which is a major tool in empirical studies of demand.

In indifference theory, however, the income effect is removed by changing money income until the original level of satisfaction—the original indifference curve—can just be achieved. This results in a slightly different measure of the income effect, but the principle involved in separating the total change into an income effect and a substitution effect is exactly the same as in the text.[3]

The separation of the two effects according to indifference theory is shown in Figure 7A-7. The figure shows in greater detail part of the price-consumption line first drawn in Figure 7A-6. Points E_0 and E_2 are on the price-consumption line for carrots. We can think of the separation occurring in the fol-

lowing way. After the price of the good has fallen, we reduce money income *until the original indifference curve can just be obtained.* This leads the household to move from point E_0 to an imaginary point E_1, and this response is defined as the substitution effect. Then, to measure the income effect, we restore money income. The household moves from the point E_1 to the final point E_2, and this response is defined as the income effect.

Now compare this indifference theory definition with the Slutsky definition used in Chapter 7. In the text we measure the substitution effect of any price change by altering money income until the original bundle of goods can just be purchased. In this appendix we measure the substitution effect by altering

---

[3] The approach used in the text (see page 128) defines constant real income as constant purchasing power. The introduction of indifference curves allows a slightly more sophisticated concept of constant real income—constant satisfaction as captured by the original indifference curve. However, the two are very similar in practice and, indeed, in most applications the approach taken in the chapter (the Slutsky equation) is used.

FIGURE 7A-8   Income and Substitution Effects for Inferior Goods

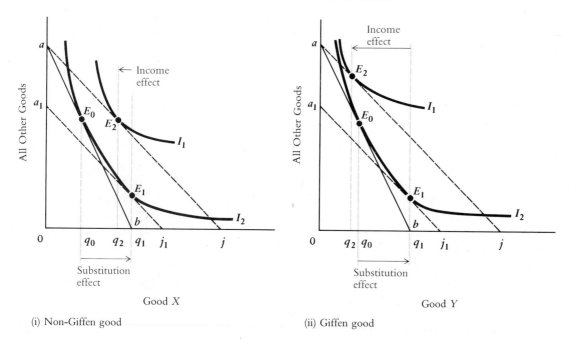

(i) Non-Giffen good

(ii) Giffen good

Inferior goods have negative income effects. A large enough negative income effect can outweigh the substitution effect and lead to a decrease in consumption in response to a fall in price. In each part of the figure the household is in equilibrium at E_0, consuming a quantity q_0 of the good in question. The price then decreases, and the budget line shifts to aj, with a new equilibrium at E_2 and quantity consumed being q_2. In each case the substitution effect is to increase consumption from q_0 to q_1. In (i) there is a negative income effect of q_1q_2. Because this is less than the substitution effect, the latter dominates, so good X has a normal, downward-sloping demand curve. In (ii) the negative income effect q_1q_2 is larger than the substitution effect, and quantity consumed actually decreases. Good Y is thus a Giffen good.

money income until the original level of satisfaction—the original indifference curve—can just be attained.

The advantage of the Slutsky definition is that it is operational; the change in money income required to allow the original bundle to be purchased at the new prices can be simply calculated. The disadvantage is that this change does not leave unchanged the household's real income, defined as its level of satisfaction. The advantage of the indifference curve approach is that the change does leave the household's level of satisfaction unchanged and hence defines the substitution effect as the response to changes in relative prices with real satisfaction unchanged. The disadvantage is that the measurement is not easily made operational; we have to know each household's tastes to be able to make the required change in money income.

In Figure 7A-7 the income and substitution effects are in the same direction, both tending to increase quantity demanded when price falls. Is this necessarily the case? The answer is no. While it follows from the convex shape of indifference curves that the substitution effect is always in the same direction, income effects can be in either direction. The direction depends on the distinction we drew earlier between normal and inferior goods.

The Slope of the Demand Curve for a Normal Good

For a normal good, an increase in real income due to a decrease in the price of the commodity leads to its increased consumption, reinforcing the substitution effect. Because quantity demanded increases, the demand curve slopes downward.

The Slope of the Demand Curve for an Inferior Good

Figure 7A-8 shows indifference curves for inferior goods. The income effect is negative in each part of the diagram. This follows from the nature of an inferior good: As income rises, less of the good is consumed. In each case the substitution effect serves to increase the quantity demanded as price decreases and is offset to some degree by the negative income effect. The final result depends on the relative strengths of the two effects. In part (i) the negative income effect only partially offsets the substitution effect, and thus quantity demanded increases as a result of the price decrease, though not as much as for a normal good. This is the typical pattern for inferior goods, and it too leads to downward-sloping demand curves, often relatively inelastic ones.

In part (ii) the negative income effect actually outweighs the substitution effect and thus leads to an upward-sloping demand curve. This is the Giffen case. For this to happen the good must be inferior, but that is not enough; the change in price must have a negative income effect *strong enough* to offset the substitution effect. A combination of circumstances that makes this possible is not often expected, and therefore an upward-sloping market demand curve is at most an infrequent exception to the rule that demand curves slope downward.

SUMMARY

1. While the budget line describes what the household *can* purchase, indifference curves describe the household's tastes and, therefore, refer to what it *would like* to purchase. A single indifference curve joins combinations of commodities that give the household equal satisfaction and among which it is therefore indifferent. An indifference map is a set of indifference curves.

2. The basic hypothesis about tastes is that of a diminishing marginal rate of substitution. This hypothesis states that the less of one good and the more of another the household has, the less willing it will be to give up some of the first good to get a further unit of the second. This means indifference curves are downward sloping and convex to the origin.

3. The household achieves an equilibrium that maximizes its satisfactions, given its budget line at the point at which an indifference curve is tangent to its budget line.

4. The income-consumption line shows how quantity consumed changes as income changes with relative prices being held constant.

5. The price-consumption line shows how quantity consumed changes as relative prices change. When prices change, the household will consume more of the commodity whose relative price falls.

6. The price-consumption line relating the purchases of one particular commodity to all other commodities contains the same information as an ordinary demand curve. The horizontal axis measures quantity, and the slope of the budget line measures price. Transferring this price-quantity information to a diagram whose axes represent price and quantity leads to a conventional demand curve.

7. The effect of a change in price of one commodity, all other prices and money income being held constant, changes not only relative prices but also real incomes. A price decrease can affect consumption both through the substitution effect and through the income effect.

8. Demand curves for normal goods slope downward because both income and substitution effects work in the same direction, a decrease in price leading to increased consumption.

9. For an inferior good, a decrease in price leads to more consumption via the substitution effect and less consumption via the income effect. In the extreme case of a Giffen good, the negative income effect more than offsets the substitution effect, and the consumption of the commodity decreases as a result of a price decrease. This is a theoretical possibility that has seldom, if ever, been observed in fact.

Appendix B to Chapter 7

Marginal Utility Theory

In this second appendix to Chapter 7 we study the marginal utility theory of household demand.

Marginal and Total Utility

We confine our attention for the moment to the consumption of a single commodity. The satisfaction that a consumer receives from consuming that commodity is called its **utility. Total utility** refers to the total satisfaction resulting from the consumption of that commodity by a consumer. **Marginal utility** refers to the change in satisfaction resulting from consuming a little more or a little less of that commodity. For example, the total utility of consuming 14 eggs per week is the total satisfaction that those 14 eggs provide. The marginal utility of the fourteenth egg consumed is the additional satisfaction provided by the consumption of that egg. Thus marginal utility is the difference in total utility gained by consuming 13 eggs and by consuming 14.[1]

The Hypothesis of Diminishing Marginal Utility

The basic hypothesis of utility theory, sometimes called the *law of diminishing marginal utility,* is as follows:

The utility that any household derives from successive units of a particular commodity diminishes as total consumption of the commodity increases while the consumption of all other commodities remains constant.

Consider water. Some minimum quantity is essential to sustain life, and a person would, if neces-

sary, give up all of his or her income to obtain that quantity of water. Thus the marginal utility of that much water is extremely high. More than this bare minimum will be drunk, but the marginal utility of successive glasses of water drunk over a period of time will decline steadily.

Evidence for this hypothesis will be considered later, but you can convince yourself that it is at least reasonable by asking a few questions. How much money would induce you to cut your consumption of water by one glass per week? The answer is very little. How much would induce you to cut it by a second glass? By a third glass? To only one glass consumed per week? The answer to the last question is quite a bit. The fewer glasses you are consuming already, the higher the marginal utility of one more or one less glass of water.

Water has many uses other than for drinking. A fairly high marginal utility will be attached to some minimum quantity for bathing, but much more than this minimum will be used only for more frequent baths or for having a water level in the bathtub higher than is absolutely necessary. The last weekly gallon of water that is used for bathing is likely to have a low marginal utility. Again, some small quantity of water is necessary for brushing teeth, but many people leave the water running while they brush. The water going down the drain between wetting and rinsing the brush surely has a low utility. When all the extravagant uses of water by the modern consumer are considered, it is certain that the marginal utility of the last, say, 30 percent of all units consumed is very low, even though the total utility of *all* the units consumed is extremely high.

Utility Schedules and Graphs

The schedule in Table 7B-1 is hypothetical. It is constructed in order to illustrate the assumptions that have been made about utility, using movie attendance as an example. The table shows that total utility rises as the number of movies attended each month rises. Everything else being equal, the more movies the

---

[1] Here and elsewhere in elementary economics it is common to use interchangeably two concepts that mathematicians distinguish. Technically, *incremental* utility is measured over a discrete interval, such as from 9 to 10, whereas *marginal* utility is a rate of change measured over an infinitesimal interval. However, common usage applies the word *marginal* when the last unit is involved, even if a one-unit change is not infinitesimal. **[11]**

TABLE 7B-1	Total and Marginal Utility Schedules	
Number of movies attended per month	Total utility	Marginal utility
0	0	
1	30	30
2	50	20
3	65	15
4	75	10
5	83	8
6	89	6
7	93	4
8	96	3
9	98	2
10	99	1

Total utility rises, but marginal utility declines as this household's consumption increases. The marginal utility of 20, shown as the second entry in the last column, arises because total utility increases from 30 to 50—a difference of 20—with attendance at the second movie. To indicate that the marginal utility is associated with the change from one rate of movie attendance to another, the figures in the third column are recorded between the rows of the figures in the second column. When plotting marginal utility on a graph, it is plotted at the midpoint of the interval over which it is computed.

household attends each month, the more satisfaction it gets—at least over the range shown in the table. However, the marginal utility of each additional movie per month is less than that of the previous one even though each movie adds something to the household's satisfaction. The schedule in Table 7B-1 shows that marginal utility declines as quantity consumed rises. [12] The same data are shown graphically in the two parts of Figure 7B-1.

Maximizing Utility

A basic assumption of the economic theory of household behavior is that households try to make themselves as well off as they possibly can in the circumstances in which they find themselves. In other words, the members of a household seek to maximize their total utility.

The Equilibrium of a Household

How can a household adjust its expenditure so as to maximize its total utility? Should it go to the point

at which the marginal utility of each commodity is the same, that is, the point at which it would value equally the last unit of each commodity consumed? This would make sense only if each commodity had the same price per unit. However, if a household must spend $3 to buy an additional unit of one commodity and only $1 to buy one unit of another, the first commodity would represent a poor use of its money if the marginal utility of each were equal. The household would be spending $3 to get satisfaction from what it could have acquired for only $1.

The household that is maximizing its utility will allocate its expenditures among commodities so that the utility of the last dollar spent on each is equal.

Imagine that the household is in a position in which the utility of the last dollar spent on carrots yields three times the utility of the last dollar spent on brussels sprouts. In this case total utility can be increased by switching a dollar of expenditure from brussels sprouts to carrots and by gaining the difference between the utilities of a dollar spent on each.

The utility-maximizing household will continue to switch its expenditure from brussels sprouts to carrots as long as a dollar spent on carrots yields more utility than a dollar spent on brussels sprouts. This switching, however, reduces the quantity of brussels sprouts consumed and, given the law of diminishing marginal utility, raises the marginal utility of brussels sprouts. At the same time, the switching increases the quantity of carrots consumed and thereby lowers the marginal utility of carrots.

Eventually the marginal utilities will have changed enough so that the utility of a dollar spent on carrots is just equal to the utility of a dollar spent on brussels sprouts. At this point there is nothing to be gained by a further switch of expenditure from brussels sprouts to carrots. If the household persists in reallocating its expenditure, it will further reduce the marginal utility of carrots (by consuming more of them) and raise the marginal utility of brussels sprouts (by consuming less of them). Total utility will no longer be at its maximum because the utility of a dollar spent on brussels sprouts will exceed the utility of a dollar spent on carrots.

Let us now consider the conditions for maximizing utility in a more general way. Denote the marginal utility of the last unit of commodity X by MU_x

FIGURE 7B-1   Total and Marginal Utility Curves

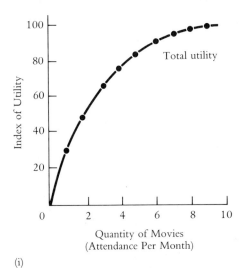

(i)

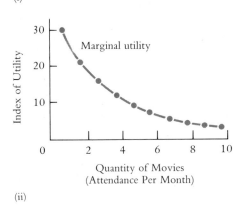

(ii)

The total utility curve rises, but the marginal utility curve falls as the quantity consumed rises. The dots correspond to the points listed in Table 7B-1; smooth curves have been drawn through them.

and its price by p_x. Let MU_y and p_y refer, respectively, to the marginal utility of a second commodity Y and its price. The marginal utility per dollar of X will be MU_x/p_x. For example, if the last unit adds 30 units to utility and costs $2, its marginal utility per dollar is $30/2 = 15$.

The condition required for a household to maximize its utility is, for any pair of commodities,

$$\frac{MU_x}{p_x} = \frac{MU_y}{p_y} \qquad [1]$$

This says that the household will allocate its expenditure so that the utility gained from the last dollar spent on each commodity is equal.

This is the fundamental equation of the utility theory of demand. Each household demands each good (for example, movie attendance) up to the point at which the marginal utility per dollar spent on it is the same as the marginal utility of a dollar spent on another good (for example, water). When this condition is met, the household cannot shift a dollar of expenditure from one commodity to another and increase its utility.

An Alternative Interpretation of Household Equilibrium

If we rearrange the terms in Equation 1, we can gain additional insight into household behavior.

$$\frac{MU_x}{MU_y} = \frac{p_x}{p_y} \qquad [2]$$

The right side of this equation states the *relative* price of the two goods. It is determined by the market and is outside the control of the individual household; the household reacts to these market prices but is powerless to change them. The left side states the relative ability of the goods to add to the household's satisfaction and is within the control of the household. In determining the quantities of different goods it buys, the household determines also their marginal utilities. (If you have difficulty seeing why, look again at part (ii) of Figure 7B-1.)

If the two sides of Equation 2 are not equal, the household can increase its total satisfaction by rearranging its purchases. Assume, for example, that the price of a unit of X is twice the price of a unit of Y ($p_x/p_y = 2$), while the marginal utility of a unit of X is three times that of a unit of Y ($MU_x/MU_y = 3$). Under these conditions it is worthwhile for the household to buy more of X and less of Y. For example, if the household reduces its purchases of Y by two units, enough purchasing power is freed to buy a unit of X. Since one extra unit of X bought yields 1.5 times the satisfaction of two units of Y foregone, the switch is worth making. What about a further switch of X for Y? As the household buys more of X and less of Y, the marginal utility of X falls and the marginal utility of Y rises. The household will go on rearranging its purchases—reducing Y consumption and increasing X consumption—until, in this example, the marginal utility of X is only twice that of Y. At this point, total satisfaction cannot be further increased by rearranging purchases between the two commodities.

Now consider what the household is doing. It is faced with a set of prices that it cannot change. The household responds to these prices and maximizes its satisfaction by adjusting the things it can change—the quantities of the various goods it purchases—until Equation 2 is satisfied for all pairs of commodities.

This sort of equation—one side representing the choices that the outside world gives decision makers and the other side representing the effect of those choices on their welfare—recurs in economics. It reflects the equilibrium position reached when decision makers have made the best adjustment that they can to the external forces that limit their choices.

When it enters the market, every household faces the same set of market prices. When all households are fully adjusted to these prices, each will have identical ratios of its marginal utilities for each pair of goods. Of course, a rich household may consume more of each commodity than a poor household. However, the rich and the poor households (and every other household) will adjust their *relative* purchases of each commodity so that the relative marginal utilities are the same for all. Thus, if the price of X is twice the price of Y, each household will purchase X and Y to the point at which the household's marginal utility of X is twice its marginal utility of Y. Households with different tastes will, however, have different marginal utility schedules and so may consume differing relative quantities of commodities, even though the ratios of their marginal utilities are the same for all households.

Derivation of the Household's Demand Curve

To derive the household's demand curve for a commodity, it is only necessary to ask what happens when there is a change in the price of that commodity. As an example, let us do this for candy. Take

Equation 2 and let X stand for candy and Y for all other commodities. What will happen if, with all other prices remaining constant, the price of candy rises? The household that started from a position of equilibrium will now find itself in a position in which[2]

$$\frac{MU \text{ of candy}}{MU \text{ of } Y} < \frac{\text{price of candy}}{\text{price of } Y} \qquad [3]$$

To restore equilibrium, it must buy less candy, thereby raising its marginal utility until once again Equation 2 (where X is candy) is satisfied.[3] The common sense found in this is that the marginal utility of candy *per dollar* falls when its price rises. The household began with the utility of the last dollar spent on candy equal to the utility of the last dollar spent on all other goods, but the rise in candy prices changes this. The household buys less candy (and more of other goods) until the marginal utility of candy rises enough to make the utility of a dollar spent on candy the same as it was originally.

This analysis leads to the basic prediction of demand theory.

A rise in the price of a commodity (with income and the prices of all other commodities being held constant) will lead to a decrease in the quantity of the commodity demanded by each household.

If this is what each household does, it is also what all households taken together do. Thus, the theory predicts a downward-sloping market demand curve.

[2] The inequality sign ($<$) points to the smaller of two magnitudes. When the price of candy rises, the right side of Equation 2 increases. Until the household adjusts its consumption patterns, the left side will stay the same. Thus Equation 2 is replaced by Inequality 3.

[3] For most consumers candy absorbs only a small proportion of their total expenditures. If, in response to a change in its price, expenditure on candy changes by $5 per month, this represents a large change in candy consumption but only a negligible change in the consumption of other commodities. Hence, in the text we proceed by assuming that the marginal utilities of other commodities do not change when the price and the consumption of candy change.

SUMMARY

1. Marginal utility theory distinguishes between the total utility gained from the consumption of all units of some commodity and the marginal utility resulting from the consumption of one more unit of the commodity.
2. The basic assumption made in utility theory is tht the utility the household derives from the consumption of successive units of a commodity per period of time diminishes as the consumption of that commodity increases.
3. Households are assumed to maximize utility and thus reach equilibrium when the utility derived from the last dollar spent on each commodity is equal. Another way of putting this is that the marginal utilities derived from the last unit of each commodity consumed will be proportional to their prices.
4. Demand curves slope downward because when the price of one commodity, X, falls, each household restores equilibrium by increasing its purchases of X sufficiently to restore the ratio of x's marginal utility to its now lower price (MU_X/p_x) to the same level as it has achieved for all other commodities.

Chapter 8

Using Demand Theory

In Chapter 7 we covered some basic material concerning the theory of demand. In this chapter we go further and develop some important applications of this theory. We start by showing the link between the household demand curves that we discussed in Chapter 7 and the market demand curves that we discussed in earlier chapters.

Market and Individual Demand Curves

Market demand curves tell how much is demanded by all purchasers. For example, in Figure 4-1 (page 57) the market demand for carrots is 90,000 tons when the price is $40 per ton. This 90,000 tons is the sum of the quantities demanded by millions of different households. It may be made up of 4 pounds for the Carsons, 7 pounds for the Chows, 1.5 pounds for the Smiths, and so on. The demand curve in Figure 4-1 also tells us that when the price rises to $60, aggregate quantity demanded falls to 77,500 tons per month. This quantity too can be traced back to individual households. The Carsons might buy only 3 pounds, the Chows, 6.5 pounds, and the Smiths, none at all. Notice that we have now described two points, not only on the market demand curve but also on the demand curves of each of these households.

The market demand curve is the horizontal sum of the demand curves of individual households.

It is the horizontal sum because we wish to add quantities demanded at a given price, and quantities are measured in the horizontal direction on a conventional demand curve. This is illustrated in Figure 8-1.

Some Applications of Consumers' Surplus

In subsequent chapters we will find many uses for the concept of consumers' surplus. In this chapter we show how it can be used to resolve some very old problems.

The Paradox of Value

Early economists, struggling with the problem of what determines the relative prices of commodities, encountered what they

FIGURE 8-1   The Relationship Between Household and Market Demand Curves

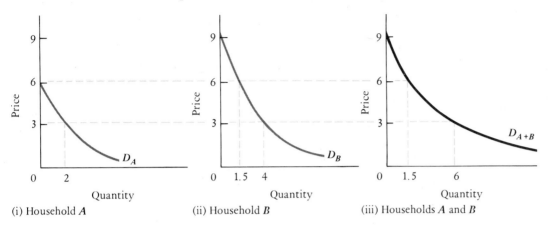

(i) Household *A*   (ii) Household *B*   (iii) Households *A* and *B*

An aggregate demand curve is the horizontal sum of the individual demand curves of all households in the market. The figure illustrates aggregation over only two households. At a price of $3, household *A* purchases 2 units and household *B* purchases 4 units; thus together they purchase 6 units. No matter how many households are involved, the process is the same.

called the *paradox of value:* Many necessary commodities, such as water, have prices that are low compared with the prices of luxury commodities, such as diamonds. Water is necessary to our existence, whereas diamonds are used mostly for frivolous purposes and could disappear from the face of the earth tomorrow without causing any real hardship. Does it not seem odd, then, these economists asked, that water is so cheap and diamonds are so expensive? It took a long time to resolve this apparent paradox, so it is not surprising that even today analogous confusions cloud many policy discussions.

The key to solving this "paradox" lies in the important distinction between what one would pay to avoid having one's consumption of a commodity reduced to zero and what one would pay to gain the use of one more unit of that commodity. This point involves a distinction between total and marginal values that is frequently encountered in many branches of economics.

We have seen already that the area under the demand curve shows what the household would pay for the commodity if it had to purchase it unit by unit. It is thus a measure of the total value that the household places on *all* of the units it consumes. In Figure 7-7 on page 138, the *total* value of q_0 units is the entire shaded area (light and dark) under the demand curve.

What about the *marginal value* that the household places on one more, or one less, than the q_0 units it is currently consuming? This is given by the commodity's market price, which is p_0 in this case. Faced with a market price of p_0, the household buys all the units that it values at p_0 or greater but does not purchase any units that it values at less than p_0. It follows that the household places on the last unit consumed of any commodity a value that is measured by the commodity's price.[1]

Now look at the *total* market value of the commodity. This is the amount that everyone spends to purchase it. It is price multiplied by quantity. In Figure 7-7 this is the dark shaded rectangle with sides p_0 and q_0.

We have seen that the total value that consumers place on a given amount of a commodity, as measured by the relevant area under the demand curve, is different from the total market value of a commodity, as given by the commodity's price multi-

---

[1] In terms of indifference theory (Appendix A to Chapter 7), the price measures the rate at which the household is prepared to substitute the good in question for money—that is, the slope, at the equilibrium point, of the indifference curve drawn with the quantity of the good on one axis and consumption of all other goods, measured in money units, on the other axis. In terms of utility theory (Appendix B to Chapter 7), the price measures the marginal utility of the last unit that the household purchases.

plied by the quantity consumed. Being different, the two values do not have to be related to each other. Figure 8-2 illustrates a case in which a good with a total high value has a low market value, and vice versa.

The resolution of the paradox of value is that a good that is very plentiful, such as water, will have a low price and will thus be consumed to the point where all households place a low value on the last unit consumed, whether or not they place a high value on their total consumption of the commodity.

By contrast, a commodity that is relatively scarce will have a high market price, and consumption will therefore stop at a point where consumers place a high value on the last unit consumed, regardless of the value that they place on their total consumption of the good.

We have now reached an important conclusion:

Because the market price of a commodity depends on demand and supply, there is nothing paradoxical in there being a commodity on

---

FIGURE 8-2   Total Value Versus Market Value

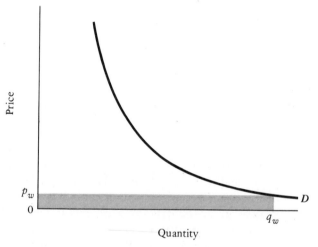

(i) Water

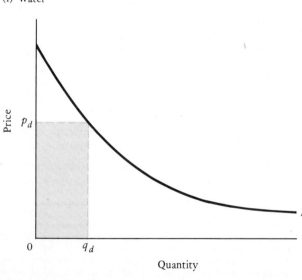

The market value of the amount of some commodity bears no necessary relationship to the total value that consumers place on that amount. The diagram presents hypothetical demand curves for water and diamonds that are meant to be stylized versions of the real curves. The total value that households place on water, as shown by the area under the demand curve, is great—indeed, we do not even show the curve for very small quantities because people would pay all they had rather than be deprived completely of water. The total valuation that households place on diamonds is shown by the area under the demand curve for diamonds. This is clearly less than the total value placed on water.

The low supply of diamonds makes diamonds scarce and keeps diamonds high in price, as shown by p_d in the figure. Thus, the total market value of diamonds sold, indicated by the dark shaded area of p_dq_d, is high.

The large supply of water makes water plentiful and makes water low in price, as shown by p_w in the figure. Thus, the total market value of water consumed, indicated by the dark shaded area of p_wq_w, is low.

which consumers place a high total value but that sells for a low price, and hence has only a low amount spent on it.

Necessities, Luxuries, and Elasticity

In ordinary discussions people often distinguish between necessities and luxuries, necessities being commodities that are difficult to do without and luxuries being commodities that could be fairly easily dispensed with. The distinction is somewhat arbitrary; for example, are eggs a necessity or a luxury? Nonetheless, some sense can be made of the distinction by understanding it in order to compare the *total* values that households place on their consumption of different commodities. Earlier in this chapter we learned to measure these total values by the areas under demand curves. Using this terminology, we would say that a necessity has a very large area under its demand curve; a luxury has a smaller area under its demand curve.

A frequent error occurs when people try to use knowledge of total values to predict demand elasticities. It is sometimes argued that, since luxuries can be given up, they have highly elastic demands; when their prices rise, households can stop purchasing them. It is likewise argued that necessities have highly inelastic demands because, when prices rise, households have no choice but to continue to buy them.

However, elasticity of demand depends on how consumers value commodities at the margin, not on how much they value the total consumption of the commodity. The relevant question for the determination of elasticity is, "How much do households value a bit more of some commodity?," not "How much do they value *all* of the commodity that they are now consuming?"

Demand theory leads to the prediction that when the price of a commodity rises, each household will reduce its purchases of that commodity until it values the last unit consumed of the commodity at the price that it must pay for that unit. Will the reduction in quantity required to raise the valuation be a little or a lot? This depends on the shape of the demand curve in the relevant range. If the demand curve is flat, a large change in quantity is required, and demand will be elastic. If the curve is steep, a small change will suffice, and demand will be inelastic. Figure 8-3 pre-

FIGURE 8-3   The Relationship of Elasticity of Demand to Total Value

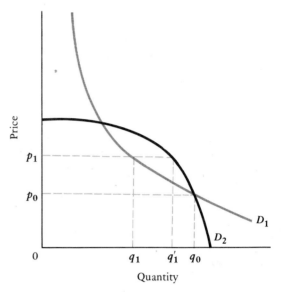

Elasticity of demand is determined by marginal valuation in the relevant range, not total value. Consider two alternative demand curves for a commodity, D_1 and D_2. Suppose price is p_0. Given either demand curve, the household consumes the quantity q_0, where the last unit consumed is valued at p_0. When the price rises to p_1, households cut their consumption.

If the black line D_2 is the demand curve, consumption only falls to q_1' and the demand for the product is quite inelastic. If, however, the grey line D_1 is the demand curve, consumption falls to q_1 and the demand for the product is less inelastic.

Although the shape of the demand curve in the relevant range is important, its shape outside of this range is irrelevant for determining elasticity. However, total value depends on the whole area under the curve. Depending on the shape of the curve up to q_0, either curve can show more or less total value than the other. Thus, total value has no influence on market behavior in response to a change in price from p_0 to p_1.

sents two possible responses to a doubling in price. It leads to this important conclusion:

The size of the response of quantity demanded to a change in price depends on the value that households place on having a bit more or a bit less of the commodity and has no necessary relationship to the value that they place on their total consumption of the quantity in question.

Box 8-1 provides an example from outside the field of economics of the importance of distinguishing between the total value that people get from some activity and the value that they would place on doing a bit more or a bit less of it.

Free, Scarce, and Freely Provided Goods

A **free good** is one for which the quantity supplied exceeds the quantity demanded at a price of zero. Such goods therefore will not command positive prices in a market economy. A household can become better off by increasing its consumption of free goods as long as it places a positive value on the extra units consumed. It follows that free goods will be consumed up to the point at which the value that households place on another unit consumed is zero. At some times in some places, air, water, salt, sand, and wild fruit have been free goods. Note that a good may be free at one time or place but not at another.

A **scarce good** is one for which the quantity demanded exceeds the quantity supplied at a price of zero. If all such goods had zero prices, the total amount that people would want to consume would greatly exceed the amount that could be produced. Such goods therefore will command positive prices in a market economy. Most goods are scarce goods.

Many people have strong views about the prices that are charged for certain commodities. These views are often an emotional reaction to the total values of the goods rather than to their marginal values. Here is an example: "Because water is such a complete necessity of life to rich and to poor, it is wrong to make people pay for water. Instead, the government should provide free water for everyone."

When deciding between a zero price and a modest price for water, the relevant question for the consumer is, "Are the marginal uses of water so important that we are willing to use scarce resources to provide the necessary quantities?" The question is not, "Is water so necessary that we want everyone to be provided with some of it?" The distinction is important because the two questions will have different answers.

The evidence that we have about the consumption of water at various prices suggests that the demand curve for water is shaped like the curve shown in part (i) of Figure 8-2. If so, the difference in consumption that results from providing water free or charging a modest price for it will be large. The additional water consumed, however, is costly to provide, and its provision requires scarce resources that could have been used to produce other commodities. If the value that households place on the commodities foregone is higher than the value that they place on the extra water consumed, households are worse off as a result of receiving water free. A charge for water would release resources from water production to produce commodities that households value more highly at the margin. Of course, some minimum quantity of water could be provided free to every household, but the effects of this would be quite different from the effects of making all water free.

It follows that neither the gain to consumers of encouraging a little more consumption of some commodity nor the loss from inducing a little less can be inferred from a knowledge of the total value placed on all of the consumption of that commodity.

Similar considerations apply to food, medical services, and a host of other commodities that are necessities of life but that also have numerous low-value uses that will be encouraged if a scarce commodity is provided at a zero price.

Household Behavior Under Uncertainty[2]

In the previous chapter we studied how households choose between alternatives that are *certain*. As we have seen earlier in this chapter, the theory of demand that results from this approach is very powerful in explaining many real-world events that we observe. However, many, if not all, of the choices that households make involve *uncertainty*. Of course, for many problems, the role of uncertainty is incidental and the standard analysis assuming certainty is perfectly adequate. However, there are some situations, such as whether to buy lottery tickets or insurance, in which uncertainty is central to the issue.

---

[2] The remainder of this chapter can be skipped without loss of continuity.

BOX 8-1

What Do Attitude Surveys Measure?

Consider a type of survey that is popular, both in the daily newspapers and in sociology and political science. These surveys take the form of asking such questions as these:

"Do you like the Republicans more than the Democrats?"

"In deciding to live in area *A* rather than area *B*, what factors influenced your choice? List the following in order of importance: neighbors, schools, closeness to swimming area, price and quality of housing available, play areas for children, general amenities."

"In choosing a university, what factors were important to you? List the following in order of importance: environment, academic excellence, residential facilities, parents' opinion, school opinion, athletic facilities, tuition."

You should be able to add other examples to this list. The three survey questions cited, and most of those you might add, attempt to measure the *total* value that households place on some activity rather than the *marginal* value that they would place on a little more or a little less of that activity.

The total value being measured includes the consumers' surplus. There is, of course, nothing illegal or immoral about this. People are free to measure anything that interests them, and in some cases knowledge of total valuation may be useful. But, in most cases, actual behavior is determined by marginal valuation, and anyone who attempts to predict such behavior from a knowledge of total valuation, even if it is a correct knowledge of total valuation, will be hopelessly in error.

Where the behavior being predicted involves an either-or decision, such as a vote for the Republicans or the Democrats in a two-party contest, total value attached to each choice will indeed be what matters because the voters are choosing one or the other. Where the decision is marginal, between a little more and a little less, total value, however, is not what will determine behavior.

A recent newspaper poll that was taken in a large U.S. city showed that two-thirds of the city's voters rated its excellent school system as an important asset. Yet in a subsequent election the voters turned down a school bond issue. Is this irrational behavior, as the newspaper editorials charged? Does it show a biased sample in the poll? It demonstrates neither. The poll measured the people's assessment of the total value derived from the school system (high), whereas the school bond issue vote was a result of the people's assessment of the marginal value of a little more money being spent on the school system (low). There is nothing contradictory in anyone's feeling that the total value of the city's fine school system is high but that the city (or the taxpayer) has other needs that have a higher value at the margin than further money being spent on schools.

A recent survey showed—paradoxically, it claimed—that many Canadians are getting more pleasure from their families just at the time that they are electing to have smaller families. There is nothing paradoxical about a shift in tastes that increases the marginal value of one or two children and reduces the marginal value of each additional child, nor is there anything paradoxical about a parent's getting a high total value from the total time being spent with the children but assigning a low marginal value to the prospect of spending additional time with them each evening.

In the remainder of this chapter we examine how the theory of demand deals with uncertainty.[3]

What are the sources of uncertainty? How does uncertainty influence household decisions? How do markets cope with uncertainty? Is the market for insurance different from the market for carrots?

Sources of Uncertainty

Uncertainty arises whenever decisions are made with imperfect information about the alternatives. It is present in virtually all aspects of economic life. Any action, some of whose effects will be felt in the future, will of necessity have some uncertainty attached to it. This is true for such apparently "safe" decisions as holding on to one's money in anticipation of a summer holiday next year; since you are uncertain about what prices will be next year, the purchasing power of the money you save is also uncertain. It is obviously true of speculative purchases of gold, real estate, or stocks. It is also true when you buy a consumer durable; for example, since you cannot be sure about the reliability and durability of a new automobile, you are uncertain about the value of the services that the car will deliver. Box 8-2 takes up the interesting problems that this poses for the used-car market.

Uncertainty obviously complicates the household's decisions. For example, a household may be uncertain about the quality of the products from among which it is choosing. The household may think that the more expensive Brand X will last longer and require less maintenance expenditure than the cheaper Brand Y, but how much longer will Brand X last, and how much less maintenance is involved? Another household may be deciding between buying a condominium in the ritzy part of town or buying a cheaper one "on the wrong side of the tracks." Buying the expensive one may reduce the chances of being broken into, as may installing bars on the ground-floor windows, but by how much?

Consider a household choosing between Bundle A (10 units of food and 5 units of clothing) and Bundle B (6 units of food and 12 units of clothing). The household may know with certainty the con-

tents of each bundle, but it may be unsure of what the weather will be or whether relatives might drop by for the weekend. Hence, it does not know for certain what the relative merits of each bundle of food and clothing will turn out to be. In this case, it knows with certainty what is in each bundle, but it is uncertain about the circumstances that will occur while the goods are being consumed. These circumstances are often called either the "state of the world" or the "state of nature." If different commodities or bundles of commodities have different values in different states of the world, then uncertainty about the state of the world introduces an important element of uncertainty into the problem of household choice.[4]

This chapter is about households, so we shall concentrate on household behavior under uncertainty. However, firms also make choices under uncertainty; production takes time and involves spending money now to produce goods that will be sold in the uncertain future. Indeed, all decision makers operate under conditions of significant uncertainty much of the time.

Many of the principles discussed in this chapter were first developed by analyzing games of chance such as roulette or coin tossing. The same principles arise in consumption and production decisions involving uncertainty, but it is often easier to appreciate them in the context of the kind of games that were first studied. The discussion in this chapter gives only an intuitive overview of the principles that are involved.[5]

The Characterization of Risky Events

Much of what is involved in making risky choices can be captured in two measures: the *expected value* of the choice and the *degree of risk* attached to making the choice.

Expected value.   Let us say that you are playing a game in which a fair coin is tossed once every minute. (A fair coin is one for which there is an equal

---

[3] For the purposes of this chapter we follow convention and use the terms "risk" and "uncertainty" synonymously, although more advanced treatments sometimes distinguish between the two.

[4] The "state of the union" might matter also, since particular clothes will have different merits depending upon whether one is in Texas or Alaska, but it is unlikely to be a source of uncertainty unless one is in a "state of confusion"!

[5] You should be warned at the outset that many of the ideas are quite subtle. To handle them rigorously requires careful definitions and some complex analysis. Indeed, game theory has become an exciting but very technical area of economic research.

BOX 8-2

Used-Car Prices: The Problem of "Lemons"

It is common for people to regard the large loss of value of a new car in the first year of its life as a sign that consumers are overly style conscious and will always pay a big premium for the latest in anything. Professor George Akerlof of the University of California suggests a different explanation based upon the proposition that the flow of services expected from a 1-year-old car that is *purchased on the used-car market* will be lower than those expected from an average 1-year-old car on the road. Consider his theory.

Any particular model year of automobiles will include a certain proportion of "lemons"—cars that have one or more serious defects. Purchasers of new cars of a certain year and model take a chance on their car's turning out to be a "lemon." Those who are unlucky and get a "lemon" are more likely to resell their car than those who are lucky and get a quality car. Hence, in the used-car market there will be a disproportionately large number of "lemons" for sale. (Also, not all cars are driven in the same manner; those that are driven for long distances or

under bad conditions are much more likely to be traded in or sold as used cars than those that are driven on good roads and for moderate distances.)

Thus buyers of used cars are right to be on the lookout for low-quality cars, while salespeople are quick to invent reasons for the high quality of the cars they are selling ("It was owned by a little old lady who drove it only on Sundays"). Because it is difficult to identify a "lemon" or a badly used car before buying it, the purchaser is prepared to buy a used car only at a price that is low enough to offset the increased probability that it is of poor quality.

This is a rational consumer response to uncertainty and may explain why 1-year-old cars typically sell for a discount that is much larger than can be explained by the physical depreciation that occurs in 1 year in the *average* car of that model. The large discount reflects the lower services that the purchaser can expect from a used car because of the higher probability that it will be a "lemon."

chance that either heads or tails will turn up; that is, a coin with a probability of 0.5 that it will turn up heads and a probability of 0.5 that it will turn up tails.) The game is defined as follows: You win $1 if the result is heads, and you lose $1 if the result is tails.

The expected value of the outcome of any game can be expressed by adding up the various possible outcomes, each multiplied by its probability of occurrence. The amount that you would expect to win in this coin toss game, the *expected value of the game*, is zero. The probability of winning $1 is one-half, and the probability of losing $1 is one-half. Thus, the expected value of any toss of the coin is

$$\$1(0.5) - \$1(0.5) = \$0.5 - \$0.5 = \$0.$$

If you play the game for 10 minutes, you may be lucky and win $10. There is an equal chance that you will be unlucky and lose $10. It is much more likely,

however, that you will get some heads and some tails and end up winning or losing a sum much smaller than $10. The single most likely outcome is that you will exactly break even; that is, you will receive the expected value of the game. The two next most likely results are that you will win $2 (six heads and four tails) or that you will lose $2 (six tails and four heads). Outcomes with larger gains and larger losses become less and less likely until you get to the two least likely results: winning $10 and losing $10.

Now consider playing the game repeatedly day after day, for several months. It is still possible that you will end up winning $10 or losing $10. After all, if you break even after many days of play, you still may encounter 10 heads in a row in your last 10 plays. As you go on playing, however, it is more likely that your gain or loss will be close to the expected outcome of zero and less likely that your gain or loss will be high.

More generally, the expected value of any choice is the average outcome.

Degree of risk.   In the preceding game you stood to win $1 per toss or to lose $1 per toss. If you contract to play for 10 minutes, your maximum possible loss is $10. Now suppose that you play the same game but that you win $100 on heads and lose $100 on tails. This still seems to be a fair game since it has an expected outcome of zero, but because the stakes are higher you now risk more if you play it for any given amount of time. There is the same chance that you will encounter an unlucky run of 10 tails, but now you stand to lose $1,000. Clearly there is more risk attached to the second game than to the first.

Risk refers to the dispersion of the possible results. In the first game the possible results from 10 minutes of play are dispersed over a range running from +$10 to −$10; in the second game the possible results are dispersed over a range running from +$1,000 to −$1,000.

The risk attached to any choice refers to the dispersion of the possible outcomes resulting from making that choice.[6]

Fair and Unfair Games

The coin toss games that we have considered so far are fair games in the sense that, if you play them, you have just as much chance of winning as of losing. A lottery in which all of the ticket revenues are paid out is also a fair game. Say, for example, that 100 lottery tickets are sold for $1 each and that a draw then determines which of the ticket holders wins $100. This is a fair game, because each ticket holder has 1 chance in 100 of winning $99 (the person's own $1 back and the $99 in winnings) and 99 chances in 100 of losing $1. The expected value of buying the lottery ticket is $99(1/100) − $1(99/100) = $.99 − $.99 = $0. A **fair game** is one for which the expected value of the outcome is zero.

If you play a fair game repeatedly, you may end up winning or losing, depending on the "luck of the toss," but the *average gain or loss per play*

will tend to approach zero as the number of times that the game is repeated increases.

Now consider playing the coin toss game under the rule that if you toss heads you win $2 and if you toss tails you lose $1. The expected value of the outcome of each toss is $2(0.5) − $1(0.5) = $1 − $0.50 = $.50. If you play the game only once, you will either win $2 or lose $1. If you play it repeatedly, however, your average gain will tend toward $.50 per toss. This is not a fair game; instead, it is biased in your favor (and hence biased *against* whomever you are playing with).

Finally, consider lotteries. In most cases, the organizers—be they a firm, a charity, or the government—take a proportion of the ticket revenue as their profit and distribute the rest as prize money. Such lotteries are *not* fair games. They are biased against the participants, because the expected value of participating in the game is negative.

To illustrate this point, take our previous example of a lottery in which 100 tickets are sold at $1 each. Now, however, assume that the organizers take $50 as their profit and pay the other $50 to the winning ticket. The expected value of a lottery ticket is now $49(1/100) − $1(99/100) = $.49 − $.99 = −$.50. The negative value shows that this is not a fair game; instead, it is biased against anyone who plays it. (Another way of seeing this is to ask yourself what would happen if you bought all the tickets. You would spend $100 and win $50, thus incurring a loss of $50. This is a loss of $.50 per ticket, which, as we have seen already, is the expected value of each ticket.)

Preferences Toward Risk

How do people behave when they are faced with risky choices? Some people dislike risk and would pay to avoid or to eliminate it. Others like risk and, everything else being equal, would choose a more risky alternative over a less risky one. Still others are indifferent about it, so the relative risk of two alternatives will not influence their choice.

Risk neutral individuals are indifferent about risk. They care only about the average return that a given activity is expected to yield, and they will engage in the activity only if the expected return is positive. Thus, they are indifferent about playing a fair game, would willingly play one that is biased in their favor, and would not play one that is biased against them.

---

[6] For many purposes, the dispersion can be satisfactorily measured by the range of possible outcomes; in other situations it can be better measured by what is called the *variance* of the possible results.

Risk averse individuals do not like risk. They will engage in a risky activity only if the expected return is high enough to compensate them for the risk that they will have to take. (The required increase in the expected return is often called the *risk premium*.) Thus risk averse individuals will only play games that are sufficiently biased in their favor to overcome their aversion to risk; they will be unwilling to play fair games, let alone ones that are biased against them.

Risk lovers like risk. They will engage in some risky activities simply in order to get some of the pleasure that the risk entails. Thus risk takers will not only gladly play fair games and games biased in their favor but also willingly play some games that are biased against them, the extent of the love of risk being measured by the degree of bias that a person is willing to accept. (No one would knowingly buy a ticket for a lottery in which the prize were zero, but some extreme risk lovers might enter a lottery in which only 10 percent of the ticket money would be paid out as prize money.)

How do these differences influence the reaction to the fair coin toss game that we studied? Recall that each play offers an equal chance of winning or losing $1. Risk neutral people are indifferent about playing the game. Thus they must value the chance of winning $1 the same as they value the chance of losing $1; that is, their valuation of a $1 change in their wealth is the same for small increases or decreases to their wealth. Risk averse people would choose not to play the game. Thus they value the chance of winning $1 less than they value the chance of losing $1; that is, their valuation of a $1 change in their wealth is larger for decreases than for increases. Risk lovers would choose to play the game. Thus they must value the chance of winning $1 more than they value the chance of losing $1; that is, their valuation of a $1 change in their wealth is larger for increases than for decreases.[7]

---

[7] In terms of the concepts introduced in Appendix B to Chapter 7, risk neutrality arises when there is constant marginal utility of income. Similarly, risk aversion arises when there is diminishing marginal utility of income, and risk loving arises when there is increasing marginal utility of income. The basis for this classification comes from the pathfinding 1940s analysis by two Princeton University professors, John von Neumann and Oscar Morgenstern, who developed the *expected utility hypothesis*. This hypothesis holds that consumer evaluation of a risky prospect can be described by calculating the expected value of the utility that would be obtained in each of the possibilities.

The Market for Insurance

What role do preferences toward risk play in the market for insurance? We shall first study household demand for insurance, and then we shall look briefly at the behavior of insurance firms.

The Demand for Insurance

Suppose there is 1 chance in 100 that some unfavorable outcome will happen in which you will lose some asset (possibly your house) that you value at $100,000, and supposed there are 99 chances in 100 that nothing will happen at all to this asset. Thus, the most likely outcome is that nothing will happen, but there is a small chance that you will incur a very big loss.

Suppose that someone now offers you an insurance policy that costs $1,000. If nothing else happens, you simply lose the $1,000. However, if the disaster occurs and you suffer the loss of $100,000, you will be fully compensated.

If you buy the policy, you give up $1,000 for certain, but you are no longer at risk. If you do not buy the policy, you are taking a risk. The possible outcomes from having no insurance are 1 chance in 100 of losing $100,000 and 99 chances in 100 of losing nothing. This gives an expected value of $-\$100,000(1/100) + \$0(99/100) = -\$1,000$. The insurance policy represents a "fair game" because the expected values of both courses of action are the same—a loss of $1,000.

Although the expected values of the two choices are the same, not buying the insurance is a much riskier choice than buying it. If you do not buy the insurance and are lucky, you save the $1,000 insurance premium; however, if you are unlucky, you lose $100,000. If you buy the insurance, you lose $1,000 for certain.

Someone who is risk averse would buy the policy, whereas someone who is a risk lover would not. Since both courses have the same expected value, a risk neutral person would be indifferent to either buying the insurance policy or not buying it—if there were no other considerations.

This discussion assumes that the insurance policy offers a fair bet, but insurance companies must themselves make money, so they do not offer their policyholders mathematically fair policies. In the preceding case, in which the risk was 1 chance in 100 of losing $100,000, the policy would actually cost more

BOX 8-3

The Economics of Gambling

Gambling and insurance both represent market activities that involve uncertainty. They differ from each other in that when one buys insurance one pays a certain sum to avoid the chance of incurring a larger loss, whereas when one gambles one pays a certain sum to obtain the chance of incurring a larger gain. That is, buying insurance reduces the risk that an individual faces, whereas gambling increases the risk that an individual faces. Buying insurance and gambling thus appear to be inconsistent; the former requires risk averse behavior, whereas the latter requires risk taking behavior. Yet we observe both insurance and gambling in our society. How can we explain this? To answer this question, we must first look at the demand to gamble.

The Demand to Gamble

Consider any situation in which one has an option to pay money to purchase the chance of a gain. This could be a lottery ticket, a bet on a football game, an investment of money by a firm in a new technological development that might produce profits in the future, or a purchase by an individual of a share in a firm on the stock market.

Consider first a mathematically fair possibility.

You are offered the chance to buy a ticket in a lottery consisting of 100 tickets, each being sold for $1, with a single prize of $100 to the winning ticket. As we saw earlier, this is a fair bet; if you are risk averse you would not buy a ticket, and if you are risk neutral you would be indifferent about it. Only a risk lover would be anxious to participate in the game.

Most gambling games, however, are not mathematically fair. Instead, they are biased against the player. The organizer of the game takes out some of the money wagered as profit (if the game is legal, the government may also take some in the form of a tax); only what is left is distributed as prize money. This is true of lotteries, pari-mutuel betting on horse races, casino gambling, and every commercial gambling operation.

Gambling on any event in which the organizers take a profit or on which the government levies a tax has a negative expected value. We would not expect to see risk averse or risk neutral individuals take such gambles.

Reconciling Insurance and Gambling

Why is it that we observe both gambling, which appeals only to risk lovers, and insurance, which

than $1,000. Say it costs $1,200. Now the expected return from holding the policy remains at $1,000, but the cost of the policy is $1,200; thus, the expected value of buying the policy is negative, and a risk neutral person would not buy it. If the excess of the cost of insurance over the expected return is not too large, some risk averse individuals would still buy the insurance.

In a market in which insurance companies must charge a premium that is large enough to provide them with an expectation of profit, neither a risk lover nor a risk neutral person would buy insurance; only some risk averse individuals would.

Most people choose to buy insurance for a large number of activities. This can be explained by assuming that most people are sufficiently risk averse. Although the cost of the policy exceeds the expected value of the loss without insurance, most feel that this is compensated for by eliminating the risk that has to be borne if they are uninsured. Box 8-3 explores the problems that arise in reconciling this explanation with the observation that many people engage in the risky activity of gambling.

The Supply of Insurance

When households buy insurance, they are essentially "trading" in risk with those who sell them the in-

appeals only to risk averters? One possibility is that although most people are risk averse, some people are risk takers. This would explain why the latter gamble on games that have negative expected values. It would, however, be inconsistent with their buying of insurance policies with negative expected values, so this explanation does not help us understand why *the same person* would both buy insurance and gamble.

A second possibility is that people are not risk lovers in terms of their evaluations of the expected monetary gains and losses involved but they do get some pleasure simply from "playing the game," or at least from "playing some *particular* games." Betting on "the home team" or on "the sentimental favorite" is common, even though the odds offered may not adequately reflect the team's realistic chances; this is often described as "betting with one's heart rather than with one's head"; you probably know some people who usually behave in a risk averse fashion but who bet "irrationally" on their favorite baseball team. Others may bet on horse races because they think that they are good enough handicappers to overcome the odds or because they get real pleasure from watching a horse race in which they have a financial stake. People who get pleasure from *particular* gambles might still

buy insurance, as long as their risk aversion was a stronger force than the satisfaction attached to the particular risks of being uninsured.

A third possibility is that, although people are not risk lovers in general, they get some utility from the dreams that they have attached to even a remote possibility of winning a lottery or a similar bet. In this case, they know that the average participant will lose, but they are sustained by the mere thought that, against all the odds, they might win a sum large enough to transform an otherwise dull, or even hopeless, life. This may go a long way toward explaining why people buy tickets for lotteries in which only a few very large prizes are to be won. It is a less satisfactory explanation of why people bet on horse races, in which winnings, although more frequent, are not enough to change their whole life-style.

A further possibility is of course that people are just badly informed. They may not know the expected value of the gambles that they take. It is probably true that many people do not realize the magnitude of the negative expected value of many of their gambles.

surance. We now complete the story of insurance by explaining why firms are willing to supply insurance to households who demand it.

An insurance firm takes your money and agrees to pay out a certain sum should the unlucky event strike you. It expects to make profits on the difference between the premiums it charges and the amount of claims it expects to pay to its customers. These profits, however, are not guaranteed. Conceivably, the insurance firm itself could have a run of bad luck in which many of the people it insures suffer losses at the same time. Indeed, conceivably, it could even incur losses sufficiently large to cause it to go bankrupt.

How can insurance companies afford to absorb

their customers' risks? The main explanation of insurance company behavior relies on their ability to engage in *risk pooling* and *risk sharing* in order to reduce the total amount of risk that has to be borne by them and their customers.

Risk pooling. To see what is involved in the pooling of risks, consider two individuals who receive an income that varies according to the toss of a coin. (Once again the coin toss is simply an example used to illustrate the principles that apply for any source of uncertainty.) Each individual tosses a coin each month. If heads comes up John receives $500; if tails comes up he receives nothing. The same applies to June: she receives $500 if she tosses heads and nothing

TABLE 8-1	Incomes When Risks Are and Are Not Pooled		
	Risks are not pooled		**Risks are pooled**
	John	June	Both get
T-T	0	0	0
T-H	0	$500	$250
H-T	$500	0	$250
H-H	$500	$500	$500

Pooling of independent risks reduces risk. Each person gets an income of $500 if he or she tosses a head and nothing if he or she tosses a tail. There are four possible results. In two of them one head an one tail occurs. In the other two, either two tails or two heads occurs. When each accepts his or her own risks, each expects an income of $500 half the time and zero the other half. When the incomes are pooled and then split, only one combination in four gives them zero income, while half of the time they will get $250. The deviations of their monthly incomes from the expected value of $250 is decreased by pooling, but the expected value itself is unchanged.

if she tosses tails. The expected value of each person's income is $500(0.5) = $250 per month. Over a long period of time, each person's monthly income will indeed average close to $250, but John and June may not like the possibility of going from $500 to nothing on the toss of a coin each month.

Suppose they decide to pool their incomes each month and each take one-half of the resulting amount. The expected value of each person's income is still $250 per month, but now the variation from month to month will be diminished.[8] The result is shown in Table 8-1. When they were operating on their own, each person's income deviated from its expected value by $250 each month; in good months it was $250 above the expected value and in bad months it was $250 below the expected value. When the two incomes are pooled, the expected value is reached whenever one person is lucky and the other is unlucky, which will be about one-half the time. Only in one-quarter of the outcomes will income be $250 above, and only in one-quarter of the outcomes

will it be $250 below. These results each require that both be lucky or unlucky at the same time.

The key to this result is that the events must be independent. The result of John's coin toss was independent of the result of June's. In the case in which their incomes were not pooled, the extreme result occurs to one of them when one of them is unlucky. The probability of the extreme result is less likely when they pool their incomes, because it requires that both be unlucky at the same time.

If 3 people pool their incomes, the extreme cases of each receiving $500 or each receiving zero occur only when all 3 are lucky or unlucky at the same time. These cases each occur with a probability of 1 chance in 8. (There is 1 chance in 2 that any one will toss heads, but a (1/2)(1/2)(1/2) = 1/8 that all 3 will toss heads at once.) If 4 people pool their incomes, the extreme cases of each receiving either $500 or $0 income will occur only with a probability of 1/64. By the time 10 people are involved, the extreme cases will occur only 1 time in 2 raised to the tenth power, which is a very small fraction indeed.

The larger is the number of independent events that are pooled, the less and less likely it is that extreme results will occur.

The same reasoning applies to all kinds of events that may be regarded as chance events, as long as they are independent of each other. Suppose that there is 1 chance in 1,000 that any given house in the country will burn down in any given year, and suppose that an insurance company collects a premium from the owners of these houses and offers them full compensation if their house burns down.

If the company is so small that it can only insure 10 houses, it may be unlucky in having 10 owners who just happen to be careless at the same time and have their houses burn down accidentally. This is unlikely but not impossible. A bad bit of luck that destroys all 10 insured houses would ruin the company, since it could not meet all of its insured risks at the same time. Suppose, however, that the company is large enough to insure 100,000 houses. Now it is pooling its risk over a large number, and the chances are high that something very close to 1 house in 1,000 insured will burn down. With 100,000 houses insured, the most likely outcome is that 100 houses will burn down. The company might be unlucky and have 110 burn down or lucky and have

---

[8] This can be seen by evaluating the four possible outcomes: there is a 0.25 chance of each individual's share of the pool being $500, a 0.5 chance of it being $250, and a 0.25 chance of it being $0. This sums to $500(0.25) + $250(0.5) + $0(0.25) = $125 + $125 + $0 = $250.

only 90 burn down, but to have even 150 burn down is very unlikely indeed, as long as the chance of a fire burning down one house is independent of the chance of a fire burning down another. (Insurance companies are careful to spread the houses that they insure over a wide geographic area!)

This requirement of independence is why insurance policies normally exclude wars and other situations in which some common cause acts on all the insured units. A war may lead to a vast number of houses being destroyed. Since the cause of the loss of one house is not independent of the cause of the loss of another, the insurance company has a high probability that it may suffer losses on a large proportion of its insured properties, and this could ruin the insurance company.

The basic feature in insurance is the pooling of independent events, which is what makes extreme outcomes unlikely. A common cause that has a similar effect on all insured items defeats the principle on which insurance is based.

The typical insurance company, therefore, deals with repeated events such as fires or death in which the probability that any individual insured item will become a claimant is independent of the probability that any other insured item will become a claimant.

Risk sharing.   Let us say that a famous concert pianist wants to insure her hands against any event that would end her career as a performer. The amount insured would be colossal, amounting to all the income that she would have earned over her life if her hands had not been harmed. The company can calculate the chances that any randomly chosen person in the population will suffer such a loss. It is not insuring an entire population, however; only one person is involved. If there is no catastrophe, the company will gain its premium; if there is a catastrophe, the company will suffer a large loss.

The trick in being able to insure the pianist, or any unique person or thing posing the risk of a large loss, lies in what is called *risk sharing*. One company writes a policy for the pianist and then breaks the policy up into a large number of subpolicies. Each subpolicy carries a fraction of the pay out and earns a fraction of the premium. The company then sells each subpolicy to a different firm.

Assume, for the purposes of illustration, that 100 firms each write one such primary policy, for example, one on a pianist's hands, one on a football player's legs, one on a rare painting being flown to Japan for an exhibit, and so on. Each then breaks its primary policy up into 100 subpolicies and sells each subpolicy to the other 99 firms. Each firm ends up holding risks that are independent of each other, no one of which is large enough to threaten the firm should it give rise to a claim. This is what Lloyds of London does. It is a syndication of a large number of insurance underwriters. Each one is prepared to insure almost anything as long as a claim would not bankrupt all of the firms when the risk is spread over a large number of them.[9]

As with risk pooling, the possibilities for risk sharing require that the events being insured against are independent of each other. An insurance company that takes one-tenth of the risk for each of 10 events that are closely related and hence likely to occur together if they occur at all is no better off than the insurance company that simply insures against one of the events.

Moral Hazard and Adverse Selection

Insurance markets work quite well at reducing the risk that individuals must contend with *and* at reducing the overall risk in the economy. However, there are problems that reduce the ability of insurance companies to exploit the principles of risk pooling and risk sharing to insure households against some risks. Two of the most interesting are *moral hazard* and *adverse selection*.

Having insurance often affects people's behavior. How often have you heard someone say—or have you said yourself—"Don't worry about it; it's insured"? When having insurance leads people to behave less carefully, thus raising the insurance company's expected costs, the situation is described as displaying **moral hazard.** For example, car owners might be much more willing to park their cars in an unsavory part of town where the risk of it being stolen is high and might be less diligent about locking it

---

[9] This is also what bookies do when they cannot control the odds themselves. When they take bets at odds set by others, one large bet could ruin them by requiring a pay out that is greater than their current assets. To avoid such risks, they "lay off" part of the bet with other bookies. In this way no single bookie ends up holding bets that are big enough to threaten his solvency if he suffers an unlucky series of pay outs.

regularly, if their cars are insured against theft. If this effect is strong enough, insurance companies will not find it profitable to offer insurance against the particular event, and hence car owners will have to bear the risk themselves. Often the problem is sufficient to make it impossible for the car owners to obtain complete insurance; the insurance company offers only *partial coverage* by requiring that the car owner pay the first, say, $250 dollars in the event of a claim.

Another problem is that not everyone buys insurance, so the full benefits of risk pooling are not available to the insurance company. In particular, for any policy that is offered, *those most likely to make a claim are also most likely to purchase the policy.* This is referred to as **adverse selection,** since from the insurer's viewpoint the wrong people have chosen to buy the policy.

If insurance companies can distinguish among different potential customers, they can "customize" policies to suit each group's characteristics. For example, life insurance companies usually require that applicants have a medical examination, and they charge higher premiums to those who are thus demonstrated to be higher risks.

When insurance companies cannot distinguish among different potential customers and thus have to make any policy available to all potential customers, they will have to charge a high enough premium to allow for the increased risks created by adverse selection. This may mean that potential customers who know themselves to be low-risk individuals will choose not to buy the policy. If these people could convince the insurance company that they are low risks, there is a price at which the insurance company would be able to sell them insurance and still make a profit, but, of course, everybody would like to convince the insurance company that they are low-risk individuals and hence benefit from the lower premiums.

Thus, adverse selection can create a situation in which some individuals cannot purchase insurance. One way insurance companies deal with this problem is to identify characteristics—often age or sex or occupation—that are related to risk and then to offer different policies to individuals with different characteristics; however, in many states legislation has been introduced that makes such discrimination illegal.

This completes our introductory study of the importance of risk. We shall have occasion to return to these problems and to build on the present discussion at several points later in this book.

SUMMARY

1. Market demand curves reflect the aggregate of the consumption behavior of the millions of households in the economy.
2. It is important to distinguish between total and marginal values because choices concerning a bit more and a bit less cannot be predicted from a knowledge of total values. The paradox of value involves a confusion between total value and market value.
3. Elasticity of demand is related to the marginal value that households place on having a bit more or a bit less of some commodity; it bears no necessary relationship to the total value that households place on all of the units consumed of that commodity.
4. Households will consume any good that has a zero price up to the point where the marginal value that they place on further consumption is zero.
5. Risky events can be characterized in terms of their expected value and the degree of risk that they involve. A risky event that has a zero expected value is called a fair game.
6. Risk neutral individuals are indifferent toward risk and hence are indifferent about participating in a fair game. Risk averse people avoid risk and would choose not to participate in a fair game. Risk lovers like risk and would participate in a fair game.
7. Risk averse people would choose to buy insurance as long as the premium does not exceed the expected value of the risky alternative by too much. Insurance companies can absorb risk from such people

and then reduce the risk that they themselves bear by exploiting the principles of risk pooling and risk sharing. These principles operate when the risky events being insured are independent of one another.

8. Insurance markets may fail to operate effectively if there are serious problems of moral hazard or adverse selection. Moral hazard arises when having insurance causes people to behave in a manner that increases the chance of bad outcomes occurring, thus reducing the expected profits of the insurance company. Adverse selection arises when potential customers have different risk characteristics and insurance companies cannot easily distinguish the various groups.

TOPICS FOR REVIEW

Market demand and individual household demand curves
The paradox of value
Total value versus marginal value
Necessities and luxuries
Free goods and scarce goods
Expected value and degree of risk
Fair and unfair games
Risk neutral, risk averse, and risk loving behavior
The market for insurance
Risk pooling and risk sharing
Moral hazard and adverse selection

DISCUSSION QUESTIONS

1. Why is market demand the horizontal sum of individual demand curves? Is the vertical sum different? What would a vertical sum of individual demand curves show? Can you imagine any use of vertical summation of demand curves?
2. Which of the choices implied below involves a consideration of marginal values, and which involves a consideration of total values?
   a. Congress debates whether 17-year-olds should be given the vote.
   b. A diet calls for precisely 1,200 calories per day.
   c. My doctor says I must give up smoking and drinking or else accept an increased chance of getting a heart attack.
   d. When Armand Hammer decided to buy the Rembrandt painting *Juno* for $3.25 million, he called it the "crown jewel of my collection."
   e. I enjoyed my golf game today, but I was so tired that I decided to stop at the seventeenth hole.
3. Explain the transactions described in the following quotations in terms of the value of the commodity. Interpret "worthless" and "priceless" as used here.
   a. "Bob Koppang has made a business of selling jars of shredded U.S. currency. The money is worthless, and yet he's sold 53,000 jars already and has orders for 40,000 more—at $5 a jar. Each jar contains about $10,000 in shredded bills."
   b. "In February 1987 Vincent Van Gogh's priceless painting *Sunflowers* sold at auction for $39 million."
4. The *New York Times* called it the great liver crisis. Chopped liver is a delicacy on the table, particularly the kosher table, but not long ago there was a glut of it on the market. Prices had sunk to a 20-year low as supplies had risen to an all-time high due to a high

slaughter of cattle. What do the following quotations from the *New York Times* tell you about the marginal and total value of liver?

a. "Grade A-1 liver is being used for cats and dogs instead of people. It's unheard of, it's a waste," says the manager of Kosher King Meat Products. "Even Israel is drowning in chopped liver."

b. "They're falling all over their feet to sell to me," said the president of Mrs. Weinberg's Kosher Chopped Liver Co., which uses 3,500 pounds of liver daily. "I've been offered prices so low I can't believe them."

c. "The nature of people being what they are, even though they like a good bargain, they're not going to eat something that doesn't agree with their taste."

5. Mary is willing to pay $10 for the first widget that she purchases each year, $9 for the second, $8 for the third, and so on down to $1 for the tenth and nothing for the eleventh. How many widgets will she buy, and what will be her consumers' surplus if widgets cost $3 each? What will happen if the price of widgets rises to $5? Can you state a generalization about the relationship between consumers' surplus obtained and price of a commodity?

6. What do you think about someone who buys two lottery tickets instead of one and tells you that he does this in order "to increase my chances of coming out a winner"?

7. Describe the difference in behavior at a cocktail party at which drinks are free between someone who imbibes up to the point where the *marginal* value of more alcohol consumed is zero and someone who imbibes up to the point where the *average* value of alcohol consumed is zero.

Chapter 9

The Role of the Firm

Ask almost anyone you know to name 10 American firms. The odds are overwhelming that the list will include some of these firms: General Motors, IBM, General Electric, CITICORP, EXXON, Prudential Insurance, American Telephone and Telegraph, and CBS. Drive around Ypsilanti, Michigan, and note at random 10 firms that come into view. They will likely include a Kroger's supermarket, Richardson's Pharmacy, a Shell service station, an Ace Hardware store, Haabs, and the National Bank of Detroit. Drive through Iowa or Nebraska and look around you: Every farm is a business, or firm, as well as a home.

Firms develop and survive because they are efficient institutions for organizing resources to produce goods and services and for organizing their sales and distribution. It is not difficult to count ways in which General Motors, Haabs, and the Iowa farm are different. However, we can gain insight by treating them all under a single heading, that is, by seeing what they have in common. This is what economic theory does. Economists usually assume that the firm's behavior can be understood in terms of a common motivation. Whether the firm is Ma and Pa's Bar and Grill or the Ford Motor Company and whether a particular decision is made by the board of directors, the third vice-president in charge of advertising, or the owner-manager are regarded as irrelevant to predicting what decisions are made. Criticisms that economic theory neglects differences among firms will be considered in Chapter 16.

Before studying how the firm is treated in economic theory, we shall examine more closely the firm in America today.

The Organization of Production

Forms of Business Organization

There are three major forms of business organization: the single proprietorship, the partnership, and the corporation. In the **single proprietorship,** one owner makes all the decisions and is personally responsible for all of the firm's actions and debts. In the **partnership,** there are two or more joint owners, each of whom may make binding decisions and is personally responsible for all of the firm's actions and debts. In the **corporation,** the firm has a legal existence separate from that of the owners. The owners are the firm's shareholders, and they risk only the amount that they put up to purchase their shares. The owners elect a board of directors, who hire managers to run the firm under the board's supervision.

In the United States today there are about 7 million single proprietorships (not counting farms), 1 million partnerships, and nearly 2 million corporations.

Corporations account for more than two-thirds of the nation's privately produced income.

In manufacturing, transportation, public utilities, and finance, corporations do almost all of the nation's business. In trade and construction they do about one-half of the total business. Only in agriculture and in services (such as hairstyling, medicine, and accounting) is the corporation relatively unimportant.

The Single Proprietorship and the Partnership

The major advantage of the single proprietorship is that the owner is the boss who maintains full control over the firm. The disadvantages are, first, that the size of the firm is limited by the amount of capital that the owner can personally raise and, second, that the owner is personally responsible by law for all debts of the firm.

The partnership overcomes to some extent the first disadvantage of the single proprietorship but not the second. Ten partners may be able to finance a much bigger enterprise than could one owner, but they are still subject to unlimited liability. Each partner is fully liable for all of the debts of the firm.

Because of unlimited liability, people with substantial personal assets are unwilling to enter into a partnership unless they have complete trust in the other partners and a full knowledge of all the obligations of the firm. Investors may be willing to risk a specific sum but unwilling to jeopardize their entire fortune; if, however, they join a partnership in order to do the former, they may also do the latter.

There are certain professions in which a general partnership is traditional. These include law, medicine, and (until recently) brokerage. Partnerships survive in these professions partly because they all depend heavily on a relationship of trust between owners and clients, and the partners' unlimited liability for one another's actions is thought to enhance public confidence in the firm.

The **limited partnership,** which has two classes of partners (general and limited), provides protection against some of the risks of the general partnership. The firm's *general partners* have unlimited liability; the firm's *limited partners* have liability only for the amount that they have invested. Limited partners can neither participate in the running of the firm nor make agreements on its behalf. In effect, the limited partnership permits some division of the functions of decision making and risk taking.

The Corporation

The corporation is regarded by law as an entity separate from the individuals who own it. It can enter into contracts, sue and be sued, own property, contract debts, and generally incur obligations that are the legal obligations of the corporation *but not of its owners.* The corporation's right to be sued may not seem to be an advantage, but it is, because it allows others to enter into enforceable contracts with the corporation.

Although some corporations are owned by just a few persons, who also manage the business, the most important type of corporation is one that sells shares to the general public. The company raises the funds that it needs for the business by selling stock, and those who invest their money by buying its stock, called its **stockholders,** or its **shareholders,** are the company's owners. All profits belong to the stockholders. Those profits that are paid out to them are called **dividends;** those profits that are retained to be reinvested in the firm's operations are called **undistributed profits.** If the corporation is liquidated, stockholders share any assets that remain after all the debts are paid.

Diffuse ownership of corporate shares means that the owners cannot all be managers. Stockholders, who are entitled to one vote for each share that they own, elect a board of directors. This board of directors defines general policy and hires senior managers whose job it is to translate this general policy into detailed decisions.

Should the corporation go bankrupt, the personal liability of any one stockholder is limited to whatever money that stockholder has actually invested in the firm. This is called **limited liability.**

From a stockholder's viewpoint, the most important aspect of the corporation is its limited liability.

The advantage to the corporation is that it can raise capital from a large number of individuals. Each of these individuals who invest money in the firm shares in the firm's profits but has no personal liability beyond risking the loss of the amount that he or she has invested. Thus investors know how much they have at risk. Because shares are easily transferred from one person to another, a corporation has a continuity of life that is unaffected by frequent changes in investors.

From the individual investor's point of view, there are disadvantages in investing in a corporation. First, the investor may have little to say about the management of the firm. For example, if those who hold a majority of the shares decide that the corporation should not pay dividends, an individual investor cannot compel the payment of his or her share of the earnings. Second, the income of the corporation is taxed twice. Corporations are taxed on their income before dividends are paid. Dividends are paid out of the after-tax income and are then taxed as part of the stockholders' incomes. This *double taxation* of corporate income is viewed by some as unfair and discriminatory; others see it as the price to be paid for the advantage of incorporating.

The Rise of the Modern Corporation

The direct predecessors of the modern corporation were the English chartered companies of the sixteenth century. The Muscovy Company, granted a charter in 1555, the East India Company, first chartered in 1600, and the Hudson's Bay Company, chartered in 1609 and still going strong in Canada nearly 400 years later, are famous examples of early joint-stock ventures with limited liability. Their needs for many investors to finance a ship that would not return with its cargo for years—if it returned at all—made this exceptional form of organization seem desirable.

In the next three centuries, the need to commit large amounts of capital for long periods of time and to diversify risks were felt in other fields, and charters were granted for insurance, turnpikes and canals, and banking, as well as for foreign trade. Exploiting the new techniques of the Industrial Revolution required the growth of large firms in many branches of manufacturing. The growing need for large firms led to the passage of laws permitting incorporation with limited liability *as a matter of right rather than as a special grant of privilege.* Such laws became common in England and in the United States during the late nineteenth century.

Today incorporation is relatively routine, although it is subject to a variety of state laws. Moderate incorporation fees are charged, and competition among the states for these fees has liberalized the conditions for incorporation throughout the country. Delaware is an example of a small state that has a disproportionate share of incorporations because of its permissive laws. In insurance, Connecticut took the lead; most insurance companies founded before 1930 have Connecticut charters.

Financing of Firms

The money that a firm raises for carrying on its business is sometimes called its **financial** (or *money*) **capital.** This is distinct from its **real** (or *physical*) **capital,** the physical assets of the firm that constitute plant, equipment, and inventories. Money capital may be broken down into **equity capital,** which refers to funds provided by the owners of the firm, and **debt,** which refers to the funds that have been borrowed from persons or institutions who are not owners of the firm.

The use of the term *capital* to refer to both an amount of money and a quantity of goods can be confusing, but it is usually clear from the context in which it is discussed which of these is being referred to. The two uses are not independent, for much of the money capital raised by a firm will be used to purchase the capital goods that the firm requires for production.

There are two basic methods by which a firm raises financial capital: equity financing and debt financing.

Equity Financing

We have seen that the owners of the firm are its stockholders. They make their money available to the firm and risk losing it in return for a share of the firm's profits. Stockholders usually have the right to one vote for each of their shares in the election of a board of directors. The board of directors in their turn set broad company policy and select senior management personnel.

There are two ways in which the firm can raise equity capital. One way is to sell newly issued shares. The other is to reinvest, or plow back, some of its own profits. Although shareholders do not receive reinvested profits directly as their dividend income, they benefit from the rise in value of their shares that occurs if the funds are reinvested profitably. Reinvestment has become an important source of funds in modern times. The amounts vary greatly from year to year. Nonfarm, nonfinancial American corporations reinvested amounts, ranging from a high of $54 billion to a low of $16 billion, each year in the 1980s.

Debt Financing

Firms also can raise money by issuing debt, for example, by selling bonds to the public or by borrowing from financial institutions. A **bond** is a promise to pay interest each year and to repay the principal at a stated time in the future (say, 20 years hence). Bank loans are often short term; sometimes the firm even commits to repaying the principal *on demand.* Debtholders are creditors, not owners, of the firm: They have loaned money to the firm in return for the firm's promise to pay interest on the loan and, of course, to repay the principal. The commitment to make interest payments is a legal obligation that must be met whether or not profits have been made. Many a firm that would have survived a temporary crisis had all its capital been equity financed has been forced into liquidation because it could not meet its contractual obligations to pay interest to its debtholders. The debtholders, and all other creditors, then have the first claims on the firm's funds. Only when they have been repaid in full can the stockholders attempt to recover anything for themselves.

The Firm in Economic Theory

IBM and the Main Street Deli certainly make decisions in different ways. Indeed, within a single, large corporation not all decisions are made by the same people or in the same way. To use an example, someone at IBM decided to introduce a small computer in 1981. Someone else decided to call it the IBM personal computer and market it for home use. Someone else decided how and where to produce it. Someone else decided its price. Someone else decided how best to promote its sales. The common aspect of these decisions is that all were in pursuit of the same goal—the manufacture and sale of a product to earn profits for IBM.

Economic theory assumes that the same principles underlie each decision made within a firm and that the decision is uninfluenced by who makes it. The assumption that a single theory of decision making can be applied to all firms is further discussed in Box 9-1.

Motivation: Profit Maximization

In building a theory of how firms behave, economists usually assume that firms try to make their profits as large as possible. In other words, firms are assumed to *maximize their profits,* which are the difference between the value of sales and the costs to the firm of producing what is sold.

Why is this assumption made? First, it is necessary to make *some* assumption about what motivates decision makers if the theory is to predict how they will act. Second, a great many of the predictions of theories based on this assumption have been confirmed by observation. Third, no single alternative assumption has been shown yet to yield more accurate predictions. However, the assumption has been criticized, and alternatives have been suggested (see Chapter 16).

The assumption of profit maximization provides a principle by which a firm's decisions can be predicted.

Economists predict the behavior of firms by studying the effect that making each choice available to the firm would have on profits. They then predict that firms will select the alternative that yields the largest profits.

This theory does not say that profit is the *only* factor that influences the firm's behavior; rather, it says only that profits are important enough that assuming profits to be the firm's sole objective will produce predictions that are substantially correct.

Factors of Production

Firms seek profits by producing and selling commodities. Production may be compared to a sausage machine. Certain elements, such as raw materials and the services of capital and labor, are fed in at one end, and a product emerges at the other end. The materials and services of factors of production, called **factor services,** that are used in the production process are called **inputs,** and the goods and services that result from the production process are called

BOX 9-1

Kinds of Firms

In economic theory the firm is defined as the unit that makes decisions with respect to the production and sale of commodities. This single definition covers a variety of business organizations, from the single proprietorship to the corporation, and a variety of business sizes, from inventors operating in their garages and financed by whatever they can extract from reluctant bank managers to vast undertakings with tens of thousands of stockholders and creditors. We know that in large firms decisions are actually made by many different individuals. We can nonetheless regard the firm as a single, consistent decision-making unit because of the assumption that all decisions are made to achieve the common goal of maximizing the firm's profits.

Whether a decision is made by a small independent proprietor, a plant manager, or a board of directors, that person or group is the firm for the purposes of that decision. This is a truly heroic assumption; it amounts to saying that for purposes of predicting those aspects of their behavior that interest us, we can treat a farm, a corner grocery, a department store, a small law partnership, General Motors, and a giant multinational corporation all under the umbrella of a single theory of the behavior of the firm. If this turns out to be even partially correct, it will prove enormously valuable in revealing some unity in behavior where to the casual observer there is only bewildering diversity.

We should not be surprised, therefore, if at the first encounter the theory appears rather abstract and out of touch with reality. To generalize over such a wide variety of behavior, the theory must ignore many features with which we are most familiar and that distinguish the farmer from the grocer and each of them from the Exxon Corporation. Any theory that generalizes over a wide variety of apparently diverse behavior necessarily has this characteristic, because it ignores those factors that are most obvious to us and that create the appearance of diversity. If it were not possible to do this, it would be necessary to have dozens of different theories, one for each type of firm. The task of learning economics would then be much more complex than it is now!

outputs. One way of looking at the production process is to regard the inputs as being combined to produce the outputs. Another equally useful way is to regard the inputs as being used up, or sacrificed, to gain the outputs.

Hundreds of inputs enter into the output of most goods and services. Among the inputs entering into the output of automobiles are sheet steel, rubber, spark plugs, electricity, machinists, cost accountants, forklift operators, managers, and painters. These inputs can be grouped into four broad classes: (1) those that are inputs to the automobile manufacturer but outputs to some other manufacturer, such as spark plugs, electricity, and sheet steel; (2) those that are provided directly by nature, such as the land used by the automobile plant; (3) those that are provided directly by households, such as the services of workers; and (4) those that are provided by machines, such as drill presses and robots.

Inputs in the first group just mentioned are called *intermediate products.* They are goods that are produced by other firms. They appear as inputs only because the stages of production are divided among different firms so that, at any one stage, a firm is using as inputs goods produced by other firms. If these products are traced back to their sources, all production can be accounted for by the services of only three kinds of inputs, which are called *factors of production:* Economists call all gifts of nature, such as land and raw materials, **land;** all physical and mental contributions that are provided by people, **labor;** and all manufactured aids to further production, such as machines, **capital.**

Extensive use of capital is one distinguishing feature of modern production. Instead of making consumer goods with only the aid of simple natural tools, productive effort goes into the manufacture of tools, machines, and other goods that are desired not in themselves but as aids to making other goods.

The Meaning of Cost

Profits are the difference between the value of the goods that a firm sells and the cost of producing these goods. In later chapters we shall look at the firm's sales revenues. Here we are concerned with cost. **Cost,** to the producing firm, is the value of inputs used to produce its output.

Notice the use of the word "value" in the definition. A given output produced by a given technique, say, 6,000 cars produced each week by General Motors with its present production methods, has a given set of inputs associated with it—so many working hours of various types of laborers, supervisors, managers, and technicians, so many tons of steel, glass, and aluminum, so many kilowatt-hours of electricity, and so many hours of the time of various machines. The cost of each can be calculated, and the sum of these separate costs is the total cost to General Motors of producing 6,000 cars per week.

Opportunity Cost

Although the details of economic costing vary, they are governed by a common principle that is sometimes called *user cost* but is more commonly called *opportunity cost*. We introduced this concept in Chapter 1.

The cost of using something in a particular venture is the benefit foregone by not using it in its best alternative use.

Box 9-2 considers some general applications of the principle of opportunity cost.

The Measurement of Opportunity Cost

To measure opportunity cost, the firm must assign to each input that it uses a monetary value equal to what it has sacrificed to use the input. Applying this principle to specific cases is not quite as easy as it may seem at first.

Purchased and Hired Factors

Assigning costs is a straightforward process when inputs purchased in one period are used up in the same period and when the price that the firm pays is determined by forces beyond its control. Inputs of intermediate products purchased from other firms fall into this category. If a firm pays $110 per ton for coal, it has sacrificed its claims to whatever else the $110 can buy, and thus the purchase price is a reasonable measure of the firm's opportunity cost of using 1 ton of coal.

Inputs of hired factors of production are also in this category. Firms hire labor, and the opportunity cost is the price that must be paid for these labor services. This includes the wage rate and all related expenses, such as contributions to pension funds, unemployment and disability insurance, and other fringe benefits. Firms also use borrowed money. Interest payments measure the opportunity cost of borrowed funds because the money paid out as interest could have been used to buy something else of equivalent monetary value.

Imputed Costs

Some of the inputs that the firm uses are neither purchased nor hired for current use. Their use requires no payment to anyone outside the firm, so the costs of using them are not obvious. Nonetheless, their use does entail a cost. The opportunity cost of these inputs is the amount that the firm would earn if it were to shift the inputs to their next best use. When these costs are calculated, they are called **imputed costs,** which refers to a cost that must be inferred because it is not made as a money payment. The following examples all involve imputed costs.

Using the firm's own money.   Let us consider a firm that uses $100,000 of its own money, which instead it could have loaned out at 10 percent per year yielding $10,000 per year. This amount should be deducted from the firm's revenue as the cost of funds used in production. If, to continue the example, the firm earns only $6,000 over all other costs, one should not say that the firm made a profit of $6,000 but that it lost $4,000. If it had closed down completely and merely loaned out its money to someone else, it could have earned $10,000.

BOX 9-2

Opportunity Cost Beyond Economics

Opportunity cost plays a vital role in economic analysis, but it is also a fundamental principle that applies to a wide range of situations. It is one of the great insights of economics. Consider some examples:

George Bernard Shaw, on reaching his ninetieth birthday, was asked how he liked being 90. He is reputed to have said, "It's fine, when you consider the alternative."

Llewelyn Formed likes to watch both Dan Rather and Peter Jennings. If he finally decides to watch Peter Jennings, what is the opportunity cost of this decision?

Link Heartthrob, a 31-year-old bachelor, is thinking about marrying. Although he thinks Miss Piggy is a lovely girl, he realizes that if he marries her, he will give up the chance of wedded bliss with another girl he may meet next year, so he decides to wait a while. What other information do you need to determine the opportunity cost of this decision?

Serge Ginn, M.D., complains that now that he is earning large fees he can no longer afford to take the time for a vacation trip to Europe. In what way does it make sense to say that the opportunity cost of his vacation depends upon his fees?

Retired General William Russ, who is married to a wealthy woman, has decided to contribute $5,000 to the campaign of a political candidate. His lawyer points out to him that since he is in the 28% tax bracket and since political contributions are not deductible from income, the real cost of his contribution is the same as if he were giving an extra $6,950 to his favorite charity, the General Russ Foundation. Is the opportunity cost of the political contribution $5,000 or $6,950?

Costs of durable assets.   The costs of using assets owned by the firm, such as buildings, equipment, and machinery, include a charge, called **depreciation**, for the loss in value of an asset over a period of time because of its use in production, due to physical wear and tear and to obsolescence. The economic cost of owning an asset for a year is the loss in value of the asset during the year.

Accountants use several conventional methods to show depreciation based on the price originally paid for the asset, which is called its "historical cost." One of the most common is *straight-line depreciation*, in which the same amount of historical cost is deducted in every year of useful life of the asset. Although historical cost is often a useful approximation, in some cases it may differ seriously from the depreciation required by the opportunity-cost principle. Consider two examples.

Assets that may be resold. A woman buys a new automobile for $12,000. She intends to use it for six years and then sell it for $6,000. She may think that, using straight-line depreciation, this will cost her

$1,000 per year. If after one year, however, the value of her car on the used-car market is $10,000, it has cost her $2,000 to use the car during the first year. Why should she charge herself $2,000 depreciation during the first year? After all, *she* does not intend to sell the car for six years. The answer is that one of the purchaser's alternatives is to buy a one-year-old car and operate it for five years. Indeed, that is the position she is in after the first year. Whether she likes it or not, she has paid $2,000 for the use of the car during the first year of its life. If the market had valued her car at $11,500 after one year (instead of $10,000), the correct depreciation would have been only $500.

Sunk costs. In the previous example, an active used-asset market was available. At the other extreme, consider an asset that has no alternative use. This is sometimes called a *sunk cost*. Assume that a firm has a set of machines that it purchased a few years ago for $100,000. These machines were expected to last 10 years, and the firm's accountant calculates the depreciation costs of these machines by the straight-line method at $10,000 per year. Assume also that the machines can be used to make one product and nothing else. Suppose, too, that they are installed in the firm's plant, they cannot be leased to any other firm, and their scrap value is negligible. In other words, the machines have no value except to this firm in its current operation. Assume that, if the machines are used to produce the product, the cost of all other factors used will amount to $25,000, while the goods produced can be sold for $29,000.

Now, if the accountant's depreciation "costs" of running the machines are added in, the total cost of operation comes to $35,000; with revenues at $29,000, this yields an annual loss of $6,000 per year. It appears that the goods should not be made!

The fallacy in this argument lies in the adding in of a charge based on the sunk cost of the machines as one of the costs of current operation. The machines have no alternative uses whatsoever. Clearly, their *opportunity cost* is *zero*. The total cost of producing this line of goods is thus only $25,000 per year (assuming all other costs have been correctly assessed), and the line of production shows an annual return over all relevant costs of $4,000, not a loss of $6,000.

To see why the second calculation leads to the correct decision, we notice that, if the firm abandons this line of production as unprofitable, it will have no money to pay out and no revenue received on this account. If the firm takes the economist's advice and pursues the line of production, it will pay out $25,000 and receive $29,000, thus making it $4,000 per year richer than if it had not done so. Clearly, production is worth undertaking. The amount that the firm happened to have paid out for the machines in the past has no bearing whatever on deciding the correct use of the machines once they are installed on the premises.

Because they involve neither current nor future costs, sunk costs should have no influence on deciding what is currently the most profitable thing to do.

The principle of "let bygones be bygones" extends well beyond economics and is often ignored in poker, in war, and in love. Because you have invested heavily in a poker hand, a war, or a courtship does not mean that you should stick with it if the prospects of winning become very small. At every mo-

ment of decision making, maximizing behavior should be based on how benefits from this time forward compare with current and future costs.

Risk taking.   One difficulty in imputing costs has to do with risk taking. Business enterprise is often a risky affair. Uninsured risks are borne by the owners of the firm, who, if the enterprise fails, may lose the money that they have invested in the firm.

Risk taking is a service that must be provided by someone. When the firm is the risk taker, it will not carry on production unless it is compensated for the risk. If a firm does not yield a return that is sufficient to compensate for the risks involved, it will not be able to persuade people to invest in it. Those who buy the firm's shares expect a return that exceeds what they could have obtained if they had invested their money in a virtually riskless manner, say, by buying a government bond.

Suppose a businesswoman invests $100,000 in a class of risky ventures and expects that most of the ventures will be successful but that some will fail. In fact, she expects that about $10,000 will be a total loss. (She does not know which specific ventures will be the losers, because, if she did, she would not invest in them.) Suppose further that she requires a 20 percent return on her total investment. To earn a $20,000 profit and recover the $10,000 expected loss, she needs to earn a $30,000 profit on the $90,000 of successful investment. This is a rate of return of $33\frac{1}{33}$ percent. She charges 20 percent for the use of the capital plus $13\frac{1}{13}$ percent for the risk she takes.

Patents, trademarks, and other special advantages. Suppose that a firm owns a valuable patent or a highly desirable location or produces a popular brand-name product such as Coca-Cola or Miller Lite. Each of these involves an opportunity cost to the firm in production (even if it was acquired free), because if the firm does not choose to use the special advantage itself, it could sell or lease it to others.

The Meaning and Significance of Profits

Economic profits, sometimes also called *pure profits*, are the difference between the revenues received by the firm from the sale of output and the opportunity cost of the inputs used to make the output. If costs are greater than revenues, such "negative profits" are called *losses*.

TABLE 9-1 The Calculation of Economic Profits: An Example

Gross revenue from sales	$1,000
Less direct cost of production (materials, labor, electricity, etc.)	650
"Gross profits" (or "contributions to overhead")	350
Less: indirect costs (depreciation, overhead, management salaries, interest on debt, etc.)	140
"Net profits"	210
Income taxes payable	74
After-tax "net profits"	136
Less: normal profits (i.e., imputed charges for own capital used and for risk taking)	130
Economic profits	$ 6

Economic profits are less than net profits. The main difference between economic profits and what a firm calls its net profits is in the subtraction of normal profits, which are the imputed charges for use of capital owned by the firm and for risk taking. Income tax is levied on whatever definition of profits the taxing authorities choose, usually closely related to net profits. Although economic profits are necessarily less than net profits, they can be greater or less than normal profits. (In this example they are much less.)

This definition *includes* in costs (and thus *excludes* from profits) the imputed returns to capital and to risk taking. By doing so, it gives a special meaning to the words *profits* and *losses*—a meaning that differs somewhat from everyday usage. Table 9-1 illustrates how the terms *cost* and *profit* are used by economists.

Other Definitions of Profits

Firms define *profits* as the excess of revenues over the costs as measured by the conventions of accounting. In the appendix to this chapter we explore some of the differences between accountants' and economists' views of business transactions. Some of these differences affect the meaning of profits. Accountants do not charge for risk taking and use of the owner's own capital as costs, and thus these items are recorded by the firm as part of its profits. When a firm says it *needs* a certain amount of profits to stay in business, it is making sense within its definition, for its "profits" must be large enough to pay the costs of those of its inputs that accounting conventions do not include as costs.

Economists would express the same notion by saying that the firm needs to cover *all* of its costs, including those that are not employed in accounting. If the firm is covering all of its opportunity costs, it could not do better by using its resources in any other line of activity than the one currently being followed.

There is an alternative usage of *profits* that is sometimes encountered. In it the term **normal profits** is used by some economists to refer to the opportunity costs of capital and risk taking. When this definition is used, we would say that the firm must earn normal profits if it is to be willing to stay in the industry. Whatever we call the opportunity costs of capital and risk taking—costs or normal profits—they must be covered if the firm is to be willing to remain in production in that industry.

A situation in which revenues equal costs (economic profits of zero) is satisfactory, because all factors, hidden as well as visible, are being rewarded at least as well as they would be in their *best* alternative uses.

The income-tax authorities have yet another definition of *profits,* which is implicit in the thousands of rules as to what may and may not be included as a deduction from revenue in arriving at taxable income. In some cases the taxing authorities allow more for costs than accountants recommend; in other cases they allow less than accountants recommend.

It is important to be clear about different meanings of the term *profits,* not only to avoid fruitless semantic arguments, but also because a theory that predicts that certain behavior depends on profits defined in one way will not necessarily predict behavior accurately if *profits* is defined in another way. For example, the prediction that new firms will seek to enter an industry whenever profits are earned will not stand up if it is tested against the accountants' definition of *profits.* Firms may be earning accounting profits but economic losses because they are not covering the full opportunity costs of their capital. In this case the tendency will be for firms to be leaving rather than entering the industry.

The definition of *economic profits* as an excess over all opportunity costs is for many purposes the most useful, but in order to apply it to business behavior or to tax policy, appropriate adjustments must be made. Conversely, to apply accounting or tax data to particular economic theories requires the reverse set of adjustments. Henceforth, when we use the word *profits*, unless otherwise noted, we mean *economic* profits.

Profits and Resource Allocation

When resources are valued by the opportunity-cost principle, their costs show how much these resources would earn if used in their best alternative uses. If there is an industry in which revenues exceed opportunity costs, the firms in that industry will be earning profits. Thus the owners of factors of production will want to move resources into that industry because they could earn more there than in their present uses. Conversely, if in some other industry firms are incurring losses, resources in that industry could earn more revenues in other uses, and their owners will want to move them to those other uses. Only when economic profits are zero is there no incentive for resources to move into or out of an industry.

Profits and losses play a crucial signaling role in the workings of a free-market system.

SUMMARY

1. The firm is the economic unit that produces and sells commodities. The economist's definition of the firm abstracts from real-life differences in size and form of the organization of firms.
2. The single proprietorship, the partnership, and the corporation are the major forms of business organization in the United States today. The corporation is by far the most common wherever large-scale production is required. The corporation is recognized as a legal entity; its owners, or shareholders, have a liability that is limited to the amount of money that they have invested in the organization. Corporate ownership is readily transferred by the sale of shares of the company's stock in securities markets.
3. Firms can raise money through equity financing or debt financing. A firm's owners provide equity capital either when they purchase newly issued shares or when the firm reinvests its profits. The firm obtains debt financing from creditors either by borrowing from financial institutions or by selling bonds to the public.
4. Economic theory assumes that the same principles underlie each decision made within the firm and that the actual decision is uninfluenced by who makes it. The key behavioral assumption is that the firm seeks to maximize its profit.
5. Production consists of transforming inputs (the services of factors of production) into outputs (goods and services). It is often convenient to divide factors of production into categories. One common classification is land, labor, and capital. Land includes land and natural resources, labor means all human services, and capital denotes all manufactured aids to further production. An outstanding feature of modern production is the use of capital goods.
6. The opportunity cost of using a resource is the value of that resource in its best alternative use. If the opportunity cost of using a resource in one way is less than, or equal to, the gain from using the resource in this way, there is no superior way of using it.
7. Measuring opportunity cost to the firm requires imputing the cost of resources not purchased or hired for current use. Among these imputed costs are those for the use of the owners' money, depreciation, risk taking, and any special advantages, such as trademarks, that the firm possesses.
8. A firm that is maximizing profits, defined as the difference between revenue and opportunity cost, is making the best allocation of the resources under its control, according to the firm's evaluation of its alternatives.

9. Economic profits and losses provide important signals concerning the reallocation of resources. Profits earned in an industry provide a signal that more resources can profitably move into the industry. Losses show that resources have more profitable uses elsewhere and serve as a signal that some of these resources should be transferred out of that industry.

TOPICS FOR REVIEW

Role of profit maximization
Single proprietorship, partnership, and corporation
Advantages of the corporation
Debt and equity financing
Inputs and factors of production
Opportunity costs
Imputed costs
Alternative definitions of profits
Profits and resource allocation

DISCUSSION QUESTIONS

1. Can the economic theory of the firm be of any help in analyzing the decisions of such nonprofit organizations as governments, churches, and colleges? What, if any, role does the notion of opportunity cost play for them?

2. Until 1988 not-for-profit private colleges and universities were not required to impute depreciation of their facilities as part of their costs of operation. However, the Financial Accounting Standards Board (FASB) now requires these institutions to depreciate their fixed assets, just as private businesses do. Comment on the following quotation from *Forbes* magazine (April 4, 1988): "Like tire factories and headquarters buildings, lecture halls and chapels wear out over time. If college administrators ignore depreciation, aren't they cheating future students by undercharging today's?"

3. "There is no such thing as a free lunch." Can anything be free? In earlier decades, gasoline stations routinely provided many free services, including windshield cleaning, air pumps for tire inflation, and road maps. Now, many sell road maps and have discontinued free services. Indeed, self-service stations are becoming increasingly popular with motorists who like the lower gasoline prices of these stations. Under what conditions will profit-maximizing behavior lead to the coexistence of full-service and self-service gasoline stations? What would determine the proportions in which each occurred?

4. What is the opportunity cost of the following?
   a. Fining a politician $10,000 and sending her to prison for one year
   b. Lending $500 to a friend
   c. Not permitting a $116 million electric power dam to be built because it would destroy the snail darter, a rare 3-inch-long fish found only in that particular river
   d. Towing icebergs to Saudi Arabia to provide drinking water at the cost of $.50 per cubic meter

5. According to *Forbes* magazine (June 13, 1988) "Unredeemed frequent-flyer coupons, the bright promotional idea dreamed up first by American Airlines in 1981 and subsequently copied by just about everyone else . . ." mean that ". . . the industry owes passengers about 25 billion miles of free travel . . . [and] if all the miles earned were cashed in, it would cost the airlines $1.7 billion." How would you go about estimating the cost to the airlines of the 25 billion frequent-flyer miles that are now outstanding?

6. Having bought a used car from Smiling Sam for $2,000, you drive it for two days, and it stops. You now find that it requires an extra $1,500 before it will run. Assuming that the car is not worth $3,500 fixed, should you make the repairs?

7. "To meet the legislated standard of 3.4 grams of carbon monoxide per mile driven, General Motors has calculated that it will cost $100 million and prolong 200 lives by one year each, thus costing $500,000 per year of extra life. Human lives are precious, which is why it is so sad to note another use of that money. It has been estimated that the installation of special cardiac-care units in ambulances could prevent premature deaths each year at an average cost of only $200 for each year of extra life."

   Assume that the facts in this quotation are correct. If the money spent on carbon monoxide control would have been spent on cardiac-care units instead, what is the opportunity cost of the carbon monoxide requirement? If the money would not have been so spent but simply reduced automobile companies' costs, what is the opportunity cost? In either case, do the facts tell us whether the regulation of carbon monoxide to the 3.4 gram level is desirable or undesirable?

8. Which concept of profits is implied in the following quotations?
   a. "Profits are necessary if firms are to stay in business."
   b. "Profits are signals for firms to expand production and investment."
   c. "Accelerated depreciation allowances lower profits and thus benefit the company's owners."

Appendix to Chapter 9

Balance Sheets, Income Statements, and Costs of Production: Two Views

Accounting is a major branch of study in and of itself. Many students of economics will want to study accounting at some stage in their careers. It is not our intention to give a short course in accounting in this appendix but rather to acquaint you with the kinds of summary statements that are used by both economists and accountants. **Balance sheets** are a financial report of the status of a firm at a particular moment in time. They balance in the sense that they show the assets (or valuable things) owned by the firm on one side and the claims against those assets on the other side. **Income statements** summarize the flows of resources through the firm in the course of its operations over a specified period of time (for example, a year). Balance sheets thus measure a stock; income statements measure a flow. (See page 20 for the distinction between stock and flow variables—which has nothing to do with company stocks!)

To illustrate what balance sheets and income statements are, the same example will be treated from two points of view: that of the accountant and that of the economist.

An Example

Late in 1989, James Maykby, the second vice-president of Acme Artificial Flower Corporation (at a salary of $50,000 per year), decided he would go into business for himself. He quit his job and organized the Maykby Leaf Company. He purchased suitable plant and equipment for $160,000 and acquired some raw materials and supplies. By December 31, 1989, he was in a position to start manufacturing. The funds for his enterprise were $80,000 raised as a bank loan on the factory (on which he is obligated to pay interest of $10,000 per year) and $110,000 of his own funds, which had previously been invested in common stocks. He also owed $10,000 to certain firms that had provided him with supplies.

Maykby, who is a trained accountant, drew up a balance sheet showing his company's position as of December 31, 1989 (see Table 9A-1).

Maykby showed this balance sheet to his sister-in-law, an economist, and was pleased and surprised[1] to find that she agreed that this was a fair and accurate statement of the position of the company as it prepared to start operation.

During 1990 the company had a busy year. The following points summarize these activities of the 12-month period.

1. The firm hired labor and purchased additional raw materials in the amount of $115,000, of which it still owed $20,000 at the end of the year.[2]
2. The firm manufactured artificial leaves and flowers whose sale value was $200,000. At year's end it had sold all of these and still had on hand $30,000 worth of raw materials.
3. The firm paid off the $10,000 owed to suppliers at the beginning of the year.
4. At the very end of 1989 the company purchased a new machine for $10,000 and paid cash for it.
5. The company paid the bank $10,000 interest on the loan.
6. Maykby paid himself $20,000 "instead of a salary."

An Accountant's Balance Sheet and Income Statement

Taking account of all these things and also recognizing that he had depreciation on his plant and equipment,[3] Maykby spent New Year's Day 1991 prepar-

---

[1] He usually finds that he and his sister-in-law disagree about everything.

[2] In this example all purchased and hired factors of production are treated in a single category.

[3] The tax people told him that he could charge 15 percent of the cost of his equipment as depreciation during 1990, and he decided to use this amount in his own books as well. No depreciation was charged on the new machine.

TABLE 9A-1   Maykby Leaf Company, Balance Sheet, December 31, 1989

Assets		Liabilities and equity	
Cash in bank	$ 10,000	Owed to suppliers of factors	$ 10,000
Plant and equipment	160,000	Bank loan	80,000
Raw materials and supplies	30,000	Equity	110,000
Total assets	$200,000	Total liabilities and equity	$200,000

TABLE 9A-2   Maykby Leaf Company, Accountant's Balance Sheet, December 31, 1990

Assets		Liabilities and equity	
Cash in bank (See Exhibit 1)	$ 65,000	Owed to suppliers of factors of production (See Exhibit 4)	$ 20,000
Plant and equipment (See Exhibit 2)	146,000	Bank loan	80,000
Raw materials and supplies (See Exhibit 3)	30,000	Equity (See Exhibit 5)	141,000
Total assets	$241,000	Total liabilities and equity	$241,000

TABLE 9A-3   Maykby Leaf Company, Exhibits to Balance Sheet of December 31, 1990

Exhibit 1. Cash

Balance, January 1, 1990	$ 10,000	
+Deposits		
Proceeds of sales of goods	200,000	$210,000
−Payments		
Payments to suppliers (1990 bills)	10,000	
Payments for labor and additional raw materials	95,000	
Salary of Mr. Maykby	20,000	
Purchase of new machine	10,000	
Interest payment to bank	10,000	−145,000
Balance, December 31, 1990		65,000

Exhibit 2. Plant and Equipment

Balance, January 1, 1990	$160,000	
+New machine purchased	10,000	170,000
−Depreciation charged		− 24,000
Balance, December 31, 1990		146,000

Exhibit 3. Raw Materials and Supplies

On hand January 1, 1990	$ 30,000	
Purchases in 1990	115,000	145,000
Used for production during 1990		−115,000
On hand December 31, 1990		30,000

Exhibit 4. Owed to Suppliers

Balance, January 1, 1990	$ 10,000	
New purchases, 1990	115,000	125,000
Paid on old accounts	10,000	
Paid on new accounts	95,000	−105,000
Balance, December 31, 1990		$ 20,000

Exhibit 5. Equity

Original investment	$110,000
+Income earned during year (See income statement)	31,000
Balance, December 31, 1990	$141,000

TABLE 9A-4	Maykby Leaf Company, Accountant's Income Statement for the Year 1990		

Sales			$200,000
Costs of operation			
Hired services and raw materials	$115,000		
Depreciation	24,000		
Mr. Maykby	20,000		
Interest to bank	10,000		− 169,000
Profit			$ 31,000

TABLE 9A-5	Maykby Leaf Company, Economist's Income Statement for the Year 1990		

Sales		$200,000
Cost of operations		
Hired services and raw materials	$115,000	
Depreciation[a]	36,000	
Interest to bank[b]	10,000	
Imputed cost of capital	11,000	
Services of Mr. Maykby	50,000	− 222,000
Loss		$(22,000)

[a] Market value on January 1 less market value on December 31.
[b] Because the bank loan is secured by the factory, its opportunity cost seems to the economist to be properly measured by the interest payment.

ing three financial reports (see Tables 9A-2, 9A-3, and 9A-4).

These reports reflect the operations of the firm as just described. The bookkeeping procedure by which these various activities are made to yield both the year-end balance sheet and the income statement need not concern you at this time, but you should notice several things.

1. Some transactions affect the balance sheet but do not enter into the current income statement. Examples of these are the purchase of a machine, which is an exchange of assets—cash for plant and equipment—and which will be entered as a cost in the income statements of some future periods as depreciation is charged; and the payment of past debts, which enter the income statements in the period in which the things purchased are used in production.[4]
2. The net profit from operations increased the owner's equity, since it was not "paid out" to him. A loss would have decreased his equity.
3. The income statement, covering a year's operation, provides a link between the opening balance sheet (the assets and the claims against assets at the beginning of the year) and the closing balance sheet.
4. Every change in a balance sheet between two dates can be accounted for by events that occurred during the year. (See the exhibits to the balance sheet, Table 9A-3.)

After studying these records, Maykby felt that it had been a good year. The company had money in the bank, it had shown a profit, and it was able to sell the goods it produced. He was bothered, however, by the fact that he and his wife felt poorer than

[4] Beginning students often have difficulty with the distinction between *cash* flows and *income* flows. If you do, analyze item by item the entries in Exhibit 1 in Table 9A-3 and in Table 9A-4, the income statement.

in the past years. Probably the cost of living had gone up!

An Economist's Balance Sheet and Income Statement

When Maykby's sister-in-law reviewed the December 31, 1990, balance sheet and the 1990 income statement, she criticized them in three respects.

1. Maykby should have charged the company $50,000 for his services, since that is what he could have earned outside.
2. Maykby should have charged the company for the use of the $110,000 of his funds. He computes that had Maykby left these funds in the stock market, he would have earned $11,000 in dividends and capital gains.
3. Maykby's depreciation figure is arbitrary. The plant and equipment purchased for $160,000 a year ago now has a *market value* of only $124,000. (Let us assume that he is correct about this fact.)

The sister-in-law prepared three revised statements. (See Tables 9A-5, 9A-6, and the exhibit, Table 9A-7.)

It was not hard for Maykby to understand the difference between the accountant's profit of $31,000 and the reported economist's loss of $22,000. The difference of $53,000 is made up as follows:

Extra salary	$30,000
Imputed cost of capital	11,000
Extra depreciation	12,000
	$53,000

What Maykby did *not* understand was how he *lost* $22,000 during the year. To explain this, his sister-in-law prepared the report shown in Table 9A-8.

Although Maykby spent the afternoon muttering to himself and telling his wife that his sister-in-law was not only totally lacking in any business sense but unpleasant as well, he was observed that evening at the public library asking the librarian whether there was a good "teach yourself economics" book. (We do not know his answer.)

The next day Maykby suggested to the economist that they work out together the expected economic profits for next year. "After all," he said, "dwelling on what might have been doesn't really help to decide whether I should continue the Maykby Leaf Company next year." The economist agreed. Because of expected sales increases, they concluded, the prospects were good enough to continue for at least another year. They dipped deep in the bowl of New Year's cheer to toast those stalwart pillars of society, the independent businessperson and the economist.

TABLE 9A-6   Maykby Leaf Company, Economist's Balance Sheet, December 31, 1990

Assets		Liabilities and equity	
Cash	$ 65,000	Owed to suppliers of factors	$ 20,000
Plant and equipment	134,000	Bank loan	80,000
Raw materials and supplies	30,000	Equity (see exhibit, Table 9A-7)	129,000
	$229,000		$229,000

TABLE 9A-7   Exhibit to Balance Sheet, December 31, 1990: Equity to Mr. Maykby

Original investment		$110,000
New investment by Mr. Maykby		
Salary not collected	$30,000	
Return on capital not collected	11,000	41,000
		151,000
Less loss from operations		22,000
Equity		$129,000

TABLE 9A-8   Mr. Maykby's Situation Before and After

	(1) As second vice-president of Acme Flower Company	(2) As owner-manager of Maykby Leaf Company	(3) Difference (2) − (1)
Salary paid	$ 50,000	$ 20,000	−$30,000
	11,000	0	− 11,000
Earnings on capital, invested in stocks		129,000 (equity in Maykby Leaf Co.)	
Assets owned	110,000 (stocks)		+ 19,000
Net change			−$22,000

Chapter 10

Production and Cost in the Short Run

Every firm knows that its total costs of production are positively related to its output. If it produces more, it must pay more to hire additional workers and to buy more of other inputs. Perhaps, more interestingly, many firms also find that their costs *per unit of output* are systematically related to their outputs. Both very low and very high levels of output are usually associated with high unit costs, while intermediate levels that are near the plant's normal output capacity are typically associated with lower unit costs of production.

In the previous chapter we defined costs of production. In this chapter we see how and why costs vary with the level of production and with changes in factor prices.

Choices Open to the Firm

Consider a firm that is producing a single product in a number of different plants. If its rate of sales has fallen off, should production be reduced correspondingly, or should production be held at the old rate and the unsold amounts stored up against an anticipated future rise in sales? If production is to be reduced, should a single plant be closed or should some plants be operated for shorter periods of time? Such decisions concern how best to use *existing* plant and equipment. They involve time periods that are too short in which to build new plants or to install more equipment.

Rather different decisions must be made when managers make their long-range plans. Should the firm adopt a highly automated process that will greatly reduce its wage bill, even though it must borrow large sums of money to buy the necessary equipment, or should it continue to build new plants that use current techniques? These matters concern what a firm should do when it is changing or replacing its plant and equipment. Such decisions may take a long time to put into effect.

In the examples just given, managers make decisions from known possibilities. Large firms also have research and development (R&D) staffs whose job it is to discover new products and new methods of production. Such firms must decide how much money to devote to R&D and in what areas the payoff for new development will be largest. If, for example, a shortage of a particular labor skill or raw material is anticipated, the research staff can be told to try to find ways to economize on that input or even to eliminate it from the production process.

Time Horizons for Decision Making

Economists organize all of the decisions that firms are constantly making into three classes: (1) how best to employ existing plant and equipment—the *short run;* (2) what new plant and equipment and production processes to select, given the framework of known technical possibilities—the *long run;* and (3) how to encourage, or adapt to, the invention of new techniques—the *very long run.*

The Short Run

The **short run** is a time period in which the quantity of some inputs, called **fixed factors,** cannot be increased.[1] A fixed factor is usually an element of capital (such as plant and equipment), but it might be land, the services of management, or even the supply of skilled labor. Inputs that can be varied in the short run are called **variable factors.**

The short run does not correspond to a specific number of months or years. In some industries it may extend over many years; in others it may be only a matter of months or even weeks.

In the electric power industry, for example, it takes three or more years to acquire and to install a steam-turbine generator. An unforeseen increase in demand will involve a long period during which the extra demand must be met with the existing capital equipment. In contrast, a machine shop can acquire new equipment or sell existing equipment in a few weeks. An increase in demand will have to be met with the existing stock of capital for only a brief time, after which the stock of equipment can be adjusted to the level made desirable by the higher demand.

The Long Run

The **long run** is a time period in which all inputs may be varied but in which the basic technology of production cannot be changed. As with the short run, the long run does not correspond to a specific length of time.

The long run corresponds to the situation facing the firm when it is planning to go into business, to expand the scale of its operations, to branch out into new products or new areas, or to change its method of production. The firm's *planning decisions* are long-run decisions because they are made from given technological possibilities but with freedom to choose from a variety of production processes that will use factor inputs in different proportions.

The Very Long Run

Unlike the short and long run, the **very long run** is a period of time in which the technological possibilities available to a firm will change. Modern industrial societies are characterized by continuously changing technologies that lead to new and improved products and production methods.

Some of these technological advances are made by the firm's own research and development efforts. For example, much of the innovation in cameras and films has been made by Kodak and Polaroid. Other firms adopt technological changes developed by others. For example, the transistor and the electronic chip have revolutionized dozens of industries that had nothing to do with developing them. Firms regularly must decide how much to spend in efforts to change technology either by developing new techniques or by adapting techniques that have been developed by others.

Connecting the Runs: The Production Function

The various "runs" are simply different aspects of the same basic problem: getting output from inputs efficiently. They differ in terms of what the firm is able to change.

The **production function** describes the precise physical relationship between factor inputs and output. A simplified production function in which there are only two factors of production, labor and capital, will be considered here, but the conclusions apply equally when there are many factors. (Capital is

---

[1] Sometimes it is physically impossible to increase the quantity of a fixed factor in a short time. For instance, there is no way to build a hydroelectric dam or a nuclear power plant in a few months. At other times it might be physically possible but prohibitively expensive to increase the quantity of a fixed factor in a short time. For example, a suit manufacturing firm could conceivably rent a building, buy and install new sewing machines, and hire a trained labor force in a few days if money were no consideration. Prohibitive costs, along with physical impossibility, are both sources of fixed factors.

taken to be the fixed factor, and labor is taken to be the variable one.) This chapter deals with the short-run situations in which output and cost change as different amounts of the variable input, labor, are used. Long-run situations in which both factors can be varied, and very long-run situations in which the production function changes, are both covered in the next chapter.

Short-Run Choices

Total, Average, and Marginal Products

Assume that a firm starts with a fixed amount of capital (say, 4 units) and contemplates applying various amounts of labor to it. Table 10-1 shows three different ways of looking at how output varies with the quantity of the variable factor. As a first step, some terms need defining.

Total product (TP) is the total amount that is produced during a given period of time. If the inputs of all but one factor are held constant, total product will change as more or less of the variable factor is used. This variation is shown in columns 1 and 2 of Table 10-1, which gives a total product schedule. Figure 10-1(i) shows such a schedule graphically. (The shape of the curve will be discussed shortly.)

Average product (AP) is the total product divided by the number of units of the variable factor used to produce it. If we let the number of units of labor be denoted by L, the average product can be written as:

$$AP = \frac{TP}{L}$$

Notice in column 3 of Table 10-1 that as more of the variable factor is used, average product first rises and then falls. The level of output at which average product reaches a maximum (34 units in the example) is called the **point of diminishing average productivity.** Up to that point, average productivity is increasing; beyond that point, average productivity is decreasing.

Marginal product (MP), sometimes called *incremental product* or **marginal physical product**

TABLE 10-1   Variation of Output with Capital Fixed and Labor Variable

(1) Quantity of labor (L)	(2) Total product (TP)	(3) Average product (AP)	(4) Marginal product (MP)
0	0	—	
			15
1	15	15.0	
			19
2	34	17.0	
			14
3	48	16.0	
			12
4	60	15.0	
			2
5	62	12.4	

The relationship between changes in output and changes in the quantity of labor can be looked at in three ways. Capital is assumed to be fixed at 4 units. As the quantity of labor increases, the level of output (the total product) increases. Average product increases at first and then declines. The same is true of marginal product.

Marginal product is shown between the lines because it refers to the *change* in output from one level of labor input to another. When graphing the schedule, marginal products are plotted at the midpoint of the interval. For example, the marginal product of 12 would be plotted to correspond to quantity of labor of 3.5.

(MPP), is the change in total product resulting from the use of one unit more of the variable factor:[2] **[13]**

$$MP = \frac{\Delta TP}{\Delta L}$$

Computed values of marginal product are shown in column 4 of Table 10-1. The figures in this column are placed between the other lines of the table to stress that the concept refers to the *change* in output caused by the *change* in quantity of the variable factor. For example, the increase in labor from 3 to 4 units ($\Delta L = 1$) raises output by 12 from 48 to 60 ($\Delta TP = 12$). Thus, the MP equals 12, and it is recorded between 3 and 4 units of labor. Note that the MP in the example first rises and then falls as output increases. The level of output at which marginal product reaches a maximum is called the **point of diminishing marginal productivity.**

Figure 10-1(ii) plots average product and marginal product curves. Although three different sched-

---

[2] Δ is read "change in." For example, ΔL is read "change in quantity of labor."

ules are shown in Table 10-1 and three different curves are shown in Figure 10-1, they are all aspects of the same single relationship described by the production function. As we vary the quantity of labor, with capital being fixed, output changes. Sometimes it is interesting to look at total output, sometimes at the average output, and sometimes at the marginal change in output.

Finally, bear in mind that the schedules in Table 10-1 and the curves in Figure 10-1 all assume a specified quantity of the fixed factor. If the quantity of capital were, say, 10 units instead of the 4 that were assumed, there would be a different set of total product, average product, and marginal product curves. The reason is that if for any specified amount of labor there is more capital to work with, labor can produce more output; that is, the total product will be greater.

The Shape of Marginal Product and Average Product Curves

The Law of Diminishing Returns

The variations in output that result from applying more or less of a variable factor to a given quantity of a fixed factor are the subject of a famous economic hypothesis. Usually it is called the **law of diminishing returns.** (Sometimes it is also called the *law of variable proportions.*)

The law of diminishing returns states that if increasing amounts of a variable factor are applied to a given quantity of a fixed factor, eventually a situation will be reached in which each additional unit of the variable factor adds less to total product than did the previous unit; that is, the marginal product of the variable factor will decline.

The commonsense explanation of the law of diminishing returns is that, as output is increased in the short run, more and more of the variable factor is combined with a given amount of the fixed factor. As a result, each unit of the variable factor has less and less of the fixed factor with which to work. When the fixed factor is capital and the variable factor is labor, each unit of labor gets a declining amount of capital to assist it as the total output grows. It is

FIGURE 10-1   Total Product, Average Product, and Marginal Product Curves

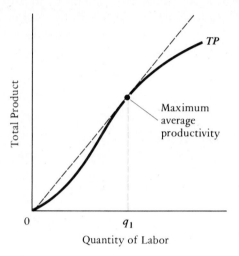

(i) Total product curve

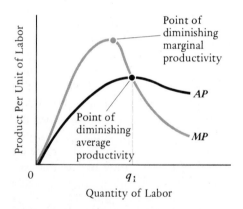

(ii) Average and marginal product curves

Total Product (*TP*), average product (*AP*), and marginal product (*MP*) curves often have the shapes shown here. (i) The total product curve shows the total product steadily rising, first at an increasing rate and then at a decreasing rate. This causes both the average and the marginal product curves in (ii) to rise at first and then to decline. The point of diminishing average productivity (also called the point of maximum average productivity) is q_1. At this point $MP = AP$.

not surprising, therefore, that, sooner or later, equal increases in labor eventually begin to add diminishing amounts to total output.

It is possible that marginal product might diminish from the outset, so that the first unit of labor contributes most to total production and each successive unit contributes less than the previous unit. It is also possible for the marginal product to rise at first and to decline only at some higher level of output. In this case the law of diminishing marginal returns might more accurately be described as the law of *eventually diminishing marginal returns*.

To illustrate this second case, consider the use of workers in a manufacturing operation. If there is only one worker, that worker must do all the tasks, shifting from one to another and becoming competent in each. As a second, third, and subsequent workers are added, each laborer can specialize in one task, becoming expert at it. This process, as we noted in Chapter 1, is called the *division of labor*. If additional workers allow for more efficient divisions of labor, marginal product will rise: each newly hired worker will add more to total output than did each previous worker. However, according to the law of diminishing returns, the scope for such economies must eventually disappear, and, sooner or later, the marginal products of additional workers must decline. When this happens, each additional worker that is hired will increase total output by less than did the previous worker. This case, in which marginal product rises at first and then declines, is the one illustrated in Figure 10-1.

Eventually, as more and more of the variable factor is employed, marginal product may reach zero and then become negative. It is not hard to see why, if you consider the extreme case in which there would be so many workers in a limited space that additional workers simply would get in the way.

So far we have spoken of diminishing marginal returns, but average returns also are expected to diminish. The *law of diminishing average returns* states that if increasing quantities of a variable factor are applied to a given quantity of fixed factors, the average product of the variable factor will eventually decrease. Both diminishing marginal and average products are illustrated in Table 10-1. **[14]**

The Significance of Diminishing Returns

Empirical confirmation of both diminishing marginal and diminishing average returns occurs frequently. Some examples are illustrated in Box 10-1. One might wish that it were not so. There would then be no reason to fear a food crisis caused by the population explosion in less developed countries. If the marginal product of additional workers applied to a fixed quantity of land were constant, food production could be expanded in proportion to population growth merely by keeping a constant fraction of the population on farms. With fixed techniques, however, diminishing returns dictate an inexorable decline in the marginal product of each additional laborer because an expanding population has a fixed supply of agricultural land.

Thus, unless there is a steady improvement in the techniques of production, continuous population growth will bring with it, according to the law of diminishing returns, declining average living standards and eventually widespread famine. This gloomy prediction of the nineteenth century English economist Thomas Malthus is discussed further in Box 11-2 on page 210.

The Relationship Between Marginal and Average Curves

Notice that in Figure 10-1(ii) the *MP* curve cuts the *AP* curve at the *AP*'s maximum point. It is important to understand how these curves are related. **[15]**

The average product curve slopes upward as long as the marginal product curve is *above* it; whether the marginal product curve is itself *sloping* upward or downward is irrelevant. This makes sense, because, if an additional worker is to raise the average product of all workers, that additional worker's output must be greater than the average output of all the other workers. It is immaterial whether the new worker's contribution to output is greater or less than the contribution of the worker hired immediately before; all that matters is that the new worker's contribution to output exceeds the average output of *all workers hired previously*. (The relationship between marginal and average measures is illustrated further in Box 10-2.)

Short-Run Variations in Cost

We now shift our attention from the firm's production function to its costs. The majority of firms cannot influence the prices of the inputs that they em-

BOX 10-1

Diminishing Returns

The following examples show the law of diminishing returns operating in a wide range of circumstances.

When Southern California Edison was required to modify its Mojave power plant to reduce the amount of fly ash emitted into the atmosphere, it discovered that a series of filters applied to the smokestacks could do the job. A single filter eliminated one-half of the discharge. Five filters in series reduced the fly ash discharge to the 3 percent allowed by law. When a state senator proposed a new standard that would permit no more than 1 percent fly ash emission, the company brought in experts who testified that this would require at least 15 filters per stack and would triple the cost.

British Columbia's Campbell River, a noted sport fishing area, has become the center of a thriving, well-promoted tourist trade. As fishing has increased, the total number of fish caught has steadily increased, but the number of fish per person fishing has decreased and the average hours fished for each fish caught has increased.

Public opinion pollsters, as well as all students of statistics, know that you can use a sample to estimate characteristics of a very large population. Even a relatively small sample can provide a useful estimate—at a tiny fraction of the cost of a complete enumeration of the population. However, sample estimates are subject to sampling error. If, for example, 38 percent of a sample approves of a certain policy, the percentage of the population that approves of it is likely to be close to 38 percent, but

it might well be anywhere from 36 to 40 percent. The theory of statistics shows that the size of the expected sampling error can always be reduced by increasing the sample size. The 4 percent interval (in the preceding example) could be cut in half—to 2 percent—by *quadrupling the sample size;* that is, if the original sample had been 400, a new sample of 1,600 would halve the chance of an error of any given size from occurring. To reduce the interval to 1 percent, the new sample would have to be quadrupled again—to 6,400. In other words, increasing the sample size means that diminishing marginal returns in terms of accuracy are encountered.

During the early days of World War II there were so few naval ships available that each North Atlantic convoy had only a few escort vessels to protect it from German submarines. The escorts dashed about from one side of the convoy to another and ended up sinking very few submarines. As the construction program made more ships available, the escorts could stay in one position in the convoy: some could close in on the various flanks; others could hunt farther afield. Not only did the total number of submarines sunk per convoy crossing rise, but also the number of submarines sunk per escort vessel rose. Still later in the war, as each successive convoy was provided with more and more escort vessels, the number of submarines sunk per convoy crossing continued to rise, but the number of submarines sunk per escort vessel began to fall sharply.

ploy; instead they must pay the going market price for their inputs. For example, a shoe factory in New Orleans, a candy manufacturer in Boston, a rancher in Wyoming, and a boat builder in Seattle are each too small a part of the total demand for the factors that they use to be able to influence their prices significantly. The firms must pay the going rent for the land that they need, the going wage rate for the labor that they employ, and the going interest rate that banks charge for loans to other similar customers. As it is with these firms, so it is with most other

firms.[3] Given these prices and the physical returns summarized by the product curves, the costs of different levels of output can be calculated.

---

[3] The firm that is a large enough employer of labor, or user of land or capital, that it is able to set its own prices for its factor services, is the exception rather than the rule. The exceptions are found in very large firms, such as General Motors, and firms in one-company towns. (Even such firms cannot set just any wage they wish, because their workers always have the option of moving to another town.) The important problems that arise when a firm can influence the wage rate that it pays to its employees are considered in Chapter 18.

BOX 10-2

Pete Rose's Batting Statistics

The relationship between the concepts of marginal and average measures is very general. An illuminating example comes from the *Baseball Encyclopedia*. The table below gives the average batting percentage—that is, the number of hits (output) divided by official times at bat (input)—of Pete Rose during his illustrious career in the National League, during which he set all kinds of batting records. For each year column 1 gives his lifetime batting percentage as of the opening day of that season. Column 2 gives his batting percentage during the year. Column 3 gives his lifetime batting percentage at the end of the season, which, of course, is also the entry in column 1 for the next year.

The columns of the table provide an interesting example of the general relationship between average and marginal values: *whenever his performance during a season was better than his lifetime batting average at the start of the season, his lifetime batting average rose.* For example, in the years 1975, 1976, and 1977, Rose raised his lifetime batting average because each was an above-average year. *Whenever his performance during a season was worse than his lifetime batting average at the start of the season, his lifetime batting average fell.* For example, during the 1971, 1974, and 1980 seasons his performance was below his lifetime batting average going into those seasons, and hence in each case his lifetime batting average fell.

If the average is to rise, all that matters is that the marginal is above the average; if the average is to fall, all that matters is that the marginal is below the average.

	Pete Rose's Batting Record*		
	(Old average)	**(Marginal)**	**(New average)**
Year	Lifetime batting percentage at start of season	Batting percentage during season	Lifetime batting percentage at end of season
1963	0.0000	0.2729	0.2729
1964	0.2729	0.2694	0.2713
1965	0.2713	0.3119	0.2863
1966	0.2863	0.3135	0.2935
1967	0.2935	0.3009	0.2949
1968	0.2949	0.3355	0.3019
1969	0.3019	0.3477	0.3085
1970	0.3085	0.3159	0.3095
1971	0.3095	0.3038	0.3088
1972	0.3088	0.3070	0.3087
1973	0.3087	0.3382	0.3116
1974	0.3116	0.2837	0.3092
1975	0.3092	0.3172	0.3098
1976	0.3098	0.3233	0.3108
1977	0.3108	0.3115	0.3109
1978	0.3109	0.3023	0.3103
1979	0.3103	0.3312	0.3115
1980	0.3115	0.2824	0.3099
1981	0.3099	0.3248	0.3104
1982	0.3104	0.2713	0.3084
1983	0.3084	0.2454	0.3061
1984	0.3061	0.2830	0.3054
1985	0.3054	0.2642	0.3042

* Baseball fans will note that in order to allow changes in lifetime percentages to show up in all cases, the figures are reported to four decimal places rather than to the customary three decimal places.

Cost Concepts Defined

The relevant cost concepts are closely related to the product concepts just introduced.

Total cost (*TC*) is the total cost of producing any given level of output. Total cost is divided into two parts, *total fixed cost (TFC)* and *total variable cost*

(TVC). **Total fixed cost** does not vary with the level of output; it will be the same whether output is one unit or a million units. Such a cost is also referred to as an *overhead cost* or *unavoidable cost*. A cost that varies directly with output, rising as more output is produced and falling as less output is produced, is called a **total variable cost** (also a *direct* or *avoidable*

TABLE 10-2   Variation of Costs with Capital Fixed and Labor Variable

(1) Labor (L)	(2) Output (q)	Total cost ($)			Marginal cost ($ per unit)	Average cost ($ per unit)		
		(3) Fixed (TFC)	(4) Variable (TVC)	(5) Total (TC)	(6) (MC)	(7) Fixed (AFC)	(8) Variable (AVC)	(9) Total (ATC)
0	0	100	0	100		—	—	—
					0.67			
1	15	100	10	110		6.67	0.67	7.33
					0.53			
2	34	100	20	120		2.94	0.59	3.53
					0.71			
3	48	100	30	130		2.08	0.62	2.71
					0.83			
4	60	100	40	140		1.67	0.67	2.33
					5.00			
5	62	100	50	150		1.61	0.81	2.42

The relationship of cost to level of output can be looked at in several different ways. These cost schedules are computed from the product curves of Table 10–1, given the price of capital of $25 per unit and the price of labor of $10 per unit. Marginal cost (in column 6) is shown between the lines of total cost because it refers to the *change* in cost divided by the *change* in output that brought it about. For example, the *MC* of $.71 is the $10 increase in total cost (from $120 to $130) divided by the 14-unit increase in output (from 34 to 48). In constructing a graph, marginal costs should be plotted midway in the interval over which they are computed. The *MC* of $.71 would be plotted at an output of 41.

---

cost). In the example in Table 10-1, since labor is the variable factor of production, wages are a variable cost.

Average total cost (ATC), also called **average cost (AC),** is the total cost of producing any given number of units of output divided by that number. Average total cost is divided into **average fixed costs (AFC),** fixed cost is divided by quantity of output and **average variable costs (AVC),** variable cost is divided by quantity of output in the same way that total costs are.

Although average *variable costs* may rise or fall as production is increased (depending on whether output rises more rapidly or more slowly than total variable costs), it is clear that average *fixed costs* decline continuously as output increases. A doubling of output always leads to a halving of fixed costs per unit of output. This is a process popularly known as *spreading one's overhead.*

Marginal cost (MC), sometimes called **incremental cost,** is the increase in total cost resulting from raising the rate of production by one unit. Because fixed costs do not vary with output, marginal fixed costs are always zero. Therefore, marginal costs are necessarily marginal variable costs, and a change in fixed costs will leave marginal costs unaffected. For example, the marginal cost of producing a few more potatoes by farming a given amount of land more intensively is the same, whatever the rent paid for the land. [16]

Short-Run Cost Curves

Using the production relationships found in Table 10-1, assume that the price of labor is $10 per unit and that the price of capital is $25 per unit. The cost schedules that result from these values are shown in Table 10-2.

Figure 10-2 shows cost curves that are similar in shape to those arising from the data in Table 10-2. Notice that the marginal cost curve cuts the average total cost curve and the average variable cost curve at their lowest points. This is another example of the relationship between a marginal and an average curve. The *ATC* curve, for example, slopes downward as long as the *MC* curve is below it; it makes no difference whether the *MC* curve is itself sloping upward or downward.

To see this, consider an example in which 10 units are produced each week at an average cost of $5 per unit (total cost equals $50). The average cost of producing 11 units will exceed $5 if the eleventh unit adds more than $5 to the output (*MC* exceeds *AC*) and will be less than $5 if the eleventh unit adds less than $5 to the cost (*MC* is less than *AC*). The marginal cost of the tenth unit does not matter for this calculation. (It could be above, below, or equal to the eleventh unit's marginal cost.)[4]

---

[4] If you do not see where any of the numbers come from, review Table 10-1 and the definitions of cost just given.

FIGURE 10-2   Total Cost, Average Cost, and Marginal Cost Curves

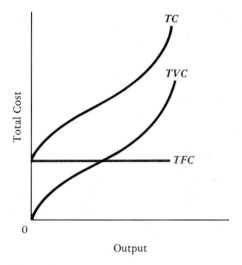

(i) Total cost curves

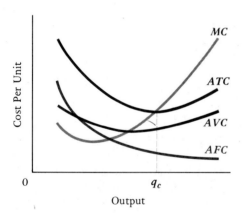

(ii) Marginal and average cost curves

Total cost (*TC*), average cost (*AC*), and marginal cost (*MC*) curves often have the shapes shown here. (i) Total fixed cost does not vary with output. Total variable cost and the total of all costs ($TC = TVC + TFC$) rise with output, first at a decreasing rate and then at an increasing rate. The total cost curves in (i) give rise to the average and marginal curves in (ii). Average fixed cost (*AFC*) declines as output increases. Average variable cost (*AVC*) and average total cost (*ATC*) fall and then rise as output increases. Marginal cost (*MC*) does the same, intersecting *ATC* and *AVC* at their minimum points. Capacity output is q_c, the minimum point on the *ATC* curve.

Short-run average variable cost. In Figure 10-2 the average variable cost curve reaches a minimum and then rises. With fixed factor prices, when average product per worker is at a maximum, average variable cost is at a minimum. **[17]** The common sense found in this proposition is that each additional worker adds the same amount to cost but a different amount to output, and when output per worker rises, the cost per unit of output must fall, and vice versa.

Eventually diminishing average productivity implies eventually increasing average variable costs.

Short-run average total cost curve. Short-run *ATC* curves are often U-shaped. This reflects the assumptions that (1) average productivity increases when output is low, but (2) at some level of output, average productivity begins to fall fast enough to cause average variable costs to increase faster than average fixed costs are falling. When this happens, *ATC* increases.

Marginal cost curves. In Figure 10-2(ii) the marginal cost curve is shown as a declining curve that reaches a minimum and then rises. This is the reverse of the shape of the marginal product curve in Figure 10-1(ii). The reason for the reversal is as follows. If extra units of a variable factor that is bought at a fixed price per unit result in increasing quantities of output (marginal *product rising*), the cost per unit of extra output must be falling (marginal *cost falling*). On the other hand, if marginal product is falling, then marginal cost will be rising. Thus the hypothesis of eventually diminishing marginal product implies eventually increasing marginal cost. **[18]**

Total variable cost. In Figure 10-2(i) total variable cost is shown as an upward-sloping curve, indicating that total variable cost rises with the level of output. This is true as long as marginal cost is positive, since the total variable cost of producing any given level of output is the area under the marginal cost curve up to that level of output. **[19]**

Definition of Capacity

The level of output that corresponds to the minimum short-run average total cost is often called the **capacity** of the firm. In this sense capacity is the largest output that can be produced without encountering rising average costs per unit. In Figure 10-2(ii) capacity output is q_c units, but higher outputs can be achieved, provided the firm is willing to accept the higher per unit costs that accompany any level of output that is "above capacity." A firm that is producing at an output less than the point of minimum average total cost has **excess capacity.**

The technical definition gives the word *capacity* a meaning that is different from the one used in everyday speech, in which it often means an upper limit that cannot be exceeded. The technical definition is, however, a useful concept that is widely used in economic and business discussions.

Shifts in Short-Run Cost Curves

So far we have seen how costs vary as output varies, with input prices being held constant. Figure 10-3 shows the effect on a firm's cost curves of a change in the price of any variable input. A rise in the price of any input used by the firm must raise the price of producing any given quantity of output. A fall in the price of any input has the opposite effect. This is a very simple relationship but nonetheless one that is important.

A change in the price of any variable input used by the firm will shift its variable and total cost curves—upward for a price increase and downward for a price decrease.

A Family of Short-Run Cost Curves

A short-run cost curve shows how costs vary with output for a given quantity of the fixed factor, say, a given size of plant.

FIGURE 10-3   The Effect of a Change in Input Prices

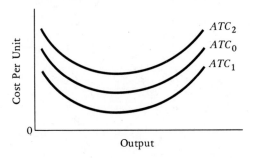

A change in any input price shifts the entire cost curve. The original average total cost curve is shown by ATC_0. A rise in the price of a variable input used by the firm must raise the price of producing each level of output. In the figure it shifts the average total cost curve upwards to ATC_2. Conversely, a fall in the price of a variable input used by the firm shifts the average total cost curve downward; in the figure this shift is to ATC_1.

There is a different short-run cost curve for each given quantity of the fixed factor.

A small plant that manufactures nuts and bolts will have its own short-run cost curve. A medium-size plant and a large plant will each have its own short-run cost curve. If a firm expands and replaces its small plant with a medium-size plant, it will move from one short-run cost curve to another. This change from one plant size to another is a long-run change. We shall discuss how short-run cost curves of plants of different sizes are related to each other in the next chapter.

SUMMARY

1. A firm's production decisions can be classified into three groups: (a) how best to employ existing plant and equipment—the short run, (b) what new plant and equipment and production processes to select, given the framework of known technical possibilities—the long run, and (c) how to encourage or to adapt to technological changes—the very long run.

2. The short run involves decisions in which one or more factors of production are fixed. The long run involves decisions in which all factors are variable but technology is given. The very long run involves decisions in which technology can change.

3. The production function shows the output that results from each possible combination of inputs. Short-run and long-run situations

can be interpreted as implying different kinds of constraints on the production function. In the short run the firm is constrained to·use no more than a *given* quantity of some fixed factor; in the long run it is constrained only by the available techniques of production.

4. The theory of short-run costs is concerned with how output varies as different amounts of the variable factors are combined with given amounts of the fixed factors. The concepts of total, average, and marginal product represent alternative relationships between output and the quantity of the variable factor of production.

5. The hypothesis of diminishing returns asserts that if increasing quantities of a variable factor are combined with given quantities of fixed factors, the marginal and the average products of the variable factor will eventually decrease. If factor prices are fixed, this hypothesis implies that marginal and average costs will eventually rise.

6. Given physical productivity schedules and the prices of inputs, it is a matter of simple arithmetic to develop the whole family of short-run cost curves, one for each quantity of the fixed factor.

7. Short-run average total cost curves are U-shaped. Average productivity increases at low levels of outputs but eventually declines sufficiently and rapidly to offset advantages of spreading overheads. The output corresponding to the minimum point of a short-run average total cost curve is called the plant's capacity.

8. Changes in factor prices shift the short-run cost curves—upward when prices rise and downward when prices fall. Thus, there is a whole family of short-run curves—one for each set of factor prices.

TOPICS FOR REVIEW

Short run, long run, and very long run
Total product, average product, and marginal product
The law of diminishing returns
Marginal product curves and average product curves
Relationship between productivity and cost
Total cost, marginal cost, and average cost
Short-run cost curves
Capacity and excess capacity

DISCUSSION QUESTIONS

1. Does the short run consist of the same number of months for increasing output as for decreasing it? Must the short run in an industry be the same length for all firms in the industry? Under what circumstances might the short run actually involve a longer time span than the very long run for one particular firm?

2. Use the distinction between long and short run to discuss each of the following.
    a. A guaranteed annual employment contract of at least forty-eight 40-hour weeks of work for all employees
    b. A major economic recession during which there is substantial unemployment of labor and in which equipment is being used at well below capacity levels of production
    c. A speeding up of delivery dates for new easy-to-install equipment

3. In 1921 experimenters who were working with chemical fertilizers at the Rothampsted Experimental Station, an agricultural research institute in Hertfordshire, England, applied different amounts of a particular fertilizer to 10 apparently identical quarter-acre plots of

land. The results for one test, using identical seed grain, are listed in the following table. Compute the average and marginal product of fertilizer, and identify the (approximate) points of diminishing average and marginal productivity.

Plot	Fertilizer dose	Yield index*
1	15	104.2
2	30	110.4
3	45	118.0
4	60	125.3
5	75	130.2
6	90	132.4
7	105	131.9
8	120	132.3
9	135	132.5
10	150	132.8

*Yield without fertilizer = 100

4. Indicate whether each of the following conforms to the hypothesis of diminishing returns and, if so, whether it refers to marginal or average returns, or to both.
   a. "The bigger they are, the harder they fall."
   b. As more and more of the population receive smallpox vaccinations, the reduction in the smallpox disease rate for each additional 100,000 vaccinations becomes smaller.
   c. Five workers produce twice as much today as 10 workers did 40 years ago.
   d. Diminishing returns set in last year when the rising rural population actually caused agricultural output to fall.

5. Consider the education of a human being as a process of production. Regard years of schooling as one variable factor of production. What are the other factors? What factors are fixed? At what point would you expect diminishing returns to set in? For an Albert Einstein, would diminishing returns set in during his lifetime?

6. Suppose that each of the following news items is correct. Discuss each in terms of its effects on cost. (You will have to decide which concept of cost is most likely to be affected.)
   a. A state board of education reports that the increasing level of education of youth has led both to higher productivity and to increases in the general level of wages.
   b. During the winter of 1977, because of fuel shortages, many factories were forced to reduce production and to operate at levels of production far below capacity.
   c. NASA, the U.S. agency for space exploration, reports that the space program has led to development of electronic devices that have brought innovations to many industries.

7. "Because overhead costs are fixed, increasing production lowers costs. Thus small business is sure to be inefficient. This is a dilemma of modern society, which values both smallness *and* efficiency." Discuss.

Chapter 11

Production and Cost in the Long and Very Long Runs

In this chapter we shall look first at *long-run* behavior, in which firms are free to vary all factors of production. Should firms use a great deal of capital and only a small amount of labor? Should they use less capital and more labor? What effects do these decisions have on firms' costs?

In the second part of the chapter we shall examine the *very long run*. The discussion concerns the improvements in technology and productivity that have dramatically increased output and incomes in all industrial countries during the past 100 years.

 ## The Long Run: No Fixed Factors

In the short run, in which only one factor varies, the only way to produce a given output is to adjust the input of the variable factor until the desired level of output is achieved. Thus, once the firm has decided on a rate of output, there is only one possible way of achieving it. In the long run, all factors can be varied, so there are numerous technically possible ways to produce any given output. Thus, the firm must decide both on a level of output *and* on how to produce that output. Specifically, this means that firms in the long run must choose the nature and amount of plant and equipment, as well as the size of their labor force.

In making this choice, the firm will wish to avoid being technically inefficient, which means using more of *all* inputs than are necessary. Being technically efficient is not enough, however. To be economically efficient, the firm must choose from among the many technically efficient ways of producing its output the one that produces that output at the lowest possible cost. Achieving the lowest possible opportunity cost means producing the output at the least possible sacrifice in the value of other outputs that could have been produced instead. (The distinction between various types of efficiency sometimes causes confusion, particularly when engineers and economists are involved in the same decision-making process. Box 11-1 elaborates on this distinction for those who wish to study it further.)

Long-run planning decisions are important. A firm that decides to build a new steel mill and to invest in machinery that will go into it will choose among many alternatives. Once installed, that equipment is fixed for a long time. If the firm makes a wrong choice, its survival may be threatened; if it estimates shrewdly, it may be rewarded with large profits.

BOX 11-1

Various Concepts of Efficiency

In popular discussion, in business decision making, and in government policies, three different types of efficiency concepts are often confused. These are engineering, technical, and economic efficiency. Each is a valid concept, and each conveys useful information. However, the use of one concept in a situation in which another is appropriate is a potential source of error and waste.

Engineering efficiency refers to the *physical* amount of some *single key input*. It is measured by the ratio of that input to output. For example, the engineering efficiency of an engine refers to the ratio of the amount of energy in the fuel burned by the engine to the amount of usable energy produced by the engine. The difference goes in friction, heat loss, and other unavoidable sources of waste. Saying that a steam engine is 40 percent efficient means that 40 percent of the energy in the coal that is burned in the boiler is converted into work that is done by the engine, while the other 60 percent is lost.

Technical efficiency (or technological efficiency) is related to the *physical* amount for *all factors* used in the process of producing some commodity. The production of a given output is technically inefficient if there exist other ways of producing the output that will use less of all inputs. Production is technically efficient if there exists no alternative that will use less of all inputs. (Economists often call technical inefficiency *X-inefficiency*.)

Economic efficiency is related to the *value* of *all inputs* used in producing a given output. The production of a given output is economically efficient if there is no other way of producing the output that will use a smaller total value of inputs.

What is the relationship between economic efficiency and these other two concepts? Technical efficiency is desirable as long as inputs are costly to the firm in any way. If a technically inefficient process is replaced by a technically efficient process, there is a saving of *all* inputs. We do not need to put a precise value on the cost of each input to make this judgment. All we need to know is that

inputs have some positive cost to the firm, so that saving on all of these costs is desirable.

Usually, however, any given output may be produced in any one of many alternative, technically efficient ways in the long run. Avoiding technical inefficiency is clearly a necessary condition for producing any output at the least cost. The existence of technical inefficiency means that costs can be reduced by reducing all inputs. Avoiding technical efficiency is not, however, a sufficient condition for producing at lowest possible cost. The firm must still ask: Which of the many technically efficient methods should it use? Here is where the concept of economic efficiency comes in. The method to be used is the one that uses the least value of inputs. When this is done, the firm has spent as little as possible on its given output, and, using the meaning of opportunity cost, the firm has sacrificed the least possible value in terms of other things that it might have done with the inputs used.

We have seen that engineering efficiency measures the efficiency with which a single input is used. Although knowing the efficiency of any given steam, electric, or diesel engine is interesting, increasing this efficiency is not necessarily economically efficient, because doing so usually requires the use of other valuable resources. For example, by using more and stronger steel in the firebox and the boiler, the engineering efficiency of a steam engine can be increased. Similar gains can be made in all types of engines in existence today. Raising the engineering efficiency of an engine saves on fuel, but at the cost of using more of other inputs. To know whether this is worth doing, the firm must compare the value of the fuel saved with the value of the other inputs used. Maximizing engineering efficiency is never desirable. The optimal level of engineering efficiency is achieved by increasing efficiency, as long as the value of the input saved exceeds the value of the extra resources used, but not by increasing efficiency into the range where the costs exceed the value of the input saved.

Long-run decisions are risky because the firm must anticipate what methods of production will be efficient not only today but also for many years ahead, when costs of labor and raw materials will no doubt have changed. The decisions are risky, too, because the firm must estimate how much output it will want to produce. Is the industry to which it belongs growing or declining? Will new products emerge to render its existing products, such as typewriters or records, less useful than an extrapolation of past sales suggests?

Profit Maximization and Cost Minimization

Any firm that is trying to maximize its profits should, in the long run, select the economically efficient method, which is the method that produces its output at the lowest possible cost. This implication of the hypothesis of profit maximization is called **cost minimization:** From the alternatives open to it, the profit-maximizing firm will choose the least costly way of producing whatever specific output that it chooses.

Choice of Factor Mix

If it is possible to substitute one factor for another to keep output constant while reducing total cost, the firm is not using the least costly combination of factors. In such a situation the firm should substitute one factor for another factor, as long as the marginal product of the one factor *per dollar* expended on it is greater than the marginal product of the other factor *per dollar* expended on it. The firm cannot minimize its costs as long as these two magnitudes are unequal. For example, if an extra dollar spent on labor produces more output than an extra dollar spent on capital, the firm can reduce costs by spending less on capital and more on labor.

If we use K to represent capital, L to represent labor, and p to represent the price of a unit of the factor, the necessary condition of cost minimization may be stated as follows:

$$\frac{MP_K}{p_K} = \frac{MP_L}{p_L}$$ [1]

Whenever the two sides of Equation 1 are not equal, there are possibilities for factor substitutions that will reduce costs.[1]

To see why this equation must be satisfied if costs of production are to be minimized, suppose that the left side of Equation 1 is equal to 10, showing that the last dollar spent on capital added 10 units to output, while the right side of Equation 1 is equal to 4, showing that the last dollar spent on labor added only 4 units to output. In such a case the firm, by using $2.50 less of labor, would reduce output by 10 units. It could regain that lost output, however, by spending $1.00 more on capital. Making such a substitution of capital for labor would leave output unchanged and reduce costs by $1.50. Thus the original position was not cost-minimizing.[2]

By rearranging the terms in Equation 1, we can look at the cost-minimizing condition a bit differently.[3]

$$\frac{MP_K}{MP_L} = \frac{p_K}{p_L}$$ [2]

The ratio of the marginal products on the left side of the equation compares the contribution to output of the last unit of capital and the last unit of labor. If the ratio is 4, this means that 1 unit more of capital will add 4 times as much to output as 1 unit more of labor. The right side of the equation shows how the cost of 1 unit more of capital compares to the cost of 1 unit more of labor. If the ratio is also 4, the firm cannot reduce costs by substituting capital for labor or vice versa. Now suppose that the ratio on the right side of the equation is 2. Capital, although twice as expensive, is four times as productive. It will pay the firm to switch to a method of production that uses more capital and less labor. If, however, the ratio on the right side is 6 (or *any* number more than 4), it will pay to switch to a method of production that uses more labor and less capital.

[1] Readers who read Appendix B to Chapter 7 should notice that Equation 1 is analogous to the condition for the utility-maximizing household, given on page 153, in which the household equated the ratio of the marginal utilities of each pair of goods with the ratio of their prices.

[2] The argument in this paragraph assumes that the marginal products do not change when expenditure changes by a small amount.

[3] The appendix to this chapter provides a graphical analysis of this condition, which is similar to the analysis of household behavior in Appendix A to Chapter 7.

How much should inputs be changed? We have seen that when the ratio MP_K/MP_L is 4, while the ratio P_K/P_L is 2, the firm will substitute capital for labor. How far does the firm go in making this substitution? There is a limit, because as the firm uses more capital, its marginal product falls, while as it uses less labor, the marginal product of labor rises. Thus the ratio MP_K/MP_L falls. When it reaches 2, the firm need substitute no further. The ratio of the marginal products is equal to the ratio of the prices.

Equation [2] shows how the firm can adjust the elements over which it has control (the quantities of factors used, and thus the marginal products of the factors) to the prices of the factors given by the market.

Long-Run Equilibrium of the Firm

The firm will have achieved long-run equilibrium factor proportions when there is no opportunity for cost-reducing substitutions. This occurs when the marginal product per dollar spent on each factor is the same (Equation 1), or, equivalently, when the ratio of the marginal products of factors is equal to the ratio of their prices (Equation 2).

The Principle of Substitution

Suppose that a firm is meeting the cost-minimizing conditions shown in Equations 1 and 2 and that the cost of labor increases while the cost of capital remains unchanged. The least-cost method of producing any output will now use less labor and more capital than was required to produce the same output before the factor prices changed.

Methods of production will change if the relative prices of factors change. Relatively more of the cheaper factor and relatively less of the more expensive factor will be used.

This is called the **principle of substitution,** and it follows from the assumption that firms minimize their costs.

The principle of substitution plays a central role in resource allocation, since it relates to the way in which individual firms respond to changes in relative

factor prices that are caused by the changing relative scarcities of factors in the economy as a whole. Individual firms are motivated to use less of factors that become scarcer to the economy and more of factors that become more plentiful. Here are two examples of the principle of substitution in action.

In recent decades, construction workers' wages have risen sharply relative to the wages of factory labor and the cost of machinery. In response, many home builders have shifted from on-site construction to panelization, which is a method of building that uses standardized modules. The wiring, plumbing, insulation, and painting of these standardized modules are all done at the factory. The bulk of the factory work is performed by machinery and by assembly line workers whose wages are only half those of on-site construction workers.

Some countries have plentiful land and small populations. Their land prices are low, and, because their labor is in short supply, their wage rates are high. In response, their farmers make lavish use of the cheap land while economizing on expensive labor; thus their production processes use low ratios of labor to land. Other countries are small in area but have large populations. The demand for land is high relative to its supply, and land is relatively expensive while labor is relatively cheap. In response, farmers economize on land by using much labor per unit of land; thus their production processes use high ratios of labor to land.

Once again we see the price system functioning as an automatic control system. No single firm needs to be aware of national factor surpluses and scarcities. These are reflected by market prices, so individual firms that never look beyond their own profits are led to economize on factors that are scarce to the nation as a whole.

This discussion suggests why methods of producing the same commodity differ among countries. In the United States, where labor is highly skilled and expensive, a farmer with a large farm may use elaborate machinery to economize on labor. In China, where labor is abundant and capital is scarce, a much less mechanized method of production is appropriate. The Western engineer who believes that the Chinese are inefficient because they are using methods long ago discarded in the West is missing the truth about efficiency in the use of resources. The notion that to aid underdeveloped countries we have only to export Western "know-how" is misleading.

Cost Curves in the Long Run

There is a best (least-cost) method of producing each level of output when all factors are free to be varied. In general, this method will not be the same for different levels of output. If factor prices are given, a minimum achievable cost can be found for each possible level of output; if this cost is expressed as a quantity per unit of output, we can obtain the long-run average cost of producing each level of output. When this least-cost method of producing each output is plotted on a graph, the result is called a **long-run average cost (LRAC) curve.** Figure 11-1 shows one such curve.

This cost curve is determined by the technology of the industry (which is assumed to be fixed) and by the prices of the factors of production. It is a "boundary" in the sense that points below it are unattainable; points on the curve, however, are attainable if sufficient time elapses for all inputs to be adjusted. To move from one point on the long-run average cost (LRAC) curve to another requires an adjustment in all inputs, which may, for example, require building a larger, more elaborate factory.

The LRAC curve is the boundary between those cost levels that are attainable with known technology and given factor prices from those that are unattainable.

The Shape of the Long-Run Average Cost Curve

The long-run average cost curve shown in Figure 11-1 first falls and then rises. This curve is often described as U-shaped, although "saucer-shaped" might be more accurate.

Decreasing costs. Over the range of output from zero to q_m the firm has falling long-run average costs: An expansion of output permits a reduction of costs per unit of output. These are referred to as **economies of scale.** (Of course, when output is increased, such economies of scale will be realized only after enough time has elapsed to allow changes in all factor inputs.) Since the prices of factors are assumed to be constant, the reason for the decline in long-run average cost must be that output is increasing *more than* in proportion to inputs as the scale of the firm's production expands. Over this range of output the

decreasing-cost firm is often said to enjoy long-run **increasing returns.**[4]

Increasing returns may occur as a result of increased opportunities for specialization of tasks made possible by the division of labor. Adam Smith's classic discussion of this important point is given in Box 3-1 on page 43. Even the most casual observation of the differences in production techniques used in large and small plants will show that larger plants use greater specialization.

These differences arise because large, specialized equipment is useful only when the volume of output that the firm can sell justifies employment of that equipment. For example, assembly line techniques, body-stamping machinery, and multiple-boring engine-block machines in automobile production are economically efficient only when individual operations are repeated thousands of times. Use of elaborate harvesting equipment (which combines many individual tasks that would otherwise be done by hand and by tractor) provides the least-cost method of production on a big farm but not on a few acres.

Typically, as the level of planned output increases, capital is substituted for labor and complex machines are substituted for simpler machines. Robotics is a contemporary example. Electronic devices can handle huge numbers of operations quickly, but unless the level of production requires such a large volume of operations, robotics or other forms of automation will not provide the least-cost method of production.

The preceding discussion refers to the technology of production, which is one major source of increasing returns to scale. A second source lies in the geometry that is intrinsic to the three-dimensional world in which we live. To illustrate how geometry may matter, consider a firm that wishes to store a gas or a liquid. The firm is interested in the *volume* of storage space. However, the materials cost of a storage container is related to the *area* of its surface. When the size of a container is increased, the storage capacity, which is determined by its volume, increases faster than its surface area.

Consider, for example, a cubic container with metal sides, bottom, and lid, all of which measure 1 foot by 1 foot. To build this container, 6 square feet

---

[4] Economists shift back and forth between speaking in physical terms (i.e., *increasing returns to scale*) and cost terms (i.e., *decreasing costs of production*). As we have seen in the text, the same relationship can be expressed in either terms.

of metal are required (six sides, each of which is 1 square foot), and it will hold 1 cubic foot of gas or liquid. Now increase all of the lengths of each of the container's sides to 2 feet. Twenty-four square feet of metal are now required (six, each of which is 4 square feet), and the container will hold 8 cubic feet of gas or liquid (2 feet × 2 feet × 2 feet). So, increasing the amount of metal in the container's walls by fourfold has the effect of increasing its capacity by eightfold. This is a genuine case of increasing returns—the output, in terms of storage capacity, increases more proportionately than the increase in the costs of the required construction materials.

A third source of increasing returns is inputs that do not have to be increased as the output of a product is increased, even in the long run. For example, there are often large fixed costs in developing new products, such as a new generation of airplanes or a more powerful computer. These R&D costs have to be incurred only once for each product and hence are independent of the scale at which the product is subsequently produced.

Even if the product's total *production costs* increase in proportion to output in the long run, average total costs, including *product development costs,* will fall as the scale of output rises. This phenomenon is popularly referred to as "spreading one's overheads." It is similar to what happens in the short run when average fixed costs fall with output. The difference is that fixed short-run production costs are variable long-run production costs. If the firm increases its scale of output for some product, it will incur more capital costs in the long run as a larger plant is built. However, its costs of developing that product are not affected. The influence of such once-and-for-all costs is, other things being equal, that they cause average total costs to be falling over the entire range of output. (The significance of such once-and-for-all costs is discussed in several places throughout the next three chapters.)

Increasing costs.   Over the range of outputs greater than q_m the firm encounters rising long-run costs. An expansion in production, even after sufficient time has elapsed for all adjustments to be made, will be accompanied by a rise in average costs per unit of output. If costs per unit of input are constant, the firm's output must be increasing *less than* in proportion to the increase in inputs. When this happens the increasing-cost firm is said to encounter long-run

decreasing returns.[5] Decreasing returns imply that the firm suffers some diseconomy of scale. As its scale of operations increases, diseconomies are encountered that increase its per unit cost of production.

These diseconomies may be associated with the difficulties of managing and controlling an enterprise as its size increases. For example, planning problems do not necessarily vary in direct proportion to size. At first, there may be scale economies as the firm grows, but, sooner or later, planning and coordination problems may multiply more than in proportion to the growth in size. If so, management costs per unit of output will rise. Other sources of scale diseconomies concern the possible alienation of the labor force as size increases and the difficulties of providing appropriate supervision as more and more tiers of supervisors and middle managers come between the person at the top and the workers on the shop floor. Control of middle-range managers may also become more difficult. As the firm becomes larger, managers may begin to pursue their own goals rather than devote all of their efforts to making profits for the firm. (This is the principal-agent problem that is discussed in detail on page 317.)

Constant costs.   In Figure 11-1 the firm's long-run average costs fall until output reaches q_m and rises thereafter. Another possibility should be noted. The firm's *LRAC* curve might have a flat portion over a range of output around q_m. With such a flat portion, the firm would be encountering constant costs over the relevant range of output. This means that the firm's long-run average costs per unit of output do not change as its output changes. Since factor prices are assumed to be fixed, the firm's output must be increasing *exactly in proportion to* the increase in inputs. A firm in this situation is said to be encountering **constant returns.**

Relationship Between Long-Run and Short-Run Costs

The family of short-run cost curves mentioned at the conclusion of Chapter 10 and the long-run curve

---

[5] Long-run decreasing returns differ from the short-run diminishing returns. In the short run at least one factor is fixed, and the law of diminishing returns ensures that returns to the variable factor will eventually diminish. In the long run all factors are variable, and it is possible that physically diminishing returns would never be encountered—at least as long as it was genuinely possible to increase inputs of all factors.

FIGURE 11-1   A Long-Run Average Cost Curve

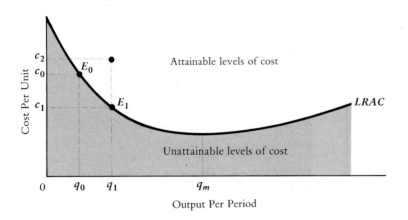

The long-run average cost ($LRAC$)
curve provides a boundary between attainable and unattainable levels of
costs. If the firm wishes to produce output
q_0, the lowest attainable cost level is c_0 per
unit. Thus, point E_0 is on the $LRAC$ curve.
E_1 represents the least-cost method of producing q_1. Suppose that a firm is producing
at E_0 and desires to increase output to q_1. In
the short run it will not be able to vary all
factors, and thus costs above c_1, say, c_2,
must be accepted. In the long run a plant
optimal for output q_1 can be built, and the
cost of c_1 can be attained. At output q_m the
firm attains its lowest possible per unit cost
of production for the given technology and
factor prices.

studied in this chapter are all derived from the same
production function. Each curve assumes given
prices for all factor inputs. In the long run all factors
can be varied; in the short run some must remain
fixed. The long-run average cost ($LRAC$) curve
shows the lowest cost of producing any output when
all factors are variable. Each short-run average total
cost ($SRATC$) curve shows the lowest cost of producing any output when one or more factors are held
constant at some specific level.

No short-run cost curve can fall below the long-
run curve because the $LRAC$ curve represents the
lowest attainable cost for each possible output. As the
level of output is changed, a different size plant normally is required to achieve the lowest attainable
costs. This is shown in Figure 11-2, where the
$SRATC$ curve lies above the $LRAC$ curve at all
outputs except q_0.

As we observed at the end of Chapter 10, an
$SRATC$ curve, such as the one shown in Figure
11-2, is one of many such curves. Each curve shows
how costs vary as output is varied from a base output, holding the fixed factor at the quantity most
appropriate to that output. Figure 11-3 shows a family of short-run average total cost curves, along with
a single long-run average cost curve. The long-run
average cost curve sometimes is called an **envelope**
because it encloses, by being tangent to, a series of

short-run average total cost curves. Each short-run
average total cost curve is tangent to (touches) the
long-run average cost curve at the level of output for
which the quantity of the fixed factor is optimal and
lies above it for all other levels of output.[6]

Shifts in Cost Curves

The cost curves derived so far show how cost varies
with output, given constant factor prices and fixed
technology. Changes in either technological knowledge or factor prices will cause the entire family of
short-run and long-run average cost curves to shift.
Loss of existing technological knowledge is rare, so
technological change normally causes change in only
one direction, to shift cost curves downward. Improved ways of making existing commodities mean
that lower-cost methods of production become available. (Technological change is discussed in more detail in the next section of this chapter.)

Changes in factor prices can exert an influence in
either direction. If a firm has to pay more for any

---

[6] Notice that, since all costs are variable in the long run, we do
not need to distinguish between AVC, AFC, and ATC, as we did
in the short run; in the long run there is only one $LRAC$ for any
given set of input prices.

FIGURE 11-2   Long-Run Average Cost and Short-
            Run Average Cost Curves

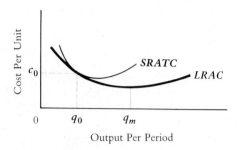

The short-run average total cost (*SRATC*) curve is
tangent to the long-run average cost (*LRAC*) curve
at the output for which the quantity of the fixed
factors is optimal. If output is varied around q_0 units
with plant and equipment fixed at the optimal level for
producing q_0, costs will follow the short-run cost curve.
Whereas *SRATC* and *LRAC* are at the same level for
output q_0, where the fixed plant is optimal for that level,
for all other outputs there is too little or too much plant
and equipment, and *SRATC* lies above *LRAC*. If some
output other than q_0 is to be sustained, costs can be reduced to the level of the long-run average cost curve
when sufficient time has elapsed to adjust the plant and
equipment.

factor that it uses, the cost of producing each level
of output will rise; if the firm has to pay less for any
factor that it uses, the cost of producing each level
of output will fall.

A rise in factor prices shifts the family of short-
run and long-run average cost curves upward.
A fall in factor prices, or a technological advance, shifts the entire family of average cost
curves downward.

   Although factor prices usually change gradually,
sometimes they change suddenly and drastically. For
example, in the mid-1980s oil prices fell dramatically;
the effect was to shift downward the cost curves of
all users of oil and oil-related products.

The Very Long Run

In the long run, profit-maximizing firms do the best
they can to produce known products with the techniques and the resources currently available. This
means being *on*, rather than above, their long-run
cost curves. In the very long run the techniques
and resources that are available change. Such
changes cause *shifts* in long-run cost curves.
These shifts, along with the development of new
products, are major sources of economic growth—
the long-run rise in output that accounts for rising
living standards.
   The decrease in costs that can be achieved by
choosing wisely among available factors of production, known techniques, and alternative levels of output is necessarily limited, since a firm can never do
better in the long run than to select the best available

FIGURE 11-3   The Envelope Relationship Between the Long-Run
            Average Cost Curve and All the Short-Run
            Average Cost Curves

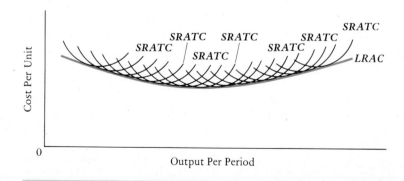

To every point on the long-run average
cost (*LRAC*) curve there is an associated short-run average total cost
(*SRATC*) curve tangent at that point.
Each short-run curve shows how costs vary
if output varies, with the fixed factor being
held constant at the level that is optimal for
the output at the point of tangency.

technique. Improvements by invention and innovation are potentially limitless, however, and for this reason, sustained growth in living standards is critically linked to technological change.

Kinds of Technological Change

Three kinds of change dominate production and cost in the very long run. All are related to technology, broadly defined.

New techniques. Throughout this century, changes in the techniques available for producing existing products have been dramatic. About the same amount of coal is produced in America today as was produced 50 years ago, but the number of coal miners is less than one-tenth of what it was then. Eighty years ago roads and railways were built by gangs of workers who used buckets, spades, and draft horses. Today bulldozers, steam shovels, giant trucks, and other specialized equipment have banished the workhorse completely from construction sites and to a great extent have displaced the pick-and-shovel worker. Generally, capital has been substituted for labor.

New products. New goods and services constantly are being invented and marketed. Television, polio vaccine, nylon, personal computers, and many other current consumer products did not exist 50 years ago. Other products have changed so dramatically that the only connection they have with the "same" commodity that was produced in the past is the name. A 1990 Ford automobile is very different from a 1920 Ford. It is even different from a 1970 Ford in size, safety, and gasoline consumption. Modern jets are revolutionary compared with the DC-3, which was the workhorse of the airlines during the 1930s and 1940s. In turn, the DC-3 bore little resemblance—beyond having wings and an engine—to the Wright brothers' airplane, which made its historic flight during the lifetime of some living Americans.

Improved inputs. Improvements in such intangibles as health and education raise the quality of labor services. Today's workers and managers are healthier and better educated than their grandparents. Many of today's unskilled workers are literate and competent in arithmetic, and their managers are apt to

be trained in modern scientific methods of business management and computer science.

Similarly, improvements in raw materials occur. For example, the type and quality of metals have changed. Steel has replaced iron, and aluminum substitutes for steel in a process of change that makes a statistical category such as "primary metals" seem unsatisfactory. Even for a given category, say, steel, today's product is lighter, stronger, and more flexible than the "same" product manufactured only 15 years ago.

Sources of Technological Change

Technological change refers to all changes in the available techniques of production. To measure its extent, economists use the notion of **productivity,** defined as a measure of output produced per unit of resource input. The rate of increase in productivity provides a measure of the progress caused by technological change. Growth in productivity highlights society's ability to get more and better output from given resources. The significance of such growth is explored further in Box 11-2. Here are some of the major historical sources of productivity increase.

One widely used measure of productivity is output *per hour* of labor. This is the measure we shall use. Other possible measures include output *per worker,* output *per person,* and output *per unit* of inputs, measured by an index number.

Substitution of Capital for Labor

Manufacturing, transportation, communications, mining, and agriculture all have seen a steady substitution of capital for labor over the years. This substitution is measured by changes in the **capital-labor ratio**—the amount of capital per worker in an economy—which has increased continually for more than 100 years.

Three reasons for this substitution can be identified. First, the price of labor has risen relative to capital goods. As predicted by the principle of substitution, this has led to the use of more capital and less labor per unit of output. Second, machines have become more and more productive over time, so a laborer working with a typical machine will produce much more now than in the past. Third, growing demand—due to a rising population and a rising per capita income—has allowed each industry to produce

BOX 11-2

The Significance of Productivity Growth

Economics used to be known as "the dismal science" because some of its predictions were dismal. Malthus and other classical economists predicted that the pressure of more and more people on the world's limited resources would cause a decline in output per person due to the operation of the law of diminishing returns. Human history would see more and more people living less and less well and the surplus population that could not be supported dying off from hunger and disease.

This prediction has proven wrong for the developed countries, for two main reasons. First, their populations have not expanded as rapidly as foreseen by early economists, who were writing before birth control techniques were widely used. Second, pure knowledge and its applied techniques have expanded so rapidly during the past 150 years that the ability to squeeze more out of limited resources has expanded faster than the population. We have experienced sustained growth in productivity that permits increases in output per person.

Productivity increases are a powerful force for increasing living standards. To our great-grandparents, the standard of living that exists today in most industrialized countries would have been inconceivable. An apparently modest rate of increase in productivity of 2.0 percent per year leads to a doubling of output per hour of labor every 35 years. American productivity increased at a rate somewhat greater than this throughout most of the twentieth century.

The growth rates of other countries have been even higher. Between 1945 and 1980 German productivity increased at 5 percent per year, doubling its output every 14 years. In Japan it increased at more than 9 percent per year, a rate that doubles output per hour of labor approximately every 8 years! In many countries, a stable rate of productivity growth came to be taken for granted as an automatic source of ever-increasing living standards.

During the 1970s the American rate of productivity growth dropped sharply below its historical trend. From 1977 to 1982 American nonagricultural productivity did not increase at all. Since 1982 productivity growth has resumed at about 2 percent per year, only to falter again later in the decade—the rate being well under 1 percent in 1988. It remains to be seen whether the slowdown was a one-time occurrence or whether the accustomed doubling of productivity in every generation is now a thing of the past.

A permanent slowdown in productivity growth would have severe consequences. Declining productivity growth means that living standards rise more slowly, or actually decline.

larger outputs by using more capital, thereby taking advantage of economies of scale.

Energy Substitution

Related to the substitution of capital for labor has been the increasing reliance on inanimate energy for production. Energy to plow fields, to turn machines, to move goods, to provide heat, and to transform natural resources is a major determinant of the productive power of an economy. In 1900 more than one-half of all American energy requirements was supplied by human beings, horses, mules, and oxen. By 1990 human and animal power provided well under 10 percent of all energy that was consumed; they have been replaced by coal, oil, gas, nuclear power, and hydroelectric power.

Invention and Innovation

Invention is the discovery of something new, such as a production technique or a product. **Innovation**

is the introduction of an invention into methods of production. Invention is thus a precondition to innovation.

Invention is cumulative in effect. A useful invention is adopted; a useless one is discarded. The cumulative impact of many small, useful devices and techniques may be as great as the impact of one occasional dramatic mechanism such as the steam engine, the cotton gin, or the sewing machine. Indeed, few famous inventions have sprung from a single act of creative inspiration; usually each builds on the contributions of prior inventors. The backlog of past inventions constitutes society's technical knowledge, and that backlog in turn feeds innovation.

Innovation depends on a steady supply of new inventions. However, new methods, machines, materials, and products do not come into use simply because they have been invented. They are introduced if and when it appears profitable to do so, and they flourish if their production proves to be profitable.

The Endogenous Nature of Technological Change

Technological change once was thought to be mainly a random process, brought about by inventions made by crackpots and eccentric scientists working in garages or basements. We now know better.

Changes in technology are often *endogenous responses* to changing economic signals; that is, they are responses to the same things that induce the substitution of one factor for another within a given technology. In our discussion of long-run demand curves in Chapter 5, we looked at just such technological changes in response to rising relative prices when we spoke of the development of smaller, more fuel-efficient cars in the wake of rising gasoline prices. Similarly, much of the move to substitute capital for labor in industry in response to rising wage rates has taken the form of inventing new, labor-saving methods of production.

Invention frequently can be produced on demand; the development of the atomic bomb in the 1940s is a dramatic example of this. Money and determination can buy invention. Major technological changes are often the result of expenditures on research and

development (R&D). In the United States in 1988, just over $100 billion was devoted to such expenditures, of which roughly 40 percent was expended by the federal government, 40 percent by private firms, and the rest by universities and other research institutions.

Current evidence indicates that productivity growth to a significant degree is a response to investment in research. Those countries, particularly Germany and Japan, that have stepped up R&D expenditures have experienced much higher levels of productivity growth than those countries (e.g., the United States, Canada, and the United Kingdom) that have let such expenditures lag. Similarly, industries that are major R&D spenders (e.g., chemicals, electrical equipment, air transport) have maintained productivity growth at a much higher level than industries that do little research (e.g., steel and construction). Some sectors that do little research, such as coal mining and farming, may buy their inputs (such as equipment, fertilizer, and seed) from industries that do much R&D, achieving gains in productivity as a result. These sectors buy invention and innovation through the price they pay for inputs.

Innovation has an unmistakably endogenous component, rising as profit incentives increase, declining as they fall. Profit incentives in turn are affected by many aspects of the economic climate, among them the rate of growth of the economy, the cost and availability of money for investment, and all sorts of government policies from taxes to regulations. Some of the important lessons that can be learned from the slackening in productivity growth a decade ago are discussed in Box 11-3.

How Much Productivity Growth Do We Want?

There remains an important question about social values. Progress has come to mean growth, and growth usually has meant industrialization. Applied to the economy as a whole, industrialization, and its accompanying changes in productivity, have changed our material well-being vastly and have permitted ever more people to escape hunger and poverty.

Paradoxically, however, slowdowns in productivity growth are sometimes a part of the growth

BOX 11-3

Causes of Decline in Productivity Growth

The rate of productivity growth in the United States slackened in the 1970s and early 1980s. Not surprisingly, this raised fears that the slowdown might be permanent. The partial recovery of productivity growth in the mid-1980s showed that the more extreme views of the end of productivity-driven growth were unfounded. Here we shall discuss some of the possible sources of such a slowdown in productivity growth.

Exhaustion of growth opportunities. When a country starts to industrialize, labor is generally employed in labor-intensive, low-productivity industries. As labor shifts into high-productivity, capital-intensive industries, productivity rises. As a country becomes industrialized, there is less possibility for further gains in productivity, since most of the labor has already shifted from low- to high-productivity sectors.

Abundance of energy. Falling energy prices assisted American productivity growth for a century. Each worker was supplied with more and more of ever cheapening energy, so each could produce more output. In the early 1970s oil became scarce and expensive. Rising energy costs slowed productivity increases by reducing the amount of energy that it was profitable to combine with each worker. Now that energy costs are again falling, productivity is rising.

Demographic changes. Growth of per capita income is easier to achieve in a moderately increasing population than in a static or a declining one. When relatively few industries and firms are expanding, less investment will take place and firms will tend to keep the existing plant and equipment in place. Every time a firm undertakes new investment, it is likely to adopt the most modern technology available. A growing industry often has profitable opportunities for investment geared to a larger scale of output.

Similarly, it is easier for labor to adapt to the changing requirements of growth when the population is growing rather than when it is remaining static. It is harder to retrain existing workers than to train new workers in newly needed skills—and the faster the population is growing, the more new workers there will be in any one year. Moreover, a fall in the growth rate also causes a fall in the rate at which new occupations and promotion opportunities are being developed. This, in turn, may discourage young people from acquiring the fresh skills that contribute to further productivity growth.

Shifts in the composition of output. During recent decades in the United States there has been a major shift of demand from high-productivity manufacturing to lower-productivity services. Fast-food

process itself. The current shift to the provision of services with high income elasticities but low productivity levels is the most obvious example. People spend much of the increases in their income that growth has provided on entertainment, travel, education, and other services and less and less on manufactured products.

Few things in this world come without some cost. Growth in productivity is often accompanied by increased pollution and more industrial accidents. The gasoline engine, the steel mill, the jet airplane, DDT, plastics, and the skyscraper with its hundreds

of thousands of electric lights are the artifacts of our progress over the last century. Many believe that some of these have in some ways lowered the real quality of life, while at the same time they have raised the measured standard of living.

Just as members of a society can benefit (at some stage of economic development) from more luxuries and fewer basic necessities, so, too, they may sometimes benefit from more amenities and a lower productivity growth. To the extent that they can, a slower rate of productivity growth may reflect a better life, not a worse one.

and other services—such as garbage collection, clean air, police protection, libraries, and medical and hospital care—tend to have a lower value of output per worker than is typical in manufacturing industries. The shifts of labor from sectors with relatively high levels of productivity (largely due to abundant capital per worker) to those with much lower levels has decreased average productivity. This has nothing to do with the skill or dedication of the librarian compared to the factory worker; it is related to the nature of their tasks and the tools at their disposal. In the librarian's production of services there is no counterpart to the highly automated assembly line where automobiles are produced.

Low saving and investment.   For some time now, the United States has had one of the lowest ratios of private savings to national income among the world's advanced countries. Thus, a significant amount of investment has had to be financed out of foreign-owned funds. This in itself need not reduce the U.S. growth rate, although it will, over the years, increase the proportion of U.S. income accruing to foreign residents. Of more importance to the growth rate is the declining amount of investment. The ratio of net private investment to national income (as measured by GNP) has declined in every single decade since World War II. From

nearly 8 percent of GNP in the 1950s, net private investment fell to an average of just under 5 percent for the first eight years of the 1980s.

Institutional climate.   The profits from innovation depend, among other things, on tax laws and regulatory requirements. If innovators are allowed to reap large gains from successful innovations, they will be more likely to take the risks of innovating. Innovation can be encouraged by investment tax credits, strong patent laws, low tax rates, government subsidies, and government-assisted R&D. It can be discouraged by regulatory burdens such as environmental impact statements, safety regulation, and the hassle and delays involved in meeting government requirements.

Many believe that the institutional climate in the United States became increasingly hostile to private innovation during the 1960s and 1970s and that high taxes, government regulations, and economic protection all added to the forces inhibiting innovation and growth. Part of the supply-side economic revolution of the 1980s was an attempt to make the economic climate more favorable to innovation.

SUMMARY

1. There are no fixed factors in the long run. Profit-maximizing firms choose from the alternatives open to them the least-cost method of achieving any specific output. A long-run cost curve represents the boundary between attainable and unattainable levels of cost for the given technology.
2. The principle of substitution says that efficient production will use cheaper factors lavishly and more expensive ones economically. If the relative prices of factors change, relatively more of cheaper factors and relatively less of more expensive ones will be used.
3. The shape of the long-run cost curve depends on the relationship of inputs to outputs as the whole scale of a firm's operations changes. Increasing, constant, and decreasing returns lead to decreasing, constant, and increasing long-run average costs.

4. The long-run and short-run cost curves are related. Every long-run cost corresponds to *some* quantity of each factor and is thus on some short-run cost curve. The short-run cost curve shows how costs vary when that particular quantity of a fixed factor is used to produce outputs greater than or less than the output for which it is optimal.

5. Cost curves shift upward or downward in response to changes in the prices of factors or changed technology. Increases in factor prices shift cost curves upward. Decreases in factor prices, or technological advances, shift cost curves downward.

6. Over extended periods, the most important influence on costs of production and on standards of living has been the very-long-run increases in output made possible by new technology, which has led to new techniques, new products, and improved inputs.

7. Major sources of productivity growth in industrializing countries include the substitution of capital for labor (an increasing capital-labor ratio), increased energy use, and invention and innovation.

8. Innovation is the key to productivity growth. It requires invention but also profitable opportunities for the introduction of available knowledge. Thus innovation and the changes in technology it brings are partly endogenous. The state of the economy, the institutional climate, and differences in technological possibilities in sectors where demand is growing and declining all affect the opportunities for innovation.

9. Material progress leads both to more goods and services per person and to opportunities for better living. Yet such progress is a mixed blessing; pollution and an increased number of injuries and accidents accompany growth in productivity. Expenditures to control pollution and increase safety are examples of things that may decrease measured productivity, while improving the quality of life.

TOPICS FOR REVIEW

Implication of cost minimization
Interpretation of $MP_K/MP_L = p_K/p_L$ and $MP_K/p_K = MP_L/p_L$
The principle of substitution
Increasing, decreasing, and constant returns
Economies of scale
Envelope curve
Distinction between production and productivity
Level of productivity and rate of growth of productivity
Sources of increasing productivity
Invention and innovation
Determinants of innovation
Causes of the slowdown in growth of productivity

DISCUSSION QUESTIONS

1. Why does the profit-maximizing firm choose the least-cost method of producing any given output? Might a nonprofit-maximizing organization such as a university, church, or government intentionally choose a method of production other than the least-cost one?

2. In Dacca, Bangladesh, where gasoline costs $3.00 per gallon and labor is typically paid less than $.20 per hour, Abdul Khan pedals a bicycle-ricksha (pedicab) for his living. It is exhausting work that is coming under increasing attack by those who feel it is an inhumane practice. "We really want to get rid of them and move to

motorized taxis, but I'm afraid it will take a long, long time," says a Bangladesh information officer. Ricksha drivers earn $2.00 per day, which is more than a skilled worker gets in Dacca. Explain the use of pedicabs in Dacca but not in New York or Tokyo. Comment on the information officer's statement.

3. Use the principle of substitution to predict the effect of each of the following.

   a. During the 1960s salaries of professors rose much more rapidly than those of teaching assistants. During the 1970s salaries of teaching assistants rose more than those of professors. During the 1980s the relative salaries of these two groups did not change greatly.

   b. The cost of land in big cities increases more than the cost of high-rise construction.

   c. Gold leaf is produced by pounding gold with a hammer. The thinner it is, the more valuable it is. The price of gold is set on the world market, but the price of labor varies among countries.

   d. Wages of textile workers and shoe machinery operators rise more in New England than in South Carolina.

4. The long-run average cost curve can be thought of as consisting of a series of points, one pulled from each of a number of short-run average total cost curves. Explain in what sense any point on the long-run average cost curve is also on some short-run average total cost curve. What is the meaning of a move from one point on a long-run average cost curve to another point on the same curve? Contrast this with a movement along a short-run average total cost curve.

5. During the "energy crisis" of the 1970s, the director of federal energy programs urged the American people to make necessary "long-run adjustments to the energy shortage by reducing energy input per unit of output." How exactly might this be done? Is this use of *long run* also the economists' use of *long run*? During the 1980s the price of many types of energy fell relative to the price level. What effects would this have?

6. Israel, a small country, imports the "insides" of its automobiles, but it manufactures the bodies. If this makes economic sense, what does it tell us about cost conditions of automobile manufacturers?

7. Name five important modern products that were not available when you were in grade school. Make a list of major products that you think have increased their sales at least tenfold during the past 30 years. Check your judgment by consulting the *Statistical Abstract of the United States, Business Statistics* (a biennial publication of the U.S. Department of Commerce), or similar sources. Consider to what extent the growth in each list may reflect product or process innovation.

8. Each of the following is a means of increasing productivity. Discuss which groups within a society might oppose each one.

   a. A labor-saving invention that permits all goods to be manufactured with less labor than before

   b. Rapidly increasing growth of population in the economy

   c. Removal of all government production safety rules

   d. Reduction in corporate income taxes

   e. Reduction in production of services and increase in agricultural production

9. Mobil Oil Chairman Rawleigh Warner, Jr., was quoted in the press as saying: "Our government has adopted a gratuitously hostile attitude. Industry has been compelled to spend more and more of its research dollars to comply with environmental, health and safety regulations—and to move away from longer-term efforts aimed at major scientific advance." Suppose this is true. Is it necessarily a sign that government policies are misguided?

Appendix to Chapter 11

Isoquants: An Alternative Analysis of the Firm's Input Decisions

The production function gives the relationship between the factor inputs that the firm uses and the output that it obtains. In the long run the firm can choose among many different combinations of inputs that will yield the same output. The production function and the long-run choices open to the firm can be represented graphically using what are called *isoquants*.

A Single Isoquant

Table 11A-1 illustrates a hypothetical example in which several different combinations of two inputs (labor and capital) can produce a given quantity of output. The data from Table 11A-1 are plotted

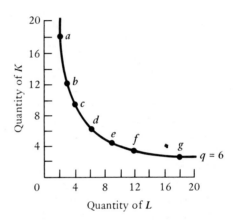

FIGURE 11A-1   An Isoquant for Output of 6 Units

Isoquants are downward sloping and convex. The downward slope reflects the requirement of technological efficiency. A method that uses more of one factor must use less of the other factor if it is to be technologically efficient. The convex shape of the isoquant reflects a diminishing marginal rate of substitution. The lettered points on the graph are plotted from the data in Table 11A-1. Starting from point *a*, which uses relatively little labor and much capital, and moving to point *b*, 1 additional unit of labor can substitute for 6 units of capital (while holding production constant). However, from *b* to *c*, 1 unit of labor substitutes for only 3 units of capital. This diminishing rate is expressed geometrically by the flattening of the slope of the isoquant.

TABLE 11A-1	Alternative Methods of Producing 6 Units of Output: Points on an Isoquant			

Method	K	L	ΔK	ΔL	Rate of substitution ΔK/ΔL
a	18	2			
b	12	3	−6	1	−6.0
c	9	4	−3	1	−3.0
d	6	6	−3	2	−1.5
e	4	9	−2	3	−0.67
f	3	12	−1	3	−0.33
g	2	18	−1	6	−0.17

An isoquant describes the firm's alternative methods for producing a given output. The table lists some of the methods indicated by a production function as being available to produce 6 units of output. The first combination uses a great deal of capital (*K*) and very little labor (*L*). As we move down the table, labor is substituted for capital in such a way as to keep output constant. Finally, at the bottom, most of the capital has been replaced by labor. The rate of substitution between the two factors is calculated in the last three columns of the table. Note that as we move down the table, the absolute value of the rate of substitution declines.

graphically in Figure 11A-1. A smooth curve is drawn through the points to indicate that there are additional ways, which are not listed in the table, of producing 6 units.

This curve is called an **isoquant.** It shows the whole set of technologically efficient factor combinations for producing a given level of output—6 units in this case. This is an example of graphing a relationship among three variables in two dimensions. It is analogous to the contour line on a map, which shows all points of equal altitude, and to an indifference curve, which shows all combinations of commodities that yield an equal utility.

As we move from one point on an isoquant to another, we are *substituting one factor for another* while holding output constant. If we move from point *b* to point *c,* we are substituting 1 unit of labor for 3 units of capital. The marginal rate of substitution measures the rate at which one factor is substituted for another with output being held constant. Graphically, the marginal rate of substitution is measured by the slope of the isoquant at a particular point. Table 11A-1 shows the calculation of some rates of substitution between various points of the isoquant. [20]

The marginal rate of substitution is related to the marginal products of the factors of production. To see how, consider an example. Assume that at the present level of inputs of labor and capital the marginal product of 1 unit of labor is 2 units of output, while the marginal product of capital is 1 unit of output. If the firm reduces its use of capital and increases its use of labor to keep output constant, it needs to add only ½ unit of labor for 1 unit of capital given up. If, at another point on the isoquant with more labor and less capital, the marginal products are 2 for capital and 1 for labor, then the firm will have to add 2 units of labor for every unit of capital it gives up. The general proposition is

The marginal rate of substitution between two factors of production is equal to the ratio of their marginal products.

Isoquants satisfy two important conditions: They are downward sloping, and they are convex viewed from the origin. What is the economic meaning of these conditions?

The downward slope indicates that each factor input has a positive marginal product. If the input of one factor is reduced and that of the other is held constant, output will be reduced. Thus, if input of one factor is decreased, production can be held constant only if input of the other factor is increased. The marginal rate of substitution has a negative value. Decreases in one factor must be balanced by increases in the other factor if output is to be held constant.

To understand convexity, consider what happens as the firm moves along the isoquant of Figure 11A-1 downward and to the right. Labor is being added and capital is being reduced to keep output constant. If labor is added in increments of exactly 1 unit, how much capital may be dispensed with each time? The key to the answer is that both factors are assumed to be subject to the law of diminishing returns. Thus the gain in output associated with each additional unit of labor added is *diminishing,* whereas the loss of output associated with each additional unit of capital foregone is *increasing*. It therefore takes ever smaller reductions in capital to compensate for equal increases in labor. This implies that the isoquant is convex viewed from the origin.

An Isoquant Map

The isoquant of Figure 11A-1 is for 6 units of output. There is another isoquant for 7 units, another for 7,000 units, and a different one for every rate of output. Each isoquant refers to a specific output and connects combinations of factors that are technologically efficient methods of achieving that output. If we plot a representative set of these isoquants from the same production function on a single graph, we

FIGURE 11A-2   An Isoquant Map

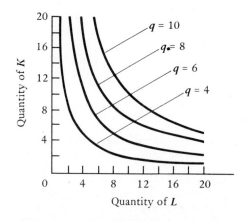

An isoquant map shows a set of isoquants, one for each level of output. The figure shows four isoquants drawn from the production function and corresponding to 4, 6, 8, and 10 units of production.

get an **isoquant map** like that in Figure 11A-2. The higher the level of output along a particular isoquant, the farther the isoquant is from the origin.

Conditions for Cost Minimization

Finding the efficient way of producing any output requires finding the least-cost factor combination. To do this requires that, when both factors are variable, factor prices be known. Suppose, to continue the example, that capital is priced at $4 per unit and labor at $1 per unit. In Chapter 8 a budget line was used to show the alternative combinations of goods that a household could buy; here an *isocost line* is used to show alternative combinations of factors that a firm can buy for a given outlay. Four different isocost lines appear in Figure 11A-3. The slope of each reflects *relative* factor prices, just as the slope of the budget line in Chapter 8 represented relative product prices. For given factor prices a series of parallel isocost lines will reflect the alternative levels of expenditure on factor purchases that are open to the firm. The higher is the level of expenditure, the farther the isocost line is from the origin.

FIGURE 11A-3   Isocost Lines

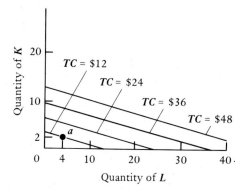

Each isocost line shows alternative factor combinations that can be purchased for a given outlay. The graph shows the four isocost lines that result when labor costs $1 per unit and capital $4 per unit and when expenditure is held constant at $12, $24, $36, and $48, respectively. The line labeled $TC = $12 represents all combinations of the two factors that the firm could buy for $12. Point *a* represents 2 units of *K* and 4 units of *L*.

In Figure 11A-4 the isoquant and isocost maps are brought together. The economically most efficient method of production must be a point on an isoquant that just touches (i.e., is tangent to) an isocost line. If the isoquant cuts the isocost line, it is possible to move along the isoquant and reach a lower level of cost. Only at a point of tangency is a movement in either direction along the isoquant a movement to a higher cost level. The lowest attainable cost of producing 6 units is $24. This cost level can be achieved only by operating at *A,* the point where the $24 isocost line is tangent to the 6-unit isoquant. The lowest average cost of producing 6 units is thus $24/6 = $4 per unit of output.

The least-cost position is given graphically by the tangency point between the isoquant and the isocost lines.

Notice that point *A* in Figure 11A-4 indicates not only the lowest level of cost for 6 units of output but also the highest level of output for $24 of cost. Thus, we find the same solution if we set out *either* to minimize the cost of producing 6 units of output *or* to maximize the output that can be obtained for $24. One problem is said to be the "dual" of the other.

The slope of the isocost line is given by the ratio of the prices of the two factors of production. The slope of the isoquant is given by the ratio of their marginal products. When the firm reaches its least-cost position, it has equated the price ratio (which is given to it by the market prices) with the ratio of the marginal products (which it can adjust by varying the proportions in which it hires the factors). In symbols,

$$\frac{MP_K}{MP_L} = \frac{p_K}{p_L}$$

This is equivalent to Equation 2 on page 203. We have now derived this result by use of the isoquant analysis of the firm's decisions. [21]

The Principle of Substitution

Suppose that with technology unchanged, that is, with the isoquant map being held fixed, the price of one factor changes. Suppose that with the price of capital unchanged at $4 per unit, the price of labor

FIGURE 11A-4   The Determination of the Least-Cost Method of Output

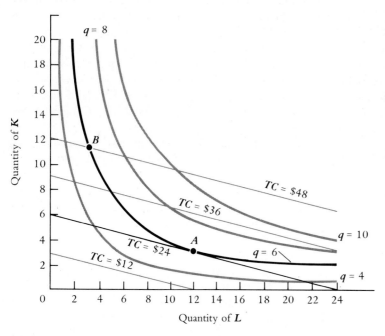

Least-cost methods are represented by points of tangency between isoquant and isocost lines. The isoquant map of Figure 11A-2 and the isocost lines of Figure 11A-3 are brought together. Consider point A. It is on the 6-unit isoquant and the $24 isocost line. Thus, it is possible to achieve the output $q = 6$ for a total cost of $24. There are other ways to achieve this output, for example, at point B, where $TC = $48. Moving along the isoquant from point A in either direction increases cost. Similarly, moving along the isocost line from point A in either direction lowers output. Thus, either move would raise cost per unit.

rises from $1 to $4 per unit. Originally, the efficient factor combination for producing 6 units was 12 units of labor and 3 units of capital. It cost $24. To produce that same output in the same way would now cost $60 at the new factor prices. Figure 11A-5 shows why this is not efficient. The slope of the isocost line has changed, which makes it efficient to substitute the now relatively cheaper capital for the relatively more expensive labor.

This illustrates the principle of substitution.

Changes in relative factor prices will cause a partial replacement of factors that have become relatively more expensive by factors that have become relatively cheaper.

Of course, substitution of capital for labor cannot fully offset the effects of a rise in cost of labor, as Figure 11A-5(i) shows. Consider the output attainable for $24. In the figure there are two isocost lines representing $24 of outlay—at the old and new prices of labor. The new isocost line for $24 lies inside the

old one (except where no labor is used). The isocost line must therefore be tangent to a lower isoquant. This means that if production is to be held constant, higher costs must be accepted. However, because of substitution, it is not necessary to accept costs as high as those that would accompany an unchanged factor proportion. In the example 6 units can be produced for $48 rather than the $60 that would be required if no change in factor proportions were made.

This leads to the predictions that

A rise in the price of one factor with all other factor prices being held constant will (1) shift upward the cost curves of commodities that use that factor and (2) lead to a substitution of factors that are now relatively cheaper for the factor whose price has risen.

Both of these predictions were stated in Chapter 11; now they have been derived formally by using the isoquant technique.

FIGURE 11A-5   The Effects of a Change in Factor Prices on Costs and Factor Proportions

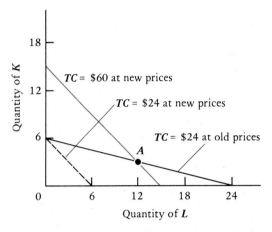

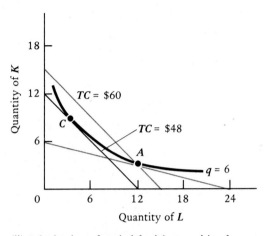

(i) The effect on the isocost line of an increase in the price of labor

(ii) Substitution of capital for labor resulting from an increase in the price of labor

An increase in the price of labor pivots the isocost line inward and thus increases the cost of producing any output. It also changes the slope of the isocost line and thus changes the least-cost method of producing. (i) The rise in price of L from $1 to $4 per unit (with price of K being held constant at $4) pivots the $24 isocost line inward to the dashed line. Any output previously produced for $24 will cost more at the new prices if it uses any amount of labor. The new cost of producing A rises from $24 to $60. (ii) The steeper isocost line is tangent to the isoquant at C, not A. Costs at C are $48, higher than they were before the price increase, but not as high as they would be if the factor substitution had not occurred.

P·A·R·T

4

MARKETS
AND
PRICING

12

Competitive Markets

Market Structure and Firm Behavior

Does Shell compete with Texaco in the sale of gasoline? Does American Express compete with Diners Club? Does a wheat farmer from Wheatland, Iowa, compete with a wheat farmer from North Platte, Nebraska? If we use the ordinary meaning of the word *compete*, the answers to the first two questions are plainly yes, and the answer to the third question is probably no.

Shell Oil Company and Texaco both advertise extensively to persuade car drivers to buy *their* product. Everything from new mileage-stretching additives to free dishes is used to tempt drivers to buy one brand of gasoline rather than another. A host of world travellers in various tight spots attest on television to the virtues of American Express, while discreet ads in many magazines tell us that the Diners Club card is *the* prestigious credit card to carry.

When we shift our attention to firms producing wheat, however, we see that there is nothing that the Iowa farm family can do to affect either the sales or the profits of the Nebraska farm family. They would not want to do so even if they could, since the sales and profits of the Nebraska farm have no effect on those of the Iowa farm.

Behavior and Market Structure

To sort out the questions of who is competing with whom and in what sense, it is useful to distinguish between the *behavior* of individual firms and the *type of market* in which they operate. In everyday use, the word *competition* usually refers to competitive behavior. Economists, however, are interested both in the competitive behavior of individual firms and in a quite distinct concept, competitive market structure.

The term **market structure** refers to all the features of a market that may affect the behavior and performance of the firms in that market. Examples are the number of firms in the market and the type of product that they sell.

Competitive market structure. The competitiveness of the market refers to the extent to which individual firms have power to influence market prices or the terms on which their product is sold. The less power an individual firm has to influence the market in which it sells its product, the more competitive is that market.

• KEY IDEAS IN •

MICROECONOMICS

This section provides important diagrams and captions from the text as reminders of basic economic concepts at a glance. If you need to refresh your memory concerning a principle being shown here, look in the appropriate chapter for a full explanation. The figure number of each diagram indicates the chapter from which it is taken (e.g., Figure 23-4 means the fourth figure in Chapter 23).

FIGURE 1-2   A Production Possibility Boundary

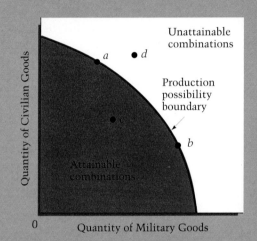

The downward-sloping boundary shows the combinations that are just attainable when all of the society's resources are efficiently employed.

FIGURE 4-8   The Equilibrium Price

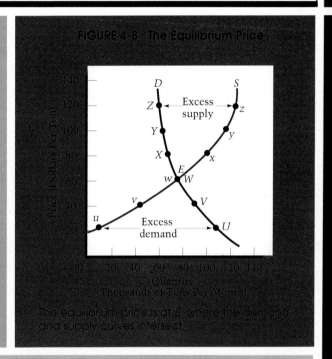

The equilibrium price is at E where the demand and supply curves intersect.

FIGURE 4-9   The Laws of Demand and Supply

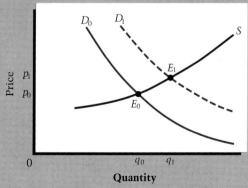

(i) The effect of shifts in the demand curve

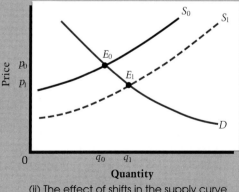

(ii) The effect of shifts in the supply curve

The effects on equilibrium price and quantity of shifts in either demand or supply are called the *laws of demand and supply*. Price and quantity change in the *same* direction when demand shifts and in the *opposite* direction when supply shifts.

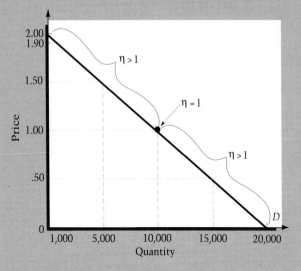

FIGURE 5-4   Elasticity of Demand and Total Expenditure

(i) Demand curve

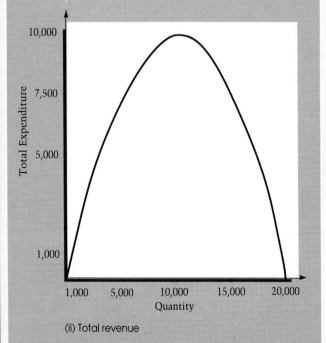

(ii) Total revenue

The change in total expenditure on a commodity in response to a change in price depends upon the elasticity of demand.

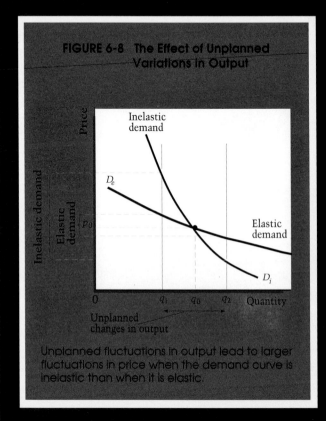

FIGURE 6-8   The Effect of Unplanned Variations in Output

Unplanned fluctuations in output lead to larger fluctuations in price when the demand curve is inelastic than when it is elastic.

FIGURE 7-4   The Income and Substitution Effects

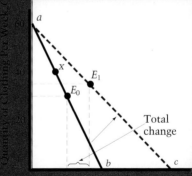

(i) A fall in the price of food

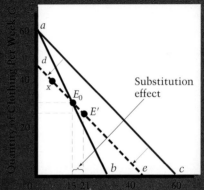

(ii) The substitution effect

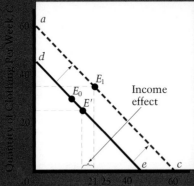

(iii) The income effect

The effect of a change in price can be broken into (1) a substitution effect, measuring the response to a change in relative prices, with purchasing power being held constant, and (2) an income effect, measuring the response to the change in purchasing power caused by the price change.

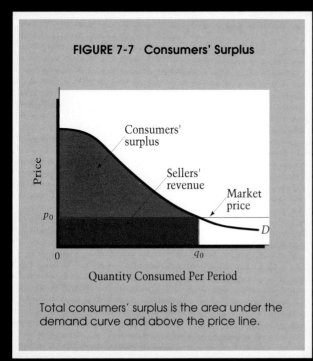

FIGURE 7-7   Consumers' Surplus

Total consumers' surplus is the area under the demand curve and above the price line.

FIGURE 10-1 Total Product, Average Product and Marginal Product Curves

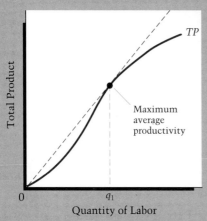

(i) Total product curve

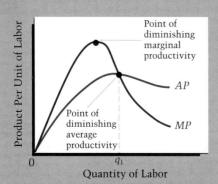

(ii) Average and marginal product curves

Total product (*TP*), average product (*AP*), and marginal product (*MP*) curves often have the shapes shown here.

FIGURE 10-2 Total Cost, Average Cost, and Marginal Cost Curves

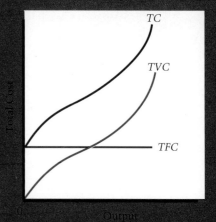

(i) Total cost curves

(ii) Marginal and average cost curves

Total cost (*TC*), average cost (*AC*), and marginal cost (*MC*) curves often have the shapes shown here.

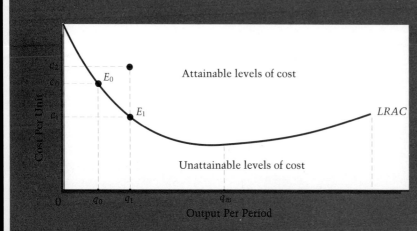

FIGURE 11-1 A Long-Run Average Cost Curve

The long-run average cost (*LRAC*) curve provides a boundary between attainable and unattainable levels of cost when all long-run adjustments have been made.

The extreme form of competitiveness occurs when each firm has zero market power. In such a case, there are so many firms in the market that each must accept the price set by the forces of market demand and market supply. The firms perceive themselves as being able to sell as much as they choose at the prevailing market price and as having no power to influence that price. If the firm charged a higher price, it would obtain no sales; so many other firms would be selling at the market price that buyers would take their business elsewhere.

This extreme is called a *perfectly competitive market structure*. In it, there is no need for individual firms to compete actively with one another, since none has any power over the market. One firm's ability to sell its product does not depend on the behavior of any other firm. For example, the Iowa and the Nebraska wheat farmers do not engage in active *competitive behavior* with each other. They are firms that are operating in a perfectly competitive market over which they have no power. Neither firm can change the market price for its wheat by altering its own behavior, so neither one needs to indulge in competitive behavior against the other.

Competitive behavior. In everyday language, the term *competitive behavior* refers to the degree to which individual firms actively compete with one another. For example, Shell and Texaco certainly engage in competitive behavior. It is also true, however, that both companies have real power over their market. Either firm could raise its prices and still continue to attract customers. Each has the power to decide, within limits set by buyers' tastes and the prices of competing products, the price that drivers will pay for their gasoline and oil. Thus, although they compete actively with each other, they do so in a market that is not perfectly competitive.

Behavior versus structure. The distinction that we have just made explains why firms in perfectly competitive markets (e.g., the Iowa and the Nebraska wheat producers) do not actively compete with each other, while firms that do compete actively with each other (e.g., Shell and Texaco) do not operate in perfectly competitive markets.

The Significance of Market Structure

Shell and Texaco are two of several large firms in the oil *industry*. They produce petroleum products and sell them in various *markets*. The italicized words in the previous two sentences are familiar enough from everyday use. However, economists give them precise definitions that we need to understand.

From the point of view of buyers, a **market** consists of the firms from which a well-defined product can be purchased; from the point of view of firms, a market consists of the buyers to whom a well-defined product can be sold. A group of firms that produces a well-defined product or a closely related set of products constitutes an **industry.** In previous chapters we have developed and used market demand curves. Notice that the market demand curve for any particular product is the demand curve facing the *industry* that produces that product.

When the managers of a firm make their production and sales decisions, they need to know what quantity of a product their firm can sell at various prices that it could charge for the product. Their concern is not so much, therefore, with the *market* demand curve for their industry's product as with their firm's *own* demand curve for that product. If they know the demand curve that their own firm faces, they know the sales that their firm can make at each price it might charge, and thus they know its potential revenues. If they also know their firm's costs for producing the product, they can calculate the profits that would be associated with each rate of output and can, therefore, choose the output that maximizes profits.

We have seen that economists define market structure to mean the characteristics that affect the behavior and performance of firms that sell in that market. These characteristics determine, among other things, the relationship between the market demand curve for the industry's product and the demand curve facing each firm in that industry.

The number of sellers and the nature of the product are significant aspects of market structure. There are others as well, such as the ease of entering the industry, the nature and the number of the purchasers of the firm's products, and the firm's ability to influence demand by advertising.

To reduce the analysis of market structure to manageable proportions, economists focus on four theoretical market structures that represent a high proportion of actual cases. These are called perfect competition, monopoly, monopolistic competition, and oligopoly. Perfect competition will be dealt with in the rest of this chapter, while the others will be dealt with in the chapters that follow.

BOX 12-1

Demand Under Perfect Competition: Firm and Industry

Since all products have negatively sloped market demand curves, *any* increase in the industry's ouput will cause *some* fall in the market price. As the calculations in the table show, however, any conceivable increase that one wheat farm could make in its output has such a negligible effect on the industry's price that the farmer correctly ignores it.

The table calculates in two steps the elasticity of demand facing one wheat farmer. Step 1 shows that a 200 percent variation in the firm's output leads to only a very small percentage variation in the world's price. Thus, as step 2 shows, the firm's elasticity of demand is very high: 71,428!

Although the arithmetic used in reaching these measures is unimportant, understanding why the wheat farmer is a price taker in these circumstances is vital.

Here is the argument that the table summarizes. The market elasticity of demand for wheat is approximately 0.25. This means that, if the quantity of wheat supplied in the world increased by 1 percent, the price would have to fall by 4 percent to induce the world's wheat buyers to purchase the entire increase in the crop.

Even huge farms produce a very small fraction

of the total world crop. In a recent year, one large American farm produced 1,750 metric tons of wheat. (World wheat production is measured in metric tons. A metric ton is a little larger than a U.S. ton.) This was only 0.0035 percent of the world production of 500 million metric tons. Suppose that the farm decided in one year to produce nothing and in another year managed to produce twice its normal ouput of 1,750 metric tons. This is an extremely large variation in output. Indeed, it is an impossibly large variation for a farm that can normally produce 1,750 metric tons.

The increase in output from zero to 3,500 metric tons is a 200 percent variation that is measured around the farm's average output of 1,750 metric tons. Yet the percentage increase in world output is only (3,500/500 million)100 = 0.0007 percent. The table shows that this increase would lead to a decrease in the world price of 0.0028 percent (2.8 cents in $1,000) and give the firm's own demand curve an elasticity of over 71,000! This is an enormous elasticity of demand; the farm would have to increase its output by over 71,000 percent to bring about a 1 percent decrease in the price of wheat! Because the farm's output cannot be varied this

Elements of the Theory of Perfect Competition

The perfectly competitive market structure—usually referred to simply as perfect competition—applies directly to a number of real-world markets. It also provides an important benchmark for comparison with other market structures.

Assumptions of Perfect Competition

The theory of **perfect competition** is built on a number of key assumptions relating to the firm and to the industry.

Assumption 1: All the firms in the industry sell an identical product. Economists describe this by saying that the firms sell a **homogeneous product.**

Assumption 2: Customers know the nature of the product being sold and the prices charged by each firm. They will, therefore, be indifferent about which firm they will buy the product from.

Assumption 3: The level of a firm's output at which its long-run average total cost reaches a minimum is small relative to the industry's total output (when price is such that firms are covering all costs).

Assumption 4: The *firm* is assumed to be a **price taker.** This means that the firm can alter its rate of production and sales without significantly affecting the market price of its product. Thus, as stated earlier, a firm that is operating in a perfectly

---

The Calculation of the Firm's Elasticity of Demand (η_F) from Market Elasticity of Demand (η_M)

Given:
$\eta_M = 0.25$
World output = 500 million metric tons
A large farm with an average output of 1,750 metric tons varies its output between 0 and 3,500 tons.
The variation of 3,500 tons on an average output of 1,750 metric tons = 200%.
This causes world output to vary by (3,500/500 million)100 = 0.0007%.

Step 1. Find the percentage change in world price.

$$\eta_M = -\frac{\text{percentage change in world output}}{\text{percentage change in world price}}$$

$$\text{Percentage change in world price} = -\frac{\text{percentage change in world output}}{\eta_M}$$

$$= -\frac{0.0007}{0.25}$$

$$= -0.0028$$

Step 2. Compute the firm's elasticity of demand.

$$\eta_F = -\frac{\text{percentage variation in firm's output}}{\text{percentage change in world price}}$$

$$= -\frac{+200}{-0.0028} = +71,428$$

---

much, it is not surprising that the farmer regards the price of wheat as unaffected by any change in output that this one farm could conceivably make.

For all intents and purposes, the wheat-producing firm is faced with a perfectly elastic demand curve for its product; *it is a price taker.*

competitive market has no power to influence that market through its own individual actions. It must passively accept whatever happens to be the ruling price, but it can sell as much as it wants at that price.[1]

Assumption 5: The *industry* is assumed to be characterized by *freedom of entry and exit;* that is, any new firm is free to set up production if it so wishes, and any existing firm is free to cease production and leave the industry. Existing firms cannot bar the entry of new firms, and there are no legal

prohibitions or other artificial barriers to entering or exiting the industry.

An Illustration

The Iowa and the Nebraska wheat farmers whom we considered earlier provided us with good illustrations of firms that are operating in a perfectly competitive industry.

Since each individual wheat farmer is just one of a very large number of producers who are all growing the same product, one firm's contribution to the industry's total production is only a tiny drop in an extremely large bucket. Each firm will correctly assume that variations in its output have no significant

---

[1] To emphasize its importance, we identify price taking in a separate assumption, although, strictly speaking, it is implied by assumptions 1, 2, and 3. What really matters for perfect competition is that the firm perceive itself to be a price taker and that the industry have freedom of entry and exit.

effect on the world price of wheat. Thus, each firm, knowing it can sell as much or as little as it chooses at that price, accepts the market price of wheat. Furthermore, anyone who has the capital can become a wheat farmer. There is nothing that existing farmers can do to stop another farmer from growing wheat, and there are no legal deterrents to becoming a wheat farmer.

The difference between the wheat farmers and the Shell Oil Company is in *degree of market power*. Each firm that is producing wheat is an insignificant part of the whole market and thus has no power to influence the price of wheat. The oil company does have power to influence the price of gasoline because its own sales represent a significant part of the total sales of gasoline in the U.S. market.

Box 12-1 explores further the reasons why each firm that is producing wheat finds the world price of wheat to be beyond its power of influence.

Demand and Revenue for a Firm in Perfect Competition

A major distinction between firms operating in perfectly competitive markets and firms operating in any other type of market is in the shape of the firm's own demand curve.

The demand curve facing a single firm in perfect competition is horizontal, because variations in **the firm's output over the range that it needs to consider have no noticeable effect on price.**

The horizontal (perfectly elastic) demand curve does not mean that the firm could actually sell an infinite amount at the going price. It means, rather, that the variations in production *that it will normally be possible for the firm to make* will leave price virtually unaffected because its effect on total industry supply will be insignificant.

Figure 12-1 contrasts the demand curve for a competitive industry and for a single firm in that industry.

Total, average, and marginal revenue. To study the revenues that firms receive from the sales of their products, we define three concepts—total, average, and marginal revenue—that are the revenue counterparts of the concepts of total, average, and marginal cost that we considered in Chapter 10.

Total revenue (TR) is the total amount received by the seller from the sale of a product. If q units are sold at p dollars each,[2] $TR = p \cdot q$.

Average revenue (AR) is the amount of revenue *per unit sold*. This is equal to the price at which the product is sold.

---

[2] Three common ways of indicating that any two variables such as p and q are to be multiplied together are $p \cdot q$, $p \times q$, and pq.

FIGURE 12-1 The Demand Curve for a Competitive Industry and for One Firm in the Industry

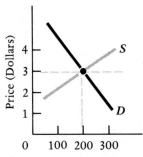

(i) Competitive industry's demand curve

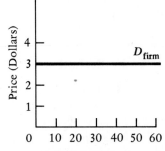

(ii) Competitive firm's demand curve

The industry's demand curve is downward sloping; the firm's demand curve is virtually horizontal. Notice the difference in the quantities shown on the horizontal scale in each part of the figure. The competitive industry has a price of $3 and an output of 200 million tons. The individual firm takes that market price as given to it and considers producing up to, say, 60 thousand tons. The firm's demand curve in (ii) appears horizontal because of the change in the quantity scale compared to the industry's demand curve in (i). The firm's output variation has only a tiny percentage effect on industry output. If we plotted the industry demand curve from 199,970 thousand tons to 200,030 thousand tons on the scale used in (ii), the D curve would appear virtually horizontal.

Marginal revenue (*MR*), sometimes called *incremental revenue*, is the change in a firm's total revenue resulting from a change in its rate of sales by one unit. Whenever output changes by more than one unit, the change in cost must be divided by the change in output to calculate marginal revenue. For example, if an increase in output of three units per month is accompanied by an increase in costs of $1,500, then the marginal cost of producing *one extra unit* per month is $1,500/3, which is $500. At any existing level of sales, marginal revenue shows what revenue the firm would gain by selling one unit more and what revenue it would lose by selling one unit less. **[22]**

To illustrate each of these revenue concepts, consider a firm that is selling an agricultural commodity in a perfectly competitive market at a price of $3 per ton. Total revenue rises by $3 for every ton sold. Since every ton brings in $3, the average revenue per ton sold is clearly $3. Furthermore, since each *additional* ton sold brings in $3, the marginal revenue of an extra ton sold is also $3. Table 12-1 shows calculations of these revenue concepts for a range of outputs between 10 and 13 tons.

The important point that is illustrated in Table 12-1 is that, as long as the firm's output does not affect the price of the product it sells, marginal revenue is equal to average revenue (which is always equal to price). Graphically, as shown in part (i) of Figure 12-2, average revenue and marginal revenue are the same horizontal line drawn at the level of market price. Since the firm can sell any quantity it chooses at this price, the horizontal line is also the *firm's demand curve;* it shows that any quantity that

FIGURE 12-2 Revenue Curves for a Price-taking Firm

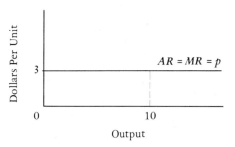

(i) Average and marginal revenue

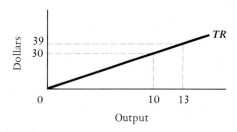

(ii) Total revenue

This is a graphical representation of the revenue concepts in Table 12-1. Because price does not change, neither marginal nor average revenue varies with output. When price is constant, total revenue is an upward-sloping straight line starting from the origin.

the firm chooses to sell will be associated with this same market price.

If the market price is unaffected by variations in the firm's output, then the firm's demand curve, its average revenue curve, and its marginal revenue curve all coincide in the same horizontal line.

This result can be stated in a slightly different way that turns out to be important for our later study:

For a firm in perfect competition, price equals marginal revenue.

This means, of course, that total revenue rises in direct proportion to output, as shown in part (ii) of Figure 12-2.

TABLE 12-1	Revenue Concepts for a Price-taking Firm			
Price p	Quantity q	$TR = p \cdot q$	$AR = TR/q$	$MR = \Delta TR/\Delta q$
$3.00	10	$30.00	$3.00	
3.00	11	33.00	3.00	$3.00
3.00	12	36.00	3.00	3.00
3.00	13	39.00	3.00	3.00

When the firm is a price taker, $AR = MR = p$. Marginal revenue is shown between the lines because it represents the change in total revenue (e.g., from $33 to $36) in response to a change in quantity (from 11 to 12 units): $MR = (36 - 33)/(12 - 11) = $3 per unit.

Short-Run Equilibrium

The Firm's Equilibrium Output

We learned in Chapter 11 how each firm's costs vary with its output. In the short run the firm has one or more fixed factors, and the only way in which it can vary its output is by using more or less of the factors that it can vary. Thus, the firm's short-run cost curves are relevant to its decision regarding output.

We have just learned how the revenues of each price-taking firm vary with its output. The next step is to combine the firm's costs and revenues to determine the level of output that will maximize its profits. We start by stating two rules that apply to *all* profit-maximizing firms, whether or not they operate in perfectly competitive markets. The first determines whether or not the firm should produce at all, and the second determines how much it should produce.

Rules for All Profit-maximizing Firms

Should the firm produce at all?   The firm always has the option of producing nothing. If it exercises this option, it will have an operating loss that is equal to its fixed costs. If it decides to produce, it will add the variable cost of production to its costs and the receipts from the sale of its product to its revenue. Therefore, it will be worthwhile for the firm to produce as long as it can find some level of output for which total revenue exceeds total variable cost. However, if total revenue is less than total variable cost at *every* level of output, the firm will actually lose more by producing than by not producing.

Rule 1: A firm should not produce at all if the total variable cost of producing its output exceeds the total revenue derived from selling it, or, equivalently, if its average variable cost exceeds its price. [23]

How much should the firm produce?   If a firm decides that (according to rule 1) production is worth undertaking, it must decide how much to produce. Common sense dictates that on a unit-by-unit basis, if any unit of production adds more to revenue than it does to cost, producing and selling that unit will increase profits. However, if any unit adds more to cost than it does to revenue, producing and selling it will decrease profits. Using the terminology introduced earlier, a unit of production raises profits if the marginal revenue obtained from selling it exceeds the marginal cost of producing it; it lowers profits if the marginal revenue obtained from selling it is less than the marginal cost of producing it.

Now let the firm with some existing rate of output consider increasing or decreasing that output. If a further unit of production will increase the firm's profits, the firm should expand its output. However, if the last unit produced reduced profits, the firm should contract its output. From this it follows that the only time the firm should leave its output unaltered is when the last unit produced adds the same amount to costs as it does to revenue.

If we put the results in these two paragraphs together, we will get the following important result:[3]

Rule 2: Assuming that it is worthwhile for the firm to produce, the firm should produce the output at which marginal revenue equals marginal cost. [24]

The two rules that we have stated refer to each firm's own costs and revenues, and they apply to all profit-maximizing firms, whatever the market structure in which they operate.[4]

The $MC = MR$ Rule Applied to Price-taking Firms

Rule 2 tells us that any profit-maximizing firm that produces anything will produce at the point at which marginal cost equals marginal revenue. However, we have already seen that for price-taking firms marginal revenue is the market price. It follows that:

A firm that is operating in a perfectly competitive market will produce the output that equates its marginal cost of production with the

---

[3] Formal proofs of the propositions that are discussed in the text are given in the Mathematical Notes, which appear at the back of this book.

[4] There is also a third rule that is needed to distinguish between profit-*maximizing* and profit-*minimizing* positions: The marginal cost curve must cut the marginal revenue curve from below. This rule is not, however, needed for the discussion that follows, so we say nothing further about it.

cost with the price of its product that is given to it by the market.

FIGURE 12-3   The Short-Run Equilibrium of a Competitive Firm

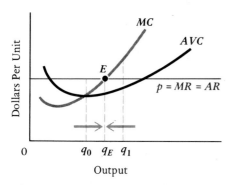

The firm chooses the output for which $p = MC$ above the level of AVC. When $p = MC$, as at q_E, the firm would decrease its profits if it either increased or decreased its output. At any point to the left of q_E, say, q_0, price is greater than the marginal cost, and it is worthwhile for the firm to increase output (as indicated by the arrow on the left). At any point to the right of q_E, say, q_1, price is less than the marginal cost, and it is worthwhile for the firm to reduce output (as indicated by the arrow on the right). The short-run equilibrium output for the firm is q_E.

market price of its product (as long as price exceeds average variable cost).

Equilibrium Output

In a perfectly competitive industry, the market determines the price at which the firm sells its product. The firm then picks the quantity of output that maximizes its profits. This is the output for which $p = MC$.

When the firm is maximizing profits, it has no incentive to change its output. Therefore, unless prices or costs change, the firm will continue to produce this output because it is doing as well as it can do, given the market situation. The firm is said to be in *short-run equilibrium*, as illustrated in Figure 12-3.

In a perfectly competitive market, each firm is a mere quantity adjuster. It pursues its goal of profit maximization by increasing or decreasing quantity until it equates its short-run marginal

cost with the price of its product that is given to it by the market.

Short-Run Supply Curves

We have seen that in a perfectly competitive market the firm responds to a price that is set by the forces of demand and supply. By adjusting the quantity it produces in response to the current market price, the firm helps to determine the market supply. The link between the behavior of the firm and the behavior of the competitive market is provided by the *market supply curve*.

The supply curve for one firm.   The firm's supply curve is derived in part (i) of Figure 12-4, which shows a firm's marginal cost curve and four alternative prices. The horizontal line at each price is the firm's demand curve when the market price is at that level. The firm's marginal cost curve gives the marginal cost corresponding to each level of output. We require a supply curve that shows the quantity that the firm will supply at each price. For prices below average variable cost, the firm will supply zero units (rule 1). For prices above average variable cost, the firm will equate price and marginal cost (rule 2, modified by the proposition that $MR = p$ in perfect competition). This leads to the following conclusion:

In perfect competition the firm's supply curve is the firm's marginal cost curve above average variable cost.

The supply curve of an industry.   Figure 12-5 illustrates the derivation of an industry supply curve for only two firms. The general result is as follows.

In perfect competition the industry supply curve is the horizontal sum of the marginal cost curves (above the level of average variable cost) of all firms in the industry.

The reason for this is that each firm's marginal cost curve shows how much that firm will supply at each given market price, and the industry supply curve is the sum of what each firm will supply. This supply curve, based on the short-run marginal cost curves of all the firms in the industry, is the industry's supply curve that was first introduced in Chapter 4. We have now shown the profit-maximizing behavior of

FIGURE 12-4   Derivation of the Supply Curve for a Price-taking Firm

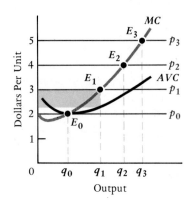

(i)   Marginal cost and average variable cost curves

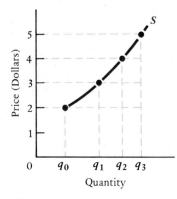

(ii)   Supply curve

The supply curve of the price-taking firm, shown in part (ii), is the same as its MC curve, shown in part (i). For prices below $2, output is zero, because there is no output at which AVC can be covered. Thus, the point E_0, where the price of $2 is just equal to AVC, is the point at which the firm will shut down. As price rises to $3, $4, and $5, equilibrium shifts to E_1, E_2, and E_3, taking output to q_1, q_2, and q_3. At any of these prices, the firm's revenue exceeds its variable costs of production. An example of the excess is shown in part (i) of the figure by the shaded area associated with price p_1 and output q_1. This amount is available to help cover fixed costs and, should these be covered, to provide a profit.

individual firms that underlies this curve. It is sometimes called a **short-run supply curve** because it is based on the short-run, profit-maximizing behavior of the firms in the industry. This distinguishes it from a *long-run supply curve*, which relates quantity supplied to the price that rules in long-run equilibrium (which we will study later in this chapter).

Short-Run Equilibrium Price

The market price of a product sold in a perfectly competitive market is determined by the interaction of the industry's short-run supply curve and the market demand curve. Although no one firm can influence the market price significantly, the collective actions of all firms in the industry (as shown by the industry supply curve) and the collective actions of households (as shown by the market demand curve) together determine the equilibrium price. This occurs at the point where the market demand curve and the industry supply curves intersect.

At the equilibrium price, each firm is producing and selling a quantity for which its marginal cost equals price. No firm is motivated to change its output in the short run. Since total quantity demanded equals total quantity supplied, there is no reason for market price to change in the short run; the market and all the firms in the industry are in short-run equilibrium.

Short-Run Profitability of the Firm

We know that when an industry is in short-run equilibrium each firm is maximizing its profits. We do not, however, know *how large* these profits are. It is one thing to know that a firm is doing as well as it can, given its particular circumstances; it is another thing to know how well it is doing.

Figure 12-6 shows three possible positions for a firm in short-run equilibrium. In all cases the firm is maximizing its profits by producing where $p = MC$, but in part (i) the firm is suffering losses, in part (ii) it is just covering all of its costs (breaking even), and in part (iii) it is making profits in excess of all costs. In part (i) we could say that the firm is minimizing its losses rather than maximizing its profits, but both statements mean the same thing. The firm is doing as well as it can, given its costs and the market price.

Long-Run Equilibrium

Although Figure 12-6 shows three possible short-run equilibrium positions for the firm in perfect competition, not all of them are possible long-run equilibrium positions.

FIGURE 12-5   Derivation of the Supply Curve for a Competitive Industry

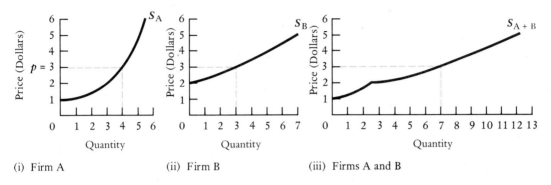

(i) Firm A   (ii) Firm B   (iii) Firms A and B

The industry's supply curve is the horizontal sum of the supply curves of each of the firms in the industry. At a price of $3, firm A would supply 4 units and firm B would supply 3 units. Together, as shown in part (iii), they would supply 7 units. If there are hundreds of firms, the process is the same. Each firm's supply curve (derived in the manner shown in Figure 12-4) shows what the firm will produce at any given price p. The industry supply curve relates the price to the sum of the quantities produced by each firm. In this example, because firm B does not enter the market at prices below $2, the supply curve S_{A+B} is identical to S_A up to price $2 and is the sum of $S_A + S_B$ above $2.

FIGURE 12-6   Alternative Short-Run Equilibrium Positions of a Competitive Firm

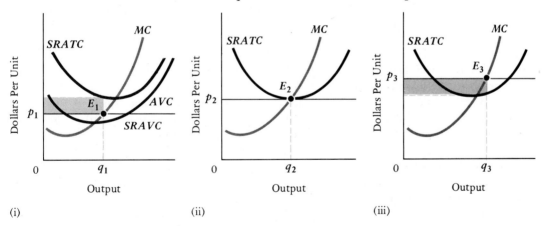

(i)   (ii)   (iii)

When it is in short-run equilibrium, a competitive firm may be suffering losses, breaking even, or making profits. The diagrams show a firm with given costs that is faced with three alternative prices p_1, p_2, and p_3. In each part of the diagram equilibrium occurs at the point at which $MC = MR$ = price. Since in all three cases price exceeds AVC, the firm is in short-run equilibrium at E_1, E_2, and E_3, respectively, in parts (i), (ii), and (iii).

In (i) price is p_1 and the firm is suffering losses, shown by the color shaded area, because price is below average total cost. Since price exceeds average variable cost, it is worthwhile for the firm to keep producing, but it is *not* worthwhile for it to replace its capital equipment as the capital wears out.

In (ii) price is p_2 and the firm is just covering its total costs. It is worthwhile for the firm to replace its capital as it wears out, since it is covering the full opportunity cost of its capital.

In (iii) price is p_3 and the firm is earning profits, shown by the gray shaded area, in excess of all its costs.

The Effect of Entry and Exit

The key to long-run equilibrium under perfect competition is entry and exit. We have seen that when firms are in *short-run equilibrium*, they may be making profits, suffering losses, or just breaking even. Since costs include the opportunity cost of capital, firms that are just breaking even are doing as well as they could do by investing their capital elsewhere. Thus there will be no incentive for such firms to leave the industry, and there will be no incentive for new firms to enter the industry, since capital can earn the same return elsewhere in the economy. If, however, existing firms are earning profits over all costs, including the opportunity cost of capital, new capital will enter the industry to share in these profits. If existing firms are suffering losses, capital will leave the industry because a better return can be obtained elsewhere in the economy. Let us now consider this process in a little more detail.

First, let all firms in the competitive industry be in the position of the firm shown in part (iii) of Figure 12-6. New firms, attracted by the profitability of existing firms, now will enter the industry. Suppose that, in response to the high profits that 100 existing firms have made, 20 new firms enter the industry. The market supply curve that formerly added up the outputs of 100 firms now must add up the outputs of 120 firms. At any price, more will be supplied because there are more producers.

This shift in the short-run industry supply curve, with an unchanged market demand curve, means that the previous equilibrium price will no longer prevail. The shift in supply will lower the equilibrium price, and both new and old firms will have to adjust their output to this new price. This is illustrated in Figure 12-7. New firms will continue to enter, and the equilibrium price will continue to fall, until all firms in the industry are just covering their total costs. Firms will then be in the position of the firm shown in part (ii) of Figure 12-6, which is called a *zero-profit equilibrium*.

Profits in a competitive industry are a signal for the entry of new firms; the industry will expand, pushing price down until the profits fall to zero.

Now let the firms in the industry be in the position of the firm shown in part (i) of Figure 12-6. Although the firms are covering their variable costs, the return on their capital is less than the opportunity

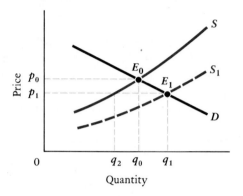

FIGURE 12-7   The Effect of New Entrants

New entrants shift the supply curve to the right and lower the equilibrium price. Initial equilibrium is at E_0. The entry of new firms shifts the supply curve to S_1. Equilibrium price falls to p_1, while output rises to q_1. Before the entry of new firms only q_2 would have been produced at price p_1. The extra output is supplied by the new productive capacity.

cost of this capital. They are not covering their total costs. This is a signal for the exit of firms. Old plant and equipment will not be replaced as it wears out. As a result, the industry's short-run supply curve shifts leftward, and the market price rises. Firms will continue to exit, and the market price will continue to rise, until the remaining firms can cover their total costs, that is, until they are all in the zero-profit equilibrium illustrated in part (ii) of Figure 12-6. The exit of firms then ceases.

Losses in a competitive industry are a signal for the exit of firms; the industry will contract, driving the market price up until the remaining firms are covering their total costs.

Since firms exit because they are motivated by their losses and enter because they are motivated by their profits, it follows that:

The long-run equilibrium of a competitive industry is a zero-profit equilibrium.

In all of this we see that profits serve the function of providing signals that guide the allocation of scarce resources among the economy's industries.

Conditions for Long-Run Equilibrium

There are four major conditions for a competitive industry to be in long-run equilibrium.

First, existing firms must be doing as well as they can, given their existing capital. This means that short-run marginal costs of production must be equal to market price.

Second, existing firms must not be suffering losses. If they are suffering losses, they will not replace their capital. In this case, the size of the industry will shrink over time.

Third, there must be no incentive for new firms to enter the industry. The absence of an incentive for entry requires that existing firms are not earning profits on their existing plants; if they were, new entrants could duplicate these facilities and earn profits themselves.

Fourth, existing firms must not be able to increase their profits by changing the size of their production facilities. This implies that each existing firm must be at the minimum point of its long-run cost curve. This is a new condition; to understand it, assume that it does not hold and see that firms could then increase their profits. This is shown in Figure 12-8. Although the firm is in short-run equilibrium, where it is just covering all of its costs, there are unexploited economies of scale. By increasing its size (for example, by building a new plant with a larger capacity than its existing plant), the firm can reduce its average cost. Since, in its present position, average cost is just equal to price, any reduction in average cost must yield profits.

The only way in which a price-taking firm can be in long-run equilibrium with respect to its size is by producing at the minimum point on its *LRAC* curve.

The level of output at which *LRAC* reaches a minimum is known as the firm's **minimum efficient scale (MES)** or its *minimum optimal scale*.

When all firms in the industry are producing at the minimum point of their long-run average cost curve and just covering costs (i.e., they are in the position shown in Figure 12-9), the whole industry is in equilibrium. Because marginal cost equals price, no firm can improve its profits by varying its output in the short run. Because *LRAC* is above price at all possible outputs except the current one, where it is equal to the price, there is no incentive for any ex-

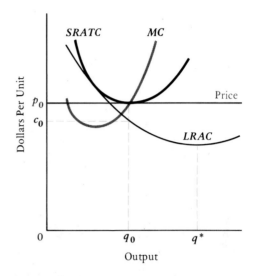

FIGURE 12-8   Short-Run Versus Long-Run Equilibrium of a Competitive Firm

A competitive firm that is not at the minimum point on its *LRAC* curve cannot be in long-run equilibrium. A competitive firm with short-run cost curves *SRATC* and *MC* faces a market price of p_0. The firm produces q_0, where *MC* equals price and total costs are just being covered. However, the firm's long-run cost curve lies below its short-run curve at output q_0. The firm could produce output q_0 at cost c_0 by building a larger plant so as to take advantage of economies of scale. Profits would rise, because average total costs of c_0 would then be less than price p_0. The firm cannot be in long-run equilibrium at any output below q^* because, with any such output, average total costs can be reduced by building a larger plant. The output q^* is the *minimum efficient scale* of the firm.

isting firm to move along its long-run cost curve by altering the scale of its operations. Because there are neither profits nor losses, there is no incentive for entry into, or exit from, the industry.

In long-run competitive equilibrium the firm's cost is the lowest attainable cost, given the limits of known technology and factor prices.

To summarize, the conditions for long-run equilibrium for a competitive industry are as follows: (1) existing firms produce at the point at which marginal cost equals price; (2) existing firms have no incentive to exit (existing firms are not making losses); (3) new

FIGURE 12-9   **The Equilibrium of a Firm When the Industry Is in Long-Run Equilibrium**

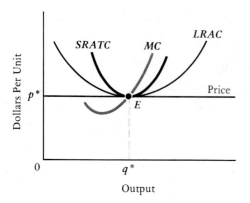

In long-run competitive equilibrium the firm is operating at the minimum point on its *LRAC* curve. In long-run equilibrium each firm must be (1) maximizing short-run profits, $MC = p$; (2) earning profits of zero on its existing plant, $SRATC = p$; and (3) unable to increase its profits by altering the scale of its operations. These three conditions can only be met when the firm is at E, the minimum point on its *LRAC* curve, with price p^* and output q^*.

firms have no incentive to enter (existing firms are not making profits); and (4) existing firms produce at the minimum point on their long-run average cost curve.[5] This is the position shown in Figure 12-9. (Note that conditions 2 and 3 can be collapsed into a single condition that the total revenues of existing firms should exactly equal their total costs.)

The Long-Run Industry Supply Curve

Consider a competitive industry that is in the type of long-run equilibrium that we have just studied. The market demand for the industry's product then increases. The reactions to this demand shift are a familiar story by now. First, price will rise, and, in response, existing firms will increase their outputs

and earn profits. New firms, attracted by the profits, will enter the industry. As the industry's capacity expands, price will fall, and this process will continue until profits have been eliminated. At that time, existing firms will once again be just covering their full costs.

This is familiar ground, but there is one further question that we could ask. When all the dust has settled, will the new long-run equilibrium price be higher or lower than, or the same as, the original price? A similar analysis could be made for a fall in demand, and the same question could be asked: When all adjustments have been made, will the new long-run equilibrium price be higher or lower than, or the same as, the original price?

The adjustment of a competitive industry to the types of changes that we have just discussed is shown by the **long-run industry supply (*LRS*) curve.** This curve shows the relationship between the market price and the quantity supplied by a competitive industry when it is in long-run equilibrium. Note, however, that the curve does not take very long-run reactions into account and so is drawn on the assumption that technological knowledge is constant. (Very long-run changes in technology will *shift* the *LRS* curve.) The derivation of this curve, and its various possible shapes, are shown in Figure 12-10.

In part (i) of the figure, the *LRS* curve is horizontal. This indicates that the industry will adjust its size to provide whatever quantity is demanded at a constant price. An industry with a horizontal *LRS* curve is said to be a *constant-cost industry*. This situation occurs when the long-run expansion of the industry, due to the entry of new firms, leaves the long-run cost curves of existing firms unchanged. Since new firms have access to the same technology and face the same factor prices as do existing firms, their cost curves will be the same as those of existing firms. It follows that all firms, new or old, will have cost curves that are unaffected by an expansion (or a contraction) of the industry. Thus, long-run, zero-profit equilibrium can only be reestablished when price is returned to its original level—which was, and still is, equal to each firm's unchanged minimum long-run average total cost. In other words, since cost curves are unaffected by the expansion or contraction of the industry, each firm must start from, and return to, the long-run equilibrium position shown in Figure 12-9, *which means that market price must do the same.*

---

[5] Since all costs are variable in the long run, there is no need to distinguish long-run average variable cost from long-run average total cost. They are identical, and we refer to them merely as long-run average costs (*LRAC*).

Changing factor prices and rising long-run supply curves.
When an industry expands its output, it needs more
inputs. The increase in demand for these inputs may
bid up their prices.[6]

If costs rise with increasing levels of industry
output, so too must the price at which the producers
are able to cover their costs. As the industry expands,
the short-run supply curve shifts outward, but the
firms' *SRATC* curves shift upward because of rising
factor prices. The expansion of the industry comes
to a halt when price is equal to minimum *LRAC* for
existing firms. This must occur at a higher price than
ruled before the expansion began, as illustrated in
part (ii) of Figure 12-10. A competitive industry with
rising long-run supply prices is often called a *rising-
cost industry*.

[6] In a fully employed economy, the expansion of one industry
implies the contraction of some other industry. What happens to
factor prices depends on the proportions in which the expanding
and the contracting industries use the factors.

Can the long-run supply curve decline?   So far we have
suggested that the long-run supply curve may be
constant or rising. Could it ever decline, thereby
indicating that higher outputs were associated with
lower prices in long-run equilibrium?

It is tempting to answer yes, because of the opportunities of more efficient scales of operation using
greater mechanization and more effective specialization of labor. However, this answer would not be
correct for perfectly competitive industries, because
each firm in long-run equilibrium must already be
at the lowest point on its *LRAC* curve. If a firm
could lower its costs by building a larger, more
mechanized plant, it would be profitable to do so
without waiting for an increase in demand. Since any
single firm perceives that it can sell all it wishes at
the going market price, it will be profitable for the
firm to expand the scale of its operations as long as
its *LRAC* is falling.

The scale economies that we have just considered

FIGURE 12-10   Long-Run Industry Supply Curves

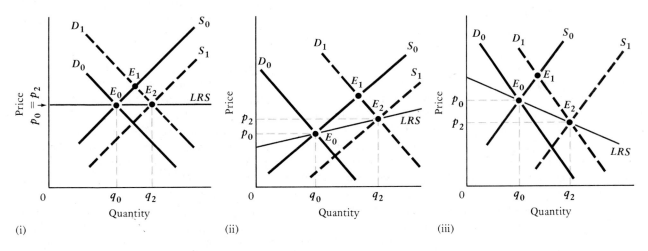

The long-run industry supply curve may be horizontal, slope upward, or slope downward. In
all three parts, the initial curves are at D_0 and S_0, yielding equilibrium at E_0, with price p_0 and quantity
q_0. A rise in demand shifts the demand curve to D_1, taking the short-run equilibrium to E_1. New
firms now enter the industry, shifting the supply curve outward, pushing down price until pure profits
are no longer being earned. At this point the supply curve is S_1 and the new equilibrium is E_2, with
price at p_2 and quantity q_2.

In part (i) price returns to its original level, making the long-run supply curve horizontal. In part
(ii) profits are eliminated before price falls to its original level, giving the *LRS* curve a positive slope.
In part (iii) the price falls below its original level before profits return to normal, giving the *LRS* curve
a negative slope.

are within the control of the firm; they are said to be **internal economies of scale.** A perfectly competitive industry might, however, have falling long-run costs if industries that supply its inputs have increasing returns to scale. Such effects are outside the control of the perfectly competitive firm and are called **external economies of scale.** Whenever expansion of an industry leads to a fall in the prices of some of its inputs, the firms will find their cost curves shifting downward as they expand their outputs.

As an illustration of how the expansion of one industry could cause the prices of some of its inputs to fall, consider the early stages of the growth of the automobile industry. As the output of automobiles increased, the industry's demand for tires grew greatly. This, as was suggested earlier, increased the demand for rubber and tended to raise its price, but it also provided the opportunity for tire manufacturers to build larger plants that exploited the scale economies available in tire production. These economies were large enough to offset any factor price increases, and tire prices charged to automobile manufacturers fell. Thus automobile costs fell, because of lower prices of an important input. This case is illustrated in part (iii) of Figure 12-10. An industry that has a declining long-run supply curve is often called a *falling-cost industry*.

Notice that, although the economies were external to the automobile industry, they were internal to the tire industry. This, in turn, requires that the supplying industry not be perfectly competitive. If it were, all its scale economies would already have been exploited, so this case refers to a perfectly competitive industry that uses an input produced by a non-perfectly-competitive industry, whose own scale economies have not yet been fully exploited because demand is insufficient. An example is provided by perfectly competitive agricultural industries who buy their farm machinery from an industry that is dominated by a few large firms.

We now can use our long-run theory to understand two commonly encountered but often misunderstood real-world situations.

Changes in Technology

Consider an industry in long-run equilibrium. Since the industry is in equilibrium, each firm must be in

zero-profit equilibrium. Now assume that technological development lowers the cost curves of newly built plants. Since price is just equal to the average total cost for the existing plants, new plants will be able to earn profits, and some of them will now be built. The resulting expansion in capacity shifts the short-run supply curve to the right and drives price down.

The expansion in capacity and the fall in price will continue until price is equal to the short-run average total cost of the *new* plants. At this price, old plants will not be covering their long-run costs. As long as price exceeds their average variable cost, however, such plants will continue in production. As the outmoded plants wear out, they will gradually disappear. Eventually, a new long-run equilibrium will be established in which all plants will use the new technology.

What happens in a competitive industry in which technological change occurs not as a single isolated event but more or less as a continuous event? Plants built in any one year will tend to have lower costs than plants built in any previous year.[7] This common occurrence is illustrated in Figure 12-11.

Industries that are subject to continuous technological change have a number of interesting characteristics. One of them is that plants of different ages and at different levels of efficiency exist side by side. This characteristic is dramatically illustrated by the variety of vintages of steam turbine generators found in any long-established electric utility.

Critics who observe the continued use of older, less efficient plants and urge that "something be done to eliminate these wasteful practices" miss the point of economic efficiency. If the plant is already there, the plant can be profitably operated as long as it can do more than cover its variable costs. As long as a plant can produce goods that are valued by consumers at an amount above the value of the resources currently used up for their production (variable costs), the value of society's total output is increased by using that plant to produce goods.

A second characteristic of a competitive industry that is subject to continuous technological change is that price is governed by the *minimum ATC* of the

---

[7] This statement refers to real resource costs, which tend to fall due to technological change. Of course, in times of general inflation, *money costs* of plants may well be rising. In the comparisons made here, we are assuming that costs have been adjusted for changes in the general price level.

FIGURE 12-11   Plants of Different Vintages in an Industry with Continuing Technological Progress

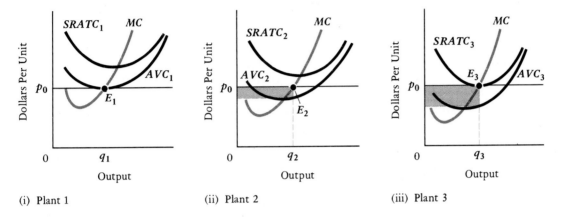

(i) Plant 1   (ii) Plant 2   (iii) Plant 3

Entry of progressively lower-cost firms forces price down, but older plants with higher costs remain in the industry as long as price covers average variable cost. Plant 3 is the newest plant with the lowest costs. Long-run equilibrium price will be determined by the average total costs of plants of this type, since entry will continue as long as the owners of the newest plants expect to earn profits from them. Plant 1 is the oldest plant in operation. It is just covering its AVC, and if the price falls any further it will be closed down. Plant 2 is a plant of intermediate age. It is covering its variable costs and earning some contribution toward its fixed costs. In parts (ii) and (iii), the excess of revenues over variable costs is indicated by the shaded area.

most efficient plants.[8] Entry will continue until plants of the latest vintage are just expected to earn normal profits over their lifetimes. The benefits of the new technology are passed on to consumers because all of the units of the commodity, whether they are produced by new or old plants, are sold at a price that is related solely to the ATCs of the new plants. Owners of older plants find that their returns over variable costs fall steadily as more and more efficient plants drive the price of the product down.

A third characteristic is that old plants are discarded (or "mothballed") when the price falls below their AVCs. This may occur well before the plants are physically worn out. In industries with continuous technological progress, capital is usually discarded because it is *economically obsolete*, not because

it has physically worn out. Old capital is obsolete when the market price does not even cover its average variable cost of production.

Declining Industries

What happens when a competitive industry in long-run equilibrium begins to suffer losses due to a permanent and continuing decrease in the demand for its products? As demand declines, price falls and firms that were previously covering average total costs are no longer able to do so. They find themselves in the position shown in part (i) of Figure 12-6. Firms suffer losses instead of breaking even, and the signal for the exit of capital is given, but exit takes time.

The Response of Firms

The economically efficient response to a steadily declining demand is to continue to operate with existing equipment as long as its variable costs of pro-

---

[8] Price will not necessarily equal minimum ATC. If firms anticipate the future changes, they will install new capital only when they expect to cover costs over the lifetime of the capital. This means that there must be sufficient profits in early years to match the losses in later years. Thus price will exceed average costs of the most efficient plants.

duction can be covered. As equipment becomes obsolete because it cannot cover even its variable cost, it will not be replaced unless the new equipment can cover its total cost. As a result, the capacity of the industry will shrink. If demand keeps declining, capacity must keep shrinking.

Declining industries typically present a sorry sight to the observer. Revenues are below long-run total costs, and, as a result, new equipment is not brought in to replace old equipment as it wears out. The average age of equipment in use thus rises steadily. The untrained observer, seeing the industry's plight, is likely to blame it on the old equipment.

The antiquated equipment in a declining industry is often the effect rather than the cause of the industry's decline.

An interesting illustration of the importance of the distinction between fixed and variable costs—one that is familiar to most hotel users—is given in Box 12-2.

The Response of Governments

Governments are often tempted to support declining industries because they are worried about the resulting job losses. Experience suggests, however, that propping up genuinely declining industries only delays their demise—at significant national cost. When the government finally withdraws its support, the decline is usually more abrupt and hence more difficult to adjust to than it would have been had the industry been allowed to decline gradually under the market force of steadily declining demand.

Once governments recognize the decay of certain industries and the collapse of certain firms as an inevitable aspect of economic growth, a more appropriate response is to provide welfare and retraining schemes that cushion the blow of change. These can moderate the effects on the incomes of workers who lose their jobs and make it easier for them to transfer to expanding industries. Intervention that is intended to increase mobility and reduce the social and personal costs of mobility is a viable long-run policy; trying to freeze the existing structure by shoring up an inevitably declining industry is not.

Although this advice is good in principle, few things are ever perfectly simple in practice. Following this advice requires that governments be able to separate firms and industries that are genuinely declining from those that are in temporary trouble that might be overcome effectively by short-term government assistance. The classic example is the federal government's support of the Chrysler Motor Company in 1980. Without this support, the firm probably would have gone bankrupt. Its assets might then have been sold to an existing automobile company—possibly one of the foreign companies that wanted a larger presence in the United States. As it was, however, the company received substantial temporary support from the government and restored its prosperity within a few years.

A striking example of the confusion of cause and effect in a declining industry occurred during the debate over the nationalization of the coal industry in Great Britain during the period between World Wars I and II. The view that public control was needed to save the industry from the hands of third-rate, unenterprising private owners was commonly held and was undoubtedly a factor that led to its eventual nationalization. Sir Roy Harrod, a leading British economist from the 1920s to the 1960s, shocked many people by taking the opposite view, arguing that the run-down state of the coal industry in some parts of the country represented the correct response of the owners to the signals of the market. He wrote:

> Economic efficiency does not consist in always introducing the most up-to-date equipment that an engineer can think of. . . . In not introducing new equipment, the managements may have been wise, not only from the point of view of their own interest, but from that of national interest, which requires the most profitable application of available capital. . . . It is right that as much should be extracted from the inferior mines as can be done by old-fashioned methods [with equipment already installed] and that they should gradually go out of action.[9]

The general point that Harrod makes is important. Capital resources are scarce; to install new plant and equipment in a genuinely declining industry is to use the nation's scarce resources where they will not lead to the largest possible increases in the value

---

[9] Roy Harrod, *The British Economy* (New York: McGraw-Hill, 1963), p. 54.

BOX 12-2

A Parable of Seaside Inn

Why do some resort hotels stay open during the off-season, even though to do so they must offer bargain rates that do not even cover their "full costs"? Why does the management of other hotels allow them to fall into disrepair even though they are able to attract enough customers to stay in business? Are the former being overly generous, and are the latter being penny pinchers?

To illustrate what is involved, consider an imaginary resort hotel called Seaside Inn. Its revenues and costs of operating during the four months of the season and during the eight months of the off-season are shown in the table below. When the profit-maximizing price for its rooms is charged, the hotel earns a return over its total variable costs of $22,000 during the season, as shown in the table. This surplus goes toward meeting the hotel's fixed costs of $24,000.

If it were to charge the same rates during the off-season, it could not attract enough customers even to cover its costs of maids, bellhops, and managers. The hotel discovers, however, that by charging lower rates during the off-season, it can rent some of its rooms and earn revenues of $18,000. Its costs of staying open are $16,000, and if it allocates the same portion of its fixed costs of $24,000 to each month that it stays open, it will not be covering its total costs (fixed plus variable costs) in the off-season, but it will be earning a surplus of $2,000 over variable costs. This surplus, though relatively small, can go toward covering some part of the fixed costs. Therefore, the hotel stays open during the whole year by offering bargain rates to grateful guests. (Indeed, if it were to close during the winter months, it would not be able to cover its total fixed and variable costs solely through its season operations.)

Now assume that the off-season revenues fall to $19,000 (everything else being the same). The short-run condition for staying open, $TR > TVC$, is met both for the season and for the off-season. However, the long-run condition is not met, since the TR over the whole year of $77,000 is less than the total cost of $78,000, all of which are variable in the long run. The hotel will remain open as long as it can do so with its present capital—it will produce in the short run. However, it will not be worthwhile for the owners to replace the capital as it wears out.

It will become one of those run-down hotels about which guests ask, "Why don't they do something about this place?"—but the owners are behaving optimally. They are operating the hotel as long as it covers its variable costs, but they are not putting any more investment into it, since it cannot cover its fixed costs. Sooner or later, the fixed capital will become too old to be run or, at least, to attract customers, and the hotel will be closed.

The Seaside Inn (*total costs and revenues*)			
	Total Revenue	**Total Variable Cost**	**Contribution to Fixed Costs**	
Season	TR	TVC	$TR - TVC$	Total Fixed Costs
Season	$58,000	$36,000	$22,000	
Off-season	$20,000	$18,000	$ 2,000	
Total	$78,000	$54,000	$24,000	$24,000

of national output. It is in the public and private interest for methods that appear to be antiquated to be employed in declining industries.

The Appeal of Perfect Competition

Consider an economy in which all markets are perfectly competitive. In this economy there are many firms and many households. Each is a price taker, responding as it sees fit to signals that are sent to it by the market. No single firm or consumer has any power over the market; instead, each is a passive quantity-adjuster who merely responds to market signals. Yet the impersonal force of the market produces an appropriate response to all changes. If tastes change, for example, prices will change, and the allocation of resources will change in the appropriate direction. Throughout the entire process, no one firm will have any power over any other firm. Dozens of firms will react to the same price changes, and if one firm refuses to react, there will be countless other profit-maximizing firms that will be eager to make the appropriate changes.

Market reactions, not public policies, eliminate shortages or surpluses. There is need neither for regulatory agencies nor for bureaucrats to make arbitrary decisions about who may produce what, how to produce it, or how much it is permissible to charge for the product. If there are no government officials to make such decisions, no bribes will be necessary to influence one decision rather than another.

In the impersonal decision-making world of perfect competition, neither private firms nor public officials wield economic power. The market mechanism, like an invisible hand, determines the allocation of resources among competing uses.

The theory of perfect competition is an intellectual triumph in showing how a price system can work to coordinate decentralized decision making by allowing all necessary adjustments to occur, in spite of the fact that no one foresees them or provides any overall plan for them.

The famous British historian Thomas Macaulay once said, "Power tends to corrupt; absolute power corrupts absolutely." To someone who fears power either in the hands of the state or in such private organizations as large firms, the perfectly competitive model has a strong appeal. It describes an economy that functions efficiently without any private or public group exercising any significant market power.

Economic and social policy would be much simplified if the entire economy were perfectly competitive. Although the price system often allocates resources in ways that are quite similar to the perfectly competitive economy, and although some markets are indeed perfectly competitive, in our world many groups have power over many markets. Large firms often set prices, determine what will be produced, and decide what research will take place. Labor unions often influence wages by offering or withdrawing their labor services. Governments influence many markets by being the dominant purchaser, as well as by regulating many others. As it is, those who fear the concentration of market power can only regret that the perfectly competitive model does not describe the world in which we live; so many problems would disappear if only it did.

SUMMARY

1. Market behavior is concerned with the degree to which individual firms compete against one another; market structure is concerned with the type of market in which firms operate. Market structure affects the degree of power that individual firms have to influence such market variables as the price of the product. Under the market structure known as perfect competition, individual firms are price takers.

2. Five key assumptions of the theory of perfect competition are that (a) all firms produce a homogeneous product; (b) purchasers know the nature of the product and the price(s) charged for it; (c) each

firm's *MES* occurs at a level of output that is small relative to the industry's total output; (d) firms are price takers; and (e) the industry displays freedom of entry and exit. A firm that is a price taker will adjust to varying market conditions by altering its output.

3. A profit-maximizing firm will produce at a level of output at which (a) price is at least as great as average variable cost and (b) marginal cost equals marginal revenue. In perfect competition, firms are price takers, so marginal revenue is equal to price. Thus, a profit-maximizing firm operating in a perfectly competitive market equates marginal cost to price.

4. Under perfect competition, each firm's short-run supply curve is identical with its marginal cost curve above average variable cost. The perfectly competitive industry's short-run supply curve is the horizontal sum of the supply curves of the individual firms (i.e., the horizontal sum of the firms' marginal cost curves).

5. If a profit-maximizing firm is to produce at all, it must be able to cover its variable cost. However, such a firm may be suffering losses (price is less than average total cost), making profits (price is greater than average total cost), or just breaking even (price is equal to average total cost).

6. In the long run, profits or losses will lead to the entry or the exit of capital from the industry. This entry or exit of capital will push a competitive industry to a long-run, zero-profit equilibrium and move production to the level that is consistent with minimum average total cost.

7. The long-run response of a growing, perfectly competitive industry to steadily changing technology is the gradual replacement of less efficient plants and machines by more efficient ones. Older plant and equipment will be utilized as long as price exceeds average variable cost; only when average variable costs rise above price will they be discarded and replaced by more modern ones. The long-run response of a declining industry will be to continue to satisfy demand by employing its existing machinery as long as price exceeds average variable cost. Despite its antiquated appearance, it is correct to use the existing machinery when faced with a steadily falling demand.

8. The great appeal of perfect competition as a means of organizing production lies in the decentralized decision making of myriad firms and households. No individual firm or household exercises power over the market. At the same time, it is not necessary for the government to intervene to determine resource allocation and prices. Although modern economies have some markets that are perfectly competitive, overall they are not perfectly competitive economies.

TOPICS FOR REVIEW

Competitive behavior and competitive market structure
Rules for maximizing profits
Perfect competition
Price taking and a horizontal demand curve
Average revenue, marginal revenue, and price under perfect competition
Relationship of supply curves to marginal cost curves
Short-run and long-run equilibrium of firms and industries
Entry and exit in achieving long-run equilibrium

DISCUSSION QUESTIONS

1. Consider the suppliers of the following commodities. What elements of market structure might you invoke to account for differences in their market behavior? Could any of these be characterized as perfectly competitive industries?
   a. Television broadcasting
   b. Automobiles
   c. Sand and gravel
   d. Medical services
   e. Mortgage loans
   f. Retail fruits and vegetables
   g. Soybeans

2. Which of the following observed facts about an industry are inconsistent with its being a perfectly competitive industry?
   a. Different firms use different methods of production.
   b. There is extensive advertising of the industry's product by a trade association.
   c. Individual firms devote 5 percent of their sales receipts to advertising their own product brand.
   d. There are 24 firms in the industry.
   e. The largest firm in the industry makes 40 percent of the sales, and the next largest firm makes 20 percent of the sales, but the products are identical, and there are 61 other firms.
   f. All firms made large profits in 1989.

3. In which of the following sectors of the American economy might you expect to find competitive behavior? In which might you expect to find industries that are classified as operating under perfectly competitive market structures?
   a. Manufacturing
   b. Agriculture
   c. Transportation and public utilities
   d. Wholesale and retail trade
   e. Criminal activity

4. In the 1930s the U.S. coal industry was characterized by easy entry and price taking. Because of large fixed costs in mine shafts and fixed equipment, however, exit was slow. Faced with declining demand, many firms were barely covering their variable costs but not their total costs. As a result of a series of mine accidents, the federal government began to enforce mine safety standards, which forced most firms to invest in new capital if they were to remain in production. What predictions would competitive theory make about market behavior and the quantity of coal produced? Would coal miners approve or disapprove of the new enforcement program?

5. Suppose entry into an industry is not artificially restricted but takes time because of the need to build plants, to acquire technical know-how, and to establish a marketing organization. Can such an industry be characterized as perfectly competitive? Does ease of entry imply ease of exit, and vice versa?

6. What, if anything, does each one of the following tell you about ease of entry into or exit from an industry?
   a. Profits have been very high for two decades.
   b. No new firms have entered the industry for 20 years.
   c. The average age of the firms in the 40-year-old industry is less than 7 years.

    d. Most existing firms are using obsolete equipment alongside newer, more modern equipment.

    e. Profits are low or negative; many firms are still producing but from steadily aging equipment.

7. In the 1970s grain prices in North America rose substantially relative to other agricultural products. Explain how each of the following may have contributed to this result.

    a. Crop failures caused by unusually bad weather around the world in several years

    b. Rising demand for beef and chicken because of rising population and rising per capita income

    c. Great scarcities in fishmeal, a substitute for grain in animal diets, because of a mysterious decline in the anchovy harvest off Peru

    d. Increased Soviet purchases of grain on the world market

8. It is often alleged that, when all firms in an industry are charging the same price, this indicates an absence of competition and the existence of some form of price-setting agreement. Assess this allegation.

Chapter 13

Monopoly

Is Consolidated Edison a monopoly? Are IBM, U.S. Steel, the National Football League, or the Coca-Cola Company monopolies? The word *monopoly* comes from the Greek words *monos polein,* which mean "alone to sell." Economists say that a **monopoly** occurs when the output of an entire industry is produced and sold by a single firm, called a **monopolist** or a *monopoly firm.*

A Single-Price Monopolist

In the first part of this chapter we shall deal with a monopoly firm that charges a single price for everything that it sells. The firm's profits will depend, as with all firms, on the relationship between its production costs and its sales revenues.

Cost and Revenue in the Short Run

We saw in Chapter 10 that the shape of a firm's short-run cost curves is a consequence of the law of diminishing returns. Since this law is not related to market structure, monopoly firms will have U-shaped cost curves that are generally similar in shape to those of perfectly competitive firms.

What distinguishes a monopoly firm from a firm that operates under any other market structure is the firm's demand curve. Because the monopoly firm is the only producer of a particular product, its demand curve is identical with the market demand curve for that product. The market demand curve, which shows the total quantity that buyers will purchase at each price, also shows the quantity that the monopolist will be able to sell at each price that it might set. Thus the monopoly firm, unlike the perfectly competitive firm, faces a negatively sloped demand curve. This means that it faces a trade-off between price and quantity: Sales can be increased only if price is reduced, whereas price can be increased only if sales are reduced.

Average and Marginal Revenue

Starting with the market-demand curve, the monopoly firm's average and marginal revenue curves can be readily derived. When the monopoly firm charges the same price for all units sold, average revenue per unit is identical with price. Thus, the market demand curve is also the firm's *average revenue curve.*

Now consider the monopoly firm's *marginal revenue* resulting from the sale of an additional (or marginal) unit of production. Because its demand curve is negatively sloped, the monopoly firm must lower the price that it charges on *all* units in order to sell an *extra* unit. **[25]** It follows that the addition to its revenue resulting from the sale of an extra unit is less than the price that it receives for that unit (less by the amount that it loses as a result of cutting the price on all the units that it was selling already).

The monopoly firm's marginal revenue is less than the price at which it sells its output.

This proposition, which is explored numerically in Table 13-1 and graphically in Figure 13-1, provides an important contrast with perfect competition (in which, you will recall, the firm's marginal revenue from selling an extra unit of output is equal to the price at which that unit is sold). The reason for the difference is not difficult to understand. The perfectly competitive firm is a price taker, selling all it wants at the given market price; the monopoly firm faces a negatively sloped demand curve and drives the market price down when it increases its sales.

FIGURE 13-1   Effect on Revenue of an Increase in Quantity Sold

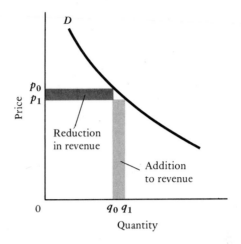

For a downward-sloping demand curve, marginal revenue is less than price. A reduction of price from p_0 to p_1 increases sales by one unit from q_0 to q_1. The revenue from the extra unit sold is shown as the lighter shaded area. To sell this unit, however, it is necessary to reduce the price on all of the q_0 units previously sold. The loss in revenue is shown as the darker shaded area. The marginal revenue associated with increasing output from q_0 to q_1 is equal to the *difference* between the two areas.

TABLE 13-1   Relationship Between Average Revenue and Marginal Revenue: A Numerical Example

Price $p = AR$	Quantity q	$TR = p \times q$	$MR = \Delta TR/\Delta q$
$9.10	9	$81.90	
9.00	10	90.00	$8.10
8.90	11	97.90	7.90

Marginal revenue is less than price because price must be lowered to sell an extra unit. In this example, to increase sales from 10 to 11 units, the monopolist must reduce the price on all units sold from $9.00 to $8.90. The extra unit sold brings in $8.90, but the firm sacrifices $.10 on each of the 10 units that it could have sold at $9.00 had it not wanted to increase sales. The net addition to revenue is the $8.90 minus $.10 times 10 units, or $1.00, making $7.90 altogether. Thus, the marginal revenue resulting from the increase in sales from 9 to 10 units is $7.90, which is less than the price at which the 10 units are sold.

Marginal revenue is shown displaced by half a line to emphasize that it represents the effect on revenue of the *change* in output between the two amounts shown in the first column.

Marginal Revenue and Elasticity

The top part of Figure 13-2 illustrates the average and marginal revenue curves for a monopoly firm that faces a negatively sloped, straight-line demand curve.[1] In Chapter 5 we discussed the relationship between the elasticity of the market demand curve and the total revenue derived from selling the product. Figure 13-2 summarizes this earlier discussion and extends it to cover marginal revenue:

When the demand curve is elastic, total revenue rises as more units are sold; marginal revenue

---

[1] It is helpful when you are drawing these curves to remember that if the demand curve is a downward-sloping straight line, the *MR* curve also slopes downward but is twice as steep. Its price intercept (where $q = 0$) is the same as that of the demand curve, and its quantity intercept (where $p = 0$) is one-half that of the demand curve.

FIGURE 13-2   Relationship Between Total, Average, and Marginal Revenue and Elasticity of Demand

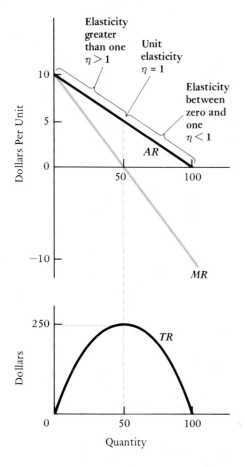

For a monopolist, *MR* is always less than price; when *TR* is rising, *MR* is greater than zero and elasticity is greater than one. The monopoly firm's demand curve is its *AR* curve; the *MR* curve is below the *AR* curve because the demand curve has a negative slope.

In the example shown, for outputs from 0 to 50, marginal revenue is positive, elasticity is greater than one, and total revenue is rising. For outputs from 50 to 100, marginal revenue is negative, elasticity is less than one, and total revenue is falling.

must, therefore, be positive. When the demand curve is inelastic, total revenue falls as more units are sold; marginal revenue must, therefore, be negative.

Short-Run Monopoly Equilibrium

To show the profit-maximizing position of a monopolist, we need only to bring together information about the monopolist's revenues and costs and then to apply the two rules developed in Chapter 12. Recall that these two rules are: (a) the firm should not produce at all unless its price is at least equal to its total variable cost, and (b) if the firm does produce, its output should be set at the point at which marginal cost equals marginal revenue.

When the monopoly firm equates marginal cost with marginal revenue, it reaches the equilibrium shown in Figure 13-3. Because marginal revenue is less than price for the monopoly firm, when marginal revenue is equated with marginal cost, both are less than price.

Marginal revenue equals price for the perfectly competitive firm, while it is less than price for the monopoly firm; marginal cost equals price in a perfectly competitive equilibrium, while it is less than price in a monopolistic equilibrium.

The relationship between elasticity and revenue just discussed has an interesting implication for the monopoly firm's equilibrium. Since marginal cost is always greater than zero, a profit-maximizing monopoly (which produces where *MR* = *MC*) will always produce where marginal revenue is positive, that is, where demand is elastic. If the firm were producing where demand was inelastic, it could reduce its output, thereby both increasing its total revenue and reducing its total costs.

A profit-maximizing monopoly will never push its sales into the range where the demand curve is inelastic.

Monopoly profits.   The fact that a monopoly firm produces the output that maximizes its profits tells us nothing about how large these profits will be or even whether there will be any profits at all. Profits may exist, as shown in part (i) of Figure 13-3. As part (ii) of Figure 13-3 shows, however, the profit-maximizing monopolist may break even or suffer losses. Nothing guarantees that a monopoly firm will make profits in the short run, but if it suffers persistent losses, it will eventually go out of business.

FIGURE 13-3   Profit-maximizing Position of a Monopolist

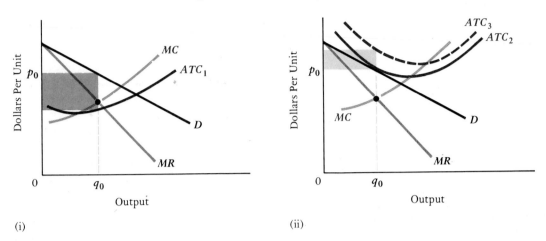

(i)

(ii)

Profit-maximizing output is q_0, where $MR = MC$; price is p_0, which is above MC at that output. The rules for profit maximization require $MR = MC$ and $p > AVC$. (AVC is not shown in the diagram, but it must be below ATC.) Whether or not there are profits depends on the position of the ATC curve. In part (i), where average total cost is ATC_1, there are profits, as shown by the gray shaded area. In part (ii), where average total cost is ATC_2, profits are zero. If average total costs were ATC_3, the monopolist would suffer the losses shown by the color shaded area.

No supply curve for a monopoly. In describing the monopolist's profit-maximizing behavior, we did not introduce the concept of a supply curve, as we did in the discussion of perfect competition. In perfect competition the industry short-run supply curve depends only on the marginal cost curves of the individual firms. This is because under perfect competition profit-maximizing firms equate marginal cost with price. Given marginal costs, it is possible to know how much will be produced at each price. This is not the case, however, with a monopoly.

In a monopoly there is no unique relationship between market price and quantity supplied.

Let us see why this is so. Like all profit-maximizing firms, a monopoly firm equates marginal cost with marginal revenue, but, unlike firms in perfect competition, the monopoly firm's marginal revenue does not equal its price. Because marginal revenue depends on the slope of the demand curve and not on the price, a given price can be associated with many different demand curves and hence many dif-

ferent levels of output. If the same output can be associated with different prices, there is no unique relationship between price and output that is required for a supply curve.

Firm and industry. Since the monopolist is the only producer in an industry, there is no need for separate theories about the firm and the industry, as is necessary with perfect competition. The monopolist *is* the industry. Thus, the short-run, profit-maximizing position of the firm, as shown in Figure 13-3, is also the short-run equilibrium of the industry.

Long-Run Monopoly Equilibrium

In a monopolized industry, as in a perfectly competitive one, losses and profits provide incentives for exit and entry.

If the monopoly firm is making losses in the short run, it will continue to operate as long as it can cover its variable costs. In the long run, however, it will leave the industry unless it can find a scale of operations at which its full opportunity costs can be covered.

If the monopoly firm is making profits, other firms will wish to enter the industry in order to earn more than the opportunity cost of their capital. If such entry occurs, the equilibrium position shown in part (i) of Figure 13-3 will change and the firm will cease to be a monopolist.

Entry Barriers

Impediments that prevent entry are called **entry barriers;** they may be either natural or created.

If a monopoly's profits are to persist in the long run, the entry of new firms into the industry must be prevented by effective entry barriers.

Natural Barriers

Natural barriers most commonly arise as a result of economies of scale. When the long-run average cost curve is negatively sloped over a large range of output, big firms have significantly lower average total costs than small firms.

You will recall from Chapter 11 that the *minimum efficient scale (MES)* is the smallest sized firm that can reap all of the economies of large-scale production. It occurs at the level of output where the firm's long-run average total cost curve reaches a minimum.

Now suppose that the technology of an industry is such that one firm's *MES* would be 10,000 units per week at an average total cost of $10 per unit. Further, assume that at a price of $10, the total quantity demanded is 11,000 units per week. Under these circumstances, only one firm can operate at or near its *MES*.

A **natural monopoly** occurs when, as in the preceding example, the industry's demand conditions allow only one firm, at most, to operate at its *MES*. If a second firm tried to enter an industry that was a natural monopoly, it could not achieve sales large enough to obtain costs that would be competitive with those of the existing firm.

Another type of natural barrier is *set-up cost*. If a firm could be catapulted fully grown into the market, it might be able to compete effectively with the existing monopolist. The cost to the new firm of entering the market, developing its products, and establishing such things as its brand image and its dealer network may, however, be so large that entry would be unprofitable.

Created Barriers

Some barriers to entry can be created by the conscious action of governments and are therefore condoned by it. Patent laws, for instance, may prevent entry by conferring on the patent holder the sole right to produce a particular commodity. A firm may also be granted a charter or a franchise that prohibits competition by law.

Other barriers can be created by the firm or firms already in the market. In extreme cases, the threat of force or sabotage can deter entry. (The most transparent entry barriers of this type are seen in the field of organized crime, where legal prohibitions do not prevent the use of a whole battery of crude but potent barriers to new entrants.) Most legitimate firms use less crude tactics. These may range from the threat of price cutting, which would impose unsustainable losses on a new entrant, to activities such as heavy brand-name advertising, which would increase a new entrant's set-up costs. (These and other created entry barriers will be discussed in much more detail in Chapter 14.)

The Significance of Entry Barriers

When there are no entry barriers, firms will enter an industry whenever they judge that the market is sufficiently large enough to support at least one more firm. Thus, in perfect competition, where there are no entry barriers, profits cannot persist in the long run. In monopoly, however, profits may persist in the long run but only if there are effective barriers to the entry of new firms.

Profits attract entry, and entry erodes profits.

Entry barriers frustrate this adjustment process.

The Persistence of Entry Barriers in the Very Long Run

In the very long run technology changes. New ways of producing old products are invented, as well as new products to satisfy both familiar and new wants. What has this to do with entry barriers? The answer to this question is that a monopoly that succeeds in preventing the entry of new firms to produce its own commodity may find its barriers circumvented by innovations. One new firm may be able to use new processes that avoid some patent or other barrier that the monopolist relies on in order to bar entry of firms that can produce the same commodity. Another new firm may compete by producing a newly invented product that satisfies the same need as does the monopoly firm's product.

"Creative Destruction"

The distinguished Austrian—and later American—economist Joseph Schumpeter took the view that entry barriers were not a serious problem in the very long run. He argued that monopoly profits provide one of the major incentives for people who risk their money by financing inventions and innovations. In his view, the large, short-run profits of a monopoly provide a strong incentive for others to try to usurp some of these profits for themselves. If a frontal attack on the monopolist's barriers to entry is not possible, then the barriers will be circumvented by such means as the development of similar products against which the monopolist will not have protection from another firm's entry.

Schumpeter called the replacing of one monopoly by another through the invention of new products or new production techniques the *process of creative destruction*. He argued that this process precludes the very long-run persistence of barriers to entry into industries that earn large profits.

He pushed this argument further and argued that, because creative destruction thrives on innovation, the existence of monopoly profits is a major incentive to economic growth. A key part of his argument can be found in the following words:

What we have got to accept is that it [monopoly] has come to be the most powerful engine of progress and in particular of the long-run expansion of total output not only in spite of, but to a considerable extent through, this strategy [i.e., creating monopolies] which looks so restrictive when viewed in the individual case and from the individual point of time. In this respect, perfect competition is not only impossible but inferior, and has no title to being set up as a model. It is hence a mistake to base the theory of government regulation of industry on the principle that big

business should be made to work as the respective industry would work in perfect competition.[2]

Schumpeter was writing at a time when the two dominant market structures studied by economists were perfect competition and monopoly. His argument easily extends, however, to any market structure that allows profits to exist in the long run. Today there are few examples of pure monopolies, but there are many industries in which profits can be earned for long periods of time. Such industries are candidates for the operation of the process of creative destruction.

Examples of creative destruction abound. In the nineteenth century, railways began to compete with wagons and barges for the carriage of freight. Then, in the twentieth century, trucks operating on newly constructed highways began competing with trains. Later, during the 1950s and 1960s, airplanes began to compete seriously with trucks and trains. The ballpoint pen eclipsed the ink-filled fountain pen, which in its day had driven out the quill pen along with its inkstand. Movie theaters competed with vaudeville and were in turn hard pressed when TV first brought visual entertainment into the home.

The slide rule (a crude method of dividing and multiplying that uses two pieces of wood that are calibrated with a logarithmic scale) provides us with a typical example of one product that has had its market destroyed by a new one, which resulted in the elimination of a firm's monopoly power. By the 1960s Keuffel & Esser had achieved a dominant position in the manufacture and the sale of slide rules, an essential tool of the engineer and the applied scientist. Its dominant position and highly profitable operations were wiped out, not by a better slide rule, but by the pocket calculator. When they were first introduced in the early 1970s, pocket calculators were relatively expensive, often costing over $100. They were also relatively crude in their capabilities. Nonetheless, they proved to be popular; sales and profits rose, and firms rushed to enter the lucrative new field. Competition led simultaneously to product improvement and price reduction. Today calculators that perform basic calculations can be bought for a few dollars, and sophisticated scientific and pro-

[2] Joseph Schumpeter, *Capitalism, Socialism and Democracy,* 3rd ed. (New York: Harper & Row, 1950), p. 106.

grammable pocket calculators can be bought for under $50. Few of today's college students have heard of Keuffel & Esser, but most of them know about Texas Instruments.

Similarly, during the 1980s microcomputers for the home and the office showed signs of sweeping away the markets of many important products and services. For instance, in-store computers are being used to answer customer questions and decrease the need for salespeople. One day computers may even displace the college textbook.

Another example of this process of creative destruction is discussed in more detail in Box 13-1.

Cartels as Monopolies

Up to this point in this chapter a monopoly has meant a firm that is the only seller of a product in an industry. A second way in which a monopoly can arise is for many firms in an industry to agree to cooperate with one another, to behave *as if* they were a single seller, in order to maximize joint profits, thus eliminating competition among themselves. Such a group of firms is called a **cartel.** A cartel that includes *all* of the firms in the industry can behave in the same way as would a single-firm monopoly that owned all of these firms. The firms can agree among themselves to restrict their total output to the level that maximizes their joint profits.[3]

The Effects of Cartelization

The incentive for firms to form a cartel lies in the cartel's ability to restrict output, thereby creating profits. The incentive exists whenever an industry is producing more than the output that would maximize the joint profits of the firms in the industry, which is always the case in equilibrium under perfect competition.

It is *always* profitable for all of the firms in perfectly competitive equilibrium to increase their

[3] In this chapter we deal with the simple case in which all of the firms in a perfectly competitive industry form a cartel in order to act as if they were a monopoly. Cartels are sometimes formed by a group of firms that account for a significant part, but not all, of the total supply of some commodity. The effect is to create what is called an *oligopoly*. We shall return to this type of cartel in Chapter 14.

profits by means of an agreement that restricts output.

The intuitive reasoning behind this result is as follows. Because perfectly competitive firms are price takers, they accept the market price as given and increase their production until their marginal cost equals price. The monopoly firm, however, faces the market demand curve as its own demand curve and, as a result, knows that increasing output forces the market price downward. To take account of this, the monopolist stops increasing output when marginal revenue is equal to marginal cost. If all the firms in a perfectly competitive industry get together in a cartel, they too will be able to take account of the effect of their joint output on price. They can agree to restrict output until they have reached the output that maximizes their joint profits (where the industry's marginal cost is equal to the industry's marginal revenue).

When a perfectly competitive industry is cartelized, the firms agree to restrict their joint output to the profit-maximizing level. One way to do this is to establish a quota for each firm's output. Say, for example, that the profit-maximizing output is two-thirds of the perfectly competitive output. When the cartel is formed, each firm could be given a quota equal to two-thirds of its competitive output. The effect of cartelizing a perfectly competitive industry and of reducing its output through production quotas is shown in more detail in Figure 13-4.

Problems That Cartels Encounter

Cartels encounter two characteristic problems. The first of these is how to ensure that each firm in the industry follows the behavior that will maximize the firms' *joint* profits, and the second of these is how to prevent these profits from being eroded by the entry of new firms. To study these problems, let us look at the formation of a cartel among the firms in an industry that was perfectly competitive.

Enforcement of output restrictions. The managers of any cartel want the industry to produce its profit-maximizing output. Their job is made more difficult if individual firms either stay out of the cartel or enter and then cheat on their output quotas. Any one firm, however, does have an incentive to do just this: to be either the one that stays out of the organization or the one that goes in and cheats. For the sake of

BOX 13-1

Erosion of a Monopoly

The great strength of the incentive to share in a monopoly's profits can be illustrated by the case of the ball-point pen, in which a monopoly was created by product innovation.

In 1945 Milton Reynolds developed a new type of pen that wrote with a ball bearing rather than with the then conventional nib. He formed the Reynolds International Pen Company, which he capitalized at $26,000, and began production on October 6, 1945.

The Reynolds pen was introduced with a good deal of fanfare by Gimbels, which guaranteed that the pen would write for two years without needing refilling. The price was set at $12.50. Gimbels sold 10,000 pens on October 29, 1945, the first day that they were on sale. In the early stages of production the cost of producing the pens was estimated to be around $.80 per pen.

The Reynolds International Pen Company quickly expanded its production. By early 1946 it employed more than 800 people in its factory and was producing 30,000 pens per day. By March 1946 it had $3 million in the bank.

Macy's, Gimbels' traditional rival, introduced an imported ball-point pen from South America. Its price was $19.98 (production costs are unknown).

The heavy sales from this pen quickly elicited a response from other pen manufacturers. Eversharp introduced its first model in April 1946, which was priced at $15.00. In July 1946 *Fortune* magazine reported that Sheaffer was planning to sell a pen for $15.00, and Eversharp announced its plan to produce a "retractable" model that would be priced at $25.00. Reynolds introduced a new model but kept the price at $12.50. Costs were estimated at $.60 per pen.

The first signs of trouble now emerged. The Ball Point Pen Company of Hollywood put a model for $9.95 on the market, and a manufacturer named David Kahn announced his plans to introduce a pen that would sell for less than $3.00. *Fortune* reported that there were fears in the industry of an impending price war in view of the growing number of manufacturers and the low cost of production. In October Reynolds introduced a new model, priced at $3.85, that cost about $.30 to produce.

By late December 1946 approximately 100 manufacturers were in production, some of whom were selling pens for as little as $2.98. By February 1947 Gimbels was selling a ball-point pen that was made by the Continental Pen Company for $.98. Reynolds introduced a new model that was priced to sell at $1.69, but Gimbels sold it for $.88 in a price war with Macy's. Reynolds felt betrayed by Gimbels. Reynolds introduced a new model that was listed at $.98. By this time ball-point pens had become economy rather than luxury items, but they were still a highly profitable item to sell.

In mid-1948 ball-point pens were selling for as little as $.39 and costing about $.10 to produce. In 1951 prices of $.25 were common. Within six years the power of the monopoly was gone forever. Since that time, the market has been saturated with a wide variety of models and prices of pens ranging from $.19 and up. The firms that manufacture them cover the full opportunity costs of their capital, but they have long since ceased to earn pure profits.

Of course there can still be strong incentives to gain monopoly power and profits, even if the effort is sure to fail eventually. The lag between an original monopoly and its subsequent erosion by competition may be long enough to ensure large profits to the monopolist. It is estimated, for example, that Milton Reynolds earned profits as high as $500,000 in a single month—about 20 times his original investment.

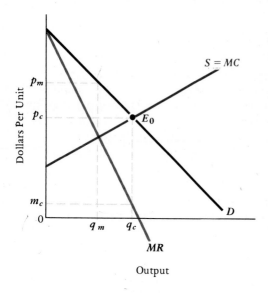

FIGURE 13-4 Effect of Cartelizing an Industry in Perfectly Competitive Equilibrium

Cartelization of a perfectly competitive industry can always increase that industry's profits.
Equilibrium for a perfectly competitive industry occurs at E_0, where the supply and the demand curves intersect. Equilibrium price and output are p_c and q_c. Because the industry demand curve slopes downward, marginal revenue is necessarily less than price. In the diagram, marginal revenue is m_c at the competitive equilibrium output of q_c.

If the industry is cartelized, profits can be increased by reducing output. All units between q_m and q_c add less to revenue than to cost—the marginal revenue curve lies below the marginal cost curve. (Recall from Figure 12-5 that the industry's supply curve is the sum of the supply curves, and hence of the marginal cost curves, of each of the firms in the industry.) If the units between q_m and q_c are not produced, output is reduced to q_m and price rises to p_m. This price-output combination maximizes the industry's profits because it is where marginal revenue equals marginal cost.

then reap the benefit of the other firms' restraint and sell all that it wishes at the high price that has been set by the cartel's actions. However, if all of the firms cheat, the price will be pushed back to the competitive level and all of the firms will be back to their zero-profit position.

This conflict between the interests of the group and the interests of the individual firm is the cartel's dilemma. Provided enough people cooperate in restricting output, all firms are better off than they would be if the industry remained perfectly competitive. Any one firm, however, is even better off if it remains outside or enters and cheats. However, if all firms act on this incentive, all will be worse off than if they had joined the cartel and restricted output.

Cartels tend to be unstable because of the incentives for individual firms to violate the output quotas that are needed to enforce the monopoly price.

The conflict between the motives for cooperation and for independent action is analyzed in more detail in Figure 13-5.

Cartels and similar output-restricting arrangements have a long history. For example, schemes to raise farm incomes by limiting crops bear ample testimony to the accuracy of the predicted instability of cartels. Agreements concerning crop restriction often break down, and prices fall as individual farmers exceed their quotas. The bitterness and the occasional violence that are sometimes exhibited against cheaters by members of crop restriction plans are readily understandable.

Restricting entry. A cartel must not only police the behavior of its members but also be able to prevent the entry of new producers. An industry that can support a number of individual firms must have no overriding natural entry barriers. Thus, if it is to maintain its profits in the long run, a cartel of many separate firms must create barriers that prevent the entry of new firms that are attracted by the cartel's profits. Successful cartels often are able to license the firms in the industry and to control entry by restricting the number of licenses. At other times the government has operated the quota system and has given it the force of law. If no one can produce without a quota and the quotas are allocated among existing producers, entry is precluded. Box 13-2 provides an

simplicity, assume that all firms enter the cartel, so enforcement problems are concerned strictly with the cheating of its members.

If firm X is the only firm to cheat, it is in the best of all possible situations. All other firms restrict output and drive up the industry price. They earn profits but only by restricting output. Firm X can

FIGURE 13-5   Conflicting Forces Affecting Cartels

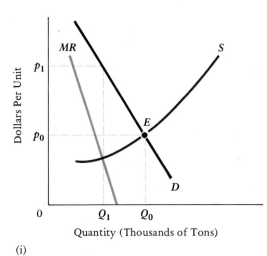
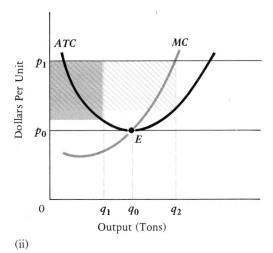

(i)   (ii)

Cooperation leads to the monopoly price, but individual self-interest may lead to production in excess of the monopoly output. Market conditions are shown in part (i), and the situation of a typical firm is shown in part (ii). (Note the change of scale between the two graphs.) Initially, the market is in competitive equilibrium with price p_0 and quantity Q_0. The individual firm is producing output q_0 and is just covering its total costs.

The cartel is formed and then enforces quotas on individual firms that are sufficient to reduce the industry's output to Q_1, the output where the supply curve cuts the marginal revenue curve. Q_1 is thus the output that maximizes the joint profits of the cartel members. Price rises to p_1 as a result. The typical firm's quota is q_1. The firm's profits rise from zero to the amount shown by the gray shaded area in part (ii). Once price is raised to p_1, however, the individual firm would like to increase output to q_2, where marginal cost is equal to the price set by the cartel. This would allow the firm to earn profits shown by the diagonally striped area. However, if all firms increase their outputs above their quotas, industry output will increase beyond Q_1, and the profits earned by all firms will fall.

example of the typical fate of a cartel that cannot control entry.

A Multiprice Monopolist: Price Discrimination

So far in this chapter we have assumed that the monopoly firm charges the same price for every unit of its product, no matter to whom or where it sells. However, other situations are common. Raw milk is often sold at one price when it is to be used as fluid milk but at a lower price when it is to be used to make ice cream or cheese. Doctors often charge for their services according to the incomes of their patients. Movie theaters may have lower admission prices for children than for adults. Railroads charge different rates per ton per mile for different products. Electric companies sell electricity at one rate to homes and at another, lower rate to firms. Airlines often charge less to people who stay over a Saturday night than to those who come and go within the week.

Price discrimination occurs when a producer charges different prices for different units of the same commodity for reasons not associated with differences in cost. Not all price *differences* represent price *discrimination*. Quantity discounts, differences between wholesale and retail prices, and prices that

BOX 13-2

Does Price Fixing Raise Profits?

Assume that there are many barber shops and freedom of entry into barbering: Anyone who qualifies can set up as a barber. Assume that the going price for haircuts is $20 and that at this price all barbers believe their incomes are too low. The barbers hold a meeting and decide to form a trade association. They agree on the following points: First, all barbers in the city must join the association and abide by its rules; second, any new barbers who meet certain professional qualifications will be required to join the association before they are allowed to practice their trade; third, the association will recommend a price for haircuts that no barber shall undercut.

The barbers intend to raise the price of haircuts in order to raise their incomes. You are called in as a consulting economist to advise them of the probable success of their plan. Suppose you are persuaded that the organization does have the requisite strength to enforce a price rise to, say, $25. What are your predictions about the consequences?

You now need to distinguish between the short-run and the long-run effects of an increase in the price of haircuts. In the short run the number of barbers is fixed. Thus, in the short run, the answer depends only on the elasticity of the demand for haircuts.

If the demand elasticity is less than 1, total expenditure on haircuts will rise and so will the incomes of barbers; if demand elasticity exceeds 1, the barbers' revenues will fall. Thus you need some empirical knowledge about the elasticity of demand for haircuts.

Suppose on the basis of the best available evidence that you estimate the elasticity of demand over the relevant price range to be 0.45. You then predict that barbers will be successful in raising income in the short run. A 25 percent rise in price will be met by an 11.25 percent fall in business, so the total revenue of the typical barber will rise by about 11 percent.*

---

* Let p and q be the price and quantity before the price increase. Total revenue after the increase is then given by $TR = (1.25p)(.8875q) = 1.108375pq$.

---

vary with the time of day or the season of the year may not represent price discrimination, because the same product sold at a different time, in a different place, or in different quantities may have different costs. If an electric power company has unused capacity at certain times of the day, it may be cheaper for the company to provide service at those hours than at peak demand hours. If price differences reflect cost differences, they are not discriminatory.

When a price difference is based on different buyers' valuations of the same product, it is discriminatory. It does not cost a movie theater operator less to fill seats with children than with adults, but it may be worthwhile for the movie theater to let the children in at a discriminatory low price if few of them would attend at the full adult fare and if they take up seats that otherwise would be empty.

Why Price Discrimination Is Profitable

Why should a firm want to sell some units of its output at a price that is well below the price that it receives for other units of its output? The simple answer is because it is profitable to do so. Why should it be profitable?

Persistent price discrimination is profitable either because different buyers are willing to pay different amounts for the same commodity or because one buyer is willing to pay different amounts for different units of the same commodity. The basic point about price discrimination is that in either of these circumstances sellers may be able to capture some of the consumers' surplus that would otherwise go to buyers. (You should review the discussion of consumers' surplus on pages 136–138.)

Now what about the long run? If barbers were just covering costs before the price change, they will now be earning profits. Barbering will become an attractive trade relative to others requiring equal skill and training, and there will be a flow of barbers into the industry. As the number of barbers rises, the same amount of business must be shared among more and more barbers, so the typical barber will find business—and thus profits—decreasing. Profits may also be squeezed from another direction. With fewer customers coming their way, barbers may compete against one another for the limited number of customers. The association does not allow them to compete through price cuts, but they can compete in service. They may spruce up their shops, offer their customers expensive magazines to read, and so forth. This kind of competition will raise operating costs.

These changes will continue until barbers are just covering their opportunity costs, at which time the attraction for new entrants will vanish. The industry will settle down in a new long-run equilibrium in which individual barbers make incomes only as large as they did before the price rise. There will be more barbers than there were in the original situation, but each barber will be working for a smaller fraction of the day and will be idle for a larger fraction (the industry will have excess capacity). Barbers may prefer this situation; they will have more leisure. Customers may or may not prefer it: They will have shorter waits even at peak periods, and they will get to read a wide choice of magazines, but they will pay more for haircuts.

You were hired, however, to report to the barbers with respect to the effect on their incomes, not the effect on their leisure. The report that you finally present will thus say, "You will succeed in the short run (because you face a demand curve that is inelastic), but your plan is bound to be self-defeating in the long run unless you are able to prevent the entry of new barbers."

Discrimination among units of output.   Look back to Table 7-2 on page 136, which showed the consumers' surplus received by one consumer when she bought 8 glasses of milk at a single price. If the firm could sell her each glass separately, it could capture this consumers' surplus. It would sell the first unit for $3.00, the second unit for $1.50, the third unit for $1.00, and so on until the eighth unit was sold for $.30. The firm would get total revenues of $8.10 rather than the $2.40 obtained from selling 8 units at the single price of $.30 each. In this example, the firm is able to discriminate perfectly and to extract the entire consumers' surplus.

Perfect price discrimination occurs when the entire consumers' surplus is obtained by the firm. This usually requires that each unit be sold at a separate price. In practice, perfect discrimination is seldom possible. Suppose, however, that the firm could charge two different prices, one for the first four units sold and one for the next four units sold. If it sold the first four units for $.80 and the next four units for $.30, it would receive $4.40—less than it would receive if it could discriminate perfectly but more than it would receive if it sold all units at any single price.

Discrimination among buyers.   Think of the demand curve in a market that is made up of individual buyers, each of whom has indicated the maximum price that he or she is prepared to pay for a single unit. Suppose, for the sake of simplicity, that there are only four buyers, the first of whom is prepared to pay any price up to $4, the second of whom is prepared to pay $3, the third, $2, and the fourth, $1.

Suppose the product has a marginal cost of production of $1 per unit for all units. If the seller is limited to a single price, it will maximize its profits by charging $3, sell two units, and earn profits of $4. If the seller can discriminate among units, it could charge the first buyer $4 and the second $3, thus increasing its profits from the first two units to $5. Moreover, it could also sell the third unit for $2, thus increasing its profits to $6.

Price discrimination more generally.   Demand curves slope downward because different units are valued differently, either by one individual or by different individuals. This fact, combined with a single price for a product, gives rise to consumers' surplus.

The ability to charge multiple prices gives a seller the opportunity to capture some (or, in the extreme case, all) of the consumers' surplus.

In general, the larger the number of different prices that can be charged, the greater is the firm's ability to increase its revenue at the expense of consumers. This is illustrated in Figure 13-6.

It follows that, if a seller is able to price discriminate, it can increase revenues received (and thus also profits) from the sale of any given quantity. **[26]**

However, price discrimination is not always possible, even if there are no legal barriers to its use.

When Is Price Discrimination Possible?

Discrimination among units of output sold to the same buyer requires that the seller be able to keep track of the units that a buyer consumes each period. Thus, the tenth unit purchased by a given buyer in a given month can be sold at a price that is different from the fifth unit *only* if the seller can keep track of who buys what. This can be done by an electric company through its meter readings or by a magazine publisher by distinguishing between renewals and new subscriptions. It can also be done by a firm's distributing of certificates or coupons that allow, for example, a car wash at a reduced price on a return visit.

Discrimination among buyers is possible only if the buyers who face the low price cannot resell the goods to the buyers who face the high price. However, even though the local butcher might like to charge the banker twice as much for buying his steak as he charges the taxi driver, he cannot succeed in doing so. The banker can always shop for meat in the supermarket, where her occupation is not known. Even if the butcher and the supermarket

---

FIGURE 13-6   Price Discrimination

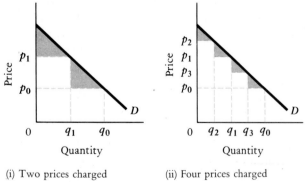

(i) Two prices charged   (ii) Four prices charged

Multiple prices permit a seller to capture consumers' surplus. Suppose in either graph that if a single price were charged, it would be the price p_0. Quantity q_0 would be sold, and consumers' surplus would be the entire area above p_0 and below the demand curve. In part (i) two prices are charged: p_1 for the first q_1 units and p_0 for the remaining $q_1 q_0$ units. Consumers' surplus is reduced to the two shaded areas, and the seller's revenue is increased accordingly. In part (ii) four prices are charged: p_2 for the first q_2 units, p_1 for the units between q_2 and q_1, and so on. Consumers' surplus is further reduced to the shaded areas, and the seller's revenue is increased accordingly. At the extreme, if a different price could be charged for each unit, producers could extract every bit of the consumers' surplus, and the price discrimination would be perfect.

agreed to charge her twice as much, she could hire the taxi driver to shop for her. The surgeon, however, may succeed in discriminating (especially if other reputable surgeons do the same) because it will not do the banker much good to hire the taxi driver to have her operation for her.

Price discrimination is possible if the seller can either distinguish individual units bought by a single buyer or separate buyers into classes such that resale among classes is impossible.

The ability to prevent resale tends to be associated with the character of the product or the ability to classify buyers into readily identifiable groups. Services are less easily resold than goods; goods that require installation by the manufacturer (e.g., heavy equipment) are less easily resold than movable goods such as household appliances. An interesting example of nonresalability occurs in the case of plate glass. Small pieces of plate glass are much cheaper to buy per square foot than bigger pieces, but the person who needs glass for a picture window that is 6 by 10 feet cannot use four pieces of glass that are 3 by 5 feet. Transportation costs, tariff barriers, and import quotas separate classes of buyers geographically and may make discrimination possible.

It is, of course, not enough to be able to separate buyers or units into separate classes. The seller also must be able to control the supply to each group. This is what makes price discrimination an aspect of the theory of monopoly.

Consequences of Price Discrimination

The consequences of price discrimination are summarized in the following two propositions.

Proposition 1: **For any given level of output, the most profitable system of discriminatory prices will provide higher total revenue to the firm than the profit-maximizing single price.**

This proposition was illustrated in Figure 13-6. All that it requires is a downward-sloping demand curve. To see that the proposition is reasonable, remember that a monopolist with the power to discriminate *could* produce exactly the same quantity as a single-price monopolist and charge everyone the same price. Therefore, it need never receive *less* rev-

enue, and it can do better if it can raise the price on even one unit sold.

Proposition 2: **Output under price discrimination will generally be larger than under a single-price monopoly.**

Remember that a monopoly firm that must charge a single price for a product will produce less than would all the firms in a perfectly competitive industry, because producing and selling more of the product would drive down the price against itself. Price discrimination allows it to avoid this disincentive. To the extent that the firm can sell its output in separate blocks, it can sell another block without spoiling the market for the block that is already being sold. In the case of *perfect price discrimination,* in which every unit of output is sold at a different price, the profit-maximizing monopolist will produce every unit for which the price charged is greater than or equal to its marginal cost. It will, therefore, produce the same quantity of output as the firm in perfect competition does.

Normative Aspects of Price Discrimination

The predicted combination of higher average revenue and higher output does not in itself have any *normative* significance. It will typically lead to a different distribution of income and a different level of output than when the seller is limited to a single price. The ability of the discriminating monopolist to capture some of the consumers' surplus will seem undesirable to consumers but not to the monopolist. How outsiders view the transfer may depend on who gains and who loses. For instance, when railroads discriminated against small farmers, the results aroused public anger. However, when doctors in private practice discriminate by giving low-priced service to poor patients, it is taken to be necessary since lower-income people would not be able to afford medical care if doctors charged all their patients the same fees. Not everyone will judge it to be bad for airlines to discriminate by giving senior citizens and vacationers lower fares than business travelers. Further examples are explored in Box 13-3.

There are two quite separate issues involved in evaluating any particular example of price discrimi-

BOX 13-3

Is Price Discrimination Bad?

The consequences of price discrimination differ from case to case. No matter what an individual's values are, he or she is almost bound to evaluate individual cases differently from one another.

Secret rebates. A large oil-refining firm agrees to ship its product to market on a given railroad, provided that the railroad gives the firm a secret rebate on the transportation cost and does not give a similar concession to rival refiners. The railroad agrees and is thereby charging discriminatory prices. This rebate gives the oil company a cost advantage that it uses to drive its rivals out of business or to force them into a merger on dictated terms. (John D. Rockefeller was accused of using such tactics in the early years of the Standard Oil Company.)

Use of product. When the Aluminum Company of America (ALCOA) had a virtual monopoly on the production of aluminum ingots, it sold both the raw ingots and the aluminum cable that was made from the ingots. At one time ALCOA sold aluminum cable at a price that was 20 percent *below* its price for ingots. (Of course, the cable price was above ALCOA's variable cost of producing the cable.) It did so because users of cable could substitute copper cable, but many users of ingot had no substitute for aluminum. In return for its "bargain price" for cable, ALCOA made the purchasers of cable agree to use it only for transmission purposes. (Without such an agreement, any demander of aluminum might have bought cable and melted it down.)

Covering costs. A product that many people want to purchase has a demand and a cost structure such that there is no single price at which a producing firm can cover total costs. However, if the firm is allowed to charge discriminatory prices, it will be willing to produce the product and it may make a profit. This is illustrated in the figure.

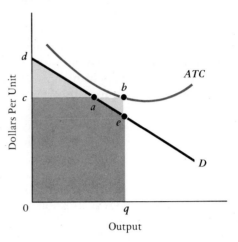

Because the average total cost *(ATC)* curve is everywhere higher than the demand curve *(D)*, no single price would lead to revenues equal to costs. A price-discriminating monopolist may be able to cover total costs. The total cost of output q is the area $0cbq$. The maximum revenue attainable at any output by perfect discrimination is the area under the demand curve. For output q this area, shown as the dark and light gray shaded areas, exceeds total cost, since the light gray shaded triangle cda is greater than the color shaded triangle abe.

Equitable fares. For many years British railways were not allowed to discriminate among passengers in different regions. To prevent discrimination, a fixed fare per passenger mile was specified and charged on all lines, whatever their passenger traffic and whatever the elasticity of demand for the services of the particular line. In the interests of economy, branch lines that could not cover costs closed down. Some lines stopped operating, even though their users preferred rail transport to any alternatives and the strength of their preference was such that they would have willingly paid a price that would have been sufficient for the line to yield a profit. However, the lines were closed because it was thought to be inequitable to discriminate against the passengers on these lines.

nation. One concerns the effect of discrimination on the level of output, and the other concerns the effect of discrimination on the distribution of income. Discrimination usually results in a higher output than would occur if a single price were charged. Often, however, it is the effect of discrimination on income distribution that accounts for people's strong emotional reactions to it. By increasing the monopoly's profits, price discrimination transfers income from buyers to sellers. When buyers are poor and sellers are rich, this may seem undesirable to many of us. However, as we saw in the case of doctors' fees and senior citizens' discounts, discrimination sometimes allows lower-income people to buy a product that they would be unable to afford if it were sold at the single price that maximized the producers' profits.

Systematic and Unsystematic Price Discrimination

So far the discussion has been concerned with persistent, systematic price discrimination. Systematic price discrimination most often consists of classifying buyers according to age, location, industry, income, or the use they intend to make of the product and then of charging different prices to the different "classes" of buyers. It may also take other forms, such as charging more for the first unit bought than for subsequent units.

Another sort of price discrimination is common. Any firm that occasionally gives a favorite customer a discount or reduces its price to land a new account is also engaged in price discrimination. If these practices are used irregularly, they are called *unsystematic* discrimination. Such discrimination is not really part of the equilibrium structure of prices, but it does play a major role both in the dynamic process by which prices change in response to changing market conditions and in rivalrous behavior among competing firms. For example, a tacit agreement among a number of producers to refrain from competing with each other may begin to break down when firms offer discriminatory price reductions to favored customers. If this signals the outbreak of competition among firms that were previously behaving as if they were a monopoly, it may be in the public interest to allow such discriminatory behavior.

The causes and consequences of systematic price discrimination are very different from those of unsystematic price discrimination.

The legal system generally is unable to distinguish between systematic and unsystematic price discrimination and so hits at both. Legislation, motivated solely by a desire to attack systematic discrimination, may have unforeseen and possibly undesired effects on unsystematic discrimination. Because unsystematic price discrimination is important for market adjustment and the process of competition, prohibiting it may slow market adjustments and help to maintain the power of the monopoly.

SUMMARY

1. Monopoly is a market structure in which an entire industry is supplied by a single firm. The monopoly firm's own demand curve is identical with the market demand curve for the product. The market demand curve is the monopoly firm's average revenue curve, while its marginal revenue curve always lies below its demand curve.
2. When a single-price monopoly is maximizing its profits, marginal revenue is positive and thus elasticity of demand is greater than unity. The amount of profits that a monopoly earns may be large, small, zero, or negative in the short run, depending on the relationship between demand and cost. For monopoly profits to persist in the long run, there must be effective barriers to the entry of other firms. Entry barriers can be natural or created.
3. Monopoly power is limited by the presence of substitute products, the development of new products, and the entry of new firms. In the very long run it is difficult to maintain entry barriers in the face of the process of creative destruction—the invention of new processes and new products to attack the entrenched position of an existing monopolist.

4. A group of firms may form a cartel by agreeing to restrict their joint output to the monopoly level. Cartels tend to be unstable because of the strong incentives for each individual firm to cheat by producing more than its quota allows.

5. A price-discriminating monopolist can capture some of the consumers' surplus that exists when all of the units of a product are sold at a single price. Successful price discrimination requires that the firm be able to control the supply of the product offered to particular buyers and to prevent the resale of the product.

6. For any given level of output, the best system of discriminatory prices will provide larger profits and higher output than occur under a single-price monopoly.

TOPICS FOR REVIEW

Relationship between price and marginal revenue for a monopolist
Relationships among marginal revenue, total revenue, and elasticity for a monopolist
Potential monopoly profits in perfectly competitive equilibrium
Natural and created entry barriers
Cartels as monopolies
The instability of cartels
Systematic and unsystematic price discrimination
Causes and consequences of price discrimination

DISCUSSION QUESTIONS

1. Suppose that only one professor teaches economics at your school. Would you say that this professor is a monopolist who can exact any "price" from her students in the form of readings assigned, tests given, and material covered? Suppose now that two additional professors have been hired. Has the original professor's monopoly power been decreased?

2. Imagine a monopoly firm that has fixed costs but no variable or marginal costs, for example, a firm that owns a spring of water that can produce indefinitely once certain pipes are installed in an area where no other source of water is available. What would be the firm's profit-maximizing price? What elasticity of demand would you expect at that price? Would this seem to be an appropriate pricing policy if the water monopoly were municipally owned?

3. Which of these industries—licorice candy, copper wire, outboard motors, coal, or the local newspaper—would you most like to monopolize? Why? Does your answer depend on several factors or on just one or two? Which would you as a consumer least like to have monopolized by someone else? If your answers to the two questions are different, explain why.

4. A movie exhibitor, Aristotle Murphy, owns movie theaters in two Indiana towns of roughly the same size, and they are 50 miles apart. In Monopolia he owns the only chain of theaters; in Competitia there is no theater chain, and he is but one of a number of independent operators. Would you expect movie prices to be higher in Monopolia than in Competitia in the short run? In the long run? If differences occur in his prices, would Mr. Murphy be discriminating in price?

5. While liquor retailing is a competitive industry in most American states, it is a government monopoly in most Canadian provinces.

What differences would you expect to find between the industry in the two countries?

6. Airline rates to Europe are higher in summer than in winter. Some railroads charge lower fares during the week than on weekends. Electric companies charge consumers lower rates, the more electricity they use. Are these all examples of price discrimination? What additional information would you like to have before answering this question?

7. Discuss whether each of the following represents price discrimination. In your view, which are the most socially harmful?

   a. Standby airline fares that are less than full fare

   b. Standby fares available only to bona fide students under 22 years of age

   c. First-class fares that are 50 percent greater than tourist fares, recognizing that two first-class seats use the space of three tourist seats

   d. Discounts negotiated from list price, for which sales personnel are authorized to bargain and to get as much in each transaction as the traffic will bear

   e. Higher tuition for out-of-state students at state-supported colleges and universities

   f. Higher tuition for law students than for history students

Chapter 14

Patterns of Imperfect Competition

The two market structures that we have studied so far are important "polar" cases. They define the extremes of market power over an industry, just as the North and the South poles define the limits of "traveling north" and "traveling south." Under perfect competition, firms are price takers; price is driven to the level of marginal cost and profits are zero, which means that firms are just covering the opportunity cost of their capital. The monopoly firm is a price setter; it sets price above marginal cost, and it may earn more than the opportunity cost of its capital.

The Structure of the American Economy

Although they provide important insights, these two polar theories are insufficient for an understanding of the behavior of all American firms. On the one hand, in the many industries that contain enough firms to be perfectly competitive, each firm sells its own distinctive set of products. As a result, each firm has some control over the price that it charges, unlike a perfect competitor. This is true in many branches of retailing and in some branches of manufacturing, such as clothing and fabrics. On the other hand, most industries in which a few large firms have market power contain more than one firm. These firms compete vigorously with each other, so they cannot be monopolies. Most of the major manufacturing industries, such as automobiles, aircraft, and household appliances, fall into this category.

Two Groupings of American Industries

Much of American industry can be divided into two broad groups: industries with a large number of relatively small firms and industries with a small number of relatively large firms.

Industries with Many Firms

About 65 percent of the American national product is produced by industries that are made up of firms that are either small in absolute size, as are most independent retailers, or small relative to the size of the market in which they sell, as are many of even the very largest American farms.

The perfectly competitive model, extended to allow for the impact of government intervention where necessary, does quite well in explaining the behavior of some of these industries. These are the ones in which individual firms produce more or less identical products and so are price takers. Foreign exchange markets and stock exchanges are notable examples. Agriculture also fits fairly well in most ways: the individual farmer is clearly a price taker; entry into farming is easy; and exit does occur, often making news when it happens on a large scale. Many basic raw materials, such as iron ore, tin, and copper, are sold on world markets where most individual firms lack significant market power and prices fluctuate continually in response to changing market conditions.

Other industries, however, do not exhibit the behavior that is predicted by the perfectly competitive model, even though they contain many firms. In retail trade and in services, for example, most firms have some influence over prices. The local grocery, supermarket, discount house, and department store not only consider weekend specials and periodic sales to be important to their success but also spend a good deal of money advertising them—something they would not have to do if they faced perfectly elastic demand curves. Moreover, each store in these industries has a unique location that may give it some local monopoly power over nearby customers. In wholesaling, the sales representative is regarded as a key figure who must compete with other representatives to sell to reluctant purchasers.

We are, as the American Professor R. L. Bishop long ago observed, "a race of eager sellers and coy buyers, with purchasing agents getting the Christmas presents from the salesmen rather than the other way around." This would not be true if each firm could sell all it wished at the going market price.

Thus, the first group of industries—those with many relatively small firms—contains some whose behavior can be understood and predicted by the perfectly competitive model and others to which the perfectly competitive model does not apply in all of its key aspects.

Industries with a Few Firms

About 35 percent of the American national product is produced by industries that are dominated by either a single firm or a few large ones.

Few American industries, however, are true monopolies. Many railway companies once enjoyed monopolies of service over rural areas (although seldom between major cities, which were normally served by several companies). In this century, however, airlines, trucking, and automobiles have provided intense competition to the railroads.

In the past, monopolies have dominated certain American manufacturing industries. The Aluminum Company of America (ALCOA) was the sole producer of primary aluminum in the United States from 1893 until World War II. The United Shoe Machinery Company had a monopoly on certain types of shoe machinery until antitrust decrees limited its exercise of monopoly power. The National Cash Register Company, the International Nickel Company, the Climax Molybdenum Company, and International Business Machines all had control, at one time or another, over more than 90 percent of the output of the industries in which they operated. Today, however, public utilities, such as power companies and the Post Office, provide almost the only examples of single-firm monopolies.

Even with the public utilities, however, monopoly sometimes exists only because of government regulations. For example, if a legal monopoly were not enforced by the government, ordinary letter delivery services would long ago have become more competitive, as is suggested by the competition that exists among Federal Express, Emery, and other carriers for rapid, reliable delivery of packages and overnight mail. In other cases, a monopoly that at one time seemed quite unassailable has been broken by technological developments, just as Schumpeter's theory that was discussed on page 251 predicts. Technological breakthroughs have made voice communication an industry with significant competition, in contrast to the monopoly that once existed of AT&T. Recently the Fax machine has removed the Post Office's monopoly over the delivery of written communications.

Most industries that are dominated by large firms contain more than one firm. The names of these firms are part of the average citizen's vocabulary. In this category fall many major transportation firms (e.g., the two rail giants, Amtrak and Conrail, United Airlines, American Airlines, Greyhound), communications (e.g., AT&T, NBC, CBS, Western Union), local public utilities, and much of the manufacturing sector (e.g., General Motors, Chrysler, Boeing, USX, IBM, and Westinghouse). Many service industries that used to be dominated by small, independent producers have, in recent decades, seen the development of large firms that are operating on a worldwide basis. In accounting, for example, firms such as Price, Waterhouse and Touche, Ross are enormous and clearly have some market power.

Patterns of Concentration in Manufacturing

To measure the extent to which the individual firms in an industry have market power, economists calculate what are called *concentration ratios*. A **concentration ratio** is the fraction of total market sales controlled by some specified number of the industry's largest sellers. Common types of concentration ratios cite the share of an industry's total market sales made by the largest four or eight firms, but it could be any other number of firms, such as two or ten. For example, the four-firm concentration ratio for soaps and detergents is 60 percent. This means that the largest four firms in that industry account for 60 percent of the industry's total sales.

It is important when we are measuring market power through concentration ratios that we calculate the ratios over the relevant market. In many cases, the country is separated into many regional markets, so that national concentration ratios understate the degree of market power that individual firms have over their real markets. For example, concentration ratios in national sales of cement are low, but heavy transportation costs divide the cement industry into a series of regional markets, in each of which there are relatively few firms, each with significant power over their local markets.

In other cases, international trade means that the appropriate market is much wider than the national market. For example, the national four-firm concentration ratio for U.S. firms in the American private-car market is 100 percent. Competition from foreign-car producers, however, means that General Motors and Ford have far less market power than this national ratio might at first suggest.

To measure market power appropriately, concentration ratios need to measure the fraction of sales over the relevant market—which may be larger or smaller than the entire United States—made by the largest firms operating in that market, whether they are American or foreign owned.

Table 14-1 shows the four-firm concentration ratios in selected industries that together account for about 40 percent of all manufacturing sales. Table

TABLE 14-1 Concentration Ratios in Selected Manufacturing Industries, 1982	
Industry	Four-firm concentration ratio (percentage)
Automotive	
Vehicles	92
Parts	61
Office machines	50
Tires and tubes	66
Soaps and detergents	60
Aircraft	
Planes	64
Engines and parts	72
Aluminum	
Primary	64
Rolling and drawing mills	83
Radio and television	
Sets	49
Equipment	22
Steel mills and blast furnaces	42
Chemicals	
Organic industrial	36
Plastics	22
Pharmaceutical	26
Machinery	
Farm	53
Construction	42
Forest products	
Paper mills	22
Pulp mills	45
Nonferrous wire	30
Petroleum refining	28
Foods	
Cereals	86
Bread and cake	34
Fluid milk	16
Canned fruit and vegetables	21
Soft drinks	14
Clothes	
Men's and boy's suits and coats	25
Women's and misses' dresses	6
Fur goods	12
Metal stamping	10
Commercial printing, lithography	6

Source: U.S. Department of Commerce, *1982 Census of Manufactures,* 1986.

Concentration ratios vary greatly among manufacturing industries. These data show the share of the industries' shipments accounted for by the four largest firms. All industry data in this chapter are based on the 1982 *Census,* which was the latest available at our time of publication.

14-2 gives more detail. It shows that, in nearly three-quarters of American manufacturing industries, the four largest firms control between 20 and 80 percent of the value of sales.

Industries at the top of Table 14-2 have high concentration ratios. In most of these, such as automobiles, aluminum, and cereals, a few firms with undoubted market power compete vigorously with one another.

Industries toward the bottom of Table 14-2 contain enough firms to be almost perfectly competitive, *if* they are producing a homogeneous product. Instead, however, almost all of the firms sell products or provide services that are differentiated from those provided by their competitors. This gives them some control over their selling prices. For example, because of variations in style, quality, and design, manufacturers of women's clothing can vary their prices in ways that are not open to firms in perfectly competitive industries. Metal stamping firms, print shops, and soft-drink bottlers, although they are numerous nationally, operate in small regional and local markets. In each of these industries a few sellers are in direct rivalry with one another and do not regard themselves as price takers.

Imperfectly Competitive Market Structures

Neither the theories of perfect competition nor of monopoly can explain the behavior of firms that compete actively with each other. (Recall the discussion on pages 224–225 in Chapter 12.) Intermediate market structures that are designed to help us understand such behavior are called *imperfectly competitive*. The word *competitive* emphasizes that we are not dealing with monopoly, while the word *imperfect* emphasizes that we are not dealing with perfect competition (in which firms are price takers and do not need to compete actively with each other).

Before studying specific market structures that are imperfectly competitive, we note certain patterns of behavior that are more or less common patterns to all such industries.

Firms Select Their Products

If a new farmer enters the wheat industry, the full range of products that can be produced is already in

TABLE 14-2   Manufacturing Industries, Classified by 1982 Concentration Ratios

Concentration ratio (percentage)	Number of industries listed by the census	Percentage of value of total shipments of all manufacturing industries
80–100	18	6
60–79	54	12
40–59	120	18
20–39	163	44
Less than 20	86	20
Total	441	100

Source: U.S. Department of Commerce, *1982 Census of Manufactures,* 1986

Notice the importance measured both in numbers and in value of shipments of industries in the three middle groups. These data were computed from the 1982 census of manufactures. The concentration ratios are those for the four largest firms in each industry.

existence. If a new firm enters the cigarette industry, that firm must decide what the characteristics will be of the new cigarettes that it is to produce. It will not produce types of cigarettes that are identical to those already in production. Rather, it will develop, possibly at substantial cost, one or more new cigarettes, each of which will have its own distinctive characteristics. As a result, firms in the cigarette industry sell an array of differentiated products, no two of which are identical.

A **differentiated product** refers to a group of commodities that are similar enough to be called the same product but dissimilar enough that all of them need not be sold at the same price. For example, although one brand of soap is similar to all others, soaps differ from each other in their chemical composition, color, smell, softness, brand name, reputation, and a host of other characteristics that matter to customers. So face soap is a distinct product from detergents, and face soaps are a differentiated product.

Most industries in imperfectly competitive market structures sell differentiated products. In such industries, the firm itself must decide on what characteristics to give the products that it will sell. Having done so, it must then develop such a product and then market it.

Firms Administer Their Prices

Because firms in perfect competition sell a homogeneous product, they face a market price that they are quite unable to influence. They then adjust their quantities to this price (firms are price takers and quantity adjusters).

In perfect competition, changes in market conditions are signaled to firms by changes in the market prices that they face.

In all other market structures, firms have negatively sloped demand curves and thus face a trade-off between the price that they charge and the quantity that they sell. Whenever different firms' products are not perfect substitutes for each other, firms must decide on a price to quote. If they are unsatisfied with the sales that they achieve at this price, they can change their quote, but quote a price they must. In such circumstances, economists say that firms *administer* their price. The term *administered price* refers to a price set by the conscious decision of an individual firm rather than by impersonal market forces.

There is no market that sets a single price for razor blades or television sets, for example, by equating overall demand with overall supply. Instead, it is in the nature of such products that each producer must state a price at which it is willing to sell each of its own products. (Of course, a certain amount of "haggling" is possible, particularly at the retail level, but this is usually within well-defined limits that have been set by the price that was initially quoted by the seller.) What is true for razor blades and for television sets is also true for virtually all consumer goods—they are *differentiated products*. Any one firm typically will have several product lines that differ more or less from each other and from the competing product lines of other firms. Each product has a price that must be set by its seller. Of course, the firm has some idea of how much it can sell at each price that it might set. Unexpected market fluctuations will nonetheless take the form of unexpected variations in the quantities that are sold at the administered prices.

In market structures other than perfect competition, firms set their prices and then let demand determine their sales. Changes in market conditions are signaled to the firm by changes in the quantity that the firm can sell at its current administered price.

The changed conditions may or may not then lead firms to change their prices.

Other Aspects of the Behavior of Firms

Several other important aspects of the observed behavior of firms that are the subject of the theories of imperfect competition are inconsistent either with perfect competition or monopoly.

Unexploited scale economies.   Many firms appear to be operating on the downward-sloping portion of the long-run average cost curves for many of their products. For example, it has been observed several times that when international trade has been liberalized, firms that were able to increase their sales found that their average costs were falling. Although this is possible under monopoly, firms in perfect competition must, in the long run, be at the minimum point of their long-run average cost curves. (See Figure 12-9 on page 236.) The puzzle is why scale economies should not be fully exploited under conditions of imperfect competition.

Prices are sticky in the short term.   Many firms do not alter their prices in response to every shift in demand or costs. Instead their prices alter less frequently than do prices in perfectly competitive markets.

Nonprice competition.   Many firms spend large sums of money on advertising. They do so in an attempt both to shift the demand curves for the industry's products and to attract customers from competing firms. Any kind of advertising is inconsistent with perfect competition, while advertising directed at competing firms in the same industry is, by definition, inconsistent with monopoly.

Many firms engage in a variety of other forms of nonprice competition, such as giveaway contests, variation in quality, and varying product guarantees.

Entry prevention.   Firms in many industries that contain more than one firm engage in activities that appear to be designed to hinder the entry of new firms, thereby preventing existing pure profits from being eroded by entry.

The market structures of monopolistic competition and oligopoly, which will be discussed in the rest of this chapter, are designed for the analysis of industries that are neither monopolies nor perfectly competitive and for an explanation of the behavior just outlined.

Monopolistic Competition

The theory of **monopolistic competition** was developed many years ago to deal with the phenomenon of product differentiation.[1] This market structure is similar to perfect competition in that the industry contains many firms and exhibits freedom of entry and exit. It differs, however, in one important respect. Whereas firms in perfect competition sell a *homogeneous product* and are price takers, firms in monopolistic competition sell a differentiated product and have some power over the price of their own product.

Product differentiation leads to, and is enhanced by, the establishment of brand names and advertising, and it gives each firm a degree of monopoly power over its own product. Each firm can raise its price, even if its competitors do not, without losing all its sales. This is the "monopolistic" part of the theory. Each firm's monopoly power is severely restricted, however, by the presence of similar products that are sold by many competing firms and by easy entry and exit. As a result, each firm's demand curve is much flatter than the industry's demand curve. This is the "competition" part of the theory.

Assumptions of Monopolistic Competition

The theory of monopolistic competition is based on three key assumptions, the first of which is what distinguishes monopolistic from perfect competition. First, each firm produces one specific variety, or brand, of the industry's differentiated product. Each firm thus faces a demand curve that, although it is

negatively sloped, is highly elastic, because other varieties of the same product that are sold by other firms provide many close substitutes.

Second, the industry contains so many firms, each of which is in close competition with many others, that each one ignores the possible reactions of its many competitors when it makes its own price-output decisions. In this way, firms in monopolistic competition are similar to firms in perfect competition. They make decisions based on their own demand and cost conditions and do not consider interdependence between their own decisions and those of the other firms in the industry. (There are too many firms for it to be possible for any one firm to try to take the other firms' separate reactions into account.)

Third, there is freedom of entry and exit in the industry. If profits are being earned by existing firms, new firms have an incentive to enter. When they do, the demand for the industry's product must be shared among more brands, and this is assumed to take demand equally from all existing firms. Entry continues until profits fall to zero, just as they do under perfect competition.

Predictions About Behavior

The only thing that makes monopolistic competition different from perfect competition is the differentiated product. However, product differentiation has important consequences for behavior in both the short and the long run.

The Short-Run Equilibrium of the Firm

In the short run, a firm that is operating in a monopolistically competitive market structure is similiar to a monopoly. It faces a negatively sloped demand curve and maximizes its profits by equating marginal cost with marginal revenue. If the demand curve cuts the average total cost curve, as is shown in part (i) of Figure 14-1, the firm can make pure profits over and above the opportunity cost of its capital.

The Long-Run Equilibrium of the Industry

The existence of profits, as shown in part (i) of Figure 14-1, provides an incentive for new firms to enter the industry. As they do so, the total demand for the industry's product must be shared among this larger number of firms, so each gets a smaller share of the

---

[1] This theory was first developed by the American economist Edwin Chamberlin in his path-breaking book, *The Theory of Monopolistic Competition* (Cambridge, MA: Harvard University Press, 1933).

FIGURE 14-1   Equilibrium of a Firm in Monopolistic Competition

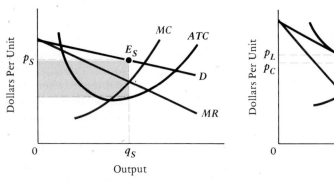

(i) Short-run equilibrium

(ii) Long-run equilibrium

Short-run equilibrium of a monopolistically competitive firm is the same as for a monopolist. In the long run, a monopolistically competitive industry has zero profits and excess capacity. Short-run equilibrium occurs in part (i) at E_S, the output for which $MR = MC$. Price is p_s and quantity is q_s. Profits may exist; in this example they are shown by the shaded area. Starting from the short-run equilibrium shown in part (i), entry of new firms shifts the firm's demand curve to the left and eliminates profits. In part (ii), point E_L, where demand is tangent to ATC, is the long-run equilibrium. Price is p_L and quantity is q_L. Price is greater and quantity is less than the perfectly competitive equilibrium price and quantity (p_C and q_C). At equilibrium, the monopolistically competitive firm has excess capacity of $q_1 q_C$.

total market. This shifts the demand curve for each existing firm's product to the left. Entry, and the consequent leftward shifting of the existing firms' demand curves, continues until profits are eliminated. When this has occurred, each firm is in the position shown in part (ii) of Figure 14-1. Its demand curve has shifted to the left until the curve is *tangent* to the average total cost curve. At this output the firm is just covering all of its costs. At any other output, it would be suffering losses, because average total costs would exceed average revenue.[2]

The excess capacity theorem.   Part (i) of Figure 14-1 makes it clear that monopolistic competition results

in a long-run equilibrium of zero profits, even though each individual firm faces a negatively sloped demand curve. It does this by forcing each firm into a position in which it has excess capacity; that is, each firm is producing to the left of the lowest point on its average total cost curve. If the firm were to increase its output, it would reduce its cost per unit, but it does not do so, because selling more would reduce revenue by more than it would reduce cost. This result is called the **excess capacity theorem.**

In monopolistic competition, commodities are produced at a point where average total costs are falling, in contrast to perfect competition, where they are produced at their lowest possible cost.

Evaluation of the Theory of Monopolistic Competition

Alleged inefficiency.   The excess capacity theorem once aroused passionate debate among economists

[2] If the demand curve *nowhere touched* the average total cost curve, there would be no output at which costs could be covered and exit would occur. If the demand curve were to *cut* the average total cost curve, there would be levels of output at which profits could be earned and entry would occur. Thus, the only possible long-run equilibrium, consistent with there being neither entry nor exit, is one where the demand curve is tangent to the average total cost curve (i.e., the demand curve just touches the average total cost curve at one output and lies below it at all other outputs).

because it seemed to show that all industries that sell differentiated products would produce them inefficiently at a higher cost than was necessary. Since product differentiation is a characteristic of virtually all modern consumer goods industries, this suggested that modern market economies were systematically inefficient. A few decades ago, many critics of market economies called for state intervention to eliminate unnecessary product differentiation, thus ensuring efficient (i.e., cost-minimizing) levels of production in consumer goods industries.

A more modern analysis by economists such as William Baumol, Kelvin Lancaster, and Joseph Stiglitz has shown that the charge of inefficiency has not been proven. The "excess capacity" of monopolistic competition does not necessarily indicate inefficiency (and waste of resources), because when firms can choose the characteristics of their own products, minimizing costs of producing a given set of products is not necessarily the most efficient thing to do. Differentiated products provide consumers with a choice among a variety of products, and it is clear that consumers have different tastes with respect to differentiated products. For example, each brand of breakfast food, running shoes, personal computers, and cameras has its devotees.

From society's point of view, there is a trade-off between producing more brands to satisfy diverse tastes and producing fewer brands at a lower cost per unit.

Monopolistic competition produces a wider range of products but at a somewhat higher cost per unit than perfect competition. It cannot be proven, however, that consumers necessarily will be worse off with 10 brands of a differentiated product to choose from than with 1 standard brand, or vice versa. Since consumers clearly value variety, the extra cost that variety imposes must be matched against the benefits of variety in judging the social efficiency of monopolistic competition, in order to find the *optimum amount* of product differentiation. Product differentiation is wasteful only if the costs of providing variety exceed the benefits conferred by providing that variety.

The optimum number of varieties of a differentiated product is attained when the gain to consumers from adding one more variety equals the loss from having to produce each existing variety at a higher cost because less of each is produced.

Empirical relevance. A long controversy raged in economics over several decades as to the empirical relevance of monopolistic competition. Of course, product differentiation is an almost universal phenomenon in consumer goods and in many other industries. Nonetheless, some economists maintained that this market structure was almost never found in practice.

To see why, we need to distinguish between products and firms. In many manufacturing industries a host of differentiated products are produced by only a few firms. In breakfast foods, for example, a vast variety of products is produced by a mere three firms (Kelloggs, Nabisco, and General Foods). Similar circumstances exist in soap, chemicals, cigarettes, and numerous other industries in which many more or less competing products are produced by a few very large firms. These industries clearly are neither perfectly competitive nor monopolies. Are they monopolistically competitive? The answer is no, because they contain only a few firms that often take account of each others' reactions when they are determining their own behavior. Furthermore, they often earn large profits without attracting new entry. In fact, these firms operate under a market structure that is called *oligopoly,* which we shall consider in the next section.

While accepting that many differentiated products are produced by industries that are not monopolistically competitive, some economists find that the theory is useful for analyzing industries where concentration ratios are low and the product is differentiated.

Oligopoly

The data in Tables 14-1 and 14-2 show that many American industries are characterized by a small number of firms, each of which accounts for a significant fraction of each industry's production. These firms—typically, from 3 to 12—tend to dominate such industries, and newcomers find it hard to establish themselves. The market structure that embraces such industries is called *oligopoly,* from the Greek words *oligos polein,* meaning "few to sell." An **oligopoly** is an industry that contains two or more firms, at least one of which produces a significant portion of the industry's total output. Whenever there is a high concentration ratio for the firms that are serving one particular market, that market is oligopolistic.

Characteristics of Oligopoly

An oligopolistic firm has a downward-sloping demand curve. It is large enough to realize that its competitors may respond to anything that it does. In other words, oligopolists are aware of the interdependence among the decisions taken by the various firms in the industry, and they engage in the type of rivalrous behavior discussed on pages 224–225.

Oligopolistic industries are of many types. In some there are only a few firms in the entire industry (8, in the case of cigarettes). In others there are many firms, but only a few dominate the market. For example, there are 282 petroleum refiners, but the 232 smallest firms together account for only 7 percent of the aggregate value of output. There are 108 tire and tube manufacturing companies, of which the 100 smallest supply less than 14 percent of the market. Oligopoly is consistent with a large number of small sellers, called a "competitive fringe," as long as a "big few" dominate the industry's production.

In oligopolistic industries, prices typically are administered. Products usually are differentiated. The intensity and the nature of rivalrous behavior vary greatly from industry to industry and from one period of time to another. This variety has invited extensive theoretical speculation and empirical study.

Why Bigness?

Why are so many industries dominated by a few large firms? It turns out that there is more than one answer to this question.

Much factory production uses the principle of the division of labor that we first studied in Chapter 1. The production of a commodity is broken up into hundreds of simple, repetitive tasks. This type of division of labor was the basis of the assembly line, which revolutionized the production of many goods

earlier in this century, and it still underlies economies of large-scale production in many industries. Such division of labor is, as Adam Smith observed long ago, dependent on the size of the market. (See Box 3-1 on page 43.) There is no point in dividing the production of a commodity up into a number of tasks, each of which can be done in a few minutes, if only a few units of the product can be sold each day.

Modern industries produce many differentiated products that give rise to a different type of scale economy. To develop a new product is costly, and it may be only a matter of a few years before it is replaced by some superior version of the same basic product. These fixed costs of product development must be recovered by the revenues from sales of the product. The larger are the firm's sales, the less is the cost that has to be recovered from each unit sold. Consider a product that costs $10 million to develop and to market. If 1 million units are to be sold, then $1 of the selling price of each unit must go toward recovering the development costs. If, however, the firm expects to sell 10 million units, then each unit need only contribute $.10 to these costs, and the market price can be lowered accordingly. With the enormous development costs of some of today's "high-tech" products, firms that can sell a large volume have a distinct pricing advantage over firms that sell a smaller volume.

Other scale economies are related to financing and to marketing. It is costly to enter a market, to establish a sales force, and to make consumers aware of a product. These costs are often nearly as high when a small volume is being marketed as when a large volume is being marketed. Thus, the smaller is the volume of the firm's sales, the higher must be the price per unit sold, if the firm is to cover all of these costs.

For these and other similar reasons, there are major advantages of being a large size for firms in many industries. Where size confers a cost advantage, there may be room for only a few firms, even when the total market is quite large. This cost advantage of size will dictate that the industry be an oligopoly unless some form of government regulation prevents the firms from growing to their efficient size.

In other cases, as we shall see later in this chapter, the existing firms in the industry may create barriers to entry where natural ones do not exist. The industry will then be dominated by a few large firms only because they are successful in preventing the entry of new firms that would lower the industry's concentration ratio.

The Basic Dilemma of Oligopoly

Oligopolists face a basic dilemma between competing against each other and cooperating with each other.

The firms in an oligopolistic industry will make more profits as a group if they cooperate with each other; any one firm, however, may make more profits for itself if it competes with the others.

This is the same result that we established in Chapter 13 for the cartelization of a perfectly competitive industry. In a perfectly competitive industry, however, there are so many firms that they cannot reach the cooperative equilibrium unless some central governing body is formed, by either themselves or the government, to enforce the necessary behavior on all firms. In contrast, the few firms in an oligopolistic industry cannot help but recognize their mutual interdependence. As a result, they see the possibility of reaching a cooperative solution by tacitly agreeing to avoid competitive behavior.

The Cooperative Equilibrium

If the firms in an oligopolistic industry cooperate with one another, either overtly or tacitly, to produce among themselves the monopoly output, they can maximize their joint profits. If they do this, they will reach what is called the **cooperative equilibrium,** which is the equilibrium that a single monopoly firm would reach if it owned all the firms in the industry.

The Noncooperative Equilibrium

If all the firms in an oligopolistic industry are at the cooperative equilibrium, it will usually be worthwhile for any one of them to cut its price or to raise its output, as long as the others do not do so. However, if everyone does the same thing, they will be worse off as a group and may all be worse off individually. An equilibrium that is reached by firms when they proceed by calculating only their own gains, without worrying about the reactions of others, is called **noncooperative equilibrium.**

An Example from Game Theory

A typical situation of this sort is illustrated in Figure 14-2 for the case of a two-firm oligopoly, called a **duopoly.** This figure shows what is called a *payoff matrix.* It takes us into the realm of *game theory,* which analyzes optimal strategies for games in which players compete with each other while knowing that they need to take account of each others' reactions.

When game theory is applied to oligopoly, the players are firms, their game is played in the market, their strategies are their price or output decisions, and the *payoffs* are their profits.

Now look closely at the payoff matrix in Figure 14-2, which shows a simplified version of an oligopoly game. The simplified game, adopted for the purposes of illustration, allows only two strategies: produce an output equal to one-half of the monopoly output or two-thirds of that output. Even this simple game, however, is sufficient to illustrate several key ideas in the modern theory of oligopoly.

The data in the matrix show that if both sides cooperate, each producing one-half of the monopoly output, they achieve the cooperative equilibrium and jointly earn the monopoly profits. As a group, they can do no better.

Once the cooperative position is attained, the data in the figure show that if A cheats and produces more, its profits will increase. However, B's profits will be reduced: A's behavior drives the industry's prices down so that B must earn less from its unchanged output. Since A's cheating takes the firms away from the joint profit-maximizing, monopoly output, their joint profits must fall, which means that B's profits will fall by more than A's will rise.

Figure 14-2 shows that similar considerations also apply to B: It is worthwhile for B to depart from the joint maximizing output, as long as A does not. So both A and B have an incentive to depart from the joint profit-maximizing level of output.

Finally, Figure 14-2 shows that when either firm does depart from the joint maximizing output, the other has an incentive to do so as well. As a result of such "selfish" behavior, they reach a noncooperative equilibrium, in which each has profits that are lower than in the cooperative equilibrium.

Nash equilibrium. The noncooperative equilibrium shown in Figure 14-2 is called a *Nash equilibrium,* after the American mathematician John Nash, who developed it some 40 years ago. A **Nash equilibrium** is one in which each firm's best strategy is to maintain its present behavior *given the present behavior of the other firm.* It is easy to see that there is one Nash equilibrium in Figure 14-2. In the bottom right-hand square, the best decision for each firm, given that the other firm is producing two-thirds of the monopoly output, is to produce two-thirds of the monopoly output itself. Neither player has a self-interest in departing from this position, except through cooperation with the other.

The basis of a Nash equilibrium is rational decision making in the absence of cooperation. Its particular importance in oligopoly theory is that it is the only self-policing equilibrium. If it is established—by any means whatsoever—the individual firms have no incentive to depart from it by altering their own individual behavior.

The equilibrium in perfect competition is a Nash equilibrium, since no firm has any incentive to alter its output, given the behavior of all other firms, which collectively determine the market supply and hence the current market price. The equilibrium established by a cartel that has been formed by formerly perfectly competitive firms by cooperation among oligopolists is not a Nash equilibrium, since, as we have already seen, each individual firm has an incentive to depart from it.

Recognition of interdependence. We have seen how the Nash equilibrium in Figure 14-2 can be arrived at when firms cheat on an agreement to reach the cooperative equilibrium. The same equilibrium will be attained if each firm decides independently what its optimal strategy will be, taking into account what the other firm may do. Let us see how this works.

First, assume that firm A reasons as follows: "What if B produces one-half of the monopoly output? If I do the same, I receive a profit of 20, but if I produce two-thirds of the monopoly output, I receive 22." Next, A asks itself: "What if B produces two-thirds of the monopoly output? If I produce one-half of the monopoly output, I receive a profit of 15, whereas if I produce two-thirds, I receive 17.

FIGURE 14-2 The Oligopolist's Dilemma: To Cooperate or to Compete

		A's Output	
		One-half monopoly output	Two-thirds monopoly output
B's Output	One-half monopoly output	20 20	15 22
	Two-thirds monopoly output	22 15	17 17

Cooperation to determine the overall level of output can maximize joint profits, but it leaves each firm with an incentive to alter its production. The figure gives what is called a payoff matrix for a two-person duopoly game. Only two levels of production are considered in order to illustrate the basic problem facing oligopolists. A's production is indicated across the top of the matrix, and its profits (measured in millions of dollars) are shown in the white circles within each square. B's production is indicated down the left side of the matrix, and its profits (in millions of dollars) are shown in the colored circles within each square. For example, the top, right-hand square tells us that if B produces one-half, while A produces two-thirds, of the monopoly output, A's profits will be $22 million, while B's will be $15 million.

If A and B cooperate, they can each produce one-half the monopoly output and can each earn profits of $20 million. This is shown in the upper left-hand box. However, at the position, known as the cooperative equilibrium, each firm can raise its profits by producing two-thirds of the monopoly output, provided that the other firm does not do the same.

Now assume that A and B make their decision noncooperatively. A may reason that whether B produces either one-half or two-thirds of the monopoly output, A's best output is two-thirds. B may reason similarly. In this case they reach the noncooperative equilibrium, as shown in the bottom, right-hand square. Each produces two-thirds of the monopoly output, and each makes less than it could if they had cooperated.

Clearly, my best strategy is to produce two-thirds in either case." B reasons in the same way. As a result, they end up producing $1\frac{1}{2}$ times the monopoly output between themselves, and each earns a profit of 17.

We have now seen in detail how oligopolists have an incentive to cooperate but may be driven, through their own individual decisions, to produce more and earn less than they would in a cooperative equilibrium. Our next step is to look in more detail at the types of cooperative and rivalrous behavior that oligopolists may adopt. We can then go on to study the forces that influence the balance between cooperation and competition in actual situations.

Types of Cooperative Behavior

When firms agree to cooperate in order to restrict output and to raise prices, their behavior is called **collusion.** Collusive behavior may occur with or without an actual agreement to collude. Where explicit agreement occurs, economists speak of *overt* or *covert collusion,* depending on whether the agreement is open or secret. Where no explicit agreement actually occurs, economists speak of **tacit collusion** (while lawyers speak of *conscious parallel action*). In this case, all firms behave cooperatively without an explicit agreement to do so. They merely understand that it is in their mutual interests to restrict output and to raise prices. In terms of Figure 14-2, firm A decides to produce one-half of the monopoly output, hoping that firm B will do the same. Firm B does what A expects, and they achieve the cooperative equilibrium without ever explicitly cooperating.

Explicit Cooperation

The easiest way for firms to ensure that they all will maintain their joint profit-maximizing output is to make an explicit agreement to do so. Such collusive agreements have occurred in the past in the United States, although they have been illegal for a long time. When they are discovered today, they are rigorously prosecuted. We shall see, however, that such agreements are not illegal everywhere in the world, particularly when they are supported by national governments.

We saw in Chapter 13 that when a group of firms gets together to act in this way, it is called a *cartel.* Cartels show in stark form the basic conflict between cooperation and competition that we just discussed.

Full cooperation always allows the industry to achieve the result of monopoly. It also always presents individual firms with the incentive to cheat. The larger is the number of firms, the greater is the temptation for any one of them to cheat. After all, the cheating of one small firm may not be noticed, since it will have a negligible effect on price. The problems facing all cartels are seen most vividly, therefore, in the case that we studied in Chapter 13, in which the number of firms is so large that most of them are price takers. This is why cartels that involve firms in industries that would otherwise be perfectly competitive tend to be unstable. Cartels also may be formed by a group of firms that would otherwise be in an oligopolistic market. The smaller is the group of firms that forms a cartel, the more likely it is that the firms will let their joint interest in cooperating guide their behavior. Although cheating may still occur, the few firms in the industry can easily foresee the outcome of an outbreak of rivalrous behavior among themselves.

OPEC as an Example of a Cartel

The most famous modern example of a cartel that engaged in cooperative behavior is the Organization of Petroleum Producing Countries (OPEC). This cartel illustrates the power of cooperative behavior to create short-run profits, as well as the problems of trying to exercise long-run market power in an industry without substantial entry barriers.

OPEC did not attract worldwide attention until 1973, when its members voluntarily restricted their outputs by negotiating quotas among themselves. In that year, OPEC countries accounted for about 70 percent of the world's supply of crude oil and 87 percent of the world's oil exports. So, although it was not quite a complete monopoly, the cartel came close to being one. By reducing output, the OPEC countries were able to drive up the world price of oil and to earn massive profits both for themselves and for non-OPEC producers, who obtained the high prices without having to limit their outputs. After several years of success, however, OPEC began to encounter the characteristic problems of cartels.

New entry. New entry became a problem. The high price of oil encouraged the development of new supplies, and within a few years new productive capacity was coming into use at a rapid rate in non-OPEC countries.

Long-run adjustment of demand.   There was not too much that consumers could do in the short run, and the short-run demand for oil proved to be highly inelastic. Over time, however, adaptations to reduce the demand for oil were made within the confines of existing technology. Homes and offices were insulated more efficiently, and smaller, more fuel-efficient cars became popular. This is an example of the distinction between the short- and the long-run demand for a commodity, which was first introduced on pages 80–82.

Innovation in the very long run.   Innovation further reduced the demand for oil in the very long run. Over time, technologies that were more efficient in their use of oil, as well as alternative energy sources, were developed. Had the oil prices stayed up longer than they did, major breakthroughs on solar energy and heat from the interior of the earth would have been registered.

This experience in both the long and the very long run shows the price system at work, signaling the need for adaptation and providing the incentives for that adaptation. It also provides an illustration of Schumpeter's concept of creative destruction, which we first discussed on pages 251–252. In order to share in the profits generated by high energy prices, new technologies and new substitute products were developed, and these destroyed much of the market power of the original cartel.

Cheating.   At first, there was little incentive for OPEC to violate quotas. OPEC countries found themselves with such undreamed-of increases in their incomes that they found it difficult to use all of their money productively. As the output of non-OPEC oil grew, however, OPEC's output had to be reduced to hold prices high. Incomes in OPEC countries declined sharply, as a result.

Many OPEC countries had become used to their enormous incomes, and their attempts to maintain them in the face of falling output quotas brought the instabilities inherent in all cartels to the surface. In 1981 the cartel price reached its peak of $35 per barrel. In real terms, this was about five times as high as the 1972 price, but production quotas were less than one-half of OPEC's capacity. Eager to in-

crease their oil revenues, many individual OPEC members gave in to the pressure to cheat and produced in excess of their production quotas. By late 1984 Saudi Arabia indicated that it would not tolerate further cheating by its partners and demanded that others share equally in reducing their quotas yet further. However, agreement proved to be impossible. In December 1985, OPEC decided to eliminate production quotas and let each member make its own decisions about output.

After the collapse.   OPEC's collapse as an output-restricting cartel led to a major reduction in world oil prices. Early in 1986 the downward slide took the price to $20 per barrel, and it fell to $11 per barrel later in the year. Allowing for inflation, this was about the price that had prevailed just before OPEC introduced its output restrictions in 1973. Prices have been volatile since then. They have oscillated between about $10 per barrel, which is close to the perfectly competitive price, and $18 per barrel, which seems to be all that can be sustained with the modicum of agreement on output restrictions that can currently be obtained.

Tacit Cooperation

While collusive behavior that affects prices is illegal in the United States, a small group of firms that recognize the influence that each has on the others may act without any explicit agreement to achieve the cooperative equilibrium. In such tacit agreements, the two forces that we just analyzed are still evident. The firms have a common interest in cooperating to maximize their joint profits at the cooperative equilibrium.

Each firm is, however, interested in its own profits, and any one of them usually can increase its profits by behaving in a rivalrous fashion. Although the most obvious way in which to do this is for one firm to produce more than its share of the joint profit-maximizing output, there are, as we shall soon see, other ways in which rivalrous behavior may break out.

Even if *joint* profits are maximized, there is the problem of market shares. How is the profit-maximizing level of sales to be divided among the competing firms? Competition for market shares may upset the tacit agreement to hold to joint maximizing behavior. In an industry that has many differentiated products and in which sales are often by contract between buyers and sellers, cheating may be covert rather than overt. Secret discounts and rebates can allow a firm to increase its sales at the expense of its competitors, while appearing to hold to the tacitly agreed monopoly price.

Another reason why the monopoly level of profits may not be achieved, even if the monopoly price is maintained, is that firms often compete for market shares by various forms of nonprice competition, such as advertising and variations in the quality of their product. Such costly competition may reduce industry profits.

Very long-run considerations also may be important. In a world in which technology and product characteristics are being changed constantly, a firm that chooses to behave in a rivalrous way may be able to maintain a larger market share and to earn larger profits than it would if it behaved in a cooperative way, even though all the firms' joint profits are lower.

For these and for other reasons, often there are strong incentives for oligopolistic firms to compete with each other rather than to maintain the cooperative equilibrium, even when they understand the risks that are involved to their joint profits.

Cooperation or Competition?

Empirical research by such economists as the late Jo Bain and Nobel Laureate Herbert Simon suggests that the relative strengths of the incentives to cooperate and to compete vary from industry to industry in a systematic way, depending on observable characteristics of firms, markets, and products. What are some of the characteristics that will affect the strength of the two incentives?

1. *The tendency toward joint maximization of profits is greater for smaller numbers of sellers than for larger numbers of sellers.* This involves both motivation and ability. When there are few firms, they will know that one of them cannot gain sales wthout inducing retaliation by its rivals. Also, a few firms can tacitly coordinate their policies with less difficulty than can many firms.

2. *The tendency toward joint maximization of profits is greater for producers of similar products than for producers of sharply differentiated products.* The more nearly identical are the products of sellers, the closer will be the direct rivalry for customers, and the less will

be the ability of one firm to gain a lasting advantage over its rivals. Such sellers will tend to prefer joint efforts to achieve a larger pie to individual attempts to increase their own shares.

3. *The tendency toward joint maximization of profits is greater in a growing than in a contracting market.* When demand is growing, firms can produce at full capacity without any need to "steal" customers from their rivals. When firms have excess capacity, they are tempted to give price concessions to attract customers. When their rivals retaliate, price cuts become general.

4. *The tendency toward joint maximization of profits is greater when the industry contains a dominant firm rather than a group of more or less equal competitors.* A dominant firm may become a *price leader,* which is a firm that sets the industry's price while all other firms fall into line. Even if a dominant firm is not automatically a price leader, other firms may look to it for judgment about market conditions, and its decisions may become a tentative focus for tacit agreement.

5. *The tendency toward joint maximization of profits is greater when nonprice rivalry is absent or limited.* When firms seek to suppress their basic rivalry by avoiding price competition, rivalry will tend to break out in other forms unless it is expressly curtailed. Firms may seek to increase their market shares through extra advertising, changes in the quality of the product, the establishment of new products, giveaways, and a host of similar schemes that leave their prices unchanged but increase their costs and so reduce their joint profits.

6. *The tendency toward joint maximization of profits is greater when the barriers to entry of new firms are greater.* The high profits of existing firms attract new entrants, who will drive down price and reduce profits. The greater are the barriers to entry, the less this will occur. Thus, the greater are the entry barriers, the closer the profits of existing firms can be to their joint maximizing level without being reduced by new entrants.

Short-Run Price Stickiness

We have seen that all firms that sell differentiated products, whether they are under monopolistic competition, oligopoly, or monopoly, must administer their prices. One striking contrast between perfectly competitive markets, on the one hand, and markets for differentiated products, on the other hand, concerns the behavior of prices. In perfect competition, prices change continually in response to changes in demand and supply. In markets where differentiated products are sold, prices change less frequently. Manufacturers' prices for radios, automobiles, television sets, and men's suits do not change with anything like the frequency that prices change in markets for basic materials or stocks and bonds.

Since the bulk of manufacturing industries that sell differentiated products are oligopolies, this phenomenon is often referred to as the *stickiness* of oligopolistic prices.

Before considering possible explanations of why prices may be sticky, it is important to recognize that administered prices do change.

Changing prices.   Oligopolistic prices usually change when there are major changes in costs of production. Sometimes a specific set of costs will rise, as when the two OPEC oil shocks pushed up the prices of oil, gasoline, and all oil-related products. Sometimes most costs will be rising, as with a general inflation. In either set of cases, increases in input costs are passed on quite quickly by means of rises in output prices. This is because such increases in costs threaten to eliminate profits unless they are passed on, at least in part, in terms of higher prices. By the same token, major reductions in costs, as when a new product such as the personal computer is being developed, are usually followed by reductions in prices. This is because of the rivalry among oligopolistic firms. If one firm fails to cut prices when costs fall, another firm will do so, seeking thereby to increase its market share.

Oligopolistic prices also often change in response to large, unexpected shifts in demand. If an industry finds itself faced with an apparently permanent downward shift in demand, firms will often cut prices in an attempt to retain their markets until long-term adjustments can be made. For example, the American automobile industry was faced with declining demand from 1980 to 1982 due to its lag in developing small, fuel-efficient cars that would be competitive with Japanese imports. It offered big rebates that slashed prices to levels that could not have been maintained in the long run.

Sticky prices.   The stickiness of administered prices occurs mainly in the face of cyclical and seasonal fluctuations in demand. The existence of business

cycles (i.e., alternating periods of high and low demand for output) is well known to firms, even if the precise course of each cycle cannot be predicted in advance. Oligopolistic (and monopoly) firms tend to adjust to these changes more by varying quantities than by varying prices.

Price stickiness is short-term behavior that need not affect our long-term view of how the economy functions. Nonetheless, the stickiness is an interesting problem in its own right, and it also has important implications for macroeconomics.[3]

Three main explanations of oligopolistic price stickiness have been offered: tacit collusion, fear of competitors' reactions, and the cost of changing prices. Each may have validity in certain circumstances.

Tacit Collusion

We have seen that it is worthwhile for oligopolistic firms to avoid price competition and therefore maximize their joint profits by achieving the monopoly price and output for the industry as a whole. We have also seen that such agreements will be fragile because of the incentive for individual firms to cheat.

Realizing this, oligopolistic firms that do have some effective tacit cooperation on price and output will be reluctant to alter prices or outputs in response to small or temporary changes in demand. They will fear that other firms will misinterpret their actions and react in a rivalrous way, causing an outbreak of competitive behavior that will reduce everyone's profits.

Where rivalrous price and output behavior is being restrained by tacit cooperation, caution may restrain firms from changing prices as a result of changes in demand that might otherwise lead them to alter prices.

This theory may explain some price stickiness in situations in which firms are tacitly cooperating and fear rivalrous competitive behavior. It does not explain the observed price stickiness on the part of monopolists who have no competitors to worry

[3] A major problem of macroeconomics is understanding why in the short run it is mainly output, rather than prices, that responds to changes in the total demand for goods and services across the whole economy. The oligopolistic behavior that we have studied in this section provides one part of the explanation of this phenomenon.

about: those oligopolists who either feel that their cooperation is secure or who do not cooperate at all and so are already in the noncooperative equilibrium; or those monopolistic competitors who are, by definition, unconcerned about the reaction of the numerous firms in their industry.

Fear of Competitors' Reactions: The Kinked Demand Curve

A second explanation also considers each firm's anticipation of its competitors' reactions. This time, however, the competitors are assumed to react in a very specific manner.

According to this theory, each oligopolist conjectures that its rivals will match any price decreases that it makes but will not match any price increases that it makes. If one firm raises its price and no one follows, it will lose its market share and its sales will fall off rapidly. Thus, its demand curve for price *increases* will be rather flat. On the other hand, if one firm lowers its price and everyone follows, it will not increase its market share. Its sales will expand only in proportion to the expansion in the industry's sales. Thus, the demand curve for price *reductions* will be steeper than the demand curve for price increases. The resulting **kinked demand curve** is shown in Figure 14-3.

Whenever oligopolists make these assumptions about their competitors' reactions, they will be reluctant to change prices in response to shifts in costs. Their profit-maximizing strategy will be to hold prices constant in the face of significant shifts in marginal costs, even though the cooperative equilibrium calls for a rise in price and a fall in output.

The theory does less well in explaining responses to changes in demand. If the demand curve shifts, the firm will be led to change its price unless, by coincidence, the kink on the new demand curve occurs at the same price as the kink on the original demand curve. Such a coincidence is not impossible, but it is hardly likely to be an explanation of any *general tendency* for oligopolistic prices to be sticky in the face of fluctuations in demand.

This theory may well explain oligopolistic price stickiness in specific circumstances in which oligopolists make the stated assumptions about their competitors' reactions. The earlier discussion makes it clear, however, that oligopolists' assumptions about their competitors' reactions may vary with the mar-

FIGURE 14-3   The Kinked Demand Curve

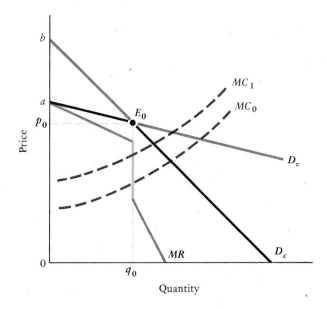

Price stickiness in the case of varying costs can result if the firm assumes that its competitors will match its price reductions but not its price increases. The firm is in equilibrium at E_0 by charging a price of p_0 and selling at q_0. Its demand curve, drawn on the assumption that all other firms follow any price changes it makes, is the curve D_c. The firm's market share is constant along this curve. (This curve is labeled D_c for *constant* market share.) The firm's demand curve, drawn on the assumption that all other firms hold their prices constant, is D_v. Along this curve the firm's market share varies negatively with the price it charges: The higher is its price, the lower is its market share. (This curve is labeled D_v for *variable* market share.)

Since the firm assumes that its competitors will match its price cuts but not its price increases, its demand curve is given by D_c below E_0 and D_v above E_0. Thus, the whole demand curve runs from a to E_0 to b with a kink at E_0, where there is a change in the demand curve that is relevant to the duopolist's decisions. The marginal revenue curve for this kinked demand curve takes a jump at quantity q_0. For lower quantities, where the demand curve D_v is relevant, its MR curve is high up and relatively flat. For larger quantities, where the demand curve D_c is relevant, its MR curve is lower down and steeper.

The marginal cost curves of MC_0 and MC_1 both give equilibrium output at q_0 with price p_0, because both pass through the point where the marginal revenue curve "jumps."

ket circumstances in which they find themselves. Thus a theory based on the assumption of one particular reaction is unlikely to explain all cases. Also, the theory has the same limitations as those discussed in connection with the first explanation given previously: It does not explain the observed price stickiness among monopolies and monopolistic competitors.

Cost of Changing Prices

The third explanation of sticky prices concerns the cost for multiproduct firms of making price changes. Modern firms that sell differentiated products typically have hundreds, and sometimes even thousands, of distinct products in their price lists. Changing such a long list of administered prices, at the same frequency that competitive market prices change, would be physically impossible. Changing them at all is costly. These costs include those of printing new list prices, notifying all customers, the difficulty in accounting and billing of keeping track of frequently changing prices, and the loss of customer and retailer goodwill due to the uncertainty caused by frequent changes in prices. These costs are often a significant consideration to multiproduct firms.

Maintaining sticky prices in the face of fluctuating demand and output would cause large losses to firms whose costs varied greatly with output, as shown by the U-shaped curve in Figure 14-4. However, a firm with a flat cost curve of the type that also is shown in Figure 14-4 can maintain prices without suffering large losses. Part of the explanation of sticky prices in the presence of the costs of price adjustments is found, therefore, in the rather flat cost curves that are encountered by many manufacturing firms: monopolistic competitors, oligopolists, and monopolists.

Cost curves that are steep at either extreme and flat over a long middle portion are often referred to as being *saucer shaped*. Box 14-1 discusses the reason for this shape.

Although the saucer-shaped cost curves that are typically found in manufacturing do not *force* firms to adopt sticky pricing policies, they do make it possible for such policies to be profitable.

The explanation of sticky prices based on a combination of flat cost curves and the cost of changing

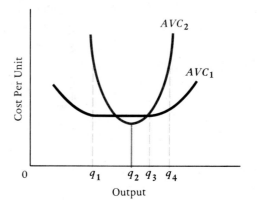

FIGURE 14-4   U-shaped Versus Saucer-shaped Cost Curves

A firm that anticipates fluctuating output may choose a plant with a flat-bottomed cost curve. AVC_1 and AVC_2 are alternatives based on how a plant is designed and built. While AVC_2 achieves lower unit costs than does AVC_1 if output is very close to q_2, it is much less adaptable to either higher or lower outputs. If the firm could count on producing q_2 every period, it would prefer the plant yielding AVC_2. However, if it anticipates outputs ranging from q_1 to q_4, it would prefer AVC_1.

prices is as follows. Firms estimate their *normal* demand curve, that is, the average of what they can expect to sell at each price over the business cycle. Having built a plant that is consistent with this normal demand and with the expected fluctuations in output, they adopt the profit-maximizing price derived from their normal demand curve as their "normal price." Short-run fluctuations in demand are met by holding price constant and varying output. This avoids the costs involved in repeated price changes and is profit-maximizing behavior *if* costs of changing prices are high enough and *if* production cost curves are flat enough. The best thing that a firm can then do, whether it is monopolistically competitive, oligopolistic, or a monopoly, is to set the price that maximizes profits for average demand and adjust output rather than price as demand fluctuates cyclically.

Changes in costs such as those that accompany an inflation are, however, passed on through price increases. Since few firms expect inflationary price increases to be reversed, they know that they must raise their prices to cover them. Even in these cases, however, they do so periodically, rather than continuously, because of the costs incurred in making such changes.

Long-Run Behavior: The Importance of Entry Barriers

Suppose firms in an oligopolistic industry succeed in raising prices above long-run average total costs and earn substantial profits that are not completely eliminated by nonprice competition. In the absence of significant barriers to entry, new firms will enter the industry and erode the profits of existing firms, as they do in monopolistic competition.

Natural barriers to entry were discussed in Chapter 13 (see pages 250–251). Where such natural barriers do not exist, oligopolistic firms can earn profits in the long run only if they can create entry barriers. To the extent to which this is done, existing firms can move toward joint profit maximization without fear that new firms, attracted by the high profits, will enter the industry. We discuss next some types of created barriers.

Brand Proliferation

By varying the characteristics of a differentiated product, it is possible to produce a vast array of different variations on the general theme of that product. Think, for example, of cars with a little more or a little less acceleration, braking power, top speed, cornering ability, gas mileage, and so on, compared with existing models. Although the multiplicity of existing brands is no doubt partly a response to consumers' tastes, it can have the effect of discouraging the entry of new firms.

To illustrate why brand proliferation may be a formidable barrier to a small, potential entrant, assume that the product is the type for which there is a substantial amount of brand switching by consumers. In this case, the larger is the number of brands sold by existing firms, the smaller are the expected sales of a new entrant. Say that an industry contains 3 large firms, each selling one brand of cigarettes, and say that 30 percent of all smokers change brands in a random fashion each year. If a new firm enters the industry, it can expect to pick up 25 percent of the smokers who change brands (the smoker has

available 1 out of the new total of 4 brands). This would give the new firm 7.5 percent (25 percent of 30 percent) of the total market the first year merely as a result of picking up its share of the random switchers, and it would keep increasing its share thereafter. If, however, the existing 3 firms have 5 brands each, there would be 15 brands already available, and a new firm selling 1 new brand could expect to pick up only one-sixteenth of the brand switchers, giving it less than 2 percent of the total market the first year, with smaller gains also in subsequent years. This is an extreme case, but it illustrates a general result.

The larger is the number of differentiated products that are sold by existing oligopolists, the smaller is the market share available to a new firm that is entering with a single new product.

Set-up Costs

Existing firms can create entry barriers by imposing significant fixed costs on new firms that enter their market. This is particularly important if the industry has only weak natural barriers to entry, because the minimum efficient scale occurs at an output that is low relative to the total output of the industry.

Advertising is one means by which existing firms can impose heavy set-up costs on new entrants. Advertising, of course, serves purposes other than that of creating barriers to entry. Among them, it may perform the useful function of informing buyers about their alternatives, thereby making markets work more smoothly. Indeed, a new firm may find that advertising is essential, even when existing firms do not advertise at all, simply to call attention to its entry into an industry in which it is unknown.

Nonetheless, advertising can also operate as a potent entry barrier by increasing the set-up costs of new entrants. Where heavy advertising has established strong brand images for existing products, a new firm may have to spend heavily on advertising to create its own brand images in consumers' minds. If the firm's sales are small, advertising costs *per unit sold* will be large and price will have to be correspondingly high to cover those costs.

Figure 14-5 illustrates how heavy advertising can shift the cost curves of a firm with a low minimum efficient scale (*MES*) to make it one with a high *MES*. In essence, what happens is that a scale advantage of advertising is added to a low *MES* of pro-

BOX 14-1

Saucer-shaped Industry Cost Curves

Ever since economists began measuring the cost curves of manufacturing firms some 50 years ago, they have reported flat, short-run variable cost curves. The evidence is now clear that in most manufacturing industries, and in some others, cost curves are shaped like the black curve (AVC_1) shown in Figure 14-4, with a long, flat portion in the middle and sharply rising sections at each end. For such a saucer-shaped curve, there is a large range of output over which average variable costs are constant. Over this range, marginal costs are equal to average variable costs, and thus they, too, are constant per unit of output.

Why are many cost curves saucer-shaped rather than U-shaped? The answer is that firms design plants to have this property so that they can accommodate the inevitable seasonal and cyclical swings in demand for their products. As Professor George Stigler (the 1982 Nobel Laureate in Economics) pointed out, a firm that is faced with two possible average variable cost curves, such as those shown in Figure 14-4, might well prefer to build a plant that results in the saucer-shaped curve if it anticipates widely fluctuating demand. The saucer-shaped curve then leads *on average* to lower costs,

even if at some output the U-shaped cost curve dips below it.

To see why a firm can choose the shape of its short-run average cost curve, consider again the law of diminishing returns that we first encountered in Chapter 10. The U-shaped, short-run cost curve arises when a variable amount of one factor, say, labor, is applied to a fixed amount of a second factor, say, capital. Imagine starting from zero output and zero use of the variable factor and then increasing output. As more of the variable factor is used, a more nearly optimal combination with the fixed factor is achieved. Once the optimal combination is arrived at, the use of further units of the variable factor leads to too much of the variable factor being used in combination with the fixed factor. This causes average variable costs to begin to rise. Only one quantity of labor leads to the least-cost factor proportions.

These changing combinations of fixed and variable factors must occur in the short run whenever all of the fixed factor must be used all of the time; in other words, when the fixed factor is *indivisible*. This is not always the case, however. Even though the firm's plant and equipment may be fixed in the

duction, with the result that the overall *MES* is raised. Thus,

A new entrant with small sales but large set-up costs finds itself at a substantial cost disadvantage relative to its established rivals.

Any once-and-for-all cost of entering a market has the same effect as a large, initial advertising expenditure. For example, with many consumer goods, the cost of developing a new product that is similar, but not identical, to existing products may be quite substantial. Even if there are few economies of scale in the production of the product, its large fixed development cost can lead to a falling long-run average total cost curve over a wide range of output.

An Application

The combined use of brand proliferation and advertising as an entry barrier can help to explain one apparent paradox of everyday life—that one firm often sells multiple brands of the same product, which compete directly against one another as well as against the products of other firms.

The soap and cigarette industries provide classic examples of this behavior. Since all available scale economies can be realized by quite small plants, both industries have few natural barriers to entry. Both contain a few large firms, each of which produces an array of heavily advertised products. The numerous existing products make it harder for a new entrant to obtain a large market niche with *one* new product.

short run, so that *no more* than what exists is available, it is often possible to utilize *less* than this amount. For this reason, the flat cost curve is not inconsistent with the law of diminishing returns. The divisibility of the "fixed factor" means that diminishing returns does not apply, because variations in output below full capacity are accomplished by reducing the input of both labor and capital.

Consider, as a simple example, a factory that consists of 10 sewing machines in a shed, each of which has a productive capacity of 20 units per day when operated by 1 operator for 1 shift. If 200 units per day are required, then all 10 machines would be operated by 10 workers on a normal shift. If demand falls to 180, then 1 operator could be laid off. There is no need, however, to have the 9 remaining operators dashing about trying to work 10 machines. Clearly, 1 machine could be "laid off" as well, and the ratio of *employed* labor to *employed* machines could be held constant. Production could go from 20 to 40 to 60 all the way to 200 units per day without any change in the proportions in which the employed factors would be used. In this case, we would expect the factory to have constant marginal and average variable costs from 20 to 200 units

per day. Only beyond 200 units per day would it begin to encounter rising costs, since production would have to be extended by overtime and other means of combining more labor with the maximum available supply of 10 machines.

In such a case, the fixed factor is *divisible*. Since some of it can be left unemployed, there is no need to depart from the most efficient ratio of *labor used* to *capital used* as production is decreased. Thus, average variable costs can be constant over a large range, up to the point at which all of the fixed factor is used.

A similar situation occurs when a firm has many plants. For example, a plywood manufacturer with 10 plants may choose to reduce its output by temporarily closing one or more plants (or operating them on a limited-time basis) while operating the rest at normal-capacity output. The *firm's* short-run variable costs tend to be constant over a large range of output because there is no need to depart from the optimal combination of labor and capital in those plants that are kept in operation.

The heavy advertising, although it is directed against existing products, creates an entry barrier by increasing the *set-up costs* of a new product that seeks to gain the attention of consumers and to establish its own brand image.

Predatory Pricing

A firm that is considering entry will not do so if it is faced with the expectation of losses after entry. One way in which existing firms can create such a situation is to cut prices below costs whenever entry occurs and to keep them there until the entrant goes bankrupt. The existing firms sacrifice profits while doing this, but they send a discouraging message to

potential future rivals, as well as to present ones. Economists use the term *reputation effects* to refer to the effects of a strategy against new entrants of predatory price cutting. Even if this strategy is costly in terms of lost profits in the short run, it may pay for itself in the long run by deterring the entry of new firms at other times or in other markets that the firm controls.

There is controversy concerning predatory pricing. Some economists argue that pricing policies that appear to be predatory can be explained by other motives and that existing firms only hurt themselves when they engage in such practices instead of accommodating new entrants. Others argue that predatory pricing seems to have been observed and that it is in

FIGURE 14-5   A Theory of Sticky Prices in the Face of Fluctuating Demand

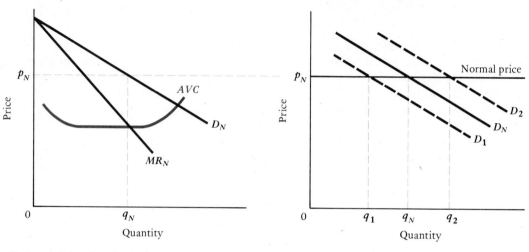

(i) Determining normal price   (ii) Adjusting to demand fluctuations

If it is costly to make price changes, a profit-maximizing firm may fix a price based on average sales and vary quantity in the face of fluctuating demand. In part (i) the firm with normal capacity q_N and a normal (average) demand curve D_N with a marginal revenue curve MR_N sets p_N as the profit-maximizing price, where $MR_N = MC$ (which equals AVC, because average variable cost is constant at q_N). This price becomes its normal price. As shown in part (ii), when demand slumps to D_1, the firm reduces output to q_1 but keeps price unchanged. When demand peaks at D_2, it also maintains prices and increases output to q_2.

the long-run interests of existing firms to punish the occasional new entrant even when it is costly to do so in the short run.

Whatever the outcome is of this debate among economists, the courts have taken the position that predatory pricing does occur. A number of firms have been convicted of using it as a method of eliminating competition.

Oligopoly and the Functioning of the Economy

We have seen that oligopoly is the most commonly encountered market structure in large parts of the American economy. How does this observation affect our views of the working of the price system?

Oligopolies do not fulfill the technical conditions of allocative efficiency that we shall study in Chapter 15. In many industries, however, scale economies make perfect competition impossible. There is just

not enough room for a large number of firms all of which are operating at or near their minimum efficient scales. Important issues for public policy thus concern how to evaluate the performance of oligopolistic industries. In doing this, two questions are important. First, in their price and output behavior, where do oligopolistic firms typically settle between the extreme outcomes of monopoly and perfect competition? Second, how much do oligopolists contribute to economic growth by encouraging innovative activity in the very long run?

Short-Run Price-Output Decisions

We have seen that under perfect competition prices are set by the impersonal forces of demand and supply, while firms in oligopolistic markets administer their prices. The market signaling system works slightly differently when prices are administered rather than determined by the market. Changes in

BOX 14-2

Contestable Markets

Professors William Baumol of Princeton University, Robert Willig of Princeton University, and John Panzer of Northwestern University have recently developed a theory of what they call **contestable markets.** This theory shows that markets do not have to contain many firms or to experience actual entry for profits to be held near the competitive level. Potential entry can do the job just as well as actual entry, as long as (1) entry can be easily accomplished and (2) existing firms take potential entry into account when they are making their price and output decisions.

Entry is usually costly to the entering firm. It may have to build a plant; it may have to develop new versions of the industry's differentiated product; or it may have to advertise heavily in order to call attention to its product. These and many other costs of entry are often called *sunk costs of entry.* A sunk cost of entry is a cost that a firm must incur to enter the market and that cannot be recovered if the firm subsequently exits. For example, if an entering firm builds a product-specific factory that has no resale value, this is a sunk cost of entry. However, the cost of a factory that is not product specific and that can be resold for an amount that is close to its original cost is not a sunk cost of entry.

A market in which new firms can enter and leave without incurring any sunk costs of entry is called a *perfectly contestable market.* A market can be perfectly contestable even if the firm must pay some costs of entry, as long as these can be recovered when the firm exits. Since all markets require at least some sunk costs of entry, contestability must be understood as a variable. The lower are the sunk costs of entry, the more contestable is the market.

In a contestable market, the existence of profits, even if they are due to transitory causes, will attract entry. Firms will enter to gain a share of these profits and will exit when the transitory situation has changed.

Consider, for example, the market for air travel between two cities. It will be quite contestable as long as counter and loading space is available to new entrants at the two cities' airline terminals. An airline that is not currently serving the cities in question can shift some of its existing planes to the market with little sunk costs of entry. Some training of personnel may be needed for them to become familiar with the route and the airport. This is a sunk cost of entry that cannot be recovered if the cities in question are no longer to be served. However, most of the airline's costs are not sunk costs of entry. If it subsequently decides to leave the city, the rental of terminal space will stop, and the airplanes and the ground equipment can be shifted to another location.

Sunk costs of entry constitute a barrier to entry, and the larger these are, the larger can the profits of existing firms be without attracting new entrants. The flip side of this coin is that firms operating in markets without large sunk costs of entry will not earn large profits, because, if they do, firms will enter to capture the profits while they last and then exit.

Contestability, where it is possible, is a force that limits the profits of existing oligopolists. Even if entry does not occur, the ease with which it can be accomplished will keep oligopolists away from the cooperative equilibrium.

Contestability is just another example, in somewhat more refined form, of the key point that the possibility of entry is the major force preventing the exploitation of market power to restrict output and to raise prices. As we shall see in Chapter 15, however, there is reason to think that many oligopolistic markets are not highly contestable because of large sunk costs of entry. In these cases, potential entry cannot be relied on to hold profits close to zero.

the market conditions for both inputs and outputs are signaled to the perfectly competitive firm by changes in the prices of its inputs and its outputs. Changes in the market conditions for inputs are signaled to oligopolistic firms by changes in the prices of their inputs. Changes in the market conditions for the oligopolist's output are typically signaled, however, by changes in the sales at administered prices.

Increases in costs of inputs will shift cost curves upward, and oligopolistic firms will be led to raise prices and lower outputs. Increases in demand will cause the sales of oligopolistic firms to rise. Firms will then respond by increasing output, thereby increasing the quantities of society's resources that are allocated to producing that output. They will then decide whether or not their administered prices need to be altered.

The market system reallocates resources in response to changes in demands and costs in roughly the same way under oligopoly as it does under perfect competition.

Some oligopolies succeed in coming close to joint profit maximization. Others compete so intensely among themselves that they come close to achieving competitive prices and outputs. The consequences for the behavior of the economic system vary accordingly. Box 14-2 discusses one recent theory that outlines some of the conditions under which oligopoly can be pushed toward the competitive equilibrium by potential, rather than actual, entry.

Innovation

An important defense of oligopoly relates to Schumpeter's concept of creative destruction (see pages 251–253). Some economists have theorized that intermediate market structures, such as oligopoly, would lead to more innovation than would occur in either perfectly competitive or monopolistic industries. They argue that the oligopolist is faced with clear and present competition from existing rivals

and cannot afford the more relaxed life of the monopolist. At the same time, however, the oligopolistic firm expects to keep a good share of the profits that it earns from any innovative activity that it undertakes. The empirical evidence is broadly consistent with this view. Professor Jesse Markham of Harvard University concluded a survey of empirical findings by saying:

> If technological change and innovational activity are, as we generally assume, in some important way a product of organized R&D activities financed and executed by business companies, it is clear that the . . . payoffs that flow from them can to some measurable extent be traced to the doorsteps of large firms operating in oligopolistic markets.

Everyday observation provides some confirmation of this finding. Leading North American firms that operate in highly concentrated industries, such as Kodak, IBM, du Pont, Xerox, General Electric, and 3M, have been highly innovative over many years.

A Final Word

Oligopoly is an important market structure in modern economies because there are many industries in which the minimum efficient scale is simply too large to support a large group of competing firms. Although oligopoly usually will not achieve the same efficiency as perfect competition, rivalrous oligopoly may also be effective in producing very long-run adaptations that develop both new products and cost-reducing methods of producing old ones.

The defense of oligopoly as a market structure is that it may be the best of the available alternatives when minimum efficient scale is large. The challenge to public policy is to keep oligopolists competing, rather than colluding, and using their competitive energies to improve products and to lower costs, rather than merely to erect entry barriers.

SUMMARY

1. Although some American industries fit the perfectly competitive model and a few are monopolies, many have intermediate market structures that are called imperfectly competitive.
2. Most of the firms that are operating in these market structures sell differentiated products whose characteristics they chose themselves. They also administer their prices, sometimes have unexploited econ-

omies of scale, do not change their prices as often as prices in perfectly competitive markets change, engage in nonprice competition, and sometimes take actions designed to prevent the entry of new firms.

3. Monopolistic competition has the same characteristics as perfect competition, except that the firms sell a differentiated, rather than a homogeneous, product. Firms face negatively sloped demand curves and may earn monopoly profits in the short run. In the long run, new firms enter the industry whenever profits can be made and the equilibrium requires that each firm earns zero profits. Each firm's demand curve is tangent to its average total cost curve, which means that each firm is producing less than its minimum-cost level of output.

4. Monopolistic competition does not necessarily result in inefficiency. Even though each firm produces at a cost that is higher than the minimum attainable cost, the resulting product choice is valued by consumers and so may be worth the extra cost.

5. Oligopolies are dominated by a few large firms that usually sell differentiated products and have significant market power. They can maximize their joint profits if they cooperate to produce the monopoly output. By acting individually, each firm has an incentive to depart from this cooperative equilibrium, but rivalrous behavior reduces profits and may lead to a noncooperative, Nash equilibrium from which no one firm has an incentive to depart.

6. OPEC is an example of overt cooperation to limit supply. It suffered from all the problems of cartels. It raised profits initially, but this set up a chain of market reactions that greatly reduced its market power. Demand fell over the long and the very long runs; new entry raised supply from nonmember countries; and cheating increased the outputs of member countries.

7. Tacit cooperation is possible but often tends to break down as firms struggle for market shares, indulge in nonprice competition, and seek advantages through the introduction of new technology. Oligopolistic industries are likely to come closer to the joint profit-maximizing, cooperative position: (a) The smaller is the number of firms in the industry, (b) the less differentiated are their products, (c) when the industry's demand is growing rather than shrinking, (d) when the industry contains a dominant firm, (e) the less is the opportunity for nonprice competition, and (f) the smaller are the barriers to entry.

8. Oligopolistic prices do not change continually in the way that free-market prices do. As a result, the first effect of a change in demand is a change in output rather than a change in price. This price stickiness applies to most differentiated products. Three main explanations concern the desire not to upset tacit price-setting agreements, the fear that competitors will match one's price cuts but not one's price increases, and the maximization of profits in the face of flat cost curves and costly price changes.

9. Oligopolistic industries will exhibit profits in the long run only if there are significant barriers to entry. Natural barriers relate to scale economies in production and in entry costs. Firm-created barriers can relate to proliferation of competing brands, heavy brand-image advertising, and the threat of predatory pricing when new entry occurs. Contestable market theory shows that potential entry may

be sufficient to hold profits down and emphasizes the importance of sunk costs and an entry barrier.

10. In the presence of major scale economies, oligopoly may be the best of the feasible alternative market structures. Evaluation of oligopoly depends on how much interfirm competition (a) drives the firms away from the cooperative, profit-maximizing equilibrium and (b) leads to innovations in the very long run.

TOPICS FOR REVIEW

Concentration ratios
Reasons for the persistence of large firms
Administered prices
Product differentiation
Imperfect competition
Monopolistic competition
The excess capacity theorem
Types of collusion
The cooperative, joint profit-maximizing equilibrium
The noncooperative, Nash equilibrium
OPEC as a cartel
Firm-created entry barriers
Contestable markets

DISCUSSION QUESTIONS

1. The Canadian market is one-tenth the size of the U.S. market, and when similiar industries are compared, national concentration ratios are much higher in Canada than in the United States. Does this mean that Canadian firms typically have more market power than their U.S. counterparts?

2. Does the consumer benefit from lower prices, higher quality, more product variety, or advertising? If trade-offs are necessary (more of one means less of another), how would you evaluate their relative importance with respect to the following products?
   a. Vitamins
   b. Beer
   c. Cement
   d. Bath soap
   e. Women's dresses
   f. Television programs

3. Tires with white sidewalls cost a little more to manufacture than tires with black sidewalls, and they lower the durability of the tires somewhat. They sell for a markup over black tires that is about five times the difference in their costs. Yet well over one-half of all tires in passenger cars that are manufactured in the United States have white sidewalls. What, if anything, do these facts tell you about the market structure of the manufacture, distribution, or marketing of automobile tires? If white sidewalls are found to be somewhat more likely to suffer blowouts, should their use be prohibited by law?

4. It is sometimes said that there are more drugstores and gasoline stations than are needed. In what sense might this statement be correct? Does the consumer gain anything from this plethora of retail outlets?

5. Might any of the following industries be monopolistically competitive?
    a. Textbook publishing (Note: There are over 50 elementary economics textbooks in use somewhere in the United States this year.)
    b. College education
    c. Cigarette manufacture
    d. Restaurant operation
    e. Automobile retailing

6. What bearing did each of the following have on the eventual inability of OPEC to maintain a monopoly price for oil?
    a. Between 1979 and 1985 OPEC's share of the world oil supply decreased by one-half.
    b. "Saudi Arabia's interest lies in extending the life span of oil to the longest possible period," said Sheik Yamani.
    c. The Soviet Union, in order to earn Western currency to pay for grain, increased its oil exports to the West during the late 1970s, thereby becoming the world's second largest oil exporter.
    d. The Iran-Iraq war decreased oil production in the Middle East from 1979 to 1981 by 4.5 million barrels per day.
    e. U.S. government policies during the 1970s protected American consumers from oil price shocks by holding domestic prices well below OPEC levels.

7. How did these headlines, which are all from 1985, foreshadow the collapse of OPEC?
    a. "Saudis threaten to double oil production if OPEC does not accept its terms"
    b. "Britain's price cut adds to OPEC's predicament"
    c. "Saudi economy is ailing after three years of recession"
    d. "New oil discovery adds Colombia to world's producers"
    e. "OPEC oil ministers meet amid discord on pricing policy"

8. "The OPEC experience proved to the world that there were many available substitutes for gasoline, among them bicycles, car pools, moving closer to work, cable TV, and Japanese cars."
    Discuss how each of these may be a substitute for gasoline.

9. It has been estimated that if automobile companies did not change the models of their cars for 10 years, the cost of production would be reduced by approximately 30 percent. In view of this fact, why are there annual changes in their models? Which, if any, of the reasons that you have suggested depend on the industry's being oligopolistic? Should frequent changes in models be forbidden by law?

10. Compare the effects on the automobile and the wheat industries of each of the following. In the light of your answers, discuss general ways in which oligopolistic industries fulfill the same general functions as do perfectly competitive industries.
    a. Large rise in demand
    b. Large rise in costs of production
    c. Temporary cuts in supplies coming to market due to a three-month rail strike
    d. Rush of cheap foreign imports

11. Some analysts of the beer industry believe that the big national brewing companies are going to get bigger and that the smaller companies will disappear relatively rapidly. Their reasoning is that

big national brewers have decisive advantages over local and regional brewers. What are these analysts assuming about the cost and the demand conditions in the beer industry? Is this assumption consistent with the report by *Fortune* that indicated that a small regional brewery has higher labor productivity than the newest but larger plant of Anheuser Busch? If the efficient size of a *plant* in the industry is small, might there be reasons to expect multiplant firms to predominate?

Chapter 15

Public Policy Toward Monopoly and Competition

Monopoly has long been regarded with suspicion. In *The Wealth of Nations* (1776), Adam Smith developed a stinging attack on monopolists. Since then, most economists have criticized monopoly and advocated competition.

In this chapter we first consider what economic theory has to say about the relevant advantages of the two polar market structures of monopoly and competition. Next, we consider intermediate market forms and then go on to consider some details of public policy that are directed at encouraging competition and discouraging monopoly.

Part of the appeal of competition and the distrust of monopoly is noneconomic, being based on a fear of concentration of power. This was discussed in Chapter 12. Much of the attraction of competition and dislike of monopoly, however, has to do with the understanding that competition is efficient in ways that monopoly is not. This argument over *efficiency* constitutes the classic case against monopoly. To understand the arguments, we must first define *efficiency*.

The Theory of Efficiency

Economic efficiency requires avoiding the waste of resources. When labor is unemployed and factories lie idle (as occurs in serious recessions), their potential current output is lost. If these resources could be employed, total output would be increased and hence everyone could be made better off. However, full employment of resources by itself is not enough to prevent the waste of resources. Even when resources are being fully used, they may be used inefficiently. Let us look at three examples of inefficiency in the use of resources.

1. If firms do not use the least costly method of producing their chosen outputs, they waste resources. For example, a firm that produces 30,000 pairs of shoes at a resource cost of $400,000 when it could have been done at a cost of only $350,000 is using resources inefficiently. The lower-cost method would allow $50,000 worth of resources to be transferred to productive uses.
2. If some firms produce at high cost while other firms produce at low cost, the industry's overall cost of producing its output is higher than necessary.

3. If too much of one product and too little of another product are produced, resources are being used inefficiently. To take an extreme example, suppose that so many shoes are produced that every consumer has all the shoes he or she could possibly want and so places a zero value on obtaining an additional pair of shoes. Further assume that fewer coats are produced relative to demand, so that each consumer places a positive value on obtaining an additional coat. Now each consumer can be made better off by reallocating resources from shoe production (where the last shoe produced has a low value in the eyes of consumers) to coat production (where one more coat produced would have a higher value to consumers).

These examples suggest that we must refine our ideas of the waste of resources beyond the simple notion of ensuring that all resources are employed. The sources of inefficiency just outlined suggest important conditions that must be fulfilled if economic efficiency is to be attained. These conditions are conveniently collected into two categories, called *productive efficiency* and *allocative efficiency,* which were studied long ago by the great Italian economist Vilfredo Pareto (1848–1923). Indeed, efficiency in the use of resources is often called *Pareto-optimality* or *Pareto-efficiency* in his honor.

Productive Efficiency

Productive efficiency has two aspects: one concerning production within each firm and one concerning the allocation of production among the firms in an industry.

The first condition for productive efficiency is that each firm should produce any given output at the lowest possible cost. In the short run, with only one variable factor, the firm has no problem of choice of technique. It merely uses enough of the variable factor to produce the desired level of output. In the long run, however, more than one method of production is available. Productive efficiency requires that the firm use the least costly of the available methods of producing any given output. This means that firms will be located on, rather than above, their long-run average cost curves.

In Chapter 11 (page 203) we studied the condition for production efficiency within the firm:

Production efficiency requires that each firm produces its given output by combining factors

of production in such a way that the ratios of the marginal products of each pair of factors is made equal to the ratio of their prices.

This is the same thing as saying that $1 spent on every factor should yield the same output. If this is not so, the firm can reduce its resource costs of producing its given output by substituting the input for which $1 of expenditure yields the higher output for the input for which $1 of expenditure yields the lower output.[1]

The second condition for productive efficiency ensures that the total output of each industry is allocated among its individual firms in such a way that the total cost of producing the industry's output is minimized. If an industry is productively inefficient, it would be possible to reduce the industry's total cost of producing any given total industry output by reallocating production among the industry's individual firms.

Productive efficiency requires that all firms in an industry must produce where they have the same level of marginal cost.

To see the importance of this condition, assume that it is not fulfilled. Suppose that the Jones Brothers shoe manufacturing firm has a marginal cost of $40 for the last shoe of some standard type that it produces, while Gonzales, Inc., has a marginal cost of only $35 for the same type of shoe. If the Jones plant produces one less pair of shoes while the Gonzales plant produces one more, total shoe output is unchanged, but total industry costs are reduced by $5. Thus $5 worth of resources will be freed to increase the production of other commodities.

Clearly, this cost saving can go on as long as the two firms have different marginal costs. However, as the Gonzales firm produces more shoes, its marginal cost rises, while as the Jones firm produces fewer shoes, its marginal cost falls. (By producing

[1] As we saw in Box 11-1, producing at least cost within the firm also involves a more obvious type of efficiency, called *technical efficiency*. Technical efficiency means that the firm does not adopt any method of production when there exists another method that uses less of all inputs. Productive (economic) efficiency then ensures that the firm chooses the one method that uses the lowest *value* of resources from among the technically efficient methods. Professor Harvey Leibenstein has developed a theory of why firms, particularly those in less developed countries, may often adopt technically inefficient methods. When a firm is technically inefficient for any one of the reasons given in his theory, he speaks of it as being *X-inefficient* rather than technically inefficient.

more, the Gonzales firm is moving upward to the right along its given MC curve, while by producing less, the Jones firm is moving downward to the left along its given MC curve.) Say, for example, that after Gonzales, Inc., increases its production by 1,000 shoes per month, its marginal cost *rises* to $37, while when Jones Brothers reduces its output by the same amount, its marginal cost *falls* to $37. Now there is no further cost saving to be obtained by reallocating production between the two firms.

Figure 15-1 shows a production possibility curve of the sort that was first introduced in Figure 1-2 on page 6. Productive inefficiency implies that the economy is at some point inside the curve. In such a situation it is possible to produce more of some goods without producing less of others.

Productive efficiency implies being on, rather than inside, the economy's production possibility curve.

Allocative Efficiency

Productive efficiency ensures that any given volume of an industry's output is produced at the lowest possible cost. Allocative efficiency concerns the relative quantities of the different commodities to be produced. Achieving allocative efficiency ensures that the bundle of goods actually produced is an efficient one. **Allocative efficiency** refers to a situation in which it is impossible to change the allocation of resources in such a way as to make someone better off without making someone else worse off. Changing the allocation of resources implies producing more of some goods and less of others, that is, changing the mix of production.

From an allocative point of view, resources are said to be used *inefficiently* when using them to produce a different bundle of goods would make it *possible* for at least one person to be better off while making no other person worse off. Conversely, resources are said to be used *efficiently* when it is *impossible*, by using them to produce a different bundle of goods, to make any one person better off without making at least one other person worse off.

Reallocating resources to produce a different bundle of goods means moving from one point on the economy's production possibility curve to another point. This is also shown in Figure 15-1.

This tells us what is meant by allocative efficiency, but how is it achieved? How do we find the

FIGURE 15-1   Productive and Allocative Efficiency

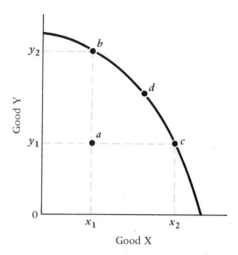

Any point on the production possibility curve is productively efficient; not all points on this curve are allocatively efficient. The curve shows all combinations of two goods X and Y that can be produced when the economy's resources are fully employed and being used with productive efficiency.

Any point inside the curve, such as a, is allocatively inefficient. If the inefficiency exists in industry X, production could be reallocated among firms in that industry in such a way as to raise production of X from x_1 to x_2. This would take the economy from point a to point c, raising production of X without any reduction in production of Y. Similarly, if the inefficiency exists in industry Y, production of Y could be increased from y_1 to y_2, which would take the economy from point a to point b. If both industries are allocatively inefficient, production can be increased to take the economy to some point on the curve *between* b and c, thus increasing the production of *both* commodities.

Allocative efficiency concerns being at the most efficient point on the production possibility curve. Assessing allocative efficiency means judging among points on the curve, such as b, c, and d. Usually only one such point will be allocatively efficient, while all others will be inefficient.

efficient point on the production possibility curve? For example, how many shoes should be produced to achieve allocative efficiency? How many dresses should be produced? How many hats should be produced?

The answer is as follows:

The economy's allocation of resources is efficient when, for every good produced, marginal cost of production is equal to its price.

To understand the reasoning behind this answer, we need to recall a point that was established in our discussion of consumers' surplus in Chapter 7. The price of any commodity indicates the value that each consumer places on the last unit of that commodity that is consumed. Faced with the market price of some commodity, the consumer goes on buying units until the last one is valued the same as its price. Consumers' surplus arises because the consumer would be willing to pay more than the market price for all but the last unit that is bought. On the last unit bought (i.e., the marginal unit), however, the consumer only "breaks even," because the valuation placed on it is just equal to its price.

Now assume that some commodity, say, shoes, sells for $30 per pair but has a marginal cost of $40. If one less pair of shoes were produced, the value that all households would place on the pair of shoes not produced would be $30. Using the concept of opportunity cost, however, we see that the resources that would have been used to produce that last pair of shoes could instead produce another good (say, a coat) valued at $40. If society can give up something that its members value at $30 and get in return something that its members value at $40, the original allocation of resources is inefficient. Someone can be made better off, and no one need be worse off.

This is easy to see when the same household gives up the shoes and gets the coat, but it follows even when different households are involved, for the gaining household could compensate the losing household and still come out ahead.

Assume next that shoe production is cut back until the price of a pair of shoes rises from $30 to $35, while its marginal cost falls from $40 to $35. Efficiency is achieved in shoe production because $p = MC = 35. Now if one less pair of shoes were produced, $35 worth of shoes would be sacrificed, while, at most, $35 worth of other commodities could be produced with the freed resources.

In this situation the allocation of resources to shoe production is efficient because it is not possible to change it to make someone better off without making someone else worse off. If one household were to sacrifice the pair of shoes, it would give up goods worth $35 and would then have to obtain for itself all of the new production of the alternative commodity produced just to break even. It cannot gain without making another household worse off. The same argument can be repeated for every commodity, and it leads to the conclusion that we have stated already: The allocation of resources is efficient when each commodity's price equals its marginal cost.

Allocative efficiency is assured for the whole economy if $p = MC$ in all industries.

Efficiency in Perfect Competition and in Monopoly

We now know that for productive efficiency marginal cost should be the same for all firms in any one industry and that for allocative efficiency marginal cost should be equal to price in all industries. Do the market structures of perfect competition and monopoly lead to productive and allocative efficiency?

Perfect Competition

Productive efficiency. We saw in Figure 12-9 that, in the long run under perfect competition, all firms produce at the lowest point on their long-run average cost curves. Therefore, no one firm could lower its costs by altering its own production.

We also know that in perfect competition all firms in an industry face the same price of their product and that they equate marginal cost to that price. It follows immediately that marginal cost will be the same for all firms. Because all firms in the industry have the same cost of producing their last unit of production, no reallocation of production among the firms could reduce the total industry cost of producing a given output.

Productive efficiency is achieved under perfect competition because all firms in an industry face the same price and so have identical marginal costs at all times and achieve the same level of minimized costs in long-run equilibrium.

Allocative efficiency. We have seen already that perfectly competitive firms maximize their profits by equating marginal cost to price. Thus, when perfect competition is the market structure for the whole economy, price is equal to marginal cost for all production.

Allocative efficiency is achieved when perfect competition prevails across the whole economy because price will be equal to marginal cost in all industries.

Monopoly

Productive efficiency. Monopolists have an incentive to be productively efficient because their profits will be maximized when they adopt the lowest-cost method that can be used to produce the level of output that is chosen. Thus, monopolists will operate on their *LRAC* curves.

Allocative efficiency. Although any profit-maximizing monopoly is productively efficient, its level of output will be too low to achieve allocative efficiency. We have seen that the monopolist chooses an output at which the price charged is greater than marginal cost. This violates the conditions for allocative efficiency because the amount that consumers pay for the last unit of output exceeds the opportunity cost of producing it.

Consumers would be prepared to buy additional units for an amount that is greater than the cost of producing these units. Some consumers could be made better off, and none need be made worse off, by shifting extra resources into production of the monopolized commodity, thus increasing the production of the product. As a consequence, the monopolist produces an output that is *not* allocatively efficient.

From this follows the classic, efficiency-based preference for competition over monopoly.

Monopoly is not allocatively efficient, since the monopolist's price always exceeds its marginal cost.

This result has important policy implications for economists and for political leaders, as we shall see later in this chapter.

Efficiency in Other Market Structures

Note that the result just stated extends beyond the case of a simple monopoly. Whenever a firm has any power over the market in the sense that it faces a downward-sloping rather than a horizontal demand curve, its profit-maximizing behavior will lead it to produce where *MC* equals *MR,* not where *MC*

equals price. Thus, strictly speaking, both oligopoly and monopolistic competition are allocatively inefficient.

Oligopoly is an important market structure in today's economy, because there are many industries in which the minimum efficient scale is simply too high to support a large group of competing firms. Although oligopoly does not achieve the conditions for allocative efficiency, it may produce more satisfactory results than monopoly. As we observed in Chapter 14, oligopoly may also be effective in producing very long-run adaptations that result in both new products and cost-reducing methods of producing old ones.

The defense of oligopoly as a market form is that it may be the best of the available alternatives when minimum efficient scale is large. The challenge to public policy is to keep oligopolists competing and using their competitive energies to improve products and to lower costs rather than to restrict interfirm competition and to erect entry barriers. As we shall see later in this chapter, much public policy has just this purpose. What economic policymakers call monopolistic practices include not only output restrictions operated by firms with complete monopoly power but also anticompetitive behavior among firms that are operating in oligopolistic market structures.

Allocative Efficiency: An Elaboration

The previous section gave the basic results needed to understand productive and allocative efficiency. A fuller interpretation of the normative significance of allocative efficiency can, however, be given by using the concepts of consumers' and producers' surplus.

Consumers' and Producers' Surplus

We have seen that consumers' surplus is the difference between the total value that consumers place on all the units consumed of some commodity and the payment that they actually make for the purchase of that commodity. Consumers' surplus is shown once again in Figure 15-2.

Producers' surplus is analogous to consumers' surplus. It occurs because all units of each firm's output are sold at the same market price, while, given a rising supply curve, each unit except the last is produced at a marginal cost that is less than the market price.

FIGURE 15-2 Consumers' Surplus and Producers' Surplus

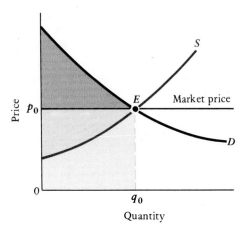

Consumers' surplus is the area under the demand curve and above the market price line. Producers' surplus is the area above the supply curve and below the market price line. The equilibrium price and quantity in this competitive market are p_0 and q_0, respectively. The total value that consumers place on q_0 of the commodity is given by the sum of the three shaded areas. The amount that they pay is $p_0 q_0$, the rectangle that consists of the two lighter shaded areas. The difference, shown as the dark shaded area, is *consumers' surplus*.

The receipts to producers from the sale of q_0 units are also $p_0 q_0$. The area under the supply curve, the color shaded area, is total variable cost, the minimum amount that producers require to supply the output. The difference, shown as the light gray shaded area, is *producers' surplus*.

Producers' surplus is defined as the amount that producers are paid for a commodity less their total variable cost of producing the commodity. The total variable cost of producing any output is shown by the area under the supply curve up to that output.[2]

[2] The marginal cost shows the addition to total cost, caused by producing one more unit of output. Summing these additions over each unit of output, starting with the first, yields the total variable cost of output. For example, the sum of the marginal costs of producing the first 10 units of output is the total variable cost associated with 10 units of output. Graphically, this process of summation is shown by the whole area under the marginal cost curve. Since, as we have already seen, the industry supply curve is merely the sum of the marginal cost curves of all the firms in the industry, the area under that supply curve up to some given output is the total of all the firms' variable costs of producing that output.

Thus, producers' surplus is the area above the supply curve and below the line giving market price. Producers' surplus is also shown in Figure 15-2.

The Allocative Efficiency of Perfect Competition Revisited

If the sum of consumers' and producers' surplus is not maximized, the industry could be moved to the point where it was, and the extra surplus that is available could be used to make some household better off without making anyone worse off.

Allocative efficiency occurs at the point where the sum of consumers' and producers' surplus is maximized.

The point where the sum of consumers' and producers' surplus is maximized is where the demand curve intersects the supply curve, that is, the point of equilibrium in a competitive market. This is shown graphically in Figure 15-3. For any output that is less than the competitive output, the demand curve is above the supply curve, which means that consumers value the last unit at an amount that is greater than its marginal cost of production. Suppose, for example, that the current output of shoes is such that consumers value at $45 an additional pair of shoes that adds $35 to costs. If it is sold at any price between $35 and $45, both producers and consumers gain; there is $10 of potential surplus to be divided between the two groups. In contrast, the last unit produced and sold at competitive equilibrium adds nothing to either consumers' or producers' surplus, since consumers value it at exactly its market price, and it adds the full amount of the market price to producers' costs.

If production were pushed beyond the competitive equilibrium, the sum of the two surpluses would be diminished. Assume, for example, that firms were forced to produce and sell further units of output at the competitive market price and that consumers were forced to buy these extra units at that price. (Note that neither group would do so voluntarily.) Firms would lose producers' surplus on those extra units because their marginal costs of producing the extra output would be above the price that they received for it. Purchasers would lose consumers' surplus because the valuation that they placed on these extra units, as shown by the demand curve,

FIGURE 15-3   The Allocative Efficiency of Perfect Competition

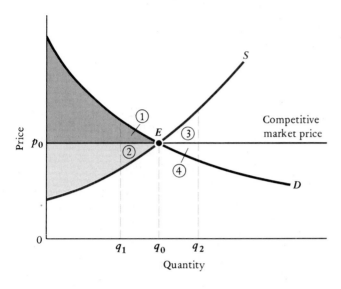

Competitive equilibrium is allocatively efficient because it maximizes the sum of consumers' and producers' surplus. The competitive equilibrium occurs at the price-output combination, p_0q_0. At this equilibrium consumers' surplus is the dark shaded area above the competitive market price line, while producers' surplus is the light shaded area below the competitive market price line.

For any output that is less than q_0, the sum of the two surpluses is less than at q_0. For example, reducing output to q_1 but keeping price at p_0 lowers consumers' surplus by area 1 and lowers producers' surplus by area 2.

For any output that is greater than q_0, the sum of the surpluses is also less than at q_0. For example, if producers are forced to produce output q_2 and to sell it to consumers, who in turn are forced to buy it at price p_0, producers' surplus is reduced by area 3 (the amount by which variable costs exceed revenue on those units), while the amount of consumers' surplus is reduced by area 4 (the amount by which expenditure exceeds consumers' satisfactions on those units).

Only the competitive output, q_0, maximizes the sum of the two surpluses.

would be less than the price that they would have to pay.

The sum of producers' and consumers' surplus is maximized *only at the competitive output,* which is thus the only output that is allocatively efficient.

The Allocative Inefficiency of Monopoly Revisited

Since, as we have just seen in Figure 15-3, the perfectly competitive equilibrium output maximizes the sum of consumers' and producers' surplus, it follows immediately that the lower monopoly output must result in a smaller total of consumers' and producers' surplus.

Why would producers and consumers agree to reduce their surpluses? The answer is that the monopoly equilibrium is not the outcome of voluntary agreement between the one producer and the many consumers. Instead, it is imposed by the monopolist by virtue of the power it has over the market. When

the monopolist reduces output below the competitive level, market price rises. As a result, consumers' surplus is diminished, and producers' surplus is increased. In this way the monopoly firm gains at the expense of consumers. This is not the whole story, however.

When output is lowered from the competitive level, there is always a *net* loss of surplus. More is given up by consumers than is gained by the monopolist. Some surplus is lost, because output between the monopolistic and the competitive levels is not produced. This loss of surplus is called the *deadweight loss of monopoly.* This is illustrated in Figure 15-4.

Major Policy Issues

Monopolies, cartels, and price-fixing agreements among oligopolists, whether explicit or tacit, have

FIGURE 15-4   The Allocative Inefficiency of Monopoly

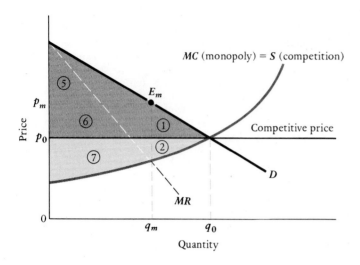

Monopoly is allocatively inefficient because it produces less than the competitive output and thus does not maximize the sum of consumers' and producers' surplus. If this market were perfectly competitive, price would be p_0, output would be q_0, and consumers' surplus would be the sum of areas 1, 5, and 6 (the dark shaded area). When the industry is monopolized, price rises to p_m, and consumers' surplus falls to area 5. Consumers lose area 1 because that output is not produced; they lose area 6 because the price rise has transferred it to the monopolist.

Producers' surplus in a competitive equilibrium would be the sum of areas 7 and 2 (the light shaded area). When the market is monopolized and price rises to p_m, the surplus area 2 is lost because the output is not produced. However, the monopolist gains area 6 from consumers (6 is known to be greater than 2 because p_m maximizes profits).

While area 6 is transferred from consumers' to producers' surplus by the price rise, *areas 1 and 2 are lost*. They represent the deadweight loss resulting from monopoly and account for its allocative inefficiency.

met with public suspicion and official hostility for over a century. These and other noncompetitive practices are collectively referred to as *monopoly practices*. Note that such practices go far beyond what actual monopolists do and include noncompetitive behavior of firms that are operating in other market structures. The laws and other instruments that are used to prevent monopoly practices comprise **antitrust policy.** In addition to antitrust policy, governments at all levels employ *economic regulation,* which prescribes the rules under which firms can do business and, in some cases, determines the prices that businesses can charge for their output. Electric power and local telephone service are examples of services that are subject to this kind of regulation.

In the last decade antitrust policy and economic regulation have been very much in the public eye and have directly affected almost every household and firm in the United States. In 1982 one of the largest monopolies in the United States was broken up. In settlement of an antitrust case, the American Telephone and Telegraph Company (AT&T) agreed

to divest itself of all local telephone companies. Prior to 1978, airlines had to ask the federal Civil Aeronautics Board (CAB) for permission to change any air fare or to add or to drop service on any route. Under current law the airlines are subject only to the discipline of the marketplace in setting prices and routes. Economic analysis and economists played major roles in both of these changes, as they did also in a wave of economic deregulation that affected financial institutions, trucking, and a number of other industries.

The 1980s also saw an enormous increase in the number of **conglomerate mergers,** in which one firm purchases either the physical assets or the controlling share of ownership of another firm that generally is in an unrelated industry. These will be discussed in Chapter 16.

The goal of economic efficiency provides rationales both for antitrust policy and for economic regulation. Antitrust policy can be used in an attempt to promote efficiency by increasing competition in the marketplace. Where effective competition is not possible (as in the case of a natural monopoly, such as an electric power company), economic regulation can be used as a substitute for competition. Consumers could then be protected from the high prices and reduced output that result from the use of monopoly power.[3]

As we shall see in the remainder of this chapter, public policies are indeed used in these ways, but they are often used in ways that reduce economic efficiency. Why? The answer is partly that economic efficiency is not the only thing that policymakers have been concerned with in the design and implementation of antitrust policy. Partly it is an example of a more general phenomenon that we shall discuss in Chapter 21: When public policies that have the potential to redistribute income and wealth are available, various private interests will try to use them for private gain, regardless of their original public purpose. We shall see in the remainder of this chapter that antitrust policy and economic regulation often have been used in ways that reduce efficiency by protecting firms from the consequences of competition. Protection of U.S. firms from competition comes in many forms, including protection of firms from foreign competition, protection of small firms from bigger, often more efficient rivals, protection of large firms from smaller, more efficient rivals, and protection of firms generally from "unfair" competition.

In the remainder of this chapter we shall look at a variety of ways in which American policymakers have chosen to intervene in the workings of the un-regulated market economy through antitrust policy and economic regulation.

Antitrust Policy Against Monopoly

Earlier in this chapter we showed how the theory of monopoly leads to three principal predictions: (1) Where monopoly power exists in an industry, fewer resources will be employed than where competitive conditions exist; (2) firms with monopoly power will earn profits in excess of opportunity costs; (3) their

owners thus will command a larger share of the national income than they would under conditions of competition. In short, an economy in which many firms exercise monopoly power will have a different (and usually less efficient) allocation of resources and a different distribution of income than will an economy that is composed largely of competitive industries.

Antitrust laws attempt to prohibit the acquisition or the exercise of monopoly power by business firms.

The first American antitrust law, the Sherman Antitrust Act, was passed in 1890, in an era in which economists believed that perfect competition both produced ideal results and was the feasible alternative to monopoly. The Sherman Act prohibits firms from restraining trade through the use of monopoly, through attempts to monopolize, and through combinations, conspiracies, and certain kinds of contracts. Additional antitrust laws prohibit other commercial practices and give the courts the power to stop such practices and to impose remedies to prevent their recurrence.

The Nature of Antitrust Policy

The dominant theme of antitrust policy has been to foster competition against those who seek to achieve or to exercise monopoly power or to restrain trade in other ways.[4]

The anticompetitive results that antitrust policy seeks to redress may arise or be perpetuated in many different ways. Some are purely behavioral; others involve changing market structures. Any of them may lead to monopoly profits that will persist if there are barriers that prevent new competition from arising. Among these ways are the following:

1. Collusive agreements among firms to restrict output, raise prices, divide markets, or otherwise to not compete among themselves
2. Contractual agreements that limit buyers in their choice of sellers, such as exclusive dealing arrangements or tying contracts

---

[3] A second kind of regulation, *social regulation,* involves a government's rules that require firms to consider the health, safety, environmental, and other social consequences of their behavior. Social regulation will be discussed in Chapter 22.

[4] There are also noneconomic motives for dealing with the "monopoly problem." Many people fear the political influence of those who have substantial economic power.

3. Mergers or acquisitions that reduce the number of independent firms in a market or an industry
4. Predatory behavior by those with substantial market power against rival sellers to force them into bankruptcy, cooperative behavior, or merger
5. Price discrimination
6. A firm that finds monopoly "thrust upon it" (in the words of U.S. Appeals Court Judge Learned Hand) either by its natural efficiency as a single producer or by successful innovation

The first five of these ways involve behavior that has been the object of antitrust legislation. The sixth does not, because, as we shall see, merely being a monopoly is not illegal under U.S. antitrust law. All of these practices may be civil offenses, and many are criminal offenses as well. Under criminal law, a firm that is found guilty may be fined, and its officers also may be fined or sentenced to jail.

Civil (noncriminal) cases may be brought against firms by the government or by private parties. A firm that is found in violation of the law may be required by the court to abandon certain practices, or it may be forced to dissolve itself into a number of separate companies. In private cases a firm may be obliged to pay injured parties an amount that is up to three times the amount of damages caused by the violation. Such *treble damages* are designed to provide a substantial incentive to private firms to root out violations of the law that might escape the notice of government prosecutors, as well as to provide a powerful deterrence to violations.

Antitrust Policies in Practice

As can be seen in Box 15-1, the principal laws that govern antitrust policy contain language that provides great latitude in interpretation. The courts have interpreted words and phrases such as "restraint of trade," "monopolize," "substantially lessen competition," and "unfair method of competition" to mean different things at different times. The vagueness of the antitrust statutes also has permitted considerable variation in the vigor with which the Justice Department and private plaintiffs have chosen to pursue antitrust cases. As a result, the overall effect of antitrust policy has changed greatly over time.

Laws Promoting Competition

The Sherman Antitrust Act (1890) was enacted in response to the growth in the size of firms during the last half of the nineteenth century. Section 1 of the act declares illegal every contract, combination, or conspiracy in restraint of trade. Section 2 makes it illegal to monopolize or to attempt to monopolize. It also prohibits conspiracies or combinations that result in monopolization. The language of the Sherman Act was strong but vague. It was some time before the courts defined the act's scope more specifically.

The Clayton Antitrust Act (1914) was an attempt to be more precise and to strengthen the powers of the antitrust prosecutors by allowing them to strike at potentially anticompetitive practices before they did too much damage. It also identified certain practices as illegal "where the effect may be substantially to lessen competition." Its most important provisions were: Section 7, applying to the acquisition of stock in a competing company; Section 2, limiting the practice of price discrimination; and Section 3, regulating exclusive dealing and tie-in contracts. (A tie-in contract requires a buyer to purchase other items in order to purchase the item that it wants.) An important provision in the Clayton Act specifically exempted collective bargaining by labor unions from the antitrust provisions. The Clayton Act was strengthened in 1950 by passage of the Celler-Kefauver Act, which applied the same provisions (Section 7) to acquisitions of physical assets that had previously applied only to acquisitions of stock.

The Federal Trade Commission Act (1914) prohibited "unfair methods of competition" and also created a regulatory agency, the Federal Trade Commission (FTC) with substantial powers of enforcement. The FTC has proved to be much less important relative to the courts than was anticipated in 1914, because FTC decisions can be appealed to the courts.[5]

Variation in Judicial Interpretation

The rule of reason. The first important series of antitrust prosecutions occurred at the beginning of the

---

[5] Under federal antitrust law, government cases originate either within the antitrust division of the Department of Justice or within procedures of the FTC. Many cases never go to trial because they are settled by agreement between the Department of Justice or the FTC and the companies. Cases of the Department of Justice and private cases go to trial before federal district courts. Cases are heard first by the FTC. In all cases appeal is to the appropriate Circuit Court of Appeals and then to the Supreme Court. Supreme Court decisions, here as elsewhere, stand until they are modified by other decisions of this highest court.

BOX 15-1

Principal Antitrust Provisions

Sherman Antitrust Act (26 Stat 209, 1890, as amended)

1. Every contract, combination in the form of trust or otherwise, or conspiracy, in restraint of trade or commerce among the several States, or with foreign nations, is hereby declared to be illegal. . . . Every person who shall make any contract or engage in any combination or conspiracy shall be deemed guilty of a felony and on conviction thereof, shall be punished by a fine not exceeding one million dollars if a corporation, or, if any other person, one hundred thousand dollars, or by imprisonment not exceeding three years, or by both . . . in the discretion of the Court.
2. Every person who shall monopolize, or attempt to monopolize, or combine or conspire with any other person or persons, to monopolize any part of the trade or commerce among the several States, or with foreign nations, shall be deemed guilty of a felony. . . .
8. That the word "person," or "persons," wherever used in this act shall be deemed to include corporations.

Clayton Antitrust Act (38 Stat 730, 1914, as amended)

2. (Including Robinson-Patman Amendments, 1948.) (a) That it shall be unlawful for any person engaged in commerce, in the course of such commerce, either directly or indirectly, to discriminate in price between different purchasers of commodities of like grade and quality . . . where the effect of such discrimination may be substantially to lessen competition or tend to create a monopoly in any line of commerce. . . . *Provided,* that nothing herein contained shall prevent differentials which make only due allowance for differences in the cost . . . resulting from the differing methods or quantities in which such commodities are . . . sold or delivered. . . .
3. That it shall be unlawful for any person engaged in commerce, in the course of such commerce, to lease or make a sale or contract . . . on the condition, agreement, or understanding that the lessee or purchaser thereof shall not use or deal in the . . . commodities of a competitor . . . where the effect of such . . . agreement . . . may be to substantially lessen competition or tend to create a monopoly in any line of commerce.
4. Any person who shall be injured in his business or property by reason of anything forbidden in the antitrust laws may sue therefor . . . and shall recover threefold the damages by him sustained, and the cost of suit, including a reasonable attorney's fee. . . .
7. (As amended by Celler-Kefauver Act of 1950.) That no corporation engaged in commerce shall acquire . . . the whole or any part . . . of another corporation engaged also in commerce, where in any line of commerce in any section of the country, the effect of such acquisition may be substantially to lessen competition, or to tend to create a monopoly. . . .
16. That any person, firm, corporation, or association shall be entitled to sue and have injunctive relief, in any court of the United States having jurisdiction over the parties, as against threatened loss or damage by a violation of the antitrust laws. . . .

Federal Trade Commission Act (38 Stat 717, 1914, as amended)

5. (a) (1) Unfair methods of competition . . . and unfair or deceptive acts or practices in or affecting commerce, are hereby declared unlawful.
(6) The Commission is hereby empowered and directed to prevent . . . using unfair methods . . . or deceptive acts or practices in commerce.
5. (1) Any person . . . who violates an order of the Commission to cease and desist . . . shall pay a civil penalty of not more than $10,000 for each violation . . . each day of continuance . . . shall be deemed a separate offense.

twentieth century. In 1911 the Supreme Court enunciated the "rule of reason" when it forced John D. Rockefeller's Standard Oil Company and the American Tobacco Company to divest themselves of a large share of their holdings of other companies. Not all trusts, but only *unreasonable* combinations in restraint of trade, merited conviction under the Sherman Act.

Because the rule of reason was so broad, a conservative Court gave the Sherman Act a very narrow interpretation for 25 years. In the famous *U.S. Steel* case (1920), the Court found that the company had not violated the law, even though it found that the organizers of the company had *intended* to monopolize the industry and earlier had conspired to fix prices. The Court held that U.S. Steel had not succeeded in *achieving* a monopoly. (Indeed, its vain attempts at price fixing proved that!) The decision said in part, "The law does not make mere size an offense. It . . . requires overt acts."

In related decisions the Court not only reiterated that mere size was not an offense but also added that the existence of unexerted monopoly power was not an offense, no matter how impressive was that power. Under this interpretation, which lasted until World War II, the antitrust laws were virtually unenforceable so far as attacks on the structure of heavily concentrated industries were concerned.

The "new" Sherman Act.   A sharp break in antitrust practice occurred in a series of cases that were prosecuted during the late 1930s, which reached the Court both before and just after World War II. A landmark decision in *United States* v. *Socony-Vacuum Oil Co.* (1940) enunciated a strong rule against price fixing: "Under the Sherman Act a combination formed for the purpose and with the effect of raising, depressing, fixing, pegging or stabilizing the price of a commodity in interstate commerce is illegal *per se*." Thus, where price fixing was concerned, no test of reasonableness or sound social purpose would be applied. Price fixing was a violation of the law regardless of its consequences.

An even more basic attack on the rule of reason was enunciated in the *Aluminum Company of America* case, decided in 1945. The decision reversed the *U.S. Steel* decision and found ALCOA to be an illegal monopoly, even though it had not engaged in "unreasonable behavior." The decision suggested that beyond some point mere size would, in itself, be an offense if the defendants had not done everything possible to avoid becoming dominant.

This case and others led some people to speak of the "new" Sherman Act. Subsequent decisions have modified the strongly anti-big-business aspects of the *ALCOA* case, but the retreat from *ALCOA* has stopped short of the *U.S. Steel* decision. The conduct of firms with large market power, such as IBM, Kodak, and AT&T, has continued to be closely scrutinized in order to distinguish between competitive and monopolistic behavior.

The Warren Court (1953–1969).   The modification of Section 7 of the Clayton Act in 1950, together with the advent of the Warren Court—so named for its chief justice, Earl Warren, a former Republican governor of California—ushered in a period of virtually unbroken triumphs for the government in its antitrust cases. Justice Potter Stewart, a frequent dissenter, wryly remarked that the only principle he could discern in the Court's decisions was that "the government always wins."

In particular, the Warren Court's antitrust decisions greatly restricted the ability of large corporations to merge. The Court's antimerger bias rested upon the implicit assumption that merger was not an appropriate way to achieve economies of scale. A **horizontal merger** involves the combination of firms in the same line of business, and thus the market share of the new, merged firm is always increased. But the Warren Court opposed mergers even when market shares were relatively small. For example, in the *Von's Grocery* case (1965), a merger of two supermarkets was ruled illegal even though the merged firms would have had only a 7.5 percent share of the local (Los Angeles) market. In a **vertical merger** one of the firms that join together is a supplier of the other firm. The merger of Brown Shoe Company with a chain of retail stores (Kinney) is an example of a vertical merger that the Warren Court found to be illegal. The threat to competition is hard to find (Kinney sold less than 2 percent of the nation's shoes, and Brown supplied only 8 percent of Kinney's needs). In other areas as well, the Warren Court was highly critical of any business practice that might appear to increase the market power of individual firms.

The Burger and Rehnquist Courts (1969–).   Chief Justice Warren was replaced by Warren Burger, after which the Court's composition changed quite rapidly. Four of its nine members were appointed by President Nixon (1969–1974), one of its members was appointed by President Ford (1974–1977), and three of its members were appointed by President Reagan (1981–1989). The Court's views on antitrust matters became much more tolerant of normal business practices, even if these practices might restrict competition. The Court greatly reduced the list of actions that are illegal *per se*. Moreover, in the 1980s both the FTC and various lower courts allowed a *contestable markets* theory, which we studied in Chapter 14, as a defense against actions that led to high market shares. Box 15-2 further discusses the attitudes of economists toward this development.

The Supreme Court has not overturned these decisions based on an alleged contestability of markets. Further, a 1986 Court ruling (*Cargill* v. *Monfort of Colorado*) made it much more difficult for private parties to succeed in blocking mergers on antitrust grounds. In 1986 Chief Justice Burger retired and was replaced by Associate Justice William Rehnquist. The Rehnquist Court is not expected to return to a more aggressive antitrust stance.

The Vigor of Prosecution

Courts, whatever their predilections, decide only those cases that come before them. Whether to bring cases to court, and which cases to bring, are matters that are largely decided by the antitrust division of the Department of Justice, whose head is a presidential appointee, and by private plaintiffs.

As with judicial interpretation, the nature of prosecution has changed repeatedly throughout the century. President Theodore Roosevelt set up the antitrust division in the Justice Department in 1903, and his administration initiated the series of major prosecutions that led to the *Standard Oil, American Tobacco,* and *U.S. Steel* decisions.

There was relatively little antitrust activity from World War I until 1937. After a brief flurry of prosecutions, including the *ALCOA* and *Socony-Vacuum* cases, World War II and the Korean War pushed antitrust policy to the sidelines until the 1950s. A more vigorous antitrust policy was pursued during the Eisenhower, Kennedy, and Johnson administrations. It reached a climax in the mid-1960s decisions of the Warren Court. During the same period, various barriers to private plaintiffs were greatly reduced. During the Nixon, Ford, and Carter administrations, the vigor of enforcement did not increase, but the level of both government and private prosecutions remained high.

Antitrust policy in the Reagan administration. With the advent of the Justice Department Merger Guidelines that were issued in 1982 and revised in 1984, the Reagan administration began a brisk march in the other direction. The guidelines embody a good deal of economic theory and take as their underlying principle a concern that market power should not be used to raise prices above competitive levels. The guidelines also reflect the economic thinking that underlies the theory of *contestable markets*. Thus, even in cases in which a proposed merger would cause a new firm to have a high market share, the guidelines suggest that the merger would be permitted if other firms, actual *or potential,* would be induced to enter the industry should prices be raised.

One commentator has characterized the use of contestable market theory as an antitrust "defense home run." If the defense can plausibly argue that new competition would emerge if prices were raised, it can win the case, even when the firm's market share is currently very high. The theory is thus valuable to defendants in antitrust merger cases, because it adds a defense that is hard to disprove.

In practice the Guidelines have been even more permissive than they are in principle. Since their promulgation, the Justice Department and the FTC have all but ignored vertical and conglomerate mergers, concentrating instead on a relatively small number of horizontal mergers. At one point the head of the antitrust division indicated his view that most restrictive practices other than price fixing are not anticompetitive. The Reagan administration tolerated mergers of giant corporations that surely would have been attacked a decade earlier, for example, Texaco's acquisition of Getty Oil and General Electric's acquisition of RCA. Indeed, the secretary of commerce went so far as to suggest repeal of Section 7 altogether, a suggestion that Congress has not followed.

By the mid-1980s the antitrust pendulum had swung back from the antibusiness attitude of the Warren Court; many believed it had swung too far in the other direction. In Box 15-4 we shall discuss one industry, air transport, in which there is currently a good deal of pressure for stricter antitrust enforcement.

BOX 15-2

Antitrust Policy and the Theory of Contestable Markets

Until quite recently, the dominant method of assessing whether a firm had market power in an industry was to look at the firm's share of sales. The greater was the share of sales (in the limit of pure monopoly it is 100 percent), the greater was the firm's market power. A new, alternative view, known as *contestable market theory,* was discussed in Chapter 14. There we saw that the basic idea behind contestable markets is that what is required to limit market power is *potential* competition. Actual competition is irrelevant. Thus, even if one observes, say, an airline that has all of the market between point A and point B, as long as it is *possible* for some other airline to compete on that route, the first airline is limited to earning normal profits. Why? The answer is that if the incumbent sets prices too high, others will come in, cut prices, and competition will continue until the profits disappear. In short, *if there are no barriers to entry,* market concentration is irrelevant. Outcomes will be perfectly competitive as a result, whether or not competition among many existing firms is actually observed in the industry.

Most economists take the view that, although contestable markets are an elegant extension of competitive markets in theory, there are at least *some* barriers to entry in almost all real markets—and very large ones in some markets. Setting up an effective organization to produce or to sell almost anything requires the incurring of fixed costs. In the case of airlines, for instance, the new company at a given airport must hire and train staff, advertise extensively to let customers know that it is in the market, set up baggage-handling facilities, and overcome whatever loyalties customers have to the preexisting firms. New firms face entry costs that are analogous to these in almost all industries.

At the same time that economists have become increasingly skeptical of contestability theory, both the Department of Justice and many antitrust decisions have adopted the theory as applying in a variety of antitrust settings. This has led Richard Schmallansee to observe that "the position . . . that entry is almost always nearly perfectly free, is doing a lot better in antitrust decisions these days than in economics journals."* The relevant question to ask when we are assessing the importance of contestability involves determining how costly it would be for a firm to overcome whatever barriers to entry exist in a given market. These provide the limit to the pure profits that an incumbent firm can earn.

Let us return to the example of the airline industry. It is striking that even in that case the evidence indicates that the barriers may be quite large. On the face of it, airlines look like an ideal case for contestability. All a firm must do to compete is to fly an airplane to point A, sell some tickets, and fly on to point B. It is hard to think of a more mobile factor of production than an airplane! As we have seen, however, the plane is not the only factor of production that is needed to serve a particular air route. This, in turn, suggests that contestability, in practice, is something to be measured, rather than simply asserted.

* Richard Schmallansee, "Ease of Entry: Has the Concept Been Applied Too Readily? *Antitrust Law Journal,* 56:1 (1987), p. 42.

The Deviant Theme in Antitrust Policy

Antitrust was given two meanings from its earliest days. One of these was "antimonopoly," and the other was "antibig firm." Some of the supporters of the original Sherman Act saw its purpose as the protecting of small, independent businesses from the tyranny of markets in which large corporations were coming to play such a big role. When the Sherman Act was not interpreted in this way, the supporters rallied behind passage of the Federal Trade Commission Act (1914), which legislated against "unfair methods of competition." From at least that time until the 1970s, when Justices Black and Douglas left the Supreme Court, the populist view had its voice on the Court, and that view often was protective of small firms in its effect. In *Chicago Board of Trade* (1918), the Court supported restrictions on price competition in order to let traders enjoy a more tranquil life. In *Appalachian Coals* (1933), small coal producers, who had been devastated by the Great Depression, were allowed to restrict output in order to protect their revenues. In *Von's Grocery* (1965), cited earlier, the underlying concern was the plight of the "Ma and Pa" grocery stores that were being displaced by the ever growing presence of the chain stores.

Policymakers always have been concerned about the effects of monopoly on the distribution of income. The deviant theme in antitrust policy is probably best understood in this light. In the industrial sectors of the economy, corporate managers and stockholders typically have above average incomes. Monopoly power, when it is exercised by those who are relatively poor rather than relatively rich, frequently has been supported rather than opposed by the government. For example, the efforts of farmers to increase farm income not only have been approved but also have been actively promoted by public policies of crop restriction, price supports, and exemption of producers' cooperatives from antitrust laws. (Ironically, the farmers who have benefitted most from these policies have been those with the highest incomes.) Labor unions are exempt from antitrust prosecution, not because wage fixing is less anticompetitive than price fixing but because public policymakers have chosen to help laborers increase their income by encouraging unions and by giving those unions the opportunity to act as labor cartels.

Protection against bigness *per se* in antitrust is currently on the wane. The Fair Trade laws, which allowed manufacturers to set retail prices, have been repealed, and both Congress and the courts have restricted the FTC's ability to impose limitations on "unfair" competitive practices. During the Reagan administration the antitrust division devoted much of its attention to prosecuting cases of price fixing, a plainly anticompetitive practice in which firms in the same industry agree upon the prices that they will charge. At the same time, the Justice Department downplayed prosecution of other practices, for example, price discrimination, which, while apparently restrictive, may sometimes be procompetitive.

The Success of Antitrust Policy

Economists do not generally agree on how much the *structure* of American industry has been influenced by nearly a century of antitrust policy. American manufacturing industries remain highly concentrated (see Chapter 14), but empirical studies have shown no tendency for the concentration either to increase or to decrease drastically. Would the pattern be very different if there were no antitrust laws or if the existing laws were more vigorously enforced? We do not know for sure.

Many economists and antitrust lawyers believe that U.S. antitrust laws have been quite successful in inhibiting price fixing and certain restrictive practices. At the same time, the laws have done little to alter the basic structure of the economy. Whether this constitutes a signal success or a brave failure depends on one's diagnosis of the health of the American market system. Here people disagree sharply. The role of economic analysis in antitrust policy is discussed briefly in Box 15-3.

Public Utility Regulation of Natural Monopoly

Natural monopoly arises because of economies of scale (as discussed on page 250). Policymakers have not wanted to compel the maintenance of several smaller, less efficient producers when a single firm would be much more efficient; neither have they wanted to give a monopolist the opportunity to restrict output, raise prices, and appropriate as profits the gains made available by virtue of large-scale production.

How might these values be reconciled with the view, dominant during the late nineteenth century, that government should not interfere with the free market? The answer is to identify certain natural monopoly products as *public utilities,* whose provision ought to be supervised by the government.

The concept of public utilities grew out of a recognition that when there are major economies of large-scale production, forcing competition among a number of firms may not foster economic efficiency.

BOX 15-3

Economics and Antitrust Law

Economic concepts such as competition, monopoly, and markets lie at the heart of antitrust policy. Economists are employed in the Justice Department, by the Federal Trade Commission, and by lawyers for private companies. Market definition, for example, plays a critical role in antitrust merger litigation: Section 7 of the Clayton Act requires evaluation of a merger by asking whether "in any line of commerce, in any section of the country the effect of such acquisition may be substantially to lessen competition or to tend to create a monopoly."

The words "line of commerce" and "section of the country" involve product and geographical market definitions, because competition occurs only within sensibly defined markets. A great many antitrust cases have turned on market definition, and some have even utilized such economic concepts as cross-elasticity of demand.

Here are a few of the questions that the courts have asked and answered.

Is cellophane in the same market as wax paper, Saran wrap, and other flexible wrapping materials? (Yes, said the Supreme Court.)

Are glass jars and tin cans in the same market? (Yes, said the Supreme Court.)

Are insulated aluminum and copper cable in the same market? (Yes, said the U.S. District Court; no, said the Supreme Court.)

Are New York and Philadelphia banks in the same market and thus in competition with one another? (No, said the courts in 1963.)

Do different grades of coal in Illinois constitute an economic market? (No, said the U.S. District Court, in part because it found the relevant market to be energy. The Supreme Court did not reverse the decision.)

Even though courts decide these matters, the matters themselves involve economic questions, and economic studies or witnesses were introduced by both parties in each of these litigations.

While antitrust policies use economic theory and economic expertise, our antitrust laws ignore certain distinctions that economists think are important. In particular, the role of big business, even monopoly, in promoting dynamic advances, as argued by Joseph Schumpeter, has many adherents, yet it is largely ignored by antitrust policies. Some decisions have protected smaller competitors against larger, more efficient rivals. The distinction between injury to *competition* and injury to *competitors* has not always been made clearly by the courts. Finally, the courts have had a difficult time in coming to grips with oligopoly. They sometimes regard it favorably because it is much more competitive than monopoly, and sometimes they regard it unfavorably because it is much less competitive than perfect competition.

Economists themselves are divided as to whether these distinctions are important. Some believe that public policy ought to be based on things such as size and market share, without regard for actual conduct or performance. Others offer their own "rule of reason," called *workable competition*. They argue that the real choice is between more or less oligopoly and that the positive effects of a given market share, or merger, on prices, on profits, and on costs should be determined in each individual case. The question at hand is not whether oligopoly is "good" or "bad," but which of the feasible alternatives will come closest to achieving economic efficiency.

This seems reasonable. Why do some people object to it? They object because they believe that workable competition will lead to endless studies and no action. Because economists do not speak with a unified voice on such matters, it is perhaps not surprising that the basic nature of antitrust policy for a long time has been set by lawyers. The economic point of view is, however, receiving increased attention today. Economists (albeit quite conservative ones) played a major role in the Justice Department's Merger Guidelines, and, increasingly, judicial opinions on antitrust matters use economic as well as legal analysis.

One response to this problem is for government to assume ownership of the single firm and to delegate to government-appointed managers of the *nationalized* industry decisions about how much to produce and what price to charge, in each case being guided by the national interest. Many countries have done precisely this with regard to telephone and railroad services, among others. The characteristic response in the United States since the late nineteenth century has been to allow private enterprise but to regulate its behavior.

Public utility regulation gives to appropriate public authorities (usually specially constituted regulatory commissions) control over the price and the quantity of service provided by a natural monopoly. The object is to achieve the efficiency of a single seller without the output restriction of the monopolist.[6]

In return for giving a company a franchise or a license to be the sole producer, the public utility regulators reserve the right to regulate its behavior.

Regulation of this kind began with the establishment of the Interstate Commerce Commission (ICC) in 1887. Its primary function was to regulate railroad rates. Public utility regulation by both federal and state governments subsequently spread to other forms of transportation (airlines and pipelines) as well as to the standard utilities: telephone, electricity, water, and gas.

Although regulatory commissions were first created to deal with problems resulting from natural monopoly, much regulatory activity today is no longer of this kind. In particular, environmental and health and safety regulations arise from different motives. We shall discuss these kinds of regulation in Chapter 22. In this section, however, we are concerned only with regulation of natural monopoly.

Regulation of Price

The dilemma of natural monopoly is illustrated in Figure 15-5. To achieve low costs, a single large

---

[6] In some cases, the structure of costs is such that there would be a "natural oligopoly," rather than a natural monopoly. The argument for public utility regulation made here extends to such cases.

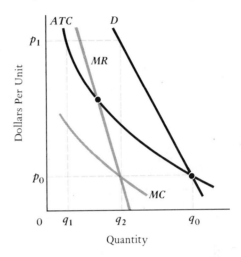

FIGURE 15-5 The Problem of Natural Monopoly

Cost conditions in a situation of natural monopoly are such that a single firm is needed to achieve the economies of scale, but a monopolist finds it profitable to restrict output to maximize profits. ATC and MC are the cost curves of an efficient firm. D is the market demand curve, and MR is the marginal revenue. Because ATC declines sharply, efficiency is served by having a single firm. Clearly, one firm producing at q_0 would be more efficient than several firms each producing at q_1 at a cost of p_1 per unit. However, an unregulated monopoly would restrict output to q_2 and charge price p_1, thereby depriving consumers of the advantages of large-scale production.

producer is necessary, but an unregulated, profit-maximizing monopoly would restrict output, raise price, and fail to provide the large volume of output at a low price that the technology makes possible.

What price should a regulatory commission permit a monopoly to charge? It might wish to set price equal to marginal cost in order to achieve allocative efficiency ("the way it would be in perfect competition"), but such a price and quantity may well lead to losses, for marginal cost is necessarily below average cost when average cost is falling. This is illustrated in Figure 15-6. Such a pricing scheme would require a continuing subsidy of the resulting losses.

Alternatively, a commission could employ a **two-part tariff,** in which the utility would charge two prices. Customers would pay one price merely

FIGURE 15-6   Pricing Strategy of a Regulatory Commission

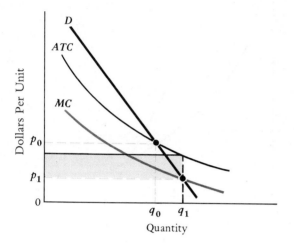

Average cost pricing is the goal of regulatory commissions that seek low prices but no losses for natural monopolies. Allocative efficiency requires a quantity q_1 where price equals marginal cost. However, at the price-quantity combination p_1 and q_1, a firm would suffer losses (shown as the shaded area). A regulatory commission could not insist on price p_1 unless it was prepared to subsidize the firm. However, it might require price p_0, which permits the firm to produce q_0 and to cover all costs. The output q_0 achieves some, but not all, of the cost advantages of large-scale output. Pricing where demand crosses ATC is called *average cost pricing*.

to have access to the utility and a second price for each unit consumed. In principle, the hook-up fee could cover fixed costs, and use of the utility could be priced at marginal cost. In practice, some electric utilities use a modified form of the two-part tariff, in which each customer pays a high price for the first few kilowatts of electricity consumed each month and then pays a price that is closer to marginal cost for the remaining consumption. Two-part tariffs sometimes are also used by nonregulated firms that have marginal cost below average total cost. The advantage of two-part tariffs is that they allow the firm to price marginal output at marginal cost but still to cover (with the access fee) total costs.

Two-part tariffs are relatively rare in the United States. More often, regulation has aimed at setting prices high enough to permit firms to cover all their costs, yet low enough to achieve the large sales that are required to reap the scale economies that characterize natural monopoly. If a regulatory commission knew the demand curve and the cost curves exactly, it could simply pick the price indicated by the intersection of the demand curve and the average total cost curve. This is called *average cost pricing*. Average cost pricing will not, in general, lead to allocative efficiency, because price is not equal to marginal cost, as was shown in Figure 15-3. However, average cost pricing would give lower prices and larger outputs than a monopolist's, and the differences could be very large, depending on the shape of the demand and average cost curves.

Of course, regulators do not have enough data to determine exact demand and cost curves, and regulatory commissions often do not have even reasonably accurate demand and cost information. In the absence of these, commissions have tended to judge prices according to the level of profits that they produce. Generally, once they have set prices, regulatory agencies permit price increases when profits fall below "fair" levels and require price reductions if profits exceed such levels. Thus, what started as price regulation becomes instead profit (or what is called *rate-of-return*) regulation. Meanwhile, concepts of marginal cost and economic efficiency often are ignored in regulatory decisions.

Problems in Regulation

If average cost regulation is successful, only a normal rate of return will be earned; that is, economic profits will be zero. Unfortunately, the reverse is not necessarily true. Profits can be zero for any of a number of reasons, including inefficient operation and misleading accounting. Thus, commissions that rely on rate of return as their guide to pricing must monitor a number of other aspects of the regulated firm's behavior in order to limit the possibility of wasting resources.

Definition of costs.   If a company is to be allowed to charge a price that is determined as "cost plus a fair profit" (as the regulators say) and if that price is below the profit-maximizing one, it is clearly in the firm's interest to exaggerate costs. One major activity of regulatory commissions has been to define rules of allowable costing. Cost supervision is an important activity of public utility regulation for another reason as well. Without it, managers of the regulated industries might have little incentive to be efficient and might simply let costs drift upward.

Rate base. Average total cost includes an appropriate rate of return on the capital that has been invested in the business. Suppose that it is agreed that a firm should be allowed to earn a rate of return of 11 percent on its capital. The **rate of return** is defined as the ratio of net profits to total invested capital. The value of the capital to which 11 percent is to be applied is called the **rate base.** In practice, much of public utility regulation has turned on what should count as part of the rate base.

The precise nature of regulatory rules is important, because the rules affect the incentives of those who are regulated. Economists Harvey Averch and Leland Johnson have shown that a regulated utility has less incentive to resist excessive capital costs than an unregulated one and that in some circumstances it is worthwhile for the regulated utility to buy relatively unproductive equipment. This can occur because, by acquiring expensive capital goods, the firm will increase its rate base. Thus, the notion of "necessary and prudent investments" enters into regulatory rules. This is only one example of the tendency for one regulation to lead to a need for yet further regulation.

Fair return. The permitted rate of return that is implicit in the theory of public utility regulation is the opportunity cost of the owners' capital, with allowances for risk. This is what economists call a position of zero profits. Regulatory commissions have paid some attention to overall earnings rates in the economy, and the level of permitted earnings has changed slightly over time. However, "fairness" and tradition have played a much larger role than considerations of opportunity cost, and regulatory commissions have been slow to adjust permitted rates of return to changing market conditions. For decades, permitted rates of return of 6 to 9 percent were employed, but, when market interest rates soared to double-digit figures during the late 1970s, the traditional levels were not sufficient to induce new investment. Yet regulatory commissions were reluctant to permit the large increases in prices that would result from sharp increases in permitted rates of return.

Curtailment of service. While regulatory commissions regulate prices with an eye on profits, they do not guarantee any minimum rate of return. A regulated utility in a declining industry may have a serious problem. If it is failing to earn the permitted rate, it may apply for permission to increase its prices. In many cases, the price increase will do more harm than good. It will certainly lead to falling sales; whether profits rise or fall depends on the elasticity of demand and the behavior of variable costs. When demand is elastic, a rise in rates will lead to a reduction in revenues. Moreover, for most public utilities, the saving in cost from reducing output is relatively small: Marginal cost is less than average cost. The problem has been especially severe for privately owned urban-transit systems and passenger rail lines. These firms have faced secularly declining demand as people have shifted to substitutes: private cars and airplanes. Given elastic demand curves, when transport companies raise fares (hoping to increase revenues), they find that they only lose more customers (and revenues) to other means of transport.

At this point, a local bus company, for example, may look to its costs to see how it can avoid losses. Often it finds that some parts of its service (such as routes to outlying neighborhoods) no longer cover even the variable costs of providing them, and it proposes to the regulatory authority that this service be dropped. Often the regulators say no. The reason is that they see other considerations in abandoning the bus service (such as increased congestion in the downtown area as even more people use their own cars) that are important to the regulators, but not to the bus company.

The regulators want the regulated company to "cross-subsidize" the less popular routes with profits from the more popular routes; at the same time, they do not want to force the company into bankruptcy. Thus, each time that a curtailment of service is proposed, regulators must make the difficult determination of whether the company is merely trying to increase its profits at the expense of consumers or whether it is truly in trouble.

The Success of Natural Monopoly Regulation

The moral of our discussion of public utilities is that what in theory looks like a simple and straightforward activity of regulating natural monopoly turns

BOX 15-4

Airline Deregulation

Prior to 1978 airlines that flew interstate routes were subject to economic regulation. The Civil Aeronautics Board (CAB) determined the fares that could be charged and the routes that each carrier could fly. All airlines that were permitted to fly a given route were required to charge the same fare. The only way that airlines could compete with each other was on the *quality* of service. By offering many flights on a given route, they could provide relatively uncongested, comfortable seating. Having more airplanes than needed for the traffic both enhanced an airline's quality and increased its rate base, just as the Averch-Johnson analysis (see p. 309) predicts. The average load factor (the percentage of seats filled per flight) was under 50 percent in 1970. An additional dimension of quality was the provision of direct flights—flights on which passengers did not have to change airplanes.

Deregulation has led to tremendous turmoil in the industry, but with this turmoil have come both growth and enormous improvements in efficiency. There now are far fewer direct flights. In their place is the now familiar "hub and spoke" technology: Each of the major airlines has a few hubs, where people often change airplanes, which serve many smaller airports (spokes). Northwest, for example, has hubs at Detroit and Minneapolis; U.S. Air, at Pittsburgh and Philadelphia; and Delta, at Atlanta. Flights to and from relatively small markets

(spokes) can operate at much higher load factors, since they can carry passengers from many different origins to many different destinations via changes in airplanes at the hubs. Adoption of this technique has been largely responsible for the increase in average load factors, which rose to 60 percent by the mid-1980s. Increases in load factors directly reduce average costs, since the cost of flying an aiplane is essentially independent of the number of passengers.

Those who remember the "good old days" of half-empty, direct flights may argue that the reductions in quality inherent in fuller airplanes and more frequent changes of airplanes outweigh any cost advantages, but a careful study by Steven Morrison and Clifford Winston reaches the opposite conclusion. Indeed, Morrison and Winston found that in 1985 the net benefits of deregulation to all travelers (including those who would not have traveled at the higher prices under regulation) were $10 billion. Compared to the regulated industry, fares were lower, traffic and profits were higher, and both business and tourist travelers were better off.

While airline deregulation can be used to make a powerful case for deregulating other industries that are not natural monopolies, there is also a case to be made for further increasing economic efficiency by vigorously enforcing the antitrust laws as they apply to airlines. The past few years have

out in practice to be highly complex and to have spawned a maze of bureaucratic rules and procedures. In large part this is because regulated companies adapt their behavior to the rules that are imposed on them and thus begin a chain of adaptation and change by regulators and regulated companies that ends up producing a complex and cumbersome apparatus. The costs of regulation are high and include the costs of running regulatory commissions, the costs imposed on the courts by frequent appeals, and the costs imposed on businesses (and, hence,

their customers) that must strive to comply with required paperwork.

There has been a loss of confidence in natural monopoly regulation during the last decade or two. While many people believe that, as long as competition is not possible, there are benefits to traditional public utility regulation, increasing numbers have come to doubt that the benefits exceed the costs. Such costs include not only all the regulatory red tape but also the possible loss of the innovative zeal that unregulated firms might bring to the industries

seen a wave of mergers that have greatly increased market shares at hub airports. By the spring of 1986, for example, American had 61.8 percent of enplanements at Dallas-Fort Worth; U.S. Air had 82.3 percent at Pittsburgh; Piedmont had 78.6 percent at Charlotte; and Delta had 54.2 percent at Atlanta. Recent work by Severin Borenstein indicates that dominant airlines that are operating at hubs charge substantially higher prices per mile for flights originating or terminating at the hub than they charge for flights that pass through the hub. On average, Borenstein finds that after controlling for many other variables that might affect the cost of flights and their value to consumers, an increase in market share of 10 percent at an airport leads to an increase of 4.2 percent in the fares paid by passengers who begin or end their trips at that airport.

Many economists view these results with some suspicion, because, under deregulation, entry into the market at most airports seems to be quite easy. As we have seen, free entry could prevent the earning of monopoly profits. Borenstein suggests that dominant firms have a number of ways in which to create barriers to entry, including frequent-flier programs, bonuses to travel agents, and, because a large firm offers more total flights, increased choice of round-trip packages. Whatever the causes, the data suggest that airlines with large market shares at individual airports are able to exert some monopoly power. Does this finding imply that deregulation has been a bad idea? Many economists would say no. Rather, the experience of monopoly power suggests that antitrust policy may have a role to play in blocking future mergers that increase market shares at individual airports. Antitrust policy could also be used to limit the ability of firms to create entry barriers, such as frequent-flier programs. Less likely but imaginable is the possibility that in a different political climate some airlines would be forced to "un-merge," or to divest parts of their operations.

Finally, it is worth noting that airlines have been subject to safety regulation, a form of social regulation, since their inception, and this form of regulation has been essentially unaffected by economic deregulation. While a few economists have argued that the forces of competition would be sufficient to assure that the optimal level of safety would obtain in an unregulated market, this is very much a minority view. The majority view among observers of the industry is that, although economic deregulation has been a success, safety regulations should be maintained and it is too soon to tell whether antitrust policy should be brought to bear on the industry. The issue is not whether government should play a role in the private marketplace; it is what government's role should be.

now regulated. This Schumpeterian view would allow short-run monopoly profits as a price that must be paid to reap very long-run gains that can be achieved by innovation. The question then becomes: Do the benefits arising from innovation exceed the costs imposed by monopoly pricing?

Perhaps a more widely held view is that regulation, even when it is effective at first, becomes too rigid and unresponsive to change and, as a result, fails to recognize and to permit such competition as is possible. Given changing technology, yesterday's natural monopoly of a single railroad may become only one mode of transportation in today's competitive transportation industry. Wire telephone communications are no longer a unique means of voice communication, given radio and satellites. The Post Office is not the only way to send written messages and parcels from one place to another. Further, the local bank is now in competition with other financial institutions around the country and around the world. Thus, the appropriate scope of natural monopoly regulation keeps changing, but regulators tend to cling to—and in some cases are legally committed to—rules and assumptions that may no longer fit the world that they are regulating.

An even more basic source of disenchantment with public utility regulatory commissions is that they have changed their function. In many cases, they have largely abandoned protection of the consumer from natural monopoly and have become protectors of firms *from* competition.

Anticompetitive Policies of Regulatory Commissions

In antitrust, procompetitive and anticompetitive tendencies have existed side by side. In public utility regulation, it is often argued, protection of the regulated firms has replaced protection of the consumer. This view, which has been articulated by economists for decades, is partly responsible for the widespread wave of deregulation during the last two decades. The transportation industry—rail, trucking, and airlines—is perhaps *the* classic example of how regulation got out of hand and thus led to deregulation.

Originally, the ICC regulated railroad rates in order to keep them down. By the 1930s, however, the ICC had become concerned over the depressed economic condition of the railroads, the potentially destructive competition among them, and the emerging vigorous competition from trucks and barges. The ICC became the protector of the railroads, permitting them to establish *minimum* rates for freight of different classes, allowing price discrimination, and encouraging other restrictive practices. Moreover, it became a leading advocate of bringing motor carriers under the regulatory umbrella.

Restricting entry into trucking and setting *minimum* rates for trucks was unmistakably anticompetitive. The only reason for regulating the large interstate carriers was to control their competition with the railroads. The big interstate carriers were limited in where they could go and how *low* a price they could quote. As a result, they became targets for small, unregulated truckers who could cut rates and thus draw away customers without fear of retaliation. To eliminate the competition over rates, regulation was extended to small truckers. At the same time, the ICC set minimum rates for bulk cargo that was shipped by rail. The purpose was to allow truckers to compete for a market in which rail had a natural advantage.

Airlines were never a natural monopoly, although, when the Civil Aeronautics Board began regulating routes and fares, there was arguably so little demand that competition might not have been effective. By the 1960s, regulation was plainly protectionist and was designed to shield the major carriers from competition. Indeed, part of the impetus for deregulation was provided by the fact that in the late 1960s unregulated airlines, which were exempt from CAB regulation because they operated only in one state, charged an average of 45 percent less than did regulated interstate carriers operating along the same routes.

What accounted for the turn toward protection of industries by regulatory commissions whose original mandate was protection of consumers from natural monopolists? One thesis, the "capture hypothesis," is that the regulatory commissions came to adopt the perspectives of those that they were supposed to regulate. Another is that the protectionist policies of the 1930s really reflected the public's mood and a genuine fear that competition was destructive. The depression of the 1930s deeply affected a whole generation. It shook public confidence in many long-held beliefs, including the "received wisdom" that competition was in the public's interest. Faith in competition was greatly shaken by bank and business failures and by the massive unemployment of workers and factories. With the emergence of new generations, for whom the Great Depression is only one of many episodes in past history and not a remembered nightmare, some degree of faith in competition has returned. It is fragile, however, as was demonstrated by the calls for more protection during the recession of 1981–1983.

Deregulation

The renewed belief in the value of competition has manifested itself in widespread deregulation of industries during the 1980s. Airlines, motor carriers, financial institutions, natural gas producers, and long-distance telephone companies are among those that have been substantially unleashed from close regulatory supervision of both prices and entry. Not surprisingly, adjusting to the competitive marketplace has led to considerable turmoil in many of these industries. With the withdrawal of the protection from competition that regulation afforded them, many companies have gone out of business, which is what we would expect if regulation had encouraged inefficiency. Moreover, many industries that still enjoy regulatory protection have been able to bring substantial political pressure to bear in favor of the current status. For the past decade, however, the trend toward repealing economic regulation that affects industries where there is no natural monopoly has been a strong one that shows every sign of continuing. Most economists would argue that the overall effects of deregulation have been positive. Deregulation of the airline industry is discussed in Box 15-4.

Economic deregulation during the 1980s was part of a more general increase in reliance on the market-place and a reduction in reliance on government. The 1980s witnessed considerable *privatization* of activities that previously were provided by governments, especially at the state and local level. At the same time, there was much sentiment for review and limitation of *social regulation,* which is broadly aimed at assuring that firms take the health and safety consequences of their behavior into account. Just how much account should be taken and what the best regulatory mechanisms may be to enforce this are subjects of vigorous debate among both economists and policymakers. We shall discuss these issues in Chapter 22.

SUMMARY

1. Productive efficiency is obtained when any given output is produced at the lowest possible cost, which is another way of saying that a firm is on, rather than above, its relevant cost curve. Productive efficiency within the firm requires that the firm substitute factors of production until the ratio of their marginal productivities equals the ratio of their prices. It also requires that production be allocated among the firms in any one industry so that all firms have the same marginal cost. When an economy is allocatively efficient, it is on, rather than inside, its production possibility boundary.

2. Allocative efficiency relates to the bundle of goods produced, that is, to the specific point that is reached on the production possibility boundary. When allocative efficiency obtains, it would be impossible to produce a different bundle of goods and, as a result, to make everyone in the economy better off. The condition for allocative efficiency is that marginal cost should be equal to price in all lines of production.

3. All profit-maximizing firms will achieve productive efficiency, since profits cannot be maximized if the firm's output, whatever its amount, is produced at a higher cost than is necessary.

4. Only perfect competition is allocatively efficient, because only in perfect competition is marginal cost equal to price. Whenever firms face downward-sloping demand curves, they will equate marginal cost with marginal revenue and hence reach equilibrium where marginal cost is less than price.

5. American policy regarding competition has had three strands: antitrust policy to prevent the acquisition or exercise of monopoly power; public utility regulation of natural monopoly; and protection of firms against excessive competition.

6. The basic tool of antitrust policy is the series of laws that seeks to eliminate practices that lead to monopoly. The overall effect of antitrust policy at any time rests on three things: the nature of the laws themselves, the attitude and interpretation of the courts, and the vigor with which prosecutions are brought by the government and by private plantiffs. These things have varied greatly over time, and thus there have been swings in the antitrust climate.

7. Antitrust policy has been an important feature of the last 40 years. Most observers believe that antitrust laws have been more nearly successful in inhibiting restrictive practices than in altering the basic structure of the economy.

8. The original philosophy of public utility regulation was to grant a monopoly where necessary to achieve the advantages of large-scale production but to prevent the monopolist from restricting output and raising price. The most common regulatory approach has been to regulate prices. This is done by watching profits: allowing price increases only if necessary to permit the regulated utility to earn a fair return on its capital and requiring price decreases if profits rise above the approved level.

9. During implementation of this straightforward theory difficulties are encountered because any set of rules becomes a set of signals that induces patterns of response from those firms that are regulated. Thus it has been necessary for regulators to define carefully "proper" costs, how the costs should be measured, the appropriate rate base, what constitutes "necessary and prudent" additions to capital equipment, and what constitutes a fair return. They have also been forced to determine when and whether utilities can discontinue providing services to groups in the community.

10. Public utility regulation appears to most observers not to have been an unqualified success. Among the reasons are the high costs of regulation and the loss of innovative zeal. Additionally, critics charge that regulators have tended to shift their focus from protection of consumers to protection of the firms that are being regulated.

11. From the earliest days of antitrust and public utility regulation, protection of firms *from* competition has been a theme parallel to protection *of* competition. During the Great Depression protection emerged as a dominant theme, and some believe that it has permanently transformed the regulatory environment.

12. There is a danger that protectionist policies will protect firms from the normal rigors of competition and thus prevent or delay the reallocation of resources that is necessary to achieve efficiency.

13. The entire regulatory apparatus has come under close scrutiny in recent years. How effective deregulation has been and how far the deregulation movement will go is sure to continue to be a major political issue during the 1990s.

TOPICS FOR REVIEW

The meaning of productive and allocative efficiency
The conditions for productive and allocative efficiency
The efficiency of perfect competition
The inefficiency of monopoly
Purposes of antitrust legislation
Difficulties of public utility regulation
Protection of competition versus protection of competitors
Deregulation
Contestable markets and antitrust

DISCUSSION QUESTIONS

1. Would antitrust laws be necessary in an economy of perfect competition? Would they be beneficial in an economy of natural monopoly?

2. What are the arguments for and against exemption from antitrust prosecution of the following:
   a. Labor unions
   b. Farmers
   c. Professional baseball teams (but not professional football teams)

3. Evaluate the wisdom of having the antitrust division use profits as a measure of monopoly power in deciding whether to prosecute a case. Would such a rule be expected to affect the behavior of firms with high profits? In what ways might any changes induced by such a rule be socially beneficial and in what ways might they be socially harmful?

4. Price-fixing agreements are (with some specific exemptions) violations of the antitrust laws. Consider the effects of the following. In what way, if at all, should the following be viewed as being similar to price-fixing agreements?
   a. A manufacturer "recommends" minimum prices to its dealers.
   b. A manufacturer publishes a product price list that is changed only every three months.
   c. A trade association publishes "average industry total costs of production" every month.
   d. A manufacturer prints the "Manufacturer's Suggested Retail Price" (MSRP) on the packaging material for a retail product.

5. Under what circumstances might it be sensible to treat some aspect of market structure or market conduct as *illegal per se,* that is, without considering the effect in the particular case?

6. It is often asserted that when a regulatory agency such as a public utilities commission is established, ultimately it will become controlled by the people whom it was intended to regulate. (This argument raises the question of who regulates the regulators.) Can you identify why this might happen? How might the integrity of regulatory boards be protected?

7. "In a competitive market the least-cost production techniques are revealed by entry and exit, while in public utility regulation they are revealed by commission hearings on rates. It is easier to fool the commission than the market. Therefore, wherever possible, competition should be permitted." Discuss.

8. The effect of the breakup of AT&T's telephone monopoly and deregulation of telephone rates is still controversial. Discuss how each of the following facts might affect the evaluation:
   a. On average, cost of telephone service has increased for residential users and has decreased for large business users.
   b. The price of long-distance telephone calls has declined, while that of local telephone service has increased.
   c. Prices of individual services have been brought more in line with costs of providing those services.
   d. The share of households with one or more phones has decreased from 95 percent to about 92 percent.

9. Consider the following quotation from the *New York Times.* Suppose that the belief expressed in the first paragraph proves to be correct. Discuss whether it would mean that deregulation of airlines was a mistake.

   "Six huge airlines with the power to control fares and routes could emerge from turbulent forces that are reshaping the industry, many Wall Street analysts and airline executives believe.

   "If they are right, such a concentration in a business that now has a dozen or so major participants would severely undercut the competitive forces that legislators sought to unleash when they approved deregulation of the airline industry in 1978."

Chapter 16

The Nature of the Firm and the Market for Corporate Control

How are we to judge the record number of takeovers of large firms during the 1980s? Should government encourage, discourage, or just leave such activity alone? Do increasing levels of corporate debt pose a threat to the health of the economy? Is profit maximization a good description of what firms do; of what they should do?

None of these questions can be answered or even easily discussed in terms of the simple model of the firm that we have developed in the preceding chapters. In that model, firms are users of factors of production and producers of commodities. They face cost and demand curves that are largely determined by forces beyond their control. They seek to maximize their profits by keeping their costs as low as possible and by producing to satisfy consumers' demands. Those who manage firms care only about profits, and their decisions are uninfluenced by the way in which they are organized to do business. Thus, they contribute to our high living standards by producing, as cheaply as possible, goods that satisfy consumers' demands.

In this chapter, we look *inside* the firm and examine the standard assumption that firms always maximize profits. We introduce a number of alternative *behavioral* models of firms. We also examine the great takeover boom of the 1980s—what has come to be known as the market for corporate control. It turns out that the two sets of issues are related; the internal organization and the day-to-day behavior of firms are greatly influenced by the market for corporate control. In particular, a firm that deviates too far from profit maximization becomes an attractive candidate for takeover.

What Do Firms Maximize?

The view that many firms maximize something other than profits is made plausible by the nature of the modern corporation. One hundred years ago the single-proprietor firm, whose manager was its owner, was common in many branches of industry. In such firms the single-minded pursuit of profits would be expected. Today, however, ownership is commonly diversified among thousands of stockholders, and the firm's managers are rarely its owners. Arranging matters so that managers always act in the best interests of stockholders is, as we shall see, anything but straightforward. Thus, there is potential for managers to maximize something other than profits.

The Separation of Ownership from Control

Writing in 1932, A. A. Berle and Gardiner Means hypothesized that, because of diversified ownership and the difficulty of assembling or organizing stockholders, the managers rather than the stockholders or the directors exercise effective control over the corporation.

The hypothesis of the separation of ownership from control is that managerial control occurs and leads to different behavior than would direct control by the firm's owners.

In the modern corporation the stockholders elect directors, who appoint managers. Directors are supposed to represent stockholders' interests and to determine broad policies that the managers will carry out. In order to conduct the complicated business of running a large firm, a full-time professional management group must be given broad powers of decision. Although managerial decisions can be reviewed from time to time, they cannot be supervised in detail. The links between the directors and the managers typically are weak enough so that top management often truly controls the corporation over long periods of time.

As long as directors have confidence in the managerial group, they accept and ratify their proposals, and stockholders elect and reelect directors who are proposed to them. If the managerial group does not satisfy the directors' expectations, it may be removed and replaced, but this is a disruptive and drastic action, and it is seldom employed.

Within wide limits, then, effective control of the corporation's activities resides with the managers. Although the managers are legally employed by the stockholders, they remain largely unaffected by them. Indeed, the management group typically asks for, and gets, the **proxies** of enough stockholders to elect directors who will reappoint it, and thus it perpetuates itself in office. (A proxy authorizes a person who is attending a shareholder meeting to cast a shareholder's vote. In the vast majority of cases, almost all of the votes cast are in the form of proxies.)

None of this matters unless the managers pursue different interests from those of the stockholders. Do these interests in fact diverge?

Principal-Agent Analysis

Principal-agent problems are everywhere. For example, if you (the principal) hire the kid down the block (your agent) to mow your lawn while you are away, all you can observe is how the lawn looks when you come back. She *could* have mowed it every 10 days, as you agreed, or she could have waited until 2 days before you were due home and mowed it only once. By prevailing on a friend or a neighbor to *monitor* her behavior, you could find out what she did, in fact, but only at some cost.

When you hire a physician to diagnose and to treat your lower back pain, it is almost impossible for you to monitor the physician's effort and diligence on your behalf. You have not been to medical school, and much of what the physician does will be a mystery to you. This situation is close to the relationship that exists between stockholders and managers. The managers have information and expertise that the stockholders do not—indeed, that is *why* they are the managers. The stockholders can observe profits, but cannot directly observe the managers' efforts. To make matters worse, even when the managers' behavior can be observed, the stockholders do not generally have the expertise to evaluate whether that behavior was the best available. It takes very detailed knowledge of the firm and the industry to know how well the firm *could* do. Boards of directors, who represent the firm's stockholders, can acquire some of the relevant expertise and monitor managerial behavior, but, again, this is costly.

These examples illustrate the **principal-agent problem:** the problem of designing mechanisms that will induce agents to act in their principals' interests. In general, unless there is costly monitoring of the agent's behavior, the problem cannot be completely solved. Hired managers (like hired gardeners) will generally wish to pursue their own goals. They cannot ignore profits, of course, because if they perform badly enough they will lose their jobs. Just how much latitude they have to pursue their own goals at the expense of profits will depend on many things, including the degree of competition in the industry and the possibility of takeover by more profit-oriented management.

Principal-agent analysis shows that, when ownership and control are separated, profits will be lower than in a "perfect," frictionless world in which principals act as their own agents.

Sales maximization.   Even though we may know that the modern corporation is unlikely always to maximize profits, this does not tell us what *is* maximized. Whatever may be maximized, managers are not entirely free to pursue their own private ends. Instead, their goals, whatever they are, will be maximized subject to the constraint that profits are high enough so that stockholders will not revolt and so that others will not be tempted to take over the firm.

Suppose that the managers need to make some minimum level of profits to keep the stockholders satisfied. After this they are free to maximize sales, unhampered by profit considerations. This is a sensible policy on the part of management, the argument runs, because salary, power, and prestige all rise with the size of a firm as much as with its profits. Generally, the manager of a large, normally profitable corporation will earn a salary that is considerably higher than the salary earned by the manager of a small but highly profitable corporation.

The sales-maximization hypothesis says that managers of firms seek to maximize their sales revenue, subject to a profit constraint.

Sales maximization subject to a profit constraint leads to the prediction that firms will sacrifice some profits by setting price below and output above their profit-maximizing levels (see Figure 16-1).

Failure to minimize costs.   The sales-maximization hypothesis assumes that firms minimize the cost of producing any output but choose to produce more than the profit-maximizing level of output. As was noted in Chapter 15, it is also possible that firms will produce their chosen output at greater than minimum cost. Why would a firm fail to minimize costs? There are many possible answers, but the most straightforward one is that minimizing costs can demand a great deal of detailed managerial attention, so if management can avoid doing so, it would prefer not to make the necessary effort. Moreover, as we shall see later in this chapter, it may be costly for a firm to change its routine behavior. If this is so, one firm may operate at a higher cost than another, but it will still not be worthwhile for the first firm to copy the behavior of the second firm. The *transaction costs* of making the change could outweigh the benefits. As with sales maximization, stockholders and competition will limit the extent to which economic

or technological inefficiency can survive, but they may not eliminate inefficiency.

Alternative Theories of the Firm

Many students of corporate behavior criticize the profit-maximization assumption from a different perspective. They ignore principal-agent problems by assuming that managers do not intentionally pursue their own private interests at stockholders' expense. These critics then argue that there are other reasons for doubting that modern corporations are "simple profit-maximizing computers." They believe that corporations are profit-oriented in the sense that, other things being equal, more profits are preferred to less profits. They do not believe, however, that firms are profit maximizers.

Nonmaximization Due to Ignorance

The critics in one group say that profit-maximizing theory is inadequate because firms, however hard they may try, cannot reach decisions in the way that the theory predicts. We consider two such criticisms—one crude, the other more sophisticated.

Failure to understand marginal concepts.   One of the crudest criticisms is based on the observation that people who run businesses do not calculate in the manner that is assumed by the theory. When managers are interviewed, it is sometimes discovered (apparently to the surprise of the interviewer) that they are unaware of the concepts of marginal cost and marginal revenue. It is then argued that: (1) the theory assumes that firms equate marginal cost to marginal revenue; (2) empirical observations show that many managers have not heard of marginal cost and marginal revenue; (3) therefore, the theory is refuted, because managers cannot be employing concepts of which they are unaware.

This observation, assuming it is correct, does refute the theory that managers of firms make decisions by calculating marginal values and by consciously equating them. It does not, however, refute the theory that firms maximize profits.

The mathematical concepts of marginal cost and marginal revenue are used by economic theorists to discover what will happen as long as, by one means or another—guessing, clairvoyance, luck, or good judgment—firms succeed in maximizing their profits. If firms do so, then economic theory will predict correctly how firms will react to certain changes (e.g., the introduction of a tax). These predictions are independent of the thought process by which managers actually reach their decisions.

Inadequate information.   More sophisticated critics point out that the information available to decision makers is simply not adequate to permit them to reach the decisions that economists predict they will reach. This argument generally takes one of three forms: (1) that firms are the victims of their accountants and base their decisions on accounting concepts, which differ from economic ones; (2) that the natural lag between accumulating and processing data is such that important decisions must be made on fragmentary and partially out-of-date information; or (3) that firms cannot afford to acquire as much information as economists assume they have. These criticisms boil down to the observation that firms in the real world must base their decisions on imperfect information. This insight comes as no surprise to either economists or managers. (See Chapter 8.) As long as firms maximize *expected profits*, the predictions that arise from the economic theory of the firm will still be correct on average.

Nonmaximization by Choice

Alternatives to maximizing theories usually are based on observations of actual firms. The observations, and the theories built on them, often have in common the implication that firms *choose* not to be profit maximizers. Rather, the firms are observed to use explicit rules for decision making that appear to be inconsistent with profit maximization.

Full-Cost Pricing

Most manufacturing firms are price setters: They must quote a price for their products rather than accept a price that has been set in some impersonal competitive market. Simple profit-maximizing theory predicts that these firms will change their prices in response to every change in demand and cost that they experience. Yet students of large firms have

long observed that, except during periods of rapid inflation, this much price flexibility rarely is observed. In the short run, prices of manufactured goods do not appear to vary in response to every shift in demand. Instead, they appear to change less often.

This short-run behavior is consistent with the hypothesis of **full-cost pricing,** which was originally advanced in the 1930s by Robert Hall, a British economist, and Charles Hitch, an American economist, following a series of detailed case studies of actual pricing decisions. Case studies in the intervening decades have continued to reveal the widespread use of full-cost pricing procedures.

The full-cost pricer, instead of equating marginal revenue with marginal cost, sets price equal to average cost at normal-capacity output plus a fixed markup.

The full-cost pricing firm changes its prices when its average costs change substantially (as a result of such events as a new union contract or a sharp change in the prices of key raw materials), and it may occasionally change its markup. However, its short-run pricing behavior is rather unresponsive to changes in demand.

A nonmaximizing interpretation of full-cost pricing. Some modern critics of profit-maximizing theory hold that the prevalence of conventional full-cost practices shows that prices typically are not at their profit-maximizing level. They also hold that full-cost pricing shows that firms are creatures of custom that make only occasional, profit-oriented changes at fairly infrequent intervals.

A profit-maximizing interpretation of full-cost pricing. We saw in Chapter 14 that the short-term stickiness of oligopolistic prices can be accounted for under profit-maximizing theory by saucer-shaped cost curves and by the fact that it is costly for a multi-product firm to change its list prices. The possible conflict between full-cost and profit-maximizing theory then concerns only the setting of the markup that relates prices to costs. If markups are arbitrary and only rarely revised, then there is conflict. If, however, the markup is the profit-maximizing one for normal-capacity output, then full-cost pricing can be consistent with profit maximization.

Organization Theory

A common criticism of profit-maximizing theory is that the behavior of firms is influenced seriously by their organizational structure. **Organization theory** argues that the size and form of the organization within firms affects the substance of the decisions. One way in which the decision-making process varies among firms is the extent to which this process is centralized. Some firms require that everything be approved by "headquarters." Other firms allow smaller operating units to make decisions. Firms of the first type generally respond to new situations more slowly, but also more consistently, than firms of the second type.

The central prediction of organization theory is that different decisions will result from different kinds of organizations, even when all else is unchanged.

One proposition that follows from this theory is that large and diffuse organizations find it necessary to develop standard operating procedures to help them in making decisions. These rules for decision making arise as compromises among competing points of view and, once adopted, are changed only reluctantly. Even if a particular compromise were the profit-maximizing strategy in the first place, it would not remain so when conditions changed. Thus, it is predicted that profits usually will not be maximized.

Another prediction is that decision making by means of compromise will lead firms to adopt conservative policies that avoid large risks. Smaller firms that are not faced with the necessity of compromising competing views will take bigger risks than large firms.

Organization theorists have suggested an alternative to profit maximization that they call **satisficing**. The theory of satisficing was first put forward by Professor Herbert Simon of Carnegie-Mellon University, who in 1978 was awarded the Nobel Prize in economics for his work on the behavior of firms. He wrote, "We must expect the firm's goals to be not maximizing profits but attaining a certain level or rate of profit, holding a certain share of the market or a certain level of sales." In general, a firm is said to be satisficing if it does not change its behavior, provided a *satisfactory* (rather than optimal) level of performance is achieved.

According to the satisficing hypothesis, firms will strive to achieve certain target levels of profits, but, having achieved them, they will not strive to improve their profit position further. This means that the firm could produce any one of a range of outputs that yield at least the target level of profits rather than the unique output that maximizes profits. An example of this behavior is sales maximization, which is illustrated in Figure 16-1.

The theory of satisficing predicts, not a unique equilibrium output, but a range of possible outputs that includes the profit-maximizing output somewhere within it.

Evolutionary Theories

The modern evolutionary theories advanced by such economists as Richard Nelson and Sidney Winter of Yale University build on the earlier theories of full-cost pricing and satisficing. Nelson and Winter argue that firms do not—indeed, could not—behave as profit-maximizing theory predicts. They see firms

FIGURE 16-1 Output of the Firm Under Profit Maximizing, Sales Maximizing, and Satisficing

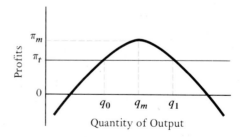

The "best" level of output depends on the motivation of the firm. The curve shows the level of profits associated with each level of output. A profit-maximizing firm produces output q_m and earns profit π_m. A sales-maximizing firm, with a minimum profit constraint of π_t, produces the output q_1.

A satisficing firm (see page 320), with a target level of profits of π_t is willing to produce any output between q_0 and q_1. Thus, satisficing allows a range of outputs on either side of the profit-maximizing level, whereas sales maximizing results in a higher output than does profit maximizing.

operating cautiously with imperfect information in an uncertain world and so making only gradual changes toward the profit-maximizing position. However, since the conditions are constantly changing, firms are best seen as evolving toward a moving target that they never reach. Thus, although firms are profit oriented, they never, except by accident, succeed in maximizing their profits, either locally or globally.

Evolutionary theorists have gathered much evidence to show that tradition seems to be important in firms' planning. The basic effort at the early stages of planning is directed, they argue, toward the problem of performing reasonably well in established markets and maintaining established market shares. They quote evidence to show that suggestions that are made in preliminary planning documents to do something entirely new in some areas, even on a 10-year horizon, are usually weeded out in the reviewing process. They believe that most firms spend little effort on plans to enter entirely new markets and still less on plans to leave or even to reduce their share in long-established markets. These attitudes were illustrated by one firm that, although faced with obviously changing circumstances, reported that "we have been producing on the basis of these raw materials for more than 50 years with success, and we have made it a policy to continue to do so."

The evolutionary theory of the firm draws many analogies with the biological theory of evolution. Here are two.

The genes. In biological theory some behavior patterns are transmitted by genes. Rules of behavior fulfill the same function in the evolutionary theory of the firm. In Professor Winter's words, "A great deal of firm decision behavior is routinized. Routinized decision procedures cover decision situations from pricing practices in retail stores to such 'strategic' decisions as advertising or R and D effort, or the question of whether or not to invest abroad." Winter talks of firms "remembering by doing" according to repetitive routines. He adds that government policymakers tend to have unrealistic expectations about firms' flexibility and responsiveness to changes in market incentives. These expectations arise from the maximizing model, whose fatal flaw, Winter alleges, is to underestimate the difficulty "of the task of merely continuing the routine performance, i.e., of preventing undesired deviations."

The mutations. In the theory of biological evolution, mutations are the vehicle of change. In the evolutionary theory of the firm, this role is played by innovations. Some innovations are the introduction of new products and new production techniques. However, a further important class of innovations in evolutionary theory is the introduction of new rules of behavior. Sometimes innovations are thrust on the firm; at other times the firm consciously plans for and creates innovations.

According to maximizing theory, innovations are the result of incentives—the "carrot" of new profit opportunities. In evolutionary theory the firm is much more of a satisficer, and it usually innovates only under the incentive of the "stick" of unacceptably low profits or of some form of external prodding. Firms change routines when they get into trouble, not when they see a chance to improve an already satisfactory performance. For example, in the growing markets of the 1960s, many firms continued all sorts of wasteful practices that they shed fairly easily when their profits were threatened in the more difficult economic climate of the 1970s and 1980s.

Profit Maximization as an Evolutionary Equilibrium

The economist Armen Alchian has suggested that in long-run equilibrium firms will evolve to become profit maximizers. The basic argument is based in the principle of "survival of the fittest." In a competitive environment, firms that pursue goals or adopt rules that are inconsistent with profit maximization will be unable to stay in business; firms that either choose or happen upon rules that are closer to profit maximization will undersell and displace those that do not. Eventually, only the profit-maximizing firms will survive in the marketplace.

A similar kind of argument can be applied to firms that operate in oligopolistic or monopolistic markets. Here it is not competition that forces the firm toward profit maximization in the long run but the possibility of a takeover. A firm that does not maximize profits will be less valuable than one that does maximize profits. Thus, the nonmaximizing firm can be bought by maximizing managers, who will increase its value as they increase its profits. (This possibility is discussed at length in the second part of this chapter.)

BOX 16-1

Do Firms Control the Market?

John Kenneth Galbraith has argued that it is *not* consumers' wants that create the market signals that provide profit opportunities and motivate business behavior. On the contrary, Galbraith argues, large corporations have the power to create and to manipulate demand in the interest of reducing their own uncertainty.

The key to Galbraith's hypothesis is the power of advertising, whereby corporations persuade consumers to buy what the corporations want them to buy, rather than what the consumers themselves want. Being responsive to consumers, he argues, would require more investment. It is much safer and cheaper merely to make consumers into corporate puppets through the power of advertising. Corporations are also alleged to manipulate the government in order to provide a favorable environment in which to control the market.

There is much superficial support for this view. Large corporations spend a good deal of money on advertising, and they also exert considerable influence on all levels of government. There have been many cases in which this influence has been blatantly corrupt.

Still, the bulk of the evidence, both theoretical and empirical, suggests that in the end, it is consumers who dictate what firms must do to survive, rather than the other way around. Consider the recent history of the U.S. automobile industry. In spite of the industry's enormous financial and political power and in spite of billions of dollars of advertising, the advent of the small, fuel-efficient car, introduced by foreign competitors, nearly brought the industry to its knees. The cars of today are safer, more comfortable, and more efficient than those of 10 years ago, at least in part because the industry had to meet the competition and to serve the desires of its customers.

Turnover in the list of leading companies is revealing. Only one company, Exxon (Standard Oil of New Jersey), was in the top 10 both in 1910 and in 1985. Consider these giants of 1910, none of which are among the largest 250 today: International Mercantile Marine (today United States Lines), United States Cotton Oil, American Hide and Leather, American Ice, Baldwin Locomotive, Cud-ahy, International Salt, and United Shoe Machinery. They have slipped or disappeared from the marketplace largely because of the relative decline in the demand for their products. Today's giants

---

Alchian's argument suggests that even if no firm starts out with the intention of maximizing profits, in the long run each firm that survives in the marketplace will be a profit-maximizing firm.

This view provides an apparent synthesis of maximizing and evolutionary theories of the firm. The distinction between the theories is not so stark as it might seem. On the other hand, many organization theorists point out that evolutionary equilibrium is unlikely ever to be achieved. As technology and tastes change over time, so too does profit-maximizing behavior. Without a fixed target, a firm's behaviors will continually evolve (generally toward profit

maximization) but will never reach an equilibrium. The target refuses to stay put.

Should Firms Maximize Profits?

The preceding discussion has operated under the implicit assumption that by maximizing profits the firm is acting in the best interests of society. There are at least two reasons why profit maximization might not be desirable, however. One is that firms may use their power to manipulate consumer tastes. If they are successful in doing so, one of the basic ideas of standard economics—that of consumer sovereignty—is called into question. We treat this possi-

include automobile, oil, airline, computer, and electric power companies, for the obvious reason that demand for these products is strong.

Are these shifts in demand explained by the corporate manipulation of consumers' tastes through advertising or by more basic changes? Advertising has two major aspects: It seeks to inform consumers about available products, and it seeks to influence consumers by altering their demands. The first aspect, informative advertising, plays an important part in the efficient operation of any free-market system; the second aspect is one through which firms seek to control, rather than be controlled by, the market.

About the second aspect, there can be no question—advertising *does* influence consumers' demand. If GM were to stop advertising, it would surely lose sales to Ford, Chrysler, and Toyota, but it is hard to believe that the automotive society was conjured up by Madison Avenue. When you are persuaded to "fly the friendly skies of United," your real alternative is not a Conestoga wagon, a bicycle, or even (usually) a Greyhound bus; more likely you are foregoing American, Texas Air, or Northwest Airlines.

Careful promotion can influence the success of one rock group over another, but could it sell the waltz to today's teenager? Taste making through advertising unquestionably plays a role in shaping demand, but so do more basic human attitudes, psychological needs, and technological opportunities. When existing companies are cautious about adopting new technologies, new companies will take the risk in order to make a profit. The case of the personal computer is an excellent example. A small number of unknown entrepreneurs invented and successfully marketed the first personal computers. When they did so, advertising was irrelevant. What mattered was that they took a technology and developed a product that they could sell at a price that would earn them a profit. When they had done so, a whole industry followed their lead. Only then did advertising begin to play a role.

The evidence suggests that the allocation of resources among major product groups owes far more to the tastes and the values of consumers than it does to corporate advertising and related activities.

bility, which is associated with the writings of John Kenneth Galbraith, in Box 16-1. Another line of thought argues that firms should take the public interest into account, especially with regard to the environmental consequences of their production. (We shall discuss pollution at some length in Chapters 21 and 22.)

Consumerism is a movement that asserts that there is a conflict between the interests of firms and the public interest. Consumerists hold that the conflict should be removed by pressuring firms to be motivated by the public interest rather than by their stockholders' desires for maximum profits.

Consumerists believe, for example, that GM's directors should be made to recognize that automo-

biles pollute and cause accidents and that GM's resources should be invested in the development and installation of safety and antipollution devices. This, they argue, would be a proper use of GM's funds, even if GM's stockholders do not agree and even if automobile purchasers do not want to pay for the extra safety and antipollution devices.

What are the main arguments *for* this view? First, only the company can know the potentially adverse effects of its actions. Second, by virtue of holding a corporate charter, the corporation assumes the responsibility to protect the general welfare while pursuing private profits.

What are the main arguments *against* the consumerist view? Managers of companies have neither the knowledge nor the ability to represent the general public interest; they are largely selected, judged, and promoted according to their ability to run a profit-oriented enterprise, and the assumption that they are especially competent to decide broader *public* questions is unjustified. Moral, as distinct from economic, decisions—such as whether to use nuclear power, to make or use internal combustion engines, to manufacture or smoke cigarettes, and to manufacture or utilize insecticides or aerosol sprays—cannot properly be delegated to corporations or their executives. Some are individual decisions; others require either the expertise or the authority of a public regulatory agency. Whoever makes decisions on behalf of the public must be potentially responsible to the public. Neither corporate managers nor consumer activists meet this criterion.

Those who oppose the consumerist view hold that most required changes in corporate behavior should be accomplished, not by exhorting business leaders to behave responsibly or by placing consumer representatives on a corporation's board of directors, but by regulations or incentives that force or induce the desired corporate behavior. Let corporations pursue their profits but be subject to public laws. For example, Congress can require that all cars have seat belts or have air bags, or have antipollution devices or meet specific standards of emission levels. Congress can prohibit the use of DDT; it can fine companies that pollute above a specified level; it can regulate the use of nuclear power and aerosols. Congress can also make it easier for private parties to bring lawsuits that would either enjoin certain behavior or force corporations to pay for the damages that their products cause. By adopting strategies like these, the profit motive itself can be harnessed on behalf of public-policy goals. Firms that do not act in accordance with the law will lose profits through the fines and damages that they must pay.[1]

The Market for Corporate Control

We have just seen that there are many reasons why firms may seek to do things other than maximize their profits. However, the owners of the firm—the

stockholders—want the firm to maximize profits, because the profits belong to them. There are at least three things that the owners can do in order to induce managers to act in their interests. (1) The owners can try to design their contracts with managers so as to minimize *agency* costs (including monitoring costs) that arise from the principal-agent problem. Even so, minimum agency costs will always exceed zero. (2) In cases in which it is clear that the managers are not doing as well with the firm's assets as they could, the stockholders can fire the managers. This possibility limits the extent to which firms depart from profit maximization. (3) Even if the owners (acting through their boards of directors) lack the expertise to evaluate the performance of their firms, other firms and other potential managers will be on the lookout for assets that can be employed more profitably. When a firm is badly managed, its stock price will tend to be low relative to its *potential value*, making it a natural target for a takeover. Thus, the possibility of a takeover that is hostile to the current management will tend to limit departures from profit maximization.

Takeovers and takeover bids can be interpreted as transactions in a **market for corporate control.** This market, like any other, has both buyers (those who would acquire the rights to control a firm) and sellers (the current owners of stock in the firm). Also, as in other markets, the expected outcome is that the resource (control) winds up in the hands of those who value it most. In the market for corporate control, the value of the firm will be maximized when the firm is in the control of the best possible managers.

The wave of takeover activity that began during the 1980s has been interpreted in just this light—as an efficiency-enhancing response to unrealized profit opportunities that improves the overall quality of management and the productivity of the target firms. It has also been interpreted as a speculative binge of no intrinsic value that poses a number of longer-term threats to the health of the economy. In this section we summarize the emerging debate and its implications for public policy.

A *takeover* begins when the management of the acquiring firm makes a **tender offer** to the stockholders of the target firm. The takeover is called a *hostile takeover* when current management does not approve of it. Tender offers are promises to purchase stock of a specified price for a limited period of time, during which the acquiring firm hopes to gain con-

---

[1] The costs of enforcing laws and regulations are discussed in Chapters 21 and 22.

trol of the target company. Typically, the prices offered are considerably higher than the prevailing stockmarket price (a 50 percent premium has been the average in recent years). Box 16-2 provides a discussion of how takeovers and leveraged buy outs work.

The Effects of Takeovers

The heart of the argument in favor of takeovers is that, after a takeover, new management can make more efficient use of the target firm's assets. The acquiring firm should be able to exploit profit opportunities that target management is not exploiting. If this is true, the value of the target firm will rise in response to a takeover, reflecting the new profits to come. Additionally, if the *acquiring* firm's managers are acting in the best interest of *their* stockholders, the value of the acquiring firm also should rise when it is successful in a takeover bid.

Returns to Shareholders of Target Companies

Evidence on the effects of takeovers strongly supports the proposition that they benefit the stockholders of target firms. Estimates of the magnitude of the gains varies, but even the low estimates exceed 20 percent of pretakeover stock value during the period from 1962 through 1985. More recent takeovers seem to yield higher returns to stockholders in target companies. Estimates of the average gains in successful tender offers during the 1980s range from about 30 percent to more than 50 percent.

The natural economic interpretation of these gains would imply that markets perceive the acquiring management as able to greatly improve the profitability of target firms. F. M. Scherer and David Ravenscraft have done a number of careful studies of acquired firms both before and after a takeover. Strikingly, although the stock market value of the acquired firms rose after a takeover, Scherer and Ravenscraft found that the firms' actual economic performance was not significantly changed by the takeovers. This is a puzzling result, and it casts doubt on the proposition that takeovers enhance economic efficiency.[2]

[2] See F. M. Scherer, "Corporate Takeovers: The Efficiency Arguments," *Journal of Economic Perspectives,* 2:1 (Winter, 1988), pp. 69–82.

Returns to Stockholders of Acquiring Companies

The benefits to stockholders in the acquiring firms seems to be much smaller than to those in the target firms. Indeed, the best evidence is that the average benefit during the 1980s was slightly negative. How could this be? One possibility, suggested by Andrei Schleifer and Robert Vishny, is that the takeovers result from non-profit-maximizing motivations on the part of the *acquiring* firms' managements.

Consider the position of the top management of a firm in an industry that is slowly declining. The firm may be highly profitable. Indeed, to the extent that the slow decline allows the firm to forego some investments to replace old equipment, the firm may be very profitable in an accounting sense and may have a good deal of cash on hand. In this case, optimal behavior of the firm on behalf of the stockholders often will be to pay large dividends or to repurchase stock—either of which strategies transfers the firm's cash to its owners. However, if management also is interested in its own perquisites and power, it may want to move into areas that are growing, even if it has no expertise in these areas. Moreover, management may be willing to pay a high premium to get into new areas, thus reducing the value of the acquisition for its stockholders, while increasing it for the stockholders of the target firm. Notice the irony here. The threat of takeover acts as a disciplining device for one set of managers by reducing the agency costs that arise from the separation of ownership and control. At the same time, the takeover provides an opportunity for another set of managers to engage in behavior that does not benefit their stockholders.

Increases in Corporate Debt

The recent wave of takeovers and leveraged buy outs largely have been financed by borrowing and have thus greatly increased the extent to which U.S. corporate assets are financed by debt, rather than by stock. (See Chapter 9 for a discussion of corporate financing methods.) A firm must pay interest on its debt, whether or not it is earning profits. If a firm fails to make its required interest payment, it goes bankrupt. The higher is a firm's *leverage,* or ratio of debt to total value, then the greater is its chance of going bankrupt.

Bankruptcy imposes real costs on the owners of the firm. The firm must be reorganized, and its physical assets must be productively reemployed. Trust-

BOX 16-2

The Mechanics of Takeovers and Leveraged Buy Outs

When a takeover bid is made, the management of the target firm may respond in a number of ways. It can recommend that stockholders accept the tender offer. It can look for or organize an alternative buyer—one that would be more sympathetic to management's interests. It can promise to put in place reforms that improve the operation of the firm, thus increasing its profits and removing the motivation for takeover. It can resist the takeover by employing financial devices (discussed later in this box) that make the target firm unattractive for takeover.

Acceptance.   In many cases, target management will decide that the takeover bid is in the best interests of its stockholders, and they will choose to work with the acquiring firm in reorganizing the target firm's operation. (Note that such agreement is almost always desirable. Target management will always possess a good deal of information that can help new management to improve the firm's operations.) In this case, the takeover is no longer hostile and becomes indistinguishable from a merger.

Acceptance of takeover bids by target management can be facilitated by *golden parachutes.* These are contracts that assure that, in the event of successful takeovers, managers of the target firms will receive generous severance pay. Properly imple-

mented, they can reduce the conflict between managers, who want to keep their jobs, and stockholders, who want to see the price of their stock rise—something that the acquiring management promises. Improperly implemented, they can reduce incentives for management to run the firm well: If a manager knows that after the takeover he or she will be set for life, why should the manager work hard to prevent the firm from becoming a takeover target? Finally, with or without golden parachutes, target management sometimes will approve the takeover in accordance with an ancient economic principle: "If you can't lick 'em, join 'em."

Resistance.   There are two basic ways in which target management can resist a takeover. One is to look for a takeover on terms that are more favorable to management (and, perhaps, to the stockholders). Often, this will involve searching for a *white knight,* a company that the target management finds to be a more congenial merger partner. Sometimes, especially recently, management may use the technique of the *leveraged buyout (LBO)* and take over the firm itself. (See below.) The second form of resistance is to make the target firm unattractive to the acquiring firm. A number of financial mechanisms, loosely called *poison pills,* can be used for this purpose. The idea behind a poison pill is im-

ees, lawyers, accountants, and courts all take their cut along the way. The benefits of long-standing organizational routines both within firms and between them may be lost during bankruptcy. These costs, however, are largely borne by stockholders and bondholders, and the risk that these costs will be incurred should be accounted for in the price of the stocks and bonds that finance the firm. If a firm is seen as having an increased risk of going bankrupt because it is carrying a lot of debt relative to its value,

it will compensate new investors by paying a higher rate of return on investments. As long as everyone is assessing the risks accurately (see Chapter 8), the recent increase in the ratio of debt to value in the corporate sector poses no special problems. To be sure, risk has increased, but so have expected returns increased. This is exactly the sort of trade-off that stock markets and bond markets have always offered to investors.

The economy as a whole, however, may suffer

plicit in its name. It is a device that makes the target firm difficult or impossible to digest. One form of poison pill works by requiring that after a successful takeover the (new) firm must buy back stock from existing shareholders at well above the market price. Such a commitment would make the target firm very unattractive to new owners (it would have a contractual commitment to buy assets for more than they are worth) and thus discourage a takeover bid. Poison pills have been challenged in the courts, and the challenges have met with mixed success. To the extent that poison pills are legal, they very much reduce the attractiveness of firms that employ them as takeover targets.

Reform.   By the time a tender offer is made, it is unlikely that target management can implement profit-enhancing reforms in time to resist the takeover bid. However, the threat of takeover may work as an incentive for existing management to implement the changes that would have been implemented after a takeover. Indeed, it is this unseen effect (no takeover bid will take place because current management is acting in the best interests of stockholders) that is at the heart of the argument in favor of takeover activity. The argument is that the activity that we see serves to discipline the behavior of corporate managers in general.

Leveraged Buy Outs

In its classic form, the **leveraged buy out (LBO)** permits the management of the firm, usually in conjunction with a group of other investors, to buy the firm from the stockholders. This is the ultimate defense against a hostile takeover. The way in which LBO's work is that the takeover group borrows ("leverage" is nothing more than a finance term for *debt*) almost all of the money that is needed to buy out the stockholders, thus turning a large, public corporation into a private one. (The largest LBO offer to date is over $20 billion for RJR Nabisco.) Much of the borrowing is often in the form of so-called *junk bonds*, which are high yield and relatively high risk. The large amounts of debt involved put a great deal of pressure on management. They must run the firm well enough to meet regular interest payments at a relatively high rate. If they are successful and the value of the firm is increased, they can sell the firm, or parts of it, in the future and make money on the transaction. The great advantage of LBO's that are initiated by management is that they solve the principal-agent problem: Management becomes a major stockholder in the firm and has strong incentives to perform well. The advantages of LBO's that are initiated by external investor groups are less obvious.

effects that are not accounted for in the behavior of individual firms, their stockholders, and bondholders. The reason for this is that when one firm goes bankrupt it may adversely affect the performance of other firms. These effects will not be taken into account by investors in the first firm. They are a form of *externality*, a subject that is discussed at length in Chapter 21. Consider an example. Suppose that in the event of a recession many firms that have increased their leverage will find it difficult to continue to meet the interest payments on their outstanding debt. Some of these firms will go bankrupt, while others will postpone productivity-enhancing investment in order to get the money needed to pay their creditors. Making these adjustments will adversely affect other firms (suppliers, most notably), which will increase the possibility that they, too, will fail. The affected firms, in turn, will lay off workers and reduce orders to *their* suppliers, further increasing the severity of the recession.

Much criticism of the recent takeover movement is based on the possibility that acquiring firms are incurring risks to the economy as a whole in excess of the risks that they themselves bear. Whether this problem will be as serious as some observers believe awaits the evidence of another recession.

Public Policy Toward Takeovers

The recent sharp increases in the level of takeover activity have spawned a great many proposals, at both the national and state levels, to make takeovers more difficult. To the extent that takeovers are merely a mechanism that permits assets to be used in the way that maximizes their economic value, such proposals, like poison pills (see Box 16-2), simply stand in the way of progress. They increase the agency costs that are intrinsic to the separation of ownership and control.

Indeed, current law already limits the efficacy of takeovers. Under current law, an acquiring firm must file a report with the Securities and Exchange Commission within 10 days of the date that it acquires 5 percent of the target firm's stock. Once the report is filed, the target firm's stock price generally increases, so that the benefits from the takeover go to the stockholders of the target firm. To the extent that the acquiring firm can make money on the deal, it will be on the stock that it can buy during the 10-day grace period. Proposals to shorten this period (to as little as 1 day) will tend to weaken the positive effects of takeovers.

Andrei Schleifer and Robert Vishny have proposed a different sort of reform.[3] Their proposal would act directly on the principal-agent problem, rather than on the takeover process. They would strengthen the incentives of boards of directors to monitor managers by requiring that the directors be compensated through stock in the firm, rather than in cash. Upon election to the board, directors would be given stock that is equal in value to their salaries for their terms in office and would be required to hold the stock for a period of years. They would then have a direct incentive to see that managers maximized the value of the firm.[4]

---

[3] Andrei Schleifer and Robert Vishny, "Value Maximization and the Acquisition Process," *Journal of Economic Perspectives,* 2:1 (Winter, 1988), pp. 7–20.

[4] One possible defect of this scheme is that directors' fees are often a rather small part of directors' incomes, in which case the incentive effects would also be small.

Most economists believe that takeovers provide a useful discipline on the ability of managers to act in nonmaximizing ways, but the case is not conclusive, and many of the potential costs of takeover activity will not be measurable until the economy enters its next recession. In the absence of evidence to show that takeovers do not increase efficiency, however, most economists would probably favor leaving the market for corporate control free of further government control.

Conclusion: The Importance of Nonmaximizing Theories

An impressive array of empirical and theoretical evidence can be gathered in support of various non-profit-maximizing theories. What would be the implications if they were accepted as being better theories of the behavior of the economy than the "standard model," which is based on the assumption of profit maximization?

To the extent that existing non-profit-maximizing theories are correct, the economic system does not perform with the delicate precision that follows from profit maximization. Firms will not always respond quickly and precisely to small changes in market signals from either the private sector or government policy. They are not certain either to make radical changes in their behavior even when the profit incentives to do so are large.

Generally, the nonmaximizing theories imply that in many cases firms' responses to changes in market signals will be of uncertain speed and direction.

There are limits, however, to the extent that the nonmaximizing behavior can survive in the marketplace. According to all of the existing theories, maximizing and nonmaximizing, firms will tend to sell more when demand goes up and less when it goes down. They will also tend to alter their prices and their input mixes when they are faced with sufficiently large changes in input prices. Moreover, as we have seen, failure to respond to profit opportunities can lead to takeover by a more profit-oriented management. While this does not mean that profits are being precisely maximized at all times, it does put real limits on the extent to which firms can ignore profits.

Profits are a potent force in the life and death of firms. The resilience of profit-maximizing theory and its ability to predict the economy's reactions to many major changes (such as the dramatic variations in energy prices that have occurred over the last two decades) suggest that firms are at least strongly motivated by the pursuit of profits.

In the last decade or so, the question of how firms behave in detail has received renewed attention from both economists and organization theorists. Almost everyone in the field agrees that firms do not exactly maximize profits. At the same time, almost everyone agrees that firms cannot stray "too far" from the goal of profit maximization. Just how far is "too far" depends on the circumstances in which firms operate and the mechanisms that firms' owners can use to influence managers. These areas are at the frontier of current economic research.

SUMMARY

1. The widespread ownership of the modern corporation leads to the question: Who really controls the corporation?
2. Principal-agent theory strongly supports the idea that corporate managers will not always operate corporations in the best interests of the stockholders; that is, the managers will pursue their own interests, rather than simply maximizing profits. Sales maximization is an example of such a pursuit.
3. An alternative set of hypotheses denies that firms seek to maximize any well-defined objective:
   a. Some theories hold that firms do not have sufficient information to maximize their profits. Other theories hold that firms consciously choose to do something other than maximize their profits.
   b. The full-cost hypothesis states that firms determine price by adding a customary—and infrequently changed—markup to full costs. This also makes pricing behavior relatively insensitive to short-term fluctuations in demand.
   c. Organization theorists see firms as insensitive to short-term fluctuations in market signals. The reason lies in the decision-making structure of large organizations, which must rely on routines and rules of thumb rather than on fresh calculations of profitabilities as each new situation presents itself. Organization theorists also emphasize that different decision-making structures will lead to different responses to market signals.
   d. Evolutionary theorists build on full-cost and organizational theories. They see the firm as a profit-oriented entity in a world of imperfect information, making small changes in response to new information but being more resistant to large "structural changes."
4. In recent years serious concern has developed over whether corporations should represent the interests of their owners and managers or whether they should be responsible to a broader public interest. Consumerism argues for the latter point of view; others prefer to rely on markets and government control to protect the public interest.
5. Firms that are not run in stockholders' interests—that do not maximize profits—are attractive targets for takeover, because their value will be low compared to their potential, profit-maximizing value. This possibility will limit the ability of managers to pursue their own ends instead of maximizing profits.

6. The last decade has seen an unprecedented wave of corporate takeovers and buy outs in a developing market for corporate control. Successful takeovers have greatly benefited the stockholders of acquired firms. Stockholders in acquiring firms have not done as well.

7. Many observers fear that the increase in corporate debt that has financed the largest takeovers has increased the risk that the next recession will lead to costly and widespread business failures.

8. Under both maximizing and nonmaximizing theories, profits are an important driving force in the economy, and changes in demand and costs cause changes in profits, which cause firms to reallocate resources. The speed and precision, but not the general direction, of the reallocations are what is different between maximizing and nonmaximizing theories.

TOPICS FOR REVIEW

Principal-agent analysis
Sales maximization
Full-cost pricing
Organization theory
Satisficing
Evolutionary theories
Consumerism
Effects of takeovers

DISCUSSION QUESTIONS

1. Assume that each of the following assertions is factually correct. Taken together, what would they tell you about the prediction that big business is increasing its control of the U.S. economy?
   a. The share of total manufacturing assets owned by the 200 largest corporations has been rising steadily for the last 25 years.
   b. The number of new firms begun every year has grown steadily for the last 25 years.
   c. The share of manufacturing in total production has been decreasing for 40 years.
   d. Profits as a percentage of national income are no higher now than they were a half century ago.

2. Comment on this excerpt from an Allied Chemical Corporation advertisement:
   "Our economy, like an engine, must have fuel to operate. And the fuel our economy runs on is profit. Profits keep it going—and growing. But there is strong evidence that the economy's fuel supply is running low. Profits of U.S. corporations today are about 5 percent on sales—less than the 1965 rate.
   "We Americans have become accustomed to a quality of life that can survive only through profits. For profits not only create jobs and goods, they furnish essential tax revenues. Federal, state, and local taxes finance the countless programs that our citizens demand—from paving the roads on which we drive to building our country's defense forces . . . to helping millions of Americans who need some form of assistance."

3. "The business of the corporate manager is to run his or her business so as to make profits. If he or she does so, the public interest is better served than if managers try to decide what is good for society.

Management is neither elected nor appointed to that task." Discuss this quote.

4. "Our list prices are really set by our accounting department: They add a fixed markup to their best estimates of fully accounted cost and send these to the operating divisions. Managers of these divisions may not change those prices without permission of the Board of Directors, which is seldom given. Operating divisions may, however, provide special discounts if necessary to stay competitive." Does this testimony by the president of a leading manufacturing company support the full-cost pricing hypothesis?

5. The leading automobile tire manufacturers sell original equipment (OE) tires to automobile manufacturers at a price that is below the average total cost of all the tires that they make and sell. This happens year after year. Is this consistent with profit-maximizing behavior in the short run? In the long run? If it is not consistent, what does it show? Do OE tires compete with replacement tires?

6. In light of principal-agent theory, why might physicians and attorneys be required to subscribe to professional codes of ethics that prevent (or at least limit) their ability to sell unneeded services to their clients? Why do we not see similar codes of ethics for automobile mechanics?

7. Comment on the following quote from the *New York Times* on October 26, 1988:

"While many stockholders are rejoicing at the flurry of huge corporate takeover attempts, bondholders are wincing at the damage inflicted on their holdings. . . . Buyers of new and old industrial bonds are balking because, when companies are taken over by buying out shareholders with huge amounts of new debt, existing bondholders are left holding securities that are not as safe as before. Suddenly, the chance of an economic downturn could make it impossible for the company to pay interest on all the debt it owes."

8. *The Economist* ran the following on October 29, 1988, under the headline "Someone's Wrong:"

"Notice the curious paradox involved in the biggest and third biggest takeover deals in history? Kohlberg Kravis Roberts is offering $20.3 billion so RJR Nabisco can split its tobacco companies away from the food-making parts of its empire by taking Winston, Camel and Salem private, while selling off Nabisco and Del Monte. [*Note:* Kohlberg's eventual winning bid was billions higher.] Over at Philip Morris, the exact opposite is going on: The company is willing to pay $11.5 billion to add another food company, Kraft, to its existing tobacco and food business (Marlboro, Benson and Hedges, General Foods). More than $30 billion is therefore riding on two flatly contradictory views of the best future for the food and tobacco business. LBOs may be fashionable, but no one can accuse the American investors of herd instinct."

a. Why does *The Economist* find these behaviors so puzzling?

b. Think of some explanations for the puzzle and discuss them.

P·A·R·T

5

THE DISTRIBUTION OF INCOME

Chapter 17

Factor Mobility and Factor Pricing

Are the poor getting poorer and the rich getting richer, as Karl Marx thought they would? Are the rich becoming relatively poorer and the poor becoming relatively richer, as Alfred Marshall hoped they would? Is the distribution of income affected by social changes, such as the increased participation of women in the labor force? Is it affected by changes in public policy toward poverty? Should we reject the view held by the great Italian economist Vilfredo Pareto (inventor of indifference curves and student of income distribution) that inequality of income is a social constant determined by forces that are possibly beyond human understanding and probably beyond human influence?

The Functional and the Size Distribution

The founders of classical economics, Adam Smith and David Ricardo, were concerned with the distribution of income among what were then the three great social classes: workers, capitalists, and landowners. They defined three factors of production as labor, capital, and land. The return to each factor was treated as the income of the respective social class.

Smith and Ricardo were interested in what determined the income of each class relative to the total national income. Their theories predicted that, as society progressed, landlords would become relatively better off and capitalists would become relatively worse off. Karl Marx had a different theory. He predicted that, as growth occurred, capitalists would become relatively better off and workers would become relatively worse off (at least until the whole capitalist system collapsed).

These nineteenth century debates focused on what is now called the **functional distribution of income,** defined as the distribution of total income among the major factors of production. Table 17-1 shows data for the functional distribution of income in the United States in 1987.

Although functional distribution categories (wages, rent, profits) pervade current statistics, economists have shifted to another way of looking at differences in incomes. At the beginning of the century, Pareto studied what is now called the **size distribution of income,** which is the distribution of income among different households without reference to the source of the income or the social class of the households. He discovered that inequality in

TABLE 17-1	The Functional Distribution of National Income in the United States, 1987		
Type of income		Billions of dollars	Percentage of total
Employee compensation		$2,932.5	73.3
Corporate profits		323.8	8.1
Proprietor's income		322.1	8.0
Interest		397.7	10.0
Rental income		20.1	0.6
Total		$3,996.2	100.0

Source: *Survey of Current Business,* November 1988.

Income is classified here according to the nature of the factor service that earned the income. While these data show that employee compensation is about three-quarters of national income, this does not mean that workers and their families receive only that fraction of national income. Many households will have income in more than one category listed in the table.

TABLE 17-3	Inequality in Family Income Distribution, 1987
Family income rank	Percentage share of aggregate income
Lowest fifth	4.6
Second fifth	10.9
Middle fifth	16.8
Fourth fifth	24.0
Highest fifth	43.7
	100.0
Top 5 percent	17.0

Source: *Statistical Abstract of the United States,* 1988.

While far from showing overall equality, income distribution is relatively equal for the middle 60 percent of the distribution. If the income distribution were perfectly equal, each fifth of the families would receive 20 percent of aggregate income. These data are plotted in Figure 17-1.

income distribution was substantial in all countries and, more surprisingly, that the degree of inequality was quite similar from one country to another. Tables 17-2 and 17-3 show that in the United States in 1984 there was substantial inequality in the size distribution of income.

Inequality in the distribution of income is also

TABLE 17-2	Incomes of American Families,[a] 1987
Income class (thousands of dollars)	Percentage of families
Less than 10	19.1
10.0 to 19.9	21.4
20.0 to 34.9	26.1
35.0 to 49.9	16.6
50.0 or more	16.8

Source: *Statistical Abstract of the United States,* 1988.

[a] The census definition of a family is two or more persons related by blood, marriage, or adoption who are residing together.

Although median family income in 1987 was just over $30,000, many received much less than this comfortable level of income, and some received a great deal more. While nearly 17 percent of American families had very comfortable incomes of over $50,000, a full 19 percent had to subsist on incomes that were below $10,000.

shown graphically in Figure 17-1. This curve of income distribution, called a **Lorenz curve,** shows how much of total income is accounted for by given proportions of the nation's families. (The farther the curve bends away from the diagonal, the more unequal is the distribution of income.) Today the bottom 20 percent of all U.S. households receive less than 5 percent of all income earned; therefore, the present size distribution of income is virtually unchanged from what it was 20 years ago.

There are good reasons why much of the attention of modern economists is devoted to the size, rather than the functional, distribution of income. After all, some capitalists (such as the owners of small retail stores) are at the lower end of the income scale, while some wage earners (such as skilled athletes) are at the upper end of the income scale. Moreover, if someone is poor, it matters little whether that person is a landowner or a worker.

To understand the distribution of income, we must first study how the income of households is determined. Superficial explanations of differences in income, such as, "People earn according to their ability," are clearly inadequate. Incomes are distributed much more unequally than any *measured* index of ability, whether it be IQ, physical strength, or typing skill. In what sense is Curtis Strange five times as able a golfer as Dave Barr? His average score is only 1 percent better, yet he earns five times as much. However, if answers that are couched in terms of worth and ability are refuted easily, so are answers such as, "It's all a matter of luck," or "It's just the system."

The Theory of Income Distribution

How does economic theory explain the distribution of income more satisfactorily than these superficial explanations? In this chapter, using the basic tools of supply and demand, we provide an answer to this question.

Factor Markets and Factor Incomes

Workers' incomes depend on their wage rates and on the hours that they work. Similarly, all incomes have two components: prices paid and quantities supplied. We look at each of these.

Factor prices.   Consider the money wage of $5 per hour. Does someone who earns this money wage expect to get a large or a small share of the nation's total production? In 1930, when a bus ride cost $.05 in many cities and a restaurant meal could be bought for $.25, $5 per hour offered command over what most people would have regarded as a very satisfactory share of the nation's output. In 1990, when a bus ride costs over $1 in many cities and even a modest restaurant meal costs over $5, a wage rate of $5 per hour offers command over what most people would regard as a quite unsatisfactory share of the nation's output.

What this example illustrates is that a factor's real income depends on the price that it can command *relative to* all the other prices in the economy. "Expensive" and "cheap" are relative concepts. A factor becomes more expensive and commands a larger share of the nation's total output when its price rises relative to most other prices. It becomes cheap and commands a smaller share of the nation's total output when its price falls relative to most other prices. The theory of factor pricing is concerned with relative prices, with what makes a factor become more or less expensive relative to the prices of other

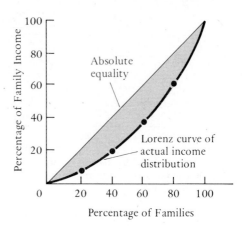

FIGURE 17-1   A Lorenz Curve of Family Income in the United States

The size of the shaded area between the Lorenz curve and the diagonal is a measure of the inequality of income distribution. If there were complete income equality, the bottom 20 percent of income receivers would receive 20 percent of the income, and so forth, and the Lorenz curve would coincide with the diagonal line. Because the lower 20 percent receive only 5 percent of the income, the Lorenz curve lies below the diagonal line. The extent to which it bends away from the straight line indicates the amount of inequality in the distribution of income.

goods and services in the economy, so that the factor will command a larger or smaller share of the nation's total output.[1]

Factor quantities.   There is no point in being offered a high wage rate if little or no work can be found at that rate. This emphasizes that a factor's share of the national income depends not only on the price that its services command but also on the quantity of those services that are sold.

---

[1] The theory of inflation is concerned with why all prices change; that is, it is concerned with the absolute level of all prices. The theory of market prices of goods and factor services is concerned with why some prices change relative to others; that is, it is concerned with relative prices. If we assume that all prices other than the one under consideration are constant, then a change in a factor's money price is a change in its relative price. If all other prices are rising, then a change in relative price requires that the factor's money price rise faster or slower than the average of all prices. See Chapter 4, pages 67–69 for a fuller discussion of this.

Factor income. To discover a factor's income, we need to know the price of its services and the amount of them that are sold. This is something that we have done already for final goods and services that are sold in competitive and in monopolistic markets.

According to the neo-Classical theory of distribution, *determining* **a factor's income is just a particular application of price theory.**

This determination is shown for a competitive market in Figure 17-2. (Look again at Figure 4-8 on page 66 to see why this analysis is familiar.) This is all there is to the essence of the neo-Classical theory of distribution in competitive markets. The theory applies to all factors that are priced and sold in any market. To apply it to any particular factor, such as labor, we need only to allow for any special forces that influence the demand or the supply of labor. To apply the theory of noncompetitive markets, we need merely to apply what we have learned already about pricing in markets under monopoly or oligopoly.

FIGURE 17-2   The Determination of Factor Price and Income in a Competitive Market

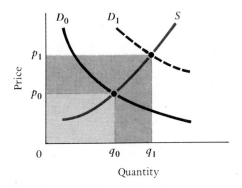

In competitive factor markets, demand and supply determine factor prices, quantities of factors used, and factor incomes. With demand and supply curves D_0 and S, the price of the factor will be p_0 and the quantity employed will be q_0. The total income earned by the factor is the light gray shaded area. A shift in demand from D_0 to D_1 raises equilibrium price and quantity to p_1 and q_1, respectively. The income earned by the factor rises by an amount equal to the dark gray shaded area.

In this chapter and the next, we shall study some interesting applications of this theory that can be made to competitive markets. In Chapter 19, we shall study the market for labor in some detail; to do so, we consider now a number of special forces that influence the demand and the supply of labor, and we extend the theory to cover noncompetitive market structures.

The Demand for Factors

Firms require inputs, not for their own sake, but as a means to produce goods and services. For example, the demand for computer programmers and technicians is growing as we use more and more computers. The demand for carpenters and building materials rises or falls with the amount of housing construction. Anything that increases the demand for new housing—population growth, lower interest rates on mortgages, and so on—will increase the demand for the inputs that are required to build the houses. The demand for any input depends on the existence of a demand for the goods or services that it helps to produce; the demand for a factor of production is therefore called a **derived demand.**[2] Typically, one input will be used in making many commodities. Steel is used in dozens of industries, as are the services of carpenters.

The total demand for an input will be the sum of the derived demands for it in every activity in which it is used.

The theory of income distribution rests in part on the demand by firms for land, labor, and capital to be used as inputs. Firms also use products that are produced by other firms as their inputs, such as steel, plastics, and electricity. If we investigate the production of these inputs, we will find that they, too, are made by using land, labor, capital, and other produced inputs. If we continue following through the chain of outputs used as inputs, we will find that we can account for all of the economy's output in terms of inputs of the three basic factors of production—land, labor, and capital.

[2] In the next chapter we shall look in detail at the role of marginal productivity theory in understanding the derived demand for the services of factors of production.

The Total Supply of Factors

To what extent do economic forces determine the *total supply* of a factor to the whole economy? To what extent do economic forces determine the *supply available to a particular industry?*

In this section we look at total supply. At any one time, the total supply of each factor of production is given. For example, in each country the labor force is of a certain size, there is so much arable land available, and there is a given known supply of petroleum. However, these supplies can and do change in response to both economic and noneconomic forces. Sometimes the change is very gradual, as when a climatic change slowly turns arable land into desert or when a medical discovery lowers the rate of infant mortality and hence increases the rate of population growth, thereby eventually increasing the supply of adult labor. Sometimes the changes can be quite rapid, as when a boom in business activity brings retired persons back into the labor force or a rise in the price of oil greatly encourages the discovery of new oil supplies, or when a rise in the price of agricultural produce encourages the draining of marshes to add to the supply of arable land.

Although people worry about depleting natural resources, complete exhaustion of a given resource is quite rare. Frequently, newly discovered or previously unexploited sources of a resource maintain the supply, although perhaps at a higher cost than existing supplies. Ultimately, of course, there is an upper limit, and resources can be exhausted; worse, they can be contaminated or otherwise despoiled before they are consumed. However, even when the supply of one resource is exhausted, substitutes usually are developed. The exhaustion of high-grade iron ore reserves in the Mesabi Range of northern Michigan did not end steel production in the United States, partly because ways to use low-grade iron ores once thought worthless were discovered and partly because new supplies in Labrador and in the Caribbean were developed.

Shortages often lead to their own correction. When oil became scarce over a decade ago, its price rose; users turned to substitutes to meet their demands; synthetic oil was developed; and oil companies explored for new sources.

Time is an important element in the determination of the total supply of a factor. The longer is the time period, the more responsive the total supply of any factor will be to economic forces.

Now consider the total supply of each of the three key factors of production.

Total Supply of Capital

The supply of capital in a country consists of the stock of existing machines, plant, equipment, and so on. Capital is a manufactured factor of production, and its total supply is in no sense fixed, although it changes only slowly. Each year the stock of capital goods is diminished by the amount that becomes physically or economically obsolete and is increased by the amount that is produced. On balance, the trend has been for the capital stock to grow over the past decades. In Chapter 18 we shall consider the theory of investment that deals with long-term changes in the stock of capital.

Total Supply of Land

The total area of dry land in a country is almost completely fixed, but the supply of *fertile* land is not fixed. Considerable care and effort are required to sustain the productive power of land. If the return to land is low, its fertility may be destroyed within a short time. Moreover, scarcity and high prices may make it worthwhile to increase the supply of arable land by irrigation and other forms of reclamation.

Total Supply of Labor

The *total supply of labor* means the total number of hours of work that the population is willing to supply. This quantity is often also called the **supply of effort.** It has many obvious determinants, such as the rewards for working, the ages at which people enter the labor force and retire from it, and the length of the conventional work week. It also has many less obvious ones. For example, a social trend, such as the women's liberation movement, affects labor force participation. For another, the whole pattern of tax rates, unemployment insurance, and welfare payments affects the relative advantages of working and not working.

As is discussed in Box 17-1, the evidence shows some, but relatively small, adverse effects of taxes on the supply of effort. However, welfare schemes sometimes have been a severe disincentive to work.

BOX 17-1

Taxes, Welfare, and the Supply of Effort

Taxes

Many people believe that high income taxes tend to reduce the supply of effort by lowering the incentive for people to work. Such objective evidence as exists, however, suggests that tax cuts do not always increase the supply of effort. Even when they do, the aggregate effect may be small.

A tax cut sets up two opposing forces, and the final effect on the amount of work that is done by people depends on the relative strengths of each. An example will suggest why this is so. Consider Barry Bluecollar, who has a job on an assembly line. He typically takes off 5 hours per week and so works only 35 hours, receiving a take-home pay of $8.50 per hour, or $297.50 per week. Now suppose that there is a tax cut, so that his take-home pay rises to $10.00 per hour. He might elect to work a little more, since every hour that he works now nets him $10.00 instead of $8.50. If he raises his average weekly hours to 37, he will raise his take-home pay by $72.50 to $370.00. Economists call the tendency to work more because the reward for an hour's work has risen the *substitution effect*.

However, Bluecollar might elect to work a little less, since, with the rise in his hourly take-home pay, he can have more income *and* get more leisure. Suppose that he takes off an extra 3 hours per week. His take-home pay is now $320.00 per week (32 hours at $10.00 per hour, as compared to 35 hours at $8.50 per hour before the tax cut). Now he has 3 more hours of leisure a week *and* $22.50 more in income. Economists call the tendency to work less because it is possible to have more income *and* more leisure the *income effect*.

If the substitution effect dominates, people respond to a tax cut by working more. If the income effect dominates, they respond by working less.

Either result is possible, so a tax cut may raise or lower the amount of work that people want to do.

A good deal of research has been done on the effect of changes in tax rates. It has shown that, in response to a rise in taxes, some people work fewer hours because the reward is less, while others feel poorer and work more to maintain their after-tax income. The most recent research, however, suggests that there is at most a small net disincentive up to a level of marginal tax rate of 50 percent, such as existed in the United States until 1987. The sharp decrease in maximum rates that became effective then will provide important additional evidence within a few years.

Welfare

Do welfare payments and other aids to the poor make them less willing to take jobs? While many of those who receive welfare payments are unable to find work, there is no doubt that some welfare rules discourage work because they result in heavy taxes to welfare recipients on much or all of any income that they might earn. If a family's welfare payment of, say, $500 per month, is decreased dollar for dollar by any earnings, this amounts to a 100 percent tax on the first $500 of earnings per month. The person who could earn $400 through part-time work would have no economic incentive to do so.

In recent years, many welfare schemes have recognized this problem and have allowed persons on welfare to keep a major portion of any extra money that they earn. Thus, although some disincentive to work will exist with any welfare scheme, the disincentive can be minimized when the financial aids are structured so as to leave those who can work with some incentive to do so.

Although most people prefer working to being on welfare, it is not surprising that they respond rationally to an incentive system that severely penalizes any work done by welfare recipients.

The Supply of Factors for a Particular Use

Most factors have many uses. A given piece of land can be used to grow any one of several crops, or it can be subdivided for a housing development. A computer programmer in Washington, D.C., can work for one of several firms, for the government, or for Georgetown University. A lathe can be used to make many different products, and it requires no adaptation when it is turned for one use or another. Plainly, it is easier for any one user to acquire more of a scarce factor of production than it is for all users to do so simultaneously. One user can bid resources away from another user, even though the total supply may be fixed.

The total supply of any factor must be allocated among all the different uses to which it can possibly be put.

Factor Mobility

When we are considering the supply of a factor for a particular use, the most important concept that we should keep in mind is *factor mobility*. A factor that shifts easily between uses in response to small changes in incentives is said to be *mobile*. It will be in elastic supply in any one of its uses, because a small increase in the price offered will attract many units of the factor from other uses. A factor that does not shift easily from one use to another, even in response to large changes in remuneration, is said to be *immobile*. It will be in inelastic supply in any one of its uses, because even a large increase in the price offered will attract only a small inflow from other uses. Often a factor may be immobile in the short run but mobile in the long run.

An important key to factor mobility is time. The longer is the time interval, the easier is it for a factor to convert from one use to another.

Consider the factor mobility among particular uses of each of the three key factors of production.

Capital.   While some kinds of capital equipment—lathes, trucks, and computers, for example—can be shifted readily among uses, many others are comparatively unshiftable. A great deal of machinery is utterly specific: Once built, it must be used for the purpose for which it was designed, or it cannot be used at all. (It is the immobility of much fixed capital equipment that makes the exit of firms from declining industries the slow and difficult process that we studied on pages 239–240 of Chapter 12.)

In the long run, however, capital is highly mobile. When capital goods wear out, firms may simply replace them with identical goods, but the firm has many other options. It may buy a newly designed machine to produce the same goods, or it may buy machines to produce totally different goods. Such decisions lead to changes in the long-run allocation of a country's stock of capital among various uses.

Land.   Land, which is physically the least mobile of factors, is one of the most mobile in an economic sense. Consider agricultural land. Within one year, one crop can be harvested, and a totally different crop can be planted. A farm on the outskirts of a growing city can be sold for subdivision and development on short notice.

Once land is built on, its mobility is much reduced. A site on which a hotel has been built can be converted into an office building site, but it takes a large differential in the value of land use to make it worthwhile, because the hotel must be torn down.

Although land is highly mobile among alternative uses, it is completely immobile as far as location is concerned. There is only so much land within a given distance of the center of any city, and no increase in the price paid can induce further land to be located within that distance. This locational immobility has important consequences, including high prices for desirable locations and the tendency to build tall buildings to economize on the use of scarce land, as in the center of large cities.

Labor.   Labor is unique as a factor of production in that the supply of the service requires the physical presence of the person who supplies it. Absentee landlords, while continuing to live in the place of their choice, can obtain income from land that is located in remote parts of the world. Investment can be shifted from iron mines in South Africa to mines in Labrador, while the owners commute between San

Francisco and Hawaii. However, when a worker who is employed by a firm in Duluth, Minnesota, decides to supply labor service to a firm in Cincinnati, Ohio, the worker must physically travel to Cincinnati. This has an important consequence.

Because of the need for labor's physical presence, nonmonetary considerations are much more important in the allocation of labor than in the allocation of other factors of production.

People may be satisfied with or frustrated by the kind of work that they do, where they do it, those with whom they do it, and the social status of their occupations. Since these considerations influence their decisions about what they will do with their labor services, they will not always move just because they could earn a higher wage. Nevertheless, occupational and job movement do occur when there are changes in the wage structure.

The mobility that does occur depends on many forces. For example, it is not difficult for a secretary to shift from one company to another in order to take a job in Boise, Idaho, instead of in Tacoma, Washington, but it can be difficult for a secretary to become an editor, a model, a machinist, or a doctor in a short period of time. Those who lack ability, training, or inclination find certain kinds of mobility to be difficult or impossible.

Some barriers may be virtually insurmountable once a person's training has been completed. It may be impossible for a farmer to become a surgeon or for a truck driver to become a professional athlete, even if the relative wage rates change greatly. However, the children of farmers, doctors, truck drivers, and athletes, when they are deciding how much education or training to obtain, are not nearly as limited in their choices as their parents, who have already completed their education and are settled in their occupations.

Thus, the labor force as a whole is mobile, even though many individual members in it are not. At one end of the age distribution are people who enter the labor force directly from school; at the other end are those who leave it through retirement or death. The turnover in the labor force due to these causes is about 3 or 4 percent per year. Over a period of 10 years, a society could create a totally different occupational distribution merely by directing new entrants to jobs other than the ones that were left vacant by workers who left the labor force, without a single individual ever changing jobs. The role of education in helping people to adapt to available jobs is great. In a society in which education is provided to all, it is possible to achieve large increases in the supply of any needed labor skill within a decade or so.

Factor Price Differentials

If every laborer were the same, and if all benefits were monetary, then the price of labor would tend to be the same in all uses. Workers would move from low-priced jobs to high-priced ones. The quantity of labor supplied would diminish in occupations in which wages were low, and the resulting labor shortage would tend to force those wages up; the quantity of labor supplied would increase in occupations in which wages were high, and the resulting surplus would force wages down. The movement would continue until there were no further incentives to change occupations, that is, until wages were equalized in all uses.[3]

In fact, however, wage differentials commonly occur. These differentials may be divided into two distinct types: those that exist only in disequilibrium situations and those that persist in equilibrium.

Disequilibrium Differentials

Some factor price differentials reflect a temporary state of disequilibrium. They are brought about by circumstances such as the growth of one industry and the decline of another. The differentials themselves lead to reallocation of factors, and such reallocations in turn act to eliminate the differentials.

Consider the effect on factor prices of a rise in the demand for air transport and a decline in the demand for rail transport. The airline industry's demand for factors increases while the railroad industry's demand for factors decreases. Relative factor prices will go up in airlines and down in railroads. The differential in factor prices causes a net movement of factors from the railroad industry to the airline industry, and this movement causes the differentials to lessen and eventually to disappear. How long this process takes will depend on how easily factors can be reallocated from one industry to the other, that is, on the degree of factor mobility.

---

[3] Similar remarks also apply to all other factors of production.

Equilibrium Differentials

Some factor price differentials persist in equilibrium, without any generating forces that will eliminate them. These **equilibrium differentials** can be explained by intrinsic differences in the factors themselves, by differences in the cost of acquiring skills, or by different nonmonetary advantages of different occupations.

Intrinsic differences.   If various units of a factor have different characteristics, the price that is paid may differ among these units. If intelligence and dexterity are required to accomplish a task, intelligent and manually dexterous workers will earn more than less intelligent and less dexterous workers. If land is to be used for agricultural purposes, highly fertile land will earn more than poor land. These differences will persist even in long-run equilibrium.

Acquired differences.   If the fertility of land can be increased by costly methods, then that land must command a higher price than less fertile land. If it did not, landlords would not incur the costs of improving fertility. The same holds true for labor. It is costly to acquire most skills. For example, a mechanic must train for some time, and unless the earnings of mechanics remain sufficiently above what can be earned in less skilled occupations, people will not incur the cost of training.

Nonmonetary advantages.   Whenever working conditions differ among various uses for a single factor, that factor will earn different equilibrium amounts in its various uses. The difference between a test pilot's wage and a chauffeur's wage is only partly a matter of skill; the rest is compensation to the worker for facing the higher risk of testing new planes as compared to driving a car. If they both were paid the same, there would be an excess supply of chauffeurs and a shortage of test pilots.

Academic researchers commonly earn less than they could earn in the world of commerce and industry because of the substantial nonmonetary advantages of academic employment. If chemists were paid the same in both sectors, many chemists would prefer academic to industrial jobs. Excess demand for industrial chemists and excess supply of academic chemists would then force chemists' wages up in industry and down in academia until the two types of jobs seemed equally attractive on balance.

The same forces account for equilibrium differences in regional earnings of otherwise identical factors. Welders and carpenters earn more in Point Barrow, Alaska, than they do in Phoenix, Arizona. Without higher pay, not enough people would be willing to work in unattractive or remote locations. Similarly, if enough people preferred living in New England to living in Gary, Indiana, equilibrium wages in comparable occupations would be lower in New England than in Gary, Indiana.

Differentials and Factor Mobility

The distinction between equilibrium and disequilibrium differentials is closely linked to factor mobility.

Disequilibrium differentials lead to, and are eroded by, factor movements; equilibrium differentials are not eliminated by factor mobility.

Equalizing net advantage.   The behavior that causes the erosion of disequilibrium differentials is summarized in the assumption of *the maximization of net advantage:* The owners of factors of production will allocate them to uses that maximize the net advantages to themselves, taking both monetary and nonmonetary rewards into consideration. If net advantages were higher in occupation A than in occupation B, factors would move from B to A. The increased supply in A and the lower supply in B would drive factor earnings down in A and up in B until net advantages would be equalized, after which no further movement would occur. This prediction is summarized in the hypothesis of *equal net advantage:* Units of each kind of factor of production will be allocated in equilibrium among alternative possible uses in such a way that the net advantages in all uses are equalized.

While nonmonetary advantages are important in explaining differences in levels of pay for labor in different occupations, they tend to be quite stable over time. As a result, monetary advantages, which vary with market conditions, lead to changes in *net advantage.*

A change in the relative price of a factor between two uses will change the net advantages of the uses. It will lead to a shift of some units of that factor to the use whose relative price has increased.

This implies a rising supply curve for a factor in any particular use. When the price of a factor rises in that use, more will be supplied to that use. This factor supply curve (like all supply curves) can *shift* in response to changes in other variables. For example, a change in laws that relate to safety or a new union agreement that alters working conditions will shift the curve of labor to that use, showing a new quantity supplied at each wage.

Policy issues.   The distinction between equilibrium and dynamic factor price differentials raises an important consideration for policy. Trade unions, governments, and other bodies often have explicit policies about earnings differentials, often seeking to eliminate them in the name of equity. The success of such policies depends to a great extent on the kind of differential that is being attacked.

Consider a policy that resists a disequilibrium differential. Only a short time ago large differentials opened up between earnings in the Sun Belt and those in the industrial Midwest. These were disequilibrium differentials that were associated with an economic boom in the Sun Belt. The wage differentials could have been narrowed by imposing similar wages for similar jobs done everywhere in the country—as is done by national unions in some countries, and has been proposed by some advocates of equal pay legislation. If successful, such policies would have slowed the movement of labor to the Sun Belt and thus would have prolonged the period during which there would be excess labor in the Midwest and a shortage in the Sun Belt.

Policies that attempt to eliminate equilibrium differentials will encounter even more severe difficulties. A recent example is legislation requiring *equal pay for work of equal value*. Whatever the social value of such laws, they run into trouble whenever they require equal pay for jobs that have different nonmonetary advantages.

Say that two jobs demand equal skills, training, and everything else that is taken into account when deciding what is work of equal value but that, in a city with an extreme climate, one is an outside job and the other is an inside job. If some "pay commission" requires equal pay for both jobs, there will be a shortage of workers who work outside and an excess of people who want to work inside. Employers will seek ways to compensate those who work outside through monetary advantages. Higher pen-

sions, shorter hours, longer holidays, overtime paid for but not worked, and better working conditions may be offered. If these are allowed, they will achieve the desired result but will defeat the original purpose of equalizing the monetary benefits of the inside and the outside jobs; they will also cut down on the number of outside workers that employers will hire, since the total cost of an outside worker to an employer will have risen. If the jobs are unionized, or if the pay commission prevents such "cheating," the shortage of workers for outside jobs will remain. The issue of equal pay for work of equal value is further considered in Chapter 19. The main point is that policies designed to achieve this concept of equality run into a series of problems—which may or may not be surmountable—whose existence is to be understood by the hypothesis of equal net advantage.

Factor price differentials are a natural market consequence of the conditions of supply and demand. Movement of factors among alternative uses tends to establish equilibrium levels of factor prices at which disequilibrium differentials are eliminated and equilibrium differentials are restored. Policies that seek to eliminate factor price differentials without consideration of what caused them or how they affect the market for the factor are likely to have perverse results.

Economic Rent

One of the most important concepts in economics is that of *economic rent*. A factor must earn a certain amount in its present use to prevent it from moving to another use.[4] If there were no nonmonetary advantages in alternative uses, the factor would have to earn its opportunity cost (what it could earn elsewhere) to prevent it from moving elsewhere. This is usually true for capital and land. Labor, however, gains important nonmonetary advantages in various jobs, and what it must earn in one to prevent it from moving to another is enough to equate the two jobs' total advantages—monetary and nonmonetary. *Any excess that it earns over this amount* is called its **economic rent.**

[4] Following Alfred Marshall, this amount is sometimes called the *factor's transfer earnings.*

BOX 17-2

Origin of the Term *Economic Rent*

In the early nineteenth century there was a public debate about the high price of wheat in England. The price was causing great hardship because bread was a primary source of food for the working class. Some argued that wheat had a high price because landlords were charging high rents to tenant farmers. To pay these rents for land, the prices that farmers charged for their wheat also had to be raised to a high level. In short, it was argued that the price of wheat was high because the rents of agricultural land were high. Some of those who held this view advocated restricting the rents that landlords could charge.

David Ricardo, a great British economist who was one of the originators of Classical economics, argued that the situation was exactly the reverse. The price of wheat was high, he said, because there was a shortage, which was caused by the Napoleonic wars. Because wheat was profitable to produce, there was keen competition among farmers to obtain land on which to grow wheat. This competition in turn forced up the rent of wheat land. Ricardo advocated removing the tariff so that imported wheat could come into the country, thereby increasing its supply and lowering both the price of wheat and the rent that could be charged for the land on which it was grown.

The essentials of Ricardo's argument were these. The supply of land was fixed. Land was regarded as having only one use, the growing of wheat. Nothing had to be paid to prevent land from

transferring to a use other than growing wheat because it had no other use. No self-respecting landowner would leave land idle as long as he could obtain some return, no matter how small, by renting it out. Therefore, all the payment to land, that is, rent in the ordinary sense of the word, was a surplus over and above what was necessary to keep it in its present use.

Given a fixed supply of land, the price of land depended on the demand for land, which depended upon the demand for wheat. *Rent,* the term for the payment for the use of land, thus became the term for a surplus payment to a factor over and above what was necessary to keep it in its present use.

Later, two facts were realized. First, land often had alternative uses, and, from the point of view of any one use, part of the payment made to land would necessarily have to be paid to keep it in that use. Second, factors of production other than land also often earned a surplus over and above what was necessary to keep them in their present use. Television stars and great athletes, for example, are in short and fairly fixed supply, and their potential earnings in other occupations often are quite moderate. However, because there is a huge demand for their services as television stars or athletes, they may receive payments greatly in excess of what is needed to keep them from transferring to other occupations. This surplus is now called *economic rent,* whether the factor is land, labor, or a piece of capital equipment.

Economic rent is analogous to the economists' concept of profit as a surplus over the opportunity cost of capital. The concept of economic rent is crucial in predicting the effects that changes in earnings have on the movement of factors among alternative uses. However, the terminology of rent is confusing because economic rent is often called, simply, *rent,* and *rent* also means the price paid to hire something, such as a machine or a piece of land. How the same

term came to be used for these two different concepts is explored in Box 17-2.

The Division of Factor Earnings

In most cases economic rent makes up part of the actual earnings of a factor of production. The distinction is most easily seen, however, by examining

FIGURE 17-3   The Determination of Rent in Factor Payments

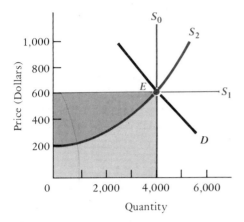

The amount of rent in factor payments depends on the shape of the supply curve. A single demand curve is shown with three different supply curves. In each case the competitive equilibrium price is $600, and 4,000 units of the factor are hired. The total payment ($2.4 million) is represented by the entire shaded area.

When the supply curve is vertical (S_0), the whole payment is economic rent, because a decrease in price would not lead any unit of the factor to move elsewhere.

When the supply curve is horizontal (S_1), none of the payment is rent, because even a small decrease in price offered would lead all units of the factor to move elsewhere.

When the supply curve rises to the right (S_2), part of the payment is rent. As shown by the height of the supply curve, at a price of $600 the 4,000th unit of the factor is receiving just enough to persuade it to offer its services in this market, but the 2,000th unit, for example, is earning well above what it requires to stay in this market. The aggregate of economic rents is shown by the dark gray shaded area, and the aggregate of what must be paid to keep 4,000 units in this market is shown by the light gray shaded area.

two extreme cases. In one, everything a factor earns is rent; in the other, none is rent.

The possibilities are illustrated in Figure 17-3. When the supply curve is perfectly inelastic (vertical), the same quantity is supplied, whatever the price is. Evidently, there is no minimum that the factor needs to be paid to keep it in its present use, since the quantity supplied does not decrease, no matter how

low the price goes. In this case the whole of the payment is an economic rent. The price actually paid allocates the fixed supply to those who are most willing to pay for it.

When the supply curve is perfectly elastic (horizontal), none of the price paid is economic rent. If any lower price is offered, nothing whatsoever will be supplied. All units of the factor will transfer to some other use.

The more usual situation is that of a gradually rising supply curve. A rise in the factor's price serves the allocative function of attracting more units of the factor into the market in question, but the same rise provides additional economic rent to all units of the factor that are already employed. We know the extra pay that is going to the units already employed is an economic rent because the owners of these units were willing to supply them at the lower price. The general result for a positively sloped supply curve is stated as follows.

If the demand for a factor in any of its uses rises relative to the supply available to that use, its price will rise in that use. This will serve the allocative function of attracting additional units into that use. It will also increase the economic rent to all units of the factor already in that use, since their transfer earnings were already being covered.

Determinants of the Division

The proportion of a given payment to a factor that is economic rent varies from situation to situation. We cannot point to a factor of production and assert that some fixed fraction of its income always is its economic rent. The proportion of its earnings that is rent depends on the alternatives that are open to it.

Focus first on a narrowly defined use of a given factor, say, its use by a particular firm. From that firm's point of view, the factor will be highly mobile, since it could readily move to another firm in the same industry. The firm must pay the going wage or risk losing that factor. Thus, from the perspective of the single firm, a large proportion of the factor payment is a transfer payment.

Focus now on a more broadly defined use, for example, the factor's use in an entire industry. From the industry's point of view, the factor is less mobile, because it would be more difficult for it to gain

BOX 17-3

Economic Rent as a Component of Factor Earnings

Labor

How much has to be paid to keep labor in its present use depends on the use of that labor.

First, consider movement *among firms in one industry*. Assume, for example, that carpenters receive $160 for working a normal 8-hour day. A construction firm will have to pay $160 per day or it will not obtain the services of any carpenter. To that one firm, none of the $160 is an economic rent; if it were not paid, carpenters would not remain with that firm.

Second, consider movement *among industries*. Assume that there is a decline in demand for buildings and that all construction firms reduce the wages that are offered to carpenters. Now carpenters cannot move to other construction firms to get more money. If they do not like the wages that are offered, they have to move to another industry that employs carpenters. If the best that they can do elsewhere is $125 per day (and nonmonetary advantages are the same in the two uses), they will not begin to leave the construction industry until wages in that industry fall below $125 per day. When carpenters were receiving $160 (presumably because there was a heavy demand for their services), the additional $35 per day was an economic rent from the point of view of the construction *industry,* even though it was not an economic rent from the point of view of an individual construction firm.

Third, consider movement *among occupations*. Assume that there is a decline in the demand for carpenters in all industries. The only option that a carpenter has is to move to another occupation, say, truck driving. If no carpenters are induced to leave carpentry until the wage falls to $110 per day, then $110 is what must be paid to keep people in the occupation. From the point of view of that occupation, any payment over $110 is an economic rent.

Consider how this applies to the often controversial large salaries that are received by some highly specialized types of laborers, such as superstar singers and professional athletes. These performers have a style and a talent that cannot be duplicated, whatever the training. The earnings that they receive are mostly economic rent from the viewpoint of the occupation: These performers enjoy their occupations and would pursue them for much less than the high remuneration that they actually receive. For example, John Ellway would choose football over other alternatives even at a much lower salary. However, because of Ellway's amazing skills as a quarterback, most NFL teams would pay handsomely to have him on their rosters, and he is able to command a high salary from the team he does play for. From the perspective of the firm, the Denver Broncos, most of Ellway's salary is required to keep him from switching to another team and hence is not an economic rent. From the point of view of the football industry, however, much of his salary is an economic rent.

Land

The analysis for land is similar to the analysis for labor. First, consider the case of an *individual* wheat farmer. In order to have the use of the land, she must pay the land's going price to prevent it from being transferred to another wheat farmer. From her point of view, therefore, none of the payment that she makes is an economic rent.

Second, consider the wheat *industry*. To secure land for wheat production, it will be necessary to offer at least as much as the land could earn when put to other uses. From the point of view of the industry, the payment made for land that is equal to what it could earn in its next most remunerative use is not an economic rent. Unless that much is paid, the land will be transferred to the alternative use. If, however, land that is particularly suitable for growing wheat is scarce relative to the demand for it, then the actual payment for the use of this land may be above this amount; the additional payment is the economic rent.

Third, consider the choice between *agricultural* and *urban uses*. Land is highly mobile among agricultural uses because its location is usually of little importance. For urban uses, however, location is critical. From this point of view, land is, of course, completely immobile. If there is a shortage of land in New York City, any land that is available will command a high price, but, no matter what the price, land in rural areas will not move into New York City. The high payments made to urban land are thus well in excess of what is necessary to prevent it from being transferred back to agricultural uses; the payment is thus economic rent.

Capital

If a piece of capital equipment has several uses, the analysis of land or labor can be repeated. Much equipment, however, has only one use. For capital that is virtually immobile, any income arising from its use is an economic rent.

Assume, for example, that when some machine was installed, it was expected to earn $5,000 per year in excess of all its operating costs, and assume also that the machine has no scrap value. If the demand for the product falls so that the machine can earn only $2,000 per year, it will still be worthwhile to keep it in operation rather than to scrap it. Indeed, it will be worthwhile to do so as long as it yields any return at all over its operating costs. Thus, all the return that is earned by the installed machine is economic rent because it will still be allocated to its present use—it has no other—as long as it yields even $1 above its operating costs. *Once the machine has been installed,* any net income that it earns is economic rent.

The machine will, however, wear out eventually, and it will not be replaced unless it is expected to earn a return over its lifetime that is sufficient to make it a good investment for its owner. Thus, in long-run equilibrium, the revenue earned by the machine is not an economic rent; if the revenue is not earned, a machine will not continue to be allocated to that use.

employment quickly outside the industry. From the perspective of the particular *industry* (rather than the specific *firm* within the industry), a larger proportion of the payment to a factor is economic rent.

From the even more general perspective of a particular *occupation,* mobility is likely to be less, and the proportion of the factor payment that is economic rent is likely to be more. It may be easier, for example, for a carpenter to move from the construction industry to the furniture industry than to retrain as a computer operator.

As the perspective moves from a narrowly defined use of a factor to a broadly defined use of a factor, the mobility of the factor decreases; as mobility decreases, the share of the factor payment that is economic rent increases.

Examples of how these considerations apply to each of the key factors of production are given Box 17-3.

Do Factors Move in Response to Changes in Earnings?

The theory that has been developed in this chapter predicts that factors move among uses, industries, and places, taking both monetary and nonmonetary rewards into account. It predicts that they will move in such a way as to maximize the net advantages to the owners of factors.

Does the world behave in the way that theory predicts? Because there are impediments to the mobility of factors, there may be lags in the response of factors to changes in relative prices, but the question remains: Do adjustments occur even though there are impediments?

Land and Capital

The most casual observation reveals to us that the allocative system works pretty much as described by the theory with respect to land and capital. Land is transferred from one crop to another in response to changes in the relative profitabilities of the crops. Land on the edge of town is transferred from rural to urban uses as soon as it can earn substantially more as a building site than as a cornfield. Materials and

capital goods move from use to use in response to changes in relative earnings in those uses.

This is hardly surprising. Nonmonetary benefits do not loom large for factors other than labor, and the theories of both competition and monopoly predict that quantities supplied will respond to increases in earnings generated by increased demand.

In the case of nonhuman factors—land and capital—there is strong evidence that factors move in response to earnings differentials.

Labor

Labor can be mobile in many ways, moving among occupations, industries, firms, skill categories, and regions. These categories are not exclusive; in order to change occupation from a farm laborer to a steelworker, for example, a person will also have to change industry and probably place of residence.

There are, of course, barriers to labor mobility. Unions, pension funds, and other institutions inhibit labor mobility in various ways. State governments have erected barriers to mobility in the form of occupational licensing, differential training requirements, and the like.

Nevertheless, the documented mobility of labor is impressive. When wages in manufacturing areas soared during World War II, workers flocked to those areas to take lucrative jobs in the rapidly expanding industries producing aircraft, ships, and other materials of war. When new oil fields were discovered in northern Alaska and northern Canada, high wages attracted welders, riveters, and the many other types of labor that the oil fields required.

During the period 1950–1970 American workers migrated steadily from the South to the North in search of jobs. During the 1970s this trend slowed, and in the late 1970s and early 1980s it was reversed as the movement of many American firms to the Sun Belt created new jobs in the South.

Figure 17-4 illustrates another dimension of labor mobility. The shifts among sectors that have occurred during the postwar period indicate the substantial adaptability of the labor force to changing patterns of demand for the outputs of various sectors. The process of "deindustrialization" that is evident in this figure is discussed further in Box 17-4.

FIGURE 17-4   The Changing Composition of the Nonagricultural Labor Force

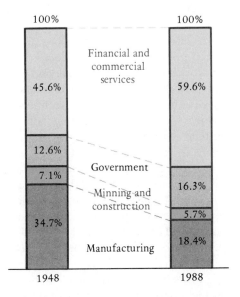

In less than half a century a major shift has occurred in labor utilization. In 1948 over 40 percent of the nonagricultural labor force was in the industrial sectors (largely blue collar), including manufacturing, mining, and construction. This figure had decreased to less than 25 percent by 1988. The shift was to the public and private service-oriented sectors (largely white collar). This process of deindustrialization was especially dramatic in the 1970s. In that period there was a net increase of 19 million jobs in the United States, 87 percent of which were in the service sector.

From decade to decade, labor is highly mobile in response to changes in demand.

Of course, labor does not always move promptly in response to changes in earnings. Thus, not all behavior is neatly explained by the theory. For example, despite the recent relative decline in academic salaries and academic job opportunities, many more students persist in getting Ph.D.'s in fields such as history and English than can reasonably expect to find jobs that will require or make use of their training. Economists can speculate about such behavior, for example, by saying that for many students graduate education is a consumption good as well as an

investment or that the nonmonetary advantages of an academic position are large enough to be worth the gamble of finding a job. Such possibilities, however, take us beyond elementary economics. At this stage, we have to be satisfied with a theory that explains much, but not all, behavior.

The Pricing of an Exhaustible Resource

So far, we have discussed the pricing of factors, such as labor and capital, that can be replaced as they "wear out." As older people leave the labor force due to retirement and death, young persons, seeking their first jobs, enter. As existing capital equipment is retired due to depreciation or obsolescence, it is replaced by new capital. Such resources are called **renewable resources.**

We now consider factors of production that are available in fixed amounts. For each such factor, the total stock is given and every unit that is used today permanently reduces the stock that is available for future use. Such a factor is called a **nonrenewable resource** or an **exhaustible resource.** (It is usually a subclass of the broadly defined factor of production that economists call *land*.)

In practice few, if any, resources are completely nonrenewable. Although there is only a fixed stock of oil, coal, or iron ore that is known to exist at any moment in time, new discoveries add to the known stock, while extraction subtracts from it. It is, however, possible to imagine exhausting all of the world's supplies of oil, natural gas, or coal. In this sense, these are closer to being exhaustible resources than renewable resources.

An Example

To focus on the basic issues, it is easiest to think of an imaginary resource that is completely nonrenewable: There is just so much "zube oil" in existence, and every unit that is used permanently diminishes the available stock by one unit.

Assume that many firms own the land that contains the zube oil supply. They have invested money in discovering the oil, in drilling wells, and in laying pipelines. Their current extraction costs are virtually

BOX 17-4

Deindustrialization: From Blue Collar to White Coat

The growth of employment in services and retail trade over the past two decades has been dramatic in all industrialized nations. The growth has been concentrated in several areas: transportation and communication, eating and drinking, health care, education, retail services such as hotels and entertainment, and a host of business services. In the United States in 1989, *total employment* in all manufacturing industries (under 20 million persons) was less than the *increase* in employment in services over the previous decade.

In one sense this is good news, for without these new job opportunities, overall employment would not have been as high as it was. However, many people worry about deindustrialization. They fear that productivity is lower and that the opportunities for growth are much more limited in service industries than in goods-producing industries. They argue that the possibilities for using more and more capital per unit of labor employed, which raises labor productivity, are less in selling hamburgers than in producing metal and metal products.

There are reasons to be cautious about accepting some of the popular views concerning the growth of services. First, the trend toward services has been going on for over 100 years in advanced industrial societies, although the speed of the shift seems to have accelerated since 1970.

Second, to a considerable extent, the decrease in the share of manufacturing in total employment is a result of that sector's dynamism. More and more manufactured goods have been produced by fewer and fewer workers, leaving more workers to produce services. Incomes that are earned in the service sector provide the demand to buy manufactured goods, which have been falling in relative price because of their high productivity growth.

This movement is analogous to the shift out of agriculture earlier in the century. At the turn of the century nearly 45 percent of the American labor force worked on farms.* Today less than 3 percent do so, yet they produce more total output than did the 45 percent in 1900. The "deagriculturalization" of the United States freed workers to move into manufacturing, thereby raising our living standards and transforming our way of life. So also deindustrialization is freeing workers to move into services, and, by replacing the grimy blue-collar jobs of the pollution-creating smokestack industries with white-collar jobs in the relatively clean service industries, it too will transform our way of life.

Third, to a considerable extent, the decrease in the share of manufacturing in total employment follows from consumers' tastes. Just as consumers in the first half of the century did not want to go on consuming more and more food products as their incomes rose, today's consumers do not wish

* Data from *Historical Statistics of the United States*.

---

zero; all they have to do is turn their taps on, and the oil flows at any desired rate to the zube oil markets.[5]

[5] It is, of course, a simplification of any real case to assume that current production costs are actually zero. The assumption, however, is not too far from reality in the case of such a resource as oil, where the fixed costs of discovery, extraction, and distribution account for the bulk of total costs. When extraction costs are nonzero, all statements about prices in the text refer to the margin by which price *exceeds* the current opportunity cost of extraction.

Optimal Firm Behavior

What should each firm do? It could extract all of its oil in a great binge of production this year, or it could husband the resource for some future rainy day and produce nothing this year. In practice, it is likely to adopt some intermediate policy, producing and selling some oil this year and holding stocks of it in the ground for extraction in future years. This much is easy, but *how much* should it extract this year

to spend all of their additional incomes on manufactured products. Households have chosen to spend a high proportion of their increased incomes on services, thus directing employment in that direction.

Fourth, although some service industries—particularly personal services and fast foods—do generate low-paying jobs, so do many manufacturing industries. Three decades ago pessimists worried that the new industrial revolution of automation and computerization was going to destroy most of the jobs available for unskilled workers. However, the growth in the service sector fully compensated for the low-skilled jobs that were lost in manufacturing.

Thus we need to keep a sense of perspective about the low-paying service jobs. Disposable income per employed person has been rising in all of the industrialized countries, including the United States. As a nation, we are getting wealthier, not poorer. Since the size distribution of income is not much more skewed than it was two decades ago, it follows that this increased wealth has been enjoyed by most of the nation's employed citizens.

Finally, it is easy to underestimate the scope for quality, quantity, and productivity increases in services. As just one example of productivity increases, compare your local bank with one that you see in a movie that was made no more than 20 years ago. As another, note that since 1950 output per full-time worker has grown about twice as fast in the communications industry as it has in manufacturing.

Also, many quality improvements in services go unrecorded. Today's hotel room is vastly more luxurious than a hotel room of 40 years ago, yet this is unlikely to show up in our national income statistics as a quantity improvement. All that the statistics are likely to reflect is that the price of a hotel room has risen.

Measuring such technological improvements is even more difficult when they take the form of entirely new products. Airline transportation, telecommunications, fast food chains, and financial services are prominent examples. The resulting increase in output often is not properly captured in our existing statistics.

It is easy to get depressed by looking at the official statistics for slow growth rates and at the low wages earned in some service jobs. If we look at the growth in the real standard of living, there is little reason to think that the worldwide shift in employment from industries to services in the second half of the twentieth century—which, after all, is driven by our rising real incomes—will be any less beneficial to industrialized nations than was the shift from agriculture to manufacturing in the first half of this century.

and *how much* should it carry over for future years? What will the decision imply for the price of oil over the years?

The firms that own the zube oil land are holding a valuable resource. Holding it, however, has an opportunity cost: It could have been extracted and sold this year, yielding revenue to the firms (and value to consumers) in the same year. The firms will only be willing to leave the resource in the ground if it earns a return equal to what the firm can earn in other investments. This is measured by the interest rate. So, if next year's price is expected to rise by less than the interest rate, the firms will extract more oil this year. Because the demand curve has a negative slope, raising the extraction rate will lower this year's price. Production will be curtailed, and the price will fall, until the expected price rise between this year and next year is equal to the interest rate. The firms will then be indifferent at the margin between producing another barrel this year and holding it for production next year. If, on the other hand, next year's price is expected to rise over this year's price by more than the interest rate, the firms will produce less oil this year. They will prefer to leave more barrels in the ground, where they earn a higher return than could be earned by selling the oil this year and investing the proceeds at the current interest rate. This will raise this year's price, until the gap between the current price and next year's expected price is equal to the interest rate.

In a perfectly competitive industry, the profit-maximizing equilibrium for a nonrenewable resource occurs when the last unit produced would have earned just as much for the firm as if it had been left in the ground.

Say, for example, that a barrel produced this year sells for $1.00 and that next year's price is expected to be $1.05. If the rate of interest is 5 percent, zube oil producers make the same amount of money whether they leave $1.00 worth of oil in the ground to be worth $1.05 next year or they sell the oil for $1.00 this year and invest the proceeds at a 5 percent interest rate.

Optimal Social Behavior

Zube oil is a valuable social resource, and the value to consumers of one more barrel produced now is the price that they would be willing to pay for it, which is the current $1.00 market price of the oil. If the oil is extracted this year and the proceeds are invested at the rate of interest (they might be used to buy a new capital good), they will produce $1.05 worth of valuable goods next year. If that barrel of oil is not produced this year and is left in the ground for extraction next year, its value to consumers at that time will be next year's price of oil. It is not socially optimal, therefore, to leave the oil in the ground unless it will be worth $1.05 next year. More generally, society obtains increases in the value of what is available for consumption by conserving units of a nonrenewable resource to be used in future years only if the price of these units is expected to rise at a rate that is at least as high as the interest rate.

This answer to the question, "How much of a nonrenewable resource should be consumed now?" was provided many years ago by the American economist Harold Hotelling. His answer is very simple,

yet it specifically determines the optimal profile of prices over the years. It is interesting that the answer applies to all nonrenewable resources. It does not matter whether there is a large or a small demand or whether that demand is elastic or inelastic. In all cases the answer is the same:

The rate of extraction of any nonrenewable resource should be such that its rate of price increase is equal to the interest rate, and this is the rate of extraction that will be produced by a competitive industry.

The Amount of Extraction

Now, what about the actual rate at which the resource is extracted? The answer to this question *does* depend on market conditions. Specifically, it depends on the position and the slope of the demand curve. If the quantity demanded at all prices is small, the rate of extraction will be small. The larger is the quantity demanded at each price, the higher will the rate of extraction tend to be.

Now consider the influence of the slope of the demand curve. A steep demand curve suggests that there are few substitutes and that purchasers are prepared to pay large sums rather than do without the resource. This will produce a relatively even rate of extraction, with small reductions each period being sufficient to drive up the price at the required rate. A relatively flat demand curve suggests that people can easily find substitutes once the price rises. This will encourage a great deal of consumption now and a rapidly diminishing amount over future years, since large reductions in consumption are needed to drive the price up at the required rate.

Figure 17-5 illustrates this working of the price mechanism with a simple example in which the whole stock of zube oil must be consumed in only two periods, this year and next year. The general result that is illustrated in this example is:

The steeper is the demand curve, the more even will be the rate of extraction (and hence the rate of use) over the years; the flatter is the demand curve, the more uneven will be the rate of extraction over the years.

A flat demand curve will lead to a large consumption now and a rapid fall in consumption over the years. A steep demand curve will lead to a smaller

FIGURE 17-5   The Extraction Rate for a Nonrenewable Resource

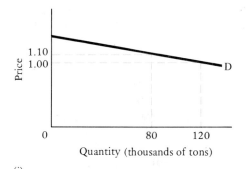

(i)

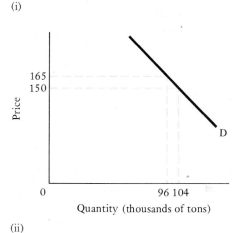

(ii)

The shape of the demand curve determines the extraction profile over time. In the example in this figure, the interest rate is assumed to be 10 percent and there is a fixed supply of 200,000 tons of zube oil that can be extracted from the ground at zero variable cost. (All of its costs are fixed costs.) The zube oil is available for extraction either in the current period or in the next period, after which it spoils.

In part (i) of the figure, the demand curve is rather flat. The two conditions—that the whole supply be used over two periods and that the price rise by 10 percent between the two periods—dictate that the quantities be 120,000 tons in the first period, with a price of $1.00 per ton, and 80,000 in the second period, with a price of $1.10 per ton.

In part (ii) the demand curve is rather steep. The same two conditions now dictate that the quantities be 104,000 tons in the first period, with a price of $1.50 per ton, and 96,000 tons in the second period, with a price of $1.65 per ton.

consumption now and a less rapid fall in consumption over the years.

Resources Rents

The incomes earned by the owners of the zube oil resources are *rents:* The owners would be willing to produce the oil at any price that covers the direct costs of extraction, which in this example is zero.[6] Although these incomes serve no function in getting the product produced, since any nonzero price would do the job, they do fulfill an *intertemporal* allocative function. As we have seen, the price profile determines the use of the resource and hence the amount of resources allocated to its production *over time*.

The Price System as a Conservation Mechanism

In all of the preceding discussion we see the price system playing its now familiar role of coordinator. By following private profit incentives, the firm is led to conserve the resource in a manner that is consistent with people's needs.

The Role of Rising Prices

The optimal profile for a totally nonrenewable resource is for its price to rise at a constant rate each year. This may seem unsatisfactory to the casual observer, but, if price is prevented from so rising, the resource will be depleted much faster. The rising price fulfills a number of useful functions.

First, the rising price encourages conservation. As the resource becomes scarcer and its price rises, users will be motivated to be more and more economical in its use. Uses that yield low values may be abandoned altogether, and uses that yield high values may be pursued only as long as their value at the margin is enough to compensate for the high price.

Second, the rising price encourages the discovery of new sources of supply—at least in those cases in which the world supply is not totally fixed and known.

Third, the rising price encourages innovation. New products that will do the same job may be developed, as well as new processes that use alternative resources.

---

[6] In real cases the direct cost of extracting the resource is positive and the rent is the income earned above that amount.

How Might the Price System Fail?[7]

There are three basic ways in which the price system might fail to produce the optimal rate of resource extraction: First, firms may not know enough to make the correct calculations; second, deficiencies in property rights may result in firms having incentives to extract the resource too fast; and, third, markets may not correctly reflect social values. We look at examples of each of these and ask if they justify government intervention.

Ignorance.   Private owners might not have enough knowlege to estimate the rate at which prices will rise. If they do not know the world stocks of their commodity and the current extraction rate, they may be unable to estimate the rate of the price rise and so will not know when to raise or lower their current rates of production. For example, if all firms mistakenly think that prices will not rise greatly in the future, they will all produce too much now and conserve too little for future periods.

There is no reason to think that the government could do better, unless it has some special knowledge that private firms do not have. If it does have such knowledge, the government needs only to make it public; further intervention is unnecessary. In practice, such knowledge that does exist about both the proven reserves of nonrenewable resources and their current extraction rates is usually freely and openly available.

Inadaquate property rights.   Some nonrenewable resources have the characteristics of what is called *common property*. This is property that cannot be exclusively owned and controlled by one person or firm. For example, one person's oil-bearing land may be adjacent to another person's, and the underground supplies may be interconnected. In such a case, if one firm holds off producing now, the oil may end up being extracted by its neighbor. In such cases, which are sometimes found with petroleum, there is a tendency for a firm to extract the resource too fast, because a firm's oil that has been left in the ground may not be available to that firm at a future date.

This is a problem of inadaquate property rights. Since the resource will be worth more in total value

when it is exploited at the optimal extraction rate than when overly small firms exploit it too quickly, there will be an incentive for individual owners to combine until each self-contained source of supply is owned by only one firm. The problem of over exploitation will not then arise. Government ownership is not necessary to achieve this result. What is needed, at most, is intervention to ensure that markets can work to provide the optimal size of individual units so that proper extraction management can be applied by the private owners.

Political uncertainty can provide another source of inadequate property rights. For example, the owners of the resource may fear that a future election, or revolution, will establish a government that is determined to confiscate their property. They will then be motivated to exploit the resource too quickly, on the grounds that a certain revenue now is more valuable than a highly uncertain revenue in the future. The current rate of extraction will tend to increase, until the expected rate of price rise exceeds the interest rate by a sufficient margin to compensate for the risks of future confiscation of supplies left in the ground.

Divergences between market and social values.   Normally, in a competitive world, the market interest rate indicates the rate at which it is optimal to discount the future over the present. Society's investments are valuable if they earn the market rate of return and are not valuable if they earn less (because the resources could be used in other ways to produce more value to consumers). In certain circumstances, however, the government may have reasons to adopt a different rate of discount. It is then said that the *social rate of discount*—the discount rate that is appropriate to the society as a whole—differs from the private rate, as indicated by the market rate of interest. In such circumstances, there is reason for the government to intervene to alter the rate at which the private firms would exploit the resource.

Critics are often ready to assume that profit-mad producers will despoil most exhaustible resources by using them up too quickly. They argue for government intervention to conserve the resource by slowing its rate of extraction. Yet—unless the social rate of discount is clearly below the private rate—there is no clear social gain in investing by holding resources in the ground where they only will yield, say, a 2 percent return, when, say, 5 percent can be gained on other investments.

[7] This discussion partly anticipates some of the analysis in Part 6, which investigates market successes and market failures in more general terms.

Actual Price Profiles

Many nonrenewable resources do not seem to have the steadily rising profile of prices that the theory predicts. The price of oil, having been raised artificially by the OPEC cartel, returned in the late 1980s to an inflation-adjusted level that was not far from where it was in 1970. Indeed, it has since been held somewhat above that price only insofar as the producing countries have succeeded in intermittently enforcing some output restrictions. The price of coal has not soared; neither has the price of iron ore. In many cases the reason for this lies in the discovery of new supplies, which have prevented the total known stocks of many resources from being depleted. In the case of petroleum, for example, the ratio of known reserves to one year's consumption is no lower now than it was two or even four decades ago. Furthermore, most industry experts believe that large quantities of undiscovered oil exist under both the land and the sea.

In other cases the invention of new substitute products has reduced the demand for some of these resources. For example, plastics have replaced metals in many uses, while ceramics have replaced copper wire in some types of message transmission.

In yet other cases, the reason is to be found in government pricing policy. An important example of this type is water for irrigation in much of the United States. Vast underground reserves of water lie in aquifers beneath many areas of the United States. Although these reserves were accumulated over millenia, they are being used up at a rate that will exhaust them in a matter of decades. The water is often supplied by government water authorities at a price that covers only a small part of its total cost and that does not rise steadily to reflect the dwindling stocks.

Such a constant-price policy for any nonrenewable resource creates three characteristic problems. First, the resource will be exhausted much faster than if price were to rise over time. A constant price will lead to a constant rate of extraction to meet the quantity demanded at that price, until the resource is compeletely exhausted. Second, no signals will go out to induce conservation, innovation, and exploration. Third, when the supply of the resource is finally exhausted, the adjustment will have to come all at once. If the price had risen steadily each year under free-market conditions, adjustment would have taken place little by little each year. The controlled price, however, gives no signal of the ever diminishing stock of the resource, until all at once the supplies run out. The required adjustment will then be much more painful than it would have been if it had been spread over time in response to steadily rising prices.

The dwindling water supplies under much of the country would long ago have led to price rises close to those predicted by Hotelling's theory and hence to a series of gradual adjustments, had the price been set on a free market. As it is:

The present generation of water users is, in effect, obtaining a subsidy from future water users who, if present policies continue, will have to make many adjustments abruptly while paying much higher prices for their water.

SUMMARY

1. The functional distribution of income refers to the shares of total national income going to each of the major factors of production; it focuses on sources of income. The size distribution of income refers to the shares of total national income going to various groups of households; it focuses only on the size of income, not its source.
2. The income of a factor of production is composed of two elements: the price paid per unit of the factor and the quantity of the factor used. The determination of factor prices and quantities is an application of the same price theory that is used to determine product prices and quantities.
3. The demand for any factor of production is a derived demand because the factor is used as an input into the production of goods and services. The total demand for a factor of production will be the sum of the individual derived demands for it in each activity in which it is used. The total supply of any factor must be allocated among all the uses to which it can possibly be put.

4. Factor mobility is the ease with which a factor can move to alternative uses. Land is mobile between uses but cannot change its geographical location. Capital equipment is durable, but firms regularly replace discarded or worn-out machinery with totally different machines and so change the composition of the nation's capital stock gradually but steadily. Labor mobility is greatly affected by nonmonetary considerations. The longer is the period of time, the more mobile is a factor.

5. In competitive factor markets, prices are determined by demand and supply, but factor price differentials occur. Disequilibrium differentials in the earnings of different units of factors of production induce factor movements that eventually remove the differentials. Equilibrium differentials reflect differences among units of factors as well as nonmonetary benefits of different jobs; they can persist indefinitely.

6. The hypothesis of equal net advantage is a theory of the allocation of the total supply of factors to particular uses. Owners of factors will choose the use that produces the greatest net advantage, allowing for monetary and nonmonetary advantages of a particular employment. In so doing, they will cause dynamic factor price differentials to be eliminated.

7. Some amount *must* be paid to a factor in order to prevent it from transferring to another use. Economic rent is the difference between that amount and a factor's actual earnings. Whenever the supply curve is upward sloping, part of the factor's total pay is transfer earnings, and part of it is rent. The proportion of each depends on the mobility of the factor: The more narrowly defined is the use, the larger is the fraction that is transfer earnings, and the smaller is the fraction that is economic rent.

8. Factor mobility is typically greater for nonhuman factors than it is for labor. Even where impediments to mobility exist, factors (including labor) tend to move in response to persistent differences in earnings or employment opportunities.

9. The socially optimal rate of exploitation for a nonrenewable resource occurs when its price rises at a rate that is equal to the rate of interest. This is also the rate that will be established by a profit-maximizing, competitive industry.

10. Resources for which the demand is highly elastic will have a high rate of exploitation in the near future and a fairly rapid fall off over time. Resources for which the demand is highly inelastic will have a lower rate of exploitation in the near future and a smaller fall off over time.

11. Rising prices act as a conservation device by rationing the consumption over time according to people's preferences. As prices rise, conservation, discovery of new sources of supply, and innovation to reduce demand are all encouraged.

12. The price system can fail to produce optimal results if (a) people lack the necessary knowledge, (b) property rights are inadequate enough to protect supplies left for future use by their owners, or (c) the social rate of discount differs significantly from the market rate.

13. Controlling the price of an exhaustible resource at a constant level speeds up the rate of exploitation and removes the price incentives to react to the growing scarcity, until the resource is completely exhausted.

TOPICS FOR REVIEW

Functional distribution and size distribution of income
Derived demand
Factor mobility
Disequilibrium and equilibrium differentials
Hypothesis of equal net advantage
Economic rent

DISCUSSION QUESTIONS

1. Other things being equal, how would you expect each of the following to affect the size distribution of after-tax income? Do any of them lead to clear predictions about the functional distribution of income?
   a. An increase in unemployment
   b. Rapid population growth in an already crowded city
   c. An increase in food prices relative to other prices
   d. An increase in social insurance benefits and taxes
   e. Removal of the deductibility for personal income tax purposes of interest paid on mortgages
2. Consider the effects on the overall level of income inequality of each of the following.
   a. Increasing participation of women in the labor force as many women shift from work in the home to full-time jobs
   b. Increasing use by California produce growers of migrant workers who are in the United States illegally
   c. Increasing numbers of minority group members studying law and medicine
   d. Cuts in the rates of income tax, together with the elimination of many personal income tax deductions, effected under the Reagan administration
3. How much of the following payments for factor services is likely to be economic rent?
   a. The $750 per month that a landlord receives for an apartment leased to students
   b. The salary of the president of the United States
   c. The $1,000,000 annual salary of Patrick Ewing
   d. The salary of a window cleaner who says, "It's dangerous, dirty work, but it beats driving a truck"
4. Which of the following are disequilibrium and which are equilibrium differentials in factor prices?
   a. Differences in earnings of hockey coaches and wrestling coaches
   b. A "bonus for signing on" offered by a construction company seeking carpenters in a tight labor market
   c. Differences in monthly rental charged for three-bedroom houses in different parts of the same metropolitan area
   d. Higher prices per square foot of condominium space in Los Angeles compared with Topeka, Kansas
5. Equal pay for equal work is a commonly held goal, but "equal work" is hard to define. What would be the consequences of legislation that enforces equal pay for what turns out to be unequal work?
6. Rent controls often succeed in reducing rents paid by tenants in the short run but at the cost of a growing housing shortage in the long run. What does this tell us about the nature of the earnings of landlords in the short and the long run?
7. Look again at the data in Figure 17-4. What economic forces might have given rise to the labor movements described there? What would you predict about the pattern of wages in the various categories in

the figure? (Check the facts to see if your predictions were correct.) For occupations that saw an increase in wages, did the increases represent increased transfer payments or economic rents?

8. Can you think of any resources that are renewable if they are exploited at one rate and nonrenewable if they are exploited at other, higher rates?

9. Some Canadians opposed the Free Trade Agreement that was signed in 1988 between Canada and the United States because they wished to prohibit the export of Canadian oil and natural gas to the United States and instead to save it for use by future generations of Canadians. Some Americans opposed the same Free Trade Agreement because they wished to restrict the import of cheap Canadian natural gas into the United States. What would have been the economic gains and losses resulting from following the courses of action advocated by these groups?

10. Outline some of the main events that would follow if no further significant discoveries of oil were ever made after 1995.

Chapter 18

More on Factor Markets

Why is the demand for steel quite inelastic, while the demand for cedar shakes and shingles is highly elastic? Why is the relative price of oil quite volatile, while the relative price of construction workers has remained relatively stable? To deal with these and many related subjects, we need to inquire further into the determinants of the demand for and supply of factors of production.

The Demand for Factors of Production

We saw in Chapter 17 that the demand for any factor depends on the demand for the goods that it helps to produce. For this reason the demand for a factor is called a *derived demand*. What are the economic forces that influence this demand?

Marginal Productivity Theory

All profit-maximizing firms, whether they are selling under conditions of perfect competition, monopolistic competition, oligopoly, or monopoly, produce to the point at which marginal cost equals marginal revenue. Similarly, all profit-maximizing firms hire units of the variable factor up to the point at which the last unit employed adds as much to revenue as it does to cost. Thus it is a simple implication of profit maximization that *firms* hire units of a variable factor up to the point at which the marginal cost of the factor (i.e., the addition to the total cost resulting from the employment of one more unit) equals the marginal revenue produced by the factor.

Because we use the term *marginal revenue* to denote the change in revenue that results when the rate of product sales is increased by one unit, we shall use another term, **marginal revenue product (MRP),** to refer to the change in revenue caused by the sale of the increased output resulting from using *an additional unit of the variable factor.* [27] Using this term, the implication of profit maximization, which was stated in the previous paragraph, can be written:

Marginal cost of the variable factor = **Marginal revenue product of that factor**

If the firm is unable to influence the price of the variable factor by buying more or less of it (i.e., if the firm is a price taker when it is *buying factors*), the marginal cost of the factor is its price. The cost, for example, of adding an extra worker to such a firm's work force is the wage that must be paid to that worker. The firm will continue to add workers to its labor force until the marginal revenue product of the last worker added is equal to the wage that the firm pays to that last worker.

A profit-maximizing firm that is a price taker in factor markets hires a factor up to the point at which the price of the factor equals the factor's marginal revenue product.

If we let w stand for the market-determined price of the variable factor, we can write this as:

$$w = MRP$$

For example, if the wage rate is $10 per hour, it will be profitable for a firm to take on more workers as long as each additional worker adds more than $10 to its revenue per hour. Once an additional hour worked adds only $10, the firm will stop hiring more workers. It will be in equilibrium.

The proposition that in equilibrium factors will be paid the value of their respective marginal products is often called the **marginal productivity theory of distribution.**[1] This is nothing more than an implication of profit maximization. Over the years, however, the theory has been the subject of many emotional attacks and defenses and has often been seriously misunderstood. Some of these issues are taken up further in Box 18-1.

Slope of the Derived Demand Curve

So far we have drawn all factor demand curves to indicate that the price of a factor and its quantity demanded are negatively related. Three reasons for this are worth noting.

Diminishing Returns

Because of the operation of the law of diminishing returns, each equal additional unit of a variable factor that is combined with a given amount of a fixed factor adds smaller and smaller amounts to total output. Thus, if a factor's price rises, each firm will reduce the amount of factors that it hires until the marginal revenue product of the last unit is large

enough to cover the now higher price of hiring it. Similarly, if a factor's price falls, each firm will hire more factors until the MRP of the last unit hired is reduced to the now lower price of hiring it.

Substitution

A second influence operates by means of the principle of substitution. When the price of one factor goes up, other relatively cheaper factors will be substituted. For example, if carpenters' wages rise relative to those of factory workers, some factory-prefabricated door and window frames will be used to replace on-the-job carpenters.

Derived Demand

A third influence arises because the demand for a factor of production depends on the demand for the commodity that it helps to make (i.e., it is a *derived* demand). A negatively sloped demand for a commodity implies a negatively sloped demand for the factors that help to make it.

For example, a rise in carpenters' wages will raise the cost of producing houses, thus shifting the supply curve of houses to the left. This leads to a rise in the price of houses and, because of the negatively sloped demand curve for houses, to a decrease in the number of houses sold. If fewer houses are sold, fewer will be built, and fewer carpenters will be needed. A decrease in carpenters' wages has the opposite set of effects: The cost of producing houses falls; the supply curve shifts to the right; more houses are built; and more carpenters are demanded.

Elasticity of Factor Demand

The elasticity of demand for a factor measures the *degree* of the response of the quantity demanded to a change in its price. The three influences that were discussed in the previous sections explain the *direction* of the response; that is, the quantity demanded is negatively related to price. You should not be surprised, therefore, to hear that the degree of the response depends on the strength with which these three influences operate.

Diminishing Returns

The first influence on the slope of the demand curve is the diminishing marginal productivity of a factor. If marginal productivity declines rapidly as more of

---

[1] The way in which marginal productivity theory can be used to derive the demand curve for a factor is discussed in the appendix to this chapter.

BOX 18-1

The Marginal Productivity Theory of Distribution

The marginal productivity theory of distribution is simply an implication of profit maximization: Any firm that is maximizing its profits must hire each variable factor up to the point at which the last factor hired adds just as much to costs (the price of the factor) as it does to revenue (the marginal revenue product). Nonetheless, misconceptions about the theory persist. Indeed, in certain quarters the marginal productivity theory of distribution is avoided. It has been criticized on the grounds that it is inhumane and that it falsely implies that the market leads to factor prices that, however low they might be, are "just." Both criticisms rest on misconceptions of what the theory says and implies.

Inhumanity?

Marginal productivity theory does not make a distinction between human services and other services. Some think that the theory is inhumane because it treats human labor as it treats a ton of coal or a wagon load of fertilizer.

The marginal productivity theory is only a theory of the *demand* for a factor. It explains only what profit-maximizing employers would like to buy. According to the theory, desired purchases of a factor depend on the price of the factor, the technical conditions of production, and the demand for the product produced using the factor. *Supply* conditions undoubtedly differ between human and nonhuman factors, but these differences are accommodated within the theory of distribution. No evidence has been gathered to indicate that it is necessary to have separate theories of the demand for human and nonhuman factors of production.

Justice?

The theory predicts that, given perfectly competitive factor markets, in equilibrium all factors re- ceive payment that is equal to the values of their marginal products. Some eminent economists in the past spoke as if this led to a just distribution, because factors were rewarded according to the value of their own contributions to the national product. "From each according to his ability; to each according to his own contribution" might have been the slogan for these economists. Many critics of the low levels of wages that then prevailed reacted passionately to a theory that was claimed to justify those low wages.

According to the marginal productivity theory of distribution, each worker receives the value of what one more worker would add to production if that worker were hired while all other factors were held constant. If 1 million similar workers were employed, each of the 1 million workers would receive a wage that would be equal to the extra product that would have been contributed by the millionth worker if he or she had been hired while capital and all other factors remained unchanged. Whether such a distribution of the national product is or is not "just" may be debated. The marginal productivity theory of distribution does not, however, contribute to that debate; it does not say that each unit of a factor receives as income the value of *its own* contribution to production. Indeed, where many factors cooperate in production, it is generally impossible to divide total production into the amounts contributed by each unit of each factor of production. It is possible both to hold that marginal productivity tends to determine how people get paid and to believe that government policies that change the distribution of income are desirable. Many economists hold both positions.

a variable factor is employed, a fall in the factor's price will not induce many more units to be employed. Conversely, if marginal productivity does not fall rapidly as more of a variable factor is employed, there will be a large increase in quantity demanded as price falls.

Substitution

The second influence on the slope of the demand curve is the ease with which one factor can be substituted for another. The greater is the ease of substitution, the greater is the elasticity of demand for the factor. The ease of substitution depends on the substitutes that are available and on the technical conditions of production. Even in the short run it is possible to vary factor proportions in surprising ways. For example, in automobile manufacture and in building construction, glass and steel can be substituted for each other simply by varying the dimensions of the windows. Another example is that construction materials can be substituted for maintenance labor in the case of most durable consumer goods. This is done by making the product more or less durable and more or less subject to breakdowns by using more or less expensive materials in its construction.

Such short-run substitutions are not the end of the story. In the long run, plant and equipment are being replaced continually, which allows more or less capital-intensive methods to be built into new plants in response to changes in factor prices. Similarly, engines that use less gasoline per mile tend to be developed when the price of gasoline rises severely.

Derived Demand

The third influence on the slope of the demand curve is related to derived demand. When we come to discuss how a factor's elasticity of demand is affected by the fact that it is derived from the demand for the product that it helps to make, we find that two separate influences are at work: how much the supply curve of a commodity shifts when a factor's price changes and how much this shift affects the price of the commodity that the factor helps to make.

Importance of the factor.   The larger is the fraction of the total costs of producing some commodity that are made up of payments to a particular factor, the greater is the elasticity of demand for that factor. To

see this, suppose that wages account for 50 percent of the costs of producing a good, while raw materials account for 15 percent. A 10 percent rise in the price of labor raises the cost of producing the commodity by 5 percent (10 percent of 50 percent), but a 10 percent rise in the price of raw materials raises the cost of the commodity by only 1.5 percent (10 percent of 15 percent). The larger is the increase in cost, the larger is the shift in the commodity's supply curve, and hence the larger are the decreases in the demand for the commodity and for the factors that were used to make it.

Elasticity of demand for the commodity produced. Other things being equal, the more elastic the demand is for the commodity that the factor helps to make, the more elastic the demand for the factor will be. If an increase in the price of the commodity causes a large decrease in the quantity demanded, that is, if the demand for the commodity is elastic, there will be a large decrease in the quantity of a factor needed to produce it in response to a rise in the factor's price. However, if an increase in the price of a commodity causes only a small decrease in the quantity demanded, that is, if the demand for the commodity is inelastic, there will be only a small decrease in the quantity of the factor required in response to a rise in its price.[2]

Let us summarize the effect that works through derived demand.

An increase in the price of a factor that produces a particular commodity causes the supply curve for that commodity to shift to the left, which reduces its equilibrium quantity and, in turn, reduces the quantity of the factor that is demanded. The fall in quantity of the factor demanded will be greater (1) the greater is the proportion of total costs accounted for by that

---

[2] All of these propositions are qualified by *the usual condition of other things being equal.* For example, the smaller is the proportion of a commodity's total costs that is accounted for by the cost of one particular factor, the lower is the elasticity of demand for that factor, *other things being equal.* Other things are not equal, for example, if we compare two factors, both of which account for small parts of total cost but one of which can easily be dispensed with because it has many good substitutes while the second has few good substitutes. The first will have elasticity of demand (the ease of substitution will be what matters), while the second will have a low elasticity (its unimportance in total cost will be what matters).

factor, since this proportion determines the amount that the commodity's supply curve shifts, and (2) the more elastic is the demand curve for the commodity, since this elasticity determines the amount by which the commodity's output falls when its supply curve shifts to the left.

Distribution Theory: Some Evidence

Does the theory of distribution satisfactorily explain the allocation process in our economy? In Chapter 17 we reviewed the impressive array of evidence that showed that, despite the presence of impediments to factor mobility, such as licensing and union restrictions for labor, safety requirements for capital equipment, and zoning laws for land, factors do move in response to changes in factor prices. In the following section we examine whether market forces do in fact determine factor prices and factor earnings.

Capital and Land

Many nonhuman factors are sold on competitive markets. The theory predicts that changes in the earnings of these factors will be associated with changes in market conditions. The evidence overwhelmingly supports this prediction, as illustrated by the following examples.

The prices of plywood, tin, rubber, cotton, and hundreds of other materials fluctuate daily in response to changes in their demand and supply. The responses of factor markets to the many shortages that characterized the American economy during the 1970s provide dramatic confirmation of this. When the price of agricultural commodities shot up following a grain shortage, farm income soared. When oil became scarce, prices rose, and oil producers and owners of oil properties found their profits and incomes rising rapidly. Not only did the relative prices of oil products rise, the relative prices of numerous other commodities, such as chemical fertilizers and air travel, which make use of petroleum products, rose as well. When oil became abundant in the mid-1980s, these trends were reversed.

Land in the heart of growing cities provides another example. Such land is fixed in supply, and values rise steadily in response to increasing demand for it.[3] Land values may even be high enough to make it worthwhile for people to destroy durable buildings in order to convert the land to more productive uses. The high rise is a monument to the high value of urban land. The increase in the price of land on the periphery of every growing city is an observable example of the workings of the market.

Similar results occur in markets that are far from being perfectly competitive. In 1979 the price of power in virtually all its forms rose sharply in response to the energy shortage that caused a doubling of the price of oil. Oligopolists, producing key metals such as zinc, molybdenum, steel, and aluminum, raised prices when their costs of production rose. Further examples can be found in almost every issue of the *Wall Street Journal* and the *New York Times*, but the point should now be clear:

The prices and earnings of nonhuman factors are successfully predicted by market theories of factor pricing.

Labor

When we apply the theory of distribution to labor, we encounter two important complications. First, because labor is the human factor of production, nonmonetary considerations loom large in its incentive patterns, and this may redirect the effect of market signals. Second, the competitive and noncompetitive elements of labor markets occur in different proportions from market to market. These complications make it harder to see if market conditions determine factor earnings. Nevertheless, there is a mass of evidence to support the view that they do.

Market Fluctuations

The evidence shows that earnings often respond to normal fluctuations of demand and supply. For example, with the advent of the automobile, skilled carriage makers saw the demand for their services decline rapidly. Earnings fell, and many older workers found that they had been earning substantial economic rents for their scarce but highly specific skills. They suffered large income cuts when they moved to other industries. Workers who acquired skills that

---

[3] A friend is fond of saying, "Nobody buys land any more; its price is much too high because everybody wants it."

were wanted in the newly expanding automotive industry found that the demands for their services and their incomes rose rapidly.

More recently, there has been a large increase in the earnings of premier professional athletes. In part this has resulted from rising demand due to an expansion in the number of major league teams. In part it has resulted from increased revenues to the teams and leagues from televising sports, which has increased the marginal revenue product of the athletes. Further, in part it has resulted from athletes' acquiring the right to offer their services to more than one employer, thereby reducing the ability of employers to hold down wages by eliminating competition among themselves.

One group that has been suffering the consequences of factor price determination on competitive markets is college graduates. In recent years the earnings of college graduates have fallen relative to other workers as employment opportunities have dropped sharply, especially for new graduates. The downturn is explained partly by slackening demand due to changes in industrial structure (e.g., substituting sophisticated computers for college-trained persons) and partly by continued growth of supply as the "baby-boomers" finish college.

Wage changes that are induced by market conditions have little to do with abstract notions of justice or merit. If you have some literary talent, why is it that you can make a lot of money writing copy for an advertising agency but very little money writing poems? It is not because an economic dictator or a group of philosophers has decided that advertising is more valuable than poetry. It is because in the economy there is a large demand for advertising but a small demand for poetry.

Monopoly Elements

A strong union—one that is able to bargain effectively with management and to control entry of labor into its market—can raise wages well above the competitive level. These high earnings attract others to the occupation or the industry, and the privileged position can be maintained only if the supply of labor can be restricted effectively. Highly skilled plasterers, plumbers, and electricians have all managed to restrict entry into their trades and, as a result, maintain wages well above what they would be in a compet-

itive market. Many similar cases have been documented.

Monopoly elements not only can raise incomes above their competitive levels but also can prevent wages from falling in response to decreases in demand. (Of course, if the demand disappears more or less overnight, there is nothing that any union can do to maintain incomes.)

From 1945 to 1965 the production of coal declined as oil, gas, and electricity were steadily substituted for it. The coal that was produced was mined by ever more capital-using and labor-saving techniques. Both these forces led employment to shrink steadily. Coal miners offered their labor in a declining labor market from 1945 until 1965. Competitive theory would predict relatively low wages and low incomes, followed by exit of the most mobile coal miners and hard times for those who decided to stick it out.

This is precisely what happened in many countries. In Canada, for example, average coal miners' wages, which in 1945 had been 36 percent above those in manufacturing, fell steadily until 1965, when they were 8 percent below those in manufacturing, and mining employment declined to 35 percent of its previous level. In the United States, however, this was *not* the pattern. Faced with a similar decline in production, relative wages actually rose in U.S. coal mining, from 18 percent above manufacturing in 1945 to 34 percent above it in 1965. Employment did fall—indeed, by 1965 employment was only 30 percent of the 1945 level—but those who kept jobs did relatively well.

What happened was that a powerful American union, the United Mine Workers, prevented wages from falling. By raising wages despite falling demand, the union actually accelerated the decline in employment. The lower employment that accompanied the "high-wage" policy of the United Mine Workers discouraged the young from waiting for jobs in the industry. As workers left the industry because of retirement, ill health, or death, they were not replaced.

In the 1970s the demand for coal miners rebounded as the demand for coal to produce electricity surged. As a result, as theory predicts, employment and relative wages in coal mining rose sharply, not only in the United States but also in many other countries.

All of these examples support the following general proposition:

Earnings of labor respond to significant changes in market conditions.

Implications for Economic Efficiency

The theory and evidence presented so far can be summarized in two important propositions.

1. **Factors will move between alternative uses in order to maximize the net advantage to the factors' owners.**
2. **Profit-maximizing employers will hire any factor up to the point at which the last unit hired adds as much to revenue as it does to cost (i.e., its *MRP* equals its *MC*).**

Taken together, the two propositions just stated have an important implication for economic efficiency. To see this implication, we study the case of labor, although the argument applies equally to all factors.

No nonmonetary advantages.   Suppose—to consider the simplest case first—that workers of one type all derive the same satisfaction (or dissatisfaction) from all jobs; the only thing that distinguishes one job from another is the wage rate. Whenever wage rates differ among jobs, workers move from low- to high-paying jobs. This movement continues until the wages paid for that type of labor have been equalized among the various jobs.

Since competitive firms equate the wage rate with labor's marginal revenue product (proposition 2), the *MRP*s of this type of labor are equalized in all its uses. When this is true, the value of total output cannot be increased by reallocating labor. If a worker were to move from one firm to another, the value that the worker would add to the output of the new firm would be exactly equal to the value of the fall in output in the old firm.

If the nonmonetary advantages are the same in all possible uses of a factor, competitive markets equalize that factor's marginal revenue products in all uses; as a result, the value of total output is maximized.

The effect of nonmonetary advantages.   We can now allow for the fact that workers derive different levels of satisfaction from different jobs. When workers compare different jobs, they compare both the wage rates and the other satisfactions (or dissatisfactions) that the jobs offer. They then move among jobs until the net advantages of each—both monetary and nonmonetary—are equalized. As a result, wages are higher in jobs with low levels of nonmonetary satisfaction than they are in jobs with high satisfaction levels.

In the presence of nonmonetary advantages, the competitive market does not equalize wage rates.

It follows that, when competitive firms equate wage rates with marginal revenue products, *MRP*s are not equalized in all the jobs that are occupied by this type of labor. As a result, output does not achieve its maximum possible value. Instead, it is possible to increase output by moving labor from a job where its wage and the value of its *MRP* are low (because the job has a high nonmonetary advantage) to a job where its wage and the value of its *MRP* are high (because the job has a low nonmonetary advantage). However, the increase in output of goods and services would be offset by the "psychic" cost to the worker in moving from a more preferred activity to a less preferred one. For example, a carpenter in Phoenix, Arizona, may earn a lower wage and have a lower marginal revenue product than one in Fargo, North Dakota. If the carpenter from Arizona moves to North Dakota, the economy's value of output of carpentry services would go up. However, if the initial difference in wages and hence in marginal revenue products reflects the net nonmonetary satisfaction to the carpenter of living in Phoenix, the increase in value of output of carpentry services would be exactly matched by the decrease in nonmonetary returns to the carpenter.

The general message is that the market prices of all factors reflect the values of factors in alternative uses and thus play a key role in their efficient allocation.

If factors are not priced according to their scarcity, there will be no easy means of allocating them efficiently among competing uses.

This is not just idle speculation. In the early years of the Communist experiment in Russia, interest, which is the price paid for capital, was banned for ideological reasons. The resulting misallocation of capital among its various uses led to such serious waste that the policy had to be abandoned. This and related ideological issues concerning interest and capital are discussed in Box 18-2.

Capital and Interest

We begin by exploring an important complication that arises because factors of production are durable—a machine lasts for years, a laborer for a lifetime, and land more or less forever. It is convenient to think of a factor's lifetime as being divided into shorter periods that we refer to as *production periods* or, equivalently, *rental periods*.

The durability of factors makes it necessary to distinguish between the factor itself and the flow of services that it provides in a given production period. We can, for example, rent the use of a piece of land for some period of time, or we can buy the land outright. This distinction is just a particular instance of the general distinction between flows and stocks that we first encountered on page 20.

Although what follows applies to any durable factor, applications to capital are of most importance, so we confine the remainder of our text discussion to capital. Box 18-3 discusses some of these issues as they apply to labor.

Two Prices of Capital

If a firm hires the use of a piece of capital equipment for some period of time, for example, one truck for one month, it pays a price for the privilege of using that piece of capital equipment. If the firm buys the truck outright, it pays a different (and higher) price for the purchase. Consider each of these prices—rental price and purchase price—in turn.

Rental Price

The *rental price of capital* is the amount that a firm pays to obtain the services of a capital good for a given period of time. The rental price of one week's use of a piece of capital is analogous to the weekly wage rate and the weekly rent bill that are the prices of hiring the services of labor and land.

Just as a profit-maximizing firm continues to hire labor until its *marginal revenue product (MRP)* equals its wage (see page 360), so will the firm go on hiring capital until its *MRP* equals its rental price, *R*. Since, in a competitive market, all firms will face the same rental price, all firms that are in equilibrium will have the same *MRP* of capital.

As a result of profit maximization, the rental price of capital will be equated with its *marginal revenue product (MRP)*, which is the net addition to the firm's revenue that is contributed by the use of the capital services over the rental period.

A capital good also may be used by the firm that owns it. In this case the firm does not pay out any rental fee. However, the rental price is the amount that the firm could charge if it leased its capital to another firm. It is thus the *opportunity cost* to the firm of using the capital good itself. This rental price is the *implicit* price that reflects the value to the firm of the services of its own capital that it uses during the current production period.

Whether the firm pays the rental price explicitly or calculates it as an implicit cost of using its own capital, the rental price of a capital good over the production period is equal to its marginal revenue product, which in turn is the stream of net income that the capital good produces over that period.

Purchase Price

The price that a firm pays to buy a capital good is called the *purchase price of capital*. When a firm buys a capital good outright, it obtains the use of the good's services over the whole of that good's lifetime. What the capital good will contribute to the firm is a flow that is equal to the expected marginal revenue product of the good's services over the good's lifetime. The price that the firm is willing to pay is, naturally enough, related to the total value that it places now on this stream of *expected* receipts to be received over future time periods.

The term "expected" emphasizes that the firm is usually uncertain about the prices at which it will be able to sell its outputs in the future. For the sake of

BOX 18-2

Capital, Capitalists, and Capitalism

A capitalist is someone who owns capital goods. The role of the capitalist is interpreted differently in different economic philosophies. For example, to many Marxists the capitalist is a villain; to many socialists the capitalist is at best a dispensable drone; to many conservatives the capitalist is a hero who steers the economy through the risky channels that lead to ever higher living standards.

Ideology aside, if there is capital, someone must own it. Capital may be predominantly in private hands, in which case the economy is sometimes described as *capitalist,* or capital may be predominantly owned by the state, in which case the economy is described as *socialist* or *communist.* In virtually all economies ownership is mixed: Some capital is owned privately, and some is owned publicly.

No matter who owns the capital goods, such goods are indispensable in the productive process. A primitive society in which there are no capital goods—no spears, no levers, no stones for grinding grain, no jugs for carrying water—has never occurred in recorded human history.

Since resources must be used in the manufacture of capital goods, such goods have scarcity value. Any economic system that is interested in maximizing production will want to allocate scarce capital to its most productive uses. One effective way of doing this is to assign a rental price to capital that reflects its opportunity cost and to allow firms

to use more capital only if the capital earns enough to cover this price. A charge that is levied on producers for use of capital serves such an important function that it is hard to eliminate it without serious consequences.

Early Communist rulers in Russia thought differently. Payments for the use of capital were officially barred during the years following the Russian Revolution of 1917 on the grounds that a Communist society should purge itself of this reminder of capitalism. However, this left no way of deciding how to allocate scarce capital efficiently among its many competing uses. Indeed, prices are such an efficient allocative device that today all Communist states use them for allocating scarce capital among competing uses. Furthermore, planners in Communist states give a good deal of attention to setting the correct rental price for capital. If capital is privately owned and a price is charged for its use, the payments go to the capitalists and become their income. In Communist countries capital is owned by the state, and payments for its use go to the state. The desirability of private versus public ownership of the *means of production* (the term often used in socialist and communist literature to describe capital) is still debated in some circles. The issue of ownership, however, is quite a separate issue from that of whether to charge a rental price for the use of capital.

---

simplicity we confine ourselves to the special case in which the firm knows the future *MRP*s.

Present Value of Future Returns

The amount that the stream of future income that is provided by a capital good is worth *now* is called the good's present value. In general, **present value (PV)** refers to the value *now* of one or more payments to be received *in the future.*

Present Value of a Single Future Payment

One period hence.   To learn how to find the present value, we start with the simplest possible case. How much would a firm be prepared to pay *now* to purchase a capital good that will produce a single marginal revenue product of $100.00 in 1 year's time, after which time the good will be useless? One way to answer this question is to discover how much the firm would have to lend out in order to have $100.00

BOX 18-3

The Rental and Purchase Price of Labor

If you wish to farm a piece of land, you can buy it yourself, or you can rent it for a specific period of time. If you want to set up a small business, you can buy your office and equipment, or you can rent them. The same is true for all capital and all land; a firm often has the option of buying or renting.

Exactly the same would be true for labor if we lived in a slave society. You could buy a slave to be your assistant, or you could rent the services either of someone else's slave or of a free person. Fortunately, slavery is illegal throughout most of today's world. As a result, the labor markets that we know deal only in the services of labor; no one goes to a labor market to buy a worker body and soul. However, one can buy the services of a laborer for a long period of time. In professional sports multiyear contracts are common, and 10-year contracts are not unknown. Some symphony orches-

tras have appointed their famous conductors for life. Herbert von Karajan, for example, was appointed "conductor for life" of the Berlin Philharmonic Orchestra. Publishers sometimes tie up their authors in multibook contracts, and entertainment firms, such as movie and television production units, often sign up their actors on long-term contracts. In all cases of such *personal services contracts* the person is not a slave, and his or her personal rights and liberties are protected by law. The purchaser of the long-term contract is, nonetheless, buying ownership of the factor's services for an extended period of time. If the contract is transferable, the owner can sell these services for a lump sum or rent them out for some period. As with land and capital goods, the price paid for this *stock* of labor services is the present value of the expected rental prices over the contract period.

a year from now. Suppose for the moment that the interest rate is 5 percent, which means that $1.00 invested today will be worth $1.05 in 1 year's time.[4]

If we use PV to stand for this unknown amount, we can write $PV(1.05) = \$100.00$ (which means PV *multiplied by* 1.05). Thus $PV = \$100.00/1.05 = \$95.24$. This tells us that the present value of $100.00, receivable in 1 year's time, is $95.24 when the interest rate is 5 percent. Anyone who lends out $95.24 for 1 year at 5 percent interest will receive $95.24 back plus $4.76 in interest, which makes $100.00 in total. When we calculate this present value, the interest rate is used to *discount* (i.e., reduce to its present value) the $100.00 to be received 1 year hence. The maximum price that a firm would be willing to pay for this capital good is $95.24 (assuming that the relevant interest rate is 5 percent).

To see why, let us start by assuming that firms

are offered the capital good at some other price. Say that the good is offered at $98. If, instead of paying this amount for the capital good, a firm lends its $98.00 out at 5 percent interest, it would have at the end of 1 year more than the $100.00 that the capital good will produce. (At 5 percent interest $98.00 yields $4.90 in interest, which, together with the principal, makes $102.90.) Clearly, no profit-maximizing firm would pay $98.00—or, by the same reasoning, any sum in excess of $95.24—for the capital good. It could do better by using its funds in other ways.

Now say that the good is offered for sale at $90.00. A firm could borrow $90.00 to buy the capital good and could pay $4.50 in interest on its loan. At the end of the year, the good yields $100.00. When this is used to repay the $90.00 loan and the $4.50 in interest, then $5.50 is left as a profit to the firm. Clearly, it would be worthwhile for a profit-maximizing firm to buy the good at a price of $90.00 or, by the same argument, at any price less than $95.24.

---

[4] Readers who are familiar with this type of reasoning will recognize that the analysis in the rest of this chapter assumes *annual* compounding of interest.

The actual present value that we have calculated depended on our assuming that the interest rate is 5 percent. What if the interest rate had been 7 percent? At that interest rate, the present value of the $100.00 receivable in 1 year's time would be $100.00/1.07 = $93.46.

These examples are easy to generalize. In both cases we have found the present value by dividing the sum that is receivable in the future by 1 plus the rate of interest.[5] In general, the present value of R dollars 1 year hence at an interest rate of i per year is

$$PV = \frac{R}{(1 + i)} \qquad [1]$$

Several periods hence.   Now we know how to calculate the present value of a single sum that is receivable 1 year hence. The next step is to ask what would happen if the sum were receivable at a later date. What, for example, is the present value of $100.00 to be received *two* years hence when the interest rate is 5 percent? This is $100.00/(1.05)(1.05) = $90.70. We can check this by seeing what would happen if $90.70 were lent out for two years. In the first year the loan would earn an interest of $(0.05)(\$90.70) = \$4.54$, and hence after 1 year the firm would receive $95.24. In the second year the interest would be earned on this entire amount; interest earned in the second year would equal $(0.05)(\$95.24) = \$4.76$. Hence, in 2 years the firm would have $100.00. (The payment of interest in the second year on the interest income earned in the first year is known as *compound interest*.)

In general, the present value of R dollars after t years at i percent is

$$PV = \frac{R}{(1 + i)^t} \qquad [2]$$

All that this formula does is to discount the sum, R, by the interest rate, i, repeatedly, once for each of the t periods that must pass until the sum becomes available. If we look at the formula, we see that the higher is i or t, the higher is the whole term $(1 + i)^t$. This term, however, appears in the denominator, so that PV is *negatively* related to both i and t.

[5] Notice that in this type of formula the interest rate is expressed as a decimal fraction where, for example, 7 percent is expressed as 0.07, so $(1 + i)$ equals 1.07.

The formula $PV = R/(1 + i)^t$ **shows that the present value of a given sum payable in the future will be smaller the further away the payment date is and the higher the rate of interest is.**

Present Value of a Continuous Stream of Payments

Finally, consider the present value that the firm would place on a capital good that is producing a stream of marginal revenue products which continues forever. In effect, this means that the capital good is not subject to depreciation. This simplifies the argument while still retaining the essence of the nature of capital.

Say that some capital good will produce $100 each year forever and that the interest rate is 10 percent. To find the present value of $100 payable every year in the future, we ask how much money would have to be invested now at an interest rate of 10 percent per year to obtain $100 every year in the future. This present value is simply $0.1(PV) = \$100$, where PV is the sum required. In other words, $PV = \$100/0.1 = \$1,000$. This tells us that $1,000 invested at 10 percent interest forever would yield a constant stream of income of $100 per year; or, put the other way around, when the interest rate is 10 percent, the present value of $100 per year forever is $1,000.

To generalize for any interest rate, we merely write i for the interest rate and R for the revenue to be received each year. Now we wish to find the amount PV that, invested at i, will yield R per year forever. This is $i(PV) = R$, or

$$PV = \frac{R}{i} \qquad [3]$$

Here, as before, PV is related to the rate of interest: The higher is the interest rate, the less is the (present) value of any stream of future receipts and hence the lower is the price that the firm would be prepared to pay to purchase the capital good.

Conclusions

From the previous discussion we can put together the following important propositions about the rental and the purchase prices of capital.

1. **The rental price of capital is the flow of net receipts that the capital good is expected to produce over the rental period, that is, the marginal revenue product of the capital good.**
2. **The maximum purchase price that a firm would pay for a capital good is the discounted present value of the flow of net receipts, that is, rental values, that the good is expected to produce over its lifetime.**
3. **The maximum purchase price that a firm would pay for a capital good is positively associated with its rental price and negatively associated with the interest rate and amount of time that the owner must wait for payments to accrue.**

The Equilibrium of the Firm

An individual firm faces a given interest rate and a given purchase price of capital goods. The firm can vary the quantity of capital that it employs, and, as a result, the marginal revenue product of its capital varies; the law of diminishing returns entails that the more capital the firm uses, the lower is its *MRP*.

The Decision to Purchase Capital

Price exceeds present value.   Suppose that for $8,000 a firm can purchase a machine that yields $1,000 per year into the indefinite future. Also, suppose that the firm can borrow (and lend) money at an interest rate of 10 percent. The present value of the income stream earned by the machine is $R/i = \$1,000/0.10 = \$10,000$. It is profitable for the firm to purchase the machine, since it obtains something worth $10,000 for a price of only $8,000.

It is always worthwhile for a firm to buy another unit of capital whenever the present value of the stream of *MRP*s that the capital provides exceeds its purchase price.

Marginal efficiency exceeds the interest rate.   Another way to see the profitability for the firm of the purchase of a unit of capital is to suppose that the firm has only two uses for its money: to buy the machine or to lend out the $8,000 at 10 percent interest. It will be worthwhile for the firm to buy the machine,

because the firm can do so and earn $1,000 per year, whereas, if it lends the $8,000 at 10 percent interest, it will earn only $800 per year. In this example, each dollar invested in the machine yields a return of 12.5 percent ($1,000/$8,000 = 0.125$), whereas each dollar lent out produces a return of only 10 percent. The concept of the **marginal efficiency of capital (MEC)** generalizes this result. It is defined as the return on capital per dollar invested in that capital. For the type of capital that we are considering—one that produces a perpetual stream of net revenue of *R* per period—the *MEC* is:

$$MEC = \frac{R}{P} \qquad [4]$$

It is always worthwhile for the firm to buy another unit of capital whenever the *MEC* exceeds the interest rate.

The two previous statements in color are just two ways of stating the same condition for a profitable purchase of capital. To say that the present value, which is R/i, should exceed the purchase price, *P*, is the same as saying that the *MEC*, which is R/P, should exceed the interest rate, *i*. So now we know when it is worthwhile for a firm to buy capital, but how much will it buy?

The Size of the Firm's Capital Stock

Since the *MRP* declines as the firm's capital stock rises, the firm will eventually reach an equilibrium with respect to its capital stock. The firm will go on adding to its capital until the present value of the flow of *MRP*s conferred by the last unit added is equal to the purchase price of the capital. If we continue to use *R* for the *MRP* per period, we can write it as

$$PV = \frac{R}{i} = P$$

The equilibrium capital stock of the firm is such that the present value of the stream of net income that is provided by the marginal unit of capital is equal to its purchase price.

A second way of stating the same result is that the firm will go on adding to its capital until the *MEC* falls to the level of the rate of interest: that is,

$$MEC = i$$

Saying that R/P (the *MEC*) should equal i in equilibrium is the same as saying that R/i (the *PV* of the capital's stream of marginal revenue products) should equal P.[6]

The negative relationship between the *MRP* and the stock of capital implies that the firm's desired capital stock falls when the rate of interest rises and that it rises when the rate of interest falls.

The Equilibrium for the Whole Economy

The term **capital stock** refers to some aggregate amount of capital. The *firm's capital stock* has a marginal revenue product, showing the increase in the firm's revenue when another unit of capital is added to its capital stock. The *economy's capital stock* also has a marginal revenue product. This is the addition to total national output (GNP) that is caused by adding another unit of capital to the economy's total stock. This capital stock also has an average product, which is total output divided by the total capital stock (i.e., the amount of output per unit of capital).[7]

If the industries that produce capital goods are perfectly competitive, the price of these goods will equal their marginal cost of production. We take this as it is given by the cost conditions in these industries and beyond the control of the firms that purchase and use capital goods. Thus there is a given price of producing one more unit of capital.

The Marginal-Efficiency-of-Capital Schedule

Now consider how the marginal efficiency of capital varies for the whole economy as the existing capital stock is varied. The law of diminishing returns tells us that the larger the capital stock that is applied to the economy's given supplies of land and labor, the lower will be the marginal revenue product of a marginal unit of capital. Thus, as we vary the size

---

[6] In this chapter we assume that the rate of interest reflects the opportunity cost of capital to the firm. We saw in Chapter 9 that this may not always be the case. When the market rate of interest and the firm's own opportunity cost of capital diverge, the *MEC* must be equated with the latter, not the former.

[7] The idea of a capital stock being measured by a single number is a simplification (just as is the idea of a total quantity of labor being measured by a single number). Society's stock of capital goods is made up of a diverse array of aids to production such as factories, machines, bridges, and roads. Also, the marginal and average products referred to in the text relate to the *flow of services* provided by the capital goods rather than to the *goods themselves.*

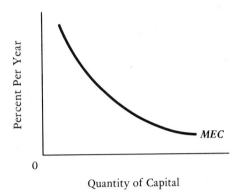

FIGURE 18-1 The Marginal Efficiency of Capital

Percent Per Year (vertical axis)

MEC

0

Quantity of Capital

The marginal efficiency of capital (*MEC*) curve shows the relationship between the size of the capital stock and the rate of return on the marginal unit of capital. Because of diminishing returns each successive unit of capital adds less to output than each previous unit. Thus, the *MEC* curve, which relates the value of the additional output of each additional dollar's worth of capital added to the capital stock, is negatively sloped.

---

of the capital stock, the *MRP* in Equation 4 varies and so, therefore, does the *MEC*. Specifically, as the capital stock grows, the *MEC* falls. This negative relationship between these two magnitudes is shown in Figure 18-1.

Short-Run Equilibrium

In the short run, the economy's capital stock is given, but, for the economy as a whole, the interest rate is variable. Whereas the firm reaches equilibrium by altering its capital stock, the whole economy reaches equilibrium through variations in the interest rate. Let us see how this comes about.

For the economy as a whole, the condition that *MEC* = *i* determines the equilibrium interest rate.

If the market interest rate were below the *MEC*, which is the same thing as saying that the price of capital is less than the present value of its stream of future *MRP*s, it would be worthwhile for all firms to borrow money to invest in capital. For the economy as a whole, however, the stock of capital cannot

FIGURE 18-2   The Equilibrium Interest Rate

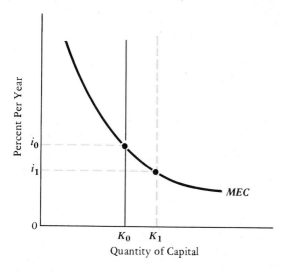

The economy's equilibrium interest rate is negatively related to the quantity of capital. The *MEC*
curve is reproduced from Figure 18-1. If the capital stock
is K_0, the equilibrium interest rate is i_0. If the actual rate
were below i_0, all firms would wish to borrow in order
to invest in capital, and this would drive the interest rate
upward to i_0. If the actual rate were above i_0, no firm
would wish to borrow in order to invest in capital, and
this would drive the interest rate down to i_0.

An increase in the capital stock to K_1 lowers the equilibrium interest rate to i_1.

change quickly, so the effect of this demand for borrowing would be to push up the interest rate until it
equaled the *MEC*. Conversely, if the *MEC* were
below the interest rate—that is, if the price of capital
were above its present value—no one would wish to
borrow money to invest in capital, and the rate of
interest would fall. This is illustrated in Figure 18-2.

The Accumulation of Capital in the Long Run

As more capital is accumulated over time, the economy's stock of capital grows slowly. As this happens,
the *MEC* falls. This will cause the equilibrium interest rate to fall over time, as shown in Figure 18-2.

Changing Technology in the Very Long Run

In the very long run, technology changes. As a result, capital becomes more productive, which shifts

FIGURE 18-3   The Effect of Changing Technology and Capital Stock

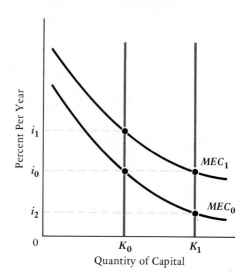

Increases in technological knowledge and in the
capital stock have opposite effects on the equilibrium interest rate. The original capital stock is K_0, and
the original state of technology gives rise to the marginal
efficiency of capital schedule MEC_0. Thus, the equilibrium interest rate is i_0. Technological improvements shift
the marginal efficiency of capital curve to MEC_1 and,
with a constant stock of capital, would raise the interest
rate to i_1. The capital stock increases to K_1. If the *MEC*
had remained at MEC_0, the equilibrium interest rate
would have fallen to i_2. In the figure, the two effects
exactly offset each other, and i remains unchanged at i_0,
where K_1 and MEC_1 intersect.

the *MEC* curve outward. This tends to increase the
equilibrium interest rate associated with any one
stock of capital. The accumulation of capital moves
the economy downward to the right along any given
MEC curve, which tends to lower the interest rate
associated with any one *MEC* curve. The net effect
on the interest rate of both of these changes may be
to raise it, to lower it, or to leave it unchanged, as
shown in Figure 18-3. The very long-run effects of
changing technology, combined with a growing capital stock, are studied further in Chapter 36 on economic growth.

SUMMARY

1. The demand for any factor is derived from the demand for the commodities that the factor is used to make. Factor demand curves slope downward, for two reasons. First, an increase in a factor's price will raise the cost of production of goods that use the factor in their production; this will increase the price of those goods and thus reduce the amount demanded. Second, an increase in a factor price will create incentives for producers to substitute cheaper factors for more expensive ones.

2. A profit–maximizing firm will hire units of any variable factor until the last unit that is hired adds as much to costs as it does to revenue. If factors are bought in a competitive market, the addition to cost will be the price of a unit of a factor. From this comes the important condition that in competitive equilibrium the price of a factor will equal its marginal revenue product. This is the marginal productivity theory of distribution.

3. The elasticity of factor demand will tend to be greater (a) the greater the elasticity of demand of the products it makes, (b) the greater the ease of substitution of one factor for another, and (c) the greater the proportion of the total cost of production accounted for by the factor.

4. Market conditions exert a powerful influence on factor earnings. This is most evident for nonhuman factors such as raw materials and land, but it is also true for labor, despite the greater role of nonmonetary considerations and the greater importance of noncompetitive markets.

5. The marginal productivity theory of factor demands has the important implication that factors will be allocated efficiently among competing uses.

6. Because capital goods are durable, we distinguish between the stock of capital goods and the flow of services provided by them and thus between their purchase price and their rental price. The linkage between them relies on the ability to assign a present value to future returns. The present value of a future payment will be lower when the payment is more distant and the interest rate is higher.

7. The rental price of capital, equal to its marginal revenue product, is the amount that is paid to obtain the flow of services that a capital good provides for a given period. The purchase price is the amount that is paid to acquire ownership of the capital, and in equilibrium it is equal to the present value of the future income stream earned by the capital.

8. The marginal efficiency of capital (*MEC*) is the ratio of the value of the additional income stream to the value of the additional capital stock that is needed to produce the increased income stream. In equilibrium, the *MEC* will equal the interest rate.

9. An individual firm will invest in capital goods as long as the *MEC* exceeds the interest rate or, equivalently, as long as the present value of the stream of future net incomes that are provided by another unit of capital exceeds its purchase price; thus the condition that $MEC = i$ determines the firm's equilibrium capital stock. In the economy as a whole, the size of the total capital stock and hence the *MEC* changes only slowly; hence the condition that $MEC = i$ determines the interest rate.

TOPICS FOR REVIEW

Derived demand
Marginal revenue product
Marginal productivity theory of distribution
Elasticity of factor demand
Efficient allocation of factors
Rental price and purchase price of durable goods
Present value
Marginal efficiency of capital
The interest rate and the capital stock

DISCUSSION QUESTIONS

1. The demands that are listed below have been increasing rapidly in recent years. What derived demands would you predict have risen sharply? Where will the extra factors of production that are demanded be drawn from?
   a. Demand for electric power
   b. Demand for medical services
   c. Demand for international and interregional travel
2. Can the following factor prices be explained by the marginal productivity theory of distribution?
   a. The actor James Garner is paid $25,000 for appearing in a 10-second commercial. The model who appears in the commercial with him is paid $500.
   b. The same jockey who is riding the same horse is paid 50 percent more money for winning a $\frac{3}{4}$-mile race with a $150,000 first prize than a $1\frac{1}{2}$-mile race with a $100,000 first prize.
   c. The manager of the New York Yankees is paid *not* to manage during the third year of a 3-year contract.
   d. The Los Angeles Kings lure hockey superstar Wayne Gretsky away from the Edmonton Oilers, which he has led to several Stanley Cup titles, by an offer that the Oilers—one of the richest clubs in the National Hockey League—are unwilling to match.
3. "One of the interesting side effects of the women's liberation movement has been a growing shortage of nurses." Why might women's liberation and the shortage of nurses be linked? Under what circumstances would the shortage persist? Under what circumstances would it be eliminated fairly quickly?
4. Consider the large-scale substitution of jumbo jets, each of which has a seating capacity of about 350, for jets with a seating capacity of about 125. What kinds of labor service would you predict will experience an increase in demand, and what kinds will experience a decrease? Under what conditions would airplane pilots (as a group) be made better off economically by virtue of this substitution?
5. A recent study has shown that, after differences in education, age, hours worked per week, weeks worked per year, and so forth are taken into account, professionally trained people earn approximately 15 percent less if they work in universities than if they work in government service. Can this be accounted for by the theory of distribution that we have been studying?
6. Discuss the implications of the suggestion that the Canadian federal government should change its policy of paying all its secretaries according to the same salary scale, regardless of location, to one that adapts the salary scale to local market conditions.
7. What light does marginal productivity theory shed on the observation that unions in industries that compete strongly with foreign imports

tend to favor trade restrictions, while unions in industries that are major exporters tend to favor free trade?

8. Suppose you are offered, free of charge, either one of each of the following pairs of assets. What considerations would determine your choice?

  a. A perpetuity that pays $20,000 a year forever or an annuity that pays $100,000 a year for 5 years

  b. An oil-drilling company that earned $100,000 after corporate taxes last year or Canada Savings Bonds that paid $100,000 in interest last year

  c. A 1 percent share of a new company that has invested $10 million in a new cosmetic that is thought to appeal to middle-income women or a $100,000 bond that has been issued by the same company

9. How would you go about evaluating the present value of

  a. The existing reserves of a relatively small oil company

  b. The total world reserves of an exhaustible natural resource whose completely fixed supply is known

  c. A perpetuity, issued by a very shaky third-world government, in which it promises to pay the bearer $1,000 per year forever

  d. A lottery ticket that your neighbor bought for $10, which was one of 1 million tickets sold for a drawing that is to be held in one year's time and that will pay $2 million to the single winning ticket

Appendix to Chapter 18

The Firm's Demand for Factors

In Chapter 18 we saw that all profit-maximizing firms will hire units of the variable factor up to the point at which the marginal cost of the factor equals the marginal revenue that is produced by the factor. For a firm that is a price taker in factor markets, this means that it hires a factor up to the point at which the factor's price equals its marginal revenue product. Consider a single firm with only one variable factor, labor, and one fixed factor, capital. Assume that the average and marginal revenue products of the labor are those shown in Figure 18A-1. The firm wishes to hire the quantity of labor that will maximize its profits.

The demand curve for a factor is the downward-sloping portion of the marginal revenue product curve where it is below the average revenue product curve.

To see why this statement is correct, let us first ask a number of questions.

Why do points on the downward-sloping portion of *MRP*, such as *a* and *b* in Figure 18A-1, belong on the demand curve? If the wage rate (the price of the variable factor) is w_2, the profit-maximizing firm will hire the factor up to the point where $w = MRP$, that is, up to q_2. This is point *a*. If the wage rate is w_1, the firm will hire up to q_1. This is point *b*. Points *a* and *b* are thus on the firm's demand curve for the factor.

What is the maximum wage rate that the firm will pay? In Chapter 12 we saw that it will never be worthwhile for the firm to produce a product when its price is below the level of average variable cost. We also saw (see page 197) that, where average product is a maximum, average variable cost is a minimum. For any wage rate above w_3, such as w_4, the average revenue that is generated by a unit of labor (shown by *ARP*) would be less than the variable cost of the unit of labor (its wage rate). For such a wage rate it is not worthwhile for the firm to hire any workers. In other words, w_3, where average revenue product

is a maximum, is the highest factor price that a firm could pay and still cover its variable costs.

Why is the downward-sloping, not the upward-sloping, portion of *MRP* the demand curve? Consider the wage rate w_2. Here $w = MRP$ at both q_4 (point *c*) and q_2 (point *a*). We have seen already that point *a* is on the demand curve. What about point *c*? For every unit of labor that is hired up to q_4, *MRP* is less than the wage rate. In other words, each unit of labor is contributing less to revenue than to cost. Thus, a profit-maximizing firm would be better off if it hired zero units rather than q_4 units. For every unit of labor

---

FIGURE 18A-1   The Demand for a Factor and Marginal Revenue Product

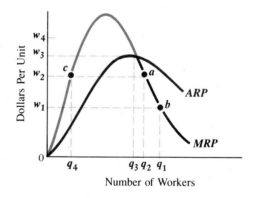

The derived demand curve for a factor is the downward-sloping portion of the *MRP* curve below the *ARP* curve as indicated by the black portion of the *MRP* curve. Suppose the factor in question is labor. The average revenue generated by a unit of labor, the average revenue product of labor, is shown by the curve *ARP*, while the revenue generated by a marginal increase in the labor force, the marginal revenue product of labor, is shown by the curve *MRP*. Only points on the black portion of the *MRP* curve are on the firm's demand curve for the factor.

from q_4 to q_2, MRP exceeds the wage rate. Thus, if a firm were hiring q_4 units, it would find each additional unit beyond q_4 (up to q_2) worth hiring. Point c, where MRP is rising when it equals the wage rate, is a point of *minimum* profit, not maximum profit. [28] A firm at point c would improve its profitability by moving in either direction—to hiring zero workers or to hiring q_2 workers. (We already know that q_2 is better than zero, because at that quantity ARP is greater than the wage rate.) Only points where MRP cuts the wage rate from above, that is, where MRP is downward sloping, are possible profit-maximizing quantities.

Will There Be a Downward-sloping Portion of *MRP*?

We may now ask, having shown that only downward-sloping portions of MRP are relevant to the demand curve for the factor, whether we have any reason to believe that MRP will slope downward. The presence of diminishing returns is sufficient to assure this result, as we can easily show. Marginal revenue product depends on two things: (1) the physical increase in output that an additional unit of the variable factor makes possible, multiplied by (2) the increase in revenue derived from that extra output. The first of these is called the marginal product (*MP*); the second of these is called marginal revenue, which by now is a familiar concept:

$$MRP = MP \times MR$$

The hypothesis of diminishing marginal returns was introduced in Chapter 10. This hypothesis says that MP has a declining section over some range of output. If marginal revenue is constant (as it is in perfect competition), MRP will have the same shape as MP and must also decline.

Marginal revenue, however, may not be constant. If MR declines as output increases (as it does in monopoly and in any other situation in which the firm's demand curve declines), MRP must decline even more sharply. The hypothesis of diminishing marginal productivity thus implies diminishing MRP and a downward-sloping demand curve for the factor.

Chapter 19

Labor Markets and Discrimination

The competitive theory of factor price determination tells us a great deal about factor prices, factor movements, and the distribution of income. Indeed, for the pricing and employment of many nonhuman factors, there is little need to modify the competitive model. Much of what is observed about labor markets is also consistent with the theory of competitive markets, but not all of it is.

The owners of capital or land need not be present when the services of factors are utilized. We observed in Chapter 18, however, that the need for workers to be physically present when their labor services are used differentiates labor from these other factors of production. As a result, nonmonetary factors, such as location of employment and other working conditions, are likely to be more important in the labor market than in markets for other factors of production.

Considerations other than material advantage enter the relationship between employer and employee, for it is a relationship among people who look for loyalty, fairness, appreciation, and justice along with paychecks and productivity. It is also a relationship that may involve discrimination on the basis of such things as sex, race, and age. The performance of labor markets will be affected by all of these "noneconomic" considerations and more.

Labor unions, employers' associations, collective bargaining, and government intervention in free-market wage determination are important features of the real world. They influence wages and working conditions and affect the levels of employment and unemployment in many industries.

The theory of factor price determination therefore must be modified somewhat before it can be applied to the full range of problems concerning the determination of wages.

Theoretical Models of Wage Determination[1]

If all workers were identical and labor markets were perfectly competitive, in equilibrium everyone would earn the same wage. We know that in the real world this is hardly the case. Some people work full time and are in poverty; others are able to live very

---

[1] Remember that, unless otherwise specified, we are dealing with real wages, that is, wages relative to the price level.

well on their wages or salaries. Generally, the more education and experience a worker has, the higher his or her wages will be. Given equal education and experience, blacks earn less than whites (on average), and women earn less than men (on average). Workers in highly unionized industries tend to get paid more than workers with similar skills and experience in nonunionized industries. These differentials arise both because all workers are not identical and because there are many important noncompetitive forces operating in labor markets. In the following sections we look more systematically at the reasons why different labor groups earn different incomes.

Wage Differences in Competitive Labor Markets

Where there are many employers (buyers) and many nonunion workers (sellers), there is a competitive factor market of the kind discussed in the previous chapter. Under competitive conditions the wage rate and level of employment are set by supply and demand. No worker or group of workers and no firm or group of firms would be able to affect the market wage. Indeed, if all workers and all jobs were identical, there would be only one market wage.

Of course, there are many kinds of workers and many kinds of jobs. Some jobs require highly specialized skills; some do not. Some jobs require that workers take great risks or work in unpleasant environments, while others can be performed in safety and comfort. In competitive equilibrium without discrimination, there will be three major sources of differences in pay.

Luck

Skills that are essentially impossible to teach and that are highly valued, for example, the physical ability to play professional football, will earn large incomes. In this case, there is a small and inelastic supply of the relevant kind of labor, and a large enough demand so that the market-clearing wage is high. There are also less extreme cases. Some people are endowed with the ability to make others feel good—they make superior salespersons and therapists. Some people seem to enjoy working hard more than others; they are thus more valuable on the job and often get paid more. In general, peoples' inheritance and early environment, both of which depend on luck, can have

important effects on their ability to earn income as adults.

Human Capital

Investment in capital usually is discussed in terms of tangible assets such as buildings or machines. Much modern production, however, requires another type of investment. Skills and attitudes that can only be acquired through education are needed to fit labor for many of today's skilled jobs. When people invest in acquiring these skills, they are investing in another sort of capital.

Consider a high school graduate who has enough schooling to get and to keep a job. Instead of taking a job, however, she elects to go to college and possibly to graduate or professional school. During her university career her contribution to society's current output is small (only a summer job perhaps), but, because of her education, her lifetime contribution to production may be substantially larger than it would have been had she taken a job after high school.

The choice of whether to take a job immediately or to continue one's education has all the basic elements of an investment decision, and it is useful to regard this situation as if the student were making an investment to acquire capital. Because the value derived from such an investment is embodied in a person—in terms of greater skills, more knowledge, better health, and the like—rather than in a machine, it is known as **human capital.** Major elements of human capital are health, training, and education of all sorts. An extended education program requires, for example, that resources be withdrawn from the production of goods for current consumption. The resources include materials in the school, services of teachers, and the time and talents of pupils. The education of an individual is a good investment if the difference between the value of the lifetime output of the trained worker and the lifetime output of the individual without that training exceeds the value of the incremental resources that are used in the education process. If it does, the education increases the value of total production of the economy. Skills that can be learned also will be rewarded in the market. Thus, engineers are highly paid, in part as compensation for undergoing many years of arduous training. During their training years, their pay is much *lower* than it would have been in some other line of work. Their high wages must compensate them both for the training itself and for the opportunity cost of acquiring it. So one cause of wage differentials is the return on human capital necessary to persuade people to acquire it. These differentials will persist in equilibrium.

Notice that in this case an increase in wages above their equilibrium value will induce an increase in the number of people choosing to become engineers. Where wages are high in order to compensate for human capital acquisition, the supply curve will be at least somewhat elastic—a further rise in the wage will encourage others to acquire the capital that is needed to earn that wage.

Notice also that experience can be an important form of human capital. An experienced worker often is more able than an inexperienced one. This will increase the experienced worker's wage relative to that of the inexperienced worker.

Compensating Differentials

Given identical skills, workers will be rewarded for working under relatively onerous or risky conditions. Thus, construction workers who work the "high iron," assembling the frames for skyscrapers, are paid more than workers who do the same kind of work at lower altitudes. Other things being equal, risk and unpleasantness will reduce the supply of labor, raising the wage above what it would otherwise be.

Because workers and jobs differ greatly, the labor market is best thought of as many related markets—one for each type of worker in each kind of job—rather than as a single market.

In competitive labor markets, supply and demand set the equilibrium wage, but the wage will differ according to the characteristics of the worker and the nonmonetary advantages of the job.

The Influence of Market Structure

One major reason for wage differences is found in the different types of market in which various groups of labor sell their services. In Chapters 12–14 we distinguished different structures for the markets in which firms sell their outputs. The inputs that firms use are also bought in markets that have different

structures. Although some markets are perfectly competitive, many show monopoly elements on either the demand or the supply side.

To study the influence of different labor-market structures (as well as to keep the analysis simple), we consider in this section the case of an industry that employs only one kind of worker for one kind of job. Furthermore, we assume that all of the workers involved have the same level of skill.

Monopoly: A Union Enters a Competitive Market

For the purposes of our discussion of labor markets, a **union** (or *trade union* or *labor union*) is an association of individual workers that is authorized to represent them in negotiations with their employers. Unions negotiate with individual employers or employers' associations.

Suppose a union enters a competitive labor market to represent all of the workers. As the single seller of labor facing many buyers, the union is a monopoly. If it uses its power, it will negotiate a wage above the competitive level. By doing so it is establishing a minimum wage below which no one will work. This changes the supply curve of labor. The industry can hire as many units of labor as are prepared to work at the union wage but no one at a lower wage. Thus, the industry (and each firm) faces a supply curve that is horizontal at the level of the union wage up to the maximum quantity of labor that is willing to work at that wage.

This is shown in Figure 19-1, where the intersection of this horizontal supply curve and the demand curve establishes a higher wage rate and a lower level of employment than the competitive equilibrium.

There will be a group of workers who would like to obtain work in the industry or occupation but cannot. This presents a problem for the union, which seeks to represent *all* the employees in the industry. A conflict of interest has been created between serving the interests of the union's employed and unemployed members. Pressure to cut the wage rate may develop among the unemployed, but the union must resist this pressure if the higher wage is to be maintained.

An alternative way to achieve the higher wage level *without* the resulting unemployment is to shift the supply curve to the left. The union may do this by restricting entry into the occupation by methods such as lengthening the required period of appren-

FIGURE 19-1   Union Wage Enters a Competitive Labor Market

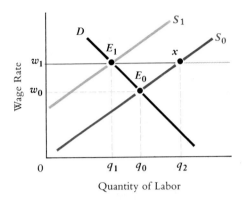

A union can raise the wages of those who continue to be employed in a competitive labor market at the expense of the level of employment. The competitive equilibrium is at E_0, the wage is w_0, and employment is q_0. If a union enters this market and sets a wage of w_1, a new equilibrium will be established at E_1. The supply curve has become $w_1 x S_0$. At the new wage, w_1, there will be $q_1 q_2$ workers who would like to work but whom the industry will not hire. Employment will be q_1. The decrease in employment due to the wage increase is $q_1 q_0$.

The wage w_1 can be achieved without generating a pool of persons who are seeking but unable to find work in the occupation. To do so, the union must restrict entry into the occupation and shift the supply curve to the left to S_1. Employment will be q_1.

This figure also can be used to illustrate the effect of government's imposing a minimum wage of w_1 on the market where the competitive equilibrium is at E_0. The q_1 workers who remain employed benefit by the wage increase. The $q_1 q_0$ workers who lose their jobs in this industry suffer to the extent that they fail to find new jobs at a wage of w_0 or more.

ticeship and reducing openings for trainees. Alternatively, the union may shift the supply curve by persuading the government to impose restrictive licensing or certification requirements on those who would work. Either way, the result is less efficient than is the competitive labor market. Workers who *could* do the work at the competitive wage are not doing it. However, these potential workers in the industry are unable to offer their services at the lower wage because of the entry restrictions.

Raising wages without restricting supply will give rise to a pool of unemployed workers who would like to work in the industry but cannot find jobs. Restricting supply will raise wages without creating a group of workers who are unemployed in the occupation at the going wage.

Raising wages by restricting entry is not, of course, limited to unions. Consider the professions of medicine and law. Because professional standards have long been regarded as necessary to protect the public from incompetent practitioners, doctors and lawyers have found it publicly acceptable to control supply by limiting entry into their professions.

American doctors' incomes are the highest of any American profession, partly because of barriers to entry, including the difficulties of getting into an approved medical school, the high costs of creating new medical schools, and various certification requirements applying to both students and schools.

Lawyers have been less successful in limiting entry into their profession (and thus in achieving high average incomes) because the supply of law schools has increased to meet the increased demand for law school admissions. Graduates of new, and even second-rate, law schools, for the most part, can satisfy certification requirements (often with the aid of "cram schools" for the bar exams) and gain access to the profession.

Monopsony: A Single Buyer in the Market

A **monopsony** is a market where there is only one buyer; it is to the buying side of the market what monopoly is to the selling side of the market. Although pure monopsony is rare, it is not uncommon to see labor markets in which there are only a few firms. Analysis of the case of a pure monopsony can shed considerable light on such cases. Imagine, then, that the firms in an industry form an employers' hiring association in order to act as a single buying unit.

Monopsonistic labor markets in the absence of unions. Suppose that there are many employees and that they are not members of a union. The employers' association can offer any wage rate that it chooses, and the laborers must either work at that rate or find a different job. Suppose that the monopsonist decides to hire some specific quantity of labor. The labor supply curve shows the wage that it must offer. To the monopsonist this wage is the *average cost curve* of labor. In deciding how much labor to hire, however, the monopsonist is interested in the marginal cost of hiring additional workers. The monopsonist wants to know how much its costs will rise if it takes on more labor.

Whenever the supply curve of labor slopes upward, the marginal cost of employing extra units will exceed the average cost. It exceeds the wage paid (the average cost) because the increased wage rate necessary to attract an extra worker must also be paid to *everyone already employed*. [29] For example, assume that 100 workers are employed at $8.00 per hour and that, in order to attract an extra worker, the wage must be raised to $8.01 per hour. The marginal cost of the one-hundred-and-first worker is not the $8.01 per hour paid to the worker, but $9.01 per hour—made up of the extra $.01 per hour paid to the 100 existing workers and $8.01 paid to the new worker. Thus, the marginal cost is $9.01, while the average cost is $8.01.

The profit-maximizing monopsonist will hire labor up to the point where the marginal cost just equals the amount that the firm is willing to pay for an additional unit of labor. That amount is determined by the marginal revenue product of labor and is shown by the demand curve. This is illustrated in Figure 19-2.

Monopsonistic conditions in a labor market will result in a lower level of employment and a lower wage rate than would rule when labor is purchased under competitive conditions.

The common sense of this result is that the monopsonistic employer is aware that by trying to purchase more, it is responsible for driving up the wage. It will, therefore, stop short of the point that is reached when the wages are negotiated by many separate firms, no one of which can exert an influence on the wage rate.

Monopoly versus monopsony: A union in a monopsonistic market. What if a wage-setting union now enters the monopsonistic market and sets a wage below which labor will not work? There will then be no point in the employer's holding off hiring for fear of driving the wage up or of reducing the quantity

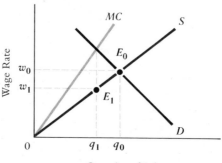

FIGURE 19-2   Monopsony in a Labor Market

A monopsonist lowers both the wage rate and employment below their competitive levels. D and S are the competitive demand and supply curves. In competition equilibrium is at E_0, the wage rate is w_0, and the quantity of labor hired is q_0. The marginal cost of labor (MC) to the monopsonist is above the average cost. The monopsonistic firm will maximize profits at E_1. It will hire only q_1 units of labor. At q_1 the marginal cost of the last worker is just equal to the value to the firm of that worker's output, as shown by the demand curve. The wage that must be paid to get q_1 workers is only w_1.

demanded in the hope of driving the wage rate down. Here, just as in the case of a wage-setting union in a competitive market, the union presents the employer with a horizontal supply curve (up to the maximum number of workers who will accept work at the union wage). As demonstrated in Figure 19-3, the union can raise wages and employment above the monopsonistic level.

Because the union turns the firm into a price taker in the labor market, it can prevent the exercise of the firm's monopsony power and thus raise both wages and employment to the competitive levels.

The union may not be content merely to neutralize the monopsonist's power. It may choose to raise wages further. If it does, the outcome will be similar to that shown in Figure 19-1. If the wage is raised above the competitive level, the employer will no longer wish to hire all the labor that is offered at

FIGURE 19-3 A Union Enters a Monopsonistic Labor Market

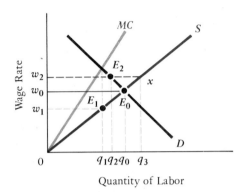

Quantity of Labor

By presenting a monopsonistic employer with a fixed wage, the union can raise both wages and employment over the monopsonistic level. The monopsony position before the union enters is at E_1 (from Figure 19-2), with a wage rate of w_1 and q_1 workers hired. A union now enters and sets the wage at w_0. The supply curve of labor becomes w_0E_0S, and wages and employment rise to their competitive levels of w_0 and q_0 without creating a pool of unemployed workers. If the wage is raised further, say, to w_2, the supply curve will become w_2xS, and the quantity of employment will fall below the competitive level, to q_2, while a pool of unsuccessful job applicants of q_2q_3 will develop.

This figure can also be used to illustrate the effect of the government's imposing a minimum wage of w_0 or w_2 on a monopsonistic labor market.

that wage. The amount of employment will fall, and unemployment will develop. This is also shown in Figure 19-3. Notice, however, that the union can raise wages substantially above the competitive level before employment falls to a level as low as it was in the preunion monopsonistic situation.

Minimum-Wage Laws

When unions set wages for their members, they are in effect setting a minimum wage. Governments can cause similar effects by legislating specific **minimum wages,** that is, wage rates that are the lowest that may legally be offered.

In the United States the federal minimum wage was $3.35 per hour in early 1989. Some industries,

employing about 20 percent of the labor force, are exempt for various reasons from the minimum wage. Of the 80 percent to which the law applies, those in *covered* industries, the minimum wage in 1989 was below the actual market wage for the great majority. In such cases the minimum wage is said to be *not binding.* However, some workers are in occupations or industries in which the free-market wage rate would be below the legal minimum, and there the minimum wage is said to be *binding* or *effective.*

Although minimum wages are an accepted part of the American labor scene, economists view their effects as less obviously beneficial than do many others. To the extent that they are effective, they raise the wages of employed workers. However, as our analysis in Chapter 6 indicated, an effective floor price (which is what a minimum wage is) may well lead to a market surplus—in this case, unemployment. Thus, minimum wages will benefit some groups while it hurts others.

The problem is more complicated than the analysis of Chapter 6 would suggest, both because not all labor markets are competitive and because minimum-wage laws do not cover all employment. Moreover, some groups in the labor force, especially youth and minorities, are affected more than the average worker.

A Comprehensive Minimum Wage

Suppose that minimum-wage laws apply uniformly to all occupations. The occupations and the industries in which minimum wages are effective will be the lowest paying in the country; they usually involve unskilled or at best semiskilled labor. In most of them the workers are not members of unions. Thus, the market structures in which minimum wages are likely to be effective include both those in which competitive conditions pertain and those in which employers exercise monopsony power. The effects on employment of minimum wages are different in the two cases.

Competitive labor markets. The consequences for employment of an effective minimum wage are unambiguous when the labor market is competitive. By raising the wage facing employers, minimum-wage legislation leads to a reduction in the quantity of labor that is demanded and an increase in the quantity of labor that is supplied. As a result the actual level of employment falls, and unemployment is generated. This situation is exactly analogous to the one that arises when a union succeeds in setting a wage above the competitive equilibrium wage, as illustrated in Figure 19-1. The excess supply of labor at the minimum wage also creates incentives for people to evade the law by working below the legal minimum wage.

In competitive labor markets, effective minimum-wage laws raise the wages of those who remain employed but also create some unemployment.

Monopsonistic labor markets.

By effectively flattening out the labor supply curve, the minimum-wage law can simultaneously increase wages and employment in monopsonistic labor markets. The circumstances in which this can be done are the same as those in which a union that is facing a monopsonistic employer succeeds in setting a wage above the wage that the employer would otherwise pay, as shown in Figure 19-3. Of course, if the minimum wage is raised above the competitive wage, employment will start to fall, as in the union case. When it is set at the competitive level, however, the minimum wage can protect the worker against monopsony power *and* lead to increases in employment.

A Noncomprehensive Minimum Wage

In the United States today, about 80 percent of all workers are in industries covered by the minimum wage. The minimum wage is binding for at least some jobs in industries in which there is no monopsony and thus causes some unemployment in the covered sectors. The displaced workers can move to the uncovered sector. If they do, they will increase the supply of labor in the uncovered sector. This will lead to lower wages and increased employment in the uncovered sector.

Overall Effect

Researchers have devoted a great deal of effort to studying the effect of minimum wages on employment. The studies show that the adverse employment effects of minimum wages fall most heavily on those who have the least education and training. This group, which includes many teenagers, women, and blacks, has fewer job opportunities as the wage rate

rises. Many of those affected could have found jobs at lower wages. Estimates of the effect of a 10 percent increase in the minimum wage on teenage unemployment rates vary from about three-quarters of a percentage point to two percentage points. More recent studies find effects at the low end of the range. Even an effect of three-quarters of a percentage point on the unemployment rate is not a small number, but it must be evaluated against an overall teenage unemployment rate of about 20 percent throughout the 1980s. The minimum wage also adversely affects the employment of young adults (aged 20 to 24) but less so. Blacks suffer a disproportionately greater loss of employment due to minimum wages than whites, as do females relative to males.

These job losses could have important long-term effects. Much acquisition of skill occurs on the job. Employees in occupations in which on-the-job training occurs frequently "pay" for their education by receiving low wages in the initial stages of their employment. Minimum-wage legislation makes this more difficult. Instead of being able to "apprentice" in jobs that will lead to productive careers, some workers may become trapped either in unemployment or in low-skill, short-term, or part-time employment. Just how important these effects are in practice is not known.

In Canada several provinces have responded to the employment problems caused by minimum wages by allowing lower minimum wages for young or inexperienced workers and for workers demonstrably in a "learning period."[2] The United States also has a lower minimum wage (85 percent of the general minimum wage) for students, but the provision is rarely used. President Reagan's proposal for a minimum wage for "youth" received little attention during his term of office.

The adverse employment effect is, however, only one element in deciding whether, overall, minimum wages are beneficial or harmful. It is clear that minimum-wage laws raise the incomes of many workers at the very lowest levels of pay. Some of those who benefit most are members of groups that are chronically poor and whom the government is anxious to aid by income redistribution. However, the lowest

---

[2] It may be objected that such exceptions are discriminatory, but, as we saw on page 260, labeling something "discriminatory" does not necessarily mean that it is bad. The argument favoring a minimum wage for youth is that it is better to be employed at a lower wage than unemployed at a higher one.

paid are not the only ones who gain. Because union wage structures maintain differentials between skill classes, an increase in minimum wages also raises wages in many occupations that are already above the minimum.

Thus, there are gainers and losers from minimum-wage laws. Labor-union members as a whole are gainers, as are both white and black adult males. Black and white females and teenagers are net losers, because the loss of earnings resulting from less employment is larger than the gains resulting from higher wage rates. Of course, there are gainers and losers within each group. The losers are the ones without jobs; the gainers are those who receive higher wages than they otherwise would. Again, recent empirical work on the subject tends to suggest that the distributional effects of the minimum wage, like the employment effects, are fairly small. A review article by Charles Brown, reviewing the literature on minimum wages, concludes that "the minimum wage is overrated: by its critics as well as its supporters."[3]

Given its mixed economic effects, support for and opposition to the minimum wage may best be understood as arising largely from political and sociological motives. Organized labor has consistently pressed for a broad, relatively high minimum wage. There is some economic reason for this, in that there is evidence that the minimum wage "trickles up" to higher wage workers, both unionized and not. Arguably, however, the support dates back to the 1930s, when organized labor was still fighting for its position in American society. Enactment of a minimum wage was then a great political victory, and the minimum wage still has symbolic significance.

The Nature and Evolution of Modern Labor Unions

Unions today represent only about 14 percent of the workers in the private sector and less than 20 percent of all workers, but union influence is greater than these percentages suggest. One reason is the impact that union wage contracts have on other labor mar-

kets. When, for example, the United Auto Workers negotiate a new contract, its provisions set a pattern that directly or indirectly affects other labor markets, both in Michigan and in many other industrial states. A second reason is the major leadership role that unions have played in the last 50 years in the development of labor-market practices and in lobbying for legislation that applies to all workers.

Labor-Market Institutions

The process by which unions and employers (or their representatives) arrive at and enforce their agreements is known as **collective bargaining.** This process has an important difference from the theoretical models with which we began this chapter. There we assumed that the union set the wage and the employer decided how much labor to hire. In collective bargaining the wage is negotiated. In terms of Figure 19-3, it may be that the employer wants the wage to be w_1 and the union wants the wage to be w_2. Depending on each side's market power and bargaining strength, the final wage that is agreed upon may be anywhere in between. In collective bargaining there is usually a substantial range over which an agreement can be reached, and the actual result in particular cases will depend on the strengths of the two bargaining parties and on the skill of their negotiators.

Unions today are an accepted part of economic life, especially in manufacturing industries and in much of government service. It was not always so. Within the lifetime of many of today's members, unions were fighting for their lives, and union organizers and members were risking theirs. In the 1930s the labor movement evoked the loyalties and passions of people as a great liberal cause in ways that seem quite extraordinary today. Indeed, some unions today appear to many as conservative (even reactionary) groups of hard hats. Why and how did the change come about?

The Development of American Labor Unions

Trade unionism had its origin in the pitifully low wages and brutal working conditions in nineteenth century factories. Box 19-1 provides a vivid picture

[3] For this and much of the preceding discussion, see Charles Brown, "Minimum Wage Laws: Are They Overrated?" *J. Econ. Perspectives,* Summer 1988.

BOX 19-1

Factory Life in the United States, 1903

Stories of workers' very real suffering during the Industrial Revolution and the years that followed could fill many volumes, but an example will at least illustrate some of the horrors that lay behind the drive for change and reform.

In the worst days of cotton-milling in England the conditions were hardly worse than those now existing in the South. Children—the tiniest and frailest—of five and six years of age rise in the morning and, like old men and women, go to the mills to do their day's labor; and when they return home, they wearily fling themselves on their beds, too tired to take off their clothes. Many children work all night—"in the maddening racket of the machinery, in an atmosphere insanitary and clouded with humidity and lint." It will be long before I forget the face of a little boy of six years, with his hands stretched forward to rearrange a bit of machinery, his pallid face and spare form showing already the physical effects of labor. This child, six years of age, was working twelve hours a day in a country which has established in many industries an eight-hour day for men. The twelve-hour day is almost universal in the South, and about twenty-five thousand children are now employed on twelve-hour shifts in the mills of the various Southern states. The wages of one of these children, however large, could not compensate the child for the injury this monstrous and unnatural labor does him; but the pay which the child receives is not enough, in many instances, even to feed him properly. If the children fall ill, they are docked for loss of time. . . . The mill-hands confess that they hate the mills, and no one will wonder at it. A vagrant who had worked in a textile mill for sixteen years once said to a friend of mine: "I done that [and he made a motion with his hand] for sixteen years. At last I was sick for two or three days with a fever, and when I crawled out, I made up my mind that I would rather go to hell than go back to the mill."*

* The quotation comes from *Poverty,* by Robert Hunter, published in 1904.

of factory conditions at the turn of the twentieth century. Out of these conditions and other grievances of working men and women came the full range of radical political movements. Out of the same conditions also came an American form of collective action called **bread-and-butter unionism,** whose goals are higher wages and better working conditions rather than political reform.

The early industrial organizer saw that 10 or 100 employees acting together had more influence than one acting alone and dreamed of the day when all would stand solid against the employer. (The word *solidarity* occurs often in the literature and songs of the labor movement.) However, employers did not sit by idly; they, too, knew that in union there was strength. "Agitators" who tried to organize workers were fired and blacklisted; in some cases they were beaten and killed.

The union movement showed its first real power among small groups of relatively skilled workers. Why? First, it was easier to control the supply of skilled workers than unskilled ones; employers could easily find replacements when unskilled labor threatened to strike. But skilled workers—the coopers (barrel makers), the boot makers, the shipwrights—controlled access to their trades by means of apprenticeships. The original craft unions were, in effect, *closed shops:* One had to belong to the union to hold a job in the craft, and the union set the rules of admission.

Second, employers were often vulnerable to the demands of a union of workers whose skills might be indispensable to the production process.

Third, because labor in a particular skilled occupation is likely to account for a relatively low proportion of total costs, the effect on the employer's overall costs of giving in to a small group's demand for a wage increase is likely to be small. The difficulty of substituting other factors for skilled labor and a relatively small contribution to total costs combined to create an inelastic demand. This gave the unions of skilled workers an advantage in fighting the employer that was not enjoyed by other groups of workers.

The New Deal: 1933–1945. In the 1930s the Great Depression created a climate of public opinion that was openly hostile to big business and tolerant of labor. These attitudes led to passage of the Wagner Act (1935), which guaranteed the *right* of workers to organize and to elect, by secret ballot, an exclusive bargaining agent. This provided unions with the ability to control the supply of even unskilled labor.

The unions won—first by force and even violence and finally by law—the right to form unions in order to articulate their grievances and to bargain in order to relieve them.

After World War II. Since 1950 union membership has declined steadily as a percentage of the labor force. The major reason is the absence of employment growth in traditionally unionized industries and in industries with large concentrations of employees. The exception is government employment, which in 1986 was 36 percent unionized. The growing service sector, however, is one of the least unionized in the country, with only about 6 percent of all employees unionized in 1986.

The main development in the nature of unionization over the last three decades—besides the steady decline in the proportion of workers covered—has been the stabilizing of union-management relations in industry after industry. Strikes still occur and always will, but the number and the duration of strikes today are relatively minor compared with the 1930s and late 1940s. In 1985 major strikes led to only one-seventh the loss in work time (adjusting for the size of the economy) of strikes in 1948.

Objectives of Modern Unions

Unions seek many goals when they bargain with management. They may push for higher wages, higher fringe benefits, more stable employment, or less onerous working conditions. Whatever their specific goals, they must deal with a fundamental dilemma, except when they face a monopsonist across the bargaining table. This is an inherent conflict between the level of wages and the size of the union itself.

The more successful a union is in raising wages, the more management will attempt to reduce the size of its work force, substituting capital for labor. This will lead to lower union membership. On the other hand, if the union does not provide some wage improvement for its members, they will have little incentive to stay around.

Wages Versus High Employment— The Fundamental Dilemma

Different unions deal with the conflict between wages and employment differently. The United Mine Workers employed a high-wage, shrinking-employment strategy for decades, and both employment and union membership declined. The longshoremen's union has achieved high wages, but it chooses to ration the available jobs among its members rather than to reduce its membership. It thus spreads the underemployment around. In the garment trades the demand for labor is relatively elastic, and in order to protect the employment of their members, the major unions traditionally have avoided pushing for big wage increases.

Growing competition for American manufactured goods from foreign production has led to a new recognition among major American industrial unions that high wages and high levels of layoffs and unemployment of their members often go hand in hand. Major unions in such industries as automobiles, steel, rubber, smelting, and airlines have accepted wage increases below the increases in the cost of living; many have even agreed to significant reductions in wages and other benefits under existing contracts. They did so in order to prevent further plant closings and to encourage the rehiring of unemployed union workers.

Wages versus employment poses a long-term problem as well as a short-term one. Unionization and rising wages in fruit picking have led to mechanization and a drop in the demand for labor. In the auto industry the traditional high-wage policy encouraged the major manufacturers to increase automation. There were 200,000 fewer jobs in the auto industry in 1987 than there had been 10 years earlier for about the same level of production.

The fundamental dilemma of choosing between high wages and high employment is splitting many unions and dividing the American labor movement. Barely one-half of the auto workers at General Motors approved a contract containing wage concessions by the union, despite intense lobbying for the contract by the union's leaders. Given seniority rules, it is not hard to guess which half voted yes.

Not all unions are acting in the same way. While the steel, auto, and many other industries are trying to preserve jobs, the electrical workers are resolutely refusing to do so, and employment in this field is shrinking.

Job security. One method of seeking job security is through *seniority rules* that require employers to lay off and to rehire on the basis of years of service. This protects existing workers, and many unions have been willing to accept lower wages in order to build seniority provisions into their contracts.

A second method of seeking job security is to resist the introduction of labor-saving innovations. During a period of heavy unemployment, the installation of a labor-saving machine in a factory is likely to mean unemployment for those whose jobs are lost by the change. It is little wonder that during and after the Great Depression new machines were opposed bitterly and that job-saving restrictive practices were adhered to with tenacity.

In the long run, however, this strategy cannot work. Mechanization increases productivity and consequently the wages and profits that are earned. After World War II the attitude of many unions slowly changed from one of resisting technological change to one of collaborating with it and trying to reduce some of its costs to individuals who would be adversely affected by it.

The 1980s saw a major change in union attitudes toward job security. Many of the current generation of leaders see the increased mechanization of Japanese, Korean, and German firms, rather than their own employers, as the principal threat to union workers' jobs. Improving the ability of American employers to compete with foreign firms is now one way in which unions attempt to increase job security for their members.

Fringe benefits. Indirect or **fringe benefits,** such as company contributions to union pension and welfare funds, sick leave, and vacation pay, as well as required payments toward social security and unemployment compensation insurance, are estimated to make up almost one-third of the total compensation of industrial workers. Why do unions and employers not simply agree to a wage and let it go at that? Why should the average employed automobile worker who earns $25,000 cost the company $40,000?

Fringe benefits appeal to employees in part because they are not subject to income taxes. Pension funds and medical benefits let employees provide for their future and that of their families more cheaply than they could by purchasing them privately, and these benefits often protect them even when they lose their jobs. A package that includes high wages and job security for the employed and unemployment benefits for those squeezed out by high wages appeals to union leaders because it provides something for everyone.

The use of fringe benefits also offers some advantages to employers. For example, pension funds tend to bind the worker more closely to the company, thereby decreasing the turnover rate among employees. If employees stand to lose part of their benefits by changing jobs, they will not be so ready to move.

Two-tier pricing. A recent innovation that is designed to resolve the wage-employment dilemma for the present generation of union members is called *two-tier pricing*. The objective of a two-tier wage structure is to protect the high wages of existing employees who have seniority in their unions but at the same time to permit employers to lower their labor costs by hiring new workers on a lower wage scale. This benefits the union—so goes the argument—because it assures the union that there will be a flow of new members who would otherwise not be hired. It benefits new employees *if* they would not otherwise have been hired, and it does not hurt the existing union members. In many cases, however, two-tier pricing has led to significant friction between workers in the two tiers. It also encourages management to replace old workers with new ones.

Discrimination in Labor Markets

There have been, and continue to be, large differences between the earnings of nonwhites and whites and between women and men. If we create an index of median wage and salary earnings with white males equal to 100, then black males today equal about 63, white females equal about 52, and black females equal about 51. These disparities in earnings have multiple causes, but they raise a concern about the existence of labor-market discrimination and the extent to which discriminatory employment practices give rise to the differences in earnings.

The first major labor-discrimination lawsuit was settled in 1973 when AT&T paid $15 million in back pay and an additional $23 million per year in raises to women and minority males against whom it had allegedly discriminated in job assignments, pay, and promotions. Since then, such suits and settlements have become commonplace. Coal companies have paid fines for denying women access to high-paying underground jobs. The construction industry has agreed to quotas for black workers to remedy the past exclusion of blacks from a variety of occupations. These lawsuits and settlements focus on what many had long suspected—that discrimination by race and by sex often has occurred in the American job market.

The economic effects of discrimination against minorities and women take many forms. Labor-market discrimination does not wholly explain, but it surely contributes to, lower wages and higher unemployment rates for those discriminated against. Both lower wages and greater unemployment lead to lower incomes for the workers involved.

Discrimination also may have powerful indirect effects on attitudes toward the work place and toward society. It affects not only the workers discriminated against but also their children, whose ability, aspirations, and willingness to undertake the education or training required to "succeed" may be adversely affected. Indeed, it may change their definition of success. There are many subtle ways in which discrimination can become part of the way in which a society functions, and these can be as important in their effects as overt (and now generally illegal) direct discrimination.

The problems of racial discrimination and sex discrimination are different from each other, but there are similarities as well as differences. It is helpful to look first at how either kind of discrimination leads to important economic effects.

A Model of Labor-Market Discrimination

To isolate the effects of discrimination, we begin by building a simplified picture of a nondiscriminating labor market and then we introduce discrimination between two sets of equally qualified workers. We phrase our discussion in terms of two artificial groups. One is called "stars," for the stars that appear on their foreheads at birth; the other is called "stripes," for an analogous reason. The analysis, however, applies to any situation in which workers are distinguished on any grounds other than their ability, such as female and male, black and white, alien and citizen, Catholic and Protestant.

Suppose that, except for the fact that half of the people are marked with stars and the other half are marked with stripes, the groups are the same; each has the same number of members, the same proportion who are educated to various levels, an identical distribution of talent, and so on. Suppose also that there are two occupations. Occupation E (for elite) requires people of above average education and skills, and occupation O (ordinary) can use anyone. If wages in the two occupations are the same, employers in occupation O will prefer to hire the above average worker. Finally, suppose that the nonmonetary advantages of the two occupations are equal.

In the absence of discrimination, the labor markets that we are studying are competitive. The theory of competitive factor markets suggests that the wages in E occupations will be bid up above those in O occupations in order that the E jobs attract the workers of above average skills. Stars and stripes of above average skill will take the E jobs, while the others, both stars and stripes, will have no choice but to seek O jobs. Because skills are equally distributed, each occupation will employ one-half stars and one-half stripes.

Now we introduce discrimination in its most extreme form. All E occupations are hereafter open only to stars; all O occupations are hereafter open to either stars or stripes. The immediate effect is to reduce by 50 percent the supply of job candidates for E occupations; candidates must now be *both* stars and above average. The discrimination also increases the supply of applicants for O jobs by 50 percent; this group now includes all stripes and the below average stars.

Wage Level Effects

Suppose that labor is perfectly mobile among occupations, that everyone seeks the best job that he or she is eligible for, and that wage rates are free to vary so as to equate supply and demand. The analysis is shown in Figure 19-4. Wages rise in E occupations and fall in O occupations. The take-home pay of those in O occupations falls, and the O group is now approximately two-thirds stripes.

FIGURE 19-4   Economic Discrimination: Wage Level Effects

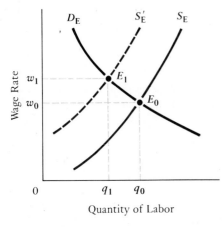

(i) Elite market (E)

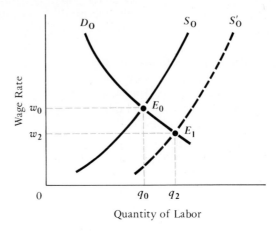

(ii) Ordinary market (O)

If market E discriminates against one group and market O does not, the supply curve will shift to the left in E and to the right in O. Market E requires above average skills, while market O requires only ordinary skills. When there is no discrimination, demands and supplies are D_E and S_E in market E, and D_O and S_O in market O. Initially, the wage rate is represented by w_0 and employment by q_0 in each market. (The actual wage in market E will be slightly higher than the wage in market O.) When all stripes are barred from E occupations, the supply curve shifts to S_E', and the wage earned by the remaining workers, all of whom are stars, rises to w_1. Stripes put out of work in the E occupation now seek work in the O occupation. The resulting shift in the supply curve to S_O' brings down the wage to w_2 in the O occupations. Since all stripes are in O occupations, they have a lower wage rate than many stars. The average star wage is higher than the average stripe wage.

Discrimination, by changing supply, can decrease the wages and incomes of a group that is discriminated against.

In the longer run, further changes may occur. Notice that total employment in the E industries falls. Employers may find ways to utilize slightly below average labor and thus lure the next best qualified stars out of O occupations. While this will raise O wages slightly, it will also make these occupations increasingly "stripe occupations." If discrimination has been in effect for a sufficient length of time, stripes will learn that it does not pay to acquire above average skills. Regardless of ability, stripes are forced by discrimination to work in unskilled jobs.

Now suppose that a long-standing discriminatory policy is reversed. Because they will have responded to discrimination by acquiring fewer skills than stars,

many stripes will be locked into the O occupations, at least for a time. Moreover, if both stars and stripes come to expect that stripes will have less education than stars, employers will tend to look for stars to fill the E jobs. This will reinforce the belief of stripes that education does not pay. This, and other kinds of subtle discrimination, can persist for a very long time, making the supply of stripes to O jobs higher than it would be in the absence of discrimination, thus depressing the wages of stripes.

Discrimination in competitive labor markets. We have seen that in the absence of discrimination, competitive markets will tend to equalize the wages of the two groups. Some economists go further than this and argue that in equilibrium discrimination cannot be sustained. This theory, propounded by Professors Gary Becker of the University of Chicago and

Thomas Sowell of the Hoover Institution, works like this: Employers of workers in E jobs who pay high wages (w_1) can increase their profits if they hire qualified stripes at any lower wage. If stripes have the same distribution of qualifications as stars, under discrimination there will be plenty of workers who will be willing to work in E jobs at any wage that is greater than the low wage level in the O market (w_2)—much less than the going wage for stars. If some employers take advantage of this opportunity, there will be competitive pressure that, all other things being equal, works against the maintenance of discrimination. As firms who hire qualified stripes at wages below w_1 (but above w_2) earn profits, they will grow, and other firms will have to imitate them or go out of business. Eventually, the discrimination will disappear in competitive equilibrium.

This theory shows the important pressures that act against discrimination in competitive markets. The idea, however, that competitive equilibrium is completely inconsistent with the practice of discrimination fails to take into account a number of important phenomena. One of these is the indirect effect of discrimination on both the acquisition of skill and on the expectations of employers. Further, the taste for discrimination, presumably arising in part from a dislike of stripes on the part of stars, will inhibit at least some firms from maximizing profits if doing so requires breaking social norms that reinforce discrimination. It is also possible that tastes for discrimination will have direct market effects. For example, consumers who dislike stripes may refrain from buying the products of firms that employ stripes in E occupations; prejudiced workers may be less productive if stripes are treated as equal in the work place. In any event, the history of both race and sex discrimination in the U.S. economy suggests that whatever competitive forces do work against discrimination, they are not strong enough to *eliminate* it.

Employment Effects

For a number of reasons, labor-market discrimination may have adverse employment effects that are even more important than effects on wage levels. Labor is not perfectly mobile; wages are not perfectly flexible downward; and not everyone who is denied employment in an E occupation for which he or she is trained and qualified will be willing to take a "de-

meaning" O job. We continue the graphical example in Figure 19-5.

If wages do not fall to the market-clearing level, possibly because of minimum-wage laws, the increase in supply of labor to O occupations will cause excess supply, which will result in unemployment in O occupations. Since stripes dominate these occupations, stripes will bear the brunt of the extra unemployment, as illustrated in Figure 19-5(i).

A similar result will occur if labor is not fully mobile between occupations. For example, many of the O occupation jobs might be in places to which the stripes are unable or unwilling to move. (Discrimination in housing markets may be one reason for this.) See Figure 19-5(ii). Potential O workers who cannot move to places where jobs are available become unemployed or withdraw from the labor force. Quite apart from any discrimination, long-term technological changes tend to decrease the demand for less skilled labor of the kind that is required in O occupations. Occupation O then becomes increasingly oversupplied. This possibility is outlined in Figure 19-5(iii).

The kind of discrimination that we have considered in our model is extreme. It is similar to the South African apartheid system, in which blacks are excluded by law from prestigious and high-paying occupations. In the United States, labor-market discrimination against a particular group usually occurs in somewhat less obvious ways. First, it may be difficult (but not impossible, as in our model) for members of the group to get employment in certain jobs. Second, members of groups subject to discrimination may receive lower pay for a given kind of work than do members of groups not subject to discrimination.

Indeed, the first type of discrimination may encourage the second type! How might this happen? First, if discrimination makes it difficult for a qualified person to get a good job, she may be more willing to accept such a job even if the pay and working conditions are poorer than those given to others in the same job. Even under relatively unfavorable terms, the job will still be better than the alternative (an O job). Second, employers who are seeking to fill E jobs and who have no taste for discrimination nonetheless will be able to hire qualified stripes at wages that, although higher than O wages, are lower than E wages. As long as there is some discrimination of the first type (in the extreme,

FIGURE 19-5   Economic Discrimination: Employment Effects

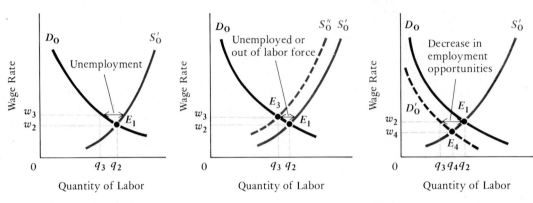

(i) Wage rigidities (or minimum wage)

(ii) Immobile labor (or withdrawal from labor force)

(iii) Declining demand

Increasing supply or decreasing demand in occupations in which those discriminated against are the major sources of labor can increase unemployment. In each part of the diagram the curves D_O and S_O' are those from Figure 19-4(ii); they show the market for O workers after the discriminatory policies are put into effect. Equilibrium is at E_1. In each case the wage w_2 would clear the market and provide employment of q_2.

(i) If the wage rate cannot fall below w_3, perhaps because of a minimum-wage law, employment will fall to q_3, and unemployment will occur in the amount shown by the arrows.

(ii) If some of the potential workers in O occupation are unable or unwilling to take employment in O jobs, the supply curve will not be S_O' but S_O''. Equilibrium will be at E_3. While O wages will rise somewhat to w_3, employment will be only q_3, and a number of workers, shown by the arrows, will not be employed. Whether they are recorded as "unemployed" or as having withdrawn from the labor force will depend on the official definitions.

(iii) If demand is declining in O occupations over time, say, from D_O to D_O', either wages and employment will fall to the new equilibrium E_4 with w_4 and q_4, or wages will be maintained but employment will fall to q_3. The arrows illustrate the latter case, where the fall in employment is q_3q_2.

apartheid), there will be pressures coming from both the supply and the demand sides of the labor market for discrimination of the second type.

These theoretical possibilities have their counterparts in the real world. We shall discuss them briefly with respect to both black-white and female-male differences in the United States.

Black-White Differentials

The differences in employment and pay rates for blacks and for whites are dramatic. During the mid-1980s, after more than two decades of vigorous equal employment activity, the median black family had earnings that were only 60 percent as high as those of the median white family. This figure reflects fewer

jobs, lower-paying jobs, more frequent part-time employment, and the fact that the proportion of black families that are headed by women is much higher than that for white families. Women, in turn, have fewer jobs, lower-paying jobs, and more frequent part-time employment than men, both black and white.

Unemployment among blacks normally runs at more than twice the level for whites—roughly 11.5 percent to 5 percent in relatively good times—and in sharp recessions the ratio increases. This pattern applies consistently to different age groups. Black teenagers (age 16–19) have unemployment rates of over 40 percent, whereas white teenagers have unemployment rates of about 20 percent. When black males aged 45–49 have an unemployment rate of 7 percent, the rate for white males of the same age is only 4 percent. Wage rates for black males average about 73 percent of those for white males. For women, the black-white differential in wages essentially has vanished, but, as we shall see later, women of both races have much lower wages than men.

We emphasize that we are talking here about averages. What is true for a group on average is not necessarily true for each individual in a group. Many blacks are highly successful economically by any standard. For example, the median income of black families that were headed by a married couple in which at least one adult was a full-time worker was almost $37,000 in 1987, 87 percent of the level for white families with the same characteristics. Moreover, this ratio has been rising more or less steadily since 1940.

Overall, there are many millions of blacks who do as well as or better than many whites in both employment and wages. Indeed, in 1987 over one-quarter of all black families had higher incomes than the median white family. In 1940 this was true of only 8 percent of black families. There is tremendous variation in the economic circumstances of black households, and there has been enormous progress since the 1940s. However, although many blacks have higher incomes than many whites, *most* blacks still have lower incomes than *most* whites.

Employed blacks are often disadvantaged relative to whites. Blacks tend to have less seniority than whites of similar ages, often because of past discrimination. The seniority that they do have tends to be in the less skilled, lower-paying job categories. A white man is more than twice as likely as a black man to have a managerial job. The odds are reversed for laborers.[4] Blacks as a group have poorer health, shorter life expectancies, and shorter working lives.

All of these characteristics contribute to lower economic status, but not all of them necessarily represent direct racial discrimination. Many of the disadvantages remain even when there is equal pay for equal work. Whites and blacks have, on average, different educational backgrounds and different sorts of professional or vocational training. Since these, too, affect employment opportunities and actual pay

rates within occupations, is it possible that they, rather than current discrimination, account for the differentials?

In trying to answer this question it is important to note that discrimination might be present, not only directly (e.g., refusing to hire blacks because they are black), but also indirectly. An example of indirect discrimination would be refusing to hire blacks who are not well trained, when training has been denied to them because they are black, or only hiring blacks for poor jobs, again because they have a lack of training.

The Effects of Discrimination

Direct discrimination has decreased during the last 35 years. For example, direct employment discrimination against black athletes ended during that period, and federal laws have resulted in equal pay for equal work in many industrial jobs. Blatant discrimination survives, however, in some occupations, and a preference for whites still exists in many others. One example was reported in the *Wall Street Journal* on October 18, 1988. According to the article, 8 of the most popular 10 athletes in 1987 were black, but 9 of the 10 athletes with the largest compensation for endorsing products were white.

One way in which we can try to measure direct discrimination is to use statistical techniques to estimate how much blacks would earn if they had the same characteristics, such as experience, education, industry, and region of employment, as whites. A recent study that did this found that the black-white earnings ratio for men would have been 0.86 in 1981 had blacks had the same characteristics as whites. The actual ratio was 0.73. This implies that about one-half of the difference between blacks and whites can be explained by differences in background. The other half (about $.14 on the dollar) can be interpreted as the effects of direct discrimination.[5]

The same study also provides us with a very rough way to estimate the effect of indirect discrimination. Differences in characteristics account for about 13 percentage points of the earnings differential between black and white males. Many of these differences in characteristics, but probably not all of them, arise from indirect discrimination. This sug-

[4] For a detailed study of the importance of race to social and economic measures, see Reynolds Farley and Walter Allen, *The Color Line and the Quality of Life in America* (New York: Russell Sage, 1987).

[5] Daniel S. Hamemesh and Albert Rees, *The Economics of Work and Pay,* 4th ed. (New York: Harper & Row, 1988), p. 360.

gests that the 13 percentage points are a maximum estimate of the effect of indirect discrimination on *employed* black males. Of course, both direct and indirect discrimination are one reason that black males are less likely to be in the labor force than white males, and there are still no estimates of this effect. The total effect of indirect discrimination could thus be larger.

The Effects of Age and Education

At every level of education, black-white wage differentials for men are lowest for the youngest age groups. Moreover, for every age group, the differentials are generally lower the higher is the level of education.[6] The first finding is probably due in part to indirect discrimination, which can be expected to play a greater role for older workers. After all, many of today's older workers began their careers during a period when the most blatant direct discrimination was legal. That apparent discrimination is less for the most educated groups could be due to any of a variety of reasons. One possibility is that employers' prejudices about blacks' abilities are more difficult to sustain, the greater is the level of employees' education.

In light of the positive role that education plays in reducing labor-market discrimination, it is troubling that rates of college attendance for blacks declined throughout the 1980s. The causes are not clear. One explanation is that the amount of financial aid that was targeted for blacks fell at about the same time that the rates of college attendance for blacks started to fall.[7]

Both direct and indirect discrimination against blacks are still important forces in the labor market. Moreover, even if all direct discrimination were to vanish, the effects of indirect discrimination would be felt for generations to come. Were all direct discrimination to end today, blacks on average would still have fewer skills and less experience than whites. They would thus have lower incomes, which would place them at a disadvantage in acquiring more skills and education. They would, on average, still live in

[6] James P. Smith and Finis R. Welch, *Closing the Gap* (Santa Monica, CA: The Rand Corporation, 1986); Hamemesh and Rees, op. cit., Table 13.3.

[7] Robert Hauser, "College Entry Among Black High School Graduates: Family Income Does Not Explain the Decline." Center for Demography and Ecology Working Paper 87–19. Madison, WI: University of Wisconsin, 1987.

segregated neighborhoods, often in areas of relatively low incomes and thus of relatively low budgets for schools. Again, discrimination, in both housing and labor markets, is part of the cause.

Female-Male Differentials

In 1987, the median earned income of women who earned income was 53 percent of the median income of men who earned income. Women are more likely than men to work part-time; when we look only at year-round, full-time workers, the ratio of median incomes rises, but only to 65 percent. Wages of females tend to be only about two-thirds those of males. The "salary gap" for females is due to a combination of causes: Women are underrepresented in high-paying occupations; proportionately fewer women than men reach higher-paying jobs in the occupations in which both work; and those who do reach higher-paying jobs do so more slowly. To what extent do these facts reflect discrimination?

Discrimination within occupations. To what extent do differences in pay levels of men and women *within* an occupation reflect direct discrimination against women, and to what extent do they reflect other sex-linked characteristics, the most important of which is the persistent difference in lifetime patterns of labor force participation? The statistics show that, on average, women have fewer years of work experience than men of the same age. The average working female is less mobile occupationally and geographically than her male counterpart. These facts reflect, at least in part, *labor-market attachment*. For example, many women withdraw from the labor force or work only part-time, in order to have and raise children.

The causes of gender differences in labor-market attachment have attracted attention from both social psychologists and from economists. There is ample evidence that *sex role socialization* is an important factor. To the extent that women and men are socialized to accept the view that women should be the primary caretakers of young children, some social scientists argue that differences in labor-force attachment arise from a form of indirect discrimination. However important this may be, it arises from differences in the way in which boys and girls are raised, not from the direct behavior of the labor market.

The extent of direct discrimination in an occupation may be measured by comparing the pay status of groups with similar characteristics. Professors Mary Corcoran and Greg Duncan analyzed pay differences between men and women and found that less than half (44 percent) of the differences could be explained by differences in education, work experience, and labor-market attachment. Other studies show much the same thing and conclude that from 10 to 25 percentage points of the pay differences are *not* explained by these variables. Analysts attribute this part of male-female pay differentials to direct discrimination.

Interoccupational discrimination. Women may tend to be employed in a different set of occupations from men. They have been refused admission, or have been discouraged from seeking entry into, certain occupations; for example, traditionally they have been urged into nursing rather than into medicine, social work rather than law, and secretarial schools rather than managerial training programs. The result of this is called *occupational segregation*. Similarly, girls who have been raised in a culture in which their education seems less important than that of their brothers or in which they are trained to think of themselves as potential homemakers are less likely to acquire the skills for many high-paying occupations that are wholly within their capabilities. This is a form of the sex role socialization that we discussed earlier.

Differences in pay among occupations reflect, as we have seen, differences in supply and demand, including nonmonetary factors. May they not also reflect discrimination, if one occupation is predominantly female and the other predominantly male? This is certainly possible, and a number of studies have shown that such an effect exists; that is, if one uses the characteristics of workers (education, training, experience, etc.) to explain their wages, the fraction of female workers in the occupation has a significant, negative effect. Moreover, this effect exists for both men and women. Men (and women) who work in predominantly female occupations are paid less than men (and women) with the same training and experience in predominantly male occupations. For this reason, many have urged that attention be paid to interoccupational pay differences under the general term "pay equity." Determining how much observed differences reflect discrimination is extremely difficult, because so many different consid-erations affect the pay levels of, say, fire fighters and librarians. A particular (but controversial) approach to this problem, called *comparable worth,* is discussed in Box 19-2.

Progress Against Discrimination

Laws that prohibit discrimination in pay and in employment have been in effect since the early 1960s. The civil rights and women's movements have been active during the intervening years. How much progress has been made? The answer is mixed and subject to continuing debate.

Consider male-female differences. Women's labor-force participation rates have increased steadily, from only about 35 percent during the late 1950s to over 55 percent during the late 1980s; labor-force participation of adult males declined from 86 to 78 percent during the same period. Moreover, unemployment rates are only slightly higher for women than for men. Thus, differences in ability to get and to hold some kind of a job have plainly been reduced, but the gap in pay has not. Partly this is the effect of differences in pay levels within occupations, partly of the continued segregation of women in lower-paying occupations, and partly of the fact that women, largely as a result of their role in child rearing, have, on average, less experience and on-the-job training than men of the same age and education.

The black-white picture is also mixed. On wages, blacks have made progress relative to whites, but the unemployment rate for blacks remains at more than twice the rate for whites. Moreover, labor-force participation of black males has dropped somewhat more than labor-force participation of white males, with the difference probably reflecting withdrawal from the labor-force of many blacks after long bouts of unemployment. At the same time, the labor-force participation rate for black women has been rising. Thus, black males have been substantially less successful than women in improving their access to jobs, although they have been substantially more successful in reducing discriminatory wage differences.

It is hard to characterize all of these differences, and we will not attempt to do so. Plainly, the way in which both indirect and direct discrimination work is different for blacks and women. This should not be surprising. For one thing, blacks and whites typically are segregated in childhood, both in their residences and in their schools, whereas boys and

BOX 19-2

Comparable Worth

In 1983 a U.S. District Court judge ruled that the state of Washington had violated the Civil Rights Act of 1964 and had discriminated on the basis of sex when it paid (predominantly female) practical nurses $739 per month and (predominantly male) campus police $1,070 per month. The ruling led to retroactive pay increases that cost the state $800 million. Perhaps more important, it gave a big boost to the notion that an occupational yardstick, called *comparable worth,* could be used to evaluate sex discrimination.

The objective in measuring comparable worth is to measure the *intrinsic* value of different occupations so as to judge whether job A is worth more than job B. One method assigns each occupation "worth points" in four categories, based on interviews by a team of experts: (1) knowledge and skills, (2) mental demands, (3) accountability, and (4) working conditions. Two occupations with comparable point totals are classified as of comparable value. Methods like this have long been used to determine pay scales within large organizations, in both the public and the private sectors. In Minnesota the results of such a calculation showed that librarians and fire fighters were of approximately comparable worth. Since librarians (mostly female) earned less than fire fighters (mostly male), the conclusion was that discrimination had occurred.

Comparable Worth Versus Supply and Demand

Consider a situation in which pay differentials are not discriminatory but reflect instead equilibrium differentials in a competitive market economy.

Suppose that two groups of city employees, call them librarians and fire fighters, have the supply and demand curves that are shown in the figure below. In competitive equilibrium librarians would earn a wage w_1, and fire fighters, a wage w_2; that is, there is an equilibrium differential in the market-clearing wages. Now, as a result of a study of

comparable worth, the city is ordered to pay equal wages to the two groups.

The mayor proposes to comply by paying both groups a compromise wage, w_c, which is somewhat higher than the wage that librarians have been receiving but lower than the current wage that fire fighters have been receiving. Librarians are pleased, and, indeed, the mayor begins to get extra applications from persons who seek to be librarians once the new wage goes into effect. (There is an excess supply of librarians, q_1q_2, at w_c.) But the head of the fire fighters' union is burned up: "You can't cut our pay. We'll quit." Indeed, some of the fire fighters do quit. (At wage w_c there is excess demand of q_3q_4.) The fire chief warns the mayor that he won't be able to fill the firehouse or meet all the calls for putting out fires. The mayor decides to go back to the court with her dilemma. The judge is unsympathetic: "All your problems come from the proposed cut in fire fighters' pay. You may pay anything you like to fire fighters; just be sure to pay the librarians the same."

The mayor then tells the city compensation director to raise the librarians' pay to w_2, the fire fighters' competitive rate.

In order to meet the extra wage bill, the city council orders that libraries be closed two days per week and lays off some librarians. While the fire fighters do not complain, the librarians who have been laid off do, and so do the citizens who want

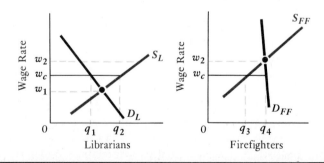

the libraries open on Fridays and Saturdays. Meanwhile, the head of the libraries is besieged with applications for the newly attractive library jobs.

In the preceding example, the problem might have been avoided had a different evaluation mechanism been used. However, it is easy to think of cases where even the best evaluation systems would not prevent conflict between comparable worth and market equilibrium. One such example comes from Professor Sharon Smith. She has pointed out that under any plausible evaluation scheme a French-English and a Spanish-English translator would score about the same. Yet it is highly likely that in, say, Miami both the supply and the demand for Spanish-English translators would be greater, with uncertain effects on the equilibrium wage. Attributing any wage difference to discrimination would be incorrect, and eliminating it through comparable worth would only cause problems of excess supply (or demand) of one type of translator or the other.

The Australian Experience

In the United States comparable worth is usually proposed as a legal remedy for pay discrimination within firms or within governments. Because much of the pay difference between men and women is associated with the fact that men tend to be more concentrated in higher-paying firms (and, for that matter, in higher-paying industries), the potential effect of comparable worth applied within enterprises has been estimated to be quite small—about 10 percent of the wage gap. During the early 1970s Australia began implementation of a much more radical form of comparable worth, one that applied across enterprises as well as within them. The system is highly intrusive—a centralized government commission has wide wage-setting powers over both the public and the private sectors. Between 1970 and 1980 the ratio of women's to men's hourly wages rose 20 percentage points, from 74 percent

to 94 percent. The effects of this on the employment of women are in dispute, but it is fair to say that most economists, including those who found that comparable worth led to lower employment of women than would otherwise have obtained, would have expected these effects to be larger than the largest current estimates.*

Evaluation

Is comparable worth "progressive pragmatism," as New York Governor Mario Cuomo called it, or is it a "profoundly and irretrievably flawed" concept, as the Commission on Civil Rights concluded? The answer depends in part on whether preexisting wage differentials are largely arbitrary or whether they reflect market conditions of supply and demand. To the extent that they are equilibrium differentials, they serve to assure an adequate supply of persons in different occupations.

Even where there *is* discrimination in existing wage scales, however, there are problems with using job evaluation formulas as a remedy. Some method of correction is appropriate, but any rigid system promises trouble. The right differential (between, say, French and Spanish translators) today will be the wrong differential next year. Comparable worth, by focusing on *intrinsic* aspects of jobs and ignoring market ones (such as that with equal pay many more people would choose to be librarians than fire fighters), builds in a rigidity that will surely cause problems in resource allocation. Many who believe in the importance of eliminating discriminatory pay differentials oppose determining wages on the basis of anything so arbitrary as worth points. Most economists believe that ever changing market conditions of supply and demand must be given a role as well.

* See Harry J. Aaron and Cameran M. Lougy, *The Comparable Worth Controversy* (Washington, D.C.: The Brookings Institution, 1986).

girls are not. On average, boys and girls thus receive roughly the same quality of education and government services. Blacks and whites do not. They have different degrees of access to a wide variety of social institutions. How these differences translate into labor-market performance is not clear, but they give wide scope for different effects, especially of indirect discrimination.

Overall, the cup is both half empty and half full. The last 25 years have seen enormous progress made against discrimination as it affects both groups. There are signs that the progress slowed down, well short of equality, during the 1980s. Discrimination against blacks and women, both direct and indirect, is still with us.

Who Loses as a Result of Discrimination?

Obviously, the victims of labor-market discrimination lose because of it, but it is a mistake to think that they are the only losers. Society loses, too, because of the losses in efficiency that discrimination causes—and in other ways as well.

Efficiency losses arise for several reasons. If women or blacks are not given pay that is equal with that of white males for equal work, the labor force will not be allocated so as to get the most out of society's scarce resources. When people are kept from doing the jobs at which they are most productive and must instead produce goods or services that society values less, the total value of goods and services that is produced is reduced. More obviously, when prejudice increases unemployment, it reduces total output.

The ones who gain from discrimination are those who earn the higher pay that results from a limited supply of jobs in their occupations, those who get the jobs that blacks and women would otherwise have held, and the bigots who gain pleasure from not having to work with "them" or from not consuming services provided by "them." But if the total output of society is less, the net losses will be borne by the society as a whole.

Beyond the efficiency losses that discrimination imposes on society are further economic and social costs. Increased welfare or unemployment payments may be required, and the costs of enforcing anti-discrimination laws must be paid.

The costs of discrimination also include increased crime, hostility, and violence. These things are all by-products of unemployment, poverty, and frustration. Discrimination, if it is not attacked and rolled back, has one more cost, perhaps the most important: a sense of shame in a society that does not do what is necessary to eliminate the barriers to equal treatment.

SUMMARY

1. In a competitive labor market, wages are set by the forces of supply and demand. Differences in wages will arise because some skills are more valued than others and because some jobs are more onerous than others.
2. A union entering a competitive market can raise wages, but only at the cost of reducing employment and creating a pool of unemployed who would like to work at the going wage but are unable to gain employment in that market.
3. If the union can limit entry into the field, it can shift the supply curve to the left and achieve a higher wage without creating unemployment in the occupation.
4. A union entering a monopsonistic market may increase both employment and wages over some range. If, however, it sets the wage above the competitive level, it will create a pool of workers who are unable to get the jobs that they want at the going wage.
5. Governments set some wages above their competitive levels by passing minimum-wage laws. The overall effects of minimum wages have now been studied extensively. It is clear that they raise the incomes of many employees, but they cause unemployment for some of those with the lowest levels of skills.

6. Labor markets have developed a wide variety of institutions, including labor unions and employers' associations. Such institutions greatly affect wage determination.

7. American unionism developed first in the skilled trades, along craft lines, where it was possible to control supply and prevent nonunion members from undercutting union wages. Widespread organization of unskilled workers did not occur until after the legal right to organize was established by the Wagner Act in 1935. The emergence of mature collective bargaining is a relatively recent development.

8. Unions face a basic conflict between the goals of raising wages and preserving employment opportunities for members and potential members. Other trade-offs concern wages and job security, and wages and fringe benefits.

9. Discrimination by race and by sex has played an important role in labor markets, as it has in other aspects of American life. Direct discrimination affects wages and employment opportunities in part by limiting labor supply in the best paying occupations and by increasing it in less attractive occupations.

10. Indirect discrimination has had an effect through limiting the opportunities for education and training available to those who are subject to discrimination and through lowering people's career aspirations.

11. Discrimination imposes costs on the victims of discrimination. In addition, it leads to inefficiency and loss of output and is costly in other ways.

TOPICS FOR REVIEW

Competitive wage differences
Monopsony power
Power of unions
Effects of minimum wages
Collective bargaining
Goals of unions
Labor-market attachment
Effects of economic discrimination on wages and employment
Direct and indirect discrimination

DISCUSSION QUESTIONS

1. American unions traditionally have supported laws restricting immigration, expelling illegal aliens, and raising the minimum wage and extending its coverage. How does each of these positions benefit or hurt the following groups: (a) the American consumer; (b) American workers as a whole; and (c) unionized workers with seniority in their jobs?

2. A union that has bargaining rights in two plants of the same company in different states almost always insists on "equal pay for equal work" in the two plants. It does not always insist on equal pay for men and women in the same jobs. Can you see any economic reasons for such a distinction?

3. Why were craft unions more successful than industrial unions in the late nineteenth century in the United States? What happened to change this during the 1930s?

4. Interpret the following statements or practices in terms of the subject matter of this chapter.
   a. A requirement that one must pass an English-language proficiency test to be a carpenter in New York City
   b. A statement by an official of a textile workers' union in Massachusetts: "Until we have organized the southern textile industry, we will be unable to earn a decent wage in New England."
   c. A statement by an official of the United Steel Workers: "Things are getting rough in our locals because the youngsters have different views about wages than the old-timers."

5. "The great increase in the number of women entering the labor force for the first time means that relatively more women than men earn beginning salaries. It is therefore not evidence of discrimination that the average wage earned by females is less than that earned by males." Discuss.

6. The American Cyanamid Corporation once had a policy of removing women of child-bearing age from, or not hiring them for, jobs that expose them to lead or other substances that could damage a fetus. Is this sex discrimination? Whether it is or is not, debate whether this sort of protective hiring rule is something that the government should require, encourage, or prohibit.

7. "One can judge the presence or absence of discrimination by looking at the proportion of the population in different occupations." Does such information help? Does it suffice? Consider each of the following examples. Relative to their numbers in the total population, there are
   a. Too many blacks and too few Jews among professional athletes
   b. Too few male secretaries
   c. Too few female judges

8. Consider the consequences of applying the notion of "equal pay for comparable worth" to compensation of:
   a. Football coaches and cross-country coaches
   b. University presidents and network anchorpersons
   c. Fashion models and poets
   d. Police in large cities and police in small towns

9. Compare the following policies designed to reduce pay differentials due to occupational segregation of women in lower-paying jobs.
   a. Making pay adjustments based on an analysis of the "comparable worth" of occupations
   b. Removing barriers to women's employment in traditionally male jobs
   c. Setting quotas based on the relevant population statistics for minimum fractions of females in each occupation

10. Actuaries are among the highest paid people of all professionals. According to *Forbes* magazine, "The biggest drag on finding new actuaries is the rarefied mathematical talents the job requires. Like fiction writing or figure skating, this is a profession you join not for the money but because you love the work." Compare the market for actuaries with that for insurance salespeople. How do demand and supply conditions differ? What might account for the high salaries of actuaries?

11. According to a recent article in *Fortune* magazine, the Vatican doubled its spending between 1981 and 1986. "In the 1960s and 1970s a docile non-union work force settled for low wages and . . .

members of the clergy earned less than lay employees. . . . Some 1700 of the Holy See's 2300 employees are members of the clergy. . . ." In 1980 lay workers threatened to strike over the right to unionize, and by 1985 members of the clergy were receiving equal pay.

a. How might the change in compensation have been a response to the supply of clergy (priests and nuns)?

b. Now that clergy earn the same as lay workers, what would you expect to happen to the composition of the work force at the Vatican?

c. Would you expect the Vatican to employ inputs in the same way as a profit-maximizing firm? Why or why not?

Chapter 20

The Problem of Poverty

Possibly the most discussed aspect of distribution concerns the proportion of national income that goes to the very poor. Who are they? Why are they poor? What can, or should, we do about it?

Poverty in the United States

Since the mid-1960s, when President Lyndon Johnson declared "War on Poverty," there have been enormous changes in both poverty and in public policy toward the poor. According to the official definition, poverty among the elderly has declined sharply, but poverty among the very young has actually increased. In 1987 20 percent of all children and 45.8 percent of all black children were poor. The 1980s also saw an increasing feminization of poverty: In 1986 just over half of all persons living in households that were headed by a woman with children were poor. This group constituted over one-third of all poor people. By the late 1980s many observers were concerned about the apparent growth of a dependent urban "underclass." Some blamed this development on federal programs; others argued that without the programs things would be much worse.

The Concept of Poverty

The statistics in the preceding paragraph rely on the definition of poverty that is used by the U.S. Census Bureau. There are other possible definitions of poverty. One is that a person simply is poorer than most members of society. If we use this definition, a certain percentage of the population will always be poor: 10 percent of the population must be poorer than the other 90 percent.

Clearly, poverty must mean more than low relative income. Some minimum income standard for families is required to define the **poverty level**—the income below which a family is said to be poor. The official government standard specifies a dollar amount based on estimates of need and the cost of living. In 1987 the American poverty level was defined by the Department of Commerce as $11,611 per year for a nonfarm family of four. This amount is based on a standard that was developed during the 1960s and has been allowed to grow with inflation since then. The 1960s standard set the poverty level at three times the cost of a cheap, but nutritionally adequate, food budget.

The concept of poverty reflects the expectations and aspirations of society as a whole as to what constitutes an acceptable minimum standard of living. Less than 100 years ago, poverty would have been defined as the lack of the minimum amounts of food, shelter, and clothing that are needed to sustain life. At one time this condition faced (or threatened) a large portion of the world's urban and rural masses. Total output was so low that all but a privileged minority lived at or near this level, and any crop failure plunged thousands into starvation. Poverty in this sense is still present in the world, even in the United States. Starvation, hunger, and malnutrition are suffered by millions of individual Americans, and some Americans born in 1990 will starve to death.

Yet in most advanced industrial countries, as in the United States, output has risen until the average family enjoys a high material standard of living, and the provision of subsistence requirements of food, shelter, and clothing is a major problem for only a small number of families. If this is so—if mere subsistence does not define the poverty level—what does the Census Bureau mean when it says that 32.5 million Americans lived in poverty in 1987?

Consider the income of a member of a family just at the poverty level. An income of $11,611 for a family of four buys enough food, shelter, and clothing to survive, yet it is only about 38 percent of the average (median) income of American families, which in 1987 was $30,850. What it does not provide is enough money for the full range of commodities that the rest of us take for granted. It comes to a little under $8.00 a day per person. One can eat on that and pay the rent for crowded and dilapidated accommodations, but one cannot do much more. Many of the poor are understandably bitter and resentful that they and their children are outsiders looking in on the comfortable way of life that is shown in advertisements and on television. "I'd like, just once," one of them said to a *Newsweek* interviewer, "to buy Christmas presents the children want instead of the presents they need."

The Extent of Poverty

The extent of poverty may be measured either by the number and percentage of persons in households who have incomes below the poverty level or by measuring the **poverty gap:** the number of dollars per year required to raise everyone's income to this level. In 1987 over 32 million persons (13.5 percent of the population) were classified as poor, and the poverty gap was approximately $52 billion.

These figures are themselves controversial. Economists Martin Anderson of Stanford University and Edgar Browning of the University of Virginia argue that the figures neglect such extras as illegal income, unreported income, and noncash (often called "in-kind") benefits such as food stamps and subsidized housing. The Census Bureau has developed estimates of the effect of noncash benefits, and adding these in reduces the incidence of poverty by two to five percentage points. The Census Bureau adjustments reduce the poverty gap by between 28 and 40 percent. The group that is most affected by these adjustments is the elderly, who receive heavily subsidized medical insurance and medical care. The Census Bureau estimates that counting the value of in-kind transfers would reduce the measured incidence of poverty among the elderly in 1986 to 8.0 percent—as low as that of any large demographic group.

The historical record.   Whatever the deficiencies of the official numbers as absolute measures of poverty, they are useful for tracing changes in the magnitude of the problem. In 1933 President Franklin D. Roosevelt spoke of a third of a nation as being in poverty. By 1959 the official definition placed 22 percent of the nation below the poverty line. Figure 20-1 charts the course of poverty in America since then. The steady downward trend from 22 percent to just about 12 percent in the decade from 1959 to 1969 is impressive, but the trend was much flatter during the 1970s. The upturn since 1978 is a major source of concern. In 1987 the percentage in poverty was 13.6, and it was over 33 for blacks. Especially disquieting was the fact that the economic recovery that began in 1983 had not succeeded in restoring poverty rates to their prerecession (1980) levels.

Explaining the changes.   A widely held view among economists (parts of which, as we shall see, the Reagan administration disputed) explains the level of poverty in a country at any time in terms of three influences:

1. *The historical record of economic growth, which raises average productivity and reduces poverty for those whose incomes depend on labor earnings.* Historically,

FIGURE 20-1   **Percentage of Americans Below the Poverty Level, 1959–1987**

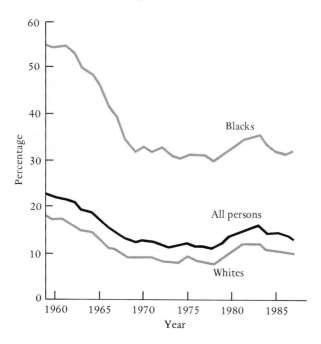

Poverty declined sharply during the 1960s but declined much less during the 1970s and has risen since 1978. The poverty level is adjusted annually to incorporate changes in the Consumer Price Index. For 1987 a family of four with an income below $11,611 was considered poor. The frequency of poverty is much higher for blacks than for whites, and there is no suggestion in the chart that this condition is likely to change soon.

economic growth has played a major role in the reduction of poverty.

2. *The number and level of government policies that redistribute income to those in poverty.* Recent experience suggests that government programs of income redistribution have become increasingly important in affecting the level of poverty in the United States. Since the mid-1970s, transfers to the nonelderly poor have grown less rapidly than inflation, increasing the number of people in poverty. Moreover, as we shall see below, a number of explicit reductions in programs occurred during the 1980s, and these account, at least in part, for the fact that the economic expansion of the 1980s did not reduce the incidence of poverty to 1979 levels.

3. *The level of unemployment in the economy, with in-*

creases in unemployment leading to increases in poverty. Unemployment has the same short-term effect that lack of general economic growth has in the long term. It reduces the ability of labor earnings to remove people from poverty.

These three influences tell us a great deal about the overall level of poverty, given the characteristics of the population, but they tell us little about who in the population will be poor. For that we need to look at individuals and households in more detail.

Who Are the Poor?

There are poor among people of all ages, races, and educational levels, among the working as well as the unemployed and the retired. Yet some groups have much higher incidences of poverty than others. Figure 20-1 shows that this is true of blacks. Table 20-1 shows that the incidence of poverty is also particularly high among families with minor children (especially if they are black), those unemployed or not in the labor force, those with limited education, and those of Hispanic origin. These data show one sharp change from a couple of decades ago, when a disproportionate number of the elderly were in poverty. In 1969, for example, 27.9 percent of persons over age 65 were in poverty. Since then, social security and other policies have significantly decreased old age as a major correlate of being poor. The poverty rate for the elderly today is now slightly lower than that for the population as a whole.

The data in Table 20-2 permit us to look at the problem somewhat differently. Instead of focusing on the prevalence of poverty among certain subgroups in the population, we look at those who are poor and describe some of their characteristics. A great many of the poor are employed; many are neither very young nor very old; many did not complete high school; and many are members of small households. These data show that there is no simple way to describe "the poor." Note also that for most categories that are shown in Table 20-2, the differences in the composition of poverty across races are small compared to the differences in the probabilities of being poor, as shown in Table 20-1.

Causes of Poverty

Poverty is almost four times as likely to occur among those families that do not have an employed head as

TABLE 20-1	The Incidence of Poverty Among American Families, 1987	

Characteristic	Percentage below poverty line
All families	11
Race and ethnic background	
White	8
Black	30
Hispanic origin	26
Families with children under 18 years of age	
All	16
White	12
Black	37
Hispanic origin	32
Employment status of head of family	
Employed (including armed forces)	6
Unemployed	35
Not in labor force	23
Families with female head	
All	34
White	27
Black	52
Hispanic origin	52
Age of family head	
15–24 years	30
25–44 years	13
45–64 years	7
65 years or more	7
Education of head of family over 24 years of age	
Elementary school or none	24
1–3 years of high school	19
4 years of high school	9
Some college	4

Source: U.S. Department of Commerce, Bureau of the Census, *Current Population Reports,* Series P-60, No. 151.

Race and ethnic background, family status, employment, and education all affect the likelihood of poverty. The numbers show the percentage of families with the designated characteristic whose incomes fall below the poverty level. Thus, while only 4 percent of families whose head had some college education were below the poverty level, more than one-half of minority families with a female head were in poverty.

among those that do. The fact that many of the poor are in families that are headed by women with minor children results in part from their having fewer opportunities for work; similarly, age and illness force many people out of the labor market, and govern-

ment transfer programs do not always compensate for the income loss. Other important groups that suffer from poverty include the rural poor, who strive in vain to earn a decent living from marginal or submarginal farmlands; the urban working poor, who often lack the skills to command a wage that is high enough to support themselves and their families above the poverty level; the immobile poor, who are trapped by age and outdated skills in areas and in occupations in which the demand for their services is declining faster than their number; and, most important, the minority (nonwhite) poor. Nonwhites constitute only one-eighth of the population but constitute almost one-third of the poor.

There is no simple explanation for the existence of individual poverty in the midst of plenty. It is partly a result of mental and physical handicaps, partly of low motivation, and partly of the raw deal that fate gives to some. Partly it is a result of current and past prejudice and discrimination. Partly, as we saw in Chapter 19, it can result from a lack of the kind of education and training that pays off in the long run. Partly it is a result of the market's valuing the particular abilities that an individual does have at such a low price that, even in good health and with full-time employment, the income that can be earned leaves that person below the poverty line. Box 20-1 provides a few profiles of individuals who were living in poverty during the 1980s.

The Persistently Poor

Fluctuations in the number who are poor as a result of swings in the economy highlight the important distinction between the *occasionally poor* and the *persistently poor.* According to a study by Mary Jo Bane and David Ellwood, about one-third of the poor at a given time can be expected to leave poverty in four years or less.[1] Slightly over half, however, are experiencing periods of poverty that will last nine years or more. Most of the poor are persistently poor. On the other hand, most of the people who ever *become* poor will leave poverty within two years, and only about 12 percent of persons who enter poverty in a given year will stay in poverty for nine years or more. While at first blush these findings may appear to be contradictory, it is easy to see that they are not.

[1] Mary Jo Bane and David T. Ellwood, "Slipping in and out of Poverty: The Dynamics of Spells" *J. Human Resources,* Sept. 1986, pp. 2–23.

TABLE 20-2 Selected Characteristics of American Families Below Poverty Level, 1987			
Characteristic	White (percentage)	Black (percentage)	Hispanic (percentage)
Employment status of head of family			
Employed (including armed forces)	41	31	40
Unemployed	10	12	8
Not in labor force	49	56	51
	100	100[a]	100[a]
Age of head of family			
Under 25 years	12	13	13
25–44 years	55	56	61
45–66 years	22	20	20
65 years and over	11	10	6
	100	100[a]	100
Education of head of family over 24 years of age			
Elementary school or none	31	23	55
1–3 years of high school	20	30	20
4 years of high school	34	37	18
Some college	15	10	7
	100	100	100
Sex of head of household			
Male	58	26	52
Female	42	74	47
	100	100	100[a]
Size of family			
2 or 3 persons	59	53	42
4 or 5 persons	31	34	40
6 or more persons	10	13	18
	100	100	100

Source: U.S. Department of Commerce, Bureau of the Census, *Current Population Reports,* Series P-60, No. 161.

Note: Hispanics may be of any race.

[a] Details may not add to totals due to rounding.

Escaping poverty is not merely a matter of employment status, age, education, or family status. In contrast to Table 20-1, this one looks at the characteristics of the poor, not the likelihood of poverty for those with a given characteristic. Many of those below the poverty level are the working poor. For example, 41 percent of white families below the poverty level have an employed head. The poor are found in all age groups and in small families as well as in large families. Over one-half of those in poverty are in families whose head did not finish high school.

Bane and Ellwood use the example of a hospital. Most of the patients who are admitted to a hospital undergo brief courses of treatment and are discharged. This group is analogous to all those who ever become poor. On the other hand, the relatively few admissions who are chronically ill stay for a long time and use a large share of the hospital's beds. These are analogous to the persistently poor.

The "Underclass"

The importance of persistent poverty has led to a large body of theoretical and empirical research regarding a group of persistently poor that is loosely termed the "underclass." The neighborhoods and families in which members of the underclass live, it is argued, promote values, behavior, and views of

BOX 20-1

Profiles of Poverty

The following are newspaper sketches of people who are living below the poverty level. Only the names are fictitious.

A 34-year-old mother of four children ranging in age from 5 to 15 waited in the Nassau County, New York, Social Services building recently for recertification for welfare.

Divorced last year from her husband, who "lived at home on and off," Glenda Rodriguez has been on welfare for 10 years. She is entitled to $450 a month in welfare grants; of that, $271 goes for rent and $67 for heating. She works as a part-time waitress whenever she can and earns $60 in a good week.

For every $60 she earns, however, her welfare grant is reduced by $40. (Changes in the law since this story was written would require that her grant be reduced dollar for dollar.)

"Right now, I don't know how I'll make it the next two days until Friday," she said. "I owe the oil company $400—money I haven't been able to pay. We're not starving, but my kids get a little tired of eating eggs and franks.

"I'm working and I'm trying to give my children a little better life, rather than being completely on assistance," she said, "but I'm not getting any place. I'm in the hole each month."

Eddie Mason, 19 years old, drank cheap wine and smoked marijuana recently in an abandoned building on Jones Street in St. Louis's slums as he told a visitor, "I've been to the employment office and they've got jobs there only in the suburbs, and I don't have a car. It wouldn't be worth my time to pay bus fare, taxes, lunch, and stuff for a job way out in the suburbs that

pays $3.35 an hour." Mr. Mason lives with his mother and admits to just enough petty thievery "to stay alive."

The old man is sitting at the bus stop, in San Francisco, "just resting." He's very old, but he's not slow witted. He's hunched a little forward, hands cupped on the top of the cane that he holds between his knees.

He wants to talk, and in a little time he covers a lot of ground. Private Julius Goldman in World War I, master sergeant in World War II, and 1929 and the depression in between. Kids, inflation, retirement, a dead wife, more inflation. The way it is and the way it was.

He is a pet food devotee. Heat it; it tastes like hash.

The cab driver in Madison, Wisconsin, is glad to talk: "Call me Tommy." He's 25, has a common law wife, Ivory, and a 2-year-old son. He gets to drive only about 80 days a year even with 2 years of seniority, but the family can almost get by on the $6,000 he earns and the welfare Ivory gets. They don't pay much in taxes. He's worried now, because it's a severe winter and fuel costs are breaking their budget. Ivory works some as a midwife, but midwifery is illegal in Wisconsin, and there's not much money in it. He dropped out of college after 2 years—it didn't seem relevant. He can't go back now, although he thinks it might make sense, because he's got a family to support. His parents could support him while he finished a degree, but they won't. His father disapproves of his long hair, his earring, and the fact that he and Ivory don't want to get married. His mother gives them money from time to time and that helps. He blames the system for forcing him to struggle in order to keep his son warm and healthy.

the world that make exit from poverty extremely difficult. For example, members of the underclass have unusually high rates of teenage pregnancy and tend, it is argued, not to believe in the efficacy of education and work as a means to improve one's lot in life. It is easy to see how these phenomena would inhibit an exit from poverty. If one adds the assumption that the values underlying such behavior and attitudes are transmitted, either through a subculture or through families, one has a model of a self-repli-

cating, permanent underclass. Many discussions assign an important role in perpetuating the underclass to the welfare system, which is alleged to foster dependency.

A major part of the debate about the underclass is over its permanence. To what extent can its members attain the ability to leave it? No one would deny that life in an urban ghetto rewards behaviors that are not ideal recipes for success in mainstream society. The question is what happens when disadvantaged residents of underclass neighborhoods are given access to the skills and the opportunities that do make for success in the mainstream. Those who argue that membership in the underclass is essentially permanent say that there would be little effect. Once underclass values are inculcated into people, it is very hard to make them go away. Many others argue that values are not at all what is at issue. Rather, they say, underclass behavior is a sensible response to life in the underclass environment. Given clear opportunities and the means to adapt, most members of the underclass could do perfectly well on their own. Economists, sociologists, psychologists, and anthropologists are engaged in lively discussion of these issues. The consequences of this discussion for public policy are potentially very large.

As we have just noted, the concept of the underclass is as yet imprecise; it has almost as many definitions as there are scholars who are studying the poor. By *all* definitions in use, however, the underclass constitutes a fairly small percentage of either the poor or the persistently poor. The idea of the underclass generally requires a concentration of poverty—that its members live in environments in which poverty is pervasive. If we adopt the arbitrary convention that census tracts (areas of roughly 5,000 in total population, which are used by the Census Bureau for analyses of population) must have a population that is at least 40 percent poor in order to sustain an underclass, we find that at most 7 percent of the poor (less than 1 percent of the total population) in 1979 could be in the underclass. More recent figures would probably be somewhat higher.

In 1987 about 10 percent of the poor at most were members of the underclass.[2]

The feminization of poverty. In 1987 more than one-half of all persons in poverty lived in households that were headed by a woman. In 1959 only about a third of the poor lived in female-headed households. This change in the composition of the poor derives from two sources. First, the incidence of poverty among female-headed households always has been higher than that for other types of households. The past three decades have seen a steady increase in the percentage of the total population that is living in such

households. Second, although poverty rates have fallen for all groups since 1959, they have fallen disproportionately little for female-headed households. Thus, the relative incidence of poverty has risen for female-headed households at the same time that the relative number of such households has also increased. The combination has led to a marked feminization of poverty and has focused concern toward children in these households, who in 1987 constituted 22 percent of all poor persons and 57 percent of all poor children. Of special concern is the fact that many of these children can be expected to be persistently poor. According to the Bane and Ellwood study, the mean duration of poverty for children who are born into poverty is between seven and eight years—nearly one-half the length of childhood itself. Childhood poverty, in turn, increases the chances of poor economic performance as an adult.

Poverty among blacks. A recent University of Michigan study found that more than three-quarters of persons who are in poverty for 9 or more consecutive years are black. Blacks represent 11 percent of the total population, 30 percent of those below the poverty level, and 77 percent of the persistently poor. Similarly, according to the Bane and Ellwood study, when a black person enters poverty, on average he or she will stay in poverty for 6.5 years. The analogous figure for whites is 3.4 years. Black children who are born into poverty will, on average, stay in poverty for almost 10 years.

The disproportionate representation of blacks among the poor stems from a variety of causes. Discrimination, which we discussed in Chapter 19, plays a direct role and contributes indirectly by making blacks, on average, less well educated than whites and overrepresented in occupations in which employment is declining. Additionally, the feminization of poverty, although important for all ethnic groups, has been more pronounced for blacks than for whites. Even so, Mary Jo Bane estimates that at most 44 percent—and probably somewhat less—of the difference between black and white poverty rates stems from differences in household composition. Put the other way around, more than one-half of the difference arises because blacks have a higher incidence of poverty for comparable types of households.[3]

---

[2] Erol Ricketts and Isabel Sawbill, "Defining and Measuring the Underclass," *Journal of Policy Analysis and Management,* Winter 1988, pp. 316–325.

[3] Mary Jo Bane, "Household Composition and Poverty," in S. Danziger and D. Weinberg, eds., *Fighting Poverty* (Boston, MA: Harvard University Press, 1986), pp. 209–231.

Policies Toward Poverty

In principle, eliminating poverty is more straightforward than eliminating air pollution or cancer, for which cures are as yet unknown. For an amount that was estimated at about $52 billion per year in 1987, every household below the poverty line could be given an income supplement that would be sufficient to remove it from poverty. Put another way, Congress could, in principle, directly eliminate the poverty gap that we discussed earlier in this chapter. Although $52 billion is a lot of money, it is less than 20 percent of the national defense budget, and it represents less than 2 percent of the total income that is earned in the nation. Of course, such a policy would not be practical, because if it were put into place it would almost surely reduce work incentives and lead to an increase in the number of households who would be poor in the absence of transfers. The size of these effects on work incentives is a subject of much research and debate and is intimately related to the question of what kinds of policies, if any, should be used to combat poverty.

Incentive Effects and Targeting

Imagine a program that would provide just enough cash income to everyone in poverty to raise their income to the poverty line and provides nothing to anyone else. Such a program would be an example of perfect *targeting*—it would reach only the poor. It would have very bad incentive effects, however, for anyone whose market income was at or below the poverty line. Since people would receive exactly poverty level income whether they worked or not, they would have no incentive to work. The number of *pretransfer poor* (people who are in poverty before they receive any government benefits) and the size of the pretransfer poverty gap would surely rise.

At the other extreme, imagine a program that would give every individual an annual cash grant that would be equal to the poverty level plus $1, no matter what the individual's earnings. The program would be financed by taxes, and as long as the taxes were not too high, it would provide incentives for everyone to work. When an individual worked, whether her wage was high or low, she would get to keep some of her income. Moreover, the cash grant from the government would be the same whether the individual worked or not. The grant itself, and the income tax, would still affect work incentives but much less than in the first program. Compared to the first program, pretransfer poverty would be less, as would be the pretransfer poverty gap. On the other hand, hundreds of billions of dollars would go to the nonpoor every year. Under this program, which would be an extreme form of a negative income tax, targeting would be very bad and incentive effects would be relatively good.

The preceding examples illustrate a fundamental dilemma in designing transfer programs to aid the poor.

In many cases the more precisely programs are targeted toward people in poverty, the worse their disincentive effects will be.

One way out of the dilemma is to target programs toward people who are not necessarily poor but who have characteristics that are correlated with poverty. Ideally, these characteristics should be difficult for an individual to acquire. The classic example of such a program is social security. Social security payments to retired workers are targeted toward people who have attained a certain age—something for which there are already ample incentive effects! As it happens, pretransfer poverty among the elderly is very high, but, largely because of social security, posttransfer poverty is lower than the average for the U.S. population. Here is a case in which targeting is fairly good (the incidence of poverty among those over 65 is reduced from over 50 percent to under 15 percent by social security and related programs) and incentive effects are quite small.[4] Similarly, Supplemental Security Income, which is a federal program that supports those aged, blind, and disabled persons who are not covered by social security, is well targeted and has good incentive properties. It simply isn't worth being poor *and* getting old, blind, or disabled in order to get the transfer payments.

---

[4] The size of incentive effects arising from social security is a matter of some debate. Social security clearly reduces the incentive to engage in private saving during one's working life, because the government is guaranteeing a pension in retirement. Less clear is the effect of social security on labor that is supplied prior to retirement age. Most studies have found this effect to be quite small.

The targeting-incentives dilemma is much more serious in the case of programs that are designed to help poor children, because it is impossible to get resources to the children without also aiding their parents, and the parents are often subject to work disincentives. Some observers of the U.S. transfer system have argued that the principal program that is designed to aid poor children, AFDC (Aid to Families with Dependent Children), has disincentive effects that do more harm than good. They argue that the program provides an incentive for poor young women to have children, making them eligible for the program, and no incentive for either the mothers or the fathers to work their way off welfare.

Charles Murray, whose work had an important influence on the Reagan administration's thinking about poverty programs, has blamed much of the increase in pretransfer poverty rates during the 1970s on the generosity of the welfare system. Most observers find little support in the data for this view. For one thing, most people who receive welfare leave the system in under two years, suggesting that the disincentive effects are not overwhelming in the majority of cases. For another, the welfare system became less generous, after accounting for inflation, during the 1970s. It is hard to see how its disincentive effects could have been increasing at the same time. Finally, most studies of the labor supply of AFDC mothers indicate that they are not very responsive to work incentives and disincentives.[5]

Disincentive effects are of obvious importance in designing transfer programs to help the poor. The bigger these effects are, the more expensive it will be to accomplish any given degree of poverty reduction. One of the most important ways that economists can help both policymakers and the poor is to improve the measurement of these effects. To the extent that transfer programs can be aimed at groups who are not subject to disincentive effects, such as the disabled, they can be a very efficient means of reducing poverty for members of those groups. However, not all of the poor are in such groups, suggesting that different kinds of antipoverty programs should apply to different groups of poor people.

[5] David T. Ellwood and Lawrence Summers, "Poverty in America: Is Welfare the Answer or the Problem?" in S. Danziger and D. Weinberg, eds., *Fighting Poverty* (Boston, MA: Harvard University Press, 1986), pp. 78–105.

The more subject a group is to work disincentives, the more expensive it is to provide income support to that group.

Antipoverty Programs

Two organizing principles in the development of antipoverty programs have been, first, that the able-bodied should work and, second, that heads of households should support their families whenever possible.

The traditional strategy for dealing with poverty is to provide job opportunities for all who are able to work and income-support programs for those who are unable to work.

Some programs provide **social insurance** that is related to work. Insurance benefits are paid when there is temporary unemployment, disability, or retirement. These programs are not aimed directly at poverty but at any household that loses labor income through no fault of its own. Typically, social insurance programs are financed by a tax on wages. In the language of the preceding discussion, they are not targeted. A second set of programs are called *means-tested programs*. These are designed to provide monetary assistance and in-kind assistance to persons whose incomes are low and who are unable to work for reasons of age, health, or family status. Because the target population is unable to work, the social insurance programs cannot apply to it.

The definition of who is unable to work, however, has changed a good deal over time. A generation ago mothers of young children were expected to stay home, and the major welfare program for dependent children was designed to support the mother in caring for her children. This view has changed radically. Under the welfare reform act that was passed by Congress in 1988, it is intended that all mothers whose children are older than 3 years should work or be in a job training program. This change in welfare is often termed "workfare," under which able-bodied adults must work in order to receive welfare benefits.

Providing Employment Opportunities

Families with an employed member have much more of a chance of escaping poverty than those without one. Thus, providing job opportunities for the unemployed and for those who are not even looking for work is of major importance. As we have seen, providing work is not a guarantee that families will escape poverty. About 40 percent of all poor families have an employed head of household; for these *working poor,* the problem is often a lack of skills that command a wage that will allow them to rise above the poverty level.

Programs of education, training, and retraining are designed to lessen these causes of poverty by providing better job opportunities. Such programs have proven to be both expensive and limited in the number of persons that they reach. Educational opportunities for the children of the poor may free them from inheriting poverty, but such progress is measured from generation to generation, not from year to year. Still, many of these programs have proved to be effective and to provide benefits in excess of costs: They increase the lifetime incomes of their recipients by more than the costs of the program. In some cases, they may even generate enough tax revenue from the earnings of their recipients to cover the costs of the program. Among the programs that have met the benefit-cost test are Head Start, which is directed toward prekindergarten poor children; WIC (an acronym for Women, Infants, and Children), which provides nutrition for pregnant women and infants; and the Job Corps, which provides job training to disadvantaged youth.

Social Insurance

Table 20-3 shows the major income-support programs that existed in 1987. Social insurance programs added up to over $333 billion dollars. The Social Security Act (first passed in 1935) provides Old Age, Survivors, and Disability Insurance (OASDI) to millions of Americans who are old and to the widows, widowers, and orphans of eligible workers. Medicare provides medical expenses for those who are receiving OASDI benefits. Unemployment insurance is paid, for a limited time, to those covered workers who lose their jobs. These expenditures keep millions off the poverty rolls and reduce the size of the poverty gap for many others, but it should be noted that none of them is primarily a *poverty* program. Middle-income and wealthy individuals also share in such benefits and, indeed, receive the great majority of them.

TABLE 20-3   Major Income-Support Programs, 1987

Program	Expenditures (billions of dollars)
Social insurance	333.2
Cash benefits	
Social Security (OASDI)	201.7
Unemployment Insurance	14.3
Worker's Compensation	16.0
Other	20.9
In-kind benefits	
Medicare	80.3
Income assistance (welfare)	95.6
Cash benefits	
Aid to Families with Dependent Children and General Assistance	16.5[a]
Supplementary Security Income (SSI)	14.8[a]
In-kind benefits	
Medicaid	44.0[a]
Food stamps	10.6
Housing assistance	6.5
School lunches	3.2
Total	428.8

Source: Social Security Bulletin, Dec. 1988; and U.S. Bureau of the Census, Technical Paper No. 58, 1988.

[a] Includes federal and state government payments.

In 1987 the income-support programs cost $429 billion, about 9.5 percent of GNP. The table shows the range and the size of programs in 1987. Note that over three-quarters of the expenditures were not for welfare; that is, they are not need related but rather are categorical entitlements to the aged, unemployed, and others regardless of their other sources of income. Less than one-quarter of the expenditures were in welfare programs targeted to the poor. AFDC and food stamps, the most publicized programs, are a relatively small part of the total cost of income-support programs. OASDI and Medicare—"social security"—represent two-thirds of the total.

Successive increases in eligibility for coverage and in the size of benefits, including increases to match rises in the cost of living, make social insurance an increasingly effective preventative from poverty for the majority of Americans. Indeed, it is largely because of social security that poverty rates among the elderly have fallen so dramatically since 1970. During the early 1980s the social security system was in some danger of bankruptcy, following decades of tremendous growth in both coverage and generosity. Recent reforms, including both tax increases and reductions in the growth of benefits, assure that under reasonable assumptions about economic growth the program will stay solvent well into the next century.

Means-tested Programs (Welfare)

A second group of income transfer programs is highly targeted. In order to be eligible to receive cash benefits under most of these programs, one must both have low income and fall into some other category of need. In order to receive cash welfare payments from the federal government, one must either be in a family with dependent children (AFDC) or be aged, blind, or disabled (Supplemental Security Income), as well as meet a low-income standard. Food stamps are available to anyone who meets the relevant low-income standard. A striking feature of most of these programs is that they are administered by the states, which set widely varying benefit levels. In 1988 the average monthly AFDC payment for a family was $366.85. California paid $574.00; Mississippi paid $114.00. Medicaid benefits and standards also vary by state, although not by as much. Supplemental Security Income (SSI) eligibility standards are uniform, and there is a federal floor on the amount of the payments, but some states choose to provide supplementary benefits, while others do not. States also provide some of the financing for Medicaid and AFDC, according to a formula that is set by the federal government.

In 1987 these programs cost $95.6 billion, about one-quarter of which was paid by state governments. The largest program by far was Medicaid, costing about $44 billion. AFDC, which is the program that most people have in mind when they use the word *welfare,* was received by 3.7 million families and accounted for $9 billion (under 1 percent) of the federal budget. Means testing works differently in the various programs. Prior to passage of the 1988 welfare reform act, if a family's income was above a certain level or if the family was ineligible for AFDC, Medicaid payments were reduced to nothing. This provided a perverse incentive for households that were near the poverty level. By working a little harder they could lose *all* of their medical coverage. It made sense for them not to do the extra work. The 1988 welfare reform provides for a "transitional" year, in which families will retain their Medicaid benefits when they work their way off welfare.

Under AFDC itself there is essentially no incentive to work: Benefits are reduced dollar for dollar with earned income. The new workfare provisions in the 1988 welfare reform act eventually will require that AFDC recipients work, but they provide no monetary benefit for working.

Antipoverty Policy

The war on poverty began with a fanfare in the mid-1960s. New programs, such as food stamps, Medicare, and Medicaid were begun, and older programs were expanded in both coverage and generosity in the succeeding decade. Most of the growth was in social security and not in programs that were directly aimed at the poor, but by any measure growth in both types of programs was large. Social security (including Medicare), for example, expanded from 14 percent of federal spending in 1965 to 26 percent in 1980. Means-tested programs grew from 4 percent to 8 percent over the same period.

By the late 1970s the growth in income-maintenance expenditures had tapered off. Social security went through the first of a series of reforms, the largest being in 1977 and 1983, that were designed to cut the growth of benefits and assure the financial health of the program. Lower economic growth in the country as a whole translated into reduced growth in income-transfer programs. Spending on Medicare and food stamps kept pace with the rapid inflation of the late 1970s, but the real value of the benefits stopped growing. AFDC benefits did not do even this well; in most states the level of cash benefits was kept constant or grew slowly, while the price level rose sharply. Thus, the quantity of goods that the typical welfare recipient could buy began to fall in the mid-1970s.

Still, as shown in Table 20-4, the overall impact of antipoverty programs between 1965 and 1980 was sizable. Between 1965 and 1980 the proportion of the population whose private-sector incomes were below the poverty line hardly changed. Over the same period money and in-kind transfers reduced the chances of being in poverty by over one-third. These transfers also reduced the poverty gap of millions of people whose incomes remained below the poverty level. The magnitude of the progress in the war on poverty, its cost, and whether the one was worth the other, were all strongly debated during the 1980 presidential election. The winner of that election, Ronald Reagan, believed that both the poor and the taxpayer

TABLE 20-4	Effectiveness of Government Income-Assistance Programs, 1965–1986

Percent of population below poverty level, measured by

	Market income (excluding transfers)	Adjusted income (including cash and in-kind transfers)
1965	21.3	16.8
1970	18.8	—[a]
1975	22.0	—[a]
1980	21.9	10.6
1983	24.2	13.3
1984	22.0	12.4
1985	20.9	12.0
1986	20.5	11.6

Source: S. Danziger, R. Haveman, and R. Plotnick, "Antipoverty Policy: Effects on the Poor and Nonpoor," in *Fighting Poverty: What Works and What Doesn't,* edited by S. Danziger and D. Weinberg (Boston, MA: Harvard University Press, 1986); and U.S. Bureau of the Census.

[a] Not available.

Income-assistance programs have had a major impact on the incidence of poverty since 1965. Market income includes no government transfer payments and thus provides a benchmark for evaluating the effect of transfers. Adjusted income adds both cash transfer payments (such as social security) and in-kind transfers (such as food stamps).

The data show that mere growth of the economy between 1965 and 1980, working by way of market income, had little effect. The percent falling below the poverty line fluctuated but did not decrease. However, government programs had a big effect in reducing the number living below the poverty level between 1965 and 1980. From 1980 to 1983 the increase in those in poverty (by either measure) reflected both a serious recession and a cutback in government transfer payments by the Reagan administration. The economic recovery that started in 1983 reduced the incidence of poverty but not enough to offset the earlier decreases in income-assistance programs.

could be made better off if spending on government transfer programs were sharply reduced.

Poverty and the Reagan Administration (1981–1989)

The Reagan administration consistently articulated a view that with a strong private economy there would be no role for government transfers except to support a small group of the "truly needy." In many cases

transfers were seen to have such negative incentive effects that they would do more harm than good. This view led to a radical revision of antipoverty policy.

Reliance on Growth Rather Than on Income Transfers

The central tenet of the new policy was that economic growth is the only generally effective weapon in the war on poverty. As President Reagan put it, "Our aim is to increase national wealth so all will have more, not just redistribute what we already have, which is just a sharing of scarcity." Indeed, the administration went further and argued that the progress made in the war on poverty prior to 1980 could be entirely attributed to economic growth and not to government programs.

If this controversial view is correct—and it is surely in conflict with the statistics presented in Table 20-4—it would make sense, even to those in poverty, to *reduce* income transfers if by so doing economic growth would be fostered. Established income-support programs became a target of Reaganomics. The general economic philosophy of the administration was that decreasing the federal government's domestic expenditures was a key to economic recovery. What better way to reduce government expenditures, the administration argued, than to cut expensive welfare programs that had not (in any case) contributed to progress! Many of these programs were the cornerstones of the traditional antipoverty strategy. The administration sharply cut funds for food stamps, AFDC, and Medicaid in the hope that the economic recovery resulting from a reduction in government spending, accompanied by reduced inflation, would ameliorate the lot of the poor. Nearly 20 percent of the recipients of welfare lost some or all of their benefits. Whether or not this strategy will work in the very long run, during the 1980s it unmistakably increased rather than alleviated poverty.

The "truly needy." The Reagan administration recognized, as had prior administrations, that not all of the poor could be rescued by economic growth, even in the long run. The "truly needy" would always require help. Here, too, changes in philosophy became apparent. A major change was the new belief that welfare and other transfers should be designed simply to assure a minimum standard of living, not to close the poverty gap. One official of the Office of Management and Budget put it succinctly: "The policy decision is that welfare is a safety-net and not an income supplement program."

What this meant was that persons whose incomes from other sources raised them above the threshold level of the safety net were to be cut off from eligibility for welfare, Medicaid, and food stamps. The first dollars earned above the threshold level caused major losses of benefits. The intent was to eliminate those who were not truly needy, including welfare cheaters, but a side effect was a sharp disincentive to continue work for those who could raise their income above the safety net only by a combination of transfers and work.

By targeting income assistance to the "truly needy," an administration whose economic policy was founded on the importance of providing incentives to work and to save dramatically *reduced* those incentives for the working poor.

The proper role of government.   The war on poverty had increased the role of both government in general and the federal government in particular in antipoverty policy. President Reagan called for an abrupt reversal of these trends. He urged private charity to fill any gap that was left by the reduction in government programs, and, more importantly, he called for a return to state and local governments of the major responsibility for aid to the poor. Most economists, whatever their views were on the appropriate level of income support, opposed this trend for a simple reason. When different states provide different levels of support, the poor will tend to migrate toward the more generous states, and the wealthy will tend to migrate toward the less generous states. As a result, economically important decisions about where people live and where production takes place are distorted. (This is an example of a fiscal externality, a subject that is discussed at length in Chapters 21 and 23.) Uniform, federal transfer programs eliminate this problem, and thus most economists have argued that income redistribution should be undertaken at the federal level. Indeed, the United States was already unusual among the world's advanced economies in permitting the level of aid to the poor to depend upon where in the country poor people live.

The impact of the Reagan approach.   The number of people living in the United States below the poverty level increased sharply between 1979 and 1987, even though by 1987 the unemployment rate was lower than it had been in 1979. Reagan supporters argue that the administration's policies were always designed to work not as a quick fix but as a gradual middle- and long-run solution. But the economy in 1987 had recovered from the recession of 1980–1982, while the poverty rate was two percentage points higher (about 5 million people) than it had been before the recession began. Unless there is a radical decline in poverty, the case that the Reagan policies will reduce poverty in the long run will become increasingly difficult to make.

Future Directions of Policy Toward Poverty

Poverty has not been eliminated, and the debate over our attitudes and policies toward poverty surely will continue for many years to come.

Successful antipoverty policies need to take account of the many different kinds of poor people. Policies that help the working poor, whether by upgrading their skills or subsidizing their wages, will do little for those who do not work. Policies that provide employment and training for persons in poverty who could work but do not will still not help those who are unable to work. Income support that is provided to groups who are easily able to work will surely have negative incentive effects. On the other hand, where children are involved, withholding such support from parents who are unable to work can negatively affect the childrens' abilities to compete when they grow up.

The current welfare system, for all of its faults, seems to work fairly well for households whose poverty is transitory—the vast majority of people who are ever poor. There is increasing evidence, however, that for a subset of the poor the welfare system has become a regular way of life and that children for whom welfare is an important income source are disproportionate users of the system as adults. This combines with concerns about the "underclass" to suggest that one area of debate in the coming years will be over policies to improve the adult opportunities of persistently poor children. One factor that will complicate this debate is that there is often no practical way of getting resources to needy children without helping parents who are viewed by many as undeserving. The dilemma is that even if the parents are in some sense undeserving of the help that they receive, their children are surely undeserving of the handicapped start that they would get in life without that help.

Programs that are designed to help both children and adults to make it on their own have been viewed with increasing favor in the last few years, and the 1988 welfare reform act requires that states provide such programs, starting over the next five years, for welfare recipients. Even proponents of this change, however, caution that for many of the poor, including many single mothers, the solutions lie elsewhere. Just where is not so clear. Work by economists that evaluates programs and calculates the incentive effects of various approaches in both the long and the short run is an essential ingredient for the design of such programs.

SUMMARY

1. The concept of poverty involves both relative and absolute levels of income and reflects the aspirations of society as well as the income needed for subsistence alone. Today roughly 13.5 percent of all Americans are classified as living in poverty.
2. Economic growth, although it has led to a reduction of poverty, will by itself never eliminate it, for many of those in need do not share directly in the fruits of growth.
3. The incidence of poverty is much greater among some groups than among others, particularly among those who are not employed and who are relatively uneducated. However, there are many poor among the working, and poverty is appreciable in all ages and among all groups in the population.
4. Poverty is particularly acute among blacks and Hispanics. This reflects in part the minority groups' lower than average stock of human capital—especially education and training—and in part the discrimination that has prevented fuller utilization of the skills and talents that the groups' members have.
5. A small but growing fraction of the poor live in urban neighborhoods where poverty is highly concentrated. This group is often referred to as the "underclass." Whether underclass behavior can be changed by improved economic opportunity is currently a matter of heated debate.
6. The incidence of poverty is especially high among households that are headed by women. An increasing fraction of the poor are in such households—a trend that is often termed "the feminization of poverty."
7. Some poverty programs are highly targeted on the poor. The advantage of such programs is that little public money goes to those who are not in need. The disadvantage is that such programs may provide powerful disincentives to work, especially if small increases in earnings lead to large reductions in program benefits.
8. The antipoverty policies that were developed between the 1930s and 1980 included attempts to expand employment opportunities; retraining programs intended to match people with available jobs; social insurance to help the able-bodied meet the risks of unemployment and retirement; and categorical assistance designed to help those unable to care for themselves. The evidence is clear that these policies greatly reduced poverty in the United States. The existence and size of their long-run disincentive effects is a matter of continuing debate.
9. The Reagan administration advocated and partially adopted policies that represented a sharp break with the trend of the previous half century. The underpinning of the Reagan policy was to seek economic growth by reducing government spending even if this meant

decreasing income transfers to the poor. The policy was designed to improve targeting, providing a safety net to protect only the truly needy. Moreover, the approach of the Reagan administration was increasingly to return poverty programs to state and local control and to private charity. The long-run effect of these controversial policies is not yet known. In the short run they have increased the incidence of poverty.

TOPICS FOR REVIEW

Poverty level and poverty gap
Correlates of poverty
Occasional poverty and persistent poverty
The "underclass"
Targeting and disincentive effects
Social insurance versus income assistance
Alternative policies toward poverty

DISCUSSION QUESTIONS

1. In what ways are the problems of poverty in the United States likely to be different from the problems of poverty in an underdeveloped, poor country, such as Bangladesh? In what ways are they easier to solve in one place than in the other?

2. The official poverty level used in the United States is based only on money income. It does not take into account food stamps or subsidized housing. It does not consider the assets of the family. It does not consider whether families with low incomes have wealthy relatives. Do these omissions lead to an exaggerated view of the poverty problem? Should the poverty level rise if average income of the American people rises, with no increase in the prices of individual items of consumption?

3. Suppose that your objectives are (first) to eradicate poverty and (second) to reduce unemployment. Evaluate the probable effectiveness of each of the following in meeting each objective.
   a. Increasing welfare payments
   b. Increasing aid to education
   c. Creating a program of public works to hire the poor
   d. Ending employment discrimination against blacks

4. A proposed program of rental allowances to the poor has been attacked in Congress as giving money to slumlords instead of to the poor and thereby worsening the distribution of income. Evaluate this position. Argue the case for and against assistance that is tied to a particular kind of expenditure rather than to giving the money to the poor to spend as they think best.

5. Comment on each of the following headlines in terms of the matters that were discussed in this chapter:
   a. "Working poor are victims of Reaganomics"
   b. "On welfare or working: Poor is poor"
   c. "Economic recovery decreases number on welfare"
   d. "War on poverty is difficult to call off"

6. In what sense does a policy that reduces welfare payments dollar for dollar for every dollar of earned income constitute "a 100 percent tax on working"? In what sense is this not accurate? (*Hint:* If the maximum welfare payment is $10,000 per family, what marginal and average "tax rate" is implicit for a welfare recipient who is offered a job that pays $8,000? What about a job that pays $13,000?)

7. News item: "On an income of $800 a month, Sharon Smith and her children cannot afford to get sick. Nor can they manage to stay well. Ms. Smith is a secretary, a single parent, who lost eligibility for AFDC, Medicaid, food stamps, and other benefits in 1981 when the Reagan budget cuts occurred. She is thinking of taking a lower paid job in order to qualify for the Medicare help her children need." Discuss the nature of the incentives that are motivating Ms. Smith and whether it makes sense for her to take a lower-paying job.

8. Children who grow up in households using welfare have a higher incidence of using welfare as adults than does the population as a whole. Children who grow up in poverty, whether or not their families use welfare, have a higher incidence of poverty as adults than does the population as a whole. What do these facts suggest about welfare dependency? About equality of economic opportunity? About the "underclass"?

THE MARKET ECONOMY: PROBLEMS AND POLICIES

Chapter 21

Benefits and Costs of Government Intervention

There are two caricatures of the American economy. One pictures the United States as the last stronghold of free enterprise, with millions of Americans in a mad and brutal race for the almighty dollar. In the other, American business people, workers, and farmers are seen as strangling slowly in a web of red tape spun by the spider of government regulation. Neither is realistic.

Many aspects of economic life in the United States are determined by the operation of a free-market system. Private preferences, expressed through private markets and influencing private profit-seeking enterprises, determine much of what is produced, how it is produced, and the incomes of productive factors.

But even casual observation makes it clear that public policies and public decisions play a large role in the economic life of the United States. Laws restrict what people and firms may do, and taxes and subsidies influence their choices. Much public expenditure is not market determined, and this influences the distribution of national product. The United States is in fact a mixed economy.

The general case for some reliance on free markets is that allowing decentralized decision making is more efficient in a number of ways than having all economic decisions made by a centralized planning body. This is a lesson that the governments of the USSR, the People's Republic of China, and Eastern Europe have learned the hard way.

The general case for some public intervention is that almost no one wants to let the market decide everything about our economic affairs. Most people's moral and practical sense argues for some state intervention to mitigate the disastrous results that the market deals out to some. Most people believe that there are areas in which the market does not function well and in which state intervention can improve the general social good. Indeed, even when there is maximum reliance on the market economy, government is needed to enforce contracts and prevent theft. For such reasons, there is no known economy in which the people have opted for complete free-market determination of all economic matters and against any kind of government intervention.

Although many nineteenth century economists advocated a policy of **laissez faire**—the minimizing of government interference with the operation of markets—the operative choice today is not between an unhampered free-market economy and a fully centralized command economy. It is, instead, the choice of what mix of markets and government intervention best suits a people's hopes and needs. Although all economies are mixed, the mixture varies greatly among economies and over time. Whether the existing mixture is wrong—and, if so, in which direction—is debated continually.

Even the most passionate advocates of free markets agree that government must provide for enforcement of the rules under which private firms and persons make contracts. Without well-defined property rights, the enforcement of contracts and a reasonable assurance that goods and services will not be stolen, market economies cannot function in practice. In the modern, mixed economy, however, government does a great deal more than act as a "traffic cop" for the private sector.

One reason that there are mixed economies lies in what an unkind critic once called the economists' two great insights: *Markets can work, and markets can fail.* A second reason is what the critic might have called the political scientists' two great insights: *Government intervention can work, and government intervention can fail.*

In this chapter we discuss the role of the government in market-based economies. Why is it there at all? What does it do well, and what does it do badly? Do we need more or less government intervention?

How Markets Coordinate

Any economy consists of thousands upon thousands of individual markets. There are markets for agricultural goods, for manufactured goods, and for consumers' services; there are markets for intermediate goods such as steel and pig iron, which are outputs of some industries and inputs of others; there are markets for raw materials such as iron ore, trees, bauxite, and copper; there are markets for land and for thousands of different types of labor; there are markets in which money is borrowed and in which securities are sold. An economy is not a series of markets functioning in isolation but an interlocking system in which an occurrence in one market affects many others.

Any change, such as an increase in demand for a product, requires many further changes and adjustments. Should the quantity produced change? If it should, by how much and by what means? Any change in the output of one product will generally require changes in other markets and will start a chain of adjustments. Someone or something must decide what is to be produced, how, and by whom, and what is to be consumed and by whom.

The essential characteristic of the market system is that its coordination occurs in an unplanned, decentralized way. Millions of people make millions of independent decisions concerning production and consumption every day. Most of these decisions are not motivated by a desire to contribute to the social good or to make the whole economy work well but by fairly immediate considerations of self-interest. The price system coordinates these decentralized decisions, making the whole system fit together and respond to the wishes of individual consumers and producers.

The basic insight into how a market system works is that decentralized, private decision makers, acting in their own interests, respond to such signals as the prices of what they buy and sell. Economists have long emphasized price as a signaling device. When a commodity becomes scarce, its free-market price rises. Firms and households that use the commodity are led to economize on it and to look for alternatives. Firms that produce it are led to produce more of it. How the price system informs these decisions has been examined at several places in this book (for example, with respect to carrots and brussels sprouts, in Chapter 3, and with respect to agriculture, in Chapter 6). When a shortage occurs in a market, price rises and profits develop; when a glut occurs, price falls and losses develop. These are *signals,* for all to see, that arise from the overall conditions of market supply and demand.

The Role of Profits and Losses

Although the free-market economy often is described as the *price system,* the basic engine that drives the economy is economic profits. Except when there is monopoly, economic profits and losses are symptoms of *disequilibrium,* and they are the driving force in the adaptation of the economy to change.

A rise in demand or a fall in production costs creates profits for that commodity's producers. Profits make an industry attractive to new investment.

They signal that there are too few resources devoted to that industry. In search of these profits, more resources enter the industry, increasing output and driving down price, until profits are driven to zero. A fall in demand or a rise in production costs creates losses. Losses signal the reverse and an excess of resources devoted to the industry. Resources will leave the industry until those left behind are no longer suffering losses.

The importance of profits and losses is that they set in motion forces that tend to move the economy toward a new equilibrium.

Individual households and firms respond to common signals according to their own best interests. There is nothing planned or intentionally coordinated about their actions, yet when, say, a shortage causes price to rise, individual buyers begin to reduce the quantities that they demand and individual firms begin to increase the quantities that they supply. As a result, the shortage begins to lessen. As it does, price begins to come back down, and profits are reduced. These signals in turn are seen and responded to by firms and households. Eventually, when the shortage has been eliminated, there are no profits to attract further increases in supply. The chain of adjustments to the original shortage is completed.

Notice that in the sequence of signal-response-signal-response no one has to foresee at the outset the final price and quantity, nor does any government agency have to specify who will increase production and who will decrease consumption. Some firms respond to the signals for "more output" by increasing production, and they keep on increasing production until the signals get weaker and weaker and finally disappear. Some buyers withdraw from the market when they think that prices are too high, and perhaps they reenter gradually, as prices become "more reasonable." Households and firms, responding to market signals, not to the orders of government bureaucrats, "decide" who will increase production and who will limit consumption. No one is forced to do something against his or her best judgment. Voluntary responses collectively produce the end result.

Because the economy is adjusting to shocks continuously, a snapshot of the economy at any given moment reveals substantial positive profits in some industries and substantial losses in others. A snapshot

at another moment also will reveal windfall profits and losses, but their locations will be different.

The price system, like an *invisible hand* (Adam Smith's famous phrase), coordinates the responses of individual decision makers who seek only their own self-interests. Because they respond to signals that reflect market conditions, their responses are coordinated without any conscious planning.

Coordination in the Absence of Perfect Competition

To say that the price system coordinates is not to imply that it always leads to the results that perfect competition would produce. The price system coordinates responses even to prices that are "rigged" by monopolistic producers or that are altered by government controls. The signal-response process occurs in a price system even when the prices have not been determined in freely competitive markets.

When an international cartel of uranium producers decided to reduce production and raise the price of uranium, they created a shortage (and a fear of worse future shortages) among those electric utilities that depend on uranium to fuel nuclear power plants. The price of uranium shot up from under $10 per pound to over $40 in less than a year. This enormous price rise greatly increased efforts among producers outside the cartel to find more uranium and to increase their existing production by mining poorer grade ores previously considered too costly to mine.

The increases in production from these actions slowly began to ease the shortage. On the demand side, high prices and short supplies led some utilities to cancel the construction of planned nuclear power plants and to delay the construction of others. Such actions implied a long-run substitution of oil or coal for uranium. Only the fact that the OPEC cartel had also sharply raised the price of oil prevented an even more rapid reversal of the previous trend from oil to nuclear powered generators. With the prices of both uranium and oil quadrupling, the demand for coal increased sharply, and its price and production rose. Thus, the market mechanism generated adjustments to the relative prices of different fuels, even though some prices were set by cartels rather than by the free-market forces of supply and demand. It also set in motion reactions that placed limits on the power of the cartel.

The Case for the Market System

In presenting the case for free-market economies, economists have used two different approaches. One of these may be characterized as the formal defense. It is based upon showing that a free-market economy consisting of nothing but perfectly competitive industries would lead to an optimal allocation of resources. The case was discussed in Chapter 15.

The other approach is at least as old as Adam Smith and is meant to apply to market economies whether they are perfectly competitive or not. It is based on variations and implications of the theme that the market system is an effective coordinator of decentralized decision making. The case is intuitive in that it is not laid out in equations representing a complete, formal model of an economy, but it does follow from some hard reasoning, and it has been subjected to much intellectual probing. What is the nature of this defense of the free market?

Flexible and Automatic Coordination

Defenders of the market economy argue that, compared with the alternatives, the decentralized market system is more flexible and leaves more scope for adaptation to change at any moment in time and for quicker adjustment over time.

Suppose, for example, that the price of oil rises. One household might prefer to respond by maintaining a high temperature in its house and economizing on its driving, while another might do the reverse. A third household might give up air conditioning instead. This flexibility can be contrasted with centralized control, which would force the same pattern on everyone, say by rationing heating oil and gasoline, by regulating permitted temperatures, and by limiting air conditioning to days when the temperature exceeded 80° F.

Furthermore, as conditions change over time, prices will change and decentralized decision makers can react continually. In contrast, government quo-

tas, allocations, and rationing schemes are much more difficult to adjust. As a result, there are likely to be shortages and surpluses before adjustments are made. The great value of the market is that it provides automatic signals *as* a situation develops, so that all of the consequences of some major economic change do not have to be anticipated and allowed for by a body of central planners. Millions of adaptations to millions of changes in tens of thousands of markets are required every year, and it would be a Herculean task to anticipate and plan for them all.

A market system allows for coordination without *anyone* needing to understand how the whole system works. As Professor Thomas Schelling put it:

> The dairy farmer doesn't need to know how many people eat butter and how far away they are, how many other people raise cows, how many babies drink milk, or whether more money is spent on beer or milk. What he needs to know is the prices of different feeds, the characteristics of different cows, the different prices . . . for milk . . . , the relative cost of hired labor and electrical machinery, and what his net earnings might be if he sold his cows and raised pigs instead.

It is, of course, an enormous advantage that all the producers and consumers of a country collectively can make the system operate without any one of them, much less all of them, having to understand how it works. Such a lack of knowledge becomes a disadvantage, however, when people have to vote on schemes for interfering with market allocation. This contrast lies at the heart of the intuitive argument in favor of market systems.

Stimulus to Innovation and Growth

Technology, tastes, and resource availability are changing all the time, in all economies. Twenty years ago there was no such thing as a personal computer or a digital watch. Front-wheel drive was a curiosity. Students carried their books in briefcases or in canvas bags that were anything but waterproof. Manuscripts only existed as hard copy, not as computer records. In order to change one word in a manuscript, one often had to retype every word on a page. Video cassettes did not exist. The next 20 years will surely also see changes great and small. New products and techniques will be devised to adapt to short-ages, gluts, and changes in consumer demands.

In a market economy individuals risk their time and money in the hope of earning profits. While many fail, some succeed. New products and processes appear and disappear. Some are passing fads or have little impact; others become items of major significance. The market system works by trial and error to sort them out and allocates resources to what prove to be successful innovations.

In contrast, planners in more centralized systems have to guess which are going to be productive innovations or products that will be in demand. Planned growth may achieve wonders by permitting a massive effort in a chosen direction, but central planners also may guess wrong about the direction and put far too many eggs in the wrong basket or reject as unpromising something that will turn out to be vital. It is striking that the last decade has seen the two largest centrally planned economies in the world, the Soviet Union and mainland China, make increasing use of markets.

Relative Prices Reflect Relative Costs

A market system tends to drive prices toward the average total costs of production. When markets are close to perfectly competitive, this movement occurs quickly and completely; but even where there is substantial market power, new products and new producers respond to the lure of profits, and their output drives prices down toward the costs of production.

The advantage of having relative prices reflect relative costs was discussed in Chapter 15. When prices are equal to marginal costs, there will be allocative efficiency, because market choices are then made in the light of opportunity costs.[1] Firms will choose methods that minimize their own cost of producing output, and in so doing automatically will minimize the opportunity cost of the resources that they use. Similarly, when households choose commodity A over commodity B, even though A uses resources of twice the total value of the resources used to produce B, they will have to pay the (differ-

ence in) price. They will only do so when they value A correspondingly more than B at the margin.

When relative prices reflect relative costs, producers and consumers use the nation's resources in a manner that is consistent with allocative efficiency.

Self-Correction of Disequilibrium

Equilibrium of the economic system is continually disrupted by change. If the economy does not "pursue" equilibrium, there would be little comfort in saying things would be bright indeed if only it reached equilibrium. (We all know someone who would have been a great surgeon if only he or she had gone to medical school.)

An important characteristic of the price system is its ability to set in motion forces that tend to correct disequilibrium.

To review the advantages of the price system in this respect, imagine operating without a market mechanism. Suppose that planning boards make all market decisions. The Board in Control of Men's Clothing hears that pleated shirts are all the rage in neighboring countries. It orders a certain proportion of clothing factories to make pleated shirts instead of the traditional men's dress shirt. Conceivably, the quantities of pleated shirts and traditional shirts produced could be just right, given shoppers' preferences. But what if the board guesses wrong and orders too many traditional shirts and not enough pleated shirts to be produced? Long lines would appear at pleated-shirt counters, while mountains of traditional shirts would pile up. Once the board sees the lines for pleated shirts, it could order a change in quantities produced. Meanwhile, it could store the extra traditional shirts for another season or ship them to a country with different tastes.

Such a system can correct an initial mistake, but it may prove inefficient in doing so. It may use a lot of resources in planning and administration that could instead be used to produce commodities. Further, many consumers may be greatly inconvenienced if the board is slow to correct its error. In such a system the members of the board may have no incentive to admit and correct a mistake quickly.

---

[1] Of course, the mechanism in the text only assures that prices tend to equal average costs, not marginal costs. Except when there is natural monopoly, long-run average costs will be near long-run marginal costs, and the mechanism in the text will generate allocations that are near to being efficient.

Indeed, if the authorities do not like pleated shirts, the board may get credit for having stopped the craze before it went too far!

In contrast, suppose that in a market system a similar misestimation of the demand for pleated shirts and traditional shirts is made by the men's clothing industry. Lines develop at pleated-shirt counters, and inventories of traditional shirts accumulate. Stores raise the prices of pleated shirts and at the same time lower them for traditional shirts. Consumers who care more about price than fashion could get bargains by buying traditional shirts. Pleated-shirt manufacturers could earn profits by raising prices and running extra shifts to increase production. Some traditional-shirt producers would be motivated to shift production quickly to pleated shirts and to make traditional shirts more attractive to buyers by cutting prices. Unlike the planning board, the producers in a market system would be motivated to correct their initial mistakes as quickly as possible. Those who would be slowest to adjust would lose the most money and might even be forced out of business.

Decentralization of Power

Another important part of the case for a market economy is that it tends to decentralize power and thus requires less coercion of individuals than does any other type of economy. Of course, even though markets tend to diffuse power, they do not do so completely; large firms and large unions clearly do have and do exercise substantial economic power.

While the market power of large corporations and unions is not negligible, it tends to be constrained both by the competition of other large entities and by the emergence of new products and firms. This is the process of creative destruction that was described by Joseph Schumpeter (see pages 251–252). In any case, say defenders of the free market, even such aggregations of private power are far less substantial than government power.

Governments must coerce if markets are not allowed to allocate people to jobs and commodities to consumers. Not only will such coercion be regarded as arbitrary (especially by those who do not like the results), but the power surely creates major opportunities for bribery, corruption, and allocation according to the tastes of the central administrators. If at the going prices and wages there are not enough apartments or coveted jobs to go around, the bureaucrats can allocate some to those who pay the largest bribe, some to those with religious beliefs, hair styles, or political views that they like, and only the rest to those whose names come up on the waiting list. This line of reasoning has been articulated forcefully by the conservative economist and Nobel Prize winner Milton Friedman, who argues that economic freedom—the ability to allocate resources through private markets—is essential to the maintenance of political freedom. Many other economists and social theorists have noted that this proposition has not been demonstrated empirically.

 ## The Case for Intervention

Free markets do all of the good things that we have just discussed and more; yet there are many circumstances in the workings of the free market that do not result in the most desirable outcomes. When this happens, we say that markets have *failed*. The case for intervening in free markets turns in large part on identifying the conditions that lead to **market failure.** Much of the following discussion is devoted to this task.

The word *failure* in this context may convey the wrong impression.

Market failure does not mean that nothing good has happened but that the *best attainable outcome* has not been achieved.

The phrase is used to apply to two quite different sets of circumstances. One is the failure of the market system to achieve efficiency in the allocation of society's resources. The other is the failure of the market system to serve social goals other than efficiency, such as a desired distribution of income or the preservation of value systems. We treat each in turn.

Failure to Achieve Efficiency

Market economies can fail to be efficient for any one of four broad types of reasons. The first is *monopoly*, which we discussed in Chapter 15. Monopoly producers will maximize profits at an output where price exceeds marginal cost, leading to inefficiency. Although some monopolies are maintained through artificial barriers to entry, others arise naturally because in some industries the least costly way to produce a good or a service is to have a single producer. The standard government remedies are antitrust policy and public utility regulation, which, as discussed in Chapter 15, present problems of their own.

There are three other broad types of phenomena that lead to inefficient market outcomes, called *externalities, collective consumption goods,* and *information asymmetries.*

As in the case of monopoly, externalities, collective consumption goods, and information asymmetries cause inefficiency to arise because in market equilibrium the marginal revenue for the producer is not equal to the marginal cost to society.

This violates the conditions for allocative efficiency that were discussed in Chapter 14.

Externalities as a Source of Inefficiency

Costs, as economists define them, concern the value of resources used in the process of production. According to the opportunity-cost principle, value is the benefit that resources would produce in their best alternative use. But who decides what resources are used when and what their opportunity cost is?

Consider the case of a student who is thinking of extending a party for one more hour at 1:00 A.M. For this student, the opportunity cost includes the psychological value of getting an extra hour of sleep, as well as the money cost of the electricity to run the stereo, whatever will be eaten and drunk, the value of repairs to the apartment, and so forth. However, there is another resource used when the party runs for an extra hour—the neighbors' sleep, and the student does not consider it when she makes her decision to keep the stereo blasting.

Private and social costs.   The difference in the viewpoint of the party thrower and the neighbors illustrates the important distinction between **private cost** and **social cost.** Private cost measures the best alternative use of the resource available to the private decision maker. The party thrower incurs private

costs equal to her best alternative use of the resources that go into an extra hour of partying. The party thrower cannot make any use of the neighbors' sleep and so values the sleep at zero. The *social cost* includes the private cost but also includes the best use of *all* resources available to society. In this case, social cost includes the cost imposed on the neighbors by an extra hour of partying.

Discrepancies between private and social cost lead to market failure.

The reason for this is that efficiency requires that prices cover social cost, but private producers and consumers, adjusting to private costs, will neglect those elements of social cost that are incurred by others. This is shown in Figure 21-1, which illustrates the case of a firm whose production process generates harmful smoke. Individuals who live and work in the neighborhood of the firm bear real costs due to the firm's production. In addition to the disutility of enduring the smoke and of any adverse health effects, they may invest in air conditioners so that they can keep the noxious fumes out. None of the resources that are used to remove the pollution are available to the firm. Therefore, the value of these resources will not be taken into account when the firm decides how much to produce. The element of social cost that the firm is ignoring in its decision is external to its decision-making process.

In general, discrepancies between social and private cost occur when there are **externalities,** which are the costs or benefits of a transaction that are incurred or received by other members of the society but not taken into account by the parties to the transaction. They are also called *third-party effects,* because parties other than the two primary participants in the transaction (the buyer and the seller) are affected. Externalities arise in many different ways, and they may be beneficial or harmful.

When I paint my house, I enhance my neighbors' view and the value of their property. When an Einstein or a Rembrandt gives the world a discovery or a work of art whose worth is far in excess of what he is paid to produce it, he confers an external benefit. Private producers will tend to produce too little of commodities that generate beneficial externalities because they bear all of the costs, while others reap part of the benefits.

Other externalities are harmful. Before we con-

FIGURE 21-1   Private and Social Cost

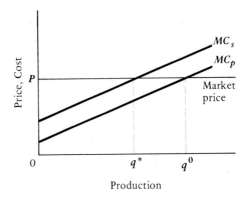

A competitive firm will produce output to the point where its private marginal cost equals the market price. In this case, every unit of output produced imposes *external costs,* equal to the distance between MC_p (private marginal cost—the marginal cost curve that is faced by the firm) and MC_s (social marginal cost). The profit-maximizing competitive firm chooses to produce q^0, the output where price equals private marginal cost. If the full social cost of production were taken into account, only q^* would be produced. Notice that for each unit of output between q^* and q^0, the cost borne by all members of society exceeds the value to consumers, which is the market price. Over this range, social cost exceeds private revenue, implying allocative inefficiency.

sider several examples, we can observe that private producers will tend to produce too much of commodities that generate harmful externalities because they bear none of the extra costs that are suffered by others.

Externalities, whether adverse or beneficial, cause market outcomes to be inefficient, because they cause marginal private revenue to differ from marginal social cost.

Pollution.   When firms use resources that they do not regard as scarce, they fail to consider the cost of those resources. This is a characteristic of most examples of pollution, including the case that is illustrated in Figure 21-1. When a paper mill produces pulp for the world's newspapers, more people are affected than its suppliers, employees, and customers. Its water-discharged effluent hurts the fishing

boats that ply nearby waters, and its smog makes many resort areas less attractive, thereby reducing the tourist revenues that local motel operators and boat renters can expect. The firm neglects these external effects of its actions, because its profits are not affected by them.

Dumping of hazardous wastes, air pollution, and water pollution may occur as a result of calculated decisions as to what and how to produce or consume. They also may occur because private producers are willing to take excessive risk when they bear only part of the costs should things go wrong. Thus, accidents, such as an oil blowout or the breakup of a tanker, which are not desired or planned by anyone, may occur more frequently because private firms devote insufficient resources to avoiding risk.

Common-property resources.   The world's oceans once teemed with fish, but today overfishing has caused a worldwide fish shortage. How could this happen?

Fish are an example of what is called a **common-property resource,** a resource that is owned by no one and may be used by anyone. No one owns the oceans' fish until they are caught. The world's international fishing grounds are common property for all who seek to catch them. If by taking more fish one person reduces the catch of others, he or she does not count this as a cost, but it is a cost to society.

It is socially optimal to add to a fishing fleet until marginal social revenue (the increase in the value of the fleet's total catch from adding the last boat) just equals the marginal social cost (the value of the resources used to operate the last boat). This is the size of the fishing fleet that a benevolent social planner would choose.

The free market will not, however, produce this result. Potential new entrants will judge entry to be profitable if the value of their own catch is greater than the cost of operating their boats. However, a new entrant's catch is *partly* an addition to total catch and *partly* a reduction of the catch of others—because of congestion, each new boat reduces the catch of all other boats. Thus, under free entry there will be too many boats in the fleet. Boats will continue to enter until there are no longer any profits for the marginal boat. In other words, boats will enter until the *average* value of the catch of a typical boat is equal to the cost of running that boat. At this point, however, the net addition to the *total* catch brought about by the last boat will be substantially less than the cost of operating the boat.

With common-property resources the level of activity will be too high because each new entrant will gain revenue, not only from the amount that it adds to total product but also from the amount that it takes away from the outputs of other producers.

This is not an untested theory. Fishing grounds and other common-property resources show a typical pattern of overexploitation. As a result, governments often use quotas and other restrictions in an attempt to hold the industry to its socially optimal size.

Congestion. The externality arising from common-property resources often takes the form of *congestion*. When a commuter drives to work during the morning rush hour, she incurs the cost of driving her car, including the opportunity cost of spending her time in traffic rather than doing something else. She is also imposing a social cost on other commuters. Because her trip adds to traffic congestion, she is making everyone else's trip on the same road take a little bit longer. If she is just indifferent between taking the trip and not, her private cost will just equal her private benefit.

The social costs imposed on others will not be taken into account by any individual commuter. At the optimum, there would be less traffic—the time and money cost of the marginal commuter, plus the extra time costs imposed on all other drivers would add up to the commuter's benefit from the trip.

Congestion externalities arise in highway traffic, air traffic (where the externality is the added risk of collision that another plane imposes on all others in the sky), and city sidewalks at lunch hour. They also occur, in the form of brownouts, when people consider only the money cost of using their air conditioners. As we shall see, some congestion externalities are relatively easy to ameliorate through government intervention, while others are not.

Myopia. Private producers and consumers making decisions today often fail to account fully for the effects that their behavior will have in the future. The externalities imposed can, again, be either positive or negative, but it is generally thought that negative cases, where current behavior imposes fu-

ture costs that are not taken into account, are the more prevalent. Long-term environmental damage (discussed at length in Chapter 22) may arise from failure to take the well-being of future citizens into account. *Myopia* is especially likely to lead to misallocation of resources when *collective consumption goods,* such as environmental quality, are involved.

Collective Consumption Goods as a Source of Inefficiency

Collective consumption goods, sometimes called **public goods,** have the peculiar property that the total cost of providing them does not increase as the number of consumers increases. The classic case is national defense. Adding to the population of the United States does not diminish the extent to which each U.S. citizen is defended by a given size and quality of the armed forces. Information is also a public good. Suppose a certain food additive causes cancer. The cost of discovering this needs to be borne only once. The information is then of value to everyone who might have used the additive, and the cost of making the information available to one more consumer is essentially zero.

Both of these examples raise what is called the *free-rider* problem. In neither case will the private market produce efficient amounts of the public good, because in both cases once the good is produced it is virtually impossible to make people pay for its use. Indeed, it is quite possible that markets will fail to produce collective consumption goods at all. The obvious remedy in these cases is government provision of the good, paid for by taxes.

How much of a public good should the government provide? It should provide up to the point where the *sum of everyone's individual valuations* of the good is just equal to the marginal cost of providing the good. To see why we must add up everyone's marginal valuation, consider a simple example. Suppose Andy, Barbara, Carol, and Dick are all thinking of renting a videotape. Watching the video will be a collective consumption good for the four of them, because the cost will be same no matter how many of them decide to watch. Suppose each honestly expresses his or her value of watching the tape. Say it is worth $1.00 to Andy, $2.00 each to Barbara and Carol, and $.50 to Dick. If the rental charge for the tape is $5.50 or less, it is worth renting, because the total value to all consumers will be at least equal to the cost.

This example can also illustrate the free-rider problem. If the cost of renting the tape is only $3, everyone will have an incentive to understate the value that they place on watching the tape, hoping to get the others to pay for their "free ride."

Inefficient exclusion. Sometimes it is possible to eliminate the free-rider problem by charging a fee for using a public good. In the example above, the videotape rental would have been covered if each member of the group were charged $1. Doing so, however, would have been inefficient. Dick, who would be willing to pay $.50 to see the video, would be excluded. The marginal benefit from letting Dick see the video is $.50, and the marginal cost is zero. It is plainly inefficient to exclude him.

Parks, roads, and bridges often are financed through fees or tolls that lead to inefficient exclusion. For an uncongested road, efficiency requires that users pay marginal cost, which is very close to zero. (Gasoline taxes typically cover maintenance costs.) Charging a toll that pays for construction of a road, as is done on some turnpikes in the East and in the Midwest, excludes users who value its use at more than marginal cost but less than the toll. There is another inefficiency involved in charging tolls. They are expensive to collect, and, as anyone who has ever driven on toll roads in large cities knows, they cause congestion of their own.

Even where getting around the free-rider problem is technically possible, it is usually inefficient. As in cases in which the private market would not produce a public good at all, the obvious remedy is government provision.

Efficient provision of public goods requires that consumers pay the marginal cost of their consumption—zero. Private markets will never provide goods at a price of zero and thus will always underprovide collective consumption goods.

Asymmetric Information as a Source of Inefficiency

The role of information in the economy has received increasing attention from economists in recent years. Information is, of course, a valuable commodity, and markets for information and expertise are well developed, as every college student is aware. Markets for expertise are conceptually identical to markets for

any other valuable service. They can pose special problems, however. One of these we have already discussed: Information is often a public good and thus will tend to be underproduced by the private sector, because once the information is known to anyone it is extremely cheap to make it available to others.

Even where information is not a public good, markets for expertise are prone to market failure. The reason for this is that one party to a transaction often can take advantage of special knowledge in ways that change the nature of the transaction itself. Here are some important examples.

Moral hazard. As we saw in Chapter 8, *moral hazard* problems often occur as a result of insurance. In general, we say that there is moral hazard when one party to a transaction has both the incentive and the ability to shift costs onto the other party. The classic example is the homeowner who does not bother to shovel snow from his walk because he knows that his insurance will cover the cost if the mail carrier should twist an ankle. The costs of the homeowner's lax behavior will be borne largely by others, including the mail carrier, the insurance company, and, indirectly, others who purchase insurance. Individuals and firms who are insured against loss generally will take less care to prevent that loss than they would in the absence of insurance. They do so because they do not bear all of the marginal cost imposed by the risk, while they do bear all of the marginal cost of taking action to reduce the risk.

As in all of the cases of market failure that we have considered, the failure arises because the marginal private benefit of an action is not equal to the marginal social cost of that action. The existence of insurance markets, which ideally merely spread risk, also will increase total risk because of moral hazard.

Insurance is not the only context in which moral hazard problems arise. Another example is professional services. Suppose you ask a physician whether you are sick or an attorney whether you need legal assistance. The doctor and the lawyer both face moral hazard, in that they both have a financial interest in giving you answers that will encourage you to buy their services, and it is difficult for you to find out if their advice is "good" advice. A similar situation occurs when you ask your mechanic what is wrong with your engine. In all of these cases, one party to the transaction has special knowledge that he or she could use to change the nature of the transaction in his or her favor. As long as the auto mechanic merely is selling her expertise in repairing cars, there is no problem, but when she uses her expertise to persuade the consumer to demand more repairs than are warranted, there is a moral hazard problem. Codes of professional ethics, and licensing and certification practices, both governmental and private, are reactions to concerns about this kind of moral hazard.

Adverse selection.   Closely related to moral hazard (see Chapter 8) is the problem of *adverse selection*—the tendency of people who are most at risk to buy the most insurance. A person who is suffering from a heart condition may seek to increase his life insurance coverage by purchasing as much additional coverage as is available without a medical examination. People who buy insurance almost always know more about themselves as individual insurance risks than do their insurance companies. The company can try to limit the variation in risk by setting up broad categories based on variables, such as age and occupation, over which actuarial risk is known to vary. The rate charged is then different across categories and is based on the average risk in each category, but there must always be much variability of risk *within* any one category.

Those who know that they are well above the average risk for their category are offered a bargain and will be led to take out more car, health, life, or fire insurance than they otherwise would. Their insurance premiums also will not cover the full expected cost of the risk that they are insuring against. Once again, their private cost is less than social cost. On the other side, someone who knows she is a low risk and pays a higher price than the amount warranted by her risk is motivated to take out less insurance than she otherwise would. In this case her private cost is more than the social cost. In both cases, resources are allocated inefficiently because the marginal private benefit of the action (taking out insurance) is not equal to the social cost.

More generally, any time either party to a transaction lacks information that the other party has or is deceived by claims made by the other party, market results will tend to be changed, and such changes may lead to inefficiency. Economically (but not legally) it is but a small step from such unequal knowledge to outright fraud. The arsonist who buys fire insurance before setting a building on fire or the business person with fire insurance who decides that

a fire is preferable to bankruptcy are extreme examples of moral hazard.

Asymmetric information is involved in many other situations of market failure. The *principal-agent* problem, which was discussed in Chapter 16, is an example. In its classic form, the firm's managers act as agents for the stockholders, who are the legal principals of the firm. The managers are much better informed than the principals are about what they do and what they can do. Indeed, the managers are hired for their special expertise. Given that it is expensive to monitor what the agents do, they have latitude to pursue goals other than the firms' profits. The private costs and benefits of their actions thus will be different from the social costs and benefits, with the usual consequences for the efficiency of the market system. Another example of market failure due to asymmetric information is the apparent overdiscounting of the prices of used cars because of the buyer's risk of acquiring a "lemon." (See the discussion of this problem in Box 8-2.)

Government remedies to problems that arise from moral hazard, adverse selection, and principal-agent problems are relatively rare. The most important is the case of Medicare, the national health insurance system for the elderly. Until the advent of Medicare in 1965, it was virtually impossible for elderly consumers to purchase health insurance that covered serious illness. Why? This was because the insurance companies were quite aware of the problem of adverse selection. They feared that only those elderly who knew themselves to be bad risks would buy health insurance. At the price that the companies thought they needed to charge to break even while covering the worst risks, no one wanted insurance at all! By providing mandatory insurance, paid for by payroll taxes, the government got around the adverse-selection problem. Whether they are good or bad risks, almost all U.S. workers *must* buy Medicare hospital insurance and have no choice about how much to buy. Thus, the insurance can be provided without any adverse selection.

Failure to Achieve Other Social Goals

Notwithstanding the real problems that are generated by externalities, information asymmetries, and public goods, the great strength of market systems is their ability to generate reasonably efficient outcomes, in a great many cases, using very decentralized organization. It should not be surprising that markets do less well at fostering goals that are held for society as a whole rather than derived from individuals' desires to improve their private circumstances. Some of these goals, for example, the desire for an "equitable" income distribution, are basically economic. Some, especially notions that people in a given society should have shared values, such as patriotism or a belief in civil liberties, are basically not economic. In either set of cases, however, markets are not very effective, precisely because the goods in question are not of the kind that can be exchanged in decentralized transactions. (Indeed, if we stretch the definition a bit, these are collective consumption goods, and we know that markets tend to underproduce such goods.)

Income Distribution

An important characteristic of a market economy is the *distribution* of the income that it determines. People whose services are in heavy demand relative to supply, such as television anchorpersons and superior football players, earn large incomes, while people whose services are not in heavy demand relative to supply, such as Ph.D.s in classics and high school graduates without work experience, earn much less.

The distribution of income produced by the market can be looked at in equilibrium or in disequilibrium. In equilibrium, in an efficiently operating free-market economy, similar efforts of work or investment by similar people will tend to be similarly rewarded everywhere in the economy. Of course, dissimilar people will be dissimilarly rewarded.

In disequilibrium similar people making similar efforts are likely to be dissimilarly rewarded. People in declining industries, areas, and occupations suffer the punishment of low earnings through no fault of their own. Those in expanding sectors earn the reward of high earnings through no extra effort or talent of their own.

These rewards and punishments serve the important function in decentralized decision making of motivating people to adapt. The advantage of such a system is that individuals can make their own decisions about how to alter their behavior when market conditions change; the disadvantage is that temporary rewards and punishments are dealt out as a result of changes in market conditions that are beyond the control of the affected individuals.

Moreover, even equilibrium differences in income may seem unfair. A free-market system rewards certain groups and penalizes others. Because the workings of the market may be stern, even cruel, society often chooses to intervene. Should heads of households be forced to bear the full burden of their misfortune if, through no fault of their own, they lose their jobs? Even if they lose their jobs through their own fault, should they and their families have to bear the whole burden, which may include starvation? Should the ill and the aged be thrown on the mercy of their families? What if they have no families? Both private charities and a great many government policies are concerned with modifying the distribution of income that results from such things as where one starts, how able one is, how lucky one is, and how one fares in the free-market world.

Often the goal of a more equitable distribution conflicts with the goal of a more efficient economy.

Some of the problems that this can create in policy debates are further discussed in Box 21-1.

Preferences for Public Provision

Police protection, even justice, might be provided by private-market mechanisms. Security guards, private detectives, and bodyguards all provide police-like protection. Privately hired arbitrators, "hired guns," and vigilantes of the Old West represent private ways of obtaining "justice." Yet the members of society may believe that a public police force is *preferable* to a private one and that public justice is preferable to justice for hire.

As another example, public schools may be better or worse than private schools; either way they are likely to be different, particularly because persons other than parents, teachers, and owners influence their policies. Much of the case for public education rests on the advantages of having other people's children educated in a particular kind of environment that is *different* from what a private school would provide. In these cases, the fact that markets provide individual choice is viewed by some as a market failure.

Protecting Individuals from Others

People can use and even abuse other people for economic gain in ways that the members of society find offensive. Child labor laws and minimum standards of working conditions are responses to such actions.

BOX 21-1

Distribution Versus Efficiency

Economists recognize that government actions can affect both the allocation of resources and the distribution of income. Resource allocation is easier to talk about, simply because economists have developed precise definitions of *efficient* and *inefficient* allocations. Distribution is more difficult, because we cannot talk about *better* or *worse* distributions of income without introducing normative considerations. Partly because of this, much of economics concerns efficiency and neglects effects on the distribution of income. Many disagreements about economic and social policy can be understood in terms of differences in emphasis on efficiency and distribution.

Consider the OPEC-induced rise in oil prices during the 1970s. From the point of view of efficiency alone, the correct policy was to let domestic oil prices in all oil-importing countries rise along with the world price. Instead, many governments held the price down. They were concerned, among other things, with the effect of rising prices on the windfall profits that were earned by large oil companies and on the welfare of poorer citizens. "We just cannot let the poor find their heating bills rise so much and so fast while the profits of the oil companies soar" was a common reaction.

Here is a genuine conflict for which economics cannot provide a solution, because, in the end, the answer must rest on value judgments. However, economics can make the consequences of various choices apparent, and it can suggest policy alternatives. The consequences of holding down the price of oil (out of concern for the effect of higher prices on the poor) was an inefficient use of the countries' resources. Total national income was reduced, and some new investment was misdirected into high-cost (oil-using) rather than low-cost (oil-saving) methods of production. Thus, in the long run average standards of living were reduced. Whether this reduction in the average standard of living was a reasonable price to pay for shielding the poor is an open question; yet it is unlikely that the question was ever posed or the calculations made.

Can one have both efficiency and desired redis-

tributions? One way is to let the price system do the job of signaling relative scarcities and costs, thereby ensuring some efficiency in the allocation of resources, but at the same time to use taxes or expenditures to transfer income to achieve redistributive goals. This method does not seek to help the poor (or other underprivileged groups) by subsidizing oil or any other price. Rather, it seeks to provide these groups with sufficient income by providing direct income transfers. Then it leaves producers and consumers free to respond to relative prices that approximately reflect relative opportunity costs.

Advocates of this method argue that it is surer, more direct, and less costly in its side effects than the method of subsidizing the prices of particular goods. Moreover, the price-subsidy method surely ends up subsidizing some who are rich and missing some who are very poor. Subsidizing gasoline prices, for example, benefits the Cadillac owner and does nothing for those too poor to own a car. Thus, even in redistribution this method of subsidization is haphazard.

Supporters of redistribution through the price system usually counter with two arguments. First, it is well and good to say we *could* let oil prices rise and simultaneously subsidize the poor and tax the rich, but the political process makes it unlikely that we *will* do so. Thus, say supporters of redistribution, holding prices down may not be the best imaginable policy, but it may be the best or even the only practical way to get a fairer distributive result.

Second, certain commodities such as food, heat, medical care, and housing are claimed to be basic to a civilized life and therefore should be provided to households cheaply, whatever their real opportunity cost. The supporters of redistribution through the price system believe that the inefficiencies resulting from prices that do not reflect opportunity costs are a burden worth bearing to ensure that even people with very low incomes can afford these basics. (Box 23-2 provides further discussion of subsidies to medical care.)

Yet direct abuse is not the only example of this kind of market failure. In an unhindered free market, the adults in a household would usually decide how much education to buy for their children. Selfish parents might buy no education, while egalitarian parents might buy the same education for all of their children, regardless of their abilities. The members of society may want to interfere in these choices, both to protect the child of the selfish parent and to ensure that some of the scarce educational resources are distributed according to the ability and the willingness to use them rather than according to a family's wealth. All households are forced to provide a minimum of education for their children, and a number of inducements are offered—through public universities, scholarships, and other means—for talented children to consume more education than they or their parents might choose if they had to pay the entire cost themselves.

Paternalism

Members of society, acting through the state, often seek to protect adult (and presumably responsible) individuals, not from others but from themselves. Laws prohibiting the use of heroin, crack, and other drugs and laws prescribing the installation and use of seat belts are intended primarily to protect individuals from their own ignorance or shortsightedness. This kind of interference in the free choices of individuals is called **paternalism.** Whether such actions reflect the wishes of the majority in the society or whether they reflect the actions of overbearing governments, there is no doubt that the market will not provide this kind of protection. Buyers do not buy what they do not want, and sellers have no motive to provide it.

Protection and paternalism are often closely related to **merit goods.** Merit goods are goods that society deems to be especially important and that individuals should be required or encouraged to consume. Housing, education, and health care are prime examples of merit goods.

Social Obligations

In a free-market system, if you can pay another person to do things for you, you may do so. If you persuade someone else to clean your house in return for $35, presumably both parties to the transaction are better off: You prefer to part with $35 rather than to clean the house yourself, and the person you hire prefers $35 to not cleaning your house. Normally society does not interfere with people's ability to negotiate mutually advantageous contracts.

Most people do not feel this way, however, about activities that are regarded as social obligations. For example, when military service is compulsory, contracts similar to the one between you and a housekeeper could also be negotiated. Some persons faced with the obligation to do military service could no doubt pay enough to persuade others to do their tour of service for them.[2] By exactly the same argument as we just used, we can presume that both parties will be better off if they are allowed to negotiate such a trade. Yet such contracts are usually prohibited. They are prohibited because there are values to be considered other than those that can be expressed in a market. In times when it is necessary, military service by all healthy males is usually held to be a duty that is independent of an individual's tastes, wealth, influence, or social position. It is felt that everyone *ought* to do this service, and exchanges between willing traders are prohibited.

Military service is not the only example of a social obligation. Citizens cannot buy their way out of jury duty or legally sell their votes to another, even though in many cases they could find willing trading partners.

Even if the price system allocated goods and services with complete efficiency, members of a society may not wish to rely solely on the market if they have other goals that they wish to achieve.

 # Government Intervention

Private collective action sometimes can remedy the failures of private individual action. (Private charities can help the poor; volunteer fire departments can fight fires; insurance companies can guard against adverse selection by more careful classification of clients.) However, by far the most common remedy for market failure is government intervention.

The previous discussion makes clear that markets

---

[2] During the Civil War it was a common practice for a man to avoid the draft by hiring a substitute to serve in his place.

do fail, thereby providing scope for governments to intervene in beneficial ways. Whether government intervention is warranted in a given case will depend both on the magnitude of the market failure that the intervention is designed to correct and on the costs of the government action itself. The benefits of some types of government intervention (e.g., the social advantages of having a publicly provided justice system) are both difficult to quantify and potentially very large. For many types of government activity, however, *benefit-cost analysis,* developed by economists to consider what sorts of economic projects ought to be undertaken by governments, can be helpful in considering the general question of when, and how much, governments ought to intervene.

The idea behind benefit-cost analysis is transparently simple: Add up the (opportunity) costs of a given action, then add up the benefits, and do the action if the benefits outweigh the costs. In practice, benefit-cost analysis can be difficult for three reasons. First, it may be difficult to ascertain what will happen when an action is undertaken. Second, many government actions involve costs and benefits that will take place only in the distant future. Just how to *discount* future events raises both technical and normative problems for the analyst. Third, some benefits and costs (e.g., the benefits of prohibiting actions that would harm members of an endangered species of animal) are at best very hard to quantify. Indeed, many people would argue that they cannot be and should not be quantified, as they involve values that are not commensurate with money. The practice then is to use benefit-cost analysis to measure the things that can be measured and to be sure that the things that cannot be measured are not forgotten when collective decisions are made. By narrowing the range of things that must be determined by informal judgment, benefit-cost analysis can still play a useful role.

In this chapter we have been working toward a benefit-cost analysis of government intervention. We have made a general case against it (free markets are great economizers on information and coordination costs). We have made a general case for it (free markets will fail to produce efficiency when there are public goods, externalities, or information asymmetries and will fail to produce other social goals as well). We now turn to the more specific questions of what governments do when they intervene, what the costs of government intervention are, and under which circumstances government interventions are

likely to fail to improve upon even imperfect private markets.

The Tools of Government Intervention

The legal power of the government to intervene in the workings of the economy is limited only by the Constitution (as interpreted by the courts), the willingness of Congress to pass laws, and the willingness of the executive branch to enforce them. There are numerous ways in which one or another level of government can prevent, alter, complement, or replace the workings of the unrestricted market economy.

Public provision.   National defense, the criminal justice system, the public schools, the interstate highway system, air traffic control, and the national parks are all examples of goods or services that are directly provided by governments in the United States. Public provision is the obvious remedy for market failure to provide collective consumption goods, but it is also often used in the interest of redistribution (e.g., public hospitals) and other social goals (e.g., public schools). In Chapter 23 we shall consider public spending in detail.

Redistribution and social insurance programs.   Taxes and spending often are used to provide a distribution of income that is different from that generated by the private market. The transfer programs that were discussed in Chapter 20 affect the distribution of income in this way. In Chapter 23 we shall examine the distributive effects of the tax system. Chapter 23 also contains a discussion of the effect of redistributive spending on government budgets.

Proscriptive rules.   Proscriptive rules take the form "Thou shalt. . . ." or "Thou shalt not. . . .": They tell people and firms what they can and cannot do. Such rules require parents to send their children to school and to have them inoculated against measles and diphtheria. Laws that prohibit gambling and pornography attempt to enforce a particular moral code on the whole society. In Chapter 15 we discussed an important form of policy by prohibition—antitrust policy.

There are many other examples. Children cannot be served alcoholic drinks legally. Prostitution is prohibited in most places, even between a willing buyer and a willing seller. In most states you must buy automobile insurance. A person who offers goods for sale, including his or her own house, cannot refuse to sell to someone because of a dislike for the customer's color or dress. There are rules against fraudulent advertising and the sale of substandard, adulterated, or poisonous foods.

Notice that proscriptive rules are used to deal with a wide range of types of market failure. In the examples just given, the rules requiring that all drivers must have automobile insurance and prohibiting the selling of poisonous food are designed to prevent negative externalities. Rules against housing discrimination support a social value of equal opportunity. Rules against serving alcohol to minors are basically paternalistic. Antitrust laws, at least some of the time, directly proscribe a type of market imperfection.

Prescriptive rules. Prescriptive rules substitute the rule maker's judgment for the firm's or the household's judgment about such things as prices charged, products produced, and methods of production. Prescriptive regulation tends to restrict private action more than proscriptive regulation because it *replaces* private decision making rather than simply *limiting* the set of acceptable private decisions. Regulation of public utilities is an important example of prescriptive regulation (see Chapter 15), but prescriptive regulation goes far beyond the natural-monopoly regulation that we have discussed. Indeed, much economic regulation, especially regarding pollution control, safety, and health, comes in the form of prescriptive rules. (See Chapter 22.)

As is the case with proscriptive rules, prescriptive rules are used to deal with essentially all types of market failure. Public-utility regulation is designed to ameliorate the consequences of natural monopoly; some health and safety regulation reduces negative externalities, and some is arguably paternalistic. Some states require that private firms provide specific fringe benefits (the consequences here are primarily redistributive). Many localities require real estate developers to donate and to develop park land when they build certain types of projects. The resulting parks are collective consumption goods that are privately provided.

Problems with rule making. Rule making often appears to be a cheap, easy, and direct way of compelling desirable behavior in the face of market failure, but this appearance is deceptive. Rules must be enforceable and enforced, and, once enforced, they must be effective in obtaining the hoped-for results. These conditions are often difficult and expensive to achieve. Moreover, difficulties in enforcement can lead to inequities.

Consider a requirement for the installation of an antipollution device that will meet a certain standard in reducing automobile exhaust emissions. Such a law may be the outcome of congressional debate on pollution control—and, having passed the bill, Congress will turn to other things. Yet certain problems must be solved before the law can achieve its purpose. Even with perfect compliance by the manufacturer, the device may not work well unless it is kept in working order by the owner. Yet the owner has no private incentive to maintain it, and it would be expensive to inspect every vehicle regularly and to force owners to keep the devices at the standard that is set by law.

Even a well-designed rule will work only to the extent to which those who are regulated cannot figure out a way to evade its intent while obeying its letter.

There will be a substantial incentive to find loopholes in regulations. Resources that could be used elsewhere will be devoted by the regulated to the search for such loopholes and then, in turn, by the regulators to counteracting such evasion.

Structuring incentives. Almost all government actions, including the kinds that we have discussed here, change the incentives facing households and firms. If the government provides a park, people will have a weakened incentive to own large plots of land of their own. If the government proscribes a certain type of behavior, the penalty that is imposed will influence people to do something else. Fixing minimum or maximum prices (as we saw in the discussion of agriculture and rent control in Chapter 6) affects privately chosen levels of output.

The government can adjust the tax system to provide subsidies to some kinds of behavior and penalties to others (see Chapter 23). Deductible mortgage interest and real estate taxes, for example, make owned housing relatively more attractive than other assets that a household might purchase. Such tax treatment sends the household different signals from those sent by the free market. Scholarships to students to become nurses or teachers may offset barriers to mobility into those occupations. Fines and criminal penalties for violating the rules that are imposed are another part of the incentive structure. By providing direct or indirect fines or subsidies, the government can correct externalities, induce private production of public goods, change the income distribution, and encourage behavior that is deemed socially valuable.

The government has many tools at its disposal and can use them singly or in combination to address different kinds of market failure.

The Costs of Government Intervention

Consider the following argument: (1) The market system is working imperfectly; (2) government has the legal means to improve the situation; (3) therefore, the public interest will be served by government intervention.

This appealing argument is deficient because it neglects two important considerations. First, government intervention is costly. For this reason not every market failure is worth correcting. Second, government intervention may be imperfect. Just as markets sometimes succeed and sometimes fail, so government intervention sometimes succeeds and sometimes fails. In this section we consider costs of intervention, neglecting government failure. Later we consider the added problem imposed by imperfect government intervention.

The *benefits* of government intervention are the value of the market failures averted. To evaluate government intervention, it is necessary to consider the costs of the intervention and compare costs with benefits.

Large potential benefits do not necessarily justify government intervention, nor do large potential costs necessarily make it unwise. What matters is the balance between benefits and costs.

There are several kinds of costs of government intervention.

Internal Costs

Government intervention uses real resources that could be used elsewhere. Civil servants must be paid. Paper, photocopying, and other trappings of bureaucracy, the steel in the navy's ships, the fuel for the army's tanks, and the pilot of Air Force One all have valuable alternative uses. The same is true of the accountants who administer the social security system and of the educators who retrain displaced workers.

Similarly, when government inspectors visit plants to monitor compliance with federally imposed standards of health, industrial safety, or environmental protection, they are imposing costs on the public in the form of the salaries and expenses of the inspectors. When regulatory bodies develop rules, hold hearings, write opinions, or have their staff prepare research reports, they are incurring costs. When the antitrust division of the Justice Department employed 40 lawyers to spend 10 years working on an antitrust case against IBM (a case that was eventually dropped), real costs were incurred. The costs of the judges, clerks, and court reporters who hear, transcribe, and review the evidence are likewise costs imposed by government regulation. All these activities use valuable resources that could have provided very different goods and services.

Whatever the form of government intervention, the intervention will impose direct internal costs.

This type of cost is fairly easy to see, as it almost always involves expenditure of public budgets. Other costs of intervention are less apparent but no less real.

External Costs

Most government interventions in the economy impose some costs on firms and households. The nature and the size of the extra costs borne by firms and households subject to government intervention vary with the type of intervention. A few examples are worth noting.

Changes in costs of production.   Federal safety and emission standards for automobiles have raised the costs of both producing and operating cars. These costs are much greater than the direct budgetary costs of administering the regulations. Taxes used to finance the provision of collective consumption goods must be paid by producers and consumers and typically increase the cost of producing or selling goods and services.

Costs of compliance. Government regulation and supervision generate a flood of reporting and related activities that often are summarized in the phrase *red tape*. The number of hours of business time devoted to understanding, reporting, and contesting regulatory provisions is enormous. Affirmative action, occupational safety, and environmental control have all increased the size of nonproduction payrolls. The legal costs alone of a major corporation sometimes can run into tens or hundreds of millions of dollars per year. While all this provides lots of employment for lawyers and economic experts, it is costly because there are other tasks such professionals could do that would add more to the production of consumer goods and services. The time and money cost of filling out individual income tax returns recently has been estimated to be about 8 percent of the total revenue that is collected.

Losses in productivity. Quite apart from the actual expenditures, the regulatory climate may reduce the incentive for experimentation, innovation, and the introduction of new products. Requiring advance government clearance before a new method or product may be introduced (on grounds of potential safety hazards or environmental impact) can eliminate the incentive to develop it. Requiring advance approval by a regulatory commission before entry is permitted into a regulated industry can discourage potential competitors. Tax policy also can have an effect. An income tax may make it less profitable to invest in specialized training that will yield a high income.

Government "Imperfection"

Our conceptual benefit-cost analysis of government intervention is almost complete. First, we calculate the social cost of each market failure. This cost is the potential benefit of intervention. Then we make our best estimate of the actual effect of the intervention—in most cases the best that we can do is less than the maximum potential benefit. Then we calculate the costs of the intervention, as outlined in the preceding

section. If the benefits exceed the costs, the intervention is warranted. Unfortunately, things are never this simple. For one thing, as we have just explained, many of the benefits of government intervention are extremely difficult to quantify. Even in the "easy" cases, however, where the benefits and the direct costs of intervention can be measured, governments, like private markets, are imperfect. Often they will "fail," in the same sense that markets do, to achieve their potential.

Causes of Government Failure

The reason for government failure is not that public-sector employees are less able, honest, or virtuous than people who work in the private sector. Rather, the causes of government failure, like the causes of market failure, are by and large natural ones. Indeed, as we show in Box 21-2, some of them are inescapable costs of democratic decision making.

Governments as monopolists. Governments face the same problems of cost minimization that private firms do, but often operate in an environment where they are monopoly producers without stockholders. Large governments (states, big cities, the federal government) face all of the organizational problems faced by large corporations. They tend to use relatively rigid rules and thus to respond only slowly to change. Building codes are an example of this type of problem. Most local governments have detailed requirements regarding the materials that must go into a new house, factory, or office. When technology changes, the codes often lag behind. For example, plastic pipe, which is cheaper and easier to use than steel pipe, was prohibited by building codes for decades after its use became feasible. Similarly, much antipollution regulation specifies the type of control equipment that must be employed. Changes in technology may make a regulation inefficient, but the regulation may stay in place for some time.

Like those of large private enterprises, a government's "organization chart" will often be out of date. In Chapter 15 we discussed the example of the regulatory commission that was charged with maintaining a healthy railroad system. With the advent of buses and trucks, the commission should have turned to developing a healthy *transportation system*. Yet for years the ICC rate structure favored railroads. The same kind of problem might well arise when the

BOX 21-2

Social Choice Theory—The Economic Analysis of Government Behavior

Economics is the study of the allocation of scarce resources. Given that many of these resources, even in market-oriented economies such as the United States, are allocated by government, it is not surprising that economists have spent a good deal of effort in the study of government provision of goods and services. The question that is asked by social choice theory is what the relationship is between the rules that governments use to reach decisions and the way in which society's real resources are allocated. There is also a growing empirical literature on social choice.

Logrolling

At the core of most people's idea of democracy is the idea that each citizen's vote should count the same. One of the insights of social choice theory is that when resource allocation is based on the principle of one-person-one-vote it generally be inefficient because it fails to take into account the *intensity of preferences.* Consider three farmers, A, B, and C, who are contemplating building access roads. Suppose that the road to A's farm is worth $7,000 to A and that the road to B's farm is worth $7,000 to B. (C's farm is on the main road, which already exists.) Suppose that, under the taxing rules in effect, each road would cost each farmer $2,000. It is plainly efficient to build both roads, since each generates net benefits of $1,000 ($7,000 gross benefits to the farmer helped, less $6,000 total cost). But each would be defeated 2-1 in a simple majority vote. (B and C would vote against A's road; A and C would vote against B's road.)

Now suppose that we allow A and B to make a deal: "I will vote for your road if you will vote for mine." Such deals, often decried by political commentators, are examples of **logrolling.** In this case, the deal enhances efficiency: Both roads now get 2-1 majorities, and both roads get built. Efficiency, however, was purchased at a potentially high price—the trading of votes. Moreover, although logrolling is a mechanism that allows inten-

sity of preferences to be acted upon in practice, it can sometimes reduce efficiency. If we make the gross value of each road $5,000, instead of $7,000, and let A and B roll their logs, each road will still command a 2-1 majority, but building the roads will now be inefficient. (The gross value of each road is now only $5,000, while the cost is still $6,000.) A and B will be using democracy to appropriate resources from C.

"**Special interests.**"   This latter case can be interpreted in a different way. Instead of being the third farmer, C might be all of the voters in the county. Instead of bearing one-third of the costs, A and B each might bear only a small portion of the costs. To the extent that A and B are able to go to the county commission (or state legislature or Congress) and forcefully articulate the benefits that they would derive from the roads, they may be able to use democracy to appropriate resources from taxpayers in general. Much of the concern with the power of "special interests" stems from the fact that the institutions of representative democracy tend to be responsive to benefits (or costs) that focus on particular, identifiable, and articulate groups. Often, costs that are borne diffusely by taxpayers or voters in general are hardly noticed. This potential bias applies to regulations, as well as to direct government provisions. Chapter 15 discussed a number of cases in which economic regulations are promulgated in the interest of the affected industry. Similarly, as we saw in Chapter 6, rent-control ordinances can be interpreted, at least in part, as benefitting existing tenants at the expense of future potential tenants; the latter group tends to have no political power at all.

Arrow's Impossibility Theorem

The economist and Nobel Laureate Kenneth Arrow has shown that it is generally impossible to construct a set of rules for making social choices that is at once comprehensive, democratic, efficient, and consistent. Arrow's theorem has led to decades of work on the part of economists, philosophers, and political scientists, who have tried to find conditions under which democracy can be expected to yield efficient (or otherwise normatively favored) allocations of resources. The news is generally not good. Unless individual preferences or their distribution in the population meet fairly unlikely criteria, either democracy or efficiency must be sacrificed in the design of social choice mechanisms.

The Arrow theorem can be illustrated by a familiar and simple case, depicted in the following table. Again, we have a society that consists of three voters. This time they are choosing how many trees to plant in the local park. The three possibilities are: (1) Plant very few trees in one corner. This would make the park suitable for frisbee and soccer but not for walks in the woods. (2) Plant trees in moderate density throughout the park. In this case, the park would be nice for tag and jogging but not usable for most sports. (3) Plant trees densely everywhere. This would make the park a pleasant place to get away from it all (for whatever reasons) but not a good place to jog in. Voter A loves jogging, hates frisbee and the noise that frisbee players make, and likes walking in the woods. His ranking of the alternatives is 2-3-1. Voter B likes the wide open spaces. His ranking is 1-2-3. Voter C likes to play frisbee, likes solitude even more, and has little taste for a park that provides neither. Her ranking is 3-1-2.

Suppose that the electorate gets to choose between alternatives that are presented two at a time. What does majority rule do? It depends on which two alternatives are presented. In a choice of 1 versus 2, 1 wins, getting votes from B and C. When the choice is between 2 and 3, 2 wins, getting votes from A and B. When 3 is pitted against 1, 3 wins with the support of A and C. Thus, the *social choice mechanism* of *majority rule* is inconsistent. It tells us that 1 is preferred to 2, 2 is preferred to 3, and 3 is

| | | *Voter* | | |
		A	**B**	**C**
Density of	Sparse	3	1	2
Trees	Medium	1	2	3
	Thick	2	3	1

preferred to 1. There is no way to make a choice without arbitrarily (nondemocratically) choosing which set of alternatives to offer the electorate.

Bureaucracy and "Leviathan"

Another area that has received the attention of social choice theorists is the behavior of government agencies, which, after all, are not subject to the disciplines of the marketplace. William Niskanen has proposed that bureaucrats will act like revenue-maximizing monopolists, trying to make their agencies as large as possible and using their monopoly power to do so. Other economists have noted that competition among agencies will limit but not eliminate the power of government agencies to do this. Another limitation arises from the fact that politicians who give too much power to bureaucrats reduce their chances of being reelected.

An extreme model, in which neither of the two checks on bureaucracy that were just noted is assumed to apply, was proposed by Gerald Brennan and Nobel Laureate James Buchanan. In effect, Brennan and Buchanan assume that the bureaucrat-politicians' ability to gain control over economic resources only can be limited by the taxing power granted to them in the Constitution. This leads Brennan and Buchanan to advocate limiting the range of activities that the government may tax and also to advocate imposing the requirement of balanced budgets.

The "New" Political Economy

The rise of social choice theory has added greatly to the economist's ability to analyze the institutions that affect the allocation of resources. The study of social choice blurs the distinction between economics and political science. From the economist's perspective, once it is recognized that there is a role for government, it follows that, even within government, economic incentives will matter. In order to make an informed choice about what should be privately and publicly provided in a society, one must look in detail at the nonmarket mechanisms

that determine public resource allocation. Political scientists have known this for years, but they have not had available to them the economist's tools for undertaking the investigation. The application of these tools has revealed much, not the least of which is that social institutions have a profound effect on the allocation of economic resources. The study of social choice is likely to be a growth industry for some time to come.

purchasing division in a large corporation, which uses typewriters exclusively, is confronted with modern word-processing technology. In the private sector, there are usually market forces pushing the corporation into revising its view of the problem at hand. Usually there is no market mechanism tending to force governments toward the use of relatively efficient rules of thumb and organizational structures. Put in the language of Chapter 16, the scope for satisficing governments to depart from optimal behavior is generally greater than that for satisficing firms. Put in another way, much government failure arises precisely because governments do not have competitors.

Principal-agent problems in government.   Governments face the same kinds of *principal-agent problems* (see Chapter 16) that firms do, but the problem in the case of governments can be more serious for two reasons. First, the possibility of a hostile takeover, although quite powerful as applied to elected officials (they can be removed from office), is very weak as applied to bureaucracies. Second, the principal in the case of government is all of its citizens, and this group will in general be unable to agree on what it is that government *should* do. Stockholders can all agree that the firm should maximize stock value. Citizens who vote, by contrast, are not expected to agree on any simple mission for their elected representatives. This lack of agreement makes it that much more difficult for the agents to serve their principals and that much easier for agents who do not perform well to get away with it.

Rent seeking.   A different kind of problem arises from the mere existence of government and its potential to use its tools in ways that affect the distri-

bution of economic resources. The example of the ICC and railroads will serve again. Once the government is in the business of setting prices for private firms, it will be rational for these firms to spend real resources trying to influence the regulators. The opportunity cost of these resources might be the development of cost-saving technology in the industry. Similar cases arise with collective consumption goods, externalities, and taxes. Given that the government *can* act in ways that transfer resources to private entities and given that government's behavior can be influenced, whether by voting, campaign contributions, lobbying, or bribes, real resources will be used in trying to influence government behavior. Taken to its logical conclusion, this argument suggests that the mere existence of government imposes a negative externality. More practically, some have used the problem raised by rent-seeking behavior as an argument for limiting the size and scope of government.

The Effect of Government Failure

Suppose, for any of the reasons that we have just discussed, that the government makes a mistake in regulation. Say the government mistakenly specifies a method of pollution control that is less effective than the best method. This will increase the cost of achieving any given level of prevention. If the government insists on the level of control that is appropriate to the correct method but requires the incorrect method, it can convert a social gain from control into a social loss.

To generalize from the specific example, it is clear that any form of government failure adds to the costs of or decreases the benefits of government intervention. Thus, the lower is the public's confidence in government's ability to do the right thing, the lower will be its willingness to have government intervention.

How Much Should Government Intervene?

The theoretical principles for determining the optimal amount of government intervention are individually accepted by almost everyone. What they add up to, however, is more controversial. Does government intervene too little or too much in response to market failure? This question reflects one aspect of the ongoing argument about the role of government in the economy.

Much of the rhetoric of our concern with ecology urges government intervention against heartless, profit-hungry, giant corporations that destroy the environment for their own crass purposes. Such feelings lead to the demand for more—and more stringent—government regulation.

At the same time, others see the heavy hand of government regulation as burdening private companies with regulations that add to costs and impede innovation and thus keep prices and wages artificially high. Even perfect intervention would be costly, but imperfect intervention makes it much too costly. In this view, the deregulation movement that started during the 1980s was long overdue.

Evaluating the costs and the effectiveness of government intervention requires a comparison of the unregulated economic system as it is working (not as it might work ideally) with the pattern of government intervention as it is likely to perform (not as it might perform ideally).

The Role of Analysis

Economic analysis and measurement can help to eliminate certain misconceptions that cloud and confuse the debate on the "proper" role of government. One mistake is the notion that the invisible hand of free markets will always lead to an efficient allocation of resources. Externalities, public goods, and moral-hazard problems are features of real market econo-

mies, and they lead to inefficiency whenever they appear.

Another mistake is to equate market failure with the greed of profit-motivated corporations. Externalities do not require callous, thoughtless, or deliberately deceptive practices of private, profit-seeking firms; they occur whenever the signals to which decision makers respond do not include social as well as private benefits and costs. Such situations are not limited to private firms in a capitalist system. Cities and nationalized industries pollute just as much as privately owned industries when they neglect externalities in their operations, as they often do.

A third mistake is to think that the profits of a corporation tell something about neglected externalities. It is possible for either a profitable firm or an unprofitable one to spend too little on pollution control or on safety, but it is also possible for it to spend too much. The existence of profits provides no clue as to which is the case.

The Role of Ideology

While positive analysis has a role to play, there are several reasons why ideology plays a bigger role in evaluating government intervention than in other areas. First, much of what government does is in the realm of "other social goals," rather than economics. Economic analysis can be useful in helping to find ways to achieve such goals, but at bottom political and social ideology must always play a large role in defining the shape and the role of government.

Second, measuring the costs of government intervention is difficult, particularly with respect to external costs, because some of the trade-offs are inherently uncertain. How important and how unsafe is nuclear power? Does the ban on some pesticides cause so much malnutrition as to offset the environmental gains that it brings? Costs that cannot be measured readily can be alleged to be extremely high (or low) by opponents (or supporters) of intervention. The numerous findings by scholars on both sides of each of these subjects has led one economist to the cynical conclusion that "believing is seeing."

Third, classifying the actual pattern of government intervention as successful or not is in part subjective. Has government safety regulation been (choose one) useful if imperfect, virtually ineffective, or positively adverse? All three views have been expressed and "documented."

Fourth, specifying what constitutes market failure is difficult. Does product differentiation represent market success (by giving consumers the variety they want) or failure (by foisting expensive and useless variations on them)?

In the United States in 1990 it seems safe to conclude that confidence in the existing mix of free-market and government regulation is at a relatively low ebb. Both specific policy suggestions and the whole philosophy of intervention are being argued hotly. There is as yet no consensus as to what is wrong; the pressures for changes are strong in *both* directions.

What government actually *does* should have some bearing on the debate, regardless of ideology. In Chapter 15 we discussed government action that is designed to affect monopoly and competition. In the next two chapters we shall discuss in some detail three other important types of intervention in the U.S. economy today: environmental and safety regulation, taxation, and public spending.

SUMMARY

1. The various markets in the economy are coordinated in an unplanned, decentralized way by the price system. Profits and losses play a key role in achieving a coordinated market response. Changes in prices and profits, resulting from emerging scarcities and surpluses, lead decision makers to adapt to a change in any one market of the economy. Such responses tend to correct the shortages and surpluses as well as to change the market signals of prices and profits.

2. Important features of market coordination include voluntary responses to market signals, the limited information required by any individual, and the fact that coordination will occur under any market structure.

3. A widely held argument in favor of the free market goes beyond its ability to provide automatic coordination. Many believe that its flexibility and adaptability make it the best coordinator and also encourage innovation and growth. The tendency of the market to push relative prices toward the costs of production fosters efficient allocation of resources and self-correction of disequilibrium. Furthermore, the market economy tends to be impersonal, to decentralize power, and to require relatively little coercion of individuals.

4. Markets do not always work perfectly. Dissatisfaction with market results often leads to government intervention. Four main kinds of market failure are: (a) externalities arising from differences between private and social costs and benefits, (b) the inability of markets to produce collective consumption goods, (c) information asymmetries, and (d) failure to achieve social goals other than efficiency.

5. Pollution is an example of an externality. An important source of pollution is producers' use of water and air that they do not regard as scarce. Since they do not pay all of the costs of using these resources, they are not motivated to avoid the costs. Individual use of common-property resources causes congestion and also gives rise to externalities.

6. National defense is an example of a collective consumption good, often called a public good. Markets fail to produce collective consumption goods because the benefits of such goods are available to people whether they pay for them or not.

7. Information asymmetries cause market failure when one party to a transaction is able to use his or her expertise to manipulate the transaction in his or her own favor. Moral hazard, adverse-selection, and principal-agent problems are all consequences of information asymmetries.

8. Changing the distribution of income is one of the roles for government intervention that members of a society desire. Others include values that are placed on public provision for its own sake, on protection of individuals from themselves or from others, and on recognition of social obligations.

9. Microeconomic policy concerns activities of the government that alter the unrestricted workings of the free-market system in order to affect either the allocation of resources or the distribution of income. Major tools of microeconomic policy include (a) public provision, (b) redistribution, (c) rule making, and (d) structuring incentives. (The first two are the subject of Chapter 23.) Both prescriptive and proscriptive rule making occur in a variety of forms. Incentives can be structured in a number of ways, including the use of fines, subsidies, taxes, and effluent charges (which are discussed in Chapter 22). Each of these is a means of internalizing externalities and thus of avoiding market failure.

10. The costs and benefits of government intervention must be considered in deciding whether, when, and how much intervention is appropriate. Among the costs are the direct costs that are incurred by the government; the costs that are imposed on those who are regulated, direct and indirect; and the costs that are imposed on third parties. These costs are seldom negligible and are often large.

11. If government intervention fails, the costs of intervention are incurred without realizing the benefits of avoiding market failure. The possibility of government failure must be balanced against the potential benefits of removing market failure. It is neither possible nor efficient to correct all market failure; neither is it always efficient to do nothing.

TOPICS FOR REVIEW

Market coordination
Differences between private and social valuations
Market failure
Rule making
Externalities
Collective consumption goods
Benefit-cost analysis
Information asymmetries
Benefits and costs of government intervention
Government failure

DISCUSSION QUESTIONS

1. Should the free market be allowed to determine the price for the following, or should government intervene? Defend your choice for each.
   a. Transit fares
   b. Plastic surgery for victims of fires
   c. Garbage collection
   d. Postal delivery of newspapers and magazines
   e. Fire protection for churches
   f. Ice cream

2. The following activities have known harmful effects. In each case identify any divergence between social and private costs.
   a. Cigarette smoking
   b. Driving a car at the national (rural) speed limit of 65 mph
   c. Private ownership of guns
   d. Drilling for offshore oil

3. Suppose all the following statements are true. Should they trigger government intervention? If so, what policy alternatives are available?
   a. Hospital costs have been rising at about four times the rate of increase of personal income, and proper treatment of a serious illness has become extraordinarily expensive.
   b. The cost of an average one-family house in Washington, D.C., is now over $230,000—an amount that is out of the reach of most government employees.
   c. Cigarette smoking tends to reduce life expectancy of the smoker by eight years.
   d. Saccharin in large doses has been found to cause cancer in mice.

4. Consider the possible beneficial and adverse effects of each of the following forms of government intervention.
   a. Charging motorists a tax for driving in the downtown areas of large cities and using the revenues to provide peripheral parking and shuttle buses
   b. Prohibiting juries from awarding large malpractice judgments against doctors
   c. Mandating no-fault automobile insurance, in which the automobile owner's insurance company is responsible for damage to his or her vehicle no matter who causes the accident
   d. Requiring automobile manufacturers to warrant the tires on cars that they sell instead of (as at present) having the tire manufacturer be the warrantor

5. The president of Goodyear Tire and Rubber Company complained that government regulation had imposed $30 million per year in "unproductive costs" on his company, as listed below. How would one determine whether these costs were "productive" or "unproductive"?
   a. Environmental regulation, $17 million
   b. Occupational safety and health, $7 million
   c. Motor vehicle safety, $3 million
   d. Personnel and administration, $3 million

6. Your local government probably provides, among other things, a police department, a fire department, and a public library. What are the market imperfections, if any, that each of these works to correct? Which of these are closest to being collective consumption goods? Which are farthest?

7. What market failure(s) does public support of higher education seek to remedy? How would you go about evaluating whether the benefits of this support outweigh the costs?

Chapter 22

Social and Environmental Regulation

In almost everything we do, we are subject to some form of government regulation. The system of criminal law regulates our interactions with people and property. Local zoning ordinances regulate the ways in which the land that we own may be used. Insurance commissions must approve both the insurance contracts that we sign and the rates that are charged. Public utility commissions set rates for electricity, natural gas, local telephone service, and a host of other goods and services. Seat belts, brake lights, turn signals, air bags, internal door panels, bumpers, and catalytic converters are all subjects of regulation in just one industry. The number of electrical outlets per room, the material used for plumbing, and the spacing of the vertical supports in an interior wall are dictated by local building codes. The list goes on and on. A good case can be made that governments in the United States have more effect on the economy through regulation than through taxing and spending.

In the previous chapter, we identified a number of types of market failure that might be addressed by government policy. Regulation of economic activity is used to address all of them. Market failure arising from *natural monopoly* has led to public utility regulation, as discussed in Chapter 15. *Externalities*, especially the negative externalities of industrial pollution, are the motivation for environmental regulation, a major topic of this chapter.

Regulation of advertising, and much health and safety regulation, are designed to deal with market failures arising from *information asymmetries*. There is no easy way for a consumer to know whether the paint on a child's toy can cause lead poisoning, so the Consumer Product Safety Commission regulates the market for children's toys. Occupational licensing is defended on the same grounds; in most states professionals as different as barbers and psychiatrists must undergo specified courses of training before they are allowed to ply their trades. The idea is to prevent "just anyone" from claiming and abusing alleged expertise.

Information about a professional's training is a *public good*: Once the information is available to one consumer, it can be made available to all very cheaply. Occupational licensing is a way to produce this public good—in the form of the familiar diploma that hangs on the wall of the barbershop, physician's office, or repair garage.

Regulations also can be used to change the *distribution of income*. This is the purpose of, among other regulations, rent controls, minimum wages, and agricultural pricing rules. Finally, the laws and regulations that enforce private contracts are a pure public good that is essential to the operation of a market economy. Without reliably enforceable contracts, many transactions would be so risky that they would not take place.

The principal topic of this chapter is **social regulation.** Social regulation does not mean the regulation of social behavior (e.g., dress and speech). Rather, it is the regulation of economic behavior to advance social goals in circumstances in which neither competition nor economic regulation can be expected to do the job.

In this chapter we consider both the market failures that social regulation addresses and the effectiveness of different kinds of regulation in correcting these market failures. We start by extending Chapter 21's analysis of negative externalities to the problem of environmental pollution.

The Economics of Pollution and Pollution Control

Pollution is a negative externality. As a consequence of producing or consuming goods and services, "bads" are produced as well. Steel plants produce heat and benzene, in addition to steel. Farms produce chemical runoff, as well as food. Households produce human waste and garbage as they consume goods and services. In all of these cases, the technology of production and consumption automatically generates pollution. Indeed, there are few human endeavors that do not have negative pollution externalities.

The Economic Rationale for Regulating Pollution

Figure 22-1 illustrates a typical case. A profit-maximizing competitive firm sets its marginal cost equal to the market price of output. When the firm's production generates pollution, however, there is an *external cost* that is not borne by the firm. If we add the marginal private cost that the firm bears (MC_p) and the external cost that it imposes on others (EC), we get the *marginal social cost curve* of the firm's production (MC_s).

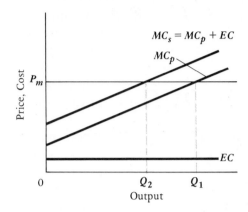

FIGURE 22-1   Pollution Externalities

Internalizing an externality can correct market failure. The private marginal cost curve, MC_p, is the conventional marginal cost for a firm that is producing output in a competitive market. The external cost curve, EC, depicts marginal cost that the firm's production imposes on people other than its owners, employees, and customers. Since the firm is maximizing profits, it will ignore EC and produce output Q_1, where the market price P_m equals marginal cost. Adding EC and MC_p yields *social marginal cost, MC_s.* The socially optimal level of output is Q_2, where price is equal to MC_s. Here the price is sufficient to pay for the private marginal cost of production, MC_p, *and* to compensate others for the external marginal cost imposed on them, EC.

Suppose that the firm is required to pay a tax of $EC per unit of output. Its MC_p curve will now become the MC_s curve. The externality will be *internalized,* and the profit-maximizing firm will be motivated to reduce its output to the socially optimal level, Q_2. It does this because with the tax added to its private marginal cost, Q_2 is the profit-maximizing level of output.

Allocative efficiency requires that the price (the value that consumers place on the marginal unit of output) be just equal to the marginal social cost (the value of resources that society gives up to produce the marginal unit of output).

By producing where price equals marginal private cost and thereby ignoring the externality, the firm is maximizing profits but producing too much output. The price that consumers pay just covers the marginal private cost but does not pay for the external damage. The **social benefit** of the last unit of output (the market price) is less than the social cost (MC_s). Reducing output by one unit would reduce

Chapter 22 Social and Environmental Regulation   **447**

social benefit by P and reduce social cost by MC_s for a net gain just equal to the pollution externality. The market fails to achieve efficiency because of the externality.

Making the firm bear the entire social cost of its production is called **internalizing** the externality. This will cause it to produce at a lower output. Indeed, at the optimal output, consumer prices would just cover all of the marginal social cost of production—marginal private cost plus the externality. We would have the familiar condition for economic efficiency that marginal benefits to consumers are just equal to the marginal cost of producing these benefits. The difference here is that some of the marginal social cost takes the form of an externality.

Suppose that Warthog Industries, Inc., manufactures kitchen cabinets and that residue from painting the cabinets is washed into a stream that runs outside of the plant. The stream is part of the municipal water supply, which is treated at a water purification plant before it is sent into people's homes. Suppose that each cabinet produced increases the cost of running the water treatment plant by $.01. Then, in terms of the previous analysis, EC is $.01. and MC_s will be exactly $.01 above MC_p.

In practice, the external cost (EC) is often quite difficult to measure. This is especially so in the case of air pollution, where the damage is often spread over hundreds of thousands of square miles and can have real but small effects upon millions of people. Another difficulty arises because the cost that is imposed by pollution generally will depend on the mechanisms that are used to undo the damage that it causes. Control mechanisms are themselves costly, and their costs also must be counted as part of the social cost of pollution. Nevertheless, the basic analysis of Figure 22-1 applies to these more difficult cases.

The socially optimal level of output is at the quantity where *all* marginal costs, private plus external, equal the marginal benefit to society.

Notice that the optimal level of output is not the level at which there is *no* pollution. Rather, it is the level at which the beneficiaries of pollution (the consumers and producers of Warthog Industries' kitchen cabinets, in our example) are just willing to pay the marginal social cost that is imposed by the pollution.

Unregulated markets generally will produce excessive amounts of environmental damage. Zero environmental damage, however, is neither technologically possible nor economically efficient.

Pollution Control in Theory and Practice

Figure 22-2 depicts the benefits and costs of pollution control. The figure might be thought of as applying, say, to water pollution in a specific watershed. It is drawn from the perspective of a public authority that has been charged with maximizing social welfare. The horizontal axis shows the amount of *pollution*

FIGURE 22-2   The Optimal Amount of Pollution Abatement

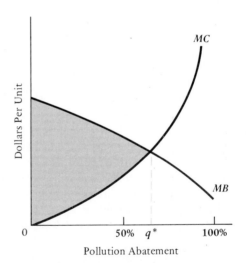

The optimal amount of pollution abatement occurs where the marginal cost of reducing pollution is just equal to the marginal benefits from doing so. *MB* represents the marginal benefit that is achieved by pollution prevention in some activity. *MC* represents the marginal cost of preventing pollution; it rises sharply as more and more pollution is eliminated. The optimal level of pollution control is q^*, where $MB = MC$. *Notice that not all pollution is eliminated.* For all units up to q^*, the marginal benefits derived from pollution abatement exceed the marginal costs. Net benefits are shown by the total shaded area. Any further reductions in pollution would add more to costs than to benefits.

abated (or prevented). Thus, zero on the horizontal axis represents the amount of pollution that would occur in an unregulated market. The greater is the distance from the origin, the greater is the amount of pollution that has been prevented and the smaller is the amount of pollution that is remaining. The reason that we put pollution that has been prevented on the horizontal axis is that pollution abatement is a good of economic value, and we are used to looking at supply and demand analyses for such goods.

The marginal cost curve is the marginal cost of preventing pollution. It is shown as starting low and rising steeply. There are two reasons for believing that this shape is generally accurate. First is the familiar logic behind increasing marginal costs. For each firm that pollutes, there will be some antipollution measures that can be taken fairly easily, so the first portion of pollution reduction will be cheap relative to later portions. In addition, it is likely that pollution reduction of any degree will be easier for some firms than for others. New facilities are likely to run cleaner than old ones, for example. Reducing pollution from a factory that was designed in the era of environmental concern may be much easier than obtaining similar reductions from an older factory. After some point, however, the easy plants and the easy fixes are exhausted, and the marginal cost of reducing pollution further rises steeply.

The marginal benefit of pollution reduction is depicted as falling, for much the same reason that the typical demand curve slopes downward. Starting at any nonlethal level of pollution, people will derive some benefit from reducing the level of pollution, but the marginal benefit from a given amount of reduction will be lower, the lower is the level of pollution.[1]

The optimal amount of pollution reduction occurs where the marginal benefit is equal to the marginal cost—where "supply" and "demand" in Figure 22-2 intersect. In trying to reach this optimum, the pollution control authority, the Environmental Protection Agency (EPA) in the United States, faces

three serious problems. First, although Figure 22-2 looks like a supply-demand diagram, we have already seen that the private sector will not create a market in pollution control. Thus, the EPA must intervene in private sector markets if the optimal level of control that is shown in Figure 22-2 is to be attained.

The second problem is that q^* generally is not easily known, because the marginal benefit and the marginal cost curves that are shown in Figure 22-2 generally are not observable. In practice, the EPA (or the relevant state or local authority) can only estimate these curves, and accurate estimates are often difficult to obtain, especially when the technology of pollution control is changing rapidly and the health consequences of various pollutants (e.g., chemicals that are new to the marketplace) are not known.

Determining the optimal level of pollution control in the real world is often very difficult.

The third problem is that the available techniques for regulating pollution are themselves imperfect. Even when the optimal level of pollution control is known, there are both technical and legal impediments to achieving that level through regulation.

Direct Controls

Direct control is the form of environmental regulation that is used most often. Automobile emissions standards are direct controls that are familiar to most of us. The standards must be met by all new cars that are sold in the United States. They require that emissions per mile of a number of noxious chemicals and other pollutants be less than certain specified amounts. The standards are the same no matter where the miles are driven. The marginal benefit of reducing carbon monoxide emissions in rural Iowa, where there is relatively little air pollution, is almost certainly much less than the marginal benefit in New York City, where there is already a good deal of carbon monoxide in the air. Yet the standard is the same in both places.[2]

Direct controls also often require that specific techniques be used in order to reduce pollution.

[1] This argument does not work in the case of toxic pollutants. There the marginal benefit of pollution reduction is small or zero if the level of emissions is above some dangerous threshold and is very large when pollution is reduced below the threshold. The marginal benefit curve in these cases would be strongly kinked at the threshold. The health consequences of most pollution, however, are of a kind that is consistent with the shape of the "demand" curve that is shown in Figure 22-2.

[2] California, which has the worst air pollution problems, has tougher standards than the rest of the country. Even there, residents of rural Humboldt County must meet the same standards that apply to Los Angeles.

Thus, coal-fired utility plants are required to use devices called "scrubbers" in order to reduce sulfur dioxide emissions.

Another form of direct control is the simple prohibition of certain polluting behaviors. Many cities and towns, for example, prohibit the private burning of leaves and other trash because of the air pollution problem that the burning would cause. A number of communities have banned the use of wood stoves. Similarly, the EPA gradually has reduced the amount of lead that is allowed in leaded gasoline.

Problems with direct controls. Economists consistently have criticized the use of direct controls on efficiency grounds. Suppose that pollution of a given waterway is to be reduced by a certain amount. Regulators typically will apportion the required reduction among all of the polluters according to some roughly equitable criterion. The regulators might require that every polluter reduce its pollution by the same percentage. Alternatively, every polluter might be required to install a certain type of control device or to assure that each gallon of water that is dumped into the watershed meets certain quality criteria. While any of these rules might seem reasonable, unless the polluters face identical pollution abatement costs, each of them will be inefficient.

To see this, consider two firms that face different costs of pollution abatement, as depicted in Figure 22-3. Suppose that firm A's marginal cost of pollution abatement is everywhere below firm B's. Such a circumstance is quite likely when one recalls that in the real world pollution comes from many different industries. It may be easy for one industry to cut back on the amount that it uses of some pollutant; in another industry the pollutant may be an integral part of the production process. Clearly, the most efficient way to reduce pollution would be to have firm A cut back on its pollution until the marginal cost of further reductions is just equal to firm B's marginal cost of reducing its first (and cheapest to forego) unit of pollution. Once their marginal costs of reducing pollution are equalized, *further* reductions in pollution will be efficient only if this equality is maintained. To see this, suppose that the marginal costs of abatement are different for the two firms. By reallocating some pollution abatement from the high marginal cost firm to the low-cost firm, total pollution abatement could be kept constant while the real resources used to abate pollution would be re-

duced. Alternatively, one could hold the resource cost constant and increase the amount of abatement.

Direct pollution controls are usually inefficient in that they do not minimize the cost of a given amount of pollution abatement.

When direct controls require that firms adopt specific techniques of pollution abatement, a second type of inefficiency arises. Regulations of this kind tend to change only slowly: The regulators often will mandate today's best techniques tomorrow, even if something more effective has come along.

Both of these sources of inefficiency in direct controls are examples of "government failure," as discussed in Chapter 21. In both cases, the government does not do as well as it could in pursuing its valid social objectives. In terms of Figure 22-2, government failure would add to the marginal cost of pollution reduction. Thus, the socially optimal level of pollution will be higher, the less efficient is the method used to control pollution.

A final problem that arises with direct controls in practice is that they are expensive to monitor and to enforce. The regulatory agency has to check, factory by factory, farm by farm, how many pollutants of what kinds are being emitted. It then also needs a mechanism for penalizing offenders. Accurate monitoring of all potential sources of pollution requires a level of resources that is much greater than has ever been made available to the relevant regulatory agencies. Moreover, the existing system of fines and penalties, in the view of many critics, is not nearly harsh enough to have much effect. A potential polluter, required to limit emissions of a pollutant to so many pounds or gallons per day, will take into account the cost of meeting the standard, the probability of being caught, and the severity of the penalty before deciding how to behave. If the chances of being caught and the penalties for being caught are small, the direct controls may have little effect.

Monitoring and enforcement of direct pollution controls is costly, which reduces the effectiveness of the controls.

Emissions Taxes

An alternative method of pollution control is to levy a tax on emissions at the source. The great advantage

BOX 22-1

Charging for Emissions at Home*

Nov. 21—Tossing out the household trash here requires care and ingenuity these days, because residents of this town of 4,000 must now pay for garbage disposal by the bag.

In an effort to control disposal rates that have soared across most of the nation, High Bridge has stopped charging households a flat $280 annual fee for garbage collection. In January, the town began charging for the amount of trash residents actually discard.

Each 30-gallon can or 30-gallon bag set out at curbside each week must carry a town sticker. Households are charged $140 for 52 stickers, and additional stickers cost $1.25 each.

Environmental Result

The switch to billing by the bag has also had an environmental impact, reducing High Bridge's residential trash volume by 25 percent, officials say. At a time when the United States throws away

* The following article, by Robert Harley, ran under the headline, "Pay-by-Bag Trash Disposal Pays, New Jersey Town Discovers." *New York Times,* November 24, 1988, National Edition, p. 8. © 1988 by The New York Times Company. Reprinted by permission.

more trash than any nation in the world, the switch has heightened awareness of recycling programs for newspapers, aluminum cans and glass bottles and has ended careless ways at the kitchen trash bin.

The new system has also placed this hilly town 16 miles east of the Pennsylvania border in the forefront of a growing movement. About three dozen New Jersey communities—all anguished about soaring trash-disposal costs as the state closes landfills—have called the High Bridge Town Clerk, Claire Knapp, to hear how its system works. Centerville, Utah, and Afton, Minn., have also expressed interest.

People here quickly began sorting and recycling their trash.

"I've been doing it for years, but many of my friends and neighbors said they couldn't be bothered," said Emily Bruton, who has seven children. "But now they bother because it's hitting them in the pocketbook."

Neighborly Sharing

Some people whose garbage can is only two-thirds full on the eve of the weekly collection share their

---

of such a procedure is that it internalizes the pollution externality, so that decentralized decisions can lead to efficient outcomes. Again, suppose that firm A can reduce emissions cheaply, while it is more expensive for firm B to reduce emissions. If all firms are required to pay a tax of t on each unit of pollution, profit maximization will lead them to reduce emissions to just the point where the marginal cost of further reduction is just equal to t. This means that firm A will reduce emissions much more than firm B and that in equilibrium both will have the same marginal cost of further abatement, which is required for efficiency. This is illustrated in Figure 22-4.

Note that if the regulatory agency is able to ob-

tain a good estimate of the marginal damage that is done by pollution, it could set the tax rate just equal to that amount. In such a case, polluters would be forced by the tax to internalize the full pollution externality.

A second great advantage of using emissions taxes is that they do not require the regulators to specify anything about *how* polluters should abate pollution. Rather, polluters themselves can be left to find the most efficient abatement techniques. The profit motive will lead them to do so, because they will want to avoid paying the tax.

Emissions taxes can, in principle, perfectly internalize pollution externalities, so that profit-

empty space with neighbors whose can is overflowing.

"I've heard of people taking bags of garbage home from parties to help the hostess out," said Mary Briggs, the Town Council member who organized the new collection system.

Trash compactors are going into more and more kitchens. And outdoor compost piles, common generations ago, are popping up in many yards.

Sixteen-year-old Peter Butkosky tends his family's compost on Wood Glen Drive. Anything that's biodegradeable goes on the pile, including potato peels, melon rinds, spoiled fruits and vegetables, even the innards of fish that Peter and his father catch in the Atlantic.

"We let it all rot in sections for a year and then use it as fertilizer for the lawn," Peter said.

Volume of Trash Declines

Since billing by the garbage bag started, the trash collected by the town truck has dropped to an average of 6.3 tons a day from 8.5, according to William Newell, a Town Councilman.

The town's 4,000 residents include many older people on fixed incomes. Many are retirees of a now-defunct iron foundry that manufactured weapons for all the nation's wars since the Revolution. Most retirees, said Miss Knapp, the Town Clerk, produce far less trash than young families with children. But under the old system, everybody paid the same flat rate.

Under the new system, households that put out just one can a week pay only $140; those that put out more buy more stickers in strips of 10 for $12.50.

Extra stickers are required for bulky disposable items, like stuffed chairs (2) and sofa beds (6).

The value of the stickers appears to be inspiring some communal sacrifice.

"We wanted to throw out an old sofa, and they wanted four stickers on it," said Janet Nazif. "We didn't want to part with them, so we looked extra hard and found a school that wanted a used couch for a classroom."

maximizing behavior on the part of firms will lead them to produce the efficient amount of pollution abatement at minimum cost.

Box 22-1 provides an example of a pollution tax that seems to be both economically and politically successful. In this case, the polluters are ordinary households, and the pollution is ordinary household trash. Yet the principles we have discussed are very much in evidence. By using an emissions tax, an externality is internalized; individual decision makers are forced to take social costs into account.

Difficulties in using emissions taxes.   Emissions taxes can only work if it is possible to measure emissions accurately. For some types of pollution, this does not pose much of a problem, but, for many other types of pollution, good measuring devices that can be installed at reasonable cost do not exist. Obviously, in these cases emissions taxes cannot work. One important example of such a case is automotive pollution. It would be very expensive to attach a reliable monitor to every car and truck and then to assess taxes due based on readings from the monitor. In this case, as in many others, direct controls are the only feasible approach.

When there is good reason to prohibit a pollutant altogether, direct controls are obviously better than taxes. Municipal bans on burning of leaves fall in this category, as do the occasional emergency bans on some kinds of pollution that are invoked during an air pollution crisis in cities such as Los Angeles and Denver.

Another problem with emissions taxes involves setting the tax rate. Ideally, the regulatory agency would obtain an estimate of the marginal social damage caused per unit of each pollutant and set the tax equal to this amount. This would perfectly internalize the pollution externality. However, the information that is needed to draw the curves shown in Figures 22-1 and 22-4 is often difficult to obtain. If society is currently far away from the optimum, it may be very difficult to estimate what the marginal social damage *will be* at the optimum. If the regulatory agency sets the tax rate too high, too many resources will be devoted to pollution control—the equilibrium will be beyond q^* in Figure 22-2. If the tax is set too low, there will be too much pollution. In many practical cases, regulators may have a much better idea of the acceptable level of pollution than of the tax rate that would lead to that result.

A potentially serious problem with emissions taxes is that information necesary to determine the optimal tax rate is often unavailable.

A final argument against pollution taxes is more political than economic, but it is certainly important in explaining why such taxes are so rare. The argument is that by taxing pollution, rather than by outlawing it above some amount, the government is selling licenses to commit crimes against society. Direct controls, according to this argument, have much greater normative force, because they say that violating the standards is simply wrong. Taxes, on the other hand, make violating the standards just one more element of cost for the firm to consider as it pursues its private goals. Most economists find arguments of this kind unpersuasive. An absolute ban on pollution is impossible, and in choosing how much pollution to allow, society must trade pollution abatement against other valuable things. Economic analysis has a good deal to say about how a society might minimize the cost of *any* degree of pollution abatement.

Tradeable Emissions Permits

The great advantage of direct controls is that the regulators can set the standards to limit the total quantity of pollution in a given geographic area. This can be done without knowing the details of either the marginal benefit or the marginal cost curves in Figure 22-2. The great advantage of emissions taxes is that they allow for decentralized decision making, providing firms with an incentive to internalize the negative externality of pollution. *Tradeable emissions permits* can combine both of these advantages.

In Figure 22-3, we noted that direct pollution controls generally would be inefficient because the marginal cost curves for pollution abatement would vary across firms. Tradeable permits can solve this problem. To see this, we must first figure out how much pollution to allow. This involves reformulating the regulator's problem. Start with the same conditions as those in Figure 22-3, and permit each firm to pollute exactly the same amount as would be allowed by the direct controls in Figure 22-3. Instead of saying to each firm, "Thou shalt abate pollution by Q_R," however, the regulators say, "Thou shalt not pollute more than you would if you abated by Q_R." The statements are identical in meaning. All that we have done is to describe a glass that is two-thirds empty as one-third full.

Now suppose that the firms are allowed to buy and to sell **tradeable emissions permits**—rights to pollute. At the initial permitted amounts of pollution (Q_R), the marginal cost of pollution for firm A is lower than that for firm B. Firm B would be willing to pay up to C_B for the right to pollute one more unit, and firm A would be willing to sell that right for any amount that exceeded C_A. Notice that, if such a trade were made, the total amount of pollution would be unchanged, the total cost of abating pollution would fall (by $C_B - C_A$), and both firms would be at least as well off as before. We would thus have a clear efficiency improvement. No one is made worse off, and at least one party is made better off.

Once the firms are allowed to exchange rights to pollute, they will do so until their marginal abatement costs are equalized. At this point, there is no further gain from trading permits. Notice that the new equilibrium is identical to that depicted in Figure 22-4, with the equilibrium *price* of an emissions permit just equal to the emissions *tax* shown in that figure.

Tradeable emissions permits can be used to achieve the same allocation of resources as would occur with emissions taxes.

FIGURE 22-3   Inefficiency of Direct Pollution Controls

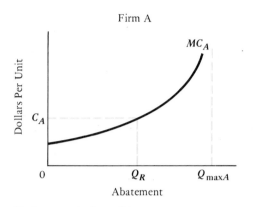
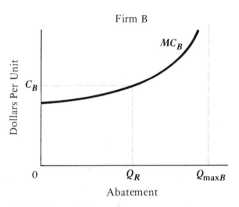

(i) Low marginal cost firm   (ii) High marginal cost firm

Requiring equal amounts of pollution abatement from different polluters is likely to be inefficient. Firm A is able to reduce its emissions according to the marginal cost curve MC_A. Firm B, which operates at the same scale but in a different kind of factory, has a higher marginal cost of abatement, MC_B. Suppose that a regulatory authority requires that the two firms reduce pollution by the same amount, Q_R. Firm A will have a marginal cost of pollution abatement of C_A, while firm B's marginal cost will be C_B, a greater amount.

To see that this outcome is inefficient, consider what happens if firm A increases its pollution abatement by one unit, while firm B is allowed to pollute one unit more. Total pollution remains the same, but total costs fall. Firm A incurs added costs of C_A, and firm B saves a greater amount, C_B. Since the total amount of pollution is unchanged, the total social cost of pollution and pollution abatement would fall.

Tradeable emissions permits in practice.   Both the EPA and a number of state regulatory agencies allow limited trading of emissions and have done so for over a decade. According to a recent study, the trading programs have had essentially no effect on environmental quality. The study estimates that savings in pollution control costs from these programs amounted to over $4 billion for the period 1974 through 1985. Although this is a considerable sum, most economists who specialize in environmental economics would argue it is but a small percentage of the savings that could be realized if trading in emissions permits became more widespread.

President Bush has indicated an interest in expanding the use of economic incentives for pollution reduction. A bipartisan group of legislators recently (early 1989) produced a report suggesting a number of ways, including the expansion of tradeable permits, that market forces could be used to internalize environmental externalities. As this book goes to press, extensive use of tradeable permits looks to be an idea whose time may be coming.

Tradeable permits and emissions taxes pose formidable problems of implementation. Some of these involve technical difficulties in measuring pollution and in designing mechanisms to assure that firms and households comply with regulations. Additionally, the potential efficiency gains arising from tradeable permits cannot be realized if regulatory agencies are prone to change the rules under which trades may take place. This has been a problem in the past, but it is a problem that can be corrected.

Governmental creation of a "market" in "bads" may become one of the most promising strategies for efficiently overcoming the market failure that leads to environmental pollution.

Much environmental pollution is caused by the failure of markets to account for externalities. At the

FIGURE 22-4   A Tax on Pollution

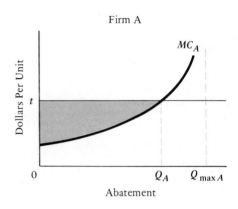 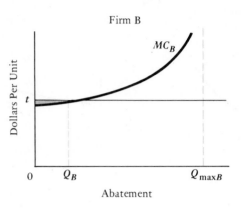

Taxes on pollution can lead to efficient pollution abatement. As in Figure 22-3, firm A faces a lower marginal cost of pollution abatement than does firm B. Suppose that the regulatory authority imposes a tax of t per unit of pollution. Firm A will choose to reduce its pollution by Q_A. Up to this point, the tax saved by reducing pollution exceeds the marginal cost of reducing pollution. If firm A chooses not to abate pollution at all, it would pay t times Q_{max} in pollution taxes, where Q_{max} is the firm's total pollution if it does nothing to prevent pollution. By reducing its pollution to $Q_{max} - Q_A$ (the same thing as abating pollution by Q_A), firm A saves an amount that is given by the shaded area in panel A.

Firm B chooses to abate only a small amount of pollution, Q_B. Any further abatement would require that the firm incur costs along MC_B, which would be greater than the benefits of taxes saved, t.

Note that in equilibrium both firms have the same marginal cost of abatement, and marginal reallocation of abatement between firms would not affect total social costs of pollution plus abatement.

If the regulatory agency wished to reduce pollution further, it could raise the tax rate; there would still be equality of marginal abatement costs between firms.

---

same time, market-like mechanisms can be effective in internalizing the externalities. Pollution is an example of a problem in which markets themselves can be used to correct market failure.

Regulation for Health and Safety

The Food and Drug Administration (FDA) must approve the marketing of both prescription and non-prescription drugs. The National Highway Transportation Safety Administration (NHTSA) requires that automobiles have brake lights and seat belts. A requirement that new automobiles be equipped with

air bags has been a source of controversy for a decade. The Consumer Product Safety Commission (CPSC) can remove dangerous goods from the marketplace. It can also set standards for product safety, such as requiring "dead man" controls that automatically stop engines in lawn mowers when the operator lets go of the handle. The Occupational Safety and Health Administration (OSHA) is broadly responsible for health and safety in the work place. It sets detailed standards that are designed to reduce workers' exposure to injury and to health risks, such as those imposed by asbestos. The Federal Trade Commission, in addition to its antitrust role, which we discussed in Chapter 15, regulates "truth in advertising."

What all of these examples have in common is

that the market failure that they address is in the market for information. A consumer has no way of knowing if a cold remedy has dangerous side effects, what the effect of brake lights is on the chances of having an accident, or how likely a child's pajamas are to catch fire. An individual worker may be in no position to assess the risks of working on a given machine and may not be able to find out easily whether there are toxic chemicals in the work place.

Health and Safety Information as a Public Good

In the previous chapter, we saw that information is likely to be underproduced in private markets, because information is an example of a (nearly) *pure public good*. Once the flammability of different materials that are used in children's pajamas is known, making the information available to interested parents can be done at negligible marginal cost. A private firm that develops the information would be unable to recoup its investment. Unless the government intervenes, product information would tend to be either unavailable or available only at inefficiently high prices. Most economists would agree that information about safety in the work place and product safety is a public good; this provides a rationale for the government either to produce or to require private firms to produce such information.[3]

Is Good Information Enough?

In practice, most health and safety regulation goes well beyond the simple provision of information. Rather, firms are required to meet standards of work place and product safety. Many economists have argued that given good information, private markets

will assure efficient levels of work place safety. In order to evaluate this argument, we present here a very simple example of what would happen if there were no standards and everyone had accurate information about safety risks.

Consider a worker who can take a job at either firm A or firm B. Suppose that the worker knows that accidents at firm A will lead the typical worker to miss two weeks of work per year, while the average time lost to injury at firm B is one week per year. There is no compensation paid for the time spent at home due to inury. In order to keep the example simple, suppose that lost pay is the only cost of accidents that is borne by workers. (These must be pretty trivial accidents!)

Equilibrium in the labor market can only occur if workers at firm A have a higher wage than workers at firm B. Assume that full-time work in both firms is 50 weeks per year. Workers in firm A can expect to be laid up and unable to work for an average of one week per year more than those at firm B. They will thus require a wage that is 50/49 times the wage paid to workers in firm B (assuming that they get no pleasure from spending a week at home in bed).

Notice that in this example all that is required for equilibrium to occur is that the workers know the probability of accidents at each firm and that markets respond to conditions of demand and supply. No government standard needs to be set. Rather, workers who work in the firm that is less safe will demand a compensating wage differential in order to work there. Thus, the greater is the chance of an accident at work, the higher are the wages that a firm must pay. This is illustrated by the upward-sloping curve shown in Figure 22-5. From the perspective of the employer, the curve represents the marginal wage cost (per worker) of increasing the probability of accidents. As accidents become more likely (moving along the horizontal axis), the firm must pay higher wages.

There is also a corresponding marginal benefit curve facing the firm. Returning to our example, suppose that firm A could be just as safe as firm B if it spent C dollars per year per worker on improved lighting and more frequent cleanup of potentially hazardous debris on the shop floor. If C is greater than one week's pay, the extra costs would not be worth it. The firm would be spending C per worker per year and saving less than C. If the costs of reducing the probability of lost time at work by one

[3] Those who do not agree would rely on the legal system to compel private producers and employers to develop the information. If someone is hurt by an unsafe product, the person can sue the manufacturer for damages. If the manufacturer has provided accurate information about the risks inherent in using the product, the consumer's chance of winning the lawsuit is much reduced. Thus, the manufacturer has an interest in developing accurate information. A similar case can be made regarding worker health and safety. In practice, however, many lawsuits of this kind are defended on the grounds that manufacturers had no knowledge of or reason to be concerned about their products' hazards. That such defenses often succeed suggests that there is an incentive to *fail* to develop relevant information about health and safety.

FIGURE 22-5   The "Market" for Occupational Safety

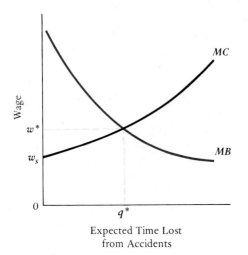

The labor market can induce firms to provide work place safety. Suppose that a perfectly safe work place would have to pay a wage of only w_s. As the expected time lost because of accidents increases, the required wage rises in order to compensate workers for the risk of injury. The curve that shows the higher wages is labelled MC, because it gives the (per worker) marginal cost to the firm of letting the work place become less safe.

The marginal benefit to the firm of reducing safety is given by the MB curve, which shows the *savings* (per worker) that the firm can obtain by reducing safety-related expenditures. At the axis, time that is lost through accidents is zero; the work place is perfectly safe. The MB curve starts very high, because the cost of making a safe work place safer is likely to be very high. Thus, reducing safety by a small amount from perfect safety would sharply reduce the firm's costs.

Where the two curves intersect, the marginal cost of making the work place safer is just equal to the marginal benefit from doing so. To the left of q^*, reducing safety in the work place saves MB and costs only MC.

Given that the MC curve is derived from the preferences of workers who are well informed about work place risks, the market solution of q^* and w^* will be cost-minimizing for the firm and socially efficient.

week per worker (C) were less than one week's pay, however, a cost-minimizing firm would incur those costs. In general, the marginal benefit to the firm of increasing the probability of accidents is the saving in safety-related costs. This is shown as the downward-sloping MB curve in Figure 22-5.

In equilibrium, firms will choose a level of safety such that the savings in nonwage costs of reducing safety a little bit is just equal to the increase in the wages that the firm would have to pay. Notice that the optimal rate of accidents, much like the optimal level of pollution, is not zero. Rather, it depends on the cost of reducing the level of accidents.

In the oversimplified world of Figure 22-5, there is no need for safety standards; if workers are perfectly informed about the risk of accidents (and about the costs that they would bear when accidents occur) and firms minimize costs, the private market will generate efficient solutions. This argument also can be extended to product safety, given the strong assumption that consumers are perfectly informed about the risks inherent in consuming the products that they buy.

With perfect information, private markets will produce efficient levels of occupational and product safety.

In spite of this, there are a number of arguments for government intervention to promote health and safety.

Perfect information may be impossible to obtain or to evaluate.   Our example of firm A and firm B could work quite well for, say, an experienced machinist who is comparing two machine shops. Such a worker will have a good sense of what can be expected on the shop floor and may be able to estimate quite accurately the chances of injury. If the government requires all firms to publish their accident histories every year, the worker can make an informed choice. Such a choice may be impossible, however, when the cause of harm in the work place is a chemical that might cause cancer. Evaluation of carcinogens often takes many years; there is likely to be uncertainty in the medical literature; and it is very likely that the typical worker will have a difficult time interpreting the information, even if it is made easily available.

Information about safety risks in offices is also unlikely to be available, at least in some cases. Most white-collar workers have no idea what their buildings are made of, how quickly the buildings would burn, or what kind of emergency lighting would be available in case of a fire. Further, it would not be easy for them to decode the blueprints of different buildings to make informed choices about fire safety.

Similar problems arise with product safety. The typical automobile driver is not able to make informed choices about the benefits of collapsing steering columns, reinforced door panels, or dual-braking systems. A complete maintenance report on each airplane that you fly on would probably be of little help to you in assessing the safety of the airplane. Less dramatically, it would be prohibitively expensive for the government to develop accident data for every consumer product and then to let consumers sift through the information as they decided what to buy.

Safety standards can free workers and consumers from making difficult calculations that they are ill equipped to make. When information is costly or impossible to process, standards can enhance efficiency.

Paternalism and merit goods.   One of the most cost-effective regulations in existence involves collapsing steering columns in automobiles. (The idea is that, in the case of a front-end collision, the steering column breaks before impaling the driver.) According to a recent estimate, the protection afforded by the collapsing steering column saves about 1,300 lives per year at a cost (in 1985) of $100,000 per life. On pure efficiency grounds, matters might be further improved if automobile manufacturers offered the collapsing steering column as an option and were required to provide data on the hazards of noncollapsing steering columns. Only very ardent proponents of laissez faire would argue for such a policy.

Another safety regulation requires that children's sleepwear meet a nonflammability standard. (The standard requires that the fabric not burst into flame when it is lit.) This regulation is less cost effective than the requirement of collapsing steering columns. In 1985 the cost *per life saved* was estimated to be about $1.3 million. Still, few people would wish to permit parents to choose flammable pajamas at somewhat lower cost. It is hard to think of a government regulation that is more literally paternalistic!

Health and Safety Regulation in Practice

In Chapter 21 we noted that even when there is market failure, the case for government intervention is weakened by the possibility of government failure. Perhaps the most widely cited examples of government failure arise in the area of health and safety regulation.

A notorious example of regulatory failure is the short-lived ban on saccharin. Saccharin was banned under the Delaney Amendment, which requires that the Food and Drug Administration ban any product that has been shown to cause cancer in laboratory animals. When huge doses of saccharin caused rats to get cancer, the FDA followed the law. Saccharin was so popular that Congress passed a special law exempting it from the Delaney Amendment. But the Delaney Amendment still applies generally, and it is used to ban products from the marketplace even when the risk of cancer is very low and the cost of alternative products is high.[4]

As with pollution, health and safety regulators often take an engineering approach to their task. Rather than specifying a particular outcome or providing incentives for increased safety, they mandate that certain kinds of equipment be used to perform certain functions. The Occupational Safety and Health Administration, for example, requires that handrails be of a certain height and a certain distance from the wall, and have supports of specified spacing and diameter.

In principle, the case for the engineering approach may be stronger for safety regulation than it is for pollution control, because the alternative of a "safety tax" generally is not feasible. Unfortunately, the problems inherent in all engineering standards—that they may become obsolete and that they may be much more effective in some settings than in others—remain. To the extent possible, efficiency dictates that standards be expressed in terms of required performance, rather than required design and materials. The reason for this is that it provides an incentive for firms to find inexpensive ways of meeting the standards, thus reducing the cost of complying with them. An example is the standard requiring that lawn mowers be equipped with "dead man" controls. Basically, the requirement is simply that the controls must work; the manufacturers may choose the design.

The overall record on health and safety regulation

---

[4] The Delaney Amendment does not apply to tobacco products, which are not officially considered to be either foods or drugs. Thus, tobacco is permitted to be sold even though it is known to cause cancer.

is mixed. After a shaky start (one that included requiring, among other things, that cowboys have access to portable toilets), the Occupational Safety and Health Administration lately has been found to have a modest positive impact on worker health and safety.[5] The same study, however, has concluded that "most available cost studies fail to show examples where the benefits of OSHA standards exceed the costs. . . ."

Benefit-Cost Analysis of Social Regulation

Economics often has been called the "dismal science," and evaluation of health, safety, and pollution regulation can be dismal indeed. The social purpose of such regulation is obvious. No one wants unsafe products, hazardous work places, and ugly or dangerous environments. However, even for as wealthy a society as the United States in the 1990s, the goals of health and safety cannot be absolute ones. There is no such thing as a completely safe work place or product; it is impossible to establish that a prescription drug can never be harmful; it is hard to think of any human activity that does not generate some minimum amount of waste. Given that these problems always will be with us to some degree, the relevant question is *to what degree*. Economics can help provide an answer to the question by evaluating costs as well as benefits—an answer that has been a recurring theme of both this book and this chapter.

For economic efficiency, environmental, health, and safety risks should be reduced to the point where the marginal social cost of further reduction is just equal to the marginal social benefit of further reduction.

Many critics of the economic approach to social regulation rightly point out that these costs and benefits are often very difficult to measure. True as this may be in certain cases, the logic of the benefit-cost criterion still holds. Unless public policies attempt to equate marginal benefits and marginal costs, scarce social resources will be wasted.

Cost-effectiveness analysis is a procedure that is much easier to perform than cost-benefit analysis. In cost-effectiveness analysis, the analyst holds constant the *outputs* of a policy and looks for the cheapest (most cost-effective) way of pursuing those outputs. Such analysis is particularly useful when it is difficult to measure the value of outputs. A prominent example involves the cost of saving lives. We do not presume to put a dollar value on a human life. Cost-effectiveness analysis, however, tells us that in designing programs to save human lives, we should implement those programs that do so at lowest cost first. If we do not, we will be wasting resources that could be devoted to saving lives and thus will be reducing the number of lives saved compared to what could be accomplished.

A recent study of regulations designed to save lives reveals an extraordinary range in the cost per life saved of actual and proposed regulations. The most cost-effective is the collapsing steering column, at $100,000 per life, in 1984. The least cost-effective regulation in place at the time of the study involved the use of DES in cattle feed and was calculated to cost $132 million per life saved, over a thousand times as much.[6] Begging the question of the value of human life, there are surely thousands of ways to spend $132 million and save more than one life. Consider, for example, the hiring of crossing guards who would work during rush hours, policing the most travelled street corners that do not have crossing guards. Assuming a wage of $13,200 per year per guard (surely high for a part-time job such as this one), 10,000 such guards could be hired for one year. They would surely save more than one life.

The rationale for seeking efficiency in social regulation comes from the same source as the rationale for seeking economic efficiency in other areas. The more efficiently the goals of social regulation are pursued, the more resources will be available to pursue other things of value.

Regulatory Reform

The agenda for regulatory reform that is implicit in this analysis is clear. Indeed, it has been adopted, in

[5] W. Kip Viscisi, "The Prospect of Occupational Safety and Health Regulation, 1973–1983," *Rand Journal of Economics,* Winter 1986, pp. 567–580.

[6] John F. Morral III, "A Review of the Record," *Regulation,* Nov./Dec. 1986, pp. 25–34.

varying degrees and with limited success, by the Ford, Carter, Reagan, and Bush administrations.

1. Regulations should be subject to formal benefit-cost analysis. The question of how much we are willing to pay for social goals is properly political and not purely economic. If the goals are to be pursued rationally, however, it is essential that society be able to measure the costs accurately. Unfortunately, many of the relevant statutes do not allow for regulators to consider costs. For example, the law that created OSHA mandated that the government "assure so far as possible every working man and woman in the nation safe and healthful working conditions." The phrase "so far as possible" says nothing about cost, and indeed the Supreme Court has ruled that technical feasibility alone should be relevant to OSHA's behavior.

2. To the extent possible, regulations should specify required levels of performance, rather than specific techniques. This would leave firms to decide how best to comply with the standards. The firms, in turn, would have an incentive to shop for inexpensive techniques, which the private sector would have an incentive to develop.

3. The use of market and marketlike policies should be much more extensively explored. Where all parties to a transaction are well informed, private markets will tend to reduce risk to efficient levels. Where there is an externality present, the regulators themselves should be encouraged to design incentives to internalize them, as in the case of tradeable emissions permits.

Most economists would support the preceding agenda for reform. Even if it is fully adopted, however, difficult social choices and difficult technical problems, of both measurement and program design, will remain. Moreover, when health, life, and safety are at stake, there are many who will never be comfortable with the results of decentralized decision making, no matter how well informed are the parties to private transactions. The desire to protect people from the negative consequences of their actions extends well beyond an interest in internalizing externalities or providing efficient levels of information.

Economic analysis can help society to examine the costs and the consequences of social regulation. Most important, it can help regulators to achieve desired consequences at minimum cost and thus reduce the level of government failure. It can help us to decide how best to intervene in the interest of health and safety, but it cannot tell us how much we should intervene.

SUMMARY

1. Almost all economic activity is subject to at least some government regulation. Government regulation is used to deal with every type of market failure—public goods, externalities, natural monopoly problems, information asymmetries, and social values.

2. Economic regulation refers to the regulation of natural monopoly, which was discussed in Chapter 15. Social regulation is the regulation of economic behavior to advance social goals where neither competition nor economic regulation can be expected to do the job.

3. Most pollution problems can be analyzed as negative externalities. Polluting firms and households going about their daily business do harm to the environment and fail to take account of the costs that they impose on others.

4. The economically efficient level of pollution in any activity is generally not zero; it is the level where the marginal cost of further pollution reduction is just equal to the marginal damage done by a unit of pollution. If a firm or a household faces incentives that cause it to internalize the costs that pollution imposes, it will choose the economically efficient level of pollution.

5. Pollution can be regulated either directly or indirectly. Direct controls are used most often. Direct controls are often inefficient, because they require that all polluters meet the same standard regardless of the benefits and costs of doing so. Indirect controls, such as taxes on emissions, are more efficient; ideally, they cause firms to internalize

perfectly the pollution externality. Tradeable emissions permits could have the same effect.

6. Health and safety regulation covers work place health and safety and product safety. Some economists have argued that regulation of this kind is unnecessary, because, if people are well informed about health and safety risks, the level of resources devoted to safety and health will be efficient.

7. Perfect information about health and safety risks is often difficult to obtain or to evaluate. Society may also choose not to permit people to face certain kinds of risks. In either of these cases, health and safety regulation addresses a real market failure. Government failure is common in the areas of health and safety regulation.

8. Cost-effectiveness analysis is a method of evaluating regulations when the benefits are hard to measure. It is particularly helpful for evaluating regulations that are designed to save lives, where the most cost-effective regulation is the one that saves the most lives per dollar of cost.

9. Increased use of benefit-cost and cost-effectiveness analysis could reduce the social costs imposed by social regulation. Alternatively, holding social cost constant, it could increase the benefits from social regulation. Economics, however, cannot tell society what should and should not be regulated.

TOPICS FOR REVIEW

Costs and benefits of pollution abatement
Emissions taxes
Direct controls
Efficient level of pollution
Tradeable emissions permits
Regulatory failure
Cost-effectiveness analysis
Regulatory reform

DISCUSSION QUESTIONS

1. Many occupations are licensed, either by governments or by professional organizations (such as state medical boards, which are run by physicians). Are economists licensed? Should they be? Why or why not?

2. "Pollution is wrong. When a corporation pollutes, it commits assault on the citizens of the country and it should be punished." Comment on this quotation in light of the discussion in this chapter.

3. Assume that the following statements are true. What do they imply about the argument that health and safety regulations are necessary to promote economic efficiency?

   a. Welders who work on the upper stories of unfinished skyscrapers are paid more than welders who work only indoors.

   b. Following a commercial airplane crash, the stock market value of the airline company tends to fall.

   c. Within a city, housing of a given structural quality tends to sell for less, the greater is the health risk that is posed by air quality in the neighborhood.

   d. For decades, asbestos was widely used as insulation. Installers of asbestos insulation routinely breathed asbestos fiber in concentrations that are now known to be potentially lethal. For some years, asbestos producers were aware that asbestos was dangerous but did not share this information with installers.

e. Until recently, the upholstery in airline seats emitted lethal fumes when they were burning.

4. Consider the following (alleged) facts about pollution control and indicate what, if any, influence they might have on policy determination.

   a. In the mid-1980s the cost of meeting federal pollution requirements was about $100 per person per year.

   b. More than one-third of the world's known oil supplies lie under the ocean floor, and there is no known blowout-proof method of recovery.

   c. Sulfur removal requirements and strip-mining regulations have led to the tripling of the cost of a ton of coal used in generating electricity.

   d. Every million dollars that is spent on pollution control creates 67 new jobs in the economy.

5. During a Pittsburgh air pollution alert, a 69-year-old retired steelworker was interviewed. He said, "I've got a heart condition myself, and I know that when I look out the window and see the air like it was this morning, I've got to stay inside. Yesterday, I tried to drive to the store, and I couldn't see 50 feet ahead of me, it was so thick, so I just came home. I remember that when I was young, we never thought about pollution. Everybody was working, and everybody had money, and the smokestacks were smoking, and the air was dirty, and we were all happy. I think the best air we ever had in Pittsburgh was during the Depression. That's when nobody was working." Comment on this statement in terms of the issues discussed in this chapter.

6. Suppose you were given the job of drafting a law to regulate water pollution over the entire length of some river.

   a. How would you determine how much total pollution to permit?

   b. What control mechanism would you use to regulate emissions into the river? Why?

   c. Would you impose the same rules on cities as on farms?

   d. Would the answers to any of the preceding questions depend on the quality of information that would be available to you? How and why?

Chapter 23

Taxation and Public Expenditure

All governments spend money, and they must raise revenue in order to do so. American governments—federal, state, and local—are no exception. Today however, spending and taxation at all levels of government go far beyond the minimum required to provide such essentials as a system of justice and protection against foreign enemies. Spending and taxing are also key tools of economic policy.

In Chapter 21 we saw that there were a number of reasons why the scope of government extends beyond the minimum. Public spending is the obvious way to provide collective consumption goods. It is also one way (via transfer programs) to affect the distribution of income. Taxation is needed to raise money for public spending. It also can play a policy role in its own right. Taxes can affect the distribution of income—some people get taxed more than others. Moreover, by taxing some activities heavily and others lightly or not at all, the tax system can influence the allocation of resources. In some cases tax policy is carefully designed with such effects in mind.

In this chapter we are concerned with public expenditure and taxation. We ask how these activities of government affect the allocation of resources and the distribution of income. We ask about the extent to which they are effective tools of public policy. We also consider the question of which governmental services (and associated taxes) should be the responsibility of which levels of government.

Taxation

There is a bewildering array of taxes, some highly visible (such as sales taxes and income taxes) and others all but invisible to the consumer because they are imposed on producers of raw materials and intermediate products. People are taxed on what they earn, on what they spend, and on what they own. Firms are taxed as well as households. Aggregate taxes from all levels of government amount to roughly one-third of the total value of goods and services that are produced in the United States each year. The diversity and the yield of various taxes are shown in Table 23-1.

Although one-third of national output may seem like a great deal, it puts the United States near the bottom of the list of industrialized countries. In recent years the share of GNP paid in taxes in the United States has been slightly higher than that in Japan and much lower than that in Western Europe and Canada.

Progressivity of Taxation

The effect of taxes on the income distribution can be summarized by classifying taxes as *progressive, proportional,* or *regressive.* A **progressive tax** takes a higher proportion of income, the higher is the taxpayer's income. A **proportional tax** takes a constant proportion of income at all levels of income. A **regressive tax** takes a lower proportion of income, the higher is the taxpayer's income.

The differences can be illustrated by an example. Suppose we have a (very) small town with 100 taxpayers, half of whom make $20,000 a year and half of whom make $40,000 a year. The town's budget (for street repair) is $10,000 per year.

Now consider three alternative tax systems. First, if the tax system simply were to assess $100 per year from each taxpayer (as it would with a *head tax,* under which each person pays the same tax), the outcome would be highly regressive. The lower-income taxpayers would be paying 0.5 percent of their incomes, and the higher-income taxpayers would be paying 0.25 percent of theirs. If, instead, the repairs were paid for by a proportional tax, everyone would pay 0.33 percent of income. Finally, a scheme whereby the first $20,000 of income would be subject to a 0.1 percent rate of tax and all

income above $20,000 would be subject to a 0.8 percent rate of tax would be progressive. The low-income taxpayers would pay only 0.1 percent of their incomes, while taxes would average 0.45 percent for the high-income group. Note that in all these examples the total tax revenues add up to the requisite $10,000.

Tax Expenditures

Sometimes taxes are used in ways that are very similar to spending programs. For example, until recently the federal government allowed an *investment tax credit* on private investment. The way in which the credit worked was that any qualified investment would permit the relevant taxpayer to reduce his or her income taxes by 10 percent of the amount of the investment. Now imagine a program in which, instead of allowing the tax credit, the U.S. Treasury simply wrote a (nontaxable) check to the taxpayer for 10 percent of the value of the investment. The effect would be identical to the investment tax credit: Every qualified investment would receive a 10 percent rebate from Uncle Sam.

When the tax system provides rewards of this kind for specified activities, the lost revenues often are called **tax expenditures.** The difference between a tax expenditure and an ordinary budgetary expenditure is that a tax expenditure *reduces* the revenue side of the budget, instead of increasing the expenditure side. As a practical matter, tax expenditures often receive little scrutiny from Congress. Their effects are usually harder to discern and harder to evaluate than those of direct spending programs.

In many cases, tax expenditures are difficult to distinguish from tax "loopholes." The distinction is often in the eye of the beholder. The investment tax credit, for example, was considered by many, especially in the business community, to be a means of enhancing economic growth by encouraging investment. It was seen by others as a way of allowing the richest and most successful businesses (and, indirectly, their stockholders) to avoid paying taxes that they were plainly able to pay.

The U.S. Tax System

The term "U.S. tax system" is something of a misnomer. Taxes are collected by the federal government, by each of the 50 states and the District of

TABLE 23-1	Federal, State, and Local Tax Revenue, 1987 (*billions of dollars*)	
	Federal	State and local
Personal income	$405.6	$164.7
Sales and excises	54.0	312.3
Corporate income	105.8	27.9
Payroll	351.0	48.1
Total	916.5	553.0

Source: 1989 *Economic Report of the President.*

Federal, state, and local governments have very different revenue sources. In 1987 sales and excise taxes, including property taxes, accounted for almost one-half of state and local tax revenue but less than 10 percent of federal revenue. Income and social insurance (payroll) taxes were much more important for the federal government than for state and local governments.

Columbia, and by tens of thousands of cities, towns, villages, counties, and special districts. The federal government collects about one-and-a-half times as much revenue as all of the other governments put together. The states, in turn, collect about twice as much as do local governments. Income and payroll taxes are the main sources of revenue for the federal government. Sales taxes are the most important for states, with income taxes being a close second. Local governments rely heavily on property taxes.

The Federal Personal Income Tax

The federal personal income tax accounts for about 42 percent of federal revenues. The tax was greatly changed by the Tax Reform Act of 1986, which reduced income-tax rates overall and greatly reduced (but did not eliminate) tax expenditures and loopholes. The income tax is paid on all types of income, including wages, salaries, dividends, interest, rents, and capital gains. Most income comes in the form of wages and salaries. Tax on wages and salaries is *withheld* by employers from employees' paychecks. On April 15 (or before, for the unusually well-organized) people file tax returns with the Internal Revenue Service. Most people will have had enough tax withheld over the year so that they either receive a refund or pay no additional tax.

The federal income tax is a progressive tax: The percentage of income paid in taxes rises with income. This is accomplished in two ways: First, by exempting some minimum income from any tax. Second by making the tax rate itself dependent upon the amount of income. Table 23-2 reports on two types of tax rates, the **average tax rate** and the **marginal tax rate.** The average tax rate is just total taxes paid divided by income. As Table 23-2 shows, it rises smoothly from zero (for incomes below $12,800 in 1988) to 28 percent. The marginal tax rate is the amount that must be paid on the *last* dollar of income. It is the relevant amount to consider when a person decides whether or not to put in an extra hour

---

TABLE 23-2   The U.S. Personal Income Tax, 1988 (*married couples with two children*)

(1)	(2)	(3)	(4)
		Average tax rate	
	Personal income	(percentage)	Marginal tax rate
Income	tax	(2 ÷ 1)	(percentage)
$ 10,000	$ 0	0	0
12,800	0	0	0
15,000	330	2.2	15.0
20,000	1,080	5.4	15.0
30,000	2,580	8.6	15.0
40,000	4,080	10.2	15.0
50,000	6,549	13.1	28.0
75,000	13,548	18.1	28.0
100,000	21,313	21.3	33.0
200,000	54,313	27.1	33.0
1,000,000	278,600	27.9	28.0

The average income-tax rate rises with income; thus the U.S. income tax is progressive in structure. These data give the amount of federal tax to be paid at different income levels by a married couple with two dependent children in 1988. They assume that the couple takes the "standard deduction" of $5,000. Each member of the household is also entitled to a $1,950 personal exemption. Thus, the first $12,800 of actual income is exempt from tax [$5,000 + (4 × $1,950) = $12,800]. Higher-income households often are able to deduct more than $5,000 from income, in which case the effective average tax rates on income are lower, especially at high incomes, than those shown in column 3.

of work. The marginal tax rate under the U.S. federal income tax starts at zero, rises to 15 percent, then to 28 and 33 percent, and falls back to 28 percent for couples with taxable incomes over $192,930 and for single individuals with incomes that exceed $100,480.

Prior to the 1986 tax reform, the tax rate schedule contained many more tax brackets, with marginal tax rates ranging from 11 to 50 percent. (Before 1981, the top rate was 70 percent.) The old system was somewhat more progressive at the highest levels of income, but it actually taxed low-income taxpayers more than does the current system. If the old system were still in place, it would raise only slightly more revenue than the new system. The reason for this is that, although the old system taxed most income at higher rates, there were also many more loopholes and tax expenditures than exist under the reformed system.

Exemptions and deductions.   The way in which most tax loopholes and tax expenditures work is either by *exempting* certain types of income from taxation or by allowing certain types of expenditures to be *deducted* from taxable income. An example of an exemption—one that is still allowed—is interest income from state and local bonds. This income is not taxed by the federal government. An example of a deduction that is still permitted is that for mortgage interest payments.

Tax expenditures and tax loopholes generally will make a progressive income tax less progressive in practice than it appears to be on paper.

There are two related reasons for this. First, an exemption or a deduction is worth more the higher is the tax bracket. Consider two couples, each of which pays $10,000 in mortgage interest per year. Bob and Carol make $50,000 per year and are in the 28 percent marginal tax bracket. The $10,000 mortgage interest deduction reduces their taxes by 28 percent of $10,000, or $2,800. Ted and Alice make only $30,000 per year. The mortgage interest deduction saves them only 15 percent of $10,000, or $1,500. The effect of the deduction is plainly regressive: It reduces taxes by more, both absolutely and as a percentage of income, for the higher-income

household. The income tax is still progressive but less so than if mortgage interest were not deductible.[1]

The second effect of tax expenditures arises from the first. Because they are of greater value to those who face higher marginal tax rates, they will be sought out by them. The tax exemption on municipal bonds, for example, is worth very little to someone in the 15 percent bracket. In fact, it may be worth nothing at all. As this edition goes to press, the interest rate on taxable, high-grade corporate bonds is about 10 percent, while the rate on tax-free municipal bonds is about 7.8 percent. For a taxpayer who is in the 28 percent bracket, the municipal bonds are a better buy: The yield is 7.8 percent, while the *after-tax* yield on the taxable bonds is only 7.2 percent (10 percent minus 0.28×10 percent). The taxpayer in the 15 percent bracket gets a net return of 8.5 percent on the taxable bonds (10 percent minus 0.15×10 percent) and only 7.8 percent on the municipal bonds. It is not surprising, then, that almost everyone who takes advantage of this tax exemption is in the higher tax brackets. This is another way in which tax expenditures and loopholes operate to reduce the overall progressivity of the tax system.

Payroll taxes.

The payroll tax is the second most important source of federal revenue, and its importance has grown greatly over the last 20 years.

In 1969 payroll taxes accounted for about 25 percent of federal revenues. By 1988 the figure had risen to 40 percent. Most of this growth can be attributed to the sharp growth in social security taxes, which account for the bulk of payroll taxes.

Federal payroll taxes are levied directly on wages and salaries—on payrolls. They are proportional up to a *ceiling*, which makes them slightly regressive. For example, in 1988 social security taxes (for retire-

---

[1] This example also illustrates a difficulty in interpreting the mortgage interest deduction as a beneficial tax expenditure designed to encourage home ownership. It encourages home ownership more for high-income households than for low-income households. It is hard to imagine Congress enacting an expenditure program that would give nothing to help married couples with two children who earned less than $12,800 to help own their own homes, something to those between $12,800 and $42,550, and a lot to those above $42,500. But this is what current tax law does!

ment, disability, and Medicare) were about 15 percent (7.5 percent each from employers and from employees) of wages and salaries below $45,000. The marginal tax rate on wage income above $45,000 was zero. Thus, the very highest income workers paid lower average payroll tax rates than did lower-income workers.

The corporate income tax.   Corporate income taxes are levied directly on the *accounting profits* (see Chapter 9) of corporations. The tax rate is now a flat 34 percent on all corporate income after a small exempt amount. Prior to the Tax Reform Act of 1986, the tax rate was 46 percent, but because tax reform also reduced or eliminated various *corporate* tax expenditures, the tax reform actually increased the revenue from the corporate income tax.

The corporate income tax is much less important today than it was 20 years ago. In 1969 taxes on corporate profits were 18 percent of federal revenue, compared to 11 percent in 1988. It is difficult to determine the effect of corporate taxation on income distribution, for there is great controversy over the extent to which it is "shifted" to consumers.[2]

Excise and sales taxes.   An excise tax is levied on a particular commodity (e.g., liquor); a sales tax is levied on all or most sales. If two families spend the same proportion of their income on a certain commodity that is subject to a sales or an excise tax, the tax is proportional in its effects on them. If the tax is on a commodity, such as food, that takes a larger proportion of the income of lower-income families, it is regressive. If it is on a commodity, such as jewelry, on which the rich spend a larger proportion of their income than do the poor, it is progressive. A general sales tax is regressive because poorer families tend to spend a larger proportion of their incomes than do richer ones.

All but a handful of states in the United States have general sales taxes. The federal government does not use a general sales tax, but it imposes a number of excise taxes, the most important of which are on cigarettes, alcoholic beverages, gasoline, and rubber tires. Compared to the other major categories of federal taxes, excise taxes are of minor significance. The gasoline tax, however, finances a trust fund for construction and repair of federal highways. The alcohol and cigarette taxes perhaps are intended to induce people to behave in certain ways as well as to raise revenue. All three of these taxes in 1989 were in the news as possible sources of "revenue enhancement."

Commodities such as tobacco, alcohol, and gasoline usually account for a much greater proportion of expenditure by lower-income than higher-income groups, so the taxes on them are regressive.

The sales and excise taxes that are used in the United States today are, as a whole, regressive.

State and Local Taxes

State and local governments use the same kinds of taxes as the federal government but in very different proportions. They also use property taxes, which the federal government does not. The most important source of revenues at the state level is the general sales tax, which is a tax on the value of most sales of goods, usually excluding food, medicine, and housing. Because the share of income that is consumed is highest at low incomes, general sales taxes tend to be regressive. Most states also have personal income taxes but at much lower rates than the federal income tax. Corporate taxes at the state level account for relatively little revenue, although their importance has been increasing.

The property tax.   Many large cities levy income taxes, and some have their own sales taxes, but by far the most important tax for local governments is the property tax. Property taxes are based on the value of taxable property, including residential housing (both owner-occupied and rented), farms, factories, and business equipment. At any time a local government will have a total *assessed value* of property. The tax rate (often called a *millage,* and expressed as the tax due per $1,000 of property) is then multiplied by the assessed value to calculate the amount of tax. This procedure is quite straightforward, yet the property tax is the most controversial of all U.S. taxes. During the late 1970s and early 1980s, many states experienced a "property tax revolt," in which property taxes were reduced or limited statewide.

---

[2] The question of tax shifting is called *the problem of incidence,* that is, who really pays a tax imposed on any one group. It is discussed later in this chapter.

The property tax is different from any other major U.S. tax because taxpayers do not need to buy or sell anything in order to incur a tax liability. It is the only important U.S. tax that is based on wealth.

In order to owe income tax, one must generate income (sell labor, capital services, or whatever). In order to owe sales or excise taxes, one must buy or sell something. But to owe property tax, one must merely *own* property. This leads to two difficulties. First, before the tax is collected, someone (the local *assessor*, in practice) must make an estimate of what the property is worth. For a house or a factory that was last sold 20 years ago, such estimates may be difficult to make. Second, it is perfectly possible to own valuable property, and thus owe a good deal of tax, but not have the cash on hand to pay the tax.

These two problems make the property tax especially vulnerable to political controversy. Property owners can often claim, with some justice, that *their* property is overassessed compared to a neighbor's property. People who have low income in a given year, especially elderly home owners, may be put in the position of having to sell their houses in order to raise the money to pay the taxes that are due.

The property tax is widely thought to be regressive, but many economists believe that the tax is much closer to being proportional. An important reason that the tax might look regressive is that many retired people still live in the homes that they bought while they were working. Their current incomes may be low compared to the value of their houses, although their lifetime incomes will be in line with the value of their houses. If the progressivity or regressivity of the property tax is calculated on lifetime incomes, the tax looks much more progressive.

The political consequences of forcing elderly home owners to choose between paying high taxes and leaving their family homes are hard for governments to bear. As a result, many states now have special provisions that forgive property taxes for elderly home owners when the tax that is assessed exceeds a few percent of total income. These provisions often are called *circuit breakers* because the usual property tax rules are "broken" if the ratio of taxes to income is above a threshold amount. The Canadian province of British Columbia has a different method of dealing with the same problem. There,

home owners who are over 65 are allowed to stop paying property taxes altogether. When the home owner dies, the government is paid the taxes due when the house is sold. In effect, the government is lending the property taxes to the home owner.

Evaluating the Tax System

Many people use a very simple rule for evaluating taxes—the lower the better. This view does not provide a helpful guide for designing a tax system. Once the level of taxes is chosen, the important question is the following: *Holding the amount of revenue to be raised constant*, what makes one tax system better (or worse) than another? Economists try to answer this question by considering two aspects of taxation—efficiency and equity. If you have gotten this far in this book, you should have a pretty good idea of what economists mean by efficiency, and you can probably guess that taxes affect efficiency by distorting free-market allocations of resources. We will investigate this in some detail later in this chapter. As we discussed in Chapter 21, equity is another matter, because notions of fairness are very much in the eye of the beholder.

Equity

The ability-to-pay principle. Most people view an equitable tax system as being based on people's *ability to pay* taxes, although some have argued, as we shall see, that taxes should be based, instead, on how much people benefit from public expenditure. In considering equity that is based on ability to pay, two concepts need to be distinguished. *Vertical equity* concerns equity across income groups; it focuses on comparisons between individuals or families with different levels of income. This concept is central to discussions of the progressivity of taxation. Proponents of progressive taxation argue as follows. (1) Taxes should be based on ability to pay. (2) The greater is one's income, the greater is the percentage of income that is available for goods and services beyond the bare necessities. (3) Thus, the greater is one's income, the greater is the proportion of income that is available to pay taxes. Thus, (4) an ability-to-pay standard of vertical equity requires progressive taxation.

Horizontal equity concerns equity within a given income group; fundamentally it is concerned with establishing just who *should* be considered equal to whom in their ability to pay taxes. Two households with the same income may have different numbers of children to support. One of the households may have greater medical expenses, leaving less for both life's pleasures and for taxes. One of the households may have just lost its house in a fire. One of the households may incur greater expenses that are necessary for earning income (e.g., requirements to buy uniforms or to pay union dues). All of these examples involve horizontal equity; there is simply no objective way to decide how much these and similar factors affect the ability to pay taxes. In practice, the income-tax law makes some allowance for these difficulties (as well as others) by permitting taxpayers to exempt some of their income from tax. However, the corrections are rough, at best, and the amount that can be exempted for children ($1,950 per child in 1988) is much less than the average cost of feeding, housing, and clothing a child.

The benefit principle.   There is a second strand in the theory of equitable taxation that is often in conflict with the ability-to-pay principle. According to the *benefit principle*, taxes should be paid in proportion to the benefits that taxpayers derive from public expenditure. From this perspective the ideal taxes are *user charges*, such as those that would be charged if private firms provided the government services. The benefit principle is the basis for the gasoline tax, which is used entirely to build and to maintain roads. There is also a special excise tax on airline tickets that is used for airport operations, air traffic control, and airport security. Although there are other examples, especially at the local level, the benefit principle has historically played only a minor role in the design of the U.S. tax system.

It is difficult to see how the benefit principle could be applied to many of the most important categories of government spending. Who gets how much benefit from national defense or from the interest on the national debt? It is even more difficult to imagine applying the benefit principle to programs that redistribute income.

How Progressive Is the U.S. Tax System?

It is more difficult to assess the overall impact of a tax system than the impact of any particular tax, but in assessing equity this is the important question: To what extent does the whole array of taxes tend to increase or to decrease the degree of inequality of the income distribution? One aspect of this question depends upon the mix of different kinds of taxes. Federal taxes (chiefly income taxes) tend to be somewhat progressive. State and local authorities rely heavily on property and sales taxes and thus have tax systems that tend to be regressive.

The difficulty in determining overall progressivity is increased by the fact that income from different sources is taxed at different rates. For example, under the federal individual tax in 1988, royalties on oil wells were taxed more lightly than royalties on books; interest on municipal bonds was tax exempt, while most other interest income was taxed. To evaluate progressivity, one needs to know the way in which different levels of income correlate with different sources of income. The best method for finding such relationships involves examining large numbers of individual tax returns.

The net effect of the federal tax system is progressive, except at the very lowest income levels, where the regressivity of excise taxes outweighs the progressivity of the income tax. According to the Congressional Budget Office, the tax reforms of 1986 increased the progressivity of the system somewhat but not as much as the tax changes that took place in the early 1980s reduced it. When federal, state, and local taxes are combined, the overall effect is roughly proportional, although it is regressive at the lowest levels of income. The reason is that the progressive income tax has only a small effect at low incomes (little or no tax is due), but regressive sales and excises apply at even the lowest levels of consumption. One proposed method of increasing the progressivity of the income tax at the lowest levels of income is discussed in Box 23-1.

The federal tax system is somewhat progressive. The U.S. tax system as a whole is roughly proportional.

In evaluating the progressivity of the tax system, how the money is spent is just as important as how it is collected. A regressive tax may provide funds

BOX 23-1

The Negative Income Tax

A tax is negative when the government pays "the taxpayer" instead of the other way around. The so-called **negative income tax (NIT)** is a policy tool designed to increase progressivity and combat poverty by making taxes negative at very low incomes. Such a tax would extend progressivity to the very lowest incomes.

Many versions of the NIT have been proposed; the one described here illustrates the basic idea. The underlying belief is that a family of a given size should be allowed a minimum annual income. The aim is to guarantee this income without eliminating the incentive to become self-supporting. This is done by combining a grant with a tax. As an example (see the figure), consider a system in which each household is guaranteed $6,000 per year. For each dollar earned above that amount, the household loses $.50—the marginal tax rate on the grant is 50 percent. The household breaks even at $12,000, the amount at which it receives no grant and pays no tax. Below this break-even level, the family is paid by the government; that is, the family pays a negative tax. Above this level, it pays a positive tax.

The scheme illustrated here works as if every family is given an untaxed grant of $6,000 and then taxed at a rate of 50 percent on all other income. (Of course, only the *difference* between the grant and the tax payable actually is paid or collected.) A family with $12,000 in taxable income breaks even. A family with income below $12,000 in taxable income is paid by the government. A family with taxable income above $12,000 pays taxes. The heavy black line shows the after-tax income for different levels of taxable income under this particular scheme. The 45° line shows the income before tax. Therefore, the vertical distance between it and the heavy black curve shows the payments by or to the government at any level of income under this scheme.

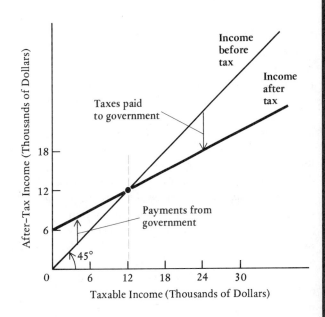

Supporters of the negative income tax believe that it would be a particularly effective tool for reducing poverty. It provides a minimum level of income as a matter of right, not of charity, and it does so without removing the incentive to work from those who are eligible for payments. Every dollar earned adds to the after-tax income of the family.

As a potential replacement for many other welfare programs, it promises to mitigate the most pressing cases of poverty with much less administrative cost and without the myriad exceptions that are involved in most programs. An incidental advantage is that it removes whatever incentive people might have to migrate to states with better welfare programs, but it does not discourage migration to places where work may be available.

for increasing welfare payments and thus redistribute income to the poor. It is the combined overall effect of taxes and spending that is important, and it may be easier for those who want to redistribute income to get Congress to enact progressive expenditure programs than to adopt more progressive taxes.

Efficiency

The tax system influences the allocation of resources by changing the *relative* prices of different goods and factors and the *relative* profitability of different industries and of different uses of factors of production.

While it is theoretically possible to design a neutral tax system—one that leaves all relative prices unchanged—actual tax policy leads to a different allocation of resources than would occur without it. The reason for this is that the taxes themselves change the relationship between prices and marginal costs, and shift consumption and production toward goods and services that are taxed relatively lightly (and away from those that are taxed more heavily). Usually, this *distortion* of free-market outcomes causes economic inefficiency. In a world without taxes (and without other market imperfections), prices would equal marginal costs, and society's resources could be efficiently allocated.

Of course, in a world without taxes, there would be other problems—it would be impossible to pay for government programs desired by society. Also there would be no way to provide public goods that enhance economic efficiency. In practice, then, the relevant objective for tax policy is to design a tax system that minimizes inefficiency, given the amount of revenue to be raised. In designing such a tax system, a natural place to start would be with taxes that both raise revenue and enhance efficiency. These are the fines and emissions taxes that we discussed in Chapter 22. When taxes are imposed on negative externalities, marginal social benefit moves closer to marginal social cost, *and* government revenue is raised. Unfortunately, such taxes cannot raise nearly enough revenue to finance all of government expenditure.

In the absence of externalities, a tax normally does two things. It takes money from the taxpayers, and it changes their behavior. Taxpayers typically are made worse off by both of these things. Economists call the first, the revenue collected, the **direct burden** of the tax. The value to taxpayers of the changed behavior is called the **excess burden.** The excess burden is hard to measure in practice but easy to measure in principle. It is the amount of money that the taxpayers would have to receive, over and above the tax paid, in order to be just as well off as if there were no tax.

An example may make this clear. Suppose that your state imposes a $2 excise tax on the purchase of rock records. If you are so attached to listening to rock music that you still buy your usual 10 records a week, there is no excess burden upon you. The direct burden on you is equal to the total burden, $20 a week. There is also no economic inefficiency; the cost of raising $20 a week for the state is just the $20 a week that you pay in taxes.

When taxes cause no changes in behavior, there is no excess burden and no economic inefficiency.

Suppose that your friend down the block is also a rock fan but not quite so fanatical. The tax leads her to cut back on her consumption of rock records from two a week to none. In this case, no revenue is raised, but your friend is clearly worse off. We do not know by how much, but we do know that some amount of money greater than zero (in fact, exactly her consumer surplus from buying two untaxed records per week) would be needed to make her as well off as she was before the tax was imposed.

When a tax is imposed, some people behave like the rock fanatic and do not change their behavior; others cease engaging in the taxed behavior altogether, and still others cut back on it. There will be excess burden for members of both of the latter two groups. This means that the revenue collected will understate the total cost to taxpayers, actual and potential, of generating that revenue. An efficient tax system will be one that minimizes the amount of excess burden. Usually, this will be the tax system that changes behavior the least.

The taxes that change behavior the least are taxes that apply to the goods for which the price elasticity of demand is least. Indeed, a good that is perfectly inelastically demanded (that has a vertical demand curve) can be taxed with no excess burden at all. Unfortunately, many of life's necessities have very price-inelastic demand curves, so a tax system that taxed only goods that had inelastic demand curves would prove to be very regressive.

Efficiency and equity are often competing goals in the design of tax systems.

"Supply-Side" Effects of Taxation

In principle, taxes on some activities can be so high that reducing the tax rate would actually increase tax revenue. This is the idea behind the **Laffer curve,** named for the economist Arthur Laffer, whose views were influential during the early years of the Reagan administration. Its essential feature is that tax revenues reach a maximum at some rate of taxation well below 100 percent (see Figure 23-1).

The general shape of the Laffer curve is argued as a matter of simple logic. At a zero tax rate no revenue would be collected. Similarly, at a 100 percent tax rate, revenue again would be zero because no one would bother to earn taxable income just to support the government. At intermediate rates people would both earn income and pay taxes. Government tax revenue would reach an upper limit at some rate of taxation below 100 percent. For rates higher than the rate that produces this maximum, every increase in tax rates will lead to a decrease in tax revenue.

Just where this maximum occurs—whether at average tax rates of 40 percent or 80 percent or 95 percent—is an important empirical matter. Laffer believed that by the 1970s the United States had already increased taxes past the point where higher tax rates yielded more revenue. As a result, he argued, any attempt to increase revenues by raising income-tax rates would be self-defeating.

Many other economists disagreed. Although they might concede that some countries may have reached such a point, they argued that this has not happened in the United States. A number of careful studies show that the then current U.S. top marginal tax rate of 50 percent was still short of being self-defeating in terms of tax revenue. These studies suggest that Laffer identified a potential rather than an actual problem.

Capital gains taxes. The Laffer curve has undergone something of a revival lately, this time applied to *capital gains taxes.* Capital gains occur when an asset (say, stock in a corporation) is sold for more than the purchase price. Until the 1986 tax reform, capital gains were taxed at much lower rates than ordinary income. From 1987 until at least late 1989 (when this book went to press), capital gains were treated in the same way as any other income. Many economists, and some politicians, notably George Bush, have argued that a reduction in capital gains rates would lead to such a large increase in capital gains that revenue would actually be increased. This is at least somewhat plausible, because people can choose when to sell assets and thus when to *realize* their capital gains. If they believe that the tax rate is going to fall, it will make sense for them to wait until it does so. Indeed, in 1987, when it was known that the capital gains rate would *rise* in 1988, there was an enormous increase in the sales of capital assets. The evidence on the long-term relationship between the capital gains tax rate and revenues from the tax is mixed, but if President Bush gets his way, new evidence will be forthcoming.

Tax Incidence

The major unresolved question about taxes and allocation is empirical: Just how different is the allocation because of tax policy? Perhaps surprisingly, there is no consensus on this question. The reason is that we are not sure who really pays the taxes that

---

FIGURE 23-1 A Laffer Curve

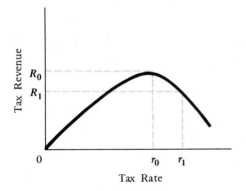

Increases in tax rates beyond some level will decrease rather than increase tax revenue. The curve relates the government's tax revenue to the tax rate. As drawn, revenue reaches a maximum level of r_0 at average tax rate r_0. If tax rates were r_1, *reducing* them to r_0 would increase revenue to the government.

are levied. This is called the problem of **tax incidence,** or the identification of who ultimately bears the burden of a tax. It is currently a very active area of economic research.

When a tax is imposed on a firm, does the firm bear the burden of the tax, or does it pass the burden on to the consumer in the form of higher prices? To see why this is a difficult question to answer, consider two examples.

Do Landlords or Tenants Pay the Property Tax?

Landlords characteristically protest that the crushing burden of property taxes makes it impossible for them to earn a reasonable living from renting buildings to tenants who as often as not abuse the property. Tenants are likely to reply that landlords typically shirk their responsibilities for building maintenance and that the whole burden of the tax is passed on to the tenants in the form of higher rents. Both sides cannot be right in alleging that they each bear the entire burden of the tax!

To examine the incidence, suppose that a city imposes a property tax. The thousands of landlords in the city decide to raise rents by the full amount of the tax. This scenario is shown graphically in Figure 23-2. There will be a decline in the quantity of rental accommodations that are demanded as a result of the rent increase.

The decline in the quantity demanded without any change in the quantity supplied will cause a surplus of rental accommodations at the higher prices. Landlords will find it difficult to replace tenants who move out, and the typical unit will remain empty longer between tenancies. Prospective tenants will find alternative sites from which to choose and will become very particular in what they expect from landlords.

Some prospective tenants, seeing vacant apartments, will offer to pay rents below the asking rent. Some landlords will accept the offer rather than earn nothing from vacant premises. Once some landlords cut rents, others will have to follow suit or find that their properties are staying unrented for longer periods of time.

Eventually, rentals will reach a new equilibrium at which the quantity demanded equals the quantity supplied. The equilibrium rental price will be higher than the original before-tax rent but lower than the rent that passes the entire tax on to the tenants.

FIGURE 23-2   The Incidence of a Tax on Rental Housing

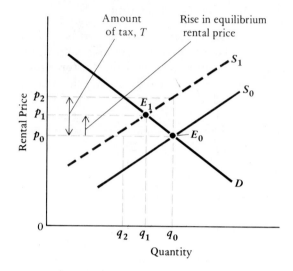

Since the equilibrium rent rises by less than the amount of the tax, landlords and tenants share the burden. The supply schedule S_0 reflects the landlords' willingness to supply rental housing at different levels of rents received. Before the tax, equilibrium is at E_0. When a tax of T is imposed on landlords, the supply curve shifts up by the full amount of the tax to S_1. Suppose landlords attempt to raise rents by the full amount of the tax, from p_0 to p_2. There will be an excess supply of housing of q_2q_0 at p_2, and rents will fall. At the new equilibrium E_1, with rental price p_1, landlords have succeeded in raising the rental price by p_0p_1, less than p_0p_2, the full amount of the tax. Thus, landlords are paying p_1p_2 of the total tax on each unit that is rented.

The incidence of the property tax is shared by landlords and tenants.

Just how it is shared by the two groups will depend on the elasticity of the demand and supply curves.[3] These elasticities, in turn, will depend on how much landlords and tenants can react to changes.

---

[3] We suggest that you draw a series of diagrams with demand and supply curves of different slopes to see how this works. In each case shift the supply curve up by the same vertical amount—to represent the property tax—and see what proportion of the increase is reflected in the new equilibrium price.

Notice that the question of incidence does not depend on who writes the check to pay the tax bill. In many European countries, the tenant rather than the landlord is sent the tax bill and pays the tax directly to the city; even in this case, however, the landlord bears part of the burden. As long as the existence of the tax reduces the quantity of rental accommodations demanded below what it otherwise would be, the tax will depress the amount that is received by landlords. In this way landlords will bear part of the burden.

Notice also that this result emerges even though neither landlords nor tenants realize it. Because rents are changing for all sorts of other reasons, no one will have much of an idea of what equilibrium rentals would be in the absence of the tax. It does not do much good just to look at what happens immediately after tax rates are changed because, as we have seen already, landlords may begin by raising rents by the full amount of the tax. Although they think that they have passed the tax on, this creates a disequilibrium. In equilibrium, prices will have risen by less than the full amount of the tax.

Do Taxes on Profits Affect Prices?

Economic theory predicts that a general percentage tax on profits, *as defined by economists,* will have no effect on price or output, and thus the full incidence of such a tax will fall on producers. To see this quickly, suppose that one price-quantity combination gives the firm higher profits (without considering taxes) than any other. If the government imposes a 20 percent profits tax, the firm will have only 80 percent as much profits after tax as it had before; *this will be true for each possible level of output.* The firm may grumble, but it will not be profitable for it to alter its price or output.

Notice that this argument is independent of the tax rate. **[30]** It applies equally whether the tax rate is 10 percent or 75 percent.

A tax on corporation income. Corporate income taxes are taxes on profits *as defined by the tax laws.* The definitions make them a tax on a combination of economic profits, plus some of the return to capital and to risk taking. Capital returns and returns to risk taking in the noncorporate sector are subject to different and, generally, lower taxes. One effect of the corporate income tax, then, is to shift resources out of the corporate sector. This certainly causes some economic inefficiency.

Just who pays the corporate income tax is much less clear. The tax could be paid, in whole or in part, by owners of capital, by labor, or by consumers. (Labor would bear some of the tax if the tax causes total capital investment to fall: With a smaller capital stock, wages would be lower.) Economists have been puzzling over this problem for years and have reached no consensus on the incidence of the tax.

Public Expenditure

Federal, state, and local governments in the United States spend about 35 percent of the nation's annual output. The share of national output that is spent by government has risen slowly since 1980, when it was 32.6 percent. It hardly changed in the 1970s, having grown rapidly (from 26.6 percent) during the 1960s. The federal government accounts for about 62 percent of this spending. For the federal government, defense and social security are the largest items; between them they make up more than one-half of the total. Education and highways are the major expenditures at the state and local levels. They account for slightly less than one-half of the total.

Table 23-3 shows the major spending categories for the different levels of government in 1987. There are four broad categories of spending, shown in the table. Government *purchases of goods and services* often are called "exhaustive" government expenditures. When a government buys a missile or a paper clip, when it pays a bureaucrat or hires a consulting firm to help reduce the deficit, when it uses fuel to run the Navy's ships or uses paint to maintain them, it is *using real resources that could be used elsewhere.* Some government purchases occur when the government acts like a firm and produces output. The armed services and public education are important examples of this. In other cases, the government hires private-sector workers and firms (most highways are built this way). In both cases, however, the government is the final purchaser of the resources.

The other categories of government spending are different from purchases and from each other. *Transfer payments* are payments made to individuals *without* the receipt of anything in return. The individuals use

TABLE 23-3	Major Categories of Government Spending, 1987 (*billions of dollars*)	
	Federal	State and local
Purchases of goods and services	$382.0	$542.8
Transfer payments	402.0	118.7
Grants-in-aid	102.7	—
Net interest	143.0	−44.6

Source: Economic Report of the President, 1989.

Different levels of government spend their money in different ways. State and local governments spend the great majority of their budgets on purchases of goods and services, whereas the federal government spends more on transfer payments than on any other category. The *negative* entry for state and local net interest arises from the fact that state and local governments earn more from their assets (mostly held to support their employees' pension plans) than they pay on their debt.

the transfer payments to make purchases, but the transfer payments themselves are not used by the government to purchase anything. Interest on government debt is like interest on any other debt; it is the cost that government incurs for having borrowed in the past. *Grants-in-aid* to state and local governments are similar to transfer payments, although the recipients are governments. Grants made by the federal government eventually are spent by lower levels of government.

Figure 23-3 shows that there has been a striking change in the composition of federal spending. Until 1974 the largest category of federal expenditures was purchases of goods and services. Transfer payments have been the largest category since 1975, although their lead has been eroded in the 1980s. This is due in part to the defense buildup and in part to the Reagan administration's reductions in social programs.

No such change has taken place with state and local governments. In 1987 over 89 percent of state and local government spending was for purchases of goods and services. In 1955 the figure was 92 percent.

Transfer Payments

Transfer payments are defined generally as payments to private persons or institutions that are not payments for current productive activity. (They do not include grants-in-aid, which are transfers from

one level of government to another, nor do they include interest on the national debt.) Welfare payments, social security payments, pensions, veterans' benefits, fellowships, and unemployment insurance are all transfer payments. Some federal transfers are made to foreigners as part of foreign-aid programs. Some transfer payments are private, such as private pensions and charitable contributions by individuals and corporations. Many are made by state and local governments, often by using funds that they have received as federal grants-in-aid.

The largest category of transfer payments is that made by the federal government to individuals. In

FIGURE 23-3   The Changing Form of Major Federal Expenditures (*selected years, 1955–1988*)

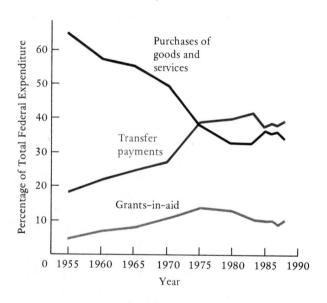

From 1955 until the 1980s, transfer payments and grants-in-aid grew steadily in importance. In 1955 two-thirds of all federal expenditures were purchases of goods and services. By 1980 the fraction was only one-third. Transfer payments to persons in the United States and grants-in-aid to state and local governments increased from less than one-fourth to more than one-half of the total between 1955 and 1980. The Reagan administration halted the trend. The three categories of expenditure that are graphed here account for 83 percent of total federal expenditures. The largest item not shown on the graph is net interest paid by the government, which in 1988 was 14 percent of the total.

1987 such transfer payments amounted, in the aggregate, to $402 billion. Most of these transfer payments are part of public income-maintenance programs of the kind that were examined in Chapter 20. The percentage of all personal income received in the form of government transfer payments increased sharply, from under 5 percent in 1955 to 7 percent in 1965 and to more than 14 percent in 1983. Since 1983 the percentage has stayed roughly constant.

Social security.   The major source of growth in transfer payments has been in social security, including Medicare. In 1965 just under 15 percent of federal outlays were for social security. By 1980 social security accounted for 20 percent and Medicare (which provides medical benefits to social security recipients) used up nearly 6 percent of the federal budget. In 1987 social security and Medicare together constituted over 28 percent of federal spending.

Social security has two important effects on the income distribution. Historically, although it has been billed as an "insurance" program, it has redistributed income from young to old. To date, every group of social security recipients has received much more from the social security system than the taxes that they paid to social security could have supported, even if they had been invested wisely. This generous financial arrangement was made possible by the underlying growth of the social security system. When many people are paying in and few are drawing out, a low tax rate can support generous benefits. One way in which the system grew was to add new categories of eligible recipients. For example, when social security was started in the 1930s, farm workers, government workers, and many service workers were not covered. Every time a new group was added, the number of people who were paying payroll taxes grew sharply, but the number of eligible recipients grew only slowly—as the newly eligible recipients retired.

Population growth has had a similar effect. The more rapidly a population grows, the larger will be the fraction of the population below any given age. Thus, the number of social security recipients, who by definition were born many years ago, is always much less than the number of taxpayers, who are both younger and from larger birth cohorts (i.e., there are many more 25-year olds today than there were 40 years ago).

Except for normal population growth, there will be no further increases in the number of social security taxpayers. Almost all U.S. workers are covered by social security, in part as a result of the 1983 financing reforms that were designed to assure that the system would remain financially viable. Moreover, the population is now growing only very slowly, so normal population growth will not contribute much in the future.

The second source of redistribution in the social security system comes from the formula that is used to calculate retirement and disability benefits. The formula is quite progressive. Benefits are higher the more social security taxes an individual pays over his or her lifetime, but the ratio of benefits to taxes falls quite sharply as earnings rise. To see what is involved, consider the notion of the expected value of social security benefits divided by social security taxes (appropriately adjusted for time and inflation). For someone who is starting work today, this ratio is less than one for high-wage earners and greater than one for low-wage earners. An interesting implication of this is that although the social security tax is by itself regressive, the effect of the system over an individual's lifetime is progressive—the combination of a very progressive benefit formula with a slightly regressive tax.

The financial solvency of the social security system was in serious doubt during the early 1980s. The tax rates and payment formulas then in effect would have led the social security system to be unable to make all of its promised payments before the end of the decade. In 1983 a number of reforms were enacted that had the effect of both lowering benefits and increasing taxes. An important way in which benefits were reduced was by slowly increasing the retirement age from 65 to 67. The extra two years of paying taxes rather than receiving benefits make a great difference to the projected financial health of the system. The 1983 reforms make it likely that the system will remain solvent for decades to come (although the outlook for Medicare is not as hopeful). Even so, the general aging of the population that is a consequence of low birth rates means that the number of workers whose output must support each retiree will continue to fall. Currently, there are about 3.3 workers for every retired person. By 2040— about the time that many readers of this book will be contemplating retirement—current trends suggest that there will be only 1.9 workers producing output for each retiree.[4] This may require yet another set of reforms in order to assure that the social security system remains financially solvent.

Means-tested programs.   The other major category of transfer programs are means-tested programs, which have grown from 4.5 percent of the federal budget in 1965 to 7.4 percent in 1987. The biggest source of growth is Medicaid, the federal share of which grew from essentially nothing in 1965 to $27.4 billion (2.7 percent of the federal budget) in 1987. As we discussed in Chapter 20, states also pay over a third of the cost of Medicaid and welfare. In addition, many states provide general assistance to persons who are not eligible for federal welfare programs.

Purchases of Goods and Services

In 1988 U.S. governments at all levels spent $964 billion on purchases of goods and services. This means that about 20 percent of the nation's output for the year ultimately was used by governments. The majority of government purchases ($584 billion in 1988) is spent by state and local governments. Two areas of expenditure—education and highways—account for nearly half of this expenditure. Recalling our discussion in Chapter 21, we see that highways are collective consumption goods. Public schools have important private benefits to students, but public education is widely believed to be an important institution in a democratic society. The rest of state and local purchases are for police and fire protection, trash collection, hospitals, prisons, transit subsidies, and libraries, among (many) other things. Again, many of these are collective consumption goods, and many fill other gaps in what is provided by private markets.

Fully three-fourths of federal purchases of goods and services are for defense. The remaining quarter of federal purchases (about 8 percent of all federal spending—under $85 billion in 1988) pays for the Federal Bureau of Investigation (FBI), the national parks, the federal civil service, the highway program, construction of federal office buildings, the search for a cure for cancer, the computers that the Internal Revenue Service (IRS) uses to audit income taxes—everything that the federal government *buys* or *pro-*

duces in the course of the business of governing. One area in which all three levels of government expend significant resources is that of health care. This is one of the fastest growing areas of both public and private expenditure. Some of the reasons for this are discussed in Box 23-2.

State and local governments spend about seven times as much as the federal government does on nondefense goods and services.

Grants-in-Aid and Fiscal Federalism

The federal government spends over $100 billion per year making grants to state and local governments. State governments, in turn, spend a large amount of their revenues in the form of grants to local governments. Why do governments share their revenues in these ways? How do we determine which levels of government will have responsibility for which governmental functions? How *should* we? The subject of *fiscal federalism*, or intergovernmental budgetary relationships, is at least as old as the U.S. Constitution.

Different public services are best delivered to different-sized areas. At one extreme is national defense: It is difficult to see what role a city or a state could efficiently play in its provision. At the other extreme is a firehouse. If fire protection is to be effective, it is necessary that there be firehouses serving fairly small geographic areas. The concept of a "state fire station," with an enormous building and thousands of firefighters working at one location, makes very little sense.

Most public finance economists who have studied fiscal federalism would agree that there is a fairly natural association of levels of government with many governmental functions. Defense and international relations belong at the national level. So does income redistribution, because if this is left to subnational governments there will tend to be migration problems. (The poor will tend to move toward generous states, and the rich will tend to move away from them.) Police and fire protection belong at the local level; roads belong at the state or local level, depending on the type of road.

Education is tricky. To the extent that there is a public role for higher education, much of it is arguably at the national level—the development of knowledge is a public good. Thus, the rationale for state universities would appear to be historical, or

---

[4] Immigration policy could have an important effect on the ratio of workers to retirees in the future.

perhaps related to football. At the elementary and secondary levels, the provision of some minimum standard is arguably a national role (in part because education is so important to earning income and in part because the general level of education in a society is a public good). Administrative control over what schools do, however, should surely be decentralized. It is hard to think of important economies of scale in the provision of education at even the state level, much less the national one.

When economies of scale are unimportant, there is a public choice argument for decentralizing the provision of public goods and services. Especially in large metropolitan areas, competition among local governments can solve some of the problems created by the existence of public goods. Suppose, for example, that Edville has high property taxes and good public schools, while Deadville has low property taxes and mediocre public schools. Citizens who care a lot about public education will tend to live in Edville, while those who do not will tend to live in Deadville. The existence of the two suburbs, offering different tax and expenditure packages, creates something of a market in local public services. With enough suburbs, and enough variation in the packages offered, many of the advantages of competitive markets can be realized, even though the markets are only implicit, and the commodities being produced and sold are public goods.

The same logic can be extended somewhat to state governments, although it is hard to hold other features, such as climate and economic environment, so constant across states. Still, Michigan and Indiana, for example, border each other. Michigan basically offers relatively high taxes and state expenditures, while Indiana has much lower taxes and a much lower level of public services. Many citizens of both states are better off, since they have a choice, than they would be if "Michiana" offered an intermediate package. (Some citizens, those who prefer the intermediate package, will be worse off.)

Intergovernmental Grants

Suppose Mytown is considering widening Main Street. Most of the benefits of the wider street will be realized by residents of Mytown, but some residents of Yourtown will be able to get home faster or to shop more easily because of the improvement. At the same time, Yourtown may be building a new

public park, which residents of Mytown will make use of; or Yourstate might improve a road that is used by many citizens of Mystate; or the city of Upstream may be dumping raw sewage into a river that is used as the water supply for the village of Downstream. All of these are examples of intergovernmental *spillovers*, which work essentially in the same way as externalities. The only real difference is that spillovers occur among governments, rather than among firms and consumers.

Spillovers provide an important rationale for intergovernmental grants. If, for example, most local roads get about 20 percent of their use from people who live out of town, a state *matching grant* of 20 percent, paying local governments 20 percent of their road expenditures, will perfectly internalize the spillover. The analysis, shown in Figure 23-4, is the same as the analysis of externalities that was presented in Chapters 21 and 22. In this case, however, the preferred policy instrument is a subsidy, rather than a tax, because the spillover (externality) is a beneficial one. The 20 percent subsidy reduces the marginal cost of building roads and will cause local governments to build more roads.

In practice, intergovernmental grants, at least federal grants to states and localities, do not often appear to be consistent with the spillover rationale. Many intergovernmental grants have very high matching rates (up to 90 percent) up to some ceiling and then provide no marginal incentive at all. Such grants often appear to restrict the uses to which they are put, but if the grant is for $100,000 on highways and the local government is going to spend $200,000 anyway, there will be very little real effect. In essence, the higher level of government simply will have given $100,000 to the local government. The latter simply can reduce its own highway budget by $100,000 and do what it pleases with the money.

Much of the motivation for intergovernmental grants appears to be distributional. The federal government has a more progressive tax system than do the lower levels of government, and the federal government also has a more efficient tax collection system. Thus, some have argued, it makes sense for the federal government to collect money that can then be redistributed to the states and localities.

Most economists would argue that, if the federal government is interested in equalizing the income distribution, it would be more efficient to redistribute directly to people, rather than to governments.

BOX 23-2

The Rising Cost of Health Care

The rising cost of health care is an emotional and provocative issue. Almost everyone would agree that in a wealthy society, such as the United States in the 1990s, some minimum level of health care should be available to all citizens by right. At the same time, there is public concern over the high current cost of medical care. Economic analysis shows that these two elements—the belief in the right to free medical care and the clamor over its high social cost—are not unrelated.

Explaining the High Cost of Medical Care

Without health insurance, a single major operation can be an enormous financial burden, and a prolonged illness will impoverish even the most prudent middle-income household. Why has health care become so costly?

One reason is that health care is highly labor-intensive. The wages of nurses, physicians, laboratory technicians, and other medical personnel have risen substantially relative to their productivity. (The number of temperatures taken, beds made, and meals served per employee do not increase much over time.)

A second reason is the steadily rising quality of medical care. Available knowledge, techniques, equipment, and the training of new physicians all have improved over time. Thus, it becomes possible not only to provide quicker, surer cures for common and recurring ailments but also to prevent and treat other, less common ailments and complications.

A third reason for rising medical costs is that the way in which most medical care is provided and paid for has tended to weaken incentives to economize on its use or to keep costs down. Doctors (in their role as experts) often prescribe expensive medical care that they or other doctors provide. Will the patient contradict the doctor? Usually, the patient will not.

Most insurance and publicly provided medical programs have eliminated significant *marginal* charges to the patient for the incremental medical or hospital care that is consumed. Instead, they charge either the patient or the insurance company something that is closer to the average cost. An individual has no incentive to economize on the quantity or quality of his or her own elective care, because doing so will not lower the average cost of total care significantly.

Either free public provision or comprehensive prepaid (or employer-paid) health insurance is virtually sure to lead to higher costs. This is an example of moral hazard, which was discussed in Chapter 8 and in Chapter 21. In the free-market system, individual patients would choose medical care (as they choose housing) from a wide variety of price-quality alternatives.

If patients had to pay their own bills and if they could make fully informed choices, many might prefer to pay less and not have the best available equipment and doctors in all circumstances. However, at zero marginal cost, patients naturally will prefer to have the extra benefits of the best possible care, no matter what the extra cost is to the insurance company, employer, or state. They will consume hospital and medical services that are free at the margin until the marginal utility from these services is zero.

Also, doctors and hospitals do not always have strong incentives to hold costs down. They can pass along the higher costs of advanced modern techniques to insurers in higher fees, especially if they do not have to worry that these higher fees may cause a reduction in the quantity of their services demanded. They may well reason: Our job is to give the best treatment; let others worry about the costs. Indeed, unscrupulous doctors can prescribe unnecessary surgery or other medical care to increase the demand for their services. Of course, the insurance companies have to pass on higher claims in the form of higher premiums, and thus they might exercise cost control. If the government or a giant employer pays most of the bill, however (as it does for many patients), insurers may not feel too much resistance to rising insurance rates, at least for a long time.

What Is the Right Quantity and Quality of Health Care?

While almost everyone agrees that some minimum level of health care should be provided to all who need it, the definition of this minimum is controversial. No doubt the acceptable minimum level of health care has risen over time; accordingly, we have had increasing public intervention in the health sector.

The issue provokes more emotion than a discussion of housing or clothing, however. After all, human lives are at stake. This is true enough, but it does not end the matter. A first response is that much (although, of course, not all) medical and hospital care is elective and has almost nothing to do with life or death. By way of analogy, to say that no one should starve is not to say that all people should receive all the free food that they want to eat. Nonvital medical attention accounts for a large part of our demand for health care. If it is offered at little or no marginal cost to users, it will be consumed beyond the point where marginal benefit is equal to the cost of providing it.

Even when life is at stake, however, do we really always want the very best? Suppose the extra cost of the very best pays off in a small increased probability of survival. How much would we pay to have, say, 9 instead of 10 people in 10,000 die from a particular disease? Surely, few would want to spend $1 billion per life saved; most would say that the opportunity cost is too high; the resources represented by these large amounts of money could be put to better use elsewhere. Yet doctors in hospitals often make a different decision implicitly by ordering the best of everything. This then passes the costs on to society as a whole through increased resource allocation to the health sector. The issue is not whether to save lives but the opportunity cost of doing so. Money that is spent to save lives here is money that is not available to save lives (or improve the quality of life) elsewhere.

Controlling the Cost

Under many current payment schemes, neither providers nor patients have strong incentives to keep down the costs of medical care. The most obvious solution is to place enough of a marginal charge on users so that they will ask themselves whether this doctor's visit, this extra day in the hospital, this use of the most expensive health-monitoring system, is worth the cost to them.

The spread of health maintenance organizations (HMOs) that agree to provide specified levels of care for a fixed fee have created institutions with some incentives to bargain hard with doctors and hospitals to keep their costs down. At the same time, many large employers now offer their employees a choice of health care plans. When employees choose a relatively inexpensive plan (usually one that limits the patient's choice of doctors and hospitals and requires the patient to pay a "deductible" amount on covered services), they get a commensurate increase in take-home pay. The effect of these efforts to add some competition to the medical-care business are not yet clear.

Another proposed solution is to ask the government to regulate the quantity, quality, and prices of services provided or the rates that insurance companies may charge. The regulation of rates gives insurance companies the motivation to exercise cost control. Many states do regulate health insurance rates. In addition, the federal government has toughened its standards for payments under Medicare, and many insurance companies have begun to follow the federal rules for reimbursements. These efforts have, at best, slowed the rate of cost increases, and many observers have argued that the effect has been quite small.

In health care, as elsewhere, if the price paid by users is kept below the marginal cost of providing the services, the private market will have excess demand. The government must either provide the services demanded directly or subsidize others to do so, or a way must be found to limit the demand to the quantity available. In countries with national health services, rationing is accomplished in part by long lines at doctors' offices and long waits for hospital admissions and in part by a lower average quality of medical services, which then reduces demand. (The lines are much longer in England, which spends about 6 percent of national output on health care, than in Sweden, which spends nearly 10 percent.) These forces are powerful. The United States spends more on health care per capita than any country in the world. It also has among the least well-developed systems for rationing health

care. Almost all health care is provided privately, although much of it is paid for publicly. From a cost perspective, this is the worst of both worlds. Unlike the case in Western Europe, the government cannot limit directly the amount of care provided (thus creating long lines), because the government is generally not providing the care.

In adopting a policy toward health care, there are at least three separable decisions: how much care to provide, how to allocate the costs of that care, and how to ration the supply. In the free-market system, prices do all three. When we elect to have the government intervene because we do not like the free-market results, someone has to make these decisions.

Evaluating the Role of Government

Almost everyone would agree that the government has some role to play in the economy because of the many sources of possible market failure. Yet there is no consensus that the present level and role of government intervention are about right.

One aspect of the contemporary debate about the efficient level of government intervention was discussed in Chapter 22. There we asked when and to what degree government is justified in attempting to modify private-market behavior, say, by affecting the way in which a paper mill discharges its wastes. Other issues arise when government provides goods and services that the private sector does not and will not provide.

Do Benefits of Public Programs Exceed Costs?

For some government programs, such as flood control, there are well-defined benefits and costs, and it is relatively easy to decide whether the project is beneficial.

However, consider the evaluation of a program such as the great space adventure of the 1960s, which placed a man on the moon before the end of the decade. The budgetary costs were easily defined. At its peak in 1966, the program absorbed (in 1989 dol-

lars) somewhat more than $20 billion per year. Unmistakably, the project succeeded—it met its stated objective—but was the "giant step for mankind" worth the billions of dollars it cost? The benefits certainly included the psychological lift that the moon walks gave the American people and the substantial advances in technology and knowledge that the space program spawned. The real costs are those things that the expenditure replaced. What was the alternative: more arms to Vietnam; massive urban redevelopment; a return of funds to private spenders to use as they saw fit? Most of us will evaluate the worth of the space program very differently, depending on what we see as the alternative uses of the resources that were involved.

Such questions can never be answered unambiguously. As a result, the evaluation of government programs is inherently political and controversial. Economic analysis of benefits and costs is involved, but it does not play the sole or even the dominant role in answering some big questions.

What Is the Correct Balance Between Private and Public Sectors?

When the government levies taxes and spends the money, it increases the size of the public sector and decreases that of the private sector. Since the public sector and the private sector spend money on different things, the government is changing the allocation

This section provides important diagrams and captions from the text as reminders of basic economic concepts at a glance. If you need to refresh your memory concerning a principle being shown here, look in the appropriate chapter for a full explanation. The figure number of each diagram indicates the chapter from which it is taken (e.g., Figure 23-4 means the fourth figure in Chapter 23).

FIGURE 12-4   Derivation of the Supply Curve for a Price-taking Firm

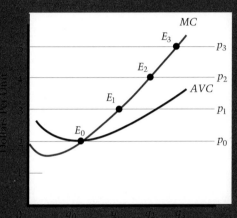

Above the AVC curve, the supply curve of the price-taking firm, shown in part (ii), is the same as its MC curve, shown in part (i).

FIGURE 12-9:   Equilibrium of a Firm When a Perfectly Competitive Industry Is in Long-Run Equilbrium

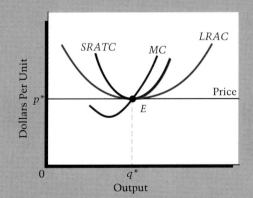

In long-run, perfectly competitive equilibrium, the firm is operating at the minimum point on its $LRAC$ curve.

FIGURE 13-3   Equilibrium Under Monopoly

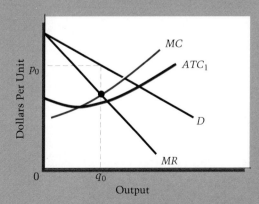

Profit-maximizing output is q_0, where $MR = MC$; price is p_0, which is above MC at that output.

FIGURE 14-1 Equilibrium Under Monopolistic Competition

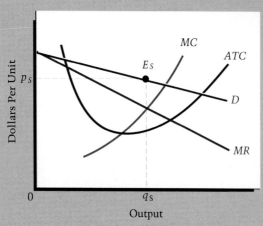

(i) Short-run equilibrium   (ii) Long-run equilibrium

Short-run equilibrium of a monopolistically competitive firm is the same as for a monopolist. In the long run, a monopolistically competitive industry has zero profits and excess capacity.

FIGURE 14-2 The Oligopolist's Dilemma: To Cooperate or to Compete

Cooperation to determine the overall level of output can maximize joint profits, but it leaves each firm with an incentive to alter its production. (B's profits are represented by orange circles; A's profits are represented by blue circles.)

		A's output	
		One-half monopoly output	Two-thirds monopoly output
B's output	One-half monopoly output	20 20	15 22
	Two-thirds monopoly output	22 15	17 17

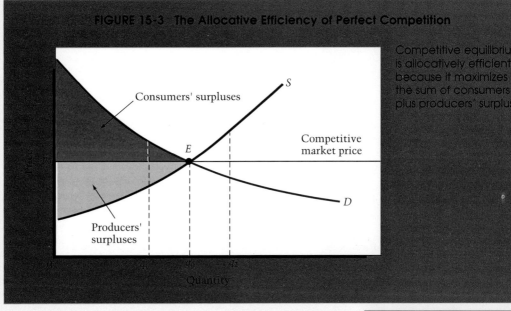

FIGURE 15-3 The Allocative Efficiency of Perfect Competition

Competitive equilibrium is allocatively efficient, because it maximizes the sum of consumers' plus producers' surplus.

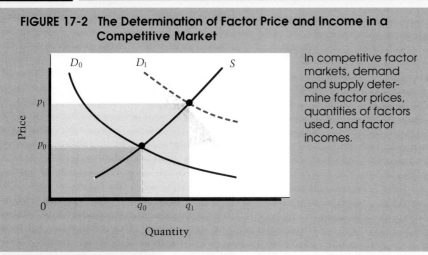

FIGURE 17-2 The Determination of Factor Price and Income in a Competitive Market

In competitive factor markets, demand and supply determine factor prices, quantities of factors used, and factor incomes.

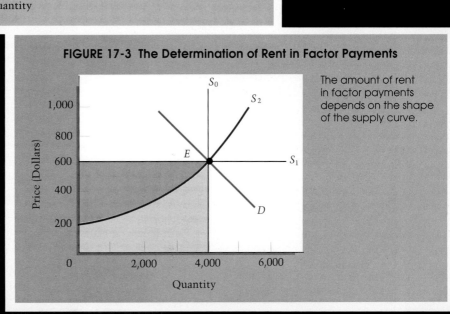

FIGURE 17-3 The Determination of Rent in Factor Payments

The amount of rent in factor payments depends on the shape of the supply curve.

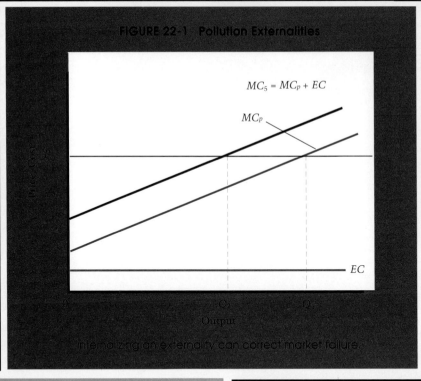

FIGURE 22-1   Pollution Externalities

$MC_S = MC_P + EC$

MC_P

Price, Cost

EC

O Q_1 Q_2

Output

Internalizing an externality can correct market failure.

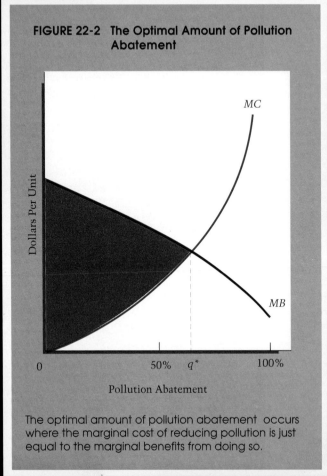

FIGURE 22-2   The Optimal Amount of Pollution
Abatement

MC

Dollars Per Unit

MB

0   50% q^* 100%

Pollution Abatement

The optimal amount of pollution abatement occurs
where the marginal cost of reducing pollution is just
equal to the marginal benefits from doing so.

FIGURE 23-4 Benefit Spillovers and Intergovernmental Grants

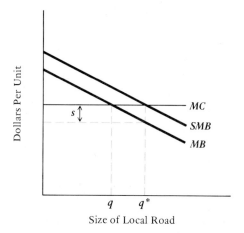

Size of Local Road

Intergovernmental grants can internalize benefit spillovers. The figure depicts a local government's demand and cost of adding to the size of a road. The *MB* curve shows the marginal benefit to the residents of the locality. *MC* is the marginal cost of making the road larger. Left to its own devices, the government will choose a road of size q, where marginal benefit equals marginal cost. This neglects the *SMB* curve, which adds the demands of *nonresident* users of the road to that of local users, yielding the social marginal benefit. If the state government offers a subsidy of s per unit of road built, the local government will choose q^*, where marginal benefit equals the marginal cost it faces, $MC - s$. If s is chosen optimally by the state government, this will be the size of road at which social marginal benefit equals social marginal cost.

of resources. Is this good or bad? How do we know if the country has found the right balance between the public and private sectors? Should there be more national parks and fewer houses or more houses and fewer national parks?

Because automobiles and houses are sold on the market, consumer demand has a significant influence on the relative prices and quantities produced of these commodities and thus on the allocation of the nation's resources. This is true for all goods that are produced and sold on the market. But there is no market that provides relative prices for private houses versus the Coast Guard; thus, the choice be-

tween allowing money to be spent in the private sector and allowing it to be spent for public goods is a matter to be decided by Congress and other legislative bodies.

John Kenneth Galbraith's best seller *The Affluent Society* proclaimed the "liberal" message that a correct assignment of marginal utilities would show them to be higher for an extra dollar's worth of expenditure on parks, clean water, and education than for an extra dollar's worth of expenditure on television sets and deodorants. In this view, the political process often fails to translate preferences for public goods into effective action; thus, more resources are devoted to the private sector and fewer to the public sector than would be the case if the political mechanism were as effective as the market.

The "conservative" view has many supporters who agree with Professor James Buchanan that society already has gone beyond the point where the value of the marginal dollar spent by the government (especially the federal government) is greater than the value of that dollar left in the hands of households or firms that would have spent it had it not been taxed away. Because bureaucrats, the conservatives argue, are spending other people's money, they don't care very much about a few million (billion) dollars here or there. They have no sense of the opportunity cost of public expenditure and thus tend to spend beyond the point where marginal benefits equal marginal costs. Note that this argument makes more sense the higher the level of government is to which it is applied. For the 70 percent of Americans who live in urban areas, there is often a good deal of effective competition among local governments.

One of the most difficult problems for the student of the U.S. economic system is to maintain a perspective about the scope of government activity in the market economy. There are literally tens of thousands of laws, regulations, and policies that affect firms and households. Many believe that significant additional deregulation would be possible and beneficial.

Private decision makers still have an enormous amount of discretion about what they do and how they do it. One pitfall is to become so impressed (or obsessed) with the many ways in which government activity impinges on the individual that one fails to see that these only make changes—sometimes large but often small—in market signals in a system that basically leaves individuals free to make their own decisions. It is in the private sector that most individuals choose their occupations, earn their livings, spend their incomes, and live their lives. In this sector, too, firms are formed, choose products, live, grow, and sometimes die.

Another pitfall is to fail to see that some, and perhaps most, of the highly significant amounts paid by the private sector as taxes to the government also buy goods and services that add to the welfare of individuals. By and large, the public sector complements the private sector by doing things that the private sector would leave undone or do very differently. To recognize this is not to deny that there is often waste, and sometimes worse, in public expenditure policy, nor does it imply that whatever is, is, just what people want. Social policies and social judgments evolve and change.

Yet another pitfall is the failure to recognize that the public and private sectors compete in the sense that both make claims on the resources of the economy. Government activities are not without opportunity costs, except in those rare circumstances in which they use resources that have no alternative use.

Public policies in operation at any time are not the result of a single master plan that specifies precisely where and how the public sector shall seek to complement or to interfere with the workings of the market mechanism. Rather, as individual problems arise, governments attempt to meet them by passing ameliorative legislation. These laws stay on the books, and some become obsolete and unenforceable. This is true of systems of law in general. As a result, it is easy to find outrageous examples of inconsistencies and absurdities in any system. A distinguished professorship at Harvard gives its incumbent the right to graze a cow in Harvard Yard; laws still exist that permit the burning of witches.

Many anomalies exist in our economic policies; for example, laws that were designed to support the incomes of small farmers have created some agricultural millionaires, and commissions that were created to assure competition often end up creating and protecting monopolies. Neither individual policies nor entire programs are above criticism.

In a society that elects its policymakers at regular intervals, however, the majority view on the amount and type of government that is desirable will have some considerable influence on the things that governments actually do. The size of government and the extent of government regulation were major political issues of the 1980s. Fundamentally, a free-market system is retained because it is valued for its lack of coercion and its ability to do much of the allocating of society's resources. However, we are not mesmerized by it; we feel free to intervene in pursuit of a better world in which to live. At the same time, we recognize that, even where there are real problems, government is not always able to provide effective solutions.

SUMMARY

1. Two of the most powerful tools of microeconomic policy are taxation and public expenditure.
2. Although the main purpose of the tax system is to raise revenue, tax policy is potentially a powerful device for income redistribution. Personal income-tax rates are progressive, but their effect on progressivity is reduced by other provisions of the tax law. Sales and excise taxes are likely to be regressive.
3. Tax expenditures are provisions in the tax law that provide favorable tax treatment for certain economic behavior. They are called tax "expenditures" because their effects usually could be achieved by appropriating money on the spending side of the budget, instead of by reducing revenues on the tax side. Tax expenditures in the income tax reduce the progressivity of the tax system. The 1986 tax reform sharply cut back on the number and importance of tax expenditures but did not eliminate them.
4. The total American tax structure is roughly proportional except for very low-income groups (for whom it is regressive). The 1986 tax reforms increased progressivity but not by as much as the 1981–1983 tax reforms reduced it.

5. Evaluating the effects of taxes on resource allocation requires first that we determine tax incidence, that is, determine who really pays the taxes. For most taxes, the incidence is shared. Excise taxes, for example, affect prices and are thus partially passed on but partially absorbed by producers. The actual incidence depends on such economic considerations as demand and supply elasticities.

6. A large part of public expenditure is for the provision of goods and services that private markets fail to provide. State and local governments spend most of their budgets on the provision of goods and services.

7. The major redistributive activities of the federal government take the form of direct transfer payments to individuals and grants-in-aid to state and local governments for economic welfare payments. The largest single transfer program is social security, which, with Medicare (the social security medical-insurance program for the elderly), accounts for nearly 30 percent of all federal spending.

8. Government expenditure of all kinds has a major effect on the allocation of resources. The government determines how much of society's total output is devoted to national defense, education, and highways. It is also influential in areas in which private provision of goods and services is common; health care is a notable example.

9. Grants-in-aid to state and local governments are a key form of public expenditure policy; they lead to a different allocation of resources than would occur without them. Grants-in-aid are used to promote economic efficiency, by internalizing intergovernmental spillovers, and also to redistribute income.

10. Evaluating public expenditures involves reaching decisions about absolute merit (Do benefits exceed costs?) and about the relative merit of public and private expenditures.

11. The U.S. economy is a mixed economy and a changing one. Each generation faces anew the choice of which activities to leave to the unfettered market and which to encourage or to repress through public policy.

TOPICS FOR REVIEW

Tax expenditures
Progressive, proportional, and regressive taxes
Vertical and horizontal equity
Tax incidence
Transfer payments to individuals
Intergovernmental spillovers
Grants-in-aid to state and local governments
Choosing between private and public expenditures

DISCUSSION QUESTIONS

1. Under federal tax law certain kinds of income are tax exempt. One of these is interest on municipal bonds. Who benefits from such an exemption? What are its effects on the distribution of income and on the allocation of resources? In what sense is this a "tax expenditure"?

2. The 1986 Tax Reform Act lowered every taxpayer's marginal tax rate, with the maximum rate dropping from 50 percent to 33 percent, but increased the tax base so that total tax revenue was essentially unchanged.

   a. Is it possible that everyone's average tax *rate* fell?

 b. Is it possible that everyone's tax *bill* fell?

 c. Suppose contributions to universities and colleges were tax deductible under the original tax law but not under the revised one. Would you predict such contributions to increase, decrease, or remain the same?

 d. If such contributions are fully deductible under both the original and the revised tax law, would the amount of such contributions be expected to increase, decrease, or remain the same?

 e. Consider now taxpayers whose marginal tax rate falls from 50 percent to 33 percent and whose tax bills are less after the revision. What would happen to their charitable contributions?

3. Rank the following taxes by their likely ratio of excess burden to revenue raised, starting from the tax with the lowest ratio.

 a. A sales tax on one brand of breakfast cereal

 b. A sales tax on all food

 c. A flat fee of $5 per day, paid by all employed persons

 d. A low (1 percent) tax on videocassette rentals

 e. A high (50 percent) tax on videocassette rentals

4. How might each of the following affect the incidence of a real estate property tax imposed on central-city rental property?

 a. The residents of the community are largely blacks who face racial discrimination in neighboring areas.

 b. The city installs a good, cheap rapid transit system that makes commuting to the suburbs less expensive and more comfortable.

 c. The income-tax laws are changed to eliminate the deductibility of property taxes on owner-occupied housing from taxable income for those who itemize deductions.

5. Under the federal tax laws all state and local income taxes can be deducted from income in computing the federal tax liability. Suppose, given the tax schedule that is shown in Table 23-2, two local communities each impose a 10 percent tax on personal incomes. Richville is composed of families who earn $100,000 or more per year. Uniontown consists mainly of families who earn about $20,000 per year. Who really pays how much of the taxes in each case? What, if anything, prevents Richville from raising its taxes?

6. The Tax Reform Act of 1986 originally had the word *Simplification* in the title, but it wound up being 1,811 pages long. Who benefits from a complicated tax code? Who loses? What does this suggest about the political viability of tax simplification?

7. Develop the case for and against having the federal government (rather than state and local governments) provide

 a. Police protection

 b. Teachers' salaries

 c. Highways

 d. Welfare payments to the poor

8. Classify each of the following programs as a transfer payment, a grant-in-aid, a purchase of goods and services, or none of these. Which ones clearly tend to decrease the inequality of income distribution?

 a. Payments of wages and family living allowances to soldiers who are serving overseas

 b. Unemployment insurance payments to unemployed workers

 c. Payments to states for support of highway construction

 d. A negative income tax

  e. Pensions of retired Supreme Court justices
  f. An excess-profits tax on oil companies

9. "I believe the spirit of volunteerism lives in America. We see examples of it on every hand: the community charity drive, the rallying around whenever disaster strikes. The truth is, we've let Government take away many things we once considered were really ours to do voluntarily, out of the goodness of our hearts and a sense of neighborliness. I believe many of you want to do those things again." Discuss the probable effects of getting the government out of all activities that once were covered by private charity. The quotation is from a speech by former President Reagan.

10. Medical and health costs were 4.5 percent of GNP in 1950 and over 10 percent in 1985. Is 10 percent necessarily too much? Is it necessarily a sign that we are providing better health care? How might an economist think about what is the right percentage of GNP to devote to medical care?

P·A·R·T

7

NATIONAL INCOME AND FISCAL POLICY

Chapter 24

An Introduction to Macro-economics

Inflation, unemployment, recession, and economic growth are everyday words. Full employment, price stability, and economic growth were adopted as national goals in the Employment Act of 1946. Since then, governments have worried about how to prevent recessions, reduce inflation, and stimulate growth. Households are anxious to avoid the unemployment that comes with recessions, to protect themselves against the hazards of inflation, and to obtain the rising incomes that are brought about by economic growth. Firms are concerned about how inflations and recessions affect their profits.

What Is Macroeconomics?

Each of the concerns just mentioned plays a major role in macroeconomics.

Macroeconomics is the study of how the economy behaves in broad outline without dwelling on much of its interesting, but sometimes confusing, detail. In contrast, *microeconomics* deals with the detailed behavior of individual markets, such as the market for wheat, coal, or strawberries.

The difference between the two branches of economics is illustrated by different aspects of recent changes in oil prices.

A microeconomic issue. For decades oil prices fell in relation to the prices of most other commodities. Beginning in the 1970s this trend was reversed. Oil became increasingly expensive relative to many other goods and services. Then, in the mid-1980s, oil prices fell dramatically—although they remained somewhat above their pre-1970s levels relative to other prices. These price changes had an impact on countless individual markets, from those for fertilizers and plastics, which are made from petroleum, to cars and air travel, which use it as fuel. Explaining the causes and effects of such changes in terms of *relative prices* are microeconomics issues.

A macroeconomic issue. The average of all prices is called the **price level.** As well as changing relative to other prices, oil prices have tended to follow the rising trend of all prices. Dramatic rises in oil prices helped to accelerate inflation in 1974–1975 and 1979–1980. In both cases inflation was followed by a major recession, with a rise in the nation's rate of unemployment. Explaining the causes and consequences of changes in the general price level, the overall level of business activity, and the rate of unemployment are macroeconomic issues.

Major Macroeconomic Issues

The economy tends to move in a series of ups and downs, called *business cycles,* rather than in a steady pattern. Why did the 1930s see the greatest economic depression in recorded history, with up to one-fifth of the American labor force unemployed and with massive unemployment in all major industrial countries? Why were the 25 years following World War II a period of sustained economic growth, with only minor interruptions from modest recessions? Why did the early 1980s see the onset of the worst worldwide recession since the 1930s? What fueled the recovery of the mid-1980s?

Why, during the 1970s and early 1980s, did inflation reach levels never before seen in peacetime in many advanced Western nations? Has our attitude toward inflation permanently changed? In the early 1970s, when inflation crept up to 4 percent, concern was so great that emergency measures were adopted by the Nixon administration. By the mid-1980s the government was claiming credit for having *reduced* inflation to 4 percent!

Earlier in the century, alternating bouts of inflationary boom and deflationary recession caused many headaches for policymakers. Booms still tend to be accompanied by inflationary pressures, but it can be assumed no longer that recessions will bring deflations. Why were the recessions of the 1970s and early 1980s accompanied not only by their familiar companion, high unemployment, but also by an unexpected fellow traveler, rapid inflation? Will **stagflation**—simultaneous high unemployment and rapid inflation—return?

Both total output and output per person have risen for many decades in most industrial countries. These long-term trends have meant rising average living standards. Did the slowdown in worldwide growth rates over the 1970s and 1980s represent a basic change in underlying trends, or was it just a reflection of a prolonged downturn? Can governments do anything to influence growth rates?

Throughout most of the 1980s, the United States was plagued with the problem of the "twin deficits." The first deficit was the enormous discrepancy between what the federal government spent and what it raised in taxes. This *budget deficit* had to be financed by borrowing funds, thus adding to the national debt. The second deficit was the *trade deficit*—the difference between the value of what American producers sell abroad and what American purchasers buy from abroad.

Did the high trade deficit reflect an underlying loss of American international competitiveness, as some economists believe? Is the trade deficit primarily the consequence of the government's budget deficit, as other economists insist?

In today's internationalized world, American citizens own assets all over the world. They own shares in foreign companies, they hold bills and bonds issued by foreign governments and firms, they have balances in foreign banks, and they possess all kinds of real estate, from hotels and apartment buildings to country cottages. In 1980 the value of foreign assets that were owned by all Americans exceeded the value of American assets that were owned by foreigners. The difference was enough to make the United States the world's largest creditor country. By 1990 the United States had become the world's largest debtor country. Its net foreign liabilities—the excess of foreign holdings of American assets over American holdings of foreign assets—greatly exceeded those of any of the other large debtor countries such as Mexico, Brazil, and Argentina. Is it true that this dramatic turnaround was the direct result of the government's persistent budget deficits: Since enough domestic funds were not available to finance the government's budget deficit, funds had to be attracted from foreign sources?

Key Macroeconomic Variables

The price level, employment, total output, and the interest rate are key macroeconomic variables for the domestic side of the economy. The exchange rate and the balance of payments are key variables on the international side. We hear about them on the nightly news and read about them in newspapers; politicians give campaign speeches about them; economists theorize about them. Why are so many people concerned about them? How have these variables behaved over time?

The Price Level and Inflation

Everyone knows what inflation is. Most people complain about its effects when the inflation rate is high and worry that it is just around the corner when the inflation rate is low. To most of us inflation means that prices are going up—not just the price of gasoline, blue jeans, or chewing gum, but all prices.

To study inflation, economists use two concepts. The first is the *price level,* which refers to the average level of all prices in the economy and is given the symbol *P.* The second is the *rate of inflation,* which is the rate at which the general price level is rising. The price level and the inflation rate are measured by an index number, and to understand them we need to study the meaning and interpretation of index numbers in some detail.

Calculating Index Numbers

Macroeconomists frequently ask such questions as "How much have prices risen this year?" There is no perfectly satisfactory way to answer such questions, because all prices do not move together. Yet these are not foolish questions. There *are* trends in prices trends that can be measured.

If you want to know about the trend in prices over some period of time, it is not helpful to be given a list of changes in, say, 4,682 individual prices. **Index numbers** are statistical measures that are used to give summary answers to the inherently complex questions of the kind that have just been suggested; they measure the percentage change that has occurred in some broad average or aggregate over some particular time span. They point to overall tendencies or general drifts, not to detailed facts. They are an essential tool of macroeconomics.

A **price index** measures the average of some group of prices at any given time, called the *given period,* relative to what it was at some initial time, called the *base period.* Price indexes provide measures of the price level and the rate of inflation. Later we shall use other indexes. Although each index measures something different, the principles of their construction are the same in all cases.

Two important questions must be answered when any price index is to be constructed. First, what group of prices should be used? This depends on the index. The Consumer Price Index (CPI), which is calculated by the Bureau of Labor Statistics, covers prices of commodities that are commonly bought by households. Changes in the CPI are meant to measure changes in the typical household's *"cost of living."* Other indexes, such as the wholesale price index, cover the prices of different groups of commodities.

Second, what kind of average should be used? If all prices change in the same proportion, this would not matter: A 10 percent rise in each and every price would mean a 10 percent rise in the average of all prices, no matter how the average was constructed. However, different prices usually change in different proportions. It then matters how much importance we give to each price change. Changes in the price of bread, for example, are much more important to the average consumer than changes in the price of caviar. In calculating a price index, each price is given a *weight* that reflects its importance.

Let us see how this is done for the CPI. Government statisticians periodically survey a group of households in what is called the Consumer Expenditure Survey. This shows how consumers spend their incomes. The average bundle of goods that is bought is determined, along with the proportion of expenditure that is devoted to each good. These proportions become the weights attached to the individual prices in calculating the CPI. As a result, the CPI weights rather heavily the prices of commodities on which consumers spend much of their income and weights rather lightly the prices of commodities on which consumers spend only a little of their income. Table 24-1 provides a simple example of how these weights are calculated.

Once the weights are chosen, the average price can be calculated for each period. This is done, as shown in Table 24-2, by multiplying each price by its weight and summing the resulting figures. However, a single average price is not informative. Suppose, for example, you were told that the average price of all goods that were bought by consumers last year was $89.35. "So what?" you might well ask, and the answer would be, "So, not very much; by itself, this tells you nothing of value." Now suppose you are told that this year's average price for the same set of consumers' purchases is $107.22. Now you do know something. You know that, on average, prices paid by consumers have risen sharply over the year. In fact, the increase is 20 percent.[1]

---

[1] The change is $17.87, which is 20 percent of the initial average price of $89.35.

TABLE 24-1   Calculation of Weights for a Price Index

Commodity	Price	Quantity	Expenditure (price × quantity)	Proportional weight
A	$5	60	$300	0.50
B	1	200	200	0.33
C	4	25	100	0.17
Total			$600	1.00

The weights are the proportions of total expenditure that are devoted to each commodity. This simple example lists the prices of three commodities and the quantities bought by a typical household. Multiplying price by quantity gives expenditure on each, and summing these gives the total expenditure on all commodities. Dividing expenditure on each good by total expenditure gives the proportion of total expenditure that is devoted to each commodity, as shown in the last column. These proportions become the weights for the price indexes that are calculated in Table 24-2.

The average for each period is divided by the value of the average for the base period and multiplied by 100. The resulting series is called an index number series; by construction, the base period value in this series equals 100. If prices in the next period average 20 percent higher, the index number for that period will be 120. A simple example of how these calculations are carried out is given in Table 24-2.

Price indexes are constructed by assigning weights to reflect the importance of the individual items being combined. The value of the index is set equal to 100 in the base period.

There is one added complication with respect to the CPI. Table 24-2 shows the calculation of what is called a *fixed-weight* index. The weights are the pro-

---

TABLE 24-2   Calculation of a Price Index

Commodity	Weight	Price 1988	Price 1989	Price 1990	Price × weight 1988	Price × weight 1989	Price × weight 1990
A	0.50	$5	$6.0	$14.0	$2.50	$3.00	$7.00
B	0.33	1	1.5	2.0	0.33	0.495	0.66
C	0.17	4	8.0	9.0	0.68	1.36	1.53
Total	1.00				$3.51	$4.855	$9.19

$$\text{Index} \quad 1988 \quad \frac{3.51}{3.51} \cdot 100 = 100$$

$$1989 \quad \frac{4.855}{3.51} \cdot 100 = 138.3$$

$$1990 \quad \frac{9.19}{3.51} \cdot 100 = 261.8$$

A price index expresses the weighted average of prices in the given year as a percentage of the weighted average of prices in the base year. The prices of the three commodities in each year are multiplied by the weights from Table 24-1. Summing the weighted prices for each year gives the average price in that year. Dividing the average price in the given year by the average price in the base year, and multiplying by 100, gives the price index for the given year. The index is, of course, 100 when the base year is also taken as the given year.

portion of income that is spent on the three goods in the first year. These weights are then applied to the prices in each subsequent year. Problems arise with a fixed-weight index because consumption patterns change over the years. The fixed weights then less and less represent the importance that consumers *currently* place on each of the commodities.

The CPI used to be calculated using fixed weights that were changed only every decade or so. Recently, however, there has been a change in this procedure. The Bureau of Labor Statistics now updates its Consumer Expenditure Survey continually. The weights used in the CPI are now an average of several past surveys, with the most recent one counting for 20 percent of the total weight. This avoids the problem of the fixed-weight index becoming steadily less representative of current expenditure patterns.

Interpreting Price Indexes

A price index is meant to reflect the broad trend in prices rather than the details. It gives valuable information, but it must be interpreted with care. People often treat these numbers as though they had an accuracy and a significance that their compilers do not claim for them, but being aware of their limitations should not lead people to neglect index numbers for the useful information that they can give: The average changes over time.

Although the weights will reflect the average importance of each commodity across the nation, they will not be typical of how each and every household spends its money. Rich, poor, young, old, single, married, urban, and rural households typically will consume goods in different proportions. An increase in air fares, for example, will raise the cost of living of a middle-income traveler while not affecting that of a nontraveling member of a poor household.

In the hypothetical example of Table 24-2, from 1988 to 1989 the cost of living would have risen by 20 percent, 50 percent, and 100 percent, respectively, for three different families, one of which consumed only commodity A, one of which consumed only B, and one of which consumed only C. The index in the table shows, however, that the cost of living went up by 38.3 percent for a family that consumed all three goods in the proportions indicated.

The more an individual household's consumption pattern conforms to that of the typical pat- tern used to weight the index, the better the index will reflect changes in that household's cost of living.

Measuring the Rate of Inflation

At the end of 1988 the CPI was 120.3 (1982–1984 = 100). This means that at the end of 1988 it cost just over 20 percent more to buy a representative bundle of goods than it did in the base period, which, in this case, is taken as the average of prices prevailing in the years 1982–1984. In other words, there was a 20.3 percent *increase* in the price level over that period as measured by the CPI. The *percentage change* in the cost of purchasing the bundle of goods that is covered by any index is thus the level of the index minus 100.

The *inflation rate* between any two periods of time is measured by the percentage increase in the relevant price index from the first period to the second period. In the rare event of a drop in the price level, we speak of a *deflation*. When the amount of the rise in the price level is being measured from the base period, all that needs to be done is to subtract the two indexes, as we have just done. When two other periods are being compared, we must be careful to express the change as a percentage of the index in the first period.

If we let P_1 indicate the value of the price index in the first period and P_2 its value in the second period, the inflation rate is merely the difference between the two, expressed as a percentage of the value of the index in the first period:

$$\text{Inflation rate} = \frac{(P_2 - P_1)}{P_1} \times 100$$

(When P_1 is the base period, its value is 100 and the expression shown above reduces to $P_2 - 100$.) In other cases the full calculation must be made. For example, the index went from 115.3 in October 1987 to 120.2 in October 1988, indicating a rate of inflation of 4.2 percent over the year. The rise of 4.9 points in the index is a 4.2 percent rise over its initial value of 115.3.

If the two values being compared are not a year apart, it is common to convert the result to an *annual rate*. For example, the CPI was 115.7 in January 1988 and 116.0 in February 1988. This is an increase of 0.26 percent over the month ($0.3 \div 115.7 \times 100$). It is also an *annual rate* of approximately 3.12 percent

(0.26 × 12) over the year.[2] This means that *if* the rate of increase that occurred between January and February 1988 did persist for a year, the price level would rise by approximately 3.12 percent over the year.

Inflation: The Historical Experience

Figure 24-1 shows one measure of the price level and the inflation rate from 1947 to 1988. The price level is measured by the Consumer Price Index (CPI), and the inflation rate is measured by the annual rate of change in the CPI. What can we learn from Figure 24-1? First, we learn that the price level is constantly changing.

Second, we learn that in only 2 out of the 41 observations did the price level fall; in the other 39 years the inflation rate was positive. The cumulative effect of this sequence of small, but repeated, price increases is quite dramatic; in 1988 the price level was six times higher than it was in 1946.

Third, we learn that, while the long-term increasing trend stands out when we look at the price level, the short-term fluctuations stand out when we look at the inflation rate. From 1965 to 1974 inflation averaged 3.8 percent, while from 1975 to 1984 it averaged 8.5 percent! The sharp swings in the inflation rate in the late 1970s and the early 1980s were even more dramatic. The increase in the inflation rate into double-digit levels in 1974, and again in 1979, were associated with major shocks to the world prices of oil and foodstuffs, while the declines in inflation that followed were delayed responses to major recessions. (Note that even when the inflation rate *falls*, as it did in 1982, for example, the price level continues to rise as long as inflation remains *positive*.)

Why Inflation Matters

Money is the universal yardstick in our economy. We measure economic values in terms of money, and we conduct our economic affairs by using money. Things as diverse as wages, bank balances, the value of a house, and a university's endowment all are stated in terms of money. We value money, however, not for itself but for what we can purchase with it. The terms **purchasing power of money** and *real value of money* refer to the amount of goods and services that can be purchased with a given amount of money.

A change in the price level affects us because it changes the real value of money.

The purchasing power of money is negatively related to the price level.

For example, if the price level doubles, a dollar will buy only one-half as much, whereas if the price level halves, a dollar will buy twice as much. Figure 24-1 shows that inflation has reduced the purchasing power of money over each of the last five decades.

If inflation reduces the real value of a given sum of money, it also reduces the real value of anything else whose price is *fixed* in money terms. Thus, the real value of a money wage, a savings and loan account, or the balance that is owed on a student loan is reduced by inflation.

A fully anticipated inflation. It is possible to imagine an inflation that has no real effects of any kind. What is required for this to happen is, first, that everyone who is making any sort of financial arrangement should know what the inflation rate will be over the life of the contract and, second, that *all* financial obligations be stated in real terms. The real behavior of the economy then would be exactly the same with, and without, an inflation. Say, for example, that both sides of a wage contract agree that wages should go up by 3 percent in real terms. If the inflation rate is expected to be zero, they would agree to an increase in money wages of 3 percent. If a 10 percent inflation is expected, however, they would agree to an increase in money wages of 13 percent. Ten percent would be needed to maintain the purchasing power of the money wages that would be paid, while 3 percent would be needed to bring about the desired increase in purchasing power.

Loan contracts would specify that the amount of a loan to be repaid would be increased over the amount borrowed by the rate of inflation. Thus, if $100 is borrowed and the price level rises by 10 percent, then $110 would have to be returned (quite apart from any interest that might be paid on the loan). This would ensure that the real value of what

---

[2] We say *approximately* because a 0.32 percent rise each month *compounded* for 12 months will give rise to an increase over the year that is greater than 3.12 percent. The appropriate procedure is to increase the index in January by 0.32 twelve times rather than just to multiply it by 12. The two results are the difference between simple and compound interest rates.

FIGURE 24-1   The Price Level and the Inflation Rate, 1947–1988

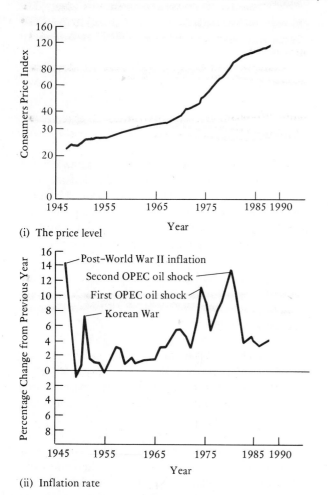

(i) The price level

(ii) Inflation rate

(i) The trend in the price level has been upward over the past half century. The data are for the Consumer Price Index from 1947 to 1988 with the average of 1982–1984 equal to 100. They are plotted on a semilog scale where equal vertical distances represent equal percentage changes. The price level rose by 100 percent over the 25 years from 1947 to 1973. In the next 15 years, the price level rose by 250 percent. (*Source:* Department of Labor, Bureau of Labor Statistics.)

(ii) The rate of inflation has varied from −1 percent to +14 percent since 1947. Prices fell dramatically during the onset of the Great Depression. They rose sharply during and after World War II and during the Korean War. The inflation rate was variable but had no discernible trend from the end of the Korean War to the mid-1960s. The period starting in the mid-1960s experienced a strong upward trend in the inflation rate. In 1983, however, the inflation rate fell to the lowest figure since the early 1970s, and it stayed in the 3–4 percent range through 1988.

is borrowed stays equal to the real value of what is returned.

Tax allowances would also have to be adjusted. For example, an exemption of $2,000 per child would be raised to $2,200 after the 10 percent inflation to keep the real value of the exemption constant.

The result of all this would be a 10 percent increase in everyone's money incomes and money assets, combined with a 10 percent increase in all money prices and all money liabilities. Nothing real would have changed. People's higher money incomes would buy the same amount as before, and the real value of their assets and liabilities would be unchanged.

Another way of making this point is to observe

that the economy can function just as well with a price level of 110, or for that matter of 200, as with a price level of 100.

Once everything has been adjusted, any one price level is as good as any other price level.

This is just as it ought to be, since it would indeed be magic if altering the number of zeros that we use when stating monetary values could change anything real.

A completely unanticipated inflation.   At the opposite extreme from a fully anticipated inflation is a completely unanticipated inflation. No one sees it coming; no one is prepared to offset its consequences. The real value of all contracts that are specified in money terms will change unexpectedly. Who will gain and who will lose?

An unexpected inflation benefits anyone who has an obligation to pay specific amounts of money and harms anyone who is entitled to receive specific amounts.

For example, consider a wage contract that specifies a wage increase of 3 percent on the assumption that the price level will remain constant. Both employers and employees expect that the purchasing power of wages paid will rise by 3 percent as a result of the new contract. Now assume, however, that the price level unexpectedly rises by 10 percent over the life of the wage contract. The 3 percent increase in money wages now means a reduction in the purchasing power of wages of about 7 percent. Employers gain because their wage payments represent a smaller part of the value of their output than they expected them to. Workers lose because their wages represent a smaller receipt of purchasing power than they expected to get.

People who have borrowed money will pay back a smaller real amount than they borrowed. By the same token, people who have lent money will receive back a smaller real amount than they lent. Say, for example, that Gerald lends Hernando enough money to buy a medium-sized house. The price level then doubles, and Hernando then pays back the money that he borrowed. Gerald now finds himself with only one-half of what is required to buy the house.

Wage earners and lenders will be able to adjust to the new price level when they make new contracts, but some people will be locked into their old money contracts for the rest of their lives. The extreme case is suffered by those who live on fixed money incomes. For example, pensions that are provided by the private sector often promise to pay a fixed money income for life. On retirement, this sum may look adequate, even generous. Twenty years later, however, inflation may have reduced its purchasing power to the poverty level. A family that retired on a fixed money income in 1967 would find the purchasing power of that income reduced year by year, until in 1987 it would have been only 29 percent of its original value. To understand the impact of this, imagine that, for every dollar that you now spend, only $.29 can be spent in the future.

Intermediate cases.   There are several reasons why most real inflations fall somewhere between the two extremes that we have just discussed.

First, the inflation rate is usually variable and seldom foreseen exactly, even though its general course may be anticipated. Thus, the actual rate will sometimes be higher than expected—to the benefit of those who have contracted to pay money. At other times the inflation rate will be lower than expected—to the benefit of those who have contracted to receive money. Given the lack of certainty, different people will have different expectations.

Because it is hard to foresee accurately, inflation adds to the uncertainties of economic life. Highly variable inflation rates cause great uncertainty.

Second, even if the inflation rate is foreseen, all adjustments to it cannot occur at the same speed. As a result, inflation redistributes income and does so in a haphazard way. Losers are those whose money incomes adjust more slowly than prices are rising; gainers are those whose money incomes keep ahead of the inflation.

Third, even if the inflation rate is foreseen, the full set of institutions that would be needed for everyone to take full avoiding action do not exist. For example, many private pension plans are stated in money terms. Employees have little choice but to take the only plan that their employers make available to them.

Fourth, much of the tax system is defined in nominal money terms, causing its effects to vary with the price level. For example, if someone sells an asset for more money than was paid for it, the difference is called a capital gain. Under present U.S. tax laws, such gains are regarded as income and are taxed fully as such. If there is no inflation, a capital gain does represent a real increase in purchasing power. The tax will absorb part of the increase, leaving the rest for the investor. In inflationary circumstances, however, the capital gain may be a purely nominal gain that does not represent a real increase in purchasing power. Consider an investor who buys $1,000 worth of stock in a company. The price level then doubles, after which the stock is sold for $2,000. The investor has made no real gain from the investment. The $2,000 received will buy no more than the original $1,000 that was paid out. The tax authorities will, however, call the $1,000 increase in nominal value a capital gain. If the gain is subject to a 33 percent income tax, the investor will only net $1,667. This is a less real value that was invested, and the capital gains tax has turned out to be a tax levied on the real value of capital, rather than the income earned by capital.

During inflationary periods capital gains taxes that are levied on nominal money gains are taxes on the real value of capital rather than taxes on current income.

Indexation. Some of the real effects of inflation can be avoided by indexing. **Indexation** means linking the payments that are made under the terms of a contract to changes in the price level. For example, a retirement pension might pay the beneficiary $15,000 per year starting in 1990, and it might specify that the amount paid will increase each year in proportion to the increase in the CPI. Thus, if the CPI rises by 10 percent between 1990 and 1991, the pension that is payable in 1991 would rise by 10 percent to $16,500. This holds the real purchasing power of the pension constant.

Indexing is valuable as a defense against unforeseen changes in the price level, as a method of reducing uncertainty, and as a way of adapting institutions so that contracts can be made in real terms.

Output and Income Variables

The value of a nation's total production of goods and services is called its *national product*. Since all the value that is produced must ultimately belong to someone in the form of a claim on that value, the national product is equal to the total income claims generated by the production of goods and services. Hence, when we study national product, we are also studying *national income*.

In fact, there are several related measures of the nation's total output and total income. Their various definitions, and the relationships among them, are discussed in detail in the next chapter. In this chapter we use the generic term *national income* to refer to both the value of total output and the value of the income generated by the production of that output.

Aggregating Total Output

To measure total output, quantities of a variety of different goods are *aggregated*. To construct such to-

tals, we add up *values of the different products*. We cannot add tons of steel to loaves of bread, but we can add the money value of steel production to the money value of bread production. Hence, by multiplying the physical output of a good by its price per unit and then summing this value for each good produced in the nation, we can find the quantity of total output *measured in dollars*.

Real and Nominal Values

The total that was just described gives the *money value* of national output, often called **nominal national income.** This measure can change because of a change in either the physical quantities or the prices on which it is based. To discover the extent to which any change is due to quantities or to prices, economists calculate **real national income.** This is a measure of total output in which the value of individual outputs is not measured at current prices but at the prices that prevailed in some base period that was chosen for this purpose.[3]

Real national income is denoted by the symbol Y. It tells us the value of current output measured at base period prices, that is, the sum of the quantities valued at prices ruling in the base period. Comparing real national incomes of different years provides a measure of the change in real output that has occurred during the interval between the years.

Since its calculation holds prices constant, real national income changes only when quantities change.

Since our interest is primarily in the *real* output of goods and services, we shall use the term *national income* (and output) to refer to *real national income* unless otherwise specified. (An example, illustrating this important distinction, is given in Box 25–3 on page 523.)

National Income: The Historical Experience

To study national income, we look at one of its most commonly used measures, called *gross national product,* or GNP. GNP can be measured in either real or nominal terms; we focus here on real GNP. The details of its calculations will be discussed in Chapter 25.

---

[3] Nominal national income is often referred to as *money national income* or *current-dollar national income*. Real national income is often called *constant-dollar national income*.

Figure 24-2(i) shows real GNP produced by the American economy since 1929; Figure 24-2(ii) shows its annual percentage change for the same period. The GNP series in Figure 24-2(i) shows two kinds of movement. The major movement is a trend increase that increased real output by over 350 percent in the half century from 1939 to 1989. Since the trend generally has been upward in the modern era, it is referred to as *economic growth.*

Long-term growth in real national income is reflected in the increasing trend in real GNP.

Not only has national income grown throughout this century, but also real income per person (also called per capita real income) has grown. Indeed, roughly it has tripled in the last 60 years.

The growth in real, per capita GNP is the basis of the enormous increase in living standards that Americans have enjoyed during this century.

A second feature of the real GNP series is the short-term fluctuations around the trend, often described as cyclical fluctuations. Overall growth so dominates the real GNP series that the fluctuations are hardly visible in Figure 24-2(i). However, as can be seen in Figure 24-2(ii), cyclical fluctuations in real GNP have been significant in the past.

The cyclical behavior of real national income is reflected in the annual fluctuations in the growth rate of real GNP.

The business cycle.   The **business cycle** refers to the continual ebb and flow of business activity that occurs around the long-term trend after seasonal adjustments have been made.[4] Such cyclical fluctuations can be seen in many economic series; in particular, they are obvious from the continual oscillations in GNP that we have seen in Figure 24-2.

Although recurrent fluctuations in economic activity are neither smooth nor regular, a vocabu-

lary has developed to denote their different stages. Figure 24-3 shows stylized cycles that illustrate some useful terms, and Box 24-1 further discusses this terminology.

It is important to realize that no two cycles are exactly the same. There are variations in duration and magnitude. Some expansions are long and drawn out, as was the one that began in 1983; others come to an end before high employment of labor and industrial capacity is reached. Nonetheless, fluctuations are systematic enough that it still seems useful to identify common factors in the four phases, which are outlined in Box 24-1.

Potential Income and the GNP Gap

Actual national income is what the economy does, in fact, produce. An important related concept is potential national income. It measures what the economy could produce if all resources—land, labor, the productive capacity—were fully employed at their normal levels of utilization. It is usually referred to as just **potential income,** but it is also sometimes called *high-employment income.*[5] We give it the symbol Y^*, to distinguish it from actual national income, which is indicated by Y.

What is variously called the **output gap** or the **GNP gap** measures the difference between what would have been produced if potential, or high-employment, national income had been achieved and what is actually produced, as measured by the current GNP. It is calculated by subtracting actual national income from potential income ($Y^* - Y$).

The gap is positive when potential income is greater than actual income. The gap then measures the market value of goods and services that *could have been produced* if the economy's resources had been fully employed but that actually went unproduced. This is sometimes referred to as the *deadweight loss* of unemployment.

Recessions are associated with large positive GNP gaps. In booms the gap may become negative, indicating that actual national income *exceeds* potential income. A negative GNP gap is possible because

[4] When economists wish to analyze monthly or quarterly data, they often remove fluctuations that can be accounted for by a regular seasonal pattern. This *seasonal adjustment* is made because many economic series show a marked seasonal pattern over the year. For example, logging activity tends to be low in the winter months and high in the summer months, whereas sales of fuel oil tend to have the reverse seasonal pattern. Retail sales are highest in December.

[5] The words *real* and *actual* have similar meanings in everyday usage. In national income theory, however, their meanings are quite distinct. Real national income is distinguished from *nominal* national income, while *actual* national income is distinguished from *potential* national income. The latter both refer to real measures, so that the full descriptions are actual real national income and potential real national income.

FIGURE 24-2   National Income and Growth, 1929–1985

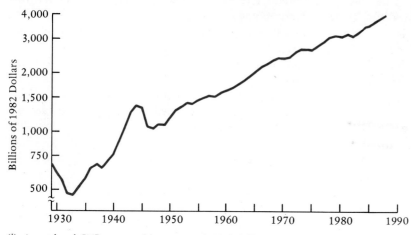

(i) Annual real GNP measured in constant (1982) dollars

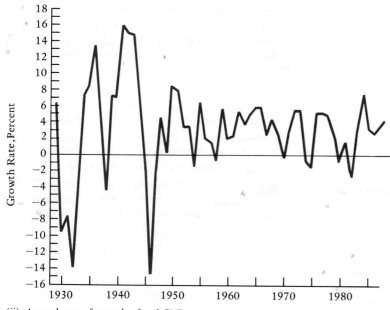

(ii) Annual rate of growth of real GNP

(i) Real GNP measures the quantity of total output produced by the nation's economy over the period of a year. Real GNP, plotted in (i) in semilog form, has risen steadily since the early 1930s, with only a few interruptions. This demonstrates the growth of the American economy. Short-term fluctuations are obscured by the long-term growth trend in (i) but are highlighted in (ii), which plots changes in real GNP. (*Source: Economic Report of the President,* various years.)

(ii) Fluctuations in the annual rate of growth of real GNP reflect cyclical changes in the level of activity in the economy. The growth rate fluctuates considerably from year to year. High growth rates occur during war years (such as World War II in the early 1940s and the Korean War in the early 1950s). Peacetime expansions (such as the mid-1960s and the last half of the 1980s) are reflected by sustained periods of above average growth rates. Low growth rates often occur during recessions. The long-term upward trend of real GNP still shows up in (i) because the majority of the observations in (ii) are positive.

potential income is defined for a *normal rate of utilization* of factors of production, and there are many ways in which these normal rates can be exceeded temporarily. Labor may work longer hours than normal; factories may operate an extra shift or not close for routine repairs and maintenance. Although these expedients are only temporary, they are effective in the short term.

Figure 24-4(i) shows potential income for the years 1955 through 1988. The rising trend reflects the growth in the productive capacity of the American economy over this period. The figure also shows actual real national income, which has kept approximately in step with potential income. The distance between the two, which is the GNP gap, is plotted in Figure 24-4(ii). Fluctuations in economic activity are apparent from fluctuations in the size of the gap. The deadweight loss from unemployment over any time span is indicated by the overall size of the gap over that time span. It is shown in part (ii) of Figure 24-4 by the colored shaded area between the curve and the horizontal axis, which represents the level at which actual output equals potential output.

Why National Income Matters

Policymakers care about short-term fluctuations in national income. Recessions cause unemployment and lost output. A large GNP gap means that actual national income falls short of potential, and it thus signals economic waste and human suffering as a result of a failure to use the economy's resources (including its human resources) at their normal intensity of use.

Booms, although associated with high employment and high output, can bring problems of their own. A negative GNP gap, indicating that actual national income exceeds potential income, usually signals the outbreak of strong inflationary pressures. These will cause serious concern for any government that is committed to keeping the inflation rate low.

The long-run trend in real national income is even more important than its short-term fluctuations. When income per person grows, each generation can expect, on average, to be substantially better off than preceding ones. For example, if real income per capita grows at the relatively modest rate of 1.5 percent per year, the average person's lifetime income expectancy will be *twice* that of his or her grandparents. Indeed, the low living standards that prevailed at the start of the Industrial Revolution are no longer with

us, primarily because economic growth has resulted in more and more output for less and less work over the last century. (It is important to remember, however, that although growth makes people better off on average, it does not necessarily make every individual better off.)

Labor Force Variables

Employment denotes the number of adult workers (defined in the United States as workers aged 16 and over) who hold full-time jobs. **Unemployment** denotes the number of adult workers who are not employed and are actively searching for a job. The **labor force** is the total number of those who are employed plus the number of unemployed. The **unemployment rate,** usually represented by the symbol U, is unemployment expressed as a percentage of the labor force.

$$U = \frac{\text{unemployed}}{\text{labor force}} \times 100 \text{ percent}$$

The number of unemployed persons in the United States is estimated from the Current Population Survey that is conducted each month by the Bureau of the Census. Persons who are currently without a job but who say they have searched actively for one during the sample period are recorded as unemployed. The total number of estimated unemployed is then expressed as a percentage of the labor force (employed plus unemployed) to obtain the figure for percentage unemployment. Some problems connected with this measurement are discussed in Box 24-2.

Consideration of employment and unemployment suggests another concept, that of *full employment* or *high employment.* One confusing thing about "full employment" is that it does *not* mean no unemployment. This is why the concept is now more often called *high employment,* although the long history of the use of the term *full employment* in economics guarantees that it will be heard for some time to come. There are two main reasons why full employment is always accompanied by some unemployment.

First, there is a constant turnover of individuals in given jobs and a constant change in job opportunities. New members enter the work force; some people quit their jobs; and others are fired. It may take some time for these people to find jobs. So, at any

FIGURE 24-3   **A Stylized Business Cycle**

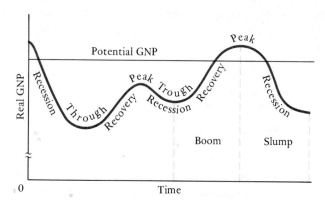

Although the phases of business fluctuations are described by a series of commonly used terms, no two cycles are the same. Starting from a lower turning point, a cycle goes through a phase of recovery, or expansion, reaches an upper turning point, and then enters a period of recession. Cycles differ from one another in the severity of their troughs and peaks and in the speed with which one phase follows another. Sometimes, the entire rising half of the cycle is loosely referred to as a *boom,* while the entire falling half is called a *slump.*

point in time, there is unemployment due to the normal turnover of labor. Such unemployment is called **frictional unemployment.**

Second, because the economy is constantly changing and adapting, at any moment in time there will always be some mismatching between the characteristics of the labor force and the characteristics of the available jobs. This is a mismatching between the *structure* of the supplies of labor and the *structure* of the demands for labor. The mismatching may occur, for example, because labor does not have the skills demanded or because labor is not in the part of the country where the demand is located. Unemployment that occurs because of a mismatching of the characteristics of the supply of labor and the demand for labor, even when the overall demand for labor is equal to the overall supply, is called **structural unemployment.** We will have more to say about these two types of unemployment in Chapter 35.

High or **full employment** is said to occur when

the only existing unemployment is frictional and structural. At less than full employment, other types of unemployment are present as well. One major reason for lapses from full employment lies with the business cycle. During recessions unemployment rises above the minimum avoidable amount of frictional and structural unemployment. This excess amount is called **cyclical unemployment** (or, sometimes, *deficient-demand unemployment*).

The measured unemployment rate when the economy is at full employment is often called the **natural rate of unemployment** or the **NAIRU.** Estimates of this rate are difficult to obtain and are often a source of disagreement among economists. Nevertheless, such estimates are a useful benchmark against which economists can gauge the current performance of the economy, as measured by the actual unemployment rate. Estimates indicate that the natural rate of unemployment rose throughout the 1970s from around 4 percent to a high of around 7 percent in the early 1980s, and it has now fallen to between 5 and 6 percent. (We shall discuss the reasons for these changes in Chapter 35.)

Unemployment: The Historical Experience

Figure 24-5(i) shows the trends in the labor force, employment, and unemployment since 1929. Despite booms and slumps, employment has grown roughly in line with the growth in the labor force and in the total population. In the 1980s, however, the labor force and employment grew faster than the total population in response to the increasing participation of youths and women in the labor force.

Although the long-term growth trend dominates the employment figures, some unemployment is always present. Figure 24-5(ii) shows that the short-term fluctuations in the unemployment rate have been quite marked. The unemployment rate has been as low as 1.2 percent in 1944 and as high as 24.9 percent in 1933; in the post–World War II period, the unemployment rate fell as low as 2.9 percent in 1953 and rose as high as 9.7 percent in 1982.

The high unemployment rate of the Great Depression in the early 1930s tends to dwarf the fluctuations in unemployment that have occurred since then. Nonetheless, the fluctuations in unemployment in recent decades have been neither minor nor unimportant.

Unemployment can rise either because employ-

BOX 24-1

The Terminology of Business Cycles

Economics is a developing subject, and the terms that are used to describe economic fluctuations are constantly evolving. The meanings of some of the main terms that you are likely to encounter are outlined below.

Trough

A trough is characterized by high unemployment and a level of demand that is low in relation to the economy's capacity to produce. There is thus a substantial amount of unused productive capacity. Business profits are low; for some individual companies they are negative. Confidence about economic prospects in the immediate future is lacking, and, as a result, many firms are unwilling to risk making new investments.

Recovery

The symptoms of a recovery, or expansion, are many: Run-down equipment is replaced; employment, income, and consumer spending all begin to rise; expectations become more favorable as a result of increases in production, sales, and profits. Investments that once seemed risky now may be undertaken as the climate of business opinion starts to change from one of pessimism to one of optimism. As demand rises, production can be increased with relative ease merely by reemploying the existing unused capacity and unemployed labor.

Peak

A peak is the top of a cycle. At the peak there is a high degree of utilization of existing capacity; labor shortages may develop, particularly in categories of key skills; and shortages of essential raw materials are likely. As shortages develop in more and more markets, a situation of general excess demand develops. Costs rise, but since prices rise also, business remains profitable.

Recession

A **recession,** or contraction, is a downturn in economic activity. Common usage defines a recession as a fall in the real GNP for two quarters in succession. Demand falls off, and, as a result, production and employment fall. As employment falls, so do households' incomes. Profits drop, and some firms get into difficulties. Investments that looked profitable with the expectation of continual rising demand now appear unprofitable. It may not even be worth replacing capital goods as they wear out, because unused capacity is increasing steadily. In historical discussions, a recession that is deep and long lasting is often called a **depression.**

Booms and Slumps

Two nontechnical but descriptive terms are often used. The whole falling half of the cycle often is called a *slump,* and the whole rising half often is called a *boom.* These are useful terms for us to use when we do not wish to be more specific about the economy's position in the cycle.

ment falls or because the labor force rises. In recent decades the number of people entering the labor force has exceeded the number leaving it. The resulting rise in the labor force has meant that unemployment has sometimes grown even in periods when employment was also growing.

Why Unemployment Matters

The social and political significance of the unemployment rate is enormous. The government is blamed when it is high and takes credit when it is low. Few macroeconomic policies are planned with-

FIGURE 24-4   Potential National Income and the GNP Gap, 1955–1988

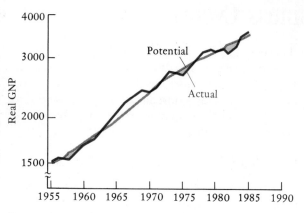

(i) Potential national income

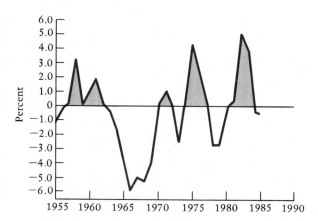

(ii) The GNP gap

(i) Potential and actual GNP both display an upward trend over the past half decade. Growth in the economy has been such that both potential and actual GNP have more than doubled since 1955. These are plotted in (i) in semilog form. Recall that both measures are in real terms; in the figure they are measured in 1982 dollars. The distance between the two curves represents the GNP gap. The shaded color areas indicate periods when there has been a positive GNP gap.

(ii) The GNP gap measures the difference between the economy's potential output and its actual output; it is expressed here as a percentage of potential output. The cyclical behavior of the economy is clearly apparent from the behavior of the GNP gap from 1955 to 1988. Slumps in economic activity cause large gaps; booms reduce the gaps. The shaded color area above the zero line, at which actual output equals potential output, represents the deadweight loss from unemployment. (*Source: Survey of Current Business,* March 1989.)

out some consideration of how they will affect it. No other summary statistic, with the possible exception of the inflation rate, carries such weight as a source of both formal and informal policy concern as does the percentage of the labor force unemployed.

Unemployment causes economic waste, and it causes human suffering. The economic waste is obvious. Human effort is the least durable of economic commodities. If a fully employed economy with a constant labor force has 120 million people who are willing to work in 1990, their services must either be used in 1990 or wasted. When the services of only 108 million are used because 10 percent of the labor force is unemployed, one year's potential output of 12 million workers is lost forever. In an economy in which there is not enough output to meet everyone's needs, many people feel that any waste of potential output is undesirable, and that large wastes are tragic.

Severe hardship can be caused by prolonged periods of unemployment. A person's spirit can be broken by a long period of desiring but being unable to find work. Careful research has shown that crime, divorce, and general social unrest tend to be positively associated with unemployment.

In the not so distant past, only private charity, or help from friends and relatives, stood between the unemployed and starvation. Today, welfare and un-

BOX 24-2

How Accurate Are the Unemployment Figures?

No measurements of unemployment are completely accurate. The unemployment figures that are calculated by the Bureau of Labor Statistics, however, have a number of shortcomings that tell us much about the concept of unemployment itself.

The measured figure for unemployment may overstate or understate the number of people who are involuntarily unemployed. On the one hand, the measured figure overstates unemployment by including people who are not involuntarily unemployed. For example, unemployment compensation provides protection against genuine hardship, but it also induces some people to stay out of work and collect unemployment benefits for as long as the benefits last. Such people have, in fact, voluntarily withdrawn from the labor force, although, in order to remain eligible for unemployment payments, they must make a show of looking for a job by registering at the local unemployment service office. Such people usually are included in the ranks of the unemployed because, for fear of losing their benefits, they tell the person who surveys them that they are actively looking for a job.

On the other hand, the measured figure understates involuntary unemployment by omitting some people who would accept a job if one were available but who did not actively look for one during the week in which the sample was taken. For example, people who have not found jobs after searching for a long time may become discouraged and stop seeking work. Such people have withdrawn voluntarily from the labor force and will not be recorded as unemployed. They are, however, unemployed in the sense that they would willingly accept a job if one were available. People in this category are referred to as *discouraged workers*. They have voluntarily withdrawn from the labor market because they believe that they cannot find a job under current conditions.

In addition, there are part-time unemployed people. If some workers are working 6 hours instead of 8 hours per day because there is insufficient demand for the product that they help to make, then these workers are suffering 25 percent unemployment even though none of them are reported as unemployed. Twenty-five percent of the group's potential labor resources are going unused. Involuntary part-time work is a major source of unemployment of labor resources, which are not reflected in the overall unemployment figures that are reported in the press.

The official figures for unemployment are useful, particularly because they tell us the *direction* of changes in unemployment. It is unlikely, for example, that they will be rising when unemployment is really falling. For all of the reasons that we have just discussed, however, they can at times give serious under- or overestimates of the total number of persons who would be genuinely willing to work if they were offered a job at the going rate of pay.

employment insurance have softened those effects, particularly when unemployment is for short periods, as is often the case. However, when an economic slump is deep and prolonged, as in the mid-1970s and again in the early 1980s, people begin to exhaust their unemployment insurance and must fall back on savings, welfare, or charity. In the early 1980s many people sank below the poverty level for the first time in their lives. They did so because they had used up their unemployment insurance but were unable to find jobs because of a persistently high unemployment level.

The Relationship Between Output and Employment

Output and employment (and, therefore, unemployment) are all closely related. If more is to be produced, either more workers must be used in produc-

FIGURE 24-5   Labor Force, Employment, and Unemployment, 1929–1988

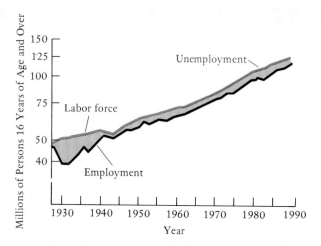

(i) Labor force, employment, and unemployment

(i) The labor force and employment have grown since the 1930s with only a few interruptions. The size of the labor force in the United States has doubled since 1930, and so has the number of the employed. These are plotted on a semilog scale. The fall in the labor force in the early 1940s was in the civilian labor force. The missing workers were in the military, and the Bureau of Labor Statistics' (BLS) definition of the labor force in use at the time did not include persons in the military. Unemployment, the gap between the labor force and employment, has fluctuated, but it has not again reached the peak of almost 13 million that occurred in 1933. As a fraction of the total labor force (see part ii), unemployment in 1933 was much higher than in any recent years. (*Source: Economic Report of the President,* various years.)

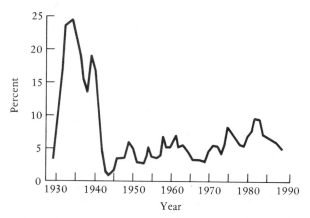

(ii) Unemployment rate

(ii) The unemployment rate responds to the cyclical behavior of the economy. Booms are associated with low unemployment; slumps, with high unemployment. The Great Depression of the 1930s produced record unemployment figures for an entire decade. During World War II unemployment rates fell to very low levels. Since 1945, however, the unemployment rate has demonstrated a slight upward trend. The recession of the early 1980s produced unemployment rates second only to those of the 1930s; these rates were extremely high by the standards of the post-World War II behavior of the American economy. After reaching a high of nearly 10 percent in 1983, the rate fell steadily throughout the rest of the decade, until it reached 5 percent in 1989. (*Source: Economic Report of the President,* various years.)

---

tion or existing workers must produce more. The first change means a rise in employment; the second means a rise in output per person employed, which is called a rise in *labor productivity*. Increases in productivity are a major source of economic growth. (Productivity was discussed in Chapter 11 and will be discussed again in Chapter 36.)

Changes in productivity and in the labor force dominate the long-term trends of output and employment, but productivity and the labor force generally change only slowly. As we study the main elements of macroeconomic theory over the next few

chapters, we will treat both the labor force and productivity as constant. Under these assumptions, a rise in output means a rise in employment and a fall in unemployment: Output is positively associated with employment and negatively associated with unemployment. Taking productivity and the labor force as constant not only greatly simplifies our discussion but also is a reasonable approximation of reality when we are dealing with the *short-term* behavior of the economy. In later chapters we shall study changes in both productivity and the labor force.

Other Important Macro Variables

In addition to the macro variables that we have just discussed, three other variables warrant our attention at this stage. They are the interest rate, the exchange rate, and the balance of payments.

The Interest Rate

If a bank loans you money, it will usually ask you to agree to a schedule for repayment. Furthermore, it will charge you interest for the privilege of borrowing the money. If, for example, you are lent $1,000 today, repayable in one year's time, you may also be asked to pay $10 per month in interest. This makes $120 in interest over the year, which can be expressed as an interest rate of 12 percent per annum [(120/1,000) × 100 percent].

The **interest rate** is the price that is paid to borrow money for a stated period of time and is expressed as a percentage amount per dollar borrowed. For example, an interest rate of 12 percent per annum means that the borrower must pay $.12 per year for every dollar that is borrowed.

Just as there are many prices of goods in the economy, so there are many interest rates. The bank will lend money to an industrial customer at a lower rate than it will lend money to you—there is a lower risk of not being repaid. The rate charged on a loan that is not to be repaid for a long time will usually differ from the rate on a loan that is to be repaid quickly.

When economists speak of *the* interest rate, they mean a rate that is typical of all the various interest rates in the economy. Dealing with one interest rate suppresses much detail, but it does allow us to deal with overall changes in the level of interest rates. The prime rate of interest, the rate that banks charge to their regular business customers, may be thought of as *the* interest rate, since, when the prime rate changes, most other rates change in the same direction.

The interest rate and inflation. How does inflation affect the rate of interest? In order to begin developing an answer, imagine that your friend lends you $100 and that it is repayable in one year. The amount that you pay her for making this loan, measured in money terms, is the **nominal interest rate.** If you

pay her $108 in one year's time, $100 will be repayment of the amount of the loan (which is called the *principal*) and $8 will be payment of the interest. In this case, the nominal interest rate is 8 percent [(8/100) × 100 percent].

How much purchasing power has your friend gained or lost as a result of making this loan? The answer will depend on what happens to the price level during the year. The **real rate of interest** tells us the return on a loan, measured in terms of purchasing power. It is given by the nominal rate of interest minus the inflation rate. This is because, as the preceding examples have illustrated, a percentage payment equal to the inflation rate is needed just to compensate for the reduction in purchasing power of the amount loaned before any real return has been earned on the investment.

If the price level remains constant over the year, then the real rate of interest that your friend earns would also be 8 percent, because she can buy 8 percent more goods and services with the $108 that you repay her than with the $100 that she lent you. However, if the price level rises by 8 percent, the real rate of interest would be zero, because the $108 that you repay her buys the same quantity of goods as the $100 that she originally gave up. If she is unlucky enough to lend money at 8 percent in a year in which prices rise by 10 percent, the real rate of interest that she earns is −2 percent.

If lenders and borrowers are concerned with real costs, measured in terms of purchasing power, the nominal rate of interest will be set at the real rate to which they agree as a return on their money *plus* an amount to cover any expected rate of inflation. Consider a one-year loan that is meant to earn a real return to the lender of 5 percent. If the expected rate of inflation is zero, the nominal interest rate set for the loan will be 5 percent. If a 10 percent inflation is expected, the nominal interest rate will be 15 percent.

To provide a given expected real rate of interest, the nominal interest rate must be set at the desired real rate of interest plus the expected annual rate of inflation.

Because they overlook this point, people often are surprised at the high nominal rates of interest that exist during periods of rapid inflation. For example, when the nominal interest rates rose drastically in 1980, many commentators expressed shock at the "unbearably" high rates. Most of them failed to notice that with inflation running at about 12 percent, an interest rate of 15 percent represented a real rate of only 3 percent. Had the Federal Reserve given in to the pressure to hold interest rates to the more "reasonable" level of 10 percent, it would have been imposing a *negative* real rate of interest. The purchasing power that lenders would get back, including interest, would be less than the purchasing power of the amount that was originally lent.

Concern about the burden of borrowing should be directed at the real, not the nominal, rate of interest.

For example, a nominal interest rate of 8 percent, combined with a 2 percent rate of inflation, is a much greater real burden on borrowers than a nominal rate of 16 percent, combined with a 14 percent rate of inflation.

Figure 24-6 shows the nominal and the real rate of interest paid on short-term government borrowing since 1950. Interest rates were both high and volatile during the early part of the 1980s. Later, rates fell somewhat and became somewhat less variable.

The Exchange Rate and the Balance of Payments

The exchange rate. If you are going on a holiday to Mexico, you will need Mexican pesos to pay for your purchases. Many of the larger banks, as well as any foreign-exchange bureau, will make the necessary exchange of currencies for you. They will sell you pesos in return for your dollars. If you get 2,000 pesos for each dollar that you give up, then these two currencies are trading at a rate of $1 = 2,000 pesos or, what is the same thing, 1 peso = 0.0005 dollars.

The exchange rate refers to the rate at which different currencies are traded for each other.

In particular, the **exchange rate** between the U.S. dollar and any foreign currency is the quantity of U.S. dollars that is needed to buy one unit of that foreign currency. For example, at the beginning of April 1989, it cost 0.00042 U.S. dollars to buy 1 peso, or, put the other way, 1 U.S. dollar was worth 2,380 pesos.

The term **foreign exchange** refers to foreign

FIGURE 24-6   Real and Nominal Interest Rates, 1950–1988

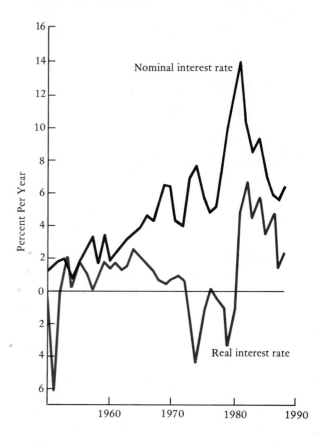

The inflationary trend over the last four decades has meant that the real interest rate has almost always been less than the nominal interest rate. The data for the nominal interest rate show the average rate of interest on three-month treasury bills in each year from 1950. The real interest is calculated in this case as the nominal interest rate minus the actual rate of inflation over the same period. With the exception of the early 1980s, the real interest rate has been below 3 percent throughout the period. Through much of the 1970s, the real interest rate was negative, indicating that the inflation rate exceeded the nominal interest rate. The 1980s saw real interest rates rise to heights that were unprecedented in the past. Later in the decade, as inflation moderated, both real and nominal interest rates fell.

currencies or claims to foreign currencies, such as bank deposits, checks, and promissory notes, that are payable in foreign money. The **foreign-exchange market** is the market where foreign exchange is traded—at a price that is expressed by the exchange rate.

The value of the U.S. dollar can be looked at in two ways. The **internal value of the dollar** refers to its power to purchase goods in American domestic markets. We have already seen that the price level and the internal value of the dollar are negatively related. The higher is the price level, the lower is the purchasing power of a dollar. The **external value of the dollar** refers to its power to purchase foreign currencies. This external value is negatively related to the exchange rate, which, as you will recall, measures the dollar cost of a unit of foreign exchange.

The lower is the dollar's external value—that is, the less foreign currency it will buy—the higher is the exchange rate—that is, the higher is the number of U.S. dollars that must be used to purchase a unit of foreign exchange.

Figure 24-7 shows two indicators of the external value of the U.S. dollar since 1970. The falling trend in the value of the dollar-yen exchange rate over most of the decade is really a reflection of the strength of the yen. The yen slowly rose in value against almost all of the world's currencies. Looked at from the point of view of any of these currencies, including the U.S. dollar, the strength of the yen showed up as a fall in the value of that currency *relative to the yen*. A more general indicator of the external value of the U.S. dollar is shown by the dollar's *trade-weighted exchange rate*. This measures the external

FIGURE 24-7   Exchange Rates for the U.S. Dollar, 1970–1988

(i) Price of U.S. dollar in yen

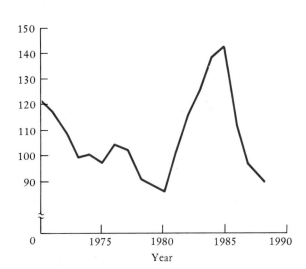

(ii) Trade-weighted exchange rate of U.S. dollars

The trend over the past two decades has been for the U.S. dollar to fall in terms of Japanese yen while fluctuating around a more stable value in terms of an average of most important foreign currencies. Part (i) shows the number of Japanese yen that are required to buy one U.S. dollar over the 1970s and 1980s. The fall in the value of the dollar relative to the yen is shown by the fact that one U.S. dollar could be bought for about 360 yen in 1970 and for only a little over 100 yen in 1988. Part (ii) shows the exchange rate of the U.S. dollar against all other major currencies, each being weighted by the importance of trade between the U.S. and expressed as an index number with 1973 equal to 100. Although interrupted by shorter-term fluctuations, the dollar fell throughout the 1970s, then rose dramatically through the first half of the 1980s, and fell equally dramatically through the latter part of the decade. (*Source: Economic Report of the President, 1989.*)

value of the dollar against an average of the currencies of the major trading nations. This series clearly shows the dramatic rise in the exchange rate in the first half of the 1980s, with the dollar rising to a high external value and then falling back again.

The balance of payments. In order to know what is happening to the course of international trade and international capital movements, governments keep an account of the transactions among countries. These accounts are called the **balance-of-payments accounts.** They record all international payments that are made for the buying and selling of both goods and services, as well as financial assets such as as stocks and bonds.

Figure 24-8 shows one part of the balance of payments that caused much controversy throughout the 1980s. This is the balance of payments on the *trade account,* or, as it is sometimes called, the *merchandise account.* This covers all trade in visible goods. (Services are recorded in another part of the account.) The balance is the difference between the value of U.S. exports and the value of U.S. imports. As we can see from Figure 24-8, American exports and imports rose fairly closely in step with each other until the second half of the 1970s. Then a small, negative net export balance appeared and persisted throughout the latter half of the decade. In the 1980s the shortfall of exports below imports became a massive amount that exceeded $100 billion in several years. In spite of some fluctuations, these negative net exports persisted throughout the end of the decade.

As we shall see in later chapters, a negative balance of trade (imports exceed exports), which is also called a *trade deficit,* is not always undesirable. During the 1980s, however, many commentators expressed the fear that the large trade deficit indicated that there was a serious reduction in the ability of U.S. industry to compete against stiffening foreign competition. Others saw in the trade deficit a mere reflection of the large government budget deficit that existed all throughout the 1980s. The trend in the data is clear and striking. The interpretation of it must wait until we have studied quite a bit of macroeconomics.

Cycles and Trends

Why are the price level, national income, and employment what they are today? What causes them to

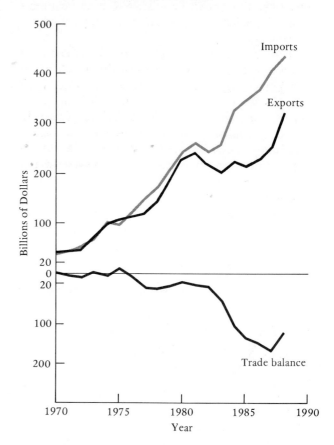

FIGURE 24-8 **U.S. Imports, Exports, and Balance of Trade, 1970–1988**

The 1980s saw an enormous increase in the U.S. balance-of-trade deficit. The nominal values of imports and exports rose greatly over the last two decades, due partly to price increases and partly to quantity increases. The world recession during the early 1980s was marked by a fall in both exports and imports. The trade deficit grew dramatically in the first half of the 1980s, when imports quickly returned to their rising trend, while exports were much slower to recover; they did not return to their 1981 level until 1987. (*Source: Economic Report of the President,* 1989.)

change? These are some of the questions that macroeconomics seeks to answer.

Before we begin to study them, it is useful for us to make a number of assumptions that serve to simplify the analysis and that can be dropped later, once we have mastered the simpler cases. Earlier in the chapter we encountered two such assumptions: Productivity and the labor force are assumed to be constant in the short run, implying that any increase in national income will be accompanied by an increase in employment and a decrease in unemployment. Hence, the theory of national income that we will develop over the next few chapters also will explain both employment and unemployment.

As we have seen already in this chapter, national income and the price level exhibit long-term trends and short-term fluctuations around those trends. The analysis of the next few chapters is to be understood as establishing how the price level and national income will behave *relative to their trend*. A fluctuation that takes the price level or national income above its long-term trend will be indicated by an increase in its value, while a fluctuation that takes the price level or national income below its trend will be indicated by a decrease in its value.

Much of macroeconomics studies relatively short-term movements in the economy (that is, in terms of months or, at most, a few years). In order to concentrate on these movements, it is easiest to treat the longer-term trends of income, prices, and all other macrovariables as zero. Thus, in the next few chapters, when we talk about national income falling by 3 percent, we mean that it falls by 3 percent *relative to its growth trend*. If, for example, its long-term trend is to grow at 2 percent per year, a 3 percent fall (relative to that trend) actually would mean an observed fall of only 1 percent. Similarly, a force that causes the price level to fall by 4 percent below its trend will cause the price level to rise by 2 percent when its long-term trend is to rise at 6 percent per year. For the sake of simplicity, we call such a change a 4 percent fall in the price level, but it is important to remember that this means a 4 percent fall below its trend.

SUMMARY

1. Macroeconomics examines the behavior of such broad aggregates and averages as the price level, national income, potential national income, the GNP gap, employment, and unemployment.
2. Index numbers are summary measures that give the average percentage change in a set of related items between a base year and another given year.
3. The price level has displayed a continual upward trend since 1929. The inflation rate measures the rate of change of the price level. Although it fluctuates considerably, the inflation rate has been consistently positive.
4. The value of total production of goods and services is called national product. Since production of output generates income in the form of claims on that output, it is common also to talk of national income. One of the most commonly used measures of national income is gross national product (GNP). Nominal national income evaluates output in current prices. Real national income evaluates output in base period prices. Changes in real national income reflect changes in quantities of output produced.
5. Fluctuations of national income around its potential level are associated with the business cycle. Recoveries pass through peaks and turn into recessions, which in turn pass through troughs to become recoveries. Although these movements are systematic rather than random, they are by no means predictably regular.
6. Potential real national income measures the capacity of the economy to produce goods and services when factors of production are employed at their normal intensity of use. The GNP gap is the difference between potential and actual real national income.

7. The unemployment rate is the number of workers over 16 who are not employed and who are actively searching for a job; it is expressed as a percentage of the labor force. The labor force and employment both have grown steadily for the past half century. The unemployment rate fluctuates considerably from year to year. Unemployment imposes serious costs on the economy in the form of economic waste and human suffering.

8. Other important macroeconomic variables include nominal and real interest rates, exchange rates, which refer to the cost of a unit of foreign currency in terms of U.S. dollars, and the balance of payments, which is a record of all international transactions made by U.S. firms, households, and governments. The trade balance is a part of the balance of payments that refers to the difference between the value of exports and the value of imports of visible goods.

9. The dominant historical trends of the economy are growth of the price level, real output, and employment over the long term. This growth has never been entirely smooth; there have always been fluctuations in the price level, output, and unemployment around their trend growth rates. The study of these fluctuations is simplified by always stating and explaining the differences between the actual value of each variable and its trend value. Stated values, therefore, give deviations from the trend value; the actual, observed value is obtained by adding the trend value to the stated value. (If the trend value were zero, each stated value would be the same as that variable's actual value.)

TOPICS FOR REVIEW

The price level and rate of inflation
Real and nominal national income
Potential and actual national income and the GNP gap
Employment, unemployment, and labor force
The exchange rate
The real and nominal interest rates
The exchange rate and the balance of payments
The effects of anticipated and unanticipated inflation

DISCUSSION QUESTIONS

1. Classify as microeconomic or macroeconomic (or both) the issues that are raised in the following newspaper headlines.
   a. "Lettuce crop spoils as strike hits California lettuce producers."
   b. "Analysts fear rekindling of inflation as economy recovers toward full employment."
   c. "Index of Industrial Production falls by 4 points."
   d. "Price of bus rides soars in Centersville as city council withdraws transport subsidy."
   e. "A fall in the unemployment rate signals the beginning of the end of the recession in the Detroit area."
   f. "New computer technology brings falling prices and growing sales of microcomputers."
   g. "Rising costs of imported raw materials cause most American manufacturers to raise prices."
2. Explain carefully what has happened to the CPI to justify each of the following newspaper headlines.
   a. "Prices on the rise again after a year of stability"
   b. "Inflation increases for three successive months"

   c. "CPI breaks 200!"

   d. "President pleased at moderation in inflation rate"

   e. "Cost-of-living increases devastating pensioners"

   f. "Union leader warns that inflation is plateauing out at a disturbingly high level"

3. What might lie behind the allegation that "inflation is legalized government robbery" and the reply that "inflation only hurts the ignorant because no one with reasonable foresight needs to lose through inflation"?

4. Most of the films on the list of 10-biggest-ever money makers have been made in the recent past. Does this mean that the best films are the most recent ones?

5. In the good old days at the turn of the century you could buy a drink for $.05 and a full meal for $.25. Were they, then, good old days of high purchasing power for the average person?

6. Discuss the following statements about unemployment.

   a. "Unemployment is a personal tragedy and a national waste."

   b. "No one needs to be unemployed these days; just look at the help wanted ads in the newspapers and the signs in the stores."

   c. "Unemployment insurance is a boondoggle for the lazy and unnecessary for the industrious."

7. How could you make a sure profit in a year in which the interest rate was 10 percent and you knew that the inflation rate was going to be 15 percent? Use the current *Economic Report of the President* to discover the real interest rate in the latest year for which figures are available. A friend's mother has just become a widow and has been left government bonds by her late husband as her only means of support. Explain to her why she cannot regard all of the interest that she receives as current income. What will happen if she does treat all of her interest receipts as current income and spends all of it each year?

8. If you thought the inflation rate was going to be 10 percent next year, why should you be unwilling to lend money at 6 percent interest? Say 6 percent was all you could get and you had money that you did not want to spend for a year. Would you do better just to hold the money? What could you do that would be better than lending your money at 6 percent?

Chapter 25

Measuring Macro-economic Variables

Our goal is to understand the type of macroeconomic events that were outlined in the previous chapter. Our first step is to look in some detail at the measurement and interpretation of one key set of variables—those relating to national output and national income.[1] We need to study national output and national income in order to develop the concepts used in macroeconomic theory and also to be able to interpret measures that play a prominent role in everyday discussion.

National Output Concepts

We are concerned in this chapter with measuring the nation's output and the income that is generated by its production. We start by asking two questions: What do we mean by output, and how do we distinguish real from nominal changes in output (and income)?

Value Added as Output

It may seem strange to ask what we mean by output. Surely the town bakery knows what it produces, and if GM does not know its own output, what does it know? If each firm knows the value of its total output, all the national income statisticians have to do is to add up each separate output value to get the nation's output—or is that all?

The reason that getting a total for the nation's output is not quite so simple as it seems is that one firm's output is another firm's input. The local baker uses flour that is the output of the flour milling company, and the flour milling company in turn uses wheat that is the farmer's output. What is true in bread production is true of most commodities.

Production occurs in stages: Some firms produce outputs that are used as inputs by other firms, and these other firms, in turn, produce outputs that are used as inputs by yet other firms.

If we merely added up the market values of all outputs of all firms, we would obtain a total that was greatly in excess of the value of the economy's actual output.

[1] We saw in Chapter 24 how to measure the price level through a price index. The measurement of labor-force variables also was discussed briefly in that chapter, and a more detailed discussion is postponed until Chapter 35.

The local baker provides an example. If we added the total value of the sales of the wheat farmer, the flour mill, and the baker, we would be counting the value of the wheat three times, the value of the milled flour twice, and the value of the bread once.

The error that would arise in estimating the nation's output by adding all sales of all firms is called **double counting.** *Multiple counting* would be a better term, since if we added up the values of all sales, the same output would be counted every time that it was sold from one firm to another.

The problem of double counting is solved by distinguishing between two types of output. **Intermediate goods** are outputs of some firms that are in turn inputs for other firms. **Final goods** are goods that are not, in the period of time under consideration, used as inputs by other firms. The term **final demand** refers to the purchase of final goods for consumption, for investment (including inventory accumulation), for use by governments, and for export. It does not include goods that are purchased by firms for use as inputs during the period under consideration.

If the sales of firms could be readily disaggregated into sales for final use and sales for further processing by other firms, measuring total output would still be straightforward. It would equal the value of all *final goods* produced by firms, excluding all intermediate goods. However, when U.S. Steel sells steel to the Ford Motor Company, it does not care, and usually does not know, whether the steel is for final use (say, construction of a new warehouse) or whether it is for use as an intermediate good in the production of automobiles.[2] The problem of double counting must therefore be resolved in some other manner.

To avoid double counting, statisticians use the important concept of **value added.** Each firm's value added is the value of its output minus the value of the inputs that it purchases from other firms (and which in turn were the outputs of those other firms). Thus, a steel mill's value added is the value of its output minus the value of the ore that it buys from the mining company, the value of the electricity and fuel oil that it uses, and the values of all other inputs that it buys from other firms. A bakery's value added

is the value of the baking products that it produces minus the value of the flour and other inputs that it buys from other firms.

The total value of a firm's output is the gross value of its output. The firm's value added is the net value of its output. It is this latter figure that is the firm's true contribution to the nation's total output. It is what its own efforts add to the value of what it takes in as inputs.

Value added is useful in avoiding the statistical problem of double counting; it is the correct measure of each firm's contribution to total output, the amount of market value that is produced by that firm.

The concept of value added is further illustrated in Box 25-1. In this simple example, as in all more complex cases, the value of total output of final goods is obtained by summing all the individual values added.

The sum of all values added in the economy is a measure of the economy's total output. This measure of total output is called gross domestic product (GDP). It is a measure of all final output that is produced by all productive activity in the economy.

Table 25-1 gives the GDP by major industry groups for the U.S. economy in 1987.

National-Income Accounting: Gross National Product

Our most important task in this chapter is to study the concepts that lie behind the system of National Income and Product Accounts (NIPA). These are produced by the Division of Economic Analysis of the Department of Commerce, and they provide us with the framework for analyzing the generation of national income.

Look again at Figure 3-1, on page 50, which shows the circular flow of expenditure and income. The bottom half of the figure focuses on expenditure

---

[2] Even if we use our earlier example of bread, a bakery cannot be sure that its sales are for final use, since the bread may be further "processed" by a restaurant prior to its final sale to a customer for eating.

BOX 25-1

Value Added Through Stages of Production

Because the output of one firm often becomes the input of other firms, the total value of goods sold by all firms greatly exceeds the value of the output of final products. This general principle is illustrated by a simple example in which firm R starts from scratch and produces goods (raw materials) valued at $100; the firm's value added is $100. Firm I purchases raw materials valued at $100 and produces semimanufactured goods that it sells for $130. Its value added is $30 because the value of the goods is increased by $30 as a result of the firm's activities. Firm F purchases the semimanufactured goods for $130, works them into a finished state, and sells the final products for $180. Firm F's value added is $50. The value of the final goods, $180, is found either by counting only the sales of firm F or by taking the sum of the values added by each firm. This value is much smaller than the $410 that we would obtain if we merely added up the market value of the commodities sold by each firm.

	Transactions at three different stages of production			
	Firm R	*Firm I*	*Firm F*	*All firms*
A. Purchases from other firms	$ 0	$100	$130	$230 Total interfirm sales
B. Purchases of factors of production (wages, rent, interest, profits)	100	30	50	180 Total value added
A + B = value of product	$100	$130	$180	$410 Total value of all sales

to purchase the nation's output in product markets, and the top half focuses on factor markets through which the receipts of firms are distributed to factors of production.

Corresponding to the two halves of the circular flow are two ways of measuring national income: by determining the value of what is produced and by determining the value of incomes generated by production. Both of these measures yield the same total, which is called **gross national product (GNP)**. When it is calculated by adding up the total expenditure for each of the main components of final output, the result is called *GNP on the expenditure side.* When it is calculated by adding up all the incomes generated by the act of production, it is called *GNP on the income side.*

The conventions of double-entry bookkeeping require that all value produced must be accounted for by a claim that someone has to that value. Thus, the two values calculated from the income and the expenditure sides are identical conceptually and differ in practice only because of errors of measurement.

Any discrepancy arising from such errors is then reconciled so that one common total is given as *the* measure of GNP. Both calculations are of interest, however, because each gives a different and useful breakdown. Also, having two independent ways of measuring the same thing provides a useful check on the statistical procedures and on unavoidable errors in measurement.

GNP from the Expenditure Side

GNP is calculated from the expenditure side by adding up the expenditures needed to purchase final output. Total expenditure on final output is the sum of four broad categories of expenditure: consumption, investment, government, and net exports.

Consumption Expenditure

Consumption expenditure includes expenditure on all goods and services produced and sold to their final users during the year (with the exception of

TABLE 25-1 Gross Domestic Product, 1987

	Billions of dollars	Percent of GDP
Value added by sector		
Agriculture, forestry, and fisheries	$ 94.9	2.1
Mining	85.4	1.9
Manufacturing	853.6	19.0
Construction	218.5	4.8
Transportation and public utilities	408.2	9.1
Retail and wholesale trade	740.4	16.4
Financial insurance and real estate	775.4	17.2
Services	793.5	17.6
Government and government enterprises	535.3	11.9
Statistical discrepancy	−8.1	
GDP	$4,497.1	100.0
Investment income received from nonresidents less investment income paid to nonresidents	29.5	
GNP	$4,526.6	

Source: *Survey of Current Business,* 1989.

GDP measures total output produced in the United States by summing the value added by each industry. As can be seen, manufacturing and trade (retail and wholesale) are major components of GDP, contributing 19 percent and 16 percent, respectively. GDP measures output *produced in,* and hence income *generated in,* the United States. To obtain GNP, which is income *earned by U.S. residents,* it is necessary, as pointed out on page 520 of the text, to subtract income generated in the United States but earned by foreign residents and to add income generated abroad but earned by U.S. residents.

residential housing, which is counted as investment). It includes services such as haircuts, medical care, and legal advice; nondurable goods such as fresh meat, clothing, cut flowers, and fresh vegetables; and durable goods such as cars, television sets, and air conditioners. We denote actual, measured, consumption expenditure by the symbol C^a.

Investment Expenditure

Investment expenditure is expenditure on the production of goods not for present consumption, including inventories, capital goods such as factories, machines and warehouses, and residential housing. Such goods are called **investment goods.**

Inventories.   Almost all firms hold stocks of their inputs and their own outputs. These stocks are called **inventories.** Inventories of inputs and unfinished materials allow firms to maintain a steady stream of

production in spite of short-term fluctuations in the deliveries of inputs bought from other firms. Inventories of outputs allow firms to meet orders in spite of temporary fluctuations in the rate of output or sales.

Inventories require an investment of the firm's money, since the firm has paid for the goods but has not sold them yet. An accumulation of inventories counts as current investment because it represents goods produced but not used for current consumption. A drawing down, often called a *decumulation,* counts as disinvestment because it represents a reduction in the stock of finished goods that are available to be sold.

Additions to inventories are a part of the economy's final production of investment goods. These are valued in the national-income accounts at market value, which includes the wages and other costs that the firm incurred in producing them and the profit that the firm will make when they are sold. Thus, in the case of inventories of a firm's own output, the expenditure approach measures what will have to be spent to purchase them when they are sold rather than what has so far been spent to produce them.

Plant and equipment. All production uses capital goods: manufactured aids to production such as tools, machines, and factory buildings. The economy's total quantity of capital goods is called the **capital stock.** Creating new capital goods is an act of investment and is called *fixed business investment,* or the shortened form, **fixed investment.**

Residential housing. A house is a durable asset that yields its utility over a long period of time. For this reason, housing construction is counted as investment expenditure rather than as consumption expenditure. This is done by assuming that the investment is made by the firm that builds the house and that the sale to a user is a mere transfer of ownership that is not a part of national income.

Gross and net investment. The total investment that occurs in the economy is called **gross investment.** Gross investment is divided into two parts: replacement investment and net investment. **Replacement investment** is the amount of investment that just maintains the existing capital stock intact; it is called the **capital consumption allowance** or simply **depreciation.** Gross investment minus replacement investment is **net investment.** Positive net investment increases the economy's total stock of capital, while replacement investment keeps the existing stock intact by replacing what has been used up.

All of gross investment is included in the calculation of national income. This is because all investment goods are part of the nation's total output and their production creates income (and employment) whether the goods produced are a part of net investment or are merely replacement investment. Actual, that is, measured, total investment expenditure is denoted by the symbol I^a.

Government Expenditure on Goods and Services

When governments provide goods and services that households want, such as roads and air traffic control, it is obvious that they are adding to the sum total of valuable output in the same way as do private firms that produce the trucks and airplanes that use the roads and air lanes. With other government activities, the case may not seem so clear. Should expenditures by the federal government to send a rocket to Jupiter or to pay a civil servant to refile papers from a now defunct department be regarded as contributions to national income? Some people believe that many (or even most) activities "up in Washington" or "down at City Hall" are wasteful, if not downright harmful. Others believe that it is governments, not private firms, that produce many of the important things of life, such as education and pollution control.

National-income statisticians do not speculate about which government expenditures are or are not worthwhile. Instead, they include all government expenditures on goods and services as part of national income. (Government expenditure on investment goods is included as government expenditure rather than investment expenditure.) Just as the national product includes, without distinction, the output of both gin and Bibles, it also includes bombers and the upkeep of parks, along with the services of CIA agents, senators, and even IRS investigators. Actual government expenditure on goods and services is denoted by the symbol G^a.

Government output typically is valued at cost rather than at the market value. In many cases there is really no choice. What, for example, is the market value of the services of a court of law? No one knows. We do know, however, what it costs the government to provide these services, so we value them at their cost of production.

Although valuing at cost is the only possible thing to do with many government activities, it does have one curious consequence. If, due to an increase in productivity, one civil servant now does what two used to do, and the displaced worker shifts to the private sector, the government's contribution to national income will register a decline. On the other hand, if two workers now do what one worker used to do, the government's contribution will rise. Both changes could occur even though what the government actually does has not changed. This is an inevitable but curious consequence of measuring the value of the government's output by the cost of the factors, mainly labor, that are used to produce it.

It is important to recognize that only government expenditure on currently produced goods and services counts as part of GNP. A great deal of government expenditure does not count as part of GNP.

For example, when a government agency makes social security payments to a retired person, the government is not purchasing any currently produced goods or services from the retiree. The payment itself adds neither to employment of factors nor to total output. The same is true of payments on account of social security, unemployment insurance, welfare, and interest on the national debt (which transfers income from taxpayers to holders of government bonds). All such payments are examples of **transfer payments,** which are government expenditures that are not made in return for currently produced goods and services. They are not a part of expenditure on the nation's total output, and they are not included in GNP.

Thus, when we refer to government expenditure as part of national income or use the symbol G^a, we include all government expenditure on currently produced goods and services, and we *exclude* all government transfer payments. (The term *government outlays* can be used to describe all government spending, including transfer payments.)

Net Exports

The fourth category of aggregate expenditure, and one that is increasingly important to the American economy, arises from foreign trade. How do imports and exports influence the national income?

Imports. One country's national income is the total value of final commodities produced in that country. If your cousin spends $8,000 on a car that was made in Japan, only a small part of that value will represent expenditure on American production. Some of it represents payment for the services of the American dealers and for transportation; the rest is the output of Japanese firms and expenditure on Japanese products. If you take your next vacation in Italy, much of your expenditure will be on goods and services produced by Italians and thus will contribute to Italian GNP.

Similarly, when an American firm makes an investment expenditure on an American-produced machine tool that was made partly with imported raw materials, only part of the expenditure is on American production. The rest is expenditure on the production by the countries that are supplying the raw materials. The same is also true for government expenditure on such things as roads and dams; some

of the expenditure is for imported materials, and only part of it is for domestically produced goods and services.

Consumption, investment, and government expenditures all have an import content. To arrive at total expenditure on American products, we need to subtract from total American expenditure any expenditure on imports, which is given the symbol M^a.

Exports. If American firms sell goods to German households, the goods are a part of German consumption expenditure but also constitute expenditure on American output. Indeed, all goods and services that are produced in the United States and sold to foreigners must be counted as part of American production and income; they create incomes for the Americans who produce them. To arrive at the total value of expenditure on American national product, it is necessary to add in the value of American exports. Actual exports are denoted by the symbol X^a.

It is customary to group actual imports and actual exports together as **net exports.** Net exports are defined as total exports minus total imports $(X^a - M^a)$. When the value of U.S. exports exceeds the value of its imports, the net export term is positive. When, as in recent years, the value of imports exceeds the value of exports, the net export term becomes negative.

Total Expenditures

Gross national product from the expenditure side is the sum of the four expenditure categories that we have just discussed. These are shown in Table 25-2 for the United States in 1988.

GNP, calculated from the expenditure side, is the sum of consumption, investment, government, and net export expenditures.

GNP from the Income Side

The production of the nation's output generates income. Labor must be employed, land must be rented, and capital must be used. The calculation of GNP from the income side involves adding up factor incomes and other claims on the value of output until all of it is accounted for. We have noted already that because all value produced must be owned by some-

TABLE 25-2   Components of GNP from the Expenditure Side, 1988

Expenditure category	Billions of dollars	Percentage of GNP
Consumption	$3,261	66
Government	955	20
Investment	773	16
Net exports	−80	−2
	$4,909	100

Source: Economic Report of the President, 1989.

GNP measured from the expenditure side of the national accounts gives the size of the major components of aggregate expenditure. Consumption was by far the largest expenditure category, equal to almost two-thirds of GNP. In 1988 net exports were negative, so that the other three expenditure categories added up to slightly *more* than GNP. (All national income data in this chapter are for the third quarter of 1988, expressed at an annual rate.)

one, the value of production must equal the value of income claims generated by that production.

Factor Payments

National-income accountants distinguish four main factor incomes: wages, rent, interest, and profits.

Wages. Wages and salaries (which national-income accountants call *compensation to employees,* but which are usually just called *wages*) are the payment for the services of labor. Wages include take-home pay, taxes withheld, social security, pension fund contributions, and other fringe benefits. They represent that part of the value of production attributable to labor.[3]

Rent. Rent is the payment for the services of land and other factors that are rented. For the purposes of national-income accounting, homeowners are viewed as renting accommodations from themselves. The amount of rent in the GNP thus includes payments for rented housing plus "imputed rent" for the use of owner-occupied housing. This allows national-income measures to reflect the value of all housing services used, whether or not the housing is owned by its user.

[3] The concepts of wages, rent, interest, and profits that are used in macroeconomics do not correspond exactly to the concepts with the same names that are used in microeconomics, but the details of the differences need not detain us.

Interest. Interest includes interest that is earned on bank deposits, interest that is earned on loans to firms, and miscellaneous other investment income.

Profits. Some profits are paid out as **dividends** to owners of firms; the rest are retained for use by firms. The former are called **distributed profits,** and the latter are called **undistributed profits** or **retained earnings.** Both distributed and undistributed profits are included in the calculation of GNP. For accounting purposes, total profits are reported in two separate categories—corporation profits and incomes of unincorporated businesses (mainly small businesses, farmers, partnerships, and professionals).

Profits and interest together represent the payment for the use of capital—interest for borrowed capital and profits for capital contributed by the owners of firms.

Net national income. The sum of the four components of factor incomes—wages, rent, interest, and profits—is called **net national income (NNI)** in the U.S. accounts, and *national income at factor cost* in most other countries. It represents the share of total production that goes as income to the factors of production, labor, land, and capital; the rest is capital consumption and net business taxes.

Indirect Business Taxes Net of Subsidies

When we are using the income approach, we must distinguish between national income valued *at factor cost* and national income valued *at market prices.* The difference between the two is created by two effects—those of indirect business taxes and those of subsidies.

Indirect business taxes. An important claim on the market value of output arises out of indirect business taxes, which are taxes on the production and sale of goods and services. In the United States the most important taxes of this kind are retail sales taxes.

If, for example, a good's market price of $10.00 includes $.50 in sales taxes, only $9.50 is available as income to factors of production. Fifty cents worth of market value represents some government's claim on that value. When adding up income claims to determine GNP, it is therefore necessary to include that part of the total market value of output that is the government's claim exercised through its taxes on goods and services.

Subsidies.   It is also necessary to subtract government subsidies on goods and services, since these allow incomes to *exceed* the market value of output. Suppose, for example, that a municipal bus company receives a $50,000 subsidy from a city government and sells bus rides with a value added of $100,000 on which no sales taxes are charged. The total income that is generated by the company's activities is $150,000. To get the market value of the company's output from the income side, we must take this $150,000 of income and subtract the $50,000 subsidy.

Net national product at market prices.   Adding indirect business taxes to the four components of factor incomes and subtracting subsidies gives **net national product (NNP) at market prices.** Taxes and subsidies often are combined into a single term, called *indirect taxes net of subsidies.*

Net national product at market prices equals the sum of wages, rent, interest, profits, and indirect taxes net of subsidies.

Depreciation

Another component on the income side arises from the distinction between net and gross investment. One claim on the value of final output is depreciation, or capital consumption allowance. This is the value of final output that embodies capital that has been used up in the process of its production. It is part of gross profits but, being that part needed to compensate for capital used up in the process of production, it is not part of net profits. Hence, it is not income earned by any factor of production. Instead, it is value that must be reinvested just to maintain the existing stock of capital equipment.

Total Product

Adding depreciation to net national product at market prices gives **gross national product at market prices.**

From the income side, GNP is the sum of the factor incomes that are generated in the process of producing final output *plus* indirect taxes net of subsidies *plus* depreciation.

The various components of the income side of the GNP in the American economy in 1988 are shown in Table 25-3.

TABLE 25-3   Components of GNP from the Income Side, 1988

Income component	Billions of dollars	Percent of GNP
Compensation to employees	$2,933	60
Business income	652	13
Capital-consumption allowance	508	10
Indirect business taxes net of subsidies	414	9
Interest	396	8
Rental income	20	—
Statistical discrepancy	−14	—
Total	$4,909	100

Source: Economic Report of the President, 1989.

GNP measured from the income side of the accounts gives the size of the major components of the income that is generated by producing the nation's output.   The largest category, equal to 60 percent of GNP, was compensation to employees, which includes wages and salaries plus employers' contributions to unemployment insurance, pensions, and other similar schemes. Business income includes incomes of both corporations and unincorporated businesses. The capital consumption allowance is that part of the earnings of businesses that is needed to replace capital used up during the year.

Other Income Concepts

Gross national income, however it is measured, is the most comprehensive income concept. The next most comprehensive measure is net national product (NNP). As we saw in building up the income approach, this is GNP minus the capital consumption allowance. NNP is thus a measure of the net output of the economy after deducting from gross output the amount needed to maintain intact the existing stock of capital. It is the maximum amount that could be consumed without actually running down the economy's capital stock.

Personal income is income that is earned by, or paid, to individuals before allowance for personal income taxes on that income. Some personal income goes for taxes, some goes for savings, and the rest goes for consumption. A number of adjustments to NNP are required to arrive at personal income. The most important are: (1) subtracting from NNP *indirect business taxes net of subsidies,* which are that part of the market value of output that goes directly to governments (this, as we have seen, gives net national income at factor cost); (2) subtracting from NNP profits retained by corporations; (3) subtracting from NNP income taxes paid by business; and (4) adding to NNP transfer payments to households. The first three are parts of the value of output not paid to households; the fourth is paid to households and thus is income that households have available to spend or to save, even though the payments are not part of GNP.

Disposable personal income is the amount of current income that households have available for spending and saving; it is personal income minus personal income taxes.

Disposable personal income is GNP *minus* any part of it that is not actually paid to households *minus* personal income taxes paid by households *plus* transfer payments received by households.

The relationships among GNP, NNP, personal income, and disposable income are shown in Table 25-4.

Interpreting National-Income Measures

The information provided by national-income data is useful, but unless it is carefully interpreted, it can be misleading also. Furthermore, each of the specialized measures gives different information. Thus, each may be the best statistic for studying a particular range of problems. Any statistical measure will be determined partly by some arbitrary decisions that might have been decided in another way. Some of these are discussed further in Box 25-2. The most important matters of interpretation will be dealt with now.

GDP and GNP

The main entries in Table 25-1 show the composition of GDP by industry, whereas Tables 25-2 and 25-3 show the composition of GNP by expenditure and income categories. These two totals, the GDP and the GNP, are slightly different. Is this another statistical error? The answer is that the difference does not reflect an error; rather, it reflects the difference between income generated in the United States and

TABLE 25-4   Various National Income Measures, 1988

A. GNP at market prices	$4,909
Less: capital consumption allowance	−508
B. NNP (at market prices)	4,401
Less: indirect business taxes net of subsidies	−400
C. National income (at factor cost)	4,001
Less: retained earnings, net interest, and social insurance contributions	−1,077
Plus: transfer payments to households	1,170
D. Personal income	4,094
Less: personal income taxes	−587
E. Disposable income	3,507

Source: Economic Report of the President, 1989.

Each of the five related national-income measures focuses on a different aspect of the national output. GNP measures the market value of total output. NNP measures the net value of output after an allowance has been made for maintaining the capital stock. National income (at factor cost) measures the incomes earned by the factors of production in the course of producing the national ouput. It is GNP minus the net amount taken by government through indirect business taxes and the amount needed to keep the capital stock intact. Personal income measures income "received" by persons before personal income taxes are withheld or paid by income receivers. Disposable income measures after-tax income of persons; it is the amount that they have available either to spend or to save.

income accruing to U.S. residents. The adjustment needed to reconcile these two totals is shown by the last entries in Table 25-1.

The difference between GDP and GNP arises from two sources. First, some factors of production that are located in the United States—land, buildings, factories, and so on—are owned by foreign residents, and hence the incomes earned by those factors do not go to American residents. Second, some Americans own factors of production that are located in other countries, and hence they earn income not generated by U.S. production.

The relative sizes of GDP and GNP depend on the balance between these two effects. For decades until the mid-1980s, the United States was a net creditor country. This meant that the value of foreign-based assets owned by Americans exceeded the value of American-based assets owned by foreigners. As a result, the foreign-generated incomes received by Americans exceeded the American-generated in-

BOX 25-2

The Significance of Arbitrary Decisions

National-income accounting uses many arbitrary decisions. Goods that are finished and held in inventories are valued at market value, thereby anticipating their sale, even though the actual sales price may not be known. In the case of a Ford in a dealer's showroom, this practice may be justified because the *value* of this Ford is perhaps virtually the same as that of an identical Ford that has just been sold to a customer. However, what is the correct market value of a half-finished house or an unfinished novel? Accountants arbitrarily treat goods in process at cost (rather than at market value) if the goods are being made by business firms. They ignore completely the value of the novel-in-progress. While these decisions are arbitrary, so would any others be. Clearly, practical people must arrive at some compromise between consistent definitions and measurable magnitudes.

The definition of final goods provides further examples. Business investment expenditures are treated as final products, as are all government purchases. Intermediate goods purchased by business for further processing are not treated as final products. Thus, when a firm buys a machine or a truck, the purchase is treated as a final good; when it buys a ton of steel, the steel is treated as a raw material that will be used as an input into the firm's production process. If the steel sits in inventory, however, it is regarded as a business investment and thus *is* a final good.

Such arbitrary decisions surely affect the size of measured GNP. Does it matter? The surprising answer, for many purposes, is no. In any case, it is wrong to believe that just because a statistical measure falls short of perfection (as all statistical measures do), it is useless. Crude measures often give estimates to the right order of magnitude, and substantial improvements in sophistication may make only second-order improvements in these estimates.

In the third century B.C., for example, the Al-

exandrian astronomer Eratosthenes measured the angle of the sun at Alexandria at the moment that it was directly overhead 500 miles south at Aswan, and he used this angle to calculate the circumference of the earth to within 15 percent of the distance as measured today by the most advanced measuring devices. For the knowledge he wanted—the approximate size of the earth—his measurement was satisfactory. To launch a modern earth satellite, it would have been disastrously inadequate.

Absolute figures mean something in general terms, although they cannot be taken seriously to the last dollar. In 1987, U.S. GNP was measured as $4,526.7 billion. It is certain that the market value of all production in the United States in that year was neither $100 billion nor $10,000 billion nor $500 billion, but it might well have been $4,800 billion or $4,200 billion had different measures been defined with different arbitrary decisions built in.

International and intertemporal comparisons, though tricky, may be meaningful when they are based on measures all of which contain roughly the same arbitrary decisions. American per capita GNP is a little less than three times the Spanish and 30 percent higher than the Japanese per capita GNPs. Other measures might differ, but it is unlikely that any measure would reveal that either the Spanish or the Japanese per capita GNP was higher than the per capita GNP in the United States. However, the statistics also show that per capita GNP was 4 percent higher in the United States than in Sweden, a difference too small to have much meaning. American output grew at 2.8 percent per year for the 30 years following World War II; it is unlikely that another measure of output would have indicated a 6 percent increase. Further, the Japanese output grew at about 9 percent per year over the same period. It is inconceivable that another measure would change the conclusion that Japanese national output rose faster than American national output in recent decades.

comes going to foreigners, making American GNP exceed its GDP. Income earned by Americans exceeded the value of American output.

In the 1980s foreign investment in the United States soared. Many economists argued that the federal government's large budget deficit was a major cause. Whatever the reasons were—and we shall study these in a later chapter—by the end of the decade, the United States had become the world's largest net debtor country in the sense that the value of American-based assets owned by foreigners greatly exceeded the value of foreign-based assets owned by Americans. As a result, American GNP may soon become less than its GDP. Americans then will earn incomes that are less than the value of American output. In the meantime, lags in the adjustment of earnings to current market conditions, plus the fact that many foreign investors are holding U.S. assets for capital gains rather than for income, mean that the smaller stock of U.S.-owned foreign assets is earning more current income than the larger stock of foreign-owned U.S. assets.

Real and Nominal Measures

In Chapter 24 (page 496) we distinguished between real and nominal measures of national income and output. When we add up money values of outputs, expenditures, or incomes, we end up with what are called *nominal values*. Suppose we found that a measure of nominal GNP had risen by 70 percent between 1980 and 1990. If we wanted to compare *real GNP* in 1990 to that in 1980, we would need to determine how much of that 70 percent nominal increase was due to increases in prices and how much was due to increases in quantities produced. Although there are many possible ways of doing this, the basic principle is always the same. It is to compute the value of output, expenditure, and income in each period by using a common set of *base period prices*. When this is done we speak of real output, expenditure, or income as being measured in *constant dollars*.

Total GNP or GDP that is valued at current prices is a nominal measure. GNP or GDP that is valued at base period prices is a real measure.

Any *change* in nominal GNP reflects the combined effects of changes in quantities and changes in prices. However, when real income is measured over different periods by using a common set of base period prices, changes in real income only reflect changes in real output.

The Implicit Deflator

If nominal and real GNP change by different amounts over some time period, this must be because prices have changed over that period. Comparing what has happened to nominal and to real GNP over the same period implies the existence of a price index measuring the change in prices over that period. We say "implies" because no price index was used in calculating real and nominal GNP. However, an index can be inferred by comparing these two values. Such an index is called an *implicit price index* or an *implicit deflator*. It is defined as follows:

$$\text{Implicit deflator} = \frac{\text{GNP at current prices}}{\text{GNP at base period prices}} \times 100\%$$

Implicit deflators are the most comprehensive indexes of the price level, because they cover all the goods and services that are produced by the entire economy. Although some other indexes use fixed weights, implicit deflators are variable-weight indexes. They use the current year's "bundle" of production to compare the current year's prices with those prevailing in the base period. Thus the 1986 deflator uses 1986 output weights, while the 1987 deflator uses 1987 output weights.

Box 25-3 illustrates the calculation of real and nominal GDP and an implicit deflator for a simple hypothetical economy that produces only wheat and steel.

Any change in any nominal measure of national income can be split into a change due to prices and a change due to quantities. For example, in 1987 American nominal GNP was 127 percent higher than in 1977. This increase was due to a 75 percent increase in prices and a 30 percent increase in real GNP.[4] Table 25-5 gives nominal and real income and the implicit deflator for selected years since 1940.

---

[4] The nominal change is not equal to the sum of the price and the quantity changes. Instead, the relationship is multiplicative. Prices and quantities are 1.75 and 1.3 times their original values. This makes nominal GNP $(1.3)(1.75) = 2.27$ times its original value, which is an increase of 127 percent.

BOX 25-3

Calculation of Nominal and Real National Income

To see what is involved in calculating nominal national income, real national income, and the implicit deflator, an example may be helpful. Consider a simple hypothetical economy that produces only two commodities, wheat and steel.

Table 1 gives the basic data for output and prices in the economy for two years.

TABLE 1   Data for a Hypothetical Economy

	Quantity produced		Prices	
	Wheat (bushels)	Steel (tons)	Wheat (dollars per bushel)	Steel (dollars per ton)
Year 1	100	20	10	50
Year 2	110	16	12	55

Table 2 shows nominal national income, calculated by adding the money values of wheat output and of steel output for each year. In year 1 the value of both wheat and steel production was $1,000, so nominal income was $2,000. In year 2 wheat output rose and steel output fell; the value of wheat output rose to $1,320 and that of steel fell to $880. Since the rise in value of wheat was bigger than the fall in value of steel, nominal income rose by $200.

TABLE 2   Calculation of Nominal National Income

Year 1 $(100 \times 10) + (20 \times 50) = \$2,000$
Year 2 $(110 \times 12) + (16 \times 55) = \$2,200$

Table 3 shows real national income, calculated by valuing output in each year by year 2 prices; that is, year 2 becomes the base year for weighting purposes. In year 2, wheat output rose but steel output fell. Using year 2 prices, the value of the fall in steel output between years 1 and 2 exceeded the value of the rise in wheat output, and real national income fell.

TABLE 3   Calculation of Real National Income Using Year 2 Prices

Year 1 $(100 \times 12) + (20 \times 55) = \$2,300$
Year 2 $(110 \times 12) + (16 \times 55) = \$2,200$

In Table 4 the ratio of nominal to real national income is calculated for each year and multiplied by 100. This ratio implicitly measures the change in prices over the period in question and is called the *implicit deflator* or *implicit price index*.

TABLE 4   Calculation of the Implicit Deflator

Year 1 $(2,000 \div 2,300) \times 100 = 86.96$
Year 2 $(2,200 \div 2,200) \times 100 = 100.00$

The implicit deflator shows that the price level increased by 15 percent between year 1 and year 2.

In Table 4 we used year 2 as the base year for comparison purposes, but we could have used year 1. The implicit deflator would then have been 100 in year 1 and 115 in year 2, and the increase in price level would still have been 15 percent.

Total Values and Per Capita Values

The rise in real GNP during this century has had two main causes: an increase in the amounts of land, labor, and capital used in production and an increase

in output per unit of input. In other words, more inputs have been used, and each input has become more productive. For some purposes, such as assessing a country's potential military strength or the total size of its market, we want to measure total output.

TABLE 25-5 Nominal and Real National Income (GNP)		
Year	Nominal national income (billions of current dollars)	Real national income (billions of 1982 dollars)	Implicit national income deflator (1982 = 100)
1940	$ 100.4	$ 772.9	13.0
1950	288.3	1,203.7	23.9
1960	515.3	1,665.3	30.9
1970	1,015.5	2,416.2	42.0
1980	2,732.0	3,187.1	85.7
1985	4,014.9	3,618.7	110.9
1988	4,909.0	4,009.4	122.4

Source: Economic Report of the President, various years.

Nominal national income tells us about the money value of output; real national income tells us about changes in physical output. Nominal national income (i.e. national income in current dollars) gives the total value of all final output in any year, valued in the selling prices of that year. Real national income (i.e. national income in base period constant dollars) gives the total value of all final output in any year, valued in the prices ruling in one particular year, in this case 1982.

    The ratio *national income in current dollars/national income in constant dollars* times 100 is the implicit deflator.

For other purposes, such as studying changes in living standards, we require per capita measures, which are obtained by dividing a total measure such as GNP by the population.

    There are many useful per capita measures. GNP divided by the total population gives a measure of how much GNP there is on average for each person in the country; this is called **per capita GNP.** GNP divided by the number of persons employed tells us the average output per employed worker. GNP divided by the total number of hours worked measures output per hour of labor input. A widely used measure of the purchasing power of the average person is disposable income per capita in constant dollars. This measure is shown in Figure 25-1.

The Significance of Omissions

Several types of economic activity are not included in GNP and, therefore, are also excluded from other measures based on GNP. The importance of these omissions depends on the purpose for which the data are to be used.

Illegal activities. GNP does not measure illegal activities, even though many of them are ordinary business activities that produce goods and services sold on the market and that generate factor incomes.

The liquor industry during Prohibition (1919–1933) is an important example, because it accounted for a significant part of the nation's total economic activity. Today the same is true of many forms of illegal gambling, prostitution, and the drug trade. To gain an accurate measure of the *total* demand for factors of production in the economy, of *total* marketable output, or of incomes generated, we should include these activities, whether or not we as individuals approve of them. The omission of illegal activities is no trivial matter. The drug trade alone is a multibillion dollar business in the United States.[5]

Unreported activities. An important omission from the measured GNP is the so-called underground economy. The transactions that occur in the underground economy are perfectly legal in themselves. The only illegal thing about them is that they are not reported for tax purposes. One example of this is the carpenter who repairs a leak in your roof and takes payment in cash or in kind in order to avoid

---

[5] Some of these activities do get included in the GNP, because people sometimes report their earnings from illicit activities as part of their earnings from legal activities. They do this to avoid the fate of Al Capone, a famous Chicago gangster in the 1930s, who, having avoided conviction on many counts, finally was caught for tax evasion.

FIGURE 25-1 Disposable Personal Income Per Capita in the United States, in Constant (1982) Dollars, 1929–1988

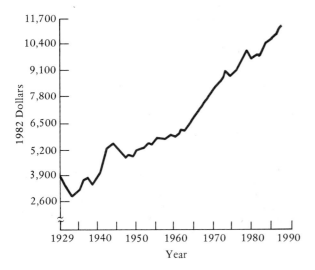

Disposable personal income per capita in constant dollars provides a measure of the real purchasing power available to the average American.
Disposable income per capita fell during the early 1930s and late 1940s, but it has risen over every decade since the 1930s, including the 1980s. It underestimates the average living standard because it leaves out the contribution of government expenditure to such items as police, fire, justice, defense, and recreation. (*Source: Economic Report of the President,* various years.)

tax. Because such transactions go unreported, they are omitted from GNP.

There are many reasons for the growth of the underground economy. Taxes, safety regulations, minimum-wage laws, antidiscrimination regulations, and social security payments all may be avoided. The growth of the underground economy also is facilitated by the rising importance of services in the nation's total output. It is much easier for a carpenter to pass unnoticed by government authorities than it is for a manufacturing establishment.

Estimates of the value of income earned in the American underground economy run from lows of 2 or 3 percent to 15 percent of American GNP. In some other countries the figures are even higher. The Italian underground economy, for example, has been estimated at close to 25 percent of that country's total GNP!

Nonmarketed activities. If a home owner hires a firm to do some landscaping, the value of the landscaping enters into GNP; if the home owner does the landscaping herself, the value of the landscaping is omitted from GNP. Such omissions also include, for example, the services of homemakers, any do-it-yourself activity, and voluntary work such as canvassing for a political party, helping to run a volunteer day-care center, or leading a Boy Scout troop.

In most advanced industrial economies the nonmarket sector is relatively small. The omissions become serious, however, when GNP or disposable-income figures are used to compare living standards in very different economies. Generally, the nonmarket sector of the economy is larger in rural than in urban settings and in less developed than in more developed economies. Be a little cautious, then, in interpreting data from a country with a very different climate and culture. When you hear that the per capita GNP of Nigeria is about $900 per year, you should not imagine living in Ohio on that income.

Other omitted factors. Many factors that contribute to human welfare are not included in GNP. Leisure is one of these. Although a shorter work week may make people happier, it will reduce measured GNP.

GNP also does not allow for the capacity of different goods to provide different satisfactions. A million dollars that is spent on a bomber or a missile makes the same addition to GNP as a million dollars that is spent on a school or on candy bars; these are expenditures that may produce very different amounts of consumer satisfaction.

Do the Omissions Matter?

If we wish to measure the flow of goods and services through the market sector of the economy or to account for changes in the opportunities for employment for those households that sell their labor services in the market, most of these omissions will not matter. If, however, we wish to measure the overall flow of goods and services available to satisfy people's wants, whatever the source of the goods and services, then the omissions are undesirable and potentially serious.

Is There a Best Measure?

To ask which is *the* best income measure is something like asking which is *the* best carpenter's tool. The answer is that it all depends on the job to be done. The decision concerning which measure to use will depend on the problem at hand, and solving some problems may require information provided by several different measures or information not provided by any conventional measures. If we wish to predict households' consumption behavior, disposable income may be the measure that we need to use. If we wish to account for changes in employment, constant-dollar GNP may be the measure that we want. For an overall measure of economic welfare, we may need to supplement or modify conventional measures of national income, none of which measure *the quality of life*. To the extent that material output is purchased at the expense of overcrowded cities and highways, polluted environments, defaced country-

sides, maimed accident victims, longer waits for public services, and a more complex life that entails a frenetic struggle to be happy, conventional measures of national income include only part of the things that contribute to human well-being.

Even if economists do come to use some new measures for some purposes, it is unlikely that GNP (and its relatives) will be discarded. Economists and policymakers who are interested in changes in market activity and in employment opportunities for factors of production will continue to use GNP and other relative measures because they are the ones that come closest to telling them what they need to know.[6]

[6] Concepts that come closer to measuring economic welfare have been developed. One was worked out by Professors William Nordhaus and James Tobin. It tries to measure consumption of things that provide utility to households rather than total production; it gives value to such nonmarketed activities as leisure and makes subtractions for such "disutilities" as pollution and congestion.

SUMMARY

1. Each firm's contribution to total output is equal to its value added. This is the gross value of its output minus the value of all intermediate goods and services—that is, the outputs of other firms—that it uses. Goods that count as part of the economy's output are called final goods; all others are called intermediate goods. The sum of all the values added produced in the economy is its total output, which is called gross domestic product (GDP).

2. Gross national product (GNP) can be calculated either from the expenditure or the income side. One gives the total value of expenditures required to purchase the nation's output, while the other gives the total value of incomes generated by the production of that output. By standard accounting conventions, these two aggregations define the same total.

3. From the expenditure side, $GNP = C^a + I^a + G^a + (X^a - M^a)$. C^a is consumption expenditures of households. I^a is investment in plant and equipment, residential construction, and inventory accumulation. Gross investment can be split into replacement investment (necessary to keep the stock of capital intact) and net investment (net additions to the stock of capital). G^a is government expenditures except transfer payments. $(X^a - M^a)$ is net exports, or exports minus imports; it will be negative if imports exceed exports.

4. GNP measured from the income side adds up all claims to the market value of production. Wages, rent, interest, profits, depreciation (or capital consumption allowance), and indirect business taxes net of subsidies are the major categories.

5. Gross domestic product (GDP) measures production that is located in the United States, and GNP measures income accruing to Americans. The difference is due to the balance between American claims to incomes that are generated abroad and foreign claims to incomes that are generated in the United States.

6. Real measures of national income are calculated to reflect changes in real quantities. Nominal measures of national income are calculated to reflect changes in both prices and quantities. Any change in nominal income can be split into a change in real income and a change due to prices. Appropriate comparisons of nominal and real measures yield implicit deflators.

7. Several related but different income measures are used in addition to the GNP. Net national product (NNP) measures total output after deducting the capital consumption allowance. Personal income is income that actually is earned by households before any allowance for personal taxes. Disposable personal income is the amount that actually is available to households to spend or to save, that is, income minus taxes.

8. GNP and related measures of national income must be interpreted with their limitations in mind. GNP excludes production resulting from activities that are illegal, that take place in the underground economy, or that do not pass through markets. Moreover, GNP does not measure everything that contributes to human welfare.

9. Notwithstanding its limitations, GNP remains a useful measure of the total economic activity that passes through the nation's markets and for accounting for changes in the employment opportunities that face households that sell their labor services on the market.

TOPICS FOR REVIEW

Value added
GDP as the sum of all values added
Intermediate and final goods
Gross national product (GNP) from the expenditure and income sides
National income measured at factor cost and at market prices
Measures of real and nominal national income
Implicit deflator
Net national income (NNI), net national product (NNP), personal income, and disposable income
The significance of omissions from measured income

DISCUSSION QUESTIONS

1. If Canada and the United States were to join together as a single country, what would be the effect on their total GNP (assuming that output in each country is unaffected)? Would any of the components in their GNPs change significantly?

2. Residents of many U.S. cities recently have become concerned about the growing proportion of their real estate that is being bought up by foreign residents. What is the effect of this transfer of ownership on the American GNP and GDP?

3. "Every time you rent a U-haul, brick in a patio, grow a vegetable, fix your own car, photocopy an article, join a food co-op, develop your own film, sew a dress, purchase a frozen dinner from a local supermarket, stew fruit, or raise a child, you are committing a productive act, even though these activities are not reflected in the gross national product." To what extent are each of these things "productive acts"? Are any of them included in GNP? Where they are excluded, does the exclusion matter?

4. In measuring American GNP from the expenditure side, which of the following expenditures are included? Why?

    a. Expenditures on automobiles by consumers and by firms

    b. Expenditures on food and lodging by tourists and by business people on expense accounts

    c. Expenditures on new machinery and equipment by American firms

    d. The purchase of one corporation by another corporation

    e. Increases in business inventories and decreases in business inventories

5. What would be the effect of the following events on the measured value of America's real GNP? Speculate on the effects of each event on the true well-being of the American people.

    a. Destruction of thousands of homes and stores in a severe earthquake.

    b. Passage of a constitutional amendment that would make abortion illegal

    c. Complete cessation of all imports from South Africa

    d. Outbreak of a new foreign conflict in which American troops become as heavily involved as they were in Vietnam

6. In the United States a Social Security Administration study, using 1972 data, found the "average American housewife's value" to be $4,705 per year. Update the total to a current-dollar figure. The study arrived at this total by adding up the hours that she spent cooking multiplied by a cook's wage, the hours spent with her children multiplied by a babysitter's wage, and so on. Should the time that a parent spends taking children to a concert be included? Are dollar amounts that are assigned to such activities a satisfactory proxy for market value of production? For what, if any, purposes would such values be excluded from or included in national income?

7. Use the table that appears on the endpapers at the back of this book to calculate the percentage increase over the most recent two decades of each of the following magnitudes. Can you account for the relative size of these changes?

    a. GNP in current dollars

    b. GNP in constant dollars

    c. Disposable income in constant dollars

    d. Disposable income per capita in constant dollars

8. Consider the effect on measured GNP and on economic well-being of each of the following:

    a. Reduction in the standard work week from 40 hours to 30 hours

    b. Hiring of all welfare recipients as government employees

    c. Increase in the salaries of priests and ministers as a result of increased contributions of churchgoers

9. A recent newspaper article reported that Switzerland was considered to be the "best" place in the world to live. In view of the fact that Switzerland does not have the highest per capita income in the world, how can it be ranked as the "best" place to live?

Chapter 26

National Income and Aggregate Expenditure

In Chapters 24 and 25 we encountered a number of important macroeconomic variables. We described how they are measured and how they have behaved over the past half century or so. We now turn to a more detailed study of what *causes* these variables to behave as they do. In particular, we study the forces that determine, first, national income (and hence employment and unemployment) and then the price level.

The first things that we want to know are what determines the size of real national income and what makes it change. Because it is easier to do things one at a time, rather than all at once, this chapter deals with these questions on the assumption that the price level is constant. In Chapter 27 we shall see what happens when the price level varies.

Our ability to explain the behavior of national income depends on our understanding of what determines the amount that households and firms spend, and why they change their spending. For this reason, we begin with an examination of the *expenditure decisions* of households and firms. As a first step, we distinguish between *desired* expenditure and *actual* expenditure.

Desired Expenditure

In Chapter 25 we discussed how national-income statisticians divide GNP, calculated from the expenditure side, into its components: consumption, C^a, investment, I^a, government, G^a, and net exports, $(X^a - M^a)$.

In this chapter we are concerned with a different concept. It is variously called *desired, planned,* or *intended* expenditure. Of course, all people would like to spend virtually unlimited amounts, if only they had the money. Desired expenditure does not refer, however, to what people would like to do under imaginary circumstances. It refers, instead, to what people want to spend out of the resources that are at their command. The *actual* values of the various categories of expenditure are indicated by C^a, I^a, G^a, and $(X^a M^a)$. We use the same letters without the superscript ^{a} to indicate the *desired* expenditure in the same categories: $C, I, G,$ and $(X - M)$.

Everyone with money to spend makes expenditure decisions. Fortunately, it is unnecessary for our purposes to look at each of the millions of such individual decisions. Instead, it is sufficient to consider four main groups of decision makers: domestic households, firms, governments, and foreign purchasers of domestically produced commodities. Their actual purchases account for the four main categories of expenditure that we have studied in the previous chapter: consumption, investment, government, and exports. Their desired expenditures, made up of desired consumption, desired investment, desired government purchases, and desired exports, account for total desired expenditure. To allow for the fact that some of the commodities desired by each group will have an import content, we subtract import expenditure. The result is total desired expenditure on domestically produced goods and services, called **aggregate expenditure**, *AE*:

$$AE = C + I + G + (X - M)$$

Desired expenditure need not equal actual expenditure, either in total or in any individual category. For example, firms may not plan to invest in inventory accumulation this year but may do so unintentionally. If they produce goods to meet estimated sales but demand is unexpectedly low, the unsold goods that pile up on their shelves are undesired, and unintended, inventory accumulation. In this case actual investment expenditure, I^a, will exceed desired investment expenditure, I.

National-income accounts measure *actual expenditures* in each of the four categories: consumption, investment, government, and net exports. The theory of national income deals with *desired expenditures* in each of these four categories.

To develop a theory of national-income determination, we need to examine the determinants of each component of desired aggregate expenditure.

In this chapter we focus on the desired consumption. It is the largest single component of aggregate expenditure, and as we will see, it provides the single most important link between desired aggregate expenditure and national income. We also look briefly at desired net exports, which provide a second link between desired aggregate expenditure and national income. For example, when residents of foreign countries decide to cut down on their purchases of American goods because their prices are too high, this reduces the desired aggregate expenditure on U.S. output.

Although desired investment and government expenditures are treated only briefly here, they will be discussed later in more detail.

Before proceeding, we need to recall the important distinction between *autonomous* and *induced* expenditure, which was first introduced in Chapter 2 (see page 20). Components of aggregate expenditure that do *not* depend on national income are called *autonomous expenditures*. Autonomous expenditures can and do change, but such changes do not occur systematically in response to changes in national income. Components of aggregate expenditure that *do* change in response to changes in national income are called *induced expenditures*. As we will see, the induced response of aggregate expenditure to a change in national income plays a key role in the determination of equilibrium national income.

Desired Consumption Expenditure

Households can do one of two things with their disposable income: spend it on consumption or save it. **Saving** is all disposable income that is not consumed.

Since by definition there are only two possible uses of disposable income, spending or saving, when the household decides how much to put to one use, automatically it has decided how much to put to the other use.

What determines the division between the amount that households decide to spend on goods and services for consumption and the amount that they decide to save? The factors that influence this decision are summarized in the consumption function and the saving function.

The Consumption Function

The **consumption function** relates the total desired consumption expenditure of all households to the factors that determine it. It is, as we shall see, one of the central relationships in macroeconomics.

While we are ultimately interested in the relationship between consumption and national income, the underlying behavior of households depends on the income that they actually have to spend—their disposable income. Therefore, we shall start with the relationship between consumption and disposable income, which we denote by Y_d, and then go on to relate consumption to national income.

Consumption and Disposable Income

It should not surprise us to hear that a household's expenditure is related to the amount of income that it has at its disposal. There is, however, more than one way in which this relationship could work. To see what is involved, consider two quite different households.

The first household is headed by the proverbial prodigal son. It spends everything it receives and puts nothing aside for a rainy day. When overtime results in a large paycheck, the household goes on a binge. When short hours are worked during periods of slack demand, the household's paycheck is small and its members cut their expenditures correspondingly. This household's expenditure each week is thus directly linked to each week's take-home pay, that is, its current disposable income.

The second household is the opposite of the first. It thinks about the future as much as the present, and it makes plans that stretch over its lifetime. It puts money aside for retirement and for the occasional rainy day when disposable income may fall temporarily—it knows that it must expect alternating bouts of good and bad times. It also knows that it will need to spend extra money while the family is being raised and educated and that its income will probably be highest later in life when the children have left home and the husband and wife have finally reached the peaks of their personal careers. The household may borrow to meet higher expenses earlier in life, paying back out of the higher income that the household expects to attain later in life. A temporary, unexpected windfall of income may be saved. A temporary, unexpected shortfall may be cushioned by spending the savings that were put aside for just such a rainy day. In short, this household's current expenditure will be closely related to its expected *lifetime income,* so that fluctuations in its *current income* will have little effect on its current expenditure, unless such fluctuations also cause it to change its expectations of lifetime income, as would be the case, for example, if an unexpected promotion came along.

John Maynard Keynes, the English economist who developed the basic theory of macroeconomics—and, incidentally, gave his name to "Keynesian economics"—inhabited his theory with prodigal

sons. For them, current consumption expenditure depended only on current income. To this day, a consumption function based on this assumption is called a *Keynesian consumption function.*

Later, two American economists, Franco Modigliani and Milton Friedman, both of whom were subsequently awarded the Nobel Prize in economics, analyzed the behavior of prudent households. Their theories, which Modigliani called *the life-cycle theory* and which Friedman called *the permanent-income theory*, explain some observed consumer behavior that cannot be explained by the Keynesian consumption function.

However, the differences between the theories of Friedman and Modigliani, on the one hand, and Keynes, on the other hand, are not as great as might seem at first sight. To see why this is so, let us return to our two imaginary households and see why their actual behavior may not be quite so divergent as we have so far described it.

Even the household that is headed by the prodigal son may be able to do some smoothing of expenditures in the face of income fluctuations. Most households have some money in the bank and some ability to borrow, even if it is just from friends and relatives. As a result, every income fluctuation will not be matched by an exactly equivalent expenditure fluctuation.

Although the second household wants to smooth its pattern of consumption completely, it may not have the borrowing capacity to do so. Its bank manager may not be willing to lend money for consumption when the security consists of nothing more than the expectation that the household's income will be much higher in later years, even if that expectation is quite reasonable. This may mean that the household's consumption expenditure fluctuates more with its current income than it would wish.

This discussion suggests that a household's consumption expenditure will fluctuate to some extent with its current disposable income and to some extent with its expectations of future disposable income. To develop our basic theory, we make the simplifying assumption that consumption expenditure is primarily determined by current disposable income. Once we understand the principles of the determination of national income, it will be an easy matter to allow for the fact that consumption expenditure is also influenced by expectations of future income.

Notice that whenever a change in current income is expected to be permanent, both current and expected future income change in the same way. This is true, for example, if households do not get an expected raise in pay this year and decide that this reflects a permanent but unforeseen downturn in the business conditions. A second example is when what is expected to be a permanent tax reform leaves households with more take-home pay. In the first case their current disposable income, and the income that they expect to receive in the future, will both fall; in the second case they both rise. Relating expenditure to changes in current or to expected future income will then give the same answer—that expenditure will rise when income rises and fall when income falls.

The term *consumption function* **describes the relationship between consumption and the variables that influence it; in the simplest theory, consumption is determined by current disposable income.**

In Chapter 26 we examined the calculation of disposable income; for the purposes of this discus-

sion, all we need to know is that disposable income tends to be a relatively constant percentage of national income.

Some consumption expenditure is autonomous, but most is induced; that is, most varies with disposable income and hence with national income. A schedule relating disposable income to desired consumption expenditure for a hypothetical economy appears in the first two columns of Table 26-1. In this example autonomous consumption expenditure is $100 billion, whereas induced consumption expenditure is 80 percent of disposable income. In what follows we use this hypothetical example to illustrate the various properties of the consumption function.

Average and marginal propensities to consume. To discuss the consumption function concisely, economists use two technical expressions.

The **average propensity to consume (APC)** is total consumption expenditure divided by total disposable income. The third column of Table 26-1 shows the APCs calculated from the data in the table.

The **marginal propensity to consume (MPC)** relates the *change* in consumption to the *change* in disposable income that brought it about. MPC is the

TABLE 26-1   The Calculation of Average Propensity to Consume (APC) and Marginal Propensity to Consume (MPC) (billions of dollars)

Disposable income (Y_d)	Desired consumption (C)	$APC = C/Y_d$	ΔY_d (Change in Y_d)	ΔC (Change in C)	$MPC = \Delta C/\Delta Y_d$
$ 0	$ 100	—			
100	180	1.800	$ 100	$ 80	0.80
400	420	1.050	300	240	0.80
500	500	1.000	100	80	0.80
1,000	900	0.900	500	400	0.80
2,000	1,700	0.850	1,000	800	0.80
3,000	2,500	0.833	1,000	800	0.80
4,000	3,300	0.825	1,000	800	0.80

APC measures the proportion of disposable income that households desire to spend on consumption; *MPC* measures the proportion of any *increment* to disposable income that households desire to spend on consumption. The data are hypothetical. We call the level of income at which desired consumption equals disposable income the break-even level; in this example it is $500 billion. *APC*, calculated in the third column, exceeds unity—that is, consumption exceeds income—below the break-even level. Above the break-even level, *APC* is less than unity. It is negatively related to income at all levels of income.

The last three columns are set between the lines of the first three columns to indicate that they refer to changes in the levels of income and consumption. *MPC*, calculated in the last column, is constant at 0.80 at all levels of Y_d. This indicates that in this example $.80 of *every* additional $1.00 of disposable income is spent on consumption and $.20 is used to increase saving.

change in disposable income divided into the resulting consumption change: $MPC = \Delta C/\Delta Y_d$ (where the Greek letter Δ, delta, means "a change in"). The last column of Table 26-1 shows the MPCs calculated from the data in the table. **[31]**

The slope of the consumption function. Part (i) of Figure 26-1 shows a graph of the consumption function plotted from the first two columns of Table 26-1. The consumption function has a slope of $\Delta C/\Delta Y_d$, which is, by definition, the marginal propensity to consume. The upward slope of the consumption function shows that the MPC is positive; increases in income lead to increases in expenditure.

Using the concepts of the average and marginal propensities to consume, we can summarize the properties of the short-term consumption function as follows:

1. There is a break-even level of income at which APC equals unity. Below this level APC is greater than unity; above it APC is less than unity.
2. MPC is greater than zero but less than unity for all levels of income.

The 45° line. Figure 26-1(i) contains a line that is constructed by connecting all points where desired consumption (measured on the vertical axis) equals disposable income (measured on the horizontal axis). Since both axes are given in the same units, this line has an upward slope of unity, or (what is the same thing) it forms an angle of 45° with the axes. The line is therefore called the **45° line.**

The 45° line makes a handy reference line. In Figure 26-1(i) it helps to locate the break-even level of income at which consumption expenditure equals disposable income. The consumption function cuts the 45° line at the break-even level of income, in this instance $500 billion. (The 45° line is steeper than the consumption function because the MPC is less than unity.)

The Saving Function

Households decide how much to consume and how much to save. As we have said, this is a single decision: how to divide disposable income between consumption and saving. It follows that, once we know the dependence of consumption on disposable income, we also automatically know the dependence

FIGURE 26-1 The Consumption and Saving Functions

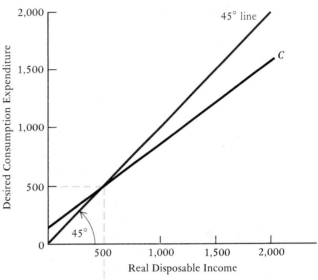

(i) Consumption function (billions of dollars)

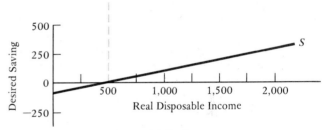

(ii) Saving function (billions of dollars)

Both consumption and saving rise as disposable income rises. Line C in part (i) relates desired consumption expenditure to disposable income by using the hypothetical data from Table 26-1. Its slope, $\Delta C/\Delta Y_d$, is the marginal propensity to consume (MPC). The consumption line cuts the 45° line at the break-even level of disposable income, $500 billion in this case.

Saving is all disposable income that is not spent on consumption ($S = Y_d - C$). The relationship between desired saving and disposable income is derived in Table 26-2, and it is shown in part (ii) by line S. Its slope, $\Delta S/\Delta Y_d$, is the marginal propensity to save (MPS). The saving line cuts the horizontal axis at the break-even level of income. The vertical distance between C and the 45° line in part (i) is by definition the height of S in part (ii); that is, any given level of disposable income must be accounted for by the amount consumed plus the amount saved.

of saving on disposable income. (This is illustrated in Table 26-2.)

Two saving concepts are exactly parallel to the consumption concepts of *APC* and *MPC*. The **average propensity to save (APS)** is the proportion of disposable income that households want to save, derived by dividing total desired saving by total disposable income, $APS = S/Y_d$. The **marginal propensity to save (MPS)** relates the *change* in total desired saving to the *change* in disposable income that brought it about, $MPS = \Delta S/\Delta Y_d$.

There is a simple relationship between the saving and the consumption propensities. *APC* and *APS* must sum to unity, and so must *MPC* and *MPS*. Since income is either spent or saved, it follows that the fractions of incomes consumed and saved must account for all income ($APC + APS = 1$). It also follows that the fraction of any increment to income consumed and saved must account for all of that increment ($MPC + MPS = 1$). **[32]**

Calculations from Table 26-2 will allow you to confirm these relationships in the case of the example given. *MPC* is 0.80, and *MPS* is 0.20 at all levels of income, while, for example, at an income of $2,000 billion *APC* is 0.85, while *APS* is 0.15.

Part (ii) of Figure 26-1 shows the saving schedule given in Table 26-2. At the break-even level of income, where desired consumption equals disposable income, desired saving is zero. The slope of the saving line $\Delta S/\Delta Y_d$ is *MPS*.

TABLE 26-2	Consumption and Saving Schedules *(billions of dollars)*	
Disposable income	Desired consumption	Desired saving
$ 0	$ 100	$ − 100
100	180	− 80
400	420	− 20
500	500	0
1,000	900	+ 100
2,000	1,700	+ 300
3,000	2,500	+ 500
4,000	3,300	+ 700

Saving and consumption account for all household disposable income. The first two columns repeat the data from Table 26-1. The third column, desired saving, is disposable income minus desired consumption. Consumption and saving both increase steadily as disposable income rises. In this example the break-even level of disposable income is $500 billion.

Consumption and Wealth

We have seen that current disposable income is an important factor in the consumption-saving decision. A second important factor is the real value of each household's wealth. By a household's **wealth** we mean the sum of all the valuable assets that it owns minus its liabilities. This includes its car, its house and contents, the value of its money in the bank, pension fund, and any stocks, bonds, or other investments that it holds.

Households save in order to add to their wealth. Many have target values for their wealth. They are willing to save now in order to be wealthier later— but only within limits. Other things being equal, an unexpected rise in their wealth will lead them to save less so that they can consume more now as well as be wealthier later. Conversely, an unexpected fall in their wealth will lead them to save more so that they can at least partially restore their targeted wealth positions. Obviously, it is the real value of wealth that matters. Should the money value of wealth and the price level change in the same proportion, leaving real wealth unchanged, the household's incentive to save will be unchanged.

A rise in wealth tends to cause a larger fraction of disposable income to be spent on consumption and a smaller fraction to be saved. This shifts the consumption function upward and the saving function downward, as shown in Figure 26-2. A fall in wealth increases the incentive to save in order to restore wealth. This shifts the consumption function downward and the saving function upward.

Individual households experience both expected and unexpected changes in wealth. For example, both planned saving and unplanned bequests will increase wealth. Similarly, both planned dissaving and unexpected declines in stock market values reduce wealth.

Many unexpected changes in wealth cancel out across households and so are unimportant for the macroeconomic consumption function. We will see, however, that inflation can be an important source of unexpected changes in wealth in most households.

Planned increases in wealth as a result of past accumulation of wealth can be important for the whole society and can lead to upward shifts in the macroeconomic consumption function as wealth accumulates. This effect operates only slowly, since wealth accumulates only slowly.

FIGURE 26-2   Wealth and the Consumption Function

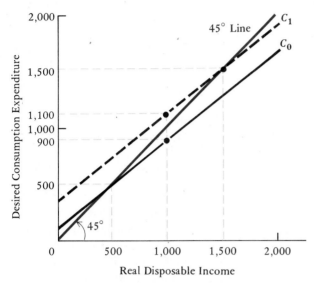

(i) The consumption function shifts upward with an increase in wealth (billions of dollars)

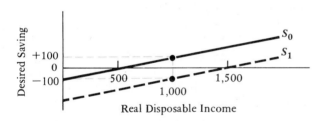

(ii) The saving function shifts downward with an increase in wealth (billions of dollars)

Changes in wealth shift consumption as a function of disposable income. In part (i) line C_0 reproduces the consumption function from Figure 26-1(i). An increase in the level of wealth raises desired consumption at each level of disposable income, thus shifting the consumption line up to C_1. In the figure the consumption function shifts up by \$200, so with disposable income of \$1,000, for example, desired consumption *rises* from \$900 to \$1,100. As a result of the rise in wealth, the break-even level of income rises to \$1,500.

The saving function in part (ii) shifts down by \$200, from S_0 to S_1. Thus, for example, at a disposable income of \$1,000, saving *falls* from plus \$100 to minus \$100.

Because for the moment we are focusing on short-term issues, the consumption function used in this chapter does not include the effects of changes in wealth.

Consumption and National Income

Desired consumption is related to *disposable* income. For a theory of the determination of national income, however, we need to know how consumption is related to national income.

The transition from a relationship between consumption and disposable income to one between consumption and national income is readily accomplished, since disposable income and national income are themselves related to each other.

The relationship between disposable income and national income. On pages 519–520 we saw how to derive disposable income from national income. Since transfer payments (the major addition to national income) are smaller than total income taxes (the major subtraction from national income), the net effect is for disposable income to be substantially less than national income. (It was about 70 percent of GNP in 1988.)

Relating desired consumption to national income. If we know how consumption relates to disposable income and how disposable income relates to national income, we can derive the relationship between consumption and national income.

As an example, assume that disposable income is always 90 percent of national income. Then, whatever the relationship between C and Y, we can always substitute $0.9Y$ for Y_d. Thus, if changes in consumption were always 80 percent of changes in Y_d, changes in consumption would always be 72 percent (80 percent of 90 percent) of Y. **[33]**

Table 26-3 shows that we can write desired consumption as a function of Y as well as of Y_d. We can then derive the marginal response of consumption to changes in Y by determining the proportion of any change in *national income* that goes to a change in desired consumption.

The marginal response of consumption to changes in *national income* ($\Delta C/\Delta Y$) is equal to the marginal propensity to consume out of *disposable income* ($\Delta C/\Delta Y_d$) multiplied by the frac-

TABLE 26-3	Consumption as a Function of Disposable Income and National Income (*billions of dollars*)	
(1) National income (Y)	(2) Disposable income ($Y_d = 0.9Y$)	(3) Desired consumption ($C = 100 + 0.8Y_d$)
$ 100	$ 90	$ 172
1,000	900	820
2,000	1,800	1,540
3,000	2,700	2,260
4,000	3,600	2,980

If desired consumption depends on disposable income, which in turn depends on national income, desired consumption can be written as a function of either income concept. The data are hypothetical. They show deductions of 10 percent of any level of national income to arrive at disposable income. Deductions of 10 percent of Y imply that the remaining 90 percent of Y becomes disposable income. The numbers also show consumption as $100 billion plus 80 percent of disposable income.

By relating columns 2 and 3, one sees consumption as a function of disposable income. By relating columns 1 and 3, one sees the derived relationship between consumption and national income. In this example the change in consumption in response to a change in disposable income (i.e., the *MPC*) is 0.8, while the change in consumption in response to a change in national income is 0.72.

tion of national income that becomes disposable income ($\Delta Y_d/\Delta Y$).

We now have a function that shows how desired consumption expenditure varies as national income varies. The relationship is defined for real income and real expenditure (i.e., income and expenditure measured in constant dollars). For every given level of real income, measured in terms of purchasing power, households desire to spend some fraction of that purchasing power and to save the rest.

Desired Net Exports

Although rich in natural resources, the United States is a major importer of raw materials and energy products, such as oil, electricity, and uranium. American households typically consume a wide range of imported goods, such as Japanese cars and Canadian furniture. The United States also exports a wide variety of American-made products to the rest of the world, such as jet airliners and plastic bags. Although foreign trade accounts for a smaller proportion of U.S. national income than it does for many other countries, U.S.-Canadian trade is the largest flow of trade between any two countries in the world today.

The Net Export Function

Exports depend on spending decisions made by foreign households that purchase American goods and services. Typically, therefore, exports will not change as a result of changes in American national income.

Imports, however, depend on the spending decisions of American households. All categories of expenditure have an import content; domestic cars, for example, use large quantities of imported components in their manufacture. Thus, imports rise when the other categories of expenditure rise. Because consumption rises with income, imports of foreign-produced consumption goods and materials that go into the production of domestically produced consumption goods also rise with income.

Desired net exports are negatively related to national income because of the positive relationship between desired expenditure on imports and national income.

This negative relationship between net exports and national income is called the *net export function*. Data for a hypothetical economy with constant exports and with imports that are 10 percent of national income are given in Table 26-4 and illustrated in Figure 26-3. In this example exports form the autonomous component and imports form the induced component of the desired net export function.

Shifts in the Net Export Function

We have seen that the net export function relates net exports ($X - M$) to national income. It is drawn on the assumption that everything that affects net exports, except domestic national income, remains constant. The major factors that must be held constant are foreign national income, domestic and foreign prices, and the exchange rate. A change in any

TABLE 26-4	A Net Export Schedule (*billions of dollars*)		
National income (Y)	Exports (X)	Imports (M = 0.10Y)	Net exports
$1,000	$240	$100	$ 140
2,000	240	200	40
2,400	240	240	0
3,000	240	300	−60
4,000	240	400	−160
5,000	240	500	−260

Net exports fall as national income rises. The data are hypothetical. They assume that exports are constant and that imports are 10 percent of national income. Net exports are then positive at low levels of national income and negative at high levels of national income.

of these will affect the amount of net exports that will occur at each level of American national income and hence will shift the net export function.

Notice that anything that affects American exports will change the values in the export column in Table 26-4 and so will shift the net export function parallel to itself, upward if exports increase and downward if exports decrease. Also notice that anything that affects the proportion of income that Americans wish to spend on imports will change the values in the import column in Table 26-4 and thus will change the slope of the net export function by making imports more or less responsive to changes in domestic income.

Foreign income. An increase in foreign income, other things being equal, will lead to an increase in the quantity of American goods demanded by foreign countries, that is, to an increase in American exports. The increase is in the constant X of the net export function, which shifts upward as a result. A fall in foreign income leads to a downward shift in the net export function.

Foreign prices. An increase in foreign prices will cause both foreign and domestic agents to substitute cheaper American goods for the now more expensive foreign goods. This will cause changes in both exports and imports. Exports will rise, and the amount of imports associated with any given level of American national income will fall. As a result, the net export function will shift upward. A fall in foreign

FIGURE 26-3   The Net Export Function

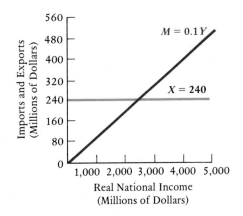

(i) Export and import functions

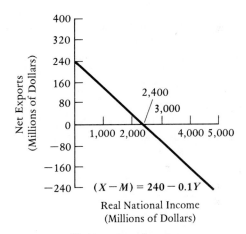

(ii) Net export function

Net exports, defined as the difference between exports and imports, are inversely related to the level of national income. In part (i) exports are constant at $240 million, while imports rise with the national income. Therefore, net exports, shown in part (ii), decline with national income. The figure is based on the hypothetical data in Table 26-4. With national income equal to $2,400 million, imports are equal to exports at $240 million and net exports are zero. For levels of national income below $2,400 million, imports are less than exports and hence net exports are positive. For levels of national income above $2,400 million, imports are greater than exports and hence net exports are negative. (Note that this is the only income-expenditure diagram with different scales on the two axes. If we had made both scales the same, the curve showing (X − M) would have been virtually indistinguishable from the income axes.)

prices has the reverse effect, with substitution away from American goods in favor of foreign goods and a downward shift in the net export curve.

Domestic prices. An increase in domestic prices leads both foreign and domestic agents to substitute foreign goods for the now more expensive American goods. The export part of net exports falls, and more imports will be associated with each level of domestic income. As a result, the net export function shifts downward. A fall in domestic prices leads to substitution in favor of American goods and an upward shift in the net export function.

The exchange rate. A depreciation of the American dollar means that foreigners must pay less of their money to buy one U.S. dollar, while Americans must pay more dollars to buy a unit of any foreign currency. As a result, expenditure shifts away from foreign goods and toward American goods. Americans will import less at each level of American national income, and foreigners will buy more of American export goods. The net export function thus shifts upward. An appreciation of the American dollar has the opposite effect, causing substitution of foreign for American goods, thus shifting the net export function downward.

Other Expenditure Categories

We have seen that desired consumption expenditure and desired net export expenditure each have an autonomous and an induced component. The induced components cause desired aggregate expenditure to depend on national income.

The relationship between desired aggregate expenditure and national income depends not only on desired consumption and net exports but also on the behavior of the other major expenditure categories, I and G. As we shall see in later chapters, changes in each of these play an important role in understanding changes in national income. For our present purposes of understanding how the equilibrium level of national income is determined, it is useful to keep things as simple as possible. Where we can, we treat these components as constant and include them in autonomous expenditure.

Desired investment expenditure. For the present it is convenient to study how the level of national income

adjusts to a fixed level of planned real investment. So we assume that firms plan to make a constant amount of fixed business investment in plant and equipment each year and that they plan to hold their inventories constant. In Chapter 29 we shall drop these assumptions and study the important effects on national income that are caused by changes in the level of desired investment.

Desired government expenditure on goods and services. Governments intend to spend, and succeed in spending, many billions of dollars on currently produced goods and services. In this chapter we take desired and actual real government expenditure as a constant. We assume that the real value of government expenditure does not change as the circumstances of the economy change. This assumption allows us to see how national income adjusts to a constant level of real government expenditure. In Chapter 30 we shall drop this assumption and study how national income responds to changes in desired and actual government expenditure.

The Aggregate Expenditure Function

The aggregate expenditure function relates the level of desired real expenditure to the level of real income. Total desired expenditure on the nation's output is the sum of desired consumption, investment, government, and net export expenditures, or

$$AE = C + I + G + (X - M)$$

Table 26-5 illustrates how such a function can be calculated, given the consumption function and the levels of desired investment, government, and net export expenditures at each level of income. In this specific case, autonomous expenditures are investment, government, exports, and the constant term in the consumption function. Induced expenditures are the induced part of consumption $(0.72Y)$ and imports $(0.10Y)$, and hence net imports $(X - M)$. The resulting aggregate expenditure function is illustrated in Figure 26-4.

The Propensity to Spend Out of National Income

Earlier we defined propensities to consume and to save that together account for all household disposable income. We now define propensities to spend

TABLE 26-5   The Aggregate Expenditure Function (*billions of dollars*)

National income (Y)	Desired consumption expenditure (C = 100 + 0.72Y)	Desired investment expenditure (I = 250)	Desired government expenditure (G = 170)	Desired net export expenditure (X − M = 240 − 0.10Y)	Desired aggregate expenditure (AE = C + I + G + [X − M])
$ 100	$ 172	$250	$170	$ 230	$ 822
400	388	250	170	200	1,008
500	460	250	170	190	1,070
1,000	820	250	170	140	1,380
2,000	1,540	250	170	40	2,000
3,000	2,260	250	170	−60	2,620
4,000	2,980	250	170	−160	3,240
5,000	3,700	250	170	−260	3,860

The aggregate expenditure function is the sum of desired consumption, investment, government, and net export expenditures. The table is based on the hypothetical data given in Tables 26-3 and 26-4. The autonomous components of desired aggregate expenditure are desired investment, desired government, desired export expenditures, and the constant term in desired consumption expenditure. The induced components are the second term in desired consumption expenditure (0.72Y) and desired imports (0.10Y).

The marginal response of consumption to a change in national income is 0.72, calculated as the product of the marginal propensity to consume (0.8) times the fraction of national income that becomes disposable income (0.9). Because this exceeds the marginal propensity to import out of national income (0.1), desired aggregate expenditure is positively related to national income, as shown in the column at the far right. The marginal response of desired aggregate expenditure to a change in national income, $\Delta AE/\Delta Y$, is 0.62.

and not to spend that together account for all national income.

The fraction of any increment to national income that will be spent on domestic production is measured by the change in aggregate expenditure divided by the change in income, symbolized by $\Delta AE/\Delta Y$. It is called the economy's **marginal propensity to spend.** The value of the marginal propensity to spend, which is something greater than zero but less than one, may be indicated by the letter z. The amount $1 - \Delta AE/\Delta Y$ is the fraction of any increment to national income that is not spent. This is the **marginal propensity not to spend.**[1] This makes the value of the marginal propensity not to spend $1 - z$.

To illustrate this, suppose that the economy produces $1.00 of extra income and that the response to this is governed by the relationships in Tables 26-3

and 26-4. Since $.10 is collected by the government as taxes, $.90 is converted into disposable income, and 80 percent of this amount ($.72) becomes consumption expenditure. However, import expenditure also rises by $.10, so expenditure on domestic goods, that is, aggregate expenditure, rises by $.62. Thus z, the marginal propensity to spend, is 0.62 (0.62/1.00). What is not spent on domestic output includes the $.10 in taxes, the $.18 of disposable income that is saved, and the $.10 of import expenditure, for a total of $.38. Hence, the marginal propensity not to spend, $1 - z$, is $1 - 0.62 = 0.38$.

Determining Equilibrium National Income

We are now ready to see what determines the *equilibrium* level of national income. Recall from Chapter 4 that equilibrium is a state of balance between opposing forces. When something is in equilibrium, there is no tendency for it to change; forces are acting on it, but they balance out, so the net result is *no*

---

[1] More fully, these terms would be called the marginal propensity to spend *on national income* and the marginal propensity not to spend *on national income*. Expenditures on imports are included in the latter. The marginal propensity not to spend $(1 - z)$ often is referred to as the *marginal propensity to withdraw*. Not spending a part of one's income amounts to a *withdrawal* from the circular flow of income, as described in Figure 3-1.

FIGURE 26-4 An Aggregate Expenditure Curve

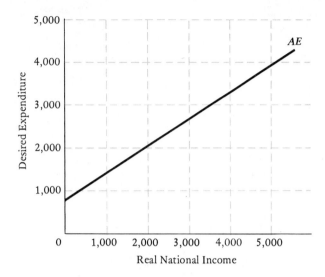

The aggregate expenditure curve relates total desired expenditure to national income. The *AE* curve in the figure plots the data from the first and the last columns of Table 26-5, which are repeated in Table 26-6. Its intercept (which in this case is $760) shows autonomous expenditure. Its slope (which in this case is 0.62) shows the marginal propensity to spend.

change. Any conditions that are required for something to be in equilibrium are called its *equilibrium conditions.*

Table 26-6 illustrates the determination of equilibrium national income for our simple hypothetical economy. Suppose that firms are producing a final output of $1,000 billion, and thus national income is $1,000 billion. According to the table, aggregate desired expenditure is $1,380 billion at this level of income. If firms persist in producing a current output of only $1,000 billion in the face of an aggregate desired expenditure of $1,380 billion, one of two things must happen.[2]

One possibility is that households, firms, and governments will be unable to spend the extra $380 billion that they would like to spend, so lines or waiting lists of unsatisfied customers will appear. These will send a signal to firms that they can in-

crease their sales if they increase their production. When the firms increase production, national income rises. Of course, the individual firms are interested only in their own sales and profits, but their individual actions have as their inevitable consequence an increase in GDP, that is the total of all firms' current production (the total of their values added).

The second possibility is that all spenders will spend everything that they wanted to spend. Then, however, expenditure will exceed current output, which can happen only when some expenditure plans are fulfilled by purchasing inventories of goods that were produced in the past. In this example the fulfillment of plans to purchase $1,380 billion worth of commodities in the face of a current output of only $1,000 billion will reduce inventories by $380 billion. As long as inventories last, more goods can be sold than are currently being produced.

Eventually, inventories will run out, but before this happens, firms will increase their output as they see their inventories being depleted. Extra sales then can be made without a further depletion of inven-

TABLE 26-6	The Determination of Equilibrium National Income (*billions of dollars*)	
National income (Y)	Desired aggregate expenditure (AE = C + I + G + [X − M])	
$ 100	$ 822	Pressure on
400	1,008	income to
500	1,070	rise
1,000	1,380	↓
2,000	2,000	Equilibrium income
3,000	2,620	↑
4,000	3,240	Pressure on
5,000	3,860	income to fall

National income is in equilibrium where aggregate desired expenditure equals national income. The data are copied from Table 26-5. When national income is below its equilibrium level, aggregate desired expenditure exceeds the value of current output. This creates an incentive for firms to increase output and hence for national income to rise. When national income is above its equilibrium level, aggregate desired expenditure is less than the value of current output. This creates an incentive for firms to reduce output and hence for national income to fall. Only at the equilibrium level of national income is aggregate desired expenditure exactly equal to the value of the current output.

---

[2] A third possibility, that prices would rise, has been excluded by assumption in this chapter.

tories. Once again, the consequence of each individual firm's behavior, in search of its own individual profits, is an increase in national income. Thus, the final response to an excess of aggregate desired expenditure over current output is a rise in national income.

At any level of national income at which aggregate desired expenditure exceeds total output, there will be pressure for national income to rise.

Next, consider the $4,000 billion level of national income in Table 26-6. At this level desired expenditure on domestically produced goods is only $3,240 billion. If firms persist in producing $4,000 billion worth of goods, $760 billion worth must remain unsold. Therefore, inventories must rise. However, firms will not allow inventories of unsold goods to rise indefinitely; sooner or later they will reduce the level of output to the level of sales. When they do, national income will fall.

At any level of income for which aggregate desired expenditure falls short of total output, there will be a pressure for national income to fall.

Finally, look at the national-income level of $2,000 billion in Table 26-6. At this level, and only at this level, aggregate desired expenditure is exactly equal to national income. Purchasers fulfill their spending plans without causing inventories to change. There is no incentive for firms to alter output. Since total output is the same as national income, national income will remain steady; it is in equilibrium.

The equilibrium level of national income occurs where aggregate desired expenditure equals total output.

This conclusion is quite general and does not depend on the numbers that are used in the specific example. **[34]**

Equilibrium Illustrated

Figure 26-5 shows the determination of the equilibrium level of national income. The line labeled *AE* graphs the aggregate expenditure function. Its slope

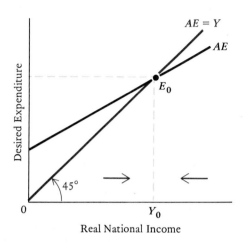

FIGURE 26-5   Equilibrium National Income

Equilibrium national income occurs at E_0, where the desired aggregate expenditure line intersects the 45° line. If real national income is below Y_0, desired aggregate expenditure will exceed national income, and production will rise. This is shown by the arrow to the left of Y_0. If national income is above Y_0, desired aggregate expenditure will be less than national income, and production will fall. This is shown by the arrow to the right of Y_0. Only when real national income is Y_0 will desired aggregate expenditure equal real national income.

is the marginal propensity to spend. The line labeled $AE = Y$ shows the equilibrium condition that desired aggregate expenditure, *AE*, equals national income, *Y*. Since the $AE = Y$ line plots points where the vertical distance equals the horizontal distance, it forms an angle of 45° with the axes. Any point on this line is a possible equilibrium.

Graphically, equilibrium occurs at the level of income at which the aggregate desired expenditure line intersects the 45° line. This is the level of income where desired expenditure is just equal to total national income and therefore is just sufficient to purchase total final output.

Now we have explained the equilibrium level of national income that arises at a *given price level*. In the next section we shall study the forces that cause equilibrium income to change. We shall see that shifts in desired consumption and investment expenditure can cause major swings in national income. We shall see also that changes in government spending and taxation policies can do the same.

Changes in National Income

Since the *AE* function plays a central role in our explanation of the equilibrium value of national income, you should not be surprised to hear that the behavior of the *AE* function also plays a central role in explaining why national income changes. (We continue to assume that the price level is constant.) To understand this influence, we must recall an important distinction first encountered in Chapter 4.

Suppose desired aggregate expenditure rises. This may be either a response to a change in national income or the result of an increased desire to spend at each level of national income. A change in national income causes a *movement along* the aggregate expenditure function. An increased desire to spend at each level of national income causes a *shift in* the aggregate expenditure function. Figure 26-6 illustrates this important distinction.

Shifts in the Aggregate Expenditure Function

For any specific aggregate expenditure function there is a unique level of equilibrium national income. If the aggregate expenditure function shifts, the equilibrium will be disturbed and national income will change. Thus, if we wish to find the causes of changes in national income, we must look for the causes of shifts in the *AE* function.

The aggregate expenditure function shifts when one of its components shifts, that is, when there is a shift in the consumption function, in desired investment expenditure, in desired government expenditure on goods and services, or in desired net exports. Such shifts were defined earlier as changes in *autonomous* aggregate expenditure.

Upward Shifts in Aggregate Expenditure Functions

What will happen if households permanently increase their levels of consumption spending at each level of disposable income; if the Ford Motor Company increases its rate of annual investment by $25 million in order to meet the threat from imported cars; if the government increases its defense spending; or if grain exports soar? (In considering these questions, re-

FIGURE 26-6   Movements Along and Shifts of the *AE* Curve

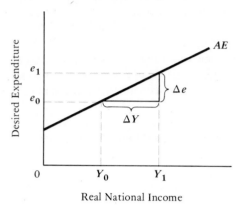

(i) A movement along the *AE* function

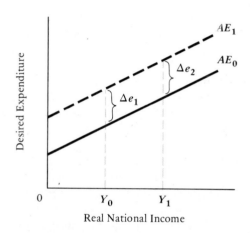

(ii) A shift of the *AE* function

A movement along the aggregate expenditure function occurs in response to a change in income; a shift of the *AE* function indicates a different level of desired expenditure at each level of income. In part (i) a change in income of ΔY, from Y_0 to Y_1, changes desired expenditure by Δe, from e_0 to e_1. In part (ii) a shift in the expenditure function from AE_0 to AE_1 raises the amount of expenditure associated with *each* level of income. At Y_0, for example, desired aggregate expenditure is increased by Δe_1; at Y_1, it is increased by Δe_2. (If the aggregate expenditure line shifts parallel to itself, $\Delta e_1 = \Delta e_2$.)

member that we are dealing with continuous flows measured as so much per period of time. An upward shift in the expenditure function means that the desired expenditure associated with each level of national income rises to and stays at a higher amount.)

Because any such increase shifts the entire aggregate expenditure function upward, the same analysis applies to all of the changes mentioned. Two types of shift in AE occur. First, if the same addition to expenditure occurs at all levels of income, the AE curve shifts parallel to itself, as shown in Figure 26-7(i). Second, if there is a change in the propensity to spend out of national income, the slope of the AE curve changes, as shown in Figure 26-7(ii). (Recall that the slope of the AE curve is z, the marginal propensity to spend.)

Figure 26-7 shows that upward shifts in the aggregate expenditure function increase equilibrium national income. After the shift in the AE curve, income is no longer in equilibrium at its original

---

FIGURE 26-7   Shifts in the AE Curve

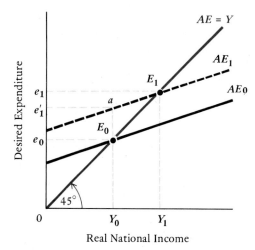

(i)   A parallel shift in AE

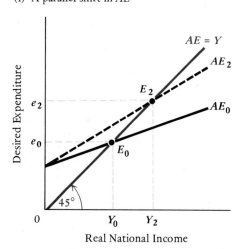

(ii)   A change in the slope of AE

Upward shifts in the AE curve increase equilibrium income; downward shifts decrease equilibrium income. In parts (i) and (ii) the aggregate expenditure curve is initially AE_0, with national income Y_0.

In part (i) a parallel upward *shift* in the AE curve from AE_0 to AE_1 means that desired expenditure has increased by the same amount at each level of national income. For example, at Y_0 desired expenditure rises from e_0 to e_1' and therefore exceeds national income. Equilibrium is reached at E_1, where income is Y_1 and expenditure is e_1. The increase in desired expenditure from e_1' to e_1, represented by a *movement along* AE_1, is an induced response to the increase in income from Y_0 to Y_1.

In part (ii) a nonparallel upward shift in the AE curve, say, from AE_0 to AE_2, means that the marginal propensity to spend at each level of national income has increased. This leads to an increase in equilibrium national income. Equilibrium is reached at E_2, where the new level of expenditure e_2 is equal to income Y_2. Again, the initial *shift* in the AE curve induces a *movement along* the new AE curve.

Downward shifts in the AE curve, from AE_1 to AE_0 or from AE_2 to AE_0, lead to a fall in equilibrium income to Y_0.

level because at that level desired expenditure exceeds national income. Equilibrium national income now occurs at the higher level indicated by the intersection of the new *AE* curve with the 45° line, along which aggregate expenditures equal real national income.

Downward Shifts in Aggregate Expenditure Functions

What will happen to national income if consumption, investment, government spending, or exports decrease? All these changes shift the aggregate expenditure function downward. A constant reduction in expenditure at all levels of income shifts *AE* parallel to itself. A fall in the marginal propensity to spend out of national income reduces the slope of the *AE* function.

Changes in Tax Rates

If tax rates change, the relationship between disposable income and national income changes.[3] For the same level of national income there will be a different level of disposable income and thus a different level of consumption. This is illustrated in Table 26-7. Consequently, *z*, the marginal propensity to spend out of national income, will have changed.

Consider a decrease in tax rates. If the government decreases its rate of income tax so that it collects $.05 less out of every dollar of national income, disposable income rises in relation to national income. Thus, consumption also rises at every level of national income. This results in a (nonparallel) upward shift of the *AE* curve, that is, a change in the slope of the curve, as shown in Figure 26-7(ii). The result of this shift will be a rise in equilibrium national income, as is also shown in Figure 26-7(ii).

A rise in taxes has the opposite effect. A rise in tax rates results in less disposable income and hence less consumption expenditure at each level of national income. This results in a (nonparallel) downward shift of the *AE* curve and thus decreases the level of equilibrium national income. This, too, is illustrated in Figure 26-7(ii).

---

[3] Effective tax rates can be changed either by changes in the percent of taxable income that is taken in taxes or by changes in the percent of national income that is taxable. For the sake of simplicity, in the text we have assumed that all national income is taxable.

The results restated. Now we have derived two important general predictions of the elementary theory of national income.

1. **A rise in the amount of desired consumption, investment, government, or export expenditure that is associated with each level of national income will increase equilibrium national income.**
2. **A fall in the amount of desired consumption, investment, government, or export expenditure that is associated with each level of national income will lower equilibrium national income.**

A change in desired consumption in relation to national income can arise, as we have seen, either because the consumption function shifts or because the relationship between disposable income and national income is altered.

The Multiplier

Now we can predict the *direction* of the changes in national income that occur in response to various shifts in the aggregate expenditure function. We would like also to be able to predict the *magnitude* of these changes.

Economists need to know the *size* of the effects of changes in expenditures in both the private and the public sectors. During a recession the government often takes measures to stimulate the economy. If these measures have a larger effect than estimated, demand may rise too much and full employment may be reached with demand still rising. This outcome will have an inflationary impact on the economy. If the government greatly overestimates the effect of its measures, the recession will persist longer than is necessary. In this case there is a danger that the policy will be discredited as ineffective, even though the correct diagnosis is that too little of the right thing was done.

Definition. A measure of the magnitude of changes in income is provided by the multiplier. We have just seen that a shift in the aggregate expenditure curve will cause a change in equilibrium national income. Such a shift will be caused by a change in any autonomous component of aggregate expenditure, for

TABLE 26-7   Tax Changes Shift the Function Relating Consumption to National Income (*billions of dollars*)

(1) National income (Y)	Disposable income equal to 80 percent of national income (tax rate = 0.2)		Disposable income equal to 90 percent of national income (tax rate = 0.1)	
	(2) Disposable income ($Y_d = 0.8Y$)	(3) Consumption ($C = 100 + 0.8Y_d$)	(4) Disposable income ($Y_d = 0.9Y$)	(5) Consumption ($C = 100 + 0.8Y_d$)
$ 100	$ 80	$164	$ 90	$172
500	400	420	450	460
1,000	800	740	900	820

The consumption function shifts if the relationship between disposable and national income changes. The table is based on the simplified hypothetical consumption function from Table 26-1 combined with the assumption that Y_d is a constant fraction of Y. Initially, $Y_d = 0.8Y$. This yields a schedule relating consumption to national income that is given in columns 1 and 3 and is described by the equation $C = 100 + 0.64Y$. Income-tax rates are then decreased so that now 90 percent of national income becomes disposable income. Column 4 indicates the Y_d that corresponds at the decreased tax rate to each level of Y shown in column 1. With an unchanged consumption function, consumption at the new tax rate is given by column 5. Columns 1 and 5 give the new schedule relating consumption to national income, described by the equation $C = 100 + 0.72Y$.

example, an increase or decrease in investment or government spending. An increase in desired aggregate expenditure increases equilibrium national income by a multiple of the initial increase in autonomous expenditure. The **multiplier** is the ratio of the change in income to the change in autonomous expenditure, that is, the change in national income *divided by* the change in autonomous expenditure that brought it about.

Why the multiplier is greater than unity. What will happen to national income if, with unchanged tax rates, the government increases its spending on road construction by $1 billion per year?

Initially, the road construction program will create $1 billion worth of new national income and a corresponding amount of employment for households and firms on which the initial $1 billion is spent, but this is not the end of the story. The increase in national income of $1 billion will cause an increase in disposable income, which will cause an induced rise in consumption expenditure. Road crews and road contractors, who gain new income directly from the government's road construction program, will spend some of it on food, clothing, entertainment, cars, television sets, and other commodities. When output

expands to meet this demand, employment will increase in all the affected industries. New incomes will then be created for workers and firms in these industries. When they, in turn, spend their newly earned incomes, output and employment will rise further. More income will be created, and more expenditure will be induced. Indeed, at this stage we might wonder whether the increases in income will ever come to an end. To deal with this concern, we need to consider the multiplier in somewhat more precise terms.

The simple multiplier. Consider an increase in autonomous expenditure of ΔA, which might be, say, $1 billion per year. Remember that ΔA stands for *any* increase in autonomous expenditure; this could be an increase in investment, in government purchases, in exports, or in the autonomous component of consumption. The new autonomous expenditure shifts the aggregate expenditure function upward by that amount. National income is no longer in equilibrium at its original level, since desired aggregate expenditure now exceeds income. Equilibrium is restored by a *movement along* the new AE curve.

The **simple multiplier** measures the change in equilibrium national income that occurs in response

FIGURE 26-8   The Simple Multiplier

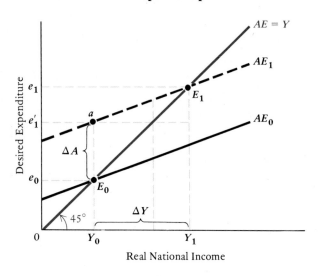

Real National Income

An increase in the autonomous component of desired aggregate expenditure increases equilibrium national income by a multiple of the initial increase. The initial equilibrium is at E_0, where AE_0 intersects the 45° line. At this point, desired expenditure, e_0, is equal to national income, Y_0. An increase in autonomous expenditure of ΔA then shifts the desired expenditure function upward to AE_1. If national income stays at Y_0, desired expenditure rises to e_1' (the coordinates of point a are Y_0 and e_1'). Since this level of desired expenditure is greater than national income, national income will rise.

Equilibrium occurs when income rises to Y_1. Here desired expenditure, e_1, equals income, Y_1. The extra expenditure of $e_1'e_1$ represents the induced increases in expenditure. It is the amount by which the final increase in income, ΔY, exceeds the initial increase in autonomous expenditure, ΔA. Since ΔY is greater than ΔA, the multiplier is greater than unity.

to a change in autonomous expenditure *at a constant price level*. We refer to it as "simple" because we have simplified the situation by assuming that the price level is fixed. Figure 26-8 illustrates the simple multiplier and makes clear that it is greater than unity. Box 26-1 provides a numerical example.

The Size of the Simple Multiplier

The size of the simple multiplier depends on the slope of the AE function, that is, on the marginal propensity to spend, z. This is illustrated in Figure 26-8.

A high marginal propensity to spend means a steep AE curve. The expenditure induced by any initial increase in income is large, with the result that the final rise in income is correspondingly large. By contrast, a low marginal propensity to spend means a relatively flat AE curve. The expenditure induced by the initial increase in income is small, and the final rise in income is not much larger than the initial rise in autonomous expenditure that brought it about.

The larger is the marginal propensity to spend, the steeper is the aggregate expenditure function and the larger is the multiplier.

The precise value of the simple multiplier can be derived by using elementary algebra. (The derivation is given in Box 26-2.) The result is that the simple multiplier, which we call K, is

$$K = \frac{\Delta Y}{\Delta A} = \frac{1}{1 - z}$$

where z is the marginal propensity to spend out of national income. (As we have seen, z is the slope of the aggregate expenditure function.)

As we saw earlier, the term $1 - z$ stands for the marginal propensity not to spend out of national income. For example, if \$.80 of every \$1.00 of new national income is spent ($z = 0.80$), then \$.20 is the amount not spent. The value of the multiplier is then calculated as $K = 1/0.20 = 5$.

The simple multiplier can be written as the reciprocal of the marginal propensity not to spend.

From this we see that, if $1 - z$ is small, the multiplier will be large (because extra income induces much extra spending). What if $1 - z$ is large? The largest possible value of $1 - z$ is unity, which arises

BOX 26-1

The Multiplier: A Numerical Example

Consider an economy that has a marginal propensity to spend out of national income of 0.80. Suppose that autonomous expenditure increases by $1 billion per year because the government spends an extra $1 billion per year on new roads. National income initially rises by $1 billion, but that is not the end of it. The factors of production involved in road building that received the first $1 billion spend $800 million. This second round of spending generates $800 million of new income. This new income, in turn, induces $640 million of third-round spending, and so it continues, with each successive round of new income generating 80 percent as much in new expenditure. Each additional round of expenditure creates new income and yet another round of expenditure.

The table carries the process through 10 rounds. Students with sufficient patience (and no faith in mathematics) may compute as many rounds in the process as they wish; they will find that the sum of the rounds of expenditures approaches a limit of $5 billion, which is five times the initial increase in expenditure. [35] The graph of the cumulative expenditure increases shows how quickly this limit is approached. The multiplier is thus 5, given the assumption about the marginal propensity to spend. Had the marginal propensity to spend been lower, say, 0.667, the process would have been similar, but it would have approached a limit of three instead of five times the initial increase in expenditure.

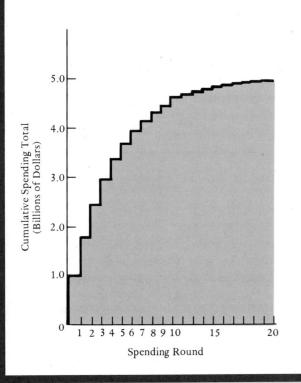

Round of spending	Increase in expenditure (millions of dollars)	Cumulative total (millions of dollars)
Initial increase	$1,000.0	$1,000.0
2	800.0	1,800.0
3	640.0	2,440.0
4	512.0	2,952.0
5	409.6	3,361.6
6	327.7	3,689.3
7	262.1	3,951.4
8	209.7	4,161.1
9	167.8	4,328.9
10	134.2	4,463.1
11 to 20 combined	479.3	4,942.4
All others	57.6	5,000.0

when z equals zero, indicating that none of any additional national income is spent. In this case the multiplier itself has a value of unity; the increase in equilibrium national income is confined to the initial increase in autonomous expenditure. There are no induced additional effects on spending, so national income only increases by the original increase in autonomous expenditure. The relation between $1 - z$ and the size of the multiplier is illustrated in Figure 26-9.

BOX 26-2

The Multiplier: An Algebraic Approach

High-school algebra is all that is needed to derive the exact expression for the multiplier. Readers who feel at home with algebra may want to follow this derivation. Others can skip it and rely on the graphical and numerical arguments that have been given in the text.

First, we derive the equation for the AE curve. Aggregate expenditure is divided into autonomous expenditure, A, and induced expenditure, N^*, so we write

$$AE = N + A \qquad [1]$$

Since N is expenditure on domestically produced output that varies with income, we can write

$$N = zY \qquad [2]$$

where z is the marginal propensity to spend out of national income. (It is a positive number between zero and unity.) Substituting Equation 2 in Equation 1 yields the equation of the AE curve.

$$AE = zY + A \qquad [3]$$

Now we write the equation of the 45° line,

$$AE = Y \qquad [4]$$

* In simple models N is mainly consumption expenditure, but in other models it may include other types of expenditure. All that matters is that there is one class of expenditure, N, that varies with income and another class, A, that does not.

which states the equilibrium condition that desired aggregate expenditure must equal national income. Equations 3 and 4 are two equations with two unknowns, AE and Y. To solve them we substitute Equation 3 in Equation 4 to obtain

$$Y = zY + A$$

Subtracting zY from both sides yields

$$Y - zY = A$$

Factoring out Y yields

$$Y(1 - z) = A$$

Dividing through by $1 - z$ yields

$$Y = A/(1 - z)$$

This tells us the equilibrium value of Y in terms of autonomous expenditures A and the propensity not to spend out of national income $(1 - z)$. The expression $Y = A/(1 - z)$ tells us that if A changes by ΔA, the change in Y, which we call ΔY, will be

$$\Delta Y = \Delta A/(1 - z)$$

Dividing through by ΔA gives the value of the multiplier, which we designate by K:

$$K = \Delta Y/\Delta A = 1/(1 - z)$$

To estimate the size of the multiplier in an actual economy, we need to estimate the value of the marginal propensity not to spend out of national income in that economy, that is, $1 - z$. Evidence suggests that the American value is larger than the 0.2 that we used in our example.

The various elements of national income that are "not spent" include income taxes, savings, and import expenditures. For the U.S. economy in the

1980s, this leads to a realistic estimate of something that is a little more than 0.5 for $1 - z$. Thus, the simple multiplier is something less than 2, not 5, as in the example.

The simple multiplier is a useful starting point for understanding the effects of expenditure shifts on national income; however, as we shall see in subsequent chapters, many complications will arise.

FIGURE 26-9   The Size of the Simple Multiplier

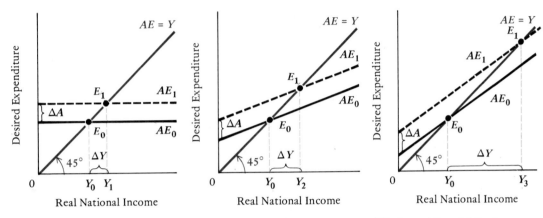

(i) Flat *AE*, multiplier unity   (ii) Intermediate case   (iii) Steep *AE*, multiplier large

The larger is the marginal propensity to spend out of national income (z), the steeper is the AE curve and the larger is the multiplier. In each part of the figure the initial aggregate expenditure function is AE_0, equilibrium is at E_0, with income Y_0. The *AE* curve then shifts upward to AE_1 as a result of an increase in autonomous expenditure of ΔA. ΔA is the same in each part. The new equilibrium is at E_1.

In part (i) the *AE* function is horizontal, indicating a marginal propensity to spend of zero ($z = 0$). The change in income ΔY is only the increase in autonomous expenditure, since there is no induced expenditure by those who receive the initial increase in income. The simple multiplier is then unity, its minimum possible value.

In part (ii) the *AE* curve slopes upward but is still relatively flat (z is low). The increase in national income to Y_2 is only slightly greater than the increase in autonomous expenditure that brought it about.

In part (iii) the *AE* function is quite steep (z is high). Now the increase in income to Y_3 is much larger than the increase in autonomous expenditure that brought it about. The simple multiplier is quite large.

SUMMARY

1. Desired aggregate expenditure includes desired consumption, desired investment, and desired government expenditures plus desired net exports. It is the amount that decision makers want to spend on purchasing the national product.

2. A change in disposable income leads to a change in consumption and saving. The responsiveness of these changes is measured by the marginal propensity to consume (*MPC*) and the marginal propensity to save (*MPS*), which are both positive and sum to one.

3. A change in wealth tends to cause a change in the allocation of disposable income between consumption and saving. The change in consumption is positively related to the change in wealth, while the change in saving is negatively related to this change.

4. Since desired imports increase as national income increases, desired net exports decrease as national income increases, other things being equal. This gives rise to a negatively sloped net export function.

5. In the simple theory of this chapter, investment expenditures, gov-

ernment expenditures, export expenditures, and the constant term in the consumption function are all autonomous expenditures, while imports and the part of consumption that responds to income are induced expenditures.

6. At the equilibrium level of national income, purchasers wish to buy neither more nor less than what is being produced. At incomes above equilibrium, desired expenditure falls short of national income, and output will sooner or later be curtailed. At incomes below equilibrium, desired expenditure exceeds national income, and output will sooner or later be increased.

7. Equilibrium national income is represented graphically by the point at which the aggregate expenditure curve cuts the 45° line, that is, where total desired expenditure equals total output.

8. With a constant price level, equilibrium real national income is increased by a rise in the desired consumption, investment, government, or export expenditure that is associated with each level of the national income. Equilibrium national income is decreased by a fall in desired expenditures.

9. Equilibrium national income is negatively related to the amount of tax revenue that is associated with each level of national income.

10. The magnitude of the effect on national income of shifts in autonomous expenditure is given by the multiplier. It is defined as $K = \Delta Y / \Delta A$, where ΔA is the change in autonomous expenditure.

11. The simple multiplier is the multiplier when the price level is constant. It is equal to $1/(1 - z)$, where z is the marginal propensity to spend out of national income. Thus, the larger z is, the larger is the multiplier. It is a basic prediction of national income theory that the simple multiplier is greater than unity.

TOPICS FOR REVIEW

Desired expenditure
Consumption function
Average and marginal propensities to consume and to save
Aggregate expenditure function
Marginal propensities to spend and not to spend
Equilibrium national income at a given price level
Shifts of and movements along expenditure curves
Effect on national income of changes in desired expenditures
Effect on national income of changes in tax rates
The simple multiplier
The size of the multiplier and slope of the AE curve

DISCUSSION QUESTIONS

1. "The concept of an equilibrium level of national income is useless because the economy is never in equilibrium. If it ever got there, no economist would recognize it anyway." Discuss this quotation.

2. Interpret each of the following statements either in terms of the shape of a consumption function or the values of *MPC* and *APC*.
   a. "Tom Green has lost his job, and his family is existing on its past savings."
   b. "The Grimsby household is so rich that they used all the extra income they earned this year to invest in a wildcat oil-drilling venture."
   c. "The widow Hammerstein can barely make ends meet by clipping

coupons on the bonds left to her by dear Henry, but she would never dip into her capital."

d. "We always thought Harris was a miser, but when his wife left him he took to wine, women, and song."

e. "The inflation has made the Schultzes feel so poor that they are adding an extra $100 a week to their account at the Savings Bank."

f. "The last stock market crash led young Ross to cancel two planned trips abroad, even though his job as a broker was never at risk."

3. Why might an individual's marginal propensity to consume be higher in the long run than in the short run? Why might it be lower? Is it possible for an individual's average propensity to consume to be greater than unity in the short run? In the long run? Can a country's average propensity to consume be greater than unity in the short run? In the long run?

4. What relationship holds along the 45° line between total expenditures and total income? In determining equilibrium graphically, are we restricted to choosing identical vertical and horizontal scales?

5. Explain carefully why national income changes when desired aggregate expenditure does not equal national income. Sketch scenarios that fit the cases of too much and too little desired expenditure.

6. Explain how a sudden unexpected fall in consumer expenditure would initially cause an increase in investment expenditure by firms.

7. What relationship is suggested by the following newspaper headline: "Auto sales soar as recovery booms"?

8. State the implied impact on the *AE* curve and hence on equilibrium national income that relates to each of the following headlines.

a. "Washington's planned spending up 10%."

b. "Soviet Union agrees to buy more American wheat."

c. "Major American companies expected to cut capital outlays."

d. "Congress considers decreasing personal-income-tax rates."

9. Locate at least two current press stories that suggest shifts in the *AE* curve.

Appendix to Chapter 26

The Permanent-Income and Life-Cycle Hypotheses of Household Consumption

In the Keynesian theory of the consumption function, current consumption expenditure is related to current income—either current disposable income or current national income. As we saw in the chapter, more recent theories relate consumption to some longer-term concept of income than the income that the household is currently earning.

The two most influential theories of this type are the **permanent-income theory** *(PIT),* developed by Professor Friedman, and the **life-cycle theory** *(LCT),* developed by Professors Modigliani, Ando, and Brumberg. Although there are differences between these, it is their similiarities that are important. In particular, we note that, in both the PIT and the LCT, household behavior tends to smooth the time pattern of consumption relative to that of disposable income. Later in this appendix we consider a potentially important difference between the two hypotheses.

In discussing this "consumption-smoothing" issue, it is important to ask: What variables do these theories seek to explain? What assumptions do they make? What are the major implications of these assumptions?

Variables

Three variables need to be considered: consumption, saving, and income. Keynesian-type theories seek to explain the amounts that households spend on purchasing goods and services for consumption. This concept is called *consumption expenditure.* Permanent-income theories seek to explain the actual flows of consumption of the *services* that are provided by the commodities that households buy. This concept is called *actual consumption.*[1]

With services and nondurable goods, expenditure and actual consumption occur more or less at the same time, and the distinction between the two concepts is not important. Consumption of a haircut, for example, occurs at the time that it is purchased, and an orange or a package of corn flakes is consumed very soon after it is purchased. Thus, if we knew when purchases of such goods and services were made, say, last year, we would also know last year's consumption of those goods and services.

This, however, is not the case with durable consumer goods. A house is purchased at one point in time, but it yields its services over a long period of time, possibly as long as the purchaser's lifetime. The same is true of a personal computer and a watch and, over a shorter period of time, of a car and a dress. For such products, if we know last year's purchases we do not necessarily know last year's consumption of the services that the products yielded.

Thus, one important characteristic of durable goods is that *expenditure* to purchase them is not necessarily synchronized with *consumption* of the stream of services that the goods provide. If in 1988 Ms. Smith buys a car for $12,000, uses it for six years, and then discards it as worn out, her expenditure on automobiles is $12,000 in 1988 and zero for the next five years. Her consumption of the services of automobiles, however, is spread out at an average annual rate of $2,000 for six years. If everyone followed Ms. Smith's example and bought a new car in 1988 and replaced it in 1993, the automobile industry would undergo wild booms in 1988 and 1993 with five intervening years of slump, even though the actual consumption of automobiles would be spread more or less evenly over time. This example is extreme, but it illustrates the possibilities, where consumer durable goods are concerned, of quite different time paths of *consumption expenditure,* which is the subject of Keynesian theories of consumption, and *actual consumption,* which is the subject of permanent-income theories.

---

[1] Because Keynes' followers did not always distinguish carefully between the concepts of consumption expenditure and actual consumption, the word *consumption* often is used in both contexts. We follow this normal practice, but where there is any possible ambiguity in the term we will refer to *consumption expenditure* and *actual consumption.*

Now consider saving. The change in emphasis from consumption expenditure to actual consumption implies a change in the definition of saving. Saving is no longer income minus consumption expenditure; it is now income minus the value of actual consumption. When Ms. Smith spent $12,000 on her car in 1988 but used only $2,000 worth of its services during that year, she was actually consuming $2,000 and saving $10,000. The purchase of a consumer-durable good is thus counted as saving, and only the value of its services actually consumed is counted as consumption.

The third important variable is income. Instead of using current income, the theories use a concept of long-term income. The precise definition varies from one theory to another, but basically it is related to the household's expected income stream over a fairly long planning period. In the LCT it is the income that the household expects to earn over its lifetime, called its *lifetime income*.

Every household is assumed to have a view of its lifetime income. This is not as unreasonable as it might seem. Students who are training to become doctors have a very different view of expected lifetime income than those who are training to become schoolteachers. Both expected income streams—for a doctor and for a schoolteacher—will be different from that expected by an assembly line worker or a professional athlete. One possible lifetime income stream is shown in Figure 26A-1.

The household's expected lifetime income is then converted into a single figure for annual **permanent income.** In the life-cycle theory this permanent income is the maximum amount that the household could spend on consumption each year into the indefinite future without accumulating debts that are passed on to future generations.[2] If a household were to consume a constant amount that was equal to its permanent income each year, it would add to its debts in years when current income was less than permanent income and would reduce its debt or increase its assets in years when its current income exceeded its permanent income. Over its lifetime, however, it would just break even, leaving neither accumulated assets nor debts to its heirs. If the interest rate were zero, permanent income would be

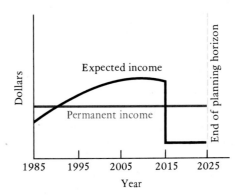

FIGURE 26A-1   Current Income and Permanent Income

Expected current income may vary greatly over a lifetime, but expected permanent income is defined to be the constant annual equivalent. The graph shows a hypothetical expected income stream from work for a household whose planning horizon was 40 years from 1985. The current income rises to a peak, then falls slowly for a while, and finally falls sharply on retirement. The corresponding permanent income is the amount that the household could consume at a steady rate over its lifetime by borrowing early against future earnings (as do most newly married couples), then repaying past debts, and finally saving for retirement when income is at its peak without either incurring debt or accumulating new wealth to be passed on to future generations.

just the sum of all expected incomes divided by the number of expected years of life. With a positive interest rate, permanent income will diverge from this amount because of the cost of borrowing and the extra income that can be earned by investing savings.

Assumption

The basic assumption of this type of theory, whether it is the PIT or LCT, is that the household's actual consumption is related to its permanent rather than to its current income. Two households that have the same permanent income (and are similar in other relevant characteristics) will have similar consumption patterns, even though their current incomes may behave differently.

[2] In the PIT the household has an infinite time horizon, and the relevant permanent-income concept is the amount that the household could consume forever without increasing or decreasing its present stock of wealth.

Implications

The major implication of these theories is that changes in a household's current income will affect its actual consumption only so far as they affect its permanent income. Consider two income changes that could occur in a household with a permanent income of $20,000 per year and an expected lifetime of 30 or more years. In the first case suppose that the household receives an unexpected extra income of $2,000 *for this year only*. The increase in the household's permanent income is small. If the rate of interest were zero, the household could consume an extra $66.66 per year for the rest of its expected life span; with a positive rate of interest, the extra annual consumption would be more because money not spent this year could be invested and would earn interest.[3] In the second case suppose that the household gets a totally unforeseen increase of $2,000 per year *for the rest of its life*. In this event the household's permanent income has risen by $2,000 because the household actually can consume $2,000 more every year without accumulating new debts. Although in both cases current income rises by $2,000, the effect on permanent income is very different.

Keynesian theory assumes that *consumption expenditure* is related to current income and therefore predicts the same change in this year's consumption expenditure in each of the cases just discussed. Permanent-income theories relate *actual consumption* to permanent income and therefore predict different changes in actual consumption in each case. In the first case there would be only a small increase in actual annual consumption; in the second case there would be a large increase.

In the LCT and the PIT, any change in current income that is thought to be temporary will have only a small effect on permanent income and hence on actual consumption.

Implications for the Behavior of the Economy

According to the permanent-income and the life-cycle hypotheses, actual consumption is not affected much by temporary changes in income. Does this mean that aggregate expenditure, $C + I + G + (X - M)$, is not affected much? This is not necessarily true. Consider what happens when households get a temporary increase in their incomes. If actual consumption is not greatly affected by this, then households must be saving most of this increase. However, from the point of view of these theories, households save when they buy a durable good just as much as when they buy a financial asset, such as a stock or a bond. In both cases actual current consumption is not changed.

Thus, spending a temporary increase in income on bonds or on new cars is consistent with both the PIT and the LCT, but it makes a great deal of difference to the short-run behavior of the economy which one of these choices is made. If households buy stocks and bonds, aggregate expenditure on currently produced final goods will not rise when income rises temporarily.[4] If households buy automobiles or any other durable consumer good, aggregate expenditure on currently produced final goods will rise when income rises temporarily. Thus, the PIT and the LCT leave unsettled the question that is critical in determining the size of the multiplier: What is the reaction of household *expenditures* on currently produced goods and services, particularly durables, to short-term, temporary changes in income?

Assume, for example, that a serious recessionary gap emerges and that the government attempts to stimulate a recovery by giving tax rebates and by cutting tax rates—both on an announced, temporary basis. This will raise households' current disposable incomes by the amount of the tax cuts, but it will raise their permanent incomes by only a small amount. According to the PIH, the flow of actual current consumption should not rise much. Yet it is quite consistent with the PIH that households should spend their tax savings on durable consumer goods, the consumption of which can be spread over many years.

In this case, even though actual consumption this year would not respond much to the tax cuts, expenditure would respond a great deal. Since current output and employment depend on expenditure rather than on actual consumption, the tax cut would

---

[3] If the rate of interest were 7 percent, the household could invest the $2,000, consume an extra $161 per year, and have nothing left at the end of 30 years.

[4] An exception to this is if there are such indirect effects as changes in interest rates; there are also a dozen other ways.

be effective in stimulating the economy. However, it is also consistent with the LCT and the PIT that households spend only a small part of their tax savings on consumption goods and seek to invest the rest in bonds and other financial assets. In this case the tax cuts may have only a small stimulating effect on the economy. It is important to note that the PIT and the LCT do *not predict unambiguously* that changes in taxes that are announced to be only short-lived will be ineffective in removing inflationary or deflationary gaps.

Chapter 27

National Income and the Price Level in the Short Run

The economy is constantly being buffeted by shocks. On the supply side, the prices of imported materials that are used by American manufacturing firms change frequently and sometimes dramatically, as when oil prices soared during 1974–1975 and 1979–1980. On the demand side, a boom in less developed countries can increase the exports of American-made goods that go to those countries, as happened during the 1970s. A domestic tax cut can lead to an increase in spending, as happened during the 1980s.

Virtually all such shocks affect both national income and the price level; that is, they have both real and nominal effects, at least initially. To understand these effects, we need to drop the assumption that the price level is constant and also to develop some further tools, called the *aggregate demand curves* and *aggregate supply curves*.

We make the transition to a variable price level in two steps. First, we study the consequences for national income of exogenous change in the price level—changes that happen for reasons that are not explained by our model of the economy. Then we use our model to *explain* movements in both national income *and* the price level.

 ## Exogenous Changes in the Price Level

What happens to equilibrium national income when the price changes for some exogenous reason, such as a rise in the price of imported raw materials? To find out, we need to understand how the change affects the desired aggregate expenditure curve.

Shifts in the *AE* Curve

There is one key result that we need to establish: A rise in the price level shifts the aggregate expenditure curve downward, while a fall in the price level shifts it upward. In other words, the price level and the desired aggregate expenditure are negatively related to each other. The explanation lies with two effects: what the change in the price level does to desired consumption expenditure and what it does to net exports.

In most cases, it is sufficient to look in detail at the implications of an increase in the price level, since a decrease merely reverses everything.

Changes in Consumption

Much of the private sector's total wealth is held in the form of assets with a fixed nominal money value. One obvious example is money itself—cash and bank deposits. Other examples are provided by many kinds of debt, including treasury bills and bonds. When a bill or a bond matures, the owner is repaid a stated sum of money. What that money can buy—its real value—depends on the price level. For this reason, a rise in the domestic price level lowers the real value of all assets that are denominated in money units, and hence lowers the wealth of their owners.

How does a fall in the real value of the private sector's wealth affect the aggregate expenditure curve?[1] As we saw in Chapter 26 (see Figure 26-2 on page 535), there is a relationship between wealth and consumption. Because households have less wealth, they increase their saving so as to restore their wealth to the level that they desire for such purposes as retirement. An increase in saving, of course, implies a reduction in consumption.

A rise in the domestic price level lowers the real value of total wealth, which leads to a fall in desired consumption; this, in turn, implies a downward shift in the desired aggregate expenditure curve. A fall in the domestic price level leads to a rise in wealth and desired consumption and thus to an upward shift in the desired aggregate expenditure curve.

We have concentrated here on the direct effect of the change in wealth on desired consumption expenditure. There is also an indirect effect that operates through the interest rate. Although this effect is potentially very powerful, we cannot study it until we have studied the macroeconomic role of money and

interest rates. Further discussion of this point must therefore be postponed until Chapter 32.[2]

Changes in Net Exports

When the domestic price level rises, American goods become more expensive relative to foreign goods. As we saw in Chapter 26, this change in relative prices causes Americans to reduce their purchases of American goods, which now have become relatively more expensive, and to increase their purchases of foreign goods, which now have become relatively less expensive. At the same time, consumers in other countries reduce their purchases of the now relatively expensive American goods. We saw in Chapter 26 that these changes can be summarized as a downward shift in the net export function.

A rise in the domestic price level shifts the net export function downward, which means a downward shift in the desired aggregate expenditure curve. A fall in the domestic price level shifts the net export function and the desired aggregate expenditure curves upward.

In simple language, if American goods become more expensive, less of them will be bought by foreigners, so total desired expenditure on American output will fall; if American goods become cheaper, more will be bought, and total desired expenditure on them will rise.

Changes in Equilibrium Income

Because it causes downward shifts in both the net export and the desired consumption curves, a rise in the price level causes a downward shift in the aggregate desired expenditure curve, as shown in Figure

---

[1] It is worth noting that changes in the real value of a person's wealth do not necessarily change the total wealth of the private sector. In many cases the change in wealth of a creditor is exactly offset by the change in wealth of a debtor. For example, a rise in the price level lowers the real wealth of a bondholder but raises the real wealth of the bond issuer, who will have to part with less purchasing power when the bond is redeemed. However, many assets held by individuals are government debt, and hence any change in the price level causes a net change in the wealth of the private sector.

[2] Here is a brief summary of what is involved. When the price level rises, firms and households need to cover their increased money expenses between one payday and the next. This means that they need to hold more money on average. The increased demand for money bids up the price that must be paid to borrow money (the interest rate). Firms that borrow money to build plants and to purchase equipment and households that borrow money to buy consumer goods and housing respond to rising interest rates by choosing to spend less on a host of items such as capital goods, housing, automobiles, and many other durable goods. This means that there is a decrease in the aggregate demand for the nation's output.

FIGURE 27-1 Aggregate Expenditure and the Price Level

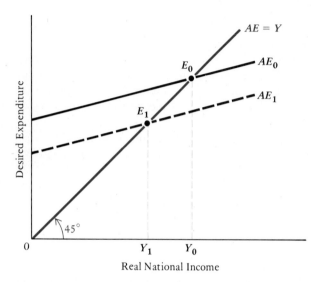

Changes in the price level cause the *AE* curve to shift and thus cause equilibrium national income to change. At the initial price level, the *AE* curve is given by the solid line AE_0, and hence equilibrium national income is Y_0. An increase in the price level reduces desired aggregate expenditure and thus causes the *AE* curve to shift downward to the dashed line, AE_1. As a result equilibrium national income falls to Y_1.

Starting with the dashed line, AE_1, a fall in the price level increases desired aggregate expenditure, shifting the *AE* curve up to AE_0 and raising equilibrium national income to Y_1.

27-1. Figure 27-1 also allows us to reconfirm what we already know from Chapter 26: When the *AE* curve shifts downward, the equilibrium level of national income falls.

Since a rise in the domestic price level causes the aggregate expenditure curve to shift downward, it reduces equilibrium national income.

Now suppose that there is a fall in the price level. Since this is the opposite of the case that we have just studied, we can summarize the two key effects briefly. First, American goods become relatively cheaper internationally, so net exports rise. Second,

the purchasing power of some existing assets that are denominated in money terms is increased, so households spend more. The resulting increase in desired expenditure on American goods causes the *AE* curve to shift upward and hence raises equilibrium national income. This is also shown in Figure 27-1.

Since a fall in the domestic price level causes the aggregate expenditure curve to shift upward, it increases equilibrium national income.

The Aggregate Demand Curve

We now know from the behavior underlying the aggregate expenditure curve that the price level and real national income are negatively related to each other; that is, a change in the price level changes equilibrium national income in the opposite direction. This negative relationship can be shown in an important new concept, called the *aggregate demand curve*.

Recall that the *AE* curve relates equilibrium national income to desired expenditure for a given price level, plotting income on the horizontal axis. The **aggregate demand (*AD*) curve** relates equilibrium national income to the price level, again plotting income on the horizontal axis. Because the horizontal axes of both the *AE* and the *AD* curves measure real national income, the two curves can be placed one above the other so that the level of national income on each can be compared directly. This is shown in Figure 27-2.

Now let us see how the *AD* curve is derived. Given a value of the price level, equilibrium national income is determined in part (i) of Figure 27-2 at the point where the *AE* curve crosses the 45° line. In part (ii) of Figure 27-2, the combination of the equilibrium level of national income and the corresponding value of the price level is plotted, giving one point on the *AD* curve.

When the price level changes, the *AE* curve shifts, for the reasons just seen. The new position of the *AE* curve gives rise to a new equilibrium level of national income that is associated with the new price level. This determines a second point on the *AD* curve, as shown in Figure 27-2(ii).

Any change in the price level leads to a new *AE* curve and hence to a new level of equilibrium income. Each combination of equilibrium in-

come and its associated price level becomes a particular point on the *AD* curve.

Note that, since the *AD* curve relates equilibrium national income to the price level, changes in the price level that cause *shifts in* the *AE* curve cause *movements along* the *AD* curve. A movement along the *AD* curve thus traces out the response of equilibrium income to a change in the price level.

The Slope of the *AD* Curve

Figure 27-2 already has provided us with sufficient information to establish that the *AD* curve is negatively sloped.

1. A *rise* in the price level causes the aggregate expenditure curve to shift downward and hence leads to a movement upward and to the left along the *AD* curve, reflecting a *fall* in the equilibrium level of national income.
2. A *fall* in the price level causes the aggregate expenditure curve to shift upward and hence leads to a movement downward and to the right along the *AD* curve, reflecting a rise in the equilibrium level of national income.

Early in our study (Chapter 4) we saw that demand curves for individual goods such as carrots or automobiles are negatively sloped. However, the reasons for the negative slope of the *AD* curve are different from the reasons for the negative slope of individual demand curves that are used in microeconomics; this important point is discussed further in Box 27-1.

Points Off the *AD* Curve

The *AD* curve depicts combinations of national income and the price level that give equilibrium between aggregate desired expenditure and actual output in the sense that aggregate desired expenditure equals actual output. These points are said to be *consistent* with expenditure decisions.

The national income given by any point on the aggregate demand curve is such that, *if* that level of output is produced, aggregate desired expenditure, at the *given price level,* will exactly equal the output.

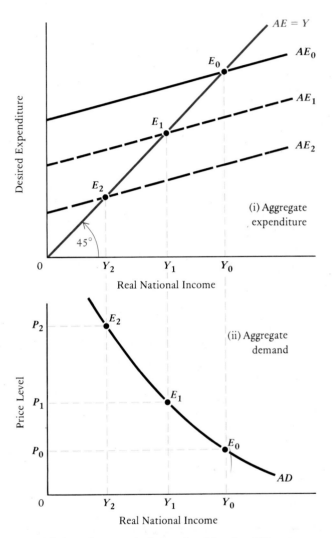

FIGURE 27-2 The *AD* Curve and the *AE* Curve

Equilibrium income is determined by the *AE* curve for each given price level; the level of income and its associated price level yield a point on the *AD* curve. When the price level is P_0, the *AE* curve is AE_0, and equilibrium income is Y_0 in part (i). (This is the initial equilibrium from Figure 27-1.) Plotting Y_0 against P_0 yields the point E_0 on the *AD* curve in part (ii).

An increase in the price level to P_1 causes AE_0 in part (i) to shift downward to AE_1, reducing equilibrium income to Y_1. Plotting this lower level of income, Y_1, against the higher price level, P_1, yields a second point, E_1, on the *AD* curve in part (ii). If the price level rises to P_2, the *AE* curve in part (i) shifts downward to AE_2, reducing equilibrium income to Y_2. Plotting Y_2 against P_2 yields a third point, E_2, on the *AD* curve in part (ii).

Thus, a change in the price level causes a shift of the *AE* curve and a movement along the *AD* curve.

BOX 27-1

The Shape of the Aggregate Demand Curve

In Chapter 4 we studied the demand curves for individual products. It is tempting to think that the properties of the aggregate demand curve arise from the same behavior that gives rise to those individual demand curves. Unfortunately, life is not so simple. Let us see why we cannot take such an approach.

If we assume that we can obtain a downward-sloping aggregate demand curve in the same manner that we derived downward-sloping individual market demand curves, we would be committing the fallacy of composition. This is to assume that what is correct for the parts must be correct for the whole.

Consider a simple example of the fallacy. An art collector can go into the market and add to her private collection of nineteenth century French paintings provided only that she has enough money. However, to assume that because any one person can do this, everyone could do so simultaneously is plainly wrong. The world's stock of nineteenth century French paintings is totally fixed. All of us cannot do what any one of us with enough money can do.

How does the fallacy of composition relate to demand curves? An individual demand curve describes a situation in which the price of one commodity changes while the prices of all other commodities and consumers' money incomes are constant. Such an individual demand curve is negatively sloped for two reasons. First, as the price of the commodity rises, each consumer's given money income will buy a smaller *total* amount of goods, so a smaller quantity of each commodity will be bought, other things being equal. Second, as the price of the commodity rises, consumers buy less of it and more of the now relatively cheaper substitutes.

The first reason has no application to the aggregate demand curve, which relates the total demand for all output to the price level. All prices and total output are changing as we move along the *AD* curve. Since the value of output determines income, consumers' money incomes will also be changing along this curve.

The second reason does have some, but very limited, application to the aggregate demand curve. A rise in the price level entails a rise in *all* domestic commodity prices. Thus, there is no incentive to substitute among domestic commodities whose prices do not change relative to each other. However, it does give rise, as we saw earlier in this chapter, to some substitution between domestic and foreign goods. Domestic goods rise in price relative to imported goods, and the switch in expenditure will lower desired aggregate expenditure on domestic output and hence will lower equilibrium national income.

Points to the left of the *AD* curve show combinations of national income and the price level that cause aggregate desired expenditure to exceed output. There is thus pressure for income to rise because firms could sell more than current output. Points to the right of the *AD* curve show combinations of national income and the price level, for which aggregate desired expenditure is less than current income. There is thus pressure for income to fall because firms will not be able to sell all of their current output. These relationships are illustrated in Figure 27-3.

Shifts in the *AD* Curve

Since the *AD* curve plots equilibrium national income as a function of the price level, anything that alters equilibrium national income *at a given price level* must shift the *AD* curve. In other words, any change other than a change in the price level that causes the *aggregate expenditure curve* to shift will also cause the *AD* curve to shift. (Recall that a change in the price level causes *a movement along* the *AD* curve.) Such a shift is called an *aggregate demand shock*. For example, in the early 1980s changes in the tax laws led to an

FIGURE 27-3   The Relationship Between the *AE* and *AD* Curves

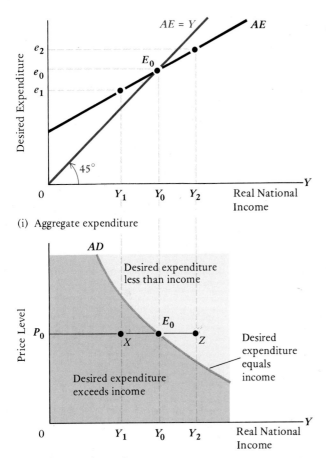

(i) Aggregate expenditure

(ii) Aggregate demand

The *AD* curve plots the price level against the level of national income consistent with expenditure decisions at that price level. The *AE* curve in part (i) is drawn for the price level P_0. The equilibrium level of national income is Y_0, as shown in part (i) by the intersection of the *AE* curve with the 45° line at E_0. At Y_0 national income is equal to desired aggregate expenditure, given by e_0. Y_0 is then plotted against P_0 in part (ii) to yield point E_0 on the *AD* curve.

With the price level constant at P_0, consider a level of national income of Y_1, which is less than Y_0. As can be seen in part (i), if national income were equal to Y_1, desired aggregate expenditure would be e_1, which is greater than Y_1. Hence, Y_1 is not an equilibrium level of national income when the price level is P_0, and the combination (P_0, Y_1) is not a point on the *AD* curve in part (ii), as shown by point X. Because desired expenditure exceeds national income at X, the pressure is for income to rise as firms expand output to meet demand.

Now consider a level of national income of Y_2, which is greater than Y_0. As can be seen in part (i), if national income were equal to Y_2, desired aggregate expenditure would be e_2, which is less than Y_2. Hence, Y_2 is not an equilibrium level of national income when the price level is P_0, and the combination (P_0, Y_2) is not a point on the *AD* curve in part (ii), as shown by point Z. Because desired expenditure is less than national income at point Z, the pressure on income is to fall as firms reduce their outputs to what they can sell.

Repeating the same analysis for each given price level tells us that, for all points to the left of the *AD* curve (dark-shaded area), income is tending to rise because desired expenditure exceeds income, while, for all points to the right of the *AD* curve (light-shaded area), income is tending to fall because desired aggregate expenditure is less than income.

---

increase in the amount of consumption expenditure that was associated with each level of national income. This was an expansionary demand shock that shifted the *AD* curve to the right.

Using our new concepts, the conclusions on page 544 now can be restated as follows:

A rise in the amount of desired consumption, investment, government, or net export expenditure that is associated with each level of national income shifts the *AD* curve to the right.

A fall in any of these expenditures shifts the *AD* curve to the left.

The Simple Multiplier and the AD Curve

We saw in Chapter 26 that the simple multiplier measures the magnitude of the *change* in equilibrium national income in response to a change in autonomous expenditure when the price level is constant. It follows that this multiplier gives the magnitude of the *horizontal* shift in the *AD* curve in response to a

FIGURE 27-4   The Simple Multiplier and Shifts in the *AD* Curve

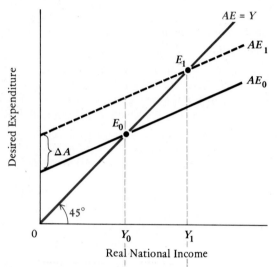

(i) Aggregate expenditure

(ii) Aggregate demand

A change in autonomous expenditure changes equilibrium national income for any given price level, and the simple multiplier measures the resulting horizontal shift in the aggregate demand curve. The original desired expenditure curve is AE_0 in part (i). Equilibrium is at E_0, with national income Y_0 at price level P_0. This yields point E_0 on the curve AD_0 in part (ii).

The AE curve in part (i) then shifts upward from AE_0 to AE_1, due to an increase in autonomous expenditure of ΔA. Equilibrium income now rises to Y_1, with the price level still constant at P_0. Thus, the AD curve in part (ii) shifts to the right to point E_1, indicating the higher equilibrium income Y_1, associated with the same price level P_0. The magnitude of the shift, ΔY, is given by the simple multiplier.

A fall in autonomous expenditure can be analyzed by shifting the AE curve from AE_1 to AE_0, which shifts the AD curve from AD_1 to AD_0 at the price level of P_0. The equilibrium value of national income falls from Y_1 to Y_0.

change in autonomous expenditure. This is shown in Figure 27-4.

The simple multiplier measures the horizontal shift in the *AD* curve in response to a change in autonomous expenditure.

If the price level remains constant and firms are willing to supply everything that is demanded at that price level, the simple multiplier also will show the change in equilibrium income that will occur in response to a change in autonomous expenditure.

Equilibrium National Income and Price Level

So far we have explained how the equilibrium level of national income is determined *when the price level is taken as given* and how that equilibrium changes as the price level is changed exogenously. By assuming that firms will produce all that is demanded at the going price level, we have effectively ignored the firms' supply decisions. We are now ready to take an important step: adding an *explanation* of the behavior of the price level. In order to do this, we need to take account of the supply decisions of firms.

The Aggregate Supply Curve

Aggregate supply refers to the total output of goods and services that firms wish to produce, assuming that they can sell all that they wish to sell. Aggregate supply thus depends on the decisions of firms to use workers and all other inputs in order to produce goods and services to sell to households, governments, and other firms, as well as for export.

An *aggregate supply curve* relates aggregate supply to the price level. It is necessary to define two types of such curves. The **short-run aggregate supply (SRAS) curve** relates the price level to the quantity that firms would like to produce and to sell *on the assumption that the prices of all factors of production remain constant*. The *long-run aggregate supply (LRAS) curve*, which we will define more fully later, relates the price level to desired sales after a full adjustment has been made to that price level. For the moment we confine our attention to the *SRAS* curve.

The Slope of the Short-Run Aggregate Supply Curve

To study the slope of the *SRAS* curve, we need to see how costs are related to output and then how prices and outputs are related.

Costs and output. Suppose that firms wish to increase their outputs above current levels. What will this do to their costs per unit of output—often called their **unit costs**? The short-run aggregate supply curve assumes that the prices of all factors of production that firms use, such as labor, remain constant. This does not, however, mean that unit costs will be constant. Less efficient standby plants may have to be used, and less efficient workers may have to be hired, while existing workers will have to be paid overtime rates for additional work. For these

and other similar reasons,[3] unit costs will tend to rise as output rises, even when input prices are constant.

Unit costs and output are positively associated with each other.

Prices and output. To consider the relationship between price and output, we need to consider firms that sell in two distinct types of markets: those in which firms are price takers and those in which firms are price setters. Some industries, including those that produce most basic industrial materials and some energy products, contain many individual firms. In these cases each one is too small to influence the market price, which is set by the overall forces of demand and supply. Each firm must accept whatever price is set on the open market and adjust its output to that price. The firms are said to be *price takers* and *quantity adjusters*. When the market price changes, these firms will react by altering their production.

Because their unit costs rise with output, price-taking firms produce more when price rises and less when price falls.

Many other industries, including most of those that produce manufactured products, contain so few firms that each can influence market prices. Most such firms sell products that differ from one another, although all are similar enough to be thought of as the single commodity produced by one industry. For example, no two kinds of automobiles are the same, but all automobiles are sufficiently alike so that we have no trouble talking about the automobile industry and the commodity, automobiles. In such cases each firm must quote a price at which it is prepared to sell each of its products; that is, the firm is a price setter. If the demand for the output of price-setting firms increases sufficiently to take their outputs into the range in which their unit costs rise (e.g., because overtime is worked and standby plants are brought into production), these firms will not increase their outputs unless they can pass at least some of these extra costs on through higher prices. When the demand falls, they will reduce output, and competition among them will tend to cause a reduction in prices whenever their unit costs fall.

[3] Those who have studied microeconomics will recognize the law of diminishing returns as a potent "other reason" why costs rise in the short run as firms squeeze more output out of a fixed quantity of capital equipment.

Price-setting firms will increase their prices when they expand output into the range in which unit costs are rising.

This is the basic behavior of firms in response to the changes in demand and prices when factor prices are constant, and it explains the slope of the *SRAS* curve, such as the one shown in Figure 27-5.

The actions of both price-taking and price-setting firms cause the price level and total output to be positively associated with each other; the graphical expression of this relationship is the positively sloped, short-run aggregate supply curve.

Shifts in the *SRAS* Curve

Shifts in the *SRAS* curve, which are shown in Figure 27-6, are called *aggregate supply shocks*. Two sources of aggregate supply shocks are of particular importance: changes in the price of inputs and increases in productivity.

Changes in input prices.   Factor prices are held constant along the *SRAS* curve, and when they change,

FIGURE 27-6   Shifts in the *SRAS* Curve

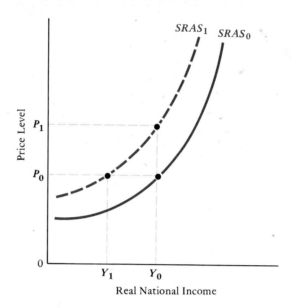

A shift to the left of the *SRAS* curve reflects a decrease in supply; a shift to the right, reflects an increase in supply. Starting from P_0, Y_0 on $SRAS_0$, suppose there is an increase in input prices. At price level P_0 only Y_1 would be produced. Alternatively, to get output Y_0 would require a rise to price level P_1. The new supply curve is $SRAS_1$, which may be viewed as being above and to the left of $SRAS_0$. An increase in supply, caused, say, by a decrease in input prices, would shift the *SRAS* curve downward and to the right from $SRAS_1$ to $SRAS_0$.

the curve shifts. If factor prices rise, firms will find the profitability of their current production reduced. For any given level of output to be produced, an increase in the price level will be required. If prices do not rise, firms will react by decreasing production.[4] For the economy as a whole, this means that there will be less output at each price level than before the increase in factor prices. Thus, if factor prices rise, the *SRAS* curve shifts upward. (Notice that when a positively sloped curve shifts upward, it also shifts to the left.)

Similarly, a fall in factor prices causes the *SRAS*

FIGURE 27-5   A Short-Run Aggregate Supply Curve

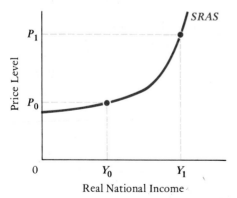

The *SRAS* curve is positively sloped. The positive slope of the *SRAS* curve shows that with the prices of labor and other inputs given, total desired output and the price level will be positively associated. Thus, a rise in the price level from P_0 to P_1 will be associated with a rise in the quantity of total output supplied, from Y_0 to Y_1.

[4] Students who have studied microeconomics already will recognize that such an upward shift in a firm's marginal cost curve leads to a decrease in the output that is profitable for the firm to produce. This was discussed in Chapter 12.

curve to shift downward (and to the right). This increase in supply means that more will be produced and offered for sale at each price level.

Increases in productivity. If labor productivity rises, meaning that each worker can produce more, the unit costs of production will fall as long as wage rates do not rise sufficiently to fully offset the productivity rise. Lower costs generally lead to lower prices. Competing firms cut prices in attempts to raise their market shares, and the net result of such competition is that the fall in production costs is accompanied by a fall in prices.

Since the same output is sold at a lower price, this causes a downward shift in the *SRAS* curve. This shift is an increase in supply, as illustrated in Figure 27-6.

A rightward shift in the *SRAS* curve, brought about, for example, by an increase in productivity with no increase in factor prices, means that firms will be willing to produce more national income with no increase in the price level. This result has been the object of many government policies that seek to encourage increases in productivity.

A change in either factor prices or productivity will shift the *SRAS* curve, because any given output will be supplied at a different price level than previously. An increase in factor prices shifts the *SRAS* curve to the left; an increase in productivity or a decrease in factor prices shifts it to the right.

Macroeconomic Equilibrium

We have now reached our objective: We are ready to see how both real national income and the price level are simultaneously determined by the interaction of aggregate demand and aggregate supply.

The equilibrium values of national output and the price level occur at the intersection of the *AD* and *SRAS* curves, as shown by the pair Y_0 and P_0 that arise at point E_0 in Figure 27-7. We describe the combination of national income and price level that is on both the *AD* and the *SRAS* curves as a *macroeconomic equilibrium*.

To see why this pair of points is the only macroeconomic equilibrium, first consider what Figure 27-7 shows would happen if the price level were below P_0. At this lower price level, the desired out-

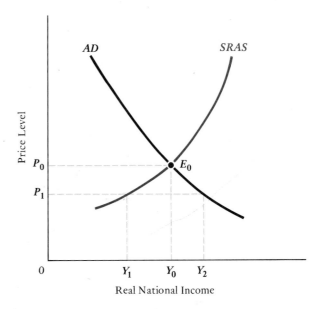

FIGURE 27-7 Macroeconomic Equilibrium

Macroeconomic equilibrium occurs at the intersection of the *AD* and *SRAS* curves and determines the equilibrium values for national income and the price level. Given the *AD* and *SRAS* curves in the figure, macroeconomic equilibrium occurs at E_0, with national income equal to Y_0 and the price level equal to P_0. At P_0 the desired output of firms, as given by the *SRAS* curve, is equal to the level of national income that is consistent with expenditure decisions, as given by the *AD* curve.

If the price level were equal to P_1, less than P_0, the desired output of firms, given by the *SRAS* curve, would be Y_1. However, at P_1 the level of output that is consistent with expenditure decisions, given by the *AD* curve, would be Y_2, greater than Y_1. Hence, when the price level is P_1, or any other level less than P_0, the desired output of firms will be less than the level of national income that is consistent with expenditure decisions.

Similarly, for any price level above P_0, the desired output of firms, given by the *SRAS* curve, would exceed the level of output that is consistent with expenditure decisions, given by the *AD* curve.

The only price level where the supply decisions of firms are consistent with desired expenditure is at macroeconomic equilibrium. At P_0 firms wish to produce Y_0. When they do so, they generate a national income of Y_0; when income is Y_0, decision makers wish to spend exactly Y_0, thus purchasing the nation's output. Hence, all decisions are consistent with each other.

put of firms, as given by the *SRAS* curve, is less than the level of output that is consistent with expenditure decisions, as given by the *AD* curve. If firms were to produce their desired level of output, desired expenditure would exceed the amount of goods supplied. Firms that found that they could sell more than their current outputs would increase their outputs, thus causing national income to change. Hence, there can be no macroeconomic *equilibrium* when the price level is below P_0.

Similarly, Figure 27-7 shows that, when the price level is above P_0, the behavior underlying the *SRAS* and *AD* curves is not consistent. In this case producers will wish to supply more than the level of income that is consistent with demand at that price level. If firms were to produce their desired levels of output, desired expenditure would not be large enough to purchase everything that would be produced.

Only at the combination of national income and price level, given by the intersection of the *SRAS* and *AD* curves, are spending behavior and supply behavior consistent.

When the price level is less than its equilibrium value, expenditure behavior is consistent with a level of national income that is greater than the desired output of firms. When the price level is greater than its equilibrium value, expenditure behavior is consistent with a level of national income that is less than the desired output of firms.

Macroeconomic equilibrium thus requires that two conditions be satisfied. The first is familiar to us because it comes from Chapter 26: At the prevailing price level, desired aggregate expenditure must be equal to national income, which means that households are just willing to buy all that is produced. The second is introduced by consideration of aggregate supply: At the prevailing price level, firms must wish to produce the prevailing level of national income, no more and no less.

Changes in National Income and the Price Level

The aggregate demand and aggregate supply curves now can be used to understand how various shocks to the economy change both national income and the price level.

A shift in the *AD* curve is called an **aggregate demand shock.** A *rightward* shift in the *AD* curve is an *increase* in aggregate demand; it means that, at all price levels, expenditure decisions will now be consistent with a *higher* level of real national income. Similarly, a *leftward* shift in the *AD* curve is a *decrease* in aggregate demand; it means that, at all price levels, expenditure decisions will now be consistent with a *lower* level of real national income.

A shift in the *SRAS* curve is called an **aggregate supply shock.** A *rightward* shift in the *SRAS* curve is an *increase* in aggregate supply; at any given price level, *more* real national income will be supplied. A *leftward* shift in the *SRAS* curve is a *decrease* in aggregate supply; at any given price level, *less* real national income will be supplied.[5]

What happens to real national income and to the price level when one of the aggregate curves shifts?

A shift in either the *AD* or the *SRAS* curve leads to changes in the equilibrium values of the price level and real national income.

Box 27-2 deals with the special case of a perfectly elastic *SRAS* curve. In that case only the aggregate supply curve determines the price level by itself, while the aggregate demand curve determines real national income by itself.

Aggregate Demand Shocks

Figure 27-8 shows the effects of an increase in aggregate demand. This increase could have occurred because of, say, increased investment or government spending; it means that more national output would

---

[5] The distinction between movements along and shifts of curves that we encountered in Chapter 4 and again in Chapter 26 is also relevant here. Recall that the phrase "a change in quantity demanded" refers to a *movement along* a demand curve, whereas "a change in demand" refers to a *shift of* the demand curve. A similar distinction applies to the supply curve.

Note that, for either the *AD* or the *SRAS* curve, a shift to the right means an increase, and a shift to the left means a decrease. If we speak of upward and downward shifts, however, the meaning differs for the two curves. An upward shift of the *AD* curve reflects an increase in aggregate demand, but an upward shift in the *SRAS* curve reflects a decrease in aggregate supply.

BOX 27-2

The Keynesian *SRAS* Curve

In this box we consider an extreme version of the *SRAS* curve that is horizontal over some range of national income. It is called the **Keynesian short-run aggregate supply curve,** after John Maynard Keynes, who in his famous book *The General Theory of Employment, Interest and Money* (1936) pioneered the study of the behavior of economies under conditions of high unemployment.

The behavior that gives rise to the Keynesian *SRAS* curve can be described as follows. When real national income is below potential national income, individual firms are operating at less than normal-capacity output. Firms respond to cyclical declines in demand by holding their prices constant at the level that would maximize profits if production were at normal capacity. They then respond to demand variations below that capacity by altering output. In other words, they will supply whatever they can sell at their existing prices as long as they are producing below their normal capacity. This means that the firms have horizontal supply curves and that their output is *demand determined.**

* The evidence is strong that firms, particularly in the manufacturing sector, do behave like this in the short run. One possible explanation for this is that changing prices frequently is too costly, so firms set the best possible (profit-maximizing) prices when output is at normal capacity and then do not change prices in the face of short-term fluctuations in demand. This is discussed further in Chapter 14.

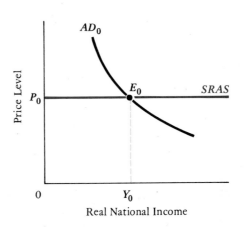

Under these circumstances, the economy has a horizontal aggregate supply curve, indicating that any output up to potential output will be supplied at the going price level. The amount that is actually produced is then determined by the position of the aggregate demand curve, as shown in the figure. Thus, we say that real national income is demand determined.

If demand rises enough so that firms are trying to squeeze more than normal output out of their plants, their costs will rise, and so will their prices. Thus, the horizontal Keynesian *SRAS* curve applies only to national incomes below potential income.

be demanded at any given price level. For now we are not concerned with the source of the shock; we are interested in its implications for the price level and real national income.[6] As is shown in the figure, following an increase in aggregate demand, both the price level and real national income rise.

Figure 27-8 also shows that both the price level and real national income fall as the result of a decrease in demand.

[6] Later (starting in Chapter 30) we shall also study how government policy can influence these variables.

Aggregate demand shocks cause the price level and real national income to change in the same direction; both rise with an increase in aggregate demand, and both fall with a decrease in aggregate demand.

An aggregate demand shock means that there is a shift in the *AD* curve (for example, from AD_0 to AD_1 in Figure 27-8). Adjustment to the new equilibrium following an aggregate demand shock involves a movement along the *SRAS* curve (for example, from point E_0 to point E_1).

FIGURE 27-8 Aggregate Demand Shocks

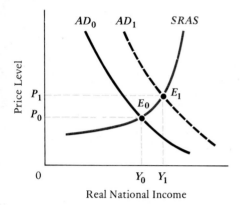

Shifts in aggregate demand cause the price level and real national income to move in the same direction. An increase in aggregate demand shifts the *AD* curve to the right, say, from AD_0 to AD_1. Macroeconomic equilibrium moves from E_0 to E_1. The price level rises from P_0 to P_1, and real national income rises from Y_0 to Y_1, reflecting a movement along the *SRAS* curve.

A decrease in aggregate demand shifts the *AD* curve to the left, say, from AD_1 to AD_0. Equilibrium moves from E_1 to E_0. Prices fall from P_1 to P_0, and real national income falls from Y_1 to Y_0, again reflecting a movement along the *SRAS* curve.

The Multiplier When the Price Level Varies

We saw earlier in this chapter that the simple multiplier gives the extent of the horizontal shift in the *AD* curve in response to a change in autonomous expenditure. If the price level remains constant and *if* firms are willing to supply all that is demanded at the existing price level, then the simple multiplier gives the increase in equilibrium national income.

Now that we can use aggregate demand and aggregate supply curves, we can answer a more interesting question: What happens in the more usual case in which the aggregate supply curve slopes upward? In this case a rise in national income caused by an increase in aggregate demand will be associated with a rise in the price level. However, we have seen that a rise in the price level (by reducing net exports and by lowering the real value of household wealth)

shifts the *AE* curve downward, which lowers equilibrium national income, other things being equal. The outcome of these conflicting forces is easily seen using aggregate demand and aggregate supply curves.

As can be seen in Figure 27-8, when the *SRAS* curve is positively sloped, the change in national income that has been caused by a change in autonomous expenditure is no longer equal to the size of the horizontal shift in the *AD* curve. A shift to the right of the *AD* curve causes the price level to rise, which in turn causes the rise in national income to be less than the horizontal shift of the *AD* curve. Part of the expansionary impact of an increase in demand is dissipated by a rise in the price level, and only part is transmitted to a rise in real output. Of course, there still is an increase in output, so a multiplier still may be calculated, but its value is not the same as that of the simple multiplier.

When the *SRAS* curve is positively sloped, the multiplier is smaller than the simple multiplier.

Why is the multiplier smaller when the *SRAS* curve is positively sloped? The answer lies in the behavior that is summarized by the *AE* curve. To understand this, it is useful to think of the final change in national income as occurring in two stages, as shown in Figure 27-9.

First, with prices remaining constant, an increase in autonomous expenditure shifts the *AE* curve upward and therefore shifts the *AD* curve to the right. This is shown by a shift upward of the *AE* curve in part (i) of the figure and a shift to the right of the *AD* curve in part (ii). The horizontal shift in the *AD* curve is measured by the simple multiplier, but this cannot be the final equilibrium position because firms are unwilling to produce enough to satisfy the extra demand at the existing price level.

Second, we take account of the rise in the price level that occurs due to the positive slope of the *SRAS* curve. As we have seen, a rise in the price level, via its effect on net exports and on wealth, leads to a downward shift in the *AE* curve. This second shift of the *AE* curve partially counteracts the initial rise in national income and so reduces the size of the multiplier. The second stage shows up as a downward shift of the *AE* curve in part (i) of Figure

FIGURE 27-9   The *AE* Curve and the Multiplier When the Price Level Varies

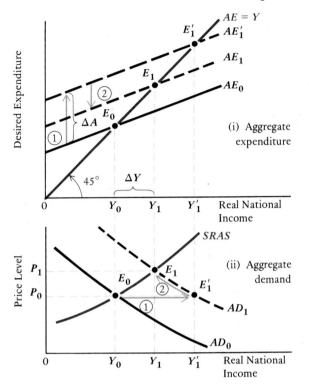

An increase in autonomous expenditures causes the *AE* curve to shift upward, but the rise in the price level causes it to shift part of the way down again. Hence, the multiplier effect on income is smaller than when the price level is constant. Originally, equilibrium is at point E_0 in both part (i) and part (ii), with real national income at Y_0 and price level at P_0. Desired aggregate expenditure then shifts by ΔA to AE_1', taking the aggregate demand curve to AD_1. These shifts are shown by arrow 1 in both parts. If the price level had remained constant at P_0, the new equilibrium would have been E_1' and real income would have risen to Y_1'. The amount Y_0Y_1' is the change called for by the simple multiplier.

Instead, however, the shift in the *AD* curve raises the price level to P_1 because the *SRAS* curve is positively sloped. The rise in the price level shifts the aggregate expenditure curve down to AE_1, as shown by arrow 2 in part (i). This is shown as a movement along the *AD* curve, as shown by arrow 2 in part (ii). The new equilibrium is thus at E_1. The amount Y_0Y_1 is ΔY, the actual increase in real income, whereas the amount Y_1Y_1' is the shortfall relative to the simple multiplier due to the rise in the price level.

The multiplier, adjusted for the effect of the price increase, is the ratio of $\Delta Y/\Delta A$ in part (i).

27-9 and a movement upward and to the left along the *AD* curve in part (ii).

The Importance of the Shape of the *SRAS* Curve

We now have seen that the shape of the *SRAS* curve has important implications for how the effects of an aggregate demand shock are divided between changes in real national output and changes in the price level. Figure 27-10 highlights this by considering *AD* shocks in the presence of an *SRAS* curve that exhibits three distinct ranges. Box 27-3 explores some possible reasons for such an increasing slope of the *SRAS* curve.

Over the *flat* range, from 0 to Y_0, any change in aggregate demand leads to little change in prices and,

as seen earlier, a response of output nearly equal to that predicted by the simple multiplier.

Over the *intermediate* range, along which the *SRAS* curve is positively sloped, from Y_1 to Y_4, a shift in the *AD* curve gives rise to appreciable changes in both real income and the price level. As we saw earlier in this chapter, the change in the price level means that real income will change by less in response to a change in autonomous expenditure than it would if the price level were constant.

Over the *steep* range, for output above Y_4, virtually nothing more can be produced, however large the demand is. This range deals with an economy near its capacity constraints. Any change in aggregate demand leads to a sharp change in the price level and to virtually no change in real national income. The multiplier in this case is nearly zero.

**FIGURE 27-10   The Effects of Increases in
Aggregate Demand**

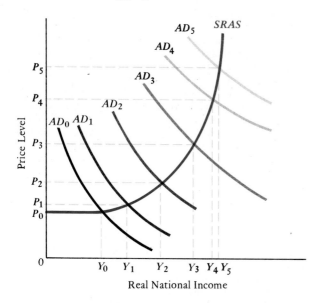

The effects of increases in aggregate demand are divided between increases in real income and increases in prices, depending on the shape of the SRAS curve. Because of the increasing slope of the SRAS curve, increases in aggregate demand up to AD_0 have virtually no impact on price. When aggregate demand increases from AD_0 to AD_1, there is a relatively small increase in price, from P_0 to P_1, and a relatively large increase in output, from Y_0 to Y_1. Successive further increases bring larger price increases and relatively smaller output increases. By the time aggregate demand is at AD_4 or AD_5, virtually all of the effect is on the price level.

How do we reconcile what we have just discovered with the AE analysis of Chapter 26, where shifts in AE *always* change national income? The answer is that each AE curve is drawn on the assumption that there is a constant price level. A rise in AE shifts the AD curve to the right. However, a steep AS curve means that the price level rises significantly, and this shifts the AE curve downward, offsetting some of its initial rise. This interaction is seen most easily if we study the extreme case, shown in Figure 27-11, where the $SRAS$ curve is vertical. An increase in autonomous expenditure shifts the AE curve upward, thus raising the amount demanded. However,

a vertical $SRAS$ curve means that output cannot be expanded to satisfy the increased demand. Instead, the extra demand merely forces prices up, and, as prices rise, the AE curve shifts downward once again. The rise in prices continues until the AE curve is back to where it started. Thus, the rise in prices offsets the expansionary effect of the original shift and, as a result, leaves both real aggregate expenditure and equilibrium real income unchanged.

The discussion of Figures 27-10 and 27-11 illustrates a general proposition:

The effect of any given shift in aggregate demand will be divided between a change in real output and a change in the price level, depending on the conditions of aggregate supply. The steeper is the SRAS curve, the greater is the price effect, and the smaller is the output effect.

For reasons discussed in Boxes 27-2 and 27-3, many economists think that the $SRAS$ curve is shaped like that in Figure 27-8, that is, relatively flat for low levels of income and becoming steeper as the level of national income increases. This shape of the $SRAS$ curve implies that at low levels of national income (well below potential), shifts in aggregate demand affect mainly output, and at high levels of national income (above potential), shifts in aggregate demand affect mainly prices.

Of course, as we have noted already, treating wages and other factor prices as constant is appropriate only when the time period under consideration is short. Hence, the $SRAS$ curve is used only to analyze short-run, or *impact,* effects. In the next chapter we shall see what happens in the *long run* when factor prices respond to changes in national income and the price level. First, however, our analysis of the short run needs to be rounded out with a study of aggregate supply shocks.

Aggregate Supply Shocks

A decrease in aggregate supply is reflected in a shift to the left in the $SRAS$ curve and means that less national output will be supplied at any given price level. An increase in aggregate supply is reflected in a shift to the right in the $SRAS$ curve and means that more national output will be produced at any given price level.

BOX 27-3

Another Look at the Shape of the *SRAS* Curve

The *SRAS* curve relates the price level to the quantity of output that producers are willing to sell. Notice two things about the shape of the *SRAS* curve that is shown in Figure 27-5. It has a positive slope, and the slope increases as output rises.

Positive Slope

The most obvious feature of the *SRAS* curve is its positive slope, indicating that a higher price level is associated with a higher volume of real output, other things being equal. Since the prices of all of the factors of production are being held constant along the *SRAS* curve, why is the curve not horizontal, indicating that firms would be willing to supply as much output as might be demanded with no increase in the price level?

You have already encountered an answer to this question. Even though *input prices* are constant, *unit costs of production* rise as output increases. Thus, a higher price level for increasing output—rising short-run aggregate supply—is necessary to compensate firms for rising costs.

The preceding paragraph addresses the question "What has to happen to the price level if national output increases, with the price of factors of production remaining constant?" One may ask a different question: "What will happen to firms' willingness to supply output if product prices rise with no increase in factor prices?" If there is an increase in the prices of products that firms sell, while the prices of the factors of production that firms use to make their products remain constant, production becomes more profitable. Since firms are interested in making profits, when production becomes more profitable, they will usually produce more.* Thus,

* Those who have studied microeconomics already can understand this in terms of perfectly competitive firms being faced with higher prices and thus expanding output *along* their marginal-cost curves until marginal cost is once again equal to price.

when the price level of final output rises while factor prices are held constant, firms are motivated to increase their outputs. This is true for the individual firm and also for firms in the aggregate. This increase in the amount that will be produced leads to an upward slope of the *SRAS* curve.

Thus, whether we look at how the price level will respond in the short run to increases in output or how the level of output will respond to an increase in the price level with input prices being held constant, we find that the *SRAS* curve has a positive slope.

Increasing slope. A somewhat less obvious but in many ways more important property of a typical *SRAS* curve is that its slope *increases* as output rises. It is rather flat to the left of potential output and rather steep to the right. Why? Below potential output, firms typically have unused capacity—some plant and equipment are idle. When firms are faced with unused capacity, only a small increase in the price of their output may be needed to induce them to expand production—at least up to normal capacity.

Once output is pushed far beyond normal capacity, however, unit costs tend to rise quite rapidly. Many higher-cost expedients may have to be adopted. Standby capacity, overtime, and extra shifts may have to be used. Such expedients raise the cost of producing a unit of output. These higher-cost methods will not be used unless the selling price of the output has risen enough to cover them. The further output is expanded beyond normal capacity, the more rapidly unit costs rise and hence the larger is the rise in price that is needed to induce firms to increase output even further.

This increasing slope is sometimes called the *first important asymmetry* in the behavior of aggregate supply. (The second, "sticky wages," will be discussed in the next chapter.)

FIGURE 27-11   Demand Shocks When the *SRAS* Curve Is Vertical

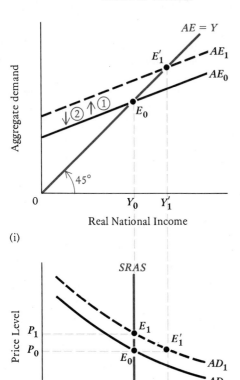

(i)

(ii)

FIGURE 27-12   Aggregate Supply Shocks

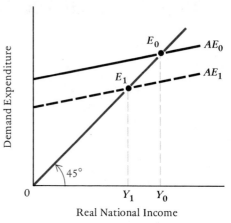

(i)

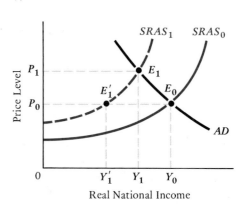

(ii)

If the *SRAS* curve were vertical, the effect of an increase in autonomous expenditure would be solely a rise in the price level. An increase in autonomous expenditure shifts the *AE* curve upward from AE_0 to AE_1, as shown by arrow 1 in part (i). Given the initial price level P_0, equilibrium would shift from E_0 to E_1', and real national income would rise from Y_0 to Y_1'. (Primes are used on these variables because these results cannot persist, since real national income cannot rise to Y_1'.) However, the price level does not remain constant. This is shown by the *SRAS* curve in part (ii). Instead, the price level rises to P_1. This causes the *AE* curve to shift back down all the way to AE_0, as shown by arrow 2 in part (i), and equilibrium income stays at Y_0. In part (ii) the new equilibrium is at E_1 with income at Y_0, which is associated with the new price level, P_1.

Shifts in aggregate supply cause the price level and real national income to move in opposite directions. The original equilibrium is at E_0, with national income of Y_0 appearing in both parts of the figure. The price level is P_0 in part (ii), and, at that price level, the desired aggregate expenditure curve is AE_0 in part (i).

An aggregate supply shock now shifts the *SRAS* curve in part (ii) to $SRAS_1$. At the original price level of P_0, firms are now only willing to supply Y_1'. The fall in supply, with no corresponding fall in demand, causes a shortage that leads to a rise in the price level along $SRAS_1$. The new equilibrium is reached at E_1, where the AD curve intersects $SRAS_1$. At the new, and higher, equilibrium price level of P_1, the *AE* curve has fallen to AE_1, as shown in part (i), which is consistent with equilibrium national income of Y_1.

Figure 27-12 illustrates the effects on the price level and real national income of aggregate supply shocks. As can be seen from the figure, following the decrease in aggregate supply, the price level rises and real national income falls. This combination of events is called *stagflation,* a rather inelegant word that has been derived by combining *stagnation* (a term that is sometimes used to mean less than full employment) and *inflation.*

Figure 27-12 also shows that an increase in aggregate supply leads to an increase in real national income and a decrease in the price level.

Aggregate supply shocks cause the price level and real national income to change in opposite directions; with an increase in supply, the price level falls and income rises; with a decrease in supply, the price level rises and income falls.

An aggregate supply shock means that there is a shift in the *SRAS* curve (for example, from $SRAS_0$ to $SRAS_1$ in Figure 27-12). Adjustment to the new equilibrium following the shock involves a movement along the *AD* curve (for example, from E_0 to E_1).

Oil prices have provided three major examples of aggregate supply shocks in recent decades. Massive increases in oil prices during 1974–1975 and 1979–1980 caused leftward shifts in the *SRAS* curve. National income fell, while the price level rose, causing stagflation. During the mid-1980s oil prices fell substantially. This shifted the *SRAS* curve to the right, increasing existing pressures for national income to rise and decreasing existing pressures for the price level to fall.

We can see now how a rightward shift in the *SRAS* curve, which is brought about by an increase in productivity without a fully offsetting increase in factor prices, raises real national income and lowers the price level. As we shall see in the next chapter, this happy combination of rising output and falling prices has proved to be difficult to achieve in practice.

SUMMARY

1. The *AE* curve shows desired aggregate expenditure for each level of income at a particular price level. Its intersection with the 45° line determines equilibrium national income for that price level, on the assumption that firms will produce everything that they can sell at the going price level. Equilibrium income then occurs where desired aggregate expenditure equals national income (output). A change in the price level is shown by a *shift* in the *AE* curve: upward when the price level falls and downward when the price level rises. This leads to a new equilibrium level of national income.

2. The *AD* curve plots the equilibrium level of national income that corresponds to each possible price level. A change in equilibrium national income following a change in the price level is shown by a *movement along* the *AD* curve.

3. A rise in the price level lowers exports and lowers consumers' spending (because it decreases consumers' wealth). Both of these changes lower equilibrium national income and cause the aggregate demand curve to have a negative slope. The *AD* curve shifts when any element of autonomous expenditure changes, and the simple multiplier measures the magnitude of the shift. This multiplier also measures the size of the change in real equilibrium national income when the price level remains constant *and* firms produce everything that is demanded at that price level.

4. The short-run aggregate supply (*SRAS*) curve, drawn for given factor prices, is positively sloped because unit costs rise with increasing output and because rising product prices make it profitable to increase output. An increase in productivity or a decrease in factor

prices shifts the curve to the right. A decrease in productivity or an increase in factor prices has the opposite effect.

5. Macroeconomic equilibrium refers to equilibrium values of national income and the price level, as determined by the intersection of the *AD* and *SRAS* curves. Shifts in the *AD* and *SRAS* curves, called aggregate demand shocks and aggregate supply shocks, change the equilibrium values of national income and the price level.

6. When the *SRAS* curve is positively sloped, an aggregate demand shock causes the price level and national income to move in the same direction. The division of the effects between a change in national income and a change in the price level depends on the shape of the *SRAS* curve. When the *SRAS* curve is flat, shifts in the *AD* curve affect mainly real national income. When the *SRAS* curve is steep, shifts in the *AD* curve affect mainly the price level.

7. An aggregate supply shock moves equilibrium national income along the *AD* curve, causing the price level and national income to move in opposite directions. A leftward shift in the *SRAS* curve causes a stagflation—rising prices and falling national income. A rightward shift causes an increase in real national income and a fall in the price level. The division of the effects between a change in national income and a change in the price level depends on the shape of the *AD* curve.

TOPICS FOR REVIEW

Effects of a change in the price level
Relationship between the *AE* and *AD* curves
Negative slope of the *AD* curve
Positive slope of the *SRAS* curve
Macroeconomic equilibrium
Aggregate demand shocks
The simple multiplier when the price level varies
Aggregate supply shocks
Stagflation

DISCUSSION QUESTIONS

1. Explain the following by shifts in either the aggregate demand curve or the aggregate supply curves, or both. Pay attention to the initial position before the shift(s) occurs.
   a. Output and unemployment rise, while prices hold steady.
   b. Prices soar, but employment and output hold steady.
   c. Inflation accelerates even as the recession in business actively deepens.

2. A survey of private economic forecasters in mid-1989 showed that the consensus economic outlook for 1990 was cautiously optimistic—most thought that real growth would remain roughly constant while unemployment would fall slightly; more worry was expressed that inflation might rise well above the 5 percent level. Explain what factors underlying the *AD* and *SRAS* curves would give rise to such a forecast. In retrospect, how accurate were these forecasts? What happened to the underlying determinants to cause actual events to differ from the forecasts?

3. During 1979–1980 the British government greatly reduced income taxes but restored the lost government revenue by raising excise and sales taxes. This led to a short burst of extra inflation and a fall in employment. Explain this in terms of shifts in the aggregate demand or aggregate supply curves, or both.

4. Indicate whether each of the following events was the cause or the consequence of a shift in aggregate demand or supply. If it was a cause, what do you predict will be the effect on the price level and on real national income?
   a. Unemployment decreases in 1989.
   b. OPEC raises oil prices in 1980.
   c. OPEC is forced to accept lower oil prices in 1985.
   d. In the late 1960s and early 1970s the United States experienced a rapid inflation under conditions of approximately full employment.
   e. In France in 1981 income and employment continue to fall while the price level is quite stable.
   f. Defense spending is cut following an arms control agreement between the United States and the USSR.
   g. U.S. exports fall in response to a high value of the U.S. dollar and intense competition from foreign suppliers.
   h. Congress slashes personal income-tax rates.
   i. Inflationary pressures build up as U.S. economic expansion continues through 1989.
   j. The Bush administration and Congress finally agree on measures to cut the federal budget deficit.
5. What would happen to employment and income if, in an attempt to lower American unemployment, Congress enacted large increases in American tariff rates? What would happen if all countries did the same?
6. Show the effects on the price level and output of income-tax cuts that make people work more in an economy that currently is experiencing an inflationary gap.
7. Following are the combinations of output and price level, given by indexes for GNP and the CPI, respectively, for some recent years. Treat each pair as if it is the intersection of an *AD* and an *AS* curve. Plot these and indicate in each case the direction of shift of the *SRAS* or *AD* curves that could have caused the changes from one year to the next. Assume that only one curve shifts unless two shifts are needed to explain the data. Why might you be uncertain about some of the shifts?

	CPI (1982–1984 = 100)	GNP (billions of 1982 dollars)
1979	72.6	3,192
1980	82.4	3,187
1981	90.9	3,249
1982	96.5	3,166
1983	99.6	3,277
1984	103.9	3,501
1985	107.6	3,619
1986	109.6	3,722
1987	113.6	3,847
1988	118.1	4,609

Chapter 28

National Income and the Price Level in the Long Run

Every labor leader knows that it is relatively easy to bargain for wage increases during a boom when the demand for labor is high. The same leaders also know that it is difficult to get any wage increases during a recession when high unemployment signals a low demand for labor. Every businessperson knows that the cost of needed materials tends to rise rapidly during business expansions and to fall—often dramatically—during recessions. It is high time, therefore, to go beyond the assumption of fixed factor prices that we used to study the initial effects of aggregate demand and aggregate supply shocks in Chapter 27. To do this we need to see what happens in a longer-term setting when changes in national income *induce* changes in factor prices.

Induced Changes in Factor Prices

The first thing we need to do is to look again at two key concepts that we first encountered in Chapter 24: potential income and the output (or GNP) gap.

Another Look at Potential Income and the Output Gap

Recall that potential income is the total output that can be produced when all productive resources—especially labor and capital equipment—are being used at their *normal rates of utilization*. When the nation's actual national income diverges from its potential income, the difference is called the output gap. (See Figure 24-4 on page 502.)

Although growth in potential income has powerful effects on all of us from one decade to another, its change from one year to another is small enough to be ignored when studying the year-to-year behavior of national income and the price level. So, in this chapter we continue with the assumption that was made in Chapter 24 that potential income is constant. This means that variations in the output gap are determined solely by variations in actual national income around a given potential national income.

Figure 28-1 shows actual national income being determined by the intersection of the *AD* and *SRAS* curves. Potential income is constant, and it is shown by identical vertical lines in the two parts of the figure. In part (i) the *AD* and *SRAS* curves intersect to produce an equilibrium national income that falls short of potential income. The result is a positive output gap. In part (ii) the *AD* and *SRAS* curves intersect to produce an equilibrium

FIGURE 28-1   Actual Income, Potential Income, and the Output Gap

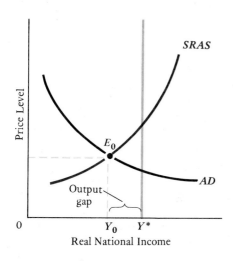

(i) A positive output gap

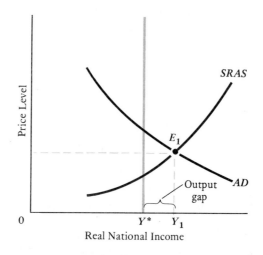

(ii) A negative output gap

The output gap is the difference between potential national income, Y^*, and the actual national income, Y. Potential national income is shown by a vertical line because it refers to a given, constant national income. Actual national income is determined by the intersection of the aggregate demand (AD) and short-run aggregate supply ($SRAS$) curves.

In part (i) the positions of the AD and $SRAS$ curves result in a positive output gap. This is because equilibrium is at E_0, so actual national income is given by Y_0, which is less than potential income. The output gap is thus $Y^* - Y_0$.

In part (ii) the positions of the AD and $SRAS$ curves result in a negative output gap. Although potential income is unchanged at Y^*, equilibrium is now at E_1, so actual national income is given by Y_1, which is greater than potential income. The output gap is thus $Y^* - Y_1$.

national income that exceeds potential income, resulting in a negative output gap.

Factor Prices and the Output Gap

The output gap provides a convenient measure of the pressure of demand on factor prices. When national income is high relative to potential income, demand for factors will also be high. When national income is low relative to potential income, demand for factors will be correspondingly low. This is true of all factors. *The discussion that follows can be simplified, however, by focusing on one key factor, labor, and on its price, the wage rate.* Earlier we referred to average costs per unit of output as *unit costs;* to focus on labor costs, we now use average wage costs per unit of output, which we refer to as *unit labor costs.*

When there is a negative output gap, the demand for labor services will be relatively high. When there is a positive output gap, the demand for labor services will be relatively low.

Each of these situations will have implications for wages. Before turning to a detailed analysis of each, we first consider our benchmark for the behavior of wages.

Upward and downward wage pressures.   In what follows we consider the *upward* and *downward* pressures on wages that are associated with various output gaps. Negative output gaps will exert upward pressure on wages, and positive output gaps will exert downward pressure on wages. To what do the upward and downward pressures relate? One answer would be that upward pressure means that wages would rise, and downward pressure means that wages would fall. However, most wage bargaining starts from the assumption that, other things being equal, workers should get the benefit of increases in their own productivity by receiving higher wages. Because of this, when national income is at its potential level, so that there are neither upward nor downward pressures on wages caused by output gaps, wages will tend to be rising at the same rate as productivity is rising.[1] When wages and productivity change proportionately, labor cost per unit of output, which we have earlier called *unit labor costs,* remains unchanged. For example, if each worker produces 4 percent more and earns 4 percent more, unit labor costs will remain constant. This, then, is the benchmark:

When there is neither excess demand nor excess supply in the labor market, wages will tend to be rising as fast as labor productivity is rising; in this case unit labor costs will remain constant.

Note that, with unit labor costs remaining constant, there is no pressure coming from the labor market for the *SRAS* curve to shift and hence no pressure for the price level to rise or to fall.

In comparison with this benchmark, upward pressure on wages means that there is pressure for wages to rise faster than productivity is rising. When this occurs, unit labor costs will also be rising. For example, if money wages rise by 8 percent while productivity rises by only 4 percent, labor cost per unit of output will be rising by about 4 percent. In this case the *SRAS* curve will be shifting leftward, and hence there will be upward pressure coming from the labor market.

Downward pressure on wages means that there is pressure for wages to rise less fast than productivity. When this occurs, unit labor costs will be falling. For example, if productivity rises by 4 percent while money wages rise by only 2 percent, labor costs per

unit of output will be falling by about 2 percent. In this case the *SRAS* curve will be shifting rightward, and hence there will be downward pressure coming from the labor market.

A negative output gap.   Sometimes the *AD* and *SRAS* curves intersect where actual output exceeds potential, as illustrated in part (ii) of Figure 28-1. Firms are producing beyond their normal capacity output, so there is an unusually large demand for all factor inputs, including labor. Labor shortages will emerge in some industries and among many groups of workers, particularly skilled workers. Firms will try to bid workers away from other firms in order to maintain the high levels of output and sales made possible by the boom conditions.

As a result of tight labor-market conditions, workers will find that they have considerable bargaining power with their employers, and they will put upward pressure on wages.[2] Firms, recognizing that demand for their goods is strong, will be anxious to maintain a high level of output. Thus, to prevent their workers from either striking or quitting and moving to other employers, firms will be willing to accede to some of these upward pressures.

The boom that is associated with a negative output gap generates a set of conditions—high profits for firms and unusually large demand for labor—that exerts upward pressure on wages.

A positive output gap.   Sometimes the *AD* and *SRAS* curves intersect where actual output is less than potential, as illustrated in part (i) of Figure 28-1. In this situation firms will be producing below their normal capacity output, so there is an unusually low demand for all factor inputs, including labor. The general conditions in the market for labor will be the opposite of those when actual output exceeds potential. There now will be labor surpluses in some industries and among some groups of workers. Firms will have below normal sales and not only will resist upward pressures on wages but also will tend to offer wage increases below productivity increases and may even seek reductions in wages.

---

[1] Ongoing inflation would also influence the normal pattern of wage changes. Wage contracts often allow for changes in prices that are expected to occur during the life of the contract. For now we make the simplifying assumption that the price level is expected to be constant; hence, changes in money wages also are expected to be changes in real wages. The distinction between changes in money wages and real wages, and the important role played by expectations of price level changes, will be discussed in Chapters 34 and 37.

[2] Additional upward pressures on the level of wages may be created by the fact that the price level, P_1, will be higher than P^*, the price level that would have prevailed had output attained its potential level.

The slump that is associated with a positive output gap generates a set of conditions—low profits for firms, unusually low demand for labor, and a desire on the part of firms to resist wage demands and even to push for wage concessions—that exerts downward pressure on wages.

Adjustment asymmetry.   At this stage we encounter an important asymmetry in the economy's aggregate supply behavior. Boom conditions, along with severe labor shortages, do cause wages (and the price level) to rise rapidly. When there is a large excess demand for labor, wage (and price) increases often run well ahead of productivity increases. Money wages might be rising by 10 or 15 percent, while productivity might be rising at only 2 or 3 percent. This means that unit labor costs will be rising rapidly.

The experience of many economies suggests, however, that downward pressures on wages during slumps often do not operate as quickly as do the upward pressures during booms. Even in quite severe recessions, when the price level is fairly stable, money wages may continue to rise, although their rate of increase tends to fall below that of productivity. For example, productivity might be rising at, say, 1½ percent, while money wages are rising at ½ percent. In this case unit labor costs are falling but only at about 1 percent per year, so the leftward shift in the *SRAS* curve and the downward pressure on the price level is correspondingly slight.[3] Money wages actually may fall, reducing unit-wage costs even more, but the reduction in unit labor costs in times of the deepest recession has never been as fast as the increases that have occurred during several of the strongest booms.

Both upward and downward adjustments to unit wage costs do occur, but there are differences in the speed at which they typically occur. Excess demand can cause unit labor costs to rise very rapidly; excess supply often causes unit labor costs to fall more slowly.

Box 28-1 discusses the wage-cost adjustment process, including its asymmetries, in terms of a famous relationship, called the *Phillips curve*.

[3] This is the second asymmetry in aggregate supply that we have encountered. The first refers to the changing slope of the *SRAS* curve, as discussed in Box 27-3.

The inflationary and recessionary gaps.   The asymmetry in the economy's speed of adjustment in response to positive and negative output gaps can be emphasized by some terminology.

Since a negative output gap normally will be accompanied by rising unit costs, the *SRAS* curve will be shifting upward. This, in turn, will push the price level up. Indeed, the most obvious event accompanying a negative output gap is likely to be a significant inflation. Large, negative output gaps will bring rapid inflations. To emphasize this salient feature, negative output gaps are referred to as **inflationary gaps.**

A positive output gap, as we have seen, will be associated with unemployment of labor and other productive resources. Unit labor costs will fall only slowly, leading to a slow downward shift in the *SRAS* curve. Hence, the price level will be falling only slowly, so that unemployment will be the positive output gap's most obvious result. Large, positive output gaps will bring high rates of unemployment. To emphasize this salient feature, positive output gaps are referred to as **recessionary gaps.**

From now on we will stick to these more vivid and descriptive terms:

When actual national income exceeds potential income, there is an inflationary gap; when actual national income is less than potential income, there is a recessionary gap.

The induced effects of output gaps on unit labor costs and consequent shifts in the *SRAS* curve play an important role in our analysis of the long-run consequences of aggregate demand shocks, to which we now turn.

The Long-Run Consequences of Aggregate Demand Shocks

We can now extend our study to cover the longer-run consequences of aggregate demand shocks, which cause factor prices to change. We need to examine separately the effect of aggregate demand shocks on factor prices for expansionary and for con-

BOX 28-1

The Phillips Curve and the Shifting *SRAS* Curve

In the early 1950s Professor A. W. Phillips of the London School of Economics was doing pathbreaking research on macroeconomic policy. He included in his early models an equation that related the rate of inflation to the difference between actual and potential income, $Y - Y^*$. Later he investigated the empirical underpinnings of this equation by studying the relationship between the rate of increase of wage costs and the level of unemployment. In 1958 he reported that a stable relationship had existed between these two variables for 100 years in the United Kingdom. This is the form in which the relationship captured world attention and

the form in which it came to be called the Phillips curve.

The Phillips curve provided an explanation, rooted in empirical data, of the speed with which wage changes shifted the *SRAS* curve by changing unit-labor costs. The empirical relationship that Phillips studied was between unemployment and wage rates. One reason he studied this was because he thought that unemployment provided a better measure of demand pressures in the labor market than did output gaps. More importantly, however, unemployment data were available as far back as the midnineteenth century, while very little data on

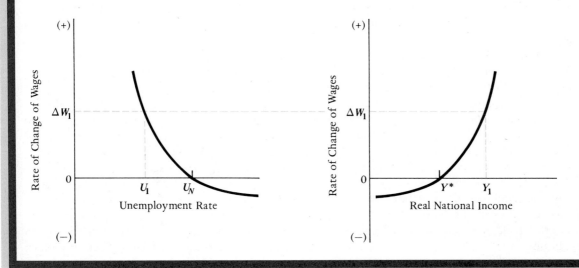

tractionary shocks, since the behavior of unit costs is not symmetrical for the two cases. In what follows we make the simplifying assumption that labor productivity is constant, so all changes in wages are also changes in unit labor costs and hence cause the *SRAS* curve to shift. Do not forget, however, that the more general result is that the *SRAS* curve shifts upward whenever money wages rise faster than productivity and downward whenever they rise more slowly than productivity.

Expansionary Shocks

Suppose that the economy starts off with a stable price level at full employment, so actual income equals potential. This is shown by the initial equilibrium in Figure 28-2(i).

Now suppose that this happy situation is disturbed by an increase in autonomous expenditure, perhaps caused by a sudden boom in investment spending. Part (i) of Figure 28-2 shows the effects of

output gaps was available when he did his pioneering empirical work.

Nonetheless, his curve can be translated into one that relates wage changes to output gaps by noting that unemployment and the gaps are negatively related to each other. A recessionary gap is associated with high unemployment, and an inflationary gap is associated with low unemployment. Thus, the Phillips curve also can be drawn with national income on the horizontal axis, as in the figures to the left.

Both figures show the same information. Inflationary gaps (which correspond to low unemployment rates) are associated with *increases* in wages, while recessionary gaps (which correspond to high unemployment rates) are associated with slow *decreases* in wages.

The Phillips curve must be clearly distinguished from the *SRAS* curve. The *SRAS* curve has the *price level* on the vertical axis, while the Phillips curve has the *rate of wage inflation* on the vertical axis. Therefore, the Phillips curve tells us how fast the *SRAS* curve is shifting when actual income does not equal potential income.

Only when $Y = Y^*$ is the *SRAS* curve not shifting on account of demand pressures. When income is at its potential level, aggregate demand for labor equals aggregate supply; the only unemployment would thus be frictional and structural.

There would be neither upward nor downward pressure of demand on wages. Thus, the Phillips curve cuts the axis at potential income Y^* and at the corresponding level of unemployment U_N. This is how Phillips drew his curve; later we shall see that things are not so simple.

The Phillips curve soon became famous. It provided a link between national-income models and labor markets. This link allowed macroeconomists to drop the uncomfortable assumption, which they had often been forced to use in many of their earlier formal models, that money wages were rigidly fixed and neither rose nor fell as national income varied. The Phillips curve relationship between money wages and national income determines (in conjunction with productivity changes) the speed at which the *SRAS* curve shifts.

Consider, for example, the situation that is shown in part (ii) of Figure 28-1, where the level of income determined by the *AD* and *SRAS* curves is Y_1. Plotting Y_1 on the Phillips curve in the figure on the right tells us that wage costs will be rising at ΔW_1. Then the *SRAS* curve in Figure 28-1(ii) will be shifting upward by that amount. The same information can be seen in the figure on the left, where national income of Y_1 corresponds to unemployment of U_1.

this aggregate demand shock in raising both the price level and national income. Now actual national income exceeds potential income, and there is an inflationary gap.

We have seen that an inflationary gap leads to increases in wages, which cause unit costs to rise. The *SRAS* curve then shifts leftward as firms seek to pass on their increases in input costs by increasing their output prices. For this reason the initial increases in the price level and in real national income

shown in Figure 28-2(i) are *not* the final effects of the demand shock. As seen in part (ii) of the figure, the leftward shift of the *SRAS* curve causes a further rise in the price level, but this time the price rise is associated with a fall in output.

The cost increases (and the consequent leftward shifts of the *SRAS* curve) go on until the inflationary gap has been removed, that is, until income returns to Y^*, its potential level. Only then is there no abnormal demand for labor, and only then do wages

FIGURE 28-2   Demand-Shock Inflation

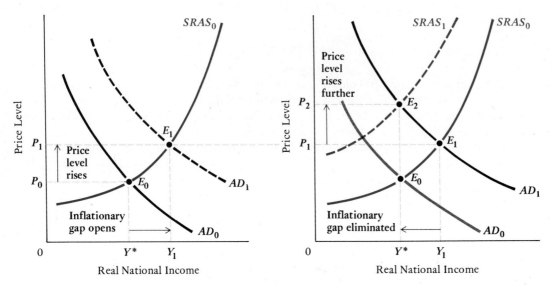

(i) Autonomous increase in aggregate demand   (ii) Induced shift in aggregate supply

A rightward shift of the *AD* curve first raises prices and output along the *SRAS* curve. It then induces a shift of the *SRAS* curve that further raises prices but lowers output along the *AD* curve. In part (i) the economy is in equilibrium at E_0, at its level of potential output, Y^*, and price level, P_0. The *AD* curve then shifts to AD_1. This moves equilibrium to E_1, with income, Y_1, and price level, P_1, and opens up an inflationary gap of $Y^* - Y_1$.

In part (ii) the inflationary gap results in an increase in wages and other input costs, shifting the *SRAS* curve leftward. As this happens, income falls and the price level rises along AD_1. Eventually, when the *SRAS* curve has shifted to $SRAS_1$, income is back to Y^* and the inflationary gap has been eliminated. However, the price level has risen to P_2.

and unit costs, and hence the *SRAS* curve, stabilize.

This important expansionary demand–shock sequence can be summarized as follows:

1. Starting from full employment, a rise in aggregate demand raises the price level and raises income above its potential level as the economy expands along a given *SRAS* curve.
2. The expansion of income beyond its normal capacity level puts heavy pressure on factor markets; factor prices begin to rise, shifting the *SRAS* curve to the left.
3. The shift of the *SRAS* curve causes national income to fall along the *AD* curve. This process continues *as long as* actual income exceeds potential income. Therefore, actual income eventually

falls back to its potential level. The price level is, however, now higher than it was after the initial impact of the increased aggregate demand, but inflation will have come to a halt.

The ability to wring more output and income from the economy than its underlying potential output (as in point 2) is only a short-term possibility. National income greater than Y^* sets up inflationary pressures that tend to push national income back to Y^*.

There is a self-adjustment mechanism that brings any inflation caused by a one-time demand shock to an eventual halt by returning

FIGURE 28-3   Demand-Shock Deflation with Flexible Wages

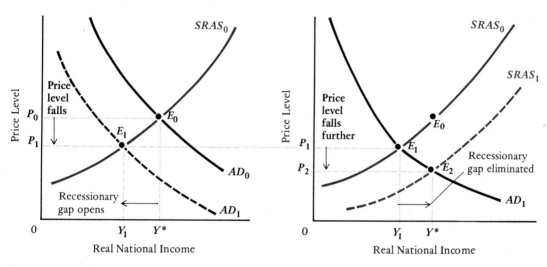

(i) Autonomous fall in aggregate demand   (ii) Induced shift in aggregate supply

A leftward shift of the *AD* curve first lowers price and output along the *SRAS* curve and then induces a (slow) shift of the *SRAS* curve that further lowers prices but raises output along the *AD* curve. In part (i) the economy is in equilibrium at E_0, at its level of potential output, Y^*, and price level, P_0. The *AD* curve then shifts to AD_1, moving equilibrium to E_1, with income Y_1 and price level P_1, and opens up a recessionary gap of $Y^* - Y_1$.

Part (ii) shows the adjustment back to full employment that would occur from the supply side of the economy if wages were sufficiently flexible downward. The fall in wages would shift the *SRAS* curve to the right. Real national income would rise, and the price level would fall further along the *AD* curve. Eventually, the *SRAS* curve would reach $SRAS_1$, with equilibrium at E_2. The price level would stabilize at P_2 when income had returned to Y^*, eliminating the recessionary gap.

output to its potential level and thus removing the inflationary gap.

Contractionary Shocks

Let us return to that fortunate economy with full employment and stable prices. It appears again in part (i) of Figure 28-3, which is similar to Figure 28-2(i). Now assume that there is a *decline* in aggregate demand, perhaps due to a major reduction in investment exenditure.

The first effects of the decline are a fall in output and some downward adjustment of prices, as shown in part (i) of the figure. As output falls, unemployment rises. The difference between potential output and actual output is the recessionary gap that is shown in Figure 28-3.

Flexible wages. What would happen if severe unemployment did cause wage rates to fall rapidly? Falling wage rates would lower unit costs, causing a rightward shift of the *SRAS* curve. As shown in Figure 28-3(ii), the economy would move along its fixed *AD* curve with falling prices and rising output until full employment was restored at potential national income Y^*. We conclude that if wages were to fall whenever there was unemployment, the resulting fall in the *SRAS* curve would restore full employment.

Flexible wages that fell when there was unemployment would provide an automatic adjustment mechanism that would push the economy

back toward full employment whenever output fell below potential.[4]

Box 28-2 takes up the interesting case of how the adjustment mechanism might work if the aggregate demand shock was anticipated in advance.

Sticky wages. Boom conditions, along with severe labor shortages, do cause wages to rise rapidly, shifting the *SRAS* curve upward. However, as we noted above when we encountered the second asymmetry of aggregate supply behavior, the experience of many economies suggests that wages typically do not fall rapidly in response to recessionary gaps and their accompanying unemployment. It is sometimes said that wages are "sticky" in a downward direction. This does not mean that wages never fall. They do. Typically, however, they do not fall as fast in response to recessionary gaps as they rise in response to inflationary gaps. If wages are sluggish in their response to recessionary gaps, unit labor costs will fall only slowly. This, in turn, means that the downward shifts in the *SRAS* curve occur slowly, and the adjustment mechanism that depends on these shifts will act sluggishly.

The weakness of the automatic adjustment mechanism does not mean that slumps must always be prolonged. What it means is that speedy recovery back to full employment must be generated mainly from the demand side. If the economy is to avoid a lengthy period of stagnation, the force leading to recovery usually must be a rightward shift of the *AD* curve rather than a rightward drift of the *SRAS* curve.

The *SRAS* curve shifts to the left fairly rapidly when national income exceeds Y^*, but it shifts to the right only slowly when national income is less than Y^*.

The asymmetry. This difference in speed of adjustment is a consequence of the important asymmetry in the behavior of aggregate supply that was noted earlier in this chapter. This asymmetry helps to explain two key facts about our economy. First, unemployment *can* persist for quite long periods with-

out causing large decreases in unit costs and prices (which, when they do occur, help to remove the unemployment). Second, booms, along with labor shortages and production beyond normal capacity, do not persist for long periods without causing large increases in unit costs and prices.

The Long-Run Aggregate Supply (*LRAS*) Curve

The automatic adjustment mechanism leads us to an important concept: the **long-run aggregate supply (*LRAS*) curve.** This curve relates the price level to real national income *after wage rates and all other input costs have been fully adjusted to eliminate any unemployment or overall labor shortages.*[5]

Shape of the *LRAS* curve. Once all the adjustments that are required have occurred, the economy will have eliminated any excess demand or excess supply of labor. In other words, full employment will prevail, and output will necessarily be at its potential level, Y^*. It follows that the aggregate supply curve becomes a vertical line at Y^*, as shown in Figure 28-4.[6]

Notice that the vertical *LRAS* curve does not represent the same thing as the vertical portion of the *SRAS* curve (see Figure 27-10). Over the vertical range of the *SRAS* curve, the economy is at its utmost limit of productive capacity, when no more can be squeezed out, as might occur in an all-out war effort. The vertical shape of the *LRAS* curve is due to the workings of an adjustment mechanism that brings the economy back to its potential output, even though it may stray away in the short run. It is called the *long-run* aggregate supply curve because it refers to adjustments that take a substantial amount of time.

Along the *LRAS* curve all the prices of *all outputs* and *all inputs* have been fully adjusted to eliminate any excess demands or supplies[7]. Proportionate

---

[4] Recall that what determines unit costs is how money wages behave relative to productivity. Since we are assuming productivity to be constant, we can talk about increases or decreases in wages. However, this must always be understood to mean increases or decreases relative to the change in productivity.

[5] Students who have studied microeconomics will notice that this use of the term *long run* appears from its meaning in microeconomics. Note, however, the key similarity that the long run has more flexibility for adjustment than does the short run.

[6] The *LRAS* curve is sometimes called the classical aggregate supply curve because the classical economists were mainly concerned with the behavior of the economy in long-run equilibrium.

[7] Strictly speaking, stocks of assets that are denominated in money terms must also be adjusted so that there are no wealth effects on spending of changes in the price level.

BOX 28-2

Anticipated Demand Shocks

Suppose that the increase in aggregate demand, which is illustrated in Figure 28-2, was widely anticipated well before it occurred. For example, as an election approached it might become widely believed that the administration would stimulate the economy in order to improve its electoral chances (as the Nixon administration did in 1972).

Further, suppose that most employers and employees believe that one of the effects of the demand stimulation will be an inflation. Now workers might press for wage increases so that the purchasing power of their earnings would not be eroded by the coming price increases. Firms, knowing that demand for their products was likely to rise, enabling them to raise their selling prices, might be persuaded to grant wage increases now and pass these on to consumers in terms of higher prices.

A demand stimulus that was widely expected to occur and whose inflationary effects were widely understood could lead to upward pressure on wages, even without any inflationary gap opening up.

If this were to occur, the leftward shift in the *SRAS* curve that is depicted in part (ii) of Figure 28-2 could occur quickly, perhaps accompanying, or even preceding, the rightward shift in the *AD* curve in part (i). Given *perfect* anticipation of the effects of the demand stimulus, and *full* adjustment to it in advance, the equilibrium would go straight from E_0 to E_2. The intermediate position, E_1, with its accompanying inflationary gap (with national income in excess of potential income), would be completely bypassed.

A similar story might be told for an anticipated fall in aggregate demand. The effects of an unanticipated fall are shown in the two parts of Figure 28-3. However, if the fall were widely anticipated and its effects were generally understood, firms might reduce their wage offers and workers might accept the decreases because they expect that prices will fall as well. In this case it is conceivable that the economy could bypass the recessionary stage and go straight to a lower price level at an unchanged level of real national income.

This possibility, that anticipated demand shocks might have no real effects on real national income and hence on unemployment, plays a key role in some important controversies concerning the effectiveness of government policies. We shall study these in detail in Chapter 37.

In the meantime, we may notice that the complete absence of real effects in the transitionary period, with the only change being in the price level, requires that everyone has full knowledge, both of the exact amount of the stimulus that the government will induce and of the new equilibrium values of the relevant prices and wages. In other words, everyone knows what the new equilibrium will be and goes directly to it. If people do not have such perfect knowledge and foresight, there may be some groping toward the equilibrium and some real effects until the final equilibrium set of wages and prices is reached.

changes in money wages and the price level (which, by definition, will leave real wages unaltered) will also leave equilibrium employment and output unchanged. The key concept is this: If the price of absolutely everything (including labor) doubles, nothing real changes. When the price of everything bought *and* sold doubles, neither workers nor firms gain any advantage and hence neither has any incentive to alter their behavior. Output, therefore, is un-

changed. The level of output will be what can be produced in the economy when all factors of production, including labor, are utilized at "normal capacity."

The vertical *LRAS* curve shows that, given full adjustment of input prices, potential income, *Y**, is compatible with *any* price level.

FIGURE 28-4   The Long-Run Aggregate Supply (*LRAS*) Curve

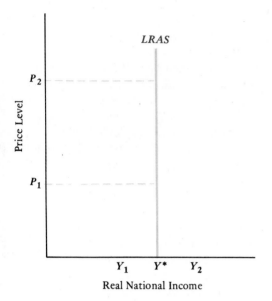

The long-run aggregate supply curve is a vertical line drawn at the level of national income that is equal to potential income, Y^*. It is a vertical line because the total amount of goods that the economy produces when all factors are efficiently used at their normal rate of utilization does not vary with the price level. If the price level were to rise from P_1 to P_2 *and* wages and all other factor prices were to rise by the same proportion, the desired output of firms would remain at Y^*.

If income were Y_1, which is less than Y^*, wages would be falling and the *SRAS* curve would be shifting rightward; hence the economy would not be on its *LRAS* curve. If income were Y_2, which is greater than Y^*, wages would be rising and the *SRAS* curve would be shifting leftward; hence the economy would not be on its *LRAS* curve.

Long-Run Equilibrium

Figure 28-5 shows the equilibrium output and the price level as they are determined by the intersection of the *AD* curve and the vertical *LRAS* curve. Because the *LRAS* curve is vertical, shifts in aggregate demand change the price level but not the level of equilibrium output, as shown in part (i). In contrast, a shift in aggregate supply changes both output and the price level, as shown in part (ii). For example, a

FIGURE 28-5   Long-Run Equilibrium and Aggregate Supply

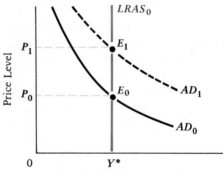

(i) A rise in aggregate demand

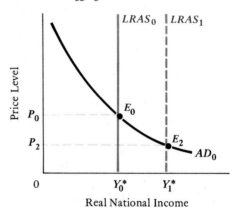

(ii) A rise in long-run aggregate supply

When the *LRAS* curve is vertical, aggregate supply determines the long-run equilibrium value of national income at Y^*. Given Y^*, aggregate demand determines the long-run equilibrium value of the price level. In both parts of the figure the initial long-run equilibrium is at E_0, so the price level is P_0 and national income is Y_0^*.

In part (i) a shift in the *AD* curve from AD_0 to AD_1, with the *LRAS* curve remaining unchanged, moves the long-run equilibrium from E_0 to E_1. This raises the price level from P_0 to P_1 but leaves national income unchanged at Y_0^* in the long run.

In part (ii) a shift in the *LRAS* curve from $LRAS_0$ to $LRAS_1$, with the aggregate demand curve remaining constant at AD_0, moves the long-run equilibrium from E_0 to E_2. This raises national income from Y_0^* to Y_1^* but lowers the price level from P_0 to P_2.

rightward shift of the *LRAS* curve increases national income and leads (eventually) to a fall in the price level.

With a vertical *LRAS* curve, output is determined solely by conditions of supply, and the role of aggregate demand is simply to determine the price level.

Of course, these are only long-term tendencies. To see the short-term impact of demand and supply shocks, we need to use the short-run aggregate supply curve. Because downward adjustments of wages, unit costs, and prices may take a long time, there may be long periods when the economy is well away from its long-run equilibrium.

Supply-Side Economics[8]

Both of Ronald Reagan's U.S. presidential campaigns featured a theory of economic policy that came to be known as *supply-side economics*. President Bush once called it "voodoo economics," but apparently he has since changed his mind. To some the policy promised a quick cure for both high inflation and low growth in real national income. To others it seemed an exercise in wishful thinking.

The theoretical tools that have been developed in this chapter can be used to explore both the theory and the doubts about it. Although supply-side economics has many aspects, here we are concerned specifically with the effects of supply-side policies on the price level and on real national income, starting from a situation with a large inflationary gap. When Ronald Reagan became president in January 1981, the inflation rate was about 10 percent and unemployment was about 7 percent; any policy that would decrease them both would have been welcomed.

How It Was Supposed to Work

The theory of supply-side economics called for adopting measures that would shift the *LRAS* curve to the right far enough to reduce inflationary pressures. In the most favorable case there would be no offsetting demand-side effects. This case is illustrated in Figure 28-6.

A major part of supply-side economics was the provision of tax incentives that would increase potential national income by increasing the nation's supplies of labor and capital. Incentives were given to firms to increase their investment, thus, it was hoped, increasing national productive capacity. Personal taxes were cut across the board to give everyone an incentive to work more. It was argued that people who were already employed would be more inclined to work longer and harder when they were able to keep a larger percentage of their pretax earnings, and people outside of the labor force would be drawn in as a result of the higher after-tax wages. Extra tax incentives were given to persons at high income levels to increase the incentives for work and risk taking on the part of the most productive people. Many argued that the resulting increases in productive capacity and in productivity would shift the *LRAS* curve to the right, thus raising equilibrium national income and further reducing inflationary pressure.

Supply siders also argued that the cuts in tax rates and increases in tax exemptions would not increase the federal government's budget deficit. They believed that the increase in national income would create an increase in the tax base that would be sufficient to generate larger tax *revenues* in spite of the lower tax *rates*. For example, if a 10 percent cut in tax rates were followed by a 10 percent increase in real national income, it would leave tax revenues approximately the same.[9]

Critics of the Theory

One major worry of critics of the theory was that demand-side effects would swamp any supply-side effects for at least the first several years. Whatever the long-term effects are on the supply side, economic theory is clear about the short-term effects of these measures on the demand side. Cuts in personal tax rates that are expected to be permanent leave households with an increase in their current and expected future disposable incomes. As a result they spend more, causing a rightward shift in the aggre-

---

[8] The rest of this chapter may be omitted without loss of continuity.

[9] Students who have read Chapter 23 and have encountered the Laffer curve (see page 471) will see that believers in that phenomenon had an even more direct reason to believe that tax cuts would increase government revenues.

FIGURE 28-6   The Theory of Antiinflationary Supply-Side Policies

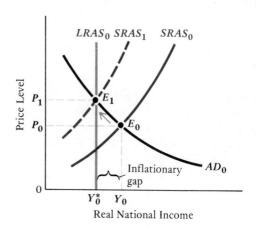 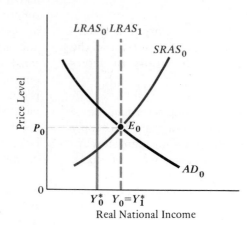

(i) An inflationary situation   (ii) Supply–side success

Supply-side policies sought to eliminate an inflationary gap by shifting the *LRAS* curve to the right without changing aggregate demand. Part (i) shows an economy in short-run equilibrium at E_0 and AD_0 and $SRAS_0$, with income Y_0 and price level P_0. As a result of the inflationary gap, $Y_0^* - Y_0$, the *SRAS* curve will shift upward, taking the equilibrium along AD_0 (as shown by the arrow), with falling national income and rising price level. Other things being equal, the inflation will come to a halt once the curve has reached $SRAS_1$ and equilibrium is established at E_1, with price level P_1 and national income at its potential level Y_0^*.

Part (ii) shows the same economy after supply-side measures shift the *LRAS* curve to $LRAS_1$. This makes Y_1^* the new level of potential income and removes the inflationary gap. The fall of income and rise in the price level shown in part (i) are both prevented.

gate demand curve. Also, we know that an increase in investment increases aggregate demand. In the short run the extra expenditure on capital goods creates new incomes for the factors of production that produce these goods and, through the multiplier process, new incomes for others as well.

Thus, the short-run effect of supply-side measures surely would be to shift the aggregate *demand* curve to the right. In the least favorable situation, if all the demand-increasing effects and none of the favorable aggregate supply effects were to occur, the result would be an increase in the inflationary gap. This possibility is illustrated in Figure 28-7.

Supply siders with training in economics knew that the short-term effects via aggregate demand would occur. However, they believed that the supply-side shifts of long-run aggregate supply would be large enough and quick enough to dominate them. Critics not only doubted this view as to timing but

also questioned whether the tax changes proposed would have the desired effects even in the long run. Economic theory makes no definite prediction about the effects of tax cuts on how much people will work. Cuts might make them work more, because they earn more for each additional hour that they work, but cuts might make them work less, because they can, if they wish, have both more disposable income and more leisure. For example, if in response to a tax cut that increased after-tax wages by 10 percent they worked 5 percent less, they would have approximately 5 percent more disposable income and 5 percent more leisure. (This is discussed in greater detail in Chapter 38.

Evaluating the Theory

It is difficult to resolve all the factual matters at issue in the supply-side debate on the basis of the Reagan

FIGURE 28-7   Demand Effects of Supply-Side Measures

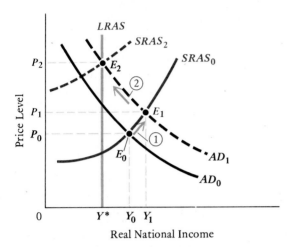

The effect of supply-side measures on aggregate demand is inflationary. The figure shows the economy in the same short-run initial equilibrium at E_0 as in Figure 28-6(i). However, it assumes that demand-side effects of the policy measures occur and are fully felt before any supply-side effects come into play. The AD curve shifts to the right to AD_1, and the economy moves toward equilibrium at E_1, as shown by arrow 1. This gives a temporary increase in output to Y_1 at the cost of an immediate rise in the price level to P_1. However, the inflationary gap is also increased, to $Y^* - Y_1$. Now the $SRAS$ curve starts to shift upward, taking the equilibrium along AD_1 in the direction shown by arrow 2, along with falling output and rising prices. If nothing else happens, the inflation will finally come to an end at price level P_2 and output Y^*. As a result of the supply-side measures, the rise in the price level, from P_0 to P_2, is *greater* than it would have been without the measures, that is, from P_0 to P_1.

administration's experiences. First, the proposed measures were never fully implemented. Second, the inflationary conditions postulated in the theory were removed by both the course of events—no further cost-side pressures from rising oil and raw material prices—and by the Federal Reserve's monetary policy (which we discuss in Chapter 33). Nonetheless, some conclusions can be ventured.

First, it is clear that the aggregate demand effects of the policy were stronger than its supply-side effects in the short term. Consumer expenditures rose dramatically. The United States enjoyed a rapid recovery from the deep recession of the early 1980s, while many other industrial countries took most of the decade to recover from the recession.

Second, it is even clearer that the induced rise in national income was not sufficient to restore the government revenue that was lost when tax rates were cut. All through the 1980s the federal government's budget deficit was a cause of concern for economists, and, by the end of the decade, the deficit remained substantially unchecked.

Finally, the anticipated supply-side effects are harder to locate. It is in the nature of these positive effects that they are diffused throughout the whole economy, which makes them difficult to identify and to measure. The incentives to business investment were accompanied by a rise in investment spending later in the decade, but it was too little and too late, and some of it would no doubt have occurred anyway. To what extent the reductions in tax rates provided effective incentives is more difficult to assess. The possibility that the supply-side reforms had major effects in improving the functioning of the economy cannot, however, be dismissed lightly. We will return to this issue in a later chapter.

SUMMARY

1. Potential income is treated as given and is represented by a vertical line at Y^*. The output gap is equal to the horizontal distance between Y^* and the actual level of income, as determined by the intersection of the AD and $SRAS$ curves.

2. A negative output gap means that demand in the labor market is relatively high. As a result, wages rise faster than productivity, causing unit costs to rise. The $SRAS$ curve shifts leftward, and the price level rises. Thus, any excess of actual national income over potential national income is called an inflationary gap.

3. A positive output gap means that demand in the labor market is relatively low. While there is some resulting tendency for wages to fall relative to productivity, asymmetrical behavior means that the

strength of this force will be much weaker than that indicated in summary point 2. Unit costs will only fall slowly, so the output gap will persist. Any shortfall of actual national income relative to potential is called a recessionary gap.

4. An expansionary demand shock creates an inflationary gap that causes wages to rise faster than productivity. Unit costs rise, shifting the *SRAS* curve to the left, resulting in a higher level of prices, with output eventually falling back to its potential level.

5. A contractionary demand shock will work in the opposite direction. If, however, factor prices are sticky, the automatic adjustment process may be slow, and a recessionary gap may not be quickly eliminated.

6. The long-run aggregate supply (*LRAS*) curve relates the price level and national income after all wages and other costs have been adjusted fully to long-run equilibrium. The *LRAS* curve is vertical at the level of potential income, Y^*.

7. Because the *LRAS* curve is vertical, output in the long run is determined by the position of the *LRAS* curve, and the only long-run role of the *AD* curve is to determine the price level.

8. Supply-side economics in an inflationary situation seeks to reduce an inflationary gap and increase output by tax cuts and other incentive measures that are designed to shift the *LRAS* curve to the right and thus increase potential output. In the short run such measures increase aggregate demand, thus adding to inflationary pressures. In the long run this may increase the rate at which the *LRAS* curve is shifting to the right due to economic growth.

TOPICS FOR REVIEW

The output gap and the labor market
Inflationary gap
Recessionary gap
Asymmetry of wage adjustment
Changes in aggregate demand shocks and induced wage changes
Wages, productivity, and unit costs
Long-run aggregate supply *(LRAS)* curve
Supply-side economics

DISCUSSION QUESTIONS

1. "Starting from a full-employment equilibrium, an increase in government spending can produce more output and employment at the cost of a once-and-for-all rise in the price level."

   "Increased spending can never lead to a permanent increase in output above its full employment level."

   Discuss these two statements in terms of short- and long-run *aggregate supply curves.*

2. Identify the effects of each of the following events on the *SRAS* and the *LRAS* curves.
   a. Increase in the price of imported raw materials that are used in key manufacturing industries
   b. Increase in the price of imported consumption goods such as coffee or bananas
   c. Increased restrictions on pollution emissions in an attempt to combat acid rain
   d. Projections of increased federal government deficits over the next five years

e. An improved economic outlook leading to an investment boom

f. Increased labor force participation rate of key sectors of the population

3. Interpret each of the following news items in terms of *AD* and *SRAS* curves. (Assume that the statements are correct for purposes of drawing your curves.)

    a. "Management representative says union wage demands are irresponsible in the face of current high unemployment rates."

    b. "Government spokesman says that although the recovery is expected to be vigorous, it will witness only modest reductions in the unemployment rate."

    c. "Wage increases have failed to keep up with inflation during the current boom."

    d. "Innovations in microelectronic technology will lead to an increase in both national output and unemployment."

    e. "Reagan's tough stance with public sector unions early in his term improved the inflation performance of the U.S. over the next few years."

4. Comment on the following newspaper headline: "More growth seen as cure for inflation."

5. Politicians are sometimes accused of adopting policies that bring "short-term gain at the cost of long-term pain," while statesmen offer "short-term pain to buy long-term gain." What policies that shifted aggregate demand or aggregate supply curves might come under one or the other of these descriptions?

6. Over 20 percent of Canadian national income is generated through exports to the United States. Why do Canadians worry that "when the U.S. gets an (economic) cold, Canada gets (economic) pneumonia"?

7. If downward flexibility of money wages would allow the automatic adjustment mechanism to eliminate recessionary gaps quickly, why do workers usually resist wage cuts during times of economic slump?

Chapter 29

Business Cycles: The Ebb and Flow of Economic Activity

Changing, always changing—that is the dominant characteristic of national income as far back as there are records. As we saw in Chapter 24, GNP—like most economic time series—exhibits two types of change. The upward trend in GNP indicates long-term change, which we call economic growth, while shorter-term oscillations in GNP represent temporary changes, which we call the business cycle.

Economic growth and the business cycle both represent changes in total real output and hence in employment and unemployment. Both are also the subject of much public debate and the object of government policies. Later in this book we shall study policy in some detail. It is therefore important at this stage to distinguish carefully between the causes and implications of long-term growth and those of short-term fluctuations.

Cycles and Growth

Figure 29-1 illustrates three alternative ways in which GNP can be increased. As shown in part (i) of the figure, an increase in aggregate demand will yield a one-time increase in real GNP. If that increase occurs when there is a recessionary gap, it pushes GNP toward potential income and thus short-circuits the working of the automatic adjustment mechanism that eventually would have achieved the same outcome by depressing wages and other costs. (The operation of this automatic adjustment mechanism is discussed in detail in Chapter 28; see especially pages 579 to 584.) If the demand shock pushes GNP beyond potential income, the rise in GNP above potential income will only be temporary; the inflationary gap will cause wages and other costs to rise, shifting the *SRAS* curve to the left. This drives GNP back toward potential so that the only lasting effect is on the price level.

Increases in aggregate supply will also lead to an increase in GNP. Here it is useful to distinguish between two possible kinds of increases that might occur—those that leave the *LRAS* curve unchanged and those that shift it.

Part (ii) of Figure 29-1 shows the effects of a temporary increase in aggregate supply due, say, to a bumper agricultural crop. This will shift the *SRAS* curve to the right but will have no effect on the *LRAS* curve or, hence, on potential income. The shock will thus cause *GNP* to rise relative to potential, but the increase will be soon reversed—in this case, possibly even before any significant impact on wages and other costs can be detected.

Part (iii) of Figure 29-1 shows the effects of permanent in-

FIGURE 29-1 Three Ways of Increasing National Income

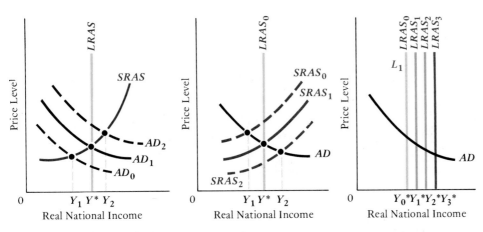

(i) An increase in aggregate
demand

(ii) A temporary increase in
aggregate supply

(iii) Permanent increases in
aggregate supply

National income will increase in response to an increase in aggregate demand or an increase in aggregate supply. The increase will be permanent if the *LRAS* curve shifts, but, if the *LRAS* curve does not shift, any divergences of GNP from potential will only be temporary; the output gap that is created will set in motion the wage adjustments that we studied in Chapter 28.

In part (i) of the figure the *AD* curve shifts to the right. If the initial level of income is Y_1, then the shift from AD_0 to AD_1 eliminates the recessionary gap and raises national income to Y^*. If the initial level of income is Y^*, then the shift from AD_1 to AD_2 raises national income to Y_2 and thereby opens up an inflationary gap.

In part (ii) the *SRAS* curve shifts to the right. If the initial level of income is Y_1, then the shift from $SRAS_0$ to $SRAS_1$ eliminates the recessionary gap and raises national income to Y^*. If the initial level of income is Y^*, then the shift from $SRAS_1$ to $SRAS_2$ raises national income to Y_2 and thereby opens up an inflationary gap.

In the cases shown in parts (i) and (ii), any increase in GNP beyond potential is temporary, since, in the absence of any additional shocks, the inflationary gap will cause wages and other factor prices to rise; this will cause the *SRAS* curve to shift upward and hence national income to converge to Y^*.

In part (iii) the *LRAS* curve shifts to the right so that potential income increases. Whether or not actual income increases immediately depends on what happens to the *AD* and *SRAS* curves. Since, in the absence of other shocks, actual income eventually converges to potential income, a rightward shift in the *LRAS* curve eventually leads to an increase in actual GNP. If the shift in the *LRAS* curve is recurring, then national income will grow continually.

creases in aggregate supply that shift the *LRAS* curve. A once-and-for-all increase due, say, to a labor-market policy that reduces the level of structural unemployment will lead to a one-time increase in potential GNP. A recurring increase that is due, say, to population growth, capital accumulation, or ongoing improvements in productivity causes a continual rightward shift in the *LRAS* curve, giving rise to a continual increase in the level of potential GNP.

A gradual but continual rise in potential GNP, or what we have called *economic growth*, contributes significantly to improvements in the standard of living. Eliminating a severe recessionary gap will cause a once-and-for-all increase in national income of perhaps 4 percent, while eliminating structural unemployment will raise it by somewhat less. However, a growth rate of 3 percent per year raises national income by 10 percent in 3 years and *doubles* it in

FIGURE 29-2 American Business Activity Since 1870

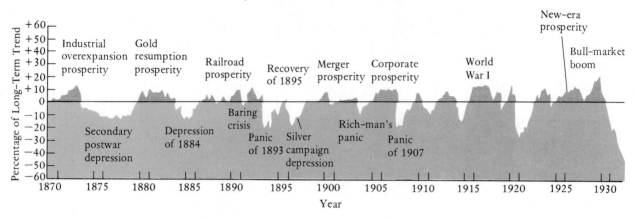

Cyclical ups and downs have dominated the short-term behavior of the U.S. economy at least since 1870. This chart is constructed by selecting one index of general economic activity, fitting a trend line to it, and plotting the deviations of the index from its trend value. It shows clearly the

about 24 years. We shall study the factors influencing economic growth in detail in Chapter 36; in this chapter we focus on *cyclical fluctuations* in GNP.

Cyclical Fluctuations

Figure 29-1 allows us to distinguish the causes of trend growth in potential GNP, which is the gradual rightward shifting of the *LRAS* curve, from the causes of cyclical fluctuations.

Cyclical fluctuations in GNP are caused by shifts in the *AD* and *SRAS* curves that cause actual GNP to deviate temporarily from potential GNP.

These shifts, in turn, are caused by changes in a variety of factors, including interest rates, exchange rates, consumer and business confidence, and government policy. While the resulting deviations of actual from potential GNP are described as "temporary," recall from the previous chapter that the automatic adjustment mechanism may work slowly enough that the deviations can persist for some time, perhaps several years.

The Concept of the Business Cycle

The business cycle was introduced in Chapter 24 (see pages 497–501), where we saw that it refers to the continual ebb and flow of economic activity.[1] The pattern of a sequence of high values for some key series followed by a sequence of low values, followed again by another sequence of high values, is the source of the term *cyclical* that is used to describe such economic fluctuations. A stylized representation of the phases of the cycle was given in Figure 24-3, and the continual oscillations in GNP were apparent in Figure 24-3. Figure 29-2 gives a longer perspective on cyclical fluctuations in real national output.

The complexity of the business cycle cannot be fully captured by a single statistic, even one as important as GNP. Figure 29-3 shows three other economic series. Each of these, as well as a dozen others that might be studied, tells us something about the general variability of the economy. It is clear that some series vary more than others and that they do not all move exactly together.

[1] We noted in Chapter 24 that, when economists wish to analyze monthly or quarterly data, they often try to remove fluctuations that can be accounted for by a regular seasonal pattern. The business cycle refers to fluctuations that remain after the seasonal adjustment has been made.

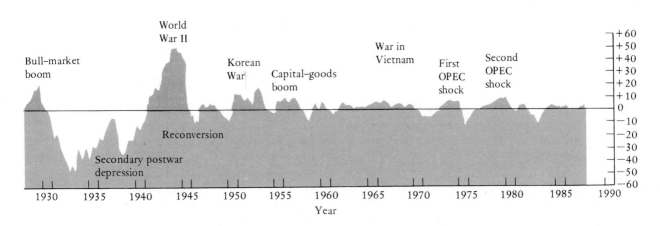

tendency for an economy to fluctuate. Major booms and slumps are unmistakable. (*Source:* The AmeriTrust Company, Cleveland, Ohio)

FIGURE 29-3   Fluctuations in Output, Selected Series, 1950–1988

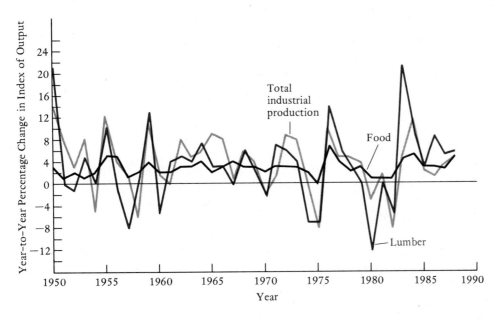

Fluctuations follow similar, but by no means identical, paths for various output series.
Fluctuations are easily seen in these series. Food tends to fluctuate much less than, and lumber fluctuates somewhat more than, the overall series for industrial production. (*Source: Economic Report of the President,* various issues)

The behavior suggested by Figures 29-2 and 29-3 is not one of occasional sharp shifts in the aggregate demand and aggregate supply curves. If it were, we would expect national income to show occasional sharp changes, followed by long periods of little or no change. Instead, the short-term situation is one of continual change at varying rates.

Evidently, there are forces at work causing economic activity to display continual short-term fluctuations around the economy's long-term growth trend.

While all cycles are not alike in duration or intensity, each appears to exhibit movements that cumulate for a while and then eventually reverse themselves. This was true long before governments attempted to intervene in order to stabilize their economies, and it is true still.

The late Alvin Hansen, a distinguished American authority on business cycles, once reported that there were 17 cycles in the U.S. economy between 1795 and 1937, with an average duration of 8.35 years. A shorter "inventory cycle" of 40 months' duration was also found, as well as longer cycles associated with building booms (15 to 20 years). The Russian economist N.D. Kondratieff thought that he could identify long cycles, associated with the introduction of major innovations, of 40 to 50 years. Some economists have argued that in many Western democracies there exists a political business cycle associated with the pattern of elections.

While the evidence is diverse, it is nevertheless possible to identify some basic characteristics of the pattern of business cycles:

1. **A common pattern of variation more or less pervades all economic series.**
2. **Economic series differ in their particular patterns of fluctuations.**
3. **Business cycles differ substantially in the length and the size of the swings involved.**

Explaining Business Cycles

An explanation of the business cycle must answer two questions: (1) What are the factors that cause GNP and other key macro variables to *fluctuate?* (2) What are the factors that cause those fluctuations

to form a *cyclical* pattern? These two questions are taken up in the two main sections that follow.

Why Do Income and Employment Fluctuate?

While there remain unresolved issues and hence points of controversy among economists who study business cycles, there is general agreement that, over the course of U.S. economic history, the business cycle has been caused mainly by fluctuations in aggregate demand. Nevertheless, particular cycles sometimes can be explained in part by aggregate supply shocks. Indeed, the oil-price shocks that occurred in the 1970s made citizens of advanced industrial countries acutely aware of supply-side causes.

Aggregate demand shocks are a major source of fluctuations in GNP; aggregate supply shocks are another source.

Figure 29-4 illustrates the two simple cases that we encountered earlier, in Chapter 27. In part (i) all fluctuations in GNP are the result of fluctuations in the AD curve, while both the $SRAS$ and $LRAS$ curves remain stationary. In part (ii) all fluctuations in GNP are the result of fluctuations in the $SRAS$ curve, while both the AD curve and the $LRAS$ curve remain stationary. These two cases form the basis for most of the discussion in this chapter. They use two key simplifications which should be noted.

First, neither of the two sources of fluctuation in Figure 29-4 affect the $LRAS$ curve nor, hence, the level of potential output. In this chapter we focus on short-term fluctuations, and hence it is useful to ignore the underlying trend of potential output and its determinants. We shall return to a discussion of economic growth in Chapter 36.[2]

Second, Figure 29-4 ignores any *induced* shifts in the $SRAS$ curve. Recall, however, that when the actual level of GNP differs from potential GNP,

---

[2] In that chapter we also encounter the possibility that the same forces that cause fluctuations also cause changes in potential output. This possibility—which essentially means that there are simultaneous shifts in the $SRAS$ and $LRAS$ curves, and hence simultaneous shifts in actual and potential GNP—is the subject of recent developments in the literature on *equilibrium business cycles* and *real business cycles.*

FIGURE 29-4   Demand- and Supply-Driven Business Cycles

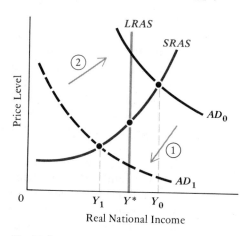

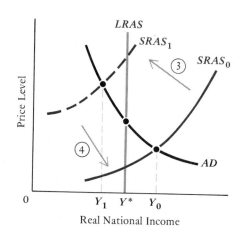

(i) *AD* fluctuations

(ii) *SRAS* fluctuations

Fluctuation in aggregate demand or aggregate supply can cause fluctuations in national income and employment. In (i) the *AD* curve oscillates regularly. Starting from a high level of demand, as depicted by AD_0 and an income level at a peak of Y_0, the *AD* curve then shifts leftward continually, as shown by arrow 1. As a result of this fall in demand, income falls—first reaching Y^* and then falling further to a trough at Y_1. The *AD* curve then starts to shift continually to the right, as shown by arrow 2. Income thus rises, first to Y^* and then reaching Y_0 again at the next peak.

In (ii) the *SRAS* curve oscillates regularly. Starting from a high level of supply, as depicted by $SRAS_0$ and an income level at a peak of Y_0, the *SRAS* curve then shifts leftward continually, as shown by arrow 3. As a result of this fall in supply, income falls—first reaching Y^* and then falling further to a trough at Y_1. The *SRAS* curve then starts to shift continually to the right, as shown by arrow 4. Income thus rises, first to Y^* and then reaching Y_0 again at the next peak.

wages and other costs will tend to adjust, causing the *SRAS* curve to shift and thus inducing further changes in actual GNP. (See Figures 28-2 and 28-3 on pages 582 and 583.) To explain why GNP *fluctuates*, we focus on why the *AD* and *SRAS* curves shift exogenously; later, in order to explain why fluctuations tend to be cyclical, we focus on *induced* shifts in the *SRAS* curve.

Sources of Aggregate Demand Shocks

What are the sources of the continual disturbances to aggregate demand? The theory of income determination suggests four main candidates: shifts in each of the four main components of aggregate expenditure.

Changes in Consumption

Consumption is the largest single component of aggregate expenditure—about two-thirds of the total. When searching for the causes of income changes, we are not concerned with changes in consumption *in response* to changes in income but, instead, with *shifts* in the function relating consumption to income. Such shifts can have many causes.

Changes in tastes.   Changes in how consumers divide their income between consumption and savings will lead to a change in desired aggregate expenditure. In the mid-1980s there was a significant increase in the demand for American cars. If the income that was spent on automobiles had been saved previously, this would have represented a significant rightward shift in the *AD* curve. Jobs and incomes would first be gained in the automobile industry. The induced increase in spending by workers in that industry would then set up a multiplier effect as increases in output, income, and spending spread throughout the economy.

Changes in expectations and interest rates. Expectations of future inflation may lead to a burst of spending to buy now while goods are cheap. On the other hand, a wave of uncertainty about the future may lead to a rise in saving and hence a cut in spending. High interest rates can be a powerful incentive to postpone buying durable goods. For example, in 1981 rates of over 20 percent helped to depress the markets for automobiles and other consumer durables; subsequent declines in interest rates led to a boom in those markets.

In an inflationary world it is important to distinguish between the real and the nominal rate of interest. (See Chapter 24, page 505, for a detailed discussion.) Recall that the real rate of interest is the difference between the nominal rate of interest and the expected rate of inflation. It is the real rate of interest that matters for most expenditure decisions.

Changes in taxes. As we saw in Chapter 27 (see page 544), tax changes can also shift the aggregate consumption function. Income-tax cuts mean that more *total* income becomes *disposable* income, leading to an increase in consumer spending; income-tax increases have the opposite effect. The large tax cuts enacted by the Reagan administration during the early 1980s are widely acknowledged to have contributed importantly to the subsequent expansion in spending and income.

Changes in transfer payments. As we also saw in Chapter 27, changes in transfer payments can influence aggregate expenditure through their effects on personal consumption. These effects can be substantial, since government transfer payments amount to roughly one-eighth of personal income.

Changes in Government Purchases

Look again at Figure 29-2. It is obvious that every war in this century has been accompanied by a rapid expansion of economic activity. Wars result in enormous increases in government purchases as people and materials are shifted from civilian to military uses. This shift is usually reversed during the postwar period. For example, federal government purchases of goods and services (measured in constant dollars at 1982 prices) rose during World War II, from $64 billion in 1940 to $723 billion in 1944, and then fell to $94 billion by 1947. Changes in government purchases of goods and services during World War II and the immediate postwar period (1941–1946), were the principal cause of changes in GNP during that period.

Such expenditures played a similar, though less dramatic, role during the Vietnam War, rising from $244 billion in 1965 to $310 billion in 1968 and falling back fairly steadily to $230 billion by 1973. The extra Vietnam War expenditures, on top of a fully employed civilian economy, helped to open up a large inflationary gap during the late 1960s and early 1970s.

The government also had a major impact on economic performance during the 1980s. During 1981–1982 the U.S. economy experienced a major recession. Unemployment reached almost 10 percent—its highest level since the Great Depression in the early 1930s. Then from 1984 through 1988 there occurred a sustained recovery, with unemployment falling below 6 percent in 1988. Many economists attributed this recovery to the growth in government expenditures (and a fall in taxes), which combined to cause a record federal government budget deficit. We shall return to a more detailed discussion of this episode in the next chapter.

Changes in Net Exports

A quarter of a century ago the United States could be studied as if it were a completely closed economy, so unimportant were imports and exports. Today, trade is a significant part of American GNP. Total exports, which were 5 percent of GNP in 1960, rose to just over 10 percent in the 1980s. Either a rise in imports, resulting from, say, a preference for foreign over American automobiles, or a fall in exports, resulting from, say, a European recession, can have a major impact on American national income and employment.

During the mid-1980s the United States experienced record trade deficits, with imports exceeding exports by $150 billion annually. Further implications of this deficit and of the possible steps that could be taken to eliminate it are discussed in Box 29-1.

Shifts in consumption, government, and net export expenditures cause major fluctuations in national income and employment.

Changes in Investment

Changes in investment expenditure are a major source of economic fluctuations. For example, the Great Depression witnessed a dramatic fall in investment. Total investment in the U.S. economy fell from $16.2 billion in 1929 (almost double the amount that was needed to replace the capital goods that were being used up in the process of producing GNP) to just $1 billion in 1932, less than one-sixth the amount that was needed just to keep the stock of capital intact. Similarly, at the trough of the recession of the early 1980s, investment expenditure was less than one-sixth its average level of the previous five years.

As Figure 29-5 shows, investment expenditure is very volatile. Quite large shocks, due to changes in investment expenditure, hit the economy frequently. The change in investment from one year to the next has been on average about three times the change in government purchases.

Changes in investment are also quite closely correlated with changes in national income, as shown in Figure 29-5. Rising investment tends to be associated with rapidly rising GNP, while falling investment tends to be associated with *slowly* rising or falling GNP. This is consistent with the view that investment shocks are a major cause of changes in national income.

Changes in investment expenditures play a key role in most theories of cyclical fluctuations.

Why Does Investment Change?

Changes in investment are a prime cause of fluctuations in the economy, but we need to know why investment fluctuates.

The Interest Rate and Investment

Empirical evidence shows that investment responds to many influencing factors. One of the most im-

portant of these factors is the rate of interest. Other things being equal, the higher is the interest rate, the higher is the cost of borrowing money for investment purposes and the less is the amount of investment expenditure.[3]

While each dollar of investment has the same consequences for aggregate demand, different types of investment respond to different sets of causes. Thus, it is useful to discuss separately the determinants of the three major types of investment expenditure: inventories, plant and equipment, and residential housing. In so doing we can see why it is that the interest rate is such an important influence on investment, and we can determine what other factors are important.

Inventories. Inventory changes represent only a small percentage of private investment in a typical year, but their average size is not an adequate measure of their importance. They are one of the more volatile elements of total investment and therefore have a major influence on shifts in investment expenditure.

Studies show that the stock of inventories that are held tends to rise as production and sales rise. Because the size of inventories is related to the level of sales, the *change* in inventories (which is current investment) is related to the *change* in the level of sales.

A firm may decide, for example, to hold inventories of 10 percent of its sales. Thus, if sales are $100,000, it will wish to hold inventories of $10,000. If sales increase to $110,000, it will want to hold inventories of $11,000. Over the period during which its stock of inventories is being increased, there will be a total of $1,000 new inventory investment.

The higher is the level of production and sales, the larger is the desired stock of inventories. Changes in the rate of production and sales cause temporary bouts of investment (or disinvestment) in inventories.

---

[3] Although in basic theory we talk of "the" interest rate, reality is not so simple. However, despite the presence of a large number of interest rates, it is usually possible to speak of movements in the general level of interest rates, since the individual interest rates tend to rise and fall together. Later in this chapter we study the complicated link between the interest rate and investment expenditure that operates through the stock market.

BOX 29-1

National Income and the Balance of Trade

Exports are an important source of demand for domestically produced goods. A key determinant of a country's exports is the level of activity in its major trading partners. When, for example, Japan and Europe experience a slump, as they did during the early 1980s, there is a reduction in their demand for American exports. In turn, via the multiplier process, the decrease in exports causes a contraction in American income. Similarly, when the United States experiences a boom, as it did during 1984–1987, American demand for foreign goods will be high. Again, the change in exports causes a multiplier effect, this time leading to an increase in foreign national incomes.

The *export multiplier* causes the business cycles of major trading partners to be closely synchronized.

As we saw in Chapter 28, expenditure on imports will grow as domestic national income grows. Imports represent spending on other countries' outputs, and therefore they raise the economy's *marginal propensity not to spend,* denoted by $(1 - z)$. As we also saw in Chapter 28, this reduces the size of the multiplier. **[36]**

A smaller multiplier is undesirable because it reduces the effectiveness of domestic policies that attempt to change the level of domestic income. It is desirable because it reduces the impact that fluctuations in autonomous expenditure (such as investment and exports) have on national income.*

Net Exports and Domestic Absorption

The model of national-income determination that we outlined in Chapter 28 provides an important perspective on the determination of net exports. Recall the basic condition for equilibrium national income:

$$Y = C + I + G + (X - M)$$

The sum of $C + I + G$ corresponds to total expenditure on all goods and services (domestic and foreign) for use within the economy; this total is often referred to as **domestic absorption (A).** The equilibrium relationship therefore can be rewritten as

$$Y = A + (X - M)$$

The right-hand side of this equation is desired aggregate expenditure on domestic goods and ser-

---

* The consequence of the latter effect is that imports act as a *built-in stabilizer.* We will encounter built-in stabilizers again in Chapter 30 in our analysis of fiscal policy.

When a firm ties up funds in inventories, those same funds cannot be used elsewhere to earn income. As an alternative to holding inventories, the firm could lend the money out at the going rate of interest. Thus, the higher is the real rate of interest, the higher will be the opportunity cost of holding an inventory of a given size; the higher is that opportunity cost, the smaller are the inventories that will be desired.

The higher is the real rate of interest, the lower is the desired stock of inventories. Changes in

the rate of interest cause temporary bouts of investment (or disinvestment) in inventories.

Residential housing construction.   Since 1970 spending on residential housing construction has varied between one-fifth and one-third of all gross private investment in the United States and between 2.5 percent and 5.5 percent of GNP. Because expenditures for housing construction are both large and variable, they exert a major impact on the economy.

Many influences on residential housing construction are noneconomic and depend on demographic

vices, represented as the sum of expenditure for internal use (domestic absorption) plus expenditure due to net external demand (net exports). Subtracting A from both sides, we get

$$Y - A = X - M$$

This makes it clear that net exports can be positive only if national income exceeds domestic absorption; that is, only if total output of goods and services in the United States exceeds total demand for goods and services to be used in the United States. Conversely, if net exports are negative, it must be the case that American national income is less than the absorption of goods and services for use within the United States.*

The record trade deficits that the U.S. economy experienced during the 1980s can then just as easily be described as record excesses of absorption relative to national income. The U.S. trade deficit simply reflected the fact that American spending exceeded American national income. This perspective led a number of commentators to describe the U.S. economy as being on a "huge spending binge" dur-

* Note that foreigners can influence the demand for American goods and services in two ways: by demanding exports and by investing in the United States.

ing this period. In part, the spending binge reflected large government budget deficits; in part, it reflected sharp increases in the level of foreign investment; and in part, it reflected high private spending. The net effect was that total spending was larger than income.

This provides an important perspective on policy alternatives to reduce the trade deficit. Substantial progress could be made by reducing the government budget deficit or by taking other measures to reduce total national spending relative to national income. A lot of attention has focused on the sharp depreciation in the U.S. dollar that occurred in 1986 and 1987. Many observers expected that this would discourage imports and encourage exports, and therefore lead to a large fall in the trade account deficit. However, as long as the forces causing spending to remain high relative to income remain, the trade deficit has to remain also. The mechanisms by which a depreciation works to lower the trade deficit are quite complicated; the change in relative prices must be accompanied by a reduction in private spending out of income for the trade deficit to fall. If the government budget deficit were also to be reduced, a smaller depreciation would then be necessary.

or cultural considerations, such as new family formation. However, households must not only want to buy houses but also be able to do so. Periods of high employment and high average family earnings tend to lead to increases in housing construction. Periods of high unemployment and falling earnings tend to lead to decreases in such construction.

Almost all houses are purchased with money that is borrowed by means of mortgages. Interest on the borrowed money typically accounts for over one-half of the purchaser's annual mortgage payments; the remainder is repayment of principal. It is for this

reason that sharp variations in interest rates exert a substantial effect on the demand for housing.

This importance was borne out by experiences from 1979 to 1982 when mortgage rates rose from less than 11 percent to just over 15 percent and housing starts fell from 1,194,000 units in 1979 to a mere 661,000 in 1982. (Since inflation fell from 1980, the increased nominal interest rates also meant increased real rates.) The construction industry itself and its major suppliers, such as the cement and the lumber industries, felt the blow of a dramatic fall in demand. Conversely, during the mid-1980s interest rates fell

FIGURE 29-5   Annual Changes in Real Gross Private Investment and GNP, 1950–1988 (*in 1982 dollars*)

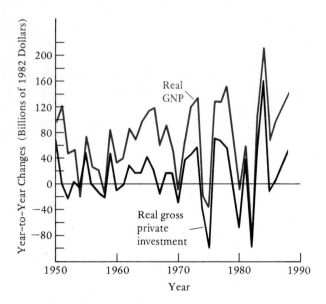

The fluctuations in gross private investment are sharp and closely related to changes in national income. The change in real GNP is repeated from Figure 24-3. Changes in private investment are closely related to changes in national income. (*Source: Economic Report of the President,* various years)

duce the volume of investment as more and more firms find that their expected profits from investment do not cover the interest on borrowed investment funds. Other firms who had cash on hand found that purchasing interest-earning assets provided a better return than investment in plant and equipment; for them, the increase in real interest rates meant that the opportunity cost of investing had risen.

A third major determinant of investment is changes in national income. If there is a rise in aggregate demand that is expected to persist and that cannot be met by existing capacity, then investment in new plant and equipment will be needed. Once the new plants have been built and put into operation, however, the rate of new investment will fall.

This further illustrates an important characteristic of investment that we have encountered already in the case of inventories:

If the desired stock of capital goods increases, there will be an investment boom while the new capital is being produced.

However, if nothing else changes, and even if business conditions continue to look rosy enough to justify the increased stock of capital, investment in new plant and equipment will cease once the larger capital stock is achieved. This aspect of investment leads to the *accelerator* theory of investment, which we look at more closely in the appendix to this chapter.

Sources of Aggregate Supply Shocks

In the previous chapter we saw that the *SRAS* curve can shift for many reasons, including changes in input prices and productivity. (See especially Figure 28-5.) When the *SRAS* curve shifts, GNP and employment fluctuate.

As we noted also in Chapter 28, one episode in which an aggregate supply shock played an important role in the U.S. economy occurred in 1974, when the members of the Organization of Petroleum Exporting Countries (OPEC) acted to raise the price of oil fourfold. Since imported oil was a major input, used by many American industries, the OPEC shock served to raise costs in those industries. As a result, the *SRAS* curve shifted up and to the left, leading to stagflation—an increase in prices and a fall in output and employment.

Changes in the foreign value of the U.S. dollar

sharply and there was a boom in the demand for new housing; that boom persisted until late 1988, when interest rates started to rise again.

Expenditures for residential construction tend to vary positively with changes in average income and negatively with interest rates.

Plant and equipment.   Investment in plant and equipment is the largest component of domestic investment. Over one-half is financed by firms' retained profits (profits that are *not* paid out to their shareholders). This means that current profits are an important determinant of investment.

A second major determinant of investment is the rate of interest. As became abundantly clear during the early 1980s, very high interest rates greatly re-

can also cause aggregate supply shocks. During the 1980s movements in the exchange rate had direct effects on costs in industries that were using imported raw materials and goods in their production. Such changes in the exchange rate also can have indirect effects on aggregate supply, since their effects on imported consumer goods can feed through to wages.

Why Do Fluctuations Exhibit Cyclical Patterns?

Explanations for the *cyclical* patterns of economic fluctuations fall into two categories. The various explanations are not necessarily competing ones, since several together often provide a better overall explanation than any one on its own. In the first category, the economy converts *random shifts* in the AD and SRAS curves into cyclical outcomes. In the second category, *cyclical shifts* in the AD curve cause cyclical fluctuations in the economy.

Random Shocks and Lags

One model of the business cycle suggests that random shifts in expenditure are transformed into systematic cycles of output and employment.

This theory begins with lags. For example, if a fall in the rate of interest makes an investment in a new project profitable, it may take 6 months to plan it, 3 months to write and sign contracts, 6 months before spending builds up to its top rate, and another 24 months to complete the project. These lags mean that changes in, say, the rate of interest will cause reactions in investment expenditure that are distributed over quite a long period of time.

Another source of lags comes from the response of production decisions to changes in demand. In many industries it takes weeks or months or even longer to bring new or mothballed capacity into production, and to hire and train new workers. As a result, changes in demand give rise to changes in output that are spread out over a substantial period of time. An increase in demand, for example, may lead to a gradual increase in output that builds up over several months. Then, as output does change, the automatic adjustment mechanism is set into ac-

tion. As an inflationary gap opens up, wages and costs start to rise and the SRAS curve shifts leftward.

Thus, a once-and-for-all demand shock gives rise to a cyclical output response, with GNP first rising because of the rightward shift in the AD curve and then falling because of the leftward shift in the SRAS curve.

Each major component of aggregate expenditure has sometimes undergone shifts large enough to disturb the economy significantly. Adjustment lags can convert such shifts into cyclical oscillations in national income.

Cyclical Spending Behavior

Several factors can cause such fluctuations in spending behavior that they themselves follow a cyclical pattern. Some explanations focus on cyclical patterns in government behavior; we examine this possibility below.

The multiplier-accelerator model, and the related theories of the inventory cycle and the construction cycle, provide some basis for expecting investment and consumption to behave cyclically. The key is that a disturbance which causes an increase in income (the multiplier process) might also trigger further expenditure increases that respond to that increase. Investment in plant and equipment, desired inventories, and spending on housing construction will all respond to the *change* in national income. Hence, an initial change will set in motion further *cumulative* changes in spending and national income. Thus, an initial positive shock to spending and income will tend to be followed by further increases, and an initial negative shock to spending will tend to be followed by further decreases. These interactions, which generate cyclical tendencies in private spending, are discussed further in the appendix to this chapter.

Policy-induced Cycles

Another theory of the business cycle is based on the allegation that government-induced demand shocks sometimes have caused cyclical fluctuations. Why should the government administer potentially disturbing demand shocks? Several reasons have been suggested.

A political business cycle. As early as 1944 the Polish-born Keynesian economist Michael Kalecki warned of a political business cycle. He argued that once governments had learned to manipulate the economy, they would engineer an election-geared business cycle. In preelection periods they would raise spending and cut taxes. The resulting expansionary demand shock would create high employment and good business conditions that would attract voters' support for the government, but the resulting inflationary gap would lead to a rising price level. So, after the election was won, the government would depress demand to remove the inflationary gap and to provide some slack for expansion before the next election.

This theory invokes the image of a cynical government manipulating employment and national income solely because it wants to stay in power. Few people believe that governments deliberately do this all the time, but the temptation to do it some of the time, particularly before elections, may prove irresistible. Indeed, Professor Alan Blinder of Princeton University has made a persuasive case that one such politically inspired demand shock was inflicted by the Nixon administration just prior to the 1972 elections.

Alternating policy goals. A variant of the policy-induced cycle does not require a cynical government and an easily duped electorate. Instead, both sides need only to be rather shortsighted and to have rather narrow vision.

In this theory, when there is a recession and relatively stable prices, the public and the government identify unemployment as the number one economic problem. The government then engineers an expansionary policy shock through some combination of tax cuts and spending increases. This, plus such natural cumulative forces as the multiplier-accelerator model, expands economic activity. Unemployment falls and income rises, but, as income rises above potential national income, the price level begins to rise. It first rises along the stable *SRAS* curve and then rises further as boom conditions raise factor prices and shift the *SRAS* curve upward. (See Figure 28-2.)

At this point the unemployment problem is declared solved. Now inflation is seen as the nation's number one economic problem. A contractionary demand shock is engineered. The natural cumulative forces again take over, causing a recession. The in-flation subsides, but unemployment rises, setting the stage once again for an expansionary shock to solve the unemployment problem.

Many economists have criticized government policy over the last few decades as sometimes causing fluctuations by alternately pushing expansion to cure unemployment and then pushing contraction to cure inflation. We shall see in Chapter 37 that this charge is particularly strong against monetary policy. But, whatever the policy, the charge is that policymakers sometimes have been too shortsighted in alternating their concern between unemployment and inflation.

Misguided stabilization policy. In a variant of the previous theory, the government tries to hold the economy at potential national income by countering fluctuations in private-sector expenditure with offsetting changes of its own through spending and taxes. The government can, in principle, dampen such cyclical fluctuations by its stabilization policies. But unless it is very sophisticated, bad timing may accentuate rather than dampen fluctuations. We shall return to this possibility in subsequent chapters.

Securities Markets (Stock Markets)

It is commonplace to observe that stock market values have sometimes displayed cumulative upward movements and at other times cumulative downward movements. The first are called *bull markets,* and the second are called *bear markets.* Most people also know that the Great Depression of the 1930s was preceded by the great stock market crash of 1929, which caused what is still the largest percentage loss of stock values ever to be suffered by American investors.

There is a clear association between fluctuations in the stock market and in the economy, but is there a causal connection? Do stock market booms help to cause business cycle booms, and do stock market slumps help to cause business cycle slumps? Before we can answer these questions, we need to learn a bit about such markets.

The Function of Securities Markets

When a household buys shares that have been newly issued by a company, it becomes one of the firm's owners. If, at some future date, the household wishes to cease being a shareholder in the firm, the firm will *not* repurchase the shares, except in the rare event that the firm is liquidated. If the household wishes to get its money back, it can only do so by persuading someone else to buy its shares in the company.

When a household buys a bond from a company, it becomes one of the firm's creditors. It cannot get its money back from the company before a specified date. For example, if you bought a 2010 bond in 1990, the bond would be redeemed by the company (i.e., the loan would be paid back) only in 2010. If you wished to get your money back sooner, all you could do would be to sell the bond to someone who was willing to become one of the company's creditors.

An organized market in which stocks and bonds are bought and sold is called a **securities market,** or a **stock market.** Two of the best known are the New York Stock Exchange and the American Stock Exchange. The trading of *existing* shares on the stock market indicates that ownership is being transferred; it does not indicate that companies are raising new money from the public, although firms also do raise funds by issuing new shares.

Securities markets are important because they allow people to put their savings into stocks and bonds that are not directly or quickly redeemable by their issuer.

For example, if I want to invest in a particular stock that I think will earn an attractive yield, I may do so, even though I know that I will want my money back after only a year. I can be confident that I will be able to sell the security a year from now. Nevertheless, while securities markets provide for the quick sale of stocks and bonds, they do not guarantee the price at which they can be sold. The price at any time is the one that equates the demand and supply for a particular security, and rapid fluctuations in stock prices are common.

Prices on the Stock Market

Figure 29-6 shows the wide swings in a well-known index of stock market prices, the Dow-Jones industrial average. The most recent swing in the period that is covered in Figure 29-6 began from a trough in May 1984 when the Dow was about 1,100. The index then rose, almost without interruption, until September 1986, when it reached a value of 1,919, a rise of 75 percent in just 28 months. After a significant fall of about 8 percent in September 1986, it then rose spectacularly, reaching 2,722 in August 1987. It then started to fall, gradually at first, and then on October 19, 1987—Black Monday—it fell by over 20 percent to 1,738. It then climbed fairly steadily, and by early 1989 it had almost reattained its August 1987 peak.

From September 1986 to early 1989, the Dow went through a series of sharp swings, first rising by almost 40 percent in 12 months, then falling by almost 40 percent in the next 2 months, and then rising again by about 40 percent in the next 16 months.

Commentators are often careless about making the key distinction between the *number of points* by which the index changes over some period and the *percentage* change in that index over the same period. For example, the fall of 984 points from August to October 1986 is the largest fall ever in terms of points. This represented a fall of 32 percent from the August peak of 2,722 points. While this is significant (it is roughly double the percentage fall that occurred in 1975–1976, when stocks lost 15 percent of their value before recovering), it remains dwarfed by the loss that everyone hopes never will be repeated: Over 80 percent of the value of stocks was lost over the three-year period from 1929 to 1933!

Causes of Stock Market Swings

What causes such rapid gains and losses, and what do they have to do with business cycles?

When investors buy a company's stocks, they are buying rights to share in the stream of dividends to be paid out by that company. They are also buying an asset that they can sell in the future for a gain or a loss.

The value of that stock thus depends on two factors: first, what people expect the stream of future dividend payments to be and, second, what capital gains or losses people expect to realize when the stocks are sold. Both influences make dealing in stocks an inherently risky operation. Will the company in which people are investing pay high dividends in future years? Will the company's value rise

FIGURE 29-6   Fluctuations in an Index of Stock Prices, 1960–1989

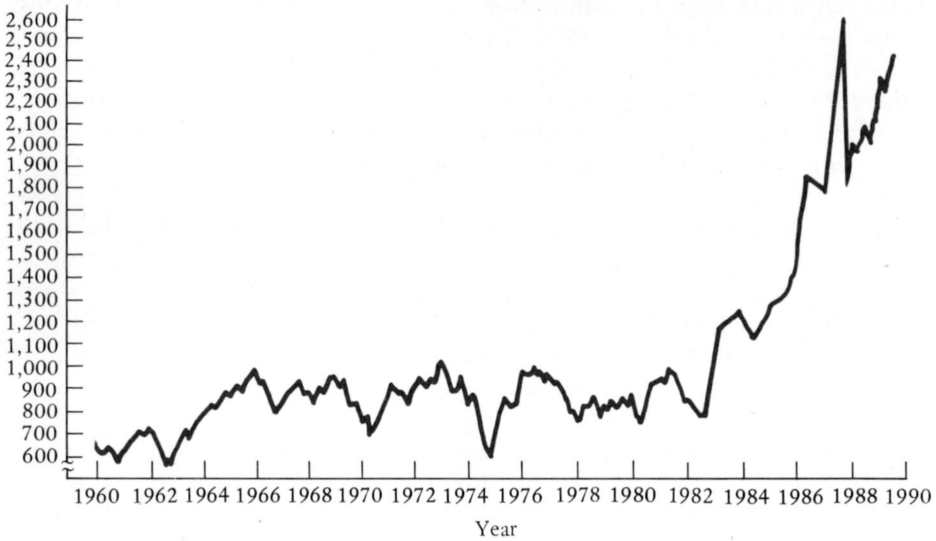

Stock market fluctuations are very sharp and irregular, and the last seven years have witnessed a sharp net increase. The chart shows quarterly variations in the Dow Jones industrial average of 30 leading stocks. The index grew steadily from 1962 to 1966 and then displayed very little trend over the next 15 years. Over that period the index did, however, fluctuate sharply; it is these fluctuations that make large speculative gains and losses possible. Three notable falls in the index occurred during the economic downturns in 1969, 1974, and 1981.

While the index was at approximately the same level in 1980 as it was in 1965, the Consumer Price Index (1967 = 100) has risen from 94.5 to 246.8, causing many commentators to believe that the market was "undervalued." The market than fell during the 1981 recession, but the economic recovery of 1982–1986 was accompanied by a dramatic sustained increase in the Dow Jones. After a downturn in September 1986, the Dow rose rapidly for 12 months. A dramatic fall of over 500 points (over 22 percent) occurred on October 19, 1987 (Black Monday). Following this, the Dow rose steadily again, almost reaching its August 1987 peak by mid-1989.

so that these people can sell their shares for more than what they bought them for? While dividend policies of most established companies tend to be fairly stable, stock prices are subject to wide swings.

The Influence of Present and Future Business Conditions

Many influences affect stock market prices; these include the state of the business cycle and the stance of government policies. Box 29-2 takes up the interesting possibility of self-reinforcing speculative booms.

Cyclical forces.   If investors expect a firm's earnings to increase, the firm will become more valuable and

the price of its stock will rise. Such influences cause stock prices to move with the business cycle, being high when current profits are high and low when current profits are low. It also causes stock prices to vary with a host of factors that influence expectations of future profits. A poor crop, destruction of trees by acid rain, an announcement of new defense spending, a change in the foreign-exchange value of the dollar, or a change in the political complexion of the administration can all affect profit expectations and hence stock prices.

Policy factors.   We shall see later in this book that major changes in monetary policy can cause major changes in interest rates. Such changes, or just the expectation of them, will have major effects on stock prices. Say, for example, that interest rates rise rapidly. Investors will see that they can now earn an increased amount by holding government bonds. As a result, they will wish to alter their investment portfolios to hold more bonds and fewer stocks. Everyone, cannot do this, however, since only so many stocks and bonds are available to be held at any given time. As all investors try to sell their stocks, prices fall. The fall will stop only when the expected rate of return to investment in stocks, based on their lower purchase price, makes stocks as attractive as bonds. Then investors will no longer try to shift out of bonds *en masse*.

Stock Market Swings: Cause or Effect of Business Cycles?

Stock markets tend often to lead, and sometimes to follow, booms and slumps in business activity. In both cases the causes usually run from real business conditions, whether actual or anticipated, to stock market prices. This is the dominant theme, the stock market as a reflector.

Stock market fluctuations are more typically a consequence than a cause of the business cycle.

It is also possible for the stock market to be a causal factor in the business cycle. The value of the stock market influences the wealth of households, which ultimately own the market, either directly or through their pension funds. Thus, stock prices can be expected to influence their consumption spending. (Recall the wealth effect from Chapter 26; see Figure 26-2.) Firms also use the stock market to issue new shares in order to finance investment spending; when stock market prices are low, they find this an unattractive way to raise new money and thus may choose to cancel, or at least postpone, investments. As a result, many people believed that the dramatic fall in stock values that were experienced in the October 1987 crash would cause households to curtail their consumption spending in response to their perceived fall in wealth. On this basis many forecasters predicted that the stock market fall of Black Monday would lead to a serious downturn in the economy. After the event such gloom-and-doom forecasts turned out to be inaccurate; apparently, people did not perceive the fall in the stock market as an indi-

cation that their permanent incomes or wealth had fallen dramatically, and hence did not reduce their consumption spending.

In many cases the stock market and the business cycle both reflect the common influence of other factors. For example, stock markets often react to changes in interest rates that may be caused by government policy; as we have seen, such interest-rate changes can also play a causal role in cyclical fluctuations in the economy. Typically, the stock market responds quicker than does the economy to such influences, and for this reason many observers look to it as a "leading indicator" of likely future economic developments.

The relationship between the stock market and the economy is further complicated by the existence of occasional speculative booms and busts. There are often real economic forces influencing expectations of stock prices, but, at least for a while, the prices may become dominated by speculative psychology. (This is discussed in Box 29-2.) Unfortunately, speculative behavior causes the stock market to react to many events that turn out to have little or no enduring implications for the economy. As one wag put it, the stock market has predicted seven out of the last two recessions!

Causes of Business Cycles: A Consensus View?

Economists have argued long and bitterly about the *best* explanation of the recurrent cyclical behavior of the economy.

Today most economists agree that there is no single cause to which all business cycles can be attributed.

In an economy that has tendencies for both cumulative and self-reversing behavior, any large shock, whether it is from without or within, can initiate a cyclical swing. Wars are important, and so are major technical innovations. A rapid increase in interest rates and a general tightening of credit can cause a sharp decrease in investment. Expectations can be changed by a political campaign or by a de-

BOX 29-2

Speculative Booms

In addition to responding to a host of factors that reasonably can be expected to influence the earnings of companies, stock prices often develop an upward or downward movement of their own, propelled by little more than speculation that feeds on itself.

In major stock market booms, people begin to expect rising stock prices and hurry to buy while stocks are cheap. This action bids up the prices of shares and creates the capital gains that justify the original expectations. This is an example of *self-realizing expectations*. Investors get rich on paper, in the sense that the market value of their holdings rises. Money-making now looks easy to others, who also rush in to buy stocks, and new purchases push up prices still further. At this stage attention to current earnings all but ceases. If a stock can yield, say, a 50 percent capital gain in one year, it does not matter much if the current earnings represent only a small percentage yield on the purchase price of the stocks. Everyone is "making money," so more people become attracted to the get-rich-quick opportunities. Their attempts to buy bid up prices still further. In such speculative booms, current earnings represent an ever diminishing percentage yield on the current price of the stocks.

Capital gains can be so attractive that investors may buy stocks on margin; that is, borrow money to buy them, using the stocks themselves as security for the loans. In doing this, many investors may be borrowing money at a rate of interest that is considerably in excess of the yield from current dividends. Even if $50,000 is borrowed at 10 percent (interest payments are $5,000 per year) to buy stocks, yielding a current dividend return of only 4 percent (dividend receipts are $2,000 per year), never mind, says the investor's logic, for the stocks

can be sold in a year or so for a handsome capital gain that will more than repay the $3,000 of interest not covered by dividends. Some people have the luck or good judgment to sell out near the top of the market, and they actually make money. Others wait eagerly for ever greater capital gains, and in the meantime they get richer and richer—on paper.

Eventually, something breaks the period of unrestrained optimism. Some investors may begin to worry about the very high prices of stocks in relation not only to current yields but also to possible future yields, even when generous allowances for growth are made. Or it may be that the prices of stocks become depressed slightly when a sufficiently large number of persons try to sell out in order to realize their capital gains. As they offer their securities on the market, they cannot find purchasers without some fall in prices. Even a modest price fall may be sufficient to persuade others that it is time to sell. However, every share that is sold must be bought by someone. A wave of sellers may not find new buyers at existing prices, causing prices to fall. Panic selling may now occur.

A household that borrowed $50,000 to buy stocks near the top of the market may find the paper value of its holdings sliding below $50,000. How will it repay its loan? Even if it does not worry about the loan, its broker will. The household may sell now before it loses too much, or its broker may "sell the customer out" to liquidate the loan. All this causes prices to fall even further and provides another example of self-realizing expectations. If enough people think that prices are going to come down, their attempt to sell out at the present high prices will create the fall in prices, the expectations of which caused the selling.

This is a very simple and stylized description of a speculative cycle, yet it describes the basic elements of market booms and busts that many believe have recurred throughout stock market history. It happened in the Jay Cooke panic of 1873 and in the Grover Cleveland panic of 1893. The biggest boom of all began in the mid-1920s and ended on Black Tuesday, October 29, 1929. The collapse was dramatic, with stocks losing about one-half of their value in about two months, nor did it stop there. For three long years stock prices continued to decline, until the average value of stock sold on the New York Stock Exchange had fallen from its 1929 high of $89.10 per share to $17.35 per share by late 1933. It also happened, although less dramatically, in the booms and busts of the 1970s and 1980s, which we discussed earlier in this section.

Speculative behavior means that stock market prices do not always just reflect the fundamentals that underlie the expected profitability of companies; in this sense, the stock market is sometimes said to be over- or undervalued. However, the extent of the over- or undervaluation is very hard to determine, and hence it is hard to predict when, and by how much, prices will "correct." For example, consider the long upswing that more than doubled stock prices in just over three years between early 1984 and October 1987. At the time the United States enjoyed a very strong recovery, and the rising stock prices no doubt reflected the resulting favorable profit outlook of companies. However, many doubted that the full increase was justified by underlying business opportunities and hence felt that there may have been a speculative component to the rise in stock values. These people argued that the dramatic fall that occurred on Black Monday represented a "correction" that removed much of the speculative component from the prices. Of course, this is easy to say after the fact. If any of us had known in advance when and by how much prices would correct, we would have been able to make a huge profit.

Stock Markets: Investment Marketplaces or Gambling Casinos?

Stock markets fulfill many important functions. It is doubtful that the great aggregations of capital that are needed to finance modern firms could be raised under a private-ownership system without them. There is no doubt, however, that they also provide an unfortunate attraction for many naive investors, whose get-rich-quick dreams are more often than not destroyed by the fall in prices that follows the occasional speculative booms that they help to create.

To some extent public policy has sought to curb the excesses of stock market speculation through supervision of security issues. This is an area of complex overlap between federal and provincial jurisdiction. Public policy seeks, among other things, to prevent both fraudulent or misleading information and trading by "insiders" (those in a company who have confidential information). Moreover, the regulators can limit the ability of speculators to trade on margin.

All in all, the stock market is both a real marketplace and a place to gamble. As in all gambling situations, players who are less well informed and less clever than the average player tend to be losers in the long term.

velopment in another part of the world. The list of possible impulses, autonomous or induced, is long.

It is probably true that the characteristic cyclical pattern involves many outside shocks that sometimes initiate, sometimes reinforce, and sometimes dampen the economy's cumulative tendencies.

Cycles differ also in terms of their structure. There are variations in timing, duration, and amplitude. In some cycles full employment of labor may be the bottleneck that determines the peak. In others high interest rates and shortages of investment funds may nip an expansion and turn it into a recession at the same time that the unemployment of labor is still

an acute problem. In some cycles the recession phase is short; in others a full-scale period of stagnation sets in. In some cycles the peak develops into a severe inflation; in others the pressure of excess demand is hardly felt, and a new recession sets in before the economy has recovered fully from the last trough. Some cycles are long in duration; others are short.

In this chapter we have suggested reasons why an economy that is subjected to periodic external shocks will tend to generate a continually changing pattern of fluctuations, as cumulative and then self-reversing forces alternatively come into play. In the next chapter we shall study how governments seek to influence the cycle and remove some of its extremes through the use of fiscal policy.

SUMMARY

1. The economy experiences continual change. Long-term change represents what is referred to as economic growth, while short-term fluctuations are referred to as the business cycle.
2. Most theories of the business cycle hold that short-term fluctuations in GNP are usually, though not always, the result of variations in aggregate demand. Overall, these fluctuations show a fairly clear pattern that is described as cyclical. Despite the overall pattern, the evidence is that the cycles are irregular in amplitude, in timing, in duration, and in the way in which they affect particular industries and sectors of the economy.
3. Any explanation of the business cycle must explain both *why* income fluctuates and *how* those fluctuations get transformed into cycles.
4. Shifts in consumption, government, investment, and net export expenditures cause fluctuations in aggregate demand and hence in national income and employment.
5. Changes in investment expenditure are a major source of fluctuations in national income. The three principal components of private investment are changes in business inventories, residential housing construction, and investment in plant and equipment. The interest rate is an important determinant of investment spending.
6. Changes in business inventories often account for an important fraction of the year-to-year changes in the level of investment. They respond both to changes in the level of production and sales and to the rate of interest.
7. Residential housing construction shows a cyclical pattern of its own. House building varies directly with the level of national income and inversely with the rate of interest.
8. Investment in plant and equipment depends on a number of variables. These include innovation, expectations about the future, level of profits, rate of interest, and changes in national income.
9. There are several explanations for the cyclical pattern of economic fluctuations. They all involve either lags, which transform random shocks into cyclical responses, or theories of systematic behavior of

spending patterns. The latter can apply both to private consumption and investment expenditure and to government purchases.

10. Securities (stock) markets allow firms to raise new capital from the sale of newly issued securities and allow the holders of existing securities to sell their securities to other investors. Prices on the stock market tend to reflect the public's expectations, both of firms' future earnings and of future changes in prices (for whatever reason). This necessarily gives a strong speculative dimension to security prices, and large speculative swings do occur. Such swings can be accentuated by the phenomenon of self-realizing expectations.

TOPICS FOR REVIEW

Economic growth and business cycles
Causes of fluctuations in GNP
Components of investment
Causes of cyclical fluctuations
Political business cycle
The stock market

DISCUSSION QUESTIONS

1. How and in what direction might each of the following shift the function relating consumption expenditure to disposable income?
   a. Introduction of free medical care
   b. A change in attitudes so that we become a nation of conspicuous conservers rather than conspicuous consumers, taking pride in how little we eat or spend for housing, clothing, and so on
   c. Increases in income taxes
   d. News that due to medical advances everyone can count on more years of retirement than ever before
   e. A spreading belief that all-out nuclear war is likely within the next 10 years
   f. Sharp increases in the down payments required on durable goods
2. Suppose that the government wished to reduce private investment in order to reduce an inflationary gap. What policies might it adopt? If it wished to do so in such a way as to have a major effect on residential housing and a minor effect on plant and equipment expenditures, which measures might it use?
3. What effect on total investment—and on which categories of investment—would you predict as a result of each of the following?
   a. Widespread endorsement of ZPG (zero population growth) by young couples
   b. A sharp increase in the frequency and duration of strikes in the transportation industries
   c. Forecasts of very low growth rates of real national income over the next five years
   d. Tax reform that eliminates deductions for property taxes in computing taxable personal income
4. When interest rates rose sharply during the early 1980s, home construction fell dramatically, but sales of mobile homes increased. How does the rise in the sale of mobile homes relate to the notion that investment responds to the rate of interest?
5. Empirical studies show that, as the volume of a firm's sales increases, the size of its inventories of raw materials tends to increase in pro-

portion. It is common for business firms to speak of such inventories in terms of "a 20-day supply of coal" rather than "52,000 tons of coal" or "$280,000 worth of coal." Why should relative size be more important than absolute quantity or dollar value?

6. Which "cause" of business investment is being relied on in each of the following quotes?

   a. An aluminum industry spokesman, justifying a $.50 per pound increase in aluminum prices: "We must have it to build the new capacity we need."

   b. Bethlehem Steel, in a newspaper ad: "We need lower taxes, not cheaper money or government deficits, to help lower barriers to capital formation."

   c. "The Reagan administration used a credit crunch to bring on a recession and reduce inflation."

7. Since different series behave differently, does it make sense to talk about a business cycle? Predict the comparative behavior of the following pairs of series in relation to fluctuations in GNP.

   a. Purchases of food and purchases of consumer durables

   b. Tax receipts and bankruptcies

   c. Unemployment and birth rates

   d. Employment in New York and employment in Michigan

   Check your predictions against the facts for the last decade.

8. The highest interest rates in American history occurred during 1981–1982. The deepest recession since the 1930s occurred in 1982. How might these facts be related? What has happened to interest rates and economic activity since?

9. An article in the 1988 Annual Report of the Federal Reserve Bank of New York stated that ". . . our international trade deficit is closely related to important imbalances in domestic assumption, saving, and investment, and a correction of those imbalances is necessary to achieve a satisfactory adjustment on the external side." Why are these external imbalances related to the internal ones? What policies might the quote give support to?

Appendix to Chapter 29

The Accelerator Theory of Investment

According to the accelerator theory, usually called the **accelerator,** investment is related to the rate of change of national income. When income is increasing, it is necessary to invest in order to increase the capacity to produce consumption goods; when income is falling, it may not even be necessary to replace old capital as it wears out, let alone to invest in new capital.

The main insight that the accelerator theory provides is the emphasis on the role of net investment as a phenomenon of *disequilibrium*—the situation in which the actual stock of capital goods differs from what firms and households would like it to be. Anything that changes the desired size of the capital stock can generate investment. The accelerator focuses on one such source of change, changing national income. This gives the accelerator its particular importance in connection with *fluctuations* in national income. As we shall see, it can itself contribute to those fluctuations.

How the Accelerator Works

To see how the accelerator theory works, suppose that there is a particular capital stock needed to produce each given level of an industry's output. The ratio of the value of capital to the annual value of output is called the **capital-output ratio.** Suppose that the industry is producing at capacity and that the demand for its product increases. If the industry is to produce the higher level of output, its capital stock must increase. This necessitates new investment.

Table 29A-1 provides a simple numerical example of the accelerator theory of investment. Working through the data step by step leads to three conclusions:

1. **Rising rather than high levels of sales are needed to call forth net investment.**
2. **For net investment to remain constant, sales must rise by a constant amount per year.**
3. **The amount of net investment will be a multiple of the increase in sales because the capital-output ratio is greater than one.**[1]

The data in Table 29A-1 are for a single industry, but if many industries behave in this way, one would expect aggregate net investment to bear a similar relationship to changes in national income. This is what the accelerator theory predicts. [37]

The accelerator theory says nothing directly about replacement investment, but it does have implications for such investment. When sales are constant (no net investment required), replacement investment will be required to maintain the capital stock at the desired level. When sales are increasing from a position of full capacity, both net investment and replacement investment will be required. When sales are falling, not only will net investment be zero, but also there will be a tendency to reduce replacement investment.

Limitations of the Accelerator

Taken literally, the accelerator posits a rigid response of investment to changes in sales (and thus, aggregatively, to changes in national income). In fact, the relationship is more subtle.

Changes in sales that are thought to be temporary will not necessarily lead to new investment. It is usually possible to increase the level of output for a given capital stock by working overtime or extra shifts. While this solution would be more expensive per unit of output in the long run, it is usually preferable to making investments in new plant and equipment that would lie idle after a temporary spurt of demand had subsided. Thus, expectations about

[1] In the example in Table 29A-1, the capital-output ratio is 5:1. Why should anyone spend $5 on capital stock to get $1 of output? It is not unreasonable to spend $5 to purchase a machine that produces only $1 of output *per year,* provided that the machine will last enough years to repay the $5 plus a reasonable return on this investment.

TABLE 29A-1   An Illustration of the Accelerator Theory of Investment

(1)	(2)	(3)	(4)	(5)
Year	Annual sales	Change in sales	Required stock of capital, assuming a capital-output ratio of 5:1	Net investment: increase in required capital stock
1	$10	$0	$ 50	$ 0
2	10	0	50	0
3	11	1	55	5
4	13	2	65	10
5	16	3	80	15
6	19	3	95	15
7	22	3	110	15
8	24	2	120	10
9	25	1	125	5
10	25	0	125	0

With a fixed capital-output ratio, net investment occurs only when it is necessary to increase the stock of capital in order to change output. Assume that it takes $5 of capital to produce $1 of output per year. In years 1 and 2 there is no need for investment. In year 3 a rise in sales of $1 requires investment of $5 to provide the needed capital stock. In year 4 a further rise of $2 in sales requires an additional investment of $10 to provide the needed capital stock. As columns 3 and 5 show, the amount of net investment is proportional to the *change* in sales. When the increase in sales tapers off in years 7–9, investment declines. When sales no longer increase in year 10, net investment falls to zero because the capital stock of year 9 is adequate to provide output for year 10's sales.

what the required capital stock will be may lead to a much less rigid response of investment to income than the accelerator suggests.

Another limitation of the accelerator theory is that it takes a limited view of what constitutes investment. The fixed capital-output ratio emphasizes investment in what economists call **capital widening,** the investment in additional capacity that uses the same ratio of capital to labor as existing capacity. It does not explain **capital deepening,** which is the increase in the amount of capital per unit of labor that occurs, say, in response to a fall in the rate of interest. Neither does the theory say anything about investments that have been brought about as a result of new processes or new products. Furthermore, it does not allow for the fact that investment in any period is likely to be limited by the capacity of the capital-goods industry.

For these and other reasons, the accelerator does not by itself give anything like a complete explanation of variations in investment in plant and equipment. It should not be surprising that a simple ac-

celerator theory provides a relatively poor overall explanation of changes in investment. Yet accelerator-like influences do exist, and empirical evidence continues to suggest that they play a role in the cyclical variability of investment.

The Multiplier-Accelerator Mechanism

The combination of the multiplier and the accelerator can make upward or downward movements in the economy cumulative. Imagine that the economy is settled into a depression, accompanied by high unemployment. Then a revival of investment demand occurs. Orders are placed for new plant and equipment, which creates new employment in the capital-goods industries. The newly employed workers spend most of their earnings. This creates new demand for consumer goods. A multiplier process is now set up, with new employment and incomes created in the consumer-goods industries.

The spending of the newly created incomes, in turn, means further increases in demand. At some stage the increased demand for consumer goods creates, through the accelerator process, an increased demand for capital goods. Once existing equipment is fully employed in any industry, extra output requires new capital equipment, and the accelerator theory takes over as the major determinant of investment expenditure. Such investment increases or, at least, maintains demand in the capital-goods sector of the economy. So the process goes on, with the multiplier-accelerator mechanism continuing to produce a rapid rate of expansion in the economy.

The Upper Turning Point

A rapid expansion can continue for some time, but it cannot go on forever. Eventually, the economy will run into bottlenecks in terms of certain resources. For example, investment funds may become scarce, and as a result interest rates rise. Firms now find new investments more expensive than anticipated, and thus some become unprofitable. Or suppose that what limits the expansion is exhaustion of the reservoir of unemployed labor. The full-employment ceiling guarantees that any sustained rapid growth rate of real income and employment eventually will be slowed.

At this point, the accelerator again comes into play. A slowing down in the rate of increase of production leads to a decrease in the investment in new plant and equipment. This decrease causes a drop in employment in the capital-goods industries and, through the multiplier, a fall in consumer demand. As consumer demand falls, investment in plant and equipment is reduced to a low level because firms already have more productive capacity than they can use. Unemployment rises, and the upper turning point has been passed.

The Lower Turning Point

A contraction, too, is eventually brought to an end. Consider the worst depression imaginable, one in which every postponable expenditure of households, firms, or governments is postponed. Even then aggregate demand does not fall to zero. Figure 26-1 shows that, as aggregate disposable income falls, households spend a larger and larger fraction of that falling income. Finally, should income fall to the break-even level, all disposable income is spent (and none is saved).

Neither does government spending fall in proportion to the fall in government tax revenues. Government expenditures on most programs continue even if tax revenues sag to low levels.

Finally, even investment expenditures, in many ways the most easily postponed component of aggregate expenditure, do not fall to zero. Industries providing basics still have substantial sales and need replacement investment. Even in the worst depression, some new processes and new products appear, and these require new investment.

Taken together, the minimum levels of consumption, investment, and government expenditure will assure a minimum equilibrium level of national income that, although well below the full-employment level, will not be zero. There is a floor below which income will not fall.

Sooner or later, an upturn begins. If nothing else causes an expansion of business activity, eventually there will be a revival of replacement investment, because, as existing capital wears out, the capital stock eventually falls below the level required to produce current output. At this stage new machines are bought to replace those that are worn out.

The rise in the level of activity in the capital-goods industries causes, by way of the multiplier, a further rise in income. The economy turns the corner. An expansion, once started, triggers the sort of cumulative upward movement that we have discussed already.

Other Endogenous Forces

The multiplier-accelerator mechanism just described is one endogenous force that contributes to cyclical fluctuations. Two other phenomena that contribute to the multiplier-accelerator mechanism are inventory and construction cycles.

Inventory Cycles

There are, as we saw in the text, good reasons to suppose that the required size of inventories is related to the level of firms' sales, and sales are related to the level of national income. If firms maintain anything like a rigid inventory-to-sales ratio, this will cause an accelerator-like linkage between investment in inventories and *changes* in national income.

Many observers believe that these sharp and somewhat periodic fluctuations lead to an "inventory cycle" of roughly 40 months' average duration.

616 Part 7 National Income and Fiscal Policy

Construction Cycles

Economists have noted some long-run, wavelike movements of roughly 20 years' duration in the statistics for expenditures on residential housing construction. These are sometimes referred to as "building cycles." Some economists suggest an accelerator-like explanation that runs from external events to demographic changes, to changes in the demand for housing and other buildings, and thence to changes in construction activity.

A major war, because males are taken away from home, tends to retard family formation and thereby tends to depress the demand for private housing. When the war ends, there is typically an increase in marriages and household formation, an increase in the demand for housing, and a boom in the construction industry.

Depending on the capacity of the building industry, the boom may last many years before the desired increases in the stock of buildings of various kinds are achieved, but eventually it ends. Then, approximately 20 years after the end of the war that triggered the boom, there is likely to be a further boom in the number of marriages and births as the new generation starts its process of family formation. Wars are not the only source of such population-induced cycles; a severe depression will lead to a similar postponement of family formation.

The evidence concerning spending for construction over the past century is thought by many economists to support the theory just outlined—a theory very much like the accelerator, though with changes in demographic factors, rather than changes in income, providing the impetus.

Conclusions

The multiplier–accelerator mechanism, acting in concert with the inventory and construction cycles, thus provides some insight into the *cyclical* nature of economic fluctuations, where initial positive (negative) shocks to spending and income tend to be followed by further increases (decreases).

Chapter 30

An Introduction to Fiscal Policy

As we saw in previous chapters, national income fluctuates continually, primarily due to shifts in aggregate demand and short-run aggregate supply. **Fiscal policy** involves the use of government spending and tax policies to pursue any of the government's many objectives. In this chapter we focus on the use of spending and tax policies, which we call *policy variables*, to influence the AD curve and, to a lesser degree, the $SRAS$ curve in order to damp fluctuations in the economy.

Any policy that attempts to stabilize national income at or near a desired level (usually potential national income) is called **stabilization policy.** This chapter deals first with the theory of fiscal policy as a tool of stabilization policy and then with the experience of using it.

Since government expenditure increases aggregate demand and taxation decreases it, the *direction* of the required changes in spending and taxation is generally easy to determine once we know the direction of the desired change in national income. However, the *timing*, *magnitude*, and *mixture* of the changes pose more difficult issues.

There is no doubt that the government can exert a major influence on national income. Prime examples are the massive increases in military spending during major wars. U.S. federal expenditure during World War II rose from 7.7 percent of GNP in 1940 to 47.3 percent of GNP in 1944. At the same time, the unemployment rate fell from 14.6 percent to 1.2 percent. Economists agree that the increase in government spending helped to bring about the rise in GNP and the associated fall in unemployment. Similar experiences occurred during the rearmament of most European countries before, or just following, the outbreak of World War II in 1939 and in the United States during the Vietnam War during the late 1960s and early 1970s.

When used appropriately, fiscal policy can be an important tool for stabilizing the economy. In the heyday of fiscal policy, from 1945 to 1970, many economists were convinced that the economy could be stabilized adequately just by varying the size of the government's taxes and expenditures. That day is past. Today most economists are aware of the many limitations of fiscal policy.

Fiscal Policy and the Budget

Changes in government expenditure and tax policies have financial implications for the government. As a result, fiscal policy is often referred to as *the government's budgetary policy* or simply as *the budget*.

The Budget Balance

The **budget balance** is the difference between total government revenue and total government expenditure. In this definition *government expenditure* includes both transfer payments and purchases of currently produced goods and services. Thus:

The budget balance is the difference between government *budget receipts* (the money it takes in as revenue) and government *budget outlays* (the money it pays out).

If receipts are exactly equal to outlays, the government has a **balanced budget.** If receipts exceed outlays, there is a **budget surplus;** if receipts are less than outlays, there is a **budget deficit.** Changes in either government spending or tax policies influence the budget balance. If the government raises its outlays without raising taxes, the extra expenditure is said to be *deficit financed.* If the extra outlays are accompanied by an increase in tax rates that yields an increase in receipts equal to the increase in outlays, we speak of a *balanced budget* change in spending.

When the government spends more than it raises, where does the money come from? If the government raises more than it spends, where does the money go? The difference between expenditure and current revenue shows up as changes in the government's debt, referred to as the *national debt.* A deficit requires that the government borrow money by selling financial instruments, usually referred to as *government bonds.*[1] A surplus allows the government to reduce its debt; it can use its excess tax revenue to redeem some of its outstanding bonds.

The Theory of Fiscal Policy

Since the stabilization objective of fiscal policy is to remove any existing GNP gaps, the appropriate fiscal

policies appear quite straightforward. All that is needed is a once-and-for-all fiscal change that will shift the *AD* curve in the appropriate direction to remove the GNP gap.

The Basic Theory of Fiscal Stabilization

A reduction in tax rates or an increase in government expenditure shifts the *AD* curve to the right, causing an increase in GNP. An increase in tax rates or a cut in government expenditure shifts the *AD* curve to the left, causing a decrease in GNP. (See Figures 27–8 and 27–9 for detailed discussions.)

A more detailed look at what is involved will provide a useful review. It will also help to show what complications might make the policy decisions more difficult.

A recessionary gap.   The removal of a recessionary gap is illustrated in Figure 30-1. There are three possible ways in which the gap may be removed.

First, the recessionary gap eventually may drive wages and other factor prices down by enough to shift the *SRAS* curve to the right and thereby reinstate full employment and potential income (at a lower price level). The evidence is, however, that this process takes a substantial period of time.

Second, the natural cyclical forces of the economy could induce a demand-side recovery for the reasons spelled out in Chapter 28 (see page 582). This would cause the *AD* curve to shift rightward, moving the economy back toward full employment and potential income. The evidence is that such recoveries do occur. Sometimes they happen quickly; often, however, a recession can be both deep and prolonged.

Third, government expenditure can be increased or taxes can be cut in order to shift the *AD* curve to the right. The advantage of using fiscal policy is that it may substantially shorten what would otherwise be a long recession. One disadvantage is that it may stimulate the economy just before private-sector spending recovers due to natural causes. If it does, the economy may overshoot its potential output, and an inflationary gap may open up.

An inflationary gap.   Figure 30-2 shows the three ways in which an inflationary gap can be removed.

First, wages and other factor prices may be pushed up by the excess demand. This will shift the *SRAS* curve to the left, eventually eliminating the

---

[1] A wide variety of financial instruments is used. Some, called treasury bills, are very short-term, promising to repay a stated amount at some specified date between 90 days and 1 year from the date of issue. A government *bond* also represents a promise to pay a stated sum of money in the future but in the more distant future than a treasury bill—as much as 25 years from the date of issue. We shall learn more about these in Chapter 32.

FIGURE 30-1   Removal of a Recessionary Gap

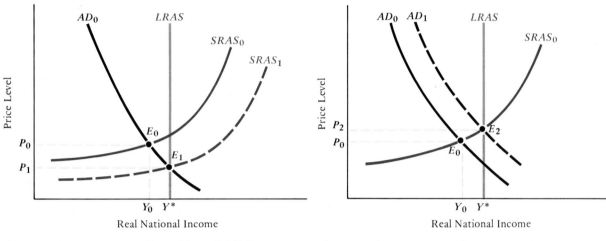

(i) A recessionary gap removed by a rightward shift in **SRAS**

(ii) A recessionary gap removed by a rightward shift in **AD**

A recessionary gap may be removed by a (slow) rightward shift of the SRAS curve, a natural revival of private-sector demand, or a fiscal policy-induced increase in aggregate demand. Initially, equilibrium is at E_0, with national income at Y_0 and the price level at P_0. The recessionary gap is Y_0Y^*.

As shown in (i), the gap might be removed by a shift in the SRAS curve to $SRAS_1$. This increase in aggregate supply could occur as a result of reductions in wage rates and other input prices. The shift in the SRAS curve causes a movement down and to the right along AD_0. This establishes a new equilibrium at E_1, achieving potential income, Y^*, and lowering the price level to P_1.

As shown in (ii), the gap might also be removed by a shift of the AD curve to AD_1. This increase in aggregate demand could occur either because of a natural revival of private-sector expenditure or because of a fiscal policy-induced increase in expenditure. The shift in the AD curve causes a movement up and to the right along $SRAS_0$. This shifts the equilibrium to E_2, taking income to Y^* and the price level to P_2.

gap, reducing income to its potential level, and raising the price level.

Second, a cyclical reduction in aggregate demand may occur for the reasons outlined in Chapter 27. This might reduce income to its potential level without the rise in the price level that is associated with a shift of the SRAS curve. However, unless aggregate demand declines quickly, rising wages and other input prices will lead to a shift of the SRAS curve to the left and hence to rising prices.

Third, the government, by raising taxes or cutting spending, may reduce aggregate demand sufficiently to remove the inflationary gap. The advantage of this approach is that it avoids the inflationary increase in prices that accompanies the first method.

One disadvantage is that if private-sector expenditures fall due to natural causes, national income may be pushed below potential, thus opening up a recessionary gap.

A key proposition.   This discussion suggests that, in circumstances in which the automatic adjustment mechanisms either fail to operate quickly enough or give rise to undesirable side effects such as rising prices, there is a potential stabilizing role for fiscal policy.

Government taxes and expenditure, by shifting the AD curve, can be used to remove persistent GNP gaps.

FIGURE 30-2   Removal of an Inflationary Gap

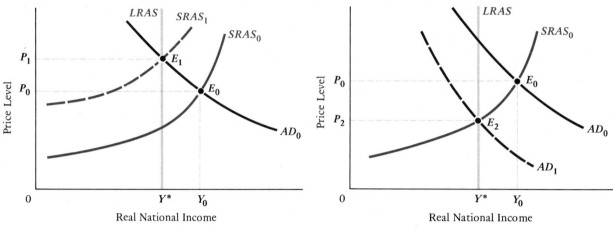

(i) An inflationary gap removed by a leftward shift in *SRAS*   (ii) An inflationary gap removed by a leftward shift in *AD*

An inflationary gap may be removed by a leftward shift of the *SRAS* curve, a natural reduction in private-sector demand, or a policy-induced reduction in aggregate demand.
Initially, equilibrium is at E_0, with national income at Y_0 and the price level at P_0. The inflationary gap is Y^*Y_0.

As shown in (i), the gap might be removed by a shift in the *SRAS* curve to $SRAS_1$. This decrease in aggregate supply could occur as a result of increases in wage rates and other input prices. The shift in the *SRAS* curve causes a movement up and to the left along AD_0. This establishes a new equilibrium at E_1, reducing income to its potential level, Y^*, and raising the price level to P_1.

As shown in (ii), the gap might also be removed by a shift in the *AD* curve to AD_1. This decrease in aggregate demand could occur either because of a natural fall in private spending or because of contractionary fiscal policy. The shift in the *AD* curve causes a movement down and to the left along $SRAS_0$. This shifts the equilibrium to E_2, taking income to Y^* and the price level to P_2.

The Paradox of Thrift

Government tax revenues are related to the performance of the economy; they are high during booms and low during slumps. Thus, if a government follows a balanced budget policy, its spending becomes procyclical. It will restrict its spending during a recession because its tax revenue is low, and it will increase its spending during a recovery when its tax revenue is rising. In other words, it rolls with the economy, raising and lowering its spending in step with everyone else.

Not long ago people generally accepted—and, indeed, many still fervently believe—that a prudent government should always balance its budget. Such thinking lies behind the desire on the part of a number of politicians to pass a constitutional amendment

requiring that the government balance its budget. This view is based on an analogy with what seems to be prudent behavior for the individual household. It is a foolish household whose current expenditure exceeds its current revenue for a prolonged period so that it goes steadily further into debt. From this commonsense observation, some people argue that, if balancing the budget is good for the individual, it must also be good for the nation. The *paradox of thrift,* however, suggests that the analogy between the government and the household may be misleading.

The theory of national income, developed in Chapters 24 through 28, predicts that, if all spending units in the economy simultaneously try to increase the amount that they save, the combined increase in thrift will shift the *AD* curve to the left and hence *reduce* the equilibrium level of income.[2] The contrary case, a general decrease in thrift and increase in expenditure, shifts the *AD* curve to the right and hence increases national income. This prediction is known as the *paradox of thrift*.[3]

The policy implication of this prediction is that substantial unemployment is correctly combatted by encouraging governments, firms, and households to spend more, *not* to save more. In times of unemployment and depression, frugality will only make things worse. This prediction goes directly against the idea that we should tighten our belts when times are tough. The notion that it is not only possible but also acceptable to spend one's way out of a depression touches a sensitive point with people raised on the belief that success is based on hard work and frugality and not on prodigality; as a result, the idea often arouses great hostility.

Applications.   As is discussed in Box 30-1, the implications of the paradox of thrift were not generally understood during the Great Depression, and most governments followed procyclical spending policies in order to balance their budgets. However, by the middle of the 1930s, many economists had concluded that such government behavior did not make the most of its potential to stabilize the economy. Why, they asked, should not the government try to stabilize the economy by doing just the opposite of what everyone else was doing—by increasing its demand when private demand was falling and by lowering its demand when private demand was rising? If completely successful, this policy could hold aggregate demand constant even though its individual components were fluctuating.

When Milton Friedman said, "We are all Keynesians now," he was referring to (among other things) the general acceptance of the view that the government's budget is much more than just the revenue and expenditure statement of a very large organization. Whether we like it or not, the sheer size of the government's budget inevitably makes it a powerful tool for influencing the economy.

---

[2] Indeed, income may fall enough that total savings falls, even though everyone's propensity to save has risen!

[3] The prediction is not actually, in fact, a paradox. It is a straightforward implication of the theory of the determination of income. The expectations that lead to the "paradox" are based on the fallacy of composition: the belief that what is true for the parts is necessarily true for the whole.

Limitations.   The paradox of thrift concentrates on shifts in aggregate demand that have been caused by changes in saving (and hence spending) behavior. Hence, it applies only in the short run, when the *AD* curve plays an important role in the determination of national income.

In the long run, when the economy is on its *LRAS* curve and hence aggregate demand is not important for the determination of national income (see Figure 28-5), the paradox of thrift ceases to apply. The more people save, the larger is the supply of funds available for investment. The more people invest, the greater is the growth of potential income. Increased potential income causes the *LRAS* curve to shift to the right.

These longer-term effects are taken up in Chapter 36 in the discussion of economic growth. In the meantime, we concentrate on the short-run demand effects of saving and spending.

The paradox of thrift is based on the short-run effects of changes in saving and investment on aggregate demand.

Balanced Budget Changes

In Figures 30-1 and 30-2 we considered the effects of changes in either government expenditure or taxes. Another policy that is available to the government is to make a balanced budget change by introducing equal changes in spending and taxes. Say the government increases tax rates enough to raise an extra $1 billion that it then uses to purchase goods and services. Aggregate expenditure would remain unchanged if, and only if, the $1 billion that the government takes from the private sector would otherwise have been spent by the private sector. If that is the case, the government's policy would reduce private expenditure by $1 billion and raise its own spending by $1 billion. Aggregate demand, and hence national income and employment, would remain unchanged.

However, this is not the usual case. When an extra $1 billion in taxes is taken away from households, they usually reduce their spending on domestically produced goods by less than $1 billion. If the marginal propensity to consume out of disposable income is, say, 0.75, consumption expenditure will fall by only $750 million. If the government spends the entire $1 billion on domestically produced

BOX 30-1

Fiscal Policy and the Great Depression

Failure to understand the implication of the paradox of thrift led many countries to adopt policies during the Great Depression that were disastrous. Failure to understand the role of built-in stabilizers also has led many observers to conclude, erroneously, that fiscal expansion had been tried in the Great Depression but had failed. Let us see how these two misperceptions are related.

The Paradox of Thrift in Action

In 1932 Franklin Roosevelt was elected president on a platform of fighting the Great Depression with government policies. His actual policies did not, however, lead to an increase in aggregate demand. They were based instead on the notion that in a recession it is necessary to "tighten our belts." In his inaugural address he urged, "Our great primary task is to put people to work. . . . [This task] can be helped by insistence that the Federal, State and local governments act forthwith on the demand that their costs be drastically reduced. . . . There must be a strict supervision of all banking and credits and investments."

Across the Atlantic, King George V told the British House of Commons in 1931, "The present condition of the national finances, in the opinion of His Majesty's Ministers, calls for the imposition of additional taxation and for the effecting of economies in public expenditure."

As the paradox of thrift predicts, these policies tended to worsen, not to cure, the depression.

Interpreting the Deficit in the 1930s

The deficits that occurred following Roosevelt's election were not the result of a program of deficit-financed public expenditure. Instead, they were the result of the fall in tax yields, brought about by the fall in national income, as the economy sank into depression. President Roosevelt and his advisers did not advocate a program of massive deficit-financed spending to shift the *AD* curve to the right. Instead, they hoped that a small amount of government spending plus numerous policies, designed to stabilize prices and to restore confidence, would lead to a recovery of private-investment expenditure that would substantially shift the *AD* curve. To

goods, aggregate expenditure will increase by $250 million. In this case the balanced budget increase in government expenditure has an expansionary effect, because it shifts the aggregate expenditure function upward and hence shifts the *AD* curve to the right.

A balanced budget increase in government expenditure will have an expansionary effect on national income, and a balanced budget decrease will have a contractionary effect.

The **balanced budget multiplier** measures these effects. It is the change in income divided by the balanced budget change in government expenditure that brought it about. Thus, if the extra $1 billion of government spending, financed by the extra $1 bil-

lion of taxes, causes national income to rise by $500 million, the balanced budget multiplier is 0.5; if income rises by $1 billion, it is 1.0.

Now compare the sizes of the multipliers for a balanced budget and a deficit-financed increase in government spending. With a deficit-financed increase in expenditure, there is no increase in tax rates and hence no consequent decrease in consumption expenditure to offset the increase in government expenditure. With a balanced budget increase in expenditure, however, the increase in tax rates and a partially offsetting decrease in consumption does occur. Thus, the balanced budget multiplier is much lower than the multiplier that relates the change in income to a deficit-financed increase in government expenditure with tax rates being held constant.

have expected a massive revival of private-investment expenditure as a result of the puny increase in aggregate demand that was instituted by the federal government now seems hopelessly naive.

When we judge Roosevelt's policies from the viewpoint of modern multiplier theory, their failure is no mystery. Indeed, Professor E. Cary Brown of MIT, after a careful study, concluded, "Fiscal policy seems to have been an unsuccessful recovery device in the 'thirties—not because it did not work, but because it was not tried." In 1933 the federal government was spending $2 billion for purchases of goods and services, compared to $1.3 billion that it spent in 1929. This increase was a small drop in a very large bucket, considering that GNP fell from $103 billion in 1929 to $46 billion in 1933! Given the deficits achieved, it would have taken a multiplier of 25 for the American economy to have approached full employment; in fact, the multiplier in the 1930s was closer to 2. Expenditures were wastefully small, not (as many people thought at the time) wastefully large.

Once the massive, war-geared expenditure of the 1940s began, income responded sharply and unemployment evaporated. Government expenditures on goods and services, which had been running at under 15 percent of GNP during the 1930s, jumped to 46 percent by 1944, while unemployment reached the incredible low of 1.2 percent of the civilian labor force.

The performance of the American economy from 1930 to 1945 is quite well explained by national income theory. It is clear that the government did not effectively use fiscal measures to stabilize the economy. War cured the Depression, because war demands made acceptable a level of government expenditure sufficient to remove the deflationary gap. Had the first Roosevelt administration been able to do the same, it might have ended the waste of the Great Depression many years sooner.

Judging the Stance of Fiscal Policy

The *stance* of fiscal policy refers to its expansionary or contractionary effects on the economy. An expansionary fiscal policy increases aggregate demand and thus tends to increase national income; a contractionary fiscal policy reduces aggregate demand and tends to lower national income. In the previous chapter and earlier in this one, we looked separately at taxes, purchases of goods and services, and transfer payments as means of influencing aggregate demand. However, people want a summary measure—one number to express the government's effect on the economy.

The Inadequacy of the Deficit as a Measure of the Fiscal Stance

Not surprisingly, people tend to focus on the government's budget deficit in order to judge the stance of fiscal policy. An increase in the government deficit is often taken as an indication of an expansionary fiscal policy, and a decrease in the deficit is often taken as an indication of a contractionary fiscal policy. However, a number of problems make the deficit an unreliable guide to judging the fiscal stance.

The deficit is the difference between the government's outlays and receipts, its receipts consisting largely of tax revenue. However, tax revenue is the result of the interaction of tax rates, which the government sets, and the level of national income, which is influenced by many forces beyond the government's control.

The major tools of fiscal policy are government expenditure and tax *rates*. The government budget balance is the relationship between government expenditure and tax *revenues*.

Assume, for example, that government expenditure is constant at $200 billion and that at current tax rates the government takes 20 percent of national income in taxes. Suppose national income is $1,000 billion (i.e., $1 trillion), so tax revenues are also $200 billion. Now assume that tax revenues sink to $150 billion, opening up a $50 billion budget deficit. This could be the result of a discretionary cut in tax rates so that now they yield only 15 percent of an unchanged national income. It could also be the result of a fall in national income itself to $750 billion, with tax rates being held constant. In the first case, a conscious change in the government's fiscal stance causes the fall in tax revenues. In the second case, a fall in national income that is not the result of fiscal policy causes tax revenue to fall; the increase in the deficit simply reflects the operation of the automatic stabilizers discussed earlier in this chapter.

This example illustrates why judging changes in the stance of fiscal policy from changes in the government's budget balance can be misleading. Doing so confuses changes in the deficit due to fluctuations in national income, which may not be the result of shifts in fiscal policy, with changes in the deficit that are the result of shifts in fiscal policy.

The Cyclically Adjusted Deficit

Changes in the stance of fiscal policy can be measured by estimating changes in the budget balance that would occur were national income held constant at some base level. Holding income constant ensures that measured changes in the budget balance are due to changes in policy. The base level most commonly used is potential national income. Because estimating the budget balance for a given level of national income controls for cyclical fluctuations in expenditures and tax revenues, it is referred to as making the *cyclical adjustment;* the resulting measure is referred to as the *cyclically adjusted budget balance,* or

cyclically adjusted deficit (CAD).[4] It is an estimate of government expenditure minus government tax revenues, not as they actually are but as they would be if national income had been at its potential level. Table 30-1 shows the actual and cyclically adjusted deficit on an annual basis since 1969.

Because they reflect *exogenous* changes in the government's policy instruments and control for *endogenous* changes in actual spending and revenues, changes in the cyclically adjusted deficit are a useful indicator of changes in the stance of fiscal policy.

Box 30-2 introduces the concept of the *budget deficit function* and discusses how using it, along with the cyclically adjusted deficit, makes it possible to avoid the errors that arise from using the current budget balance as an indicator of the stance of fiscal policy. (We encounter some related issues in Chapter 37 when we discuss some of the controversies surrounding the persistently large deficits that the federal government experienced in the 1980s.)

Implementing Fiscal Policy

The theory that we have just outlined makes the implementation of fiscal policy appear rather straightforward. However, there are complications that make the practice of fiscal policy a controversial issue.

As we saw in Chapter 27, private-expenditure functions are constantly changing. Investment expenditure shifts with business conditions, and consumption functions sometimes shift upward as the public goes on a spending spree or downward as people become cautious and increase their saving. Further, any GNP gaps that do arise set in motion

---

[4] This concept used to be called the full-employment surplus. The change from *full employment* to *cyclically adjusted* came when the amount of unemployment that is associated with potential income rose rapidly during the 1970s, and hence referring to so much unemployment as *full employment* became embarrassing. The change from *deficit* to *surplus* occurred because during the 1960s people were trying to stress possible depressing effects of surpluses, while during the 1980s people wanted to stress the alleged harmful effects of deficits.

TABLE 30-1   Actual and Cyclically Adjusted Budget Balances for the Federal Government (billions of dollars, national accounts basis)

Year	Actual deficit	Cyclically adjusted deficit
1969	8.5	4.0
1970	12.1	10.9
1971	22.0	16.8
1972	17.3	15.6
1973	5.6	13.5
1974	11.5	9.1
1975	69.3	44.4
1976	53.1	37.9
1977	45.9	42.7
1978	29.5	45.3
1979	16.1	36.3
1980	61.3	60.5
1981	63.8	55.6
1982	145.9	88.9
1983	179.4	129.5
1984	169.6	171.3
1985	196.9	202.7
1986	205.6	187.9
1987	157.8	157.6
1988	142.4	163.5

Source: Survey of Current Business, various issues.

Note: A minus indicates a surplus; that is, a negative deficit is a surplus.

Wide swings in the cyclically adjusted budget deficit indicate wide swings in the stance of fiscal policy. Because the economy operated at less than full employment during most of the 1970s, actual budget deficits were larger than cyclically adjusted deficits in most years. The large actual deficits during the mid-1970s were mainly in response to low levels of national income during the recession. Variations in the cyclically adjusted deficits show the variability of the stance of fiscal policy. The sharp increases in 1975 and after 1982 indicate expansionary fiscal policy, whereas the decreases in 1974, 1979, and 1981 indicate contractionary fiscal policy.

changes in wages and other factor costs that cause the *SRAS* curve to shift and that thus cause the gap itself to change. Further, shifts in the *LRAS* curve change potential GNP and thus make it hard to determine whether changes in actual GNP also imply that the GNP gap has changed. These, and other, considerations make stabilization policy much more difficult than it would be if it were possible simply to identify a stable inflationary or recessionary gap and then take steps to eliminate it once and for all.

Discretionary and Automatic Fiscal Policies

As a first step toward understanding some of the controversies involved in implementing fiscal policy, it is helpful to distinguish between *discretionary* and *automatic* fiscal policies.

We have seen that when identifiable, persistent GNP gaps arise, it is possible for changes in tax rates and spending to offset the gaps. **Discretionary fiscal policy** refers to such changes in policy variables when they are made in a conscious effort to stabilize the economy. **Automatic fiscal policy** does not require changes in the government policy variables; it occurs as the result of the operation of *built-in stabilizers*.

Automatic Fiscal Tools: Built-in Stabilizers

As we saw in Chapter 29 (see page 600), imports act as a *built-in stabilizer* because they reduce the marginal propensity to spend out of national income and hence reduce the value of the multiplier. In general, a **built-in stabilizer** is anything that automatically lessens the magnitude of the fluctuations in national income caused by changes in autonomous expenditures such as investment. The role of the government in the economy gives rise to a number of features that act as built-in stabilizers; note that they do so without the government's having to react consciously to each change in national income as it occurs.

Three principal government built-in stabilizers are taxes, government purchases of goods and services, and government transfer payments.

Taxes

Income taxes act as a built-in stabilizer because they reduce the marginal propensity to spend out of national income. To illustrate, consider two situations. In the first case, there are no income taxes, so every change in national income of $1 causes a $1 change in disposable income. With a marginal propensity to

BOX 30-2

The Budget Deficit Function

The distinction between changes in the budget balance due to changes in the fiscal stance and those due to cyclical changes in the economy is easily seen in what is called the government's *budget deficit function*.

The budget deficit function (curve B in the figure) expresses the difference between the government's expenditures and its tax revenues at each level of national income for given levels of government expenditure and tax rates. The curve in part (i) shows that deficits are associated with low levels of income and surpluses are associated with high levels of income; this is because at a given tax *rate* tax *revenue* rises with national income.

Changes in the government's budget balance, induced by changes in national income, are shown by *movements along* a given budget deficit function. Changes in the budget balance resulting from policy-induced changes in the level of government expenditure or tax rates are shown by *shifts* in the budget function. Such shifts indicate a different budget balance at each level of national income.

In part (ii) a fall in national income from Y_0 to Y_1 causes the actual budget to go from a surplus of D_0 to a deficit of D_1. Government expenditure and tax rates are unchanged; that is, the fiscal policy stance is unchanged. The unchanged fiscal stance is correctly captured by the constant cyclically adjusted deficit, CAD, measured at the (constant) potential level of national income, Y^*.

Part (iii) illustrates a contractionary change in the stance of fiscal policy. A government expenditure cut or a tax rate increase shifts the budget deficit *at each level of national income*. This change is correctly captured by the fall in the cyclically adjusted deficit from CAD to CAD'.

To see the misleading effects of judging changes in the policy stance from changes in the measured deficit, suppose national income had fallen from Y_0 to Y_1 at the same time that the budget deficit function shifted from B_0 to B_1. In that case, the measured balance would have gone from surplus (D)

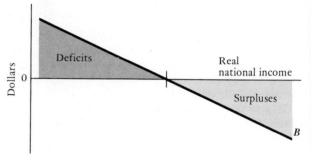

(i) The budget deficit function

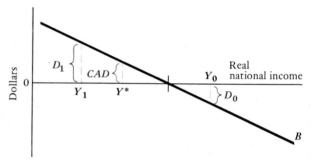

(ii) Changes in the measured deficit

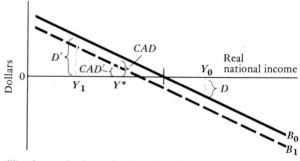

(iii) Changes in the cyclically adjusted deficit

to deficit (D') despite the fall in the cyclically adjusted deficit from CAD to CAD'. Thus, the measured balance would have indicated an expansionary fiscal policy, while the fiscal stance was actually contractionary.

TABLE 30-2   The Effect of Tax Rates on the Marginal Propensity to Spend Out of National Income

Marginal rate of tax	Change in national income (millions) ΔY	Change in tax revenue (millions) ΔT	Change in disposable income (millions) ΔY_d	Change in consumption (millions) ΔC	Marginal propensity to spend out of national income $\Delta C/\Delta Y$
0.2	$1,000	$200	$800	$640	0.64
0.4	1,000	400	600	480	0.48

The higher is the marginal rate of tax, the lower is the marginal propensity to spend out of national income. When national income changes by $1,000, disposable income changes by $800 when the tax rate is 20 percent and by $600 when the tax rate is 40 percent. Although the *MPC* out of disposable income is 0.8 in both examples, consumption changes by $640 in the first case and by only $480 in the second. Although that households' *MPC* out of their disposable income is unchanged, an increase in tax rates lowers the marginal propensity to spend out of national income on which the size of the multiplier depends.

---

consume out of disposable income (*MPC*) of, say, 0.8, consumption would change by $.80. In the second case, income taxes are positive. Now when national income changes by $1, disposable income changes by less than $1. Hence, consumption expenditure will change by less than $.80, even though the *MPC* is still 0.8.

In order to understand the second case, consider the extreme situation in which the marginal personal income-tax rate is 100 percent. If there is an autonomous rise of $1 billion in investment expenditure, none of the $1 billion will become disposable income. There are no induced rounds of secondary expenditure; the rise in national income is limited to the initial $1 billion in new investment, and the multiplier is unity. Similarly, an autonomous fall in investment expenditure of $1 billion reduces incomes that are earned in the investment industry by $1 billion and hence reduces government tax revenue by $1 billion, but it does not affect disposable income. Thus, there are no secondary rounds of induced contractions in consumption experience to magnify the initial drop in national income that has been caused by the investment decline.

Table 30-2 illustrates the stabilizing effects of taxes by comparing the effects of two different marginal tax rates on the marginal propensity to spend out of national income in otherwise identical situations. The general proposition can be stated as follows:

Income taxes reduce the magnitude of fluctuations in disposable income that are associated with any given fluctuation in national income. Hence, for a given marginal propensity to consume out of disposable income, they reduce the marginal propensity to spend out of national income.

Although tax rates fell during the 1980s, they increased greatly over this century. Although citizens complain about the burden of high taxes—perhaps with good reason—few are aware that high taxes have helped to reduce swings in national income and employment.[5]

Government Purchases

Government purchases of goods and services tend to be relatively stable in the face of cyclical variations in national income. Much of government spending is already committed by earlier legislation, so only a small proportion can be varied at the government's discretion from one year to the next, and even this small part is slow to change. In contrast, private consumption and investment expenditure tend to vary with national income.

Thus, the higher is the share of government spending in the economy, the lower is the cyclical instability of total expenditure. The twentieth century rise in the importance of the government's role

---

[5] Undistributed profits and other minor items would still hold disposable income below national income. We ignore these in the text because taxes (including subsidies and transfer payments) are the major source of the discrepancy between national income and disposable income.

in the economy may be a mixed blessing. One benefit, however, has been to put a large built-in stabilizer into the economy.

Government Transfer Payments

Government transfer payments to individuals often rise during recessions and fall during booms. This stabilizes disposable income and personal comsumption, reducing the size of the multiplier and thus acting as a built-in stabilizer.

Social insurance. The Old-Age, Survivors, and Disability Insurance program (popularly known as social security) is financed by payroll taxes that are paid jointly by employers and employees. Unemployment insurance is financed by a payroll tax on employers. During recessions these tax collections decrease and payments to the unemployed rise. Both social security and unemployment insurance support disposable income when national income falls and hold it down when national income rises.

Welfare payments. Welfare payments rise with the unemployment that accompanies falling national income. Thus, welfare programs make net additions to disposable income in times of slumps. They also make net subtractions during booms when payments are relatively low.

Transfer payments act as built-in stabilizers. They tend to stabilize disposable income, and hence consumption expenditure, in the face of fluctuations in national income.

Suppose that national income falls as a result of a fall in investment expenditure and that, in the absence of transfer payments, this would reduce disposable income by $6 billion. With an *MPC* out of disposable income of 0.8, this $6 billion reduction would cause an initial induced fall in consumption expenditure of $4.8 billion. Now assume, instead, that the fall in national income is accompanied by an increase in transfer payments of $4 billion. Instead of falling by $6 billion, disposable income now falls by only $2 billion. With the *MPC* out of disposable income still at 0.8, the initial induced fall in consumption expenditure is only $1.6 billion instead of $4.8 billion.

The Role of Built-in Stabilizers

Most built-in stabilizers are fairly new phenomena. Sixty years ago high marginal tax rates, high and stable government expenditures, and large unemployment and other social security payments were unknown in the United States. Each of these built-in stabilizers was the unforeseen by-product of policies that originally were adopted for other reasons. The progressive income tax arose out of a concern to raise government revenue while making the distribution of income less unequal. Social insurance and agricultural support programs were adopted more because of a concern with the welfare of the individuals and groups involved than with preserving the stability of the economy. Unforeseen or not, they work—even governments can be lucky.

The President's Council of Economic Advisers estimated that, with the 1970s tax system and schedules of unemployment compensation benefits, a decline in GNP automatically produced a reduction in government receipts and an increase in transfer payments that limited the decline in after-tax income to about $.65 for each $1 of reduction of GNP. Thus, roughly one-third of any decline was automatically offset by these two stabilizers alone. Tax cuts introduced during President Reagan's term decreased this automatic stabilizing effect somewhat.

No matter how lucky governments have been in finding built-in stabilizers, these stabilizers cannot reduce fluctuations to zero; they work by producing stabilizing reactions to changes in income. However, until income changes, these stabilizers are not even brought into play.

Discretionary Fiscal Policy

We have now seen that many short-term, minor fluctuations are damped automatically by built-in stabilizers. We have seen also that large and persistent gaps nevertheless sometimes appear. We can now examine the role of discretionary changes in taxes and spending in offsetting these gaps. To do this effectively, an administration must periodically make conscious decisions to alter fiscal policy. The Council of Economic Advisers, the Treasury, and the Office of Management and the Budget all study current economic trends and predict the probable course of the economy. If the predicted course is unsatisfactory, they may attempt to persuade Congress to enact the necessary legislation.

In considering discretionary fiscal policy, we first ask whether the government can expect to be able to "fine tune" the economy so as to remove virtually *all* GNP gaps.

Fine Tuning

In the heyday of Keynesian fiscal policy from 1945 to 1970, many economists advocated the use of fiscal policy to remove even minor fluctuations in national income around its potential level. Fiscal policy was to be altered frequently and by relatively small amounts to hold national income almost precisely at its potential level. This is called **fine tuning** the economy.

Fiscal fine tuning was never really possible in the United States because of the length of the **decision lag,** the period of time between perceiving a problem and deciding how to react to it. Many things contribute to the length of this decision lag. Experts must study the economy and agree among themselves on what fiscal changes are most desirable. They must persuade the president to call for the action that they endorse. The president must temper their advice with what he believes to be politically possible as well as desirable. Then Congress must be persuaded to enact the necessary legislation. A majority of the legislators must be convinced to vote for the measure, either because it is in the country's best interests or because it would be politically advantageous to do so. The time required for this process can be very long—as much as two or three years.

While the American form of government makes the decision lag rather long, both the British system—used in the rest of the English-speaking world—and the political systems in most European countries make the decision lag very short. In such countries fine tuning often has been tried. Careful assessment of the results shows that their successes, if any, have fallen far short of what was hoped. One basic reason lies in the complexity of any economy. Although economists and policymakers can identify broad and persistent trends, they do not have detailed knowledge of what is going on at any moment, of all the forces that are operating to cause changes in the immediate future, and of all the short-term effects of small changes in the various government expenditure and tax rates.

Further difficulties for fine tuning also arise because of an **execution lag,** the time that it takes to put policies in place after the decision has been made, and because of lags between the introduction of a given policy measure and its effects being felt in the economy. Often, by the time the effects of a given policy decision are felt, circumstances in the economy have changed and the policy is no longer appropriate.

Fine tuning often has done as much to encourage fluctuations in the economy as to remove them.

As a result of these experiences, fine tuning is currently out of favor. If consciously fine tuning the economy, which involves constantly changing the government's policy variables, is undesirable, must we say that nothing can be done through discretionary fiscal policy to reduce or to eliminate GNP gaps?

There is a middle ground. Rather than either doing nothing or fine tuning, one might attempt *gross tuning*—altering fiscal policy less frequently by responding only to gaps that appear to be large and persistent.

Gross Tuning

If a gap persists for a long enough period of time, its major causes can be studied and understood, and fiscal remedies can be planned and executed carefully. Such gross tuning can effectively shorten the period that it takes for the gaps to be eliminated. However, even gross tuning is not a simple matter.

The Need for Reversibility

Consider a *temporary* slump in private investment that opens up a large recessionary gap. Suppose that the government decides to adopt some combination of tax cuts and spending increases to push the economy back toward full employment. If private investment recovers to its preslump level and the government does not quickly reverse this policy, an inflationary gap will open up as the combination of rising investment expenditure and continuing fiscal stimulus takes national income into the inflationary range. The result is illustrated in Figure 30-3.

Alternatively, assume that starting from the same situation of approximately full employment, a temporary investment boom opens up an inflationary

FIGURE 30-3   Effects of Fiscal Policies That Are Not Reversed

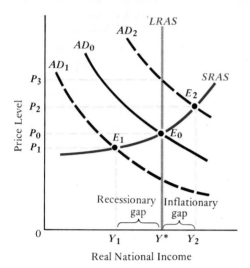

Real National Income

Fiscal policies that are initially appropriate may become inappropriate when private expenditure shifts. The normal level of the aggregate demand function is assumed to be AD_0, leaving income normally at Y^* and the price level at P_0. Suppose a slump in private investment shifts aggregate demand to AD_1, lowering national income to Y_1 and causing a recessionary gap of Y^*Y_1.

The government now introduces fiscal expansion to restore aggregate demand to AD_0 and national income to Y^*. Suppose that private investment then recovers, raising aggregate demand to AD_2. If fiscal policy can be quickly reversed, aggregate demand can be returned to AD_0 and income stabilized at Y^*. If the policy is not quickly reversed, equilibrium will be at E_2 and an inflationary gap Y^*Y_2 will open up. This will cause wages to rise and thus shift the $SRAS$ curve leftward and eventually restore Y^* at price level P_3.

Now suppose that starting from equilibrium E_0 a persistent investment boom takes AD_0 to AD_2. In order to stop the price level from rising in the face of the newly opened inflationary gap, the government introduces fiscal restraint, thereby shifting aggregate demand back to AD_0. Further assume, however, that the investment boom then comes to a halt, so that the aggregate demand curve shifts downward to AD_1. Unless the fiscal policy can be rapidly reversed, a recessionary gap will open up and equilibrium income will fall to Y_1.

gap. Rather than let the inflation persist, the government reduces expenditure and raises taxes to remove the gap. If, when the investment boom is over and investment expenditure returns to its original level, the government does nothing, a recessionary gap will open up and a slump may ensue. This, too, is analyzed in Figure 30-3.

Fiscal policies that are designed to remove persistent GNP gaps, resulting from abnormal levels of private expenditure, will destabilize the economy unless the policies can be reversed rapidly once private expenditure returns to its more normal level.

In the American economy, where decision lags for changes in government spending or taxes are measured in years, rapid reversals are not easily accomplished. This fact is a powerful argument against discretionary fiscal policy, at least as it is practiced in the United States. Even if the GNP gaps persist long enough for fiscal changes to be agreed on and to be made, subsequent rapid changes in private expenditure may require a quick reversal of the fiscal stance—a reversal that cannot easily be made, given the slow political decision-making process that is built into the American Constitution.

"Temporary" Versus "Long-lasting" Changes

Consider the attempt to remove a persistent inflationary or recessionary gap through changes in tax rates. Such a gap, though persistent, is unlikely to be a permanent feature of the economy. The relevant tax changes should therefore be advocated only for "the duration," that is, for as long as the administration thinks that the gaps would persist without the tax changes. A discretionary fiscal policy that is designed to remove such a gap might take the form, say, of a surcharge on income taxes for a two-year period. For example, the recession that began in 1974 was fought by "temporary" tax rebates that had to be renewed by Congress every six months with the clear implication that taxes would return to their "normal" levels when recovery was under way.

Such tax changes cause changes in household disposable income and, hence, in consumption expenditure. Consumption expenditure increases as tax rebates rise in times of recessionary gaps and decreases as tax surcharges rise in times of inflationary gaps.

These effects of short-term tax changes rely on the dependence of household consumption on current disposable income.

Permanent-income theories.

As we discussed in Chapter 26, some theories of the consumption function predict that a household's expected *permanent income* or *lifetime income*, rather than its *current* income, is the major determinant of consumption. (These theories were discussed in Chapter 26 and developed in detail in its Appendix.)

According to such theories, households have expectations about their lifetime incomes and adjust their consumption to those expectations. When temporary fluctuations in income occur, households maintain their long-term consumption plans and use their stocks of wealth as buffers to absorb income fluctuations. Thus, when there is a purely temporary rise in income, households will save all the extra income; when there is a purely temporary fall in income, households will maintain their long-term consumption plans by using up part of their wealth that has been accumulated through past saving.

Such behavior has serious consequences for short-lived tax changes. A temporary tax rebate raises households' disposable income, but households, recognizing it as temporary, would not revise their expenditure very much and would, instead, save most of the extra disposable income. Thus, the increase in aggregate expenditure would be smaller than hoped for. Similarly, a temporary rise in tax rates reduces disposable income, but this might lead to an almost offsetting drop in saving. Thus, total expenditure is again little changed, and a temporary surcharge fails to have much effect on the inflationary gap.[6]

The more closely household consumption expenditure is related to lifetime income rather than to current income, the smaller will be the effects on current consumption of tax changes that are known to be of short duration.

[6] The permanent-income theory is not as devastating for fiscal policy as may initially appear. As the Appendix to Chapter 26 makes clear, it is necessary to distinguish between consumption of services from durables and expenditure on durables. When a household purchases a consumer durable, such as a computer or a car, the services of which it plans to consume for many years, it is in fact saving. Thus, a transitory tax cut that leads to a transitory increase in disposable income may lead to increased saving that is also increased expenditure.

Experience that lends support to this proposition occurred in 1968, when large military expenditures that were associated with the Vietnam War gave rise to an inflationary gap. In mid-1968 a temporary tax surcharge was approved by Congress; this raised effective tax rates for a period of about 18 months and produced a substantial budget surplus. The object was to slow inflation by removing the inflationary gap. The restraining effect on inflation was disappointingly small because consumption expenditure was little affected.[7]

The advantage of having households perceive tax rate changes as long lasting is in conflict with the need for the reversibility of cuts and surcharges if they are not to destabilize the economy at a later date.

This conflict reduces the usefulness of changes in tax rates as a stabilizing tool.

Some Preliminary Policy Conclusions

What can the government reasonably expect to achieve by using fiscal policy when private-expenditure functions are shifting continually, and when lags and an uncertain response of households and firms make the timing of the effects of fiscal policy uncertain?

We have seen that the attempt to use fine tuning to eliminate the continual but small and transitory fluctuations that dominate business cycle behavior is no longer favored by most economists. However, the economy does occasionally develop severe and persistent GNP gaps. For example, an inflationary gap developed in the United States during the late 1960s as Vietnam War expenditures accelerated, and a recessionary gap developed between 1981 and 1983 when America, along with many Western countries, experienced the deepest and longest lasting recession since the 1930s. Many economists who do not believe in the value of fine tuning nevertheless do feel that fiscal policy can aid in removing such persistent gaps. These economists argue that caution dictates

[7] Of course, many other factors that influence consumption also changed during this period, and there remains a controversy whether the failure of consumption to fall was the result of these other factors or whether it was due to the *ineffectiveness* of the tax cuts.

responding only to large GNP gaps that are expected to persist and, even then, attempting to close only part of the gap in anticipation of some stabilizing change in private behavior.

Other economists believe that, even with persistent gaps, the risks that fiscal policy will destabilize the economy are still too large. They would have the government abandon any attempt at stabilization policy, instead setting its budget solely in relation to such long-term considerations as the desirable size of the public sector and the need to obtain a satisfactory long-term balance between revenues and expenditures. We shall return to this debate in Chapters 37 and 38.

Fiscal Policy in Action

We have seen that the very size of the government budget guarantees that it will have a major impact on GNP. The conscious use of the budget to influence GNP that constitutes fiscal policy is, however, not inevitable.

Fiscal *impact* is unavoidable, but fiscal *policy* is a matter of choice.

The Fiscal-Policy Record

The years following World War II were characterized in the United States by steady growth of real GNP and, once the postwar inflation had ended, by only gradual inflation. As the 1950s wore on, however, economic growth became increasingly sluggish and unemployment began to creep upward, from 2.9 percent in 1953 to 6.7 percent in 1961. Many people worried that the combination of rising prices and rising unemployment represented a new set of structural problems that could not be solved easily with the existing tools of macroeconomic policy. These fears did not prove justified, as the 1960s turned out to be relatively buoyant years. High growth continued, although both inflation and unemployment also increased toward the end of the decade.

Since the late 1960s the American economy has undergone a series of cyclical swings that fiscal

policy sometimes aggravated and sometimes resisted.

The 1960s and 1970s were years of fiscal activism, if not fiscal fine tuning. Discretionary tax and expenditure changes were repeatedly used in an attempt to stabilize the economy. Much of the reason that active fiscal policy was so in vogue was the dramatic success of tax cuts that were introduced in 1964. This episode, still cited by proponents of fiscal activism, is discussed in Box 30-3.

The experience of the 1970s indicated an impressive ability to manipulate aggregate demand. The stance of fiscal (and monetary) policy was changed several times—sometimes in pursuit of stabilization policy, sometimes for political motives, and sometimes because of unanticipated effects induced by changes in the economy (for example, when rapid inflation increased tax yields). Each time the economy responded in the direction that was predicted by economic theory. However:

While fiscal changes were able to influence the economy, fiscal policy was not always effective in stabilizing it.

Many observers came to the conclusion that cyclical fluctuations in the economy often were caused by policy reversals.[8] For example, expansionary policies, introduced in 1972 to combat unemployment, soon led to concern about inflationary pressures and were then followed in 1975 by contractionary policies that were designed to control inflation. Then, as unemployment grew again, policy became expansionary in 1975.

This experience of policy reversals was complicated further by the emergence of stagflation, which, as we have seen already, was largely due to supply-side shocks, caused by increases in the price of oil and other primary commodities. The simultaneous occurrence of rising inflation and unemployment led many to question the efficacy of using fiscal policy to stabilize the economy.

The fall of fiscal-policy activism from favor was given a further push with the election of President Ronald Reagan in 1980. The Reagan administration inherited a serious inflationary problem, which it

---

[8] Indeed, it is noteworthy that all four major downturns of the period have been attributed to explicit fiscal contraction.

BOX 30-3

Fiscal Drag and the 1964 Tax Cuts: A Fiscal-Policy Success

Fiscal drag, first diagnosed in the early 1960s, is the problem that is produced by economic growth acting on stable government expenditure and fixed tax rates. In such circumstances, growth leads to a falling cyclically adjusted budget deficit. (In terms of the figure in Box 30-2, the drag is due to a movement along the budget deficit function as potential income grows.)

Throughout the 1950s potential GNP rose between 2 percent and 3 percent per year because of economic growth. Such growth increases aggregate supply, but, since higher output means higher income earned, aggregate demand was also shifting outward. With both demand and supply increasing, it might seem that maintaining full employment would be no problem. There was a problem, however, and it lay with the tax system.

With tax rates being held constant, rising national income causes rising tax revenues. These revenues are money that does not become disposable income for households. If the government spends all its extra tax revenue, aggregate demand is not depressed. Since at the time, however, there was a relatively stable level of government expenditure,

rising tax revenues exerted a drag on the growth of aggregate demand by taking income away from households that would have spent it and by transferring it to governments that did not. There was thus a falling cyclically adjusted deficit.

This is illustrated in the figure, where we start with the curves AD_0, $LRAS_0$, and $SRAS_0$. These yield equilibrium at E_0 and potential income at Y_0^*. Economic growth now shifts the supply curves to $LRAS_1$ and $SRAS_1$. As a result of fiscal drag, however, the aggregate demand curve shifts only to AD_1 rather than to AD_2, which would have been required to sustain full employment. A GNP gap of $Y_1Y_2^*$ is thus created.

To prevent the exertion of an ever stronger depressing effect on national income by a falling CAD, it is periodically necessary either to increase government spending or to reduce tax rates. This problem arose in the American economy during the 1950s. Economic growth was producing a declining CAD. (The terminology of the time called this a rising full-employment surplus.) As a result, each cyclical upswing was weaker than the one before it, and the average level of unemployment over the cycle was creeping upward. By the beginning of the 1960s, many economists were calling for a tax cut to remove the drag and to restore full employment. Both the Kennedy and Johnson administrations advocated a large cut in tax rates. Their concern was not with cyclical stabilization of the economy but with solving a problem that is associated with long-term economic growth.

When the 1964 tax cut was enacted, the predicted effects occurred. The tax cuts increased disposable income, causing an increase in consumption expenditure that, in turn, caused an increase in national income and employment.

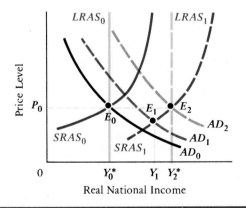

took to be economic and social enemy number one. There was a shift, however, to emphasis on monetary policy; the Reagan administration disavowed fiscal policy as a device for short-term manipulation of aggregate demand. (We shall study this episode further after we have covered monetary policy in Chapter 33.)

In spite of President Reagan's commitment to a balanced budget, the deficit grew rapidly during his first term in office. At first the rising deficit reflected the operation of the automatic stabilizers. Tax revenues fell, due to the 1981–1982 recession, and almost one-third of the 1982 increase in the deficit was due to the cyclical decline in the economy.

Without the increase in the deficit, induced by the automatic stabilizers, the 1981–1982 decline in output and rise in unemployment would both have been substantially larger.

As the economy recovered in 1983 and after, with real GNP rising and unemployment falling, the deficit continued to grow. Tax cuts, introduced to encourage saving and investment, partially offset the growth in revenues that resulted from growth in the economy, while government expenditure—in particular, military expenditures and debt service payments—grew. These increases reflected President Reagan's political agenda, which included cuts in personal and business taxes, along with a view to improving incentives for working and saving and increases in military spending. These changes, combined with the success of Congress in protecting domestic social spending, contributed to the emergence of record peacetime budget deficits.

Fiscal policy was very expansionary during the period 1983–1985, as indicated by the dramatic increase in the cyclically adjusted deficit.

Ironically, despite the Reagan administration's disavowal of fiscal *policy*, its actions had significant fiscal *effects*. Many economists believe that the dramatic increase in the deficit under President Reagan played a major role in stimulating the economy and in ending the recession. It also stimulated an extensive public debate about the consequences of persistent budget deficits, and Congress debated and passed legislation to try to reduce the deficit. (This legislation, called the Gramm-Rudman-Hollings Act, is discussed in Chapter 37.)

The final years of the Reagan administration saw some steps taken to reduce the budget deficit, but, as President Bush took office in 1989, many commentators argued that his top priority should be to cut the deficit further. This reflected their concerns about the burgeoning national debt and the persistent trade account deficit, both of which were blamed on the government budget deficit. We return to the debates surrounding this issue in Chapter 42.

SUMMARY

1. Fiscal policy uses government expenditure and tax policies to influence the economy. Changes in either government spending or tax policies also influence the budget balance.
2. Stabilization policy involves the use of government fiscal (and other) policies to damp fluctuations in the economy by trying to reduce or to eliminate GNP gaps that arise.
3. The government's budget balance is the difference between its receipts and its outlays. A budget deficit requires that the government borrow money by issuing bonds.
4. The so-called paradox of thrift is not a paradox at all. It applies to the short-run effects of saving and investment on aggregate demand. It predicts that severe recessions can be combatted by encouraging an increase in spending.
5. Changes in the stance of fiscal policy may be reasonably judged by changes in the cyclically adjusted deficit. This is the balance between revenues and expenditures as they would be if full employment prevailed.

6. Short-term stabilization by fiscal policy operates largely through such automatic stabilizers as tax revenues that vary directly with national income, expenditures on goods and services that do not vary with national income, and transfer payments that vary negatively with national income.

7. Discretionary fiscal policy also is used sometimes to attack large and persistent gaps. Such policies must be reversible; otherwise the economy may overshoot its target, once private investment recovers from a temporary slump or falls back from a temporary boom.

8. Tax changes also need to be perceived as relatively long-lived if they are to induce major changes in household spending patterns. Temporary changes may merely affect the current saving rate and not expenditure. The need to have tax changes perceived as long-lived, however, conflicts with the need to have fiscal policy easily reversible.

9. Fine tuning, the attempt to hold the aggregate expenditure function virtually constant by offsetting even small fluctuations in private expenditure, has been largely discredited. Many still believe, however, that large and persistent gaps can be offset by gross tuning, using fiscal policy.

10. Since the 1960s, the American economy has undergone a series of cyclical swings that fiscal policy has sometimes aggravated and sometimes resisted.

TOPICS FOR REVIEW

Fiscal policy
Budget balance, balanced budget, budget surplus, and budget deficit
The paradox of thrift
The stance of fiscal policy
Actual budget balance and cyclically adjusted budget balance
Built-in stabilizer
Discretionary fiscal policy
Fine tuning and gross tuning

DISCUSSION QUESTIONS

1. Consider the following questions on presidential economics.
   a. President Ford in 1975 maintained that his proposed package of a $28 billion cut in federal expenditure and a $28 billion tax cut "as a short-term measure would not affect the economy in any significant way." Does this mean that President Ford believed that the balanced-budget multiplier was zero? If so, why then might he have proposed the package? If not, what might he have meant?
   b. President Carter in 1977 said, "There will be no new programs implemented under my administration unless we can be sure that the cost of those programs is compatible with my goal of having a balanced budget before the end of that term." Does this mean that President Carter rejected fiscal policy? What might it mean?
   c. President Reagan said in 1983, "I remain committed to the idea that we can reduce budget deficits without increasing the burden on the poor, without weakening our national defense, and without destroying economic incentives by counterproductive tax increases." Are these objectives inconsistent? How does President Reagan's record stand up to his promises?

    d. In 1989 President Bush used the now famous quote, "Read my lips," to reinforce his opposition to tax increases as part of any policy package aimed at reducing the government budget deficit.

2. Which of the following would be built-in stabilizers?
   a. Food stamps for the needy
   b. Cost-of-living escalators in government contracts and pensions
   c. Income taxes
   d. Free college tuition for unemployed workers after six months of unemployment, provided that they are under 30 years old and have had five or more years of full-time experience since high school

3. In his first inaugural address, President Franklin D. Roosevelt expounded the doctrine of "sound finance"—that the government's budget should always be balanced. During his term, however, government spending rose faster than taxes, and deficits resulted. How would the effectiveness of the New Deal on employment have been changed if Roosevelt had been successful in keeping the budget balanced throughout his first term?

4. The Employment Act of 1946 made no explicit mention of price stability as an objective of national income policy. Why do you suppose this was so? What is the relationship between fiscal policy and the price level?

5. President Reagan said in 1982, "I don't place very much faith in those various deficit forecasts." Why would the president of the United States be skeptical about deficit forecasts? Does the evidence suggest that this skepticism is misplaced?

6. Look at Table 30-1 on page 625 and explain the rather different patterns that the actual and the cyclically adjusted deficits have followed for the past five years. (*Hint:* What other economic time series would you need information about in order to be able to answer this question fully?)

7. What has happened to the federal government deficit in the last two years? What role do you think the Gramm-Rudman-Hollings act has played in controlling the deficit?

8. In August 1989 the Congressional Budget Office projected a budget deficit of $127 billion for fiscal year 1991, while the White House projected a deficit of "only" $88 billion. CBO economists said that their less optimistic assumptions about the economy accounted for much of the difference. How do assumptions about the economy affect budget tax costs? Look at the data and see who was closest to being right in August 1989 about the economy and the deficit in 1990–1991.

8

MONEY, BANKING, AND MONETARY POLICY

Chapter 31

The Nature of Money and Monetary Institutions

What is the significance of money to the economy, and why are economists concerned about it? Indeed, what is money, and how did it come to play its present role? Many people believe that money is one of the more important things in life and that there is never enough of it. Yet economists argue that increasing the world's money supply would not make the average person better off. The reason for this is that, although money allows those who hold it to buy someone else's output, the total amount of goods and services that are available for everyone to buy depends on the total output that is produced, not on the total amount of money that people possess. Increasing the world's money supply would not necessarily change the total quantity of goods produced and hence available for consumption, although it would likely cause the price level to rise.

The Real and Monetary Sectors of the Economy: The Classical Dichotomy

Early in the history of economics, eighteenth century economists developed the first comprehensive theories in which the economy was conceived of as being divisible into a "real" part and a "monetary" part.

The real sector. According to these eighteenth century economists, the allocation of resources is determined in the real sector of the economy by demand and supply. Whether, for example, a lot of beef is produced relative to pork depends on the relative prices of beef and pork, not on the money price of either. If the price of beef is higher than the price of pork and both commodities cost about the same to produce, there is an incentive to produce beef rather than pork. At prices of $1 per pound for pork and $3 per pound for beef, the *relative* incentive is the same as it would be at $2 per pound for pork and $6 per pound for beef. As with beef and pork, so it is with all other commodities:

The allocation of resources among alternative uses depends on relative prices.

The monetary sector. According to the early economists, the price *level* is determined in the monetary sector of the economy. In the beef and pork example just given, an increase in the total money available might double all prices, thus raising the price of pork from $1 to $2 per pound and the price of beef from $3 to $6 per pound, but in equilibrium it would leave their *relative* prices unchanged. Hence it would have no effect on the real part of the economy, that is, on the amount of resources allocated to beef and to pork production (or to anything else).

An increase in the money supply leads to an increase in all money prices.

If the quantity of money were doubled, *other things being equal,* the prices of all commodities and money income would all double. Everyone earning an income would be made no better or worse off by the change.

Thus, in equilibrium, the real and the monetary parts of the economy were believed to have no effect on each other. The doctrine that the quantity of money influences the level of money prices but has no effect on the real part of the economy is called the **neutrality of money.** Because early economists believed that the most important questions—How much does the economy produce? What share of it does each group in the society get?—were answered in the real sector, they spoke of money as a "veil" behind which occurred the real events that affected material well-being.

The modern view.   Modern economists still accept the insights of the early economists that relative prices are a major determinant of the allocation of resources and that the quantity of money has a lot to do with determining the absolute level of prices. They accept the neutrality of money in long-run equilibrium when all forces causing change have fully worked themselves out. We shall see in Chapter 32, however, that they do not accept the neutrality of money when the economy is undergoing change from day to day, that is, when the economy is not in a state of long-run equilibrium.

In this chapter we look first at the experience of price level changes—one aspect of the importance of money—and then at the nature of money itself and the operation of the modern institutions that comprise the monetary system of our economy.

Historical Experience

In Chapter 24 (see pages 490–496) we discussed some important introductory material related to the price level itself and to inflations and deflations, that is, to changes in the price level. The material there

should be reviewed at this stage. In this chapter we present some further details of the behavior of the price levels over very long periods of time. Figure 31-1 shows the course of producer (or wholesale) prices in the United States from 1785 through 1988. Considerable year-to-year fluctuations are apparent. Despite the large fluctuations that occurred during the nineteenth century, the price trend during that period was neither upward nor downward. In contrast, so far the twentieth century has also seen large fluctuations *and* a distinct rising trend in the price level.

Although admittedly a long time, even two centuries may still not be enough to give us a clear perspective of very long-term price fluctuations. The experience of the period since 1946 looks much more dramatic and unusual when it is compared only with the nineteenth century than when it is considered in longer perspective. For an indication of the longer-term course of price levels, we can look across the Atlantic. Figure 31-2 shows the course of the price level in southern England over seven centuries. It shows that there was an overall inflationary trend but that it was by no means evenly spread over the centuries.

The Nature of Money

Inflation is a monetary phenomenon in the sense that a rise in the general level of prices is the same thing as a decrease in the purchasing power of money. But what exactly is money? More folklore and general nonsense are believed about money than about any other aspect of the economy. In this section we describe the functions of money and briefly outline its history. This will allow us to refute some of these misconceptions. In addition, continuing interest in the gold standard makes some discussion of early monetary systems relevant.

What Is Money?

In economics *money* usually has been defined as any generally accepted medium of exchange. A **medium of exchange** is anything that will be widely accepted

FIGURE 31-1 An Index of Producer Prices in the United States, 1785–1988 (1967 = 100)

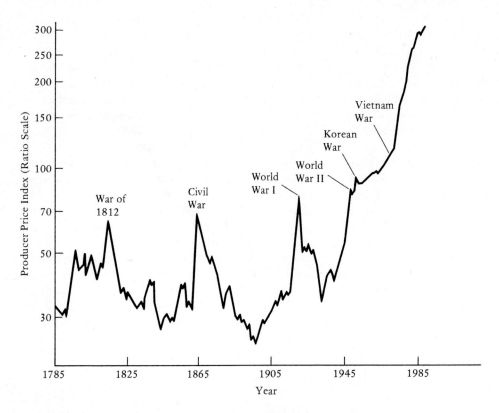

Persistent peacetime inflation only recently has become a problem in America. While the price level has fluctuated throughout American history, no long-term trend was visible during the period from the Revolutionary War to 1930. Every major war produced an inflation that was subsequently reversed. The data are plotted on a ratio scale in which equal vertical distances represent equal percentage changes. (*Sources: Historical Statistics,* 1949, p. 231; *Historical Statistics,* 1976, pp. 199, 201; *Economic Report of the President,* 1989.)

in a society in exchange for goods and services. Money is more than this, however. **Money** has several functions:

Money acts as a medium of exchange, as a store of value, and as a unit of account.

Different kinds of money vary in the degree of efficiency with which they fulfill these functions. As we shall see, the money supply is measured by using different definitions for different purposes.

A Medium of Exchange

If there were no money, goods would have to be exchanged by barter (one good being swapped directly for another). We discussed this cumbersome system in Chapter 3. The major difficulty with barter is that each transaction requires a *double coincidence of wants.* For a barter exchange to occur between Helen and Tom, not only must Helen have what Tom wants, but Tom must have what Helen wants. If all exchange were restricted to barter, anyone who spe-

· KEY IDEAS IN ·
MACROECONOMICS

This section provides important diagrams and captions from the text as reminders of basic economic concepts at a glance. If you need to refresh your memory concerning a principle being shown here, look in the appropriate chapter for a full explanation. The figure number of each diagram indicates the chapter from which it is taken (e.g., Figure 23-4 means the fourth figure in Chapter 23).

FIGURE 26-7 Shifts in the *AE* Curve

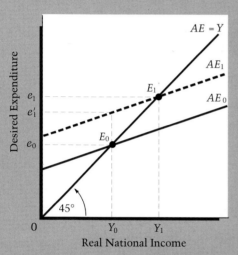

(i) A parallel shift in *AE*

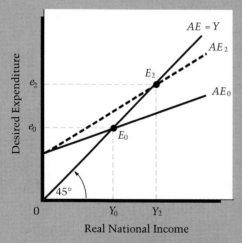

(ii) A change in the slope of *AE*

Upward shifts in the *AE* curve increase equilibrium income; downward shifts in the *AE* curve decrease equilibrium income.

FIGURE 27-2 The *AD* Curve and the *AE* Curve

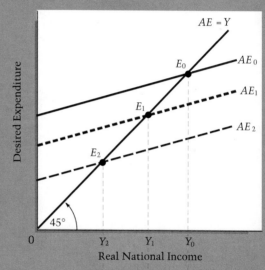

(i) Aggregate expenditure

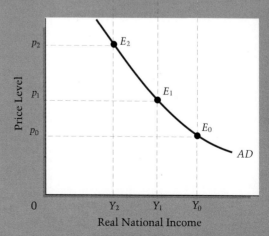

(ii) Aggregate demand

Equilibrium income is determined by the *AE* curve for each given price level; the level of income and its associated price level are then plotted to yield the *AD* curve.

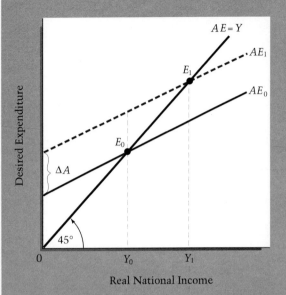

FIGURE 27-4 The Simple Multiplier and Shifts in the AD Curve

(i) Aggregate expenditure

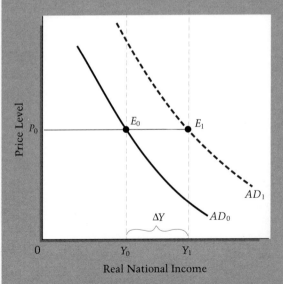

(ii) Aggregate demand

A change in autonomous expenditure changes equilibrium national income for any given price level. The simple multiplier measures the resulting horizontal shift in the aggregate demand curve.

FIGURE 27-7 Macroeconomic Equilibrium

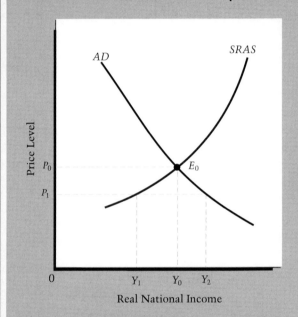

Macroeconomic equilibrium occurs at the intersection of the AD and SRAS curves and determines the equilibrium values for national income and the price level.

FIGURE 27-9 The AE Curve and the Multiplier When the Price Level Varies

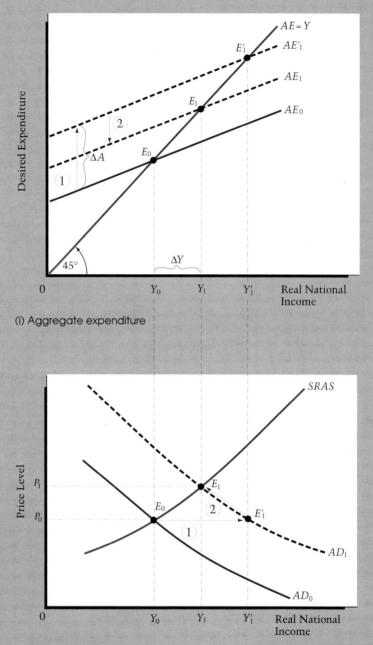

(i) Aggregate expenditure

(ii) Aggregate demand

An increase in autonomous expenditures causes the AE curve to shift upward, but the rise in the price level causes it to shift part of the way down again. Hence, the multiplier effect on income is smaller than when the price level is constant.

FIGURE 29-1 Three Ways of Increasing National Income

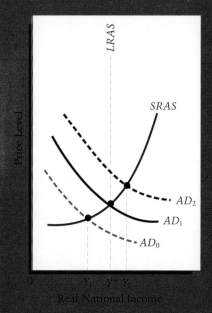

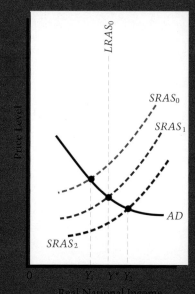

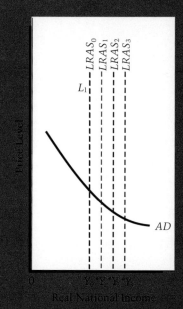

(i) Increases in aggregate demand

(ii) Temporary increases in short-run aggregate supply

(iii) Permanent increases in long-run aggregate supply

National income will increase in response to an increase in aggregate demand or an increase in aggregate supply. The increase will be permanent if the *LRAS* curve shifts, but, if the *LRAS* curve does not shift, any divergences of actual GNP from potential GNP will only be temporary.

FIGURE 31-2   A Price Index of Consumables in Southern England, 1275–1959

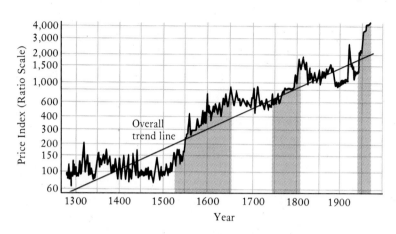

Over the last seven centuries, long periods of stable prices have alternated with long periods of rising prices. This remarkable price series shows an index of the prices of food, clothing, and fuel in southern England from 1275 through 1959. The trend line shows that the average change in prices over the whole period was 0.5 percent per year. The shaded areas indicate periods of unreversed inflation. The series also shows that even the perspective of a century can be misleading, because long periods of stable or gently falling prices tended to alternate with long periods of rising prices. (*Source: Lloyds Bank Review,* No. 58, October 1960.)

cialized in producing one commodity would have to spend a great deal of time searching for satisfactory transactions.

The use of money as a medium of exchange removes these problems. People can sell their output for money and subsequently use the money to buy what they wish from others.

The double coincidence of wants is unnecessary when a medium of exchange is used.

Without money the economic system, which is based on specialization and the division of labor, could not function, and we would have to return to primitive forms of production and exchange. It is not without justification that money has been called one of the great inventions contributing to human freedom and well-being.

To serve as an efficient medium of exchange, money must have a number of characteristics. It must be readily acceptable. It must have a high value relative to its weight (otherwise it would be a nuisance to carry around). It must be divisible, because money that comes only in large denominations is useless for transactions having only a small value. It must not be readily counterfeitable, because if money can be easily duplicated by individuals, it will lose its value.

A Store of Value

Money is a convenient way to store purchasing power; goods may be sold today, and money may be stored until it is needed. The money provides a claim on someone else's goods that can be exercised at a future date. The two sides of the transaction can be separated in time, with the obvious increase in freedom that this confers.

To be a satisfactory store of value, however, money must have a relatively stable value. When the price level is stable, the purchasing power of a given sum of money is also stable. When the price level is highly variable, this is not so, and the usefulness of money as a store of value is undermined. An extreme example is discussed in Box 31-1.

Although money can serve as a satisfactory store of accumulated purchasing power for a single individual, it cannot do so for the society as a whole. If a single individual accumulates a pile of dollars, he or she will, when the time comes to spend it, be able to command the current output of some other individual. All of society cannot do this. If all individuals were to save their money and then retire simultaneously to live on their savings, there would be no current production to purchase and consume. The society's ability to satisfy wants depends on goods and services being available; if some of this want-

BOX 31-1

Hyperinflation

Can the price level ever rise so rapidly that money loses its usefulness either as a medium of exchange or as a store of value? The answer appears to be that very occasionally this has happened. Inflation rates of 50, 100, and even 200 percent or more per year have occurred year after year and have proven to be manageable as people adjust their contracts to real terms. While there are strains and side effects, the evidence shows such situations to be possible without causing money to become useless.

Does this mean that there is no reason to fear that rapid inflation will turn into hyperinflation that will destroy the value of money completely? The historical record is not entirely reassuring. There have been a number of cases in which prices began to rise at an ever accelerating rate until the nation's money ceased to be a satisfactory store of value even for the short period between receipt and expenditure and hence ceased also to be useful as a medium of exchange.

The index of wholesale prices in Germany during and after World War I is given in the table. The index shows that a good purchased with one 100-mark note in July 1923 would have required *ten million* 100-mark notes for its purchase only four months later! While Germany had experienced substantial inflation during World War I, averaging more than 30 percent per year, the immediate postwar years of 1920 and 1921 gave no sign of an explosive inflation. Indeed, during 1920 price stability was experienced, but in 1922 and 1923 the price level exploded. On November 15, 1923, the mark was officially repudiated, its value wholly destroyed. How could this happen?

When an inflation becomes so rapid that people lose confidence in the purchasing power of their currency, they rush to spend it. People who have goods become increasingly reluctant to accept the rapidly depreciating money in exchange. The rush to spend money accelerates the increase in prices until people finally become unwilling to accept money on any terms. What was once money ceases to be money.

The price system can then be restored only by repudiation of the old monetary unit and its replacement by a new unit. This destroys the value of monetary savings and of all contracts specified in terms of the old monetary unit.

There are about a dozen documented hyperinflations in world history, among them the collapse of the continental during the American Revolution, the ruble during the Russian Revolution, the drachma during and after the German occupation of Greece in World War II, the pengo in Hungary during 1945 to 1946, and the Chinese national currency during 1946 to 1948. Every one of these hyperinflations was accompanied by great increases in the money supply; new money was printed to give governments purchasing power that they could not or would not obtain by taxation. Further, every one occurred in the midst of a major political upheaval in which grave doubts existed about the stability and the future of the government itself.

Is hyperinflation likely in the absence of civil war, revolution, or collapse of the government? Most economists think not. Further, it is clear that high inflation rates over a period of time do not mean the inevitable or even likely onset of hyperinflation, however serious the distributive and social effects of such rates may be.

Date		German wholesale price index (1913 = 1)
January	1913	1
January	1920	13
January	1921	14
January	1922	37
July	1922	101
January	1923	2,785
July	1923	74,800
August	1923	944,000
September	1923	23,900,000
October	1923	7,096,000,000
November	1923*	750,000,000,000

* The mark was repudiated on November 15, 1923.

satisfying capacity is to be stored up for the whole society, goods that are currently producible must be left unconsumed and carried over to future periods.

A Unit of Account

Money also may be used purely for accounting purposes without having a physical existence of its own. For instance, a government store in a truly communist society might say that everyone had so many "dollars" to use each month. Goods could then be assigned prices and each consumer's purchases recorded, the consumer being allowed to buy until the allocated supply of dollars was exhausted. These dollars need have no existence other than as entries in the store's books, yet they would serve as a perfectly satisfactory unit of account.

Whether they could serve also as a medium of exchange between individuals depends on whether the store would agree to transfer dollar credits from one customer to another at the customer's request. Banks will transfer dollars credited to demand deposits in this way, and thus a bank deposit can serve as both a unit of account and a medium of exchange. Notice that the use of *dollars* in this context suggests a further sense in which money is a unit of account. People think about values in terms of the monetary unit with which they are familiar.

Another related function of money is sometimes distinguished. It can be used as a standard of deferred payments. Payments that are to be made in the future, on account of debts and so on, are reckoned in money. Money is used as a unit of account with the added dimension of time because the account will not be settled until later.

The Origins of Money

The origins of money are lost in antiquity; most primitive tribes that are known today make some use of it. The ability of money to free people from the cumbersome necessity of barter must have led to its early use as soon as some generally acceptable commodity appeared.

Metallic Money

All sorts of commodities have been used as money at one time or another, but gold and silver proved to have great advantages. They were precious because their supplies were relatively limited, and they were in constant demand by the rich for ornament and decoration. Also, they did not easily wear out. Thus they tended to have a high and stable price. They were easily recognized and generally known to be commodities that, because of their stable price, would be readily accepted. They were also divisible into extremely small units.

Precious metals thus came to circulate as money and to be used in many transactions. Before the invention of coins, it was necessary to carry the metals in bulk. When a purchase was made, the requisite quantity of the metal was carefully weighed on a scale. A sack of gold and a highly accurate set of scales were the common equipment of the merchant and the trader.

The invention of coinage eliminated the need to weigh the metal at each transaction. The ruler weighed the precious metal, added some base metal for strength and durability, and made a coin out of it to which the ruler's seal was affixed, guaranteeing the amount of precious metal that it contained. If a coin was certified to contain exactly 1/16 of an ounce of gold and a commodity was priced at 1/8 of an ounce of gold, two coins could be given over without weighing the gold. This was clearly a great convenience, as long as traders knew that they could accept the coin at its "face value." The face value was nothing more than a statement that a certain weight of metal was contained therein.

Abuses of metallic money. The ruler's subjects, however, could not let a good opportunity pass. Someone soon had the idea of clipping a thin slice off the edge of the coin. If he collected a coin that was stamped as containing $\frac{1}{2}$ of an ounce of gold, he could clip a slice off the edge and pass the coin off as still containing $\frac{1}{2}$ ounce of gold. ("Doesn't the stamp prove it?") If he got away with this, he would have made a profit equal to the market value of the clipped metal.

Whenever this practice became common, even the most myopic traders noticed that things were not what they seemed to be in the coinage world. It became necessary to weigh each coin before accepting it at its face value; out came the scales again, and much of the usefulness of coins was lost. To get around this problem, the idea arose of minting the coins with a rough edge. The absence of the rough edge immediately would be apparent and would indicate that the coin had been clipped. This practice, called *milling,* survives on some coins as an interesting anachronism to remind us that there were days when the market value of the metal in the coin (if it were melted down) was equal to the face value of the coin.

Debasement of metallic money.   Not to be outdone by the cunning of their subjects, the rulers were quick to seize the chance of getting something for nothing. The power to mint placed rulers in a good position to work a *really profitable fraud.* When faced with debts that could not be paid or repudiated, rulers merely used some suitable occasion—a marriage, an anniversary, an alliance—to remint the coinage. Subjects would be ordered to bring their gold coins into the mint to be melted down and coined afresh with a new stamp. The subjects could then go away with one new coin for every old coin that they had brought in. Between the melting down and the recoining, however, the rulers had only to toss some further inexpensive base metal in with the molten gold to earn a handsome profit. If the coinage were debased by adding, say, 1 pound of new base metal to every 4 pounds of old coins, five coins could be made for every four that were turned in. For every four coins brought in, the rulers could return four and have one left as profit with which to pay off debts.

Since gold and silver are softer and more malleable than most base metals, an experienced trader could usually tell if a coin had been seriously debased by testing its hardness. This is why, in films depicting ancient markets, often you will see a merchant biting a coin to see how easily it can be bent.

The result of debasement was inflation. The subjects had the same number of coins as before and hence could demand the same quantity of goods. When rulers paid their bills, however, the recipients of the extra coins could be expected to spend them. This caused a net increase in demand. The extra demand would bid up prices. Debasing the coinage thus led to a rise in prices.

It was the experience of such inflations that led early economists to propound the *quantity theory of money and prices.* They argued that there was a relationship between the average level of prices and the quantity of money in circulation, such that an increase in the quantity of money would lead to a proportionate increase in the price level. (We shall have more to say about this theory in Chapter 32.)

Gresham's law.   The early experience of currency debasement led to the observation known as **Gresham's law,** after the Elizabethan financial expert, Sir Thomas Gresham. Gresham's hypothesis that "bad money drives out good" has stood the test of time.

When Queen Elizabeth I first came to the throne of England in the middle of the sixteenth century, the coinage had been severely debased. Seeking to help trade, Elizabeth minted new coins, which contained their full face value in gold. However, as fast as she fed these new coins into circulation, they disappeared. Why? Gresham reasoned as follows to the young queen.

Suppose that you possessed one new and one old coin, each with the same face value, and had a bill to pay. What would you do? Clearly, you would use the debased coin to pay the bill and keep the undebased one. (You part with less gold that way.) Suppose that you wanted to obtain a certain amount of gold bullion by melting down the gold coins (as was frequently done). Which coins would you use? Clearly, you would use new, undebased coins because you would part with less "face value" that way. The debased coins would thus remain in circulation, and the undebased coins would disappear. Whenever people got hold of an undebased coin, they would hold on to it; whenever they got a debased coin, they would pass it on. The example in Box 31-2 shows that Gresham's law is as applicable to the twentieth century as it was to the sixteenth century.

Paper Money

The next important step in the history of money was the evolution of paper currency. Artisans who worked with gold required secure safes, and the public began to deposit their gold with such goldsmiths for safekeeping. Goldsmiths would give their depositors receipts promising to hand over the gold on demand. When any depositor wished to make a large purchase, she could go to her goldsmith, reclaim some of her gold, and hand it over to the seller of the goods. If the seller had no immediate need for the gold, he would carry it back to the goldsmith for safekeeping.

If people knew the goldsmith to be reliable, there was no need to go through the cumbersome and risky business of physically transferring the gold. The buyer needed only to transfer the goldsmith's receipt to the seller, who would accept it, secure in

BOX 31-2

Where Has All the Coinage Gone?

Tourists who were traveling in Chile during the 1970s and in other countries with rapid inflation often wondered aloud why paper currency was used even for transactions as small as the purchase of a newspaper or a pack of matches. Metallic currency in such places was scarce and sometimes nonexistent. Similarly, the silver dollar, silver half-dollar, silver quarter, and silver dime have disappeared from circulation in the United States. The reason for these things is an example of Gresham's law.

Consider a country that has three different "tokens," each of which is legal tender in the amount of $.25. One is a silver quarter with $.10 worth of recoverable silver in it; a second is made of cheaper metals, with $.05 worth of recoverable metal in it; the third is a $.25 bill, a brightly colored piece of paper money that says plainly on its face "legal tender for all debts public and private."

If prices are stable and the government produces all three forms of money, there is no reason why they should not all circulate freely and interchangeably. Each is legal tender, and each is worth more as money than as anything else.

However, suppose an inflation starts and prices,

including proportionally the prices of silver and other metals, begin to rise sharply. By the time prices have tripled, the silver quarters will have disappeared because the silver in each one is now worth $.30, and people will hoard them or melt them down rather than spend them to buy goods priced at only $.25. Although not everyone will do this, coins passing from hand to hand eventually will reach someone who withdraws them from circulation.

What about the coins made of cheaper metal? Since prices have tripled, they now contain metal worth $.15, still less than their face value. Will they too disappear? They will if there is further inflation of, say, 100 percent. This raises the market value of the metal in the coin above its face value. The coins will disappear as they are melted down. By that time, only the paper money will be in circulation. The "bad" paper money will have driven out the "good" metal money.

Thus, inflation, and even the expectation of inflation, may make some money "good" and some money "bad" in Gresham's sense. If it does, the bad will displace the good.

---

the knowledge that the goldsmith would pay over the gold whenever it was needed. If the seller wished to buy a good from a third party, who also knew the goldsmith to be reliable, this transaction, too, could be effected by passing the goldsmith's receipt from the buyer to the seller. The convenience of using pieces of paper instead of gold is obvious.

Thus, when it first came into being, paper money represented a promise to pay on demand so much gold, the promise being made first by goldsmiths and later by banks. Banks, too, became known for their vaults ("safes"), where the precious gold was stored and protected. As long as the institutions were known to be reliable, their pieces of paper would be "as good as gold." Such paper money was *backed* by precious metal and was *convertible on demand* into this

metal. When a country's money is convertible into gold, the country is said to be on a *gold standard*.

In nineteenth century America, private banks, operating initially under either federal or state charters, commonly issued paper money nominally convertible into gold. **Bank notes** represented banks' promises to pay. In areas such as the American West, where banks were small and were often unreliable in meeting demands for payment in gold, bank notes had a shady reputation. The gold bag and scales persisted in the West well into the second half of the nineteenth century, even after paper money became widely accepted in most other parts of the country.

Fractionally backed paper money. For most transactions individuals were content to use paper currency.

It was soon discovered that it was not necessary to keep an ounce of gold in the vaults for every claim to an ounce circulating as paper money. It was necessary to keep some gold on hand because paper would not do for some transactions. If someone wished to make a purchase from a distant place where her local bank was not known, she might have to convert her paper into gold and ship the gold. Further, she might not have perfect confidence in the bank's ability to honor its pledge to redeem the notes in gold at a future time. Her alternative was to exchange her notes for gold and to store the gold until she needed it.

For these and other reasons, some holders of notes demanded gold in return for their notes. However, some of the bank's customers would receive gold in various transactions and store it in the bank for safekeeping. They accepted promises to pay (i.e., bank notes) in return. At any one time, then, some of the bank's customers would be withdrawing gold, others would be depositing it, and most would be trading in the bank's paper notes without any need or desire to convert them into gold. Thus, the bank was able to issue more money redeemable in gold than the amount of gold that it held in its vaults. This was good business, because the money could be invested profitably in interest-earning loans to households and firms.

This discovery was made by the early goldsmiths. From that time to the present, banks have had many more claims outstanding against them than they actually had in reserves available to pay those claims. We say that the currency issued in such a situation is *fractionally backed* by the reserves.

The major problem with a fractionally backed, convertible currency was maintaining its convertibility into the precious metal by which it was backed. The imprudent bank, which issued too much paper money, would find itself unable to redeem its currency in gold when the demand for gold was even slightly higher than usual. It would then have to suspend payments, and all holders of its notes would suddenly find that the notes were worthless. The prudent bank, which kept a reasonable relationship between its note issue and its gold reserve, would find that it could meet a normal range of demand for gold without any trouble.

If the public lost confidence and en masse demanded redemption of its currency, the banks would be unable to honor their pledges. The history of nineteenth and early twentieth century banking on both sides of the Atlantic is full of examples of banks that were ruined by "panics," or sudden runs on their gold reserves. When this happened, the banks' depositors and the holders of their notes would find themselves with worthless pieces of paper.

Fiat currencies. As time went on, note issue by private banks became less common, and central banks took control of the currency. Central banks, in turn, became governmental institutions. In time *only* central banks were permitted to issue notes. Originally, the central banks issued currency that was fully convertible into gold. In those days gold would be brought to the central bank, which would issue currency in the form of "gold certificates" that asserted that the gold was available on demand. The gold supply thus set some upper limit on the amount of currency.

However, central banks could issue more currency than they had in gold because in normal times only a small fraction of the currency was presented for payment at any one time. Thus, even though the need to maintain convertibility under a gold standard put an upper limit on note issue, central banks had substantial discretionary control over the quantity of currency outstanding.

During the period between World Wars I and II, almost all of the countries of the world abandoned the gold standard; their currencies were no longer convertible into gold. Money that is not convertible by law into anything valuable depends upon its acceptability for its value. Money that is declared by government order, or fiat, to be legal tender for settlement of all debts is called a **fiat money.** Some issues that are raised by the abandoning of the gold standard are discussed in Box 31-3.

Today almost all currency is fiat money.

Look at any bill in your wallet. It is not convertible into anything. Until recently much American currency bore the statement, "The United States of America Will Pay to the Bearer on Demand Twenty Dollars" (or whatever the currency was worth). The notes were signed by both the secretary of the Treasury and the treasurer. If you took this seriously and demanded $20, you could have handed over a $20 bill and received in return a different but identical $20 bill! Today's Federal Reserve $20 notes simply

BOX 31-3

Should Currency Be Backed by Gold?

The gold standard imposed an upper limit on the quantity of convertible currency that could be issued. Now that the system has been abandoned, does it matter that the central bank is not limited to its ability to issue currency?

Gold derives its value because it was scarce relative to the demand for it (the demand being derived from its monetary and its nonmonetary uses). Tying a currency to gold meant that the quantity of money in a country was determined by such chance occurrences as the discovery of new gold supplies. This was not without advantages, the most important being that it provided a check on governments' ability to cause inflation. Gold cannot be manufactured at will; paper currency can.

There is little doubt that in the past, if the money supply had been purely paper, many governments would have attempted to pay their bills by printing new money rather than by raising taxes. Such increases in the money supply in periods of full employment would lead to inflation in the same way that the debasement of metallic currency did.

Thus, the gold standard provided some check on inflation by making it difficult for the government to change the money supply. Periods of major gold discoveries, however, brought about inflations of their own. In the 1500s, for example, Spanish gold and silver flowed into Europe from the New World, bringing inflation in their wake.

A major problem that is caused by a reliance on gold is that, although it is usually desirable to increase the money supply when real national income is increasing, this cannot be done on a gold standard unless, by pure chance, gold is discovered at the same time. The gold standard took discretionary powers over the money supply out of the hands of government. Whether or not one thinks that this is a good thing depends on how one thinks governments would use this discretion.

In general, a gold standard is probably better than having the currency managed by an ignorant or irresponsible government, but it is worse than having the currency supply adjusted by a well-informed and intelligent one. The terms *better* and *worse* in this context are judged by the criterion of having a money supply that varies adequately with the needs of the economy but does not vary so as to cause violent inflations or deflations.

---

say, "The United States of America," "Twenty dollars," and "This note is legal tender for all debts, public and private." It is, in other words, fiat money pure and simple.

Legal tender is anything that by law must be accepted when offered either for the purchase of goods or services or to discharge a debt. If you are offered something that is legal tender in payment for a debt and you refuse to accept it, the debt is no longer legally collectible.

Not only is our modern currency fiat money, so is our coinage. Modern coins, unlike their historical ancestors, contain a value of metal that is characteristically a minute fraction of the value of the coin. Modern coins, like modern paper money, are merely tokens.

Why Is Fiat Money Valuable?

Today paper money and coinage are valuable because they are generally accepted. Because everyone accepts them as valuable, they *are* valuable; the fact that they can no longer be converted into anything has no effect on their functioning as a medium of exchange.

In the early days of the gold standard, paper money was valuable because everyone believed it was convertible into gold on demand. Experience during periods of crisis, when there was often a temporary suspension of convertibility into gold, and of panic, when there were bank failures, served to demonstrate that the mere *promise* of convertibility was not sufficient to make money valuable. Gradually, the realization grew that neither was convertibility necessary.

Fiat money is valuable because it is accepted in payment for the purchase of goods or services and for the discharge of debts.

Many people are disturbed to learn that present-day paper money is neither backed by nor convertible into anything more valuable—that it consists of nothing but pieces of paper whose value derives from common acceptance and from confidence that it will continue to be accepted in the future. Most people believe that their money should be more substantial than this; after all, what of the "bedrock solidity" of the Swiss franc? Yet money is, in fact, made of nothing more than pieces of paper. There is no point in pretending otherwise.

If paper money is acceptable, it is a medium of exchange; if its purchasing power remains stable, it is a satisfactory store of value; and if both of these things are true, it will also serve as a satisfactory unit of account.

Modern Money

By the twentieth century, private banks had lost the authority to issue bank notes. Yet they did not lose the power to create deposit money.

Deposit Money

Banks' customers frequently deposit coins and paper money with the banks for safekeeping, just as in former times they deposited gold. Such a deposit is recorded as an entry on the customer's account. A customer who wishes to pay a debt may come to the bank and claim the money in dollars, and then pay the money to another person. This person may then redeposit the money in a bank.

Like the gold transfers, this is a tedious procedure, particularly for large payments. It is more convenient to have the bank transfer claims to this money on deposit. The common check is an instruction to the bank to make the transfer. As soon as such transfers became easy and inexpensive, and checks became widely accepted in payment for commodities and debts, the deposits became a form of money called **deposit money,** which is defined as

money held by the public in the form of deposits in commercial banks that can be withdrawn on demand.

When individual A deposits $100 in a bank, the bank credits A's account with $100. This is the bank's promise to pay $100 in cash on demand. If A pays B $100 by writing a check that B then deposits in the same bank, the bank merely reduces A's account by $100 and increases B's by the same amount. Thus, the bank still promises to pay on demand the $100 that originally was deposited, but it now promises to pay it to B rather than to A. What makes all this so convenient is that B can actually deposit A's check in any bank, and the banks will arrange the transfer of credits.

Checks are in some ways the modern equivalent of old-time bank notes issued by commercial banks. The passing of a bank note from hand to hand transferred ownership of a claim against the bank. Similarly, a check on a deposit account is an order to the bank to pay the designated recipient, rather than oneself, money credited to the account. Checks, unlike bank notes, do not circulate freely from hand to hand; thus checks themselves are not currency. The balance in the demand deposit *is* money; the check transfers money from one person to another. Because checks are easily drawn and deposited, and because they are relatively safe from theft, they are widely used. In 1988 approximately 80 billion checks were drawn in the United States. During the last decade the number of checks drawn increased by about 7 percent per year.

Thus, when commercial banks lost the right to issue notes of their own, the form of bank money changed but the substance did not. Today banks have money in their vaults (or on deposit with the central banks) just as they always did. Once it was gold; today it is the legal tender of the times—fiat money. It is true today, just as in the past, that most of the bank's customers are content to pay their bills by passing among themselves the bank's promises to pay money on demand. Only a small proportion of the transactions made by the bank's customers is made in cash.

Bank deposits are money. Today, just as in the past, banks can create money by issuing more promises to pay (deposits) than they have cash reserves available to pay out.

The Banking System

Many types of institutions make up a modern banking system such as exists in the United States today. The **central bank** is the government-owned and -operated institution that serves to control the banking system and is the sole money-issuing authority. Through it, the government's monetary policy is conducted. In the United States the central bank is the Federal Reserve System, nicknamed "the Fed."

Financial intermediaries are privately owned institutions that serve the general public. They are called *intermediaries* because they stand between savers, from whom they accept deposits, and investors, to whom they make loans. In this chapter we focus on an important class of financial intermediaries, the *commercial banks*.[1]

Central Banks

All advanced free-market economies have, in addition to commercial banks, a central bank. Many of the world's early central banks were private, profit-making institutions that provided services to ordinary banks. Their importance, however, led to their developing close ties with government. Central banks soon became instruments of the government, though not all of them were publicly owned. The Bank of England (the "Old Lady of Threadneedle Street"), one of the world's oldest and most famous central banks, began to operate as the central bank of England in the seventeenth century, but it was not "nationalized" until 1947.

The similarities in the functions performed and the tools used by the world's central banks are much more important than the differences in their organization. Although our attention is given to the operations of the Federal Reserve System, its basic functions are similar to those of the Bank of England, the Bank of Greece, or the Bank of Canada.

[1] For many years government regulations created a sharp distinction among the various types of financial intermediaries by limiting the types of transactions that each could engage in. The past decade has seen a sweeping deregulation of the financial system, so that many of these traditional distinctions no longer apply. Nevertheless, it is useful for our purposes to focus on the commercial banks.

The Federal Reserve System

The Federal Reserve System (the Fed) began operation in 1914, following the passage of the Federal Reserve Act in 1913. Although the Fed appears, at first glance, to consist of a number of privately owned banks, controlled by the commercial banks, it actually functions as the country's central bank. The most important thing about the Fed is this:

In its role as the central bank of the United States, the Federal Reserve System is responsible for the U.S. government's monetary policy.

The basic elements in the Federal Reserve System are described in Box 31-4.

Basic Functions of a Central Bank

A central bank serves four main functions. It is a banker for commercial banks, a banker for the government, the controller of the nation's supply of money, and a regulator of money markets. The first three functions are reflected by the Fed's balance sheet, shown in Table 31-1.

Banker to commercial banks. The central bank accepts deposits from commercial banks and will, on order, transfer them to the account of another bank. In this way the central bank provides each commercial bank with the equivalent of a checking account and with a means of settling debts to other banks. The deposits made by the commercial banks with the central bank appear in Table 31-1. The reserves of the commercial banks that are deposited with the central bank are *liabilities* of the central bank, because it promises to pay them to the commercial banks on demand.

From their very beginnings, central banks have acted as "lenders of last resort" to the commercial banking system. Commercial banks with sound investments sometimes find themselves in urgent need of cash to meet the demands of their depositors. If such banks cannot obtain ready cash, they may be forced into insolvency, despite their being in a basically sound financial position. Central banks provide temporary assistance to such commercial banks by making short-term loans to them.

Loans made by the Fed to commercial banks are said to be made available through the Fed's "discount

BOX 31-4

The Federal Reserve System

The basic elements of the Federal Reserve System are: (1) the board of governors; (2) the Federal Advisory Council, which has no real power but whose 12 members advise the board of the views of commercial bankers; (3) the 12 Federal Reserve banks; (4) the Federal Open Market Committee (FOMC); and (5) the more than 25,000 member commercial banks.

The Board of Governors

The board of governors consists of seven members who are appointed by the president of the United States and confirmed by the Senate. Members serve for 14 years. The length of term is important, for it means that each member of the board serves beyond the term of the president who is making the appointment. Board members are top-level public servants who often come from the world of business or banking. In 1989 a number of its members, including Manual Johnson, Wayne Angell, and Robert Heller, were economists.

The board is responsible to Congress but works closely with the Department of the Treasury. It supervises the entire Federal Reserve System and exercises general policy control over the 12 Federal Reserve banks. The chairman of the board (Allan Greenspan in 1989) is in a powerful position to influence the country's monetary policies.

The Federal Reserve Banks

The 12 Federal Reserve banks serve the 12 districts into which the country is divided. The banks are located in Boston, New York, Philadelphia, Cleveland, Richmond, Atlanta, Chicago, St. Louis, Minneapolis, Kansas City, Dallas, and San Francisco. Each bank is nominally owned by the member banks in its district. A commercial bank that is a member of the system is required to purchase a specific amount of Federal Reserve bank stock on which it receives a flat dividend. Each Federal Reserve bank has 9 directors: 3 bankers elected by the member banks; 3 representatives of business, agriculture, or industry; and 3 public members appointed by the board of governors.

Although technically privately owned and operated, the Federal Reserve banks are actually operated under guidelines set down by the board of governors in what it deems to be the public interest.

The Federal Reserve banks have a strong tradition of service to the banking community within the policy guidelines laid down by the board of governors. Revenues that they have earned in excess of expenses and of fixed minimum profits which they can retain for their own use must be turned over to the U.S. Treasury. Most Federal Reserve banks, along with the office of the board of governors, engage in research and publish many bulletins of interest to the financial communities that they serve.

The Federal Open Market Committee

The FOMC has 12 members: the 7 members of the board of governors plus 5 presidents of various Federal Reserve banks. This committee determines the open market policy of the system, which deals principally with how many government securities the Federal Reserve banks should buy or sell on the open market. This is the group that determines the country's monetary policy.

TABLE 31-1	Federal Reserve Banks, Consolidated Balance Sheet, January 25, 1989 *(billions of dollars)*

Assets	
Gold certificates and other cash	$ 11.1
U.S. government securities	237.3
Loans to commercial banks	1.6
Other assets	44.0
	$294.0
Liabilities	
Federal Reserve notes outstanding	$230.0
Deposits of member bank reserves	41.1
Deposits of U.S. Treasury	5.8
Other liabilities	17.1
	$294.0

Source: Federal Reserve Bulletin, April 1989.

The balance sheet of the Fed shows that it serves as banker to the commercial banks and to the U.S. Treasury and as issuer of our currency; it also suggests the Fed's role as regulator of money markets and the money supply. Federal Reserve notes are currency, and the deposits of member banks give commercial banks the reserves that they use to create deposit money. The Fed's principal assets, holdings of U.S. government securities, arise from its open-market operations that are designed to regulate the money supply and also from direct purchases from the Treasury.

window." The rate of interest that the Fed charges on such loans is called the **discount rate.**

Bank for the government. Governments, too, need to hold their funds in an account into which they can make deposits and against which they can write checks. The U.S. Treasury keeps its checking deposits at the Federal Reserve banks, replenishing them from much larger tax and loan accounts kept at commercial banks. When the government requires more money than it collects in taxes, it, too, needs to borrow, and it does so by selling securities. Most are sold directly to the public, but when the central bank buys a new government bond on the open market, it is indirectly lending to the government. As of January 1989, the Federal Reserve System held over $237 billion in U.S. government securities.

Controller of the money supply. One of the most important functions of a central bank is to control the money supply. From Table 31-1 it is clear that the overwhelming proportion of a central bank's liabilities (its promises to pay) are either Federal Reserve notes or the deposits of commercial banks, which provide reserves for demand deposits that are owned by households and firms. Later in this chapter we shall study how the Fed seeks to control the money supply.

Regulator of money markets. The central bank frequently enters money markets for purposes other than controlling the money supply. For instance, it may, as an arm of the government, attempt to keep interest rates low in periods when the government is increasing its debt to reduce the government's cost of financing a given deficit.

Central banks also assume responsibility for supporting the country's financial system and for preventing serious disruption by wide-scale panic and the resulting bank failures. Various institutions are in the business of borrowing on a short-term basis and lending on a long-term basis. Examples include savings and loan associations, which take in short-term deposits from the public and lend on long-term mortgages.

Large, unanticipated increases in interest rates tend to squeeze these institutions. The average rate that they earn on their investments rises only slowly as old contracts mature and new ones are made, but they must either pay higher rates to hold on to their deposits or accept wide-scale withdrawals that could easily bring about their insolvency. The Fed sometimes helps such institutions by preventing rapid swings in interest rates. If a shortage of funds is rapidly driving up interest rates, the Fed may supply funds to the market and thus make the rise in rates more gradual.

Conflicts among functions. The several functions of the central bank are not always compatible. For example, in pursuit of an antiinflationary policy, the Fed may cause interest rates to rise. The resulting squeeze makes life uncomfortable for banks and other financial institutions and makes borrowing expensive for the government. If the Fed chooses to ease those problems, say, by lending money to banks, it is relaxing its antiinflationary policy.

The Fed must strive to balance conflicting objectives. We shall discuss a number of aspects of this conflict in Chapter 33. However, at this stage we note that many critics think that the Fed does not always succeed in finding the right balance between its conflicting objectives.

The Commercial Banks

Modern commercial banking systems are of two main types: One type has a small number of banks, each with a large number of branch offices; the other consists of many independent banks. The banking systems of the United Kingdom and Canada are of the first type, with only a few banks accounting for the overwhelming bulk of the business. The American system is of the second type. In 1988 there were approximately 15,000 independent banks, some of which (such as the Bank of America) had hundreds of branches and others of which had only a single office. Branch banking in the United States is governed by state law; interstate branching is not allowed. In some states banks are permitted to branch statewide; in other so-called unit-bank states, no branching at all is permitted; and some states permit limited branching into areas near the home office. Many of these prohibitions are under pressure and are disappearing with deregulation. Sweeping changes in banking have been occurring internationally; these developments and their interaction with domestic deregulation are discussed in Box 31-5.

There is a wide variety of banking systems in existence, but they all function in essentially the same manner.

The basic unit of the American banking system is the ordinary **commercial bank,** which is a privately owned, profit-seeking institution. All commercial banks have common attributes: They hold deposits for their customers, permit certain deposits to be transferred by check from an individual account to other accounts held in any bank in the country, make loans to households and firms, and invest in government securities.

It is these common features, in particular the holding of demand deposits, that traditionally has distinguished commercial banks from other financial institutions, each of which performed some but not all of these functions. In the past, credit unions, savings and loan associations, and mutual savings banks traditionally accepted time deposits and granted loans for specific purposes, while finance companies made loans to households for practically any purpose. While the various types of financial institutions continue to specialize to some extent, as noted earlier, sweeping deregulation over the past decade has made the distinction between the various financial institutions much less sharp.

Commercial banks differ from one another in many ways. Some are large (in 1989 the Bank of America had deposits in excess of $100 billion), and others are small; some are located in big cities, and others are located in small towns; some hold charters from the federal government (national banks), and others hold charters from state governments (state banks). Nearly 40 percent of the commercial banks, including most of the larger ones, are members of the Federal Reserve System. All national banks must be members, and any state bank may join the system by agreeing to abide by its regulations. However, nonmember banks are indirectly tied into the system, since they are invariably *correspondents* of larger member banks; that is, they have regular commercial relations with the member banks. For example, the nonmember banks keep their reserves on deposit with member banks, depend on them for loans when they are pressed for cash, and rely on them for a variety of other services that the Federal Reserve System provides for its members. In practice all commercial banks—members and nonmembers alike—have always come under the effective regulatory influence of the Fed.

Interbank Activities

Commercial banks have a number of interbank cooperative relationships. These are encouraged by special banking laws because they facilitate the smooth functioning of money and credit markets.

For example, banks often share loans. Even the biggest bank cannot meet all of the credit needs of an industrial giant such as General Motors, and often a group of banks will offer a "pool loan," agreeing on common terms and dividing the loan up into manageable segments. On a different scale, a small bank, when it is approached for a loan that is larger than it can safely handle, will often ask a larger bank to "participate" in the loan.

Another form of interbank cooperation is the bank credit card. VISA and MasterCard are the two most widely used credit cards, and each is operated by a large group of banks.

Probably the most important form of interbank

cooperation is check clearing and collection. Bank deposits are an effective medium of exchange only because banks accept each other's checks. If a depositor in bank A writes a check to someone who deposits it in bank B, bank A owes money to bank B. This, of course, creates a need for the banks to present checks to each other for payment.

There are millions of such transactions in the course of a day, and they result in an enormous sorting and bookkeeping job. Multibank systems make use of a **clearing house** where interbank debts are settled. At the end of the day, all the checks drawn by bank A's customers and deposited in bank B are totaled and set against the total of all the checks drawn by bank B's customers and deposited in bank A. It is necessary to settle only the difference between the two sums. The actual checks are passed through the clearing house back to the bank on which they were drawn. Both banks are then able to adjust the individual accounts by a set of book entries. A flow of cash between banks is necessary only when there is a net transfer of cash from the customers of one bank to those of another. For member banks, this clearing function is performed by the Federal Reserve System, and much of it is done electronically by using a system operated by the Fed called *Fedwire*.

Profit Seeking

Banks are private firms that start with invested capital and seek to "earn money" in the same sense as do firms that make neckties or bicycles. A commercial bank provides a variety of services to its customers: a safe place to store money; the convenience of demand deposits that can be transferred by personal check; a safe and convenient place to earn a modest but guaranteed return on savings; and often financial advice and estate management services. The bank earns some revenue by charging for these services, but such fees are a small part of the bank's total earnings. The largest part (typically about five-sixths) of a bank's earnings is derived from the bank's ability to invest profitably the funds placed with it.

Principal Assets and Liabilities

Table 31-2 is the combined balance sheet of the commercial banks in the United States. The bulk of a bank's liabilities are deposits that are owed to its depositors. The principal assets of a bank are the *securities* that it owns (including government bonds), which pay interest or dividends, and the *loans* that it makes to individuals and to businesses. A bank loan is a liability to the borrower (who must pay it back) but an asset to the bank. The bank expects not only to have the loan repaid but also to receive interest that more than compensates for the paperwork involved and the risk of nonpayment.

Banks attract deposits by paying interest to depositors and by providing them, for a fee that does not cover the banks' full cost, with services such as clearing checks and issuing regular monthly statements. Banks earn profits by lending and investing

TABLE 31-2 Consolidated Balance Sheet of U.S. Commercial Banks, January 25, 1989 (*billions of dollars*)				
Assets			**Liabilities**	
Reserves (cash assets including deposits with Federal Reserve banks)	$ 214.7	Deposits Demand Savings	$ 585.5 530.2	
Loans	2,022.0	Time	978.2	
U.S. government securities	533.3			
Other securities	195.0	Borrowings	491.8	
Other assets	21.5	Other liabilities	204.8	
		Capital accounts	195.8	
	$2,986.4		$2,986.4	

Source: Federal Reserve Bulletin, May 1989.

Reserves are only a small fraction of deposit liabilities. If all of the banks' customers who held demand deposits tried to withdraw them in cash, the banks could not meet this demand without liquidating $300.1 billion of other assets. This would be impossible without assistance from the Fed.

BOX 31-5

The Globalization of Financial Markets

Technological innovations in communication and the desire to avoid onerous government regulations have recently led to a globalization of the financial-service industry. Computers and satellite communications systems are the most important developments in information transfer. They put people in instantaneous contact by means of computer terminals located anywhere in the world. Reliable telephones with direct dialing, electronic mail, and fax machines are other key innovations.

As a result of these new technologies, borrowers and lenders can learn about market conditions and then move their funds instantly anywhere in search of the most favorable loan rates. Large firms need transaction balances only while banks in their area are open and can, therefore, move their transaction balances on a daily basis. Once banks close for the day in each center, the firms know that they will not need these balances until tomorrow's reopening. At the end of that market's day, the funds move on to another market, where they are used until it closes. They are then moved to yet another market. Funds are thus free to move among London, New York, and Tokyo, for example, on a daily rotation. This is a degree of global sophistication that was inconceivable before the advent of the computer, when international communication was much slower and costlier than it now is. To facilitate the movement in and out of various national currencies, increasing amounts of bank deposits are denominated in foreign rather than domestic currencies.

One of the first developments in this movement toward internationalization was the growth of the Eurobond and Eurocurrency markets in the 1960s. At first the main currency that was involved was the U.S. dollar, and hence Euro*dollar* markets were the first to develop. Today the *Eurobond* market is an international market in which bonds of various types, denominated in various national currencies, are issued and sold to customers located throughout the world. The customers are mainly public corporations, international organizations, and multinational enterprises. The *Eurocurrency* market is a market for short-term bank deposits and bank loans, denominated in various currencies. In both markets the U.S. dollar accounts for the largest single volume of transactions, but many other currencies are also used.

The original attraction of the *Eurodollar* market was the freedom from the restrictions placed by the Federal Reserve on American commercial banks. By operating in offshore markets, the banks could avoid legal reserve requirements and interest-rate ceilings imposed on various types of deposits. This allowed the banks to operate on lower reserve margins and to cut unit costs by dealing in large volume at the wholesale level (normally $1 million is the minimum unit dealt with). They could then offer rates that were higher for lenders and lower for borrowers than those prevailing in the domestic U.S. market. A further initial advantage of the Euromarkets was freedom from the exchange controls that were used by many countries to control capital movements in support of the fixed exchange rates that were imposed at that time.

The development of the Eurodollar and Eurobond markets provides an excellent example of how difficult it is to control any economic system through government regulations. Regulations that are in the collective interest of those who are being regulated—for example, those that impose desirable

money that is deposited with them for more than they pay their depositors in terms of interest and other services provided.

Competition for Deposits

Competition for deposits is active among banks and between banks and other financial institutions. Fi-

standards of safety or prudence on everyone—will tend to be successful. Regulations that go against the self-interests of those regulated tend to lead to the development of new institutions that avoid the regulations.

The abandonment of fixed exchange rates in the early 1970s, and the progressive lifting of exchange controls, interest-rate ceilings, and other capital market restrictions, led to a further globalization of the financial markets. Although this removed some of the original reasons for their growth, the Euro-markets persisted. First, they allowed banks to avoid the remaining domestic restrictions, such as minimum reserve requirements. Second, the advantage of having an international market dealing in many different national currencies was sufficient to sustain the markets.

The increasing sophistication of information transfer also led to a breakdown of the high degree of specialization that had characterized financial markets in all earlier decades. When information was difficult to obtain and analyze, an efficient division of labor called for a host of specialty institutions, each with expertise within a narrow range of transactions. As a result of the new developments in communications technology, economies of large scale came to dominate the efficiencies of a detailed division of labor. The integration of various financial operations within one firm then became increasingly common. For example, banks have moved into the markets in which securities are traded, while many security-trading firms have begun to offer a range of banking services. As the scale of such integrated firms increases, they will find it easier to extend their operations geographically as well as functionally.

It has often been difficult for government regulations to keep up with these rapid changes. Governments that relaxed their regulations first in the face of evolving realities often allowed their financial institutions to gain important advantages in international competition. The government of the United Kingdom has been quick to react to these developments, and, as a result, London has retained its strong position in the international financial world. In contrast, the U.S. government has been slow to adapt. For example, it still limits interstate banking and prevents U.S. banks from extending their operations beyond the ones that are traditionally reserved for banks. As a result, U.S. banks have lost out heavily to European and Japanese banks.

The kinds of government intervention into domestic capital markets and government control over international capital flows that characterized the regime of fixed exchange rates of the 1950s and 1960s are no longer possible. International markets are just too sophisticated. Globalization is here to stay, and, by removing domestic restrictions and exchange controls, governments in advanced countries are only bowing to the inevitable.

The banker, bending over his computer terminal in London to move funds from Hong Kong to New York in response to a change that has just occurred in the New York rate, is a long way from the British general, Sir Edward Pakenham, who on January 8, 1815, lost the battle of New Orleans (and his own life) 15 days after the war with the United States had been ended by the Treaty of Ghent but several days before the fast frigate arrived at his headquarters carrying the news that further fighting was unnecessary.

nancial deregulation that removed many restrictions on the activities of various financial institutions has contributed to this competition.

Interest paid on demand, as well as savings deposits, money market funds, high-interest certificates of deposit (CDs), advertising, personal solicitation of accounts, giveaway programs for new deposits to existing accounts, and improved services are all forms of competition for funds. Among the special services are payroll-accounting and pension-accounting schemes for industrial customers. The "lock box" is another kind of service: Banks establish locked post office boxes to which retail customers of large companies send their payments. The bank opens the remittances, deposits them to the company's account, and forwards notices of payment to the company. All of these services are costly to the bank, but they serve as inducements to customers in order to gain deposits.

Reserves

The Need for Reserves

All bankers would prefer, as a matter of convenience and prudence, to keep sufficient cash on hand to be able to meet depositors' day-to-day requirements for cash. However, just as the goldsmiths of old discovered that only a fraction of the gold that they held was ever withdrawn at any given time, and just as banks of old discovered that only a fraction of convertible bank notes was actually converted, so, too, have modern banks discovered that only a fraction of their deposits will be withdrawn in cash at any one time. Most deposits of any individual bank remain on deposit with it; thus, an individual bank need keep only fractional reserves against its deposits.

The reserves that are needed to assure that depositors can withdraw their deposits on demand will be quite small in normal times.

In abnormal times, however, nothing short of 100 percent might do the job if the commercial banking system had to stand alone. When a few bank failures cause a general loss of confidence in banks' ability to redeem their deposits, the results can be devastating. Until relatively recent times, such an event—or even the rumor of it—could lead to a "run" on banks, as depositors rushed to withdraw their money. Faced with such a panic, banks would have to close until they had borrowed enough funds or liquidated enough assets to meet the demand or until the demand subsided. However, banks could not instantly turn their loans into cash, since the borrowers would

have the money tied up in such things as real estate or business enterprises. Neither could the banks obtain cash by selling their securities to the public, since payments would be made by checks, which would not provide cash with which to pay off depositors.

The difficulty of providing sufficient reserves to meet abnormal situations can be alleviated by the central bank. Most importantly, because it controls the supply of bank reserves, the central bank can provide all the reserves that are needed to meet any abnormal situation. It can do this in two ways. First, it can lend reserves directly to the commercial banks on the security of assets that are sound but not easy to liquidate quickly. Second, it can enter the open market and buy all the securities that the commercial banks need to sell. Once the public finds that deposits can be turned into cash, the panic usually will subside and any further drain of cash out of banks will cease.

The possibility of panic withdrawals is also greatly diminished by the provision of Federal Deposit Insurance, which guarantees that depositors will get their money back, even if a bank fails completely. Most depositors will not withdraw their money as long as they are *sure* they can get it when they need it.

While deposit insurance confers a number of benefits to the operation of the financial system, it has also been subject to considerable criticism in recent years. This is taken up in Box 31-6.

Actual and Required Reserves

Look again at Table 31-2 and observe that the banking system's cash reserves are just a fraction of its deposits. If the holders of even 40 percent of its demand deposits had demanded cash sometime in January 1989, the commercial banking system would have been unable (without outside help) to meet the demand.

The American banking system is a **fractional reserve system,** with commercial banks holding reserves—either as cash or as deposits with the central bank—of much less than 100 percent of their deposits. The size of the reserves reflects not only the judgment of bankers but also the legal requirements imposed on the banks by the Fed.

A bank's **reserve ratio** is the fraction of its deposits that it holds as reserves. Those reserves that the Federal Reserve System requires the bank to hold are called **required reserves.** Any reserves held over and above required reserves are called **excess reserves.** Reserves are required by the Fed both to assure the stability of the banking system and as part of its policy arsenal for controlling the money supply, as we shall discuss at the end of this chapter.

Money Creation by the Banking System

The fractional reserve system provides the leverage that permits commercial banks and other financial institutions to create new money. The process is important, so it is worth examining in some detail.

Some Simplifying Assumptions

To focus on the essential aspects of how banks create money, assume that banks can invest in only one kind of asset, loans, and that there is only one kind of deposit, a demand deposit.

Three other assumptions listed below are provisional. When we have developed the basic ideas concerning the banks' creation of money, these assumptions will be relaxed.

1. *Fixed required reserve ratio.* It is assumed that all banks have the same required reserve ratio, which does not change. In our numerical illustration we shall assume that the required reserve ratio is 20 percent (i.e., 0.20); that is, at least $1 of reserves must be held for every $5 of deposits.
2. *No excess reserves.* It is assumed that all banks want to invest any reserves that they have in excess of the legally required amount. This implies that they always believe that there are safe investments—loans, in our example—to be made when they have excess reserves.
3. *No cash drain from the banking system.* It is assumed that the public holds a fixed amount of currency in circulation, and hence transfers of funds between individuals will not involve changes in the currency available for the banks to hold as reserves. Changes in the money supply thus will take the form of changes in deposits held at the commercial banks.

The Creation of Deposit Money

A simplified bank balance sheet is shown in Table 31-3. The Immigrants Bank and Trust Company

TABLE 31-3	The Initial Balance Sheet of the Immigrants Bank and Trust Company *(thousands of dollars)*		
Assets		**Liabilities**	
Cash and other reserves	$ 200	Deposits	$1,000
Loans	900	Capital	100
	$1,100		$1,100

The IB&T Co. has a reserve of 20 percent of its deposit liabilities. The commercial bank earns money by finding profitable investments for much of the money deposited with it. In this balance sheet, loans are its earning assets.

(IB&T Co.) has assets of $200 of reserves (all figures are in thousands of dollars), held partly as cash on hand and partly as deposits with the central bank, and $900 of loans outstanding to its customers. Its liabilities are $100 to those who initially contributed capital to start the bank, and $1,000 to current depositors. The bank's ratio of reserves to deposits is 200/1,000 = 0.20, exactly equal to its minimum requirement.

A Single New Deposit

Suppose that an immigrant arrives in the country and opens an account by depositing $100 with the IB&T Co. This is a wholly new deposit for the bank, and it results in a revised balance sheet (Table 31-4). As a result of the immigrant's new deposit, both cash assets and deposit liabilities have risen by $100. More important, the IB&T Co.'s ratio of reserves to

TABLE 31-4	The Initial Balance Sheet of IB&T Co. After an Immigrant Deposits $100 *(thousands of dollars)*		
Assets		**Liabilities**	
Cash and other reserves	$ 300	Deposits	$1,100
Loans	900	Capital	100
	$1,200		$1,200

The immigrant's deposit raises deposit liabilities and cash assets by the same amount. Since both cash and deposits rise by $100, the cash reserve ratio, formerly 0.20, increases to 0.27. The bank has more cash than it needs to provide a 20 percent reserve against its deposit liabilities.

BOX 31-6

The Crisis in the Savings and Loan Industry

In early 1989 headlines in the financial press rang the alarm that some American financial institutions were suffering staggering losses. These losses were in the so-called thrifts, primarily savings and loan institutions (or S&Ls), which accept deposits and invest in mortgages. Estimates of the potential losses ran as high as $150 billion, and some analysts thought that the entire American financial system was at risk as a result.

An article in the *Federal Reserve Bank of San Francisco Weekly Letter* argued that the problem arose because of a "confluence of economic and regulatory events" that "exposed a fatal flaw in the deposit insurance system." What were these events, and what is the "fatal flaw"?

Economic Events

S&Ls make most of their loans in the form of long-term mortgages; because of their long-term nature, the return on these assets is very slow to adjust to current economic conditions. Their deposit liabilities are, however, relatively short-term. The general level of interest rates rose steadily throughout most of 1988; as a result, the interest costs paid by the S&Ls on deposits rose quite sharply, while their interest return on assets did not.

The short-term nature of their liabilities and the long-term nature of their assets placed the S&Ls in a profit squeeze during a period of rising interest rates.

These problems were intensified by the fact that real estate values had been falling in certain areas of the country—especially in the oil-producing states of the Southwest—and S&Ls that were holding mortgages for property concentrated in these areas suffered unusually poor collections and unusually high default rates.

Regulatory and International Events

The conflicting pressures on deposit and asset rates were intensified by increased competition resulting from two, not unrelated, sources.

The first source was international. In the market for deposits, S&Ls faced increased competition from foreign institutions as a result of the ongoing "globalization" of financial markets. A variety of financial instruments evolved that provided savers with new alternatives to deposits with S&Ls, and, as a result, S&Ls had to pay more to hold or to attract deposits.

The second source was domestic. As a result of ongoing deregulation of financial markets, other domestic financial intermediaries were not only competing directly with S&Ls for deposits, but also becoming major suppliers of home mortgages. Thus, thrifts were not able to raise mortgage rates as much as they would previously have done.

Deregulation also allowed the S&Ls to expand into a new area—commercial lending—where they lacked expertise and (probably inevitably) made a disproportionate number of poor loans as they learned while they loaned.

As a result of the increases in deposit rates relative to the return on assets, the S&Ls' profit position deteriorated sharply.

The Flaw in Deposit Insurance

Deposit insurance assures depositors that their deposits are secure, independent of the losses of the institution. We saw in the text the role that this plays in stabilizing the economic system in times of financial panic. However, economists have long stressed that such insurance also creates an incentive for financial intermediaries to pursue riskier investments than they otherwise would; the existence of deposit insurance means that depositors will not be deterred much from depositing in a given institution, even if that institution is widely perceived to hold very risky assets.

What the recent experience of the S&L industry has shown is that this incentive to pursue risky investment strategies increases dramatically as an institution approaches insolvency. After a period of sustained losses such as many S&Ls experienced during the late 1980s, liabilities were as large as assets, and owner equity had been reduced to virtually zero. As a result, the owners had a powerful incentive to take risks. If a high-risk investment succeeded, the owners would reap large profits. If it failed, they lost little of their own capital and depositors were repaid by deposit insurance—in this case, the Federal Savings and Loan Insurance Corporation. As the article in the *Federal Reserve Bank of San Francisco Weekly Letter* put it, these owners faced a "heads-I-win, tails-you-lose" situation.

While some of the estimated $150 billion in losses represented losses that were sustained due to normal operations in the face of adverse circumstances, some also represented abnormal losses arising from risky strategies that were taken by decision makers who did not bear the losses themselves.

Who Pays?

If the owner-managers and the depositors do not bear the losses, then who does? Ultimately, they are borne by the taxpayers.

Some commentators have proposed that a tax be levied on the solvent S&Ls to cover the costs, but most estimates suggest that these institutions could not, in fact, cover the entire amount. Others have suggested that a tax be levied on the commercial banks, but, again, estimates suggest that the industry could not reasonably bear the entire burden without itself undergoing severe financial difficulties. In any event, there is a question of why profitable, well-managed firms should pay for the "irresponsible" behavior of others.

Thus, much of the burden will fall on general taxpayers. The Bush administration, working with a relatively conservative estimate of losses of $90 billion, identified a need of $9 billion per year to service the loss. The administration proposed that the government issue bonds to raise some of the money, but issuing bonds merely defers the taxes that must be paid; it does not replace them.

What Can Be Done?

Several reforms are possible. The implications of deposit insurance for the investment behavior of financial intermediaries suggests that, if deposit insurance is to be maintained, then other regulations concerning capital requirements and investment standards should be considered. In addition, the deposit insurance system might be reformed in order to relate the cost of insurance for a particular institution to the risks implied by that institution's asset position.

Whatever is done, it is important to ensure that in the future the risks from investment decisions made by banks and S&Ls are borne by their owners, not by taxpayers.

deposits has increased from 0.20 to 0.27 (300/1,100). The bank now has $80 in excess reserves; with $1,100 in deposits, its required reserves are only $220.

The IB&T Co. will now lend the $80 in excess reserves that it is holding. Table 31-5 shows the position after this has been done and after the proceeds of the loan have been withdrawn to be deposited to the account of a customer of another bank. The IB&T Co. once again has a 20 percent reserve ratio.

So far, of the $100 initial deposit in the IB&T Co., $20 is held by the IB&T Co. as reserves against the deposit and $80 has been lent out in the system. However, other banks have received new deposits of $80, stemming from the loans made by the IB&T Co.; persons receiving payment from those who borrowed the $80 from the IB&T Co. will have deposited those payments in their own banks. Note that, while the *banking system* suffers no cash drain (i.e., all the money that has been lent out is returned to the banking system as deposits), the IB&T Co. does suffer a cash drain (i.e., most of the $80 goes to other banks and is not redeposited at the IB&T Co.).

The banks that receive deposits from the proceeds of the IB&T Co.'s loan are sometimes called *next-generation banks* or, more specifically according to the situation, *second-generation, third-generation,* and so on. In this case the second-generation banks receive new deposits of $80, and when the checks clear, they have new reserves of $80. Because they require only $16

TABLE 31-6 Changes in the Balance Sheets of Second-Generation Banks (*thousands of dollars*)

Assets		Liabilities	
Cash and other reserves	+$16	Deposits	+$80
Loans	+ 64		
	+$80		+$80

Second-generation banks receive cash deposits and expand loans. The second-generation banks gain new deposits of $80 as a result of the loan granted by the IB&T Co., which is used to make payments to customers of the second-generation banks. These banks keep 20 percent of the cash that they acquire as their reserve against the new deposit, and they can make new loans using the other 80 percent. When the customers who borrowed the money make payments to the customers of third-generation banks, a cash drain occurs.

in additional reserves to support the new deposits, they have $64 of excess reserves. They now increase their loans by $64. After this money has been spent by the borrowers and has been deposited in other, third-generation banks, the balance sheets of the second-generation banks will have changed, as in Table 31-6.

The third-generation banks now find themselves with $64.00 of new deposits. Against these they need to hold only $12.80 in cash, so they have excess reserves of $51.20 that they can immediately lend out. Thus there begins a long sequence of new deposits, new loans, new deposits, and new loans. These stages are shown in Table 31-7. The series in the table should look familiar, for it is the same convergent process that we met when we were dealing with the multiplier in Chapter 27.

The banking system has created new deposits and thus new money, although each banker can honestly say, "All I did was invest my excess reserves. I can do no more than manage wisely the money that I receive."

If v is the reserve ratio, the ultimate effect on the deposits of the banking system of a new deposit will be $1/v$ times the new deposit. [38][2]

TABLE 31-5 The IB&T Co. Balance Sheet After a New Loan and Cash Drain of $80 (*thousands of dollars*)

Assets		Liabilities	
Cash and other reserves	$ 220	Deposits	$1,100
Loans	980	Capital	100
	$1,200		$1,200

The bank lends its surplus cash and suffers a cash drain. The bank keeps $20 as a reserve against the immigrant's new deposit of $100. It lends $80 to a customer, who writes a check to someone who deals with another bank. When the check is cleared, the IB&T Co. suffers an $80 cash drain. Comparing Tables 31-3 and 31-5 shows that the bank has increased its deposit liabilities by the $100 deposited by the new immigrant and has increased its assets by $20 of cash reserves and $80 of new loans. It has also restored its reserve ratio of 0.20.

----

[2] The "multiple expansion of deposits" that has just been worked through applies in reverse to a withdrawal of funds. Deposits of the banking system will fall by $1/v$ times any amount withdrawn from the bank and not redeposited at another.

TABLE 31-7   **The Sequence of Loans and Deposits After a Single Initial Deposit of $10.00**

Bank	New deposits	New loans	Addition to reserves
IB&T Co.	$100.00	$ 80.00	$ 20.00
Second-generation bank	80.00	64.00	16.00
Third-generation bank	64.00	51.20	12.80
Fourth-generation bank	51.20	40.96	10.24
Fifth-generation bank	40.96	32.77	8.19
Sixth-generation bank	32.77	26.22	6.55
Seventh-generation bank	26.22	20.98	5.24
Eighth-generation bank	20.98	16.78	4.20
Ninth-generation bank	16.78	13.42	3.36
Tenth-generation bank	13.42	10.74	2.68
Total for first 10 generations	446.33	357.07	89.26
All remaining generations	53.67	42.93	10.74
Total for banking system	$500.00	$400.00	$100.00

The banking system as a whole can create deposit money whenever it receives new reserves. The table shows the process of the creation of deposit money on the assumptions that all the loans made by one set of banks end up as deposits in another set of banks (the next-generation banks), that the required reserve ratio (v) is 0.20, and that there are no excess reserves. Although each bank suffers a cash drain whenever it grants a new loan, the system as a whole does not, and the system ends up doing in a series of steps what a monopoly bank would do all at once; that is, it increases deposit money by $1/v$, which, in this example, is five times the amount of any increase in reserves that it obtains.

At the end of the process that is depicted in Table 31-7, the change in the combined balance sheets of all the banks in the system is shown in Table 31-8.

Many Deposits

A more realistic picture of deposit creation is one in which new deposits accrue simultaneously to all banks, perhaps because of changes in the monetary policy of the government. (We shall study monetary policy in detail in Chapter 33.)

Say, for example, that a community contains 10 banks of equal size and that each receives new deposits of $100 in cash. Now each bank is in the position shown in Table 31-4, and each can begin to expand deposits based on the $100 of excess reserves. (Each bank does this by granting loans to customers.)

Because each bank does one-tenth of the total banking business, an average of 90 percent of any newly created deposit will find its way into other banks as the customer pays other people in the community by check. This will represent a cash drain from the lending bank to the other banks. However, roughly 10 percent of each new deposit created by every other bank should find its way into any particular bank. All banks receive new cash, and all begin creating deposits simultaneously.

The expansion can go on, with each bank watch-

TABLE 31-8   **The Combined Balance Sheets of All the Banks in the System Following the Multiple Expansion of Deposits**

Assets		Liabilities	
Cash and other reserves	+$100	Deposits	+$500
Loans	+ 400		
	+$500		+$500

The reserve ratio is returned to 0.20. The entire initial deposit of $100 ends up as reserves of the banking system. Therefore, deposits rise by (1/0.2) times the initial deposit, that is, by $500.

ing its own ratio of cash reserves to deposits, expanding deposits as long as the ratio exceeds 1/5, and ceasing when it reaches that figure. The process will come to a halt when each bank has created $400 in additional deposits, so that for each initial $100 cash deposit, there is now $500 in deposits backed by $100 in cash.

The general rule, if there is no cash drain, is that a banking system with a reserve ratio of v can change its deposits by $1/v$ times any change in reserves.

Excess Reserves and Cash Drains

Two of the simplifying assumptions that were made earlier can now be relaxed.

Excess reserves. If banks do not choose to invest their excess reserves, the multiple expansion that we discussed will not occur. Go back to Table 31-4. If the IB&T Co. had been content to hold 27 percent in reserves, it might well have done nothing more. Other things being equal, banks will choose to invest their excess reserves because of the profit motive, but there may be times when they believe that the risk is too great. It is one thing to be offered a good rate of interest on a loan, but if the borrower defaults on the payment of interest and principal, the bank will be the loser. Similarly, if the bank expects interest rates to rise in the future, it may hold off making loans now so that it will have reserves available to make more profitable loans after the interest rate has risen.

Deposit creation does not happen automatically; it depends on the decisions of bankers. If banks do not choose to use their excess reserves to expand their investments, there will not be an expansion of deposits.

The money supply is thus at least partially determined by the commercial banks in response to such forces as changes in national income and interest rates. However, the upper limit of deposits is determined by the required reserve ratio and by the reserves available to the banks, both of which are under the influence of the central bank.

Cash drain. Suppose that firms and households find it convenient to keep a fixed *fraction* of their money holding in cash (say, 5 percent) instead of a fixed *amount* of dollars. In that case, an extra $100 in money supply will not all stay in the banking system; only $95 will remain on deposit, while the rest will be added to money that is already in circulation. In such a situation, any multiple expansion of bank deposits will be accompanied by a cash drain to the public that will substantially reduce the maximum expansion below what it was when the public was content to hold all its new money as bank deposits.

The story of deposit creation when all banks receive new deposits and there is a cash drain to the public goes like this. Each bank starts creating deposits and suffers no significant cash drain to other banks. However, because approximately 5 percent of newly created deposits is withdrawn to be held as cash, each bank suffers a cash drain to the public. The expansion continues, each bank watching its own ratio of cash reserves to deposits, expanding deposits as long as the ratio exceeds 1/5 and ceasing when it reaches that figure. Because the expansion is accompanied by a cash drain, it will come to a halt with a smaller deposit expansion than in the case of no cash drain.[3]

Table 31-9 shows the consolidated balance sheets of the banking system after the deposit expansion, arising from an initial deposit of $100 when there is a 5 percent cash drain. As shown, since there is a cash drain of $20, reserves rise by only $80, loans rise by only $320, and deposits rise by only $400.

The Money Supply

The total stock of money in the economy at any moment is called the **money supply** or the **supply of money.** Economists and financial analysts use several different definitions for the money supply, most of which are regularly reported in the *Federal Reserve Bulletin*. Typically, the definitions involve the sum of currency in circulation plus some types of

---

[3] It can be shown algebraically that the percentage of cash drain must be added to the reserve ratio to determine the maximum possible expansion of deposits. **[39]**

deposit liabilities of financial institutions. Definitions vary in terms of what deposits are included. Different definitions come into or go out of favor as the importance of different types of deposits changes.

Kinds of Deposits

Most of the deposits that are held by the average person are either demand deposits or time deposits.

Demand Deposits

A **demand deposit** means that the customer can withdraw the money on demand (i.e., without giving any notice of intention to withdraw). Demand deposits are transferable by means of a check. Such a check instructs the bank to pay without delay a stated sum of money to the person to whom the check is made payable. Although banks now pay interest on demand deposits, they were legally prohibited from doing so until the 1980s.

Time Deposits

A **time deposit** is an interest-bearing bank deposit that is legally withdrawable only after a certain amount of notice, such as 30 days for a passbook account and up to 6 months on certificates of deposit. The amount of time until the deposit can be withdrawn is often called the *term* of the deposit. Until quite recently it was impossible to write a check against a time deposit. A depositor wishing to use a time deposit to pay a bill had two options. Having withdrawn her money from a savings (time) account, she could then either pay the bill in cash or deposit the funds in a demand account and then write a check against the demand account. Time deposits often are also loosely referred to as *saving deposits*.

The Disappearing Distinction

For decades interest rates on time deposits amounted to only a few percent, and people were content to keep their savings in time deposits and their reserves of cash for ordinary transactions in demand deposits. Then, interest rates available on time deposits and other safe liquid investments grew, and it became more and more expensive (in terms of lost interest) to keep cash in demand deposits, even for a week or two. Starting in the early 1970s, several devices were invented that tended to make it easier to convert interest-bearing deposits into demand deposits transferable by check.

One of the first was the **negotiable order of withdrawal (NOW),** a checklike instruction to the savings institution to transfer funds from the depositor's time deposit to another person.

A similar device is the **automatic transfer service (ATS),** which allows depositors to maintain both a demand deposit and a time deposit at the bank and to make all deposits to the time deposit. The bank automatically transfers funds to the demand deposit as needed to cover checks when they are written. This permits the customer to maintain only a small minimum amount (for example, $200) in the demand deposit account. All the rest earns interest. The ATS comes close to being both a demand deposit that pays interest and a time deposit that can be transferred by check.

Nonbank financial institutions such as brokerage firms now offer **money market mutual funds (MMMFs)** and **money market deposit accounts (MMDAs).** These accounts earn high interest and are checkable, although some are subject to minimum withdrawal restrictions and others to prior notice of withdrawal.

Finally, the Depository Institutions Deregulation and Monetary Control Act of 1980 phased out ceilings that had been imposed for decades on the interest that was allowed to be paid on various types of deposit accounts. The long-standing distinction between money and other highly liquid assets used to be that, narrowly defined, money was a medium of exchange that did not earn interest, while other liquid assets earned interest but were not media of exchange (although they were easily convertible into such). Today this distinction is much less clear than it once was.

Only notes and coins are certain to bear no interest. Although noncheckable deposits and some other liquid assets are not themselves media of exchange, they are so easily (sometimes automatically) converted into a medium of exchange that the distinction between what is and what is not legally a medium of exchange no longer has much significance.

Definitions of the Money Supply

Different definitions of the money supply include different types of deposits. The narrowly defined money supply, called **M1,** includes currency and those deposits that are themselves usable as media of exchange. Broader definitions include other deposits as well.

Prior to 1980, when the distinction between demand and time deposits was quite clear, *narrow money* was defined simply as the sum of currency plus demand deposits. The growth in ATS, NOW, and money market accounts has led to an expanded definition of M1 to include NOW, ATS, and similar accounts at credit unions and mutual savings banks, as well as the traditional currency and demand deposits.

Broader definitions include M2 and M3. **M2** is M1 plus savings and smaller time deposits of all kinds, including money market accounts and overnight loans. **M3** is M2 with the addition of several components, the most important of which are large denomination **certificates of deposit (CDs).** CDs are savings deposits, the evidence for which is a slip of paper, or certificate, rather than an entry in the saver's passbook. The most important is the large denomination, negotiable CD, which is designed to attract funds from large businesses. These pay a higher rate of interest than ordinary time deposits.

M1 concentrates on the medium-of-exchange function of money. The others include highly liquid assets that serve the temporary store-of-value function and are in practice quickly convertible into a medium of exchange at a known price ($1 on deposit in a savings account is always convertible into a $1

demand deposit or $1 in cash). Table 31-10 shows the principal components in the money supply.

Near Money and Money Substitutes

Over the past two centuries, what has been accepted by the public as money has expanded from gold and silver coins to include first bank notes and then bank deposits subject to transfer by check. Until recently, most economists would have agreed that money stopped at that point. No such agreement exists today, and an important debate centers on the defini-

TABLE 31-10	Money Supply in the United States, 1989 *(billions of dollars)* *(annual averages of daily figures)*
Currency	$ 210
Demand deposits	287
Traveler's checks	8
Other checkable deposits	279
M1	$784
Overnight repurchase agreements and Eurodollars	$ 74
Money market mutual balances	238
Money market deposit accounts	505
Savings accounts	433
Small denomination time deposits	1,019
M2	$3,053
Large denomination time deposits	$ 531
Term repurchase agreements	126
Term Eurodollars	102
Institutional money market mutual funds	87
M3	$3,889

Source: Economic Report of the President, 1989.

The three widely used measures of the money supply are M1, M2, and M3. The narrow definition of the money supply concentrates on what can be used directly as a medium of exchange. The broader definitions add in deposits that serve the store-of-value function and can be readily, and sometimes automatically, converted to a medium of exchange on a dollar-for-dollar basis.

Note that M1 includes traveler's checks held by the public, which clearly are a medium of exchange. Within M2, RPs are funds lent out on the overnight money market, and Eurodollars are U.S. dollar-denominated deposits in American banks located outside of the United States. M2 and M3 include similar items, with the difference in most cases being that the term deposits are in M3 and the demand deposits in M2.

tion of money that is appropriate to present circumstances.

If we concentrate only on the medium-of-exchange function of money, there is little doubt about what is money in America today. Money consists of notes, coins, and deposits that are subject to transfer by check or checklike instruments. These are the assets included in M1 as it is currently measured. No other asset constitutes a generally accepted medium of exchange; indeed, even notes and checks are not universally accepted—as you will discover if you try to buy a pack of cigarettes with a $1,000 bill (or even a $100 bill in a corner grocery store)—but such exceptions are unimportant.

The problem of deciding what is money arises because some media of exchange—currency that carries no interest yield and demand deposits, whose interest yield tends to be quite low—may provide relatively poor ways to meet the store-of-value function (see Table 31-11). Assets that earn a higher interest return will do a better job of meeting this function of money than will currency or demand deposits. At the same time, however, these other assets are less capable of fulfilling the medium-of-exchange function.

Near Money

Assets that adequately fulfill the store-of-value function and are readily converted into a medium of exchange but are not themselves a medium of exchange are sometimes called **near money.** Deposits at a savings and loan association are a characteristic form of near money. When you have such a deposit, you know exactly how much purchasing power you hold (at current prices) and, given modern banking practices, you can turn your deposit into a medium of exchange—cash or a checking deposit—at a moment's notice. Additionally, your deposit will earn some interest during the period that you hold it.

Why then does not everybody keep their money in such deposits instead of in currency? The answer is that the inconvenience of continually shifting money back and forth may outweigh the interest that can be earned. One week's interest on $100 (at 5 percent per year) is only about $.10, not enough to cover carfare to the bank or the cost of mailing a letter. For money that will be needed soon, it would hardly pay to shift it to a time deposit.

In general, whether or not it pays to convert cash

TABLE 31-11	The Dollar as a Store of Value Since 1965	
$1 put aside in	Had the purchasing power 5 years later of	Its average annual loss of value was
1965	$.81	4.3%
1970	.72	6.8%
1975	.65	9.0%
1980	.76	5.6%
1985	.76	5.6%
1990*	.85	3.2%

* 1990 estimate.

The dollar has not been a very satisfactory store of value over the last two decades. The second column shows the purchasing power, measured using the Consumer Price Index, of $1 five years after it was saved (assuming it earned no interest). In order for it to have maintained its real purchasing power, it would have had to earn the annual percentage return shown in the last column. (The figures in that column assume annual compounding.)

into interest-earning savings deposits for a given period of time will depend on the inconvenience and other transaction costs of shifting funds and on the amount of interest that can be earned.

There is a wide spectrum of assets in the economy that pay interest and also serve as reasonably satisfactory temporary stores of value. The difference between these assets and savings deposits is that their capital values are not quite as certain as those of savings deposits. If I elect to store my purchasing power in the form of a treasury bill that matures in 30 days, its price on the market may change between the time I buy it and the time I want to sell it, say, 10 days later. If the price changes, the purchasing power available to me changes, but, because of the short period of time to maturity, the price will not change very much. (After all, the government will pay the bond's face value in a few weeks.) Such a security is thus a reasonably satisfactory short-run store of purchasing power. Indeed, any readily salable capital asset whose value does not fluctuate significantly with the rate of interest will satisfactorily fulfill this short-term store-of-value function.

Money Substitutes

Things that serve as a temporary medium of exchange but are not a store of value are sometimes called **money substitutes.** Credit cards are a prime example of this. With a credit card, many transactions can be made without either cash or a check. The evidence of credit, the credit slip that you sign and hand over to the store, is not money, because it cannot be used to make further transactions. Furthermore, when your credit card company takes advantage of an arrangement to have your bank pay each bill as it is presented or when it sends you a bill, you have to use money to pay for the original transaction. The credit card serves the short-run function of a medium of exchange by allowing you to make purchases even though you have no cash or bank deposit currently in your possession. However, this is only temporary; money remains the final medium of exchange for these transactions when the credit account is settled.

Conclusion

Since the eighteenth century, economists have known that the amount of money in circulation is an important economic variable. As theories became more carefully specified in the nineteenth and early twentieth centuries, they included a variable called *the money supply.* For theories to be useful, however, we must be able to identify real-world counterparts of these theoretical magnitudes.

What is included in the definition of *money* has changed and will continue to change over time. NOW, ATS, MMMF, and MMDA accounts have broadened the spectrum. New monetary assets are continually being developed to serve some, if not all, the functions of money, and they are more or less readily convertible into money. There is no single, timeless definition of what is money and what is only near money or a money substitute. Indeed, as we have seen, our monetary authorities use several different definitions of money, and these definitions change from year to year.

SUMMARY

1. Early economic theorists regarded the economy as being divided into a real sector and a money sector. The real sector is concerned with production, allocation of resources, and distribution of income, determined by relative prices. The level of prices at which all transactions take place is determined by the monetary sector, that is, by the demand for and supply of money. With the demand for money being constant, an increase in the money supply would cause all equilibrium money prices to increase, but relative prices, and hence everything in the real sector, would be left unaffected.
2. Traditionally in economics, money has referred to any generally accepted medium of exchange. A number of functions of money may, however, be distinguished. The major ones are that it acts as a medium of exchange, a store of value, and a unit of account.
3. Money arose because of the inconvenience of barter, and it developed in stages from precious metal, to metal coinage, to paper money convertible to precious metal, to token coinage and paper money fractionally backed by precious metals, to fiat money, and to deposit money. Societies have shown great sophistication in developing monetary instruments to meet their needs.
4. The banking system in the United States consists of two main elements: the Federal Reserve System (which is the central bank) and the commercial banks. Each has an important effect on the money supply.
5. The central bank of the United States is the set of Federal Reserve banks and its board of governors. Although they are technically private, the Federal Reserve banks, in fact, belong to a system that functions as a central bank that administers the nation's monetary policy. Effective power is exercised by the board of governors, whose

seven members are appointed by the president of the United States for 14-year terms.

6. Commercial banks are profit-seeking institutions that allow their customers to transfer demand deposits from one bank to another by means of checks. They create and destroy money as a by-product of their commercial operations by making or liquidating loans and various other investments.

7. Because most customers are content to pay their accounts by check rather than by cash, banks need only small reserves to back their deposit liabilities. Consequently, banks are able to create deposit money. When the banking system receives a new cash deposit, it can create new deposits to some multiple of this amount. The amount of new deposits created depends on the legal minimum reserves that the Federal Reserve enforces on the banks, the amount of cash drain to the public, and whether the banks choose to hold excess reserves.

8. The money supply—the stock of money in an economy at a specific moment—can be defined in various ways. M1, the narrowest definition, includes currency, traveler's checks, and demand and other checkable deposits. M3, the widest definition, includes a number of assets, such as money market funds and overnight loans, that are readily convertible into M1 on a dollar-for-dollar basis, with or without notice.

9. Near money includes interest-earning assets that are convertible into money on a dollar-for-dollar basis but that are not currently included in the definition of money. Money substitutes are things such as credit cards that temporarily serve as a medium of exchange but are not money.

TOPICS FOR REVIEW

Real and monetary sectors of the economy
Functions of money
Gresham's law
Fully backed, fractionally backed, and fiat money
The banking system and the central bank (the Federal Reserve System)
Creation and destruction of deposit money
Reserve ratio, required reserves, and excess reserves
Demand and time deposits
The money supply
Near money and money substitutes

DISCUSSION QUESTIONS

1. "For the love of money is the root of all evil." (I Timothy 6:10). If a nation were to become a theocracy in which money was illegal, would you expect the level of national income to be affected? How about the productivity of labor?

2. Consider each of the following with respect to its potential use as a medium of exchange, a store of value, and a unit of account. Which would you think might be regarded as money?
   a. A $100 Federal Reserve note
   b. An American Express credit card
   c. A painting by Picasso
   d. A NOW account
   e. A U.S. Treasury bill payable in three months
   f. A savings account at a savings and loan association in Las Vegas, Nevada

   g. One share of General Motors stock

   h. A lifetime pass to Pittsburgh Steelers football games

3. When the Austrian government minted a new 1,000-shilling gold coin, worth $59 at face value, the 1-inch diameter coin came into great demand among jewelers and coin collectors. By law, the number of such coins to be minted each year is limited. Lines of people eager to get the coins formed outside the government mint and local banks.

   "There is exceptional interest in the new coin," said a Viennese banker. "It's a numismatic hit and a financial success." However, it has disappeared from circulation. Explain why.

4. A Canadian who receives a U.S. coin has the option of spending it at face value or taking it to the bank and converting it to Canadian money at the going rate of exchange. When the rate of exchange was near par, so that $1 Canadian was within plus or minus $.03 of $1 American, American and Canadian coins circulated side by side, exchanged at their face values. Use Gresham's law to predict which coinage disappeared from circulation in Canada when the Canadian dollar fell to $.75 American. Why did a $.03 differential not produce this result?

5. Some years ago a strike closed all banks in Ireland for several months. What do you think happened during that period?

6. During hyperinflations in several foreign countries after World War II, American cigarettes were sometimes used in place of money. What made them suitable?

7. Assume that on January 1, 1989 a couple had $25,000, which they wished to hold for use 1 year later. Calculate, using library sources, which of the following would have been the best store of value over that period. Will the best store of value over that period necessarily be the best over the next 24 months?

   a. The dollar

   b. Stocks whose prices moved with the Dow-Jones industrial average

   c. A Georgia Power 11¾ percent 2005 bond

   d. Gold

   e. Silver

8. If all depositors tried to turn their deposits into cash at once, they would find that there are not sufficient reserves in the system to allow all of them to do this at the same time. Why then do we not still have panicky runs on the banks? Would a 100 percent reserve requirement be safer? What effect would such a reserve requirement have on the banking system's ability to create money? Would it preclude any possibility of a panic?

9. What would be the effect on the money supply of each of the following?

   a. Declining public confidence in the banks

   b. A desire on the part of banks to increase their levels of excess reserves

   c. Monopolizing of the banking system into a single superbank

   d. Increased use of credit cards

   e. Transfer of deposits from banks to new nonbank institutions

Chapter 32

The Role of Money in Macroeconomics

At one time or another, most of us have known the surprise of opening our wallet and discovering that we had either more or less money than we thought. There can be pleasure in deciding how to spend an unexpected windfall in the first case, just as there can be pain in deciding what expenditure to eliminate in the second.

What determines how much money people hold in their wallets and in the bank? What happens when people discover that they are holding more, or less, money than they wish to? These turn out to be key questions for our study of the influence of money on output and prices.

 ## Financial Assets

At any one moment, households have a stock of wealth that they hold in many forms. Some of it is money in the bank or in the wallet; some is in short-term securities, such as treasury bills; some is in long-term bonds; and some is in real capital, which may be held directly (in the form of family businesses) or indirectly (in the form of shares of stock that indicate ownership of a corporation's assets).

Kinds of Assets

These ways of holding wealth may be grouped into three main categories: (1) assets that serve as a medium of exchange, that is, paper money, coins, and bank deposits on which checks may be drawn; (2) financial assets, such as bonds earning a fixed rate of interest, that will yield a fixed money value at some future date (called the *maturity date*) and that can usually be sold before maturity for a price that fluctuates on the open market; and (3) claims (i.e., stocks or shares) on capital, such as factories and machines.

To simplify our discussion, we will regroup wealth into just two categories, which we will call *money* and *bonds*. By *money* we mean M1, as defined in Chapter 31, and by *bonds* we mean all other forms of wealth. Money therefore includes currency, demand deposits, and checkable savings deposits. Bonds include all other interest-earning financial assets *plus* claims in real capital.[1]

---

[1] This simplification can take us quite a long way. However, for some problems it is necessary to treat debt and equity as distinct assets so that three categories—money, debt (bonds), and equity stocks—are used.

The Rate of Interest and the Price of Bonds

A bond is a promise by the issuer to pay a stated sum of money as interest each year and to repay the face value of the bond at some future maturity date, often many years distant. The time until the maturity date is called the **term to maturity,** often simply the **term,** of the bond. Some bonds, called *perpetuities,* pay interest forever and never repay the principal.

The **present value (PV)** of a bond, or of any asset, refers to the value now of the future payment, or payments, to which the asset represents a claim. The present value is thus the amount that someone would be willing to pay now to secure the right to the future stream of payments conferred by ownership of the asset. This amount depends critically on the rate of interest, as it is most easily seen in the case of a perpetuity. Assume that such a bond will pay $100 per year to its holder. The *present value* of the bond depends on how much $100 per year is worth, and this, in turn, depends on the rate of interest.

A bond that will produce a stream of income of $100 per year forever is worth $1,000 at 10 percent interest, because $1,000 invested at 10 percent per year will yield $100 interest per year forever. However, the same bond is worth $2,000 when the interest rate is 5 percent per year, because it takes $2,000 invested at 5 percent per year to yield $100 interest per year. The lower is the rate of interest obtainable on the market, the more valuable is a bond paying a fixed amount of interest.

Similar relations apply to bonds that are not perpetuities, though the calculation of present value must allow for the lump-sum repayment of principal at maturity. (Further details on the calculation of present value are given in Chapter 18, pages 367–369.)

The present value of any asset that yields a stream of money over time is negatively related to the interest rate.

This proposition has two important implications: (1) If the rate of interest falls, the value of an asset producing a given income stream will rise; and (2) a rise in the market price of an asset producing a given income is equivalent to a decrease in the rate of interest earned by the asset. Thus, a promise to pay $100.00 one year from now is worth $92.59 when the interest rate is 8 percent and only $89.29 when the interest rate is 12 percent: $92.59 at 8 percent interest ($92.59 x 1.08) and $89.29 at 12 percent interest ($89.29 x 1.12) are both worth $100.00 in one year's time.

The present value of bonds that are not perpetuities becomes increasingly dominated by the fixed redemption value as the maturity date approaches. For example, a rise in the interest rate from 8 to 12 percent will lower the value of $100 payable in one year's time by 3.6 percent, but it will lower the value of $100 payable in 10 years' time by 37.9 percent.[2]

The sooner is the maturity date of a bond, the less the bond's value will change with a change in the rate of interest.

Consider an extreme case. The present value of a bond that is redeemable for $1,000 in one week's time will be very close to $1,000 no matter what the interest rate is. Thus, its value will not change much, even if the rate of interest leaps from 5 percent to 10 percent during that week. This is relevant for the assets that we included in our definition of money that earn interest: They are so short-term that their values remain unchanged when the interest rate changes.

The discussion should make it clear that the present value of an asset determines its market price. If the market price of any asset is greater than the present value of the income stream that it produces, no one will want to buy it and the market price will fall. If the market value is below its present value, there will be a rush to buy it and the market price will rise. These facts lead to the following conclusion:

In a free market the equilibrium price of any asset will be the present value of the income stream that it produces.

---

[2] The example assumes annual compounding. The first case is calculated from the numbers of the previous example: (92.58 − 89.29)/92.58. The 10-year case uses the formula

Present value = Principal / $(1 + r)^n$

which gives $46.30 with 8 percent and $28.75 with 12 percent. The percentage fall in value is thus (46.30 − 28.75)/46.30 = 0.379.

Supply of Money and Demand for Money

The Supply of Money

The money supply is a stock. (It is so many billions of dollars, *not* a flow of so much per unit of time.) In January 1989, M1 was approximately $760 billion.

We saw in Chapter 31 that deposit money is created by the commercial banking system, but only within limits set by their reserves. Since, as we shall see in Chapter 33, the reserves of the commercial banking system are under the control of the Fed, ultimate control of the money supply is also in the hands of the Fed. In this chapter we simply assume that the money supply can be precisely controlled by the Fed.

The Demand for Money

The amount of wealth that everyone in the economy wishes to hold in the form of money balances is called the **demand for money.** Because households are choosing how to divide their given stock of wealth between money and bonds, it follows that, if we know the demand for money, we also know the demand for bonds. With *a given level of wealth,* a rise in the demand for money necessarily implies a fall in the demand for bonds; if people wish to hold $1 billion more money, they must wish to hold $1 billion less of bonds. It also follows that, if households are in equilibrium with respect to their money holdings, they are in equilibrium with respect to their bond holdings.

When we say that on January 1, 1989, the demand for money was $784 billion, we mean that on that date the public wished to hold money balances that totalled $784 billion, but why do firms and households wish to hold money balances at all? There is a cost to holding any money balance. The money could have been used to purchase interest-earning bonds.[3]

The opportunity cost of holding any money balance is the extra interest that could have been earned if the money had been used instead to purchase interest-earning bonds.

In terms of the distinction between the real and nominal rates of interest that were noted in Chapter 24 (see pages 505–506), it is the nominal rate of interest that is the opportunity cost of holding money. However, since in this chapter we assume that there is no ongoing inflation, the nominal and real rates of interest are the same; both are measured by the market rate of interest.

Clearly, money will be held only when it provides services that are valued at least as highly as the opportunity cost of holding it. Three important services that are provided by money balances give rise to the transactions, precautionary, and speculative motives for holding money. We examine each of these motives in detail.

The Transactions Motive

Most transactions require money. Money passes from households to firms to pay for the goods and services produced by firms; money passes from firms to households to pay for the factor services supplied by households to firms. Money balances that are held to finance such flows are called **transactions balances.**

In an imaginary world in which the receipts and disbursements of households and firms are perfectly synchronized, it would be unnecessary to hold transactions balances. If every time a household spent $10 it received $10 as part payment of its income, no transactions balances would be needed. In the real world, however, receipts and disbursements are not perfectly synchronized.

Consider, for example, the balances that are held because of wage payments. Suppose, for purposes of illustration, that firms pay wages every Friday and that households spend all their wages on the purchase of goods and services, with the expenditure spread out evenly over the week. Thus, on Friday morning

[3] As we saw in Chapter 31 (see especially Table 31-10), M1 includes some interest-bearing checkable deposits. This complicates but does not fundamentally alter the analysis of the demand for money. In particular, it means that the opportunity cost of holding those interest-bearing components of M1 is not the *level* of interest rates paid on bonds but the *difference* between that rate and the rate paid on M1 assets. For the sake of simplicity, we treat the interest rate on all M1 assets as being zero, so that we can identify the *level* of the interest rate on bonds as the opportunity cost of money.

firms must hold balances equal to the weekly wage bill; on Friday afternoon households will hold these balances.

Over the week, households' balances will be drawn down as a result of purchasing goods and services. Over the same period, the balances held by firms will build up as a result of selling goods and services until, on the following Friday morning, firms will again have amassed balances equal to the wage bill that must be met on that day.

The transactions motive arises because of the nonsynchronization of payments and receipts.

What determines the size of the transactions balances to be held? It is clear that in our example total transactions balances vary with the value of the wage bill. If the wage bill doubles for any reason, the transactions balances held by firms and households on this account will also double. As it is with wages, so it is with all other transactions: The size of the balances held is positively related to the value of the transactions.

Next, we ask how the total value of transactions is related to national income. Because of the "double counting" problem, which we first discussed in Chapter 25, the value of all transactions exceeds the value of the economy's final output. When the flour mill buys wheat from the farmer and when the baker buys flour from the flour mill, both are transactions against which money balances must be held, although only the value added at each stage is part of national income.

We now make an added assumption that there is a stable, positive relationship between transactions and national income. A rise in national income also leads to a rise in the total value of all transactions and hence to an associated rise in the demand for transactions balances. This allows us to relate transactions balances to national income. [40]

The larger is the value of national income, the larger is the value of transactions balances that will be held.

The Precautionary Motive

Many goods and services are sold on credit. The seller can never be certain when payment will be made, and the buyer can never be certain of the day of delivery and thus when payment will fall due. As a precaution against cash crises, when receipts are abnormally low or disbursements are abnormally high, firms and households carry money balances. These are called **precautionary balances;** they provide a cushion against uncertainty about the timing of cash flows. The larger such balances are, the greater is the protection against running out of money because of temporary fluctuations in cash flows.

How serious the risk of a cash crisis is depends on the penalties for being caught without sufficient money balances. A firm is unlikely to be pushed into insolvency, but it may incur considerable costs if it is forced to borrow money at high interest rates in order to meet a temporary cash crisis.

The precautionary motive arises because households and firms are uncertain about the degree to which payments and receipts will be synchronized.

The protection provided by a given quantity of precautionary balances depends on the volume of payments and receipts. A $100 precautionary balance provides a large cushion for a household whose volume of payments per month is $800 and a small cushion for a firm whose monthly volume is $25,000. Fluctuations of the sort that create the need for precautionary balances tend to vary directly with the size of the firm's cash flow. To provide the same degree of protection as the value of transactions rises, more money is necessary.[4]

The precautionary motive, like the transactions motive, causes the demand for money to vary positively with the money value of national income.

The Speculative Motive

Firms and households hold some money in order to provide a hedge against the uncertainty inherent in fluctuating prices of other financial assets. Money balances held for this purpose are called **speculative balances.** This motive was first analyzed by Keynes,

---

[4] Institutional arrangements affect precautionary demands. In the past, for example, a traveler would have carried a substantial precautionary balance in cash, but today a credit card covers most unforeseen expenses that may arise while traveling.

and the classic modern analysis was made by Professor James Tobin, the 1981 Nobel Laureate in Economics.

When a household or firm holds money balances, it foregoes the extra interest income that it could earn if it held bonds instead. However, market interest rates fluctuate, and so do the market prices of existing bonds (since their present values depend on the interest rate). Because their prices fluctuate, bonds are a risky asset. Many households and firms do not like risk; they are said to be *risk averse*.

In choosing between holding money or holding bonds, wealth holders must balance the extra interest income that they could earn by holding bonds against the risk that bonds carry. At one extreme, if a household or a firm holds all its wealth in the form of bonds, it earns extra interest on its entire wealth, but it also exposes its entire wealth to the risk of changes in the price of bonds. At the other extreme, if the household or firm holds all its wealth in the form of money, it earns less interest income, but it does not face the risk of unexpected changes in the price of bonds. Wealth holders usually do not take either extreme position. They hold part of their wealth as money and part of it as bonds; that is, they *diversify* their holdings.

Influence of wealth.   Suppose that Ms. B. Smart elects to diversify her wealth by holding 5 percent of her wealth in money and the other 95 percent in bonds. If her wealth is $50,000, her demand for money will be $2,500. If her wealth increases to $60,000, her demand for money will rise to $3,000. Thus,

The speculative motive means that the demand for money varies positively with wealth.

Although an individual's wealth may rise or fall rapidly, the total wealth of a society changes only slowly. For the analysis of short-term fluctuations in national income, the effects of changes in wealth are fairly small, and we shall ignore them for the present. Over the long term, however, variations in wealth can have a major effect on the demand for money.

Influence of interest rates.   Wealth that is held in cash earns no interest; hence, the reduction in risk involved in holding more money carries a cost in terms of foregone interest earnings. The speculative motive leads households and firms to add to their money

holdings until the reduction in risk obtained by the last dollar added is just balanced (in each wealth holder's view) by the cost in terms of the interest foregone on that dollar.

When the rate of interest falls, the opportunity cost of holding money falls. This leads to more money being held both for the precautionary motive (to reduce risks caused by uncertainty about the flows of payments and receipts) and for the speculative motive (to reduce risks associated with fluctuations in the market price of bonds). When the rate of interest rises, the cost of holding money rises. This leads to less money being held for speculative and precautionary motives.

The precautionary and speculative motives both cause the demand for money to be negatively related to the rate of interest.

Real and Nominal Money Balances

In referring to the demand for money, it is important to distinguish real from nominal values. Real values are measured in purchasing power units; nominal values are measured in money units.

First, consider the demand for money in real terms. This means the number of units of purchasing power that the public wishes to hold in the form of money balances. In an imaginary one-product wheat economy, this would be measured by the number of bushels of wheat that could be purchased with the money balances held. In a more complex economy, it could be measured in terms of the number of "baskets of goods" represented by a price index such as the CPI that could be purchased with the money balances held. When we speak of the demand for money in real terms, we speak of the amount demanded in constant dollars:

The real demand for money is the nominal quantity demanded divided by an index of the price level.

For example, in the decade from 1979 to 1989, the nominal quantity of M1 balances held in the United States doubled, rising from $380 billion to $760 billion. Over the same period, however, the price level, as measured by the CPI, rose by roughly 80 percent. This tells us that the real quantity of M1 held rose only slightly, from $380 billion to $422 billion, measured in constant 1979 dollars.

From real demand to nominal demand.   Our discussion has identified the determinants of the demand for real money balances as real national income, real wealth, and the interest rate. Notice that the real demand for money depends, among other things, on real national income; it is not influenced by the price level.

Now suppose that, with the interest rate, real wealth, and real national income being held constant, the price level doubles. Since the demand for real money balances will be unchanged, the demand for nominal balances must double. If the public previously demanded $300 billion in nominal money balances, it will now demand $600 billion. This keeps the real demand unchanged at $600/2 = $300 billion. The money balances of $600 billion at the new, higher price level represents exactly the same purchasing power as did $300 billion at the old price level.

Other things being equal, the nominal demand for money balances varies in proportion to the price level; when the price level doubles, desired nominal money balances also double.

This is a central proposition of the quantity theory of money, which is discussed further in Box 32-1.

Total Demand for Money: Recapitulation

Figure 32-1 summarizes the influences of national income, the rate of interest, and the price level, the three variables that account for most of the short-term variations in the nominal quantity of money demanded. The function relating money demanded to the rate of interest is often called the **liquidity preference (*LP*) function.**

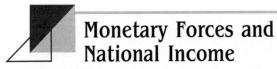

Monetary Forces and National Income

We are now in a position to examine the relationship between monetary forces, on the one hand, and the equilibrium values of national income and the price level, on the other. The first step in explaining this relationship is a new one: the link between monetary equilibrium and aggregate demand. The second is familiar from earlier chapters: the effects of shifts in aggregate demand on equilibrium values of national income and the price level.

Monetary Equilibrium and Aggregate Demand

Monetary equilibrium occurs when the demand for money equals the supply of money. In Chapter 4 we saw that, in a competitive market for some commodity such as carrots, the price will adjust so as to ensure equilibrium. The rate of interest does the same job with respect to money demand and money supply.

The Liquidity Preference Theory of Interest

Figure 32-2 shows how the interest rate will change in order to equate the demand for money with its supply. When a single household or a firm finds that it has less money than it wishes to hold, it can sell some bonds and add the proceeds to its money holdings. This transaction simply redistributes given supplies of bonds and money among individuals; it does not change the total supply of either money or bonds.

Now assume that all of the firms and households in the economy have an excess demand for money balances. They all try to sell bonds to add to their money balances, but what one person can do, all persons cannot do. At any moment the economy's total supply of money and bonds is fixed; there is just so much money and there are just so many bonds in existence. If everyone tries to sell bonds, there will be no one to buy them. Instead, the price of bonds will fall.

We saw that a fall in the price of bonds means a rise in the rate of interest. As the interest rate rises, people economize on money balances, because the opportunity cost of holding such balances is rising. This is what we saw in Figure 32-1(i), where the quantity of money demanded falls along the liquidity preference curve in response to a rise in the rate of interest. Eventually, the interest rate will rise enough that people will no longer be trying to add to their

FIGURE 32-1 The Demand for Money as a Function of Interest Rates, Income, and the Price Level

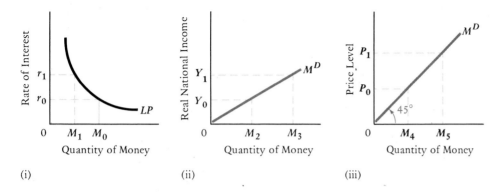

(i)   (ii)   (iii)

The quantity of money demanded varies negatively with the rate of interest and positively with both national income and the price level. In (i) the demand for money is shown varying negatively with the interest rate along the liquidity preference function. When the interest rate rises from r_0 to r_1, households and firms reduce the quantity of money demanded from M_0 to M_1.

In (ii) the demand for money is shown varying positively with national income. When national income rises from Y_0 to Y_1, households and firms increase the quantity of money demanded from M_2 to M_3.

In (iii) the demand for money is shown varying in proportion to the price level. When the price level doubles from P_0 to P_1, households and firms double the quantity of money demanded from M_4 to M_5.

money balances by selling bonds. At that point, there is no longer an excess supply of bonds, and the interest rate will stop rising. The demand for money again equals the supply.

Assume next that firms and households hold larger money balances than they would like. A single household or firm would purchase bonds with its excess balances, achieving monetary equilibrium by reducing its money holdings and by increasing its bond holdings. However, just as in the previous example, what one household or firm can do, all cannot do. At any moment the total quantity of bonds is fixed, so everyone cannot simultaneously add to personal bond holdings. When all households enter the bond market and try to purchase bonds with unwanted money balances, they bid up the price of existing bonds, and the interest rate falls. Hence, households and firms become willing to hold larger quantities of money; that is, the quantity of money demanded increases along the liquidity preference curve in response to a fall in the rate of interest. The

rise in the price of bonds continues until firms and households stop trying to convert bonds into money. In other words, it continues until everyone is content to hold the existing supply of money and bonds.

Monetary equilibrium occurs when the rate of interest is such that the existing supply of money is willingly held, that is, when the demand for money equals its supply.

The determination of the interest rate, depicted in Figure 32-2, is often described as the *liquidity preference theory* of interest and sometimes as the *portfolio balance theory*.

As we shall see, a shift either in the demand for money or in the supply of money will lead to a change in the interest rate. However, as we saw in Chapter 29, desired aggregate expenditure is sensitive to changes in the interest rate. Here, then, is a link between monetary factors and real expenditure flows.

BOX 32-1

The Quantity Theory of Money and the Velocity of Circulation

The quantity theory of money can be set out in terms of four equations. Equation 1 states that the demand for money balances depends on the value of transactions as measured by nominal income, which is real income multiplied by the price level, PY:

$$M^D = kPY \qquad [1]$$

Equation 2 states that the supply of money, M, is set by the central bank:

$$M^S = M \qquad [2]$$

Equation 3 states the equilibrium condition that the demand for money must equal the supply:

$$M^D = M^S \qquad [3]$$

Substitution produces a relationship among P, M, and Y:

$$M = kPY \qquad [4]$$

The original classical quantity theory assumes that k is a constant given by the transactions demand for money and that Y is constant because full employment is maintained. Thus, increases or decreases in the money supply lead to proportional increases or decreases in prices.

Often the quantity theory is presented by using the concept of the *velocity of circulation, V.* The **velocity of circulation** is defined as national income divided by the quantity of money:

$$V = PY/M \qquad [5]$$

Rearranging this gives us the *equation of exchange:*

$$MV = PY \qquad [6]$$

Velocity may be interpreted as showing the average amount of "work" done by a unit of money. Thus, if annual national income is \$400 billion and the stock of money is \$100 billion, on average, each dollar's worth of money is used four times to create the values added that compose the national income.

There is a simple relationship between k and V. One is the reciprocal of the other, as may be seen immediately by comparing Equations 4 and 6. Thus, it makes no difference whether we choose to work with k or V. Further, if k is assumed to be constant, this implies that V must also be treated as being constant.

An example may help to illustrate the interpretation of each. Assume that the stock of money that people wish to hold is equal to one-fifth of the value of total transactions. Thus, k is 0.2 and V, the reciprocal of k, is 5. This indicates that, if the money supply is to be one-fifth of the value of annual transactions, each dollar must be "used" on average five times.

Modern versions of the quantity theory do not assume that k is exogenously fixed. However, they do argue that k will not change in response to a change in the quantity of money.

The Transmission Mechanism

The mechanism by which changes in the demand for and the supply of money affect aggregate demand is called the **transmission mechanism.** The transmission mechanism operates in three stages: The first is the link between monetary equilibrium and the interest rate; the second is the link between the interest rate and investment expenditure; and the third is the link between investment expenditure and aggregate demand.

From monetary disturbances to changes in the interest rate.   The interest rate will change if the supply of money changes or if there is a shift in the demand

FIGURE 32-2   The Liquidity Preference Theory of Interest

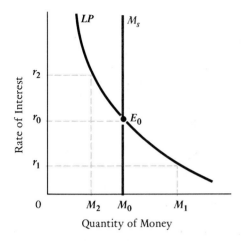

The interest rate rises when there is an excess demand for money and falls when there is an excess supply of money. The fixed quantity of money, M_0, is shown by the completely inelastic supply curve M_S. The demand for money is LP; its negative slope indicates that a fall in the rate of interest causes the quantity of money demanded to increase. Equilibrium is at E_0, with a rate of interest of r_0.

If the interest rate is r_1, there will be an excess demand for money of M_0M_1. Bonds will be offered for sale in an attempt to increase money holdings. This will force the rate of interest up to r_0 (the price of bonds falls), at which point the quantity of money demanded is equal to the fixed available quantity of M_0. If the interest rate is r_2, there will be an excess supply of money M_2M_0. Bonds will be demanded in return for excess money balances. This will force the rate of interest down to r_0 (the price of bonds rises), at which point the quantity of money demanded has risen to equal the fixed supply of M_0.

for money. For example, as shown in Figure 32-3(i), an increase in the supply of money, with an unchanged liquidity preference function, will give rise to an excess supply of money at the original interest rate. As we have seen, an excess supply of money will cause the interest rate to fall. As also shown in part (i) of Figure 32-3, a decrease in the supply of money will cause the interest rate to rise.

As shown in Figure 32-3(ii), an increase in the demand for money, with an unchanged supply of

money, will give rise to an excess demand for money at the original interest rate and will cause the interest rate to rise. As also shown in part (ii) of Figure 32-3, a decrease in the demand for money will cause the interest rate to fall.

Monetary disturbances, which can arise due to changes in either the demand for or the supply of money, cause changes in the interest rate.

From changes in the interest rate to shifts in aggregate expenditure. The second link in the transmission mechanism relates interest rates to expenditure. We saw in Chapter 29 that investment, which includes expenditure on inventory accumulation, residential construction, and business fixed investment, responds to changes in the rate of interest. Other things being equal, a decrease in the rate of interest makes borrowing cheaper and generates new investment expenditure.[5] This negative relationship between investment and the rate of interest is called the **marginal efficiency of investment (*MEI*) function**.

The first two links in the transmission mechanism are shown in Figure 32-4. We concentrate for the moment on changes in the money supply, although, as we have seen already, the process can also be set in motion by changes in the demand for money. In part (i) we see that a change in the money supply causes the rate of interest to change in the opposite direction. In part (ii) we see that a change in the interest rate causes the level of investment expenditure to change in the opposite direction. Therefore, changes in the money supply cause investment expenditure to change in the same direction.

An increase in the money supply leads to a fall in the interest rate and an increase in investment expenditure. A decrease in the money supply leads to a rise in the interest rate and a decrease in investment expenditure.

From shifts in aggregate expenditure to shifts in aggregate demand. Now we are back on familiar ground. In Chapter 27 we saw that a shift in the aggregate

---

[5] In Chapter 29 we saw that purchases of durable consumer goods also respond to changes in interest rates. In this chapter we concentrate on investment expenditure, which may be taken to stand for *all* interest sensitive expenditure.

FIGURE 32-3   Monetary Disturbances and Interest Rate Changes

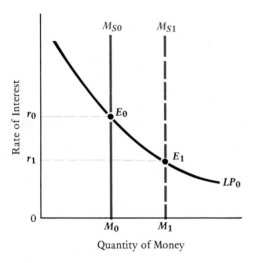

(i) A change in the supply of money

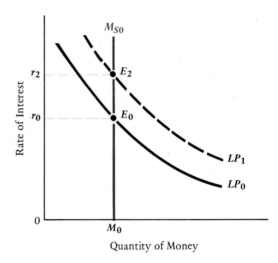

(ii) A change in the demand for money

Shifts in the supply of money or in the demand for money cause the equilibrium interest rate to change. In both parts of the figure, the money supply is shown by the vertical curve M_{S0}, and the demand for money is shown by the negatively shaped curve LP_0. The initial equilibrium is at E_0, with corresponding interest rate r_0.

In (i) an increase in the money supply causes the money supply curve to shift to the right from M_{S0} to M_{S1}. The new equilibrium is at E_1, where the interest rate is r_1, less than r_0. Starting at E_1 with M_{S1} and r_1, it can be seen that a decrease in the money supply to M_{S0} leads to an increase in the interest rate from r_1 to r_0.

In (ii) an increase in the demand for money causes the LP curve to shift to the right from LP_0 to LP_1. The new equilibrium occurs at E_2, and the new equilibrium interest rate is r_2, greater than r_0. Starting at E_2, we see that a decrease in the demand for money from LP_1 to LP_0 leads to a decrease in the interest rate from r_2 to r_0.

expenditure curve can lead to a shift in the AD curve. This is shown again in Figure 32-5.

A change in the money supply, by causing a change in desired investment expenditure and hence a shift in the AE curve, causes the AD curve to shift. An increase in the money supply causes an increase in investment expenditure and therefore an increase in aggregate demand. A decrease in the money supply causes a decrease in investment expenditure and therefore a decrease in aggregate demand.

The transmission mechanism connects monetary forces and real expenditure flows. It works from a change in the demand for or the supply of money to a change in bond prices and interest rates, to changes in investment expenditure, to a shift in the aggregate demand curve.

This is illustrated in Figure 32-6 for the case of an expansionary monetary shock, that is, a shift in money demand or money supply that tends to increase aggregate demand.

Aggregate Demand, the Price Level, and National Income

We have just seen that a change in the money supply shifts the aggregate demand curve. If we want to

---

FIGURE 32-4   The Effects of Changes in the Money Supply on Investment Expenditure

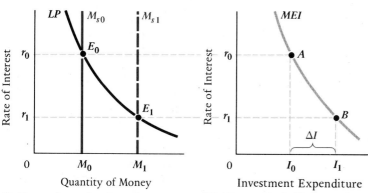

(i) Money demand and supply

(ii) The marginal efficiency of investment

Increases in the money supply reduce the rate of interest and increase desired investment expenditure. Equilibrium is at E_0, with a quantity of money of M_0 (shown by the inelastic money supply curve M_{s0}), an interest rate of r_0, and an investment expenditure of I_0 (point A). The Fed then increases the money supply to M_1 (shown by the money supply curve M_{s1}). This lowers the rate of interest to r_1 and increases investment expenditure by ΔI to I_1 (point B). A reduction in the money supply from M_1 to M_0 raises interest rates from r_1 to r_0 and lowers investment expenditure by ΔI, from I_1 to I_0.

---

know what it does to real national income and to the price level, we need to know the slope of the aggregate supply curve. This step, which is familiar from earlier chapters, is recalled in Figure 32-7.[6]

The key result is that the increase in equilibrium real income is less than the horizontal shift in the AD curve. This is because part of this shift is dissipated by a rise in the price level: Because the AD curve is negatively sloped, the rise in the price level means that the rise in real output is smaller than the horizontal shift of the AD curve.[7]

The Slope of the *AD* Curve.   We can now use the transmission mechanism to explain the negative slope of the AD curve, that is, to explain why equilibrium national income is negatively related to the price level. In Chapter 27, when we explained the

[6] Since the demand for money, in general, will depend on the level of national income, as shown in Figure 32-1(ii), our analysis at this stage is incomplete. The induced change in equilibrium national income will lead to a shift in the liquidity preference function in Figure 32-2. For the sake of simplicity, we have assumed in the text that the demand for money function does not shift in response to a change in national income. The Appendix to Chapter 38 presents a formal analysis in which this effect is allowed for and in which equilibrium levels of the interest rate and national income are determined simultaneously.

[7] If you draw the diagram, you will see that, if the AD curve were vertical, the rise in the price level would not diminish the effect on real output; real output would rise by an amount equal to the horizontal shift of the AD curve.

negative slope of the AD curve, we mentioned three reasons: the wealth (or real balance) effect, the substitution of domestic for foreign goods, and the indirect effect operating through interest rates. Up until now we have focused on the wealth effect because it was simple and direct. Now that we have developed a theory of money and interest rates, we are able to understand the indirect effect that works through the transmission mechanism.

The essential feature of this indirect effect is that a rise in the price level raises the money value of transactions. This leads to an increased demand for money, which brings the transmission mechanism into play. People try to sell bonds to add to their money balances, but, collectively, all they succeed in doing is forcing up the interest rate. The rise in the interest rate reduces investment expenditure and so reduces equilibrium national income.

This effect is important because, empirically, the interest rate is the most important link between monetary factors and real expenditure flows. Box 32-2 is for readers who wish to study the third reason for the negative slope of the AD curve in more detail.

The Monetary Adjustment Mechanism

Suppose that an economy, in equilibrium with real national income equal to its potential level, were disturbed by an increase in the money supply. Since

FIGURE 32-5   The Effects of Changes in the Money Supply on Aggregate Demand

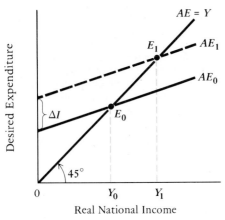

(i) Shift in aggregate expenditure

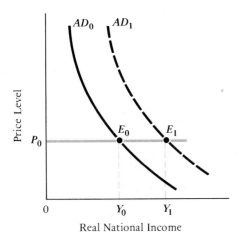

(ii) Shift in aggregate demand

Changes in the money supply cause shifts in the aggregate expenditure and aggregate demand functions. In Figure 32-4 an increase in the money supply increased desired investment expenditure by ΔI. In (i) the aggregate expenditure function shifts up by ΔI (which is the same as ΔI in Figure 32-4), from AE_0 to AE_1. At the fixed price level P_0, equilibrium income rises from Y_0 to Y_1, as shown by the horizontal shift in the aggregate demand curve from AD_0 to AD_1 in (ii).

When the supply of money falls (from M_{S1} to M_{S0} in Figure 32-4), investment falls by ΔI, thereby shifting aggregate expenditure from AE_1 to AE_0. At the fixed price level P_0, this reduces equilibrium income from Y_1 to Y_0.

FIGURE 32-6   Transmission Mechanism for an Expansionary Monetary Shock

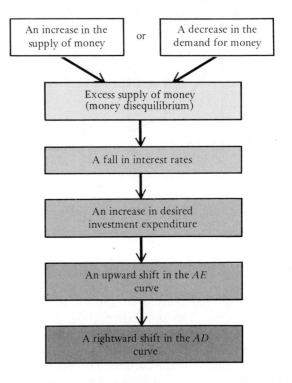

An increase in the supply of money or a decrease in the demand for money leads to an increase in aggregate demand. The excess supply of money following an expansionary monetary disturbance leads to a fall in the interest rate and an increase in investment. This causes an upward shift in the AE curve and thus a rightward shift in the AD curve.

real national income would increase, there would be an inflationary gap, as shown in Figure 32-8(i). Let us now examine the mechanism by which such an inflationary gap is eliminated. This involves an important but subtle implication of the theory.

A sufficiently large rise in the price level will eliminate any inflationary gap, provided the nominal money supply remains constant.

Operation of the monetary adjustment mechanism.   Because it causes excess demand in factor markets, the inflationary gap will cause factor prices to rise. This

**FIGURE 32-7   The Effects of Changes in the
Money Supply**

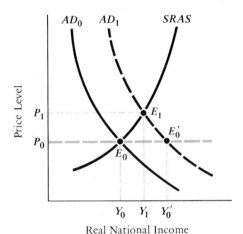

A change in the money supply leads to a change in
national income that is smaller than the horizontal
shift in the *AD* curve. An increase in the money supply causes the *AD* curve to shift to the right, from AD_0
to AD_1. With the price level being held constant,
national income would rise from Y_0 to Y_0'. With the
upward-sloping *SRAS* curve, income only rises to Y_1
while the price level rises as well—to P_1.

will shift the *SRAS* curve up and take the price level
with it. This raises the money value of transactions,
and the resulting increase in the demand for money
raises interest rates. Hence, at any level of real income, desired real expenditure falls. The fall in real
expenditure as the price level rises is shown by a
movement upward to the left *along* the *AD* curve.
This reduces the inflationary gap. When the price
level has risen enough, the inflationary gap disappears and the price level stops rising.

This mechanism, illustrated in Figure 32-8(ii),
may be called the *monetary adjustment mechanism*. It
works through the transmission mechanism.

**The monetary adjustment mechanism will
eliminate any inflationary gap, provided that
the nominal money supply is held constant.**

Thus, inflationary gaps tend to be self-correcting
as long as the money supply does not increase. They

will cause the price level to increase, but the increase
set in motion a chain of events in the markets for
financial assets that will eventually remove the inflationary gap.

The self-correcting mechanism is the reason that
price levels and the money supply have been linked
for so long in economics. Many things can cause the
price level to rise for some time. Yet, whatever the
reason for the rise, unless the money supply is expanded, the increase in the price level sets up forces
that will remove the initial inflationary gap and so
bring demand inflation to a halt.

Frustration of the monetary adjustment mechanism.
The self-correcting mechanism for removing an inflationary gap can be frustrated indefinitely if the
money supply is increased at the same rate that prices
are rising. Say that the price level is rising by 10
percent per year under the pressure of a large inflationary gap. Demand for nominal money balances
will also be rising by about 10 percent per year. Now
suppose that the Fed increases the money supply by
10 percent per year. No excess demand for money
will develop, since the extra money needed to meet
the rising demand will be forthcoming. The real
interest rate will not rise, and the inflationary gap
will not be reduced. This process is analyzed in Figure 32-9.

**If the money supply increases at the same rate
as the price level rises, the real money supply
and hence the real interest rate will remain constant, and the monetary adjustment mechanism
will be frustrated.**

An inflation is said to be *validated* when the money
supply is increased as fast as the price level, so that
the monetary adjustment mechanism is frustrated. A
validated inflation can go on indefinitely, although,
as we shall see in Chapter 34, possibly not at a constant rate.

A recessionary gap. In principle, the monetary adjustment mechanism also will operate to eliminate a
recessionary gap. If the recessionary gap led to a fall
in factor prices, the *SRAS* curve would shift to the
right, causing the price level to fall and national income to rise. However, as we saw in Chapter 28,
many economists argue that wages and other factor
costs are slow to fall in the face of a recessionary

BOX 32-2

The Slope of the Aggregate Demand Curve

The *AD* curve relates the price level to the equilibrium level of real national income. Its negative slope means that the higher is the price level, the lower is the equilibrium national income. The main reason for this negative slope is found in the transmission mechanism.

Let us look at this process in detail. Although the argument contains nothing new, it does require that you follow carefully through several steps.

We start with an initial position, depicted in part (i) of the figure. The liquidity preference schedule is LP_0, and the money supply is M_S. Equilibrium is at E_0, with the interest rate at r_0. The *MEI* sched-ule, given in part (ii), shows that, at the rate of interest r_0, desired investment expenditure is I_0. In part (iii) the aggregate expenditure curve AE_0 is drawn for that level of investment (I_0). Equilibrium is at E_0 with a real national income of Y_0. Plotting Y_0 against the initial price level (P_0) yields point A on the aggregate demand curve in part (iv).

An increase in the price level to P_1 raises the money value of transactions and increases the quantity of money demanded at each possible value of the interest rate. As a result, the liquidity preference function shifts from LP_0 to LP_1. This raises interest rates to r_1 and lowers investment expenditure by

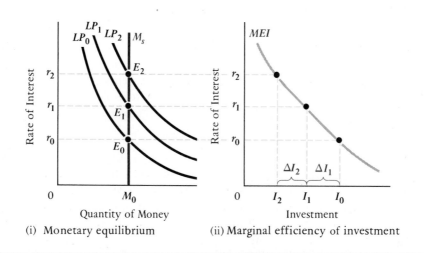

(i) Monetary equilibrium

(ii) Marginal efficiency of investment

gap. (This was referred to as the second asymmetry of aggregate supply; see the discussion surrounding Figure 28-3 on page 583.) In this circumstance the monetary adjustment mechanism will not be effective in causing national income to return quickly to its potential level. Thus, many economists argue that aggregate demand should be stimulated in the face of a recessionary gap, either through fiscal policy, which we studied in Chapter 30, or through monetary policy, which we shall study in the next chapter.

The Strength of Monetary Forces

How much will a given change in the money supply cause national income to increase? As can be seen in Figure 32-7, this will depend on both aggregate demand and aggregate supply.

The Role of Aggregate Demand

The size of the shift in the *AD* curve in response to an increase in the money supply depends on the size

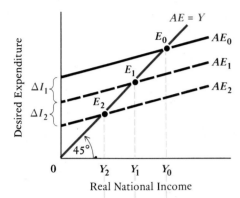

(iii) Equilibrium national income

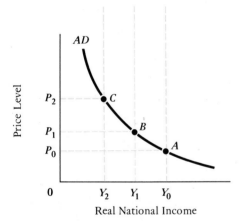

(iv) The aggregate demand curve

ΔI_1 to I_1. The fall in investment causes the AE curve in part (iii) to shift downward by an equal amount to AE_1. Equilibrium income falls to Y_1. Plotting Y_1 against P_1 produces point B on the AD curve in part (iv).

A further increase in the price level to P_2 shifts the liquidity preference function to LP_2, raises the interest rate to r_2, and lowers investment expenditure to I_2. The fall in investment shifts the AE curve in part (iii) to AE_2, and equilibrium income falls to Y_2. Plotting Y_2 against P_2 produces point C on the AD curve in part (iv).

The negative relationship between the price level and equilibrium real income shown by the AD curve occurs because, other things being equal, a rise in the price level raises the *demand for money*. Notice the qualification "other things being equal." It is important for this process that the nominal money *supply* remain constant. The transmission mechanism operates because the demand for money increases when the price level rises while the money supply remains constant. The attempt to add to money balances by selling bonds is what drives the interest rate up and reduces desired expenditure, thereby reducing equilibrium national income. (This argument is conducted in terms of the nominal supply of and demand for money. Arguing in terms of the real demand and supply of money leads to identical results.) [41]

of the increase in investment expenditure that is stimulated. This, in turn, depends on the strength of the two key linkages that make up what is called the *transmission mechanism*.

The first consideration is how much interest rates fall in response to the increase in the money supply. The more interest-sensitive is the demand for money, the less interest rates will have to fall to induce firms and households willingly to hold the increase in the money supply.

The second consideration is how much investment expenditure increases in response to the fall in interest rates. The more interest-sensitive is investment expenditure, the more it will increase in response to any given fall in the interest rate.

It follows that the size of the shift in aggregate demand in response to a change in the money supply depends on the shapes of the demand for money and marginal efficiency of investment curves. The influence of the shapes of the two curves is

FIGURE 32-8   The Monetary Adjustment Mechanism

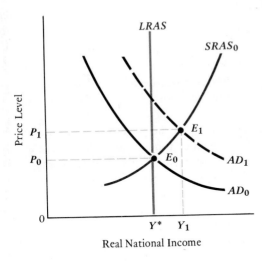

(i) Inflationary gap created

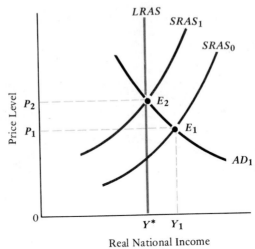

(ii) Inflationary gap eliminated

A rise in the price level will eliminate an inflationary gap. The economy is initially in long-run equilibrium at E_0, with price level P_0 and real income Y^*. In (i) some disturbance shifts the AD curve to the right, leading to equilibrium E_1, with a higher price level P_1 and an inflationary gap of Y^*Y_1.

E_1 is also shown in (ii). The inflationary gap causes wages to rise, shifting the $SRAS$ curve to the left so that the price level starts to rise. The monetary adjustment mechanism (working through a rising interest rate and falling investment) lowers aggregate expenditure so that the economy moves upward along the AD curve. Eventually, the inflationary gap is eliminated and equilibrium is reached at E_2, with income at Y^* and price level P_2.

FIGURE 32-9   Frustration of the Monetary Adjustment

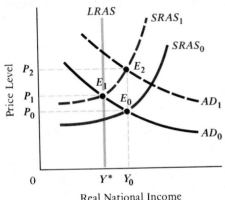

An inflationary gap can persist indefinitely if the money supply increases as fast as the price level. Suppose that the economy is at E_0, with income Y_0 and price level P_0. Since potential income is Y^*, there is an inflationary gap of Y^*Y_0. The price level now rises, which tends to shift the economy upward along any given AD curve, thereby tending to reduce the excess aggregate demand. However, the Fed increases the money supply, so that the AD curve shifts outward, thereby tending to increase excess aggregate demand. If the two forces just balance each other, by the time the price level has risen to P_2, the curve will have shifted to AD_1, leaving the inflationary gap unchanged, with equilibrium at E_2.

FIGURE 32-10   Two Views on the Strength of Monetary Changes

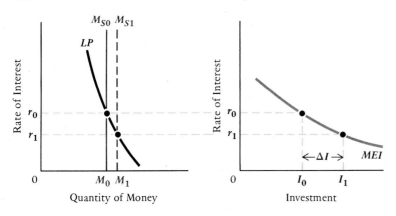

(i) Changes in the money supply effective

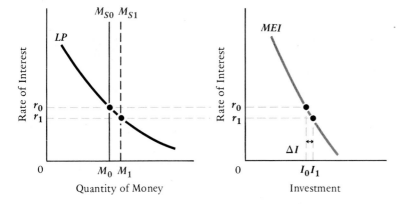

(ii) Changes in the money supply ineffective

The strength of the effect of a change in the money supply on investment and hence on aggregate demand depends on the interest elasticity of both the demand for money and desired investment expenditure. Initially, the money supply is M_{S0}, and the economy is in equilibrium, with an interest rate of r_0 and investment expenditure of I_0.

In both parts of the figure the central bank expands the money supply from M_{S0} to M_{S1}. The rate of interest thus falls from r_0 to r_1, as shown in each of the left panels. This causes an increase in investment expenditure of ΔI, from I_0 to I_1, as shown in each of the right panels.

In part (i) the demand for money is highly interest-inelastic, so the increase in the money supply leads to a large fall in the interest rate. Further, desired investment expenditure is highly interest-elastic, so the large fall in interest rates also leads to a large increase in investment expenditure. Hence, in this case the change in the money supply will be effective in stimulating aggregate demand.

In part (ii) the demand for money is interest-elastic, so the increase in the money supply leads only to a small fall in the interest rate. Further, desired investment expenditure is highly interest-inelastic, so the small fall in interest rates also leads only to a small increase in investment expenditure. Hence, in this case the change in the money supply will not be effective in stimulating aggregate demand.

shown in Figure 32-10 and may be summarized as follows:

1. **The steeper (the less interest-sensitive) is the LP function, the greater the effect a change in the money supply will have on interest rates.**
2. **The flatter (the more interest-sensitive) is the MEI function, the greater the effect a change in the interest rate will have on investment expenditure and hence on aggregate demand.**

The combination that produces the largest effect on aggregate demand for a given change in the money supply is a steep LP function and a flat MEI function. This combination is illustrated in Figure 32-10(i). It accords with the view, which we shall see later is often associated with so-called monetarists, that monetary policy is relatively effective as a means of influencing the economy. The combination that produces the smallest effect is a flat LP function and a steep MEI function. This combination is illustrated in Figure 32-10(ii). It accords with the view, which we shall see later is associated with some so-called Keynesians, that monetary policy is relatively ineffective.

The monetarist and Keynesian views that were

BOX 32-3

Two Views on the Great Depression

The stock market crash of 1929, and other factors associated with a moderate downswing in business activity during the late 1920s, caused the public to wish to hold more cash and less demand deposits. The banking system could not, however, meet this increased demand for liquidity without help from the Federal Reserve System. (As we saw in Chapter 31, banks are never able to meet from their own reserves a sudden demand to withdraw currency on the part of a large fraction of their depositors. Their reserves are always inadequate to meet such a demand.)

The Fed had been set up to provide just such emergency assistance to banks that were basically sound, but that were unable to meet sudden demands by depositors to withdraw cash. However, the Fed refused to extend the necessary help, and successive waves of bank failures followed as a direct result. During each wave, hundreds of banks failed, ruining many depositors and thereby worsening an already severe depression. In the last half of 1931 almost 2,000 American banks were forced to suspend operations! One consequence of this was a sharp drop in the money supply; by 1932 the money supply was 35 percent below the level of 1929.

To monetarists these facts seem decisive: The fall in the money supply was clearly the major cause of the fall in output and employment that occurred during the Great Depression.

While Keynesians accept the argument that the Fed's behavior was perverse, they argue that the cyclical behavior of investment and consumption expenditure was the major cause of the Great Depression. In support of this view, they point out that in Canada and the United Kingdom, where the central bank came to the aid of the banking system, bank failures were trivial during the Great Depression, and as a consequence the money supply did *not* shrink drastically as it did in the United States.

Despite these markedly different monetary histories, the behavior of the recessionary gap, investment expenditure, and unemployment was very similar in the three countries. Thus, Keynesians conclude that changes in the money supply were not necessary for the fall in output and employment.

identified in the preceding paragraph are closely related to their differing interpretations of one of the most dramatic episodes in the history of the American economy, the Great Depression. This issue is taken up in Box 32-3.

The Role of Aggregate Supply

As we saw in Chapter 28, the response of real national income and the price level to any given shift in the AD curve depends upon the behavior of aggregate supply. Two aspects of this behavior are relevant.

The slope of the SRAS curve.   As shown in Figure 27-10 on page 570, the steeper is the SRAS curve, the larger will be the change in the price level and the smaller will be the change in real national income following a shift in the AD curve. Many economists think that when the level of real national income is near (or above) its capacity level the SRAS curve is very steep. Thus:

When the economy is operating near its capacity level of output, increases in aggregate demand (including those caused by increases in the money supply) will not lead to large increases in real national income but will have a substantial effect on the price level.

Shifts in the SRAS curve.   As we saw in Figure 32-8, shifts in the SRAS curve can offset the expansionary effects of an increase in aggregate demand. In Figure

32-8 such shifts were induced by changes in factor prices that arose in response to an inflationary gap. However, many economists think that such offsetting shifts in the *SRAS* curve can also occur if the *AD* shock was caused by an increase in the money supply that was *anticipated* in advance. (In Box 28-2 on page 585 we also examined the possibility that expectations effects can cause the *SRAS* curve to shift for any anticipated shift in the *AD* curve.)

Consider Figure 32-11, which illustrates the case of an increase in the money supply that is perfectly foreseen by workers and employers alike. As in Figure 32-8, the monetary disturbance shifts the *AD* curve rightward. Workers, knowing that the prices of goods that they buy are going to rise, would demand increases in wages to compensate. Employers, knowing that the price of their output is going to rise, would be willing to grant the wage increases. Thus, the *SRAS* curve immediately shifts leftward; this *expectations effect* means that the monetary adjustment mechanism operates very quickly, thus reducing the effect of a monetary disturbance on real national income.

How far does the *SRAS* curve shift in anticipation of a future shock? In the extreme case where there was no disagreement about the extent or the implications of the initial monetary disturbance, wages would rise so as to completely offset the price increase. Real wages would thus remain unchanged. If real wages were unchanged, real output would also be unchanged, so the *SRAS* curve must shift enough to offset completely the expansionary effects on real national income, as shown in the figure. Thus:

It is possible that, in the case of a perfectly foreseen monetary disturbance, all the effects fall on money wages and prices and none fall on real wages or real national output.

Of course, most monetary disturbances are, at best, imperfectly foreseen, and typically there is considerable uncertainty about the exact nature and implications of any particular disturbance. Hence, the result that the effects on real national income are

FIGURE 32-11   Expectations and the Effects of Monetary Changes

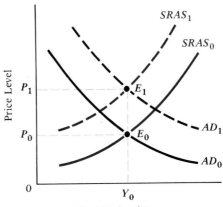

An increase in the money supply that is widely foreseen and understood might cause wages to rise, thus eliminating any effect on real national income. The economy is initially in equilibrium at E_0, with price level P_0 and real national income at Y_0. An increase in the money supply causes the *AD* curve to shift rightward from AD_0 to AD_1. Because the increase was perfectly foreseen and because workers and employers agreed that its effects would be inflationary, wages rise so that the *SRAS* curve shifts leftward. The shift will be such that the new equilibrium is at E_1, where real wages and real national income are unchanged. Hence wages rise until the *SRAS* curve reaches $SRAS_1$ and the new price level is P_1. Real national output remains unchanged at Y_0.

completely offset is extreme, and any monetary disturbance can be expected to have at least some temporary effect. However, the expectations effects complicate the analysis of the effects of monetary disturbances and create problems for economists who are trying to predict the effects of current monetary events or to advise governments on the use of monetary policy. We will encounter this issue repeatedly in the next few chapters as we study monetary policy and other macroeconomic problems and controversies.

SUMMARY

1. For the sake of simplicity, we divide all forms in which wealth is held into money, which is a medium of exchange, and bonds, which earn a higher interest return than money and can be turned into money by selling them at a price that is determined on the open market.

2. The price of bonds varies negatively with the rate of interest. A rise in the interest rate lowers the prices of all bonds. The longer is its term to maturity, the greater is the change in the price of a bond for a given change in the interest rate.

3. The value of money balances that the public wishes to hold is called the *demand for money*. It is a stock (not a flow), measured as so many billions of dollars.

4. Money balances are held, despite the opportunity cost of bond interest foregone, because of the transactions, precautionary, and speculative motives. They have the effect of making the demand for money vary positively with real national income, the price level, and wealth, and vary negatively with the rate of interest. The nominal demand for money varies proportionally with the price level.

5. When there is an excess demand for money balances, people try to sell bonds. This pushes the price of bonds down and the interest rate up. When there is an excess supply of money balances, people try to buy bonds. This pushes the price of bonds up and the rate of interest down. Monetary equilibrium is established when people are willing to hold the fixed stocks of money and bonds at the current rate of interest. The liquidity preference (*LP*) function is the relationship between money demand and the interest rate.

6. A change in the interest rate causes desired investment to change along the marginal efficiency of investment (*MEI*) function. This shifts the aggregate desired expenditure function and causes equilibrium national income to change. This means that the aggregate demand curve shifts.

7. Points 5 and 6 together describe the transmission mechanism that links money to national income. A decrease in the supply of money tends to reduce aggregate demand. An increase in the supply of money tends to increase aggregate demand.

8. The negatively sloped aggregate demand curve indicates that the higher is the price level, the lower is equilibrium national income. The explanation lies with the monetary adjustment mechanism: Other things being equal, the higher is the price level, then the higher is the demand for money and the rate of interest, the lower is the aggregate expenditure function, and thus the lower is equilibrium income.

9. The monetary adjustment mechanism that causes the aggregate demand curve to have a negative slope means that a sufficiently large rise in the price level will eliminate any inflationary gap. However, this mechanism can be frustrated if the Fed validates the price rise by increasing the money supply as fast as the price level is rising.

10. The steeper is the *LP* curve and the flatter is the investment curve, the greater is the effect of a given change in the money supply on aggregate demand. The steeper is the *SRAS* curve or the faster wages adjust, the smaller is the effect of a given shift in the *AD* curve on national income. If the change in the money supply was

widely foreseen and understood, the *SRAS* curve might shift very quickly so as to reduce any effects on national income.

TOPICS FOR REVIEW

Interest rates and bond prices
Transactions, precautionary, and speculative motives for holding money
Liquidity preference (*LP*) function
Monetary equilibrium
Transmission mechanism
Marginal efficiency of investment (*MEI*) function
Monetary adjustment mechanism
Expectations and the strength of monetary forces

DISCUSSION QUESTIONS

1. "Central banker says using monetary policy to lower interest rates now would only cause inflation to rise and lead to higher interest rates in the future." Explain how this might be so.
2. "Bond prices pressed downward by news of M1's sharp rise, economy's rebound." Does this *Wall Street Journal* headline necessarily contradict our theory about the direct link between money supply and bond prices?
3. Historically, construction of new houses has been one of the most interest-sensitive categories of spending. In 1989 the financial press carried a number of stories suggesting that, due to financial deregulation and innovations in housing finance, this interest-sensitivity had apparently decreased. If this were true, what would be the implications for monetary policy?
4. Describing a possible future "cashless society," a public report recently said, "In the cashless society of the future, a customer could insert a plastic card into a machine at a store and the amount of the purchase would be deducted from his 'bank account' in the computer automatically and transferred to the store's account. No cash or checks would ever change hands." What would such an institutional change do to the various motives for holding money balances? What functions would remain for commercial banks and for the central bank if money, as we now know it, disappeared in this fashion? What benefits and disadvantages can you see in such a scheme?
5. What motives do you think explain the following holdings?
    a. Currency and coins in the cash register of the local supermarket at the start of each working day
    b. The payroll account of the Ford Motor Company in the local bank
    c. Certificates of deposit that mature after one's retirement
    d. Government bonds held by private individuals
6. What would be the effects on the economy if Congress were to vote a once-and-for-all universal social dividend of $5,000 paid to every American over the age of 17, to be financed by the creation of new money?
7. In 1989 economists Christina and David Romer produced a study of post–World War II policies of the Federal Reserve Board. They examined six episodes in which the Fed tightened monetary policy to reduce inflation and found that each time, following the tight-

ening of monetary policy, the unemployment rate rose sharply and industrial production fell. Further, they estimated that these effects persist, so that unemployment is at its peak $2\frac{1}{2}$ years after the policy is initiated, and "there is only a limited tendency for economic activity to return to its previous path subsequently." Interpret these results in terms of the theoretical framework developed in this chapter.

8. Suppose that you alone know that the Fed is going to engage in policies that will decrease the money supply sharply, starting next month. How might you make speculative profits by purchases or sales of bonds now?

9. What would happen if, starting from a situation of a 10 percent rate of inflation and of monetary expansion, the Fed cut the rate of monetary expansion to 5 percent?

10. Trace the full sequence of events by which the monetary adjustment mechanism would work if, in the face of a constant money supply, workers and firms insisted on actions that raised prices continually at a rate of 10 percent per year. "Sooner or later in this situation something would have to give." What possible things could "give"? What would be the consequence of each "giving"?

Chapter 33

Monetary Policy

The Fed conducts monetary policy in order to influence such key macroeconomic variables as real national income, employment and unemployment, inflation, interest rates, and the exchange rate. The primary way in which it seeks to influence these variables is through control of the money supply.

Later in this chapter we study in detail how the Fed chooses to conduct monetary policy, and what is involved in choosing among different operating procedures and deciding how much emphasis to place on each of the potential policy targets. We begin by examining how the Fed controls the money supply.

 ## Control of the Money Supply

Deposit money is an important part of the money supply. Checkable deposits in the financial system account for over 75 percent of M1, the narrowest definition of money, and roughly 15 percent of M3, the broadest measure in widespread use (see Table 31-10). As we have seen, the ability of commercial banks to create deposit money depends on their reserves. The ability of the central bank to affect the money supply is critically related to its ability to affect the size and adequacy of these reserves. In the following sections we discuss four ways in which the central bank affects the money supply.

Open Market Operations

The Fed's most important tool for influencing the supply of money is its purchase or sale of government securities in financial markets. These are known as **open market operations.** Just as there are stock markets, there are active and well-organized markets for government securities. You or I, General Motors, the Chase Manhattan Bank, or the Fed can enter this market and buy or sell negotiable government securities at whatever price supply and demand establishes. When the Fed buys or sells securities, it does not know from whom it buys them or to whom it sells them.

At the start of 1989 the Federal Reserve held more than $230 billion in government securities. In a typical year the Fed adds $10 billion to $20 billion worth of government securities to its holdings by purchasing them on the open market, and during the year its total purchases and sales amount to many times this amount. What is the effect of these purchases and sales?

Purchases on the Open Market

When a Federal Reserve bank buys a bond from a household or firm, it pays for the bond with a check drawn on the central bank and payable to the seller. The seller deposits this check in its own bank. The commercial bank presents the check to the Fed for payment, and the central bank makes a book entry, increasing the deposit of the commercial bank at the central bank.

Table 33-1 shows the changes in the balance sheets of the several parties involved in a Federal Reserve bank purchase of $100 in government securities from a household. At the end of these transactions, the central bank has acquired a new asset in the form of a security and a new liability in the form of a deposit by the commercial bank. The seller has reduced its security holdings and increased its deposits. The commercial bank has increased its deposit liabilities and its reserves by the amount of the transaction.

Creation of excess reserves.   After these transactions are completed, the commercial banks have excess reserves and are in a position to expand their loans and deposits. Indeed, after the household deposits the proceeds of its sale of the security in its commercial bank account, its bank is placed in the same position as was the bank in Table 31-4 that received the new deposit from the immigrant. If the central bank buys many securities in the open market, the entire banking system will gain new reserves.

When the central bank buys securities on the open market, the reserves of the commercial banks are increased. These banks can then expand deposits, thereby increasing the money supply.

Whether the seller is a household, a firm, or a bank, the Fed's purchase of securities on the open market sets in motion a series of book transactions that increase the banking system's reserves and thus make possible a multiple expansion of credit.

The response to excess reserves.   Open market purchases by the Fed provide the commercial banks with excess reserves. These permit the banks to create new deposit money by granting new loans and purchasing securities in the manner that we analyzed in Chapter

TABLE 33-1   Balance Sheet Changes Caused by an Open Market Purchase from a Household

Private household

Assets		Liabilities	
Bonds	− $100	No change	
Deposits	+ 100		

Commercial banks

Assets		Liabilities	
Reserves (deposits with central bank)	+ $100	Demand deposits	+ $100

Central bank

Assets		Liabilities	
Bonds	+ $100	Deposits of commercial banks	+ $100

The money supply is increased when the Fed makes an open market purchase from a household. When the Fed buys a $100 bond from a household, the household gains money and gives up a bond. The commercial banks gain a new deposit of $100 and thus new reserves of $100. Commercial banks can now engage in a multiple expansion of deposit money of the sort that was analyzed in Chapter 31.

31. However, this expansion of the money supply is not automatic. Banks often hold excess reserves as a matter of policy, and the amount that they hold varies with economic conditions. For example, banks tend to hold larger excess reserves in times of business recession, when there is a low demand for loans and low interest rates, than in periods of boom, when the demand for loans is great and interest rates are high.

Changes in the commercial banks' desired excess reserves can lead to a change in the money supply without any actions on the part of the central bank. Further, if the central bank increases excess reserves through open market purchases at the same time that the commercial banks decide to hold more, then the increase in excess reserves will not lead to an increase in the money supply.

The significance of the voluntary holding of excess reserves is that it weakens the link between the creation of excess reserves and the creation of money.

However, voluntary excess reserve holding does not destroy the link, since, other things being equal, an open market purchase will lead to some undesired excess reserves and hence to some deposit creation.

Excess reserves make it *possible* for the commercial banks to expand the money supply, and an increase in excess reserves due to an open market purchase by the central bank will generally lead to some deposit creation.

Sales on the Open Market

When the central bank sells a $100 security to a household or a firm, it receives in return the buyer's check, drawn against its own deposit in a commercial bank. The central bank presents the check to the private bank for payment. Payment is made by a book entry that reduces the private bank's deposit at the central bank.

The changes in this case are the opposite of those shown in Table 33-1. The central bank has reduced its assets by the value of the security that it sold and has reduced its liabilities in the form of the deposits of commercial banks. The household or firm has increased its holdings of securities and has reduced its cash on deposit with a commercial bank. The commercial bank has reduced its deposit liability to the household or firm and has reduced its reserves (on deposit with the central bank) by the same amount. Each of the asset changes is balanced by a liability change.

The commercial bank, however, finds that, by suffering an equal change in its reserves and deposit liabilities, its ratio of reserves to deposits falls. Consider, for example, a bank with $10 million in deposits, backed by $1 million cash, in fulfillment of a 10 percent cash reserve ratio. As a result of the Fed's open market sales of $100,000 worth of bonds, the bank loses $100,000 of deposits and reserves. Reserves are now $900,000, while deposits are $9.9 million, making a reserve ratio of only 9.09 percent.

Banks whose reserve ratios are pushed below the minimum requirement must take immediate steps to restore their reserve ratios. The necessary reduction in deposits can be accomplished by not making new investments when old ones are redeemed (e.g., by not granting new loans when old ones are repaid) or by selling (liquidating) existing investments.

When the central bank sells securities on the open market, the reserves of the commercial banks are decreased. These banks, in turn, may contract deposits, thereby decreasing the money supply.

What if the public does not wish to buy the securities that the Fed wishes to sell? Can it force the public to do so? The answer is that there is always a price at which the public will buy. The Fed in its open market operations must be prepared to have the price of the securities fall if it insists on suddenly selling a large volume of them. As we have seen, a fall in the price of securities is the same thing as a rise in interest rates, so if the Fed wishes to decrease the money supply by selling bonds, it will usually also drive up interest rates.

Implications for the Money Supply

Notice in Table 31-1 that the Fed's holdings of government securities are large relative to the reserves of commercial banks. If it chooses, it can sell securities and thus reduce those reserves sharply. Similarly, it can buy securities and thereby expand its reserves.

Open market operations give the central bank a potent weapon for affecting the size of bank reserves, and thus for affecting the money supply.

Other Tools for Influencing the Money Supply

The major tool that the Fed uses in conducting monetary policy is its open market operations, but other tools are available and on occasion have been used extensively.

Reserve Requirements

One way that the Fed can control the money supply is by altering the required minimum reserve ratios. Suppose the banking system is "loaned-up"; that is, it has no excess reserves. If the Fed increases the required reserve ratio (say, from 20 percent to 25 percent), the dollar amount of reserves held by the commercial banks no longer will be adequate to support their outstanding deposits. Commercial banks

TABLE 33-2(a)	Balance Sheet for a Loaned-up Banking System with a 20 Percent Reserve Ratio		
Assets		Liabilities	
Reserves	$1,000	Deposits	$5,000
Loans	4,100	Capital	100
	$5,100		$5,100

TABLE 33-2(b)	Balance Sheet for a Loaned-up Banking System After Responding to a Change in Its Reserve Ratio to 25 Percent		
Assets		Liabilities	
Reserves	$1,000	Deposits	$4,000
Loans	3,100	Capital	100
	$4,100		$4,100

Increasing the required reserve ratio forces a loaned-up bank to reduce its deposits and thus decreases the supply of deposit money. The banking system in part (a) has a ratio of reserves to deposits of 0.20. If the Fed raises the required reserve ratio to 0.25, the reserves of $1,000 will support deposits of only $4,000. As shown in part (b), the banking system can reduce its deposits by reducing its loans. A reduction in reserve requirements from 0.25 to 0.20 would permit a banking system in the position of (b) to expand its loans and deposits to those of (a) with no increases in its dollar reserves.

then will be forced to reduce their deposits until they achieve the new, higher required reserve ratio.[1] This decrease in demand deposits is a decrease in the money supply. The process is illustrated in Table 33-2.

The effect of a reduction in required reserve ratios is also shown in Table 33-2. The reduction first creates excess reserves. Of course, if banks choose not to increase their loans, they will not respond to this increase in excess reserves. Normally, however, the profit motive will lead most banks to respond by increasing loans and deposits, and thus will lead to an increase in the money supply.

Increases in required reserve ratios force banks with no excess reserves to decrease deposits and thus reduce the money supply. Decreases in required reserve ratios permit banks to expand deposits and thus increase the money supply.

In 1934 the Federal Reserve Board was given authority by Congress to set, within limits, required reserve ratios for both demand and time deposits. The Fed frequently has changed reserve requirements, and Congress from time to time has changed the limits.

In recent years the use of reserve ratio changes has fallen out of favor. The chief argument against manipulating the reserve ratio is that it is a ponderous

weapon for changing excess reserves. Open market policy can be applied flexibly to achieve the same effects.

The Discount Rate

The *discount rate* is the interest rate at which the Fed will lend funds to member banks whose reserves are temporarily below the required level. Such loans play an important role in helping banks meet their reserve requirements when open market sales by the Fed cause a sudden contraction of bank reserves. The banks often need this temporary help to bridge the gap until they can make longer-term adjustments in their portfolios.

As a matter of policy, the Fed discourages long-term borrowing from it by commercial banks and accommodates requests at the "discount window" only on a short-term basis. Hence, the discount rate plays a relatively minor role as a policy tool. However:

The importance of a change in the discount rate is as a signal of the Fed's intentions.

Changes in the discount rate are usually associated with like changes in other interest rates. It is not always clear whether the discount rate follows or leads changes in other interest rates. One reason the discount rate sometimes follows other developments is that open market operations that apply the monetary brakes by selling bonds tend to push up interest rates. To discourage banks from turning to its discount window, the Fed must then raise the discount

---

[1] They will do this by gradually decreasing their loans or by selling some of their securities. In the short term they may borrow from the Fed to give themselves time to meet the increased reserve requirements without disrupting financial markets.

rate. One reason the discount rate sometimes leads other rates is that sharp changes in the discount rate often create expectations about future Fed policy in providing reserves to the system.

Net unborrowed reserves, often also called **free reserves,** are the total reserves of the commercial banking system minus required reserves minus the reserves that have been borrowed from the Fed, that is, excess reserves minus borrowed reserves. Net unborrowed reserves indicate the long-term ability of the banking system to support deposit money. If these free reserves are below the legal minimum, it follows that the banks are meeting their reserve requirements by using temporary borrowings from the Fed. Thus the banks will be exerting contractionary pressure on the money supply. They will be trying to reduce their deposits in order to bring their unborrowed reserves up to the legal requirements so that they will be able to pay off their loans from the Fed. If, on the other hand, the banks have an excess of net unborrowed reserves over the legal minimum, they are in a position to expand the supply of deposit money.

Selective Credit Controls

Monetary policy seeks to make money and credit *generally* scarce or *generally* plentiful. **Selective credit controls,** on the other hand, allow the Fed to decide where the initial impact of tight or plentiful credit will be felt. Margin requirements, installment-credit controls, mortgage controls, and maximum interest rates are all examples of selective credit controls that have been used since World War II. These controls can be powerful. Increasing the down payment that is required for an installment-plan purchase, for example, can cause a major fall in demand until households accumulate enough money to make the new, larger down payments.

While all of these selective credit controls have at some time been used somewhere in the Western world, their use has been steadily declining. For example, only margin requirements are currently in use in the United States. Installment-credit controls were dropped after World War II, mortgage controls after 1953, and interest rate ceilings were phased out during the 1980s.

Margin requirements. Stock market speculation can be controlled to some extent by the Federal Reserve Board through its power to regulate the **margin requirement,** which is the fraction of the price of a stock that must be put up in cash by the purchaser. (The balance may be borrowed from the brokerage firm through which the purchaser buys the security.) Since 1960 the margin requirement has varied between 50 percent and 90 percent. Such variations can have a substantial selective effect on stock market activity that is independent of the general credit picture. Thus, if the Federal Reserve Board wishes to impose moderate credit restraint generally but is particularly apprehensive about stock market speculation, it may combine a moderate amount of open market selling with a sharp increase in margin requirements.

Moral Suasion

If the commercial banking system is prepared to cooperate, the Federal Reserve banks can attempt to tighten monetary policy merely by asking banks to be conservative in granting loans. When the need for restriction is over, the commercial bankers then can be told that it is all right to grant loans and to extend deposits up to the legal maximum.

The use of "moral suasion" does not depend on pure "jawboning." Member banks depend on the Federal Reserve banks for loans, and in the long term noncooperation with the Fed's "suggestions" can prove to be costly to a bank.

The Monetary Control Act of 1980

In 1980 the American banking system began a period of substantial deregulation under the Depository Institutions Deregulation and Monetary Control Act. The general purpose of the act was "to facilitate the implementation of monetary policy, to provide for a gradual elimination of all limitations on the rates of interest which are payable on deposits and accounts, and to authorize interest-bearing transactions accounts." These deregulations were phased in during the first half of the 1980s.

The act phased out the interest rate ceilings that had existed for certain types of deposits. This increased the competitiveness of the banking system. Many economists also argued that removing the ceilings removed distortions in the system and thus made it more efficient.

The act also set the same reserve requirements

for all banks, large or small, whether they are members of the Federal Reserve System or not. This eliminated the preferential treatment that was given previously to small banks who faced lower reserve requirements. A bank's reserve requirements were set at 3 percent against its first $25 million in demand deposits (and other accounts subject to direct or indirect transfer by check) and at a ratio to be determined by the Fed (between the limits of 8 percent and 14 percent) on demand deposits in excess of $25 million. The ratio on time deposits is to be set by the Fed between the limits of 3 percent and 9 percent.

The Fed was also given the power to require that all banks hold up to 4 percent in additional reserves, provided that "the sole purpose of such requirements is to increase the amount of reserves maintained to a level essential for the conduct of monetary policy." This instrument is copied from one long used by the Bank of England to prevent deposit expansion when commercial banks unexpectedly find themselves with excess reserves at a time when the central bank does not deem monetary expansion desirable.

Instruments and Objectives of Monetary Policy

The Fed conducts monetary policy in order to influence real national income and the price level. These ultimate objectives of the Fed's policy are called **policy variables.** The variables that it controls *directly* in order to achieve these objectives are called its **policy instruments.** Variables that are neither policy variables nor policy instruments but that nevertheless can play a key role in the execution of monetary policy are called **intermediate targets;** their importance lies in their close relationship to policy variables.

Policy Variables

The Fed's twin policy variables are real national income and the price level. In practice the two are often lumped into a single variable, nominal national income.

Nominal national income as a policy variable.   Changes in nominal national income are a composite of

changes both in real national income and in the price level. In principle the central bank is concerned about how a given change in nominal national income is divided between these two components.

We saw in Chapter 32 that monetary policy operates by influencing aggregate demand, and the short-run effects of a shift in the *AD* curve will be divided between the price level and real output in a manner determined by the slope of the *SRAS* curve. This link between monetary actions by the central bank and the determination of the price level and real income is summarized in Figure 33-1.

Thus, while the central bank cares about the separate reactions of the price level and of real output, there is little that it can do in the short run to control such goals independently. For any price level response that is achieved, the real output consequence must be accepted. Alternatively, for any real output response that is achieved, the price level consequence must be accepted.

Monetary policy is not capable of pursuing two objectives of pushing the price level (*P*) and national income (*Y*) toward independently determined targets.

For this reason central banks often focus on nominal national income (*PY*) as the target for monetary policy in the short run.

The price level as the policy variable in the long run. We have seen that in the long run, when the level of wages is fully adjusted to the price level, the *LRAS* curve is vertical and hence the major impact of monetary policy will be on the price level.

While monetary policy influences both real output and the price level in the short run, its main effects in the long run are on the price level.

Policy Instruments

Having selected its policy variables and formulated targets for its behavior, the Fed must decide how to achieve these targets. How can the policy variables be made to perform in the way that the Fed wishes?

Since the Fed can control neither income nor the price level directly, it must employ its policy instruments, which it does control directly, to influence aggregate demand in the desired manner.

FIGURE 33-1 Monetary Policy and Macroeconomic Equilibrium

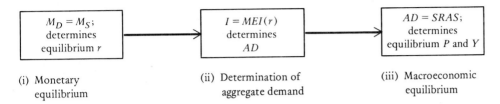

(i) Monetary
    equilibrium

(ii) Determination of
     aggregate demand

(iii) Macroeconomic
      equilibrium

Monetary policy influences aggregate demand through the transmission mechanism, and macroeconomic equilibrium determines the price level P and the level of real output Y. Monetary equilibrium requires that the interest rate be such that the money supply equal the quantity of money demanded; for a given money supply this gives rise to the liquidity preference theory of interest, as illustrated in Figure 32-2.

Monetary equilibrium is linked to the determination of aggregate demand via the transmission mechanism, as illustrated in Figure 32-6: Changes in the money market give rise to changes in interest rates and hence, via the transmission mechanism, to changes in desired aggregate expenditure.

Aggregate demand and short-run aggregate supply together determine the equilibrium values for the price level P and real national income Y. Changes in aggregate demand thus give rise to changes in P and Y; the exact combination of changes in P and Y depends on the slope of the $SRAS$ curve, as shown in Figure 27-10.

The primary instrument used by the Fed to conduct monetary policy is open market operations.

Open market operations change the size of the Fed's monetary liabilities, which are the sum of currency in circulation plus reserves of the commercial banks. Commercial bank reserves are held on deposit with the Fed, and they are the Fed's liability, because they can be redeemed on demand. The Fed's monetary liabilities, as we saw in Chapter 31, form the *base* on which commercial banks can expand and create deposits. For this reason its liabilities are often referred to as the **monetary base.** The deposit expansion process that we studied in Chapter 31 means that changes in the monetary base lead to changes in the same direction in the money supply.

The central bank cannot expect to be able to use its open market operations to control both the interest rate and the money supply independently.

This is because of the liquidity preference function, which relates the quantity of money demanded to the rate of interest. The Fed must therefore choose

between two alternative procedures in conducting its open market operations.

It may set the *price* (and hence the interest rate) at which it sells or buys bonds on the open market. In this case the quantity of bonds sold or purchased is determined by market demand. If the Fed wishes to change its policy, it must change the price at which it is willing to buy and sell bonds. This approach is called **interest rate control,** and here the interest rate is properly viewed as a policy instrument.

Alternatively, the Fed may choose to set the *quantity* of open market sales or purchases. It does this in order to set the reserves of the commercial banks. In this case it is the price of bonds, and hence the interest rate, that is determined by market demand. If the Fed wishes to change its policy, it changes the amount of its open market purchases or sales. (Of course, this means that the interest rate at which these transactions are made may also change.) In this case, in which the Fed chooses to set the quantity of its open market operations, it is directly deciding how much the monetary base will change. For this reason it is said to be using **base control,** and the monetary base is properly viewed as the policy instrument.

The operation of these two alternative policy instruments is illustrated in Figure 33-2.

FIGURE 33-2   Alternative Policy Instruments

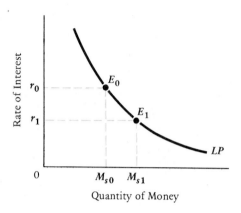

The central bank can use either the interest rate or the monetary base as its policy instrument. The demand for money is given by the negatively sloped, black liquidity preference function, LP, which is reproduced from Figure 32-2.

Suppose that the central bank chooses to set the interest rate at r_0. The money supply will then adjust to M_{s0}, the level consistent with money demand. If the money supply were larger, say M_{S1}, then at r_0 there would be an excess supply of money. Households and firms would attempt to reduce their money holding by buying bonds. In order to maintain the interest rate at r_0, the central bank would meet this demand for bonds. Thus the monetary base and the money supply would fall; this would continue until the money supply fell to its equilibrium level. If the money supply were too small, a similar process would cause it to rise to its equilibrium level. For example, suppose that the economy is in equilibrium at E_0 and that the central bank then chooses to maintain the interest rate at the lower level r_1. Then the money supply, M_{s0}, would be too small; firms and households would sell bonds in order to increase their money holdings. The central bank would buy the bonds, thus increasing the monetary base and the money supply. This would continue until the money supply reached M_{S1}.

If, instead, the central bank were to choose to control the monetary base and hence the money supply, the interest rate would then adjust to ensure monetary equilibrium. For example, if the central bank set the monetary that the money supply was M_{S1}, the interest rate would LP function, the interest rate would adjust to r_0. If, instead, the central bank were to set the monetary base so that the money supply was M_{s1}, the interest rate would adjust to r_1. This is just the liquidity preference theory of interest rates that we encountered in Figure 32-2.

Intermediate Targets

Major changes in the direction or the method of monetary policy usually are made only infrequently. Decisions regarding the implementation of policy must, however, be made almost daily. Given the values that the Fed wishes its policy variables to take on, and given the current state of the economy, is a purchase or a sale in the open market called for? How big a purchase? Or how big a sale? At what interest rate? Such questions must be answered continually by the Fed in its day-to-day operations.

Daily information about the policy variables, however, is rarely available. Inflation and unemployment rates are available only on a monthly basis and with a considerable time lag. National income figures are available even less frequently; they appear on a quarterly basis. Thus, the policymakers do not know exactly what is happening to the policy variables when they make decisions regarding their policy instruments.

How, then, does the Fed make decisions? Central banks typically have used *intermediate targets* to guide them when implementing monetary policy in the very short run. To serve as an intermediate target, a policy variable must satisfy two criteria. First, information about it must be available on a frequent basis—daily if possible. Second, its movements must be closely correlated with those of the policy variable so that changes in it can reasonably be expected to indicate that the policy variable is also changing.

The two most commonly used intermediate targets have been the money supply and the interest rate. Since the two are not independent of each other, it is important that the central bank not choose a target for one that is inconsistent with the other. By the same token, since the two are closely related, it might appear not to matter much which one is used.

For example, if the Fed wishes to remove an inflationary gap by forcing interest rates up, it will sell securities and thus drive their prices down. These open market sales will also contract the money supply. It is largely immaterial whether the Fed seeks to force interest rates up or to contract the money supply; doing one accomplishes the other. Similarly, driving interest rates down by means of open market purchases of government securities will tend to expand the money supply as the public gains money in return for the securities that it sells to the Fed.

In spite of what we have just said, there are dif-

TABLE 33-3   Assignment of Variables Under Alternative Operating Regimes of Monetary Policy

Regime	Policy instrument	Intermediate target	Policy variable
1. Monetary targeting— base control	Open market operations: regulate volume of open market sales and purchases	Quantity of money via money supply process	1. Real national income and the price level *or* 2. Nominal national income
2. Monetary targeting— interest rate control	Open market operations: regulate price at which open market sales and purchases are made (i.e., regulate interest rate)	Quantity of money via liquidity preference	
3. Interest rate targeting	Open market operations: regulate intermediate target directly	Interest rates	

Even with a given set of policy variables, central banks might adopt a variety of operating regimes. The central bank could use either the quantity of money or the interest rate as its intermediate target.

When the central bank opts for monetary targeting, it can influence its target only indirectly. Through its open market operations it can control directly either the size of the monetary base or the level of interest rates. If it controls the monetary base (regime 1), the quantity of money is influenced via the money supply process, while the interest rate is determined via monetary equilibrium, as in Figure 32-2. If the central bank controls the interest rate (regime 2), the influence on the quantity of money operates via the liquidity preference function.

Should the central bank choose to use the interest rate as an intermediate target (regime 3), it can achieve its target directly by using open market operations to control the interest rate. Although this appears to be a simpler process (and in terms of operation, it is simpler), many economists favor monetary targeting.

Other variables, such as the interest rate and the exchange rate, might also appear as policy variables. The interest rate could then appear as a policy instrument, an intermediate target, or a policy variable, depending on the policy regime.

ferences between a monetary regime, in which interest rates are taken as an intermediate target, and a regime that uses the money supply as target. As we shall see, these differences have led to changes in the Fed's use of intermediate target variables.

Operating Regime

A central bank's *operating regime* refers to the combination that it selects of intermediate targets and policy instruments used to achieve those targets.

Table 33-3 illustrates some possible operating regimes for the central bank. If the Fed chooses the money supply as its intermediate target, it can achieve its target indirectly by using either the monetary base or the interest rate as its policy instrument. If the Fed chooses the interest rate as its intermediate target, it can achieve this target directly by using interest rate control as its instrument; in this case the

distinction between intermediate target and policy instrument is superfluous. The somewhat confusing multiple roles that can be played by the various economic variables are clarified in Table 33-3 and are summarized as follows:

Nominal national income, and perhaps its composition, is a policy variable. The money supply can be an intermediate target or a policy instrument. The interest rate can be a policy variable, an intermediate target, or a policy instrument.

Monetary Policy in Action

The Federal Open Market Committee (FOMC) generally meets every 4 weeks. Its decisions are embodied in a directive, issued to the Federal Reserve Bank of New York, in which open market operations are conducted by the manager of the system's Open Market Account. In order to put current debates about monetary policy in perspective, we now turn to a review of the issues surrounding the use of monetary policy over the past 40 years. We look first at the changes that have occurred in the Fed's operating regime and then review the interaction of policy actions and the performance of the economy.

Changes in Operating Regimes

In common with many central banks, the Fed has more than once changed the variables that are its policy instruments, intermediate targets, and policy objectives.

The Accord: From Interest Rate to Income and Prices as Policy Objectives

The use of monetary policy as a tool of stabilization policy in the postwar period began in 1951 with the historic Treasury-Federal Reserve Accord. Prior to the Accord, the Fed had followed a practice, developed during World War II, of supporting the prices of treasury securities so as to hold down interest rates. This served to reduce the interest that had to be paid on the enormous amounts of government borrowing that was needed to finance the war effort. This practice meant that the Fed had to supply new money to buy any part of a government debt issue that the public would not buy at the fixed rate of interest. This policy made the interest rate the Fed's main policy goal; an implication was that the Fed had no control over the money supply. The Accord reestablished a potential for the Fed to control the money supply.

The basic concern of monetary policy since the Accord has been the achievement of full employment and price stability; this makes real national income and the price level the policy variables.

We have seen, however, that to make these objectives operational the FOMC must be able to relate them to the intermediate targets over which the Fed has a direct influence.

Changes in Intermediate Targets

From the interest rate to M1. Prior to 1970 the operating instructions of the FOMC were generally couched in terms of the net unborrowed reserve position of member banks and short-term interest rates. (Together these were referred to as money market conditions.)

Many economists, including those identified as monetarists, criticized this focus on interest rates. These economists pointed out that interest rates tended to vary directly with the business cycle, rising on the upswing and falling on the downswing. They argued that this made it difficult for the Fed to determine the impact of its monetary policy by observing the interest rate alone. Historical examples were pointed to, in which the Fed tried to restrain a boom and was lulled into thinking that its policy was pushing toward restraint by the observation that the interest rate was rising sharply. After the fact, it was concluded, however, that the expansion was so strong that it was the resulting high demand for money that was pushing up interest rates. During such periods the Fed had allowed the money supply to grow substantially, with a resulting cumulative inflationary effect.

As a result of such criticisms, the Fed turned to focusing on the money supply as its intermediate target.

In the 1970s the emphasis shifted from intermediate targets that were specified in terms of money market conditions to targets that were specified in terms of rates of growth of the money supply.

At the outset the measure that was used for this purpose was the narrowly defined money supply, M1.

Monetary targets are usually stated in nominal terms. The nominal money supply is targeted to grow by such and such a percent, which translates into an increase of so many dollars. To judge the expansionary or contractionary force of monetary policy over a particular period, it is necessary to look at the rate of growth of the money supply relative to the desired rate of growth of nominal income, which, in turn, reflects judgments about targets for real growth and inflation. If the monetary aggregate grows faster than is consistent with this desired rate, excess demand will be created and, ultimately, it will lead to inflation. If it grows slower, it will lead to a recession and, eventually, to lower inflation.

For example, suppose that real output is expected to grow at 3 percent, that inflation has been steady at 4 percent, and that this rate is viewed as acceptable. Then the target growth rate of the money supply would be approximately 7 percent.[2] If the Fed allows the money supply to grow at a faster rate, it would create an excess supply of money and put downward pressure on interest rates. This would exert expansionary pressure on the economy. If the money supply grows at a rate of less than 7 percent, interest rates will rise and this will exert a contractionary pressure on the economy.

From one to many monetary aggregates. Changes in the money supply are reliable indicators of the direction of monetary policy *only* if the demand for money is relatively stable. Experience of the past decade suggests that the demand for any particular monetary aggregate can change quite substantially and that the Fed often discovers this only after a considerable period of time. Very often the shifts are out of one type of financial instrument into another; if only the former is included in the monetary aggregate being monitored, then it appears that monetary policy is becoming tighter when, in fact, all that is happening is a substitution of one type of asset for another. In response to shifts of this type, the Fed began to monitor and target broader measures of the money supply in addition to M1.

Dissatisfaction with M1 as an intermediate target led the Fed, along with many other central banks, to regard M2 as a more important intermediate variable than M1 and to watch several monetary indicators rather than just one.

An example of the need to monitor more than one monetary aggregate is provided by the experience of the Fed following the dramatic reduction in inflation that occurred in the early 1980s. An inflation is, in effect, a tax on noninterest-bearing monetary assets, whose real value, measured in purchasing power, depreciates by the amount that prices rise.

When the inflation slows, the tax diminishes and people become much more willing to hold M1 balances for the convenience that they provide. When funds are transferred out of other assets and into M1, there is a large rise in the rate of growth of narrowly defined money. This is exactly what occurred during the 1982–1983 period.

At that time the Fed was trying to follow a rigid target for the growth of M1. Meeting this target in the face of the transfer of funds into M1 balances would have required a very restrictive monetary policy in order to halt the rapid growth of these balances. However, many economists argued that a policy of meeting rigid M1 targets would have put major contractionary pressure on the economy, because the observed growth in M1 was in response to an increase in demand for such balances and hence was not, in fact, expansionary. These critics called for an accommodating monetary policy that would allow M1 to expand to meet the new demand. This, they argued, would put neither contractionary nor expansionary pressure on the economy. In the event, the Fed accepted the counsel of these critics and allowed the money supply to expand to accommodate the increase in demand. In spite of dire predictions of an inflationary expansion from some advocates of an absolutely rigid monetary target, no inflationary increase in aggregate demand ensued.

Similar problems had arisen in earlier years. Indeed, several times during the 1970s institutional innovations caused major shifts between the demands for some of the assets that are included in the wider definitions of money but not in the narrow definition. For example, various types of money management techniques and the development of overnight markets for funds made it profitable for firms to transfer transactions balances that were unneeded, even for a matter of hours, out of demand deposits and into other highly liquid interest-earning assets. This led to major reductions in the demand for M1. In these circumstances, the growth of M1 balances was a poor indicator of the expansionary or contractionary force of current monetary policy; maintaining constant growth of M1 in the face of this declining demand would have been expansionary. Recall, as we saw in Chapter 32 (see Figure 32-6 on page 680), that a fall in the demand for money can start the transmission mechanism working in an expansionary direction, just as can an increase in the supply of money.

---

[2] The target rate would equal the rate of growth of the demand for money, which may differ slightly from 7 percent if the income elasticity of demand for money differs from 1.

Exclusive concentration on rigid targets for M1 can lead to changes in monetary policy that are contractionary when the demand for M1 increases and expansionary when the demand for M1 diminishes.

Using both monetary aggregates and the interest rate. For the reasons just enumerated, concentrating on just one measure of the money supply can be misleading. Furthermore, since there are times when the demands for all of the assets that are broadly defined as money are increasing or decreasing together, there are times when the current state of monetary policy needs to be gauged by measures other than money supply magnitudes. For example, all measures of money supply suggested that there was a fairly tight monetary policy during the last half of the 1970s, but, because of shifts in the demand for money that were not fully appreciated, monetary policy was much more expansionary than it seemed to be at the time. More attention to interest rates would have given an important signal of this. During 1977 and 1978, when the real money supply hardly grew at all, as measured by M1, and grew only modestly, as measured by M3, short-term real interest rates were negative. The rate of increase of prices exceeded the short-term interest rates, so that, in terms of purchasing power, lenders were paying borrowers for the privilege of lending money to them! A negative real interest rate will rarely, if ever, accompany a contractionary monetary policy.[3] As we argued earlier, the exclusive use of interest rates as the intermediate target can be misleading, but to ignore the information that can be obtained from the behavior of interest rates can also lead to errors.

The increased role of the exchange rate. The value of the U.S. dollar in terms of foreign currencies fluctuated a great deal during the 1980s, rising steadily throughout the first part of the decade and then falling dramatically during the period 1985 through 1988. (We shall study more about the causes and the effects of these movements in later chapters.) For the moment we merely note that the movements in the exchange rate have been of increasing interest to those who study developments in the economy and in economic policy.

It often has been suggested that the Fed should try to stabilize the exchange rate, and, indeed, the Fed itself has on occasion expressed concern about developments in the exchange rate. However, most economists believe that, while movements in the exchange rate can provide information that can be of use in guiding policy, a particular value for the exchange rate should not itself be a policy objective. Thus, in this sense, the exchange rate has become an intermediate target.

Today some central banks still try to target on a money supply figure, but most—including the Fed—try to assess their monetary stance by looking at interest rates, various money supply measures, and other intermediate targets—including the exchange rate.

Changes in Policy Instruments

1979: From interest rate to the monetary base. Prior to 1979 the Fed had relied on changes in the federal funds rate (the rate charged for interbank borrowing of reserves) to implement its desired monetary policy. When the Fed wanted to tighten monetary policy, it raised the federal funds rate, thus creating incentives for banks to increase reserve holdings and therefore to reduce deposits and loans. When it wanted to loosen monetary policy, it lowered the federal funds rate, thus creating incentives for banks to decrease reserve holdings and therefore to increase deposits and loans. In late 1979 the Fed switched from this regime of interest rate control to a regime of base control.

Under the new regime, the Fed implemented its desired monetary policy by enacting open market operations with an eye to effecting particular changes in the monetary base. Although this policy requires that interest rates be free to find their own level, many economists did not expect the degree of interest rate volatility shown in Figure 33-3. The sharp rise in interest rates in late 1980 helped to choke off the recovery that had just started. The rise in rates in early 1982 accentuated the downturn and helped to turn it into the most serious recession since the 1930s. Inflation responded dramatically, falling from about 9 percent in 1981 to about 4 percent in 1982, and this led to a significant fall in interest rates over the last half of 1982.

[3] The importance of distinguishing between nominal and real interest rates is stressed in Chapter 24 on pages 505–506.

FIGURE 33-3   Monthly Short-Term Interest Rates, 1977–1989

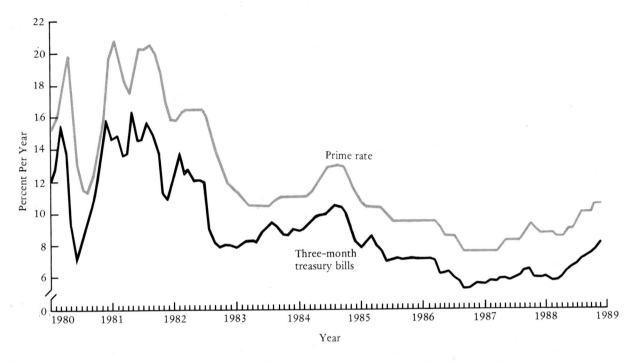

Short-term interest rates were high but variable in the period 1980 to 1982. Short-term interest rates displayed a gradual upward trend from 1978 through 1980. Tight monetary policy following the Monetary Control Act of 1980 led to sharp interest rate cycles and high average interest rates. The Fed's policy has contributed to more stable rates since 1982, and rates fell steadily through early 1988. In the middle of 1988, fears of a resurgence of inflation caused interest rates to rise. (*Source: Economic Report of the President,* various years.)

1982: From the monetary base to borrowed reserves. In response to this unprecedented variability of short-term interest rates, in late 1982 the Fed modified its operating procedures in order to pay more attention to the level of borrowed reserves that were held by member banks. An expansionary policy meant that more funds would be made available to the banking system to be held as reserves, while a contractionary policy meant that fewer funds would be made available.

This approach operates in a manner that is quite similar to the federal funds rate procedures that were used prior to 1979 in that, as can be seen in Figure 33-3, fluctuations in short-term interest rates are relatively small. However, the attention to money supply variables implicit in the borrowed-reserves approach also guards against "creeping inflation," resulting from cumulative "drift" in the money supply that many economists argued occurred under the pre-1979 procedures.

Monetary Policy Since the Accord

Figure 33-4 shows the behavior of M1 and of M2 from 1960 to 1988. Although the two measures differ sharply in behavior in any given year, two things stand out. First, by either measure monetary growth has shown sharp, short-term changes—from being quite expansive to being highly restrictive. Second, by either measure there was a steady upward trend in the rate of monetary expansion, which continued

FIGURE 33-4   Monetary Growth, 1960–1988

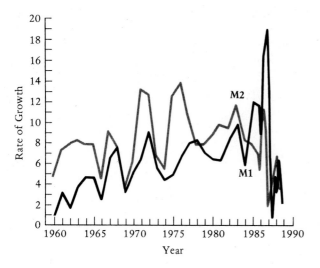

The rate of monetary expansion has shown substantial short-term variability combined with a strong
long-term upward trend. The annual rate of growth is
shown for money narrowly defined, M1, and the
broader monetary aggregate, M2. Although for any
given year fluctuations in the two are not closely related,
both exhibit the same general pattern.

   The tight monetary policy at the start of the 1980s,
the accommodation of the growth in the demand for
money during the recovery in the middle of the decade,
and the gradual tightening of monetary policy toward
the end of the decade are all evident in both series.
(*Source: Monetary Trends,* Federal Reserve Bank of St.
Louis, various issues.)

through the 1970s but was reversed in the first half
of the 1980s.

The Variability of Monetary Policy

From 1952 to 1967 the sharp variations in the rate of
growth of the money supply resulted primarily from
the Fed's attempt to use monetary policy to fine tune
the economy. Experience has shown that problems
for such a policy arise as a result of the lags between
a change in the policy instruments and the reaction
of the policy variables. The problems that these lags
can create already has been discussed in Chapter 30
in the context of fiscal policy, and it is further discussed in Box 33-1 in the context of monetary policy.

Monetary policy typically oscillated from "full
ahead" to "hard astern." The recessions of 1954–
1955, 1957–1958, 1960–1961, and 1969–1970 caused
the Fed to respond with expansionary monetary policies. Then, when inflation increased during the later
recovery phases, monetary policy typically turned
sharply contractionary. Given the lags in the effects
of monetary policy, it appears that what the Fed
thought was a stabilizing policy actually helped to
destabilize the economy, accentuating the upswings
and then contributing to the downswings of the business cycle.

   In 1976 and 1977 the Fed pursued an expansionary
monetary policy. Then, worried about renewed inflation, it turned to a severely contractionary policy
in 1979; from 1979 to 1981 the rate of growth of real
M1 was negative.

**Monetary policy appears often to have been in-
advertently perverse throughout the period
from 1950 to 1980. A series of alternating expansionary and contractionary policies augmented
the economy's natural cyclical swings.**

   Several economists have spoken of "this incredible series of self-inflicted wounds." In a detailed
study of the mid-1970s, Professor Alan Blinder of
Princeton University says that monetary policy in
the period "bears eloquent witness to the monetarists' incessant complaint that policy is too variable,
too apt to swing from one extreme to another. It is
true that whenever monetary policy departed notably
from what a fixed rule would have called for, it did
so in the wrong direction and made things worse
than they need to have been."[4]

The Rising Trend of Monetary Expansion, 1960–1979

As shown in Figure 33-4, fluctuations in monetary
expansion from 1960 to 1979 occurred around a rising trend.

**The rising trend in monetary growth accom-
panied a similar rising trend in prices, indicating
an unmistakable connection between the rate of
monetary growth and the rate of inflation.**

[4] Alan S. Blinder, *Economic Policy and the Great Stagflation* (New
York: Academic Press, 1979), p. 201.

Many economists, and certainly most monetarists, believe that monetary expansion was the main cause of inflation in the 1970s. Others believe that the monetary expansion was mainly a passive reaction to price increases caused by aggregate supply shocks in 1974 and 1979. Either way, there is no doubt that the inflation of the 1970s was accompanied by monetary expansion. Most economists argued that there was little chance of reducing inflation to the relatively modest levels of the 1950s and 1960s until the rate of monetary expansion was reduced to the more modest annual rates of those years.

Contractionary Monetary Policy, 1979–1982

In 1979, concerned over the acceleration of the inflation rate, the Fed tightened its monetary policy. As we have mentioned already, the rate of growth of M1 balances was drastically reduced, while interest rates climbed to unprecedented levels. For example, the *prime rate,* which is the rate charged by banks to their most favored customers, topped 20 percent in December 1980 and stayed over that figure for most of 1981. Combined with an inflation rate of about 9 percent, this represented a real rate of over 11 percent. As we shall study in detail in Chapter 34, inflation came down dramatically and finally fell to levels not seen since the beginning of the 1970s. This victory was bought, however, at the cost of the most severe recession since the 1930s.

A sharp reduction in monetary growth was followed by a dramatic reduction in inflation and a severe recession.

In retrospect it seems that the contractionary monetary policy was somewhat more severe than the Fed had intended. The reason lies, to some extent at least, in the unprecedented variations in the rate of growth of demand for M1 balances. The Fed used past experience to estimate how fast this demand would grow as national income grew. The Fed then set its target for the growth in the supply of M1 at a level sufficient to meet this demand at a steadily rising level of income. In this period, however, there was an unexpected surge in the growth of demand for M1 that created a severe excess demand, even though the Fed met its money supply targets. The result was rapidly rising interest rates and severe contractionary pressures on national income.

A heated debate ensued. While most observers agreed that it was desirable to stop inflation, many thought that monetary policy had been too contractionary and hence that the resulting recession was more severe than necessary. Also, shifts in the demand for money, as we have just noted, made it difficult at the time to assess just how tight monetary policy actually was.

It is clear that the performance of monetary policy would have been improved had the monetary targets been revised to accommodate the *shifts* in money demand, but separating permanent shifts from temporary shifts, or just errors in the data, is possible only after intensive study. This makes the implementation of monetary policy extremely difficult. It has also made economists, and many central bankers, pessimistic, not only about the role of monetary rules, but also about the usefulness of the money supply as an intermediate target. Indeed, the Fed temporarily abandoned explicit targets in late 1982. They were reinstated early in 1983, but with a change from M1 to M2 as the prime target. The hope was that the demand for M2 would prove to be more stable than that for M1 and hence that movements in M2 would prove to be more valuable as an intermediate target for monetary policy.

Recovery, 1983–1989

In late 1982 the economy began a long period of recovery that by mid-1986 had taken national income much of the way back toward its potential level and by mid-1989 was the longest period in peacetime of sustained growth in American history. Although painfully slow in its initial years, especially for those who were still unemployed, the American recovery was much more rapid than the recovery in many of the other developed industrial countries, including Australia, Canada, and most of the countries of Western Europe.

In a debate that we have discussed earlier, some economists advocated that the Fed stick rigidly to long-range money growth targets even during the recovery period, but the Fed did not follow this advice. Instead, it largely accommodated the major increases in the demand for money that occurred. Money demand grew for two reasons. First, the fall of inflation from two-digit to very low levels removed most of the inflationary tax on holding M1 balances and thus increased demand for M1. Second,

BOX 33-1

How Monetary Policy Can Be Destabilizing

The full effects of monetary policy occur only after quite long time lags. *Execution lags,* lags that occur after the decision has been made to implement the policy, can have important implications for the conduct of monetary policy.

Sources of Execution Lags

1. Open market operations affect the reserves of the chartered banks. The full increase in the money supply occurs only when the banks have granted enough new loans and made enough investments to expand the money supply by the full amount that is permitted by existing reserve ratios. This process can take quite a long time.
2. The division of all assets into just two categories, money and bonds, is useful for showing the underlying forces at work in determining the demand for money. In fact, however, there is a whole series of assets, from currency and demand deposits to term deposits, to treasury bills and short-term bonds, to long-term bonds and equities. When households find themselves with larger money balances than they require, a chain of substitution occurs, and households try to hold less money and more interest-earning assets. The resulting fall in interest rates, in turn, affects interest sensitive expenditures. These adjustments can take considerable time to work out.
3. It takes time for new investment plans to be drawn up, approved, and put into effect. It may take a year or more before the full increase in investment expenditure occurs in response to a fall in interest rates.
4. The increased investment expenditures set off the multiplier process that increases national income. This, too, takes some time to work out.

Furthermore, although the end result is fairly predictable, the speed with which the entire expansionary or contractionary process works itself out can vary from time to time in ways that are hard to predict. Similar considerations apply to contractionary monetary policies that seek to shift the aggregate expenditure function downward.

Monetary policy is capable of exerting expansionary and contractionary forces on the economy, but it operates with a time lag that is long and unpredictably variable.

Implications of Execution Lags

To see the significance of execution lags for the conduct of monetary policy, assume that the execution lag is 18 months. If on December 1 the Fed decides that the economy needs a stimulus, it can increase the money supply within days, and by the end of the year a significant increase may be registered. However, because the full effects of this policy take time to work out, the policy may prove to be destabilizing. By the fall of the next year, a substantial inflationary gap may have developed due to cyclical forces unrelated to the Fed's monetary policy. However, the full effects of the monetary expansion that was initiated nine months earlier are just being felt, so an expansionary monetary stimulus is adding to the existing inflationary gap.

If the Fed now applies the monetary brakes by contracting the money supply, the full effects of this move will not be felt for another 18 months. By that time a contraction may have already set in

the recovery of national income toward its potential level meant an increased demand for transactions balances.

Had the Fed chosen not to accommodate the increased demand for money that arose during the recovery, it would have put contractionary

pressure on the economy, thereby slowing the recovery or even stopping it altogether.

Through 1987 the Fed's policies had desirable results and received broad support. National income rose steadily, and inflation stayed below 4 percent. However, concern about rising inflation started to

because of the natural cyclical forces of the economy. If this is so, the delayed effects of the monetary policy may turn a minor downturn into a major recession.

The long execution lag of monetary policy makes monetary fine tuning difficult, and it may make it destabilizing.

If the execution lag were known with certainty, it could be built into the Fed's calculations, but the fact that the lag is highly variable makes this nearly impossible. Of course, when a persistent gap has existed and is predicted to continue for a long time, monetary policy may be stabilizing even when its effects occur after a long time lag.

A Monetary Rule?

The poor record of monetary policy as a short-run stabilizer has lent force to the monetarists' persistent criticisms of monetary fine tuning. Monetarists argue that (1) monetary policy is a potent force of expansionary and contractionary pressures; (2) monetary policy works with lags that are both long and variable; and (3) the Fed is, in fact, given to sudden and sharp reversals of its policy stance. Consequently, (4) monetary policy has a destabilizing effect on the economy, the policy itself accentuating rather than dampening the economy's natural cyclical swings.

Monetarists argue from this position that the stability of the economy would be much improved if the Fed stopped trying to stabilize it. What then should the Fed do? Since growth of population and

of productivity lead to a rising level of output, the Fed ought to provide the extra money needed to allow the holding of additional transactions, precautionary, and speculative balances as real income and wealth rise over time.

According to many monetarists, the Fed should expand the money supply year in and year out at a constant rate that is equal to the rate of growth of real income. When the growth rate shows signs of long-term change, the Fed can adjust its rate of monetary expansion. It should not, however, alter this rate with a view to stabilizing the economy against short-term fluctuations. Many other economists think that an appropriate monetary fine-tuning policy can, *in principle,* reduce cyclical fluctuations below what they would have been under constant-rate rule. However:

The experience of the 1970s convinced many that whatever may be true of *the best conceivable monetary policy,* the Fed's *actual* policy made cyclical fluctuations larger than they would have been under a constant-rate rule.

Subsequent experience has shown, however, that the demand for money sometimes can shift quite substantially. A stable money supply rule in the face of demand instability guarantees monetary shocks, rather than monetary stability. This undermines confidence in the appropriateness of a monetary rule. The daunting challenge that faces central banks in this situation is to offset such shifts in the demand for money while not overreacting and thereby destabilizing the economy.

emerge during the latter part of the decade. In 1987 new Fed Chairman Allan Greenspan signalled his concern about the potential for a resurgence of inflation and indicated that monetary policy would be tightened as necessary. These words were backed up with a gradual tightening of policy as the rate of growth of monetary aggregates fell (see Figure

33-4), and some increase in interest rates was experienced (see Figure 33-3).

On October 19, 1987, the stock market fell dramatically (see the discussion in Chapter 29, page 606). While no single factor can be identified as the cause of this crash, many commentators have argued that a downward revision of expectations about future economic growth in the face of a tighter monetary policy contributed to it. Many commentators also felt that the reduction in household wealth arising from the crash, combined with rising interest rates, would serve to slow the economy down. However, throughout 1988 and early in 1989 growth remained strong and inflationary pressures continued to build; the stock market crash had a smaller effect on the economy than many expected. In retrospect this was in large part because of the strong infusion of liquidity into the economy by the Fed immediately after the crash.

After the "blip" in response to the stock market crash, monetary policy continued to tighten gradually, but by mid-1989 the question remained whether, in terms of containing inflation, this was a case of "too little, too late." Could sustained growth, with steady moderate inflation, be maintained, or would inflation continue to grow, eventually evoking stronger monetary restraints that would risk throwing the economy into a policy-induced recession?

Some Tentative Conclusions

The experience of the 1980s led to a number of views becoming broadly accepted.

The role of intermediate targets.   First, it became widely acknowledged that a broader magnitude than M1 was useful, since important changes in monetary conditions were often more likely to be reflected by changes in M2 or M3 than in M1. However, the search for a single monetary aggregate to be *the* correct intermediate target was slowly abandoned. The high degree of substitutability among M1, M2, and M3 meant that all three magnitudes needed to be surveyed for the information that they could give to the Fed. Furthermore, institutional developments meant that the degree of substitutability was subject to continual change, so that no one magnitude could be taken as a proxy for all three.

It also came to be accepted that the behavior of interest rates conveyed information that might not be available from monetary aggregates alone. For example, in the mid-1980s real interest rates were high by historical standards. A goal of monetary policy, therefore, became the creation of stable conditions that would allow interest rates to return to more normal levels, but would do this without rekindling inflationary expectations.

The important lesson was also drawn from the earlier period of the 1970s that, even if all the monetary aggregates are only increasing slowly, real interest rates that are low or negative, as they often were, must indicate a loose monetary policy. Thus, the combination of low rates of growth of monetary aggregates and unusually low interest rates probably indicates major reductions in the demand for money and, hence, that monetary policy is more expansionary than the behavior of any monetary aggregate would reveal.

New goals of monetary policy, in addition to the traditional ones of income and the price level, have emerged. The two new goals of greatest importance were the health of the financial system and the behavior of the exchange rate.

1. The enormous debt that third-world countries piled up during the 1970s became unsustainable during the 1980s. (See the further discussion in Chapter 43.) Much of this debt was owed to banks in the developed countries, with the United States being the most important single debtor country. As oil revenues fell, these oil-exporting countries found it impossible to pay the interest on their debt without further loans, let alone to repay any of the principal. The Fed realized that a sudden default of these debtor countries could cause a financial crisis in the banking system. It also became aware that every time the interest rate rose 1 percent, the burden on these debtor countries was measured in billions of dollars of extra payments. For most of these countries, there is no hope that they can ever generate the revenues necessary to repay the full principal of these loans. What the banking community of the developed world could, at most, try to do was to delay the final day of reckoning by rescheduling some of the loans and by lending some of the money needed to repay the remaining interest until the major banks could adjust their portfolios sufficiently to write off enormous amounts of loans without going into insolvency.

2. The exchange rate became an important variable for the Fed in the mid-1980s. For decades most of the world's central banks have had exchange rate policies, but the Fed only recently has become concerned with the effect of the exchange rate on the competitive position of the U.S. economy. (This issue is further discussed in Chapter 43.) The Fed can no longer worry only about domestic variables. The behavior of the exchange rate influences the health of American industries that

either export or compete with imports and therefore has an important influence on domestic economic performance.

The Fed seems to have come more and more to take nominal national income as its target variable. In the past the Fed often has concentrated on the twin goals of real national income and the price level. Recently, as we noted earlier, the understanding has spread that the Fed can, at best, influence the *AD* curve; how this influence divides itself between income and the price level depends on the shape of the *SRAS* curve, which is beyond the Fed's control. The Fed is still concerned with the long-term trend in the price level as its most important goal, but in the shorter term it seems to accept that it should adjust its policies in response to the behavior of nominal national income—a composite of changes in real income and the price level.

The Fed also has been concerned about the implications of the large and persistent government budget deficit. As this deficit is reduced, there may be a need for the Fed to adopt a compensating monetary policy. The reduction in the deficit means some combination of tax increases and expenditure decreases on the part of the government. As we saw in Chapter 30, both of these changes reduce aggregate demand and tend to contract economic activity. To offset these forces, the Fed can engage in a once-and-for-all monetary expansion. As we saw in Chapter 30, this increases aggregate demand. There is no reason in theory why a change in the *mix* of macroeconomic policy to a more restrictive fiscal policy and a more expansionary monetary policy cannot leave the level of aggregate demand unchanged. This would mean that the policy changes would not significantly affect either national income or the price level.

Such a shift in the policy mix requires that the Fed be willing to play a more sophisticated role than merely following blind rules for the growth of monetary aggregates. This is a role that some would say is fraught with danger of trying to do things that are beneficial in theory but that, given the imperfections of practical policy, may turn out to be harmful in practice—harmful in the specific way of increasing inflationary pressures. Whether or not this is a serious worry should become apparent by the beginning of the 1990s; we shall take this question up again in the next chapter.

SUMMARY

1. The Fed can affect the reserves of the commercial banking system in many ways. Its major instrument is open market operations. It can also, among other things, change required reserves, change the rate of interest at which it will lend to commercial banks, and apply moral suasion.

2. The major policy instrument that is used by the Fed is open market operations. The purchase of bonds on the open market is expansionary because it increases reserves, permitting (but not forcing) a multiple expansion of bank deposits and hence of the money supply. The sale of bonds on the open market reduces bank reserves, forcing a multiple contraction of bank deposits on the part of all banks that do not have excess reserves.

3. The ultimate objectives of the Fed's monetary policy are called its *policy variables.* In principle these include real national income and the rate of change of the price level. However, in practice nominal income is often taken to be the policy variable in the short term, since the Fed cannot expect to be able to influence the composition of changes in nominal income between real growth and inflation.

4. Where the Fed cannot influence its policy variables directly, it must work through policy instruments that it can control and that will, in turn, influence its policy variables. Intermediate targets are used to guide decisions about policy instruments. The money supply and the interest rate may both be either intermediate targets or policy instruments.

5. National income can be influenced by open market operations. Since it cannot control both independently, the Fed must choose between the interest rate and the money supply as the intermediate target of such operations. When the Fed pursues a contractionary policy, it sells bonds on the open market, thereby reducing bank reserves and the money supply while driving up the rate of interest. When the Fed pursues an expansionary policy, it buys bonds on the open market, thereby increasing bank reserves and the money supply while driving down the rate of interest.

6. The modern use of monetary policy in the United States dates from the 1951 Accord between the Treasury and the Fed, by which the Fed's main objective ceased to be minimizing the cost of financing the government's debt by means of controlling interest rates. During the 1950s and 1960s, the rate of interest was the main intermediate target through which the Fed sought to influence national income. During the 1970s the emphasis shifted to influencing national income by controlling the money supply.

7. Exclusive concentration on rigid targets for M1 risks misassessing the effects of active monetary policy as the public merely shifts funds between M1 and M2 or M3. It also risks leading the Fed inadvertently into an expansionary or contractionary policy when the demand for money function shifts.

8. The Fed has been criticized for alternating too quickly between an expansionary and a contractionary policy, thereby contributing to cyclical swings in the economy. During the 1960s and 1970s, a series of strong and abrupt changes in monetary policy exerted a destabilizing force on the economy.

9. During the early 1980s the Fed pursued a target of reducing the inflation rate. Monetary tightness caused high interest rates, leading to a severe recession and eventually to a sharp fall in inflation. During the sustained recovery from that recession, the demand for M1 increased in response to the fall in the inflation rate and the growth in national income; this increase in demand was by and large accommodated by the Fed.

10. It is generally agreed that rapid changes in the money supply and interest rates can have great effects on the economy. There is disagreement, however, on how much monetary policy can and should be used as a device for stabilizing national income at its potential level or coping with temporary bouts of rising prices.

TOPICS FOR REVIEW

Open market operations
The discount rate
Policy variables, policy instruments, and intermediate targets
Variability of monetary policy and monetary rules
Appropriateness of monetary targets when money demand is shifting

DISCUSSION QUESTIONS

1. In the study of banking history, we often see the term *elastic currency*. For example, to provide an elastic currency was a purpose behind the creation of the Federal Reserve System. What do you think this term might mean, and why might it be emphasized?

2. During the recovery of the American economy from 1983 to 1985, two different views were often expressed. Some said that the adher-

ence to a long-run constant growth rate rule for monetary growth was particularly important lest inflationary expectations be rekindled by an overly fast rate of monetary expansion. Others said that encouraging the recovery required a temporary burst of monetary expansion. Discuss these two views.

3. The Federal Reserve Board runs a facility in Culpeper, Virginia, that costs $1.8 million per year to maintain and to guard against robbery, according to Senator William Proxmire of Wisconsin. Inside this "Culpeper switch," a dugout in the side of a mountain, the government has hidden $4 billion in new currency for the purpose, it says, of "providing a hedge against any nuclear attack that would wipe out the nation's money supply." Comment on the sense of this policy.

4. Describe the chief weapons of monetary policy that are available to the Federal Reserve Board and indicate whether and, if so, how they might be used for the following purposes:
   a. To create a mild tightening of bank credit
   b. To signal that the Fed favors a sharp curtailment of bank lending
   c. To permit an expansion of bank credit with existing reserves
   d. To supply banks and the public with a temporary increase of currency for Christmas shopping

5. It is often said that an expansionary monetary policy is like "pushing on a string." What is meant by such a statement? How does this contrast with a contractionary monetary policy?

6. In what situations might the following pairs of objectives come into conflict?
   a. Lowering the cost of government finance and using monetary policy to change aggregate demand
   b. Ending a deep recession and maintaining a currently achieved target for monetary growth
   c. Maintaining stable interest rates and controlling inflation
   d. Stimulating the economy and supporting the value of the dollar on foreign-exchange markets

7. Writing in 1979, Nobel Laureate Milton Friedman accused the Fed of following "an unstable monetary policy," arguing that while the Fed "has given lip service to controlling the quantity of money . . . it has given its heart to controlling interest rates." Why might the desire to stabilize interest rates create an "unstable" monetary policy?

8. Compare the reaction of the Fed to the stock market crash of 1929 with that of October 19, 1987.

9. In mid-1989, many observers forecast that the economy was moving into recession. At the same time, the cumulative effect of several years of high growth was causing inflationary forces to grow. This combination was perceived as posing a dilemma for the Fed, and a common question found in the financial press was whether the Fed could "engineer a soft-landing." Discuss the dilemma posed for the Fed, and, using the benefit of hindsight (that is, the evidence on what the Fed did and how the economy responded), evaluate the Fed's performance.

ISSUES AND CONTRO- VERSIES IN MACRO- ECONOMICS

Chapter 34

Inflation

If you look again at Figure 24-1 on page 494 you will see that, for 20 years following World War II, inflation remained low. The only exceptions were the "bubbles" immediately following World War II and during the Korean War. During the second half of the 1960s, the inflation rate slowly inched upward. It reached the double-digit range in the mid-1970s. By then inflation had been declared public enemy number one. Even more worrisome, it fell only slightly in the face of a concerted antiinflationary attack during the late 1970s, rose again to the double-digit level in 1980, and then remained quite stubborn during the recession of 1981–1982. At last, in 1983 inflation fell dramatically and then drifted down slowly to around 4 percent, where it remained through 1987. Although this was an improvement over the double-digit inflation rates experienced earlier, many observers expressed serious concern because 4 percent was historically a high inflation rate to be registered at the end of a recession. The concern was strengthened when, as national income came closer to its potential level, the inflation rate began to creep upward. By mid-1989 the rate exceeded 5 percent, and worries were being expressed that the hard-won antiinflationary successes of the early 1980s were being dissipated at the end of the decade.

What are the causes of inflation? Can inflation be prevented from skyrocketing into the double-digit range again? Can inflation ever be eliminated altogether?

Inflationary Shocks

We start by noting a key distinction.

It is important to distinguish between the forces that can cause a once-and-for-all increase in the price level and the forces that can cause a continuing (or sustained) increase.

Some terms that are sometimes used to stress this distinction are further discussed in Box 34-1.

Any event that tends to drive the price level upward is called an *inflationary shock*. To examine the causes and consequences of such shocks, we begin with an economy in long-run equilibrium: The price level is stable, and national income is at its potential level. We then study the economy as it is buffeted by different types of inflationary shocks.

Supply Shocks

Suppose that there is a decrease in short-run aggregate supply, that is, that the *SRAS* curve shifts upward and to the left. This might be caused, for example, by a rise in the costs of imported raw materials or a rise in domestic wage costs per unit of output. The price level rises, and output falls. The rise in the price level shows up as a temporary burst of inflation. (See Figure 34-1.)

What happens next depends on whether the shock to the *SRAS* curve is an isolated event or one of a series of recurring shocks. We choose import price increases as an example of an isolated supply shock because such shocks have occurred during the past two decades. We choose continued wage-cost push as an example of a repeated supply shock because, as we shall see later in this chapter and again in Chapter 38, this possibility has often worried economists.

What happens also depends on how the Fed reacts. If it responds by increasing the money supply, we say that the supply shock has been *accommodated*. If it holds the money supply constant, the shock is not accommodated. (Notice that our terminology distinguishes between the Fed's response to a supply shock, which we describe as accommodating the shock, and its response to a demand shock, which we describe as validating the shock.)

Isolated Supply Shocks

Suppose that the leftward shift in the *SRAS* curve is an isolated event; say that it is caused by a once-and-for-all increase in the cost of imported raw materials. How does monetary policy affect the economy's response to such an isolated supply shock?

No monetary accommodation. The leftward shift in the *SRAS* curve causes the price level to rise and pushes income below its full-employment level, opening up a recessionary gap. Pressure now mounts for wages and other factor costs to fall. When they do, the *SRAS* curve shifts downward, causing a return of income to full employment and a fall in the price level. In this case the period of inflation accompanying the original supply shock is eventually followed by a period of deflation, that is, a fall in the average level of all prices. The deflation continues until the original long-run equilibrium is reestablished. This is discussed in the second paragraph of

the caption to Figure 34-1. Given that wages and prices fall slowly, the recovery to full employment takes a long time.

Monetary accommodation. Now let us see what happens if the money supply is changed in response to the isolated supply shock. Suppose that the Fed reacts to the fall in national income by increasing the money supply. This shifts the aggregate demand curve to the right and causes both the price level and output to *rise*. When the recessionary gap is eliminated, the price level, rather than falling back to its original value, rises further. The effects are illustrated in Figure 34-1.

Monetary accommodation of a supply shock causes the initial rise in the price level to be

---

FIGURE 34-1   Monetary Accommodation of a Single Supply Shock

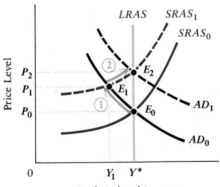

Monetary accommodation of a single supply shock causes costs, the price level, and the money supply all to move in the same direction. A supply shock causes the *SRAS* curve to shift leftward from $SRAS_0$ to $SRAS_1$, as shown by arrow 1. Equilibrium is established at E_1.

If there is no monetary accommodation, the unemployment would put downward pressure on wages and other costs, causing the *SRAS* curve to shift slowly back to the right to $SRAS_0$. Prices would fall and output would rise, until the original equilibrium was restored.

If there is monetary accommodation, the *AD* curve shifts from AD_0 to AD_1, as shown by arrow 2. This reestablishes full-employment equilibrium at E_2 but with a higher price level, P_2.

followed by a further rise, resulting in a higher price level than if the recessionary gap were relied on to reduce costs and prices.

The monetary authorities might decide to accommodate the supply shock, because relying on cost deflation to restore full employment forces the economy to suffer through an extended slump. Monetary accommodation can return the economy to full employment quickly but at the cost of a once-and-for-all increase in the price level.

Repeated Supply Shocks

We have been assuming that a recessionary gap is associated with downward pressure on wages. This implies that labor markets behave much like commodity markets, so that wages fall when there is excess supply and rise only when there is excess demand.

Now let us alter that assumption and assume instead that powerful unions are able to raise wages in the absence of excess demand for labor and even in the face of significant excess supply. Large manufacturing firms pass these higher wages on in the form of higher prices. This type of repeated supply shock causes what is called **wage-cost push inflation:** an increase in the price level due to increases in money wages that are not associated with excess demand for labor.

No monetary accommodation. Suppose that the Fed does not accommodate these supply shocks. The initial effect of the leftward shift in the *SRAS* curve is to open up a recessionary gap, as shown in Figure 34-1. If unions continue to negotiate increases in wages, subjecting the economy to further supply shocks, prices continue to rise and output continues to fall. Eventually the trade-off between higher wages and unemployment will become obvious to everyone and unions would cease forcing up wages in order to maintain jobs for those who are still employed.

Once the wage-cost push ceases, there are two possible scenarios. First, the unions may succeed in holding on to their high wages but not push for further increases. The economy then comes to rest with a stable price level and a large recessionary gap. Second, the persistent unemployment may eventually erode the power of the unions, so that wages begin to fall. In this case the supply shock is reversed,

and the *SRAS* curve shifts downward until full employment is eventually restored.

A nonaccommodated wage-cost push is self-limiting, because the rising unemployment that it causes tends to restrain further wage increases.

Monetary accommodation. Now suppose that the Fed accommodates the shock with an increase in the money supply, thus shifting the aggregate demand curve to the right, as shown in Figure 34-1. In the new full-employment equilibrium, both money wages and prices have risen. The rise in wages has been offset by a rise in prices. Workers are no better off than they were originally, although those who remained in jobs were temporarily better off in the transition after wages had risen (taking equilibrium to E_1 in Figure 34-1) but before the price level had risen (taking equilibrium to E_2).

The stage is now set for the unions to try again. If they succeed in negotiating further increases in money wages, they hit the economy with another supply shock. If the Fed again accommodates the shock, full employment is maintained but at the cost of a further round of inflation. If this process goes on repeatedly, it can give rise to a continual wage-cost push inflation. The wage-cost push tends to cause a stagflation, with rising prices and falling output. Monetary accommodation tends to reinforce the rise in prices but to offset the fall in output. This case is illustrated in Figure 34-2.

Two things are required for wage-cost push inflation to continue. First, powerful groups, such as industrial unions or government employees, must press for and employers must grant increases in money wages, even in the absence of excess demand for labor and goods. Second, governments must accommodate the resulting inflation by increasing the money supply and so prevent the unemployment that would otherwise occur. The process set up by this sequence of wage-cost push and monetary accommodation is often called a *wage-price spiral.*

Is monetary accommodation desirable? Once started, a wage-price spiral can be halted only if the Fed stops accommodating the supply shocks that are causing the inflation. The longer the Fed waits to do so, the more entrenched will be the expectations that it will continue its policy of accommodating the shocks. These entrenched expectations may cause wages to continue to rise after accommodation has ceased. Be-

FIGURE 34-2 Monetary Accommodation of a Repeated Supply Shock

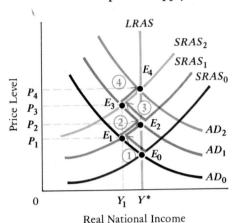

Monetary accommodation of a repeated supply shock causes a continuous inflation in the absence of excess demand. The initial equilibrium is at E_0. A supply shock then takes equilibrium to E_1, just as in Figure 34-1. This is the stagflation phase of rising prices and falling output; it is indicated by arrow 1.

The Fed then accommodates the supply shock by increasing the money supply, taking the AD curve to AD_1 and equilibrium to E_2. This is the expansionary phase of rising prices and output (arrow 2).

A second supply shock, followed by monetary accommodation, takes equilibrium to E_3 (arrow 3) and then to E_4 (arrow 4). As long as the supply shocks and the monetary accommodation continue, the inflation continues.

FIGURE 34-3 An Unvalidated Demand-Shock Inflation

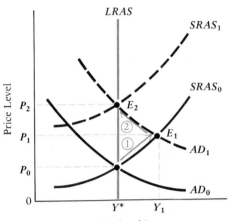

An unvalidated demand shock raises the equilibrium price level but leaves equilibrium income unchanged. The initial equilibrium is at E_0, with potential income Y^* and the price level P_0. A demand shock shifts the AD curve from AD_0 to AD_1, shifting equilibrium from E_0 to E_1, as shown by arrow 1. At E_1 income is Y_1 and the price level is P_1. The inflationary gap of Y^*Y_1 causes wages to rise, shifting the $SRAS$ curve to the left. Equilibrium moves along AD_1 to E_2, as shown by arrow 2. At E_2, income has returned to Y^*, removing the inflationary gap, while the price level has risen to P_2.

cause employers expect prices to rise, they go on granting wage increases. If expectations are firmly enough entrenched, the wage push can continue for quite some time, in spite of the downward pressure caused by the rising unemployment associated with the growing recessionary gap.

Because of this possibility, some economists argue that the process should not be allowed to begin. One way to ensure this is to refuse to accommodate any supply shock whatsoever.

To some people, caution dictates that no supply shocks should be accommodated lest a wage-price spiral be set up. Others are willing to risk accommodating isolated shocks in order to avoid the severe, though transitory, recessions that otherwise accompany them.

This key issue is discussed further in Chapter 38.

Demand Shocks

Now suppose that an initial equilibrium is disturbed by a rightward shift in the aggregate demand curve. This causes the price level and output to rise, as shown in Figures 34-3 and 34-4. The shift in the AD curve could have been caused by either an increase in autonomous expenditure or an increase in the money supply.[1] As with a supply shock, it is important to distinguish between the case in which the Fed reacts and the case in which it does not. As we have

---

[1] As we saw in Chapter 32, an increase in the money supply works through the transmission mechanism—excess supply of money, higher price of bonds, lower interest rates, increased investment expenditure—to shift the AD curve to the right.

FIGURE 34-4   A Validated Demand-Shock Inflation

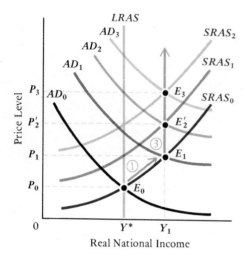

Real National Income

Monetary validation will cause the AD curve to shift rightward, offsetting the leftward shift in the SRAS curve and so leaving an inflationary gap in spite of the ever-rising price level. As in Figure 34-3, an initial demand shock shifts equilibrium from E_0 to E_1, taking income to Y_1 and the price level to P_1. The resulting inflationary gap then causes the SRAS curve to shift to the left. This time, however, the money supply is increased, shifting the AD curve to the right. By the time the aggregate supply curve has reached $SRAS_1$, the aggregate demand curve has reached AD_2. Now, instead of being at E_2 in Figure 34-3, equilibrium is at E'_2. Income remains constant at Y_1, leaving the inflationary gap constant at Y^*Y_1, while the price level rises to P'_2.

The persistent inflationary gap continues to push the SRAS curve to the left, while the continued monetary validation continues to push the AD curve to the right. By the time the aggregate supply reaches $SRAS_2$, the aggregate demand has reached AD_3. The price level has risen still further to P_3, but, because of the frustration of the monetary adjustment mechanism, the inflationary gap remains unchanged at Y^*Y_1. As long as this monetary validation continues, the economy moves along the vertical path of arrow 3.

seen, when the Fed reacts to the demand shock by increasing the money supply, it is said to be validating the shock.

No monetary validation.   The case of no monetary validation is shown in Figure 34-3. Because the initial

AD shock takes output above the full-employment level, an inflationary gap opens up. The pressure of excess demand soon causes wages and other costs to rise, shifting the SRAS curve upward and to the left. As long as the Fed holds the money supply constant, the rise in the price level brings into play the monetary adjustment mechanism (discussed in detail in Chapter 32): The economy moves upward and to the left along the fixed AD curve, and the rise in the price level acts to reduce the inflationary gap. Eventually, the gap is eliminated as equilibrium is established at a higher but stable price level and with income at its potential level. In this case the initial period of inflation is followed by further inflation that lasts only until the new equilibrium is reached.

Monetary validation.   Next, suppose that after the demand shock has created an inflationary gap, the Fed frustrates the monetary adjustment mechanism by increasing the money supply when output starts to fall. This is the case that is illustrated in Figure 34-4.[2] Two forces are now brought into play. Spurred by the inflationary gap, the wage increases cause the SRAS curve to shift to the left. Fueled by the expansionary monetary policy, the AD curve shifts to the right. As a result of both of these shifts, the price level rises, but output need not fall. Indeed, if the shift in the AD curve exactly offsets the shift in the SRAS curve, the inflationary gap will remain constant.

Validation of a demand shock turns what would have been a transitory inflation into a sustained inflation fueled by monetary expansion.

Because of the validation process, all subsequent shifts in the AD curve that perpetuate the inflation are caused by monetary forces.

Inflation as a Monetary Phenomenon

There has been heated debate among economists about the extent to which inflation is a monetary phenomenon. Does it have purely monetary causes—

---

[2] Although we distinguish between a single supply shock and a continuing one, we do not make a similar distinction with a demand shock. This is because the accommodation of a single supply shock restores full-employment equilibrium, whereas the validation of a demand shock perpetuates the disequilibrium.

BOX 34-1

Inflation Semantics

The distinction between *once-and-for-all* and *continuing* rises in the price level is important. Some economists have sought to emphasize it by reserving the term *inflation* for a continuing or sustained rise in the price level and by using other expressions such as *a rise in the price level* for a once-and-for-all increase.

One difficulty with this is that it is counter to ordinary usage, in which inflation refers to any rise in the price level. Indeed, using the restricted definition causes difficulty when communicating with the public. If we were to use it, we would have to keep saying such things as "only some of the current rise in prices is an inflation, while the rest is merely a rise in the price level" and "we won't know whether or not the current rise in the price level is an inflation or not until we see if it is sustained."

In this book we use the term *inflation,* as it is commonly used, to mean any rise in the price level. We then make the distinction by referring to *temporary* or *once-and-for-all* inflations on the one hand and to *continuing* or *sustained* inflations on the other.

No matter of substance turns on the terms that we use to refer to clearly defined concepts. We use the expressions *temporary inflation* and *once-and-for-all rise in the price level* interchangeably. We use *sustained inflation,* whereas some other economists, using the more restricted meaning, might merely talk of an inflation.

This discussion is important because students need to guard against being confused by different usages. Our selection of terms reflects only a desire to keep our language as close as possible to everyday usage.

---

changes in the demand for or the supply of money? Does it have purely monetary consequences—only the price level is affected? One slogan that states an extreme position on this issue was made popular many years ago by Milton Friedman: "Inflation is *everywhere* and *always* a monetary phenomenon."

To consider these issues, let us summarize what we have learned already. First, look at causes.

1. On the demand side, anything that shifts the *AD* curve to the right will cause the price level to rise. This includes such expenditure changes as an autonomous increase in investment or government expenditure and such monetary changes as an increase in the money supply or a decrease in money demand. On the supply side, anything that increases costs of production will shift the *SRAS* curve to the left and cause the price level to rise.
2. Such increases in the price level can continue for some time without any increases in the money supply.
3. The price level increases must eventually come to a halt, unless monetary expansion occurs.

Points 1 and 2 provide the sense in which, looking at causes, a temporary burst of inflation need not be a monetary phenomenon. It need not have monetary causes, and it need not be accompanied by monetary expansion. Point 3 provides the sense in which, looking at causes, a sustained inflation must be a monetary phenomenon. If a rise in prices is to continue, it must be accompanied by continuing increases in the money supply (or decreases in money demand). This is true regardless of the cause that set the rise in motion.[3]

Second, let us summarize the consequences of an inflation on the assumption that actual national income is initially at its potential level ($Y = Y^*$).

---

[3] The statement that inflation is everywhere and always a monetary phenomenon depends on a restricted and specific definition of the term *inflation.* To justify the statement, a temporary burst of inflation with nonmonetary causes must be called *a rise in the price level,* and the term *inflation* must be reserved for increases in the price level that are sustained long enough so that they must be accompanied by monetary expansion. Variations in the use of these terms are discussed in Box 34-1.

1. In the short run a demand-shock inflation tends to be accompanied by an increase in national income.
2. In the short run a supply-shock inflation tends to be accompanied by a decrease in national income.
3. When all costs and prices are adjusted fully (so that the relevant supply-side curve is the *LRAS* curve), shifts in either the *AD* or *SRAS* curve leave national income unchanged and affect only the price level.

Points 1 and 2 provide the sense in which, looking at consequences, inflation is not, in the short run, a purely monetary phenomenon. Point 3 provides the sense in which, looking at consequences, inflation is a purely monetary phenomenon from the point of view of long-run equilibrium.

We have now reached three important conclusions:

1. Without monetary accommodation, supply shocks cause temporary bursts of inflation, accompanied by recessionary gaps. The gaps are removed if and when wages fall, restoring equilibrium at potential income and at the initial price level.
2. Without monetary validation, demand shocks cause temporary bursts of inflation, accompanied by inflationary gaps. The gaps are removed as rising costs push the *SRAS* curve to the left, returning national income to its potential but at a higher price level.
3. With an appropriate response from the Fed, an inflation, initiated by either supply or demand shocks, can continue indefinitely; an ever increasing money supply is necessary for an ever continuing inflation.

Sustained Inflation

The price level has risen in almost all years since the end of World War II. The decade from 1972 to 1982 was one of sustained inflation, often at rates of over 10 percent per year. In the mid-1980s the inflation rate was around 4 percent. Although this was lower than had been achieved in the previous 20 years, the rate would have been judged unsatisfactory at any time in the twentieth century before 1970. Four percent is a rate of inflation that will *halve* the purchasing

power of money in about 18 years. This long-term erosion of the purchasing power of money is a serious matter for anyone who has income or wealth that is fixed in money terms.

Why do we have sustained inflations of either the rapid sort, as in the 1970s, or the more gradual sort, as in the 1980s? What are the costs and benefits of reducing or eliminating such inflations?

Before we can deal with these questions, we must look in greater detail at what is involved in a sustained inflation. We have already stressed the role of monetary validation in allowing the *AD* curve to shift up continually. We now focus on the forces that cause the *SRAS* curve to shift upward.

Upward Shifts in the *SRAS* Curve

A rise in the cost of producing each unit of output, which is called *unit cost,* will cause the *SRAS* curve to shift upward. What is it, then, that causes unit costs to rise?

Influence of wage rates and productivity.   Increases in wage rates do not necessarily cause unit costs to rise, because these costs depend on the relationship between the price of labor and labor productivity (output per unit of labor input). For example, if wage rates and productivity both rise by 3 percent, each unit of labor costs 3 percent more but also produces 3 percent more. Thus, labor costs per unit of output remain unchanged.

Wage rate increases cause unit costs to rise only when they exceed productivity increases.

In what follows, it is simplest to assume that productivity does not change, so that unit costs are positively related to money wage rates. To apply the analysis to cases in which productivity is changing, the statements "wages rise" and "wages fall" need to be understood to mean rise or fall *relative to the change in productivity.*

Why Wages Change

Let us now ask what we know about the behavior of money wages and hence of the *SRAS* curve. Up to now it has been enough to say that an inflationary gap implies excess demand for labor, low unemployment, upward pressure on wages, and, hence, an upward-shifting *SRAS* curve.

However, now we need to look in more detail at three forces that can cause wage costs to change and thus shift the *SRAS* curve upward. These are demand for labor, expectations, and random forces. Much of what we say in the case of demand forces is a recapitulation, but the points are important enough to bear repeating.

Demand Forces

The excess demand for labor that is associated with an inflationary gap puts upward pressure on wages relative to productivity. Wages rise more rapidly than productivity is rising.

The excess supply of labor associated with a recessionary gap puts downward pressure on wages relative to productivity. Wages rise more slowly than productivity is rising.

The absence of either an inflationary or a recessionary gap means that there is no demand pressure on wages. Demand forces do not exert any pressure on wages either to rise or to fall.

The NAIRU.[4] We saw in Chapter 24 that, when current national income is at its potential level $(Y = Y^*)$, unemployment is not zero. Instead, there may be a substantial amount of frictional and structural unemployment caused by the movement of people between jobs. The amount of unemployment that exists when national income is at its potential level is called the **NAIRU (U_N).** It follows from this definition that, when current national income exceeds full-employment income $(Y > Y^*)$, current unemployment will be less than the NAIRU $(U < U_N)$. When current national income is less than full-employment income $(Y < Y^*)$, current unemployment will exceed the NAIRU $(U > U_N)$.

We can now restate the three results about the pressure that is put on wage rates, and through them on the *SRAS* curve, by inflationary and recessionary gaps.

When unemployment is below the NAIRU, demand forces exert upward pressure on money wages and hence on unit costs.

When unemployment is above the NAIRU, demand forces exert downward pressure on money wages and on unit costs.

When unemployment is at the NAIRU, demand forces exert neither upward nor downward pressure on money wages and unit costs.

The influence of demand forces on wages is shown by the *Phillips curve,* discussed in Box 28-1 on pages 580–581.

Expectational Forces

A second force that can influence wages is *expectations.* Suppose, for example, that both employers and employees expect a 4 percent inflation next year. Unions will start negotiations from a base of a 4 percent increase in money wages, which would hold their real wages constant. Firms also may be inclined to begin bargaining by conceding at least a 4 percent increase in money wages, since they expect that the prices at which they sell their products will rise by 4 percent. *Starting from that base,* unions will attempt to obtain some desired increase in their real wages. At this point such factors as profits and bargaining power become important.

The general expectation of an *x* percent inflation creates pressures for wages to rise by *x* percent and hence for unit costs and the *SRAS* curve to shift by *x* percent.

Other Random Forces

Wage changes are also affected by forces that are associated with neither excess demand nor expected inflation. These forces can be positive, pushing wages higher than they otherwise would go, or negative, pushing wages lower than they otherwise would go. Furthermore, they are assumed to be many in number and independent of one another, so that they exert an overall random influence on wages—sometimes speeding wage increases up a bit and sometimes slowing them down a bit, but having a net effect that more or less is cancelled out when taken over several years. Over the long term, they may be regarded as random events and hence are referred to as *random shocks.*

One example of such forces occurs when an exceptionally strong union or an exceptionally weak management comes to the bargaining table and produces a wage increase that is a percentage point or two *above* what would have occurred under more

---

[4] These initials stand for *nonaccelerating inflationary rate of unemployment.* The reason for using this mouthful to describe the amount of unemployment associated with Y^* will become clear later in the chapter.

typical bargaining conditions. Another example is when a new government policy that is favorable to management causes this year's negotiated wage rates to be a percentage point or two *below* what they would have been.

Random shocks may be important causes of temporary bursts of inflation, but they are less important for sustained inflations. Although they may have a large positive or negative effect in any one year, over the period of a sustained inflation, positive shocks in some years will tend to be offset by negative shocks in other years, so that, in total, they contribute little to the long-term trend of the price level.

Overall Effect

The overall change in wage costs is a result of the three basic forces that we have just studied. We may express this as:

$$
\begin{array}{l}
\text{Percentage} \\
\text{increase in} \\
\text{money} \\
\text{wages}
\end{array}
=
\begin{array}{l}
\text{Demand} \\
\text{effect}
\end{array}
+
\begin{array}{l}
\text{Expectational} \\
\text{effect}
\end{array}
+
\begin{array}{l}
\text{Random-} \\
\text{shock} \\
\text{effect}
\end{array}
$$

It is important to realize that what happens to wage costs is the net effect of all three of these forces. Consider two examples. Assume that both labor and management expect a 3 percent inflation next year and are willing on this account to allow wages to increase by 3 percent. This would leave the relationship between wages and other prices unaltered. Next, assume that there is a significant inflationary gap with an associated labor shortage. The demand pressure causes wages to rise by 2 percentage points more than they otherwise would have risen. Finally, assume that there is a shock, in the form of a temporary concern on the part of labor unions with foreign competition, which moderates wage claims by 1 percentage point this year. The final outcome is that wages rise by 4 percent, which is the net effect of +3 from expectations, +2 from demand forces, and −1 from the random shock.

For the second illustration, assume that there is once again a 3 percent expected inflation but that this time there is a recessionary gap. The associated heavy unemployment exerts downward pressure on wage bargains, and hence the demand effect now works to moderate wage increases, say, to the extent of 2 percentage points. Finally, assume that some unusual cost-plus government contracts reduce employer re-

sistance to wage raises to the extent that they contribute an upward pressure on wage bargains of 1 percentage point. Wages rise by +2 percent, which is the net effect of +3 from expectations, −2 from demand forces, and +1 from shock effects.

The overall effect of the three forces acting on wage costs—demand, expectations, and random shocks—determines what happens to the SRAS curve.

Inflationary gaps, expectations of inflation, and positive random shocks put pressure on wage rates to rise relative to productivity and hence on the *SRAS* curve to shift upward. Recessionary gaps, expectations of deflation, and negative random shocks put pressure on wage rates to fall and hence on the *SRAS* curve to shift downward. What happens to the *SRAS* curve in any one year is the overall effect of all of these forces.

Inflationary Phases

We can now study some of the ways in which inflation that is generated from the demand side of the economy can become a problem for policymakers. The inflationary phases that we study here are found over and over again in actual practice. They were encountered in Chapter 33, when we discussed the experience of monetary policy, and we encounter them later in this chapter when we study recent inflationary experience. Although there is often some uncertainty about the actual inflation rate at any one moment in time—an uncertainty that is further discussed in Box 34-2—there is usually more general agreement about which phase of inflation the economy is experiencing.

The Outbreak of Inflation

Start by considering an economy that is currently experiencing a recessionary gap. That gap has persisted for long enough to remove any expectational inflation. Since there is no upward demand pressure on prices, the price level is relatively stable.

Now suppose that a recovery begins. Aggregate demand rises, pushing national income toward its potential level. The rise in income causes an increase in the amount of money that is demanded for transactions purposes. If the Fed holds the money supply constant, the increasing demand for money will bid up interest rates (as people try to sell bonds to add to their money balances). Instead, however, assume that the Fed decides to provide the additional money needed to finance the extra transactions. The Fed will enter the open market, buying bonds so as to increase the money supply at the same rate as the demand for money is rising (due to the rise in income). Now there will be no upward pressure of interest rates, because the demand for and the supply of money will expand together.

If the recovery takes national income beyond its potential level, an inflationary gap will open up and the rise in money wages and unit costs will begin to shift the *SRAS* curve upward, taking the price level upward with it. The transactions demand for money will continue to rise with nominal income, and, if the Fed goes on expanding the money supply at the same rate as money demand is rising, it will find itself accommodating the demand-shock inflation in the manner that was shown in Figure 34-4.

At this point the Fed will be urged to take steps to control the inflation. It can do so by cutting down on its rate of monetary expansion. For the sake of simplicity, assume that it now holds the money supply constant. This will stop the *AD* curve from shifting rightward and will bring the monetary-adjustment mechanism into play. The rising demand for money, in conjunction with the fixed supply, causes a money shortage. People who are trying to sell bonds in order to get additional money balances to finance the rising value of transactions will be unable to obtain funds by selling bonds to the Fed. Instead, their attempts to sell bonds merely will drive bond prices down and hence drive the interest rate up. This reduces investment expenditure, causing equilibrium national income to fall toward potential income.

Graphically, as the *SRAS* curve goes on shifting upward, equilibrium moves upward and to the left along a fixed *AD* curve, lowering national income and thus reducing the inflationary gap. (This is the path shown by arrow 2 in Figure 34-3, which shows what happens when a demand shock is not validated by an increase in the money supply.)

Interest Rates and Inflation

At this point a controversy usually breaks out over the effect of the increase in the interest rate on inflation. One group will point out that the rise in the interest rate increases business costs and that passing the extra costs on in higher prices adds to the inflation. They will condemn the Fed's tight monetary policy as being inflationary. Others will argue that the rising interest rate signifies the slowdown in rate of monetary expansion that has occurred in order to curb the inflation.

The first group is correct in pointing out that the rise in interest rates can cause a one-time increase in the price level. The rise in interest costs shifts the *SRAS* curve upward, just as does a rise in wage costs. This, however, has only a one-time effect on the price level. This group is wrong, therefore, in asserting that the Fed's policy of driving up interest rates is contributing to a long-term increase in the rate of inflation.

The second group is correct in saying that the rise in the interest rate is a necessary part of an anti-inflationary policy. If the Fed were to try to hold down interest rates, it would enter the open market and buy bonds to keep prices up. Buying bonds, however, is an open market operation that increases the money supply. This rise in the money supply shifts the *AD* curve to the right and counteracts the effects of the leftward shift in the *SRAS* curve, thus frustrating the monetary-adjustment mechanism. If the Fed is to succeed in slowing the rate of monetary expansion, it must allow the interest rate to rise as people try to sell bonds to replenish their insufficient holdings of money. The rise in the interest rate is what puts the monetary-adjustment mechanism into play. It reduces aggregate desired expenditure and takes equilibrium national income upward along a fixed *AD* curve as the price level rises. This will reduce the inflationary gap and eliminate it altogether when income falls back to its potential level. (A similar analysis appears in Figure 33-1 on page 697.)

Accelerating Inflation

If the Fed accedes to the call to hold interest rates down, it will find itself entering the open market to buy more and more bonds in order to prevent their prices from falling. This behavior expands the money supply as fast as the demand for money is rising. The result is a fully validated inflation with a

BOX 34-2

Measuring the Rate of Inflation

The Consumer Price Index (CPI) is published each month (along with monthly values for many other key macroeconomic variables). The announcement sometimes gives rise to a confusing array of interpretations about what annual inflation rate is implied by the new figure.

A hypothetical example will allow us to see what is involved in calculating annual rates. The release of the latest monthly figure for a particular price index (PI) for some country, by that country's Bureau of Statistics, elicits the following three responses: "Inflation receding," says a government spokesperson; "Inflation continues to rise," reports a TV newscaster; "Inflation unchanged," says an economist.

How can this be, if all three commentators are talking about the same announcement? The different interpretations arise from different ways of converting the new monthly statistic into an annual rate of change. (The problem can arise with any index number.)

To understand what is involved, consider the hypothetical values for the PI set out in the table. According to the table, at the end of 1984 the PI (100.0) exceeded its average for the year (95.2). At the end of 1985 it was the same (100.0) as at the start of the year and equal to its average for the year; assume that it was, in fact, constant and equal

to 100 for *each* month of 1985. In 1986 prices started to rise again.

Date	PI	Date	PI
December 1984	100.0	October 1986	106.8
1984 average	95.2	November 1986	108.9
		December 1986	110.0
December 1985	100.0	1986 average	105.0
1985 average	100.0		

Annual averages are the sum of the 12 monthly figures for the calendar year divided by 12.

Comparing Annual Averages

In stating that the inflation rate was unchanged, the economist was comparing annual averages. Comparing the 1984 average PI (95.2) and the 1985 average (100.0) gave a change of approximately 5 percent, as did comparing the 1985 average (100.0) with the 1986 average (105.0). Thus, concludes the economist, the annual inflation rate stayed constant at 5 percent over the past two years.

Comparing This Month with the Same Month Last Year

Using this procedure, we see that the annual inflation rate in December 1986 was 10 percent; in De-

---

constant inflationary gap, such as is shown in Figure 34-4.

What now happens to the rate of inflation is predicted by the **acceleration hypothesis,** which says that when the central bank engages in whatever rate of monetary expansion is needed to hold the inflationary gap constant, the actual inflation rate will accelerate. The Fed may start by validating a 3 percent inflation, but soon 3 percent will become 4 percent and, if the Fed insists on validating 4 percent, the rate will become 5 percent, and so on without limit, until the Fed finally stops trying to maintain a constant inflationary gap.

The reasoning behind this acceleration hypothesis consists of several steps. The first concerns the development of inflationary expectations.

Expectational effects. When the inflation that was shown in Figure 34-4 has persisted for some time, people will expect that the monetary validation, and hence inflation, will continue. As these inflationary expectations emerge, additional upward pressure will be put on wages as the inflationary effect comes into play. Now that the demand effect on wages has been augmented by an expectational effect, the *SRAS* curve will begin to shift upward more rapidly.

cember 1986 the PI was 10 percent higher than it was in December 1985. In November 1986 the annual inflation rate was only 9 percent, since the PI was 9 percent higher than in the previous November. Using this measure, we see that the annual inflation rate increased from 9 percent to 10 percent during the month. This procedure probably lay behind the television news report that inflation was rising.

Comparing This Month with Last Month

Using this method, we see that the annual inflation rate in December 1986 was 12 percent; the PI had risen by 1 percent over the month, and the annual rate was approximately 12 times the monthly percentage change. In November 1986 the annual inflation rate had been 24 percent, since the November PI was 2 percent higher than the October figure. This calculation would provide the basis for the government spokesperson's statement that inflation was receding.

Which Measure Is Best?

Properly understood, all three measures give useful and complementary information.

Comparing annual averages is the least erratic, but because it focuses almost entirely on underlying

trends, it is not sensitive to current changes. In our example it misses the stability in prices that prevailed throughout 1985 and the fairly sharp upturn in prices that was apparent in 1986.

Comparing this month with the same month last year gives information that is more sensitive to current events. However, it gives a lot of weight to particular events in the most recent month—events that often have little to do with the underlying trend of prices.

Comparing this month with last month gives the most erratic measure. The timing of major price changes at or near the end of the month will have a substantial accidental effect on the measure. For some purposes this sensitivity may be desirable, but for understanding the underlying trend in inflation, it can be misleading.

The three measures can be used selectively to support almost any position, but people who understand the meaning of each measure need not be fooled by such selective presentation of the data. Figures lie only to those who are uninformed about what a measure does and does not say.

More rapid monetary validation required. If the Fed still wishes to hold the level of output constant, it must increase the rate at which the money supply is growing. This is because, to hold Y constant, the AD curve must be shifted more rapidly to compensate for the more rapid shifts in the $SRAS$ curve.

An increasing rate of inflation. As a result of the increasingly rapid upward shifts in both the AD and $SRAS$ curves, the rate of inflation must now be increasing. The rise in the actual inflation rate will, in turn, cause an increase in the expected inflation rate. This will then cause the actual inflation rate to in-

crease, which will, in turn, increase the expected inflation rate, and so on. The net result is a *continually increasing rate of inflation.*[5]

According to the acceleration hypothesis, as long as an inflationary gap persists, expectations of inflation will be rising, and this will lead to increases in the actual rate of inflation.

[5] Now we see the reason for the name NAIRU. At any lower level of unemployment, national income is above Y^*, and the inflation rate tends to accelerate. So the NAIRU is the lowest level of unemployment, consistent with a nonaccelerating rate of inflation.

BOX 34-3

The Phillips Curve and Accelerating Inflation

Professor Phillips was interested in studying the short-run behavior of an economy subjected to cyclical fluctuations (see Box 28-1 on pages 580–581). Others, however, treated the curve as establishing a long-term trade-off between inflation and unemployment.

Let the government fix income at Y_1 (and thus unemployment at U_1), as shown in the figures, and validate the ensuing wage inflation of ΔW_1 per year. By doing this the government is apparently able to choose a particular combination of inflation and unemployment, with lower levels of unemployment being attained at the cost of higher rates of inflation.

In the 1960s Phillips curves were fitted to the data for many countries, and governments made decisions about where they wished to be on the trade-off between inflation and unemployment. Then, in the late 1960s, in country after country, the rate of wage and price inflation associated with any given level of unemployment began to rise. Instead of being stable, the Phillips curves were shifting upward. The explanation lay primarily in a shifting relationship between the pressure of demand and wage increases due to expectations, as discussed in the text.

In the text we noted that two important influences on wages are demand and expectations. It was gradually understood that the original Phillips curve concerned only the influence of demand and left out inflationary expectations. This proved to be an important and unfortunate omission. An increase in expected inflation shows up as an upward shift in the original Phillips curve that was drawn in Box 28-1.

The importance of expectations can be shown by drawing what is called an **expectations-augmented Phillips curve,** as shown in the figures. The heights of the Phillips curves above the axis at Y^* and at U_N show the expected inflation rate. This is the amount that wages will rise when there is neither excess demand nor excess supply pressure in labor markets. The actual wage increase is shown by the augmented curve, with the increase in wages exceeding expected inflation when $Y > Y^*$ ($U < U_N$) and falling short of expected inflation when $Y < Y^*$ ($U > U_N$). *The demand component shown by the simple Phillips curve tells us by how much wage changes will deviate from the expected inflation rate.*

Now we can see what was wrong with the idea of a stable inflation-unemployment trade-off. Tar-

The tendency for inflation to accelerate is discussed further in Box 34-3.

Constant Inflation

Must a sustained inflation always accelerate, or is it possible for an inflation to go on at a constant rate indefinitely?

The answer is that not all sustained inflations must accelerate. When the demand effect is absent and all inflation is thus expectational, inflation can persist indefinitely at a constant rate. Let us see why this is so.

When national income is at its potential level,

there is neither an inflationary nor a recessionary gap. In this case there is no demand effect operating on wage bargains. Leaving random shocks aside, the only force operating on wages is expectations. Say, for example, that both workers and employers expect a 4 percent inflation and that employers are prepared to raise wages by 4 percent per year to keep wages in line with everything else. Wages will rise by 4 percent per year, and the *SRAS* curve will shift upward by that amount each year. If the Fed validates the resulting inflation by increasing the money supply by 4 percent each year, the *AD* curve will also be shifting upward by that amount.

This case is illustrated in Figure 34-5. Here wage

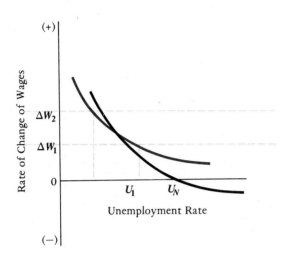

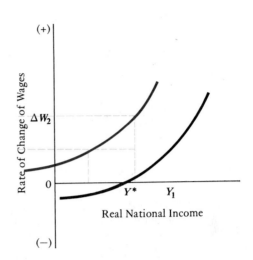

geting on income Y_1 or unemployment U_1 in the figures is fine as long as no inflation is *expected,* but, once some particular rate of inflation comes to be expected, people will demand that much just to hold their own. The Phillips curve will shift upward to the position shown in the figures. Now there is inflation ΔW_2 because of the combined effects of expectations and excess demand.

However, this higher rate is above the expected rate. Once this higher rate comes to be expected,

the Phillips curve will shift upward once again. *The expectations-augmented Phillips curve shows that the actual rate of inflation exceeds the expected rate whenever there is an inflationary gap.* Sooner or later this will cause inflationary expectations to be shifted upward. The inflation rate associated with any given level of Y or U rises over time. This is the theory of accelerating inflation that is further studied in the appendix to this chapter.

costs are rising due to expectations of inflation, and these expectations are being fulfilled.

Steady inflation at potential income results when the rate of monetary growth, the rate of wage increase, and the expected rate of inflation are all consistent with the actual inflation rate.

The key point about a pure expectational inflation at a constant rate is that there is no demand effect operating on wage bargains. Wages rise at the expected rate of inflation, and this is just enough to preserve the existing relationship between wages and all other prices. The labor shortages that accompany

an inflationary gap are absent, as are the labor surpluses that accompany a recessionary gap.

If all forces worked precisely as described in the simple theoretical model, a steady inflation would occur only when income was exactly at its potential level. In practice, however, stable inflation rates also seem to be compatible with modest recessionary gaps. In such circumstances, there is a tendency for wages to fall (relative to productivity), forcing the SRAS curve downward.

However, the negative demand effect of a recessionary gap is rather weak. Thus, when the gap is relatively small, the demand effect may be swamped by the expectational and random shock effects, so

FIGURE 34-5   Steady Inflation at the Natural Rate of Unemployment

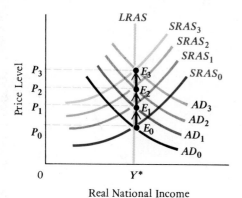

Real National Income

When income equals Y^* (and hence unemployment equals U_N), there is no demand effect on wages, and steady inflation can proceed at a rate that is consistent with inflationary expectations. With no demand effect, the $SRAS$ curve shifts upward at the expected rate of inflation. If the Fed raises the money supply at the same rate, the upward shift in the AD curve will match that of the $SRAS$ curve. Output will stay at Y^*, unemployment will be at the natural rate, and inflation will be steady. The steady inflation is shown by the rising price level as equilibrium moves along the arrows from E_0 to E_1 to E_2 to E_3 in the figure.

that an approximately stable inflation rate is the net result. This is what seems to have occurred in the mid-1980s, when a fairly stable inflation rate persisted for several years in spite of a modest recessionary gap.

Breaking an Entrenched Inflation

When an inflation has been going on for a long time, can it be reduced without inflicting major hardships in terms of unemployment and lost output?

This question greatly worried policymakers in the early 1980s when they set out to break the existing two-digit inflation. It also worried those who, later in the 1980s, were unsatisfied with the inflation rates that had persisted for several years. The issue was then, and still is, how to reduce inflation when people have come to accept the existing rate as nor-

mal and have adapted their behavior to the belief that the rate will continue.

Our analysis begins with a situation of a continuing, fully validated inflation, with actual income at its potential level ($Y = Y^*$). The inflation has been going on for some time, and people expect it to continue. Firmly held expectations of a continuation of the current inflation rate are what leads to the concept of an *entrenched inflation*.

Now suppose that the Fed decides to reduce the inflation rate by reducing its rate of monetary validation. The events that follow generally fall into three phases.

Phase 1: removing the inflationary gap.   The first phase, shown in Figure 34-6(i), consists of slowing the rate of monetary expansion below the current rate of inflation. This slows the rate at which the AD curve is shifting upward. To illustrate, we take an extreme case: the "cold turkey approach," in which the rate of monetary expansion is cut to zero so that the upward shift in the AD curve is halted abruptly.

Under the combined influence of an inflationary gap and expectations of continued inflation, wages continue to rise, and the $SRAS$ curve thus continues to shift upward. Eventually, the gap is removed. If the only influence on wages were demand, that would be the end of the story. At Y^* there is no upward demand pressure on wages. Wages would stop rising, the $SRAS$ curve would be stabilized, and the economy would remain at full employment with a stable price level.

Phase 2: stagflation.   Governments around the world many times have wished that things were really so simple. However, wages depend not only on excess demand but also on inflationary expectations. Once inflationary expectations have been established, it is not always easy to get people to revise them downward, even in the face of changed monetary policies. Thus, the $SRAS$ curve continues to shift upward, causing the price level to continue to rise and income to fall further.

Expectations may cause inflation to persist after its original causes have been removed. What was initially a demand inflation due to an inflationary gap becomes an expectational inflation.

This is phase 2, shown in Figure 34-6(ii).

FIGURE 34-6 Eliminating an Entrenched Inflation

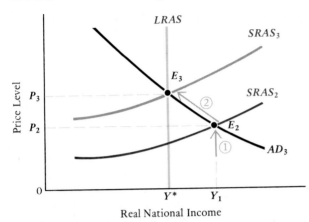

(i) Phase 1: removing the inflationary gap

(i) Phase 1: The elimination of an entrenched inflation begins with a demand contraction to remove the inflationary gap. A fully validated inflation of the type shown in Figure 34-4 is taking the economy along the path shown by arrow 1 here. When the curves reach $SRAS_2$ and AD_3, the Fed stops expanding the money supply, thus stabilizing aggregate demand at AD_3. Wages continue to rise, taking the $SRAS$ curve leftward. The economy moves along arrow 2, with income falling and the price level rising. When aggregate supply reaches $SRAS_3$, the inflationary gap is removed and equilibrium is established at income Y^* and price level P_3.

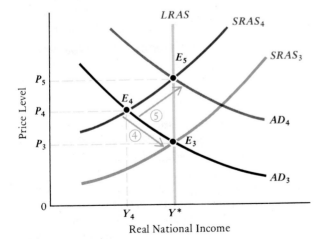

(ii) Phase 2: stagflation

(ii) Phase 2: Expectations and wage momentum lead to a stagflation, with falling output and continuing inflation. The economy moves along the path shown by arrow 3. The driving force is now the $SRAS$ curve, which continues to shift because inflationary expectations cause wages to continue to rise. The recessionary gap grows as income falls. The inflation continues but at a diminishing rate. If wages stop rising when income has reached Y_4 and the price level has reached P_4, the stagflation phase is over, with equilibrium at E_4.

(iii) Phase 3: recovery

(iii) Phase 3: After expectations are reversed, recovery takes income to Y^* and the price level is stabilized. There are two possible scenarios for recovery. In the first the recessionary gap causes wages to fall (slowly), taking the $SRAS$ curve back to $SRAS_3$ (slowly), as shown by arrow 4. The economy retraces the path originally followed in part (ii) back to E_3. In the second scenario, the Fed increases the money supply sufficiently to shift the AD curve to AD_4. The economy then moves along the path shown by arrow 5. This restores potential income at the cost of a further temporary inflation that takes the price level to P_5. Full employment and a stable price level are now achieved.

BOX 34-4

Controversies over the Length of the Stagflation Phase Needed to Break an Entrenched Inflation

Keynesian View

Keynesians cite two reasons for believing that the phase 2 stagflation in the process of breaking a sustained inflation will often tend to be long and painful. The first has to do with wage momentum, and the second has to do with expectations.

Keynesians allege the existence of a self-perpetuating momentum to wage increases. According to this view, workers are concerned about their own wage rates *relative* to rates in closely related occupations and industries. Because wage contracts fix wage rates for periods of one to three years, any particular wage will be negotiated in a situation where many related wage rates are already fixed for some time into the future (until existing contracts expire). Thus, if excess demand caused many existing wages to be raised by, say, 10 percent in contracts negotiated in the recent past, people currently negotiating new wage contracts will hold out for something close to 10 percent, even if the pressure of excess demand has weakened greatly.

This concern over wage comparability tends to give momentum to rounds of wage increases. The process is sometimes called a *wage-wage spiral*: Once started, wages tend to chase each other in a rising spiral as bargainers seek to avoid falling behind

increases that have already been agreed on for other workers.

The second main reason concerns expectations. In its simplest version, this reason is based on the so-called extrapolative theory, according to which people tend to believe that recent trends will continue and require much new evidence before they conclude that an established inflationary trend has changed. The argument is that, unless a deviation from the trend persists, people tend to dismiss a deviation—say, a fall in the inflation rate—as a transitory change and do not let it influence their long-term wage- and price-setting behavior.

The combination of the momentum of wage increases, even in the face of large recessionary gaps and slowly adjusting expectations, means that phase 2 will be long.

Monetarist View

Monetarists expect phase 2 to be over rapidly. Some say that under ideal circumstances it may never occur at all. They offer two reasons.

First, monetarists deny that significant wage-wage momentum exists. They believe that new wage bargains respond to current market conditions. Thus a large recessionary gap with unemployment above the natural rate will lead quickly

The emerging recessionary gap has two effects. First, there is rising unemployment. Thus, the demand influence on wages becomes negative. Second, as the recession deepens and monetary restraint continues, people revise their expectations of inflation downward. When they have no further expectations of inflation, there are no further increases in wage costs, and the *SRAS* curve stops shifting. The stagflationary phase is over. The inflation has come to a halt, but a large recessionary gap now exists.

Keynesians tend to be pessimistic and to expect

a severe and long-lasting slump in phase 2. Monetarists tend to be optimistic and to expect a relatively mild and short-lived recession in phase 2. These opposing views are investigated in Box 34-4.

Phase 3: recovery.   The final phase is the return to full employment. When the economy comes to rest at the end of the stagflation, the situation is exactly the same as when the economy is hit by an isolated supply shock (see Figure 34-1). The move back to full employment can be accomplished in either of

to new wage settlements well below the expected rate of inflation. The only lag in the adjustment of wage costs to current demand conditions is caused by the length of wage contracts. Thus, it will take time for *all* wages to adjust to depressed market conditions.

Second, many monetarists argue that expected inflation falls rapidly during phase 2. They accept one version of the theory of *rational expectations*, according to which people look to the government's *current* macroeconomic policy when forming their expectations of future inflation. People are assumed to understand how the economy works and to form their expectations about future inflation rates by predicting the outcome of the monetary policies currently being followed. Their expectations need not always be correct, but the rational-expectations hypothesis assumes that people do not continue to make systematic errors in forming their expectations. (This theory is considered in more detail in Chapter 38.)

Rational expectations have the effect of shortening the deflationary period. Instead of being strongly influenced by past inflation rates, people act in anticipation of the outcome of current government policies. Once they realize that the Fed has stopped validating the inflation, they will quickly revise their inflationary expectations downward, and their consequent wage- and price-setting behavior will produce a rapid slowdown in the actual inflation rate. Expected inflation falls quickly to zero, and there is no further upward push to wages arising from expectations.

This happy result occurs only if people believe that the Fed is going to stick to its restrictive policies. If they are skeptical about the Fed's resolve, they may expect the inflation to continue. They will then increase wages and prices in anticipation of the inflation, and their actions will generate the very inflation that they expected. Thus, monetarists lay heavy stress on the credibility of the Fed's monetary policy.

Keynesians argue in response that sophisticated financial-market operators may understand the underlying monetary causes of inflation, but the general public and most labor leaders and business managers hold different, sometimes crude, theories of inflation. They will tend, so the Keynesians argue, to extrapolate from past experiences and will not even know what the Fed is doing to the money supply, let alone base their expectations on it.

The experience of the early 1980s, and its relationship to this debate, is discussed later in this chapter.

two ways. First, the recessionary gap can be relied on to reduce wages, thus shifting the *SRAS* curve downward. Second, the money supply can be increased to shift the *AD* curve to a level that is consistent with full employment. These two possibilities are illustrated in Figure 34-6(iii).

Some economists worry about waiting for wages and prices to fall because they fear that the process will take a very long time. Others worry about a temporary burst of monetary expansion because they fear that expectations of inflation may be rekindled when the Fed increases the money supply. If inflationary expectations are revived, the Fed will then have an unenviable choice. Either it must let another severe recession develop to break these new inflationary expectations, or it must validate the inflation in order to reduce unemployment. In the latter case it is back where it started, with a validated inflation on its hands.[6]

---

[6] This is the so-called reentry problem that was discussed in detail on pages 705–706 of Chapter 33.

Recent Inflationary Experience

During the latter half of the 1970s, the U.S. inflation rate rose steadily. From 4.9 percent in 1976, the rate—as measured by the CPI on a December-to-December basis—rose through 6.7 and 9.0 percent in the two subsequent years, reaching just over 13 percent in 1979. In 1980 the rate was only slightly lower. Some of the pressure for the high inflation rate was coming from the cost side. The second OPEC oil price shock was working its way through the economy, pushing the *SRAS* curve upward. This supply shock was clearly being accommodated by the Fed through rapid increases in the money supply.

Controversy broke out on how much of the inflation was due to demand forces and how much was due to entrenched expectations that the inflation would continue. Everyone agreed on the goal of returning to a much lower inflation rate (zero if possible), but there was disagreement as to the means of achieving the goal. This same disagreement would occur again if the Fed advocated a policy of rapidly reducing the current rate of inflation to a much lower rate, say, as close to zero as is possible.

Monetarists advocated breaking the inflation with monetary restraint in the manner that we analyzed earlier in this chapter. Since they felt that there would be a short phase 2, they were willing to rely exclusively on monetary policy to bring about the transition from a high to a low inflationary environment.

Keynesians agreed that a low rate of monetary growth was a necessary condition for returning to a low rate of inflation. However, because they felt that phase 2 would be long—some talked in terms of 5 to 10 years—they were reluctant to use monetary policy alone during the transition. As a result, many Keynesians advocated using **incomes policies,** a term that covers any direct government intervention that is used to affect wage and price setting. They hoped that such intervention would shorten phase 2 by helping to break inflationary expectations.

The Reduction of Inflation

After some minor policy vacillations, an antiinflationary monetary policy was initiated without the addition of any incomes policy. Inflation fell from 12.5 percent in 1980 to 8.9 percent in 1981 and then to 3.8 percent in 1982. By 1983 the policy had succeeded in reducing inflation to a level that has been seen only once (1972) since the mid-1960s, but it also produced a major recession with all of its attendant costs, including unemployment, lost output, business bankruptcies, and foreclosed mortgages.

The results came out somewhere in between the extremes that had been predicted. Keynesians were right in predicting that the antiinflationary policies would induce a severe recession, but the inflation rate came down much faster than Keynesians had predicted. Jobs rather than wages quickly became the focus of many contract settlements. Not only were new wage agreements moderated in response to the excess supply of labor, but also a significant number of existing contracts were reopened and lower wages agreed upon.

Thus, as so often happens with great debates, neither the extreme pessimists nor the extreme optimists were right. The truth lay somewhere in between.

Economists still argue about why the result turned out the way it did. Monetarists have to explain why there was a significant stagflation phase at all. They argue that it resulted from the Fed's vacillation. They claim that the Fed did not take a consistently tough line on reducing the rate of monetary accommodation. This, in turn, left people uncertain as to whether or not inflation really was going to be brought down. Because of this uncertainty, inflationary expectations remained high, sustaining the stagflation phase of the adjustment.

Keynesians have to explain why the stagflation phase was so much shorter than they expected. One of their main explanations lies in the weakness at the time of the steel and automobile industries. These industries always have had strong unions, which the Keynesians claim were a major cause of the wage-price spiral. However, during the early 1980s both of these industries were in deep trouble, and no matter how hard their unions pushed for wage rises, the profits out of which extra wages would have to be paid were not there as they had been in the past. Thus, say the Keynesians, for quite fortuitous reasons, the wage push was much weaker than usual, and the stagflation phase was correspondingly shortened.

Whatever the reasons, there is little doubt that during the early 1980s inflation fell faster than many Keynesians had expected and the slump was deeper and more prolonged than many monetarists had expected.

A Stable Inflation Rate

For several years starting in 1982, the American inflation rate stabilized at just under 4 percent. This was also a time of low inflation worldwide. How is it that a relatively steady inflation rate persisted for several years with no clear tendency toward acceleration or deceleration?

The answer on the side of acceleration is that there was no inflationary gap in the economy. The inflation appears to have been an expectational inflation that was fully accommodated by the Fed's monetary policy. As such, it fulfilled the conditions for achieving a stable, rather than an accelerating, rate.

During most of this period, however, there was a significant recessionary gap. Why then did inflation not decelerate further? The answer seems to be that weak demand forces that work toward deceleration were swamped by the forces of expectational inflation and random shocks. (Recall from Chapter 28 the second asymmetry of the *SRAS* curve: The curve shifts rapidly upward when there is excess demand but only slowly downward when there is excess supply.)

In 1986 the OPEC oil cartel collapsed, and oil prices tumbled. The costs of all oil-related products, including gasoline, fuel oil, plastics, and fertilizers, fell, taking the *SRAS* curve downward with them. The inflation rate during that year was 1.1 percent. With one exception in 1964, this was the lowest rate achieved in the United States since the mid-1950s. The recovery continued, however, and by 1987 the recessionary gap had shrunk substantially. Fears were increasingly being expressed that an outbreak of demand inflation was imminent. The inflation rate, which was close to 4.5 percent in both 1987 and 1988, showed signs of accelerating further during 1989—during the first 6 months of that year, inflation was running at an annual rate over 5 percent. As a result, the Fed was being urged to tighten up its monetary policy. Once again, the old fears were being expressed that driving up interest rates would increase inflationary pressures rather than reduce them.

Inflation in the Future

At the end of the 1980s, the Fed's immediate problem was to prevent an acceleration of inflation beyond the 4–5 percent range. Its longer-term policy remains, however, to reduce the existing inflation rate slowly toward zero. This objective raises a number of important policy issues on which only the future behavior of the economy can cast further evidence.

Can an inflation of 4 percent that is entrenched in people's expectations through a decade of inflationary experience be slowly reduced by gradually cutting the rate of monetary expansion? The advantage of gradualism is that, if it can be made to work, it would largely avoid the stagflationary phase 2 that accompanies any more dramatic attack on the inflation. If gradualism does not work, so that a more drastic reduction in the rate of monetary expansion is judged to be necessary to break current expectations, how long will the stagflation phase of high unemployment and lost output last?

Is a Zero Inflation Rate Attainable?

In a static world there is no reason why the goal of price level stability should not mean just that: an unchanging price level. In a dynamic world, where relative prices are continually adjusting, a stable price level requires that some individual prices rise while others fall. Many observers believe that they have identified an asymmetry in price adjustments—prices seem to rise faster in the face of excess demand than they fall in the face of excess supply. (Note that this says nothing about equilibrium, only that the speeds of adjustment are different in different markets and for different directions of change.) As relative prices adjust continually to the forces of change, if prices rise faster in markets with excess demand than they fall in markets with excess supply, then the average level of all prices will drift upward. Under these circumstances the structure of the economy causes an inflationary bias on the order of 1 to 2 percent per year. This takes the form of a slowly shifting *SRAS* curve. In these circumstances the Fed has two choices: It can accommodate the inflation to hold income at its potential level, or it can refuse to accommodate the inflation and allow the recessionary gap slowly to open up.

This is called *the structural theory of inflation*. Its validity was debated throughout the 1950s when, in spite of a recessionary gap throughout the last half of that decade, the price level continued to rise, albeit slowly. If the inflation rate falls to the 1 or even 2 percent range, the debate will rekindle: Is this the best that policy can achieve, or is zero inflation possible?

Are Full Employment and Stable Prices Compatible?

A debate has raged on both sides of the Atlantic for many decades: Are full employment and a low, stable inflation rate compatible in the long term? As long as the *SRAS* curve shifts only because of demand, expectational, and random shock effects, as we assumed earlier in this chapter, the answer is yes. However, what worries some observers is the possibility of a cost push that pushes wages up faster than productivity once the fear of unemployment is reduced by the continued achievement of potential income. As far back as the 1940s, many Keynesians were worried that, once the government was committed to maintaining full employment, much of the discipline of the market would be removed from wage bargains. The scramble of every group that is trying to get ahead of every other group would lead to a wage-cost push inflation. The commitment to full employment would then lead to accommodating increases in the money supply.

There is evidence that something like this has happened periodically over the last 40 years in Britain and in many of the countries of continental Europe. Most economists are more skeptical that it has been a serious force in the United States. Nonetheless, some observers still worry that full employment and a low, stable inflation rate may in the end prove to be incompatible. They argue for some permanent form of incomes policy.

An interesting argument that is presented by some economists is that the best way to ensure that the two objectives can be obtained most of the time is for governments to make clear that a stable price level, rather than full employment, is their overriding commitment and that, whenever the two come into short-run conflict, price stability will be given priority over full employment! They argue that once this message has been accepted by the public, there will be two benefits. First, wage-cost push inflations may not occur, even at full employment. Second, incipient inflations of the supply or the demand shock varieties will be easy to quell with only minor recessions because inflationary expectations and inertias will never have a chance to become strongly entrenched. In this environment major policy-induced recessions will not be required to control an outbreak of inflation. Paradoxically, by abandoning its full-employment commitment, the government may make the maintenance of something close to full employment much more likely—at least, that is how the argument goes.

Throughout the history of economics, inflation has been recognized as a harmful phenomenon. This view was given renewed strength as a result of the worldwide experiences of high inflation rates during the 1970s and early 1980s. The resolve is there, at least in advanced industrial countries, to prevent another outbreak of rapid inflation, and, should one occur for reasons of unavoidable supply-side shocks, to prevent the inflation from continuing long enough to become firmly entrenched in people's expectations. The resolve is a matter that has been settled in the last decade; the success in fulfilling this resolve is a matter to be tested in the coming decade.

SUMMARY

1. Either supply shocks or demand shocks can cause a temporary inflation. For either to lead to sustained inflation, it must be accompanied by a continuing expansion of the money supply, so that the *AD* curve is shifting upward.

2. A sustained price inflation will also be accompanied by a closely

related growth in wages and other factor costs, so that the *SRAS* curve is shifting upward.

3. Factors that influence shifts in the *SRAS* curve can be divided into three main categories: demand, expectations, and random shocks.

4. The influence of demand can be expressed in terms of the inflationary and recessionary gaps, which relate national income to potential income, or in terms of the difference between the actual and natural rates of unemployment.

5. Expectations of inflation tend to cause wage settlements that preserve the expected real wage and hence lead to nominal wage increases.

6. If the Fed accommodates the increasing demand for money as the economy recovers from a serious recession, it can easily find itself validating a demand-shock inflation once the economy develops an inflationary gap. If the Fed wishes to stop the inflation, it will have to reduce its rate of monetary expansion. This will raise interest rates and reduce aggregate desired expenditure, eventually eliminating the inflationary gap. Although the rise in interest rates does cause a once-and-for-all upward shift in the *SRAS* curve, the rise is a necessary part of an antiinflationary policy that slows the rate of growth of the money supply.

7. It is impossible to have a sustained, steady inflation when income exceeds its potential level. As expectations constantly catch up to the existing inflation rate, this rate, which is the sum of the expectations and demand effects, must accelerate.

8. It is possible to have a sustained inflation at potential national income (and hence at the natural rate of unemployment). There is no demand pressure on prices, but expectations can cause wages and hence prices to grow at the same rate as the money supply.

9. Stopping an inflation through restrictive monetary policy will lead to a recession that lasts while inflation only gradually falls to a rate that is consistent with the new lower rate of money growth. The length and depth of the recession will depend on the strength of the downward pressure on wages and on the speed with which inflationary expectations adjust.

10. Keynesians tend to believe that the negative demand pressures on wages from a recessionary gap are weak and that expectations are sluggish to adjust. As a result, they believe that the typical stagflation phase will be deep and prolonged. Monetarists tend to believe that the negative demand pressures from a recessionary gap cause wages to respond quickly and that expectations are fast to adjust. As a result, they believe that the typical stagflation phase will be brief.

11. Some economists believe that zero inflation is an achievable goal of the policy of price stability; others believe that a gradual upward drift of the price level on the order of 1 to 2 percent per year must be accepted.

12. Some observers doubt that sustained full employment is compatible with stable prices. They advocate permanent incomes policies to control wage inflation and to make the two objectives compatible. Many economists are skeptical that such policies are needed in the United States and see no compelling evidence why full employment and stable prices cannot coexist in a flexible market economy.

TOPICS FOR REVIEW

Temporary and sustained inflations
Monetary accommodation of supply shocks
Monetary validation of demand shocks
Demand inflation
Expectational inflation
Natural rate of unemployment
Accelerating inflation
Entrenched inflation
Incomes policies

DISCUSSION QUESTIONS

1. On what source or sources of inflation do the following statements focus attention?
   a. "The one basic cause of inflation is the government's spending more than it takes in. The cure is a balanced budget."
   b. "Wage bargains currently being negotiated in autos, and several other basic industries, will soon cause inflation to accelerate."
   c. "Americans have become so accustomed to 4 percent inflation that it would be difficult for the Fed to induce the transition to 1 or 2 percent inflation."
   d. "As the U.S. business expansion continued for its eighth unprecedented year, inflationary pressures seemed to be building up across the country."
2. When OPEC radically increased the price of oil in 1974, the world was hit with a severe supply shock. The Bank of Canada decided to accommodate this with a rapid burst of monetary expansion, while the Fed decided on a policy of nonaccommodation. What do you think happened to the inflation rate and the national incomes of the two countries over the following two years?
3. When the entrenched inflation of the early 1980s was broken, the economies of many industrial countries came to rest with a relatively low inflation rate and high unemployment. People who feared the outbreak of inflation opposed even a temporary increase in the rate of monetary expansion. Use aggregate demand and aggregate supply analysis to show why some people felt that a *temporary* burst of monetary expansion might bring increases in employment without increases in inflation.
4. Look at the rate of increases of the money supply and the CPI over the last three years and decide whether or not the current inflation is being validated.
5. Discuss the following views that were expressed by two U.S. congressmen in 1987.
   a. "Now that inflation has been beaten to the ground, we can get on with reducing unemployment."
   b. "Eternal vigilance is the price of a low inflation rate."
6. What theory or theories of inflation are suggested by each of the following quotations?
   a. American newspaper headline in 1986: "February producer prices steady—fall in energy costs largest in 6 years."
   b. Newspaper editorial in Manchester, England: "If American unions were as strong as those in Britain, American inflationary experience would have been as disastrous as has Britain's."
   c. Study issued in 1980 by the Worldwatch Institute: "The nation's spiraling inflation reflects a global depletion of physical resources

and therefore cannot be cured by traditional fiscal and monetary tools."

    d. Article in the London *Economist*: "Oil price collapse will reduce today's inflation rate."

7. Discuss the following views on the effects of inflation.

    a. Robert D. Hersy, Jr.: "The beast [of inflation] is a luminescent specter, a killer, a threat to society, public enemy No. 1."

    b. James Tobin: "In the early 1980s inflation became the national obsession. . . . the catchall scapegoat for individual and societal economic difficulties, the symptom that diverts attention from the basic maladies."

8. In an article on the harmful effects of inflation, which was written early in the 1980s, a reporter wrote, "With the rise in mortgage interest rates to 11 percent, heaven only knows the price of what was once idealized as 'the $100,000 house.' " At the time the inflation rate was 8 percent. Did the 11 percent interest rate represent a heavy burden of inflation on the new home owner? What do you think the mortgage interest rate would have been if the inflation rate had been zero? Which situation would have meant a heavier real burden on the purchaser of a new house?

9. Discuss the apparent conflict between the following views. Can you suggest how they might be reconciled using aggregate demand and aggregate supply analysis?

    a. "A rise in interest rates is deflationary, since breaking an entrenched inflation with a tight monetary policy usually requires that interest rates rise steeply."

    b. "A rise in interest rates is inflationary, since interest is a major business cost and, as with other costs, a rise in interest will be passed on by firms in terms of higher prices."

10. Inflations cannot long persist, whatever their initiating causes, unless they are validated by increases in the money supply. Why is this so? Does it not imply that control of inflation is merely a matter of not allowing the money supply to rise faster than the rate of increase of real national income?

Appendix to Chapter 34

Sustained Inflation and the Phillips Curve

In this appendix we use the Phillips curve, introduced in Chapter 30, to analyze sustained inflations.

The Price Phillips Curve

The Phillips curve, shown in Box 28-1 on pages 580–581, described a relationship between the rate of change of *wages* and the state of demand, as measured by the level of national income. As we saw, changes in wages cause the *SRAS* curve to shift, giving rise to changes in the price level. These two steps are commonly combined to produce a new curve, relating the rate of change of the *price level* and the level of national income. Such a curve, often referred to as a *price Phillips curve,* is shown in Figure 34A-1.

The conditions under which it is possible to derive a price Phillips curve from the original relationship between wages and national income are fairly complicated.[1] However, the curve is commonly used, and we shall focus on it in this appendix. (We shall henceforth refer to the price Phillips curve simply as the Phillips curve.) The key simplification is that, once the level of income has been determined—by the intersection of the *SRAS* and *AD* curves, as before—the rate of inflation can be read *directly* from the Phillips curve.

Notice that the Phillips curve in Figure 34A-1 has the *rate of change of prices* on the vertical axis. The *SRAS* curve that appears so frequently in the text has the *level of prices* on the vertical axis. Since both curves have real national income on the horizontal axis, they might be easily confused. They must, therefore, be carefully distinguished.

Components of Inflation

Recall the three influences that cause the *SRAS* curve to shift upward and hence the price level to rise:

demand, expectations, and random shocks. In this appendix we continue to use the terms *demand* and *shock,* but we introduce the term *core inflation* as a generalization of the term *expectations* that is used in the text. The rate of increase of prices can now be written as the sum of the three components:

$$\Delta p = C + DE + SE$$

where Δp is the annual percentage rate of changes of prices (i.e., the rate of inflation), C refers to core inflation, DE refers to demand inflation, and SE refers to shock inflation. We now look at these components one at a time.

Demand Inflation

Demand inflation refers to the influence on the price level of inflationary and recessionary gaps. We have seen that an inflationary gap involves upward pressure on wages and hence on the price level, while a recessionary gap involves downward pressure. This is shown in Figure 34A-1 by the vertical distance between the Phillips curve and the horizontal axis.

The Phillips curve in Figure 34A-1 is merely a novel way of expressing relationships that we have used many times before. (It is important to remember, however, that Figure 34A-1 does not tell the whole story of inflation; it describes only the effects of *demand.*) These relationships include the following:

1. There is neither upward nor downward pressure of demand on the price level when national income is at its potential level. Graphically, the Phillips curve cuts the axis at Y^*.
2. When there is an inflationary gap, wages and other costs will rise. As we have seen, this shifts the *SRAS* curve and causes the price level to rise. The inflation continues as long as the gap persists. Graphically, the Phillips curve lies above the axis where Y exceeds Y^*.
3. When there is a recessionary gap, wages and other costs will fall. This shifts the *SRAS* curve downward and causes the price level to fall. The deflation continues as long as the gap persists. Graphically, the Phillips curve lies below the axis when Y is less than Y^*.

---

[1] For example, at any given level of income, the relationship between the rate of change of wages, given by the figure in Box 28-1, and the rate of change of prices, given by Figure 34A-1, depends on what is assumed about how fast the central bank is causing the *AD* curve to shift.

FIGURE 34A-1   Price Phillips Curve

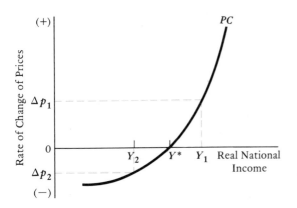

The price Phillips curve shows the positive relationship between the level of national income and the rate of increase in the *price level.* An increase in national income leads to an increase in the rate of change of wages and, other things being equal, to an increase in the rate of change of prices. A fall in income leads to a decrease in the rate of change of wages and, other things being equal, to a decrease in the rate of change of prices.

With zero core inflation and output at its capacity level Y^*, inflation is zero, as shown. When output is above Y^* at, say, Y_1, inflation is positive at Δp_1. When output is below Y^* at, say, Y_2, inflation is negative at Δp_2.

4. The speed of the upward adjustment of the price level in the face of an inflationary gap exceeds the speed of the downward adjustment in the face of a recessionary gap. Graphically, the Phillips curve becomes steeper the further to the right one moves along it. [42]

Core Inflation

The demand component cannot be the whole explanation of inflation, since, if it were, inflation would only occur if national income exceeded Y^* and inflation could be quickly removed by forcing income back to Y^*. This behavior is emphatically rejected by the recent experiences of the United States and other Western economies. To explain what we observe about inflation, we add the concept of *core inflation,* which refers to the underlying trend of in-

flation, and it is referred to by several different names: *core* inflation, *expectational* inflation, *inertial* inflation, and the *underlying rate* of inflation.

In the text we singled out expectations as a main influence on the price level, in addition to demand, but we also saw that how expectations are formed is a major source of controversy among economists. The controversy actually runs deeper than this; some analysts question whether it is explicit expectations about the future or inertia based on past experience that really dominates wage settlements. For example, past experience may matter if recent wage increases have failed to keep up with price increases; in such circumstances current wage settlements may have a "catch-up" component.

For these and other reasons, we use the general term *core inflation* to describe persistent effects that do not depend on current demand conditions. These include expectations and other elements that stem from both forward- and backward-looking behavior. Some elements may change quickly; others may change only slowly. Their total influence at any point in time is summarized in the term *core inflation.*

Core inflation operates on the *SRAS* curve through the effects of wages and other costs.[2] Core inflation also may be related to *expected future changes* in wage and capital costs, since firms that plan to change prices only infrequently must set prices on the basis of their expected costs over their planning period. If this is the case, to make our concept of core inflation operative, we need a theory of how firms form their expectations of the future movement of costs. Some of the theories on how the expectations that determine the core inflation rate are formed are discussed in Chapter 38.

Graphically, the core inflation rate is added to the demand effect by shifting the Phillips curve upward by the amount of the core inflation rate. This gives rise to a *core-augmented Phillips curve* or, more commonly, an *expectations-augmented Phillips curve,* as shown in Figure 34A-2. At any given level of income, the height of the core-augmented Phillips curve is given by the sum of the demand effect and the core rate of inflation. For example, at $Y = Y^*$, when demand inflation is zero, the height of the Phillips curve is given by the core inflation rate. At any other level of income, the rate of inflation differs

---

[2] Some variations in net profit margins can and do occur. These cause price inflation to diverge temporarily from cost inflation and are included in shock inflation.

from the demand effect by an amount equal to the core inflation rate.

Short-run Phillips curve.   Because the Phillips curve shifts upward or downward as the core rate of inflation rises or falls, it is called a **short-run Phillips curve (SRPC)** when it is drawn at any particular height above Y^* (that is, for any given level of core inflation).

The short-run Phillips curve is drawn for a given rate of core inflation.

Shock Inflation

Shock inflation refers to once-and-for-all changes that give a temporary upward or downward jolt to the price level. These include changes in indirect taxes, changes in profit margins, changes in import prices, and all kinds of other factors that are often referred to as *supply shocks*. Shock inflation includes everything that is not included in demand and core inflation.

Summary

Putting all of this together, we see that the current inflation rate depends on the influence of (1) demand as indicated by the inflationary or recessionary gap, demand inflation; (2) expected increase in costs, core inflation; and (3) a series of exogenous forces coming mainly from the supply side, shock inflation. These three components of inflation may be illustrated both numerically and graphically.

For a numerical example, assume that, in the absence of any demand pressure, prices would rise by 10 percent, because firms expect underlying costs to rise by 10 percent; that this price rise is moderated by 1 percentage point, because costs only rise by 9 percent due to heavy unemployment and that the price rise is augmented by 3 percentage points, because large increases in indirect taxes force prices up. The final inflation is 12 percent, made up of 10 percent core inflation minus 1 percent demand inflation plus 3 percent shock inflation.

Graphically, the components of inflation are illustrated in Figure 34A-3 (see page 741) for two cases with a common positive core inflation component. The curve labeled *SRPC* is the expectations-augmented Phillips curve, that is, the Phillips curve shifted by the core inflation rate. Its height above the

FIGURE 34A-2   Core Inflation and the Short-Run Phillips Curve

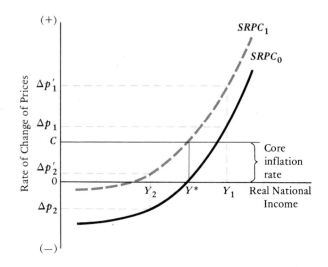

Core inflation shifts the price Phillips curve and so changes the rate of inflation that corresponds to any given level of national income. The curve $SRPC_0$, which reproduces the Phillips curve from Figure 34A-1, corresponds to a zero core inflation rate. When core inflation rises to, say, C, the Phillips curve shifts upward to $SRPC_1$. The rate of inflation at Y^* rises from 0 to C. At Y_1, which is greater than Y^*, inflation rises from Δp_1 to $\Delta p_1'$. At Y_2, which is less than Y^*, inflation was initially negative at Δp_2 but now becomes positive at $\Delta p_2'$.

axis at Y^* thus indicates core inflation. Points along *SRPC* where Y does not equal Y^* indicate how much the pressures of excess or deficient demand cause inflation to deviate from the core rate. The amount by which actual inflation lies above or below the *SRPC* shows the amount by which shocks cause the actual inflation rate to deviate from the sum of the core and the demand effects.

Expectations and Changes in Inflation

Originally, the Phillips curve in Figure 34A-1 was thought to provide the whole explanation of inflation. When it was realized that the short-run Phillips curve shifted upward or downward, the concept of

FIGURE 34A-3   The Components of Inflation Illustrated

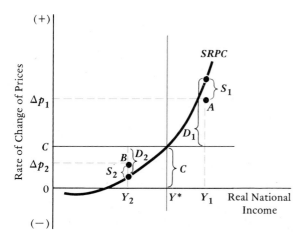

The inflation rate can be separated into three components: core inflation, demand inflation, and shock inflation. The Phillips curve is drawn for a given core rate of inflation and hence is labeled as a short-run Phillips curve. The given core rate, C, is shown by the height of the horizontal colored line.

Point A indicates a national income of Y_1, combined with an inflation rate of Δp_1. This rate is composed of the following: a core rate, C; a positive demand component, D_1 (determined by the shape of $SRPC$); and a negative shock component, S_1.

Point B indicates a national income of Y_2, combined with an inflation rate of Δp_2. This rate is composed of the following: core inflation, once again given by C; the demand component, D_2, which is now negative (since income Y_2 is less than Y^*); and a positive shock component, S_2.

core inflation was added to explain this. Changes in the core inflation rate causes shifts in the short-run Phillips curve. As a result, we have the following conclusion:

There is a family of short-run Phillips curves— one for each core rate of inflation.

This is illustrated in Figure 34A-4 (see page 742). Let us now see what governs changes in the core inflation rate and hence shifts in the $SRPC$.

Look at point Z on $SRPC_1$ in Figure 34A-5 (see page 742), which is $SRPC_1$ reproduced from Figure 34A-4 and corresponds to a core inflation rate of C_1. At point Z shock inflation is zero and demand inflation is positive (since $Y_1 > Y^*$), so the actual inflation rate is above the core inflation rate of C_1. Sooner or later this excess will come to be expected, the core rate of inflation will then rise, and the $SRPC$ will shift upward. As long as national income is held above Y^*, the actual inflation rate will exceed the core inflation rate, and, as a result, sooner or later the core inflation rate will rise. This means that the short-run Phillips curve sooner or later will shift upward, as indicated by the arrow above point Z.

Now look at point W in Figure 34A-5, where, again, core inflation is C_1 and shock inflation is zero. At W demand inflation is negative (since $Y_2 < Y^*$), so the actual inflation rate is below the core inflation rate of C_1. Sooner or later this difference will influence expectations, and the core rate of inflation will fall. As long as national income is held below Y^*, the actual inflation rate will be less than the core inflation rate, and sooner or later the core rate will fall. This means that sooner or later the short-run Phillips curve will begin to shift downward, as indicated by the arrow below W.

So we have a basic prediction of the theory:

A persistent inflationary gap sooner or later will cause the inflation rate to accelerate, whereas a persistent recessionary gap sooner or later will cause the inflation rate to decelerate.

This, of course, is the acceleration hypothesis that we encountered in the text. Let us now examine it in more detail.

Accelerating Inflation

Consider an economy with a core inflation of C_1 that has just experienced an increase in aggregate demand, so that output is above Y^*, as at point Z in Figure 34A-5. There is an inflationary gap with a positive inflation rate; the $SRAS$ curve will be shifting upward, while monetary validation by the central bank is shifting the AD curve upward. (It may be worth reiterating what is happening here: Core inflation produces the rise in prices that results from firms' expectations about the long-run trend in costs; the demand component produces the addition to infla-

FIGURE 34A-4   A Family of Short-Run Phillips Curves

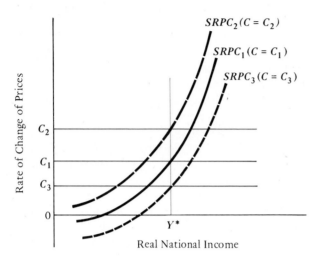

There is a separate short-run Phillips curve for each core rate of inflation. The Phillips curve of Figure 34A-3, shown here as $SRPC_1$, relates national income to inflation on the assumption that core inflation is C_1. The actual rate of inflation depends on both the core inflation rate and the level of national income (as well as on shock inflation, assumed here to be zero).

For each positive core rate of inflation, there is a short-run Phillips curve that lies above the axis at $Y = Y^*$ by the particular core inflation rate to which it relates. If the core inflation rate were C_2, greater than C_1, the Phillips curve would lie above $SRPC_1$, as shown, for example, by $SRPC_2$. If the core inflation rate were C_3, less than C_1, the curve would lie below $SRPC_1$, as shown for example, by $SRPC_3$.

FIGURE 34A-5   Shifts in the Short-Run Phillips Curve

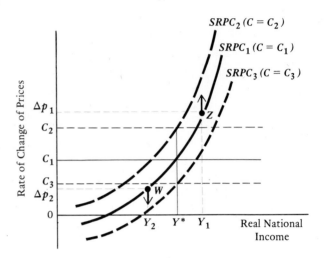

Changes in the core rate of inflation, which arise when actual inflation differs from the core rate, cause the short-run Phillips curve to shift. With a core inflation rate of C_1, the short-run Phillips curve is $SRPC_1$, reproduced from Figure 34A-4.

If income is maintained at Y_1, greater than Y^*, actual inflation will be Δp_1, greater than the core inflation rate, as indicated by point Z. Eventually, this excess of the actual inflation rate over the core inflation rate will cause the core inflation rate to rise, from C_1, say, to C_2, shifting the short-run Phillips curve to $SRPC_2$, as indicated by the arrow above point Z.

If income is maintained at Y_2, less than Y^*, actual inflation will be Δp_2, less than the core inflation rate, as indicated by point W. Eventually, the shortfall of actual inflation below the core inflation rate will cause the core inflation rate to fall below C_1, say, to C_3, causing the short-run Phillips curve to shift downward to $SRPC_3$, as indicated by the arrow below W.

tion due to what are thought to be transitory demand factors; shock inflation is still treated as zero.)

Is this situation sustainable? It is only if the Phillips curve remains stable. If the short-run Phillips curve stayed put, policymakers could conclude that they had achieved a pretty good trade-off. They would have gained a permanent increase in output of Y^*Y_1 at the cost of a permanent increase in inflation from C_1 to Δp_1.

As we have seen, however, this is not all that is happening. The persistence of a demand inflation will

eventually cause the core inflation rate to rise and hence cause the $SRPC$ to shift upward. In turn, this increases the rate at which the $SRAS$ curve is shifting upward. Let us trace this process in detail.

At point Z prices and costs are rising at Δp_1 per year, and sooner or later firms and workers will stop believing that this increase from the old rate C_1 is a transitory phenomenon. They will come to expect some of this increase to persist and incorporate it into core inflation. Let us say that after a passage of time firms come to expect wages and other costs to rise at the rate C_2 each period. This will produce a core inflation at a rate of C_2 per year in Figure 34A-5. The short-run Phillips curve now shifts upward to $SRPC_2$ in the figure. The rise in the core rate of inflation increases the actual inflation rate corresponding to each possible level of national income. If national income is maintained at Y_1, so that demand inflation remains positive, the actual inflation rate rises above Δp_1.

Now the $SRAS$ curve will be shifting upward more rapidly. If output is to be maintained at Y_1, the central bank will have to increase the rate of monetary expansion. This will cause the AD to shift upward more rapidly to match the more rapid upward shift in $SRAS$. This is illustrated in terms of the $SRAS$ and AD curves in Figure 34-4.

The actual inflation rate, Δp_2, is well above the core inflation rate, C_2. Sooner or later this will cause the core inflation rate to rise again, and the short-run Phillips curve will again shift upward. As long as output is maintained at Y_1 so that demand inflation is positive, this process of growing core inflation will continue.

From this an important conclusion follows:

If the central bank validates any rate of inflation that results from Y being held above Y^*, the inflation rate itself will accelerate continuously _and_ the rate of monetary expansion required to frustrate the monetary adjustment mechanism will also accelerate.

The Long-Run Phillips Curve

Is there any level of income in this model that is compatible with a constant actual rate of inflation? The answer is yes, potential income. When income is at Y^*, the demand component of inflation is _zero,_ as shown in Figure 34A-1. This means that, if we still let shock inflation be zero, actual inflation equals core inflation. Since the core inflation is determined by what people expect the inflation rate to be when actual inflation equals core inflation, the actual inflation rate is equal to the expected rate. There are no surprises. No one's plans are upset, so no one has

any incentive to alter plans as a result of what actually happens to inflation.

Provided that the inflation rate is fully validated and shock inflation is zero, any rate of inflation can persist indefinitely, as long as income is held at its potential level.

We now define the **long-run Phillips curve (LRPC)** as the relationship between _national income_ and _stable rates of inflation_ that neither accelerate nor decelerate. This occurs when the core and actual inflation rates are equal. According to the theory just described, the long-run Phillips curve is vertical. This is illustrated in Figure 34A-6.

Maintaining a point on the $LRPC$ leads to steady inflation at the core rate of inflation. This is illustrated in Figure 34A-7 (see page 744), where we show a situation with a positive core inflation rate and where there is full accommodation by the central bank. In part (i) the intersection of the $SRAS$ and AD curves determines Y at Y^*. In part (ii) the Phillips curve shows the rate of inflation. There is no demand effect

FIGURE 34A-6 Vertical Long-Run Phillips Curve

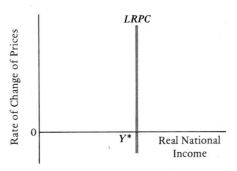

When actual inflation equals expected inflation, there is no trade-off between inflation and unemployment. In long-term equilibrium, the actual rate of inflation must remain equal to the expected rate (otherwise expectations would be revised). This can only occur at potential income Y^*, that is, along the $LRPC$.

At Y^* there is no demand pressure on the price level; hence the only influence on actual inflation is expected inflation. Any stable rate of inflation (provided it is validated by the appropriate rate of monetary expansion) is compatible with Y^* and its associated natural rate of unemployment.

FIGURE 34A-7 **Monetary Accommodation and Steady Inflation**

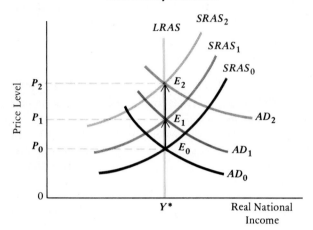

(i) Upward-shifting AD and $SRAS$ curves

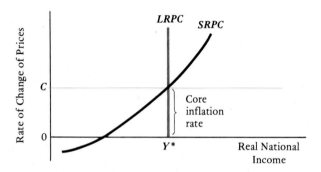

(ii) Steady inflation

Positive core inflation means that wage costs will be rising, even when output is just at its capacity level; monetary accommodation can keep output constant and sustain the inflation rate. Core inflation is shown in part (ii) by C, the height of the short-run Phillips curve above the axis at Y^*. This translates into an upward-shifting $SRAS$ curve from $SRAS_0$ to $SRAS_1$ to $SRAS_2$ in part (i). Monetary accommodation means that the AD curve in part (i) also shifts upward, from AD_0 to AD_1 to AD_2. As drawn, the monetary accommodation just keeps income constant at Y^*, so inflation persists at the core inflation rate, C.

The positive wage inflation in part (ii) is reflected in an equal rate of price increase from P_0 to P_1 to P_2 in part (i). Since we are on the $LRPC$, core inflation is constant and the $SRPC$ is stable.

on inflation, so the actual and core inflation rates are equal. As a result, the situation is sustainable (as long as the central bank continues to validate the core inflation). The increasing price level in part (i) reflects the positive inflation rate indicated in part (ii). Note that in part (ii), since the core inflation rate is not changing, the $SRPC$ will be stable, which means we are also on the $LRPC$.

We can now state a general conclusion:

The long-run Phillips curve is vertical at Y^*; only Y^* is compatible with a stable rate of inflation, and any stable rate is, if fully validated, compatible with Y^*.

The Natural Rate of Unemployment

We have talked about variations of Y from Y^*, but for every level of national income there is an associated level of unemployment. Recasting these conclusions in terms of unemployment, we have the following: As before, call the unemployment that is associated with Y^* the natural rate of unemployment or the NAIRU. Note that unemployment can be pushed below the NAIRU, but only at the cost of opening up an inflationary gap. If the government seeks to maintain this lower rate of unemployment, the inflation rate will accelerate and will have to be validated by ever increasing rates of monetary expansion.

The lowest rate of unemployment that can be maintained without a tendency for the rate of inflation to accelerate is the NAIRU.

Implications for Monetary Policy

The foregoing analysis has three major implications for the understanding and conduct of monetary policy. First, the interaction among money, inflation, and output is complex. In particular, it depends on how expectations are formulated. Monetary policies may affect expectations differently at different times. Therefore, it would be wrong to expect a simple, mechanical relationship between the money supply and the behavior of output and the price level.

Second, differences between the expected rate of inflation and the rate that is being validated by monetary policy lead to changes in the level of output and in the actual rate of inflation. Hence, changes in the rate of monetary expansion can have powerful, though not entirely predictable, effects on the economy.

Third, in the long run GDP will move to the level indicated by the long-run aggregate supply curve and the long-run Phillips curve. This means that changes in the rate of monetary expansion will cause only temporary changes in the level of output. In the long run changes in the rate of monetary expansion have their only influence on the rate of inflation.

Some Extensions

Shock inflation.   All of the foregoing analysis has been done on the assumption that shock inflation is zero. In today's world many shocks hit the price level. What we see is a much less regular experience than the simple combination of core plus demand inflation. The inflation rate varies quite substantially from period to period, due to the action of the many shocks that impinge on it. When such shocks occur, the economy's output-inflation combination will lie off the current expectations-augmented Phillips curve—above it for a positive shock and below it for a negative shock.

Asymmetrical speeds of reaction.   The shape of the Phillips curve means that it is easier to raise the core inflation rate than to lower it. The change in the core inflation rate from period to period depends on the discrepancy between the actual rate and the core rate. The steepness of the short-run Phillips curve above Y^* means that it is easy to create a substantial gap between the actual rate and the core rate by increasing the inflationary gap. This will tend to drag up the core rate fairly quickly. The flatness of the short-run Phillips curve below Y^* means that only a small discrepancy between the actual and the core rates can be created by even a large recessionary gap. Therefore, the core rate can be depressed only slowly by creating recessionary gaps.

It is an important prediction of this theory that the core rate of inflation can accelerate fairly quickly but will decelerate only slowly.

Summary

We now summarize the key points of the theory of the expectations-augmented Phillips curve and indi-

cate where there is substantial agreement and where there is controversy with competing theories.

1. *The rate of price inflation must follow the trend rate of cost inflation quite closely.* There is little disagreement over this relationship, which defines the core rate of inflation. Notice, however, that it is just a matter of simple arithmetic that the major determinant of price inflation is cost inflation. This says nothing about causes. Costs could be rising because of the pressure of excess demand in factor markets or because of the exercise of arbitrary power on the part of unions.

2. *The influence of demand on inflation is asymmetrical.* Inflationary gaps cause inflation to rise well above the core rate, whereas recessionary gaps force the actual rate only slightly below the core rate. The evidence for this asymmetry is strong, although some economists deny it.

3. *The core inflation rate falls slowly, even in the face of large recessionary gaps.* There is substantial disagreement over this point, for some economists believe that the core rate can fall quite rapidly. This key controversy underlies many differences in policy recommendations.

4. *Shocks caused by such influences as changes in indirect taxes, agricultural crop failures, or increases in import prices temporarily affect the inflation rate.* Economists do not always agree on this point; at the time of the first OPEC oil-price shocks in 1974, some said that if oil-related prices rose, other prices would fall, keeping the price level constant. As a result of the evidence of the OPEC shocks, most economists now agree that supply shocks affect the price level, causing temporary deviations in the rate of inflation from what it would otherwise be. Another example of a clear supply-shock inflation was the rise in the price level that occurred in Britain in 1979 and 1980 after income taxes were cut and value-added taxes were raised by the new Conservative government.

5. *Demand-induced rises in the inflation rate yield only temporary increases in national income.* Any departure of national income from Y^* sets in motion forces that cause a return to Y^*. Output in excess of Y^* causes an inflation that sets in motion the monetary adjustment mechanism. Frustration of the monetary adjustment mechanism by monetary expansion can sustain output above Y^*, but only if the rate of increase of wages, prices, and money is continually accelerating.

Chapter 35

Employment and Unemploy- ment

In the early 1980s unemployment in most of the world's developed economies rose to historically high levels. It remained high for many years and only began to come down—and then very slowly—during the latter half of the decade. Toward the end of 1988, unemployment rates in France, Germany, Italy, and the United Kingdom were all still high by historical standards. Although the experience in the United States was more favorable than in most other countries, the reduction in overall unemployment was still painfully slow. From a high of 9.7 percent in 1982, the civilian unemployment rate fell gradually to 5.5 percent in 1988. In the early months of 1989, the unemployment rate seemed to have stopped falling; it oscillated between 5.0 percent and 5.4 percent.

These overall U.S. unemployment figures hide, as we shall see later in this chapter, large variations in rates for specific groups. For example, in November of 1988, the unemployment rate was 4.5 percent for white males over 19 years of age and 32.4 percent for black males between the ages of 16 and 19.

Many social policies, designed to alleviate the short-term economic consequences of unemployment, have been instituted since the 1930s, and their success may be counted as a real triumph of economic policy. Being unemployed, even for a substantial period of time, is no longer the economic disaster that it once was. However, there is a wealth of evidence that long-term unemployment still has many harmful effects. Among these is a sense of disillusionment among unemployed workers who perceive a lack of opportunity in the market economy.

The case for concern about high unemployment has been put eloquently by the economist Alan Blinder:

> A high-pressure economy provides opportunities, facilitates structural change, encourages inventiveness and innovation, opens doors for society's underdogs . . . All these promote the social cohesion and economic progress that make democratic mixed capitalism such a wonderful system when it works well. A low-pressure economy slams the doors shut, breeds a bunker mentality that resists change, stifles productivity growth, and fosters both inequality and mean-spirited public policy. All this makes reducing high unemployment a political, economic, and moral challenge of the highest order.[1]

[1] Alan S. Blinder, "The Challenge of High Unemployment," *American Economic Review,* 78:2 (May 1988), p. 1.

Kinds of Unemployment

For purposes of study, the unemployed are classified in various ways. They can be grouped by personal characteristics, such as age, sex, degree of skill or education, and ethnic group. They can also be classified by geographical location, by occupation, by the duration of unemployment, or by the reasons for their unemployment.

In this chapter we are concerned mainly with the reasons for unemployment. Although it is not always possible to say why a particular unemployed person does not have a job, it is often possible to gain some idea of the total number of people unemployed for each major cause.

In Chapter 24, we distinguished three types of unemployment: *cyclical* unemployment, which is unemployment due to a recessionary gap, and *frictional* and *structural* unemployment, both of which may exist when national income is at its potential level and hence there is neither a recessionary gap nor an inflationary gap.

In this chapter we discuss each type of employment in more detail, and we also discuss *real-wage unemployment,* which may prevent an economy from reaching potential income.

Frictional Unemployment

Frictional unemployment refers to the normal turnover of labor. An important source of frictional unemployment is young people who enter the labor force and look for jobs. Another source is people who leave their jobs. Some may quit because they are dissatisfied with the working conditions; others may be fired. Whatever the reason, they must search for new jobs, which takes time. Persons who are unemployed while searching for jobs are said to be frictionally unemployed.

The normal turnover of labor would cause frictional unemployment to persist, even if the economy were at potential income and the structure of jobs in terms of skills, industries, occupations, and location was unchanging.

When Keynes examined the causes of unemploy-ment, he made a basic distinction between voluntary and involuntary unemployment. In his view, *voluntary unemployment* occurs when there is a job available but the unemployed person is not willing to accept it at the going wage rate. *Involuntary unemployment* occurs when a person is willing to accept a job at the going wage rate but cannot find one. In Box 35-1, in which we discuss *search unemployment* in more detail, we see that the distinction between voluntary and involuntary unemployment is not always as clear as Keynes suggested.

Structural Unemployment

Structural adjustments of the economy can cause unemployment. When the pattern of demand for goods changes, the demand for labor changes. Until labor adjusts fully, *structural unemployment* develops. *Structural unemployment* may be defined as unemployment that is caused by a mismatch between the structure of the labor force—in terms of skills, occupations, industries, or geographical location—and the structure of the demand for labor. In the United States today, structural unemployment exists, for example, in the oil-drilling industry in Texas and Oklahoma and in many of the older foundry and mill towns in parts of the Midwest.

Natural causes. Economic growth can cause structural unemployment. As the economy grows, the mix of required inputs changes, as do the proportions in which final goods are demanded. These changes require considerable economic adjustment. Structural unemployment occurs when such adjustments are slow enough that severe pockets of unemployment develop in areas, industries, and occupations in which the demand for factors of production is falling faster than the supply.

Changes that accompany economic growth shift the structure of the demand for labor. Demand rises in such expanding areas as southern California and falls (at least relatively) in other geographic areas. Demand rises for workers with certain skills, such as computer programming and electronics engineering, and falls for workers with other skills, such as stenography and bookkeeping. Demand rises, say, for airline pilots and short-order cooks and falls for automobile assembly line workers and railroad conductors. To meet changing demands, the structure

BOX 35-1

Search Unemployment

Some frictional unemployment is involuntary: No acceptable job in the person's occupational and skill category has yet been located. Often, however, it is voluntary. The unemployed person is aware of available jobs but is searching for better options. Voluntary frictional unemployment is often called **search unemployment.**

The existence of search unemployment shows that the distinction between voluntary and involuntary unemployment is not as clear as it might seem at first. How, for example, should we classify an unemployed woman who refuses to accept a job at a lower skill level than the one for which she feels she is qualified? What if she turns down a job for which she is trained because she hopes to get a higher wage offer for a similar job from another employer?

In one sense people in search unemployment are voluntarily unemployed, because they could find some job; in another sense they are involuntarily unemployed, because they have not yet succeeded in finding the job for which they feel that they are suited at a rate of pay that they believe exists.

Workers do not have perfect knowledge of all available jobs and rates of pay, and they may be able to gain information only by searching the market. Faced with this uncertainty, it may be sensible for them to refuse a first job offer, for the offer may prove to be a poor one in light of further market information. Too much search—for example, holding off while being supported by others in the hope of locating a job better than a job for which one is really suited—is an economic waste. Thus, search unemployment is a gray area: Some of it is useful, and some of it is wasteful.

It is socially desirable for there to be sufficient search unemployment to give unemployed people time to find an available job that makes the best use of their skills.

How long it will pay for people to remain in search unemployment depends on the economic costs of being unemployed. By lowering the costs of being unemployed, unemployment insurance tends to increase the amount of search unemployment. This may or may not increase economic efficiency, depending on whether it induces people to search beyond the point at which they acquire new and valuable information about the labor market.

---

of the labor force must change. Some existing workers can retrain and some new entrants can acquire fresh skills, but the transition is often difficult, especially for experienced workers whose skills become economically obsolete.

Increases in international competition can have effects that are similar to those of economic growth. As the geographic distribution of world production changes, so does the composition of production and labor demand in any one country. Many economists believe that increased international competition over the past two decades has contributed to increased structural employment in the United States.

Structural unemployment will increase if there is either an increase in the speed at which the structure of the demand for labor is changing or a decrease in the speed at which labor is adapting to these changes.

Policy causes.   Government policies can influence the speed with which labor markets adapt to changes. Some European countries have used policies that discourage movement among regions, industries, and occupations. These policies tend to raise structural unemployment. Others, such as Sweden, have done the reverse and have encouraged markets to adapt to change. Partly for this reason, Sweden's unemployment rates were well below the European norm during the 1980s.

Policies that discourage firms from replacing human labor with machines may protect employment in the short term. If, however, such policies lead to the decline of an industry because it cannot compete effectively with innovative foreign competitors, serious structural unemployment can result in the long run.

Minimum-wage laws can cause structural unemployment by pricing low-skilled labor out of the market. This was not much of a problem in the United States in the latter part of the 1980s, because the constant nominal minimum wage ($3.35 per hour) that prevailed from 1981 on was a very low real wage by 1989. Between 1981 and early 1989, the Consumer Price Index rose by 35 percent, implying that the real minimum wage fell by 35 percent. There is a good chance that the minimum wage will have been increased by the time this book is published, however, in which case both the positive and the negative effects of the minimum wage will be greater.[2]

The potential effect of minimum wages on employment can be illustrated by example. Consider an elderly person who may be prepared to supplement his social security pension by working for $150 per week as a caretaker of an apartment building. Suppose that the owner believes that this person is capable of doing what is needed, but the minimum wage is $170 per week. If there were no minimum wage, the elderly person would get the job. Because of the minimum wage, however, the owner has to pay more than she needs to and therefore hires someone else who can provide more services than are needed. She reasons that, since she has to pay more, she might as well get something extra for it.

The same considerations apply to an inexperienced worker, just out of school, who would accept $150 per week for a first job. A potential employer is willing to pay this wage, but the minimum wage is $170 per week. Once again the employer hires someone else who is overqualified for the job. A further unfortunate effect is that such young workers do not get on-the-job training and experience, which would enable them to hold down a stable, higher-paying job a year or two later.

Minimum-wage policies are not the only types of policies that affect the structure of relative wages, although they are by far the most important policies that are likely to have such effects in the United

States. Generally, policies that substitute imposed wage structures for market-determined ones tend to transfer employment from those whose relative wages are raised to those whose relative wages are lowered. The effect on overall employment is uncertain. However, when policies that affect the structure of wages lead to an increase in the average wage paid, they may contribute to what we will call *real-wage unemployment,* which we discuss later in this chapter.

The Relationship Between Frictional and Structural Unemployment

As with many distinctions, the one between structural and frictional unemployment becomes blurred at the margin. In a sense structural unemployment is really long-term frictional unemployment. Consider a change that requires labor to move from one sector to another. If the reallocation occurs quickly, we call the unemployment *frictional;* if the reallocation occurs slowly, we call the unemployment *structural.*

The major characteristic of both frictional and structural unemployment is that there is a job available, that is, an unfilled vacancy, for each unemployed person.

In the case of pure frictional unemployment, the job vacancy and the searcher are matched. The only problem is that the searcher has not yet located the vacancy. In the case of structural unemployment, the job vacancy and the searcher are mismatched in one or more relevant characteristics, such as occupation, industry, location, or skill requirements.

The sum of frictional and structural unemployment is what in Chapter 34 we called the *NAIRU.* Later in this chapter we consider policies that might change the NAIRU by changing the level of both frictional and structural unemployment.

Cyclical Unemployment

We have called unemployment that occurs because total demand is insufficient to purchase all the output that could be produced by a fully employed labor force *cyclical unemployment.* It is the unemployment that exists because there is a recessionary gap. As a result there are fewer available jobs than there are unemployed persons. Cyclical unemployment can be

---

[2] See Chapter 20 for a detailed discussion of the microeconomic effects of minimum wages.

measured as the number of persons currently employed minus the number of persons who would be employed at potential income. (It is thus the unemployment counterpart of the recessionary gap.) When cyclical unemployment is zero, there is some job available for every person unemployed. In this situation unemployment persists for either structural or frictional reasons. This is the level of unemployment that occurs at the NAIRU.

National-income theory seeks to explain the causes of and cures for unemployment in excess of frictional and structural unemployment. *Full employment* **does not mean zero unemployment; it means that all unemployment is frictional or structural.**

Real-Wage Unemployment

Unemployment that occurs because real wages are too high is called **real-wage unemployment** or sometimes **classical unemployment.** This latter term is used because many economists, whom Keynes dubbed "the classical economists," believed that unemployment in the 1930s was caused by excessively high real wages. The remedy that they suggested for unemployment was to reduce wages. Keynes argued that the unemployment was due to too little aggregate demand, and his remedy was to raise demand, not to cut wages. Keynesians won that debate, and the majority of economists now agree that the unemployment of the 1930s was caused primarily by deficient aggregate demand rather than excessive real wages.

Because the debates of the 1930s aroused strong emotions, some modern Keynesians have refused to believe that *any* unemployment could be caused by too high real wages. There is concern, however, that some current unemployment in Western Europe and elsewhere may be traced to excessively high real-wage levels.

When we speak of real wages that are "excessive" or "too high," we mean real wages that are so high that it does not pay private employers to provide employment for all who seek it at the going wage. How might this come about?

So far in this book we have used the term *real wages* to mean the purchasing power of money wages. This is measured by deflating the money wage by the Consumer Price Index. In this discussion we are concerned with the real cost to the employer of hiring a worker. We call this the **real product wage.** The nominal cost to the employer includes the pretax wage, any extra benefits such as pension plan contributions, and any government payroll taxes such as employers' contributions to the social security trust funds. The hourly real product wage is the nominal cost of hiring labor for one hour, divided by the value of the output produced by labor during the same time period. Thus, for example, if it costs $10 per hour to employ labor that produces output valued at $15, the real product wage is 0.667, which says that labor costs absorb two-thirds of the value of output.

Too high a real product wage can affect employment through forces operating both in the short run and in the long run. Consider the short run first. At any moment in time, many industries will have an array of plants, ranging from those that embody the oldest technologies in use and that can do little more than cover their variable costs to those that embody the latest technology and can make a handsome return over variable costs. A rise in the real product wage of 10 percent will mean that some plants can no longer cover their variable costs and so will close down. If, for example, a particular plant had wages of $.70 and other variable costs of $.25 for every $1.00 of sales, production would be worthwhile, since $.05 of every $1.00 of sales would be available as a return on already invested capital. Now suppose that the product wage rose so that $.77 for every $1.00 of sales was paid to labor. In this case, the plant would be shut down, since the product price of $1.00 would not even cover the variable costs of $1.02. The plant's employees would then lose their jobs. This analysis can be extended to the economy as a whole.

An economy-wide rise in real product wages, other things being equal, means that some plants and firms will no longer be able to cover their variable costs and will shut down. When they do, the unemployment rate will rise.

Now consider a period of time that is long enough so that the demand for labor can fully respond to an increase in the real product wage. When the real product wage rises, firms will replace old plant and equipment with new capital that requires higher capital-labor ratios. Over time, firms will adopt technologies that replace expensive labor with less expensive capital, and this will increase the amount of real-wage unemployment. Thus, when the real wage is too high across the whole economy, a structural mismatch will develop between the labor force and the capital stock. This mismatch will show up as unemployment; when the capital stock is working at full capacity, there is still unemployed labor. The unemployment will continue until one of two things happens. Unemployment may force down the real wage until it pays firms to employ all of the existing labor. Alternatively, new technologies may be invented that make profitable use of the unemployed labor, in spite of its high real product wage.

How (and for How Long) Can "Involuntary" Unemployment Persist?[3]

The existence of cyclical unemployment and real-wage unemployment poses a serious problem for both the economy and economic theory. Why do real wages fail to fall rapidly enough and far enough to eliminate all unemployment that is not frictional or structural? Indeed, the case could be made that structural unemployment would be greatly reduced if real wages were sufficiently flexible. Except in times of high cyclical unemployment, such as the Great Depression of the 1930s, someone who is unemployed because of a drop in demand for (say) skilled machinists could presumably find *some* sort of work, although the person might have to take a large cut in pay and status.

For over half a century economists have been trying to explain (or, in some cases, to deny the possibility of) involuntary unemployment. The subject is one of the most contentious and controversial in the discipline; the brief review of current thought that we present here is meant to be suggestive of the tenor of the debate, rather than to provide firm conclusions.

New theories, designed to explain involuntary unemployment, start by examining the forces that determine how quickly wages in actual labor markets will respond to changes in economic conditions. If wages do not respond quickly, then there is reason for supply and demand *not* to be equated for extended periods of time.

These theories start with the observation that la-

bor markets are not auction markets in which prices always respond to excess demand or excess supply. When unemployed workers are looking for jobs, they do not knock on employers' doors and offer to work at lower wages than are being paid to existing workers; instead, they answer want ads and hope to get the jobs offered, but often they are disappointed. Nor do employers, seeing an excess of applicants for the few jobs that are available, go to their existing workers and reduce their wages until there is no one who is looking for a job; instead, they pick and choose until they fill their needs and then hang out a sign saying "No help wanted."

Long-Term Relationships Between Employer and Employee

One set of modern theories, associated with the work of Arthur Okun and Robert Hall, among others, explains the familiar observations made in the preceding paragraph as results of the advantages to both workers and employers of relatively long-term, stable employment relationships.[4] Workers want job security in the face of fluctuating demand. Employers want a work force that understands the firm's organization, production, and marketing plans. Under these circumstances both parties care about things in addition to the wage rate, and wages become somewhat insensitive to fluctuating current economic conditions. Wages are, in effect, regular payments to workers over an extended employment relationship, rather than a device for fine tuning the supply and demand for labor. Given this situation, the tendency is for employers to "smooth out" the income of employees by paying a steady money wage and letting profits and employment fluctuate to absorb the effects of temporary increases and decreases in demand for the firm's product.

Many labor-market institutions work to achieve these results. For example, many long-term contracts provide for a schedule of money wages over a period of several years. Another example is fringe benefits, providing pensions, health care, and other benefits, which tend to bind workers to particular employers. As yet another example, pay that rises with years of service to the employer binds the employee to the

---

[3] This section can be omitted without any loss of continuity.

[4] See Robert E. Hall, "Employment Fluctuations and Wage Rigidity," Brookings Papers on Economic Activity, 1 (1980), pp. 91–123, for a review of much of this literature.

company, while seniority rules for layoffs bind the employer to the long-term worker. Such rules have become the norm in collective-bargaining agreements.

These things tend to be the adhesive that leads to long-term employment, despite the known fact that the output attributable to workers rises rapidly as they gain experience, reaches a peak, and then falls off as their age advances. Under gradually rising wages, experienced workers tend to get less than the value of the output that they produce[5] at earlier ages and more as they near retirement. But over the long pull they are paid, on average, the value of their output to the firm, just as microeconomic theory (see Chapter 19) predicts that they will be. Between wages that rise with age and dismissal in recessions in ascending order of seniority, employers and employees are held to each other, allowing payment of a more or less steady wage in the face of fluctuating economic circumstances.

In such labor markets the wage rate does not fluctuate to clear the market. Wages are written over what has been called the "economic climate" rather than the "economic weather." Because wages are thus insulated from short-term fluctuations in demand, any market clearing that occurs does so through fluctuations in the volume of employment rather than in wages. Of course, wages must respond to permanent shifts in market conditions, for example, the permanent and unexpected decline in the demand for the output of a particular industry.

Efficiency Wages

The idea of the *efficiency wage* forms the core of a second strand of thinking about why wages do not readily fall in response to excess supply in labor markets. For any of a number of reasons, employers may find that they get more output per dollar of wages paid (i.e., a more *efficient* work force) when they pay labor somewhat more than the minimum amount that would induce workers to work for them.

Suppose that it is costly for employers to monitor workers' performance on the job, so that some workers will be able to shirk some of their duties with a fairly low probability of being caught.[6] Given

the institutions of the labor market, it is generally impossible for employers to fine employees for shirking on the job. The employees could just leave their jobs rather than pay the fines. Further, if the workers can easily find new jobs that are just as good as their old ones, firing is not much of a threat. On the other hand, if there is a group of potential employees who are currently unemployed and who would like to work at the going wage, the threat of firing workers in order to discipline them is much enhanced. Under these conditions employees who are fired will be made worse off by being fired, precisely because it is difficult to find work at the going wage.

Efficiency wage theory says that firms may find it advantageous to pay high enough wages so that working is a clearly superior alternative to being laid off. This will improve the quality of workers' output without firms' having to spend large resources monitoring workers' performance.

Firms will pay efficiency wages as long as there is *some* reason that paying more than the market-clearing wage will increase the value of workers' output by more than it increases wages paid. Put this way, the idea is quite plausible. It is well established that workers who believe that they are well treated work harder than those who believe that they are treated badly.[7] This fact alone provides a potential justification for the efficiency wage idea, depending again on whether the increased output that arises from treating workers well covers the increased cost of doing so.

A variant of efficiency wage theory is especially promising as an explanation of why firms do not cut wages during recessions. If workers feel unfairly treated when their wages are reduced, wage reductions (at least in response to moderate recessions) may cost firms more (in lost output from unhappy employees) than they save in reduced wages.[8] This idea gets to the heart of the problem that we are

---

[5] For those of you who have studied microeconomics, the relevant concept is that of the value of the marginal product of labor.

[6] Those of you who have studied microeconomics will recognize this as an example of the principal-agent problem, discussed in Chapter 16.

[7] See George A. Akerlof, "Labor Contracts as Partial Gift Exchange," *Quarterly Journal of Economics,* 92 (November 1982), pp. 543–569.

[8] See Daniel Kahneman, Jack Knetsch, and Richard Thaler, "Fairness as a Constraint on Profit Seeking," *American Economic Review,* 76 (September 1986), pp. 728–741, for an interesting discussion, by a psychologist and two economists, of ways in which notions of fairness can complicate and illuminate economic analysis.

trying to account for in this discussion, explaining why real wages do not fall rapidly enough to eliminate deficient-demand and real-wage unemployment.

The basic message of new theories of unemployment is that competitive labor markets cannot be relied on to eliminate unemployment by equating current demand for labor with current supply.

Economists do not all agree on the importance of these new microeconomic explanations of why deficient-demand and real-wage unemployment can persist for long periods of time. Indeed, not all economists agree that such unemployment *can* persist. According to a number of economists, who have come to be known as *new classical* theorists (see Chapter 37), involuntary unemployment can only arise as a temporary result of unanticipated changes in economic circumstance. The new classical theorists argue that errors of this kind are quickly corrected in the labor market. Most economists have difficulty reconciling this view with the levels of unemployment that prevailed in the United States in the 1930s and the early 1980s or that prevail in much of Western Europe even today. However, to doubt the new classical interpretation as a complete explanation of unemployment is not the same thing as to embrace the new Keynesian theories that we have discussed in this subsection. Until business cycle fluctuations in unemployment are eliminated, it seems safe to say that economists will continue to search for and argue about their causes and cures.

Experience of Unemployment

Measured and Nonmeasured Unemployment

The number of unemployed persons is estimated from the Current Population Survey that is conducted each month by the Bureau of the Census. Persons who are currently without a job but who say that they have actively searched for one at any time during the past 30 days are recorded as unemployed. The total number of estimated unemployed

is then expressed as a percentage of the labor force (employed plus unemployed) to obtain the figure for the unemployment rate.[9]

The measured figure for unemployment may overstate or understate the number of people who are involuntarily unemployed.

On the one hand, the measured figure overstates unemployment by including people who are not involuntarily unemployed. For example, unemployment compensation provides protection against genuine hardship, but it also induces some people to stay out of work and to collect unemployment benefits for as long as they last. Such people have, in fact, voluntarily (if temporarily) withdrawn from the labor force, but they are usually included in the ranks of the unemployed, because they are required to check in with the local employment service in order to receive their benefits. This counts as actively looking for a job.

On the other hand, the measured figure understates involuntary unemployment by omitting some people who would accept jobs if they were available but who did not actively look for one during the 30 days prior to being interviewed. For example, people who have not found jobs by the time their unemployment benefits are exhaustd may become discouraged and stop seeking work. Such people have voluntarily withdrawn from the labor force and will not be recorded as unemployed. They are, however, truly unemployed in the sense that they would willingly accept a job if one were available. People in this category are referred to as **discouraged workers.** They have voluntarily withdrawn from the labor market because they believe that they cannot find a job under current conditions.

In addition, there is part-time unemployment. If some workers are working six hours per day instead of eight hours because there is insufficient demand for the product that they manufacture, then these workers are suffering 25 percent unemployment, even though no individual is reported as being unemployed. Twenty-five percent of the group's po-

---

[9] During the 1980s there was a change in this method for computing the unemployment rate. Members of the armed forces were added to the number of employed and to the labor force, leading to a reduction in the ratio of unemployed to the labor force. (No one in the armed forces is unemployed.) Throughout this chapter we follow the older (and internationally current) convention of using the civilian unemployment rate.

tential labor is going unused. Involuntary part-time work is a major source of unemployment of labor resources not reflected in the overall unemployment figures reported in the official statistics.

The Overall Unemployment Rate

Figure 24-5 shows the behavior of the civilian unemployment rate since 1930. Between the end of World War II (1945) and 1970, unemployment among the civilian labor force fluctuated cyclically but showed no clear rising or falling trend. During the 1950s the average unemployment rate was 4.5 percent, and during the 1960s it was 4.8 percent—not a significant difference.[10] From 1970, however, the cyclical fluctuations appear to be superimposed on a rising trend. The *low* figure of 4.9 percent unemployment for 1970–1988 was above the *average* of 4.7 percent for the previous two decades, while the *high* figure of 9.7 percent was the highest since the Great Depression of the 1930s. The low figure was achieved during the boom of 1972–1973, while the high occurred in 1982. The average rate of unemployment was 6.2 percent during the 1970s and 7.5 percent during the first nine years of the 1980s. The strong recovery that developed in the United States by the mid-1980s still left unemployment above 5 percent at the beginning of 1989.

These data strongly suggest that the NAIRU rose sometime around 1970 and that it remains higher now than it was in the 1960s. Later in this chapter, we discuss some of the reasons for movements in the NAIRU.

The contrast between the 1960s and the 1980s is even more striking for the major Western European economies. Using U.S. concepts, the average unemployment rate experienced during the 1960s in France was 1.7 percent. The average French unemployment rate from 1980 to 1987 was 9.1 percent, and the rate in 1987 was 10.8 percent. In West Germany the average unemployment rate during the 1960s was 0.65 percent. During the first eight years of the 1980s, the average rate was 6.1 percent. In the United Kingdom, the corresponding figures were 2.7 percent and 10.6 percent.

[10] Yearly figures in this section are based on annual averages of unemployment. Data are from *The Economic Report of the President,* January 1989, and *Economic Indicators,* April 1989, both of which are published by the United States Government Printing Office.

The Nature of Unemployment in the United States

By early 1989 essentially all of the cyclical unemployment that existed in the United States at the end of the recession in 1982 had been eliminated. Most economists would agree that the economy was operating approximately at potential income. Still, there were some 6 million people unemployed. To study them further, we look at some of the characteristics of the unemployed.

Figure 35-1 gives some idea of the duration of current spells of unemployment.[11] Data are given for 1982, a year of severe recession, and for March 1989, when the economy was approximately at potential income. The differences between the two sets of figures are due mainly to the reduction in cyclical unemployment over the period.

Figure 35-1 shows that the bulk of reported unemployment is relatively short term. In March 1989 over 77 percent of the unemployed had been out of work for 14 weeks or less. Really long-term unemployment, lasting longer than half a year, accounted for only 10.7 percent of the unemployed in early 1989. These figures represent considerable improvement over the recession year 1982, when 67 percent of the unemployed had been without jobs for 14 weeks or less and 16.6 percent for more than 26 weeks. Yet even the 1989 figures were not yet back to the more favorable ones for 1979, the last year before the deep recession of the early 1980s. In that year just less than 9 percent of the unemployed had been out of work for more than 26 weeks.

It seems that the potentially soul-destroying bouts of prolonged periods of unemployment are confined to a relatively small part of the labor force (but the size of that part grows significantly in recessions).

Figures 35-2 and 35-3 document some of the inequalities in unemployment rates. Males and females, the young, and the experienced have very different unemployment experiences, as Figure 35-2 shows. Even more dramatic are the differences between whites and blacks, as shown in Figure 35-3. By far

[11] The figures are based on the Current Population Survey, which asks currently unemployed individuals how long they have been out of work. Notice that this gives us the duration of currently uncompleted bouts of unemployment. It gives different and shorter figures than the duration of completed bouts of unemployment, which is obtained by asking people who have just found a job how long they were out of work.

FIGURE 35-1 Duration of Unemployment

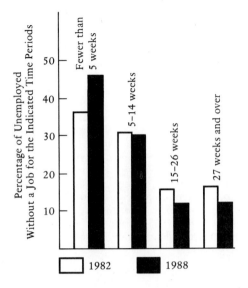

Most measured unemployment is short term, but long-term unemployment rises during prolonged recessions. The figures refer to the length of time that people who are currently unemployed have been out of a job. By far the largest single category covers those who have been out of work for fewer than five weeks. In 1982, at the trough of a serious recession, fully 16.6 percent of the unemployed had been out of a job for more than six months, while in 1988 the figure had fallen to 12 percent. (*Source: Economic Indicators,* April 1989)

the lowest unemployment rates in booms and slumps are recorded by white males 20 years of age and over. By far the highest unemployment rates occur for black males under 20 years of age.[12]

What Causes the NAIRU to Change?

Earlier in our discussion of macroeconomics, we defined potential income as the level of income that would obtain if all factors of production were employed at their normal intensity of use. The NAIRU is the unemployment rate that is associated with potential income—at the NAIRU labor is employed at its normal intensity of use, and all unemployment is

[12] Those of you who have studied microeconomics will recall some of the reasons for this from Chapter 19.

either frictional or structural. Here we consider various reasons why unemployment at potential income might change over time. By definition such changes involve changes in the level of frictional or structural unemployment.

Structural unemployment can increase because the pace of change accelerates or the pace of adjustment to change slows down. An increase in the rate of growth, for example, usually speeds up the rate at which the structure of the demand for labor is changing. The adaptation of labor to the changing structure of demand may be slowed by such diverse factors as a decline in education and state occupational licensing regulations that make it difficult for workers in a given occupation to take new jobs in other states.

Demographic changes. Because people usually try several jobs before settling into one for a longer period of time, young or inexperienced workers have higher unemployment rates than experienced workers. During the 1970s the proportion of inexperienced workers in the labor force rose significantly as the baby boom generation of the 1950s entered the labor force, along with an unprecedented number of women who elected to work outside the home. It is estimated that these demographic changes added about one-half of a percentage point to frictional and structural unemployment in 1980 relative to the 1960s. By 1987 this source of increase in the NAIRU had fallen, due to low birthrates in the 1960s.

Income-support programs. Unemployment insurance and other income-maintenance programs reduce the cost of being unemployed, thus increasing the amount of time that people are likely to spend being unemployed. Many such programs were significantly more generous by the late 1960s and early 1970s (when the NAIRU started to rise) than they had been in the 1950s and the early 1960s. By the late 1980s these programs were on average less generous, in real terms, than they had been in the early 1970s, but the levels of income support provided by such programs had not fallen all the way back to their mid-1960s levels. Some of the increase in the NAIRU during the 1970s can be attributed to the fact that social programs ameliorated the pain of being unemployed relative to earlier times. Some economists have also argued that differences in income-support programs can account for some of

FIGURE 35-2   Variations in Unemployment Rates

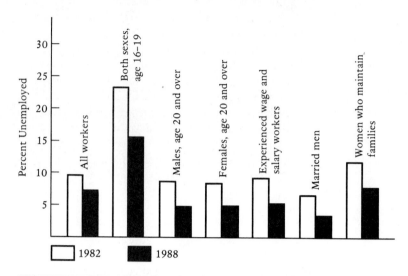

Unemployment was unevenly divided among sex and skill groups in 1982 and again in 1988. In 1982 and 1988 overall unemployment rates of 9.5 percent and 5.4 percent, respectively, concealed large variations in the unemployment rates of different groups. The recovery from 1982 to 1988 led to a fall in unemployment rates among all groups. Unemployment among married men, who typically have favorable employment experiences, fell by 63 percent from 8.8 to 3.3 percent. Unemployment among youth reached close to 25 percent (one in four) in 1982 and fell only to 15.3 percent in 1988. (*Source: Economic Indicators,* April 1989)

the difference between the recent experience of the United States and that of Western Europe. These programs are typically much more generous in Europe than they are in the United States.

Hysteresis.   In the last few years, a number of economists have proposed models of unemployment in which the level of the NAIRU is influenced by the actual rate of unemployment.[13] Such models get their name from the Greek word *hysteresis,* meaning "lagged effect." In models of this kind, the normal intensity of use of labor is affected by the actual intensity of use.

There are a number of plausible mechanisms that might lead to some hysteresis in labor markets. One mechanism, emphasized by commentators on Western Europe, which has a heavily unionized labor force, is based on the notion that in times of high unemployment people who are currently employed (insiders) use their bargaining power to assure that their own status is maintained and prevent new entrants to the labor force (outsiders) from competing effectively. In an *insider-outsider* model of this type, a period of prolonged, high unemployment—what-

[13] See, for example, Olivier Blanchard and Lawrence Summers, "Hysteresis and the European Unemployment Problem," *NBER Macroeconomics Annual,* 1986, pp. 15–78.

ever its initial cause (e.g., deficient demand)—will tend to become "locked in" to the normal functioning of the labor market. If "outsiders" are denied access to the labor market, their unemployment will fail to exert downward pressure on wages, and the NAIRU will tend to rise.

The insider-outsider mechanism is implausible in the U.S. economy, where unionization in the private sector has been falling for decades and is now under 15 percent. However, there are other mechanisms that can lead to hysteresis in labor markets, and some of these may operate in the United States. One such mechanism arises from the importance of experience and on-the-job training. Suppose, for example, that a period of deficient demand causes a significant group of new entrants to the labor force to have unusual difficulty in obtaining their first jobs. As a result, the unlucky group will be slow to acquire the important skills that workers generally learn in their first jobs. When demand increases again, this group of workers will be at a disadvantage relative to workers with normal histories of experience, and the unlucky group will tend to have unemployment rates that will be higher than average. Thus, the NAIRU will be higher than it would have been had there been no period of deficient demand.

The empirical importance of hysteresis in the

FIGURE 35-3 Unemployment by Age, Sex, and Race

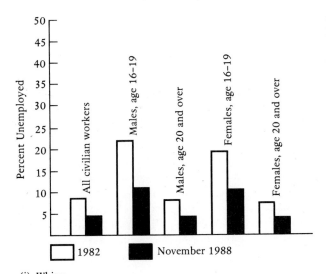

(i) Whites

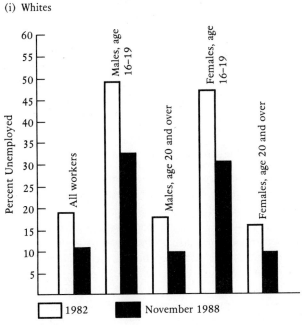

(ii) Blacks

Classification by age, sex, and race reveals large differences in the unemployment rates of these groups. Part (i) shows the unemployment experience of whites by age and gender; part (ii) shows the same data for blacks. In November, 1988 unemployment rates ranged from a high of 32 percent for black youths to a low of 4.3 percent for white males, age 20 and over. Similar inequalities were apparent in 1982, although the overall rate of unemployment was much higher. Youth unemployment is a serious problem among all groups—whites and blacks and males and females. (*Source: Economic Report of the President, 1989*)

United States has not been examined. In some countries in Western Europe, there is evidence that hysteresis may be quite important.

Increasing structural change.   The amount of resource reallocation across industries and areas seems to have increased over the last two decades. In part this is the result of the increasing integration of the U.S. economy with that of the rest of the world. Most observers feel that on balance this integration has been beneficial. However, one consequence is that changes in demand or supply conditions anywhere in the world requiring adjustments throughout the world's trading sectors increasingly affect the United States. Goods in which the United States once enjoyed world dominance (e.g., automobiles) are now made in many countries. Consumers at home and abroad benefit from the increased competition, but domestic producers and workers are now subject to changes in demand for their output that originate in events that are far removed from home.

Changes in technology also have had an effect on U.S. labor markets. The increased use of robots in factories and computer-based processes in offices has eliminated many assembly line and clerical jobs and has forced their former holders to look elsewhere for new jobs.

Another major set of forces leading to structural change arises from the shifting pattern of demand. As a result of rising income and changing social patterns, people spend a higher proportion of their income on services than they used to and a correspondingly smaller proportion on manufactured goods. Restaurant meals and day-care facilities for children are two services with rising demands. This shift is dramatically illustrated by the fact that the *increase* in employment in service industries during the past two decades exceeded the total employment in the manufacture of durable goods.

All of these developments require reallocations of labor that, while they are going on, tend to lead to increased structural or frictional unemployment.

Unemployment Policies

Every type of unemployment has costs in terms of the output that could have been produced by the

unemployed workers. Yet reducing unemployment is also costly. For example, retraining and reallocation schemes designed to reduce structural unemployment use scarce resources.

It would be neither possible nor desirable to reduce unemployment to zero. The causes of unemployment could never be removed completely, and reducing the amount of unemployment stemming from those causes is costly.

Unemployment insurance is one method of helping people to live with unemployment. Certainly, it has reduced significantly the human costs of the bouts of unemployment that are inevitable in a changing society. Nothing, however, is without cost. While unemployment insurance alleviates the suffering that is caused by some kinds of unemployment, it can itself contribute to unemployment, for, as we have observed, it encourages voluntary and search unemployment.

Supporters of unemployment insurance emphasize its benefits. Critics emphasize its costs. As with any policy, a rational assessment of the value of unemployment insurance requires a balancing of its undoubted benefits against its undoubted costs. Most Americans seem convinced that, when this calculation is made, the benefits greatly exceed the costs.

Cyclical Unemployment

We do not need to say much more about cyclical unemployment, since its control is the subject of stabilization policy, which we have studied in several earlier chapters. A major recession that occurs due to natural causes can be countered by monetary and fiscal policy to reduce cyclical unemployment.

The 1970s and 1980s saw the emergence of *policy-induced* cyclical unemployment. This occurred when, in an attempt to combat inflation, the government adopted drastic contractionary policies that opened up large recessionary gaps. As we saw in Chapter 34, a temporary bout of cyclical unemployment was the price of reducing inflation.

If hysteresis is an important cause of unemployment, there may be increased scope for stabilization policy. Indeed, the policy implications of hysteresis models are quite striking. With hysteresis in the labor market, there is the possibility that an increase in aggregate demand can bring outsiders (whatever the cause of their unemployment) into the effective labor force and, after a period of inflation, lower the NAIRU and increase potential income by increasing the normal intensity with which labor is employed. Of course, if such a policy is attempted in the *mistaken* belief that there is hysteresis, an inflationary gap may be opened up and take years for policy to remove. Until the importance of hysteresis is much more firmly established than it has been to date, it would be risky indeed for policymakers to use it as a justification for increasing aggregate demand.

Real-Wage Unemployment

If real-wage unemployment is a major problem, its cure is not an easy matter. Basically, what is required is a fall in the real product wage, combined with measures to increase aggregate demand so as to create enough total employment. However, as many European countries have discovered, the cure is slow and requires enough time to install new labor-using capital.

1. The real product wage would have to fall substantially. (In the European context, this involves, among other things, the removal of many institutional and governmental impediments to the smooth functioning of the labor market.)
2. Since wages enter into disposable income and disposable income determines consumer demand, the cut in wages would tend to reduce aggregate demand and hence reduce equilibrium national income, unless increased profits compensate for the reduced wage bill.
3. The effect on aggregate demand could (in principle) be countered by fiscal and monetary policy.

Frictional Unemployment

The turnover that causes frictional unemployment is an inevitable part of the functioning of the economy. Insofar as it is caused by ignorance, increasing the knowledge of workers about market opportunities may help, but such measures have a cost, and that cost has to be balanced against the benefits.

Some frictional unemployment is an inevitable part of the learning process. One reason that there is a high turnover rate and hence high frictional unemployment is that new entrants have to try out jobs to see if they are suitable. They typically will try more than one job before settling into one that most satisfies, or least dissatisfies, them.

Structural Unemployment

The reallocation of labor among occupations, industries, skill categories, and regions that gives rise to structural unemployment is an inevitable part of growth. There are two basic responses to increases in structural unemployment: First, try to arrest the changes that accompany growth and, second, accept the changes and try to speed up the adjustments. Throughout history labor and management have advocated, and governments have tried, both approaches.

Resisting change. Since the beginning of the Industrial Revolution, workers often have resisted the introduction of new techniques to replace the older techniques at which they were skilled. This is understandable. New techniques often destroy the value of the knowledge and experience of workers who are skilled in the displaced techniques. Older workers may not even get a chance to learn the new techniques. Employers may prefer to hire younger persons who will learn the new skills faster than older workers who often are set in their ways. From society's point of view, new techniques are beneficial, because they are a major source of economic growth. From the point of view of the workers that they displace, new techniques can be an unmitigated disaster.

Here are two characteristic ways in which economic change has been resisted. First, a declining industry may be supported with public funds. If the market would support an output of X, but subsidies are used to support an output of 2X, then jobs are provided for, say, one-half the industry's labor force who would otherwise lose their jobs in this industry and have to find jobs elsewhere. Second, the new technology may be used but an agreement reached to continue to employ workers who would otherwise be made redundant by the new technology. Each of these policies would be attractive to the people who would otherwise become unemployed. It might be a long time before they could find another job, and, in any case, their skills might not turn out to be highly valued in their new occupations.[14]

In the long term, however, such policies are not

---

[14] When employment is threatened by international competition, change is often resisted by imposing barriers to international trade. This is discussed in Chapter 40.

efficient, and they often hurt the industries that they are meant to help. Agreements to hire unneeded workers raise costs and can hasten the decline of an industry that is threatened by competitive products. An industry that is declining due to economic change becomes an increasingly large burden on taxpayers as economic forces become less and less favorable to its success. Sooner or later, public support is withdrawn, and an often precipitous decline then ensues.

In assessing these remedies for structural unemployment, it is important to realize that, although they are not viable in the long run for the economy, they may be the best alternatives for the affected workers during their lifetimes.

There is often a genuine conflict between those who are threatened by structural unemployment, whose interests lie in preserving their jobs, and the general public, whose interest is served by economic growth, which is the engine of rising living standards.

Aiding adjustments to change. Another way to deal with structural change is to accept the decline of industries and the destruction of specific jobs that go with it and to try to reduce the cost of adjustment for those who are affected. Retraining and relocation grants make movement easier and reduce structural unemployment without inhibiting economic change and growth. Retraining programs in the United States have met with mixed success at best. Relocation grants are used successfully in countries such as Sweden but have never been adopted in the United States.

By international standards the reduction in the overall level of U.S. unemployment during the recovery from the deep recession of the early 1980s was dramatic. As Figures 35-1 to 35-3 show, however, major inequalities in unemployment rates suggest that some severe structural problems will persist even when, on an overall basis, the economy is near to full employment. The Reagan administration's approach to structural unemployment was to rely mainly on the workings of market incentives. Some schemes aimed at vocational training and retraining for youth, unemployed adults, and skilled workers in declining industries and regions were introduced, but these were given only limited funding and had correspondingly limited success.

SUMMARY

1. Unemployment may be voluntary or involuntary. Involuntary unemployment is a serious social concern, both because it causes economic waste due to lost output and because it is a source of human suffering.
2. Looking at causes, it is useful to distinguish among several kinds of unemployment: (a) frictional unemployment, which is caused by the length of time that it takes to find a first job and to move from job to job as a result of normal labor turnover; (b) structural unemployment, which is caused by the need to reallocate resources among occupations, regions, and industries as the structure of demands and supplies changes; (c) cyclical unemployment, which is caused by too low a level of aggregate demand; and (d) real-wage unemployment, which is caused by too high a real product wage. Together, the amounts of frictional unemployment and structural unemployment make up what is now called *NAIRU*.
3. There is a great deal of disagreement among economists regarding the causes of persistent cyclical and real-wage unemployment. Recent theories have focused on the long-term nature of employer-worker relationships and upon the possibility that it is efficient for employers to pay wages that are above the level that would clear the labor market.
4. In 1989 the U.S. economy was approximately at potential income, and the U.S. unemployment rate was approximately the NAIRU, having fallen sharply from the high rates of the early 1980s. Unemployment rates in much of Western Europe, by contrast, had come down much less and were still above the NAIRU.

5. Measured unemployment figures may overestimate or underestimate the actual number of unemployed, for they may include some who are voluntarily unemployed and omit discouraged workers who have left the labor force.
6. Unemployment is unequally distributed across demographic groups. Married men have relatively low unemployment rates; young black men have very high unemployment rates.
7. The NAIRU rose during the 1970s and fell somewhat during the 1980s. Among the factors that affect the NAIRU are the demographic composition of the work force, the generosity of unemployment compensation and other income-support programs, and the pace of structural change in the economy. Some economists have argued that the level of actual unemployment can also affect the NAIRU.
8. Unemployment insurance helps to alleviate the human suffering that is associated with inevitable unemployment. It also increases unemployment by encouraging voluntary unemployment.
9. Unemployment can be reduced by raising aggregate demand, by making it easier to move between jobs, by slowing down the rate of change in the economy, and by raising the cost of staying unemployed. However, it is neither possible nor desirable to reduce unemployment to zero.

TOPICS FOR REVIEW

Voluntary and involuntary unemployment
Cyclical unemployment
Frictional unemployment
Structural unemployment
Real-wage unemployment
Efficiency wages
Hysteresis
Effects of demographic and structural changes on unemployment

DISCUSSION QUESTIONS

1. Interpret the following statements from newspapers in terms of types of unemployment:
   a. "Recession hits local factory; 2,000 laid off."
   b. "A job? I've given up trying," says a mother of three.
   c. "We closed down because we could not meet the competition from Taiwan," says a local manager.
   d. "When they raised the minimum wage, I just could not afford to keep all of these retired policemen on my payroll as security guards," says the owner of a local shopping center.
   e. "Slack demand puts local foundry on short time."
   f. "Of course, I could take a job as a dishwasher, but I'm trying to find something that makes use of my high school training," says a local teenager in our survey of the unemployed.
   g. "Where have all the jobs gone? They have gone to California."
   h. "Retraining main challenge in increased use of robots."
   i. "Modernization may cut U.S. textile workers."
   j. "Uneven upturn: signs of recovery hit Louisville, but not all feel its effect, as joblessness stays high."
2. What differences in approach toward the problem of unemployment are suggested by the following facts?
   a. In the 1960s and 1970s Britain spent billions of dollars on subsi-

dizing firms that would otherwise have gone out of business, in order to protect the jobs of the employees.

b. Sweden has been a pioneer in spending large sums to retrain and to relocate displaced workers.

3. Discuss the following views:

a. "American workers should resist automation, which is destroying their jobs," says a labor leader.

b. "Given the fierce foreign competition, it's a case of automate or die," says an industrialist.

4. Use the latest *Economic Report of the President* to compare the percentage of total unemployment that is long term, in the last year available, with the figures for earlier years given in the text of this chapter. Can you think of any reasons why the figures have changed?

5. What theories can you suggest to explain why unemployment rates stay persistently above average for youths and for blacks and below average for males over 20?

6. It is often argued that the true unemployment figure for the United States is much higher than the officially reported figure. What are possible sources of "hidden unemployment"? On the other side, are there reasons for expecting some exaggeration of the number of people who are reported as unemployed? Would the relative strength of these opposing forces change over the course of the business cycle? What would you expect if a short recession turned into a long and deep depression?

7. At a time when the U.S. unemployment rate stood at close to 8 percent, the press reported, "Skilled labor shortage plagues many firms—newspaper ads often draw few qualified workers; wages and overtime are up." What type of unemployment does this suggest is important?

8. A baseball writer recently predicted that the New York Mets would do well in 1989 because they gave Mookie Wilson (a part-time player) a million dollar contract. For what theory of wage setting does this observation provide evidence?

Chapter 36

Economic Growth

Popular debate is bedeviled by confusion about the various causes of change in national income. For example, some commentators argue that governments can spend their way into a rising national income, while others argue that, although expansionary government policies may stimulate the economy in the short run, they often have adverse effects on growth in the economy in the long run.

Causes of Increases in Real National Income

Figure 36-1, which reproduces Figure 29-1 on page 593, illustrates some of the most important possible ways of increasing national income. If there is a recessionary gap, raising aggregate demand will yield a once-and-for-all increase in national income. However, once potential income is achieved, further increases in aggregate demand yield only transitory increases in real income but lasting increases in the price level.

Measures that reduce structural unemployment can also increase the employed labor force and thus increase potential income. The resulting increase in income might not be very large, but there would be social gain resulting from the reduction in unemployment, especially the long-term unemployment that occurs when people are trapped in declining areas, industries, or occupations.

Over the long haul, however, what really raises national income is *economic growth*, that is, the increase in potential income due to changes in factor supplies (labor and capital) or in the productivity of factors (output per unit of factor input). The removal of a serious recessionary gap or the elimination of all structural unemployment might raise national income by, say, 6 percent. However, a modest growth rate of 3 percent per year raises national income by 10 percent in 3 years and *doubles* it in about 24 years.

Over any long period of time, economic growth, rather than variations in aggregate demand or in structural unemployment, exerts the major effect on real national income.

FIGURE 36-1   Ways of Increasing National Income

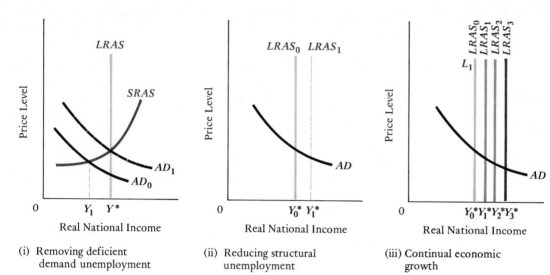

(i) Removing deficient
    demand unemployment

(ii) Reducing structural
    unemployment

(iii) Continual economic
    growth

A once-and-for-all increase in national income can be obtained by raising aggregate demand to remove a recessionary gap or by shifting the *LRAS* curve by cutting structural unemployment. Continued increases in national income are possible by shifting the *LRAS* curve through continued economic growth. In part (i), with the aggregate demand curve at AD_0, there is a recessionary gap of Y_1Y^*. An increase in aggregate demand from AD_0 to AD_1 takes equilibrium to E_1, achieving a once-and-for-all change in national income from Y_1 to Y^*.

In part (ii) potential output rises from Y_0^* to Y_1^* due to measures that reduce structural unemployment. The *LRAS* curve shifts from $LRAS_0$ to $LRAS_1$, because people who were formerly unemployed due to having the wrong skills or being in the wrong place are now available for employment.

In part (iii) increases in factor supplies and productivity lead to increases in potential income. This *continually* shifts the long-run aggregate supply curve outward. In successive periods it moves from $LRAS_0$ to $LRAS_3$, taking potential income from Y_0^* to Y_1^* to Y_3^*, *and so on, as long as growth continues.*

Effects of Investment and Saving on National Income

Short-Run and Long-Run Effects of Investment

The theory of income determination that we studied in Part 8 is a short-run theory. It takes potential income as constant and concentrates on the effect of investment expenditure on aggregate demand. Short-run national-income theory concentrates on variations of actual national income around a given potential income. This short-term viewpoint is the focus of Figure 36-1(i).

In the long run, by adding to the nation's capital

stock, investment raises potential income. This effect is shown by the continuing outward shift of the *LRAS* curve in Figure 36-1(iii).

The theory of economic growth is a long-run theory. It ignores short-run fluctuations of actual national income around potential income and concentrates on the effects of investment in raising potential income.

The contrast between the short- and long-run aspects of investment is worth emphasizing. In the short run, any activity that puts income into people's hands will raise aggregate demand. Thus, the short-run effect on national income is the same whether a firm invests in digging holes and refilling them or in building a new factory. The long-run growth of potential income, however, is affected only by the part of investment that adds to a nation's productive capacity, that is, by the factory but not by the refilled hole.

Similar observations are true of public-sector expenditure. Any expenditure will add to aggregate demand and raise national income if there are unemployed resources, but only some expenditure adds to the growth of full-employment income. Indeed, public-investment expenditure that shores up a declining industry in order to create employment may have an adverse effect on growth. Such expenditure may prevent the reallocation of resources in response to shifts both in the pattern of world demand and in the country's comparative advantage. Thus, in the long run the country's capacity to produce commodities that are demanded on open markets may be diminished.

Short-Run and Long-Run Effects of Saving

The short-run effects of an increase in saving are to reduce aggregate demand. If, for example, households elect to save more, this means that they spend less. The resulting downward shift in the consumption function lowers aggregate demand and thus lowers equilibrium national income.

In the longer term, however, higher savings are necessary for higher investment. Firms usually reinvest their own savings, while the savings of households pass to firms, either directly through the purchase of stocks and bonds or indirectly through financial intermediaries. The higher are savings, the higher is investment—and the higher is investment, the higher is the level of real income due to the accumulation of more and better capital equipment.

In the long run there is no paradox of thrift; societies with high savings rates have high investment rates and, other things being equal, high levels of real income.

The Cumulative Nature of Growth

Growth is a much more powerful method of raising living standards than the removal of either recessionary gaps or structural unemployment, *because it can*

go on indefinitely. For example, a growth rate of 2 percent per year may seem insignificant, but if it continues for a century, it will lead to a more than sevenfold increase in real national income!

The cumulative effect of small annual growth rates is large.

To appreciate the cumulative effect of what seem to be very small differences in growth rates, examine Table 36-1. Notice that, if one country grows faster than another, the gap in their respective standards will widen progressively. If, for example, countries A and B start from the same level of income and if country A grows at 3 percent per year while country B grows at 2 percent per year, A's income per capita will be twice B's in 72 years. You may not think that it matters much whether the economy grows at 2 percent or 3 percent per year, but your children and grandchildren will! (A helpful approximation device is the "rule of 72." Divide 72 by the growth rate, and the result is approximately the number of years that it will take for income to double.) [43]

To dramatize the powerful long-run effects of differences in growth rates, we included in early editions of this text a table showing students of the 1960s that, if the then current growth trends continued, the United States would not long remain the world's richest nation, for Sweden, Canada, Japan, and others were growing at a much faster rate. Many readers of that era rejected the notion as a textbook

TABLE 36-1 The Cumulative Effect of Growth

Year	Rate of growth per year				
	1%	2%	3%	5%	7%
0	100	100	100	100	100
10	111	122	135	165	201
30	135	182	246	448	817
50	165	272	448	1,218	3,312
70	201	406	817	3,312	13,429
100	272	739	2,009	14,841	109,660

Small differences in growth rates make enormous differences in levels of potential national income over a few decades. Assume that potential national income is 100 in year zero. At a rate of growth of 3 percent per year, it will be 135 in 10 years, 448 after 50 years, and over 2,000 in a century. Compound interest is a powerful force!

BOX 36-1

Case Studies of Rapid Growth: Japan and Korea

The real national income of Japan was 5.4 times as large in 1973 as it was in 1953. During this period, Japan's economic growth rate was more than double the average rate in the 10 major North American and European countries. Starting a little later and from a lower level, Korea also has experienced rapid growth in the past quarter century, and it increasingly rivals Japan in world markets for many manufactured goods. From 1960 through 1985, growth in Korea was even faster than in Japan; real per capita GNP in Korea rose from 12 percent of the U.S. level to 31 percent, while in Japan it rose from 33 to 77 percent.

Two recent studies that were done for the Brookings Institution help our understanding of what accounted for these extraordinarily rapid growth rates.* Edward Denison and William Chung found that no single factor was responsible for Japan's high postwar growth rate, and Rudiger Dornbusch and Yung Chul Park found similar results for Korea; they found, rather, that both econ-

*Edward F. Denison and William K. Chung, *How Japan's Economy Grew So Fast: The Sources of Postwar Expansion* (Washington, D.C.: Brookings Institution, 1976); and Rudiger Dornbusch and Yung Chul Park, "Korean Growth Policy," *Brookings Papers on Economic Activity*, 1987.

omies benefited from several major sources of growth: an increase in quantity and quality of labor, an increase in quantity of capital, improved technology in production, and economies of scale. For example, Japan gained more in each of these respects than any of the 10 other countries that were studied by Denison and Chung.

In addition, in both countries employment and output in manufacturing rose much faster than GNP as a whole, with resources being transferred from agriculture to manufacturing. Since productivity is generally higher in manufacturing than in agriculture, a shift of this kind raises average productivity and thereby contributes to growth even without an increase in output per person in either sector.

Both expansions have been characterized by an exceptional rise in exports and by high investment spending as a share of GNP. Both countries have pursued activist policies of import restrictions, subsidies, and credit allocation aimed at encouraging manufacturing and export industries in particular. The allocation of investment was, to a degree, centrally directed through subsidies and credit allocation; although some mistakes were made in the process, on balance, investment was concentrated

gimmick; deep down they knew that the material standard of living of the United States was and would remain the highest the world had ever known. Such a table is no longer even interesting, for by 1980 several industrial countries had indeed passed the United States in terms of per capita national income, and several more were within 10 percent of the U.S. level. The experiences of two high-growth economies, Japan and Korea, are discussed in Box 36-1.

Growth, Efficiency, and Redistribution

Without any doubt, the most important single force leading to long-run increases in living standards is

economic growth. To see this, let us compare the effects of growth with policies that increase economic efficiency or redistribute income. For the moment, we will consider a country with a constant population.

Making the economy more efficient can increase national income. However, a once-and-for-all increase of between 5 and 10 percent would be an extremely optimistic estimate of what could be obtained by removing all economic inefficiencies.

Redistributing income can make lower-income people better off at the expense of higher-income people, but increasing the incomes of the bottom 20 percent of the people by, say, 10 percent above what they are now would be a very optimistic prediction

in sectors that developed into highly competitive export industries.

Dornbusch and Park argue that Korea's success has depended on the interaction of that investment strategy with its educated work force and wage moderation. Koreans work an average of 54 hours per week, and the educational level of the work force has risen steadily since 1960. Although unit labor costs in Korean manufacturing rose sharply during the 1970s relative to those in Japan and the United States, Korea continued to expand the range and total volume of its manufacturing exports. Investment and a large pool of skilled workers allowed the Korean manufacturing sector to expand and to employ advanced technology that had been developed abroad. Although relative unit labor costs were rising on average, labor costs continued to be low in the manufacturing sectors in which Korean workers were employed with the newest technology and ample capital. This, together with a policy that maintained an undervalued exchange rate, led to improved competitiveness over a growing range of manufactured goods.

The remarkable growth records of Korea and Japan were possible partly because of their low initial *levels* of productivity. It is easier to improve from a low base than a high one. Productivity is still much lower in Japan and Korea than in the United States, even after eliminating the effects of differences between the countries in working hours, in composition and allocation of the labor force, in amounts of capital and land, in size of markets, and in the cyclical positions of the two economies. There is thus an obvious potential for still further growth in those countries relative to the United States.

A question is, then, "Can Japan's and Korea's growth rates be sustained?" While the probability of a decline in the growth rate as the various ways of securing fast growth by "catching up" are successively exhausted, the potential remains for fairly high rates of long-term growth throughout the rest of this century. (Denison and Chung's prediction of continued Japanese growth of between 5 and 8 percent per year proved accurate for the decade following the period covered by their study.) If these rates do continue, by the year 2000, Japan will be enjoying the highest standard of living of any industrialized country in the world, and Korea will not be far behind.

of what could be done with further redistribution policies. In any case, the income gains that can be achieved for lower-income groups through redistribution is limited by the size of national income.

Economic growth, however, can go on raising national income for as long as growth continues, which can be for centuries. Even the modest rate of growth of 2 percent per year takes less than five years to make it possible to raise everyone's income by the 10 percent that was suggested as the maximum that could be achieved by policies that raise efficiency once and for all. It takes just over nine years for the 2 percent growth rate to raise the living standards of the poor (and everyone else) by 20 percent—which is a very high estimate of what might be obtained through redistribution policies. Furthermore, the gain continues beyond those time horizons as long as the growth persists. The 2 percent growth rate doubles average living standards about every 35 years, so average living standards will quadruple over one biblically allotted lifetime of three score years and ten.

The continued importance of efficiency and redistribution.   When we say that, over the long term, by far the most potent force for raising living standards is economic growth rather than reducing inefficiencies or redistributing income, we are *not* asserting the unimportance of policies designed to increase eco-

BOX 36-2

Policy Options Concerning Economic Growth

As in most areas of economic policy, sharp differences arise between those who wish to let market forces determine the economy's growth and those who favor government intervention.

Conservatives feel that, in a stable environment free from government interference, growth will take care of itself. Large firms will spend a lot of money on research and development. Where they fail, or where they suppress inventions to protect monopoly positions, the genius of backyard inventors will come up with new ideas and will develop new companies to challenge the positions of the established giants. Left to itself, the economy will prosper as it has in the past, provided only that an inquiring scientific spirit and the profit motive are not suppressed.

Interventionists are less certain than conservatives about the ability of market forces to produce growth. While they recognize the importance of invention and innovation, they fear the dead hand of monopoly and cautious business practices that choose security over risk taking. Therefore, the state needs at the very least to give a nudge here or there to help the growth process along.

Interventionists thus tend to support general policies that make the macroeconomic climate favorable to growth. Thus, they typically promote subsidization or favorable tax treatment for research and development or for the purchasing of plant and equipment. Measures to lower interest rates tem-porarily or permanently are also often urged as favorable to investment and growth. Conservatives argue that such government intervention only reduces market efficiency.

The Broader Conservative Agenda

Given the large web of government rules, regulations, and perverse tax incentives that has grown over many years, the conservative agenda for promoting growth includes *opposition* to a number of existing policies that they think inhibit growth. In an assessment of the conservative proposal to eliminate each of these policies, it should be recognized that problems arise in assessing the existence and importance of the alleged harmful effects of each policy and, since the government needs revenue, in finding alternative revenue sources that will have less harmful effects than the ones being criticized.

Support for declining industries.   This policy causes resources that could be more productively employed elsewhere to leave the industry more slowly. Most economists agree that such policies are costly, harmful to growth, and self-defeating in the end.

Picking winners.   Some interventionists support what is called *picking* and *backing* winners in one way or another. Advocates of this view, such as

nomic efficiency or to redistribute income. We are simply saying that potential benefits are limited relative to what can be achieved by even a modest improvement in growth.

Interrelations among the policies.   Policies that reduce inefficiencies or redistribute income need to be examined carefully for any effects that they may have on economic growth. Any policy that reduces the growth rate may be a bad bargain, even if it increases the immediate efficiency of the economy or creates a more equitable distribution of income. Consider, for example, a hypothetical redistributive policy that raises the incomes of lower-income people by 5 percent but lowers the rate of economic growth from 2 to 1 percent. In 10 years those who gained from the

Professor Lester Thurow of MIT, want governments to pick the industries (usually new ones) that have potential for future success and then to back them with subsidies, government contracts, research funds, and all the other encouragements at the government's command.

Conservatives argue that picking winners requires foresight and that there is no reason to expect that the government will have better foresight than private investors. Indeed, since political considerations inevitably get in the way, the government may be less successful than the market in picking winners. If so, channeling funds through the government rather than through the private sector may hurt rather than help growth rates. However, some supporters respond that, since governments in other countries pursue such policies, even if our own policies are imperfect, we harm our competitive position relative to state-supported foreign producers if we fail to respond with policies of our own.

High rates of income tax.   Conservatives allege that high taxes discourage work. Yet, the effect of high taxes actually may be one of making people work either harder or less hard. Theory is silent on which is more likely, and no hard evidence has yet shown that lowering current tax rates makes people work harder. Many elements of the tax reform that was introduced in 1986, which saw tax bases broadened

and tax rates reduced, were well received by conservatives. Tax changes that encouraged saving were also widely viewed as being progrowth.

"Double taxation" of business profits.   Business profits are taxed first as income of firms and second as income of households when paid out as dividends. This and other policies that reduce business profits and hence discourage the return to investing in equities are alleged to discourage households from saving and investing in businesses that are the mainspring of economic growth.

Policy Agreement

One important potential area of agreement can be identified. As we will see later in this chapter (see especially Box 36-3), a number of economists recently have stressed the importance of "knowledge," broadly defined, as a key difference between high-growth, high-income countries and low-growth, low-income ones. If this view prevails, many conservative economists might in principle come to support government intervention that supports "learning" and technological advance.

policy would be no better off than if they had not received the redistribution of income while the growth rate had remained at 2 percent (and, of course, everyone who did not gain from the redistribution would be worse off from the beginning). After 20 years time, those who had gained from the redistribution would have 5 percent more of a national income that was 12 percent smaller than it

would have been if the growth rate had remained at 2 percent.

Of course, not all redistribution policies have unfavorable effects on the growth rate. Some may have no effect, and others—by raising health and educational standards of ordinary workers—may raise the growth rate. Some related policy issues are discussed in Box 36-2.

Theories of Economic Growth

In theoretical discussions of growth, it is useful to have a measure of the ability of an economy to convert its resources into goods and services. One widely used measure is output per hour of labor, or *productivity*. Obviously, productivity depends not only on labor input but also on the amount and kind of machinery used, the raw materials available, and so on. The focus of this measure is explained by the special emphasis that human beings place on labor.[1]

Economists today recognize that many different factors may contribute to or impede economic growth. Although our present knowledge of the relative importance of these factors is far from complete, modern economists look at the problems of growth more optimistically than did the classical economists of a century or more ago. Of particular importance are the nature and source of the investment opportunities that can lead to growth. The differences between the classical and contemporary points of view can best be understood by considering a revealing, though extreme, case.

Growth in a World with No Learning

Suppose that there is a known and fixed stock of projects that might be undertaken. Suppose also that nothing ever happens to increase either the supply of such projects or knowledge about them. Whenever the moment is right, some of the investment opportunities are utilized, thereby increasing the stock of capital goods and depleting the reservoir of unutilized investment opportunities. Of course, the most productive opportunities will be used first.

Such a view of investment opportunities can be represented by a fixed marginal-efficiency-of-capital (*MEC*) schedule of the kind presented in Chapter 18. Such a schedule is graphed in Figure 36-2. It relates the stock of capital to the productivity of an additional unit of capital. The productivity of a unit of capital is calculated by dividing the annual value of

[1] The discussion of productivity in Chapter 11 is relevant here. It should be read now and treated as part of this chapter. (Indeed, the whole section on the very long run, pages 208–213, could be usefully read now.)

FIGURE 36-2   The Marginal-Efficiency-of-Capital Schedule

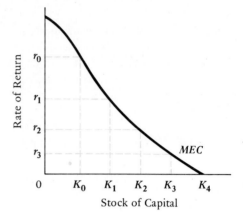

A declining *MEC* schedule shows that successive increases to the capital stock bring smaller and smaller increases in output and thus a declining rate of return. A fixed *MEC* schedule can represent the theory of growth in an economy with some unutilized investment opportunities but no learning. Increases in investment that increase the capital stock from K_0 to K_1 to . . . K_4 lower the rate of return from r_0 to r_1 to . . . zero. Because the productivity of successive units of capital decreases, the capital-output ratio rises.

the additional output resulting from an extra unit of capital by the value of that unit of capital. Thus, for example, a marginal efficiency of capital of 0.2 means that $1.00 of new capital adds $.20 per year to the stream of output.

The downward slope of the *MEC* schedule indicates that, with knowledge being held constant, increases in the stock of capital bring smaller and smaller increases in output per unit of capital; that is, the rate of return on successive units of capital declines. This shape is a consequence of the law of diminishing returns, which was discussed on pages 192–193.[2]

If, with land, labor, and knowledge being held constant, more and more capital is used, the net amount added by successive increments will dimin-

[2] This hypothesis was discussed on pages 192–193.

ish and may eventually reach zero. As capital is accumulated in a state of constant knowledge, the society will move down its *MEC* schedule. In such a "nonlearning" world, in which new investment opportunities do not appear, growth occurs only so long as there are unutilized opportunities to use capital effectively in order to increase output.

So far we have discussed the *marginal* efficiency of capital. The *average* efficiency of capital refers to the average amount produced in the whole economy per unit of capital employed. It is common in discussions of the theory of growth to talk in terms of the *capital-output ratio,* which is the reciprocal of output per unit of capital. In a world without learning, the capital-output ratio increases.

In a world without learning, growth in the capital stock will have two important consequences:

1. **Successive increases in capital accumulation will be less and less productive, and the capital-output ratio will be increasing.**
2. **The marginal efficiency of new capital will be decreasing and will eventually be pushed to zero as the backlog of investment opportunities is used up.**

Consequences of Learning

The steady depletion of growth opportunities with constant knowledge results from the fact that new investment opportunities are never discovered or created. However, if investment opportunities are created as well as used up with the passage of time, the *MEC* schedule will shift outward over time and the effects of increasing the capital stock may be different. This is illustrated in Figure 36-3.

Such outward shifts can be regarded as the consequences of "learning" either about investment opportunities or about the techniques that create such opportunities. As shown in the figure, when learning occurs, what matters is how rapidly the *MEC* schedule shifts relative to the amount of capital investment being undertaken.

Gradual reduction in investment opportunities: the classical view. If, as in Figure 36-3(i), investment opportunities are created, but at a slower rate than they

are used up, there will be a tendency toward a falling rate of return and an increasing ratio of capital to output. The predictions in this case are the same as those given for the world without learning.

This figure illustrates the theory of growth that was held by most early economists. They saw the economic problem as one of fixed land, a rising population, and a gradual exhaustion of investment opportunities. These conditions, they believed, would ultimately force the economy into a static condition, with no growth, high capital-output ratios, and the marginal return on additional units of capital forced downward toward zero.

Constant or rising investment opportunities: the contemporary view. The pessimism of the classical economists came from their failure to anticipate the possibility of really rapid innovation—of technological progress that could push investment opportunities outward as they were used up or even more rapidly, as shown in parts (ii) and (iii) of Figure 36-3.

In a world with rapid innovation:

1. **Successive increases in capital accumulation may prove highly productive, and the capital-output ratio may be constant or decreasing.**
2. **Despite large amounts of capital accumulation, the marginal efficiency of new capital may remain constant or even increase as new investment opportunities are created.**

The historical record suggests that outward shifts in investment opportunities over time lead to the reality of sustained growth. Evidently, modern economies have been successful in generating new investment opportunities at least as rapidly as old ones were used up.

A Contemporary View of Growth

The classical economists had a relatively simple theory of growth, because they viewed a single mechanism—capital accumulation—as decisively important. Contemporary theorists begin by recognizing a number of factors that influence growth, no one of which is necessarily dominant.

FIGURE 36-3   Shifting Investment Opportunities: Three Cases

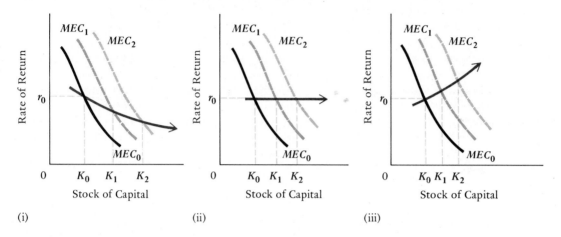

(i)   (ii)   (iii)

When both knowledge and the capital stock grow, the actual marginal efficiency of capital depends on their relative rates of growth. In each case the economy at period 0 has the MEC_0 curve, a capital stock of K_0, and a rate of return of r_0. In period 1 the curve shifts to MEC_1 and there is investment to increase the stock of capital to K_1. In period 2 the curve shifts to MEC_2 and there is new investment that increases the capital stock to K_2. It is the relative size of the shift of the MEC curve and the additions of the capital stock that are important.

In part (i) investment occurs more rapidly than increases in investment opportunities, and the rate of return falls along the black arrow. In part (ii) investment occurs less rapidly than increases in investment opportunities, and the rate of return rises along the black arrow.

Quantity of Capital Per Worker

Human beings always have been tool users. It is still true that more and more tools tend to lead to more and more output. As long as a society has unexploited investment opportunities, productive capacity can be increased by increasing the stock of capital. The effect on output per worker of "mere" capital accumulation is so noticeable that it was once regarded as virtually the sole source of growth.

However, if capital accumulation were the only source of growth, it would lead to movement down the MEC schedule and to a rising capital-output ratio and a falling rate of return on capital. The evidence does not support these predictions. The facts suggest that investment opportunities have expanded as rapidly as investments in capital goods, roughly along the pattern of Figure 36-3(ii). While capital accumulation has taken place and has accounted for much observed growth, it cannot have been the only source of growth.

Quality of Capital

New knowledge and inventions can contribute markedly to the growth of potential national income, even without capital accumulation. To see this, assume that the proportion of the society's resources that is devoted to the production of capital goods is just sufficient to replace capital as it wears out. Thus, if the old capital were merely replaced in the same form, the capital stock would be constant and there would be no increase in the capacity to produce. However, if there were a growth of knowledge, so that as old equipment wore out it was replaced by different, more productive equipment, national income would be growing.

Increases in productive capacity that are intrinsic to the form of capital goods in use are called **embodied technical change.** The historical importance of embodied technical change is clear: The assembly line and automation transformed much of manufacturing; the airplane revolutionized transportation; and electronic devices now dominate the information technology industries. These innovations plus less well known but no less profound ones—for example, improvements in the strength of metals, the productivity of seeds, and the techniques for recovering basic raw materials from the ground—create new investment opportunities.

Less obvious but nonetheless important changes occur through **disembodied technical change,** that is, changes in the organization of production that are not embodied in the form of the capital goods or raw materials used. One example is improved techniques of managerial control.

Most innovations involve both embodied and disembodied changes, but, whatever the form of innovation, the nature of the goods and services consumed and the way in which they are made change continually as innovations occur. Major innovations of the past century have resulted from the development of the telephone, the linotype, the automobile, the airplane, plastics, the assembly line, the coaxial cable, xerography, the computer, the transistor, and the silicon chip. It would be hard for us to imagine life without them.

The Quality of Labor

The "quality" of labor—or what is often called *human capital*—has several aspects. One involves improvements in the health and longevity of the population. Of course, these are desired as ends in themselves, yet they have consequences for both the size and the productivity of the labor force. There is no doubt that they have increased productivity per worker-hour by cutting down on illness, accidents, and absenteeism. At the same time, the extension of the normal life span, with no comparable increase in the working life span, has created a larger group of nonworking aged that exercises a claim on total output. Whether health improvements alone have increased output per capita in the United States is not clear.

A second aspect of the quality of human capital concerns technical training, from learning to operate a machine to learning how to be a scientist. Training clearly is required to invent, operate, manage, and repair complex machines. More subtly, there are often believed to be general social advantages to an educated population. It has been shown that productivity improves with literacy and that, in general, the

longer a person has been educated, the more adaptable, and thus, in the long run, the more productive he or she is to new and changing challenges. However, education may also increase feelings of alienation in a society that is thought to be arbitrary or unjust. Box 36-3 explores some related issues that arise from recent research on *endogenous* growth.

The Quantity of Labor

The size of a country's population and the extent of its participation in the labor force are important in and of themselves, not merely because they affect the quantity of a factor of production. For this reason it is less common to speak of the quantity of people available for work as a source of or detriment to growth than it is to speak of the quantity of capital or iron ore in the same way. Clearly, however, for any given state of knowledge and supplies of other factors of production, the size of the population can affect the level of output per capita. Every child born has both a mouth and a pair of hands; over a lifetime each person will be both a consumer and a producer. Thus, on average, it is meaningful to speak of overpopulated or underpopulated economies, depending on whether the contribution to production of additional people would raise or lower the level of per capita income.

Because population size is related to income per capita, we can define a theoretical concept, *optimal population,* that maximizes income per capita.

Many countries have or have had conscious population policies. America in the nineteenth century sought immigrants, as did Australia until recently. Greece in the 1950s and 1960s tried to stem emigration to Western Europe. All are examples of countries that believed that they had an insufficient population, though the motives were not in every case purely economic. In contrast, many underdeveloped countries of South America, Africa, and Asia desire to limit population growth.

Structural Change

Changes in the economy's structure can cause large fluctuations in its growth rate. For example, an expansion in such low-productivity sectors as agriculture and a decline in such high-productivity sectors as manufacturing will temporarily lower the measured aggregate growth rate.

When one type of energy (say, solar) supplants

BOX 36-3

Endogenous Growth Models

During the 1950s economists began to develop mathematical models to aid their understanding of economic growth. The simplest version of the resulting "neoclassical" growth model treated the economy's output as if it were a single good, produced from homogeneous capital and labor through an "aggregate production function." The stock of capital grew as a result of saving and investment, and the labor force grew with increases in the population. Because the marginal efficiency of capital was assumed to fall as the stock of capital per head rose (see Figure 36-2), balanced growth—called a "steady state"—was reached when the increases in output due to investment just balanced the growth in the labor force. Thus, the capital stock and total output both grew at the same rate as the labor force, and output per head was constant.

While this simple neoclassical growth model has proven valuable for helping to understand the behavior of growing economies, it has a number of unsatisfactory characteristics.

First, the evidence suggests that the accumulation of capital and growth in the labor force is not sufficient to account for all of the growth in total output and output per head that most advanced industrialized economies enjoyed in the post–World War II period. The residual, representing the excess of actual over "explained" growth, was dubbed "the measure of our ignorance," and it was substantial. This problem was "resolved" by assuming that the economy experienced exogenous technical progress: As time passed, productivity increased and hence growth in total output exceeded growth

in inputs, and output per head rose. (The key difference between this model and that of the first paragraph is that in the first model there is no "learning.")

Second, and related, is the criticism that the model does not really "explain" the rate of growth of the economy: Since the population and technical growth rates are both *exogenous,* so is the rate of growth. Hence, no predictions of the rate of growth or the variables that affect it are possible. For example, changes in the rate of saving in this model do not change the equilibrium rate of growth but only change per capita GNP in the steady state.

Third, since most technology can flow quite freely across borders, and since technical change plays a key role in explaining growth, the model predicts that the growth rate of per capita GDP in various countries will converge to a worldwide constant. This prediction is at odds with the evidence that there exists wide and persistent differences between individual countries' growth rates.

In reaction to these weaknesses, economists recently have developed models of *endogenous* growth.* These models stress the role of learning and investment in knowledge in influencing technical change and hence the rate of growth of the economy.

Knowledge is treated as a capital good: An individual firm's production is a function of the firm's

* For example, see Paul M. Romer, "Increasing Returns and Long-Run Growth," *Journal of Political Economy,* 94 (1986), 1002–1037; and Robert E. Lucas, Jr., "On the Mechanics of Economic Development," *Journal of Monetary Economics,* 22 (1988), 43–70.

another type (say, oil), much existing capital stock specifically geared to the original energy source may become too costly to operate and will be scrapped. New capital, geared to the new energy source, will be built. During the transition, investment expenditure is high, thus stimulating aggregate demand,

but there is little, if any, expansion in the economy's output capacity because the old capital goods have been scrapped. Gross investment is high, but net investment is low, since the capital expenditure *transforms* the capital stock but does not *increase* it. Similarly, new pollution control laws will affect invest-

own level of knowledge and of the "stock of knowledge" in the economy. The stock of knowledge creates an *externality* in production. The externality means that accumulation does not force the economy to move downward along a negatively sloped *MEC* curve, as in Figure 36-2, but, rather, along a horizontal path, such as shown by the arrow in part (ii) of Figure 36-3. For example, the accumulation of human capital by one worker, or group of workers, might increase not only their own productivity but also that of others in the economy who now work in a better trained work force. Further, those others may find that the returns to further investment in their own human capital have increased. Thus, an increase in the stock of knowledge may set up a set of actions that *permanently* increase the level and rate of growth of output.

The external effects of knowledge mean that an initial investment in human capital will make further investments more productive; thus, increased savings in the form of investment in human capital can permanently increase the economy's rate of growth.

The possibility for the level and rate of growth of output to be *permanently* affected by shocks is often referred to as *hysteresis* in the growth process.

Another possibility, captured by these models, is *learning-by-doing* in production, whereby productivity in an industry increases with the cumulative volume of production in that industry. (This is discussed in detail in Chapter 39.) Learning-by-doing means that countries with initial high levels of skill can specialize in producing products that permit faster accumulation of human capital and thus have permanently higher rates of growth than those specializing in lower-growth industries.

These models also point to ways in which economies can increase their rates of growth. Government investment in infrastructure, such as roads, airports, and other communication and transportation networks, as well as schools and training centers, can affect growth.* In particular, the models stress that the accumulation of human capital should be fostered through both specific worker training and general education. Also, an immigration policy that discriminates in favor of highly trained, skilled workers could raise the general level of productivity and enhance growth.

The importance of government investment in infrastructure highlights the fact that not all government spending is the same. For example, a government that spends less and therefore creates fewer jobs in the short run but that provides the economic underpinnings for private-sector investment may eventually produce higher standards of living through increased growth. Furthermore, too much government expenditure can reduce growth opportunities, just as too little can.

---

* The development of cities and their tremendous capacity for the generation of wealth is often cited as an example of the external effects of human capital.

---

ment expenditure but will not lead to growth in capacity. (The reduction in pollution may nonetheless be socially desirable.)

A rise in the international price of *imported* energy will also lower productivity. Although the same volume of goods can be produced with a given input of labor, a smaller portion of the output's value now accrues as income to domestic workers and firms, because more must be used to pay for the energy imports. The higher-priced imported energy input means that domestic *value added* falls and with it GDP per worker. This shows up in the statistics as a decline in productivity and a temporary fall in growth rates.

These are some of the many factors that were operative in the 1970s and early 1980s. They worked to depress growth rates for some considerable period of time, but they are not permanent factors. When the structural adjustments are complete, their depressing effects will pass. Further, many of the effects were reversed when oil prices fell in early 1986, giving a boost to the productivity of many domestic factors of production.

Institutional Considerations

Almost all aspects of a country's institutions can foster or deter the efficient use of a society's natural and human resources. Social and religious habits, legal institutions, and traditional patterns of national and international trade are all important. So, too, is the political climate.

Is There a Most Important Source of Growth?

The modern theory of growth tends to reject a dominant source of growth and to recognize that several influences singly and in interaction affect the growth rate.

Among the major contributors to rapid economic growth are a capital stock that is steadily growing and improving in quality, a healthy and well-educated labor force, and a rate of population growth that is small enough to permit per capita growth in capital.

These factors are more likely to be used effectively in some institutional settings than in others.

A complete theory of growth would do more than list a series of influences that affect the growth rate. It would include assessments of their relative importance, the trade-offs involved in having more of one beneficial influence and less of another, and the interactions among the various influences. This poses a formidable program for further empirical research.

While much remains to be learned, an important tentative conclusion of recent studies is that improvements in *quality* of capital—human as well as physical—have played a larger role than increases in the *quantity* of capital in the economic growth of the

United States since 1900. Whether quality, rather than quantity, of capital is also the more important source of growth for countries with different cultural patterns, more acute population problems, or more limited natural resources is a matter of continuing research.

Benefits and Costs of Growth

In the remainder of this chapter, we outline some more general considerations concerning economic growth. We start by looking at the benefits and then the costs of growth. Boxes 36-4 and 36-5 outline the popular arguments on both sides of the growth debate.

Benefits of Growth

Growth in Living Standards

A country whose per capita output grows at 3 percent per year doubles its living standards about every 24 years.

A primary reason for wanting growth is to raise general living standards.

The extreme importance of economic growth in raising income can be illustrated by comparing the real income of a father with the real income of the son who follows in his father's footsteps. If the son neither rises nor falls in the relative income scale compared with his father, his share of the country's national income will be the same as his father's. If the son is 30 years younger than his father, he can expect to have a real income that is nearly twice as large as the one that his father enjoyed when his father was the same age. These figures assume that the father and the son live in a country such as the United States, where the growth rate has been 2 or 3 percent per year. If they live in Japan, where growth has been going on at a rate of about 8 percent per year, the son's income will be about 10 times as large as his father's.

For those who share in it, growth is a powerful weapon against poverty. A family that is earning $15,000 today can expect an income of $22,000 within 10 years (in constant dollars), if it just shares in a 4 percent growth rate. The transformation of the life-style of blue-collar workers in North America (as well as in Europe and Japan) in a generation provides a notable example of the escape from poverty that growth makes possible.

Growth and Income Redistribution

Not everyone benefits equally from growth. Many of the poorest are not even in the labor force and thus are least likely to share in the higher wages that, along with profits, are the primary means by which the gains from growth are distributed. For this reason, even in a growing economy redistribution policies will be needed if poverty is to be averted.

Economic growth makes many kinds of redistribution easier to achieve. For example, a rapid growth rate makes it more feasible politically to alleviate poverty. If existing income is to be redistributed, someone's standard of living will actually have to be lowered. However, when there is economic growth and when the increment in income is redistributed (through government intervention), it is possible to reduce income inequalities without actually having to lower anyone's income. It is much easier for a rapidly growing economy to be generous toward its less fortunate citizens—or neighbors—than it is for a static economy.

Growth and Life-Style

A family often finds that a big increase in its income can lead to a major change in the pattern of its consumption—that extra money buys important amenities of life. In the same way, the members of society as a whole may change their consumption patterns as their average income rises. Not only do markets in a country that is growing rapidly make it profitable to produce more cars, but also the government is led to produce more highways and to provide more recreational areas for its newly affluent (and mobile) citizens. At yet a later stage, a concern about litter, pollution, and ugliness may become important, and their correction may then begin to account for a significant fraction of GDP. Such "amenities" usually become matters of social concern only when growth has assured the provision of the basic requirements for food, clothing, and housing of a substantial majority of the population.

National Defense and Prestige

When one country is competing with another for power or prestige, rates of growth are important. If our national income is growing at 2 percent, while another country's national income is growing at 5 percent, the other country will only have to wait for our relative strength to dwindle. Moreover, the faster its productivity is growing, the easier a country will find it to bear the expenses of an arms race or a program of foreign aid.

More subtly, growth has become part of the currency of international prestige. Countries that are engaged in persuading other countries of the might or right of their economic and political systems point to their rapid rates of growth as evidence of their achievements.

Costs of Growth

The benefits of growth suggest that it is a great blessing. It is surely true that, other things being equal, most people would regard a fast rate of growth as preferable to a slow one, but other things are seldom equal.

Social and Personal Costs of Growth

Industrialization can cause deterioration of the environment. Unspoiled landscapes give way to highways, factories, and billboards; air and water become polluted; and unique and priceless relics of earlier ages—from flora and fauna to ancient art and ruins—often disappear. Urbanization tends to move people away from the simpler life of farms and small towns into the crowded, slum-ridden, and often darkly evil life of the urban ghetto. Those remaining behind in the rural areas find that rural life, too, has changed. Larger-scale farming, the decline of population, and the migration of children from the farm to the city all have their costs. The stepped-up tempo of life brings joy to some but tragedy to others. Accidents, ulcers, crime rates, suicides, divorces, and murders all tend to be higher in periods of rapid change and in more developed societies.

When an economy is growing, it is also changing. Innovation renders some machines obsolete and also leaves some people partially obsolete. No matter how well trained workers are at age 25, in another 25 years most will find that their skills are at least partially obsolete. A rapid growth rate requires rapid

BOX 36-4

An Open Letter to the Ordinary Citizen from a Supporter of the Growth-Is-Good School

Dear Ordinary Citizen:

You live in the world's first civilization that is devoted principally to satisfying *your* needs rather than those of a privileged minority. Past civilizations have always been based on leisure and high consumption for a tiny upper class, a reasonable living standard for a small middle class, and hard work with little more than subsistence consumption for the great mass of people.

The continuing Industrial Revolution is based on mass-produced goods for you, the ordinary citizen. It ushered in a period of sustained economic growth that has dramatically raised consumption standards of ordinary citizens. Reflect on a few examples: travel, live and recorded music, art, good food, inexpensive books, universal literacy, and a genuine chance to be educated. Most important, there is leisure to provide time and energy to enjoy these and thousands of other products of the modern industrial economy.

Would any ordinary family seriously prefer to go back to the world of 150 or 500 years ago in its same relative social and economic position? Surely, the answer is no. However, for those with incomes in the top 1 or 2 percent of the income distribution, economic growth has destroyed much of their privileged consumption position. They must now vie with the masses when they visit the world's beauty spots and be annoyed, while lounging on the terrace of a palatial mansion, by the sound of charter flights carrying ordinary people to inexpensive holidays in far places. Many of the rich complain bitterly about the loss of exclusive rights to luxury consumption, and it is not surprising that they find their intellectual apologists.

Whether they know it or not, the antigrowth economists are not the social revolutionaries that they think they are. They say that growth has produced pollution and wasteful consumption of all kinds of frivolous products that add nothing to human happiness. However, the democratic solution to pollution is not to go back to where so few people consume luxuries that pollution is trivial, but rather to learn to control the pollution that mass consumption tends to create.

It is only through further growth that the average citizen can enjoy consumption standards (of travel, culture, medical and health care, etc.) now available only to people in the top 25 percent of the income distribution—which includes the intellectuals who earn large royalties from the books that they write in which they denounce growth. If you think that extra income confers little real benefit, just ask those in the top 25 percent to trade incomes with average citizens.

Ordinary citizens, do not be deceived by disguised elitist doctrines. Remember that the very rich and the elite have much to gain by stopping growth and even more by rolling it back, but you have everything to gain by letting it go forward.

Onward!   *A. Growthman*

---

adjustments, which can cause much upset and misery to the affected individuals.

It is often argued that costs of this kind are a small price to pay for the great benefits that growth can bring. Even if this is true in the aggregate (which is a matter of debate), these personal costs are very unevenly borne. Indeed, many of those for whom growth is most costly (in terms of jobs) share least in the fruits of growth. Yet it is also a mistake to see only the costs of growth—to yearn for the good old days while enjoying higher living standards that growth alone has made possible.

BOX 36-5

An Open Letter to the Ordinary Citizen from a Supporter of the Growth-Is-Bad School

Dear Ordinary Citizen:

You live in a world that is being despoiled by a mindless search for ever higher levels of material consumption at the cost of all other values. Once upon a time, men and women knew how to enjoy creative work and to derive satisfaction from simple activities. Today the ordinary worker is a mindless cog in an assembly line that turns out ever more goods that the advertisers must work overtime to persuade the worker to consume.

Statisticians count the increasing flow of material output as a triumph of modern civilization. You arise from your electric-blanketed bed, clean your teeth with an electric toothbrush, open a can of the sad remnants of a once-proud orange with an electric can opener, and eat your bread baked from superrefined and chemically refortified flour; you climb into your car to sit in vast traffic jams on exhaust-polluted highways.

Television commercials tell you that by consuming more you are happier, but happiness lies not in increasing consumption but in increasing the ratio of *satisfaction of wants* to *total wants*. Since the more you consume, the more the advertisers persuade you that you want to consume, you are almost certainly less happy than the average citizen in a small town in 1900 whom we can visualize sitting on the family porch, sipping lemonade, and enjoying the antics of the children as they jump rope with pieces of old clothesline.

Today the landscape is dotted with endless factories, producing the plastic trivia of the modern industrial society. They drown you in a cloud of noise, air, and water pollution. The countryside is despoiled by strip mines, petroleum refineries, acid rain, and dangerous nuclear power stations, producing energy that is devoured insatiably by modern factories and motor vehicles. Worse, our precious heritage of natural resources is being fast used up.

Now is the time to stop this madness. We must stabilize production, reduce pollution, conserve our natural resources, and seek justice through a more equitable distribution of existing total income.

A long time ago, Malthus taught us that, if we do not limit population voluntarily, nature will do it for us in a cruel and savage manner. Today the same is true of output: If we do not halt its growth voluntarily, the halt will be imposed on us by a disastrous increase in pollution and a rapid exhaustion of natural resources.

Citizens, awake! Shake off the worship of growth, learn to enjoy the bounty that is yours already, and reject the endless, self-defeating search for increased happiness through ever increasing consumption.

Upward!   *A. Nongrowthman*

The Opportunity Cost of Growth

In a world of scarcity, almost nothing is free. Growth requires heavy investments of resources in capital goods, as well as in activities such as education. Often these investments yield no immediate return in terms of goods and services for consumption; thus they imply that sacrifices have been made by the current generation of consumers.

Growth, which promises more goods tomorrow, is achieved by consuming fewer goods today. For the economy as a whole, this is the primary cost of growth.

BOX 36-6

The Brundtland Commission and "Sustainable Development"

The 1980s have seen a major increase in public awareness of the environmental problems that are facing all of the nations of the world. Problems such as global warming, ozone depletion, soil erosion, and acid rain have risen to the top of the political agenda around the world. As barges, laden with toxic waste, are shunted around the world in search of a country that is willing to accept their cargo, policymakers have come to recognize that even problems that once were considered to be purely local in nature, such as garbage disposal, have become international in scope.

In 1983 the United Nations created the World Commission on Environment and Development (called the Brundtland Commission after its Chairman Gro Harlem Brundtland) to examine global environmental and development problems and to design solutions to them. In its report, *Our Common Future,* published by Oxford University Press in 1987, the Brundtland Commission outlined a broad agenda for integrating economic development and environmental policy. The Commission stressed the view that economic growth and environmental protection are interdependent: Growth cannot long continue in the presence of the present rate of environmental degradation. Its report introduced the concept of *sustainable development,* defined as "development that meets the needs of the present without compromising the ability of future generations to meet their own needs." (Note that the concept underlying this definition can be thought of as a "broadening" of the concept of "permanent income," which was introduced in Chapter 28.)

The idea that economic growth is limited by "nature" is not new. In the early 1970s the Club of Rome focused on the limits to growth arising from the supply of natural resources: It extrapolated from the shortages in oil, caused by the formation of OPEC and the attendant price increases, that industrialized countries faced an absolute limit to growth. As we discussed in the text, this prediction was confounded by experience, as higher prices for fuel have led to both increases in supply and the efficiency with which it has been used. The bounds to growth that were envisioned by the Brundtland Commission are not absolute but, rather, a function of "the present state of technology" and the capacity of the "biosphere to absorb the effects of human activity." The environment imposes limits to growth because it is the fundamental capital upon which economic development is based. As technology and economic organization improve, the stream of wealth that flows from this stock of "environmental capital" can continue to increase. The concept of *sustainable development* stresses the role of the environment as capital, which, if exhausted, cannot be replaced.

Our Common Future is a compendium of the problems that are facing policymakers and the various ways in which national governments and international agencies can be reformed to achieve promotion of sustainable development; it addresses issues of population control, energy and food supplies, urban development, the arms race, and the management of the "global commons": the oceans, orbital space, and Antarctica.

Regardless of whether they are government agencies, small firms, or transnational corporations, the Brundtland Commission's message applies: All institutions that affect the environmental base of the economy must respect the needs of future generations. Governments need to expand their role in the collection and the dissemination of information and, where possible, should produce an annual account of the nation's environment and resource base "to complement the traditional annual fiscal budget and economic development plans." Recall from Chapter 25 that the national-income accounts measure *net* national income by subtracting depreciation of capital from *gross* national product. The Brundtland Commission's recommendations involve expanding this concept to subtract some measure of the deterioration of the environment in calculating the level and rate of growth of net national income and derivative measures such as disposable income per capita. The idea is that the environment is part of our capital, and when we degrade it, we reduce our ability to generate real income in the future, just as when a machine used for producing consumer goods depreciates.

Some of the Brundtland Commission's recommendations require more government involvement in economies, in order to produce and enforce environmental regulations. While the Brundtland Commission recognizes the value of economic incentives in generating the cost reductions that flow from more efficient use of resources, it also feels that there are limits to the ability of competitive industry to reduce waste voluntarily: "Regulations imposing uniform performance standards are essential to ensure that industry makes the investments necessary to reduce pollution and waste and to enable them to compete on an even footing." (For those who studied microeconomics first, this can be seen as intervention, justified by market failure, and a distinction between private and social costs, as discussed in Chapter 23.)

In other cases, what is required is *less* government intervention, and the report calls on governments to examine whether existing policies and subsidies contribute to resource-efficient practices. For example, agricultural policy that protects farmers in industrialized countries is criticized for being "studded with contradictions that encourage the degradation of the agricultural resource base and, in the long run, do more harm than good to the agricultural industry." The solution lies in "reducing incentives that force overproduction and noncompetitive production in the developed market economies and enhancing those that encourage food production in developing countries."

More specific recommendations are made for reforming international organizations, in which an "extensive institutional capacity exists that could be redirected towards sustainable development"; thus, most of the proposed changes "will not require additional financial resources but can be achieved through a reorientation of existing mandates, programmes, and budgets and a redeployment of existing staff." The efficacy of existing institutions is reduced by their "fragmented" nature and a "weakness of coordination." Key to these reforms is the requirement that sustainable development be made central to the mandate of all international bodies such as UN agencies and the IMF and World Bank. The United Nations Environment Program (established in 1972) should be strengthened to become a clearing house for information, and to become the "principle advocate" for cooperation on environmental issues. The funding of Non-Governmental Originations (NGOs) should be increased, and these groups should be more fully integrated into intergovernmental organizations, as NGOs can "often provide an efficient and effective alternative to public agencies."

Our Common Future is a hopeful document, but its hope is tempered with the realization that, unless major conservation initiatives are acted on quickly, the current serious rate of environmental degradation will *soon* start to harm the health and welfare of all of us.

An example will suggest the magnitude of this cost. Suppose that the fictitious economy of USSA has full employment and is experiencing growth at the rate of 2 percent per year. Its citizens consume 85 percent of the GDP and invest 15 percent. The people of USSA know that, if they are willing to decrease immediately their consumption to 77 percent, they will produce more capital and thus shift at once to a 3 percent growth rate. The new rate can be maintained as long as they keep saving and investing 23 percent of the national income. Should they do it?

Table 36-2 illustrates the choice in terms of time paths of consumption. How expensive is the "invest now, consume later" strategy? Using the assumed figures, it takes 10 years for the actual amount of consumption to catch up to what it would have been had no reallocation been made. In the intervening 10

years, a good deal of consumption is lost, and the cumulative losses in consumption must be made up before society can really be said to have broken even. It takes an additional 9 years before total consumption over the whole period is as large as it would have been if the economy had remained on the 2 percent path. [44]

A policy of sacrificing present living standards for a gain that will not begin to be reaped for a generation is hardly likely to appeal to any but the altruistic or the very young. The question of how much of its living standards one generation is prepared to sacrifice for its heirs (who are in any case likely to be richer) is troublesome. As one critic put it: Why should we sacrifice for them? What have they ever done for us?

Many governments, particularly those that are seeking a larger role in world affairs, have chosen to force the diversion of resources from consumption to investment. The Germans under Hitler, the Russians under Stalin, and the Chinese under Mao Tse-tung adopted four-year and five-year plans that did just this. Many less-developed countries are using such plans today. Such shifts in resources are particularly important when actual growth rates are small (say, less than 1 percent), for without some current sacrifice there is little or no prospect of real growth in the lifetimes of today's citizens. The very lowest growth rates are frequently encountered in the very poorest countries. This creates a cruel dilemma—the vicious circle of poverty.

Are There Limits to Growth?

Opponents of growth argue that sustained growth is undesirable; some even argue that it is impossible. Of course, all terrestrial things have an ultimate limit. Astronomers predict that the solar system itself will die as the sun burns out in another 6 billion or so years. To be of practical concern, a limit must be within some reasonable planning horizon. Best-selling books of the 1970s by Jay Forrester (*World Dynamics,* 1973) and D. H. Meadows et al. (*The Limits to Growth,* 1974) predicted an imminent growth-induced doomsday. Living standards were predicted to reach a peak about the year 2000 and then, in the words of Professor William Nordhaus of Yale University, a leading critic of these models, to "descend inexorably to the level of Neanderthal man." What lessons are there to be learned from this debate?

TABLE 36-2 The Opportunity Cost of Growth

Year	(1) Level of consumption at 2% growth rate	(2) Level of consumption at 3% growth rate	(3) Cumulative gain (loss) in consumption
0	85.0	77.0	(8.0)
1	86.7	79.3	(15.4)
2	88.5	81.8	(22.1)
3	90.3	84.2	(28.2)
4	92.1	86.8	(33.5)
5	93.9	89.5	(37.9)
6	95.8	92.9	(40.8)
7	97.8	95.0	(43.6)
8	99.7	97.9	(45.4)
9	101.8	100.9	(46.3)
10	103.8	103.9	(46.2)
15	114.7	120.8	(28.6)
20	126.8	140.3	19.6
30	154.9	189.4	251.0
40	189.2	255.6	745.9

Transferring resources from consumption to investment goods lowers current income but raises future income. The example assumes that income in year zero is 100 and that consumption of 85 percent of national income is possible with a 2 percent growth rate. It is further assumed that to achieve a 3 percent growth rate, consumption must fall to 77 percent of income. A shift from (1) to (2) decreases consumption for 10 years but increases it thereafter. The cumulative effect on consumption is shown in (3); the gains eventually become large.

The Uncontroversial Fact of Increasing Pressure on Natural Resources

The years since World War II have seen a rapid acceleration in the consumption of the world's resources, particularly fossil fuels and basic minerals. World population has increased from under 2.5 billion to over 4 billion in that period, and this alone has increased the demand for all the world's resources. However, the single fact of population growth greatly understates the pressure on resources.

Calculations by Professor Nathan Keyfitz of Harvard University and others focus on the resources used by those who can claim a life-style of the level enjoyed by 90 percent of American families. This so-called middle class, which today includes about one-sixth of the world's population, consumes 15 to 30 times as much oil per capita and, overall, at least 5 times as much of the earth's scarce resources per capita as do the other "poor" five-sixths of the population.

The world's poor are not, however, content to remain forever poor. Whether they live in the USSR, Argentina, Indonesia, or Kenya, they have let their governments understand that they expect policies to be created that will generate enough growth to give *them* the higher consumption levels that all of *us* take for granted. This upward aspiration is being fulfilled to some degree in many countries. The growth of the middle class has been nearly 4 percent per year—twice the rate of population growth—over the postwar period. The number of persons realizing middle-class living standards is estimated to have increased from 200 million to 700 million between 1950 and 1980 and is predicted almost to double again by the turn of the century.

This growth is a major factor in the recently recognized or projected shortages of natural resources. Yet the 4 percent growth rate of the middle class, which is too fast for present resources, is too slow for the aspirations of the billions who live in underdeveloped countries and who see the fruits of development all around them. Thus, the pressure on world resources of energy, minerals, and food is likely to accelerate, even if population growth is reduced.

Another way to look at the problem of increasing pressure on natural resources is to note that present technology and resources could not possibly support the present population of the world at the standard of living of today's average American family. The demand for oil would increase fivefold to tenfold. Since these calculations (most unrealistically) assume no population growth anywhere in the world and no growth in living standards for the richest one-sixth of the world's population, it is evident that resources are insufficient.

A Tentative Verdict

Most economists agree that conjuring up absolute limits to growth, based on the assumptions of constant technology and fixed resources, is not warranted. Yet there is surely cause for concern. Most agree that any barrier can be overcome by technological advances, but not in an instant, and not automatically. Clearly, there is a problem of timing: How soon can we discover and put into practice the knowledge required to solve the problems that are made ever more imminent by growth in the population, the affluence, and the aspirations of the billions who now live in poverty? There is no guarantee that a whole generation may not be caught in transition, with social and political consequences that promise to be enormous, even if they are not cataclysmic. The nightmare conjured up by the doomsday models may have served its purpose if it helps to focus our attention on these problems. One such potentially positive outgrowth is the recent attention given to the concept of "sustainable development," discussed further in Box 36-6.

SUMMARY

1. National income can increase as a result of reduction in the recessionary gap, reduction in structural unemployment, or growth in the level of potential national income.
2. Investment has short-term effects on national income through aggregate demand and long-term effects through growth in potential national income. Such growth is frequently measured by using rates of change of potential real national income per person or per hour of labor employed.

3. Savings reduce aggregate demand and therefore reduce national income in the short run, but in the long run savings finance the investment that leads to growth in potential income.

4. The cumulative effects of even small differences in growth rates become large over periods of a decade or more.

5. Understanding growth involves understanding both the utilization of existing investment opportunities and the process of creating new investment opportunities. The source of economic growth was once thought to be almost entirely capital accumulation and the utilization of a backlog of unexploited investment opportunities. Today most economists recognize that many investment opportunities can be created, and much attention is given to the sources of outward shifts in the *MEC* schedule through both embodied and disembodied technical change.

6. The most important benefit of growth lies in its contribution to the long-run struggle to raise living standards and to escape poverty. It also makes more manageable the policies that would redistribute income among people. Growth also plays an important role in a country's national defense and in its struggle for international prestige.

7. Growth, while it is often beneficial, is never costless. The opportunity cost of growth is the diversion of resources from current consumption to capital formation. For individuals who are left behind in a rapidly changing world, the costs are higher and more personal. The optimal rate of growth involves balancing benefits and costs. Most people do not wish to forego the benefits that growth can bring, but neither do they wish to maximize growth at any cost.

8. In addition to mere increases in quantity of capital per person, any list of factors affecting growth includes the extent of innovation, the quality of human capital, the size of the working population, and the whole institutional setting.

9. The critical importance of increasing knowledge and new technology in sustaining growth is highlighted by the great drain on existing natural resources, resulting from the explosive growth of the past two or three decades. Without continuing new knowledge, the present needs and aspirations of the world's population cannot come anywhere close to being met.

TOPICS FOR REVIEW

Short-run and long-run effects of investment and saving
Cumulative nature of growth
Factors affecting growth
Effects of capital accumulation with and without new knowledge
Embodied and disembodied technical change
Benefits and costs of growth

DISCUSSION QUESTIONS

1. We usually study and measure economic growth in macroeconomic terms, but in a market economy, who makes the decisions that lead to growth? What kinds of decisions and what kinds of actions cause growth to occur? How might a detailed study of individual markets be relevant to understanding economic growth?

2. Discuss the following quote from a newspaper article that appeared in the summer of 1989:

"Economics and the environment are not strange bedfellows. Environment-oriented tourism is one creative way to resolve the conflict between our desire for a higher standard of living and the realization that nature cannot absorb everything we throw at it. The growing demand for eco-tourism has placed a premium on the remaining rain forests, undisturbed flora and fauna, and endangered species of the world."

3. *Family Weekly* recently listed among "inventions that have changed our lives" microwave ovens, digital clocks, bank credit cards, freeze-dried coffee, tape cassettes, climate-controlled shopping malls, automatic toll collectors, soft contact lenses, tubeless tires, and electronic word processors. Which of these would you hate to do without? Which, if any, will have a major impact on life in the twenty-first century? If there are any that you believe will not, does this mean that they are frivolous and unimportant?

4. The Overseas Development Council recently introduced "a new measure of economic development based on the physical quality of life." Its index, called PQLI, gives one-third weight to each of the following indicators: literacy, life expectancy, and infant mortality. While countries such as the United States and Canada rank high on either the PQLI or on an index of per capita real national income, some relatively poor countries, such as Sri Lanka, rank much higher on the PQLI index than much richer countries such as Algeria and Kuwait. Discuss the merits or deficiencies of this measure.

5. "The case for economic growth is that it gives man greater control over his environment, and consequently increases his freedom." Explain why you agree or disagree with this statement by Nobel Laureate W. Arthur Lewis.

6. Consider a developed economy that decides to achieve a zero rate of growth for the future. What implications would such a "stationary state" have for the processes of production and consumption?

7. Suppose that solar energy becomes the dominant form of energy in the twenty-first century. What changes will this make in the growth rates of Africa and Northern Europe?

8. Discuss the following newspaper headlines in terms of the sources, costs, and benefits of growth.
   a. "Stress addiction: 'Life in the fast lane' may have its benefits"
   b. "Education: An expert urges multiple reforms"
   c. "Industrial radiation risk higher than thought"
   d. "Developments in the field of management design are looking ahead"
   e. "Ford urged by federal safety officials to recall several hundred thousand of its 1981–1982 front-drive vehicles because of alleged fire hazards"

9. In the late 1970s and early 1980s productivity growth was historically low, but it rebounded after 1983. How might you explain this?

10. Dr. David Suzuki recently has argued that, despite the fact that "in the twentieth century the list of scientific and technological achievements has been absolutely dazzling, the costs of such progress are so large that negative economic growth may be right for the future." Policies to achieve this include "rigorous reduction of waste, a questioning and distrustful attitude towards technological progress, and braking demands on the globe's resources." Identify some of the benefits and costs of economic growth, and evaluate Dr. Suzuki's position.

Chapter 37

Government Budget Deficits

The federal government's budget deficit soared from $16 billion in 1979 to over $200 billion in 1986, and it remained at historically record levels at the end of the 1980s. No single measure associated with the government has ever been the focus of so much attention and controversy in the media, on the campaign trail, and in coffee shops and bars across the nation. Extreme views about the deficit and its potential effects are not hard to come by. At one extreme is the view that the deficit is a "time bomb ticking away that, if unchecked, threatens the jobs and prosperity of all Americans." At the other extreme is the view that the deficit itself is not a problem at all and that the only threat it poses to Americans arises from the possible effects of severe policy actions that might be taken on the misguided advice of deficit alarmists.

The Economics of Budget Deficits

The average American has some idea of the size of the federal budget deficit (if not exactly how big, then at least that it is too big). The average Briton or West German is not likely to have any idea of the size of the government's budget deficit or a strong opinion on whether it is too large. Why is our budget deficit so large? Why do Americans worry so much about it? Is it really such a big problem?

Facts About the Deficit

In order to put the growth of the deficit in perspective, it is useful to measure it *relative* to the size of the economy, as measured by GNP. Clearly a $200 billion dollar deficit will have different implications in an economy in which GNP is also $200 billion than it will in an economy in which GNP is, say, $2 trillion.

The recent emergence of record federal budget deficits is shown in Figure 37-1. Part (i) shows total federal spending and total federal revenues since 1964, each as a share of GNP. The steady trend of increase in expenditures through 1985 is readily apparent. There has been a marked decrease in spending as a share of GNP since 1985, but the most recent figure (for 1988) is higher than that for any year in the 1960s or 1970s. Revenues display more variation and little or no trend.

FIGURE 37-1 **Federal Revenues, Expenditures, and Deficits, 1964–1988 (*as a share of GNP*)**

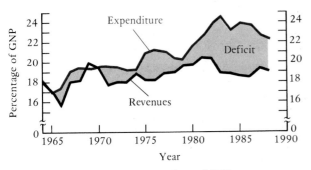

(i) Expenditures and revenues as a share of GNP

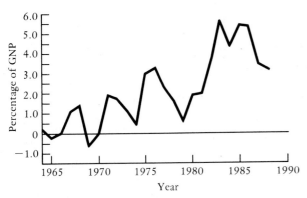

(ii) The deficit as a share of GNP

Since 1964 expenditure has grown steadily as a fraction of GNP, while revenues have fluctuated but have shown little trend. Over the period 1965 to 1970, expenditures and revenues both grew steadily. From 1970 to 1979 expenditures grew gradually, while revenues remained roughly constant. Persistent deficits emerged. Since 1979 expenditures have grown dramatically, while revenues have fallen slightly. Over that period the deficit has increased sharply, although it has fallen in the last three years. (*Source:* Congressional Budget Office: *The Economic and Fiscal Outlook* and *Economic Report of the President,* various years.)

Part (ii) of Figure 37-1 shows the deficit, also measured as a share of GNP; this is the shaded area between the two lines in part (i). The government budget had been in deficit prior to 1982, although the deficit had not been unusually large by historical standards. After 1982, however, the deficit increased dramatically as a share of GNP. By 1988 the deficit had fallen somewhat from its peak levels in the mid-1980s. Partly this was because the economy had recovered from the recession of the early 1980s and was approximately at potential GNP in 1988. For the budget deficit to be as large as 3.4 percent of GNP (the 1988 figure) with the economy at high employment is unprecedented.

Why Worry About Deficits?

Some economists have argued that deficits and public debt have no important effects on the economy. The logic underlying this *Ricardian Neutrality Proposition* position is discussed in the appendix to this chapter, where we show that the conditions required for deficits to be irrelevant are very stringent.[1] For most economists, the relevant question is not whether deficits have effects, but the form and magnitude of those effects.

One way in which deficits influence the economy is through their short-run stabilizing or destabilizing role.

This stabilization role was emphasized in Chapter 30, where we saw that there are complications that arise when measuring the deficit in order to judge the stance of fiscal policy for stabilization purposes (see pages 623–624). In particular, it is necessary to make a *cyclical adjustment,* which controls for the induced changes in spending and tax revenues caused by cyclical changes in national income. As can be seen from Table 30-1 (page 625), the *cyclically adjusted deficit (CAD)* grew even more than the actual deficit during the period from 1982 to 1985. The strength of the economic recovery meant that the GNP gap shrunk during that period and hence that the *CAD* rose relative to the actual deficit.

The persistence of a large *CAD,* along with a

---

[1] Briefly, the argument is that the government's decision of whether to finance current expenditure by levying current taxes or by issuing debt is irrelevant for the economy, since all that the latter decision does is postpone the taxes. Issuing bonds raises the current government deficit and raises current household disposable income. However, according to this theory, neither has any implications for the performance of the economy. Forward-looking consumers will know that they have to pay higher taxes later and hence will not increase their current consumption expenditures. Thus, the theory holds that there will be no stimulus to the economy from the deficit.

BOX 37-1

How Big Is the Deficit?

Another issue in measuring the size of the government budget deficit arises from what is called *the inflation adjustment*. As we have seen (pages 505–506), nominal interest rates can be divided into a real interest component and an inflation premium. The inflation adjustment involves making the same distinction when the government's debt service payments—which as we will see on page 792 constitute a significant part of total government expenditures—are assessed.

Debt service payments that are made by the government also have a real interest component and an inflation premium. While the real interest component constitutes a transfer from the government to holders of the government debt as payment for use of the principal, the inflation premium does not. This is because the inflation premium is exactly offset by a reduction in the real value of the principal.

Suppose that the current value of the government's debt is $1,000 billion. Suppose also that in the current year the government runs a deficit of $100 billion and that the current inflation rate is 10 percent. On crude measures the government has a deficit of $100 billion; this corresponds to the increase in the nominal value of the government's indebtedness. On an inflation-adjusted basis, the deficit is zero. This is because the real value—or purchasing power—of the debt is unchanged, even though the nominal stock of debt has risen by 10 percent from $1,000 billion to $1,100 billion. Because the real value of the government's indebtedness is unchanged, the "effective," or inflation-adjusted, deficit is zero.

The inflation adjustment is made by subtracting the inflation premium of government debt service payments from the measured deficit.

Whether or not making the inflation adjustment is appropriate for assessing the impact of the deficit depends upon the response of households' consumption spending to inflation-induced changes in their real wealth. Those who argue for the adjustment hold that the net effect on aggregate demand of this component of the deficit will be approximately zero: The government's outlay will be offset by an increase in private saving as wealth holders attempt to recoup the inflation-induced fall in their real wealth. Those who argue against making the adjustment hold that private-sector saving will not

large actual deficit, reinforces the concerns that many economists have about the deficit. However, other measurement issues arise, which have led a few economists to argue that the deficit is not a problem because once it has been measured properly it is not a deficit at all. Box 37-1 takes up these measurement issues and the related controversy.

A second way in which deficits can influence the economy is through their potential to affect income and welfare adversely in the long run.

People worry about the long-run effects of persistent deficits for many reasons. We will look at four of these.

Will a deficit cause inflation?   Neither economic theory nor the available evidence suggests that deficits by themselves are sufficient to cause inflation. The worry that persistent deficits may cause inflation arises out of the fear that a persistent deficit will lead to a continuous expansion of the money supply, which, as we saw in Chapter 34, is a necessary condition for a sustained inflation to occur; that is, the fear is that a persistent deficit will eventually lead to pressure on the Fed to expand the money supply and thus cause inflation. To date this has not been a problem, as the deficit has been financed by government borrowing in capital markets; only if it were financed by "borrowing" from the Fed would the money supply be steadily increased. (In effect the

rise by enough to offset the inflation component completely.* While the magnitude of the short-run response of household spending is a source of some controversy among economists, most economists hold that household spending will adjust completely in the long run and hence that, if one's concern is with the long-run effects of persistent deficits, the adjustment should be made.

Professor Robert Eisner of Northwestern University has led a small but vocal group of economists who argue on the basis of this line of reasoning that the deficit is not so large as to be considered

---

* The balanced-budget multiplier (see Chapter 30, page 622) indicates another reason for adjusting the measured deficit in order to assess its impact on the economy. The balanced-budget multiplier suggests that $1 of spending will increase aggregate demand by more than $1 of tax revenue will decrease it. Therefore, in order to properly measure the effect of fiscal actions on aggregate demand, a more sophisticated measure, which takes account of these differential effects, is required. Such a measure, called the *weighted, cyclically adjusted deficit,* is often used by economists in detailed empirical work that assesses fiscal policy.

a major problem. Indeed, Eisner and Paul Pieper have argued that, once the inflation adjustment is made and once allowance is made for the increases in the value of government assets (including gold), the *deficits* recorded for the years 1978–1980 are, in fact, *surpluses.*†

Other economists argue that long-run concerns are best captured by the evolution of the debt-to-GNP ratio. Since both real growth in the economy and inflation cause the denominator, nominal GNP, to increase, the debt-to-GNP ratio automatically allows for their effects. If the ratio increases, then the deficit was so large that it caused the stock of debt to increase faster than nominal GNP. If the ratio falls, then the deficit was small enough that the stock of debt grew slower than nominal GNP. On this basis many economists thus view the rapid run-up in the debt-to-GNP ratio that occurred in the 1980s (see Figure 37-3) as evidence that the deficit is large enough to constitute a serious problem.

---

† Robert Eisner and Paul J. Pieper, "A New View of the Federal Debt and Budget Deficits," *American Economic Review,* 74 (March 1984), pp. 11–29.

Fed would *create* the money to finance the deficit.) If this increase were too rapid, then—as we saw in Chapter 32—it would cause inflation.

Deficits financed by the continual creation of new money may cause inflation. No one believes that this is desirable.

Will the deficit crowd out private investment?   People fear that deficit spending may lead to a more or less equivalent reduction in private-sector investment spending. Government borrowing to finance its deficit can absorb a significant proportion of private savings. In 1988, for example, the federal deficit was about equal to household savings and was nearly 20

percent of total private-sector savings by households and firms. The fear is that heavy government borrowing drives up the interest rate and the higher interest rate reduces private investment expenditure. This "crowding out" process is illustrated in Figure 37-2.

If government borrowing to finance the deficit drives up the interest rate, some private investment expenditure will be crowded out.

This effect is more likely when the economy is close to full employment. When there is a large recessionary gap, the rise in income will increase the volume of savings (as households move along their

FIGURE 37-2   Crowding Out of Private Investment by Government Borrowing

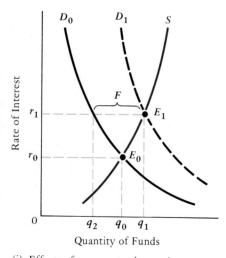

(i) Effects of government borrowing
with constant national income

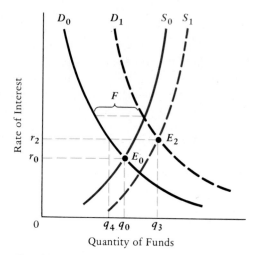

(ii) Effects of government borrowing
with increased national income

Government borrowing may crowd out private-sector borrowing and investing. Part (i) of the figure shows a supply of funds available to be lent, S, that is fairly insensitive to the interest rate. Initially, the demand to borrow funds is D_0, giving an equilibrium interest rate of r_0 and a quantity of funds borrowed for all purposes of q_0.

Government spending now increases by F, all of which is borrowed. This shifts the demand for funds to the right, from D_0 to D_1, taking equilibrium to E_1. The interest rate rises to r_1, and the quantity of funds borrowed rises to q_1. However, $q_2 q_1$ of these go to the government, so the private sector borrows only q_2, which is $q_2 q_0$ less than it was able to borrow, and hence invest, before the deficit forced the government into the market.

If, however, the extra government expenditure increases national income, it will raise saving. The savings function will then shift to the right, say, from S_0 to S_1 in part (ii) of the figure. Crowding out will then be lessened. At equilibrium E_2 the interest rate rises to r_2 and private borrowing is only $q_4 q_0$ less than before the government entered the market.

savings functions, as shown in Figure 26-2 on page 535). In this case the new savings generated by the rise in income helps to finance the deficit so that less crowding out of existing private-sector borrowing need occur.

Will the debt harm future generations?   To the extent that government borrowing to finance current expenditures crowds out private investment, there will be a smaller stock of capital to pass on to future generations. Less capital means less output; this is the long-term burden of the debt.

Despite large deficits, investment has been sus-

tained at high levels in the past few years. Does this mean that we do not need to worry about a burden arising from the large deficits? Unfortunately, the answer is no. While private investment has been maintained and deficits have had relatively little effect on interest rates, foreign lenders have supplied much of the funds.[2] Thus, while future generations of Americans may well inherit a capital stock that is not

---

[2] As we shall see in Chapter 42, the capital inflows from abroad are matched by a deficit on the current account, and the association of the current account deficit with the government budget deficit has become known as the *twin deficits problem.*

significantly reduced as a result of the deficit, they will inherit an increased stock of foreign liabilities. Either way, their wealth will have been reduced relative to what it would have been without the deficits.

Payments of interest and dividends on liabilities owed abroad will lower GNP (income owned by Americans) in relation to GDP (output produced in the United States), since some income generated by the output will accrue to foreigners. These payments will also lower GNP relative to what it would have been in the absence of the deficits.

Borrowing from abroad entails a transfer of purchasing power to domestic residents when the borrowing occurs and a transfer back to foreigners when interest payments and repayments of principal occur.

The United States slowly built up a net creditor position over the six decades before 1980. This position was completely dissipated as a result of massive foreign borrowing during Ronald Reagan's presidency. Most economists attribute this foreign borrowing to the massive government budget deficits that occurred. By 1988 the United States had become the world's largest debtor nation.[3]

Does the size of the debt hamper the operation of policy? The large interest bill on the national debt puts a strain on the budget process. For example, in 1988 a full 17 percent of all tax revenues went to pay interest on the national debt! The government's freedom of fiscal maneuvering is obviously hampered by such a large claim on the national tax revenues. When the government's interest obligations grow, it can, of course, incur an even larger deficit, at least for a while, but eventually interest on the stock of debt must be paid from new revenues. Eventually, the government must either reduce its expenditure on other programs, or it must raise taxes.

As it happened, interest on the national debt in 1988 was just about exactly the same size as the deficit itself. This means that if there had been no preexisting national debt in 1988, federal revenues and outlays would have been within a few billion

dollars of each other. The deficit (or surplus) would have been approximately zero. Instead, because past deficits led to the accumulation of a large national debt, they build in a large amount of government spending in the form of interest payments.

Although interest payments on the national debt have not yet reached crisis proportions, the large claim on existing government revenues is a cause for concern.

Deficits and the National Debt

The foregoing discussion indicates that much of the concern about government budget deficits arises from their *cumulative* effect on the national debt and therefore on the government's interest obligations. It is therefore useful to examine the recent patterns in the growth of the national debt.

Facts About the Debt

The national debt in March 1989 was $2.75 trillion, over $11,000 for every man, woman, and child in the country. About 20 percent of the debt was held by the government itself and by Federal Reserve banks; interest payments on this part of the debt are only bookkeeping transactions.[4] The debt held by the private sector at the end of 1988 was about $2 trillion.

The debt in relation to GNP. The figures for debt per person, which are often quoted in an attempt to shock the reader, require interpretation. For a government, as for a household, the significance of debt depends on what it represents and on whether the income is available to pay the interest. No one would be shocked, for example, to find that an American family of four, earning $60,000 per year, had a mortgage of $50,000 on a $120,000 home.

As with the deficit, in evaluating the national debt and the government's interest payments on it, it is useful to consider them *relative* to the size of the economy. The worries about the debt just discussed arise primarily when the debt grows faster than the

---

[3] The term *debtor nation* is widely used in this context, even though the assets and liabilities involved are not just debt instruments, such as bonds, but also include ownership of physical resources, such as real estate and plant and equipment.

[4] Federal Reserve banks buy government bonds in the course of operating monetary policy (see Chapter 33). Government departments sometimes acquire government bonds when they have funds that they do not need for short, or even long, periods of time.

economy; it is really the debt-to-GNP ratio that matters. A national debt of $2.75 trillion clearly has different implications when GNP is $500 billion and when it is $5 trillion.

Figure 37-3 shows historical data for the debt and interest payments on it as a proportion of GNP. Figure 37-3 (i) shows that national debt as a proportion of GNP started to fall at the end of World War II and continued to fall until 1976. The debt rose relative to GNP after 1977, and by 1988 the debt had reached almost 55 percent of GNP. This figure is still much less than the more than 100 percent at the postwar peak. Nevertheless, the trend is worrisome, and medium-term projections suggest that the debt-to-GNP ratio will continue to rise.

Consider next the interest payments on the debt, often called *debt service payments,* shown in Figure 37-3 (ii). Clearly, there is genuine cause for worry here. The current ratio of 3.1 percent is very high by historical standards, just below the peak of 3.2 percent that was reached in 1985 and 1986. As we pointed out earlier, in 1988 interest payments were approximately the same size as the deficit itself and limited the government's room for fiscal maneuver-

---

FIGURE 37-3   The Relative Importance of the National Debt

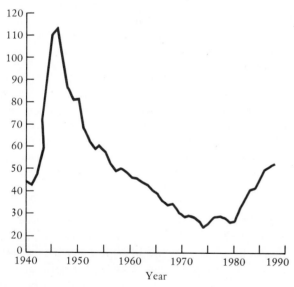

(i) National debt as proportion of GNP

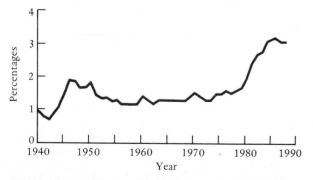

(ii) Net interest paid on national debt as proportion of GNP

The national debt has not reached alarming proportions in relation to GNP, but both the debt and interest payments on it have been growing rapidly in recent years. Stated as a proportion of the country's national income (part i), the national debt rose dramatically during World War II and again, slightly, during the major slump of 1974 to 1976. It has been growing steadily since 1977.

Net interest payments on the national debt have been a rising proportion of GNP since 1973 (part ii). The different trends in debt and debt servicing between 1973 and 1981 are accounted for by the rising cost of servicing the debt due to rising interest rates. (*Sources:* Historical tables, budget of the United States government, fiscal year 1989; *Economic Reports of the President.*)

ing. If interest payments as a share of GNP were to resume their upward trend, they could eventually put an intolerable burden on the government's taxing capacity. Ever bigger deficits would occur and, with them, even more borrowing.

The rising debt-to-GNP ratio imposes costs of two kinds. First, through some combination of crowding out and borrowing abroad, it reduces the stock of wealth that will be available to Americans in the future. Second, it creates a large and potentially growing "fixed charge," interest payments, in the budget, reducing the ability of the government to use the budget for economic stabilization or to pursue traditional governmental functions. In view of these costs, many economists and others have argued that the government's fiscal policies are imprudent and have called for a commitment to control the deficit.

Proposals to Control the Deficit

As we have seen, government deficits contribute to aggregate demand and hence can play a useful role in damping cyclical fluctuations in the economy. As we have seen also, government deficits contribute to increases in the national debt and hence in the long term might lead to a reduction in living standards of the average American. This conflict between the short-term stabilization role of deficits and the long-term adverse effects of a large public debt has been a subject of constant debate among economists and others who are concerned with government policy. Views range from those who dismiss the long-run costs of the national debt and hence are not concerned about the deficit to those who wish to eschew the short-term stabilization role for the deficit entirely and to impose a virtual straitjacket on the government, requiring it always to balance its budget. We now look at some of the specific proposals that have been put forward; some of the general options are illustrated in Figure 37-4.

An annually balanced budget. Much current rhetoric of fiscal restraint calls for a balanced budget. The Gramm-Rudman-Hollings bill, passed in late 1985 and discussed further in Box 37-2, mandates an elimination of the federal deficit by 1993. (Originally, the deficit was to have been eliminated by 1991. In 1987 Congress decided that the original goal could not be met and revised the schedule.) The discussion earlier

FIGURE 37-4 Balanced and Unbalanced Budgets

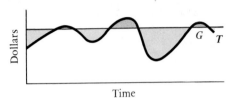
(i) A cyclically unbalanced budget

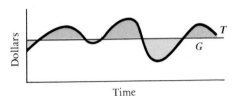
(ii) A cyclically balanced budget

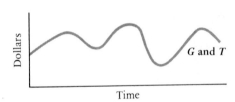
(iii) A constantly balanced budget

An annually (constantly) balanced budget is a destabilizer; a cyclically balanced budget is a stabilizer. The flow of tax receipts, T, is shown varying over the business cycle, while in parts (i) and (ii) government expenditure, G, is shown at a constant rate.

In part (i) deficits (dark areas) are common and surpluses (light areas) are rare because the average level of expenditure exceeds the average level of taxes. Such a policy will tend to stabilize the economy against cyclical fluctuations, but the average fiscal stance of the government is expansionary. This has been the characteristic U.S. budgetary position over the last several decades.

In part (ii) government expenditure has been reduced until it is approximately equal to the average level of tax receipts. The budget is now balanced cyclically. The policy still tends to stabilize the economy against cyclical fluctuations because of deficits in slumps and surpluses in booms. However, the average fiscal stance is neither strongly expansionary nor strongly contractionary.

In part (iii) a balanced budget has been imposed. Deficits have been prevented, but government expenditure now varies over the business cycle, which tends to destabilize the economy by accentuating the cyclical swings in aggregate expenditure.

BOX 37-2

Gramm-Rudman-Hollings: The Balanced Budget Act of 1985

In December 1985, the U.S. Congress passed the Balanced Budget and Emergency Deficit Control Act of 1985. This potentially far-reaching bill reflected both Congress' growing frustration with its own inability to reach a satisfactory compromise with the president on budget policy and the growing perception that unchecked deficit growth will have harmful economic and political effects. Congress' frustration is easy to understand. In 1985 it had struggled to cut one program after another, only to wind up with yet another huge deficit. The act was a response to its prevailing mood of concern.

Referred to as Gramm-Rudman-Hollings (G-R-H), after the three legislators who sponsored the bill, G-R-H initially promised to balance the budget by 1991. (A revised version of the act, passed in 1987, extended the deadline to 1993.) In both its original and its revised versions, G-R-H mandated a schedule of budget deficits, year by year, ending with a deficit of zero.

Originally, G-R-H required that the budget deficit be reduced in five equal increments (of $42 billion dollars per year) from $212 billion in fiscal 1986 to zero in fiscal 1991. The revised schedule requires that the deficit fall by $36 billion per year from fiscal 1989 through fiscal 1993, again ending at zero. The penalty for failure to agree on a plan that would meet the targets was to be automatic expenditure reductions in a large number of programs. (Notably, social security and interest on the national debt are exempt from the automatic budget cuts.) Because the automatic budget cuts are large

enough to meet the G-R-H deficit targets, G-R-H appears to be giving the government the choice of cutting the deficit either by rational action or by arbitrary formula. The idea is to force Congress to bind its own hands regarding the size of the deficit, giving it the incentive to achieve that size in the most beneficial (least harmful) way possible. For all its appeal, G-R-H suffers from a number of flaws.

The first flaw is that aiming at a zero deficit is arbitrary, perhaps dangerously so. Big cuts in the deficit may be essential, but a balanced budget is not necessary by a given date. Forcing a balanced budget could, depending on economic conditions, start a recession or stifle a healthy recovery. There is provision in the act to waive the deficit reduction schedule in the event of an economic emergency, but getting agreement on an "emergency" is not likely to be easy.

A further flaw concerns credibility. Congress may solemnly demonstrate its firm resolve with legislation, but everyone knows that Congress can act even faster in the opposite direction. As we have already pointed out, Congress revised the deficit schedule in 1987, when it became apparent that it could not meet the original schedule.* There is nothing to stop a repeat of this action as 1993 ap-

* Interestingly, the name of the act of Congress that postponed the year of reckoning under G-R-H is "The Balanced Budget and Emergency Deficit Control Reaffirmation Act of 1987." (In it, Congress reaffirmed its determination to balance the budget later rather than sooner.)

in this chapter suggests that an annually balanced budget would be extremely difficult, perhaps impossible, to achieve. With fixed tax rates, tax revenues fluctuate as national income fluctuates. Much government expenditure is fixed by past commitments, and most of the rest is hard to change quickly.

Yet, suppose an annually balanced budget, or something approaching it, were feasible. What would its effects be? Would it be desirable?

We saw earlier that a large government sector whose expenditures on goods and services are not very sensitive to the cyclical variations in national

proaches, should it be the case that budget balance looks too difficult to achieve by the target date.

Credibility is also compromised by the fact that G-R-H does not formally require that its targets be met. Rather, it requires that each summer the Office of Management and Budget (OMB) publish an economic and budgetary *forecast* that the deficit will be not more than $10 billion above the target in the fiscal year to follow. Two kinds of chicanery have flowed from the fact that the requirement takes this form. First, there has been pressure on OMB to generate very optimistic forecasts. "Shading" the forecast toward optimism is likely to be quite attractive relative to the alternatives of either cutting spending programs and raising taxes or implementing arbitrary spending cuts.

A second problem involves budgetary gimmickry. The government can meet a technical requirement that next year's budget have a deficit within range of the target by claiming that some source of revenue (e.g., proceeds from the sale of Amtrak) will become available next year. Once the forecast has been made, the required sale can be postponed and used, once again, to enhance the revenue forecast in the following year. As it happens, this trick has been performed with Amtrak at least three times, and, as of this writing, Amtrak is still firmly in government hands. The same sort of gimmick can be employed on the spending side. By postponing some category of expenditure from the last day of next fiscal year to the first day of the one after, the government can make next year's budget look unusually good. However, once the

forecast meets the G-R-H target, the government can change its plan and overspend in the coming year, making the forecast look artificially good for the year to follow.

To see that this kind of gimmickry can count, consider the budget for fiscal year 1989. That budget was determined to be in compliance with G-R-H because the OMB made a forecast during the summer of 1988 (before the start of the fiscal year) that the deficit would be within $10 billion of the target of $136 billion. In spite of the fact that the economy performed better during the fiscal year 1989 (leading to higher revenues and lower spending) than most economists expected, the most likely outcome for the fiscal year 1989 budget is a deficit of $155 billion.

For all of its difficulties, G-R-H has certainly played a role in reducing the size of the federal deficit. In part because of G-R-H, legislators are under considerable pressure to find either new revenue sources or new spending cuts when they propose new government programs. The process is arbitrary, cumbersome, and full of holes, but it has had at least some effect. Whether it can continue to be effective, given the difficulties of meeting the targets from 1990 through 1993, remains to be seen.

income is a major built-in stabilizer. To insist that annual government expenditure be tied to annual tax receipts would be to abandon the present built-in stability provided by the government. Government expenditure would then become a major *destabilizing* force. Tax revenues necessarily rise in booms and

fall in slumps; an annually balanced budget would force government expenditure to do the same. Changes in national income would then cause induced changes, not only in household consumption expenditure but also in government expenditure. This would greatly increase the economy's marginal propensity to spend and hence increase the value of the multiplier. In the terminology of Chapter 30, this would serve as a *built-in destabilizer!*

An annually balanced budget would accentuate the swings in national income that accompany changes in such autonomous expenditure flows as investment and exports.

A cyclically balanced budget.   An alternative policy—one that would prevent continual deficits (and could also inhibit the growth in the size of the government sector)—would be to balance the budget over the business cycle. This would be more feasible than the annually balanced budget, and it would not make government expenditure a destabilizing force.

Although more attractive in principle than the annually balanced budget, a cyclically balanced budget would carry problems of its own. Congress might well spend in excess of revenue in one year, leaving the next Congress the obligation to spend less than current revenue in following years. Could such an obligation to balance over a period of several years be made binding? It could be made a legal requirement through an act of Congress. However, what Congress does, Congress can undo. (This has been the history of attempts to limit the size of the national debt by legal restriction. Every time the national debt approaches the "debt ceiling," fixed in some prior year, Congress raises the ceiling and the president signs the new ceiling into law.)

Perhaps even more of a problem is that there is always room for some disagreement about the current state of the business cycle. As in the case of Gramm-Rudman-Hollings bill, a requirement to balance the budget over the business cycle can only be implemented based on some forecast of future economic conditions. Forecasting of the level of economic activity is imperfect, to say the least, and there will be genuine disagreement among economists about what stage of the business cycle the economy is in and about where the economy is headed. Compounding the difficulty that arises from such uncertainty is the fact that politicians will have a stake in the economic forecast. Those who favor increased government spending will tend to argue that *this* year is an unusually bad one and that the deficits of this year can be made up by the surpluses in (better) years to come. On the other side, some will tend always to find *this* year to be unusually good—a time to run surpluses against the hard times to follow.

While a budget, balanced over the course of the business cycle, is in principle an acceptable way of reconciling short-term stabilization and long-term prudence, the business cycle may not be defined well enough in practice to make the proposal operational.

Allowing for growth.   A further problem is that the goal of budget *balance,* whether it is applied annually or over the cycle, is, in fact, stricter than is required to avoid a rising debt-to-GNP ratio. Growth in GNP (due either to growth in real output or to inflation) means that some growth in the debt, and hence a (small) deficit, is consistent with a stable debt-to-GNP ratio.

For those who think of a stable debt-to-GDP ratio as the appropriate indicator of fiscal prudence, *budget balance* **means a deficit such that the debt grows at the same rate as nominal GNP.**

The Political Economy of the Debt

Almost all economists accept that, if the debt got so large that it could not be serviced without either putting a crushing burden on taxpayers or forcing the government to create new money to service it, there would be serious problems. However, many think that we are still a long way from that point. To them the overriding principle is that the debt should be changed according to the needs of stabilization policy.

An alternative view is what has come to be called *fiscal conservatism.* The conservative view takes a broad historical perspective: It says that during the eighteenth century spendthrift European rulers habitually spent more than their tax revenues and so created harmful inflation. By the end of the nineteenth century, the doctrine was so well established that a balanced budget was the citizen's only protection against profligate government spending and consequent wild inflation. Thus, the conservatives hold that the idea of a balanced budget was not silly and irrational, as Keynes made it out to be. Instead, it was the symbol of the people's victory in their long struggle to control the spendthrift proclivities of their nation's rulers.

The Keynesian revolution swept away that view. Budget deficits became, according to Keynesians, the tool by which benign and enlightened governments sought to ensure full employment. Nevertheless, say the conservatives, deficit spending let the tiger out of the cage. Inflationary gaps, recessionary gaps, or full employment notwithstanding, governments spent and spent and spent. Deficits accumulated, national debt rose, and inflation became the rule. In light of this analysis, it may seem somewhat odd that the greatest increase in peacetime deficits in U.S. history took place under the leadership of our most conservative modern president, Ronald Reagan. The main purpose of the Reagan administration's deficits, however, was not to provide fiscal stimulus; rather, the deficits were the result of a deliberate policy of tax reduction combined with an increase in defense spending. Concern about the resulting deficits has made it very difficult to increase spending on domestic programs, and this result is quite consistent with former President Reagan's political philosophy. It might be said that in the interest of programmatic conservatism ("the government that governs best governs least") Ronald Reagan abandoned fiscal conservatism.

The main premise of fiscal conservatives is that governments are not passive agents that do what is necessary to create full employment and maximize social welfare. Instead, governments are composed of individuals—elected officials, legislators, and civil servants—who, like everyone else, seek mainly to maximize their own well-being, and the welfare of these individuals is best served by government's hav-

ing a big role and satisfying the electorate. Thus, they tend to favor spending and to resist tax increases. This creates a persistent tendency toward deficits that is quite independent of any consideration of a sound fiscal policy.

The debate reflects deeply held views about the role of government, the nature and motivation of public officials, and the desirability of stabilization. Keynesians are more likely to emphasize the potential benefits from active fiscal policy and to regard substantial government intervention as essential to an effective and humane society. Fiscal conservatives are likely to see public intervention, however well motivated, as probably inept and ultimately destabilizing.

The deficits of the past decade also have received enough public attention so that the majority of both Keynesians and fiscal conservatives consistently argue that the deficit must be reduced. In spite of the fact that deficit reduction is politically uncontroversial in principle, it has proved to be very difficult to affect in practice. This is not entirely surprising. As we have seen, most of the harm that will arise from deficits will only appear over the very long term, in the form of potentially reduced living standards in the future. To do something about deficits, politicians must raise taxes and cut spending today, imposing real costs on today's voters, when the uncertain benefits of those actions will only be reaped in the relatively distant future.

SUMMARY

1. The recent record of persistent, large government budget deficits has attracted enormous attention and has generated heated debate over the policy options. In order to put the growth of the deficit in perspective, it is useful to measure it relative to GNP. After being roughly balanced, on average, for the 1960s and early 1970s, the government budget deficit rose from less than 1 percent of GNP at the start of the decade to over 6 percent in 1984, and it remained high throughout the remainder of the 1980s.

2. Deficits influence the economy through their short-run stabilizing or destabilizing role and through their potential to affect income and welfare adversely in the long run. The latter effects arise from the buildup of the debt-to-GNP ratio.

3. U.S. national debt and debt service payments have fluctuated as a percentage of national income, but recently they have shown a long-term upward trend. Recent increases in these ratios reflect the cumulative effect of persistently large deficits that date back to the mid-1970s. Persistent deficits are a cause for concern for several reasons, including inflation, crowding out of investment, and reducing national income in the long run.

4. An annually balanced budget would be unfeasible. Even if it were possible, it would destabilize the economy. A cyclically balanced

budget would act as a stabilizer while also curbing the growth of the government sector.

5. In a growing economy, the concept of budget balance allows for a (small but positive) deficit such that the stock of debt grows at the same rate as nominal GNP.

6. Keynesians tend to take a relatively sanguine view of the effect of active fiscal policy on the national debt. As long as the national debt does not grow rapidly as a proportion of national income, they view its short-term fluctuations as a stabilizing device and its long-term upward trend as a reasonable price to pay for economic stability.

7. Fiscal conservatives mistrust government and view insistence on a balanced budget as the only effective means of curtailing reckless government spending that wastes scarce resources and feeds the fires of inflation.

TOPICS FOR REVIEW

Short-run and long-run effects of deficits
The relationship between deficits and the national debt
Debt service payments
Debt-to-GNP ratio
Cyclically balanced budget
Keynesian and fiscal conservative views of debt

DISCUSSION QUESTIONS

1. Consider the typical annual expenditures and revenues of the organizations listed below. Comment on the appropriate debt policy for each, taking into account their respective goals, life span, and resources.
   a. Family household
   b. Two private corporations—one growing rapidly and the other, a mature firm
   c. A village of 5,000 inhabitants
   d. The U.S. government
   e. The United Nations

2. Evaluate each of the following proposals to "control the deficit" in order to avoid the long-run burden of debt.
   a. Maintaining a zero, cyclically adjusted deficit
   b. Keeping the debt-to-GNP ratio constant
   c. Limiting government borrowing from the public in each year to X percent of the national income in that year

3. Discuss the following reactions to the Gramm-Rudman-Hollings bill, all of which are quotes from newspaper articles during 1985 and 1986.
   a. "It sets up machinery that, if triggered, will slash the spending of the U.S. government like a mindless robot. There's no doubt this is a stupid way to do budgeting."
   b. "Balanced Budget Risks: Gramm-Rudman might precipitate the repetition of the fiscal blunders of the Depression."
   c. "The simple fact is that we are forced to cut expenditure if taxes are not to be raised."
   d. "Beware. The only way to balance the budget and control the deficit is to cut spending equitably, which neither the president nor Congress seems able to do; or raise taxes, which the president refuses to do, or both. No wonder everybody's racing to embrace this choice bit of balanced baloney."

4. What problems for budgetary control are posed by the fact that economic forecasting is imperfect? How might these problems be minimized?

5. How does the decision of whether to raise taxes or to issue bonds in order to finance the unusually high government expenditures incurred during a war influence "who pays" for the war?

6. Alan Greenspan, chairman of the board of governors of the Federal Reserve System, recently has expressed concern about the record government deficit and the growing level of debt in the economy. Why should this concern him?

7. In 1989, Congressional Budget Office Director Robert Reischaner said: "We have a long way to go before the [government budget] deficit is brought down to a level where Americans should feel comfortable." Arguing that the borrowing caused by the deficit erodes living standards for future generations, "How well do you want your children and grandchildren to live?" he asked. Write a critique either supporting or challenging Mr. Reischaner's views.

Does the Deficit Matter? The Ricardian Neutrality Proposition

Analysts who focus on the deficit as a summary description of the government's influence on the economy presuppose that tax-financed government expenditure contributes less to aggregate demand than bond-financed government expenditure, since the latter leads to a larger deficit. Note that deficit financing of government expenditure can be viewed as a deferral of taxes, increasing current disposable income and reducing future disposable income. This rearrangement of the timing of taxes may leave expected permanent income basically unchanged compared with the case in which taxes are levied at the same time as the government expenditure occurs. While the Keynesian consumption function predicts that consumption would increase with the increase in current disposable income, the permanent-income hypothesis (PIH), discussed in the appendix to Chapter 26, predicts that households' consumption is related to their lifetime or permanent income, not their current disposable income. If the PIH is an accurate description of behavior, deficit finance will have little effect on consumption behavior.

Thus, it is possible to identify a set of conditions that would mean that government expenditure has the same effect on the economy whether it is financed by raising current taxes or by issuing government bonds. This imaginary world, first considered by David Ricardo in 1817 and recently revived by Professor Robert Barro, is populated by far-sighted individuals whose consumption decisions depend on their "permanent" income only. Thus, changes in the time pattern of income receipts that leave their permanent income unchanged would have no effect on private-sector expenditure decisions.

In this world government bonds would not be net wealth, because the financial value of a bond would be matched exactly by a corresponding liability for future tax payments needed to service the debt. Specifically, households would be indifferent between paying $1 of current taxes and paying a stream of future taxes that has a present value of $1 when discounted at the market interest rate. In this case the government deficit would not matter; bond rather than tax finance would merely represent a rearrangement in the timing of income receipts that the private sector could (and would) offset in capital markets. Issuing bonds now and raising taxes later would be viewed as equivalent to raising taxes now.

The theory underlying this analysis requires that households have an infinite planning horizon, as in the PIH that was discussed in the appendix to Chapter 26. Otherwise taxes accruing after the household's lifetime would not offset interest payments received during the household's lifetime, and government bonds would be viewed as net wealth by the household. Hence, deficits would increase households' perceived net wealth, households would increase their consumption, and deficit-financed government expenditure would be more expansionary than tax-financed expenditure.

Barro's contribution was to show that debt neutrality could arise even in the context of the life-cycle theory if the household's concern for its heirs caused its planning horizon to extend beyond its own lifetime. Suppose that the typical household, when it is making its own lifetime consumption plans, also plans for a positive bequest that it intends to leave to its heirs. Now consider the effects of a government decision to sell bonds rather than to increase taxes in order to finance previously announced government expenditure; this, of course, increases the government budget deficit. (Thus, we are focusing on the effects of the method of financing the expenditure, not on the effects of the expenditure itself.) If the household wishes, it could simply spend the increased disposable income that results from not having to pay current taxes to finance the government expenditure, thus leaving the next generation with a liability to pay the taxes that will have to be levied when the government redeems the bonds. If the recipients behave in this manner, the fiscal authority's decision to rely on deficit financing will have stimulated the economy by inducing an increase in spending.

However, this behavior would reduce the net value of the bequest that the typical household would be leaving to its heirs, since the heirs now face an increased tax liability. This violates the notion that the members of a typical household make a rational plan that includes targets for its own consumption and for the bequest that it wishes to leave to its heirs, since the government action does not change the options open to current households. The current household could have achieved this redistribution away from future generations toward itself without the government action simply by increasing its own consumption and reducing the value of the estate that it leaves to its heirs.

If the current household wishes to preserve its initial plan, all that it needs to do is maintain its spending plans and increase saving by the full amount of the increase in its disposable income, that is, by the increase in the government budget deficit. The resulting increase in the value of the next generation's inheritance will exactly offset the increase in tax liabilities that it faces. Thus, a government deficit that issues bonds now and "promises" taxes in the future would have no effect even if the taxes were expected only after the current generation were dead.

Note that the level of government expenditure is still important in this model—only the method of financing is irrelevant. However, there are a number of reasons to believe that future taxes that have a present value of $1 are not equivalent to present taxes of $1 and thus that this debt-neutral Ricardian model does not provide an accurate description of the working of a modern economy. (Ricardo himself rejected it.) Let us cite only three reasons.

The private sector borrows on different terms than the government sector. This is perhaps the most important reason why deficit financing is not neutral in practice. In many circumstances households and, to some extent, firms face constraints that prevent them from borrowing all that they would like to at the prevailing market interest rate. Alternatively, they may be able to borrow but at a much higher interest rate than that facing the government. Consequently,

when the government substitutes future taxes for present taxes by running a deficit, these "constrained" private-sector agents will feel wealthier and, consequently, will spend more.

Myopic perception. If some households imperfectly perceive the future tax liabilities implied by the government deficit, they will not offset government dissaving with private saving.

Finite lifetimes. Another reason why households might view future taxes as not equivalent to current taxes is that future taxes may extend beyond the expected lifetime of the household. Thus, the household may anticipate escaping taxes by dying! As Barro points out, this would make no difference if households "care about their heirs"; in this case living households would simply alter any bequests that they had planned to leave to their heirs by an amount equal to the expected increase in future taxes borne by their heirs. However, if households that currently are alive do not care or are unable to alter their bequests (perhaps because such bequests cannot be reduced below their current zero level), living households will, in fact, react to a change in the deficit in a manner that does not completely offset it.

Conclusions

The basic feature of the economy that makes government deficits and the public debt matter is that, to a significant extent, current private-sector expenditure is tied to current private-sector income. The government deficit influences the current income of the private sector, since for a given level of government expenditure a larger deficit means lower current taxes and hence larger current private disposable income. In the first instance, this debt finance simply causes an intertemporal rearrangement of private-sector income. However, for the reasons noted, the private sector is not indifferent to this rearrangement of its income receipts. In particular, current private-sector expenditure rises in response to the increase in current income. This influence of government deficits on private spending not only creates the potential for a stabilizing role for deficits over the business cycle but also creates the mechanism by which persistent deficits become costly and undesirable in the longer run.

Chapter 38

Macro-economic Controversies

How well do markets work? Can government improve market performance? In various guises these two questions are the basis of most disagreements over economic policy. We shall see that different answers to these questions imply big differences in macroeconomic policy prescriptions.

Conservatives and Interventionists

Broadly speaking, we can identify a noninterventionist view and an interventionist view with respect to the various economic policy goals that we have encountered throughout this book. The noninterventionist view says that the unaided market economy functions well and needs little help from government. The interventionist view says that government policy can substantially improve the economy's performance. *Conservatives* are noninterventionist on all issues, whereas *interventionists* support government intervention at all times. A few people may actually be conservative or interventionist in this sense. Most, however, would favor intervention on some issues and oppose it on others.

Conservative Views

Conservatives believe that the free-market economy performs quite well on balance. Although shocks do hit the system, they lead rather quickly, and often painlessly, to the adjustments dictated by the market system. For example, relative prices in booming sectors rise, drawing in resources from declining sectors or regions. As a result, resources (and particularly labor) usually remain fully employed, so there is no need for full-employment policies.

Conservatives hold that macroeconomic performance will be most satisfactory if it is determined primarily by the workings of the free market.

Of course, few believe that the market system functions perfectly. However, whereas interventionists call for discretionary policies to improve economic performance, the conservative view is that the market system works well enough to preclude any significant constructive role for policy. Indeed, many conservatives believe that policies are often so crude and their effects so uncertain, with regard to both strength and timing, that their use may impair rather than improve the economy's performance.

In a modern economy, some government presence is inevitable. Thus, a stance of *no* intervention is impossible; rather, what is advocated by conservatives is minimal direct intervention in the market system. This involves the government's bearing responsibility for providing a *stable environment* in which the private sector can function. This has given rise to a debate that is popularly known as *rules versus discretion,* which is discussed further in Box 38-1.

Providing a Stable Environment

Creating a stable environment, as the conservatives advocate, may be easier said than done. One major problem is that macro variables are interrelated. The stability of one may imply the instability of another. In such cases, a choice often must be made. How much instability of one aggregate can we tolerate to secure stability in another related aggregate? We now consider the prescriptions for establishing stable fiscal and monetary policies.

Fiscal rules. Suppose that the government decides to adopt the goal of stability in the budget balance as part of the stable environment. This "stability" would require great *instability* in tax and expenditure policy. Tax revenues depend on the interaction between tax rates and the level of national income. With given tax rates, tax revenues change with the ebb and flow of the business cycle. A stable budget balance would require that the government raise tax rates and cut expenditures in slumps and lower tax rates and raise expenditures in booms.

Not only does this squander the budget's potential to act as a stabilizer (see the discussion in Chapter 37, pages 793–796), but also great instability of the fiscal environment is caused by continual changes in tax rates and expenditure levels. A stable fiscal environment requires stability in government expenditures and tax rates so that the private sector can make plans for the future in a climate of known patterns of tax liabilities and government demand.

Any target budget balance must be some average over a period long enough to cover a typical cycle. Stability from year to year should be found in tax rates and expenditure programs, *not* in the size of the budget balance.

This, in turn, requires that the budget deficit vary cyclically, showing its largest deficits in slumps and its largest surpluses in booms.

Monetary rules. Advocates of a stable monetary environment are actually advocating stable inflation. (Whether a *zero* rate is feasible or not is discussed on page 733.) The central bank is urged to set a target rate of increase in the money supply and to hold it. To establish the target, the central bank estimates the rate at which the demand for money would be growing if actual income equalled potential income and the price level were stable. This then becomes the target rate of growth of the money supply. The key proposition is that the money supply should be changing gradually along a stable path that is independent of short-term variations in the demand for money caused by cyclical changes in the economy. This is referred to as a **k percent rule.**

Will the k percent rule really provide monetary stability? The answer is, not necessarily. Assuring a stable rate of monetary growth does not assure a stable monetary environment. Monetary shortages and surpluses depend on the relationship between the supply of and the demand for money. Problems for the k percent rule arise when the demand for money shifts. For example, payment of interest on checking deposits increases the demand for M1. In this event, if the central bank adheres to a k percent rule, there will be an excess demand for money and interest rates will rise. Thus, contractionary pressure will be put on the economy.

One disadvantage of a monetary rule is that it may set up speculative behavior. If, for example, there is too much money when weekly money supply figures are announced, speculators know that in the future the price of bonds most likely will fall, because the central bank will sell more bonds to reduce the surplus. Speculators are thus induced to sell bonds now, hoping to rebuy them at bargain prices later when the central bank acts.

Monetary rules can introduce instability into interest rate behavior.

A second disadvantage of a monetary rule is that, to preserve its credibility, the central bank may fail to take discretionary action that would otherwise be appropriate. For example, after an entrenched inflation is broken, the economy may come to rest with

BOX 38-1

Rules Versus Discretion

Three of the main issues that are involved in the rules versus discretion debate are problems that are created by lags, the type of stabilization needed, and the adequacy of information.

Lags

Economists who are hostile to discretionary policy emphasize the long and variable lags of both fiscal and monetary policy. Monetary policy can be put into effect quickly, but it takes 6 to 18 months for the full effects of a change in interest rates to be felt in terms of altered private-sector expenditures. It often takes a long time to put fiscal policy into effect, since federal budgets are usually several months in the making. Once the changes are made, however, their effects spread quickly throughout the economy.

Conservatives feel that these lags destroy the presumption that discretionary full-employment policy usually will be stabilizing. Interventionists feel that, although the lags are serious, discretionary policies can be effective in reducing persistent recessionary gaps. Few interventionists, however, now call for fine tuning.

A Stable Climate for Planning

Supporters of rules emphasize the need for a stable climate so that firms and households can plan for the future. They argue that continual changes in tax rates and the money supply, which are designed to stabilize the economy, are destabilizing, because they create a climate of uncertainty that makes long-term planning difficult.

Supporters of discretionary policy argue that they want discretion exercised only when the occasional serious recession develops and that large fluctuations in income and employment can be as upsetting to long-term planning as the occasional changes in tax rates and expenditures that are required by stabilization policy.

Do We Know Enough?

Discretionary stabilization policy requires that we forecast what the state of the economy will be in the absence of that policy. Generally, actual information is available only when there is a lag. Policymakers know approximately what the GDP was last quarter and what unemployment was last month. (The first preliminary figures for many economic variables can be subject to substantial errors. Often these estimates are revised several times over subsequent months and even years.) On the basis of these data, projections of future behavior of the economy must be made and policy must be set.

Supporters of discretionary policy accept that errors in projections may be large in relation to the recessionary gaps that are created by minor recessions, but they believe that the errors are small in relation to major recessions. They argue that in major recessions policymakers will not be in doubt about the existence of a large recessionary gap or the need for some significant stimulus, even though the exact amount of the gap or the stimulus cannot be precisely determined.

substantial unemployment and a stable price level. There is then a case for a once-and-for-all discretionary expansion in the money supply to get the economy back to full employment. The *k* percent rule precludes this, condemning the economy to a slump. (This possibility is discussed in detail on pages 705–706.)

Despite these problems, conservatives believe that the *k* percent rule is superior to any known alternative. Some would agree that in principle the central bank could improve the economy's performance by occasional bouts of discretionary monetary policy to offset such things as major shifts in the demand for money. However, they also believe that, once given any discretion, the central bank would abuse it in an attempt to fine tune the economy. The resulting instability would, they believe, be much more than any instability resulting from the application of a *k* percent rule in an environment subject to some change.

Interventionist Views

Interventionists believe that the functioning of the market economy is often far from satisfactory. Sometimes markets show weak self-regulatory forces, and the economy settles into prolonged periods of heavy unemployment. At other times markets tend to "overcorrect," causing the economy to lurch between the extremes of large recessionary and inflationary gaps.

Interventionists believe that the outcomes that arise from the workings of the market system can be improved upon by the judicious use of government intervention.

Even though interventionist policies may be imperfect, they may be good enough to improve the functioning of the economy with respect to all three main goals of macro policy.

Interventionist Prescriptions

Interventionists call for discretionary fiscal and monetary policies to offset significant inflationary and recessionary gaps, and thus to stabilize national income at its capacity level. Interventionists also support government policies to control inflation. Some interventionists, particularly a group called *post-Keynesians,* believe that control of the money supply may not be enough to achieve full employment and stable prices simultaneously. This is because they accept the wage-cost push theory of inflation, which was discussed in Chapter 34.

Some interventionists call for incomes policies to restrain the wage-cost push and so make full employment compatible with stable prices. They believe that such policies should become permanent features of the economic landscape. Many economists accept that wage-price controls might work as *temporary* measures to break inflationary inertias (see Chapter 34) but that they would introduce inefficiencies and rigidities as permanent features.

More permanent incomes policies might be of two types. The first type, commonly used in Europe in past decades but now out of favor, is often called a *social contract*. Labor, management, and the government consult annually and agree on target wage changes. These are calculated to be noninflationary, given the government's projections for the future and its planned economic policies. Such a scheme is most easily initiated in a centralized economy such as West Germany's, where a few giant firms and unions exert enormous power, or in a country such as Great Britain, where the party in power during much of the period in which social contracts were used had strong official links with the labor unions.

The other main type of incomes policy is **tax-related incomes policy (TIP),** which we first encountered in Chapter 34. TIPs provide tax incentives for management and labor to conform to government-established wage and price guidelines. For example, increases in wages and prices in excess of the guidelines would be taxed heavily. TIPs have not yet been tried, although they have been strongly advocated by some economists.

TIPs rely on tax incentives to secure voluntary conformity with wage and price guidelines, whereas wage and price controls try to impose conformity by law.

Advocates of TIPs argue that their great advantage is that decisions on wages and prices are left in the hands of labor and management while they influence behavior by altering the incentive system. Critics, however, argue that they would prove to be an administrative nightmare.

Monetarists Versus the Keynesians

For almost 40 years following World War II, disagreements among macroeconomists were dominated by the ongoing debate between two groups—the monetarists and the Keynesians. As was noted in Chapter 32, monetarists often are identified with conservative views, and Keynesians often are identified with intervention. Both groups accepted the key features of the macroeconomic model of the economy, which we have outlined in previous chapters of this book.[1] The relevant features are:

1. In the long run, national income is equal to its capacity level, as determined by the position of the vertical *LRAS* curve. The level of income at this *full-employment* position is not influenced by fluctuations in aggregate demand.
2. In the short run, national income is determined by the intersection of the *SRAS* and *AD* curves. This level can deviate from the capacity level, giving rise to either an *inflationary gap* or a *recessionary gap*. In the short run, national income can be influenced by aggregate demand, which, in turn, can be influenced by monetary and fiscal policies.
3. Deviations of national income from its capacity level give rise to changes in wages and prices, which, if allowed to operate, would eventually restore full employment. (This was referred to as the *automatic adjustment mechanism*.)

Given that both groups apparently accept these "core" propositions, how is it that they disagree about the behavior of the economy and about the appropriate role of policy? To understand the sources of the disagreements, we examine each group's views about the business cycle and inflation and then turn to a consideration of the differences in their views about the strength of the automatic adjustment mechanism.

Business Cycles

We saw in Chapter 24 that real national income fluctuates about its trend or capacity value. Monetarists and Keynesians differ in their explanations of these fluctuations.

Monetarist Views

Monetarists believe that the economy is inherently stable, because private-sector expenditure functions are relatively stable. In addition, they believe that

shifts in the aggregate demand curve are mainly due to policy-induced changes in the money supply.[2]

The view that business cycles have mainly monetary causes relies heavily on the evidence advanced by Milton Friedman and Anna Schwartz in their monumental study, *A Monetary History of the United States, 1867–1960.* They establish a strong correlation between changes in the money supply and changes in the level of business activity. Major recessions have been associated with absolute declines in the money supply, and minor recessions have been associated with the slowing of the rate of increase in the money supply below its long-term trend.

Friedman and Schwartz maintain that changes in the money supply cause changes in business activity. They argue, for example, that the severity of the Great Depression was due to a major contraction in the money supply, which shifted the aggregate demand curve far to the left. The Great Depression is also discussed in Box 32-3.

According to monetarists, fluctuations in the money supply cause fluctuations in national income.

This leads the monetarists to advocate a policy of stabilizing the growth of the money supply. (This is the *k* percent rule that we discussed earlier in this chapter.) In their view this would avoid policy-induced instability of the aggregate demand curve.

Keynesian Views

The Keynesian view on cyclical fluctuations in the economy has two parts. In the first part, it emphasizes variations in investment as a cause of business cycles and stresses the nonmonetary causes of such variations.[3]

---

[1] The fullest presentation of the model is in Chapter 32; see especially pages 674–682. The appendix to this chapter presents the widely used *IS/LM* model of the influence of monetary and fiscal policy, which essentially formalizes the features of the model in Chapter 32.

[2] The view that fluctuations often have monetary causes is not new. The English economist R. G. Hawtrey, the Austrian Nobel Laureate F. A. von Hayek, and the Swedish economist Knut Wicksell are prominent among those who have given monetary factors an important role in explaining the turning points in cycles or the tendency for expansions and contractions, or both, once begun, to become cumulative and self-reinforcing. Modern monetarists carry on this tradition.

[3] Like the monetarists, the Keynesians are modern advocates of views that have a long history. The great Austrian (and later American) economist Joseph Schumpeter stressed such explanations early in the present century. The Swedish economist Knut Wicksell and the German Speithoff both stressed this aspect of economic fluctuations before the emergence of the Keynesian school of thought.

According to Keynesians, fluctuations in national income are often caused by fluctuations in expenditure decisions.

Keynesians reject what they regard as the extreme monetarist view that *only* money matters in explaining cyclical fluctuations; they believe that both monetary and nonmonetary forces are important in explaining the cyclical behavior of the economy. Although they accept mismanagement of monetary policy as one potential source of economic fluctuations, they do not believe that it is the only or even the major source of fluctuations. Thus, they deny the monetary interpretation of business cycle history given by Friedman and Schwartz.

A second part of the Keynesian view on cyclical fluctuations concerns the correlation between changes in the money supply and changes in the level of economic activity cited by Friedman and Schwartz. While most Keynesians accept the validity of the correlation and also agree that policy-induced changes in the money supply can cause national income to change, their explanation of the correlation reverses the causality suggested by the monetarists.

Most Keynesians believe that fluctuations in national income cause many of the fluctuations in the money supply that have been cited by Friedman and Schwartz.

The main reason for this belief can be seen as follows. Keynesians point out that, from 1945 to the early 1970s, most central banks tended to stabilize interest rates as an objective of monetary policy. When an expansion got under way, the demand for money tended to increase, and if there was no increase in the money supply, interest rates would rise. The central bank would prevent this rise in interest rates by buying bonds offered for sale at current prices, but in so doing it would increase banks' reserves and thereby inject new money into the economy. Similarly, in a cyclical contraction, interest rates would tend to fall, unless the central bank stepped in and sold bonds to keep interest rates up. Generally, it did so, thereby decreasing the money supply. Thus, central banks increased the money supply during upswings and decreased it during downswings, thereby creating the positive correlation on which the monetarists rely.

Inflation

As we saw in Chapter 34, sustained inflation requires a sustained expansion of the money supply. Motives for such excessive monetary expansions have varied from time to time and place to place. Sometimes central banks have increased the money supply rapidly in an effort to end a recession. Then, when the economy expanded due to its own natural recuperative forces, the increased money supply allowed a significant inflation during the boom phase of the cycle. At other times central banks have tried to hold interest rates well below their free-market levels. To do this they buy bonds to hold bond prices up. We have seen that these open market operations increase the money supply and so fuel an inflation. At still other times, central banks have helped governments finance large budget deficits by buying up the new public debt. These open market operations provide what is popularly known as *printing-press finance*. The steady increase in the money supply fuels a continuous inflation.

Monetarist Views

As we have seen already, many monetarists hold that inflation is everywhere and always a monetary phenomenon. They thus focus on changes in the money supply as the key source of shifts in the *AD* curve.

According to monetarists, all inflations are caused by excessive monetary expansion and would not occur without it.

Keynesian Views

Keynesians agree that a sustained rise in prices cannot occur unless it is accompanied by continued increases in the money supply. Keynesians also emphasize, however, that temporary bursts of inflation can be caused by shifts in the *AD* curve, brought about by increases in private- or public-sector expenditure. If such inflations are not validated by monetary expansion, they are brought to a halt by the monetary adjustment mechanism.

Keynesians also accept the importance of supply-shock inflations. Again, they accept that such inflations cannot go on indefinitely unless they are accommodated by monetary expansion.

Keynesians argue that "temporary" inflation, due to either *AD* or *SRAS* shifts, can go on long enough to be a matter of serious policy concern.

Many Keynesians also take seriously the possibility of wage-cost push inflation that we studied in Chapter 34. This type of inflation, if it exists, makes full employment incompatible with a stable price level. Again, the central bank is faced with the agonizing choice of whether or not to accommodate.

The Role of the Automatic Adjustment Mechanism

While different views on the relative strengths of monetary and real forces, and on the causal relationship between money and income, play an important role in the debate between the monetarists and the Keynesians, an important difference also emerges in their views about the strength of the automatic adjustment mechanism. This raises the question, "What behavior in the individual markets for goods and factors of production is implied by the macroeconomic model?" This issue concerns what are called the *micro foundations,* or *micro underpinnings,* of macro models.

Monetarist Views

Most monetarists view markets as competitive. They realize, of course, that perfect competition does not exist everywhere in the economy, but they believe that the forces of competition are strong enough that analysis based on the theory of perfect competition will be close to the real behavior of the economy.

One important characteristic of competitive markets is that prices and wages are flexible; they adjust to establish equilibrium at all times. When a competitive market is in equilibrium (see Chapter 4), the market is said to have *cleared.* Competitive markets clear only at the equilibrium price. At any other price, there are either unsatisfied purchasers (excess demand) or unsatisfied sellers (excess supply).

When a competitive market has cleared, every purchaser has been able to buy all that he or she wishes at the going price and every seller has been able to sell all that he or she wishes at that price. When each and every market is in equilibrium, there is full employment of all resources. The prices that clear markets are called **market-clearing prices.**

According to the monetarists, strong forces ensure that departures from full-employment equilibrium are quickly rectified; that is, monetarists believe that the automatic adjustment mechanism works quite efficiently.

While monetarists recognize the existence of cyclical fluctuations in output and unemployment, and the role of aggregate demand in influencing them, they argue that, for purposes of interpreting the behavior of the economy and for formulating policy recommendations, it is best to treat the economy *as if* there were continuous full employment.

Further, according to Friedman and his followers, long and variable lags in the operation of monetary policy not only doom it to failure but also make it counterproductive. In their view monetary policy actually has served to destabilize the economy in the past. Given this, and given the belief that the economy's automatic adjustment mechanism works quickly, the best course for monetary policy is to follow the *k* percent rule, that is, to set the rate of increase of the money supply at some given value and hold it there.

Keynesian Views

Keynesian micro foundations emphasize the noncompetitive nature of the economy. Most firms are seen as setting their own prices rather than as accepting those set in competitive markets. Their per unit output costs tend to be fairly constant, and they set prices by adding a relatively inflexible markup to their costs.[4] They then sell what they can at the going price. Cyclical fluctuations in aggregate demand cause cyclical fluctuations in the demand for each firm's products, which, in turn, cause individual firms to make cyclical variations in output and in employment rather than in price. A similar argument holds for labor markets in the Keynesian model. Wages respond to the price level and productivity but are relatively insensitive to short-term cyclical

---

[4] Complete cyclical inflexibility of markups is not necessary. What matters is that firms do not adjust prices continually and thus that they are willing to sell further units at the same price. This much price inflexibility need not imply an absence of profit maximization. Instead, it may follow from profit maximization when it is costly to alter prices. This is discussed further in Chapter 14.

fluctuations in demand. (This is discussed in detail in Chapter 20, and we return to these issues later in this chapter when we encounter the new Keynesian economics.)

While in the monetarist model the main impact of fluctuations in aggregate demand is on prices, in the Keynesian model their main impact is on output and employment.

Thus, Keynesians tend to believe that the economy lacks strong natural corrective forces that will always cause it easily and quickly to move back to full employment. In particular, while they believe that the price level rises quite quickly to eliminate inflationary gaps, they believe that the price level does not fall quickly to eliminate recessionary gaps. Keynesians thus stress the asymmetries, noted in Chapter 28 (see page 579). As a result:

Keynesians believe that recessionary gaps can persist for significant periods of time unless they are eliminated by active stabilization policy.

These "supply-side" issues that arise from differences concerning the operation of the automatic adjustment mechanism anticipate some of the current macroeconomic controversies that we take up next.

For many years the basic model, common to both the Keynesians and the monetarists, seemed successful both in explaining the overall behavior of the economy and in suggesting policies for controlling inflation and unemployment. While, as we have seen, differences in the size of critical elasticities, the stability of key behavioral relationships, and the speed of adjustment toward full employment gave rise to sharp disagreements, the basic model used by both groups was essentially the same.

Current Controversies[5]

A spate of recent research, stimulated by concern about the ability of the common core model to provide further insights into the operation of the economy and economic policy, has resulted in a number

of "schools" of thought that espouse models that represent sharp departures from the common core model studied so far in this book. We consider three of the most important. We note that debate about the merits of the models still rages today. The issues are important; because they are at the frontier of modern research, they are also difficult. The analysis depends on material that is treated in detail in more advanced courses. At this stage, therefore, we can discuss the issues only in broad outline.

New Classical Economics

The *new classical economists* follow Professors Robert Lucas and Thomas Sargent in holding that temporary departures from full employment occur mainly because people make mistakes. This viewpoint can be best understood in terms of the proposition, derived from microeconomics, that individual supply and demand behavior depends only on the structure of relative prices.[6]

To follow their argument, let us start by assuming that each of the economy's markets is in equilibrium; there is full employment, prices are stable, and the actual and expected rates of inflation are zero. Now suppose that the government increases the money supply by 5 percent. People find themselves with unwanted money balances, which they seek to spend.[7] For the sake of simplicity, assume that this leads to an increase in desired expenditure on all commodities; the demand for each commodity shifts to the right, and all prices, being competitively determined, rise. Individual decision makers see their selling prices go up and mistakenly interpret this increase as a rise in their own relative price. This is because they expect the overall rate of inflation to be zero. Firms will produce more, and workers will work more; both groups think that they are getting

---

[5] This section may be omitted without loss of continuity.

[6] The new classical economists espouse many of the same policy views, which we have just discussed, as the monetarists; both are essentially *conservative* in their approach to economic policy. Sometimes the new classical economists are referred to as *new classical monetarists,* and the original monetarists sometimes are referred to as *traditional monetarists.*

[7] Most monetarists (new classical and traditional) accept the theory of the transmission mechanism (discussed in Chapter 32), according to which the excess money balances are used to buy financial assets, thus driving down interest rates and stimulating expenditure *indirectly*. However, most monetarists tend to stress the relative importance of the *direct* expenditure effects created by excess money balances.

an increased *relative price* for what they sell. Thus, total output and employment rise.

When both groups eventually realize that their own relative prices are, in fact, unchanged, output and employment fall back to their initial levels. The extra output and employment occur only while people are being fooled. When they realize that *all* prices have risen by 5 percent, they revert to their initial behavior. The only difference is that now the price level has risen by 5 percent, leaving relative prices unchanged.

According to the new classical theory, deviations from full employment occur only because people make mistakes that cause markets to clear at more or less than full-employment output. People do not encounter constraints in their attempts to sell as many commodities or as much labor as they wish; the contraction or expansion in output is voluntary.

New classical economists focus on the role of changes in relative prices when they are signalling appropriate information in a world where tastes and technology are constantly changing. They hold that fluctuations in the money supply will lead to increased fluctuations in all prices. This makes it hard for households and firms to distinguish between changes in relative prices, to which they do wish to respond, and changes in the price level, to which they do not wish to respond. Such confusion, created by fluctuations in the money supply, thus leads to mistakes in supply and demand decisions.

The Lucas aggregate supply curve.   The behavior just described gives rise to the **Lucas aggregate supply curve.**

The Lucas aggregate supply curve posits that national output will vary positively with the ratio of the actual to the expected price level.

This is often also referred to as the *surprises-only supply curve,* since it implies that only changes in the price level that are unexpected (surprises) will give rise to fluctuations in aggregate supply.

To see this, consider what happens if there is again an increase in the money supply, but this time suppose that it has been widely expected in advance by firms and households. Again, prices will rise.

Most firms will now take this to mean only that the *observed* change in the price of their own output has roughly matched the *expected* change in the average of all other prices. Hence, they will not interpret it as a rise in the relative price of their own output and will maintain their production level at its normal level. National income will not rise above potential income, despite the rise in the general price level.

According to the new classical theory, expected changes in the price level do not lead to fluctuations in national income.

New classical policy views.   New classical economists support the *k* percent rule, just as the traditional monetarists do. They believe that firms and households make better decisions when monetary and fiscal policies are stable than when they are highly variable. They believe that active interventionist policies, designed to stabilize the economy, make it harder for people to interpret the signals that are generated by the price system and so lead them to make more errors in forming their expectations. This then increases rather than reduces the fluctuations of output around its full-employment level and increases rather than reduces the fluctuations of unemployment around the natural rate.

According to the new classical theory, active use of monetary policy in an attempt to stabilize the economy will lead to confusion about relative and absolute prices. This will cause people to make mistakes in their output and purchasing decisions and therefore will increase aggregate output fluctuations.

This conclusion depends on the particular view adopted by the new classical economists about how people form predictions or expectations—a subject that recently has become an important part of macroeconomic debates.

The Theory of Rational Expectations

The new classical model is augmented by the theory of *rational expectations.* People look to the government's current macroeconomic policy to form their expectations of future inflation. They understand how the economy works, and they form their expectations rationally by predicting the outcome of the policies being pursued. People learn fairly quickly from their mistakes; though random errors occur, systematic and persistent errors do not. In an obvious sense, expectations formed in this way are *forward looking.*

According to the theory of rational expectations, people do not make persistent, systematic errors in predicting the overall inflation rate; they may, however, make unsystematic errors.

This discussion highlights a controversial methodological aspect of new classical economics. The economy is assumed to be simple enough so that individual households and firms can understand it fully and can use current information to make rational forecasts. This paradigm of deterministic, fully rational, equilibrium systems is derived from the analogous view of the physical world that was propounded by Isaac Newton. However, the Newtonian paradigm recently has come under attack in many of the natural sciences; this is taken up in Box 38-2.

Policy invariance.   Rational expectations, combined with the Lucas aggregate supply curve, give rise to the *new classical policy invariance proposition,* or policy neutrality proposition, with this result:

Systematic attempts to use monetary policy to stabilize the economy will lead to systematic changes in the price level but will not influence the behavior of output.

This happens because *systematic* monetary policy will lead only to systematic aggregate demand shocks and thus will not be a source of confusion to households and firms. Only unsystematic monetary policy will have real effects. Thus, according to the new classical economists, monetary policy can do harm—by creating confusion about the source of price changes—but cannot do good, except by random chance. Thus, even in the face of major recessions, laissez faire is the best conceivable stabilization policy.

Let us review how this follows from combining the monetarist micro foundations with the theory of rational expectations.

1. According to the new classical theory's micro foundations, deviations from full employment occur only because of errors in predicting the

price level (which cause workers and firms to mistake changes in the price level for changes in relative prices).
2. According to the theory of rational expectations, only random errors in predicting the price level occur.
3. It follows from the first two points that there is no room for active government policy to stabilize the economy. The causes of fluctuations are random.[8] It is in the nature of random fluctuations that they cannot be foreseen and offset. Thus, there is no room for stabilization policy to reduce the fluctuations in the economy by offsetting the disturbances that emanate from the private sector.

For those new classical economists who espouse this model, the contrast with the Keynesians is extreme. Box 38-3 takes up some other aspects of the important differences between the two groups that play a role in the ongoing controversies.

Real Business Cycle Models

Recently, a number of economists have pursued a research strategy that gives rise to what they have termed *real business cycle theory.* As Professor Alan Stockman of the University of Rochester states, "The purpose of real business cycle (RBC) models is to explain aggregate fluctuations in business cycles without reference to monetary policy."[9]

The Research Strategy

RBC research has evolved from an attempt to explain cyclical fluctuations in the context of models in which equilibrium prevails at all times. In this sense the models can be seen as a further extension of the traditional monetarist and new classical approaches. (The early prototypes in this literature were referred to as *equilibrium business cycle models.*) The desire to model *equilibrium* outcomes reflects the researchers' dissatisfaction with the lack of a clear understanding of *how* monetary policy affects real outcomes in the traditional macromodel. The focus on *real* disturbances reflects their skepticism about the evidence,

[8] However, long lags may cause macro variables to display *cyclical* fluctuations, as was discussed in Chapter 29.
[9] Alan C. Stockman, "Real Business Cycle Theory: A Guide, an Evaluation, and New Directions," *Federal Reserve Bank of Cleveland Monthly Review,* 1988, pp. 24–47.

BOX 38-2

Nonlinear Dynamics, Chaos, and Bounded Rationality

Like economists, scientists in many other fields, including physics, biology, and ecology, use models in the form of systems of mathematical equations. By abstracting from many complications and focusing on the problem at hand, models present a simplified picture of the "real world," which is the ultimate object of study. Scientists have found that the analysis and simulation of such models can contribute greatly to the understanding of real-world events.

Recent discoveries in many fields have led to some startling discoveries about the behavior of models that involve *nonlinearities* in their structures. In a linear system, cause and effect are *proportionately* related; for example, if production is linear, then doubling all inputs that are used will result in a doubling of the output that is produced. In a nonlinear system, the relationship between cause and effect is more complicated; for example, doubling all inputs that are used may more than double the output that is produced. In a linear system, size does not matter; the behavior of a system can be replicated by the behavior of two smaller systems. However, in a nonlinear system, size plays a critical role in influencing behavior, and, typically, the behavior of a large system cannot be replicated by combining smaller systems.

The behavior exhibited by *apparently* simple nonlinear models can be very complex; indeed, it sometimes exhibits what is called *chaotic behavior.* This at first puzzled scientists, but in a number of fields the study of complex behavior has contributed to the understanding of phenomena that were previously considered anomalous. For example, the process that determines the population of a particular animal species in a stable environment appears quite simple but can exhibit behavior that is anything but simple; biologists find this to be helpful

when they are trying to understand phenomena such as the seven-year cycle of locusts.*

Recently economists have been incorporating the implications of nonlinear models into some of their research. In classical linear dynamics, a stable system either settles down at a constant rate of change or in a regular cycle; such a system's behavior also can be disturbed by random shocks, but their effects normally die out fairly quickly. For example, in a model of economic growth that is built on linear dynamic systems, real income may follow the growth path of potential income or it may also exhibit regular cyclical fluctuations around that growth path. In such models the observed time path of real national income can be decomposed into a long-term growth trend and a cyclical component (and possibly other systematic components, such as seasonal patterns), plus random shocks, whose effects do not influence the long-term behavior of the system.

Nonlinear dynamic systems do not always behave in this way. For example, a nonlinear model of economic growth may exhibit steady growth for a while, then, quite suddenly, move to regular cycles and then, quite suddenly again, produce irregular fluctuations that never repeat themselves. The laws that govern the system's behavior may be fully understood, and they may also be fully deterministic (i.e., there may be no random behavior in what drives the system). Nonetheless, the system may still exhibit an irregular pattern of fluctuations that never repeats itself and that cannot be predicted from a knowledge of its past behavior, no matter how many observations are available. In

*An excellent discussion of chaos in various physical sciences is given in Paul Davies, *The Cosmic Blueprint* (New York: Simon and Schuster, 1987).

these systems, the apparently random behavior is caused by the system's deterministic but nonlinear laws; when the system is started out twice at what *appear* to be the same initial conditions, it will trace out quite different paths.

Nonlinear systems that behave as we have just described are called *chaotic*. A chaotic system is one that has the capacity to magnify small differences in its initial conditions into two paths that diverge from each other to a point where they eventually do not resemble each other at all. For example, when water is cooled steadily, the speed of the random movement of its molecules falls continuously. Then, at freezing temperature, there is an abrupt change. The molecules stop moving about and become fixed in a definite pattern. The water has frozen. A similar *phase transition* occurs when the water is heated and goes abruptly from a liquid to a gaseous state.

The nonlinear model of economic growth that we have described went through two phase changes: first, when it began to exhibit regular cycles around its growth trend and, second, when it began to fluctuate in an irregular manner.

Positive-feedback loops occur when a given divergence from any state of the system is magnified rather than damped. A normal competitive market is a negative-feedback system. If price diverges from equilibrium, market forces push price back toward the equilibrium. However, if we reverse the labels of the D and S curves, we have a positive-feedback system. Now a slight increase in price above the equilibrium value will create excess demand, and this will cause price to rise even further.

Another example of positive feedback can occur when two different technologies that do the same job are competing with each other in the early stages of their development. The positive-feedback mechanism is that most R&D expenditure tends to be allocated toward the technology that is currently the more successful. A slight advantage of one technology over another will tend to cause more and more of the R&D effort to be directed to that technology, magnifying its lead over the other. The losing technology may be superior to the winning one in some fundamental way, but if a small—even random—advantage develops for the inferior technology, it may gain a decisive lead over the other because of the positive R&D feedback loop.

This is what may have happened when steam and gasoline competed for use in powering early automobiles. In many ways the steam engine, with its combustion outside of the cylinders, is superior to the gasoline engine, with its internal combustion. However, once the gasoline-driven car got a small advantage over the steam car—possibly due to some astute advertising by the manufacturers of gasoline-driven cars who were exploiting some early accidents with the steam car—most R&D funds were allocated mainly to the internal-combustion engine. Ten years later, the steam car was hopelessly behind.

The important point is that a positive-feedback R&D loop has the potential to magnify small, possibly random, divergences into large, irreversible divergences within relatively short periods of time. With a positive-feedback loop, it is the first, rather than the best, technology to enter the field that has the best chance of winning.

In standard economic models of rational behavior, the individual decision maker maximizes with respect to a full knowledge of the system in which he or she is operating. However, the behavior of nonlinear systems, especially if they produce chaotic behavior, cannot always be predicted, even by sophisticated mathematical models. Neither can the behavior be predicted from a knowledge of past behavior. The behavior is unlikely, therefore, to be predicted by the average business person, who is operating based on a mixture of experience, intuition, and simple analysis. This realization has led some economists to move away from the rationality that is assumed in traditional economics, to say nothing of the superrationality that is assumed in the theory of rational expectations. These economists use the theory of *bounded rationality,* which takes into account the limitations of decision makers in terms of their ability to observe and to understand the system in which they are operating.

Just as engineers still use Newtonian mechanics to build bridges, so economists will continue to use

classical equilibrium theory to analyze the behavior of markets that can be seen as being more or less isolated from outside influences and that are dominated by negative-feedback systems. Many believe, however, that the behavior of some individual markets, particularly financial markets, may be described by nonlinear, even chaotic, systems. Many also believe that large systems, such as those describing economic growth which involve invention, knowledge diffusion, and innovation in an economy containing a large number of individual markets, may be characterized by nonlinear dynamic equations, positive-feedback loops, occasional chaotic behavior, and decision making that is, at best, bounded in its rationality.

---

showing the strength of those alleged effects from both the traditional macromodel and from the new classical models.

Essentially, the view of the business cycle that arises in these models is that fluctuations in national income are caused by fluctuations in the vertical *LRAS* curve; this is illustrated in Figure 38-1. The contrast with the theory of fluctuations, which was shown in Figure 29-4 on page 597, is apparent.

The explanation of cyclical fluctuations that arises in RBC models is based on the role of supply shocks originating from sources such as oil price changes and technical progress.

Key Propositions and Criticisms

The RBC approach has proven to be very controversial. Although its proponents claim a number of major accomplishments as a result of this approach, its critics have pointed to a number of serious shortcomings.

The major claims made for the approach include the following:

1. It has been able to explain the recent behavior of the American economy quite well, while disavowing any role for *AD* fluctuations in the business cycle. The approach, therefore, obviously provides for no role for stabilization policy operating through monetary and fiscal policies that act to influence aggregate demand.

2. It suggests that an integrated approach to understanding cycles and growth may be appropriate, since both reflect forces that affect the *LRAS* curve. The distinction it makes is that some shocks are temporary (and thus have cyclical effects) and some are permanent (and therefore affect the economy's growth).

3. It provides valuable insights into how shocks, regardless of their origin, spread over time to the different sectors of the economy. By abstracting from monetary issues and from the automatic adjustment mechanism, more details concerning technology and household choice concerning intertemporal trade-offs in consumption and labor-leisure choice can be dealt with.

4. It has focused on explaining a number of stylized facts that other approaches have ignored. These include the comparison of seasonal and cyclical fluctuations, the fact that consumption varies less than output, and the procyclical movements of hours worked and of the average productivity of labor.

However, critics of the approach focus on some implausible results of the model, express concern over assumptions about underlying behavioral parameters, and, more importantly, are skeptical about a model in which monetary issues are completely ignored. For example, they point out that RBC models are unable to provide any insights into the issue of the correlation between money and output that was at the heart of the monetarist–Keynesian debate reviewed earlier in this chapter, and that they are

BOX 38-3

Unemployment in Alternative Models

One of the most important differences between the Keynesian models, on the one hand, and the monetarist and new classical models, on the other hand, relates to the distinction between voluntary and involuntary unemployment.

In the latter models, all unemployment and below-capacity output are voluntary. Workers decide to be unemployed, and firms decide to produce less than capacity output as a result of the errors that they make in predicting the general price level (and therefore the relative price of what they sell). So, if they had been surveyed, the millions of unemployed around the world during the early 1980s would have said that they could have had a job at the going wage but had refused to accept it because, given their expectations about inflation, the expected real wage was too low.

In the Keynesian model, prices and wages do not fluctuate to clear markets. Unemployment and production below capacity are involuntary, in the sense that unemployed workers would like jobs at the going wage rate but cannot find them, and firms would like to sell more at going prices but customers are not forthcoming.* So, if they had been surveyed, the millions of unemployed around the world during the early 1980s would have said that they would have accepted a job at the going wage rate but that none was available.

This distinction between voluntary and involuntary unemployment leads to a striking difference in the policy recommendations of the two schools. The new classicists and the traditional monetarists argue that monetary policy should not be used actively to stabilize the economy. This is for two reasons: (1) Fluctuations in the money supply are a major source of fluctuations in output and inflation,

and (2) there is no long-term trade-off between inflation and national income.†

One aspect of the new classical and monetarist models that is particularly controversial is the belief in downward flexibility of prices, which leads to the prediction that, as long as national income is below its full-employment level, the price level will *fall* at an ever accelerating rate. Keynesians say that the observed downward inflexibility of the price level refutes this view. They reject the prediction that the main cause of recessionary gaps is *voluntary* reductions in employment and output, due to errors in reading the signals that are provided by the price system. Most Keynesians do not believe that output deviates from its potential level *only* because workers and firms make mistakes, and thus they believe that stabilization policy should be used to eliminate recessionary gaps.

Major current research and debate center around issues such as what determines the degree of wage and price flexibility in the economy, the conditions under which people can be expected to form accurate expectations and act on them, and the potential for destabilizing the economy by pursuing an active stabilization policy. Views on how the economy behaves at both the micro and macro levels will be influenced by the progress of the debate, and so will views on the place of fiscal and monetary policy as possible ways to eliminate inflationary or recessionary gaps. We encounter a number of the most important issues in the next few pages of this chapter.

---

* Some economists argue that this unemployment is voluntary, because the workers earlier had voluntarily agreed to contracts at the going wage.

† Most economists accept the view that monetary forces are important in influencing inflation and unemployment, but many do not agree that monetary forces are the *most* important force. Most economists also agree that inflation will tend to accelerate if income is held permanently above its full-employment level; this is just a restatement of the acceleration hypothesis and the natural-rate hypothesis that we developed in detail in Chapter 34 and in its appendix.

FIGURE 38-1   Real Business Cycles

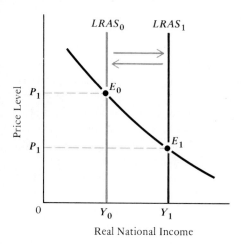

Real business cycle theory views fluctuations in national output as being caused by fluctuations in the long-run aggregate supply curve. Shocks to technology and changes in availability of key products, such as oil, cause the *LRAS* curve to shift back and forth between $LRAS_0$ and $LRAS_1$. Because the *LRAS* curve is vertical, these shifts give rise to identical fluctuations in national income; that is, national income fluctuates between Y_0 and Y_1. If the aggregate demand curve were stable, as shown by *AD,* the price level would fluctuate between P_0 and P_1. However, whatever the behavior of the *AD* curve, the behavior of national income would be unchanged.

unable to provide insights into empirical regularities involving nominal variables, such as the fact that prices apparently vary less than quantities or that nominal prices are procyclical.

Policy Implications

As we have noted, the structure of RBC models rules out any role for using policy to manage the economy via aggregate demand. However, the models do provide some basis for believing that the use of such demand management policies can be harmful and thus give rise to a conservative, *laissez faire* policy prescription.

The basis for this view is that cycles in the economy will, according to the RBC model, represent efficient responses to the real shocks that are hitting

the economy. If policymakers mistakenly interpret cyclical fluctuations as aggregate-demand-inspired deviations from full employment and therefore try to stabilize the output fluctuations, all they will succeed in doing is to distort the decisions made by households and firms. In turn, this will cause the responses to the real shocks to be inefficient.

While only a minority of economists espouse these models as complete or even reasonable descriptions of the business cycle, and thus only a minority take seriously the strict implications for policy, most accept the general message that real disturbances can play an important role in business cycles and that this mitigates against the active use of stabilization policy.

New Keynesian Macroeconomics

The first two modern research programs that we have discussed involve extensions of the market-clearing, traditional monetarist view. The third one, which we turn to now, involves a number of separate approaches to providing microfoundations for the sticky-price Keynesian model. Box 38-4 discusses one interesting recent proposal to modify wage-setting arrangements so as to circumvent some of the adjustment problems that are envisaged by the Keynesian model.

Traditional Keynesian macroeconomic theories simply assume that prices or wages, or both, are rigid in the short run; because prices change slowly, it is the quantity of output that adjusts to changes in aggregate demand. However, the price rigidity and, hence, the implications for the behavior of output and employment and for the effectiveness of stabilization policy, is not explicitly derived as optimal behavior by consumers and firms. Thus, the models are said to lack microeconomic foundations. Furthermore, the equilibrium theories just described allow no role for government intervention.

New Keynesian macroeconomics is the name that has been given to the recent attempts by some economists to develop theories of macroeconomic fluctuations that both have microeconomic foundations and allow a role for government stabilization policy. In contrast to equilibrium theories, which assume prices are flexible so all markets clear, new Keynesian theories seek explanations for rigidities that prevent markets from clearing at their optimal level and explore their macroeconomic consequences. The effect of these rigidities may either be transient—simply slowing adjustment of output toward the unique optimal level—or permanent, if the model has more than one equilibrium and shocks can cause the economy to move from one such equilibrium to another with possibly different levels of output and employment.

Explaining Slow Adjustment

Explaining how prices and wages could be slow to adjust to changes in purely nominal demand within a model of maximizing agents is difficult, as it requires an explicit model of price setting. (Equilibrium models that are based on competitive markets do not address the problem of *how* prices are set.)

For prices to be set, agents must have some degree of market power, and so new Keynesian models assume that markets for output are imperfectly competitive.[10] However, imperfect competition alone is insufficient to generate a role for government stabilization policy. If, for instance, the money supply is increased, profit-maximizing price setters will respond to the increase in demand by increasing prices; as a result, the price level will simply rise and there need be no output effects. Thus, new Keynesian models require additional features that make some price rigidity optimal. Among the possible explanations explored are menu costs, implicit contracts, and efficiency wages.

Menu costs.   When a firm incurs costs by changing its prices, it may be said to face *menu costs*. The term is an allusion to the fixed cost that a restaurant faces when it reprints its menu because it has adjusted its prices. For a firm to operate at the profit-maximizing level of output, its marginal cost will equal its marginal revenue, and hence a small change in output will create only a small effect on profits. Therefore, if the firm faces menu costs and responds to a change in demand by changing its price and its output, the cost of the change in price may well outweigh any gain in profit from its changed sales.

For example, frequent price changes for a company that sells a wide variety of small items could involve considerable costs, in terms of keeping track of customer accounts and printing new catalogues;

optimal behavior for the company may be to change prices at regular intervals, say, four times per year, rather than to adjust them constantly. Since most firms in the economy would set prices at fixed intervals, changes in nominal demand would be matched by changes in real output, and government stabilization policy would have real effects.

For an imperfectly competitive, profit-maximizing firm, sufficiently high menu costs will mean that small changes in demand will be accommodated by changes in output rather than price.

However, in order for changes in output to be large, the labor supply must vary considerably; many of the other features of new Keynesian models that we discuss next attempt to examine the conditions needed for there to be an elastic labor supply.

Implicit contracts.   Many of the models that are proposed by new Keynesian economists are characterized by a degree of attachment between agents that surpasses the atomistic behavior assumed by models of pure competition. This accords well with everyday experience; however, while many of these attachments are formalized in contracts, others are not, and so models of *implicit contracts* have been developed to explain why agents may form lasting relationships, even in the absence of formal ties.

According to implicit-contract theory, short-term wage inflexibility can stem from rational behavior on the part of firms and workers. If wage rates adjust to clear labor markets, wages will vary over the cycle. *All* workers will then bear the uncertainty that is associated with the cyclical movements in wages. However, if wages are set in response to long-term considerations but do not vary cyclically so as to clear labor markets, cyclical fluctuations in demand will cause employment to fluctuate.

Implicit contracts that give rise to wage rigidity and employment variability are viewed as a form of insurance provided by firms, who are in a better position to bear risk, to workers, who wish to avoid risk.

This insurance can increase workers' welfare *and* allow firms to reduce the wage level and thus increase profits.

Seniority can also play a role in this model. Since

---

[10] The role of imperfect competition in providing microfoundations for Keynesian macroeconomics is discussed briefly in Chapter 14; see page 280.

BOX 38-4

The Share Economy

Several times in this text we have noted that wage rigidity is widely perceived to be a major impediment to the efficient functioning of the economy. In his important book, *The Share Economy,* Professor Martin Weitzman of the Massachusetts Institute of Technology has proposed a dramatic policy that is designed to restore flexibility of wages and thus enhance economic performance.

How the Share Economy Works

The basic idea behind the *share economy* is quite simple. Under Weitzman's proposal, part of the payment that any firm makes to labor would be tied directly to that firm's net revenues. This payment, which is like an annual bonus, is called *the share wage.* In addition, workers would also receive a *base wage,* which is fixed for the duration of the labor contract and is much lower than their wage under existing, traditional labor contracts.

When the firm is prosperous and net revenues are high, the share wage paid to workers would be correspondingly high. In these circumstances the total wage, equal to the base wage plus the share wage, would exceed the initial wage that prevailed prior to the scheme's introduction. However, when the firm's sales are down and thus net revenues are low, the share wage would also be low. In these

circumstances the total wage would be below the initial wage.

Consider, for example, a firm that is currently paying its workers a fixed wage of $20 per hour. Now suppose that under the share contract it would pay them a base wage of only $10 per hour and that it also would promise to pay workers a fixed percentage of its net revenues. Finally, suppose that this percentage would be such that, if net revenues were at their average or normal level, each worker would receive a combined base plus share wage of $20 per hour, just equal to the wage in the absence of the share contract.

If the firm's net revenues turned out to be above their normal level, the share wage would rise to reflect this; thus, the total payment to workers would exceed $20 per hour, and the workers would share in the prosperity of the firm. If the firm's net revenues turned out to be below their normal level, the share wage would fall; in this case the total wage would be below $20 per hour, and the workers would "share" in the ill fortunes of the firm.

Implications of the Share Economy

Under traditional, wage-setting arrangements, rigid wages mean that a firm will lay off workers in the face of a fall in demand for its output. Under

most layoffs and rehiring are based on seniority, employment fluctuations are all borne by the 10 or 20 percent of workers who have the least seniority. The majority of workers then will have little uncertainty in the face of cyclical fluctuations in demand, since all the uncertainty will have been placed on the minority, who have the least seniority. Thus, contracts that fix wages over the cycle and allow employment to vary may be preferable to the majority of workers, compared to contracts that allow wages to vary in order to clear the labor market continually and thus prevent unemployment.

It should be noted that implicit contracts in the labor market cannot "explain" involuntary unemployment. First, all workers agree to the arrangement before demand shocks occur, and thus all those who become unemployed do so voluntarily, at least *ex ante.* If unemployment were a major concern of workers, the insurance could be against variations in employment rather than wages. Also, the predictions of these models rely heavily on the assumed attachment between firms and workers. If alternative employment were available to workers during layoffs, of course no unemployment would result; further-

a share contract, firms have less of an incentive to lay off workers during a downturn, since the total wage paid to each worker falls. Thus, in the example that we have just given, workers would face a more stable employment pattern under a share contract. However, workers would have to accept the risk of a fluctuating total wage, as compared with the initial situation, in which they would receive a fixed wage of $20 per hour *if* they remained employed.

Many observers feel that the situation under a share contract, in which each worker bears a small part of the burden of a downturn, is more equitable than the situation under a fixed total wage, in which those workers who keep their jobs bear none of the burden, while the minority who are laid off bear the total burden. Further, many observers feel that the economy would operate more efficiently in the presence of the enhanced wage flexibility that the share contracts would generate.

Weitzman proposes that tax incentives be introduced to encourage firms to enter into such contracts. For example, share wages could be subject to a special, low tax rate, with regular tax rates still applying to any income from a fixed wage rate. Firms and workers thus would have an incentive to arrange for a large fraction of the total payment to labor to be share income.

This proposal is controversial. Some unions have criticized it, arguing that if the contract specifies that a given fraction of net revenues is to be paid to all workers, firms would have an incentive to add to their work force and thus reduce each worker's share. This practice, the argument continues, would drive wages down to very low levels. Other unions reply that the expansion in employment is precisely one of the desirable features of the system, and there is no reason to expect that *total* wages would fall. Some observers fear the impact on the deficit of the special tax incentives that might be required; others reply, using reasoning reminiscent of that behind the Laffer curve (see page 471), that the improvement in the performance of the economy would be so great that total tax revenues would rise, not fall. Perhaps the highest praise of all appeared in a *New York Times* editorial, in which *The Share Economy* was referred to as "the best idea since Keynes."

more, in times of high demand, workers who are being paid a wage equal to their average productivity across the cycle could be bid away from the firm by competitors who are willing to pay them their marginal product.

It should be noted also that the rigidity that arises in these models relates to real, not nominal, wages. Thus, changes in nominal aggregate demand may not affect employment in these models. This property will change, however, if costs of changing wages, similar to the menu costs that we just discussed, make it optimal to fix nominal wages in the short run. In practice, wages are adjusted infrequently and often at quite regular time intervals, rather than as a function of the state of demand.[11]

It also has been suggested that implicit contracts

[11] The absence of agreements that are explicitly based on detailed descriptions of "the state of the world" is sometimes attributed to "bounded rationality," which refers to the limited ability of agents to understand the precise state of the world, as well as the practical difficulty of writing contracts contingent upon it. (See Box 38-2.) The first of these, as well as the related notion of asymmetric information, in which firms and workers have different information about the state of the world, can be invoked to motivate nominal wage rigidity in implicit contracts.

exist between firms and their customers. Thus, a product's price may be of only one concern to its consumers; for example, in the case of intermediate goods, purchasers may "insure" against unpredictable price fluctuations and allow delivery time to absorb demand shocks.

Efficiency wages. Efficiency wage models, which we discussed in Chapter 35, also offer an explanation of why wages may be used for purposes other than clearing the labor market. Imperfectly competitive firms paying wages above market clearing may not, in the presence of costs of changing prices and wages, adjust wages as a result of changes in nominal demand. Therefore, government stabilization policy can be effective.

Multiple Equilibria

Another class of new Keynesian models involves multiple equilibria. In these models imperfections do not necessarily retard the adjustment to equilibrium; however, the models have more than one equilibrium, and the equilibrium reached may not be optimal. Included in this class are models that are based on union behavior in the labor market and on the existence of an externality in the goods market.

Unions and the insider-outsider hypothesis.   Most models of union behavior assume that unions negotiate on behalf of their membership and recognize that, in many cases, not all of these workers may be employed. Potential workers who are not union members may enter the unions' calculations only peripherally, or not at all. This idea is formalized as the *insider-outsider hypothesis,* in which union members (insiders) negotiate in a self-interested manner, ignoring the interests of the unemployed (outsiders).

Consider a simple but extreme case, in which union membership is equated with the previous period's employment. In this case sufficient union power may result in inflexible real wages and thus in equilibrium unemployment levels that are higher than those that are considered to be optimal by policymakers. Furthermore, the unemployment is truly involuntary, as the unemployed wish to work at the union wage but cannot.

Nominal rigidities that are created by insider-outsider behavior can provide a rationale for government stabilization policy.

It is interesting to note that in this situation stabilization policy can have long-lasting effects by moving the economy to a new equilibrium; once-and-for-all changes in labor demand may alter union membership and therefore alter *insider* behavior.[12]

Thin-market externalities.   If markets for goods of services are *thin* (that is, if they involve relatively few traders), the production decisions of sellers will be very sensitive to changes in the numbers of buyers. Furthermore, since sellers in one market are buyers in another, a change in demand in one market will spill into others. For example, if workers believe that they cannot sell all of their labor services, they will reduce their demand for goods; firms, in turn, see this reduction in demand and reduce their demand for labor. Thus, in times of insufficient aggregate demand, production may reach a low-demand equilibrium. This *thin-market externality* arises because no individual agent is able to affect the state of demand significantly.

The notion of thin-market externalities was first developed in a very general model in which all agents are both producers and consumers, and production opportunities are identical, except for the fixed cost of undertaking them. As producers, agents choose a maximum cost, above which they will not undertake production. Once having produced, they then search for someone to trade with; the more agents there are who have produced, the shorter is the time spent searching for someone to trade with. A shorter search period will encourage projects with higher costs to be undertaken, and so temporary increases in aggregate demand can permanently raise the equilibrium level of production.

As government spending can be used for this temporary boost to demand, these models can yield traditional Keynesian policy prescriptions. Notice that the underemployment equilibrium and the effectiveness of government demand policy do not rely on misperceptions of agents: All decisions are optimal relative to the state of demand. Nevertheless, these models capture the Keynesian notion of "ani-

---

[12] Such permanent changes in equilibrium unemployment rates, sometimes called *hysteresis,* can also be caused by a decline in the employability of unemployed workers, due to a deterioration of their work skills, or by the cyclical dependence of unemployment insurance parameters, which adjusts the generosity of benefits countercyclically. In both of these cases, temporary changes in aggregate demand may permanently alter the equilibrium rate of unemployment.

BOX 38-5

The Progress of Economics

In this chapter we have discussed a number of current controversies about the behavior of the economy and the evidence that relates to these controversies. General acceptance of the view that the validity of economic theories should be tested by confronting their predictions with the mass of all available evidence is fairly new in economics.

Since 1936, when Keynes' *The General Theory of Employment, Interest, and Money* was published, great progress has been made in economics in relating theory to evidence. This progress has been reflected in the superior ability of governments to achieve their policy objectives. The financial aspects of World War II were handled far better than those of World War I. When President Roosevelt tried to reduce unemployment in the 1930s, his efforts were greatly hampered by the failure even of economists to realize the critical importance of budget deficits in raising aggregate demand and in injecting newly created money into the economy. When the Vietnam War forced the government to adopt expansive fiscal and monetary policies, economists had no trouble in predicting the outcome. More involvement abroad was obtained at the cost of heavy inflationary pressure at home.

The general propositions of theories are tested in such important policy areas as managing wartime economies, curing major depressions, and coping with inflations, even if all of their specific predictions are not. In some sense, then, economic theories always have been subjected to empirical tests. When they were wildly at variance with the facts, the ensuing disaster could not help being noticed, and the theories were discarded or amended in the light of what was learned.

The advances of economics in the past 50 years reflect economists' changed attitudes toward empirical observations. Today economists are much less likely to dismiss theories just because they do not like them and to refuse to abandon theories just because they do like them. Economists are more likely to try to base their theories as much as possible on empirical observation and to accept empirical relevance as the ultimate arbiter of the value of theories. As human beings, we may be anguished at the upsetting of a pet theory; as scientists, we should try to train ourselves to take pleasure in it because of the new knowledge gained thereby. It has been said that one of the great tragedies of science is the continual slaying of beautiful theories by ugly facts. It must always be remembered that when theory and fact come into conflict, theory, not fact, must give way.

---

mal spirits," in which expectations about the state of demand can cause changes in investment and thus output. If all agents are pessimistic about the time that is required to find a trading partner, this pessimism will be self-fulfilling.

Taken together, these microeconomic foundations, which underpin new Keynesian macroeconomics, are far from a unified theory. However, given that these models are still in the early stages of development, this should be expected. Only time will tell which of the ideas that we have just discussed will come to dominate the research agenda of new Keynesians. Some related issues are taken up in Box 38-5.

SUMMARY

1. Views about the role that policy plays in improving macroeconomic performance range between two extremes. The conservative view is that there is only a minimum role for policy; macroeconomic performance will be most satisfactory when the market system is allowed to function as freely as possible. The interventionist view is that active use of policy will improve macroeconomic performance.

2. Conservatives see that the role of policy is to provide a stable environment for individual decision makers. This involves maintaining a consistent set of "fiscal rules of the game," in terms of expenditure and tax rates and in terms of providing a steady but gradual growth in the money supply.

3. Interventionists have specific prescriptions for each policy variable. They advocate active use of discretionary monetary and fiscal policy to stabilize output and employment. Despite imperfections that are caused by lags and incomplete knowledge, they believe such policies are helpful. Similar policies can be combined with incomes policies to stabilize the fluctuations in the price level that arise from various sources and that are subject to an upward bias. They also support policies to promote growth through subsidization, tax favors, and more specific intervention.

4. It is common to identify monetarists with conservatives and Keynesians with interventionists. Monetarists believe that, because the economy is inherently stable, the goal of damping the business cycle is best achieved by avoiding fluctuations in policy, especially monetary policy. Hence, they advocate a k percent rule. Keynesians believe that the economy is inherently unstable, in that expenditure functions shift regularly and the economy's self-corrective mechanisms are weak. Hence, they believe in an active role for both monetary and fiscal policy as a way to stabilize the business cycle.

5. Monetarists believe that inflation is everywhere and always a monetary phenomenon, and so they advocate the same conservative policies to avoid price instability as they advocate to minimize policy-induced cycles in output. They also argue that, to control inflation, the long-term growth rate of the money supply must not be too high. Keynesians accept the view that monetary expansion is necessary for inflation to persist in the long term, but they take seriously the role of other factors in causing short-term but substantial inflation. Hence, they believe in an active role for policy as a way to offset these factors in the short term.

6. Monetarists view markets as competitive and hence believe that departures from full-employment equilibrium are quickly rectified. As a result, they believe that fluctuations in aggregate demand lead primarily to fluctuations in the price level, rather than in the level of output. They believe that the best course for monetary policy is to follow a k percent rule. For traditional monetarists, this is because they believe that long and variable lags in the effect of monetary policy mean that an interventionist monetary policy would destabilize output.

7. Keynesians emphasize the noncompetitive nature of the economy. As a result, they believe that fluctuations in aggregate demand lead primarily to fluctuations in output, rather than in the price level. In this view, an interventionist stabilization policy can be effective in stabilizing fluctuations in output.

8. New classical economists believe that departures from full-employment output occur only when people make mistakes in predicting the price level. When this belief is combined with the theory of rational expectations, it leads to the policy invariance proposition. New classical monetarists support the k percent rule because they believe that an interventionist monetary policy will not be effective in stabilizing output.

9. Real business cycle models posit that fluctuations in national income

can be explained as the result of real shocks, which cause the vertical *LRAS* curve to fluctuate; they eschew any role for *AD* fluctuations, including those caused by monetary and fiscal policies.

10. New Keynesian macroeconomics encompasses a wide variety of models that try to explain why wages and prices may be sticky and hence why aggregate demand fluctuations have an important impact on national income. These include the role of menu costs, implicit contracts, efficiency wages, the role of unions, and the externalities caused by so-called thin markets.

TOPICS FOR REVIEW

Conservatives and interventionists
Traditional Keynesians and monetarists
Micro foundations
k percent rule
New classical economics
Lucas aggregate supply curve
Theory of rational expectations
Policy invariance proposition
Real business cycle models
New Keynesian economics

DISCUSSION QUESTIONS

1. To what extent is today's unemployment a serious social problem? If people could vote in order to choose between 10 percent unemployment, combined with zero inflation, and 2 percent unemployment, combined with 10 percent inflation, which alternative do you think they would choose? Which groups might prefer the first alternative, and which groups might prefer the second?

2. Some economists urge the government to fight inflation and combat unemployment by encouraging private-sector saving and investment. How might expanded saving and investment help to reduce inflation and to combat unemployment?

3. Nobel Laureate Paul Samuelson quoted a "conservative economist friend" as saying in mid-1980, "If you're contriving a teensy-weensy recession for us, please don't bother. It won't do the job. What's needed is a believable declaration that Washington will countenance *whatever* degree of unemployment is needed to bring us back on the path to price stability, and a demonstrated willingness to *stick* to that resolution no matter how politically unpopular the short-run joblessness, production cutbacks, and dips in profit might be." Discuss the "conservative friend's" view of inflation. Does experience since 1980 suggest that his advice was followed? If so, what was the consequence?

4. An ad that appeared in the *New York Times* in the early 1980s had this to say about inflation: "First [our politicians] blamed wage increases and price hikes for inflation. Then when 'voluntary guidelines' were established, the blame shifted to OPEC oil prices. Both explanations were wrong. Government policy is responsible for inflation— paying for deficit spending by 'creating money out of thin air.'" What theories of inflation are rejected and accepted by the writers of this ad?

5. In the mid-1980s, a fervent national debate developed concerning the need to protect U.S. industries from foreign competition. How do the pro and con views of protectionism relate to the conservative and interventionist policies for promoting long-term growth?

6. In late 1989, a newspaper headline read: "Loss of consumer confidence sparks downturn in economy." What basic macroeconomic model did the writer likely have in mind?

7. A number of key microeconomic policy issues that were discussed earlier in this book are listed below. Go back and review the relevant discussion of some of them, and then present both the conservative case for "letting the market work" and the interventionist case in favor of a particular policy prescription. (Although the issues listed are "microeconomic" issues, their impact on the macroeconomic issues—in particular, economic growth—can be important.)

  a. Rent controls (Chapter 6)
  b. Deindustrialization (Chapter 17)
  c. Minimum-wage laws (Chapter 19)
  d. Increasing tariffs and other restrictions on imports (Chapter 21)
  e. Paying for social benefits (Chapter 25)
  f. Financing health care (Chapter 25)

Appendix to Chapter 38

Money in the National-Income Model

We have studied the interaction of money, interest rates, and national income in terms of the apparatus in Figures 32-3 through 32-6. A loose end in that model can best be seen by considering the impact of an increase in the money supply. This leads to a fall in interest rates, as shown in Figure 32-4(i), to increases in expenditure, as shown in Figure 32-4(ii), and to increased national income, as shown in Figure 32-5. However, increased national income, in turn, leads to an increased need for transactions balances. This increased demand for money must then be added to the liquidity preference schedule in Figure 32-4. How is the increase in demand satisfied? Does accounting for it radically alter the conclusions of the analysis of Chapter 32?

The answer to the last question is no. This appendix provides a model that integrates monetary and expenditure factors and shows how they jointly determine the interest rate and the level of national income. The British economist Sir John Hicks (awarded the Nobel Prize in economics in 1972) suggested the approach in his famous review of Keynes' *General Theory*, "Mr. Keynes and the Classics: A Suggested Interpretation." It involves identifying the relationship between income and interest rates that is imposed first by goods market equilibrium and then by money market equilibrium. We then bring the two together to determine the one combination of real national income and interest rate that satisfies both equilibrium conditions simultaneously. Finally, we use the model to examine the effects of monetary and fiscal policy.

The Interest Rate and Aggregate Expenditure: The *IS* Curve

As we saw in going from Figure 32-4(ii) to Figure 32-5(i), a fall in the rate of interest is associated with a rise in the level of real national income, due to increased investment expenditures. Figure 32A-1 depicts this relationship between interest rate and na-

tional income as the negatively sloped *IS* curve.[1] The *IS* curve shows the combinations of national income and the rate of interest for which aggregate desired expenditure just equals total production in the economy. The negative relationship is derived for *given* values of the other variables influencing the aggregate expenditure function of Figure 32-5(i).

For given settings of the relationships that underlie the aggregate expenditure function, the condition of goods market equilibrium—national income equals aggregate expenditure—means that the level of national income will vary negatively with the interest rate.

Fiscal Policy

Increases in the level of government expenditure raise the total level of aggregate expenditure *for any given interest rate*. As Figure 30-1 shows, this, in turn, leads to a multiplier effect on national income. In terms of the present model, an increase in government expenditure causes the *IS* curve to shift upward and to the right, as shown in Figure 38A-1. Combinations of national income and the interest rate that were on the original *IS* curve and hence were initially positions of equilibrium in the goods market are now positions of excess demand due to the increase in autonomous government demand. Hence, output must rise to satisfy the increased demand (in the process leading to the now familiar multiplier effect), interest rates must rise to reduce investment demand, or, as IS_1 shows, some combination of both must occur.[2]

---

[1] *IS* stands for investment and saving, since the equilibrium condition is often expressed in terms of the equality between these two aggregates.

[2] A reduction in taxes, by altering the relationship between national income and disposable income, would also lead to a rightward shift in the *IS* curve.

**FIGURE 38A-1   Goods Market Equilibrium:
The IS Curve**

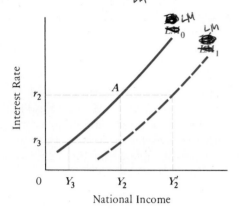

The locus of combinations of national income and
the interest rate, for which aggregate expenditure
equals output, is called the *IS* curve. The *IS* curve
slopes downward and to the right, indicating that a fall
in the interest rate from r_0 to r_1 leads, via increased investment, to an increase in the level of national income
from Y_0 to Y_0'. Expansionary fiscal policy creates excess
demand for output and causes the *IS* curve to shift to the
right to IS_1; from an initial position at *A*, the interest
rate must rise to r_0, national income must rise to Y_2, or
some combination of both along IS_1 must occur.

Expansionary fiscal policy causes the *IS* curve
to shift upward and to the right, creating a new
locus of points at which aggregate expenditure
equals national income.

By similar reasoning, cuts in government spending or tax increases shift the *IS* curve downward to
the left. [45]

Liquidity Preference and National Income: The *LM* Curve

When the money supply is held constant, if the demand for money and the supply of money are to be
equal, the *total* demand for money arising from the
transactions, speculative, and precautionary motives
must also be constant. As we have seen, the demand
for money can be expected to vary positively with
the level of national income and negatively with the

rate of interest. If there is to be monetary equilibrium
with a given money supply, any increase in national
income must therefore be accompanied by an increase in the interest rate to keep total money demand
constant. This is depicted by the positively sloped
LM curve in Figure 38A-2. The *LM* curve shows the
combinations of national income and interest rate for
which total money demand is constant at the level
of a given money supply.[3]

For a given money supply, the condition of
monetary market equilibrium means that the
level of national income will vary directly with
the interest rate.

[3] The *L* stands for liquidity preference (or demand for money),
and the *M* stands for money supply.

**FIGURE 38A-2   Monetary Market Equilibrium:
The LM Curve**

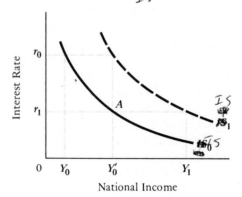

The locus of combinations of national income and
the interest rate, of which total money demand
equals a given money supply, is called the *LM*
curve. The *LM* curve slopes upward and to the right,
indicating that a fall in the rate of interest from r_2 to r_3,
which causes the demand for money to rise, must be accompanied by a fall in the level of national income, say
from Y_2 to Y_3, in order to keep money demand equal to
the constant money supply. An open-market purchase
creates an excess supply of money and causes the *LM*
curve to shift to the right to LM_1; from an initial position at *A*, the interest rate must fall to r_3, national income must rise to Y_2', or some combination of both
along *LM* must occur.

Monetary Policy

An increase in the supply of money resulting from an open market purchase by the central bank causes the LM curve to shift downward and to the right, as in Figure 38A-2. The combinations of national income and interest rate that were on the original curve, LM_0, and hence were initially positions of monetary equilibrium now correspond to excess supply, due to the increase in the supply of money. To reestablish equilibrium, the demand for money must increase to match the larger money supply; hence, national income must rise, the interest rate must fall, or, as LM_1 shows, some combination of both must occur.

An increase in the money supply causes the LM curve to shift downward and to the right, creating a new locus of points at which total money demand equals the money supply.

By similar reasoning, a decrease in the money supply causes the LM curve to shift upward and to the left. [46]

Macroeconomic Equilibrium: Determination of National Income and the Interest Rate

The model is shown in Figure 38A-3. The intersection of the LM and IS curves indicates the only combination of national income and interest rate that can occur for which aggregate expenditure equals national income *and* the demand for money is equal to the supply of money.

The intersection of the IS and LM curves gives the equilibrium levels of national income and the rate of interest in a model that combines both expenditure and monetary influences.

FIGURE 38A-3   Effects of Shifts in the IS and LM Curves

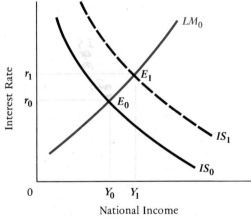

(i) A shift in the IS curve

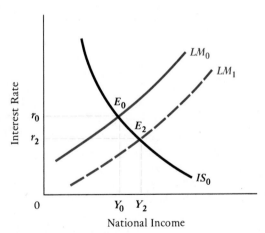

(ii) A shift in the LM curve

Similar shifts in the IS and LM curves have similar effects on national income and opposite effects on the rate of interest. The initial levels of income and interest rate are Y_0 and r_0 in both parts of the figure. In part (i) a rightward shift in the IS curve from IS_0 to IS_1 raises national income from Y_0 to Y_1 and raises the rate of interest from r_0 to r_1. In part (ii) a rightward shift in the LM curve from LM_0 to LM_1 raises national income from Y_0 to Y_2 and lowers the rate of interest from r_0 to r_2. Part (i) shows the effect of an increase in government expenditure; part (ii) shows the effect of an increase in the money supply.

Figure 38A-3 shows the effects of particular shifts in the *IS* and *LM* curves. This analysis leads to four general predictions.

1. A rightward shift in the *IS* curve raises national income and the rate of interest.
2. A leftward shift in the *IS* curve lowers national income and the rate of interest.
3. A rightward shift in the *LM* curve raises national income and lowers the rate of interest.
4. A leftward shift in the *LM* curve lowers national income and raises the rate of interest.

The Effects of Fiscal and Monetary Policy

Given our analysis of the effects of government expenditure on the *IS* curve and the effects of the money supply on the *LM* curve, we can summarize the analysis in our four basic predictions about the effects of monetary and fiscal policy.

1. An increase in government expenditure raises national income and raises the rate of interest.
2. An increase in the money supply raises national income and lowers the rate of interest.
3. A decrease in government expenditure lowers national income and lowers the rate of interest.
4. A decrease in the money supply lowers national income and raises the rate of interest.

These results represent what may be called the *Keynesian synthesis,* in which both monetary and fiscal policies have an effect on national income and interest rates.[4] [47]

At one time, debate in macroeconomics centered around the relative strengths of monetary and fiscal policy. *Monetarists* argued that monetary policy was powerful and that fiscal policy was weak; *Keynesians* tended to argue that the opposite was the case. These views, and how they are related to the underlying behavioral relations, can be understood in terms of the *IS-LM* model.

Consider first the strength of an increase in government spending. This increases expenditure directly and, as we have seen, shifts the *IS* curve rightward. The effect on national income is smaller than this rightward shift, because (1) the conditions for

monetary equilibrium summarized in the *LM* curve mean that an increase in national income must be accompanied by an increase in the interest rate, and (2) an increase in the interest rate gives rise to a fall in the level of interest-sensitive spending in the economy. The weaker either of these two effects is, the stronger the effects of the increase in government spending will be. The more interest-elastic is the demand for money, the flatter will be the *LM* curve, and hence the less the interest rate will rise in response to the fiscal stimulus. The less interest-elastic is desired expenditure, the steeper will be the *IS* curve and the smaller the "crowding out" of private investment following a fiscal expansion.

Now consider monetary policy. An increase in the money supply causes the *LM* curve to shift to the right; this leads to a fall in the interest rate and an increase in interest-sensitive expenditure. As a result, there is a movement downward and to the right along the *IS* curve, and national income rises. The rise in national income will be larger (1) the larger the fall in the interest rate is and (2) the larger the induced increase in interest-sensitive expenditure is. The less interest-elastic the demand for money is, the steeper will be the *LM* curve and the larger will be the fall in the interest rate following a monetary expansion. The more interest-elastic desired expenditure is, the flatter will be the *IS* curve and the larger will be the induced increase in interest-sensitive expenditure.

Monetarists, then, in this debate tended to think of the demand for money as relatively interest-insensitive and desired expenditure as relatively interest-sensitive; this gives rise to the combination of a steep *LM* curve and a flat *IS* curve, with the implication of effective monetary policy and ineffective fiscal policy. Keynesians, by contrast, tended to think of the opposite combination of interest-sensitive money demand and interest-insensitive desired expenditure; this gives rise to a steep *IS* curve and a flat *LM* curve, with the implication of effective fiscal policy and ineffective monetary policy.

The Price Level and Aggregate Demand

So far we have treated the price level as given and have presumed that all changes in national income were changes in *real* output. Consider now what

---

[4] As we saw in Chapters 30 and 32, a cut in tax rates has effects that are similar to an increase in *G*, and a fall in the demand for money has effects that are similar to an increase in the money supply.

would happen to the analysis if the price level were allowed to vary.

Changes in the Price Level

As we saw in Box 32-2 on pages 682–683, an increase in the price level leads to an increase in liquidity preference. For money market equilibrium to be preserved, the interest rate must rise, the level of income must fall, or, since either leads to a reduction in money demand, some combination of both must occur; that is, the *LM* curve must shift upward and to the left.

A fall in the price level reduces liquidity preference, and the *LM* curve shifts downward and to the right.

Increases in the price level cause the *LM* curve to shift upward and to the left; decreases in the price level cause the LM curve to shift downward and to the right.

However, we know that the effect in the first case is to reduce national income, while the effect in the second case is to increase national income. This is illustrated in Figure 38A-4.

Equilibrium in the money and goods markets combined implies that the price level and national income are negatively related, as summarized in the downward-sloping aggregate demand curve.

The negative relationship between the price level and national income, summarized in the aggregate demand curve, is a straightforward extension of the transmission mechanism, running from liquidity preference to the rate of interest to aggregate expenditure.

Shifts in the Aggregate Demand Curve

The *AD* curve was derived on the basis of a given money supply and given relationships underlying the *IS* curve; it is a straightforward exercise to demonstrate that fiscal and monetary policies, by influencing the *IS* and *LM* curves, cause the *AD* curve to shift. **[48]**

An increase in the money supply means that the *LM* curve corresponding to any particular price level shifts downward and to the right. Hence, that price level now corresponds to a higher level of real na-

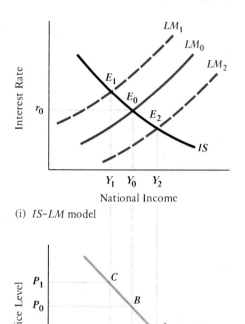

FIGURE 38A-4   Derivation of Aggregate Demand

(i) *IS-LM* model

(ii) Aggregate demand

Changes in the price level shift the *LM* curve and thus change the equilibrium level of income. An increase in the price level increases the demand for money. Alternatively, it can be seen as reducing the real value of the existing money stock. The excess demand for money leads to a leftward shift in the LM_0 curve to LM_1 and a fall in national income. A fall in the price level creates an excess supply of money and a rightward shift in the LM_0 curve to LM_2. The price level and national income are inversely related, as shown by the *AD* curve in part (ii).

tional income; that is, the *AD* curve shifts to the right as a result of an increase in the money supply.

An increase in government expenditure causes the *IS* curve to shift upward and to the right, as before; it now intersects any given *LM* curve at a higher level of national income. Again, any given price level now corresponds to a larger real national income; that is, the *AD* curve shifts to the right as a result of an increase in government expenditure.

10

INTER-
NATIONAL
ECONOMICS

Chapter 39

The Gains from Trade

Americans buy Volkswagens, Germans take holidays in Italy, Italians buy spices from Tanzania, Africans import oil from Kuwait, Arabs buy Japanese cameras, and the Japanese depend heavily on American soybeans as a source of food. *International trade* refers to exchanges of goods and services that take place across international boundaries.

The founders of modern economics were concerned with foreign-trade problems. The great eighteenth century British philosopher and economist David Hume, one of the first to work out the theory of the price system as a control mechanism, developed his concepts mainly in terms of prices in foreign trade. Adam Smith in his *Wealth of Nations* attacked government restriction of trade. David Ricardo in 1817 developed the basic theory of the gains from trade that is studied in this chapter. The repeal of the Corn Laws—tariffs on the importation of grains into Great Britain—and the transformation of that country during the nineteenth century from a country of high tariffs to one of completely free trade were, to a significant extent, the result of agitation by economists whose theories of the gains from trade led them to condemn all tariffs.

In this chapter we explore the fundamental question of what is gained by international trade, while in Chapter 40 we will deal with the pros and cons of interfering with the free flow of such trade.

Sources of the Gains from Trade

The increased output realized as a result of trade is called the **gains from trade.** The source of such gains is most easily visualized by considering the differences between a world with trade and a world without it. Although politicians often regard foreign trade differently from domestic trade, economists from Adam Smith on have argued that the causes and consequences of international trade are simply an extension of the principles governing domestic trade. What is the advantage of trade among individuals, among groups, among regions, or among countries?

Interpersonal, Interregional, and International Trade

Consider trade among individuals. Without trade each person would have to be self-sufficient; each would have to produce all

...on provides important diagrams and captions from the text as reminders of basic economic
...s at a glance. If you need to refresh your memory concerning a principle being shown
...k in the appropriate chapter for a full explanation. The figure number of each diagram
...s the chapter from which it is taken (e.g., Figure 23-4 means the fourth figure in Chapter 23).

FIGURE IN BOX 30-2 The Budget Deficit Function

The actual deficit is negatively related to real national income, but the cyclically adjusted deficit only changes when the stance of fiscal policy changes.

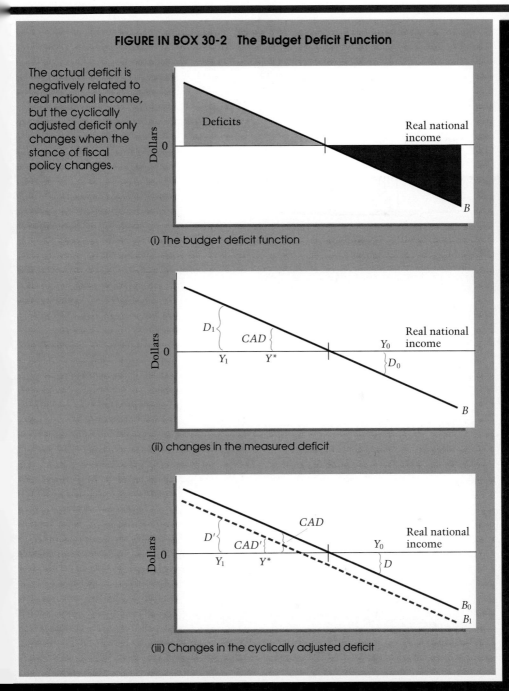

(i) The budget deficit function

(ii) changes in the measured deficit

(iii) Changes in the cyclically adjusted deficit

FIGURE 34-1   Monetary Accommodation of a
              Single Supply Shock

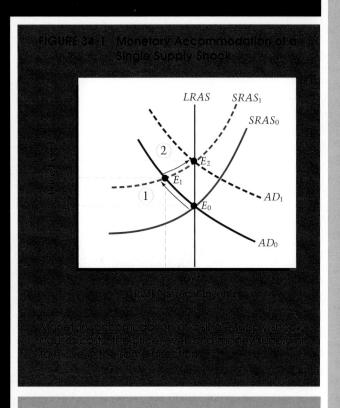

Monetary accommodation of a single supply shock
causes costs, the price level, and money supply all
to move in the same direction.

FIGURE 34-3   An Unvalidated Demand-Shock Inflation

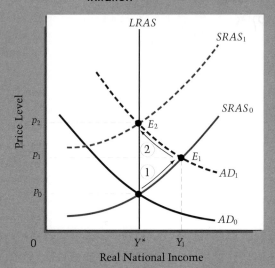

An unvalidated demand shock raises the
equilibrium price level but leaves equilibrium
income unchanged

FIGURE 32-6   The Transmission Mechanism for an Expansionary Monetary Shock

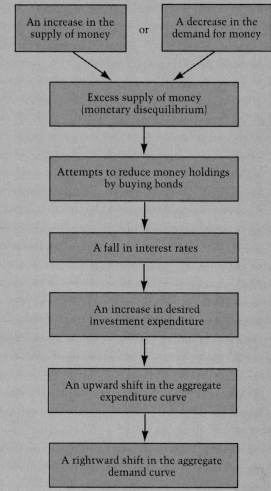

An increase in the supply of money or a decrease
in the demand for money leads to an increase in
aggregate demand. The excess supply of money
following an expansionary monetary disturbance
leads to a fall in the interest rate and an increase
in investment. This causes an upward shift in the *AE*
curve and thus a rightward shift in the *AD* curve.

FIGURE 34-6   Eliminating an Entrenched Inflation

(i) Phase 1: The elimination of an entrenched inflation begins with a demand contraction to remove the inflationary gap. A fully validated inflation is taking the economy along the path that is shown by arrow 1. When the Fed stops expanding the money supply, the economy moves along arrow 2.

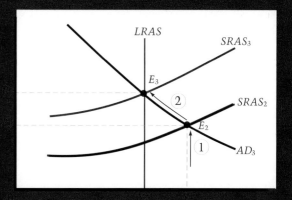

(i) Phase 1: removing the inflationary gap

(ii) Phase 2: Expectations and wage momentum lead to a stagflation, with falling output and continuing inflation. The economy moves along the path that is shown by arrow 3.

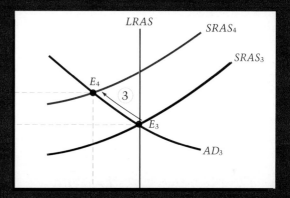

(ii) Phase 3: stagflation

(iii) Phase 3: After expectations are revised, recovery takes income to Y^* and the price level is stabilized. There are two possible scenarios for recovery: either the recessionary gap can be relied on to cause wages to fall (slowly), taking the SRAS curve back to $SRAS_2$, arrow 4; or the Fed can increase the money supply sufficiently to shift the AD curve to AD_4, arrow 5.

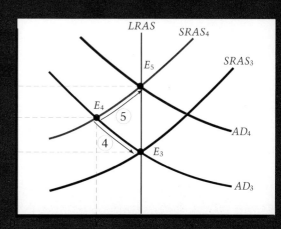

(iii) Phase 3: recovery

FIGURE IN BOX 39-1   The Gains from Trade

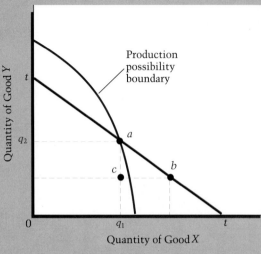

(i) Stage 1: fixed production

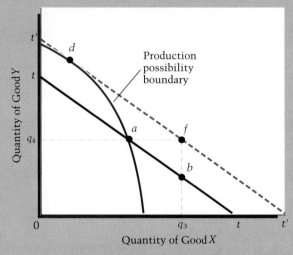

(ii) Stage 2: variable production

International trade makes it possible to trade: (1) either from the *existing production point, a* in part (i), to points beyond the production possibility boundary, such as *b* in part (i), or (2) by altering production to, say, point *d* in part (ii), to make available a set of points totally outside what could be achieved by domestic production, such as point *f* in part (ii).

FIGURE 44-1   Lorenz Curves Showing Inequalities Among the Nations of the World and Within the United States

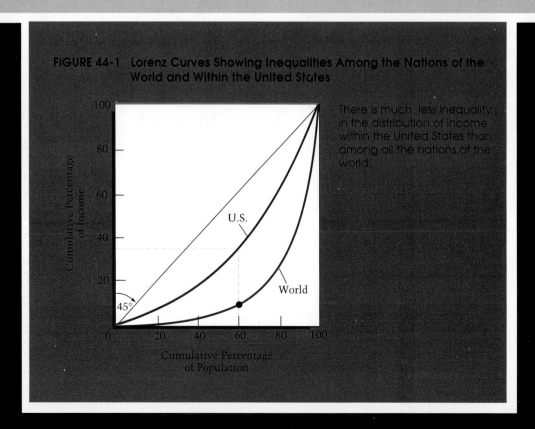

There is much less inequality in the distribution of income within the United States than among all the nations of the world.

the food, clothing, shelter, medical services, entertainment, and luxuries that he or she consumed. A world of individual self-sufficiency would be a world with extremely low living standards.

Trade among individuals allows them to specialize in those activities that they can do well and to buy from others the goods and services that they cannot easily produce. A good doctor who is a bad carpenter can provide medical services, not only for her own family, but also for an excellent carpenter who does not possess either the training or the ability to practice medicine. Thus, trade and specialization are intimately connected. Without trade individuals must be self-sufficient. With trade individuals can specialize in what they do well and satisfy other needs by trading.

The same principles apply to regions. Without interregional trade each region would be forced to be self-sufficient. With trade each region can specialize in producing commodities for which it has some natural or acquired advantage. Plains regions can specialize in growing grain, mountain regions can specialize in mining and forest products, and regions with abundant power can specialize in manufacturing. Cool regions can produce wheat and other crops that thrive in temperate climates, and hot regions can grow such tropical crops as bananas, sugar, and coffee. The living standards of the inhabitants of all regions will be higher when each region specializes in products in which it has some natural or acquired advantage and obtains other products by trade than when all regions seek to be self-sufficient.

The same principle also applies to nations. A national boundary seldom delimits an area that is naturally self-sufficient. Nations, like regions or persons, can gain from specialization and from the international trade that must accompany it. Specialization means that each country produces more of some goods than its residents wish to consume and less of others.

International trade is necessary to achieve the gains that international specialization makes possible.

This discussion suggests one important possible gain from trade:

With trade, each individual, region, or nation is able to concentrate on producing goods and ser-

vices that it produces efficiently, while trading to obtain goods and services that it does not produce.**

Specialization and trade go hand in hand because there is no motivation to achieve the gains from specialization without being able to trade the goods that are produced for goods that are desired. Economists use the term *gains from trade* to embrace the results of both.

We shall examine two sources of the gains from trade. The first source consists of differences among regions of the world in climate and resource endowment that lead to advantages in producing certain goods and disadvantages in producing others. These gains occur even though each country's costs of production are unchanged by the existence of trade. The second source is the reduction in each country's costs of production that results from the greater scale of production that specialization brings.

Gains from Specialization with Given Costs

In order to focus on differences in country's conditions of production, suppose that there are no advantages arising from either economies of large-scale production or cost reductions that are the consequence of learning new skills. In these circumstances what leads to gains from trade? To examine this question, we use an example involving only two countries and two products, but the general principles apply as well to the real-world case of many countries and many commodities.

A Special Case: Absolute Advantage

The gains from trade are clear when there is a simple situation involving absolute advantage. **Absolute advantage** concerns the quantities of a single product that can be produced using the same quantity of resources in two different regions. One region is said to have an absolute advantage over another in the production of commodity X when an equal quantity of resources can produce more X in the first region than in the second.

Suppose region A has an absolute advantage over B in one commodity, while region B has an absolute advantage over A in another. This is a case of *reciprocal absolute advantage:* Each country has an absolute advantage in some commodity. In such a situation, the total production of both regions can be increased (relative to a situation of self-sufficiency) if each specializes in the commodity in which it has the absolute advantage.

Table 39-1 provides a simple example. Total world production of both wheat *and* cloth increases when each country produces more of the good in which it has an absolute advantage. A rise in the production of all commodities entails a rise in average living standards.

The gains from *specialization* make the gains from

TABLE 39-1   Gains from Specialization with Absolute Advantage

Part A: Amounts of wheat and cloth that can be produced with one unit of resources in America and England

	Wheat (bushels)	Cloth (yards)
America	10	6
England	5	10

Part B: Changes resulting from the transfer of one unit of American resources into wheat and one unit of English resources into cloth

	Wheat (bushels)	Cloth (yards)
America	+10	− 6
England	− 5	+10
World	+ 5	+ 4

When there is a reciprocal absolute advantage, specialization makes it possible to produce more of both commodities. Part A shows the production of wheat and cloth that can be achieved in each country by using one unit of resources. America can produce 10 bushels of wheat or 6 yards of cloth; England can produce 5 bushels of wheat or 10 yards of cloth. America has an absolute advantage in producing wheat, and England, in producing cloth. Part B shows the changes in production caused by moving one unit of resources out of cloth and into wheat production in America and moving one unit of resources in the opposite direction in England. There is an increase in world production of 5 bushels of wheat and 4 yards of cloth; worldwide, there are gains from specialization. In this example the more resources are transferred into wheat production in America and cloth production in England, the larger the gains will be.

trade possible. England is producing more cloth and America more wheat than when they were self-sufficient. America is producing more wheat and less cloth than American consumers wish to buy, and England is producing more cloth and less wheat than English consumers wish to buy. If consumers in both countries are to get cloth and wheat in the desired proportions, America must export wheat to England and import cloth from England.

A First General Statement: Comparative Advantage

When each country has an absolute advantage over the other in the production of one commodity, the gains from trade are obvious. What, however, if America can produce both wheat and cloth more efficiently than England? In essence this was David Ricardo's question, posed over 170 years ago. His answer underlies the theory of comparative advantage and is still accepted by economists as a valid statement of the potential gains from trade.

To start with, assume that American efficiency increases tenfold above the levels recorded in the previous example, so that one unit of American resources can produce either 100 bushels of wheat or 60 yards of cloth. English efficiency remains unchanged (see Table 39-2). It might appear that America, which is now better at producing both wheat and cloth than is England, has nothing to gain by trading with such an inefficient foreign country, but it *does* have something to gain, as shown in Table 39-2. Even though America is 10 times as efficient as in the situation of Table 39-1, it is still possible to increase world production of both wheat and cloth by having America produce more wheat and less cloth and by having England produce more cloth and less wheat.

What is the source of this gain? Although America has an absolute advantage over England in the production of both wheat and cloth, the margin of advantage differs in the two commodities. America can produce 20 times as much wheat as England by using the same quantity of resources, but only 6 times as much cloth. America is said to have a **comparative advantage** in the production of wheat and a comparative disadvantage in the production of cloth. (This statement implies another: England has a comparative disadvantage in the production of wheat, in which it is 20 times less efficient than

TABLE 39-2   Gains from Specialization with Comparative Advantage

Part A: Amounts of wheat and cloth that can be produced with one unit of resources in America and England

	Wheat (bushels)	Cloth (yards)
America	100	60
England	5	10

Part B: Changes resulting from the transfer of one-tenth of one unit of American resources into wheat and one unit of English resources into cloth

	Wheat (bushels)	Cloth (yards)
America	+10	− 6
England	− 5	+10
World	+ 5	+ 4

When there is comparative advantage, specialization makes it possible to produce more of both commodities. The productivity of English resources is left unchanged from Table 39-1; that of American resources is increased tenfold. England no longer has an absolute advantage in producing either commodity. Total production of both commodities can nonetheless be increased by specialization. Moving one-tenth of one unit of American resources out of cloth and into wheat and moving one unit of resources in the opposite direction in England causes world production of wheat to rise by 5 bushels and cloth by 4 yards. Reciprocal absolute advantage is not necessary for gains from trade.

America, and a comparative advantage in the production of cloth, in which it is only 6 times less efficient.)

A key proposition in the theory of international trade is:

The gains from specialization and trade depend on the pattern of comparative, not absolute, advantage.

A comparison of Tables 39-1 and 39-2 refutes the notion that the absolute *levels* of efficiency of two areas determine the gains from specialization. The key is that the margin of advantage that one area has over the other must differ between commodities. As long as this margin differs, total world production

can be increased when each area specializes in the production of that commodity in which it has a comparative advantage.

Comparative advantage is necessary, as well as sufficient, for gains from trade. This is illustrated in Table 39-3, which shows a case in which America has an absolute advantage in both commodities while neither country has a comparative advantage over the other in the production of either commodity. America is 10 times as efficient as England in the production of wheat and in the production of cloth. Now, there is no way to increase the production of both wheat and cloth by reallocating resources within America and within England. Part B of the table provides one example of a resource shift that illustrates this.

Absolute advantage without comparative advantage does not lead to gains from trade.

TABLE 39-3   Absence of Gains from Specialization When There Is No Comparative Advantage

Part A: Amounts of wheat and cloth that can be produced with one unit of resources in America and England

	Wheat (bushels)	Cloth (yards)
America	100	60
England	10	6

Part B: Changes resulting from the transfer of 1 unit of American resources into wheat and 10 units of British resources into cloth

	Wheat (bushels)	Cloth (yards)
America	+100	−60
England	−100	+60
World	0	0

Where there is no comparative advantage, no reallocation of resources within each country can increase the production of both commodities. In this example America has the same absolute advantage over England in each commodity (tenfold). There is no comparative advantage, and world production cannot be increased by reallocating resources in both countries. Therefore, specialization does not increase total output.

A Second General Statement: Opportunity Costs

Much of the previous argument uses the concept of a unit of resources. It assumes that units of resources can be equated across countries, so that statements such as "America can produce 10 times as much wheat with the same quantity of resources as England" are meaningful. Measurement of the real resource cost of producing commodities poses many difficulties. If, for example, England uses land, labor, and capital in proportions that are different from those used in America, it may not be clear which country gets more output per unit of resource input. Fortunately, the proposition about the gains from trade can be restated without reference to so fuzzy a concept as units of resources.

To do this, go back to the examples of Tables 39-1 and 39-2. Calculate the *opportunity cost* of wheat and cloth in the two countries. When resources are fully employed, the only way to produce more of one commodity is to reallocate resources and produce less of the other commodity. Table 39-1 shows that one unit of resources in America can produce 10 bushels of wheat *or* 6 yards of cloth. From this it follows that the opportunity cost of producing one unit of wheat is 0.60 units of cloth, whereas the opportunity cost of producing one unit of cloth is 1.67 units of wheat. These data are summarized in Table 39-4. The table also shows that in England the

opportunity cost of one unit of wheat is 2.0 units of cloth foregone, while the opportunity cost of one unit of cloth is 0.50 units of wheat. Table 39-2 also gives rise to the opportunity costs in Table 39-4.

The sacrifice of cloth involved in producing wheat is much lower in America than it is in England. World wheat production can be increased if America rather than England produces it. Looking at cloth production, we can see that the loss of wheat involved in producing one unit of cloth is lower in England than in America. England is the lower (opportunity) cost producer of cloth. World cloth production can be increased if England, rather than America, produces it. This situation is shown in Table 39-5.

The gains from trade arise from differing opportunity costs in the two countries.

The conclusions about the gains from trade arising from international differences may be summarized:

1. Country A has a comparative advantage over country B in producing a commodity when the opportunity cost (in terms of some other commodity) of production in country A is lower. This

TABLE 39-4	Opportunity Cost of Wheat and Cloth in America and England	
	Wheat (bushel)	Cloth (yard)
America	0.60 yards cloth	1.67 bushels wheat
England	2.00 yards cloth	0.50 bushels wheat

Comparative advantages can be expressed in terms of opportunity costs that differ between countries. These opportunity costs can be obtained from Table 39-1 or Table 39-2. The English opportunity cost of one unit of wheat is obtained by dividing the cloth output of one unit of English resources by the wheat output. The result shows that 2 yards of cloth must be sacrificed for every extra unit of wheat produced by transferring English resources out of cloth production and into wheat. The other three cost figures are obtained in a similar manner.

TABLE 39-5	Gains from Specialization with Differing Opportunity Costs	

Changes resulting from each country's producing one more unit of a commodity in which it has the lower opportunity cost

	Wheat (bushels)	Cloth (yards)
America	+1.0	−0.6
England	−0.5	+1.0
World	+0.5	+0.4

Whenever opportunity costs differ between countries, specialization can increase the production of both commodities. These calculations show that there are gains from specialization, given the opportunity costs of Table 39-4. To produce one more bushel of wheat, America must sacrifice 0.6 yards of cloth. To produce one more yard of cloth, England must sacrifice 0.5 bushels of wheat. Making both changes raises world production of both wheat and cloth.

implies, however, that it has a comparative disadvantage in the other commodity.

2. Opportunity costs depend on the relative costs of producing two commodities, not on absolute costs. (Notice that the examples in Tables 39-1 and 39-2 each give rise to the opportunity costs in Table 39-4.)

3. When opportunity costs are the same in all countries, there is no comparative advantage and there is no possibility of gains from specialization and trade. (You can illustrate this for yourself by calculating the opportunity costs implied by the data in Table 39-3.)

4. When opportunity costs differ in any two countries and both countries are producing both commodities, it is always possible to increase production of both commodities by a suitable reallocation of resources within each country. (This proposition is illustrated in Table 39-5.)

Why Opportunity Costs Differ

We have seen that the sources of the gains from trade are comparative advantages, which themselves arise from differences in opportunity costs among nations. Why do different countries have different opportunity costs?

Different factor proportions. The traditional answer to this question was provided early in this century by two Swedish economists, Eli Heckscher and Bertil Ohlin. According to their theory, differences in factor endowments among nations result in different opportunity costs. For example, a country that is well endowed with fertile land but has a small population will find that land is cheap while labor is expensive. It will, therefore, produce land-intensive goods, such as wheat and corn, cheaply and labor-intensive, manufactured goods, such as watches and silicon chips, only at a high cost. The reverse will be true for a second country that is small in size but possessed with abundant and efficient labor. As a result, the first country will have a comparative advantage in land-intensive goods, and the second, in labor-intensive goods. Another country that is unusually well endowed with energy will have low energy prices and will thus have a comparative advantage in energy-intensive goods, such as chemicals and aluminum.

According to the Heckscher-Ohlin theory, countries have comparative advantages in the production of commodities that are intensive in the use of the factors of production with which their endowments are relatively abundant.

This is often called *the factor endowment theory of comparative advantage.* It assumes that all countries have the same production functions, so that equal inputs of factor services produce equal outputs in all countries, but that the supplies of factors, and hence relative factor prices, differ among nations.

Different climates. Modern research suggests that this theory explains much, but not all, of observed comparative advantages. One obvious additional influence comes from all those natural factors that can be called *climate* in the broadest sense. If we combine land, labor, and capital in the same way in Nicaragua and in Iceland, we will not get the same output of most agricultural goods. Sunshine, rainfall, and average temperature also matter. If we seek to work with wool or cotton in dry and damp climates, we will get different results. (We can, of course, artificially create any climate that we wish in a factory, but it costs money to create what is freely provided elsewhere.)

Climate, **interpreted in the broadest sense, undoubtedly affects comparative advantage.**

This explanation assumes that climatic conditions cause nations to have different production functions, so that the same inputs of factor services will produce different outputs in different climates. Countries will tend to have comparative advantages in goods for whose production their climates are particularly favorable.

Gains from Specialization with Variable Costs

So far we have assumed that unit costs are the same, whatever the scale of output, and have seen that there are gains from specialization and trade, as long as there are interregional differences in opportunity costs. If costs vary with the level of output or as experience is acquired via specialization, *additional* sources of gain are possible.

Economies of Scale[1]

Over some range of outputs, average costs of production usually fall as the scale of output increases. The larger is the scale of operations, the more efficiently large-scale machinery can be used and the more a detailed division of tasks among workers is possible. Smaller countries such as Canada, France, and Israel, whose domestic markets are not large enough to exploit all available economies of scale, would find it prohibitively expensive to become self-sufficient. They would have to produce a little bit of everything at very high cost.

Trade allows smaller countries to specialize in producing a few commodities at high enough levels of output that they will reap the available economies of scale.

Bigger countries such as the United States and the USSR have markets that are large enough to allow the production of most items at home at a scale of output that is great enough to obtain the available economies of scale. For them the gains from international trade arise mainly from specializing in commodities in which they have a comparative advantage. Yet, even for such countries, a broadening of their markets permits achieving economies of scale in subproduct lines, such as specialty steels or blue jeans.

The importance of product diversity and specialization in specific subproduct lines has been one of the important lessons that were learned from changing patterns of world trade since World War II. When the European Common Market (now called the European Community) was set up in the 1950s, economists expected that specialization would occur according to the classical theory of comparative advantage, with one country specializing in cars, another in refrigerators, another in fashion clothes, another in shoes, and so on. This is not the way it has worked out. Today one can buy French, English, Italian, and German fashion goods, cars, shoes, appliances, and a host of other goods in London, Paris, Bonn, and Rome. Ships loaded with Swedish furniture bound for London pass ships loaded with English furniture bound for Stockholm, and so on.

What European free trade did was to allow a proliferation of differentiated products, with different countries each specializing in different subproduct lines. Consumers have shown by their expenditures that they value this enormous increase in the range of choice among differentiated products. As Asian countries have expanded into American markets with textiles, cars, and electronic goods, American manufacturers have increasingly specialized their production, and we now export textiles, cars, and electronics equipment to Japan, while importing similar products from Japan.

Learning by Doing

The discussion so far has assumed that costs vary only with the *level* of output. They may also vary with the length of time that a product has been produced.

Early economists placed great importance on a phenomenon that we now call *learning by doing*. They believed that, as countries gained experience in particular tasks, workers and managers would become more efficient in performing them. As people acquire expertise, costs tend to fall. There is substantial evidence that such learning by doing does occur.

The distinction between this phenomenon and the gains from economies of scale is illustrated in Figure 36-1; it is one more example of the difference between a movement along a curve and a shift of a curve.

Recognition of the opportunities for learning by doing leads to an important implication: Policymakers need not accept *current* comparative advantages as given. Through such means as education and tax incentives, they can seek to develop new comparative advantages.[2] Moreover, countries cannot complacently assume that an existing comparative advantage will persist. Misguided education policies, the wrong tax incentives, or policies that discourage risk taking can lead to the rapid erosion of a country's comparative advantage in a particular product. So, too, can competitive developments elsewhere in the world.

A changing view of comparative advantage.   The classical theory of the gains from trade, which still has

---

[1] These are discussed in detail in Chapter 11. The classic discussion of this effect is quoted in Box 3–1 on page 43.

[2] Of course, they might foolishly use the same policies to develop industries in which they do not have, and will never achieve, comparative advantage. See the discussion in Chapter 40.

many adherents, assumes that there are given cost structures, based largely on a country's natural endowments. This leads to a given pattern of international comparative advantage. It leads to the policy advice that a government, interested in maximizing its citizens' material standard of living, should encourage production to be specialized in those goods in which it currently has a comparative advantage. When all countries follow this advice, the theory predicts that each will be specialized in a relatively narrow range of distinct products. Canadians will be farmers and producers of resource-based products, Americans will be factory workers and farmers, Central Americans will be banana growers and clothing manufacturers, and so on.

There is today a competing view. In extreme form it says that comparative advantages certainly exist but are typically acquired, not nature-given—and they change. This view of comparative advantage is *dynamic* rather than static. New industries are seen as depending more on human capital than on fixed physical capital or natural resources. The skills of a computer designer, a videogame programmer, a sound mix technician, or a rock star are acquired by education and on-the-job training. Natural endowments of energy and raw materials cannot account for Britain's prominence in modern pop music, the United States' leadership in ideas of Silicon Valley in California, or the Japanese success in the silicon-chip industry. When a country such as the United States finds its former dominance (based on comparative advantage) declining in such smokestack industries as automobiles and steel, its firms need not sit idly by. Instead, they can begin to adapt by developing new areas of comparative advantage.

There are surely elements of truth in both extreme views. It would be unwise to neglect resource endowments, climate, culture, and social and institutional arrangements. However, it also would be unwise to assume that all sources of comparative advantage are innate and immutable.

To some extent these views are reconciled in the theory of human capital that we discussed in Chapter 19. Comparative advantages that depend on human capital are consistent with the traditional Heckscher-Ohlin theory. The difference is that this type of capital is acquired by making conscious decisions relating to such matters as education and technical training.

The Terms of Trade

So far we have seen that world production can be increased when countries specialize in the production of the commodities in which they have or can acquire a comparative advantage and then trade with one another. We now ask: How will these gains from specialization and trade be shared among countries? The division of the gain depends on the terms under which trade takes place. The **terms of trade** measure the quantity of imported goods that can be obtained per unit of goods exported and are measured by the ratio of the price of exports to the price of imports.

A rise in the price of imported goods, with the price of exports remaining unchanged, indicates a *fall in the terms of trade;* it will now take more exports to buy the same quantity of imports. Similarly, a rise in the price of exported goods, with the price of imports remaining unchanged, indicates a *rise in the terms of trade;* it will now take fewer exports to buy the same quantity of imports. Thus, the ratio of prices is a measure of the amount of exported goods that are needed to acquire a given quantity of imports.

In the example of Table 39-4, the American domestic opportunity cost of one unit of cloth is 1.67 bushels of wheat. In other words, if in America resources are transferred from wheat to cloth, 1.67 bushels of wheat are given up for every 1 yard of cloth gained. However, if America can obtain its cloth by trade on more favorable terms, it is worthwhile for America to produce and export wheat to pay for cloth imports. Suppose, for example, that international prices are such that 1 yard of cloth exchanges for (i.e., is equal in value to) 1 bushel of wheat. At these prices, Americans can obtain 1 yard of cloth for 1 bushel of wheat exported. They get more cloth per unit of wheat exported than they can by moving resources out of wheat into cloth production at home. Therefore, the terms of trade favor specializing in the production of wheat and trading it for cloth in international markets.

Similarly, in the example of Table 39-4, English consumers gain when they can obtain wheat abroad at any terms of trade that are more favorable than 2

BOX 39-1

The Gains from Trade Illustrated Graphically

International trade leads to an expansion of the set of goods that can be consumed in the economy in two ways: by allowing the bundle of goods consumed to differ from the bundle produced and by permitting a profitable change in the pattern of production. The key to these gains is that international trade allows the separation of production decisions from consumption decisions. Without international trade, the choice of which bundle of goods to produce would be the same as the choice of which bundle to consume. With international trade, the consumption and production bundles can be altered independently to reflect the relative value placed on goods by international markets.

This proposition is illustrated graphically below for a simplified world in which there are only two goods, X and Y. The illustration is in two stages.

Stage 1: Fixed Production

In each part of the figure, the black curve is the economy's production possibility boundary (such a boundary was first introduced in Figure 1-2, page 6).

If there is no international trade, the economy must consume the same bundle of goods that it produces. Thus, the production possibility boundary is also the consumption possibility boundary. Suppose that the economy produces and consumes at point a, with q_1 of good X and q_2 of good Y, as in part (i) of the figure.

Next, suppose that while production stays at point a, good Y can be exchanged for good X in international markets. The consumption possibilities are now enhanced, as is shown by the line tt drawn through point a. The slope of this line indicates the world terms of trade and reflects the quantity of good Y that can be exchanged for a unit of good X in the international market.

Although production is fixed at a, consumption can now be anywhere on the line tt to the right of a. For example, the consumption point could be at b. This could be achieved by exporting ac units of good Y and importing cb units of good X. Since point b (and all others on line tt to the right of a) lies outside the production possibility boundary, there are potential gains from trade. Consumers are no longer limited by *their* country's production possibilities. Suppose that consumers prefer point b to point a. They have achieved a gain from trade by being allowed to exchange some of their production of good Y for some quantity of good X and thus to consume more of good X than is produced at home.

Stage 2: Variable Production

In stage 1 production was constant at a. An additional opportunity for the expansion of the country's consumption possibilities arises because, with trade, the production bundle may be profitably altered in response to international prices. The coun-

---

yards of cloth per unit of wheat. If the terms of trade permit exchange of 1 bushel of wheat for 1 yard of cloth, the terms of trade favor English traders' buying wheat and selling cloth in international markets. Here, both England and America gain from trade. Each can obtain the commodity in which it has a comparative disadvantage at a lower opportunity cost through international trade than through domestic production. How the terms of trade affect the

gains from trade is shown graphically in Box 39-1.

Because actual international trade involves many countries and many commodities, a country's terms of trade are computed as an index number:

$$\text{Terms of trade} = \frac{\text{index of export prices}}{\text{index of import prices}} \times 100$$

A rise in the index is referred to as a *favorable* change in a country's terms of trade. A favorable change

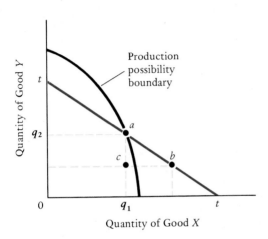

(i) Stage 1: fixed production

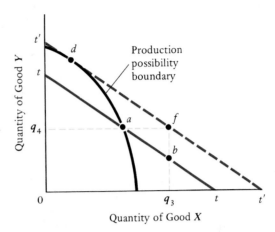

(ii) Stage 2: variable production

try may produce the bundle of goods that is most valuable in world markets, which is represented by the bundle *d* in part (ii) of the figure. The consumption possibility set is shifted to the line *t't'* by changing production from *a* to *d* and thereby increasing the country's degree of specialization in good Y. For every point on the original consumption possibility set, *tt*, there are points on the new set, *t't'*, which allow more consumption of both goods. Compare, for example, points *a* and *f*. Notice also that, except at the zero-trade point, *d*, the new consumption possibility set lies everywhere above the production possibility curve.

Many consumption bundles that cannot be produced domestically are made available by trade. The benefits from moving from a no-trade position, such as *a*, to a trading position, such as *b* or *f*, are the *gains from trade* to the country. When the production of good Y was increased and the production of good X was decreased, the country was able to move to point *f* by producing more of good Y, in which the country has a comparative advantage, and by trading the additional production for good X. Economists refer to such production changes as "exploiting the country's comparative advantage."

means that more can be imported per unit of goods exported than previously. For example, if the export price index rises from 100 to 120, while the import price index rises from 100 to 110, the terms-of-trade index rises from 100 to 109. At the new terms of trade, a unit of exports will buy 9 percent more imports than at the old terms.

A decrease in the index of the terms of trade, called an *unfavorable* change, means that the country

can import less in return for any given amount of exports or, what is the same, that it must export more to pay for any given amount of imports. For example, the sharp rise in oil prices in the 1970s led to large, unfavorable shifts in the terms of trade of oil-importing countries, including the United States. When oil prices fell sharply in the mid-1980s, the terms of trade of oil-importing countries changed favorably.

SUMMARY

1. One country (or region or individual) has an absolute advantage over another country (or region or individual) in the production of a commodity when, with the same input of resources in each country, it can produce more of the commodity than can the other.

2. In a situation of absolute advantage, total production of both commodities will be raised if each country specializes in the production of the commodity in which it has the absolute advantage. However, the gains from trade do not require absolute advantage on the part of each country, only comparative advantage.

3. Comparative advantage is the relative advantage that one country enjoys over another in production of various commodities. World production of all commodities can be increased if each country transfers resources into the production of the commodities in which it has a comparative advantage.

4. Comparative advantage arises from countries' having different opportunity costs of producing particular goods. This creates the opportunity for all nations to gain from trade.

5. The most important proposition in the theory of the gains from trade is: Trade allows all countries to obtain the goods in which they do not have a comparative advantage at a lower opportunity cost than they would face if they were to produce all commodities for themselves. This allows all countries to have more of all commodities than they could have if they tried to be self-sufficient.

6. As well as gaining the advantages of specialization arising from comparative advantage, a nation that engages in trade and specialization may realize the benefits of the economies of large-scale production and of learning by doing.

7. Classical theory regarded comparative advantage as largely determined by natural-resource endowments and climatic factors and thus as difficult to change. Economists now believe that comparative advantage can be acquired and thus can be changed. A country may, in this view, seek to influence its role in world production and trade.

8. The terms of trade refer to the ratio of the prices of goods exported to the prices of goods imported, which determines the quantities of exports needed to pay for imports. The terms of trade determine how the gains from trade are shared. A favorable change in terms of trade, that is, a rise in export prices relative to import prices, means that a country can acquire more imports per unit of exports.

TOPICS FOR REVIEW

Interpersonal, interregional, and international specialization
Absolute advantage and comparative advantage
Gains from trade: specialization, scale economies, and learning by doing
Opportunity cost and comparative advantage
Dynamic comparative advantage
Terms of trade

DISCUSSION QUESTIONS

1. Adam Smith saw a close connection between the wealth of a nation and its willingness "freely to engage" in foreign trade. What is the connection?

2. Suppose that the situation described in the following table exists. Assume that there are no tariffs and no government intervention and that labor is the only factor of production. Let X take different values,

say, $10, $20, $30, and $40. In each case in what direction will trade have to flow in order for the gains from trade to be exploited?

	Labor cost of producing one unit of	
Country	Artichokes	Bikinis
Inland	$20	$40
Outland	$15	$X

3. Suppose that the United States had an absolute advantage in all manufactured products. Should it then ever import any manufactured products?

4. Suppose that, after 1865, the United States had become two separate countries with no trade between them. What predictions would you make about the standard of living, compared with what it is today? Does the fact that Canada, the United States, and Mexico are separate countries lead to a lower standard of living in the three countries than if they were united into a new country called Northica?

5. Studies of U.S. trade patterns have shown that very high wage sectors of industry are among the largest and fastest growing export sectors. Does this contradict the principle of comparative advantage?

6. Throughout the 1980s Americans became increasingly concerned with their alleged lack of international competitiveness. Discuss the affect on (i) the volume of U.S. exports and imports, (ii) the kinds of goods exported and imported, and (iii) U.S. living standards for each of the following occurrences.
   a. The rate of U.S. productivity growth falls dramatically and equally in all industries.
   b. The rate of U.S. productivity growth falls to zero in those manufactured goods that the United States now exports but rises to high levels in those manufactured goods that the United States now imports.

7. Predict what each of the following events would do to the terms of trade of the importing country and the exporting country, other things being equal.
   a. A blight destroys a good part of the coffee beans that are produced in the world.
   b. The Japanese cut the price of the steel that they sell to the United States.
   c. A general inflation of 10 percent occurs around the world.
   d. A local inflation of 10 percent occurs in the United States, while inflation remains much lower in all other industrialized countries.
   e. Violation of OPEC output quotas leads to a sharp fall in the price of oil.

8. Heavy U.S. borrowing abroad in the early 1980s led to a high value of the dollar and thus a rise in the ratio of export prices to import prices. While this is called a favorable change in the terms of trade, are there any reasons why it may not have been a good thing for the U.S. economy?

9. Businesspersons often worry that, if their country's inflation rate exceeds the rates ruling in their major trading partners', they will be priced out of foreign markets; they worry that exports will then dwindle away, while imports of ever more competitive, foreign goods will boom. Is this worry well founded?

Chapter 40

Barriers to Free Trade

Conducting business in a foreign country is always difficult. Differences in language, in local laws and customs, and in currency all complicate transactions. Our concern in this chapter is not, however, with these difficulties but with the government's policy toward international trade, which is called its **commercial policy.** At one extreme is a policy of **free trade**, which means an absence of any form of government interference with the free flow of international trade. **Protectionism** refers to any departure from free trade designed to give some protection to domestic industries from foreign competition.

The Theory of Commercial Policy

Today debates over commercial policy are as heated as they were 200 years ago, when the theory of the gains from trade was still being worked out. Should a country permit the free flow of international trade, or should it seek to protect its local producers from foreign competition? Such protection may be achieved either by **tariffs,** which are taxes designed to raise the prices of foreign goods, or by **nontariff barriers,** which are devices other than tariffs designed to reduce the flow of imported goods. Examples include quotas and customs procedures that are deliberately made more cumbersome than necessary.

The Case for Free Trade

The case for free trade is based on the analysis presented in Chapter 39, in which we saw that, whenever opportunity costs differ among countries, specialization and trade will raise world living standards. Free trade allows all countries to specialize in producing commodities in which they have a comparative advantage.

Free trade allows the maximization of world production, thus making it *possible* for every household in the world to consume more goods than it could without free trade.

This does not necessarily mean that everyone *will* be better off with free trade than without it. Protectionism could allow the citizens of some countries to obtain a larger share of a smaller world output, so that they would benefit even though on average everyone would lose. If we ask whether it is *possible* for free trade to be advantageous to everyone, the answer is yes. But if we ask whether free trade is, in fact, *always* advantageous to everyone, the answer is not necessarily.

There is abundant evidence to show that significant differences in opportunity costs exist and that large gains are realized from international trade because of these differences. What needs explanation is the fact that trade is not wholly free. Why do tariffs and nontariff barriers to trade continue to exist two centuries after Adam Smith and David Ricardo stated the case for free trade? Is there a valid case for protectionism? Before addressing these questions, let us examine the methods that are used in protectionist policy.

Methods of Protection

The two main types of protectionist policy are illustrated in Figure 40-1. Both cause the price of the

FIGURE 40-1   Methods of Protecting Domestic Producers

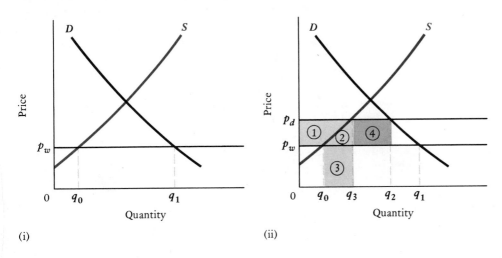

(i)   (ii)

The same reduction in imports and increase in domestic production can be achieved by using either a tariff or a quantity restriction. In both parts of the figure, D and S are the domestic demand and supply curves, respectively, and p_w is the world price of some commodity that is both produced at home and imported. Domestic consumption is q_1, domestic production is q_0, while imports are $q_0 q_1$.

Part (i) of the figure shows the situation under free trade. Part (ii) shows what happens when protectionist policies restrict imports to the amount $q_3 q_2$. When this is done by levying a tariff of T per unit, the price in the domestic market rises by the full amount of the tariff to p_d. Consumers reduce consumption from q_1 to q_2 and pay an extra amount, shown by the shaded areas 1, 2, and 4, for the q_2 that they now purchase. Domestic production rises from q_0 to q_3. Since domestic producers receive the domestic price, their receipts rise by the three light shaded areas, labeled 1, 2, and 3. Area 3 is revenue that was earned by foreign producers under free trade, while areas 1 and 2 are paid by domestic consumers because of the higher prices that they must now pay. Foreign suppliers of the imported good continue to get the world price, so the government receives as tariff revenue the extra amount paid by consumers for the $q_3 q_2$ units that are still imported (shown by the dark shaded area 4).

When the same result is accomplished by a quantity restriction, the government—either through a quota or *voluntary export agreement* (VER)—reduces imports to $q_3 q_2$. This drives the domestic market price up to p_d and has the same effect on domestic producers and consumers as did the tariff. Since the government has merely restricted the quantity of imports, both foreign and domestic suppliers get the higher price in the domestic market. Thus, foreign suppliers now receive the extra amount paid by domestic consumers (represented by the shaded area labeled 4) for the units that are still imported.

BOX 40-1

The Efficiency Effects of Import Restrictions

Students who have studied consumers' and producers' surplus in microeconomics can use these tools to study the efficiency effects of restrictions placed on imports. Others should omit this box.

The figures below reproduce the two parts of Figure 40-1, except that some different areas are shaded (where common areas are shaded, they are given the same numbers). Part (i) shows the situation under free trade, with the consumers' surplus shaded in darkly and the producers' surplus, accruing to *domestic* producers, shaded in lightly. (The white area below the S curve between 0 and q_0 is revenue to cover the variable costs of domestic producers, and the white area between q_0 and q_1 is revenue of foreign producers.)

Part (ii) shows the situation after the restriction of imports has occurred. The shaded areas, labeled 1, 2, 4, and 5, are consumers' surplus, lost by domestic consumers. The light shaded area 1 is gained as producers' surplus by domestic producers. The

dark shaded area 2 goes to pay direct costs of production on the extra amount, q_3q_0, produced at home. This represents inefficient production, since these units could have been obtained abroad at a cost that was lower by the amount indicated by area 2. The light shaded area 4 goes to the government as tariff revenue on the imports, in the case of a tariff, and to foreign producers as extra revenue, in the case of a quantity restriction. The dark shaded area 5 is gained by no one. It is lost consumers' surplus on the units no longer consumed, and, since they are not produced, there is no one to gain that surplus.

The term *deadweight loss* (of the tariff or quantity restriction) refers to the sum of the two dark shaded areas: area 5, which measures the surplus that is lost by consumers and not gained by anyone else, and area 2, which measures the unnecessary cost incurred by producing at home rather than buying abroad.

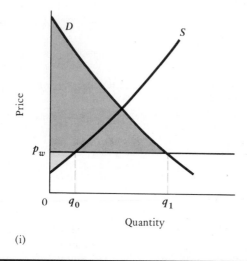

(i)

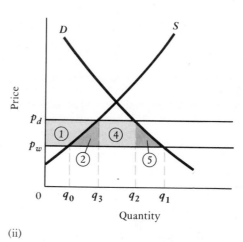

(ii)

imported good to rise and its quantity to fall. They differ, however, in how they achieve these results. The caption to Figure 40-1 analyzes the general effects of these policies, while Box 40-1 analyzes the

specific effects of these policies on economic efficiency. (The Box 40-1 is accessible, however, only to those who have studied consumers' and producers' surplus.)

Policies That Initially Raise Price

The first type of protectionist policy initially raises the *price* of the imported commodity. A tariff, also often called an *import duty,* is the most common policy of this type. Other such policies are any rules or regulations that fulfill three conditions: They are costly to comply with; they do not apply to competing, domestically produced commodities; and they are more than is required to meet any purpose other than restricting trade.

Tariffs come in two main forms: **specific tariffs,** which are levied as a specific amount of money on *each unit* of the product, and **ad valorem tariffs,** which are levied as *a percentage of the price* of the product. Tariffs raise revenues, as well as provide protection. For some less-developed countries, which have limited sources of revenue, tariffs can be an important revenue source. For developed countries, such as the United States, the revenue-raising function is relatively unimportant.

As shown in part (i) of Figure 40-1, tariffs affect both foreign and domestic producers, as well as domestic consumers. The initial effect is to raise the domestic price of the imported commodity above its world price by the amount of the tariff. Imports fall, and, as a result, foreign producers sell less and so must transfer resources to other lines of production. The price received on domestically produced units rises, as does the quantity produced domestically. On both counts domestic producers earn more. However, the extra production is achieved at a cost that is higher than the price at which the commodity could be purchased on the world market. Thus, the benefits to domestic producers come at the expense of domestic consumers, who must pay the extra cost of production in terms of higher prices. Indeed, domestic consumers lose on two counts: First, they consume less of the product because its price rises, and, second, they pay a higher price for the amount that they do continue to consume. This extra spending ends up in two places. The extra that is paid on all units produced at home goes to domestic producers, while the extra that is paid on units still imported goes to the government as tariff revenue.

Policies That Initially Lower Quantities

The second type of protectionist policy initially restricts the *quantity* of the imported commodity. A common example is the **import quota,** by which the importing country sets a maximum of the quantity of some commodity that may be imported each year. Increasingly popular, however, is the **voluntary export restriction (VER),** an agreement by an exporting country to limit the amount of a good that it sells to the importing country.

The European Community (EC) and the United States have used VERs extensively, while the EC also makes frequent use of import quotas. Japan has been pressured into negotiating several VERs with the EC and the United States in order to limit sales of some of the Japanese goods that have had the most success in international competition. For example, in 1983 the United States and Canada negotiated VERs, whereby the Japanese government agreed to restrict total sales of Japanese cars to these two countries for three years. When the agreements ran out in 1986, the Japanese continued to restrain their automobile sales by unilateral voluntary action. This episode is further considered in Box 40-2.

As shown in part (ii) of Figure 40-1, a quantity restriction of the appropriate size can have the same effects as a tariff on the domestic price and the quantities produced and consumed domestically. This means that its effects on domestic consumers and producers are the same as a tariff that has the equivalent effect in limiting imports. The major difference is in who gets the additional money that domestic consumers pay for the quantities that are still imported. When the government levies a tariff, it gets the revenue. When the government imposes (or negotiates) an import restriction, the same sum of money is transferred as additional revenue to foreign producers. This is because the quantity restriction drives up the domestic price and all of the extra amount that purchasers pay for the imported units of the commodity go to the foreign suppliers.[1]

In addition to devices that are designed to restrict imports for protectionist purposes, there is also a series of devices that are designed to prevent what are called "unfair trade practices" by foreign firms or governments. The two most common of these

---

[1] There is a third type of protectionist policy that reduces imports. This consists of anything that reduces the overall market demand for a commodity that is an imported commodity. For example, the subsidization of a domestically produced substitute product will cause a leftward shift of the product's market demand curve and thus will lower imports. Since the domestic price and the level of domestic production remain unchanged in this case, the policy is not useful as a device for protecting domestic producers; it merely works to lower imports and to raise government tariff revenue from domestic consumers who pay the tariff.

BOX 40-2

Import Restrictions on Japanese Cars: Tariffs or Quotas?

In the early 1980s, imports of Japanese cars seriously threatened the automobile industries of the United States, Canada, and Western Europe. While continuing to espouse relatively free trade as a long-term policy, the American and Canadian governments argued that the domestic industry needed short-term protection. This protection was needed in order to tide it over the period of transition that it faced as smaller cars became the typical North American household's vehicle. Once the enormous investment needed to transform the North American automobile industry had been made and new models had gained acceptance, it was hoped that free trade could be restored and the North American industry could be asked to stand up to foreign competition.

How was this protection to be achieved? Voluntary export restrictions (VERs) seemed the easiest route. An agreement was reached whereby the Japanese government agreed to limit severely the number of Japanese cars that could be exported to the U.S. and Canada.

What does price theory predict to be the economic difference between VERs and tariffs? In both cases imports are restricted and the resulting scarcity supports a higher market price. With a tariff the extra market value is appropriated by the government of the importing country—in this case the U.S. government. With a VER the extra market value accrues to the goods' suppliers—in this case the Japanese car makers and their American retailers.

Both cases are illustrated in the figure. We assume that the U.S. market provides a small enough part of total Japanese car sales to leave the Japanese willing to supply all the cars that are demanded in the United States at their fixed list price. This is the price P_0 in both parts of the figure. Given the American demand curve for Japanese cars, D, there are q_0 cars sold before restrictions are imposed.

In part (i) the United States places a tariff of T per unit on Japanese cars, raising their price in the United States to p_1 and lowering sales to q_1. Suppliers' revenue is shown by the light shaded area. U.S. government tariff revenue is shown by the dark shaded area.

In part (ii) a VER of q_1 is imposed, making the supply curve vertical at q_1. The market-clearing price is p_1. The suppliers' revenue is the whole shaded area (p_1 times q_1).

In both cases the shortage of Japanese cars drives up their price, creating a substantial margin over costs. Under a tariff the U.S. government captures the margin. Under a VER policy, however, the margin accrues to the Japanese manufacturers.

Although this is a simplified picture, it captures the essence of what actually happened. First, while sellers of North American cars were keeping prices

---

are *antidumping duties* and *countervailing duties.* Laws relating to these measures are often called **fair-trade laws** or **trade-remedy laws.** Although they are not intended as tools of protectionism, they can be used as such. For this reason they must be listed as potential protectionist devices. They are considered later in this chapter.

Nominal and Effective Rates of Tariff

The rate of tariff charged on each imported commodity, called the **nominal rate of tariff,** does not necessarily show the degree of protection given to that commodity. Nominal rates of tariff frequently understate the degree of protection offered to do-

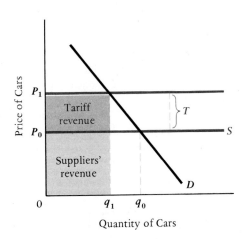

(i) Tariff of T dollars per car

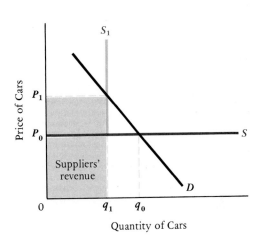

(ii) Quota of q_1 cars

as low as possible and sometimes offering rebates on slow-selling models, Japanese cars were listed at healthy profit margins. Second, while it was always possible for the buyer of a North American car to negotiate a good discount off the list price, Japanese cars usually sold for their full list price. Third, since Japanese manufacturers were not allowed to supply all of the cars that they could sell in the United States, they had to choose which types of cars to supply. Not surprisingly, they tended to satisfy fully the demand for their more expensive cars, which have larger profit margins, and to restrict

exports of the less expensive cars, which have lower profit margins. This change in the "product mix" of Japanese cars exported to the United States raised the average profit per car exported. The VERs were thus very costly to North American consumers and an enormous profit boon to Japanese car manufacturers. Indeed, it was estimated that North American consumers paid about $150,000 per year for each job that was saved in the U.S. and Canadian car industry and that most of this went to Japanese producers.

mestic manufacturing industries, and a better measure is provided by what is called the *effective tariff rate*.

The distinction between nominal and effective rates of tariff arises whenever imported raw materials or semifinished goods carry a lower rate of duty than imports of the final manufactured goods that em-

body these intermediate products. When the final good is made abroad, the duty for manufactured goods is applied to the entire price of that good, even though the price includes the values of the raw materials and semifinished goods that it embodies. When the final good is produced domestically, the raw materials and semifinished goods enter at the lower rate of tariff. For this reason a tariff of, say, 10 percent on the final good will protect a domestic producer that is much more than 10 percent less efficient than its foreign competitor.

To illustrate this important point, consider an example. A product, using a Canadian raw material, is manufactured in both Canada and the United States. Assume that the raw material enters the United States duty free but that the manufactured good is subject to a 10 percent tariff. Further assume that, when the product is manufactured in Canada, the raw material accounts for one-half the cost of the final product and the other one-half is value added by the Canadian manufacturer. Because of the 10 percent tariff, one unit of output that costs $1.00 to produce in Canada—$.50 for raw materials and $.50 for manufacturing cost—will sell in the United States for $1.10.

Now consider the position of a U.S. manufacturer that in this particular industry is less efficient than the Canadian manufacturer. (If the U.S. producer were not less efficient, there would be no need for protection.) Let the U.S. firm's production costs be 20 percent higher than those of the Canadian firm. Thus, to produce one unit of output, the raw material costs the U.S. firm $.50, but its other costs—including the opportunity costs of its capital—are $.60 (i.e., 20 percent higher than the Canadian manufacturer's costs of $.50). This gives the U.S. firm a final price of $1.10, which is just low enough to compete against the tariff-burdened Canadian import.

In this example, a tariff of 10 percent on the value of the final product is sufficient to protect a U.S. firm that is 20 percent less efficient than its Canadian competitor. To measure this effect, the **effective rate of tariff** expresses the tariff as a percentage of the *value added* by the exporting industry in question. Thus, the effective American rate of tariff on the Canadian manufacturing industry in the example is 20 percent, whereas the nominal tariff on manufactured goods is only 10 percent.

The Case for Protectionism

Two kinds of arguments for protection are commonly offered. The first concerns national objectives other than national income; the second concerns the desire to increase domestic national income, possibly at the expense of total world income.

Objectives Other Than Maximizing National Income

It is quite possible to accept the proposition that national income is higher with free trade and yet rationally to oppose free trade because of a concern with policy objectives other than maximizing per capita national income. For example, comparative advantage might dictate that a country should specialize in producing a narrow range of commodities. The government might decide, however, that there are distinct social advantages to encouraging a more diverse economy. Citizens would be given a wider range of occupations, and the social and psychological advantages of diversification would more than compensate for a reduction in living standards by, say, 5 percent below what they could be with specialization of production according to comparative advantage.

For a very small country, specializing in the production of only a few commodities—though dictated by comparative advantage—may involve risks that the country does not wish to take. One such risk is that technological advances may render its basic product obsolete. Everyone understands this risk, but there is debate about what governments can do about it. The pro-tariff argument is that the government can encourage a more diversified economy by protecting industries that otherwise could not compete. Opponents argue that governments, being naturally influenced by political motives, are, in the final analysis, poor judges of which industries can be protected in order to produce diversification at a reasonable cost.

Another risk is that cyclical fluctuations in the prices of basic commodities may cause a country to face depressed prices for years at a time and then enjoy periods of very high prices. The national income of a country that specializes in the production of such commodities will be subject to wide fluctuations. Even though the average income level over a long period of time might be higher if specialization in the production of a few basic commodities were allowed, the serious social problems associated with a widely fluctuating national income may make the government decide to sacrifice some income in order to reduce fluctuations. The government might use protectionist policies to encourage the expansion of several less cyclically sensitive industries.

Another noneconomic reason for protectionism

concerns national defense. It is sometimes argued, for example, that the United States needs an experienced merchant marine in case of war and that this industry should be fostered by protectionist policies, even though it is less efficient than that of the foreign compatititon. The Jones Act provides this protection by requiring that all cargoes moving between two U.S. ports be carried in U.S. ships. In the past (before the first OPEC shock), national defense was also used as a reason for protecting domestic oil producers. Imports of foreign oil were restricted on the grounds that national defense required a domestic oil industry of at least a certain minimum size.

Although most people would agree that, other things being equal, they would prefer more income to less, a nation may rationally choose to sacrifice some income in order to achieve other goals. Economists can do three things when they are faced with such reasons for imposing tariffs. First, they can see if the proposed tariff really does achieve the goals suggested. Second, they can calculate the cost of the tariff in terms of lowered living standards. Third, they can check policy alternatives to see if there are other means of achieving the stated goal at a lower cost in terms of lost output.

The Objective of Maximizing National Income

Next we consider five important arguments for the use of tariffs when the objective is to make national income as large as possible.

To alter the terms of trade. Trade restrictions can sometimes be used to turn the terms of trade in favor of countries that produce and export a large fraction of the world's supply of some commodity. They can also be used to turn the terms of trade in favor of countries that constitute a large fraction of the world demand for some commodity that they import.

When the OPEC countries restricted their output of oil in the 1970s, they were able to drive the price of oil up relative to the prices of other traded goods. This turned the terms of trade in their favor; for every barrel of oil exported, they were able to obtain a larger quantity of imports. When the output of oil grew greatly in the mid-1980s, the relative price of oil fell dramatically, and the terms of trade turned unfavorably to the oil-exporting companies. These are illustrations of how changes in the quantities of exports can affect the terms of trade.

Now consider a country that provides a large fraction of the total demand for some product that it imports. By restricting its demand for that product through tariffs, it can force the price of that product down. This turns the terms of trade in its favor, because it can now get more units of imports per unit of exports.

Both of these techniques lower world output. They can, however, make it possible for a small group of countries to gain, because they get a sufficiently larger share of the smaller world output. However, if foreign countries retaliate by raising their tariffs, the ensuing trade war can easily leave every country with a lowered income.

To protect against "unfair" actions by foreign firms and governments. Tariffs may be used to prevent foreign industries from gaining an advantage over domestic industries through the use of predatory practices that will harm domestic industries and hence lower national income. Two common practices are the payment of subsidies by foreign governments to their exporters and dumping by foreign firms. Such practices are called *unfair trade practices,* and the laws that deal with them are called *fair-trade laws.* The circumstances under which foreign subsidization and dumping provide a valid argument for tariffs are considered in detail later in this chapter.

To protect infant industries. The oldest valid argument for protectionism as a means of raising living standards concerns economies of scale. It is usually called the **infant industry argument.** If an industry has large economies of scale, costs and prices will be high when the industry is small but will fall as the industry grows. In such industries the country first in the field has a tremendous advantage. A newly developing country may find that in the early stages of development its industries are unable to compete with established foreign rivals. A trade restriction may protect these industries from foreign competition while they grow. When they are large enough, they may be able to produce as cheaply as foreign rivals and thus be able to compete without protection.

To encourage learning by doing. Learning by doing, which we discussed in Chapter 39, suggests that the existing pattern of comparative advantage need not be taken as immutable. If a country can learn enough by producing commodities in which it currently is at a comparative disadvantage, it may gain in the long run by specializing in those commodities and developing a comparative advantage in them as the learning process helps to lower their costs.

Learning by doing is an example of what in Chapter 39 we called *dynamic comparative advantages*. The successes of such *newly industrializing countries* (the so-called NICs) as Brazil, Hong Kong, South Korea, Singapore, and Taiwan seemed to many observers to be based on acquired skills and government policies that created favorable business conditions. This gave rise to the theory that comparative advantages can change and can be developed by suitable government policies.

Protecting a domestic industry from foreign competition may give its management time to learn to be efficient and its labor force time to acquire needed skills. If so, there may be a long-term payoff to protecting the industry against foreign competition while a dynamic comparative advantage is being developed.

Some countries clearly have succeeded in developing strong comparative advantages in targeted industries, but others have failed. One reason such policies sometimes have failed is that protecting local industries from foreign competition may make the industries unadaptive and complacent. Another reason is that it is difficult to identify the industries that will be able to succeed in the long run. All too often the protected infant industry grows up to be a weakling that requires permanent tariff protection for its continued existence, or else the rate of learning for it is slower than for similar industries in countries that do not provide protection from the chill winds of international competition. In these instances the anticipated comparative advantage never materializes.

To create or to exploit a strategic trade advantage.   A major new argument for tariffs or other trade restrictions is to create a strategic advantage in producing or marketing some new product that is expected to generate pure profits. To the extent that all lines of production earn normal profits, there is no reason to produce goods other than ones for which a country has a comparative advantage. Some goods that are produced under oligopolistic conditions may, however, yield pure profits. Where such industries are already well established, there is little chance that a new firm will replace one of the existing oligopolistic giants. The situation is, however, more fluid with

new products. The first firm to develop and to market a new product successfully may earn a substantial excess profit over all of its opportunity costs and become one of the few established firms in the industry. If protection of the domestic market can increase the chance that one of the protected domestic firms will become one of the established oligopolists in the international market, the protection may pay off. This is the general idea behind the modern concept of strategic trade policy, and it is treated in more detail in the next section.

Strategic Trade Policy

Implications of high development costs.   Many of today's high-tech industries have falling average total cost curves due to their large fixed costs of product development. For a new generation of civilian aircraft, silicon chips, computers, artificial-intelligence machines, and genetically engineered food products, a high proportion of each producer's total costs are for product development. These are fixed costs of entering the market, and they must be incurred before a single unit of output can be sold. In such industries the actual factory costs of producing each unit of an already developed product may be quite small. Even if average variable costs are constant, the large fixed development costs mean that the average total cost curve has a significant negative slope over a large range of output. It follows that the price at which a firm can recover its total cost is negatively associated with its expected volume of sales. The larger are the sales that it expects, the lower is the price that it can charge and still recover its full costs. These characteristics of many modern high-tech products have several important consequences.

First, the markets for such products are extremely risky. Vast sums often must be spent before any product is tested on purchasers. If the product fails in the market, the fixed development costs are lost.

Second, there may be room for only a few firms in the industry. The large fixed costs of entry create the conditions of natural oligopoly, and sometimes even natural monopoly. A large number of firms, each of which has a relatively small output, could not recover their fixed costs. A small number of firms, each of which has a high output, can do so.

Third, a small number of firms may make large profits. Say, for example, that two firms could make large profits but three could make losses. In this case the first two firms that become established in the market will control it and will earn the profits.[2]

The production of full-sized commercial jets provides an example of an industry that possesses many of these characteristics. The development costs of commercial jet aircraft have risen greatly with each new generation. If the aircraft manufacturers are to recover these costs, each of them must have large sales. Thus, the number of firms that the market can support has diminished steadily, until today there is room for only two or three full-sized firms in the industry.

Argument for subsidies.   The characteristics that we have just listed are used to provide arguments for subsidizing the development of such industries. Say, for example, that there is room in the aircraft industry for only two major producers of the next round of passenger jets. If a government subsidizes a domestic firm, this firm may become one of the two that succeed. In this case the profits that are subsequently earned may more than repay the cost of the subsidy. Furthermore, a third country's firm, which was not subsidized, may have been just as good as the two that succeeded. Without the subsidy, however, this firm may lose out in the battle to establish itself as one of the two firms in the market. Having lost this one battle, it loses its entire fight for existence. The firm and the country's possibility of being represented in the industry are gone for the foreseeable future.

This example is not unlike the story of the Boeing 767 and the European Airbus, which is produced by a European consortium. The European producers received many direct subsidies (and they charge that Boeing received many indirect ones). Whatever the merits of the argument, several things are clear: The civilian jet aircraft industry remains profitable; there

is room for only two or three major producers; and one of these would not have been the European consortium if it had not been for substantial government assistance.

Argument for tariffs.   The argument for tariffs is that a protected domestic market greatly reduces the risks of product development and allows successful firms to achieve sufficient scale on the domestic market to be able to sell at competitive prices abroad. The classic example here is the victory of the Japanese semiconductor producers over their American rivals. From the beginning of the industry, American firms held a large competitive edge over all others. Then the Japanese decided to develop their industry. To do so, they shielded their domestic market from penetration by U.S. firms. The Japanese, who at first were well behind the American firms, caught up and were then able to penetrate the open U.S. market. In the end the Japanese succeeded with their newest generation of silicon chips, and the once dominant U.S. industry has been eclipsed.

A combination of domestic subsidization and tariff protection allowed the Japanese semiconductor industry to score a major victory in terms of market share over their U.S. competitors. The strategy, however, entailed large costs, both for product development and aggressive, below-cost pricing policies. Currently, there is debate as to whether the long-run profits resulting from this policy will be sufficient to cover all these costs.

Debate over strategic trade policy.   Generalizing from this and similar cases, some economists advocate that the United States adopt a *strategic trade policy,* which means, for high-tech industries, government protection of the home market and government subsidization (either openly or by more subtle back-door methods) of the product development stage. These economists say that, if the United States does not follow their advice, it will lose out in industry after industry to the more aggressive Japanese and European competition—a competition that is adept at combining private innovative activity with government assistance.

Opponents argue that strategic trade policy is nothing more than a modern version of the age-old justifications for tariff protection. They argue that, once all countries try to be strategic, they will all waste vast sums trying to break into industries in

[2] The reason for this is found in the indivisibilty of product development costs. If, say, $500 million is required to develop a marketable product, the firm that spends $300 million gets nothing. To see why this creates the potential for profits, assume that the market is large enough for the product to be sold at a price that would cover variable costs of production and also pay the opportunity costs of $1.25 billion worth of capital. Further assume that the capital required for actual production is negligible. In this case two firms with a total of $1 billion of capital invested in development costs will enter the market and earn large profits. However, if a third firm entered, making the industry's total invested capital $1.5 billion, all three firms would incur losses.

which there is no room for most of them. Consumers would benefit most, they say, if their governments let other governments engage in this game. Consumers could then buy the cheap, subsidized foreign products and export traditional, lower-tech products in return. The opponents of strategic trade policy also argue that democratic governments that enter the game of picking and backing winners are likely to make as many bad choices as good ones. One bad choice, with *all* of its massive development costs written off, would require that many good choices also be made, in order to make the equivalent in profits that would allow taxpayers to break even overall.

Advocates of strategic trade policy reply that a country cannot afford to stand by while others play the strategic game. They argue that there are key industries that have major "spillovers" into the rest of the economy. If a country wants to have a high living standard, it must, they argue, compete with the best. If a country lets all of its key industries migrate to other countries, many of the others will follow. The country then risks being reduced to the status of a less developed nation.

This has been a debate about dynamic comparative advantage and the effects of key industries on growth and living standards. It is a difficult issue, and one that is strongly debated in the United States today. The debate is an important one because it concerns nothing less than the place of the United States in the world of the future. Over the next few decades, will the United States maintain its place as a leading industrial producer and innovator and as one of the world's highest income countries? Will it, instead, go the way other leading countries have gone in the past—from a burst of dynamism, when its society was young and vibrant, to a period of relative stagnation? This happened to Spain in an earlier century and to the United Kingdom in this century. Will it be the United States' turn next? What is the best way to ensure a negative answer to this question? Should unaided market forces or government assistance through strategic trade policy be relied upon?

How Much Protectionism?

So far we have seen that there is a strong case for allowing free trade in order to realize the gains from trade but that there are also some reasons for departing from completely free trade.

It is not necessary to choose between free trade, on the one hand, and absolute protectionism, on the other. A country can have some trade and some protectionism, too.

Free Trade Versus No Trade

Undoubtedly, it would be possible to grow coffee beans in Michigan greenhouses and to synthesize all of the oil that we consume (as Germany did during World War II). However, the cost in terms of other commodities foregone would be huge, because these artificial means of production require lavish inputs of factors of production. It would likewise be possible for a tropical country, currently producing foodstuffs, to set up industries to produce all the manufactured products that it consumes. However, for a small country without natural advantages in industrial production, the cost in terms of resources used could be enormous. It is thus clear that there is a large gain to all countries in having specialization and trade. The real output and consumption of all countries would be very much lower if each of them chose to produce domestically all of the goods that it consumed.

In an all-or-nothing choice, almost all countries would choose free trade over no trade.

A Little More Trade Versus a Little Less Trade

Today we have trade among nations, but this trade is not perfectly free. Table 40-1 shows the levels of tariffs on selected commodities in force today.

Would we be better off if today's barriers to trade were reduced or increased a little bit? This question shifts the focus of our discussion considerably, for it is quite a jump from the proposition that "Free trade is better than no trade" to the proposition that "A little less trade restriction than we have at present is better than a little more."

To see this latter issue more clearly, compare the effects of a 10 percent uniform effective rate of tariff with those of free trade. Tariffs of 10 percent will protect industries that are up to 10 percent less efficient than foreign competitors. If the costs of the various tariff-protected industries were spread out

TABLE 40-1   Tariffs on Selected Commodity Groups (*ad valorem rates*)

Commodity	United States	European Community	Japan
Weighted average of all manufactured items	4.4	5.5	3.6
Fruits, vegetables	1.7	3.4	14.5
Tea, coffee, and spices	5.3	1.8	34.1
Paper, paperboard	0.3	4.0	1.4
Textiles	15.9	9.0	8.0
Transport vehicles	2.5	6.2	2.1
Tobacco	13.0	0.0	54.3
Petroleum and coal products	0.0	6.3	1.4
Oil and natural gas	4.0	0.0	0.0
All commodities (trade weighted)	3.2	3.7	5.4

Source: Post-Tokyo Round tariff rates, courtesy Special Trade Representatives Office, U.S. government.

The United States is a low-tariff country overall, yet tariffs on selected items are plainly designed to be protective of important domestic industries. These tariffs, the lowest in history, result from the General Agreement on Tariffs and Trade (GATT) Tokyo Round negotiations. They were phased in during the 1980s and will apply until further tariff cuts are phased in after the end of the Uruguay Round of GATT negotiations. Notice the U.S. use of tariffs for protection on textiles and tobacco. In Japan the high tariffs on tobacco, tea, coffee, and spices are for revenue, since Japan does not produce these commodities. In contrast, the high Japanese tariffs on fruits and vegetables serve to protect a very high-cost domestic agricultural industry.

evenly, some would be 10 percent less efficient than their foreign competitors and others would be only 1 percent less efficient. Their average inefficiency would be about one-half the tariff rate, so they would be on average about 5 percent less efficient than their foreign competitors.

Suppose that, as a result of tariffs, approximately 20 percent of a country's resources are allocated to industries that are different from the ones to which they would be allocated if there were no tariffs. This means that about 20 percent of a country's resources would be working in certain industries only because of tariff protection. If the average protected industry is 5 percent less efficient than its foreign rival, approximately 20 percent of a country's resources are producing on average about 5 percent less efficiently than they would be if there were no tariffs. This

causes a reduction in national income on the order of 1 percent as a result of tariff protection.[3]

Suppose the economic costs of existing tariffs are 1 percent of our national income. Is this sacrifice of national income large or small? Expressed as a percentage of GNP, the loss seems small, yet in terms of 1988 prices, it was $50 billion *per year* in the United States. That amount every year forever could buy a lot of hospitals, schools, medical research, solar energy research—or even imported oil.

The previous calculations refer to gains from exploiting comparative advantage when costs are given and constant. More recent calculations allow for unexploited economies of scale in specific product lines and for some forms of dynamic comparative advantages. They show gains from reducing the world's remaining tariffs that are much larger than the small ones suggested before. These gains can approach 10 percent of the national incomes of small and middle-sized countries, although, for large countries such as the United States, the gains tend to be somewhat smaller, because many of the scale and dynamic economies can be exploited within the large domestic market.

Longer-run considerations. Some readers may be tempted to conclude that the seemingly small economic costs of the current amount of protectionism make it worthwhile to give in to the clamor to provide more protection for America's hard-pressed industries. Before rushing to this conclusion, however, some long-run political and economic possibilities need to be considered. The world prosperity of recent decades has been built largely on a rising volume of relatively free international trade. There are real doubts that such prosperity could be maintained if the volume of trade were to shrink steadily because of growing trade barriers. Yet the pressure to use trade restrictions in troubled times is strong. If countries give in and begin to raise barriers moderately when the initial economic costs are not large, so strong are the political forces involved that there is no telling where the process, once begun, will end.

In today's world a country's products must stand

---

[3] The above rough calculation is meant only to give some intuitive understanding of why the many careful measures of the cost of moderate tariffs commonly lead to figures that are closer to 2 than to 10 percent of the United States' national income.

up to international competition if they are to survive. Protection, by conferring a national monopoly, reduces the incentive for industries to fight to hold their own internationally. If any one country adopts high tariffs unilaterally, its domestic industries will become less competitive. Secure in its home market because of the tariff wall, it is likely to become less and less competitive in the international market. However, as the gap between domestic and foreign industries widens, *any* tariff wall will provide less and less protection. Eventually, the domestic industries will succumb to the foreign competition. Meanwhile, domestic living standards will fall relative to foreign ones, as an increasing productivity gap opens between domestic tariff-protected industries and foreign, internationally oriented ones.

While restrictive policies sometimes have been pursued following a rational assessment of the approximate cost, it is hard to avoid the conclusion that, more often than not, such policies are pursued for flimsy objectives or on fallacious grounds, with little idea of the actual costs involved. The very high tariffs in the United States during the 1920s and 1930s are a conspicuous example. The current clamor for the government to do something about the competition from Japan, Korea, and other countries of the East may well be another.

Fallacious Trade Policy Arguments

We have seen that there are gains to be had from a high volume of international trade and specialization. We have also seen that there can be valid arguments for a moderate degree of protectionism. There are also many claims that do not advance the debate. Fallacious arguments are heard on both sides, and they color much of the popular discussion. These arguments have been around for a long time, but their survival does not make them true. We examine them now to see where their fallacies lie.

Fallacious Free-Trade Arguments

Free trade always benefits all countries.   This is not necessarily so. We have just seen that some countries may gain by restricting trade in order to get a sufficiently favorable shift in their terms of trade. Such countries would lose if they gave up these tariffs and adopted free trade unilaterally.

Infant industries never abandon their tariff protection. It is argued that granting protection to infant industries is a mistake, because these industries seldom admit to growing up and will cling to their protection even when they are fully grown. However, infant industry tariffs are a mistake *only* if these industries never grow up. In this case permanent tariff protection would be required to protect a weak industry that would never be able to compete on an equal footing in the international market. However, if the industries do grow up and achieve the expected scale economies, the fact that, like any special interest group, they cling to their tariff protection is not a sufficient reason for denying protection to other genuine infant industries. When economies of scale are realized, the real costs of production are reduced and resources are freed for other uses. Whether or not the tariff or other trade barriers remain, a cost saving has been effected by the scale economies.

Fallacious Protectionist Arguments

Prevent exploitation.   According to the exploitation theory, trade can never be mutually advantageous; one trading partner *must* always reap a gain at the other's expense. Thus, the weaker trading partner must protect itself by restricting its trade with the stronger partner. However, the principle of comparative advantage shows that it is possible for both parties to gain from trade and thus refutes the exploitation doctrine of trade. When opportunity cost ratios differ in two countries, specialization and the accompanying trade make it possible to produce more of all commodities and thus make it possible for both parties to consume more as a result of trade than they could get in its absence.

Keep the money at home.   This argument says, "If I buy a foreign good, I have the good and the foreigner has the money, whereas if I buy the same good locally, I have the good and our country has the money, too." Abraham Lincoln is said to have made this argument, and it is still heard today.

The argument is based on a misconception. It assumes that domestic money actually goes abroad physically when imports are purchased and that trade flows only in one direction. However, when American importers purchase Italian-made goods, as one example, they do not send dollars abroad. They (or their financial agents) buy Italian lire and use them to pay the Italian manufacturers. They purchase the lire on the foreign exchange market by giving up dollars to someone who wishes to use them for expenditure *in the United States.* Even if the money did go abroad physically—that is, if an Italian firm accepted a shipload of dollars—it would be because that firm (or someone to whom it could sell the dollars) wanted them to spend in the only country where they are legal tender, the United States.

Dollars ultimately do no one any good except as a form of purchasing power. It would be miraculous if green pieces of paper could be exported in return for real goods; after all, the Fed has the power to create as much new money as it wishes. It is only because the green paper can buy American commodities and assets that others want it.

Protect against low-wage foreign labor.   Surely, the argument says, the products of low-wage countries will drive U.S. products from the market, and the high U.S. standard of living will be dragged down to that of its poor trading partners. Arguments of this sort have swayed many voters through the years.

As a prelude to considering them, stop and think about what the argument would imply if it were taken out of the international context and put into a local one, where the same principles govern the gains from trade. Is it really impossible for a rich person to gain from trading with a poor person? Would the local millionaire be better off if she did all her own typing, gardening, and cooking? No one believes that a rich person cannot gain from trading with those who are less rich. Why then must a rich group of people lose from trading with a poor group? "Well," you say, "the poor group will price its goods too cheaply." Does anyone believe that consumers lose from buying in a discount house or a supermarket just because the prices are lower there than at the old-fashioned corner store? Consumers gain when they can buy the same goods at a lower price. If the Koreans pay low wages and sell their goods cheaply, *Korean* labor may suffer, but we will gain because we obtain their goods at a low cost in terms of the goods that we must export in return. The cheaper our imports are, the better off we are in terms of the goods and services that are available for domestic consumption.

Stated in more formal terms, the gains from trade

depend on comparative, not absolute, advantages. World production is higher when any two areas, say, the United States and Japan, specialize in the production of the goods for which they have a comparative advantage than when they both try to be self-sufficient.

Might it not be possible, however, that Japan will undersell the United States in all lines of production and thus appropriate all, or more than all, the gains for itself, leaving the United States no better off, or even worse off, than if it had no trade with Japan? The answer is no. The reason for this depends on the behavior of exchange rates, which we shall study in Chapter 41. As we shall see, equality of demand and supply in foreign-exchange markets ensures that trade flows in both directions.

Imports can be obtained only by spending the currency of the country that makes the imports. Claims to this currency can be obtained only by exporting goods and services or by borrowing. Thus, lending and borrowing aside, imports must equal exports. All trade must be in two directions; countries can buy only if they can also sell.

In the long run, trade cannot hurt a country by causing it to import without exporting.

Trade then always provides scope for international specialization, with each country producing and exporting those goods for which it has a comparative advantage and importing those goods for which it does not.

Exports raise living standards; imports lower them.   Exports add to aggregate demand; imports subtract from it. Thus, other things being equal, exports tend to increase national income and imports tend to reduce it. Surely, then, it is desirable to encourage exports and to discourage imports. This is an appealing argument, but it is incorrect.

Exports raise national income by adding to the value of domestic output, but they do not add to the value of domestic consumption. In fact, exports are goods produced at home and consumed abroad, while imports are goods produced abroad and consumed at home. The standard of living in a country depends on the goods and services available for *consumption*, not on what is produced.

If exports were really good and imports were

really bad, then a fully employed economy that managed to increase exports without a corresponding increase in imports ought to be better off. Such a change, however, would result in a reduction in its current standards of living, because, when more goods are sent abroad and no more are brought in from abroad, the total goods available for domestic consumption must fall.

The living standards of a country depend on the goods and services consumed in that country. The importance of exports is that they permit imports to be made. This two-way international exchange is valuable because more goods can be imported than could be obtained if the same goods were produced at home.

Create domestic jobs and reduce unemployment.   It is sometimes said that an economy with substantial unemployment, such as that of the United States in the 1930s or mid-1980s, provides an exception to the case for freer trade. Suppose that tariffs or import quotas cut the imports of Japanese cars, Korean textiles, Italian shoes, and French wine. Surely, the argument maintains, this will create more employment for Detroit automobile workers, Tennessee textile workers, New York state shoe factories, and midwestern farm workers. The answer is that it will—initially. But the Japanese, Koreans, Italians, and French can buy from the United States only if they get American dollars from those who have sold goods in the United States. The decline in the sales of automobiles, textiles, shoes, and wine will decrease their purchases of American machinery, aircraft, grain, and vacations in the United States. Jobs will be lost in export industries and gained in industries that formerly faced competition from imports.

FIGURE 40-2   Tariffs in the United States, 1828–1985

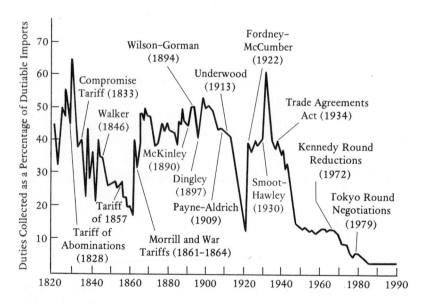

U.S. tariffs have been lower in the post-World War II period than in any other period of comparable length in American history. Throughout its history the United States has alternated between being a high-tariff country and being a modest-tariff country. The average rate of tariff has been lower since World War II than ever before. The rate fell below 10 percent in 1971 and below 5 percent when the Tokyo Round tariff reductions came into full effect in the mid-1980s. These tariffs will not be changed again until the new Uruguay Round of tariff cuts are phased in, sometime in the 1990s. (*Statistical Abstract of the United States,* selected years.)

The likely long-term effect is that overall unemployment will not be reduced but will merely be redistributed among industries. Since the export industries that contract tend to be more efficient than the import competing industries that expand, this policy tends to reallocate resources from more to less efficient lines of production and hence to reduce overall GDP.

Trade Policy in the World Today

The Importance of Trade and Tariffs

Figure 40-2 shows how tariffs have been used in U.S. history. U.S. policymakers often have been less preoccupied with foreign trade than have policymakers in such other countries as Japan, Canada, Sweden, and the United Kingdom. Part of the reason for this lies in the lesser importance of trade to the American economy. Traditionally, exports have accounted for around 5 percent of U.S. GNP. The rapid growth of foreign trade in recent decades has, however, affected the United States, along with most other nations. As a result, exports accounted for about 10 percent of American GNP in 1988. In contrast, exports accounted for between 20 and 30 percent of GNP in 1988 in Japan, Canada, Sweden, and the United Kingdom. The loss of foreign trade would have a devastating effect on any of these countries. The United States would also suffer from such a loss, but to a much smaller degree.

Although foreign trade is not a large fraction of total U.S. national income, it is vital to some of its industries. Large quantities of certain materials, for example, petroleum, bauxite, coffee beans, iron ore, lumber, and newsprint, are imported, as are large quantities of many consumer goods, such as automobiles, radios, television sets, computers, and fashion goods. The cutting off of imports of any one of these commodities would cause significant difficulties, and in some cases it would disrupt the whole economy—as Americans discovered, for example, when oil supplies were temporarily cut off in the 1970s.

Foreign trade contributes substantially to the standards of living of many countries. Even the United States, with its lower dependence on trade, would have its living standards lowered significantly if it were unable to participate in the gains from trade among nations.

International Agreements on Trade and Tariffs

In the past, any country could impose any desired set of tariffs on its imports. However, when one country increases its tariffs, the action may trigger retaliatory actions by its trading partners. Just as an arms race can escalate, so can a tariff war. Extended negotiations may then be required to undo the damage.

The General Agreement on Tariffs and Trade (GATT)

The 1930s saw a high-water mark of world protectionism, as each country sought to raise its employment by raising its tariffs. The end result was lowered efficiency, less trade, but no more employment. One of the most notable achievements of the post-World War II era was the creation of the General Agreement on Tariffs and Trade (GATT). Under this agreement, GATT countries meet periodically to negotiate bilateral cuts in tariffs that are mutually advantageous. They agree in advance that any tariff cuts negotiated in this way will be extended to all member countries under what is called the *most favored nation (MFN)* agreement. This means that each country agrees that it will not impose higher tariffs on the other country's goods than it charges on similar goods coming from any other country.

The two most recent rounds of GATT agreements have each reduced world tariffs by about one-third. The Kennedy Round negotiations were completed in 1967, and new rates were phased in over a five-year period, ending in 1972. The Tokyo Round negotiations began in 1975 and were completed in 1979. The reductions began to take effect in 1981 and were completed in 1986.

Ironically, as that new round of reductions began, pressure was mounting in many countries to protect jobs at home through trade restrictions. Protectionist policies grew alarmingly in the EC and many other areas. As time passed, even GATT itself came under attack. The worldwide recession that began in late

1981 was undoubtedly the main cause of this pressure. In addition, protectionist pressures in many countries were created by the decline in the international competitiveness of traditional industries, due to sharp changes in terms of trade. Also, under the impact of the persistent U.S. trade deficit, protectionist pressures grew through the first half of the 1980s in the United States.

In 1986 there began a new round of GATT negotiations, called the Uruguay Round. This round addressed five key issues: (1) the growing worldwide use of nontariff barriers to trade; (2) the need to develop rules for liberalizing trade in services, which is the most rapidly growing component of foreign trade; (3) the distorting effect on trade in agricultural products caused by heavy domestic subsidization of agriculture; (4) the need to develop more effective methods of settling disputes that arise from violations of GATT rules; and (5) the desire of developed nations to gain better copyright protection for intellectual property—a desire that pitted the rich, innovating nations against the poorer nations with a self-interest in gaining access to intellectual property on terms as favorable as possible. (Intellectual property is a property right resulting from mental effort, such as discovery, product development, or the creation of a work of art, and resulting in a right of ownership conferred by a document such as a patent or a copyright.)

After the mid-term review in 1988, the GATT nations were a long way from agreement. The less developed countries were reluctant to agree on protection of intellectual property, while the EC and the United States were far apart on the issue of curtailing agricultural subsidies. The final result of the negotiations will be known in 1990 or 1991.

Common Markets

A **common market** is an agreement among a group of countries to eliminate barriers to free trade among themselves and to present a common barrier to trade with the rest of the world. The most important example of this came into being in 1957, when the Treaty of Rome brought together France, Germany, Italy, Holland, Belgium, and Luxembourg in what was first called the European Common Market (ECM), then the European Economic Community (EEC), and now just the European Community

(EC). The original six countries were joined in 1973 by the United Kingdom, the Republic of Ireland, and Denmark; Greece entered in 1983, and Spain and Portugal entered in 1986.

This organization is dedicated to bringing about free trade, complete mobility of factors of production, and the eventual harmonization of fiscal and monetary policies among the member countries. Many tariffs on manufactured goods have been eliminated, and much freedom of movement of labor and capital has been achieved. Substantial monetary integration also has been achieved, but there is still a long way to go to fully integrate the monetary systems of the EC countries. At the time of writing this book, a major push was underway to remove most of the remaining restrictions by 1992. How far it will succeed was uncertain in 1989. Its full success, however, would make the EC into a genuine common market. The push toward "Europe 1992" is further discussed in Box 40-3.

Other common markets have been formed, such as the Central American Common Market and the East African Community, but none has yet achieved the success of the EC, and some have collapsed.

Free-Trade Associations

A **free-trade association** allows for tariff-free trade between the member countries, but, unlike a common market, it leaves each member free to levy its own tariffs on imports from other countries. As a result, members must maintain customs points at their common border (if they have one) to make sure that imports into the free-trade area do not all enter through the country that is levying the lowest tariff on each item.

The first important free-trade association in the modern era was the European Free Trade Association (EFTA). It was formed in 1960 by a group of European countries that was unwilling to join the EC because of its all-embracing character. Not wanting to be left out of the gains from trade, they formed an association whose sole purpose was tariff removal. They removed all tariffs on trade among themselves. Each of the EFTA countries also signed a free-trade-area agreement with the EC. This makes the EC-EFTA market the largest market in the world (over 300 million people) in which goods can move unhindered by tariff barriers.

In 1985 the United States signed a limited free-trade agreement with Israel. In 1988 a sweeping agreement was signed with Canada, instituting free trade on all goods and many services, and covering what is the largest flow of international trade between any two countries in the world. The United States was also negotiating with Mexico over a limited free-trade agreement. Australia and New Zealand have also entered into an association that removes restrictions on trade in goods and services between the two countries. (The free-trade agreement with Canada is further discussed in Box 40-4.)

Trade Remedy Laws and Nontariff Barriers

Early rounds of negotiations under the GATT concentrated on the reduction of tariffs. As these were lowered, countries that wished to protect domestic industries began using a series of trade restrictions that came to be known as nontariff barriers (NTBs). Most NTBs are ostensibly levied for purposes other than protectionism. These other purposes are often called trade relief purposes.

An effort to control the growing use of NTBs was made in the Tokyo Round of GATT negotiations. These measures were classified, and the circumstances under which their use was legitimate were laid down. The ironic result is that by making all countries aware of these measures, and by making their use respectable under some circumstances, these GATT agreements seem to have led to an increased use of NTBs for purposes of trade restrictions.

Escape clause. One procedure that can be used as an NTB is the so-called escape clause action. A rapid surge of imports may temporarily threaten the existence of domestic producers. These producers may then be given temporary relief by raising tariff rates over and above those agreed to during the GATT negotiations. The trouble is that, once imposed, these "temporary" measures are hard to eliminate.

One "temporary" measure that is still in force provides a cautionary tale. In the late 1950s, the textile and clothing industries in many advanced industrial nations saw their market shares reduced by a rising volume of trade from Hong Kong, Korea, the Philippines, and other newly industrializing nations. In response to a United States initiative, international meetings were held in 1961. Out of these meetings

came the *multifiber agreements* (MFAs), which provided maximum annual quotas for each exporting textile-producing country for a 20-year period. Starting in 1981, many of these agreements were renegotiated, generally leading to more, rather than less, restrictive policies. At the end of the decade, they were still in existence.

Dumping. When a commodity is sold in a foreign country at a price that is lower than the price in the domestic market for reasons not related to costs, this is called **dumping**. Dumping is a form of price discrimination of the kind studied in the theory of monopoly (see Chapter 13). Most governments have antidumping duties, which protect their own industries against unfair foreign pricing practices.

Dumping, if it lasts indefinitely, can be a gift to the receiving country. Its consumers get goods from abroad at less than their real cost. Dumping is more often a temporary measure, designed to get rid of unwanted surpluses, or a predatory attempt to drive competitors out of business. In either case, domestic producers complain about unfair foreign competition. In these cases it is accepted international practice to levy *antidumping duties* on foreign imports. These duties are designed to eliminate the discriminatory elements in their prices.

Unfortunately, antidumping laws have been evolving over the last two decades in ways that allow antidumping duties to become barriers to trade, rather than redresses for unfair trading practices. The United States has been a leader in making these changes, but many other countries, including those of the EC, have been quick to imitate the United States.

Two features of the antidumping system that is now in effect in many countries make it highly protectionist. First, *any* price discrimination is classified as dumping and thus is subject to penalties. Thus, prices in the producer's domestic market become, in effect, minimum prices below which no sales can be made in foreign markets, whatever the circumstances in the domestic and foreign markets. Second, following an alteration in the U.S. law in the early 1970s, many countries' laws now calculate the "margin of dumping" as the difference between the price that is charged in that country's market and the foreign producers' "full allocated cost" (average total cost). This means that, when there is global excess demand so that the profit-maximizing price for all producers

BOX 40-3

Europe 1992

1992 will see the completion of the program begun in 1958 when the Treaty of Rome set up the European Economic Community

1992 will see the creation of a single, integrated, European market of 320 million people

So, at least, goes the rhetoric, but is there substance behind it all? Are the EC's plans for 1992 revolutionary, or are the European Commission's public relations officers merely working overtime?

According to the British economist J. A. Kay, "1992 is perhaps the most successful marketing campaign of the decade. It has restored the political momentum of the European Community and broadened the horizons of many businessmen across the continent." In this sense, much of the real significance of 1992 does lie in the success of its publicity. Behind the publicity, however, lies real substance, which can be found in programs that are designed to come as close as possible to completing the liberalization of the internal European market. The three major plans for doing this are to abolish fiscal frontiers, to reduce nontariff barriers to trade, and to liberalize public procurement.

The first, and in many ways most contentious, plan is to dismantle fiscal frontiers between the member states. The Commission believes that what is needed for this is an approximate harmonization of rates of indirect taxes. The EC already has a common set of tariffs against the outside world (by virtue of its being a common market rather than a free-trade area). If it also had a common set of NTBs, this could, in principle at least, lead to the elimination of any form of border controls between the member states. In practice, differing national NTBs on imports from the rest of the world, particularly from Japan and the NICs, make some border control necessary. Even if this reason could be removed, member countries would, no doubt, still wish to maintain some border surveillance. Differences in laws (and the severity with which they are administered) on such matters as gun ownership, agricultural pests, animal diseases, and drugs would require border posts, although the surveillance would be minimal by world standards.

A second way in which the EC's market is to be integrated is through eliminating national restrictions on transportation. Airlines in Europe have not experienced the dramatic effects that deregulation brought to airlines in the United States and Canada—North American fares fell significantly, and passenger miles rose dramatically. Trucking, and some wholesale activities, are also highly regulated in some EC countries. Increasing competition in transportation should help significantly to integrate the EC market.

---

is below average total cost (but above average variable cost), foreign producers can be convicted of dumping. This gives domestic producers enormous protection whenever the market price falls temporarily below *ATC*. Furthermore, it is very difficult to allocate overheads among individual products in many multiproduct industries. This is particularly true in industries such as chemicals, where fixed costs are a high proportion of total costs and there are many individual products that have widely differing development costs.

Countervailing duties.   Countervailing duties provide another case in which a trade relief measure can sometimes become a covert NTB. The countervailing duty is designed to act, not as a tariff barrier, but rather as a means of creating a "level playing field" on which fair international competition can take place. American firms rightly complain that they cannot compete against the bottomless purses of foreign governments. Subsidized foreign exports can be sold indefinitely in the United States at prices that would guarantee losses in the absence of the subsidy.

A third way in which large potential gains might be realized is to liberalize public procurement (the purchases made by governments). Such purchases, which are now often restricted to nationals, are to be opened to international competition. However, the scope for persuading governments seriously to entertain bids from companies in other EC countries is probably limited.

The countries of the EC have been no exception to the worldwide trend toward increased use of NTBs. A significant reduction in NTBs on intra-EC trade would represent real progress in the fight to contain the use of these threats to liberalized trade. One important NTB that is signaled out for attack is the misuse of technical standards and regulations. Their purpose is consumer protection, but they are easily used to inhibit international trade, particularly in food products, pharmaceuticals, and engineering goods, as well as in financial services. The European Community's original approach to this problem was to try to impose European standards on all products. This led to complaints about bureaucratic excesses that took the distinctiveness out of such national products as beer and salami. The new approach is to set minimum common standards for consumer safety and to agree that any product meeting these standards must be admitted to the markets of all EC countries, leaving member

countries free to impose further standards on commodities produced within their own borders, if they wish to do so.

A series of barriers that restrict the entry of firms from one member country into the markets of other member countries are also to be removed. The object is to increase intracommunity competition.

For these, and many other reasons, the EC countries are looking forward to 1992, but they are not alone. The rest of the world is also waiting for 1992 and doing so with a mixture of interest and apprehension. To them, the key question is, "Will 1992 make the European Community more inward looking or more outward looking with respect to world trade?" The liberalized trading system, overseen by the GATT, has served the world well for 45 years. Now, however, it is under heavy attack. Many observers fear the advent of a new era of managed trade, with more trade taking place within various blocks and less between the blocks. By the way in which it removes its own internal barriers, Europe can make a significant difference, lending its push either to restricting, or encouraging, world trade. Which way will Europe go in 1992? At the time of this writing (1989), no one—either within the community or without—knew the answer to this momentous question.

The original object of countervailing duties was to counteract the effect on price of the presence of such foreign subsidies.

If a U.S. firm suspects the existence of such a subsidy and registers a complaint, the American government is then required to make an investigation. For a countervailing duty to be levied, the investigation must find, first, that the foreign subsidy to the specific industry in question does exist and, second, that it is large enough to be a potential injury to competing American firms.

There is no doubt that countervailing duties sometimes have been used to remove the effects of "unfair" competition that are caused by foreign subsidies. Other governments complain, however, that countervailing duties also sometimes are used as a thinly disguised barrier to trade. At the early stages of the development of countervailing duties, only subsidies whose prime effect was to distort trade were subject to countervail. Even then, however, the existence of equivalent domestic subsidies was not taken into account when decisions were made to put

BOX 40-4

The U.S.-Canada Free Trade Agreement*

January 1, 1989 was Canada-U.S. FTA-Day, the day when the historic U.S.-Canada Free Trade Agreement came into operation. The Agreement eventually will remove all tariffs on trade between the two countries.

The United States and Canada are partners in the world's largest bilateral trade flow—U.S. $268 billion worth of imports and exports . . . [in 1987]. Their far-reaching Agreement was preceded, first, by nearly two years of intense negotiations—climaxed by a walk-out of the Canadian delegation and an eleventh hour intervention by then Treasury Secretary James Baker. An intense Canadian debate then followed on how the Agreement would affect Canada's political and economic independence. The climax of the debate came during an emotional election campaign, fought primarily on the free-trade issue and won by the free-trade–supporting Progressive Conservative party.

Scope and Coverage

The U.S.-Canada Agreement covers trade in goods, a range of commercial services, and many investment practices. It removes all tariffs, curtails the use of non-tariff barriers to trade, deals with a host of detailed causes of trade-related irritants, and creates a novel set of institutions for resolving bilateral trade disputes.

The U.S.-Canada Agreement is much more comprehensive than the U.S.-Israel agreement, which is mainly confined to trade in goods. It is not, however, as embracing as the European Community, which, being a common market, imposes a uniform set of tariffs against nonmember countries, requires the free movement of labor and capital, and calls for the harmonization of many government policies.

The Agreement's fundamental principle is *national treatment*—a principle also embedded in the General Agreement on Tariffs Trade (the GATT)

* Excerpts from the article, "Handshake Across the Border," by R. G. Lipsey and R. C. York, *New York Times,* February 27, 1989. Reprinted by permission of the *New York Times.*

which has governed, since 1947, multilateral trade between its member countries which now number 96. This principle is designed to preserve, in areas covered by the Agreement, each country's policy independence while preventing discrimination based solely on nationality. In the context of the U.S.-Canada Agreement, national treatment means that each country can make whatever new laws it wishes and that these laws can differ from those of the other country on the same subject, *as long as* the laws do not discriminate between Canadian and U.S. citizens and companies operating and/or selling goods within one country (most laws already in place prior to the Agreement are not affected). For example, neither Canada nor the United States is required to harmonize its laws on pollution control with those of the other country no matter how desirable that may be; all that is required by the Agreement is that each apply its own laws equally to Canada and U.S. firms operating within its own jurisdiction. . . .

Agreement with the GATT

The U.S.-Canada Agreement provides clear evidence that the trade liberalization movement is still alive—even if not altogether well everywhere in the world. Both countries remain committed to multilateral trade liberalization negotiated through the GATT. Their Agreement is fully consistent with the GATT. It uses many GATT concepts, but it goes beyond present GATT arrangements on issues that the . . . Uruguay Round of GATT negotiations . . . [are] addressing. In so doing, the Agreement provides examples of how the GATT could deal with some of the thorny issues it now faces—such as how to improve its dispute settlement mechanism.

Nonetheless, the Agreement is also a cautionary beacon for those involved in the GATT talks. If these fail, the U.S.-Canada Agreement could provide a precedent for other bilateral, or trilateral, trade deals—a view forcefully advocated by former Treasury Secretary James Baker. In the worst-case scenario, with the world sundered into regional trading blocs, the Agreement will at least preserve regional free trade between the two countries. It might also be extended to include Mexico.

Who Will Gain?

In its most important aspects, the Agreement contains arrangements that are clear advantages to both countries. In other aspects, where the two countries' negotiating objectives differed, the Agreement represents a mixture of bargaining victories and bargaining concessions for both countries.

Removal of Barriers to Trade in Goods and Services

Both countries will gain from the removal of all bilateral tariffs. These are to be phased out in 10 equal, annual steps which began on January 1, 1989—except in the substantial number of cases where industry representatives agreed to five-year phase-out period or the immediate removal of a tariff. . . . Because each country levies its own tariffs on trade with other countries, goods must meet rules of origin requirements to qualify for preferential treatment under the Agreement.

Both countries will gain from the curtailment or removal of many nontariff barriers. These include quotas, the misuse of technical standards, certain federal procurement practices, discriminatory taxation measures, unnecessarily costly and cumbersome administrative procedures, and the misuse of trade remedy laws.

Both countries gain from an imaginative provision . . . that allows for easy temporary entry of professional, business, and service personnel. Difficulties experienced by such persons when crossing the common border in either direction had been a significant nontariff barrier to trade—to say nothing of an irritant to mutual good will.

Both countries will gain from the agreement's path-breaking liberalization of trade in those commercial services that it covers. Firms operating in "covered services" now have the right to establish themselves in both countries and the right to national treatment once established.

Both countries will gain from their commitment to refrain from increasing trade restrictions against each other and from the Agreement's requirement that each must notify and consult with the other whenever it wishes to implement changes that affect bilateral trade.

Institutional Machinery

Both countries will gain from the creation of a new, high-level Trade Commission that will oversee the working of the entire Agreement and resolve disputes arising out of its interpretation and application. Disputes will be directed first to the Commission, which will attempt to arrive at a mutually satisfactory resolution—a consensual procedure that is a familiar part of the GATT.

If a dispute cannot be settled within 30 days, an arbitration panel will be set up consisting of five members, two from each country and one selected by the Commission. The panel will operate under strict time limits. Each country will have the right to at least one hearing before the panel, to provide submissions and rebut any argument. The panel can then make binding decisions, if the two countries agree, or it can simply return recommendations to the Commission, which is then mandated to agree on a resolution of the dispute. . . .

The institutional provisions also deal with disputes arising from emergency actions used to restrict trade. Any such dispute that cannot be resolved by the Commission will be subject to compulsory binding arbitration. The Agreement also allows for cabinet-level consultations to head off any problems that might arise.

Assessment

. . . The Agreement will strengthen the long-standing friendship of the two countries. Held up for the world to see, it is testimony that, even in today's world of strained international trading relations, sovereign nations can still agree on clear, mutually advantageous, and, in many cases, binding rules governing their trade and investment practices. The Agreement is also the means through which U.S.-Canada trade and investment will grow, to the benefit of both countries' employment, incomes, and living standards.

countervailing duties on subsidized imports. Over time, the type of subsidy that is subject to countervail has evolved until almost any government program that affects industry now risks becoming the object of countervailing duty. Since all governments have many programs that provide some direct or indirect assistance to industry, the potential for the use of countervailing duties as thinly disguised trade barriers is enormous.

The Crisis in the Multilateral Trading System

At the end of World War II, the United States took the lead in forming the GATT and in pressing for reductions in world tariffs through successive rounds of negotiations. Largely as a result of this U.S. initiative, the world's tariff barriers have been greatly reduced, while the volume of world trade has risen steadily.

The 1980s saw a serious crisis evolve in this multilateral trading system. The most important single force that led toward this was a shift in the attitudes of many Americans toward protectionism. There are at least two key reasons for this shift.

The Growth of Protectionist Sentiment

First, under the impact of the persistent trade deficit, which is further discussed in Chapters 42 and 43, many influential U.S. leaders have become protectionist for the first time since the early 1930s. Second, the stiff competition coming from Japanese and European industry has led many Americans to fear a loss of U.S. competitiveness. Many seem to feel that American industry cannot compete effectively in the free market. This concern leads some to support *managed trade* as a protectionist device.

The growth of protectionist sentiments is not confined to the United States. Similar changes have been occurring in Europe for similar reasons. The great success of Japanese exporters in penetrating the EC market while helping consumers has caused trouble for many producers and has led to a search for ways to protect firms in the EC. The EC has made use of quotas, antidumping duties, and VERs. Since fighting an antidumping case can be time consuming and expensive, the mere registering of an antidumping complaint can often lead a foreign firm to raise its prices to the levels that are charged by domestic producers. This has the effect, desired by the domestic producers, of preventing a more efficient foreign supplier from underselling them.

The Pressure to Manage Trade

In the free-market system, competitive prices determine what is imported and what is exported. Under managed trade, the state has a major influence in determining the direction and magnitude of the flow of trade. The voluntary export agreement that we have just discussed is a typical example of the tools of managed trade. To fulfill a VER, the government of the exporting country must form its exporting firms into a cartel so that they can divide up the portion of the foreign market that they are allowed to serve, as well as collectively ensuring that they do not violate the export ceiling.

Another current example of the tools of managed trade is the suggestion that trade balances be judged bilaterally rather than multilaterally. Many would manage trade to reduce large bilateral balances; some would impose strict bilateral trade balances between pairs of countries. The essence of the multilateral trading system is that one country does not have to buy the same amount from another country as it sells to it, just as one country does not have to buy the same amount from each of its domestic suppliers as it sells to it. Enforcing bilateral balances would impose this requirement on each pair of trading countries. Such a requirement makes no more economic sense, however, than requiring that the barber should only cut the butcher's hair to the value of the meat that he buys from her, and so on for each supplier with whom the barber deals. To achieve bilateral balances, the state must intervene in the market to regulate exports and imports.

Regional Trading Blocks

The current trading world is dominated by the *triad countries*. These three great trading areas are (1) the countries of the European Community (EC) and the European Free Trade Area (EFTA); (2) the countries of North America (mainly the United States and Canada), who are partners in a free-trade area, plus Mexico; and (3) Japan.

Some observers are concerned with the possible growth of more and more formally negotiated regional trading blocks. Such agreements need not conflict with the multilateral trading system. The

U.S.-Canada agreement, for example, is consistent with increased trade between these two countries *and* the rest of the world. Such regional trading arrangements can, however, be inward looking, in the sense that they encourage trade between members while discouraging trade with the rest of the world. If the growth of protectionist sentiment in the United States and the EC were to leave the countries of other areas, such as the Pacific Rim, feeling excluded from the markets of Europe and North America, some of them might form their own trading block, in which they could at least trade freely with each other.

Will the Multilateral Trading System Survive?

The next decade will be critical for the future of the multilateral trading system, which has served the world so well since the end of World War II. The dangers are, first, a growth of regional trading blocks that will trade more with their own member countries and less with others and, second, the growth of state-managed trade.

It is interesting that in the United States, one of the staunchest defenders of the free-market system, there are currently so many voices that are raised in advocacy of moves that reduce the influence of market forces on international trade and increase the degree of government control over that trade. It is ironic to see enthusiasm for state-managed trade growing just at the time when the Socialist countries of Eastern Europe are at last agreeing that free markets are better regulators of economic activity than is the state. How far this movement will go will become clearer during the 1990s.

SUMMARY

1. The case for free trade is that world output of all commodities can be higher under free trade than when protectionism restricts regional specialization.

2. Domestic industries may be protected from foreign competition by tariffs and other policies, which impact on the prices of imports, or by import quotas and voluntary export agreements, which impact on the quantities of imports. Both sets of policies end up by increasing prices in the domestic market and lowering the quantities of imports. Both harm domestic consumers and benefit domestic producers of the protected commodity. The major difference is that the extra money paid for imports goes to the government under tariffs and to foreign producers under quantity restrictions.

3. Protection can be urged as a means to ends other than maximizing world living standards. Examples of such ends are to produce a diversified economy, to reduce fluctuations in national income, to retain distinctive national traditions, and to improve national defense.

4. Protection also can be urged on the grounds that it may lead to higher living standards for the protectionist country than would a policy of free trade. Such a result might come about by using a monopoly position to influence the terms of trade or by developing a dynamic comparative advantage by allowing inexperienced or uneconomically small industries to become efficient enough to compete with foreign industries.

5. Almost everyone would choose free trade if the only alternative were *no* trade. Cutting existing tariff barriers offers gains, expressed as a percentage of GNP, that may seem small but are large in terms of the total of goods and services involved.

6. Some fallacious free-trade arguments are that (a) because free trade maximizes world income, it will maximize the income of every individual country and (b) because infant industries seldom admit to growing up and thus try to retain their protection indefinitely,

the whole country necessarily loses by protecting its infant industries.

7. Some fallacious protectionist arguments are that (a) mutually advantageous trade is impossible, because one trader's gain must always be the other's loss; (b) buying abroad sends our money abroad, while buying at home keeps our money at home; (c) our high-paid workers must be protected against the competition from low-paid foreign workers; (d) imports are to be discouraged because they lower national income and cause unemployment.

8. An important recent argument for tariffs concerns strategic trade policy. This is based on the belief, held by some economists, that protecting the domestic market will allow domestic firms that are producing new products to develop quickly, so that they can then compete strongly in the hope of becoming one of a few world-scale producers of the product.

9. Trade is vitally important in the national incomes of many countries. It is relatively less important to the United States. Nonetheless, trade is vital to particular American industries, and few economists doubt that American living standards would be lowered significantly if America tried to make itself fully self-sufficient.

10. Although the most industrialized countries now have low tariffs, their recent tendency to institute nontariff barriers, either by negotiation (as in textiles) or by unilateral policies (such as the misuse of antidumping and countervailing duties), causes concern that the 50-year trend to ever freer trade is being reversed.

11. International agreements and negotiations have succeeded in lowering trade barriers from the high levels of 50 years ago. After World War II, the GATT began a series of multinational rounds of tariff reductions that have greatly lowered tariffs and are now trying to address nontariff barriers as well. Nevertheless, the recent clamor for protection in many trading nations threatens the free-trade trend that GATT has fostered. Regional common markets, such as the EC, have created substantial areas where free trade exists.

TOPICS FOR REVIEW

Free trade and protectionism
Tariff and nontariff barriers to trade
Countervail and voluntary export agreements
Fallacious arguments for free trade
Fallacious arguments for protectionism
Dumping and antidumping duties
General Agreement on Tariffs and Trade (GATT)
Common markets and free-trade associations

DISCUSSION QUESTIONS

1. "Pay $68,000, save a shoemaker," said a 1985 editorial in the *New York Times,* pointing out that a quota on shoe imports would save only 33,000 American jobs at a cost in higher shoe prices of $68,000 per job. Do consumers pay the cost? What alternatives are there to protecting jobs in the shoe industry?

2. "What unfair trade has done to an American community" was the headline of a recent full-page ad in the *New York Times.* The ad claimed that subsidized and "dumped" steel imports from unstated foreign countries were unfairly driving American steel plants out of

business. What foreign practices might justify this claim? What apparent dumping might represent perfectly fair competition? What American legislation or other practices could provide relief, whether justified or not, to the U.S. firms?

3. "U.S. consumer is seen as big loser in new restraints on imported steel," said the *Wall Street Journal* recently. The big gainers from the quota limitations on imported steel were predicted to be U.S. producers, who would sell more, and foreign producers, who would sell less but at a higher price; the big losers would be U.S. consumers. Explain carefully why each of these groups might gain or lose.

4. Suppose America had imposed prohibitive tariffs on all imported cars over the last three decades. How do you think this would have affected the following?
   a. The U.S. automobile industry
   b. The American public
   c. The kinds of cars produced by U.S. manufacturers

5. Lobbyists for many industries argue that their products are essential to national defense and therefore require protection. Suppose that supplies of a certain commodity are indeed essential in wartime. How does restricting imports solve the problem? Are there alternatives to import restrictions? If so, how might the alternatives be evaluated?

6. Import quotas are often used instead of tariffs. What real difference (if any) is there between quotas and tariffs? Explain why lobbyists for some American industries (cheese, sugar, shoes) support import quotas, while lobbyists for others (pizza manufacturers, soft drink manufacturers, retail stores) oppose them. Would you expect labor unions to support or oppose quotas?

7. There is much current concern that the United States is losing international competitiveness. Do countries that fall behind in the competitiveness race cease to reap the gains from trade?

8. The United States has greatly reduced tariffs since Congress passed trade legislation authorizing the president to negotiate tariff concessions with foreign countries. Why might Congress find it desirable to give the president this authority rather than reserve the authority to itself?

9. When France increased tariff restrictions on foreign poultry, thereby seriously hurting American chicken exporters, the United States reversed tariff reductions that had been made on brandy. Does this kind of "trade war" make any sense?

10. "An issue of *American Heritage* [reminds us] that Karl Marx was a firm, even fervent, free trader. (When he was the London correspondent for Horace Greeley's *New York Tribune,* Marx—the wicked communist—advocated free trade while Greeley—the avid capitalist—espoused protectionism.)" Reflect on what factors might have caused Marx and Greeley, given their political persuasions, to hold these views (as reported in the July 26, 1983 issue of the *Wall Street Journal*).

11. Classical economists favored free trade among nations as a means of interlocking their economies so they could not afford to fight each other. President Reagan opposed interlocking the economies of the Eastern and Western block on the grounds that this would give too much power of blockage to the Eastern countries. Discuss the "political economy" of these two opposing views.

Chapter 41

Exchange Rates and the Balance of Payments

In the mid-1980s American exporters and importers were concerned about the high value of the U.S. dollar in foreign exchange markets. The high value made it hard for American firms to sell abroad and easy for foreign firms to sell in the United States. The fall in the dollar in 1987 and 1988 eased some, but not all, of the concerns, and its strength in 1989 renewed their fears about their ability to compete with foreign producers.

The value of the dollar also concerns such varied groups as Japanese firms that want to build factories in the United States, Americans who want to buy French government bonds, German exporters who send automobiles to the United States, and Americans who hope to sell computers in Saudi Arabia. It also matters to American tourists who cash their traveler's checks in London, Athens, or Bangkok.

In this chapter we ask what it means to speak of the "price of the dollar" and what causes this price to change. The discussion will bring together material on three topics studied elsewhere in this book: the theory of supply and demand (Chapter 4), the nature of money (Chapter 31), and international trade (Chapter 39).

The Nature of Foreign Exchange Transactions

We have seen that money, which consists of any accepted medium of exchange, is vital in any sophisticated economy that relies on specialization and exchange. Yet money as we know it is a *national* matter, one that is closely controlled by the national governments. If you live in Sweden, you earn kronor and spend kronor; if you run a business in Austria, you borrow schillings and meet your payroll with schillings. The currency of a country is acceptable within the bounds of that country, but usually it will not be accepted by households and firms in another country. The Stockholm bus company will accept kronor for a fare but not Austrian schillings. The Austrian worker will not take Swedish kronor for wages but will accept schillings.

American producers require payment in dollars for their products. They need dollars to meet their wage bills, to pay for their raw materials, and to reinvest or to distribute their profits. There is no problem when they sell to American purchasers. However, if they sell their goods to Indian importers, either the Indians must exchange their rupees to acquire dollars to pay for the goods or the U.S. producers must accept rupees. They will accept rupees only if they know that they can exchange the rupees for the dollars that they require. The same holds true for producers in all countries; they must eventually receive payment for the goods that they sell in terms of the currency of their own country.

In general, trade between nations can occur only if it is possible to exchange the currency of one nation for that of another.

The exchange rate. International payments that require the exchange of one national currency for another can be made in a bewildering variety of ways, but in essence they involve the exchange of currencies between people who have one currency and require another. Suppose that an American firm wishes to acquire £3,000 for some purpose (£ is the symbol for the British pound sterling). The firm can go to its bank or to some other seller of foreign currency and buy a check that will be accepted in the United Kingdom as £3,000. How many *dollars* the firm must pay to purchase this check will depend on the price of pounds in terms of dollars.

The exchange of one currency for another is part of the process of foreign exchange. The term *foreign exchange* refers to the actual foreign currency or various claims on it, such as bank deposits or promises to pay, that are traded for each other. The *exchange rate* is the price at which purchases and sales of for-

eign currency or claims on it take place; it is the amount of home currency that must be paid in order to obtain one unit of the foreign currency. For example, if one must give up $2 to get £1, the exchange rate is 2.[1]

A rise in the price of foreign exchange (i.e., a rise in the exchange rate) is a **depreciation** of the home currency. *Foreign currencies have become more expensive; therefore, the relative value of the home currency has fallen.* A fall in the price of foreign exchange (i.e., a fall in the exchange rate) is an **appreciation** of the home currency. *Foreign currencies have become cheaper; therefore, the relative value of home currency has risen.* For example, when the dollar price of sterling rises from $2.00 to $2.50 (in other words, the sterling price of the dollar falls from £.50 to £.40), the dollar has *depreciated* and the pound has *appreciated*.

The mechanism of foreign exchange transactions. Let us see how foreign exchange transactions are carried out. Suppose that an American firm wishes to purchase a British sports car to sell in the United States. The British firm that made the car requires payment in pounds sterling. If the car is priced at £15,000, the American firm will go to its bank, purchase a check for £15,000, and send the check to the British seller. Let us suppose that this requires that the firm pay

[1] This expresses the relative values of the two currencies in terms of the dollar price of one pound sterling. Alternatively, one could consider the pound sterling price of $1.00, which in this example is £.50.

TABLE 41-1   Changes in the Balance Sheets of Two Banks as a Result of International Payments

U.K. bank			U.S. bank		
Assets	Liabilities		Assets	Liabilities	
No change	(1) Deposits of car exporter	+£15,000	No change	(1) Deposits of car importer	−$25,000
	(2) Deposits of refrigerator importer	−£15,000		(2) Deposits of refrigerator exporter	+$25,000
	Net change	0		Net change	0

International transactions involve a transfer of deposit liabilities among banks. The table records two separate international transactions at an exchange rate of $1.00 = £.60: (1) an American purchase of a British car for £15,000 (= $25,000); and (2) a British purchase of American refrigerators for $25,000 (= £15,000). The American's import of a car reduces deposit liabilities to U.S. residents and increases deposit liabilities to British residents. The Britisher's import of refrigerators does the opposite. When a series of transactions are equal in value, there is only a transfer of deposit liabilities among individuals within a country. The American refrigerator manufacturer received (in effect) the dollars that the American car purchaser gave up to get a British-made car.

$25,000.[2] (The exchange rate in this transaction is £1.00 = $1.67, or $1.00 = £.60.) The British firm deposits the check in its bank.

Now assume that in the same period of time a British wholesale firm purchases 25 American refrigerators to sell in Great Britain. If the refrigerators are priced at $1,000 each, the American seller will have to be paid $25,000. To make this payment, the British importing firm goes to its bank, writes a check on its account for £15,000, and receives a check drawn on a U.S. bank for $25,000. The check is sent to America and deposited in an American bank. The effects of these transactions are shown in Table 41-1.

The two transactions cancel each other out, and there is no net change in international liabilities. No money need pass between British and American banks; each bank merely increases the deposit of one domestic customer and lowers the deposit of another. Indeed, as long as the flow of payments between the two countries is equal (i.e., Americans pay as much to British residents as British residents pay to Americans), all payments can be managed as in the preceding example and there will be no need for a net payment from British banks to American banks.

All these calculations involve comparing magnitudes measured in different currencies. These comparisons are done by using the exchange rate. We now turn to an analysis of how such exchange rates are determined.

The Determination of Exchange Rates

For the sake of simplicity, we now consider an example involving trade between the United States and the United Kingdom and the determination of the exchange rate between their two currencies, dollars and sterling. The two-country example simplifies things, but the principles apply to all foreign transactions. *Thus, sterling stands for foreign exchange in general, and the dollar price of sterling stands for the foreign exchange rate in general.*

We can relate our example to the demand-and-supply analysis of Chapter 4. To do so, we need only

[2] Banks charge a small commission for making currency exchanges, but we will ignore this and assume that parties can exchange monies back and forth at the going exchange rate.

to recognize that *in the market for pounds sterling* the American firm that wants pounds is a demander of pounds and the British firm that is selling pounds to buy dollars is a supplier of pounds. We can also look at the *same* transaction in the market for dollars: The American firm is a supplier of dollars, and the British firm is a demander of dollars.

Because one currency is traded for another in the foreign exchange market, it follows that to demand dollars implies a willingness to supply foreign exchange, while to supply dollars implies a demand for foreign exchange.

When £1.00 = $1.67, a British importer who offers to buy $5.00 with pounds must be offering to sell £3.00. Similarly, an American importer who offers to sell $5.00 for pounds must be offering to buy £3.00. For this reason a theory of the exchange rate between dollars and pounds can deal either with the demand for and the supply of dollars or with the demand for and the supply of pounds sterling; both need not be considered. We will concentrate on the demand, supply, and price of dollars (quoted in pounds).

The Demand for Dollars

Sources of Demand for Dollars

American exports.   One important source of demand for dollars in foreign exchange markets is people who do not currently hold dollars but who wish to buy American-made goods and services. The British importer of refrigerators is such a purchaser; an Austrian couple planning to vacation in the United States is another; the Soviet government seeking to buy American wheat is a third. All are sources of demand for dollars, arising out of international trade. Each potential buyer wants to sell its own currency and buy dollars for the purpose of purchasing American exports.

Long-term capital flows.   A second source of a demand for dollars comes from foreigners who wish to purchase American assets. In recent years foreign households and firms have invested billions of dollars in American securities and real estate. This has required the conversion of foreign currencies into U.S. dollars. The resulting transactions are called *long-term* *capital movements* or *flows*. In order to buy American assets, holders of foreign currencies must first buy dollars in foreign exchange markets.

Short-term capital flows.   When interest rates in the United States soared in the early 1980s, floods of "foreign money" came into the United States to buy short-term treasury bills and notes, certificates of deposit, and so on. The buyers of these securities were seeking a high return on their liquid assets, but first these buyers had to convert their lire, guilder, marks, and francs into dollars in the foreign exchange market. When people sell financial assets in one country for foreign exchange that they then use to buy short-term financial assets in another country, the transactions are called *short-term capital movements* or *flows*.

A medium of exchange.   Certain currencies, the most important of which is the American dollar, have come to be accepted by nations, banks, and ordinary people as an international medium of exchange. These currencies are readily acceptable among buyers and sellers who might be less willing to trade with each other if they were using less well-known kinds of currency. Thus, a Norwegian exporter of smoked fish, selling to a Turkish wholesaler, may quote prices in dollars and expect payment in dollars. Most of the oil that is sold by the OPEC countries must be paid for in dollars, so a French purchaser of oil must convert francs to dollars to buy oil from Saudi Arabia.

There is therefore a demand for currencies that can act as an international medium of exchange. Some of the trading in the U.S. dollar exists to provide a medium of exchange that is quite independent of the flow of American imports or exports.

Reserve currency.   Firms, banks, and governments often accumulate and hold foreign exchange reserves, just as individuals maintain savings accounts. The government of Nigeria, for example, may decide to increase its reserve holdings of dollars and reduce its reserve holdings of pounds; if so, it will be a demander of dollars (and a supplier of pounds) in foreign exchange markets.

The Total Demand for Dollars

The demand for dollars by holders of foreign currencies is the sum of the demands for all of the purposes just discussed—for purchases of American exports, for long- or short-term capital movements, for purchases of the dollar to use in other transactions, or for adding to currency reserves.

Furthermore, since people, firms, and governments in all countries purchase goods from and invest in many other countries, the demand for any one currency will be the aggregate demand of individuals, firms, and governments in a number of different countries. Thus, the total demand for dollars, for example, may include Germans who are offering marks, Britishers who are offering pounds, Greeks who are offering drachmas, and so on. For simplicity, however, we continue with our two-country example and use only Britain and the United States.

The Shape of the Demand Curve for Dollars

The demand for dollars in terms of pounds is represented by a downward-sloping curve, such as the one shown in Figure 41-1. This figure plots the price of dollars (measured in pounds) on the vertical axis and the quantity of dollars on the horizontal axis. Moving down the vertical scale, the dollar becomes cheaper; that is, it is worth fewer pounds. Its value is depreciating in the foreign exchange market. Moving up the scale, the dollar becomes more expensive; its value is appreciating.[3]

Why does the demand curve for dollars slope downward? Consider the demand derived from purchases of American exports. If the dollar depreciates in value, the sterling price of American exports will fall. The British will buy more of the cheaper U.S. goods and will require more dollars for this purpose. The quantity of dollars demanded will rise. In the opposite case, when the dollar rises in value, the price of American exports rises in terms of foreign currency. The British will buy fewer U.S. goods and thus demand fewer U.S. dollars.

Similar considerations affect other sources of demand for dollars. When the dollar is cheaper, American assets or securities become attractive purchases, and the quantity purchased will rise. As it does, the quantity of dollars demanded to pay for the purchases will increase.

---

[3] Since we have chosen to work with the demand and supply of dollars, the vertical axis measures the pound sterling price of dollars, which is the inverse of the exchange rate as we have defined it. Thus, the exchange rate falls as we move up the vertical axis.

FIGURE 41-1   An Exchange Rate Determined on a Competitive Market

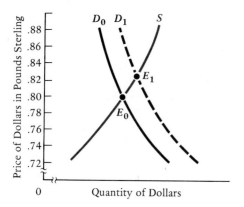

The equilibrium exchange rate equates demand and supply in the foreign exchange market. The quantity of dollars demanded is originally equal to the quantity supplied at a price of £.80 per dollar (or £1.00 = $1.25). If the demand for dollars rises to D_1, the equilibrium exchange rate will change to £.82 per dollar; that is, the dollar appreciates in value, and the pound depreciates in value.

The demand curve for dollars in the foreign exchange market is downward sloping when it is plotted against the sterling price of dollars.

The Supply of Dollars

Because of the symmetrical nature of foreign exchange markets, the sources of supply of dollars are merely the opposite side of the demand for pounds. (Recall that the *supply* of dollars by people who are seeking pounds is the same as the *demand* for pounds by holders of dollars.) Who wants to sell dollars? Americans, seeking to purchase foreign goods and services or assets, will be supplying dollars and purchasing foreign exchange for this purpose. Holders of American securities may decide to sell their American holdings and shift them into foreign assets. If they do, they will try to sell dollars; that is, they will be supplying dollars to the foreign exchange market. Similarly, a country with large dollar reserves of foreign exchange may decide that the dollar is "weak" and try to sell dollars in order to buy another currency.

Once again, people from many sources may be wishing to give up dollars and acquire foreign exchange for many purposes, but for simplicity, we continue with our two-country example.

What about the shape of the supply curve of dollars? When the dollar depreciates, the effective price of British exports to the United States rises. It takes more dollars to buy the same British good, so Americans will buy fewer of the now more expensive British goods. The amount of dollars being offered in exchange for pounds sterling in order to pay for British exports (American imports) will fall.[4]

In the opposite case, when the dollar appreciates, British exports to the United States become cheaper, more are sold, and more dollars are spent on them. Thus, more dollars will be offered in exchange for pounds, in order to obtain the foreign exchange that is needed to pay for the extra imports. Precisely the same argument, used for commodities, applies to purchases and sales of assets.

The supply curve of dollars in the foreign exchange market is upward sloping when it is plotted against the sterling price of dollars.

Equilibrium Exchange Rates in a Competitive Market

Consider a rate of exchange that is set in a freely competitive market. Like any competitive price, this rate fluctuates according to the conditions of demand and supply.

Assume that the current price of dollars is so low (say, £.76 in Figure 41-1) that the quantity of dollars demanded exceeds the quantity supplied. Dollars will be in scarce supply, some people who require dollars to make payments to America will be unable to obtain them, and the price of dollars will be bid up. The value of the dollar vis-à-vis the pound will appreciate. As the price of the dollar rises, the sterling price of U.S. exports to the United Kingdom rises and the quantity of U.S. dollars demanded to buy British goods decreases. However, as the dollar price

---

[4] As long as the elasticity of demand for imports is greater than one, the fall in the volume of imports will swamp the rise in price and hence fewer dollars will be spent on them. This elasticity condition is related to a famous, long-standing issue in international economics. In what follows, we adopt the standard case of the condition's being met. In a more general form, it is called the *Marshall-Lerner condition*, after two famous economists who first studied the problem.

of imports from the United Kingdom falls, a larger quantity will be purchased and the quantity of U.S. dollars supplied will rise. Thus, a rise in the price of the dollar reduces the quantity demanded and increases the quantity supplied. Where the two curves intersect, quantity demanded equals quantity supplied, and the exchange rate is in equilibrium.

What happens when the price of dollars is above its equilibrium value? The quantity of dollars demanded will be less than the quantity supplied. With the dollar in excess supply, some people who wish to convert dollars into pounds will be unable to do so. The price of dollars will fall, fewer dollars will be supplied, more will be demanded, and an equilibrium will be reestablished.

A foreign exchange market is like other competitive markets in that the forces of demand and supply tend to lead to an equilibrium price in which quantity demanded equals quantity supplied.

Changes in Exchange Rates

What causes exchange rates to vary? The simplest answer to this question is changes in demand or supply in the foreign exchange market. Anything that shifts the demand curve for dollars to the right or the supply curve for dollars to the left leads to an appreciation of the dollar. Anything that shifts the demand curve for dollars to the left or the supply curve for dollars to the right leads to a depreciation of the dollar. This is nothing more than a restatement of the laws of supply and demand, applied now to the market for foreign currencies.

What causes the shifts in demand and supply that lead to changes in exchange rates? There are many causes, some of which are transitory and some of which are persistent; we mention several of the most important ones.

A Rise in the Domestic Price of Exports

Suppose that the dollar price of American electronic equipment rises. What this will do to the demand for dollars depends on the foreign elasticity of demand for the American product. If the demand is elastic, perhaps because other countries supply the same product in world markets, the total amount spent will decrease and thus fewer dollars will be

demanded; that is, the demand curve for dollars will shift to the left and the dollar will depreciate.

If the demand is inelastic, say, because America is uniquely able to supply the product for which there are no close substitutes, more will be spent, the demand for dollars to pay the bigger bill will shift the demand curve to the right, and the dollar will appreciate.

A Rise in the Foreign Price of Imports

Suppose that the sterling price of Scotch whisky increases sharply. Assume also that American drinkers have an elastic demand for Scotch because they can easily switch to bourbon, rye, and other relatively close substitutes. They thus end up spending fewer pounds for Scotch whisky than they did before. Hence, they must supply fewer dollars to the foreign exchange market. The supply curve of dollars shifts to the left, and the dollar will appreciate. (If the demand for imported Scotch were inelastic, spending on Scotch would rise and the supply of dollars would shift to the right, leading to a depreciation of the dollar.)

Changes in the Overall Price Levels

Suppose that, instead of a change in the price of a specific export, such as electronic calculators, there is a change in all prices, due to inflation. What matters here is the change in the U.S. price level *relative* to the price levels of its trading partners. (In our two-country example, the United Kingdom stands for the rest of the world.)

An equal percentage change in the price level in both countries.   Suppose that there is a 10 percent inflation in both the United States and the United Kingdom. In this case, the sterling prices of British goods and the dollar prices of U.S. goods both rise by 10 percent. At the existing exchange rate, the dollar prices of British goods and the sterling prices of American goods will each rise by 10 percent. Thus, the relative prices of imports and domestically produced goods will be unchanged in both countries. There is now no reason to expect a change in either country's demand for imports at the original exchange rate, so the inflation in the two countries leaves the equilibrium exchange rate unchanged.

This argument forms the basis of what is called the *purchasing power parity* theory of exchange rates, a theory we shall study below.

A change in the price level of only one country.   What will happen if there is inflation in the United States, while the price level remains stable in the United Kingdom?[5] The dollar price of U.S. goods will rise, and they will become more expensive in the United Kingdom. This will cause the quantity of American exports, and therefore the quantity of dollars demanded by British importers in order to pay for American goods, to diminish.

At the same time, British exports to America will have an unchanged dollar price, while the price of American goods sold at home will increase because of the inflation. Thus, British goods will be more attractive compared with American goods (because they have become *relatively* cheaper), and more British goods will be bought in America. At any exchange rate, the quantity of dollars supplied in order to purchase pounds will be increased.

An American inflation, unmatched in the United Kingdom, will cause the demand curve for dollars to shift to the left and the supply curve of dollars to shift to the right. As a result the equilibrium price of dollars must fall; there is a depreciation in the value of the dollar relative to that of the pound.

Inflation at unequal rates.   The two foregoing examples are, of course, just limiting cases of a more general situation in which the price levels change in both countries. The arguments can readily be extended when we realize that it is the *relative* size of the changes in prices in two countries that determines whether home goods or foreign goods look more or less attractive. If country A's inflation rate is higher than country B's, country A's exports are becoming relatively expensive in B's markets, while imports from B are becoming relatively cheap in A's markets. This will shift the demand curve for A's currency to the left and the supply curve to the right. Each change causes the price of A's currency to fall.

If the price level of one country is rising relative to that of another country, the equilibrium value of its currency will be falling relative to that of the other country.

---

[5] When we consider price *level* changes, the elasticity of demand is relevant, as in the case just studied when a *particular* price changes. To simplify, we proceed by maintaining the assumption, outlined in footnote 4, that the foreign and domestic demands for imported goods are *elastic.*

Capital Movements

Major capital flows can exert strong influences on exchange rates. For example, an increased desire by Americans to invest in British assets will shift the supply curve for dollars to the right and depreciate the value of the dollar.

A movement of investment funds has the effect of appreciating the currency of the capital-importing country and depreciating the currency of the capital-exporting country.

This statement is true for all capital movements—short term or long term. Since the motives that lead to large capital movements are likely to be different in the short and long terms, however, it is worth considering each of them.

Short-term capital movements.   A major motive for short-term capital flows is a change in interest rates. International traders hold transactions balances just as domestic traders do. These balances are often lent out on a short-term basis rather than being left idle. Naturally, the holders of these balances will tend to lend them, other things being equal, in those markets where interest rates are highest. Thus, if one major country's short-term rate of interest rises above the rates in most other countries, there will tend to be a large inflow of short-term capital into that country in an effort to take advantage of the high rate, and this will tend to appreciate the currency. If these short-term interest rates should fall, there will most likely be a sudden shift away from that country as a source of transactions balances, and its currency will tend to depreciate.

A second motive for short-term capital movements is speculation about a country's exchange rate. If foreigners expect the dollar to appreciate, they will rush to buy assets that pay off in dollars; if they expect the dollar to depreciate, they will be reluctant to buy or to hold American securities.

Long-term capital movements.   Long-term capital movements are largely influenced by long-term expectations about another country's profit opportunities and the long-run value of its currency. A British firm would be more willing to purchase an American factory if it expected that the dollar profits would buy more pounds sterling in future years than the profits from investment in a British factory. This could happen if the American firm earned greater profits than the British firm, with exchange rates remaining unchanged. It could also happen if the profits were the same but the British firm expected the dollar to appreciate relative to the pound.

Structural Changes

An economy can undergo structural changes that alter the equilibrium exchange rate. *Structural change* is an omnibus term for a change in cost structures, the invention of new products, or anything else that affects the pattern of comparative advantage. For example, when a country's products do not improve as rapidly as those of some other country, consumers' demand (at fixed prices) shifts slowly away from the first country's products and toward those of its foreign competitors. This causes a slow depreciation in the first country's currency, because the demand for its currency is shifting slowly leftward.

The Balance of Payments

Balance-of-Payments Accounts

In order to know what is happening to the course of international trade, governments keep track of the transactions among countries. The record of such transactions is made in the *balance-of-payments accounts*. Each transaction, such as a shipment of exports or the arrival of imported goods, is classified according to the payments or receipts that would typically arise from it. Table 41-2 shows the major items in the American balance-of-payments accounts for 1987.

Current Account

The **current account** records payments arising from trade in goods and services and from income in the form of interest, profits, and dividends arising from capital owned in one country and invested in another. The current account is divided into two main sections: the *visible account* and the *invisible account*.

The first of these, the **visible account,** is var-

TABLE 41-2 U.S. Balance of Payments, 1987 *(billions of dollars)*	
Current account	
Merchandise exports	+ 250
Merchandise imports	− 410
Trade balance	− 160
Services balance	+ 10
Government grants and other transfers	− 11
Balance on current account	− 154
Capital account	
Net change in U.S. investments abroad (increase −, decrease +)	− 76
Net change in foreign investments in United States (increase +, decrease −)	+ 211
Balance on capital account	+ 135
Balance on capital plus current accounts	− 19
Official Financing	
Changes in liabilities to foreign official agencies (increase +, decrease −)	− 8
Use of official reserves (increase −, decrease +)	+ 9
Statistical discrepancy[a]	+ 18
Overall balance of payments	Always zero

Source: Economic Report of the President, 1989.

[a] In balance-of-payments accounts there is a "statistical discrepancy" item that results from the inability to measure accurately some items. For example, many capital transactions are not recorded.

The overall balance of payments always balances, but the individual components do not have to. In this example the United States shows a negative (deficit) trade balance (imports exceed exports) and a smaller negative (deficit) balance on current account. There is a positive (surplus) balance on capital account, because capital imports exceeded capital exports. This is because the United States has in recent years been a large net borrower of funds from abroad. The capital *plus* current account surplus is what is commonly referred to as the *balance of payments*. It is exactly matched by the balance in the official accounts. Note the very large statistical discrepancy of a size that is commonly found in recent years, but not in earlier ones. Evidently, some major international transactions are not now being recorded in the payments statistics.

iously called the **trade account** and the **merchandise account.** It records payments and receipts arising from the import and export of tangible goods, such as computers, cars, wheat, and shoes. American imports require the use of foreign exchange and hence are entered as debit items on the visible account. American exports earn foreign exchange and hence are recorded as credit items.

The second of these, the **invisible account,** is also called the **service account.** It records payments arising out of trade in services and payments for the use of capital. Trade in such services as insurance, shipping, and tourism is entered in the invisible account, as are payments of interest, dividends, and profits that are made for capital used in one country but owned by residents of another country.

Those items that use foreign exchange, such as purchases by American residents of foreign insurance and shipping services, travel abroad by Americans, and payments to foreign residents of interest earned in the United States, are entered as debit items. Those items that earn foreign exchange, such as foreign purchases of American insurance and shipping services, foreign travel in the United States, and payments to American residents of interest earned abroad, are entered as credit items.

Capital Account

The second main division in the balance of payments is the **capital account,** which records transactions related to international movements of financial capital. The export of funds from the United States, called a *capital export*, uses foreign exchange and so is entered as a debit item in the U.S. payments accounts. The import of funds into the United States, called a *capital import*, earns foreign exchange and so is entered as a credit item in the payments statistics.

It may seem odd that, while a merchandise export is a credit item on current account, the export of capital is a debit item on capital account. To see that there is no contradiction between the treatments of goods and capital, consider the export of American funds for investment in a German bond. The capital transaction involves the purchase, and hence the *import*, of a German bond, and this has the same effect on the balance of payments as the purchase, and hence the import, of a German good. Both items involve payments to foreigners, and both use foreign

exchange. Both are thus debit items in American balance-of-payments accounts.

The capital account often distinguishes between movements of short-term and long-term capital. Short-term capital is money that is held in the form of highly liquid assets, such as bank accounts and short-term treasury bills. If a nonresident merchant buys dollars and places them in a deposit account in New York, this represents an inflow of short-term capital into the United States, and it will be recorded as a credit item on short-term capital account. Long-term capital represents funds coming into the United States (a credit item) or leaving the United States (a debit item), to be invested in less liquid assets, such as long-term bonds, or in physical capital, such as a new automobile assembly plant.

The two major subdivisions of the long-term part of the capital accounts are *direct investment and portfolio investment*. **Direct investment** relates to changes in nonresident ownership of domestic firms and resident ownership of foreign firms. Thus, one form of direct investment in the United States is capital investment in a branch plant or a subsidiary corporation in the United States in which the investor has voting control. Another form is a takeover, in which a controlling interest in a firm, previously controlled by residents, is acquired by foreigners. **Portfolio investment,** on the other hand, is investment in bonds or a minority holding of shares that does not involve legal control.

Official Financing Account

The final section in the balance-of-payments account represents transactions in the *official reserves* that are held by a country's central bank. These transactions reflect the financing of the balance on the remainder of the accounts. The central banks of most countries hold reserves of funds that they use in order to buy and sell in the foreign exchange market. Some of these reserves are held in gold, some in foreign exchange, some as claims on various major foreign currencies, and some in an international currency, called *special drawing rights,* or *SDRs* (which we shall study in Chapter 42).

The Federal Reserve Board, operating on behalf of the government, can intervene in the market for foreign exchange to influence the dollar's exchange rate. For example, to prevent the price of dollars from falling, the Fed must buy dollars. This means that it must sell gold or foreign exchange. It can do so only if it holds reserves of these media. When the Fed wishes to stop the dollar from rising in value, it enters the market and sells dollars. In this case, the Fed buys foreign exchange, which it then adds to its reserves.

The Meaning of Payments Balances and Imbalances

We have seen that the payments accounts show the total of receipts of foreign exchange (credit items) and payments of foreign exchange (debit items) on account of each category of payment. It is also common to calculate the *balance* on separate items or groups of items. The concept of the balance of payments is used in a number of different ways, which can be confusing, so we must approach this issue in a series of steps.

The Balance of Payments Must Balance Overall

Notice two things about the payments accounts. First, they record *actual* payments, not *desired* payments. Second, they record *all* payments, whatever the reasons for which they were made. For example, it is quite possible that, at the existing exchange rate between dollars and yen, holders of yen would want to purchase more dollars than holders of dollars would want to sell in exchange for yen. In this situation, the quantity of dollars demanded exceeds the quantity supplied. However, holders of yen cannot actually buy more dollars than holders of dollars can actually sell; every yen that is bought must have been sold by someone, and every dollar that is sold must have been bought by someone.

It follows that, if we add up all the receipts arising from (1) payments received by U.S. residents on account of American exports of goods and services, (2) capital imports, and (3) purchase of foreign exchange or gold by the Fed, these must be exactly equal to all payments made by holders of dollars arising from (1) American imports of goods and services, (2) exports of capital, and (3) sale of foreign exchange or gold by the Fed.

This relationship is so important that it is worthwhile for us to write it out in symbols. We let C, K,

and F stand for current account, capital account, and official financing account, respectively, and use a P for payments (debit items) and R for receipts (credit items). Now we can write

$$C_R + K_R + F_R = C_P + K_P + F_P \qquad [1]$$

All this tells us is that, if we add up all transactions, they must balance in total.

Although the relationship given in Equation 1 is necessarily true, it often worries students who feel that it need not be true. Box 41-1 provides some examples to help clarify the issue.

Payments on Specific Parts of the Accounts Do Not Need to Balance

Although the overall total of payments must equal the overall total of receipts, the same zero balance does not have to hold on subsections of the overall accounts. We now look at the balances on *parts* of the accounts—balances that may be positive or negative. We do this first in relation to particular countries and then in relation to particular subsectors of the account.

Country balances. When all foreign countries are taken together, a country's balance of payments must balance, but a country can have bilateral surpluses or deficits with individual foreign countries or with groups of countries. In general, the **multilateral balance of payments** refers to the balance between one country's payments to and receipts from the rest of the world. When all items are considered, every country must have a zero multilateral payments balance with the rest of the world, although it can have bilateral surpluses or deficits with individual countries. This important principle is illustrated in the second part of Box 41-1.

Subsection balances. The balance on visible, or merchandise, account refers to the difference between the value of U.S. exports of goods and the value of imports of goods. A surplus occurs when exports of goods exceed imports of goods, while a deficit occurs when imports exceed exports. The balance on invisible accounts refers to the difference between the value of receipts on invisible accounts and the value of payments for invisible accounts. The *balance of payments on current account* is the sum of the balances

BOX 41-1

An Illustration of How the Balance of Payments Always Balances

Trade Between Two Countries

Suppose that the sole international transaction made this year by a small country called Myopia was an export to the United States of Myopian coconuts worth $1,000. Further suppose that the Myopian central bank issues a local currency, the stigma, but does not operate in the foreign exchange market, so there is no official financing. Finally, suppose that Myopia's self-sufficient inhabitants want no imports. Surely, then, you might think that Myopia has an overall favorable balance of $1,000, which is a current account receipt (C_R) with no balancing item on the payments side.

To see why such a conclusion is wrong, we must ask what the exporter of coconuts did with the dollars that he received for his coconuts. Let us suppose that he deposited them in a New York bank. This transaction represents a capital export from Myopia. Myopians have accumulated claims on foreign exchange, which they hold in the form of a deposit with a foreign bank. Thus, there are two entries in the Myopian accounts: One is a credit item for the export of coconuts ($C_R = $1,000$), and

the other is a debit item for the export of capital ($K_P = $1,000$). The fact that the same firm made both transactions is irrelevant. Although the current account shows a credit balance, the capital account exactly balances this with a debit item. Hence, looking at the *balance of payments as a whole*, the two sides of the account are equal. The balance of payments has balanced—as it must always do.

Consider now a slightly more realistic case. If the coconut exporter wants to turn his $1,000 into Myopian stigmas, so that he can pay his coconut pickers in local currency, he must find someone who wishes to buy his dollars in return for Myopian currency. However, we have assumed that no one in Myopia wants to import, so no one wants to sell Myopian currency for current account reasons. Assume, however, that a wealthy Myopian landowner would like to invest $1,000 in New York by buying shares in an American firm. To do so, she needs $1,000. The coconut exporter can sell his $1,000 to the landowner in return for stigmas. Now he can pay his local bills. The landowner sells her stigmas to the exporter in return for dollars. Now she can buy the American shares.

on the visible and invisible accounts. It gives the balance between payments and receipts on all income-related items.

As a carry-over from a long-discredited eighteenth century economic doctrine called *mercantilism,* a credit balance on current account (receipts exceed payments) is called a **favorable balance,** while a debit balance (payments exceed receipts) is called an **unfavorable balance.**

Mercantilists, both ancient and modern, hold that the gains from trade arise only from having a favorable balance of trade. This misses the whole point of the doctrine of comparative advantage, which states

that countries can gain from a balanced increase in trade between themselves because of the opportunity that it provides for each country to specialize according to its comparative advantage. The modern resurgence of mercantilism is discussed in Box 41-2.

The balance on capital account gives the difference between receipts of foreign exchange and payments of foreign exchange arising out of capital movements. A surplus, or "favorable" balance, on capital account means that a country is a *net* importer of capital, while a deficit, or "unfavorable" balance, means that a country is a *net* exporter of capital.

Notice that a deficit on capital account, which is

Once again, the Myopian balance of payments will show two entries, equal in size, but one is a credit and the other is a debit. There is a credit item for the export of coconuts (the sale of coconuts earned foreign exchange) and a debit item for the export of capital (the purchase of the American shares used foreign exchange).

Trade Involving Many Countries

In the preceding example, Myopia had what is called a *bilateral payments balance* with the United States. The *bilateral balance of payments* between any two countries is the balance between the payments and the receipts flowing between them. If there were only two countries in the world, their overall payments would have to be in bilateral balance; that is, one country's payments to the other would be equal to its receipts from the other. However, this is not true when there are more than two countries involved.

Suppose that in the year following the one just discussed, Myopia again sells $1,000 worth of coconuts to the United States, that the landowner does not wish to invest further in the United States, but that the Myopian people wish to buy 200,000 yens worth of parasols from Japan. (Assume also that in the foreign exchange market $1 trades for 200 yen.) Finally, assume that a Japanese importer wishes to buy $1,000 worth of skateboards from an American company.

Now what, in effect, happens is that the Myopian coconut exporter sells his $1,000 to the Japanese skateboard importer for 200,000 yen, which the coconut exporter then sells to the Myopian parasol importer in return for Myopian stigmas. (In the real world the exchanges are all done through banks, but this is what happens, in effect.) Now the Myopian payments statistics will show a $1,000 bilateral payments surplus with the United States—receipts of $1,000 from the United States on account of coconut exports, and no payments to the United States—and a bilateral deficit with Japan of 200,000 yen (equal to $1,000)—$1,000 of payments to Japan on account of parasol imports and no receipts from Japan. However, when both countries are considered, Myopia's multilateral payments are in balance.

referred to as an unfavorable balance, merely indicates that a country is investing abroad. For a rich country to invest abroad and accumulate assets that will earn income in the future may be a desirable situation. So, once again we observe that there is nothing necessarily unfavorable about having an "unfavorable" balance on any of the payments accounts.

A credit balance on official settlements account means that the Fed has bought more gold and foreign exchange than it has sold. This adds to its reserves of foreign exchange. A deficit balance means that the Fed has sold more gold and foreign exchange than it has bought. This reduces its foreign exchange reserves.

The Relationship Between Various Balances

Two important points should be noticed at this time. First, since overall payments must balance, the terms "a balance-of-payments *deficit*" and "a balance-of-payments *surplus*" refer to the balance on some part of the payments accounts. Second, because of the necessity for the balance of payments to balance overall, a deficit on any one part of the accounts implies an offsetting surplus on the rest of the ac-

BOX 41-2

The Volume of Trade, the Balance of Trade, and the New Mercantilism

Media commentators, political figures, and much of the general public often judge the national balance of payments as they would the accounts of a single firm. Just as a firm is supposed to show a profit, the nation is supposed to secure a balance-of-payments surplus, with the benefits derived from international trade measured by the size of that surplus.

This view is related to the exploitation doctrine of international trade. Since one country's surplus is another country's deficit, one country's gain, judged by its surplus, must be another country's loss, judged by its deficit.

People who hold such views today are echoing an ancient economic doctrine called *mercantilism*. The mercantilists were a group of economists who preceded Adam Smith. They judged the success of trade by the size of the trade balance. In many cases this doctrine made sense in terms of their objective, which was to use international trade as a means of building up the political and military power of the state, rather than as a means of raising the living standards of its citizens. A balance-of-payments surplus allowed the nation (then and now) to acquire foreign exchange reserves. (In those days the reserves took the form of gold. Today they are a mixture of gold and claims on the currencies of other countries.) These reserves could then be used to pay armies, composed partly of foreign mercenaries; to purchase weapons from abroad; and generally to finance colonial adventures.

People who advocate this view in modern times are called *neomercantilists*. Insofar as their object is to increase the power of the state, they are choosing means that could achieve their ends. Insofar as they

are drawing an analogy between what is a sensible objective for a business, interested in its own material welfare, and what is a sensible objective for a society, interested in the material welfare of its citizens, their views are erroneous, for their analogy is false.

If we take the view that the object of economic activity is to promote the welfare and living standards of ordinary citizens, rather than the power of governments, then the mercantilist focus on the balance of trade makes no sense. The law of comparative advantage shows that average living standards are maximized by having individuals, regions, and countries specialize in the things that they can produce comparatively best and then trading to obtain the things that they can produce comparatively worst. The more specialization there is, the more trade occurs.

On this view the gains from trade are to be judged by the volume of trade. A situation in which there is a *large volume* of trade but in which each country has a *zero balance* of trade can thus be regarded as quite satisfactory. Furthermore, a change in commercial policy that results in a balanced increase in trade between two countries will bring gain, because it allows for specialization according to comparative advantage, even though it causes no change in either country's trade balance.

To the business interested in private profit and to the government interested in the power of the state, it is the balance of trade that matters. To the person interested in the welfare of ordinary citizens, it is the volume of trade that matters.

counts. We now consider two important applications of this second statement. The first application concerns the balances on current and capital accounts, while the second concerns the balances on official settlements account and the remainder of the total accounts.

The current and capital account balances.   To make the relationship between current and capital balances clear, let us assume that the Fed does not engage in any foreign exchange transactions. This means that the official settlements account is zero, because both F_R and F_P in Equation 1 are zero.

Now any deficit or surplus on current account must be matched by an equal and opposite surplus or deficit on capital account. For example, if a country has a credit balance on current account, the foreign exchange earned must appear as a debit item in the capital account. The foreign exchange may be used to buy foreign assets or merely stashed away in foreign bank accounts. In either case there is an outflow of capital from the United States. It is recorded as a debit item, because it uses foreign exchange.

We can see this clearly if we return to Equation 1 and set F_R and F_P equal to zero to indicate no transactions by the Fed. This gives us

$$C_R + K_R = C_P + K_P \qquad [2]$$

Now subtract C_P and K_R from both sides of the equation to get

$$C_R - C_P = K_P - K_R \qquad [3]$$

This expresses in equation form what we have just stated in words: A surplus on current account must be balanced by a deficit on capital account (i.e., an outflow of capital), while a deficit on current account must be matched by a surplus on capital account (i.e., an inflow of capital).

One important implication relates to capital transfers. A country that is importing capital has a surplus on capital account, so it *must* have a deficit on current account. This is the position that the United States was in during the mid-1980s. Because of the borrowing requirements of a massive government budget deficit, and because the boom made the United States an attractive place in which to invest, there was a massive capital inflow into the United

States. This inflow made a current account deficit inevitable. As long as the capital inflow persisted, no policy measure could remove the current account deficit. This issue is considered in more detail in Chapter 42.[6]

Official financing and the rest of the accounts.   When people speak of a country as having an overall balance-of-payments deficit or surplus, *they are usually referring to the balance of all accounts, excluding official financing.* A balance-of-payments surplus means that the central bank is adding to its holdings of foreign exchange reserves; a balance-of-payments deficit means that the central bank is reducing its reserves.

If the central bank does not operate in the foreign exchange market, there can be no overall balance-of-payments deficit or surplus on current plus capital account. Suppose that holders of dollars are trying to buy more foreign exchange than holders of foreign currencies wish to sell in return for dollars. There will be an excess supply of dollars and an excess demand for foreign exchange. The dollar will depreciate in the foreign exchange market until demand equals supply. At this point both desired and actual international payments are in balance.

If exchange rates are completely free to vary, balance-of-payments deficits and surpluses will be eliminated through exchange rate adjustments.

In today's world, while no country need have a balance-of-payments problem, many still do have one. As long as governments intervene in foreign exchange markets, there will be balance-of-payments deficits and surpluses. Surpluses will occur whenever the currency is held below its equilibrium level. Persistent deficits will cause a persistent loss of reserves; they are evidence that the government is trying to resist longer-term trends for changes in the exchange rate.

[6] If we allow for the Fed's transactions, the relationship that is given in Equation 3 does not need to hold exactly. The current and capital account balance can diverge from zero by the balance on official settlements account ($F_R - F_P$). Since this balance is almost always small relative to net payments on current and capital account, the relationship between the two major accounts, shown in Equation 3, is always approximately true.

SUMMARY

1. International trade can occur only when it is possible to exchange the currency of one country for that of another. The exchange rate between two currencies is the amount of one currency that must be paid in order to obtain one unit of another currency. Where more than two currencies are involved, there will be an exchange rate between each pair of currencies.

2. The determination of exchange rates in the free market is simply an application of the laws of supply and demand, which we studied in Chapter 4; the item being bought and sold is a nation's money.

3. The demand for dollars arises from American exports of goods and services, long-term and short-term capital flows into the United States, and the desire of foreign banks, firms, and governments to use American dollars as an international medium of exchange or as part of their reserves.

4. The supply of dollars to purchase foreign currencies arises from American imports of goods and services, capital flows from the United States, and the desire of holders of dollars to decrease the size of their holdings.

5. A depreciation of the dollar lowers the foreign price of American exports and increases the quantity of dollars demanded; at the same time, it raises the dollar price of imports from abroad and thus lowers the quantity of dollars supplied to buy foreign exchange to be used to purchase foreign goods. Thus, the demand curve for dollars is downward sloping and the supply curve of dollars is upward sloping when the quantities demanded and supplied are plotted against the price of dollars, measured in terms of a foreign currency.

6. A currency will tend to appreciate in foreign exchange markets if there is a shift to the right of the demand curve or a shift to the left of the supply curve for its currency. Shifts in the opposite directions will tend to depreciate the currency. Such shifts are caused by such things as the prices of imports and exports, the rates of inflation in different countries, capital movements, structural changes, expectations about future trends in earnings and exchange rates, and the level of confidence in the currency as a source of reserves.

7. Actual transactions among the firms, households, and governments of various countries are kept track of and reported in the balance-of-payments accounts. In these accounts any transaction that uses foreign exchange is recorded as a debit item and any transaction that produces foreign exchange is recorded as a credit item. If all transactions are recorded, the sum of all credit items necessarily equals the sum of all debit items, since the foreign exchange that is bought must also have been sold.

8. Major categories in the balance-of-payments account are the balance of trade (exports minus imports), current account, capital account, and official financing. The so-called balance-of-payments account is the balance of the current plus capital accounts; that is, it excludes the transactions on official account. Ignoring official settlements, a balance on current account must be matched by a balance on capital account of equal magnitude but opposite sign.

9. There is nothing inherently good or bad about deficits or surpluses. Persistent deficits or surpluses cannot be sustained, because the former will eventually exhaust a country's foreign exchange reserves and the latter will do the same to a trading partner's reserves.

TOPICS FOR REVIEW

Foreign exchange and exchange rates
Appreciation and depreciation
Sources of the demand for and supply of foreign exchange
Effects on exchange rates of capital flows, inflation, interest rates, and
  expectations about exchange rates
Balance of trade and balance of payments
Current and capital account
Official-financing items
Mercantilist views on the balance of trade and volume of trade

DISCUSSION QUESTIONS

1. What is the probable effect of each of the following on the exchange rate of a country, other things being equal?
    a. The quantity of oil imports is greatly increased, but the value of imported oil is higher due to price decreases.
    b. The country's inflation rate falls well below that of its trading partners.
    c. Rising labor costs of the country's manufacturers lead to a worsening ability to compete in world markets.
    d. The government greatly expands its gifts of food and machinery to underdeveloped countries.
    e. A major boom occurs with rising employment.
    f. The central bank raises interest rates sharply.
    g. More domestic oil is discovered and developed.
2. During the mid-1980s the United States became a major importer of capital, partly to finance the large internal budget deficit and partly because the American boom and the European slump made the United States a highly attractive place in which to invest foreign funds. Predict the effects of this large capital inflow on the U.S. dollar exchange rate and on the balance of payments on current account. Would these developments have anything to do with the upsurge of protectionist sentiment in the Congress during the latter part of the 1980s?
3. In recent years money wages have risen substantially faster in Canada than in the United States. Many Canadians have expressed the fear that their rapidly rising costs will price them out of U.S. markets. Did this fear make sense when the Canadian exchange rate was fixed relative to the American dollar? Does it make sense today, when exchange rates are free to vary on the open market?
4. Indicate whether each of the following transactions increases the demand for dollars, the supply of dollars, or neither in foreign exchange markets.
    a. IBM moves $10 million from bank accounts in the United States to banks in Paris to expand operations there.
    b. The U.S. government extends a grant of $3 million to the government of Peru, which Peru uses to buy farm machinery from a Chicago firm.
    c. Canadian investors, responding to higher profits of U.S. rather than Canadian corporations, buy stocks through the New York Stock Exchange.
    d. Several countries stop interest payments on their large debts to U.S. banks.

e. Lower interest rates in New York than in London encourage British firms to borrow in the New York money market, converting the proceeds into pounds sterling for use at home.

5. "The necessity of the government to stabilize the balance of payments through the settlement account is a relic of the past. It was a by-product of the adherence to a policy of fixed exchange rates." Do you agree?

6. "If a country solves its balance-of-payments problems, it will have solved its foreign trade problems." Discuss this statement.

7. Outline the reasoning behind the following 1989 newspaper headline: "Sterling strengthens as British interest rates rise."

8. In discussing the U.S. current account deficit, the magazine the *Economist* said, "The U.S. hopes to become slim by encouraging its trading partners to grow." How would economic growth in Europe and Japan affect the U.S. current account?

Chapter 42

Alternative Exchange Rate Systems

The nations of the world have tried many different international monetary systems. No system has been fully satisfactory, and periods of crisis have alternated with periods of stability.

The twentieth century began with a system of fixed exchange rates under the gold standard. This system suffered periodic crises in the post–World War I years but did not collapse until the onset of the Great Depression. The 1930s was a period of experimentation with flexible, market-determined exchange rates. This ended with World War II, when governments again fixed exchange rates.

In 1944 the fixed exchange rate regime was formalized by international agreement at a conference in Bretton Woods, New Hampshire. The Bretton Woods system lasted for over a quarter of a century, but its shortcomings and the periods of crisis that it induced finally prevailed over its advantages and the periods of stability that it afforded. After several attempts to patch it up in the 1970s, the system finally broke down and was gradually abandoned, as countries turned one by one to market-determined, flexible exchange rates.

Fixed and Flexible Exchange Rates

Among the principal international monetary systems, two extremes can be distinguished. The first is a system in which exchange rates are fixed at announced par values. The gold standard was such a system, and so was Bretton Woods. (The operation and decline of both systems are discussed in the appendix to this chapter.)

The second is a system of freely fluctuating rates, determined by market demand and supply, in the absence of government intervention. Some countries have come close to this system, first in the 1930s and then since 1971.

Between these two "pure" systems are a variety of possible intermediate cases. The two that we will encounter are known as the *adjustable peg* and the *managed float*. In the adjustable peg system, governments set and attempt to maintain par values for their exchange rates, but they explicitly recognize that circumstances may arise in which they will change the par value. In a managed float, the central bank seeks to have some stabilizing influence on the exchange rate but does not try to fix it at some publicly announced par value.

The International Monetary Fund (also called the IMF and the Fund) was created as part of the Bretton Woods system. Under its original charter, the Fund had several tasks. It tried to ensure that countries kept their exchange rates fixed in the short run. It was supposed to ensure that any exchange rate change was really needed to remove a persistent payments disequilibrium and that a single devaluation did not set off a self-canceling round of devaluations. It also made loans—out of funds subscribed by member nations—to governments to support their exchange rates in the face of temporary payments deficits.

The Bretton Woods system has been abandoned, but the Fund survives, although its tasks have changed. For example, the Jamaica Agreement of 1976 amended the IMF charter to ratify the adoption of floating exchange rates and deemphasize gold as a basis for the international payments system. More recently, the Fund has played a major role in "managing" the international debt crisis.

A Fixed Exchange Rate System

In a system of **fixed exchange rates,** each country's central bank intervenes in the foreign exchange market to prevent its country's exchange rate from going outside a narrow band on either side of its par value.

This system presents one immediate difficulty in that one country must take a passive role with respect to its exchange rate. This is because there is one less exchange rate to be determined than there are countries. In a two-country world, containing only Japan and the United States, for example, if the Bank of Japan fixes the exchange rate at 150 yen to the dollar, the U.S. Federal Reserve cannot fix a different rate, making the dollar worth, say, 200 yen. Under the Bretton Woods system, all foreign countries fixed their exchange rate against the U.S. dollar. The Fed adopted the passive role; it was the only central bank in the world that did not have to intervene to support a particular value of its currency.

Having picked a fixed exchange rate for its currency against, say, the U.S. dollar, each foreign central bank then had to manage matters so that the chosen rate could actually be maintained. The bank had to be prepared to offset imbalances in demand and supply by government sales or purchases of foreign exchange. In the face of short-term fluctuations

in market demand and supply, each central bank could maintain its fixed exchange rate by entering the market and buying and selling as required.

To do this the central bank has to hold reserves of acceptable foreign exchange. When there is an abnormally low demand for its country's currency in the foreign exchange market, the bank keeps the currency from depreciating by selling foreign exchange and buying up domestic currency. This depletes its reserves of foreign exchange. When there is an abnormally high demand for its country's currency in the foreign exchange market, the bank prevents the currency from appreciating by selling domestic currency for foreign exchange. This action increases its stocks of foreign exchange.

As long as the central bank is trying to maintain an exchange rate that equates demand and supply for its currency *on average,* the policy can be successful. Sometimes the bank will be buying, and other times it will be selling, but its reserves will fluctuate around a constant average level.

If, however, there is a permanent shift in demand for or supply of a nation's currency in the foreign exchange market, the long-term equilibrium rate will move away from the **pegged rate,** that is, its par value. It will then be difficult to maintain the pegged rate. For example, if there is a major inflation in France while prices are stable in the United States, the equilibrium value of the franc will fall. In a free market, the franc would depreciate and the U.S. dollar would appreciate. However, a fixed exchange rate is not a free-market rate. If the Bank of France persists in trying to maintain the original exchange rate, it will have to meet the excess demand for U.S. dollars by selling from its reserves. This policy can persist only as long as the bank has reserves that it is willing to spend to maintain an artificially high price of francs. However, the Bank cannot do this indefinitely. Sooner or later the reserves that it has, and those that it can borrow, will be exhausted.

The management of a fixed rate is illustrated in Figure 42-1. The example used is the maintenance by the Bank of England of a fixed exchange rate between the pound sterling and the U.S. dollar.

When the fixed rate is not near the free-market equilibrium rate, controls of various sorts may be introduced, in an attempt to shift the demand curve for foreign exchange so that it intersects the supply curve at a rate close to the fixed rate. This is usually

FIGURE 42-1 A Fixed Exchange Rate

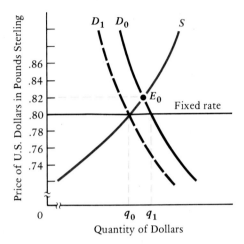

When an exchange rate is fixed at other than the equilibrium rate, either excess demand or excess supply will persist. Suppose that demand and supply curves of dollars in the absence of government controls are D_0 and S; equilibrium is at E_0, with a price of £.82 per dollar. The equilibrium price of the pound is $1.22. Now the British authorities peg the price of the pound at $1.25; that is, they fix the price of the dollar at £.80. They have overvalued the pound and undervalued the dollar. As a result there is an excess of dollars demanded over dollars supplied of q_0q_1. To maintain the fixed rate, it is necessary to shift either the demand curve or the supply curve (or both) so that the two intersect at the fixed rate. For example, demand might be shifted to D_1 by the British government's limiting imports. If the curves are not shifted, the fixed rate will have to be supported by the British government's supplying dollars in the amount of q_0q_1 per period out of its reserves.

done by restricting imports of goods and services or by restricting the export of capital. If the central bank cannot shift demand and supply in order to keep the equilibrium rate approximately as high as the fixed rate, it will have no alternative but to devalue its currency.

Problems with Fixed Exchange Rates

Three problems typically arise in a system of fixed exchange rates: (1) providing sufficient reserves, (2) adjusting to long-term trends, and (3) dealing with speculative crises.

Providing sufficient reserves. Reserves are needed to accommodate short-term balance-of-payments fluctuations arising from the current and the capital accounts. On current account, trade is subject to many short-term variations—some systematic and some random. This means that, even if the value of imports does equal the value of exports on average over several years, there may be considerable imbalances over shorter periods.

With a market-determined exchange rate, fluctuations in current and capital account payments would cause the exchange rate to fluctuate. To prevent such fluctuations when rates are fixed, the monetary authorities buy and sell foreign exchange as required. These operations require that the authorities hold reserves of foreign exchange. If they run out of reserves, they cannot maintain the pegged rate.

As discussed in the appendix to this chapter, the Bretton Woods system had difficulty in providing sufficient reserves. This was because the ultimate reserve was gold and there was not enough of it. As a result, the world's central banks held much of their reserves in U.S. dollars and British pounds sterling. Currencies that are widely held for this purpose are called **reserve currencies.**

This system worked well enough as long as these reserve currencies had a stable value. However, in the mid-1960s fear of an impending devaluation of the pound sterling arose, and in the early 1970s a similar fear arose regarding the U.S. dollar. In both cases the fears were well founded: The pound sterling was devalued in late 1967, and the dollar was devalued in 1971 and again in 1973.

The devaluation of a reserve currency reduces the value of the reserves of that currency held by the world's central banks. Fear that a devaluation will occur reduces the acceptability of a currency as a means of holding reserves. This is discussed further in Box 42-1.

The problem of providing reserves, although serious, need not be insurmountable in any future system of fixed rates. After all, a balanced portfolio, composed of some holdings of a number of currencies, could be held as reserves. This would reduce the risks from holding reserves, since whenever one

BOX 42-1

Problems for Nations Whose Currency Is Held as a Reserve

While it is prestigious to have one's currency held as a reserve currency—and even advantageous, as long as other countries are willing to increase their holdings of one's paper money without making claims on current output—there are disadvantages for the country whose currency is involved. Such a country is placed under great pressure not to devalue its currency. If it does devalue its currency, all countries holding its currency will find the value of their reserves diminished. Further, a devaluation may create a loss of confidence in the currency, and other countries will become reluctant to hold it. The result may well be that the domestic policy of the country whose currency is the reserve becomes unduly subservient to the overriding need to maintain its exchange rate.

The Loss of Confidence in the U.S. Dollar as a Reserve Currency

In the 1950s and 1960s America had frequent deficits on its overall balance of payments. This resulted largely from American loans, investments, and contributions to other nations who were rebuilding their economies after World War II. As long as other nations were willing to accumulate dollar holdings, this caused no problem; indeed, the buildup of dollars provided foreign exchange reserves that were needed to finance the increased volume of world trade.

The dollar devaluations of the early 1970s. Had everyone believed that the devaluations of 1971 (7.9

percent) and 1973 (11 percent) were just isolated adjustments, they might well have licked their wounds and gone on as before. However, many believed that these devaluations were only preludes to inevitable future ones. Fear of further devaluations led many prudent holders to want to decrease their reliance on such a shaky reserve. As people tried to get rid of U.S. dollars, the exchange rate began to slide. Between 1970 and 1973, the U.S. dollar declined 22 percent against the Japanese yen and 30 percent against the German mark. The lower value of the U.S. dollar reduced the real value of most countries' reserves and threatened their financial stability.

Attempts to flee from the dollar. While one country (or one bank) can readily reduce its holdings of U.S. dollars by buying gold or other currencies, for every country to do so requires major changes in the value of the dollar and its alternatives. In the late 1970s, the dollar fell sharply relative to the yen and the mark, and the desire to flee from U.S. dollars to gold contributed to the startling rise in the price of gold in 1979–1980 from $250 to over $900 an ounce.

The return to stable prices in the United States restored some faith in the dollar; indeed, during the period 1981–1984, most observers felt that the dollar was overvalued, so its sharp decline in the mid-1980s was welcomed. While the use of *SDRs* and other currencies has increased, the dollar still remains a key currency, and the problems that are discussed in this box remain.

currency fell in value against a second currency, the second currency would rise in value against the first.

Adjusting to long-term trends. With fixed exchange rates, long-term disequilibria can be expected to de-

velop because of lasting shifts in the demands for and supplies of foreign exchange. There are three important reasons for these shifts. First, different trading countries have different rates of inflation. Chapter 41 explained how these varying rates produce changes in the equilibrium rates of exchange; if the rate is fixed, the differences in inflation rates would produce excess supply or excess demand in each country's foreign exchange market. Second, changes in the demands for and supplies of imports and exports are associated with long-term economic growth. Because the economies of different countries grow at different rates, their demands for imports and their supplies of exports can be expected to shift at different rates. Third, structural changes, such as major new innovations or a change in the price of oil, cause major changes in imports and exports.

The associated shifts in demand and supply in the foreign exchange market imply that there is no reason to believe that the exchange rate consistent with equilibrium in the market for foreign exchange will remain unchanged.

The exchange rate consistent with balance-of-payments equilibrium will change over time; over a decade the change can be substantial.

Governments may react to long-term disequilibria in at least three ways.

1. The exchange rate can be changed whenever it is clear that a balance-of-payments deficit or surplus is the result of a long-term shift in demands and supplies in the foreign exchange market and not the result of some transient factor.

2. Domestic price levels can be allowed to change in an attempt to make the present fixed exchange rate become the equilibrium rate. To restore equilibrium, countries with overvalued currencies need to have deflations and countries with undervalued currencies need to have inflations. However, changes in domestic price levels have all sorts of domestic repercussions. Deflations are difficult and costly to accomplish (e.g., reductions in aggregate demand, intended to lower the price level, are likely to raise unemployment), and often an explicit goal of government policy is to avoid inflation. Often governments will be more willing to change exchange rates than to try to change their price levels.

3. Restrictions can be imposed on trade and foreign payments. Imports and foreign spending by tourists and governments can be restricted, and the export of capital can be slowed or even stopped. Surplus countries are often quick to criticize such restrictions on international trade and payments. However, as long as exchange rates are fixed and

price levels prove difficult to manipulate, deficit countries have little option but to restrict the quantity of foreign exchange that their residents are permitted to obtain.

Since restrictions on trade and foreign payments are undesirable in a world economy that is characterized by large-scale international trade and foreign investment, and since deflations of the price level are difficult and costly to bring about, most countries will want to preserve the possibility of making occasional changes in their exchange rates, even if fixed rates are the main rule of the day.

Under the Bretton Woods system, although most countries defended their exchange rates in the face of crises, there were still major rounds of exchange rate adjustments. Because exchange rates did have to be changed from time to time, the system of fixed rates under the Bretton Woods agreement was called an **adjustable peg system.**

Handling speculative crises.   When enough people begin to doubt the government's ability to maintain the current exchange rate, speculative crises develop. The most important reason for such crises is that over time, equilibrium exchange rates get further and further away from any given set of fixed rates. When the disequilibrium becomes obvious to everyone, traders and speculators come to believe that a realignment of rates is due. There is a rush to buy currencies that are expected to be revalued and a rush to sell currencies that are expected to be devalued. Even if the authorities take drastic steps, there may be doubt that these measures will work before the exchange reserves are exhausted. Speculative flows of funds can reach large proportions, and it may be impossible to avoid changing the exchange rate under such pressure.

Under an adjustable peg system, opportunities often arise for speculators to make large profits; this occurs when everyone knows the direction in which an exchange rate will be changed, if it is to be changed at all.

As the equilibrium value of a country's currency changes, possibly under the impact of high inflation, it becomes obvious that the central bank is having more and more difficulty holding the pegged rate. So when a crisis arises, speculators sell the country's currency. If it is devalued, they can buy it back at a lower price and earn a profit. If it is not devalued, they can buy it back at the price at which they sold it and lose only the commission costs on the deal. This asymmetry, with speculators having a chance to make large profits by risking only a small loss, eventually destroyed the Bretton Woods system.

Flexible Exchange Rates

Under a system of flexible exchange rates, demand and supply determine the rates without any government intervention. (This was illustrated in Figure 41-1 on page 874.) Such rates are called free, **flexible,** or **floating exchange rates.** Since the foreign-exchange market always clears, the government can turn its attention to domestic problems of inflation and unemployment, leaving the balance of payments to take care of itself—at least so went the theory before flexible rates were introduced.

For reasons that we analyze later in this chapter, this optimistic picture did not materialize when the world went over to flexible exchange rates. Free-market fluctuations in rates were far greater and hence potentially more upsetting to the performance of national economies and to the flow of international trade than many economists had anticipated. As a result, central banks have felt the need to intervene quite frequently and extensively to stabilize exchange rates.

Managed Floats

A major difference between the present system and the Bretton Woods system is that central banks no longer publicly announce values for exchange rates that they are committed in advance to defend, even at a heavy cost. Central banks are thus free to adjust their exchange rate targets as circumstances change. Sometimes they leave the rate completely free to fluctuate, and at other times they interfere actively to alter the exchange rate from its free-market value. Such a system is called a **managed float** or a **dirty float.**

Some countries have opted for what is called a *currency block* by pegging their exchange rates against each other and then indulging in a joint float against the outside world. The best-known currency block is the **European monetary system (EMS).** Under this arrangement the countries of the EC, with the exception of the United Kingdom, maintain fixed

rates among their own currencies but allow them to float as a block against the dollar. As Europe moves toward increased economic integration in 1992, momentum also is building for the creation of a common currency area, with one European currency issued by a European central bank.

What Determines the Exchange Rate in a Floating System?

One surprise to supporters of floating exchange rates has been the degree of exchange rate volatility. Why have rates been so volatile?

The average value of exchange rates over the long term depends on their **purchasing power parity (PPP)** values. The PPP exchange rate is the one that holds constant the relative price levels in two countries *when it is measured in a common currency.* For example, assume that the U.S. price level rises by 20 percent, while the German price level rises by only 5 percent over the same period. The PPP value of the German mark then appreciates by approximately 15 percent. This would mean that in Germany the prices of all goods (both German-produced and imported American goods) would rise by 5 percent, measured in German marks, while in the United States the prices of all goods (both American-produced and imported German goods) would rise by 20 percent, measured in U.S. dollars.

The PPP exchange rate adjusts so that the relative price of the two nations' goods (measured in the same currency) is unchanged, because the change in the relative values of two currencies compensates exactly for differences in national inflation rates.

If the actual exchange rate equals the PPP rate, the competitive positions of producers in the two countries will be unchanged. Firms that are located in countries with high inflation rates will still be able to sell their outputs on international markets, since the exchange rate adjusts to offset the effect of the higher domestic prices.

Figure 42-2 shows that the exchange rate between U.S. dollars and three major currencies has followed the PPP rate over the long run. Notice also, however, the large fluctuations around the PPP rate.

During the Bretton Woods period of fixed exchange rates, the advocates of floating rates argued

FIGURE 42-2   The Dollar and Purchasing Power Parity, 1973–1988

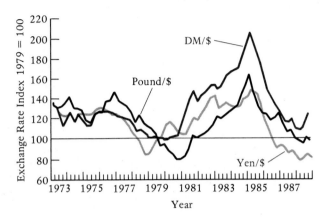

While deviations from PPP are substantial in the short run, there is some tendency for exchange rates to converge to their PPP values over the long run. The figure shows the bilateral real value of the dollar in terms of three major currencies—the Japanese yen, the West German deutsche mark, and the U.K. pound sterling. The series are calculated by multiplying the nominal exchange rate by the relative price levels of the two countries, and an index number is then calculated by setting the value for 1979 equal to 100. (In 1979 the U.S. current account was roughly in balance, and many economists argue that PPP can be assumed roughly to hold then.)

If PPP were always to hold, the series would be constant. However, as can be seen, in the early 1980s the real value of the U.S. dollar rose sharply in terms of all three currencies. This reflected a sharp rise in the foreign-exchange value of the dollar that was not offset by relatively high foreign inflation. As a result, there was a "real appreciation" of the U.S. dollar, and U.S. goods became very expensive relative to those produced in the other countries. In 1985 the real value of the dollar started to fall, and by mid-1988 it had returned to its 1979 value in terms of the pound sterling *adjusted for changes in the relative price levels*. Further, at the end of 1988, the U.S. dollar was actually lower in real terms relative to the yen than it had been in 1979, and it had almost fallen to its 1979 real value in terms of the deutsche mark.

---

that speculators would stabilize the actual rates within a narrow band around the PPP rates. The argument was that, since everyone knew the normal value was the PPP rate, speculators who were seek-

ing a profit when the rate deviated from its PPP level would quickly force the rate back to that level. To illustrate, suppose the PPP rate is U.S. $1.25 = £1.00 and that the actual rate falls to U.S. $1.15 = £1.00. Speculators would rush to buy pounds at U.S. $1.15 each, expecting to sell them for U.S. $1.25 when the rate returned to its PPP level. This very action would raise the demand for the pound and help push its value back toward U.S. $1.25.

Such speculative behavior would stabilize the exchange rate near its PPP value if speculators could be sure that the deviations would be small and short-lived. However, in practice, the swings around the PPP rate have been wide and have lasted for long periods. Thus, if the pound fell to U.S. $1.15, speculators would know that it could go as low as U.S. $1.05 and stay there for quite a while before returning to U.S. $1.25. In that case it might be worth speculating on a price of U.S. $1.10 next week rather than a price of U.S. $1.25 in some indefinite future.

The wide swings in exchange rates that have occurred show that speculative buying and selling cannot be relied on to hold exchange rates close to their PPP values.

Why have these wide fluctuations occurred? One of the most important reasons is associated with international differences in interest rates.

Exchange Rate Overshooting

Suppose that American interest rates rise above those ruling in other major financial centers. A rush to lend money at the profitable rates found in the United States will lead to an appreciation of the U.S. dollar.

This process will stop only when the rise in value of the U.S. dollar in foreign exchange markets is large enough that investors will expect the dollar subsequently to fall in value. This expected future depreciation then just offsets the interest premium from lending funds in U.S. dollars.

To illustrate, assume that interest rates are 4 percentage points higher in New York than in London, due to a restrictive monetary policy in the United States. Investors believe that the PPP rate is U.S. $1.60 = £1.00, but as they rush to buy dollars to take advantage of the higher U.S. interest rates, they drive the rate to, say, U.S. $1.40 = £1.00. (Since

BOX 42-2

Beggar-My-Neighbor Policies, Past and Present

The Great Depression of the 1930s brought an end to the long-standing stability of the gold standard and ushered in a period of experimentation in exchange regimes. Experiments were tried with both fixed and fluctuating rates.

But the overriding feature of the decade was that considerations of massive unemployment came to dominate economic policies in almost every country, and all devices, including exchange rate manipulations, seemed fair game for dealing with unemployment. Many of the policies adopted at this time were acts of desperation that would have made long-term sense only if other countries had not also been in crisis. Governments, hoping to gain short-term advantages before their policies provoked the inevitable reaction from others, tended not to consider the long-term effects on trade or on their trading partners of the policies that they adopted.

The use of devaluations to ease domestic unemployment rested on a simple and superficially plausible line of analysis: If a country has unemployed workers at home, why not substitute home production for imports and thus give jobs to one's citizens instead of to foreigners? One way to do this is to urge, say, Americans to "buy American." Another, probably more effective, way is to lower the prices of domestic goods relative to those of imports. The devaluation of one's currency does this by making foreign goods much more expen-

sive. Of course, if this policy works, other countries will find *their* exports falling and unemployment rising as a consequence. Because such policies attempt to solve one country's problems by inflicting them on others, they are called **beggar-my-neighbor policies** and are described as attempts to "export one's unemployment."

In a situation of inadequate world demand, a beggar-my-neighbor policy on the part of one country can work only in the unlikely event that other countries do not react by changing their policies to protect themselves. A situation in which all countries devalue their currencies in an attempt to gain a competitive advantage over one another is called a situation of **competitive devaluations.**

This is what happened during the 1930s. One country would devalue its currency in an attempt to reduce its imports and stimulate exports, but, because other countries were suffering from the same kinds of problems of unemployment, retaliation was swift and devaluation followed devaluation. The simultaneous attempt of all countries to cut imports without suffering a comparable cut in exports is bound to be self-defeating.

These policies, along with other restrictive trade policies, such as import duties, export subsidies, quotas, and prohibitions, led to a declining volume of world trade and brought no relief from the worldwide depression. Moreover, they contributed to a loss of faith in the economic system and in the

£1.00 now buys fewer U.S. dollars, the pound has depreciated, and since it takes fewer U.S. dollars to buy £1.00, the dollar has appreciated.) They do not believe this rate will be sustained and, instead, expect the U.S. dollar to lose value. If foreign investors expect it to depreciate at 4 percent per year, they will be indifferent between lending money in New York and doing so in London. The extra 4 percent per year of interest that they earn in New York is exactly offset by the 4 percent that they expect to lose when they turn their money back into their own currency.

Any policy that raises domestic interest rates above world levels will cause the external value of the domestic currency to appreciate enough to create an expected future depreciation that will be sufficient to offset the interest differential.

A central bank that is seeking to meet a monetary target may have to put up with large fluctuations in the exchange rate. If, in the example, the high U.S. interest rates were the result of a restrictive monetary

ability of either economists or politicians to cope with economic crises.

To avoid a recurrence of the beggar-my-neighbor policies of the 1930s, trading nations designed some important institutions. The International Monetary Fund (IMF) was supposed to reduce the chances of competitive devaluations, and the General Agreement on Tariffs and Trade (GATT) was supposed to reduce the chances of competitive increases in tariffs and other trade restrictions. These institutions worked well for over 30 years.

In 1980 the United States embarked on a tight monetary policy, driving up U.S. interest rates and the external value of the U.S. dollar. Just as expansionary monetary policy in the face of world recession tends to "export unemployment" by leading to a depreciation of the home currency and by reducing the demand for foreign goods, tight monetary policy in the face of the world inflation tends to "export inflation" by leading to an appreciation of the home currency and by raising the demand for foreign goods.

Most other governments, notably Germany and Japan, were worried about the implications of this for their own inflation rates and reacted by also adopting tight monetary policies. This monetary tightness helped to lead the world into the serious recession of 1981–1983.

Under the extreme pressures of this difficult economic situation, beggar-my-neighbor pressures

surfaced, and many governments found them hard to resist politically. Throughout the 1980s American voters showed strong support for advocates of increased tariffs. Many countries, including the United States, negotiated unofficial quotas that restricted the importation of Japanese cars. European agricultural protectionism nearly wrecked the GATT negotiations in December 1982 and remain the focus of considerable debate in the United States and elsewhere. Less-developed countries sought covert ways of protecting their own infant industries and complained, with some justice, that the developed nations paid lip service to, rather than really acted on, the slogan of "trade, not aid." It was clear that great pressure was being put on the whole postwar fabric, designed to encourage trade and discourage beggar-my-neighbor policies.

The sustained economic recovery in the second half of the decade meant that, as the decade ended, some but not all of the pressures abated. However, most observers were still worried about the threat of beggar-my-neighbor policies and the protectionist mood in the United States.

policy, the overshooting of the U.S. dollar beyond its PPP rate may put export- and import-competing industries under temporary but severe pressure from foreign competition.

The other side of this coin is that the high value of the U.S. dollar creates inflationary pressure in other countries. U.S. goods become much more expensive abroad, thus putting upward pressure on foreign prices and wages. Authorities in other countries are faced with the uncomfortable choice of accepting this increased inflation or raising their own

interest rates and thus maintaining their exchange rates in terms of the U.S. dollar. In the early 1980s, many foreign central banks chose this latter option, and tight monetary policies, initiated in the United States, were quickly imitated in other countries. This combined monetary contraction contributed to the severity of the world recession, as discussed further in Box 42-2.

The overvaluation of the dollar meant that the recession was particularly severe in the United States and that U.S. export- and import-competing industries suffered enormously. Not surprisingly, this spurred many calls for protectionist measures to save jobs in those sectors. The relatively low values of many foreign currencies and, in particular, the Japanese yen, contributed to the view that foreign competition in such traded-goods sectors was indeed unfair and hence protection was justified.

As the U.S. economy recovered during the rest of the decade, it might have been expected that the pressures for protection would have subsided. However, the U.S. current account remained in deficit, and pressures for protection remained strong. As we saw in Chapter 40, major protectionist legislation was passed in 1988, and, as the 1990s begin, it remains to be seen what further protectionist measures will be introduced.

Current Problems[1]

The Lack of an Alternative to the Dollar as a Reserve Currency

Governments that operate dirty floats need reserves, just like governments that operate adjustable pegs. The search for an adequate supply of reserves has continued unabated since the demise of the Bretton Woods system.

One major form in which reserves are held is U.S. dollars; another form—one that is growing in size—is the **special drawing rights (SDRs),** held with the IMF. First introduced in 1969, SDRs were designed to provide a supplement to existing reserve assets. The Special Drawing Account of the IMF was set up and kept separate from all other operations of the Fund. Each member country was assigned an *SDR* quota that was guaranteed in terms of a fixed gold value. Each country could use its quota to acquire an equivalent amount of convertible currencies from other participants. *SDRs* could be used without prior consultation with the Fund, but only to cope with balance-of-payments difficulties. *SDR* allocations grew from about $10 billion in 1970 to over $50 billion in 1986.

The commitment to lower inflation, initiated by

the Reagan administration in 1981, has restored some confidence in the U.S. dollar as a reserve asset, but overall these developments have not been seen as long-term solutions to the reserve problem. Other national currencies could take over the reserve role played by the U.S. dollar, but this is not likely.

Why does the world not turn to an international paper reserve system based on *SDRs* or some similar creation? Such a solution has much support from academic economists, who see an appropriate international institution managing the supply of international currency to accommodate growth and to avoid inflation.

Critics of such a system—among them most of the world's central bankers—distrust the concept of an international paper currency, pointing out that few countries have managed their own money supplies effectively. However difficult the task of the U.S. Federal Reserve may be, the task of a World Reserve Bank would be even more difficult. Further, private acceptance and use of the *SDR* has been virtually nonexistent, indicating the enormous difficulties inherent in creating a new currency.

Some who are skeptical of an international paper monetary standard have urged a return to the gold standard. This approach has critical disadvantages. In fact, the IMF and the U.S. government have at various times taken the lead in an attempt to "demonetarize" gold completely.

For the moment at least, the world cannot agree on an international monetary reserve. Until it does, there will be crises whenever there is a desire to shift from one to another of the multiple sources of reserves: dollars, gold, *SDRs*, marks, francs, and yen. The speculative opportunities inherent in such a system remain large, as evidenced by the recent behavior of the price of gold, shown in Figure 42-3.

The Impact of OPEC

One issue that affects the future payments system—and indeed the whole of international economic relations—is the variability of the price of oil.

Oil Price Increases

The OPEC cartel raised the price of oil dramatically in 1974 and again in 1979. In total these events led to a tenfold increase, which generated a massive payments surplus for the oil producers and a correspond-

---

[1] The rest of this chapter can be omitted without loss of continuity.

FIGURE 42-3   Price of Gold, 1971–1989

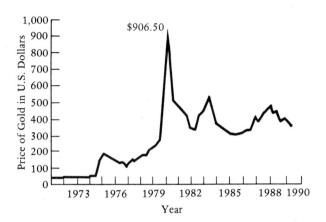

Gold soared in value and proved to be highly volatile after convertibility of the dollar was suspended in 1973. The two devaluations of the U.S. dollar in terms of gold that occurred under the adjustable peg system are barely visible. (These devaluations are discussed in the appendix to this chapter.) The effects of speculation on the price of gold is seen in subsequent experience. The price of gold more than quadrupled from 1977 to 1979, reaching a peak of over $900 per ounce. It subsequently fell to around $300 by 1982. Since that time it has fluctuated around the $400 level, sometimes rising above it and sometimes falling below it.

ing deficit for the oil-importing countries. The excess purchasing power in the hands of oil producers came to be called **petrodollars.** The cumulative stock of petrodollars may have exceeded $500 billion. Petrodollars caused several different kinds of problems.

Short-term problems of industrialized countries.   Most petrodollars were eventually used for the purchase of consumption goods and services or investment goods from industrialized countries. However, the oil-producing countries did not spend their oil revenues on goods and services as fast as they were earned. Thus, in the short term the OPEC countries had excess dollars, which they invested in the advanced industrialized nations, thereby returning on capital account the purchasing power that was extracted from the current accounts of the oil-importing nations. This created havoc in foreign exchange markets when surplus oil funds were switched between currencies, in response to changes in interest rates and expected capital gains, arising from possible exchange rate changes. Surplus petrodollars were used speculatively, and many observers believed that a good part of the sharp rise and fall in gold prices in 1979–1981 was due to just such a use of petrodollars.

Short-term problems of underdeveloped countries.   For an oil-importing country such as Kenya, the OPEC price increase turned a small trade surplus into a massive deficit overnight. The country was unable

to generate revenues quickly enough to pay its oil bill, yet it could only decrease its use of oil at the cost of a sharp slowdown in its domestic economy.

The IMF stepped in with loan arrangements to help countries that were most severely affected by the rising oil prices, the repayments of maturing loans were deferred, and the OPEC nations established a fund for short-term loans to such countries. Thus, the purely short-term problems were solved through international cooperation and recognition of the need for accommodation on the part of creditor nations. However, many of the loans made during this period are now part of the debt crisis that faces many less developed countries. (See Chapter 44, page 936.)

Oil Price Decreases

Many oil-exporting countries also borrowed heavily, based on their expectations that oil prices would rise. In early 1983, however, OPEC lost control of the market, and the price of oil started to fall. In early 1986 the price of crude oil fell sharply from over $30 per barrel to around $12 per barrel. Many international loans were threatened, including those that were made by large private banks to less-developed countries such as Mexico, which is heavily dependent on oil exports for repayment. Although oil prices recovered near the end of the decade, the risk of a major default still hangs over the system, and the

BOX 42-3

Proposals for International Monetary Reform

The high degree of variability and persistent misalignment of exchange rates that plagued the flexible exchange rate system for the first 20 years of its operation led during the mid-1980s to a number of proposals for reform.

Fixed Exchange Rates

Some observers advocated a return to fixed exchange rates. In fact, some even wanted the new system to be based on gold or some other group of commodities. This proposal was apparently motivated by the belief that *ruling out* exchange rate changes would allow some of the problems that we have noted in this text to be avoided.

This proposal has not received wide support among economists, since most believe that the flaws that led to the demise of the Bretton Woods system were indeed fatal and that a system of fixed exchange rates would have performed worse, not better, than flexible exchange rates did in the face of the shocks that have disturbed the world economy since Bretton Woods was abandoned. Proponents of fixed exchange rates counter that many of those shocks were, in fact, the result of bad policies that were made possible only by the freedom for independent domestic policy that exists under flexible exchange rates. They argue that the discipline imposed by fixed exchange rates would have improved the performance of policy over the period.

Target Exchange Rate Zones

Another proposal was for establishing *target zones* for exchange rates. Some advocates proposed "hard" zones, that is, narrowly defined zones with automatic intervention required whenever exchange rates moved outside the defined limits. This amounts to a fixed exchange rate system, and, not surprisingly, debate on this type of proposal paralleled that on fixed exchange rates.

Alternatively, some advocates proposed "soft" zones, defined more loosely, and departures from which simply served as a signal to authorities that some policy reaction might be appropriate. Although these "soft" zones were more acceptable to some observers, many expressed a good deal of skepticism about what such weak arrangements might accomplish.

"Sand in the Gears"

The enormous variability of exchange rates led to proposals to "throw sand in the gears of international financial markets" in order to limit the international mobility of capital. These proposals were motivated by the view that exchange rate variability is the result of large pools of liquid capital that move from currency to currency in anticipation of capital gains that are due to exchange rate changes. Such movements, of course, could themselves give rise to dramatic exchange rate changes—sometimes

---

IMF again finds itself facing the problem of rescheduling repayments of large international loans. (This is discussed further in Box 44-1 on page 936.)

The Management of Exchange Rates

The 1970s witnessed the replacement of a system of managed fixed exchange rates with a system of managed flexible exchange rates. The problems of the latter may have been revealed by the events

of the decade, but they cannot be said to have been solved.

Policy Problems

Managing floating rates poses several potential problems for the international monetary system.

Inconsistent exchange rate policies.   Different governments may try to fix their exchange rates at levels that are inconsistent with each other. For example,

self-fulfilling, and sometimes self-defeating, but always disruptive to international trade and investment. The "sand in the gears" would involve levying taxes on "unproductive" capital movements, in an attempt to discourage them and therefore to stabilize exchange rates. (These proposals were also sometimes called *dual exchange rates,* since the tax means that, effectively, a different exchange rate is used for taxed transactions than for untaxed ones.)

Many economists, however, oppose such schemes. They express worries about the problems of identifying "unproductive" capital movements and the potential distortions that would arise if the taxes were misapplied. They also argue that black markets would evolve that would allow many capital movements to avoid the taxes, thereby rendering them largely ineffective, but still burdening the economy with the administrative costs of trying to enforce them. They also question whether the scheme would achieve its goal, even if it could be implemented, citing markets such as real estate, rare art, and fine wine in which transactions costs are high but prices are still volatile.

Objective Indicators

Other participants in the debate promoted the idea that "objective indicators" be calculated to provide a signal to authorities when policies become mutually inconsistent. Such indicators, which might involve measures of performance, such as real growth and inflation, as well as policy measures, such as money growth rates and fiscal deficits, are an extension of the "soft" zone for exchange rate targets in that they serve merely as an indicator and do not themselves trigger automatic policy responses.

Though many commentators were sympathetic to this idea, there was little consensus as to how to calculate such indicators or how exactly indicators might work to avoid the problems in the system. Indeed, proponents of all these reforms conceded that the high variability and persistent misalignment of exchange rates were really just symptoms of the real problems in the international economy and that any real reform must address the root causes of such problems. Many of those root causes are beyond the control of policymakers, but some of the problems result from undesirable economic policies in the industrialized countries. Recognizing this, Western leaders who attended the economic summit that was held in Tokyo in May 1986 reached an agreement to establish objective indicators in an effort to improve international cooperation in formulating economic policies. That initiative, however, appears to have lost much of its momentum. As we have discussed in the text, a number of economists have argued that the extensive list of indicators to be monitored should be reduced to just one—nominal national income.

---

if the Fed's target is that the U.S. dollar should be worth 150 yen, while the Bank of Japan's target is that the yen should be worth .005 U.S. dollars, both policies cannot succeed. If both banks persist in trying to meet such inconsistent targets, they can destabilize exchange markets.

Competitive devaluations.   Countries may get involved in bouts of competitive devaluations that are similar to those that destabilized exchange markets during the 1920s and 1930s. For example, if one country devalues its currency in order to get a competitive advantage for its exports and other countries respond by devaluing their currencies, the rounds of successive devaluations will destabilize the exchange market without giving any country's exports a permanent advantage.

Destabilizing speculation.   Speculative behavior can destabilize exchange markets. Before the system of floating exchange rates was adopted, many economists felt that rates would stay fairly close to their equilibrium values. Economists expected that speculators would then stabilize rates even further by buying currencies that seemed temporarily low in price and by selling those that seemed temporarily high in price. In that event, however, very large and persistent deviations of exchange rates from the long-run equilibrium values occurred. This left speculators less clear on which way a particular rate was likely to go in the near future. When a particular currency started to fall in value, speculators might conclude that a large and persistent fall was just beginning. In this case their rush to sell the currency before its expected further fall would bring the fall about.

Policy Responses

To help avoid these problems, the IMF has issued guidelines for exchange rate management. The guidelines emphasize that exchange rate policy is a matter for international consultation and surveillance by the IMF and that intervention practices by individual central banks should be based on three principles:

1. Exchange authorities should prevent sudden and disproportionate short-term movements in exchange rates and ensure an orderly adjustment to longer-term pressures.
2. In consultation with the IMF, countries should establish a target zone for the medium-term values of their exchange rates and keep the actual rate within that target zone.
3. Countries should recognize that exchange rate management involves joint responsibilities and is not just the responsibility of the individual country in question.

The experiences of the 1970s have underlined one of the most important unsolved problems of managed floating rates: coping with the massive volume of short-term funds that can be switched rapidly between financial centers. Short-term capital flows forced the abandonment of exchange rates that had been agreed on in 1971 and have often caused violent fluctuations in floating rates since then. Severe "currency misalignments" have arisen and persisted, rendering uncompetitive on world markets the export- and import-competing sectors in countries with overvalued currencies, while creating enormous profit opportunities in countries with undervalued currencies.

Capital flows often prevent the quick return of exchange rates to their PPP values. Various attempts have been made to limit such capital flows. Italy has adopted a two-tier foreign-exchange market, with one price for foreign exchange to finance current account transactions and another price (and another set of controls) for foreign exchange to finance capital movements. Germany has used direct controls on overseas borrowing. There also has been a considerable extension of arrangements under which central banks in surplus countries lend the funds that they are accumulating back to central banks in deficit countries. Through such arrangements, the ability of banks to maintain stable exchange rates in the face of short-term speculative flights of capital is enhanced.

The major problem in managing speculative flows is to identify them accurately. Experience suggests that exchange rate management can smooth out temporary fluctuations but cannot resist underlying trends in equilibrium rates, caused by relative inflation rates, structural changes, and persistent nonspeculative capital flows. In day-to-day management, it is not always easy to distinguish among them.

Nevertheless, the excessive variability and persistent misalignment of exchange rates that continued to plague the flexible exchange rate system led to a number of proposals for reform. These are discussed further in Box 42-3.

The Need for Cooperation

One of the most impressive aspects of the international payments history of the past 30 years has been the steady rise of effective international cooperation. When the gold standard collapsed and the Great Depression overwhelmed the countries of the world, "every nation for itself" was the rule of the day. Rising tariffs, competitive exchange rate devaluations, and all forms of beggar-my-neighbor policies abounded.

After World War II, the countries of the world cooperated in bringing the Bretton Woods system and the IMF into being. The system itself was far from perfect, and it finally broke down as a result of its own internal contradictions. Nevertheless, the international cooperation that was necessary to set up the system survived. The joint cooperative actions of central banks allowed them to weather speculative crises during the 1970s that would have forced them to devalue their currencies during the 1950s.

Thus, the collapse of the Bretton Woods system did not plunge the world into the same chaos that followed the breakdown of the gold standard. The world was also better able to cope with the terrible strains that were caused by the sharp rise in oil prices during the 1970s. Of course, enormous oil-related problems remain, and they are matters for continuing international dialogue. Further, it is not yet clear how well the world economy will weather the upsurge of American protectionism of the mid-1980s. Prior to this upsurge, the United States provided essential leadership as it worked for lower restrictions on international trade. It is a serious question, then, whether other nations will now follow the American lead to *increased* protectionism and thus join in a mutually destructive round of competitive tariff increases and other restrictions.

Whatever the problems of the future will be, the world has a better chance of solving them—or even of just learning to live with them—when countries cooperate through the IMF and other international organizations than when each country seeks its own solution without concern for the interests of other countries.

SUMMARY

1. Various systems of international monetary arrangements have been tried. All involve aspects of the two extremes of fixed exchange rates and flexible exchange rates.
2. Under fixed exchange rates, the central bank intervenes in the foreign exchange market to maintain the exchange rate at or near an announced par value. To do this the central bank must hold sufficient stocks of foreign exchange reserves. Reserves historically have been held in the form of gold or reserve currencies, particularly the U.S. dollar. The *SDR* is a relatively new international paper money that is meant to provide additional international reserves, linked neither to gold nor to the U.S. dollar.
3. Any fixed exchange rate system will face three major problems: (a) providing sufficient international reserves, (b) adjusting to long-term trends in receipts and payments, and (c) handling periodic speculative crises.
4. Under a system of flexible, or floating, exchange rates, the exchange rate is market-determined by supply and demand for the currency.
5. Since their adoption in the mid-1970s, flexible exchange rates have fluctuated substantially. As a result central banks often have intervened to stabilize the fluctuations. Thus, the present system is called a *managed,* or *dirty, float.*
6. Fluctuations in exchange rates can be understood as fluctuations around a trend value that is determined by the purchasing power parity (PPP) rate. The PPP rate adjusts in response to differences in national inflation rates.
7. Current problems include the need to find an adequate reserve that is not tied to a national currency, to accommodate both the short-term and the longer-term impact of OPEC, and to develop rules for managing flexible exchange rates. A continuing commitment to international cooperation will help the world cope with these problems.

TOPICS FOR REVIEW

Fixed and flexible exchange rates
Managed floats
Adjustable peg system
Bretton Woods system
International Monetary Fund (IMF)
Exchange rate overshooting

DISCUSSION QUESTIONS

1. From mid-1985 through the end of 1986, the U.S. dollar fell sharply in terms of the Japanese yen and the major European currencies. However, the U.S. current account deficit did not fall. Can you think of any reasons why? What happened to the Canadian dollar over this period? What were the implications for Canada?

2. The U.S. dollar is no longer convertible into gold because of a change in U.S. policy. Does this lack of convertibility make the dollar any less useful as an international medium of exchange?

3. Are Americans benefited or hurt when the U.S. dollar is the standard form of international reserves?

4. "Under a flexible exchange rate system no country need suffer unemployment, for if its prices are low enough there will be more than enough demand to keep its factories and farms fully occupied." The evidence suggests that flexible exchange rates have not generally eliminated unemployment. Can you explain why? Can changing exchange rates ever cure unemployment?

5. The OPEC oil price increases during the 1970s caused grave problems in international payments and increased the need for IMF loans. Why did market adjustment of exchange rates not solve the problem?

6. In November 1985 the five major industrialized countries met and agreed that a major realignment of the world's currencies was appropriate. Why? What did they do about it? What was the result?

7. What role in international payments does or did gold play under (a) the gold standard, (b) the adjustable-peg Bretton Woods system, and (c) the present system?

8. Might a person who regards inflation as the number one economic danger favor a return to the pre-1914 gold standard? Would you predict noninflationary results if, in order to restore the gold standard, the price of gold had to be set at U.S. $1,600 per ounce, either all at once or gradually?

9. Discuss the following quote made in 1989 by a senior economist in the U.S. government: "It's unseemly to have the richest nation of the world drawing the resources of the rest of the world to support consumption."

Appendix to Chapter 42

The Gold Standard and the Bretton Woods System

Two episodes with fixed exchange rates occurred during the twentieth century. Each ultimately failed. The gold standard, whose origins are as old as currency itself, was used until the late 1920s and early 1930s. The Bretton Woods system, which was the only payments system ever to be designed and established by conscious action, was born out of World War II and collapsed a little less than 30 years later. Their histories are instructive, not least because many people continue to propose returning to one or the other of these systems.

The Gold Standard

The gold standard was not *designed;* it just happened. It arose out of the general acceptance of gold as the commodity to be used as money. In most countries paper currency was freely convertible into gold at a fixed rate. In 1914 the U.S. dollar was worth 0.053 standard ounces of gold, while the British pound sterling was worth 0.257 standard ounces of gold. This meant that the pound was worth 4.86 times as much as the dollar in terms of gold, thus making £1 worth U.S. $4.86. (In practice the exchange rate fluctuated within narrow limits set by the cost of shipping gold.) As long as all countries were on the gold standard, a person in one country could be sure of being able to make payments to a person in another.

The Gold-Flow, Price-Level Mechanism

The gold standard was supposed to maintain a balance of international payments by causing adjustments in price levels within individual countries. Consider a country that had a balance-of-payments deficit because the value of its imports (i.e., purchases) from other countries exceeded the value of its exports (i.e., sales) to other countries. The demand for foreign exchange would exceed the supply in this country's foreign exchange market. Some

people who wished to make foreign payments would need to convert their domestic currency into gold and ship the gold. Therefore, some people in a surplus country would receive gold in payment for exports. Thus, deficit countries would be losing gold, while surplus countries would be gaining it.

Under the gold standard, the whole money supply was linked to the supply of gold. The international movements of gold would therefore lead to a fall in the money supply in the deficit country and a rise in the money supply in the surplus country. If full employment prevailed, changes in the domestic money supply would cause changes in domestic price levels. Deficit countries would thus have falling price levels, while surplus countries would have rising price levels. The exports of deficit countries would become relatively cheaper, while those of surplus countries would become relatively more expensive. The resulting changes in quantities bought and sold would move the balance of payments toward equilibrium.

Actual Experience of the Gold Standard

The half century before World War I was the heyday of the gold standard. During this relatively trouble-free period, the adjustment mechanism just described seemed to work well.

Subsequent research has suggested, however, that the gold standard succeeded during that period mainly because it was not called on to do much work. No major trading country found itself with a serious and persistent balance-of-payments deficit, so no major country was called on to restore equilibrium through a large change in its domestic price level.

During the 1920s the gold standard was called on to do a major job. It failed utterly, and it was abandoned. How did this happen? During World War I most belligerent countries had suspended convertibility of currency (i.e., they went off the gold standard). Most countries suffered major inflations, but the degree of inflation differed from country to country. As we have seen, this led to changes in the equilibrium exchange rates.

After the war countries returned to the gold standard (i.e., they restored convertibility of their currencies into gold). Many returned to the prewar rates. This meant that some countries' goods were overpriced and other countries' goods were underpriced. Large deficits and surpluses in the balance of payments inevitably appeared, and the adjustment mechanism required that price levels should change in each of the countries in order to restore equilibrium. Exchange rates were not adjusted, and price levels changed very slowly. By the onset of the Great Depression, equilibrium price levels had not yet been attained. The financial chaos brought on by the Depression destroyed the existing payments system.

Major Disabilities of a Gold Standard

We may ask whether an altered gold standard, based on more realistic exchange rates, might not have succeeded. Some economists think that it would; most others believe that the gold standard suffered from the key weakness that the price adjustment process worked too slowly and too imperfectly to cope with large and persistent disequilibrium.

Furthermore, gold as the basis for an international money supply suffered several disadvantages. These included a supply that could not be expanded as rapidly as increases in the volume of world trade required, an uneven distribution of existing and potential new gold supplies among the nations of the world, and a large and volatile speculative demand for gold during periods of crisis. These factors could cause disruptive variations in the supply of gold that was available for international monetary purposes.

The Bretton Woods System

The one lesson that everyone thought had been learned from the 1930s was that a system of either freely fluctuating exchange rates or fixed rates with easily accomplished devaluations was a sure route to disaster. In order to achieve a system of orderly exchange rates that would facilitate the free flow of trade following World War II, representatives of many major countries met at Bretton Woods, New

Hampshire, in 1944. In the words of Charles Kindleberger of MIT, the Bretton Woods meeting was "the biggest constitution-writing exercise ever to occur in international monetary relations."

The Bretton Woods system had three objectives: (1) to create a set of rules that would maintain fixed exchange rates in the face of short-term fluctuations; (2) to guarantee that changes in exchange rates would occur only in the face of "fundamental" deficits or surpluses in the balance of payments; and (3) to ensure that, when such changes did occur, they would not spark a series of competitive devaluations. The basic characteristic of the system was that U.S. dollars, held by foreign monetary authorities, were made directly convertible into gold at a price fixed by the U.S. government, while foreign governments fixed the prices at which their currencies were convertible into U.S. dollars. It was this characteristic that made the system a **gold exchange standard.** Gold was the ultimate reserve, but other currencies were held as reserves, because directly or indirectly they could be exchanged for gold.

To maintain the convertibility of their currencies at fixed exchange rates and to be able to support the exchange market, the monetary authorities had to have reserves of acceptable foreign exchange.[1] In the Bretton Woods system, the authorities held reserves of gold and claims on key currencies, mainly the U.S. dollar and the British pound sterling. When a country's currency was in excess supply, its authorities would sell dollars, pounds sterling, or gold. When a country's currency was in excess demand, its authorities would buy dollars or pounds sterling. If they then wished to increase their gold reserves, they would use the dollars to purchase gold from the Fed, thus depleting the U.S. gold stock.

The problem for the United States was that it needed to have enough gold to maintain fixed price convertibility of the dollar into gold, as demanded by foreign monetary authorities. The problem for all other countries was that they needed to maintain convertibility (on either a restricted or unrestricted basis) between their currency and the U.S. dollar at a fixed rate of exchange.

---

[1] The exchange rates were not quite fixed; they were permitted to vary by 1 percent on either side of their par values. Later the bands of permitted fluctuation were widened to 2.25 percent on either side of par value.

Problems of the Adjustable Peg System

Here we see how the three problems of the Bretton Woods system, discussed in the text, actually worked out during the period after World War II.

Reserves to accommodate short-term fluctuations.
It is generally believed that the average size and frequency of the gaps between demand and supply in the foreign exchange market, created when central banks peg their exchange rates, will increase as the volume of international payments increases. Since there was a strong upward trend in the volume of overall international payments, there was also a strong upward trend in the demand for foreign exchange reserves.

The ultimate reserve in the Bretton Woods system was gold. The use of gold as a reserve caused two serious problems during the 1960s and early 1970s. First, the world's supply of monetary gold did not grow as fast as the volume of trade. The fixed price of gold, rising costs of gold production, and rising commercial uses for gold combined to cause the world's stock of monetary gold during the 1960s to grow at less than 2 percent per year, while trade grew at nearly 10 percent per year. Gold, which had been 66 percent of the total monetary reserves in 1959, was only 30 percent by 1972. Over this period reserve holdings of dollars and pounds sterling rose sharply. Clearly, the gold backing needed to maintain convertibility of these currencies was becoming increasingly inadequate.

Second, during the 1960s the United States lost substantial gold reserves to other countries that had acquired dollar claims through their balance-of-payments surpluses with the United States. By the late 1960s, the reduction in U.S. reserves was sufficiently large to undermine confidence in America's continued ability to maintain dollar convertibility.

Adjusting to long-term disequilibria.
The second characteristic problem of a fixed-rate system is the adjustment to long-term disequilibria that develop because of secular shifts in the demand for and supply of foreign exchange.

These disequilibria developed slowly. At first they led to a series of speculative crises, as people expected a realignment of exchange rates to occur. Finally, they led to a series of realignments that started in 1967. Each occurred amid quite spectacular flows of speculative funds that thoroughly disorganized normal trade and payments.

Speculative crises.
The adjustable peg system often leads to situations in which speculators are presented with one-way bets. In these disequilibria situations, there is an increasing chance of an exchange rate adjustment in one direction, with little or no chance of a movement in the other direction. Speculators then have an opportunity to secure a large potential gain, with no corresponding potential for loss. Speculative crises, associated with the need to adjust to fundamental disequilibria, were the downfall of the system.

Collapse of the Bretton Woods System

The Bretton Woods system worked reasonably well for nearly 20 years. Then it was beset by a series of crises of ever increasing severity that reflected the system's underlying weaknesses.

Speculation against the British pound.
Throughout the 1950s and 1960s, the British economy was more inflation prone than the U.S. economy, and the British balance of payments was generally in deficit. Holders of pounds sterling thus had reason to worry that the British government might not be able to keep pounds sterling convertible into dollars at a fixed rate. When these fears grew strong, there were speculative rushes to sell the pound before it was devalued. For example, by the mid-1960s it was clear to everyone that the pound was seriously overvalued, and in 1967 it was devalued in the midst of a speculative crisis. Many other countries with balance-of-payments deficits followed, bringing about the first major round of adjustments in the pegged rates since 1949.

Speculation against the American dollar.
The U.S. dollar was not devalued in 1967. The lower prices of the currencies that were devalued in 1967, plus the increasing Vietnam War expenditures, combined to produce a growing deficit in the American balance of payments. This deficit led to the belief that the dollar itself was becoming seriously overvalued. People rushed to buy gold because, under the Bretton

Woods system, a devaluation of the U.S. dollar would take the form of raising its gold price.

The first break in the Bretton Woods system came in 1968, when the major trading countries were forced to stop pegging the free-market price of gold. Speculative pressure to buy gold could not be resisted, and from that point on there were two prices of gold: the official price, at which monetary authorities could settle their debts with each other by transferring gold, and the free-market price, determined by the forces of private demand and supply independent of any intervention by central banks. The free-market price quickly rose far above the official U.S. price of $35 per ounce (see Figure 42-3).

Once the free-market price of gold was allowed to be determined independently of the official price, speculation against the dollar shifted to those currencies that were clearly undervalued relative to the dollar.[2] The German mark and the Japanese yen were particularly popular targets, and, during periods of crisis, billions and billions of dollars flowed into speculative holdings of these currencies. The ability of central banks to maintain pegged exchange rates in the face of such vast flights of funds was in question; on several occasions all exchange markets had to be closed for periods of up to one week.

Devaluation of the dollar. By 1971 the American authorities had concluded that the dollar would have to be devalued. However, because the Bretton Woods system required each foreign country to fix its exchange rate against the dollar, the American authorities could not independently fix their exchange rate against other currencies.[3] While any other country with an overvalued currency would merely unilaterally devalue, the only way that the

required U.S. devaluation could be brought about was for all other countries to agree to revalue their currencies relative to the dollar.

Prompted by continuing speculation against the dollar, President Nixon suspended gold convertibility of the dollar in August 1971. He also announced the intention of the United States to achieve a de facto devaluation of the dollar by persuading those nations whose balance of payments were in surplus to allow their rates to float upward against the dollar.

By ending the gold convertibility of the dollar, the U.S. government brought the gold exchange standard aspect of the Bretton Woods system officially to an end. The fixed-exchange-rate aspect of the system lasted a little longer.

The immediate response to the announced intention of devaluing the dollar was a speculative run against that currency. The crisis was so severe that for the second time that year foreign exchange markets were closed throughout Europe. When the markets reopened after a week, several countries allowed their rates to float. The Japanese, however, announced their intention of retaining their existing rate. Despite severe Japanese controls, $4 billion in speculative funds managed to find its way into yen during the last two weeks of August, and the Japanese were forced to abandon their fixed-rate policy by allowing the yen to float upward.

An agreement among the major trading nations was signed at the Smithsonian Institution in Washington, D.C., in December 1971. The main element of the agreement was a 7.9 percent devaluation of the dollar against their currencies.

De facto dollar standard. Following the Smithsonian agreement, the world was on a de facto **dollar standard.** Foreign monetary authorities held their reserves in the form of dollars and settled their international debts with dollars. However, the dollar was not convertible into gold or anything else. The ultimate value of the dollar was given, not by gold, but by the American goods, services, and assets that dollars could be used to purchase.

One major problem with such a system is that the kind of American inflation that upset the Bretton Woods system can be just as upsetting to a dollar standard, because the real purchasing-power value of the world's dollar reserves is eroded by such an inflation.

---

[2] When the free-market price of gold was the same as the official price, a devaluation of the dollar entailed a rise in the free-market price—and hence profit for all holders of gold. Once the free-market price was left to be determined by the forces of private demand and supply, independent of central bank intervention, there was no reason to believe that a rise in the official price of gold would affect the (much higher) free-market price. Speculators against the dollar then had to hold other currencies whose price would rise in the event of a devaluation of the dollar.

[3] If, for example, the British authorities pegged the pound sterling at $2.40, as they did in 1967, the dollar was pegged at £.417, and the Fed could not independently decide on another rate. Similar considerations applied to all other currencies.

Final breakdown of fixed exchange rates. The Smithsonian agreements did not lead to a new period of international financial stability. The U.S. inflation continued unchecked, and the U.S. balance of payments never returned to the relatively satisfactory position that had been maintained throughout the 1960s. Within a year of the agreements, speculators began to believe that a further realignment of rates was necessary. In January 1973 speculative movements of capital once again occurred. In February 1973 the United States proposed a further 11 percent devaluation of the dollar. This was to be accomplished by raising the official price of gold to $42.22 per ounce and by not keeping other currencies tied to the dollar at the old rates. Intense speculative activity followed the announcement.

Five member countries of the European Community then decided to stabilize their currencies against each other but to let them float together against the dollar. This joint float was called the *snake*. Norway and Sweden later joined the snake arrangement. The other EC countries (Ireland, Italy, and the United Kingdom) and Japan announced their intention to allow their currencies to float in value. In June 1972 the Bank of England had abandoned the de facto dollar standard with the announcement that it had "temporarily" abandoned its commitment to support the pound sterling at a fixed par value against the U.S. dollar. The events of 1973 led "temporarily" to become "indefinitely."

Fluctuations in exchange rates were severe. By early July 1973, the snake currencies had appreciated about 30 percent against the dollar, but by the end of the year they had nearly returned to their February 1973 values.

The dollar devaluation formally took effect in October 1973. Most industrialized countries maintained the nominal values of their currencies in terms of gold and *SDR*s, thereby appreciating them in terms of the U.S. dollar by 11 percent. The devaluation quickly became redundant, for, despite attempts to restore fixed rates, the drift to flexible rates had become irresistible by the end of 1973.

Chapter 43

Macro-economic Policy in an Open Economy

When we shift our attention to an *open* economy, we encounter a number of features that are of particular interest to the study of macroeconomic policy. These include the behavior of the terms of trade and their influence on net exports and national income, the nature and extent of foreign borrowing, and changes in foreign interest or inflation rates. The response of the economy to various policies is altered. For example, as we saw in Chapter 29 (see page 600), the size of the simple multiplier is smaller than that in a closed economy. Also, as we shall see in this chapter, since interest rates are closely tied to those prevailing in foreign markets, the mechanism by which macroeconomic policies influence the economy can differ sharply from the closed-economy mechanisms studied so far in this book.

Consideration of the openness of the economy also introduces some new policy targets that may be in conflict with policy targets arising solely from domestic considerations. In the next section we will introduce the study of macroeconomic policy in an open economy by considering these possibly conflicting targets.

Internal and External Balance

In this chapter we summarize the domestic policy objectives in terms of a target level of real national income. Restricting our attention to one domestic policy target is done primarily for simplicity. However, it is perhaps more general than would first appear. For example, if one objective is to reduce the domestic rate of inflation, we know from our analysis in Chapter 34 that this can be accomplished by choosing a target level of real national income below the capacity level. When real national income is at its target level, we say the economy has achieved **internal balance.**

In this section we focus on the trade account as the external policy target. As we saw in Chapter 41, the trade account is related to the current and capital accounts. Hence, such things as the level of interest payments that must be paid to foreigners, the need to accumulate or decumulate foreign exchange reserves, or the need for capital flows to finance new investment may influence the target level of the trade balance.[1] When the trade account is equal to its target level, we say the economy has achieved **external balance.**

In this section we also treat the exchange rate as fixed. Later in the chapter, we study the complications that arise when the capital account and a flexible exchange rate are considered.

The conditions for internal and external balance are illustrated in Figure 43-1.

Conflict Between Objectives

When policies that are used to move the economy closer to one objective move the economy further from the other objective, the objectives are said to be in *conflict*.

Policies to eliminate a recessionary gap will also influence the trade account by causing a movement along the net export function (which is negatively sloped—see Figure 26-3). Whether there is a conflict between the objectives of internal and external balance depends on how the trade account and real national income compare to their target values.

For the sake of simplicity, we now make the assumption that the target level of real national income is the capacity level of output and that the target for the trade account is a zero balance.[2] Hence, we can identify the initial situation relative to the targets simply in terms of the signs of the output gap and the trade account balance. There are four possible cases:

1. A trade account *deficit* combined with an *inflationary gap* poses no conflict, because the contraction of aggregate demand to eliminate the inflationary gap leads to a reduction in imports and hence reduces the trade deficit.
2. A trade account *deficit* combined with a *recessionary gap* does pose a conflict, because the expansion

of aggregate demand to eliminate the recessionary gap leads to an increase in imports and hence a worsening of the trade deficit.
3. A trade account *surplus* combined with a *recessionary gap* poses no conflict, because the expansion of aggregate demand to eliminate the recessionary gap increases imports and hence reduces the trade surplus.
4. A trade account *surplus* combined with an *inflationary gap* does pose a conflict, because the contraction of aggregate demand to eliminate the inflationary gap leads to a reduction in imports and hence an increase in the trade surplus.

The four cases are depicted in Figure 43-2.

In case 2 the trade account deficit calls for a decrease in national income, but the recessionary gap calls for an increase. In case 4 the trade account surplus calls for an increase in national income, but the inflationary gap calls for a decrease.[3]

A conflict arises between the objectives of internal and external balance when the two call for opposite changes in the level of national income.

Basically, the conflicts arise from *movements along* the net export function; we now see that resolution of such conflict arises from *shifts in* the net export function.

Expenditure-changing and Expenditure-switching Policies

We start by repeating the basic equilibrium condition, that national income equals aggregate desired expenditure.

$$Y = C + I + G + (X - M) \qquad [1]$$

The total $C + I + G$ is often referred to as *domestic absorption,* or simply *absorption.* This concept, which was discussed in Box 29-1 on page 600, refers to total expenditure on goods for use in the economy.

---

[1] For example, a nation with a large undeveloped natural resource base may have a low current national income yet anticipate a high future national income when the resource base is developed. High current investment to develop the resource base and high current consumption in anticipation of that high future income together will lead to high imports and a trade account deficit. Hence, the *target* trade account in such a circumstance may well be a deficit.

[2] We emphasize that this assumption is made only to simplify the discussion and that the actual targets often may differ from these. The same principles apply, regardless of the actual values of the targets.

[3] Case 2 traditionally has attracted the most attention, perhaps because a trade deficit is generally viewed as being a more serious problem than a trade surplus and—at least in the past—because unemployment has been considered to be a more serious problem than inflation. Case 2 is often referred to as a situation in which there is a "balance-of-payments constraint" on domestic stabilization policy.

FIGURE 43-1   Internal and External Balance

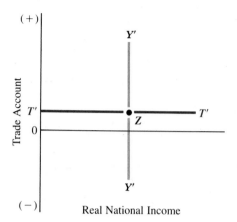

Internal and external balance are simultaneously attained at point Z. Internal balance is defined in terms of a target level of real national income and is depicted by the vertical line $Y'Y'$. External balance is defined in terms of a target level of the trade account and is depicted by the horizontal line $T'T'$. Only at the intersection, point Z, are both internal and external balance attained.

Denoting absorption by the letter A, we can rewrite the national income equilibrium condition as

$$Y = A + (X - M) \qquad [2]$$

This condition states that equilibrium national income is equal to aggregate desired expenditure, which in turn is equal to domestic absorption plus net exports.

Equation 2 is useful in distinguishing between two types of policies that might be used to maintain internal and external balance. Policies that maintain the level of aggregate desired expenditure but influence its composition between domestic absorption and net exports are called **expenditure-switching policies**. Policies that change aggregate desired expenditure are called **expenditure-changing policies**.

Expenditure-changing policies involve moving along a given net export function, so changes in the trade balance and national income will be *negatively* related. If the initial situation calls for them to move

in the same direction, the use of expenditure-changing policies necessarily involves a conflict.

The conflicts between the objectives of internal and external balance arise from the use of expenditure-changing policies.

An expenditure-switching policy shifts the net export function. As we shall see, this can lead to *positively* related changes in the trade balance and national income. Devaluation or revaluation of the domestic currency, restrictions on international trade such as tariffs or quotas, and domestic inflation or deflation relative to foreign conditions are all expenditure-switching policies.[4]

A Trade Account Deficit

As we have seen, a trade account deficit means that national income is less than domestic absorption. Now consider policies to eliminate the trade account deficit; to be successful, the policies must raise national income *relative* to absorption.

Case 1: A deficit combined with an inflationary gap—no conflict.   If the economy already has an inflationary gap, national income should not be increased further. The trade account deficit indicates that domestic absorption is above the current level of national income and hence, by virtue of the inflationary gap, above the full-employment level. To eliminate the deficit, absorption must be lowered. In other words, if net exports are to rise, resources must be released through a reduction in domestic usage. This calls for *expenditure-reducing* policies, such as reductions in the money supply, cuts in government expenditure, and increases in taxes. No conflict for expenditure-changing policies arises in this case, because the expenditure reduction cuts the inflationary gap and improves the trade account by inducing a movement along the net export function.

Case 2: A deficit combined with a recessionary gap—conflict.   When national income is below its capacity level, income can be expanded. However, an expan-

---

[4] When restrictions on international trade, such as tariffs or quotas, are used in this manner, they are referred to as *commercial policy*. Commercial policy may, in some circumstances, be useful for macroeconomic purposes, but it is never the case that commercial policy *must* be used; other expenditure-switching policies will have the same macroeconomic effects.

FIGURE 43-2   Conflicts Between Internal and External Balance

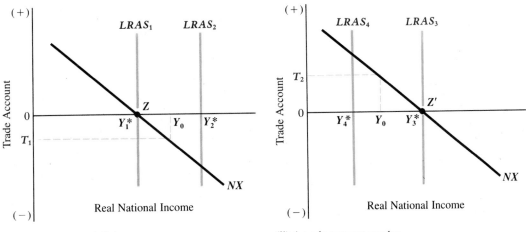

(i) A trade account deficit

(ii) A trade account surplus

Of the four different possible combinations of signs of the output gap and the trade account, only two pose conflicts. In both parts of the figure, the net export function, which relates the trade account to real national income, is shown by the black line, labeled NX. The actual level of income is given by Y_0, so in part (i) there is a trade account deficit of T_1, while in part (ii) there is a trade account surplus of T_2.

In part (i), if potential output is given by Y_1^* so that there is an inflationary gap (case 1), there is no conflict, since adjustment of actual real national income to achieve one target will also achieve the other target, at point Z. However, if potential output is given by Y_2^* so that there is a recessionary gap (case 2), there is a conflict, since movement of actual real national income to achieve either target will cause a movement away from the other target.

In part (ii), if potential income is given by Y_3^* so that there is a recessionary gap (case 3), there is no conflict, since adjustment of actual real national income to achieve one target will also achieve the other target, at point Z'. However, if potential output is given by Y_4^* so that there is an inflationary gap (case 4), there is a conflict, since a change in actual real national income to achieve either target will cause a movement away from the other target.

sion in national income with a fixed net export function would worsen the trade account, so expenditure-increasing policies are not appropriate. A reduction in national income to reduce the deficit would worsen unemployment, so expenditure-reducing policies are not appropriate. What is needed is a switch in expenditure away from foreign goods (thus reducing the trade deficit) and toward domestic goods (thus reducing the recessionary gap).

Policies to induce a *switch* of some expenditure from foreign goods to domestic goods—thereby *shifting* the net export function rightward and raising national income—will alleviate the con- flict posed by a recessionary gap combined with a trade deficit.

Such policies include devaluation of the currency and protective measures, such as tariffs and quotas. This is illustrated in Figure 43-3.[5]

---

[5] From the discussion in Chapter 41, it would appear that there should be two shifts in the NX function. The first is due to the switch in expenditure; the second, which will be in the opposite direction to the first, is due to the induced change in the price of domestic goods as national income changes. The analysis in Figure 43-3, and in this chapter, incorporates this second effect in the response of NX national income by using the $SRAS$ curve to capture the price effect. **[49]**

FIGURE 43-3   A Trade Deficit and a Recessionary Gap

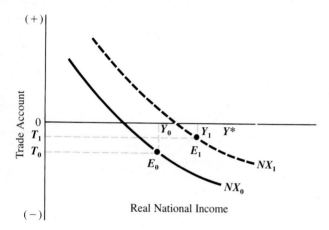

(i) Net export function

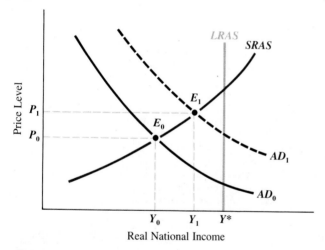

(ii) Determination of national income

A policy to switch expenditure away from foreign goods and toward domestic goods can be used to resolve the conflict that is posed by a trade deficit combined with a recessionary gap. Initially, the net export function is given by NX_0 in part (i), and aggregate demand is given by AD_0 in part (ii). Equilibrium is at E_0, with real national income equal to Y_0. There is a recessionary gap of Y_0Y^* and a trade deficit of T_0.

An expenditure-switching policy raises net exports at each level of income, so the net export function shifts rightward to NX_1 in part (i). The policy also raises aggregate demand, so the AD curve shifts rightward to AD_1 in part (ii). The new equilibrium is at E_1, with real national income of Y_1 and a trade deficit of T_1. Hence, both the recessionary gap and the trade deficit are reduced.

A Trade Account Surplus

Cases 3 and 4 in our list both involve a trade account surplus. An expansion of national income will therefore cause a move toward external balance by raising imports. Hence, in case 3, where there is a recessionary gap, no conflict arises, and expenditure-raising policies will lead to movement toward both targets. In case 4, where there is an inflationary gap, a conflict does arise; external balance calls for expenditure increases, but internal balance calls for expenditure reduction. What is needed is a *switch* in expenditure away from domestic goods (thus reducing the inflationary gap) and toward foreign goods (thus reducing the trade account surplus).

Policies to induce a switch of expenditure from domestic goods to foreign goods—thereby *shifting* the net export function leftward and lowering national income—will alleviate the conflict posed by an inflationary gap combined with a trade surplus.

This is illustrated in Figure 43-4.

FIGURE 43-4   A Trade Surplus and an Inflationary Gap

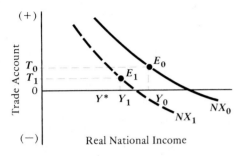

(i) Net export function

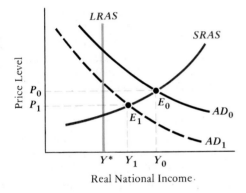

(ii) Determination of national income

A policy to switch expenditure away from domestic goods and toward foreign goods can be used to solve the conflict posed by a trade surplus combined with an inflationary gap. Initially, the net export function is given by NX_0 in part (i), and aggregate demand is given by AD_0 in part (ii). Equilibrium is at E_0 with real national income equal to Y_0. This is an inflationary gap of Y^*Y_0 and a trade surplus of T_0.

An expenditure-switching policy lowers net exports at each level of income, so the net export function shifts leftward to NX_1 in part (ii). The policy also lowers aggregate demand, so the aggregate demand curve shifts leftward to AD_1 in part (ii). The equilibrium moves from E_0 to E_1, real national income falls to Y_1, and the trade surplus falls to T_1. Hence, both the inflationary gap and the trade surplus are reduced.

A General Statement

We have now seen the difference in the effects of the two types of expenditure policies in an open economy.

To achieve internal and external balance, a combination of expenditure-changing and expenditure-switching policies is generally required.

In the conflict situations, expenditure-switching policies will result in movement *toward* both targets. However, they alone cannot be expected to achieve exactly both internal and external balance. Hence, both types of policies are generally required. Expenditure-switching policies are necessary to shift the net export function in order to make the two objectives consistent. In terms of Figures 43-3(i) and 43-4(i), this means that expenditure-switching policies should be used to ensure that the NX curve cuts the horizontal axis at Y^*. There is no assurance, however, that the effects of such policies on the aggregate demand curve will give rise to actual real national income of Y^*. Then expenditure-changing policies—which shift the aggregate demand curve but not the net export curve—can be used to attain both internal and external balance simultaneously.

Some long-run aspects of such policies are taken up in Box 43-1.

Macroeconomic Policy and the Capital Account

The capital account of the balance of payments records international movements of investment funds. When foreign investors buy securities that are issued by American corporations or governments or invest in American industry, this capital inflow is recorded as a receipt in the balance of payments, because it gives rise to an increase in the amount of foreign currency that is offered for American dollars in the foreign exchange market. Conversely, the acquisition of foreign assets by Americans represents a capital outflow and is recorded as a payment, because foreign currency is used up by such transactions.

The primary means by which capital flows can be influenced by the policy authorities is through domestic interest rates. International traders hold

BOX 43-1

Expenditure-switching Policies in the Long Run

Use of expenditure-switching policies, such as devaluation, has often been very controversial. Supporters point to the increase in output and the reduction in the trade account deficit, shown in Figure 43-3. Opponents focus on the inflationary impact indicated by the rise in the price level, also shown in Figure 43-3. The controversy often hinges on disagreement about the relative size of these two effects. Some of the controversy can be defused by distinguishing between the long-run and short-run effects of such policies.

In the text we focused on the short-run effects of expenditure-switching policies, treating the *SRAS* curve as fixed and studying the shifts in the *NX* and *AD* curves. One alternative to using such policies is to do nothing and to let the monetary adjustment mechanism, which we studied in Chapter 32, operate to eliminate the recessionary gap. (Similar automatic mechanisms also exist that establish external balance in the long run.) Justification for using devaluation, for example, in the face of a recessionary gap and a trade deficit is that such automatic adjustment mechanisms are very slow to operate. Hence, support for devaluation and other expenditure-switching policies focuses on their ability to influence output and the trade account *in the short run*.

Note, however, that such policies do not alter potential output (they do not shift the *LRAS* curve), and, hence, they have no effect on output in the long run. However, by circumventing the monetary adjustment mechanism and stimulating aggregate demand, expenditure-switching policies ensure that, when potential income is attained in the long run, the price level will be higher than it would have been in their absence. Opponents of such policies focus on this price-level effect, since it is the only long-run effect that the policies have. Typically, these opponents believe that the automatic adjustment mechanisms are strong enough so that the long-run effect can be achieved fairly quickly without intervention or that devaluations set up expectations of price rises that quickly feed into wages and hence create very little real response of output and employment, even in the short run.

The key policy implication of this debate is that devaluation and other expenditure-switching policies should be directed toward the external target but should be combined with expenditure-changing policies that focus on the internal target. In particular, a devaluation should be accompanied by expenditure-reducing policies to offset any inflationary gap caused by the devaluation in the short run and hence to avoid the price-level increase that would otherwise ensue in the long run.

---

transactions balances just as domestic traders do. These balances are often lent out on a short-term basis, rather than being left idle. Naturally enough, holders of these balances will tend to lend them, other things being equal, in markets where interest rates are highest. If short-term interest rates are raised in the United States, this will induce an inflow of short-run capital to take advantage of the higher American rates. A lowering of American interest rates will have the opposite effect, as capital moves elsewhere to take advantage of the now relatively higher foreign rates.

Long-term capital flows are typically less sensitive to interest-rate differentials, but they are nevertheless likely to show some response. In particular, American corporations and governments attempt to minimize the cost of long-term borrowing by selling bonds in foreign markets when the foreign interest rate is lower than the American rate.

In discussing the trade account in the first part of this chapter, we did not distinguish between the effects of monetary and fiscal policy. However, capital flows respond to interest rates, and monetary and fiscal policies that have the same influence on income have opposite effects on interest rates. As we saw in Chapter 32, in a closed economy, expansionary monetary policy exerts its influence on income by reducing interest rates. Fiscal policy influences aggregate demand directly, and fiscal-policy-induced increases in national income create an excess demand for money, which, in a closed economy, causes interest rates to rise. In discussing capital flows in an open economy, we must therefore distinguish between the operation of monetary and fiscal policies.

Fiscal Policy and the Capital Account

The effects of fiscal policy on the capital account of an open economy are related to the interest rate effects that it would have in a closed economy. Expansionary fiscal policy, for example, leads to increased federal government borrowing in domestic capital markets. In a closed economy, this forces interest rates up; in an open economy, it forces other domestic borrowers to import their capital requirements from foreign financial centers. In summary:

An expansionary fiscal policy will put upward pressure on interest rates and lead to an inflow of foreign capital, thereby moving the capital account toward a surplus. A contractionary fiscal policy will have the opposite effects.

Monetary Policy and the Capital Account

Since monetary policy influences interest rates in a closed economy, it will also influence the capital account in an open economy:

An expansionary monetary policy will put downward pressure on interest rates and lead to an outflow of capital, thereby moving the capital account toward a deficit. A contractionary monetary policy will have the opposite effects.

An Alternative Target for External Balance

Earlier in this chapter we used *external balance* to mean achieving the target level of the trade account. Consideration of international capital flows suggests an expansion of this target to incorporate the capital account and interest payments on the foreign debt as well.

We now specify external balance in terms of a target level of the overall balance of payments.

For the sake of simplicity, we take *external balance* to mean a zero overall balance of payments, so that any current account imbalance is exactly offset by capital account transactions.

Before turning to a discussion of how monetary and fiscal policy might be combined to achieve internal and external balance in this circumstance, it will be useful to examine the relationship between the money supply and the overall balance of payments.

The Balance of Payments and the Money Supply

Suppose that the United States is experiencing a balance-of-payments deficit and that the Fed intervenes in the foreign exchange market to maintain the value of the U.S. dollar. The Fed will be selling foreign currency in exchange for U.S. dollars and thereby running down its stock of official reserves. Payment for the foreign currency, acquired by private participants in the market, normally will be made in the form of a U.S. dollar check that has been drawn on one of the commercial banks. This check will be cleared by reducing the deposits of the bank at the Fed. These transactions are summarized in Table 43-1.

If there are no offsetting transactions, a balance-of-payments deficit will lead to a decrease both in bank reserves and in bank deposits equal to the amount of foreign exchange that has been sold by the central bank. A surplus will lead to an increase in bank reserves and deposits.

Thus, a balance-of-payments deficit will lead to a contraction of the money supply. Of course, the central bank has the option of preventing this from happening by undertaking other offsetting transactions. For example, the decrease in bank reserves can be offset by an open market purchase of bonds, which will have the effect of increasing bank reserves. This procedure of insulating the domestic

TABLE 43-1	Balance Sheet Changes Caused by a Sale of Foreign Currency by the Central Bank

Nonbank private sector

Assets		Liabilities
Foreign currency (equivalent value in U.S. dollars)	+ 100	
Deposits	− 100	

Commercial banks

Assets		Liabilities	
Reserves (deposits with central bank)	− 100	Demand deposits	− 100

Central bank

Assets		Liabilities	
Foreign currency	− 100	Deposits of commercial banks	− 100

The money supply is reduced when the central bank sells foreign currency to maintain a fixed exchange rate when there is a balance-of-payments deficit. A deficit of 100 leads to an excess demand for foreign currency of 100, which is met by a reduction of official reserves by this amount. When the central bank receives payment in the form of a check that has been drawn on a chartered bank, bank reserves fall by 100. There will then be a multiple contraction of deposit money through the process that was analyzed in Chapter 31.

money supply from the effects of balance-of-payments deficits or surpluses is known as **sterilization.**

Fixed Exchange Rates

Monetary Policy

To see the limitations of monetary policy under a fixed exchange rate, consider the following sequence of events. Suppose that interest rates in the United States are at levels similar to those in the rest of the world, and thus there is no inducement for large international movements of capital. Suppose now that the Fed, faced with a large recessionary gap, seeks to stimulate demand through an expansionary monetary policy. The Fed buys bonds in the open

market, thereby increasing the money supply and reducing interest rates.

Lower interest rates stimulate an outflow of capital from the United States and thus a deficit on the capital account.[6] To the extent that national income rises, movement along the net export function creates a deficit on the trade account. Thus, the overall balance of payments moves into deficit. To maintain the fixed exchange rate, the Fed will have to intervene in the foreign exchange market and sell foreign currency. This will have the effect of *reducing* the money supply and thus *reversing* the increase that was brought about by the initial open market operation.

If no other transactions are initiated by the Fed, national income and the money supply will fall and domestic interest rates will rise, until they all return to their initial levels. Thus, the deficit will be self-correcting, and the Fed's expansionary policy will be nullified.

Suppose now that the Fed attempts to sterilize the impact on the money supply of the balance-of-payments deficit. The difficulty with this strategy is that it can be continued only as long as the Fed has sufficient reserves of foreign exchange. If capital flows are highly sensitive to interest rates, as a great deal of evidence suggests is the case, these reserves will be run down at a rapid rate and the Fed will be forced to abandon its expansionary policy.

Under a fixed exchange rate, there is little scope for the use of monetary policy for domestic stabilization purposes, because of the sensitivity of international capital flows to interest rates. The central bank will be forced to maintain domestic interest rates close to the levels existing in the rest of the world, and it will not be able to exercise independent control of the domestic money supply.

Fiscal Policy

Consider now the effectiveness of fiscal policy under fixed exchange rates. Suppose again that U.S. interest rates are in line with those of the rest of the world when an expansionary fiscal policy, aimed at reduc-

[6] Typically, a fall in U.S. interest rates will lead to a fall in interest rates in many foreign countries. However, the interest rate differential still leads to a deficit on capital account. For the sake of simplicity, we can thus safely ignore changes in foreign interest rates in this and subsequent discussions.

ing a large recessionary gap, is introduced. The fiscal expansion raises the level of domestic interest rates and national income.

Higher interest rates stimulate a flow of capital into the United States, thereby leading to a surplus on the capital account. If the capital flows are large, the surplus on capital account will exceed the current account deficit arising from the increased national income. Hence, there will be an overall balance-of-payments surplus.

To maintain the fixed exchange rate, the Fed will have to intervene in the foreign exchange market and buy foreign currency. This will have the effect of increasing the money supply, thus reinforcing the initial fiscal stimulus.

Under a fixed exchange rate, interest-sensitive international capital flows stabilize the domestic interest rate and enhance the effectiveness of fiscal policy.

Combining Monetary and Fiscal Policy

Consider an attempt to increase employment with an expansionary monetary policy that reduces interest rates and thereby stimulates investment and other interest-sensitive expenditure. The decline in domestic interest rates makes it more attractive to invest short-term capital abroad rather than at home. The outflow of short-term capital to be invested at more attractive rates in foreign financial centers worsens the balance of payments on the short-term capital account. Of course, if the expansionary policy succeeds in raising income, there will be additional strain on the balance of payments on current account, as a consequence of the increased expenditure on imports caused by the rise in income.

In principle, the conflict can be removed by an appropriate combination of monetary and fiscal policy. Consider a country with full employment and a balance-of-payments deficit. It could eliminate the deficit by following a tighter monetary policy to increase domestic interest rates and attract short-term capital. At the same time, the contractionary effect of tight money on domestic expenditure and employment could be offset by raising government expenditures or by cutting taxes. Thus, the two goals can both be achieved through a combination of tight monetary policy and expansionary fiscal policy.

This strategy is unlikely to be a satisfactory solution to a persistent current account deficit. The country will find it increasingly difficult to maintain its exchange rate by importing short-term capital. Short-term international capital flows are extremely volatile, and they are particularly sensitive to shifts in expectations concerning exchange rates. If investors lose confidence in a country's ability to maintain its existing exchange rate, capital outflows will build up, and ultimately a devaluation will be required to reduce the deficit and to restore confidence.

Flexible Exchange Rates

A major advantage of a flexible exchange rate is that it removes any conflict between domestic stabilization objectives and the balance of payments, because deficits or surpluses can be eliminated through movements in the exchange rate. In addition, a flexible rate often cushions the domestic economy against cyclical variations in economic activity in other countries. If, for example, the U.S. economy goes into a recession, the decline in U.S. income will lead to a reduction in demand for goods exported from Canada. The fall in exports will reduce income in Canada through the multiplier effect. However, if the value of the Canadian dollar is allowed to respond to market forces, there will also be a depreciation of the Canadian dollar. This fall in the external value of the Canadian dollar will stimulate demand for Canadian exports and encourage the substitution of Canadian goods for imports. Thus, the depreciation will provide a stimulus to demand in Canada that will, at least partially, offset the depressing effect of the U.S. recession.

Fiscal Policy

Suppose that the government seeks to remove a recessionary gap by expansionary fiscal policy. An increase in government expenditures or a reduction in taxes, or both, will increase income through the multiplier effect and reduce the size of the gap. This also will tend to cause a movement along the net export function, leading to a deterioration of the trade account. However, this is not the whole story, for there also will be repercussions on the capital account and the exchange rate.

Capital flows and the crowding-out effect. In a closed economy, fiscal policy causes domestic interest rates to rise. This causes interest-sensitive private expenditures to fall, thus partially offsetting the initial expansionary effect of the fiscal stimulus. As we saw in Chapter 37, this *crowding-out effect* plays an important role in the analysis of fiscal policy in a closed economy. In an open economy, the crowding-out effect will operate differently, due to international capital flows.

Higher domestic interest rates will induce a capital inflow and cause the domestic currency to appreciate. If capital flows are highly interest-elastic, the external value of the currency is likely to rise substantially. This will depress demand by discouraging exports and by encouraging the substitution of imports for domestically produced goods. The initial fiscal stimulus will be *offset* by the expenditure-switching effects of currency appreciation.

Under flexible exchange rates, there will be a strong crowding out of net exports that will greatly reduce the effectiveness of fiscal policy.

However, it is possible to eliminate the crowding-out effect by supporting the fiscal policy with an accommodating monetary policy. Suppose that the central bank responds to the increase in the demand for money, induced by the fiscal expansion, by increasing the supply of money so as to maintain domestic interest rates at their initial level. There will then be no capital inflow and no tendency for the currency to appreciate. Income will expand by the usual multiplier process.

The effectiveness of fiscal policy under flexible exchange rates can be enhanced by an accommodating monetary policy.

Monetary Policy

We have seen that there is little scope under fixed exchange rates for the use of monetary policy for domestic stabilization purposes. Under flexible exchange rates, the situation is reversed, and monetary policy becomes a very powerful tool.

Suppose that the Fed seeks to stimulate demand through an expansionary monetary policy. The Fed buys bonds in the open market, thereby increasing bank reserves and the money supply and reducing interest rates. Lower interest rates will cause an out-

flow of capital from the United States and thus a deficit on the capital account.

Under a fixed rate, we saw that the Fed may be forced to reverse its policy in order to stem the loss of foreign reserves. Under a flexible rate, however, the U.S. dollar will depreciate. This will stimulate exports and discourage imports, so that the deficit on the capital account will be offset by a surplus on the current account.

Domestic employment will be stimulated, not only by the fall in interest rates, but also by the increased demand for domestically produced goods that has been brought about by a depreciation of the currency. The initial monetary stimulus will be *reinforced* by the expenditure-switching effects of currency depreciation.

Under flexible exchange rates, monetary policy is a powerful tool for stabilizing domestic income and employment. If capital flows are highly interest-elastic, the main channel by which an increase in the money supply stimulates demand for domestically produced goods is a depreciation of the currency.

Policy and Performance During the 1980s

Events in the U.S. economy during the 1980s provide a rich variety of experience that sheds some light on the theory outlined so far in this chapter; in turn, this theory can help us to understand and to interpret the controversies that surround those events. We have encountered already many of the key events, including the following:

1. At the start of the decade, the United States introduced sharply contractionary monetary policy in an effort to halt inflation.
2. During the decade, the federal budget deficit soared to record levels.
3. The U.S. economy went into a severe recession during 1981–1982 and then experienced a sustained recovery in output and employment. Inflation fell from its double-digit levels at the start of the decade to stabilize in the 4–5 percent range, although fears of increases in inflation were widespread as the decade came to a close.

4. During the decade, the current account deficit soared to record levels.
5. During the first half of the decade, the foreign exchange value of the U.S. dollar soared dramatically; it then fell gradually for several years, although in mid-1989 it again showed surprising strength.
6. Protectionist sentiment emerged during the decade, leading to the passage of the Omnibus Trade Bill in 1988 and to the possibility of more protectionist measures in the next few years.

We now can examine how well these events can be reconciled and explained.

Monetary Contraction and Disinflation

According to the theory that we have just outlined, monetary policy will exert a very powerful influence on the economy under flexible exchange rates. Contractionary monetary policy will operate in part through the closed-economy mechanism of higher interest rates and in part through an appreciation of the domestic currency. This accords well with what happened during the first few years of the 1980s.

The dramatic rise in interest rates in 1981–1982 curtailed consumption and investment expenditure, and the high value of the dollar placed American firms that produce traded goods (i.e., goods for export and goods that face competition from imports) at a cost disadvantage relative to foreign producers. Falling production, rising unemployment, and many business failures resulted, but inflation also fell sharply.

Monetary contraction worked as expected: High interest rates and an appreciation of the dollar led to a policy-induced recession that reduced the rate of inflation.

The appreciation of the dollar discouraged exports and encouraged imports, and thus contributed to the growth of the current account deficit.

Fiscal Deficits

The dollar became overhauled during the period of tight monetary policy that began in 1980. If a temporary *overshooting* of the exchange rate was all that was involved in that overvaluation, the dollar would

have come down shortly thereafter. Indeed, many economists expected it to do so. However, the dollar in fact remained high throughout the period 1981–1985.

Most observers believe that the dollar remained high because this period witnessed enormous capital inflows into the United States. These capital inflows were partly a result of the record U.S. government budget deficit, which at one point exceeded $200 billion (over 5 percent of GNP). Some of the deficit was financed by domestic savings, but much also had to be financed by foreign borrowing, resulting in capital inflows.

As we saw in Chapter 41, equilibrium in the foreign exchange market means that a capital inflow is *necessarily* matched by a current account deficit (see page 883). Only when these two are equal will the demand for dollars by foreign investors who wish to buy American capital assets be matched by the supply of dollars by those Americans who wish to import foreign goods and services. Thus:

The large capital inflows that occurred in the period 1980–1985 meant that there also had to be a current account deficit; from this perspective the high value of the dollar that occurred in this period was simply the mechanism by which the required current account deficit was brought about.

In a recent study, two economists estimate that about two-thirds of the U.S. current account deficit during the 1980s and about two-thirds of the appreciation of the dollar between 1980 and 1985 can be explained by the U.S. policy mix of fiscal ease and monetary tightness in the United States, combined with fiscal restraint in Germany, Japan, the United Kingdom, and France.[7]

The twin deficits. The association of the government budget deficit with a current account deficit caused many commentators to speak of the *twin deficits* problem.

The government deficit represents *negative* saving from the national viewpoint and is often referred to

[7] Peter Hooper and Catherine Mann, "The Emergence and Persistence of the U.S. External Imbalance: 1980–87," Princeton University, International Finance Section, 1988.

as *government dissaving*. Its record size thus reduced *national saving*, defined as the sum of private saving and government saving. For those who think that the government deficit was the cause of the current account deficit, the reasoning is as follows:

The fall in national savings rates, precipitated by the federal budget deficit, meant that capital had to be imported from abroad; capital inflows were accompanied by high interest rates, a strong dollar, and a current account deficit.

Others argued that the large capital inflows that occurred were primarily responding to the combination of low inflation and relative prosperity in the United States, which made the country a safe and profitable place in which to invest, and that the current account deficit was a necessary by-product of these inflows.

While there is debate about the cause of the capital inflows, it is widely acknowledged that given those inflows, a current account deficit also had to occur.

Recovery.   The evidence is that the fiscal deficits contributed to the sustained recovery that occurred during the rest of the decade. At first this seems at odds with the theory that we have just outlined, since there we argued that fiscal policy under flexible exchange rates would be "crowded out" through a reduction in net exports. In that view the increase in aggregate demand, caused by the fiscal deficit, would be offset by the decrease, caused by the fall in net exports, and thus fiscal stimulus would not be effective in increasing national income.

However, we also noted that fiscal policy can be effective if it is "accommodated" by expansionary monetary policy. It turns out that such accommodation did occur, and thus the fiscal stimulus that resulted from the federal deficit did contribute to the recovery that followed the recession of 1981–1982.

The monetary accommodation occurred in two ways. First, there was some easing of monetary policy—relative to the strong disinflationary stance of 1980–1981—on the part of the Federal Reserve Board. (See the discussion of the reentry problem in Chapter 33, page 705.) Second, the appreciation of the dollar meant that import prices were sharply lower than they would have been otherwise; this led

to an increased *real* money supply and hence an increased level of real income. As Harvard economist and former chairman of the Council of Economic Advisers, Martin Feldstein said, "While expansionary fiscal policy therefore did contribute to the greater-than-expected rise of real GNP in 1983–84, it was through the unusual channel of dollar appreciation. The fiscal expansion raised output because it caused a favorable supply shock to prices—not because it was a traditional stimulus to demand."[8]

Protectionism and the Current Account Deficit

It is useful to recall the discussion in Chapter 40 of the rise of protectionism that occurred in this period. In spite of the vigorous expansion of the economy, many traded-goods sectors remained depressed; to a considerable extent, the recovery was focused in the nontraded sectors. Not surprisingly, the plight of the import-competing and export sectors led to a call for protection. The United States put pressure on Japan, Germany, and Canada to reduce their current account surpluses and itself took many steps to curb imports. Some steps were specific, such as the tariff that was imposed in May 1986 on Canadian cedar shakes and shingles. Some were very broad in scope; the highest profile was the Omnibus Trade Bill, passed in 1988.

While the motivation for these protectionist measures was easy enough to understand, most economists felt that the measures were seriously misguided. First, they threatened to upset the fabric of international trading relations and cooperation that had been carefully built up through multilateral negotiation during the post-World War II period.

Second, the measures were likely to be largely ineffective in terms of their goal of reducing the current account deficit. As we have seen, the current account deficit is a necessary counterpart to the capital inflows that the U.S. economy is experiencing.

Unless the root causes of the capital inflows are dealt with, the current account deficit will persist with or without protectionist measures.

To see this important point, assume that import tariffs, surcharges, and quotas reduced imports by

[8] Martin Feldstein and Douglas Elmendorf, "Budget Deficits, Tax Incentives, and Inflation: A Surprising Lesson from the 1983–84 Recovery," National Bureau of Economic Research, Working Paper No. 2819, 1989.

enough to bring the current account into balance but that people still wished to bring capital into the United States. With a balanced current account, there would not be anyone willing to supply the dollars to the would-be capital importers, and, consequently, the dollar would start to appreciate. This would lead to a reduction in exports and an increase in imports until the original current account deficit was reestablished.[9]

This point extends to the role of exchange rate changes. The fact that the current account deficit remained at record levels, despite a dramatic fall in the dollar over the 1985–1988 period, was widely perceived as a challenge to the orthodox views about the relationship between the exchange rate and the current account. As we discussed in Chapter 40, economists are still studying why imports were able to maintain stable prices and large shares in many markets in the face of the depreciation of the dollar. However, part of the explanation of the persistence of the current account deficit also lies in the fact that the budget deficit remained large, and hence the need for capital inflows and an offsetting current account deficit also remained.

Whither the Dollar?

In mid-1989 the U.S. dollar was showing surprising strength in foreign currency markets, despite the persistent large current account deficit. A key question for the economy then was whether this strengthening would continue or whether the dollar would or should resume its slide against other major currencies. A related question is, "What is the appropriate policy toward the dollar?"

[9] Of course, to the extent that the tariffs create revenue and therefore reduce the government deficit, more domestic private saving would be available to finance domestic investment, and capital inflows and the current account both could be reduced correspondingly.

Some economists, such as Professor Ronald McKinnon of Stanford University, argued that the dollar would, if allowed, continue to strengthen. This view was based largely on the purchasing power parity (PPP) considerations that we discussed in Chapter 42. Calculations showed that, in terms of traded-goods prices, the dollar in 1989 was approximately 30 percent undervalued; this was largely the result of the successful antiinflation policies of the early part of the decade, and the surprising stability of import prices in the face of the 1985–1988 slide of the dollar. Hence, this group of economists felt that the dollar would, over time, strengthen and that this would not harm the competitive position of U.S. industries. Further, this group argued, if policy intervened to stabilize the dollar and thus prevent its continuation, the existing overvaluation would be corrected by increased inflation in the United States.

Other economists, including Martin Feldstein, focused on the need to correct the current account deficit. This perspective led them to believe that the dollar needed to fall substantially in terms of the major currencies in order to bring about an increase in net exports and thus reduce the current account deficit. This group advocated letting the dollar find its own value on international markets and not using monetary and fiscal policies in an attempt to achieve particular exchange rate objectives. They argued that it would be a mistake to divert macroeconomic policies from their objectives of controlling inflation and maintaining high employment and growth. For example, some argued that attempts to use monetary policy to support the dollar in early 1987 ultimately contributed to the stock market crash in October of that year and the subsequent financial disruptions.

As we enter the 1990s, we can expect that these questions will have a high profile in economic commentary, and, perhaps, we will learn which of these views will prevail.

SUMMARY

1. Policymakers in an open economy are faced with policy targets or objectives relating to the foreign sector, as well as to the domestic sector. Attainment of these targets is often called *achieving external* and *internal balance,* respectively. When policies to move the economy toward one target cause it to move away from the other, the targets are said to be *in conflict.*

2. Expenditure-changing policy, used to control the level of national income, will also influence the trade balance by altering imports.

There will be a conflict of objectives if there is a trade account deficit and a recessionary gap or if there is a trade account surplus and an inflationary gap. Expenditure-switching policies that shift the net export function can be used to deal with conflict situations.

3. In general, both expenditure-switching and expenditure-changing policies are needed to attain internal and external balance.

4. The capital account is influenced by both fiscal and monetary policy because both influence domestic interest rates.

5. Under a fixed exchange rate, there is little scope for the use of monetary policy for domestic stabilization purposes. Because of the sensitivity of international capital flows to interest rates, the central bank will be forced to maintain domestic interest rates close to the levels in the rest of the world, and it will not be able to bring about substantial changes in the domestic money supply.

6. Under a fixed exchange rate, capital flows will act to reinforce the effectiveness of fiscal policy.

7. Under a flexible exchange rate, fiscal policy actions will be offset by a crowding-out effect, unless they are accompanied by an accommodating monetary policy that prevents changes in interest rates and the exchange rate.

8. Under a flexible exchange rate, monetary policy is a powerful tool. When capital flows are highly interest-elastic, the main channel by which an increase in the money supply increases demand for domestically produced goods is a depreciation of the exchange rate.

9. Tight monetary policy during 1980–1981 had the predicted effects of high interest rates, a strong dollar, a severe recession, and a reduction in inflation. In subsequent years, fiscal deficits contributed to a recovery of output and employment and also to sustained high interest rates and the strength of the dollar.

10. Persistent, large fiscal deficits throughout the 1980s were also accompanied by persistent current account deficits. Those twin deficits remained large in the face of substantial dollar depreciation over the period 1985–1988. The persistent current account deficit thus led to concerns about the effectiveness of devaluation and to continued pressures for protectionist measures. Such measures would, however, be misguided, as they would not lead to any substantial improvements in the current account.

11. At the start of the 1990s, there was a debate about whether the dollar would strengthen toward its PPP value or whether it would weaken to help facilitate improvement in the current account. Most economists felt that it should be left free to adjust to its value, determined by the market, and that government policies should not be directed toward a target for the exchange rate.

TOPICS FOR REVIEW

Internal and external balance
Conflicts between objectives
Expenditure-changing and expenditure-switching policies
Monetary and fiscal policy under fixed exchange rates
Sterilization
Monetary and fiscal policy under flexible exchange rates
Twin deficits
The current account and protectionism

DISCUSSION QUESTIONS

1. Explain how a country can influence the external value of its currency by (a) direct intervention in the foreign exchange market, (b) fiscal policy, (c) monetary policy.

2. One message of this chapter is that, despite a formal commitment to flexible exchange rates, central banks often try to stabilize the exchange rate and to "mimic" policies of major countries. Why might a central bank oppose both a depreciation and an appreciation of its currency? Can you cite any episodes in which the Fed has faced this dilemma in the past two or three years?

3. In a speech in December 1980, Bank of Canada governor Gerald Bouey stated that "the rapid run-up of U.S. short-term [interest] rates is bound to have a major impact on Canada through increases in interest rates [in Canada] or through a fall in the foreign exchange value of the Canadian dollar, or some combination of the two." Why must one of these responses occur? What policies can the Bank of Canada follow in order to influence which of the possible responses occurs? Which is preferable?

4. Which of the following pairs of policy goals can be reached simultaneously by using an appropriate macroeconomic policy, and which involve conflicting objectives? Indicate the policies that you would advocate in each case.
   a. Lower rate of inflation and a reduced trade deficit
   b. Elimination of an inflationary gap and a trade deficit
   c. Lower rate of unemployment and a reduced trade deficit
   d. Lower rate of unemployment and a reduced balance-of-payments deficit

5. According to the analysis in this chapter, a country that maintains a fixed exchange rate will have to allow its inflation rate to adjust to the level that is occurring in the rest of the world. Is this inconsistent with the theories of demand-pull and expectational inflation that were discussed in Chapter 36?

6. Suppose that the government deficit remains high, so that national savings remain low, but that the rising U.S. national debt and the fear of inflation cause a sharp fall in the desire on the part of foreigners toward investing in the United States. Outline the key macroeconomic effects of this shift. What policies might you recommend to deal with these consequences?

7. In a column in the May 16, 1989 issue of the *Wall Street Journal*, economist Herbert Stein argues that much of the concern about the current account deficit is misplaced, since the accompanying capital inflow has resulted in a stock of productive capital in the United States that is $700 billion higher than it would otherwise have been. What is the basis for such a statement? Should we worry about the current account deficit?

8. How would you answer the question that was posed by economist Fred Bergsten in a monograph that was published in 1988, *America in the World Economy: A Strategy for the 1990s:* What would be the implications for the current account positions and policies of other countries if the U.S. current account deficit shrank from $155 billion in 1987 to $5 billion by 1992?

9. Consider the following two potential sources of dollar appreciation: (a) contractionary monetary policy followed by the Fed and (b) foreign inflation. Explain how each could lead to dollar appreciation. What are the differences for the economy? How would you distinguish between the two?

Chapter 44

Growth in the Less-Developed Countries

In the civilized and comfortable urban life of today's developed countries, most people have lost sight of the fact that a very short time ago—very short in terms of the life span of the earth—people lived like other animals, catching an existence as best they could from what nature threw their way. It has been only about 10,000 years since the first agricultural revolution, when people changed from food gatherers to food producers. Throughout most of subsequent human history, civilizations were based on a civilized life for a privileged minority and unremitting toil for the vast majority. It has been only within the last century that ordinary people have been able to expect leisure and high consumption standards—and then only in the economically developed parts of the world.

The Uneven Pattern of Development

About 5 billion people are alive today, but the wealthy parts of the world—where people work no more than 40 or 50 hours per week, enjoy substantial leisure, and have a level of consumption at or above *half* that attained by North Americans—contain less than 15 percent of the world's population. Many of the rest struggle for subsistence. Many exist on a level at or below that endured by peasants in ancient Egypt or Babylon.

Data on per capita income levels throughout the world (as in Table 44-1) cannot be accurate down to the last $100.[1] Nevertheless, such data do reflect enormous real differences in living standards that no statistical discrepancies can hide. The *development gap*—the discrepancy between the standards of living in countries at either end of the distribution—is real and large.

There are many ways to look at inequality of income distribution among the world's population. One is a Lorenz curve, as in Figure 44-1. The more the curve bends away from the straight, 45° line, the greater is the inequality in income distribution. The Lorenz curve of income distribution among Americans gives perspective on the disparity in income among countries. It is much closer to equality than the world distribution.

---

[1] There are many problems when we compare national incomes across countries. For example, home-grown food is vitally important to living standards in underdeveloped countries, but it is excluded, or at best imperfectly included, in the national income statistics of most countries. So is the contribution of a warm climate.

TABLE 44-1   Income and Population Differences Among Groups of Countries, 1983

Group	Classification (based on gross domestic product per capita in 1980 U.S. dollars) Average income level	(1) Number of countries[a]	(2) GDP (billions)	(3) Population (millions)	(4) GDP per capita	(5) Percentage of world GDP	(6) Percentage of world population	(7) Growth rate[b]
I	$400 or less	15	$ 548	2,099	$ 241	4.6	49.8	1.3
II	$401–$1,000	18	274	421	690	2.3	10.0	0.1
III	$1,001–$5,000	31	1,619	635	2,420	13.4	15.1	1.7
IV	$5,001–$10,000	13	4,175	613	6,794	34.7	14.5	2.0
V	More than $10,000	16	5,417	448	13,251	45.0	10.6	1.4

Source: IMF International Financial Statistics Yearbook, 1985; Handbook of Economic Statistics, 1984.

[a] Countries for which data are not available, and which are therefore not represented in the table, account for about 9 percent of the world's population and mostly in the poorer categories.

[b] Average annual percentage rate of growth of real GDP per capita, 1975–1983.

Over one-half of the world's population lives in poverty. Many of the very poorest are in countries that have the lowest growth rates and thus fall ever farther behind. The unequal distribution of the world's income is shown in columns 5 and 6. Groups I and II, which have about 60 percent of world population, earn less than 10 percent of world income. Groups IV and V, with 25 percent of world population, earn 80 percent of world income. Column 7 shows that the poorest countries are not closing the gap in income between rich and poor countries. Data for more recent years covers fewer of the very poor countries but tells roughly the same story.

FIGURE 44-1   Lorenz Curves Showing Inequalities Among the Nations of the World and Within the United States

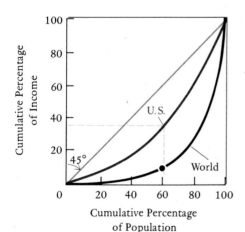

There is much less inequality in the distribution of income within the United States than among all the nations of the world. In a Lorenz curve, a wholly equal distribution of income is represented by the 45° line: 20 percent of the population would have 20 percent of the income, 50 percent of the population would have 50 percent of the income, and so on. The curve for the world indicates a very unequal distribution of income. For example, 60 percent of the world's population live in countries that earn only 10 percent of the world's income, as shown by the black dot. Contrast this with the distribution of income within the United States. The poorest 60 percent of the American population earn 36 percent of the nation's income. This is not equality, but it is much less unequal than the world distribution.

FIGURE 44-2   Countries of the World, Classified by Per Capita GNP, 1985

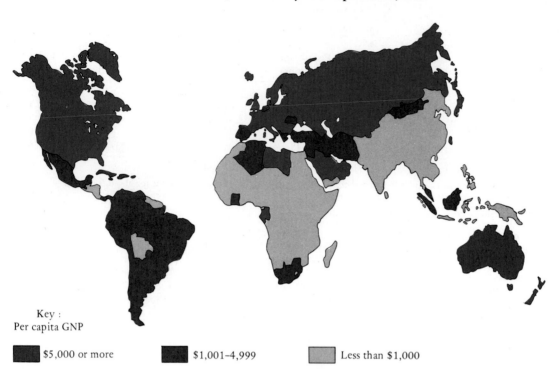

Key :
Per capita GNP

◼ $5,000 or more   ◼ $1,001–4,999   ▢ Less than $1,000

There is a sharp geographical division between "North" and "South" in the level of income per capita. The nations of the world are classified here according to three levels of measured per capita GNP. The poorest group, shown in light gray, represents 31 percent of the world's population. The middle group, shown in dark gray, represents about 41 percent of world population. The wealthiest group, shown in color, includes all of North America, Europe, the Soviet Union, and Japan and represents only 25 percent of the world's population. Areas in white indicate that no data are available. See Table 44-1 for more detail.

Another way of looking at inequality is to look at the geographic distribution of income per capita, as in Figure 44-2. Recent political discussions of income distribution have distinguished between richer and poorer nations as "North" versus "South." The map reveals why.

The consequences of low-income levels can be severe. In a rich country such as the United States, variations in rainfall are reflected in farm output and farm income. In poor countries such as those of the Sahel area of Africa, variations in rainfall are often reflected in the death rate. In these countries, many people live so close to a subsistence level that slight fluctuations in the food supply bring death by star-

vation to large numbers. Other, less dramatic characteristics of poverty include inadequate diet, poor health, short life expectancy, and illiteracy.

For these reasons, reformers in underdeveloped countries, often called **less-developed countries (LDCs)**, feel a sense of urgency not felt by their counterparts in rich countries.[2] Yet, as the first two rows of Table 44-1 show:

[2] The terminology of development is often confusing. *Underdeveloped, less developed,* and *developing* do not mean the same thing in ordinary English, yet each has been used to describe the same phenomenon. For the most part, we shall refer to the underdeveloped countries as the *less-developed countries,* or LDCs. Some of them are making progress, that is, developing; others are not.

The development gap for the very poorest countries has been widening.

As we shall see, this is a problem of both output and population. It is also an international political problem.

Obviously, underdevelopment is nothing new. Concern with it as a remediable condition, however, is recent; it has become a compelling policy issue only within the present century. One incentive behind this new attention to development was the apparent success of planned programs of "crash" development, of which the Soviet experience seemed to be the most remarkable, and the Chinese, the most recent. Observing other developing countries, people saw that it was possible to achieve better lives for themselves and their children. It is bad enough to be poor, but it is doubly galling to be poor when others are escaping poverty. Leaders in other countries asked, "If they can do it, why not us?"

What are the causes of underdevelopment, and how may they be overcome?

Barriers to Economic Development

Income per capita grows when aggregate income grows faster than population. Many forces can impede such growth.

Population and Natural Resources

Rapid Population Growth

Population growth is a central problem of economic development. If population grows as quickly as national income, per capita income does not increase. Many less-developed countries have rates of population growth that are nearly as large as their rates of growth of gross domestic product. As a result, their standards of living are barely higher than they were 100 or even 1,000 years ago. They have made appreciable gains in aggregate income, but most of the gains have been literally eaten up by the increasing population. This is shown in Table 44-2.

The population problem has led economists to talk about the *critical minimum effort* that is required, not merely to increase capital, but to increase it fast enough so that the increase in output outpaces the increase in population. When population control is left to nature, it is often achieved in a cruel way. Population increases until many people are forced to live at a subsistence level; further population growth is halted by famine, pestilence, and plague. This grim possibility was perceived early in the history of economics by Thomas Malthus.

In some ways the population problem is more severe today than it was 100 years ago, because advances in medicine and in public health have brought sharp and sudden decreases in death rates. It is ironic that much of the compassion that has been shown by wealthier nations for the poorer people of the world traditionally has taken the form of improving their health, thereby doing little to avert their poverty. We praise the medical missionaries who brought modern medicine to the tropics, but the elimination of malaria has doubled population growth in Sri Lanka. Cholera, once a killer, is now largely under control. No one argues against controlling disease, but other steps also must be taken if the children who survive the infectious illnesses of infancy are not to die of starvation in early adulthood.

Figure 44-3 illustrates actual and projected world population growth. The population problem is not limited to underdeveloped countries, but about seven-eighths of the expected growth in the world's population is in Africa, Asia, and Latin America—areas where underdevelopment is the rule rather than the exception.

Insufficient Natural Resources

A country with ample fertile land and a large supply of easily developed resources will find growth in income easier to achieve than one that is poorly endowed with such resources. Kuwait has an income per capita above that of both the United States and Canada, because by accident it sits on top of the world's greatest known oil field. A lack of oil proved to be a devastating setback to many LDCs when the OPEC cartel increased oil prices tenfold during the 1970s. Without oil, their development efforts would have been halted, but to buy oil took so much scarce foreign exchange that it threatened to cripple their attempts to import needed capital goods.

The amount of resources that is available for production is, at least in part, subject to control. Badly fragmented land holdings may result from a dowry

TABLE 44-2   The Relationship Between Population Growth and Per Capita Income, 1975–1985 *(percentages)*

Classification of countries (based on GDP per capita in 1980 U.S. dollars)			Average annual growth rate of			Population growth as percentage of real GDP growth
Group	Average income level	Percentage of world population	Real GDP	Population	Real GDP per capita	
I–II	$1,000 or less	59.8	3.2	2.6	0.6	81
III–IV	$1,001–$10,000	29.6	3.6	1.8	1.8	50
V	More than $10,000	10.6	2.7	1.3	1.4	48

Source: Calculated from *IMF International Financial Statistics Yearbook*, 1985; *Handbook of Economic Statistics*, 1984.

Growth in per capita real income depends on the difference between growth rates of real national income and population. The very poorest countries spend much of their increase in income on a rising population. Thus, their increase in income per capita is less than half that of the countries that are already richer.

or inheritance system. When farmland is divided into many small parcels, it may be much more difficult to achieve the advantages of modern agriculture than it is when the land is available in huge tracts for large-scale farming.

Lands that are left idle because of lack of irrigation or that are spoiled by lack of crop rotation are well-known examples of barriers to development. Ignorance is another. The people of the Middle East lived through recorded history alongside the Dead Sea without realizing that it was a substantial source of potash. Not until after World War I were these resources utilized; now they provide Israel with raw materials for its fertilizer and chemical industries.

Inefficient Use of Resources

Low levels of income and slower than necessary growth rates may result from the inefficient use of resources as well as the lack of key resources.

It is useful to distinguish among three kinds of inefficiency, two of which have already been discussed at length. *Allocative inefficiency* occurs when factors of production are used to make an inefficient combination of goods. There is too much of some goods and too little of others. This means that the society is at the "wrong" point on its production possibility boundary. If resources are reallocated to produce less of the former and more of the latter types of goods, some people can be made better off while no one is made worse off.

Productive inefficiency occurs when factors of production are used in inefficient combinations. Some production processes use too much capital relative to

labor, while others use too little. This means that the society is inside its production possibility boundary. If factor combinations are altered, more of all goods can be produced.

Both of these inefficiencies can occur when firms seek to maximize their profits, and owners of factors seek to maximize their material living standards, provided that either prices are not set in perfect markets or that all firms and factors do not face the same set of prices. Monopolistic and monopsonistic market structures, as well as taxes, tariffs, and subsidies, are some important sources of the distortions that lead to both allocative and productive inefficiencies.

The third type of inefficiency, which is called *X-inefficiency,* has been studied in detail by Professor Harvey Leibenstein. It occurs when either firms do not seek to maximize their profits or factor owners do not seek to maximize their material welfare.[3] X-inefficiency also puts the society inside its production possibility boundary.

X-inefficiency usually means that firms are employing productive techniques that use more of *all* factors than is necessary. A careful analysis of reactions to market prices is not needed, therefore, to identify the existence of X-inefficiency. In this sense X-inefficiency is a cruder type than the other two kinds of inefficiency.

X-inefficiency can arise when firms choose not to maximize their profits and, instead, follow routines that are dictated by custom or tradition. For example, the family members of a firm may be em-

---

[3] X-inefficiency is similar to the technological efficiency that was discussed in Box 11-1.

FIGURE 44-3   World Population Growth, 1400–2000

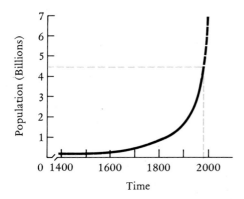

The trend of growth in the world's population is explosive. The solid line reflects present measurements. The dashed line involves projections from observed trends. It took about 50,000 years from the emergence of modern human beings for the world's population to reach 1 billion. It took 100 years to add a second billion, 30 years to add the third billion, and 15 years to add the fourth billion. If these trends continue, the population will reach 7 billion by the year 2000.

ployed by that firm even when they are less efficient than hired workers would be. The family members may behave inefficiently, not because they are intrinsically less efficient than other workers, but *because* they are employed in their families' firms. Firms may employ more factors than they need, and produce less than these factors could produce, because they are satisfied with their present situations and see no reason to try to increase their profits. (This is the type of behavior that we called *satisficing* in Chapter 16.) Firms may also avoid potentially profitable lines of endeavor because they prefer safe, customary behavior to risky, novel behavior. In this form, X-inefficiency may be the price that societies must pay for giving heavier weight to friendship, loyalty, tradition, and the quiet life than to maximizing material living standards.

Professor Leibenstein cites psychological evidence to show that nonmaximizing behavior is typical of situations in which pressure that has been placed on decision makers is either very low or very high. If the customary living standard can be obtained with little effort, according to this evidence, people are likely to follow customary behavior and spend little time trying to make optimal decisions. When pressure builds up, so that making a reasonable income becomes more difficult, optimizing behavior becomes more common. Under extreme pressure, however, such as very low living standards or a rapidly deteriorating environment, people become disoriented and once again do not adopt optimizing behavior.

In this form, X-inefficiency may be typical of industries, and whole economies, where life is either too easy or too tough. Although such environments are, no doubt, often found in some LDCs, they also are found sometimes in advanced countries. For example, the British professor, John Dunning, has studied the performance of *identical* automobile plants that are operated in the United Kingdom and in Germany. Typically, *more labor is employed* in the plants in the United Kingdom, and *less is produced* compared with Germany.

Inadequate Human Resources

A well-developed entrepreneurial class, motivated and trained to organize resources for efficient production, is often missing in less-developed countries. The cause may be that managerial positions are awarded on the basis of family status or political patronage; it may be the presence of economic or cultural attitudes that do not favor acquisition of wealth by organizing productive activities; or it may simply be the absence of the quantity or quality of education or training that is required.

Poor health is likewise a source of inadequate human resources. When the labor force is healthy, less time is lost and more effective effort is expended. The economic analysis of medical advances is a young field, however, and there is a great deal to be learned about the drag of poor health on the growth of an economy.

Cultural and Institutional Patterns

Cultural Barriers

Traditions and habitual ways of doing business vary among societies, and not all are equally conducive to productivity. Max Weber argued that the "Protestant ethic" encouraged the acquisition of wealth and

hence encouraged more growth than systems of belief that directed activity away from the economic
sphere.

Often in LDCs, cultural forces are a source of X-
inefficiency. Sometimes personal considerations of
family, past favors, or traditional friendship or en-
mity are more important than market incentives in
motivating behavior. One may find a firm that is too
small struggling to survive against a larger rival and
learn that the owner prefers to remain small because
expansion would require use of nonfamily capital or
leadership. To avoid paying too harsh a competitive
price for built-in inefficiency, the firm's owners may
then spend much of their energies in an attempt to
influence the government to prevent larger firms
from being formed or to try to secure restrictions on
the sale of output—and they may well succeed. Such
behavior will inhibit economic growth.

In an environment in which people believe that
it is more important who your father is than what
you do, it may take a generation to persuade employers to change their attitudes and another generation to persuade workers that times have changed.
In a society in which children are expected to stay in
their fathers' occupations, it is more difficult for the
labor force to change its characteristics and to adapt
to the requirements of growth than in a society in
which upward mobility is itself a goal.

Structuring incentives is a widely used form of
policy action in market-oriented economies. However, if people habitually bribe the tax collector rather
than pay taxes, they will not be likely to respond to
policies that are supposed to work by raising or lowering taxes. All that will change is the size of the
bribe.

There is lively debate on how much to make of
the significance of differing cultural attitudes. Some
analysts believe that traditional considerations dominate peasant societies to the exclusion of economic
responses; others suggest that any resulting inefficiency may be relatively small.

**The fact that existing social, religious, or legal
patterns may make growth more difficult does
not in itself imply that they are undesirable.**

Instead, it suggests that the benefits of these patterns must be weighed against the costs, of which
the limitation on growth is one. When people derive
satisfaction from a religion whose beliefs inhibit

growth, when they value a society in which every
household owns its own land and is more nearly self-
sufficient than in another society, they may be quite
willing to pay a price in terms of growth opportunities foregone.

Inadequate Infrastructure

Key services, called **infrastructure,** such as transportation and a communications network, are necessary to efficient commerce. Roads, bridges,
railways, and harbors are needed to transport
people, materials, and finished goods. The most dramatic confirmation of their importance comes in
wartime, when belligerent countries always place a
high priority on destroying each other's transportation facilities.

Phone and postal services, water supply, and san-
itation are essential to economic development. The
absence, for whatever reason, of a dependable infrastructure can impose severe barriers to economic
development.

Many governments feel that money that is spent
on a new steel mill shows more impressive results
than money that is spent on such infrastructure investments as automating the telephone system. Yet
private, growth-creating, entrepreneurial activity
will be discouraged more by the absence of good
telephone communications than by the lack of domestically produced steel. During the 1970s, for example, the Republic of Ireland spent large sums on
an unsuccessful attempt to establish a domestic steel
industry, while spending little to modernize its inefficient telephone system. Several successful firms
that moved from Ireland to the United States listed
the enormous amounts of time wasted on trying to
complete telephone calls as a major reason for their
move.

Financial Institutions

The lack of an adequate and trusted system of financial institutions is often a barrier to development.
Investment plays a key role in growth, and an important source of funds for investment is the savings
of households and firms. When banks and other financial institutions do not function well and
smoothly, the link between private saving and investment may be broken and the problem of finding
funds for investment may be greatly intensified.

Many people in LDCs do not trust banks—sometimes with good reason, but more often without. Either they do not maintain deposits, or they panic periodically, drawing them out and seeking security for their money in mattresses, in gold, or in real estate. When banks cannot count on their deposits being left in the banking system, they cannot engage in the kind of long-term loans that are needed to finance investments. When this happens, savings do not become available for investment in a productive capacity.

Developing countries not only must create banking institutions but also must develop enough stability and reliability so that people will trust their savings to such financial intermediaries.

Excessive Government Intervention

As we have just noted, the early successes of the growth policies of many Socialist countries, particularly the USSR and China, provided role models for much of the early development policies of the LDCs. Not surprisingly, the governments of many LDCs sought to copy the planning techniques that appeared to underlie these earlier Socialist successes.

In recent decades, however, most of the more developed Socialist countries have been forced into an understanding of the limitations of their planning techniques. Highly planned government intervention seems most successful in providing infrastructure and developing basic industries, such as electric power and steel, where these are needed. It is now seen to be much less successful in providing the entrepreneurial activity, risk-taking, and adaptivity to change that are key ingredients to sustained economic growth in the very long run. As a result:

The USSR, China, and most other eastern-bloc countries are putting increasing reliance on decentralized, profit-oriented decision taking, coordinated by markets rather than by central planners.

The governments of many of the world's present LDCs have learned these lessons from their own bitter experience. Others have yet to learn them. As a result, growth is often hampered by excessive and rigid bureaucratic intervention. There is room for central government planning of the outlines of growth policies, but the experience of those countries that have gone furthest with central planning is that

the limits of planning are quickly met. They find that decentralized markets are better adapted to unleashing the entrepreneurial activity that is critically important to growth in the very long run.

Some Basic Choices

There are many barriers to economic development that, singly and in combination, can keep a country poor.

Economic development policy involves identifying the barriers to the level and kind of development that is desired and then devising ways to overcome them. Although the problems and strategies vary greatly from country to country, there are common basic choices that all developing countries must face.

How Much Government Control?

How much government control over the economy is necessary and desirable? Practically every shade of opinion from "The only way to grow is to get the government's dead hand out of everything" to "The only way to grow is to get a fully planned, centrally controlled economy" has been seriously advocated.

The extreme views are easily refuted by historical evidence. Many economies have grown with very little government assistance: Great Britain in the Industrial Revolution; the Netherlands during the heyday of its colonial period; and Singapore, Hong Kong, South Korea, and Taiwan during modern times. Others, such as the Soviet Union and Austria, have sustained growth with a high degree of centralized control. Other countries have successfully used almost every conceivable mix of state and private initiative.

As we have noted in the previous section, however, the evidence strongly suggests that it is difficult to sustain growth over long periods under highly centralized planning systems. There is still room for debate, however, on the appropriate mix of government and market determination of economic decisions at various stages in the growth process.

The Case for Planning

The case for active government intervention in the management of a country's economy rests on the real or alleged failure of market forces to produce satisfactory results. The major appeal of such intervention is that it is expected to accelerate the pace of economic development.

Many barriers to development may be lowered by appropriate government actions.

For example, when living standards are low, people have urgent uses for their current incomes, so savings tend to be low. Governments can intervene in a variety of ways and force people to save more than they otherwise would in order to ease a shortage of investment funds.

Compulsory saving has been one of the main aims of most development plans of centralized governments, such as those of the USSR and China. The goal of such plans is to raise savings and thus lower current consumption below what it would be in an unplanned economy. A less authoritarian method is to increase the savings rate through tax incentives and monetary policies. The object is the same: to increase investment in order to increase growth and thus to make future generations better off.

Authoritarian central governments can be particularly effective in overcoming some of the sources of X-inefficiency. A dictatorship may suppress social and even religious institutions that are barriers to growth, and it may hold on to power until a new generation grows up that did not know and does not value the old institutions. It is much more difficult for a democratic government, which must command popular support during each election, to do currently unpopular things in the interest of long-term growth. Whether the gains in growth that an authoritarian government can achieve are worth the political and social costs is, of course, an important value judgment.

An important goal of planning is often to channel growth into industries that the planners believe will have the greatest chance of long-run success.

Unplanned growth usually will tend to exploit the country's present comparative advantages; planners may choose a pattern of growth that involves trying to change the country's comparative advantages.

Planners may seek to alter the course of a country's pattern of growth for several reasons. First, they may believe that they can evaluate the future more accurately than can the countless individuals whose decisions determine market prices. Skeptics see no reason why government bureaucrats, who are risking taxpayers' money and are responsive to politicians who worry about the next election, can be better at making such risky assessments than private entrepreneurs, who are risking their own and their shareholders' money.

Second, planners may wish to adopt a longer time horizon than would private investors. Usually, private investors require the prospect of a fairly quick payoff from those risky ventures that do succeed. Governments can worry about the state of their country decades down the line, concerning themselves with the welfare of future as well as present generations. There is a rational case for planning here. Critics argue, however, that, freed from the constraint of showing a profit in the immediate future, planners will engage in many investments that never pay off and therefore will waste the country's scarce capital.

Third, investment in changing a country's comparative advantage is in the nature of a public good. As we know from Chapter 21, if the government does not provide a public good, no one will.[4] Many skills can be acquired, some of them by formal education but some of them only through on-the-job training. Fostering an apparently uneconomic domestic industry may, by changing the characteristics of the labor force, develop a comparative advantage in that line of production, as well as in other, similar lines of production.

Supporters of this view point out that the Japanese had no visible comparative advantage in manufacturing when Commander Matthew Perry opened that feudal country to the world in 1854. Nonetheless, the Japanese became an industrial power by the end of the century and now lead the world in a range of high-tech products. Furthermore,

---

[4] In some cases private clubs can do the job, but this holds for rather specific goods and services, not a generalized activity such as altering comparative advantage.

the Asian NICs, such as Singapore, Taiwan, and South Korea, have grown dramatically under various forms of government growth policies. Supporters also point out that, during the 1920s and 1930s, Soviet planners chose to create an industrial economy out of a predominantly agricultural one and succeeded in dramatically changing the mix between agriculture and industry in a single generation.[5]

Critics of planning argue that the Soviet experience can no longer be taken as anything other than an example of the failure of planning. They also argue that the Asian countries should be seen primarily as a success of free-market capitalism. Their governments mainly provided infrastructure support, along with tariff protection that allowed infant industries to grow. Critics also point to the success of these nations relative to the more planned economies of some other Asian countries, such as India and Indonesia, and many African states. They argue that this comparison shows the limited value of any planning beyond broad framework policies that seek to set the stable background against which free-market forces can provide development. (The place of the Japanese planning board, MITI, in fostering Japanese growth remains subject to substantial debate.)

The Case for the Market

Most people would accept that government must play an important part in any development program, especially in programs concerning education, transportation, and communication. Nevertheless, what of the sectors that are usually left to private enterprise in advanced capitalist countries?

The advocates of relying on market forces in these sectors place great emphasis on human drive, initiative, and inventiveness. Once the infrastructure has been established, they argue, an army of entrepreneurs will do vastly more to develop the economy than will an army of civil servants. The market will provide the opportunities and direct their efforts. People who seem lethargic and unenterprising when held down by lack of incentives will show bursts of energy when given sufficient self-interest in economic activity.

Furthermore, the argument goes, individual capitalists are far less wasteful of the country's capital

than civil servants. A bureaucrat who is investing capital that is not his own (raised perhaps from the peasants by a state marketing board that buys cheap and sells dear) may choose to enhance his own prestige at the public's expense by spending too much money on cars, offices, and secretaries and too little on truly productive activities. Even if the bureaucrat is genuinely interested in the country's well-being, the incentive structure of a bureaucracy does not encourage creative risk taking. If his ventures fail, his head will likely roll; if they succeed, he will receive no profits—and his superior may get the medal. Thus, he will be cautious about taking risks.

What Sorts of Education?

Most studies of less-developed countries suggest that undereducation is a barrier to development and often urge increased expenditures on education. This poses a choice: whether to spend educational funds on erasing illiteracy and increasing the level of mass education or on training a small cadre of scientific and technical specialists.

To improve basic education requires a large investment in school building and in teacher training. This investment will result in a visible change in the level of education only after 10 or more years, and it will not do much for productivity even during that time span. The opportunity cost of basic education expenditures always seems high. Yet it is essential to make them, because the gains will be critical to economic development a generation later.

Many developing countries have put a large fraction of their educational resources into training a small number of highly educated men and women, often by sending them abroad for advanced study, because the results of acquiring a few hundred doctors or engineers or Ph.D.s are relatively more visible than the results of raising the school-leaving age by a year or two, say, from age 10 to age 12. It is not yet clear whether the policy of "educating the few" pays off, but it is clear that it does have some drawbacks.

Many of the educated elite become dedicated specialists who work hard for their country's welfare. Others, however, regard their education as the passport to a new aristocracy rather than as a mandate to serve their fellow citizens; and an appreciable fraction emigrate to countries where their newly acquired skills bring higher pay than they do at home.

---

[5] Box 36-1 is relevant at this point.

Of those who return home, some seek the security of a government job, which they may use to advance their own status in what is sometimes a self-serving and unproductive bureaucracy.

What Type of Population Policy?

The race between population and income has been a dominant feature of many less-developed countries.

Where population is growing rapidly, there are only two possible ways for a country to win this race. One is to make a massive effort to achieve an income growth rate that is well in excess of the population growth rate. The other is to control population growth.

The problem *can* be solved by restricting population growth. However, the issues of whether and how to restrict population growth are controversial, since considerations of religion, custom, and education are involved.

The consequences of different population policies are large. The birthrate in Sweden is 12 per 1,000, while in Venezuela it is 42 per 1,000; and the two countries have similar death rates. The variations in birthrates have economic consequences. In Venezuela the net increase of population per year is 33 per 1,000 (3.3 percent), but it is only 3 per 1,000 (0.3 percent) in Sweden. If each country were to achieve an overall rate of growth of output of 3 percent per year, Sweden's living standards would be increasing by 2.7 percent per year, while Venezuela's would be falling by 0.3 percent per year. In 1985 Sweden's income per capita ($9,000) was 2½ times as high as Venezuela's ($3,600)—and Venezuela is the wealthiest country south of the Rio Grande. The gap will widen rapidly if present population trends continue.

Population control can take forms as mild as public education programs that are designed to alter attitudes toward family size and to encourage the avoidance of involuntary pregnancies. At the other extreme are massive programs of compulsory sterilization, such as the one that was attempted in India during the mid-1970s. Between these extremes are many possibilities, most of which use various economic and legal incentives or penalties to encourage a lower birthrate.

Customs can be changed to raise the average marriage age and hence lower the birthrate. Prohibition of child labor and the establishment of compulsory education alters the costs and benefits of having children and reduces the desired family size. Changing the role of women and providing career alternatives outside the home can also lower the birthrate.

University of Maine Professor Johannes Overbeck reported recently that a comprehensive family planning program—involving the provision of a broad selection of birth control techniques, a broad range of social services, and accelerated research to develop more effective and cheaper contraceptives—would have an annual cost of $1 per capita in a typical less-developed country. Excluding mainland China, this amounts to around $2 billion per year for all LDCs combined, a relatively modest sum compared to the more than $500 billion currently spent annually on armaments. If this estimate is roughly accurate, population policy offers an extremely high return on spending to promote per capita growth in LDCs.

Different countries have adopted very different positions with respect to population. Kenya, with a birthrate of 50 per 1,000, until recently rejected any serious national policy of population control. Mexico, with nearly as high a birthrate during the early 1970s, began to dispense free contraceptives and family planning information and saw its annual rate of population growth drop from 3.2 percent to 2.5 percent in less than five years.

The Chinese—today one-quarter of the world's population—have reduced their rate of population growth from more than 3 percent to less than 1 percent in the past 25 years by promoting later marriages and exhorting parents to value daughters as well as sons and thus to be content with fewer children. In 1980 China began more aggressive steps in an announced attempt to achieve zero population growth by the year 2000. Families that have only one child receive bonuses and preferential treatment in housing and in education for their offspring. (Housing space is allocated to all families as though they had one child.) Families that do not comply with the policy have their salaries decreased and are promoted less frequently.

The political, religious, and cultural dimensions of population policy lead some governments to resist population control. Economics cannot determine whether population control is desirable, but it can describe the consequences of any choice. Economic development is much easier to achieve with population control than without it.

How to Acquire Capital?

A country can raise funds for investment in three distinct ways: (1) from the savings (voluntary or forced) of its domestic households and firms, (2) by loans or investment from abroad, and (3) by contributions from foreigners.

Capital from Domestic Saving: The Vicious Circle of Poverty

If capital is to be created at home by a country's own efforts, resources must be diverted from the production of goods for current consumption. This means a cut in present living standards. If living standards are already at or near the subsistence level, such a diversion will be difficult. At best, it will be possible to reallocate only a small proportion of resources to the production of capital goods.

Such a situation is often described as the *vicious circle of poverty:* Because a country has little capital per head, it is poor; because it is poor, it can devote few resources to creating new capital rather than to producing goods for consumption; because little new capital can be produced, capital per head remains low, and the country remains poor.

The vicious circle can be made to seem an absolute constraint on growth rates. Of course it is not; if it were, we would all still be at the level of Neanderthal man. The grain of truth in the vicious-circle argument is that some surplus must be available somewhere in the society to allow saving and investment. In a poor society with an even distribution of income, in which nearly everyone is at the subsistence level, saving may be very difficult, but this is not the common experience. Usually, there is at least a small middle class that can save and invest if opportunities for the profitable use of funds arise. Also, in most poor societies today, the average household is above the physical subsistence level. Even the poorest households will find that they can sacrifice some present living standards for a future gain. For example, presented with a profitable opportunity, villagers in Ghana planted cocoa plants at the turn of the century, even though there was a seven-year growing period before any return could be expected.

An important consideration is that in less-devel-

oped countries one resource that is often *not* scarce is labor. Profitable home or village investment that requires mainly labor inputs may be made with relatively little sacrifice in current living standards. However, this is not the kind of investment that will appeal to planners who are mesmerized by large and symbolic investments, such as dams, nuclear power stations, and steel mills.

Imported Capital

Another way of accumulating the capital that is needed for growth is to borrow it from abroad. When a poor country borrows from a rich country, it can use the borrowed funds to purchase capital goods that are produced in the rich country. The poor country thus accumulates capital and needs to cut its current output of consumption goods only enough to pay interest on its loans. As the new capital begins to add to current production, it is possible to pay the interest on the loan and also to repay the principal out of the increase in output. This method has the great advantage of giving a poor country an initial increase in capital goods that is far greater than it could possibly have created by diverting its own resources from consumption industries.

There are two main ways in which LDCs can obtain foreign capital (other than by gift). In the first way, governments, or agencies and firms that are directly under government control, may borrow it. This method was used extensively after the first OPEC oil price shock in 1974. During the next 12 years, reliance on foreign borrowing exploded to the point where it became a serious international problem for both LDCs and their creditors. During the 1970s the rising cost of oil to many oil-importing, less-developed countries, combined with overly optimistic income expectations, led to massive borrowing by the LDCs. High interest rates during the 1980s greatly raised the cost of servicing this debt. World recession and rising protectionism in the developed world made it more difficult to earn the money that was necessary to pay interest on, let alone repay, the principal. For oil-importing countries, the collapse of oil prices in 1985 provided some relief, but for oil exporters such as Mexico the oil price decline made things much worse. This problem, which had reached the dimensions of a crisis by the mid-1980s, is discussed with reference to Mexico in Box 44-1.

BOX 44-1

Debt and the LDCs

The 1970s and early 1980s witnessed explosive growth in the external debt of many LDCs. Recently, a number of these countries have experienced difficulties in making the payments that are required to service their debt. "Debt reschedulings" —putting off until tomorrow payments that cannot be made today—have been common, and many observers feel that major defaults are inevitable unless ways of forgiving the debt can be found.

The trend to increased debt started when OPEC quadrupled the world price of oil in 1973. Because many LDCs relied on imported oil, their balance of trade moved sharply into deficit. At the same time, the OPEC countries developed massive trade surpluses. Commercial banks helped to *recycle* the deposits of their OPEC customers into loans to the deficit LDCs. These loans financed some necessary adjustments and worthwhile new investment projects in the LDCs. However, not all of the funds were used wisely; wasteful government spending and lavish consumption splurges occurred in a number of borrowing countries.

A doubling of energy prices in 1979 led to a further increase in LDC debt. The severe world recession that began in 1981 reduced demand for the exports of many of the LDCs. As a result, the LDCs were unable to achieve many benefits from the adjustments and investment expenditures that they had made. Furthermore, sharp increases in real interest rates led to increased debt-service payments; as a result, many of the LDCs could not make their payments.

The lending banks had little choice but to reschedule the debt—essentially lending the LDCs the money to make interest payments while adding to the principal of the existing loans. The International Monetary Fund (IMF) played a central role in arranging these reschedulings, by making further loans and concessions conditional on appropriate policies of adjustment and restraint. These conditions presumably were intended to limit wasteful government expenditure and consumption and thus to increase the likelihood that the loans eventually would be repaid. Critics of the IMF's role, how-ever, argued that much of the restraint resulted in reduced investment, and thus the IMF conditions were counterproductive.

During the mid-1980s, the world economy recovered and interest rates fell. As a result, the LDCs' export earnings grew, their debt-service obligations stabilized, and the crisis appeared to subside. The sharp *fall* in the price of oil, which started in late 1985, further eased the problems of the oil-importing LDCs, but it also created a new debt problem.

Throughout the period of rising energy prices, a number of *oil-exporting* LDCs—including Mexico, Venezuela, and Indonesia—saw in those high prices new opportunities for investment and growth. Based on their high oil revenues, their ability to borrow improved. Their external debt grew, and they were able to avoid many of the adjustments that the oil-importing LDCs had been forced to undertake. When oil prices fell, these oil exporters found themselves in a very difficult position.

Mexico provides an illustrative case study. Its oil revenues doubled from around $8 billion in 1978 to $16 billion by 1982. This increased earning capacity led to increased borrowing, and its external debt also doubled in the same period, from $40 billion in 1978 to $80 billion in 1982. Even with its high oil revenues, however, not all was well; in the words of the British periodical, *The Economist,* "Mexico officially opened the international debt crisis in 1982."

For a number of reasons, including bad investment decisions and the world recession, Mexico's export earnings did not increase as fast as its debt. Soaring real interest rates meant that by 1982 Mexico was unable to service its debt. Only a major debt rescheduling, conditional on severe fiscal restraint and a devaluation to stimulate exports, prevented a probable default.

Continued borrowing, much of it necessary just to service its existing debt, meant that Mexico's debt continued to rise; by 1986 the debt had risen to $100 billion. For much of this period, the spending restraint in Mexico, combined with the recovery in the world economy and the fall in world interest rates, led to a gradual improvement in Mexico's prospects for growing out from under its debt burden. However, in 1986 world oil prices fell, and Mexico's oil revenues plummeted to around $8 billion. A new crisis emerged.

The situation during the late 1980s was different from the situation in 1982 in several important ways. The world economy and the international financial system were both healthier. Lower real interest rates and lower oil prices meant that other LDCs were able to repay their loans; hence, there was less fear of a collapse of the international financial system.

Nevertheless, for Mexico the 1986 crisis was worse than the 1982 one. Domestic restraint had been pushed virtually to the limit; the government deficit had been cut by over 6 percent of GNP in just two years. Headlines in the international press proclaimed, "With Mexico Focusing on Debt Repayment, Ports and Roads Suffer" and "Mexican Children Scrounge for Food as Schools Drop Free Lunch."

Projections showed that Mexico would require major foreign borrowing if it were to continue to meet its interest obligations on existing debt. Commercial banks were not eager to lend any more on their own initiative. The IMF tried to negotiate a loan package based on further restraint, and U.S. Secretary of the Treasury James Baker proposed a plan with renewed lending conditional on major economic adjustment. However, further restraint and rapid adjustment seemed politically impossible in a country that was already racked by massive restraint and plummeting export revenues; many economists argued that restraint would, in any event, retard growth and prove to be counterproductive.

A major impasse thus arose. Using the threat of default, Mexico demanded major concessions in the terms of its new borrowing. The "crisis" situation stimulated innovative proposals. One proposal was for the banks to forgive some debt in return for equity participation in Mexico's oil and other industries; this would reduce the burden of Mexico's debt-service payments while sharing some of the risks of the Mexican situation between Mexico and its creditors.

In mid-1986 an agreement was reached that provided for major new borrowing; for the first time in IMF history, the terms included not only conditions that appropriate adjustment policies be undertaken but also a provision for repayment that would be linked to the price of the borrowing country's exports, in this case oil.

After that time, the pace of economic reform accelerated. The budget deficit was brought down to 1 percent of GNP by 1989. Inflation was running at 18 percent by mid-1989 (still high but well down from the 150 percent of 1988). Tariffs had been cut, and, although imports increased greatly, so did nonoil exports.

The risks inherent in the country's economic situation were still thought to be so high that a *real* interest rate of 35 percent had to be paid to persuade Mexicans to invest their money at home rather than in the United States. This reduced investment expenditure to seriously low levels.

To help with the investment problem, rules governing foreign investment and domestic banking were liberalized. Privatization proceeded with the state airline and telephone system, some power stations, and several mining companies, which soon were to go up for sale.

With all of these reforms, stable Mexico ought to have been, in the words of The Economist, ". . . ready for sustained, non-inflationary, export-led growth and investors should be pumping money into the country. . . . This is not happening, because of the shadow cast by the country's debt." In 1989, service charges on that debt amounted to 6 percent of the country's GDP.

Unless some relief from the debt burden could be arranged, all of the reforms may count for little. As The Economist put it, "Mexico has gone through six years of austerity as the government brought order to the budget and it tried to service the debt. It now needs some relief and a breathing space." If it gets that relief, interest rates should tumble, investment should recover, and the $50 billion or so of funds that fled the country should return. A stable expansion will then be possible. Without the relief, the future is vastly more uncertain.

In early 1989 it looked as though the plan named after Treasury Secretary Brady would provide relief by providing for a write-off of substantial amounts of debt and the granting of new loans. By October, however, the Brady plan seemed in trouble as the banks, although accepting that some of their loans must be written off, balked at granting new loans that seemed no more secure than the ones to be written off. At the end of the year, a solution to the LDCs' debt problem seemed just as elusive as ever.

The second way in which foreign, nongift capital can be obtained is through capital that has been brought in by foreign companies—the so-called *multinational,* or *transnational, corporations.* Many LDCs have been suspicious of foreign capital. They have feared that foreign investors will gain control over their industries or their government.

The extent of foreign control depends on the form that foreign capital takes. When foreigners buy bonds in domestic companies, they do not own or control anything. When they buy common stocks, they own part or all of a company, but their control over management may be minimal. When foreign companies establish plants and import their own managers and technicians, they have much more control. Finally, when foreign firms subsidize an LDC government in return for permission to produce, they may feel justified in exacting political commitments.

Whatever the feelings are about foreign ownership and control, the realities of modern globalized industry are such that no country today can hope to grow from a less-developed into a developed nation without a large presence of foreign multinational corporations. These companies do too much of the world's business to be excluded from any country that hopes to become a significant player in the global marketplace. Today, more and more countries that have development plans are seeking to attract foreign multinational corporations rather than to discourage them.

Whether foreign ownership of one's industries carries political disadvantages that are sufficiently large to outweigh the economic gains is a subject of debate. In Canada, for example, there is serious political opposition to having a large part of Canadian industry owned by U.S. nationals. Many other countries actively seek increased foreign investment.

Contributed Capital

Investment funds for development are being received today by LDCs from the governments of the developed countries. These governments sometimes act unilaterally (for example, the program of the U.S. Agency for International Development and a similar Soviet program) and sometimes act through international agencies, such as the World Bank, the Export-Import Bank, and the OPEC Fund, which was established in 1980. These funds are not really outright gifts but are "soft" loans on which repayment is not demanded in the near future. It is common to label them *contributed capital* to distinguish them from hard loans, on which repayment is expected under normal commercial terms.

The heyday of contributed capital occurred during the late 1970s and early 1980s, when the United States, the Soviet Union, and others sought to win the allegiance of third-world LDCs by making "soft" loans and outright gifts. Today Japan is the largest single source of contributed capital.

 # Development Strategies

In the search for development, individual LDCs have a number of policy options. The choice of options is, in part, a matter of what the planners believe will work and, in part, a question of the nature of the society that will be created once development has occurred.

Insofar as they wish to influence the pattern of growth, governments must choose between agricultural and industrial emphases, between different kinds of industrial development, and between more or less reliance on foreign trade. Several possibilities have been widely advocated, and each has been tried. None is without difficulties.

Agricultural Development

Everyone needs food. An LDC may choose to devote a major portion of its resources to stimulating agricultural production, say, by mechanizing farms, irrigating land, and using new seeds and fertilizers. If successful, the country will stave off starvation for its current population, and it may even develop an excess over current needs and so have a crop available for export. A food surplus can earn foreign exchange to buy needed imports.

In the last two decades, India, Pakistan, Taiwan, and other Asian countries have achieved dramatic increases in food production by the application of new technology and the use of new seed in agricultural production. This has been labeled the *green revolution.*

Big, rural, poor countries are usually well advised to start with policies that are designed to increase agricultural output in order to use the existing labor force and to increase standards of living. However, the gains from this strategy, while large at first, are subject to diminishing returns. Further gains in agricultural production have an ever higher opportunity cost, in the resources needed to irrigate land and to mechanize production. Critics of sole reliance on agricultural output argue that underdeveloped economies must start at once to develop other bases for economic growth.

One problem with heavy reliance on the agricultural strategy is that it frequently requires heavy initial subsidization of agricultural production and also some means of subsidizing consumption of increased quantities of food by a poor population. A common device is to provide artificially high prices to producers and artificially low prices to consumers. Once such a program is put in place, it creates a serious potential dilemma. Continuation of the artificially high prices for producers and low prices for consumers creates a substantial drain on the government's finances. Lowering the subsidy to producers risks a

rural revolution; eliminating the subsidy to consumers risks an urban revolution. The government finds itself with an untenable policy and no room for maneuvering.

Specialization in a Few Commodities

Many LDCs have unexploited resources, such as copper, uranium, or opportunities for tourism. The principle of comparative advantage provides the traditional case for the desirability of relying on such resources. By specializing in producing products in which it has the greatest comparative advantage, the country can achieve the most rapid growth in the short run. To neglect these opportunities will result in a lower standard of living than would result from specialization that was accompanied by increased international trade.

These are cogent reasons in favor of *some* specialization, but specialization involves risks, and it may be worthwhile to reduce the risks by maintaining diversification, even at the cost of loss of some income. Specialization in a few commodities makes the economy highly vulnerable to cyclical fluctuations in world demand and supply. For example, a recession in developed countries or fear of terrorism decreases overseas travel and creates problems for an LDC that has relied on tourism for foreign exchange.

Specialization also has longer term risks. For example, when changes in technology or tastes render a product partially or wholly obsolete, a country heavily specialized in that commodity can face a major readjustment. Just as individual firms and regions may become overspecialized, so too may countries.

Import Substitution

Much of the industrialization by LDCs during the 1950s and 1960s was directed toward **import substitution industry (ISI),** that is, industry to produce at home goods that were previously imported. It is often necessary both to subsidize the home industry and to restrict imports to allow the ISI time to develop.

LDCs sometimes pursue certain lines of production on a subsidized basis for prestige purposes or because of a confusion between cause and effect. Because most wealthy nations have a steel industry, the leaders of many underdeveloped nations regard their countries as primitive until they develop a domestic steel industry. Because several LDCs have succeeded in producing consumer durables, many others assume that they should try to do so. However, if a country has a serious comparative disadvantage in steel or in making consumer durables, fostering such industries will make that country even poorer.

The ISI strategy has many problems. It fosters *inefficient* industries, and in the long run countries do not become rich by being inefficient. It aggravates inequalities in income distribution by raising the prices of manufactured goods relative to agricultural goods and by favoring profits over wages.

Export Development

Most development economists believe that industrialization should be encouraged only in areas where the country can develop a reliable and efficient industry that can compete in world markets.

Obviously, if Tanzania or Peru could develop steel, shipbuilding, and manufacturing industries that operated as efficiently as those of Korea or West Germany, they might share in the rapid economic growth that has been enjoyed by those industrial countries. Indeed, if a decade or two of protection and subsidization could give infant industries time to mature and become efficient, the price might be worth paying. After all, within living memory, Japan and Russia were underdeveloped countries.

Industrialization for export sometimes can be done by employing inexperienced workers in simple, labor-intensive enterprises, such as sewing clothing. However, it often means devoting resources to education, training, and infrastructure development for a long period, and overcoming any cultural and social barriers to efficient production. This is difficult but not impossible. Indeed, there have been some spectacular success stories. Brazil, South Korea, Hong Kong, Singapore, and Taiwan are charter members in the category of **newly industrialized countries (NICs)** that are providing vigorous competition in manufactured goods in world markets.

Their success has led to a further (and bitterly resented) problem for the industrialization strategy. When an LDC succeeds, it is likely to find the developed countries trying to protect *their* home industries from the new competition.

Import substitution and export development do not need to be seen as alternative development strategies. Many now successful trading countries used import substitution in the first stages of their development strategy. The intention was to create the domestic industrial base and the human capital that were needed for industrial success. Once that base was in place, emphasis could be shifted to export encouragement.

Canada used import substitution to build its industries behind high tariff walls in the first half of the twentieth century. Throughout the second half of the century, it has lowered tariffs to integrate its developing export industries into the world economy. Singapore and South Korea used import substitution policies in their early stages of development. Japan also did so in selected industries. The most recent example was in semiconductors (which include the chips that drive computers): The domestic industry developed behind a prohibitive Japanese tariff and then went on to lead the world in exports of semiconductors.

The challenge is not, therefore, to choose at an early stage of growth between import substitution and export development policies for all time. The challenge, if import substitution policies are adopted first, is to be able to shift into export-encouraging policies at a later stage. Such a shift will not occur if the wrong industries are chosen for import substitution so that they remain sickly infants indefinitely or if strong vested interests in the sheltered industries are able to prevent the country's later transition to an export-oriented strategy.

Cartelization

When most producers of a commodity can agree on price and output levels, they can achieve monopoly profits that are not available in competitive markets. Many LDCs are heavily committed to the production and export of one or more basic commodities such as bananas, bauxite, cocoa, coffee, copper, cotton, iron ore, jute, manganese, meat, oil, phosphates, rubber, sugar, tea, tropical timber, and tin. Why do not all producers of, say, bananas get together and create an effective cartel that gives producers the enormous profits that are potentially available?

Cartelization has been tried many times in history. Until OPEC it has always failed, yet everyone knows that OPEC transformed a handful of formerly poor LDCs into the wealthiest of nations.[6] OPEC's success was substantial, but it proved to be difficult to sustain. The special reasons for its success for almost 10 years, and its subsequent difficulties, are discussed in Chapter 14.

Wheat, coffee, cocoa, tin, rubber, and copper all have been suggested as potential subjects for similar commodity price stabilization agreements, but they lack the small number of politically cohesive producers and inelastic short-run demand and supply conditions that gave the OPEC cartel its initial successes.

Some Controversial Unresolved Issues

Development economists are currently involved in some important controversies. Among them are the following.

The Pace of Development

Reformers in less-developed countries often think in terms of transforming their economies within a generation or two. The sense of urgency is quite understandable, but, unless it is tempered by some sense of historical perspective, unreasonable aspirations may develop, only to be dashed all too predictably.

Many underdeveloped countries are probably in a stage of economic development that is analogous to that of medieval England, having not yet achieved anything like the commercial sophistication of the Elizabethan era. It took 500 years for England to develop from the medieval economic stage to its present one. Such a change would be easier now, for much of the needed technology can be imported rather than invented, but what is a feasible pace? To effect a similar growth within 50 or 100 years would require a tremendous achievement of the kind that was accomplished by the United States, Japan, and

a handful of other countries; to aspire to do it in 20 or 30 years may be to court disaster—or to invite repressive political regimes.

Population Policy

The view that has been presented in this chapter of population growth as a formidable barrier to development is neo-Malthusian and constitutes much of current conventional wisdom on development.

This view allows little place for the enjoyment value of children by their parents. Critics point out that the psychic value of children should be included as a part of the living standards of their parents. They also point out that in rural societies even young children are a productive resource, and in societies in which state help for the aged is negligible, fully grown children provide old-age security for their parents.

The neo-Malthusian theory is also criticized for assuming that people breed blindly, as animals do. Critics point out that traditional methods of limiting family size have been known and practiced since the dawn of history. Thus, they argue that large families in rural societies are a matter of choice.

The population explosion came not through any change in "breeding habits" but as a result of medical advances that greatly extended life expectancy (which surely must be counted as a direct welfare gain for those affected). Critics argue that, once an urban society has developed, family size will be reduced voluntarily. This was certainly the experience of Western industrial countries; why, critics ask, should it not be the experience of the developing countries?

The Cost of Creating Capital

Is it true that LDCs must suffer by sacrificing current consumption if they wish to grow? A recent criticism of this conventional wisdom questions the alleged heavy opportunity cost of creating domestic capital. Production of consumption and capital goods are substitutes only when factor supplies are constant and fully employed. However, critics say, the development of a market economy will lead people to substitute work for leisure.

For example, the arrival of Europeans with new goods to trade led the North American Indians to produce furs and other commodities that were needed for exchange. Until they were decimated by

---

[6] This has added to the terminological confusion. It was once fashionable to speak of a nonaligned *third world* as another term for LDCs, the first two "worlds" being the developed capitalist countries and the developed socialist countries. Now some commentators divide the LDCs into a richer (oil-producing) *third world* and a still poor *fourth world*.

later generations of land-hungry settlers, the Indians' standard of living rose steadily with no immediate sacrifice. They created the capital that was needed for their production—weapons and means of transport—in their abundant leisure time. Thus, their consumption began to rise immediately.

This, the argument says, happens in less-developed countries whenever market transactions are allowed to evolve naturally. The spread of a market economy leads people to give up leisure in order to produce the goods that are needed to buy the goods that private traders are introducing from the outside world. In this view it is the pattern of development chosen, rather than development itself, that imposes the need for heavy sacrifices.

Is There a "Best" Strategy for Development?

Each of the five strategies that we have discussed—agricultural development, specialization, import sub-stitution, export development, and cartelization—has been tried, and each has problems. Because countries differ, there is no single best strategy, but a substantial consensus exists among experts that rapid economic development requires at least three simultaneous thrusts: (1) sufficient agricultural development to provide a healthier, better-fed population and work force, (2) sufficient restraint on population growth to permit rising per capita income, and (3) sufficient development of export commodities to allow the country to trade for essentials that it must import. Whether the export commodities should be agricultural, natural resources, light manufactures, heavy manufactures, or services depends on comparative advantage.

Import substitution policies that do not lead eventually to industries that can compete in world markets and price stabilization agreements seem much less promising strategies than they did a decade ago, although there may be specific situations in which each may be helpful.

SUMMARY

1. Sustained economic development is relatively recent in history and has been highly uneven. About one-fourth of the world's population still exists at a level of bare subsistence, and nearly three-fourths are poor by American standards. The gap between rich and poor is large and not decreasing.

2. Incentives for economic development include the demonstration effect of other countries' successful transformation from peasant economy to industrial power and the opportunity to receive aid from developed countries.

3. Impediments to economic development include excessive population growth, resource limitations, inefficient use of resources particularly those that are related to X-inefficiency, inadequate infrastructure, excessive government intervention, and institutional and cultural patterns that make economic growth difficult.

4. A series of basic choices face LDCs as they contemplate development. How much should governments intervene in the economy, and how much should the economy be left to operate on the free market? History has demonstrated that the early stages of growth are possible with many mixtures of free-market and central control. Centralized planning can change both the pace and the direction of economic development; it can also prove to be highly wasteful and to destroy individual initiative. The more complex and developed an economy becomes, the greater are the advantages of decentralized markets over central planning.

5. Educational policy, while vitally important to the long-run rate of economic development, yields its benefits only in the future. Improvement of basic education for the general populace is sometimes

bypassed for the more immediate visible results of educating a selected technical and political elite.

6. The race between output and population is a critical aspect of development efforts in many countries. Different countries have different attitudes toward limiting population growth and have chosen different population policies.

7. Capital for development is invariably a major concern in development. It can be acquired from domestic savings, but the vicious circle of poverty is a problem: A country that is poor because it has little capital cannot readily forego consumption to accumulate capital because it is poor. Importing capital rather than using domestic savings permits heavy investment during the early years of development, but imported capital is available only when the LDC has opportunities that are attractive to foreign investors. A country cannot be integrated into today's global economy unless it is willing to accept the presence of foreign-owned multinational enterprises. Much foreign capital for LDCs since the 1950s has been in the form of "soft" loans or contributions by foreign governments and international institutions.

8. Development may involve choices among different strategies: agricultural development, specialization that is based on natural resources, development of import substitution industries, development of new export industries, and cartelization. None of these strategies is without problems and risks.

9. Many experts in development believe that the most appropriate approach is a multipronged strategy that includes at least some agricultural development, some development of new export commodities, and some restraint on population growth.

10. Controversial unresolved issues concern the appropriate pace of development, the neo-Malthusian view of population growth as a problem, and the cost of creating capital in terms of sacrifices of current consumption.

TOPICS FOR REVIEW

Gap between LDCs and developed countries
Barriers to development
Infrastructure
Role of planning in development
Alternative development strategies
Wealth creation versus wealth transfers

DISCUSSION QUESTIONS

1. Each of the following is a headline from the *New York Times*. Relate them to the problem of economic development.
   a. "Black Africa: Economies on the brink of collapse because of OPEC"
   b. "Hungary reforming economy to attract tourists"
   c. "Goodyear to build plant in Congo for $16 million"
   d. "Algeria's 4-year plan stresses industrial growth"
   e. "India: Giant hobbled by erratic rainfall"
   f. "Foreign banks to finance New Guinea copper mine"
   g. "Not all benefit by green revolution"

2. If you were a member of a foreign aid team that was assigned to study needed development projects for a poor recipient country, to which of the following would you be likely to give a relatively high priority, and why?
   a. Birth control clinics
   b. A national airline
   c. Taxes on imported luxuries
   d. Better roads
   e. Modernization of farming techniques
   f. Training in engineering and business management
   g. Primary education
   h. Scholarships to students to receive medical and legal training abroad

3. "This natural inequality of the two powers of population and of production in the earth . . . form[s] the great difficulty that to me appears insurmountable in the way to perfectability of society. All other arguments are of slight and subordinate consideration in comparison of this. I see no way by which man can escape from the weight of this law which pervades all animated nature. No fancied equality, no agrarian revolutions in their utmost extent, could remove the pressure of it even for a single century" (T. R. Malthus, *Population: The First Essay*, page 6).

   Discuss Malthus' "insurmountable difficulty" in view of the history of the past 100 years.

4. To what extent does the vicious circle of poverty apply to poor families that are living in developed contries? Consider carefully, for example, the similarities and differences facing a poor family living in Appalachia and one living in Ghana, where per capita income is less than $400 per year. Did it apply to immigrants who arrived on Ellis Island with $10 in their pockets?

5. "High coffee prices bring hope to impoverished Latin American peasants," reads the headline. Mexico, Kenya, and Burundi, among other LDCs, have the right combination of soil and climate to increase their coffee production greatly. Discuss the benefits and risks to them if they pursue coffee production as a major avenue of their development.

6. In 1989 some people argued that preserving future accountability for a government's own actions required that the LDCs remain responsible for their entire debt; others argued that the self-interest of the advanced countries required that some plan be adopted for relieving the LDCs of a substantial part of their indebtedness. What arguments might there be on each side of this issue? Have events since 1989 shed any light on this debate?

7. Would removing all restrictions on immigration into the advanced countries help to improve living standards in the LDCs? How might this change in policy affect living standards in the advanced countries?

8. "Just about the most important thing the advanced countries could do to help the LDCs is to remove all restrictions on imports from those countries." Is this good advice from the point of view of the LDCs? Which groups in advanced countries do you think might support such advice, and which might oppose it?

MATHEMATICAL NOTES

1. Since one cannot divide by zero, the ratio $\Delta Y/\Delta X$ cannot be evaluated when $\Delta X = 0$. However, the limit of the ratio as ΔX *approaches* zero can be evaluated, and it is infinity.

$$\lim_{\Delta X \to 0} \frac{\Delta Y}{\Delta X} = \infty$$

2. Many variables affect the quantity demanded. Using functional notation, the argument of the next several pages of the text can be anticipated. Let Q^D represent the quantity of a commodity demanded and

$$T, \overline{Y}, N, Y^*, p, p_j$$

represent, respectively, tastes, average household income, population, income distribution, its price, and the price of the jth other commodity.

The demand function is

$$Q^D = D(T, \overline{Y}, N, Y^*, p, p_j), \; j = 1, \ldots, n$$

The demand schedule or curve looks at

$$Q^D = q(p) \; \Big|_{T, \overline{Y}, N, Y^*, p_j}$$

where the notation means that the variables to the right of the vertical line are held constant.

This function is correctly described as the demand function with respect to price, all other variables being held constant. This function, often written concisely $q = q(p)$, shifts in response to changes in other variables. Consider average income. If, as is usually hypothesized, $\partial Q^D/\partial \overline{Y} > 0$, then increases in average income shift $q = q(p)$ rightward and decreases in average income shift $q = q(p)$ leftward. Changes in other variables likewise shift this function in the direction implied by the relationship of that variable to the quantity demanded.

3. Quantity demanded is a simple, straightforward but frequently misunderstood concept in everyday use, but it has a clear mathematical meaning. It refers to the dependent variable in the demand function from note 2 above:

$$Q^D = D(T, \overline{Y}, N, Y^*, p, p_j)$$

It takes on a specific value, therefore, whenever a specific value is assigned to each of the independent variables. A change in Q^D occurs whenever the specific value of any independent variable is changed. Q^D could change, for example, from 10,000 tons per month to 20,000 tons per month as a result of a *ceteris paribus* change in any one price, in average income, in the distribution of income, in tastes, or in population. Also it could change as a result of the net effect of changes in all of the independent variables occurring at once. Thus, a change in the price of a commodity is a sufficient reason for a change in Q^D but not a necessary reason.

Some textbooks reserve the term *change in quantity demanded* for a movement along a demand curve, that is, a change in Q^D as a result of a change in p. They then use other words for a change in Q^D caused by a change in the other variables in the demand function. This usage gives the single variable Q^D more than one name, and this is potentially confusing.

Our usage, which corresponds to that in all intermediate and advanced treatments, avoids this confusion. We call Q^D *quantity demanded* and refer to *any* change in Q^D as a *change in quantity demanded*. In this usage it is correct to say that a movement along a demand curve is a change in quantity demanded, but it is incorrect to say that a change in quantity demanded can occur only because of a movement along a demand curve (since Q^D can change for other reasons, for example, a *ceteris paribus* change in average household income).

4. Continuing the development of note 2, let Q^S represent the quantity of a commodity supplied and

$$G, X, p, w_i$$

represent, respectively, producers' goals, technology, the products' own price, and the price of the ith input.

The supply function is

$$Q^S = S(G, X, p, w_i), \quad i = 1, 2, \ldots, m$$

The supply schedule and supply curve looks at

$$Q^S = s(p) \Big|_{G, X, w_i}$$

This is the supply function with respect to price, all other variables being held constant. This function, often written concisely $q = s(p)$, shifts in response to changes in other variables.

5. Continuing the development of notes 2 through 4, equilibrium occurs where $Q^D = Q^S$. *For specified values of all other variables*, this requires that

$$q(p) = s(p) \qquad [1]$$

Equation 1 defines an equilibrium value of p; hence, although p is an *independent* variable in each of the supply and demand functions, it is an *endogenous* variable in the economic model that imposes the equilibrium condition expressed in Equation 1. Price is endogenous because it is assumed to adjust to bring about equality between quantity demanded and quantity supplied. Equilibrium quantity, also an endogenous variable, is determined by substituting the equilibrium price into either $q(p)$ or $s(p)$.

Graphically, Equation 1 is satisfied only at the point where demand and supply curves intersect. Thus, supply and demand curves are said to determine the equilibrium values of the endogenous variables, price and quantity. A shift in any of the independent variables held constant in the q and s functions will shift the demand or supply curves and lead to different equilibrium values for price and quantity.

6. The definition in the text uses finite changes and is called *arc elasticity*. The parallel definition using derivatives is

$$\eta = \frac{dq}{dp} \times \frac{p}{q}$$

and is called *point elasticity*. Further discussion appears in the Appendix to Chapter 5.

7. The propositions in the text are proven as follows. Letting TR stand for total revenue, we can write

$$TR = pq$$
$$\frac{dTR}{dp} = q + p\frac{dq}{dp} \qquad [1]$$

From the equation in note 6, however,

$$q\eta = p\frac{dq}{dp} \qquad [2]$$

which we can substitute in Equation 1 to obtain

$$\frac{dTR}{dp} = q + q\eta = q(1 + \eta) \qquad [3]$$

Because η is a negative number, the sign of Equation 3 is negative if the absolute value of η exceeds unity (elastic demand) and positive if it is less than unity (inelastic demand).

8. The axis reversal arose in the following way. Marshall theorized in terms of "demand price" and "supply price," these being the prices that would lead to a given quantity being demanded or supplied. Thus

$$p^d = D(q) \qquad [1]$$
$$p^s = S(q) \qquad [2]$$

and the condition of equilibrium is

$$D(q) = S(q)$$

When graphing the behavioral relationships expressed in Equations 1 and 2, Marshall naturally put the independent variable, q, on the horizontal axis.

Leon Walras, whose formulation of the working of a competitive market has become the accepted one, focused on quantity demanded and quantity supplied *at a given price.* Thus

$$q^d = q(p)$$

$$q^s = s(p)$$

and the condition of equilibrium is

$$q(p) = s(p)$$

Walras did not use graphical representation. Had he done so, he would surely have placed p (his independent variable) on the horizontal axis.

Marshall, among his other influences on later generations of economists, was the great popularizer of graphical analysis in economics. Today we use his graphs, even for Walras' analysis. The axis reversal is thus one of those historical accidents that seem odd to people who did not live through the "perfectly natural" sequence of steps that produced it.

9. The relationship of the slope of the budget line to relative prices can be seen as follows. In the two-commodity example, a change in expediture (ΔE) is given by the equation

$$\Delta E = p_C \Delta C + p_F \Delta F \qquad [1]$$

Along a budget line, expenditure is constant, that is, $\Delta E = 0$. Thus, along such a line,

$$p_C \Delta C + p_F \Delta F = 0 \qquad [2]$$

whence

$$-\frac{\Delta C}{\Delta F} = \frac{p_F}{p_C} \qquad [3]$$

The ratio $-\Delta C/\Delta F$ is the slope of the budget line. It is negative because, with a fixed budget, to consume more F one must consume less C. In other words, Equation 3 says that the negative of the slope of the budget line is the ratio of the absolute prices (i.e., the relative price). While prices do not show directly in Figure 7-3, they are implicit in the budget line: Its slope depends solely on the relative price, while its position, given a fixed money income, depends on the absolute prices of the two goods.

10. Because the slope of the indifference curve is negative, it is the absolute value of the slope that

declines as one moves downward to the right along the curve. The algebraic value, of course, increases. The phrase *diminishing marginal rate of substitution* thus refers to the absolute, not the algebraic, value of the slope.

11. The distinction made between an incremental change and a marginal change is the distinction for the function $Y = Y(X)$ between $\Delta Y/\Delta X$ and the derivative $\frac{dY}{dX}$. The latter is the limit of the former as ΔX approaches zero. Precisely this sort of difference underlies the distinction between arc and point elasticity, and we shall meet it repeatedly—in this chapter in reference to marginal and incremental *utility* and in later chapters with respect to such concepts as marginal and incremental *product, cost,* and *revenue.* Where Y is a function of more than one variable—for example, $Y = f(X, Z)$—the marginal relationship between Y and X is the partial derivative $\frac{\partial Y}{\partial X}$ rather than the total derivative.

12. The hypothesis of diminishing marginal utility requires that we can measure utility of consumption by a function $U = U(X_1, X_2, \ldots, X_n)$ where $X_1, \ldots, X_n$ are quantities of the n goods consumed by a household. It really embodies two utility hypotheses. First, $\frac{\partial U}{\partial X_i} > 0$, which says that for some levels of consumption the consumer can get more utility by increasing consumption of the commodity. Second, $\frac{\partial^2 U}{\partial X_i^2} < 0$, which says that the marginal utility of additional consumption is declining.

13. *Marginal product,* as defined in the text, is really *incremental product.* More advanced treatments distinguish between this notion and *marginal* product as the limit of the ratio as ΔL approaches zero. Marginal product thus measures the rate at which total product is changing as one factor is

varied and is the partial derivative of the total product with respect to the variable factor.

$$MP \frac{\partial TP}{\partial L}$$

14. We have referred specifically both to diminishing *marginal* product and to diminishing *average* product. In most cases, eventually diminishing marginal product implies eventually diminishing average product. This is, however, not necessary, as the accompanying figure shows.

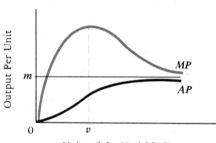

Units of the Variable Factor

In this case marginal product diminishes after v units of the variable factor are employed. Because marginal product falls toward, but never quite reaches, a value of m, average product rises continually toward, but never quite reaches, the same value.

15. Let q be the quantity of output and L the quantity of the variable factor. In the short run,

$$TP = q = f(L) \qquad [1]$$

We now define

$$AP = \frac{q}{L} = \frac{f(L)}{L} \qquad [2]$$

$$MP = \frac{dq}{dL} \qquad [3]$$

We are concerned about the relationship between these two. Whether average product is rising, at a maximum, or falling is determined by its derivative with respect to L.

$$\frac{d\frac{q}{L}}{dL} = \frac{L \frac{dq}{dL} - q}{L^2} \qquad [4]$$

This may be rewritten:

$$\frac{1}{L}\left(\frac{dq}{dL} - \frac{q}{L}\right) = \frac{1}{L}(MP - AP) \qquad [5]$$

Clearly, when MP is greater than AP, the expression in Equation 5 is positive and thus AP is rising. When MP is less than AP, AP is falling. When they are equal, AP is at a stationary value.

16. The text defines *incremental cost*. Strictly, marginal cost is the rate of change of total cost, with respect to output, q. Thus, $MC = dTC/dq$. From the definitions, $TC = TFC + TVC$. Fixed costs are not a function of output. Thus, we may write $TC = K + f(q)$, where $f(q)$ is total variable costs and K is a constant. From this we see that $MC = df(q)/dq$. MC is thus independent of the size of the fixed costs.

17. This point is easily seen if a little algebra is used:

$$AVC = \frac{TVC}{q}$$

but

$$TVC = L \times w$$

and

$$q = AP \times L$$

where L is the quantity of the variable factor used and w is its cost per unit. Therefore,

$$AVC = \frac{L \times w}{AP \times L} = \frac{w}{AP}$$

Since w is a constant, it follows that AVC and AP vary inversely with each other, and when AP is at its maximum value, AVC must be at its minimum value.

18. A little elementary calculus will prove the point:

$$MC = \frac{dTC}{dq} = \frac{dTVC}{dq}$$

$$= \frac{d(L \times w)}{dq}$$

If w does not vary with output,

$$MC = \frac{dL}{dq} \times w$$

However, referring to note 15, Equation 3, we see that

$$\frac{dL}{dq} = \frac{1}{MP}$$

Thus,

$$MC = \frac{w}{MP}$$

Since w is fixed, MC varies negatively with MP. When MP is a maximum, MC is a minimum.

19. As we saw in note 16, $MC = \frac{dTVC}{dq}$. If we take the integral of the MC from zero to q_0, we get:

$$\int_0^{q_0} MC \, dq = TVC_{q_0} + K$$

The first term is the area under the marginal cost curve, while the constant of integration, K, is fixed cost.

20. Strictly speaking, the marginal rate of substitution refers to the slope of the tangent to the isoquant at a particular point, whereas the calculations in Table 11A-1 refer to the average rate of substitution between two distinct points on the isoquant. Assume a production function

$$Q = Q(K, L) \qquad [1]$$

Isoquants are given by the function

$$K = I(L, \overline{Q}) \qquad [2]$$

derived from Equation 1 by expressing K as an explicit function of L and Q. A single isoquant relates to a particular value $(\overline{Q})$ at which Q is held constant. Define Q_K and Q_L as an alternative, more compact notation for $\partial Q/\partial K$ and $\partial Q/\partial L$, the marginal products of capital and labor. Also, let Q_{KK} and Q_{LL} stand for $\partial^2 Q/\partial L^2$ and $\partial^2 Q/\partial K^2$, respectively. To obtain the slope of the isoquant, totally differentiate Equation 1 to obtain

$$dQ = Q_K dK + Q_L dL$$

Then, since we are moving along a single isoquant, set $dQ = 0$ to obtain

$$\frac{dK}{dL} = -\frac{Q_L}{Q_K} = MRS$$

Diminishing marginal productivity implies Q_{LL}, $Q_{KK} < 0$, and, hence, as we move down the isoquant of Figure 11A-1, Q_K is rising and Q_L is falling, so the absolute value of MRS is diminishing. This is called the *hypothesis of a diminishing marginal rate of substitution*.

21. Formally, the problem is to maximize $Q = Q(K, L)$ subject to the budget constraint

$$p_K K + p_L L = C$$

To do this, form the Lagrangean

$$Q(K, L) - \lambda(p_K K + p_L L - C)$$

The first-order conditions for finding the saddle point on this function are

$$Q_K - \lambda p_K = 0; \; Q_K = \lambda p_K \qquad [1]$$

$$Q_L - \lambda p_L = 0; \; Q_L = \lambda p_L \qquad [2]$$

$$-p_K K - p_L L + C = 0 \qquad [3]$$

Dividing Equation 1 by Equation 2 yields

$$\frac{Q_K}{Q_L} = \frac{p_K}{p_L}$$

That is, the ratio of the marginal products, which is (-1) times the MRS, is equal to the ratio of the prices, which is (-1) times the slope of the isocost line.

22. Marginal revenue is mathematically the derivative of total revenue with respect to output, dTR/dq. Incremental revenue is $\Delta TR/\Delta q$. However, the term *marginal revenue* is used loosely to refer to both concepts.

23. For this and the next two notes it is helpful first to define some terms. Let

$$\pi_n = TR_n - TC_n.$$

where π_n is the profit when n units are sold.

If the firm is maximizing its profits by producing n units, it is necessary that the profits at output q_n are at least as large as the profits at output zero. If the firm is maximizing its profits at output n, then

$$\pi_n \geq \pi_0 \qquad [1]$$

The condition says that profits from producing must be greater than profits from not producing. Condition 1 can be rewritten as

$$TR_n - TVC_n - TFC_n \geq TR_0 - TVC_0 - TFC_0 \qquad [2]$$

However, note that by definition

$$TR_0 = 0 \qquad [3]$$
$$TVC_0 = 0 \qquad [4]$$
$$TFC_n = TFC_0 = K \qquad [5]$$

where K is a constant. By substituting Equations 3, 4, and 5 into Condition 2, we get

$$TR_n - TVC_n \geq 0$$

from which we obtain

$$TR_n \geq TVC_n$$

This proves Rule 1.

On a per unit basis, it becomes

$$\frac{TR_n}{q_n} \geq \frac{TVC_n}{q_n} \qquad [6]$$

where q_n is the number of units produced.

Since $TR_n = q_n p_n$, where p_n is the price when n units are sold, Equation 6 may be rewritten as

$$p_n \geq AVC_n$$

24. Using elementary calculus, we may prove Rule 2.

$$\pi_n = TR_n - TC_n$$

each of which is a function of output q. To maximize π, it is necessary that

$$\frac{d\pi}{dq} = 0 \qquad [1]$$

and that

$$\frac{d^2\pi}{dq^2} < 0 \qquad [2]$$

From the definitions,

$$\frac{d\pi}{dq} = \frac{dTR}{dq} - \frac{dTC}{dq} = MR - MC \qquad [3]$$

From Equations 1 and 3 a necessary condition of maximum π is $MR - MC = 0$, or $MR = MC$, as is required by Rule 2.

25. To prove that, for a downward-sloping demand curve, marginal revenue is less than price, let $p = p(q)$. Then

$$TR = pq = p(q) \cdot q$$
$$MR = \frac{dTR}{dq} = q\frac{dp}{dq} + p$$

For a downward-sloping demand curve, dp/dq is negative by definition, and thus MR is less than price for positive values of q.

26. A monopolist, selling in two or more markets, will set its marginal cost equal to marginal revenue in each market. Thus, the condition $MC = MR_1 = MR_2$ is a profit-maximizing condition for a monopolist that is selling in two markets. In general, equal marginal revenues will mean unequal prices, for the ratio of price to marginal revenue is a function of elasticity of demand: The higher is the elasticity, the lower is the ratio. Thus, equal marginal revenues imply a higher price in the market with the less elastic demand curve.

27. The marginal revenue produced by the factor involves two elements: first, the additional output that an extra unit of the factor makes possible and, second, the change in price of the product that the extra output causes. Let Q be output, R revenue, and L the number of units of labor hired. The contribution to revenue of additional labor is $\frac{\partial R}{\partial L}$. This, in turn, depends on the contribution of the extra labor to output $\frac{\partial Q}{\partial L}$ (the marginal product of the factor) and $\partial R/\partial Q$ (the firm's marginal revenue from the extra output). Thus,

$$\frac{\partial R}{\partial L} = \frac{\partial Q}{\partial L} \cdot \frac{\partial R}{\partial Q}$$

We define the left-hand side as marginal revenue product, MRP. Thus,

$$MRP = MP \cdot MR$$

28. The condition that for profit maximation MRP must be downward sloping at the point where $w = MRP$ is just an application of the proposition (proved in math notes 23 and 24 that for profit maximization MC must cut MR from be-

low. Consider the output added by the last unit of the variable factor. Its marginal cost is w, and its marginal revenue is MRP. Thus, w must cut MRP from below. Since w is a horizontal line, MRP must be falling.

If we put the matter in standard mathematical terms,

$$w = MRP \qquad [1]$$

is a first-order condition of *either* maximizing or minimizing. The second-order condition for maximization is

$$\frac{dw}{dq} > \frac{dMRP}{dq} \qquad [2]$$

Since

$$\frac{dw}{dq} = 0 \qquad [3]$$

the slope of MRP must be negative to satisfy [2]; that is, it must be declining.

29. The proposition that the marginal labor cost is above the average labor cost when the average is rising is essentially the same proposition proved in math note 15. Nevertheless, let us do it again, using elementary calculus.

The quantity of labor depends on the wage rate: $L = f(w)$. Total labor cost is wL. Marginal cost of labor is $d(wL)/dL = w + L(dw/dL)$. Rewrite this as $MC = AC + L(dw/dL)$. As long as the supply curve slopes upward, $dw/dL > 0$, therefore $MC > AC$.

30. Let t be the tax rate applied to the profits, π, of the firm. Thus, after-tax profits are $(1 - t)\pi$, where π is a function of output, q. To maximize profits after tax requires

$$\frac{d(1 - t)\pi}{dq} = 0 \quad \text{or}$$

$$(1 - t)\frac{d\pi}{dq} = 0$$

Dividing through by $(1 - t)$, we see that $d\pi/dq = 0$ depends on the level of q and is independent of the tax rate.

31. In the text we define MPC as an incremental ratio. For mathematical treatments it is some-times convenient to define all marginal concepts as derivatives: $MPC = dC/dY_d$, $MPS = dS/dY_d$, and so on.

32. The basic relationship is

$$Y_d = C + S$$

Dividing through by Y_d yields

$$Y_d/Y_d = C/Y_d + S/Y_d \text{ or}$$

$$1 = APC + APS$$

Next, take the first difference of the basic relationship to yield

$$\Delta Y_d = \Delta C + \Delta S$$

Dividing through by ΔY_d gives

$$\Delta Y_d/\Delta Y_d = \Delta C/\Delta Y_d + \Delta S/\Delta Y_d \text{ or}$$

$$1 = MPC + MPS$$

33. This involves using functions of functions. We have $C = C(Y_d)$ and $Y_d = f(Y)$. So, by substitution, $C = C[f(Y)]$. In the linear expressions that are used in the text, $C = a + bY_d$, where b is the marginal propensity to consume. $Y_d = hY$, so $C = a + bhY$, where bh is thus the marginal response of C to a change in Y.

34. The elementary theory of national income can be described by the following set of equations (or model):

$$Y = E \qquad \text{(equilibrium condition)} \qquad [1]$$
$$E = C + I + G + (X - M)$$
$$\qquad \qquad \text{(definition of } AE) \qquad [2]$$
$$C = a + bY_d \quad \text{(consumption function)} \qquad [3]$$
$$M = mY \qquad \text{(import function)} \qquad [4]$$
$$Y_d = hY \qquad \text{(disposable income)} \qquad [5]$$

where a, b, m, and h are parameters determined by behavior, where I, G, and X are exogenous variables (i.e., are treated as constants), and where Y, E (aggregate expenditure), C, M, and Y_d are all endogenous variables (i.e., are determined by this system of equations). Substituting Equations 3, 4, and 5 and collecting terms in Y, we can obtain the aggregate expenditure function by relating desired expenditure to income.

$$E = (a + I + G + X) + (bh - m)Y$$

where the first term (in parentheses) is autonomous expenditure and the second term is induced expenditure. Using Equation 1, we can derive the equilibrium level of income by solving

$$Y = (a + I + G + X) + (bh - m)Y$$

to obtain

$$Y = \frac{1}{1 - bh + m}(a + I + G + X) \qquad [6]$$

The z defined in the text is $(bh - m)$ in this model. The example in Table 26-5 has these values: $a = 100$, $I = 250$, $G = 170$, $X = 240$, $b = 0.80$, $h = 0.90$, and $m = 0.10$. Substituting into Equation 6 yields

$$Y = \frac{1}{1 - 0.72 + 0.10}(100 + 250 + 170 + 240)$$

$$= \frac{1}{0.38}(760) = 2,000$$

35. The total expenditure over all rounds is the sum of an infinite series. If we let A stand for the initiating expenditure and z for the marginal propensity to spend, the change in expenditure is ΔA in the first round, $z\Delta A$ in the second, $z(z\Delta A) = z^2\Delta A$ in the third, and so on. This can be written

$$\Delta A(1 + z + z^2 + \cdots + z^n)$$

If z is less than 1, the series in parentheses converges to $1/(1 - z)$ as n approaches infinity. The change in total expenditure is thus $\Delta A/(1 - z)$. In the example in the box, $z = 0.80$; therefore, the change in total expenditure is five times ΔA.

36. As we saw in Box 26-2, the simple multiplier, K, is equal to the reciprocal of the marginal propensity not to spend, $1 - z$, also called the marginal propensity to withdraw, w.

$$K = \frac{1}{w}$$

In an open economy the marginal propensity to withdraw is equal to the sum of the marginal propensity to save, $1 - b$, plus the marginal propensity to import, m. Hence, the multiplier in an open economy

$$K_o = \frac{1}{(1 - b) + m}$$

is less than that in a closed economy

$$K_c = \frac{1}{(1 - b)}$$

if the two economies had a common marginal propensity to consume, b. Note that the denominator of K_o can be written as $1 - (b - m)$ where $b - m$ is the marginal propensity to consume *home goods*.

37. The accelerator may be stated as a general macroeconomic theory. Define I_n as the volume of net investment this year and ΔY as the increase in national income from last year to this year. The accelerator theory is the relationship between I_n and ΔY.

Assume that the capital-output ratio is a constant.

$$K/Y = \alpha$$

or

$$K = \alpha Y$$

If Y changes, K must be changed accordingly:

$$\Delta K = \alpha \Delta Y$$

However, the change in the capital stock (ΔK) is net investment, so

$$\Delta K = I_n = \alpha \Delta Y$$

38. This is easily proven. In equilibrium the banking system wants sufficient deposits (D) to establish the legal ratio (v) of deposits to reserves (R). This gives $R/D = v$. Any change in D of ΔD has to be accompanied by a change in R of ΔR of sufficient size to restore v. Thus, $\Delta R/\Delta D = v$, so that $\Delta D = \Delta R/v$, and $\Delta D/\Delta R = 1/v$.

This can be shown also in terms of the deposits created by the sequence in Table 31-7. Let v be the reserve ratio. Let $e = 1 - v$ be the excess reserves per dollar of new deposits. If X dollars are initially deposited in the system, the successive rounds of new deposits will be X, eX, e^2X, e^3X. . . . The series

$$X + eX + e^2X + e^3X \cdots$$
$$= X[1 + e + e^2 + e^3 + \cdots]$$

has a limit

$$X\frac{1}{1 - e} = X\left[\frac{1}{1 - (1 - v)}\right] = \frac{X}{v}$$

This is the total new deposits created by an injection of $X of new reserves into the banking system.

39. Suppose that the public desires to hold a fraction, c, of deposits in cash. Now let the banking system receive an initial increase in its reserves of ΔR. It can expand deposits by an amount ΔD. As it does so, the banking system suffers a cash drain to the public of $c\Delta D$. The banking system can increase deposits only to the extent that the required reserve ratio v makes possible. The maximum deposit expansion can be calculated from

$$v\Delta D = \Delta R - c\Delta D$$

which, collecting terms, can be written

$$(v + c)\,\Delta D = \Delta R$$

Hence,

$$\Delta D = \Delta R/(v + c)$$

For example, when $v = 0.20$ and $c = 0.05$, the maximum expansion is $1/(0.20 + 0.05) = 4$.

40. The argument is simply as follows, where prime marks stand for first derivatives:

$$M^D = F_1(T),\ F'_1 > 0$$

$$T = F_2(Y),\ F'_2 > 0$$

therefore,

$$M^D = F_1\,(F_2(Y))$$
$$= H\,(Y),\ H' > 0$$

where H is the function of the function combining F_1 and F_2.

41. Let $L(Y, r)$ give the real demand for money measured in purchasing power units. Let M be the supply of money measured in nominal units and P an index of the price level, so that M/P is the real supply of money. Now the equilibrium condition requiring equality between the demand for money and the supply of money can be expressed in real terms as

$$L(Y, r) = M/P \qquad [1]$$

or by multiplying through by P in nominal terms as

$$PL(Y, r) = M \qquad [2]$$

In Equation 1 a rise in P disturbs equilibrium by lowering M/P, and in Equation 2 it disturbs equilibrium by raising $PL\,(Y, r)$.

42. This is expressed in functional notation as

$$DE = f(Y - Y^*)$$

where the restrictions are (a) that $f(0) = 0$, so that when $Y = Y^*$ there is no demand effect; and (b) $f' > 0$, so that as Y rises, the demand effect rises. Together (a) and (b) imply that $DE > 0$ when $Y > Y^*$ and $DE < 0$ when $Y < Y^*$.

Point 4 implies that $f'' > 0$; that is, the Phillips curve gets steeper as Y rises.

43. The "rule of 72" is an approximation, derived from the mathematics of compound interest. Any measure X_t will have the value $X_t = X_0 e^{rt}$ after t years at a continuous growth rate of r percent per year. Because $X_1/X_0 = 2$ requires $r \times t = 0.69$, a "rule of 69" would be correct for continuous growth. The "rule of 72" was developed in the context of compound interest, and, if interest is compounded only once a year, the product of $r \times t$ for X to double is approximately 0.72.

44. The time taken to break even is a function of the *difference* in growth rates, not their level. Thus, had 4 percent and 5 percent or 5 percent and 6 percent been used in the example, it still would have taken the same number of years. To see this quickly, recognize that we are interested in the ratio of two growth paths: $e^{r1t}/e^{r2t} = e^{(r1 - r2)t}$.

45. The equation for the IS curve is given by

$$y = c(y - T) + I(r) + G \qquad [1]$$

where $c'\,(y - T) > 0$ is the marginal propensity to consume $[c'(y - T) = b]$, $I_r < 0$ is the response of investment to a change in the interest rate, and T is taxes. Substituting $T = T_0 + ty$ into [1], and differentiating, we get

$$wdy = -b\,(dT_0 + ydt) + I_r dr + dG \qquad [2]$$

where w is equal to $[1 - b\,(1 - t)]$, the marginal propensity not to spend. The IS curve is drawn for $dT_0 = dt = dG = 0$. Its slope is therefore

$$\frac{dr}{dy}\bigg|_{IS} = \frac{w}{I_r} < 0 \qquad [3]$$

The horizontal shift in the *IS* curve, due to a change in any of the exogenous variables (T_0, t, or G), can be calculated from [2] by setting $dr = 0$. For example, a change in G shifts the *IS* curve by

$$\frac{dy}{dG}\Big|_{dr=0} = \frac{1}{w} > 0$$

while a change in tax rates causes a shift of

$$\frac{dy}{dt}\Big|_{dr=0} = \frac{-by}{w} < 0$$

46. The equation for the *LM* curve is given by

$$M = PL(y,r) \tag{1}$$

where $L(y,r)$ represents the demand for real money balances, which depends positively on income ($L_y > 0$) and negatively on the interest rate ($L_r < 0$). Differentiating Equation 1, we get

$$dM = L(y,r)dP + PL_y dy + PL_r dr \tag{2}$$

The *LM* curve is drawn for $dM = dP = 0$. Its slope is therefore

$$\frac{dr}{dy}\Big|_{LM} = -\frac{L_y}{L_r} > 0 \tag{3}$$

The horizontal shift in the *LM* curve, due to a change in the money supply, can be calculated from Equation 2 by setting $dr = 0$.

$$\frac{dy}{dM}\Big|_{dr=0} = \frac{1}{LP_y} > 0 \tag{4}$$

47. Equations 2 from each of the two previous math notes can be combined to give two relationships between dy and dr. Solving them simultaneously, we can derive the following expressions for the effects of monetary and fiscal policy on national income and interest rates. Restricting our analysis of fiscal policy to the effects of government expenditure (so $dT = dt = 0$), and holding $dP = 0$, these are as follows:

$$\frac{dy}{dM} = \frac{-I_r}{D} > 0 \qquad \frac{dr}{dM} = \frac{-w}{D} < 0$$

$$\frac{dy}{dG} = \frac{-PL_r}{D} > 0 \qquad \frac{dr}{dG} = \frac{PL_y}{D} > 0$$

where $D = -(I_r PL_y + wPL_r) > 0$.

48. The aggregate demand curve can be written by solving Equations 1 from each of the math notes 45 and 46 to eliminate the interest rate, thus leaving a relationship between P and y. The relationship between *changes* in P and y can be written

$$Ddy = I_r L(y, P)dP - PL_r dG - I_r dM \tag{1}$$

where D is as defined in note 47.

The *AD* curve is drawn from $dG = dM = 0$, so its slope is given by

$$\frac{dP}{dy}\Big|_{AD} = \frac{I_r L(y, P)}{D} < 0 \tag{2}$$

The horizontal shift in *AD* can be calculated from Equation 1 by setting $dP = 0$, so that the effects of monetary (dM) and fiscal (dG) policy with a constant price level can be written as follows:

$$\frac{dy}{dM}\Big|_{dr=0} = \frac{-I_r}{D} > 0$$

$$\frac{dy}{dG}\Big|_{dr=0} = \frac{-PL_r}{D} > 0$$

which, of course, are as in math note 47.

49. Net exports equals exports minus imports.

$$NX = X - M \tag{1}$$

Exports depend on foreign income, Y^f, and on the terms of trade.

$$X = X_0 + m^f Y^f - b^f\left(\frac{P}{eP^f}\right) \tag{2}$$

where X_0 is autonomous exports, m^f is the foreign marginal propensity to import, b^f is the response of exports to a change in relative prices, P is the domestic price level, e is the exchange rate, and P^f is foreign prices. Imports depend on domestic income and the terms of trade.

$$M = M_0 + mY + b\left(\frac{P}{eP^f}\right) \tag{3}$$

Combining Equations 1, 2, and 3, we can write

$$NX = (X_0 - M_0) + m^f Y^f - mY - c\left(\frac{P}{eP^f}\right) \tag{4}$$

where $c = b + b^f$. In Chapter 26 we considered this relationship in isolation, and hence the slope of the NX curve when it was drawn against national income was taken to be $dNX/dY = -m$, where the other variables in Equation 4 were held constant. Now we have to take into account the fact that P changes as Y changes.

Writing the $SRAS$ curve as

$$P = g(Y), \; g' > 0 \qquad [5]$$

and substituting Equation 5 into Equation 4, we eliminate P to yield

$$NX = (X_0 - M_0) + mY^f - mY - c\left(\frac{g(Y)}{eP^f}\right) \quad [6]$$

The slope of the NX curve is now given by

$$dNX/dY = -(m + u') < 0 \qquad [7]$$

where $u = cg'/eP^f > 0$. Hence, as Y rises, NX falls, both because of the marginal propensity to import and because of substitution away from domestic goods as P rises.

GLOSSARY

absolute advantage When a given amount of resources can produce more of some commodity in one country than in another.

absolute price The amount of money that must be spent to acquire one unit of a commodity. Also called *money price*.

acceleration hypothesis The hypothesis that when national income is held above potential, the persistent inflationary gap will cause inflation to accelerate, and when national income is held below potential, the persistent recessionary gap will cause inflation to decelerate.

accelerator The theory that relates the level of investment to the rate of change of national income.

actual GNP The gross national product that the economy, in fact, produces.

adjustable peg system A system in which exchange rates are fixed in the short term but are occasionally changed in response to persistent payments imbalances.

administered price A price set by the conscious decision of the seller rather than by impersonal market forces.

ad valorem tariff An import duty that is a percentage of the price of the imported product.

ad valorem tax See *excise tax*.

adverse selection Self-selection, within a single risk category, of persons of above average risk.

AE See *aggregate expenditure*.

aggregate demand Total desired purchases by all the buyers of an economy's output.

aggregate demand (*AD*) curve A curve showing the combinations of real national income and the price level that makes aggregate desired expenditure equal to national income; the curve thus relates the total amount of output that will be demanded to the price level of that output.

aggregate demand shock A shift in the aggregate demand curve.

aggregate expenditure (*AE*) Total expenditure on final output of the economy; $AE = C + I + G + (X - M)$, representing the four major components of aggregate desired expenditure.

aggregate expenditure (*AE*) function The function that relates aggregate desired expenditure to national income.

aggregate supply Total desired sales of all the producers of an economy's output.

aggregate supply (*AS*) curve See *short-run aggregate supply curve* and *long-run aggregate supply curve*.

aggregate supply shock A shift in the aggregate supply curve.

allocation of resources See *resource allocation*.

allocative efficiency A situation in which no reorganization of production or consumption could make everyone better off (or, as it is sometimes stated, make at least one person better off while making no one worse off).

antitrust policy Policies designed to prohibit the acquisition and exercise of monopoly power by business firms.

appreciation A rise in the free-market value of domestic currency in terms of foreign currencies; i.e., a fall in the price of foreign exchange.

a priori Literally, "at a prior time" or "in advance"; that which is prior to actual experience.

arc elasticity A measure of the average responsiveness of quantity to price over an interval of the demand curve. For analytical purposes it is usually defined by the formula

$$\eta = \frac{\Delta q/q}{\Delta p/p}$$

An alternative formula often used where computations are involved is

$$\eta = \frac{(q_2 - q_1)/(q_2 + q_1)}{(p_2 - p_1)/(p_2 + p_1)}$$

where p_1 and q_1 are the original price and quantity and p_2 and q_2 are the new price and quantity.
With negatively sloped demand curves elasticity is a negative number. Sometimes the above expressions are therefore multiplied by –1 to make measured elasticity positive.

automatic fiscal policy Fiscal policy that does not require changes in government policy variables but has its effects via the operation of *built-in stabilizers*.

automatic transfer service (ATS) A savings deposit from which funds are transferred automatically to the depositor's demand deposit to cover checks as they are drawn.

autonomous expenditure See *exogenous expenditure*.

autonomous variable See *exogenous variable*.

average cost (*AC*) See *average total cost*.

average fixed cost (*AFC*) Total fixed costs divided by the number of units of output.

average product (*AP*) Total product divided by the number of units of the variable factor used in its production.

average propensity to consume (*APC*) The proportion of income devoted to consumption; total consumption expenditure divided by total disposable income ($APC = C/Y_d$).

average propensity to save (APS) The proportion of disposable income devoted to saving; total saving divided by total disposable income ($APS = S/Y_d$).

average revenue (AR) Total revenue divided by quantity sold; this is the market price when all units are sold at one price.

average tax rate The ratio of total taxes paid to total income earned.

average total cost (ATC) Total cost of producing a given output divided by the number of units of output; it can also be calculated as the sum of average fixed costs and average variable costs. Also called *cost per unit, unit cost, average cost*.

average variable cost (AVC) Total variable costs divided by the number of units of output. Also called *direct unit cost, avoidable unit cost*.

balanced budget A situation in which current revenue is exactly equal to current expenditures.

balanced budget multiplier The change in income divided by the tax-financed change in government expenditure that brought it about.

balance-of-payments accounts A summary record of a country's transactions that involve payments or receipts of foreign exchange.

balance of trade The difference between the value of exports and the value of imports of visible items (goods).

balance sheet A financial report showing a firm's assets and the claims against those assets at a moment in time.

bank notes Paper money issued by commercial banks.

barter A system in which goods and services are traded directly for other goods and services.

base control The use of the monetary base as the instrument by which the central bank attempts to influence its target variables. See also *interest rate control*.

beggar-my-neighbor policies Policies designed to increase a country's prosperity (especially by reducing its unemployment) at the expense of reducing prosperity in other countries (especially by increasing their unemployment).

black market A situation in which goods are sold illegally at prices that violate a government price ceiling.

bond An evidence of debt carrying a specified amount and schedule of interest payments and (usually) a date for redemption of its face value.

boom A period in the business cycle characterized by high demand and increasing production at a level that exceeds potential GNP.

bread-and-butter unionism A union movement whose major objectives are higher wages and better conditions of employment rather than political or social reform.

budget balance The difference between total government revenue and total government expenditure.

budget deficit Any shortfall of current revenue below current expenditure.

budget line Graphical representation of all combinations of commodities or factors that a household or firm may obtain if it spends a specified amount of money at fixed prices of the commodities or factors. Also called *isocost line*.

budget surplus Any excess of current revenue over current expenditure.

built-in stabilizers Anything that automatically lessens the magnitude of the fluctuations in national income caused by changes in autonomous expenditures, such as investment.

business cycle Fluctuations of national income around its trend value, after seasonal fluctuations have been removed, and that follow a wavelike pattern.

C See *consumption expenditure*.

capacity The level of output that corresponds to the firm's minimum short-run average total cost.

capital A factor of production consisting of all manufactured aids to further production, including plant, equipment, and inventories.

capital account A part of the balance-of-payments accounts that records payments and receipts arising from the import and export of long-term and short-term financial capital.

capital consumption allowance An estimate of the amount by which the capital stock is depleted through its contribution to current production. Also called *depreciation*.

capital deepening Adding capital to the production process in such a way as to increase the ratio of capital to labor and other factors of production.

capitalist economy An economy in which capital is predominantly owned privately rather than by the state.

capitalized value The value of an asset, measured by the present value of the income stream that it is expected to produce.

capital-labor ratio A measure of the amount of capital per worker in an economy.

capital-output ratio The amount of capital divided by the amount of labor; it shows the amount of capital available on average to each unit of labor.

capital stock The aggregate quantity of capital goods.

capital widening Adding capital to the production process in such a way as to leave factor proportions unchanged.

cartel An organization of producers who agree to act as a single seller in order to maximize joint profits.

CD See *certificate of deposit*.

ceiling price See *price ceiling*.

central bank A bank that acts as banker to the commercial banking system and often to the government as well. In the modern world, usually a government-owned and -operated institution that controls the banking system and is the sole money-issuing authority.

certificate of deposit (CD) A negotiable time deposit carrying a higher interest rate than that paid on ordinary time deposits.

ceteris paribus Literally, "other things being equal"; usually used in economics to indicate that all variables except the ones specified are assumed not to change.

change in demand An increase or decrease in the quantity demanded at each possible price of the commodity, represented by a shift in the whole demand curve.

change in quantity demanded   An increase or decrease in the specific quantity bought at a specified price, represented by a movement along a demand curve.

change in quantity supplied   An increase or decrease in the specific quantity supplied at a specified price, represented by a movement along a supply curve.

change in supply   An increase or decrease in the quantity supplied at each possible price of the commodity, represented by a shift in the whole supply curve.

classical unemployment   See *real wage unemployment*.

clearing house   An institution where interbank indebtedness, arising from transfer of checks between banks, is computed, offset against each other, and net amounts owing are calculated.

coefficient of determination (r^2 or R^2)   A measure of how closely a relationship between two variables holds. A coefficient showing the fraction of the total variance of the dependent variable that can be associated with the independent variables in the regression equation; r^2 is used for two variables and R^2, for three or more variables.

collective bargaining   The process by which unions and employers arrive at and enforce agreements.

collective-consumption goods   Goods or services that, if they provide benefits to anyone, can, at little or no additional cost, provide benefits to a large group of people, possibly everyone in the country. Also called *public goods*.

collusion   An agreement among sellers to act jointly in their common interest, for example, by agreeing to raise prices. Collusion may be overt or covert, explicit or tacit.

command economy   An economy in which the decisions of the government (as distinct from households and firms) exert the major influence over the allocation of resources.

commercial bank   Privately owned, profit-seeking institution that provides a variety of financial services, such as accepting deposits from customers, which it agrees to transfer when ordered by a check, and making loans and other investments.

commercial policy   A government's policy involving restrictions placed on international trade.

commodities   Marketable items produced to satisfy wants. Commodities may be either *goods,* which are tangible, or *services,* which are intangible.

common market   An agreement among two or more countries to establish a single market among themselves by abolishing all tariffs on trade among themselves, by charging a common tariff on imports from nonmember countries, and by permitting a free flow of labor and capital among themselves.

common-property resource   A natural resource that is owned by no one and may be used by anyone.

common stock   A form of equity capital, usually carrying voting rights and a residual claim to the assets and profits of the firm.

comparative advantage   The ability of one nation (re-

gion or individual) to produce a commodity at a lesser opportunity cost of other products foregone than another nation.

comparative statics   Short for comparative static equilibrium analysis; the derivation of predictions by analyzing the effect of a change in some exogenous variable on the equilibrium position.

competitive devaluations   A round of devaluations of exchange rates by a number of countries, each trying to gain a competitive advantage over the other and each failing to the extent that other countries also devalue their exchange rates.

complement   Two commodities are complements when they tend to be used jointly with each other. The degree of complementarity is measured by the size of the negative cross elasticity between the two goods.

concentration ratio   The fraction of total market sales (or some other measure of market occupancy) controlled by a specified number of the industry's largest firms, four-firm and eight-firm concentration ratios being most frequently used.

conglomerate merger   See *merger*.

constant-cost industry   An industry in which costs of the most efficient size firm remain constant as the entire industry expands or contracts in the long run.

constant-dollar GNP   Gross national product valued in prices prevailing in some base year; year-to-year changes in constant-dollar GNP reflect changes only in quantities produced. Also called *real GNP*.

constant returns   A situation in which output increases in proportion to inputs as the scale of production is increased. A firm in this situation, and facing fixed factor prices, is a *constant-cost firm*.

consumerism   A movement that asserts a conflict between the interests of firms and the public interest.

Consumer Price Index (CPI)   A measure of the average prices of commodities commonly bought by households; compiled monthly by the Bureau of Labor Statistics.

consumers' durables   See *durable good*.

consumers' surplus   The difference between the total value that consumers place on all units consumed of a commodity and the payment that they must make to purchase that amount of the commodity.

consumption   The act of using commodities, either goods or services, to satisfy wants.

consumption expenditure   In macroeconomics, household expenditure on all goods and services except housing. Represented by the symbol C as one of the four components of aggregate expenditure.

consumption function   The relationship between total desired consumption expenditure and all the variables that determine it; in the simplest cases, the relationship between consumption expenditure and disposable income and consumption expenditure and national income.

contestable market   A market is perfectly contestable if there are no sunk costs of entry or exit, so that *potential* entry may hold profits of existing firms to low levels—zero in the case of perfect contestability.

cooperative equilibrium The equilibrium reached when all the firms in an industry cooperate so as to maximize their joint profits.

corporation A form of business organization in which the firm has a legal existence separate from that of the owners, and ownership and financial responsibility are divided, limited, and shared among any number of individual and institutional shareholders.

cost (of output) To a producing firm, the value of inputs used to produce output.

cost-benefit analysis A technique for evaluating government policies. The sum of the opportunity cost to all parties is compared with the value of the benefits to all parties.

cost-efficient analysis Comparison of the cost of different ways to achieve a specific government objective.

cost minimization An implication of profit maximization that the firm will choose the method that produces specific output at the lowest attainable cost.

CPI See *Consumer Price Index*.

credit rationing Rationing of available funds among borrowers in a situation of excess demand for loans at prevailing interest rates.

cross elasticity of demand (η_{xy}) A measure of the responsiveness of the quantity of a commodity demanded to changes in price of a related commodity, defined by the formula

$$\eta_{xy} = \frac{\text{percentage change in quantity demanded of one good } X}{\text{percentage change in price of another good } Y}$$

cross-sectional data Several different measurements or observations made at the same point in time.

crowding out effect The offsetting reduction in private expenditure caused by the rise in interest rates that follows an expansionary fiscal policy.

current account A part of the balance-of-payments accounts that records payments and receipts arising from trade in goods and services and from interest and dividends that are earned by capital owned in one country and invested in another.

current-dollar GNP Gross national product valued in prices prevailing at the time of measurement; year-to-year changes in current-dollar GNP reflect changes both in quantities produced and in market prices. Also called *nominal GNP*.

cyclical unemployment Unemployment in excess of frictional and structural unemployment; it is due to a shortfall of actual national income below potential national income. Sometimes called *deficient demand unemployment*.

cyclically adjusted deficit (CAD) An estimate of the government budget deficit (expenditure minus tax revenue), not as it actually is but as it would be if national income were at its potential level.

debt Generally, amounts owed to one's creditors. From a firm's point of view, that portion of its money capital that is borrowed rather than subscribed by shareholders.

decision lag The period of time between perceiving some problem and reaching a decision on what to do about it.

decreasing returns A situation in which output increases less than in proportion to inputs as the scale of a firm's production increases. A firm in this situation, with fixed factor prices, is an *increasing cost* firm.

deflationary gap See *recessionary gap*.

demand The entire relationship between the quantity of a commodity that buyers wish to purchase per period of time and the price of that commodity.

demand curve The graphical representation of the relationship between the quantity of a commodity that buyers wish to purchase per period of time and the price of that commodity, other things being equal.

demand deposit A bank deposit that is withdrawable on demand (without notice of intention to withdraw) and transferable by means of a check.

demand for money The total amount of money balances that the public wishes to hold for all purposes.

demand inflation Inflation arising from excess aggregate demand, that is, when national income exceeds potential income.

demand schedule A table showing for selected values the relationship between the quantity of a commodity that buyers wish to purchase per period of time and the price of that commodity, other things being equal.

deposit money Money held by the public in the form of demand deposits with commercial banks.

depreciation (of capital) See *capital consumption allowance*.

depreciation (of a currency) A fall in the free-market value of domestic currency in terms of foreign currency; that is, a rise in the price of foreign exchange.

depression A persistent period of very low economic activity with very high unemployment and high excess capacity.

derived demand The demand for a factor of production that results from the demand for the products that it is used to make.

differentiated product A group of commodities that are similar enough to be called the *same* product but are dissimilar enough so that all of them do not have to be sold at the same price.

diminishing marginal rate of substitution The hypothesis that the marginal rate of substitution changes systematically as the amounts of two commodities being consumed vary.

direct burden Amount of money for a tax that is collected from taxpayers.

direct investment In balance-of-payments accounting, foreign investment in the form of a takeover or capital investment in a branch plant or subsidiary corporation in which the investor has voting control.

dirty float See *managed float*.

disaggregated data Detailed data, such as investment by a single firm or all firms in one industry; in contrast to aggregated data, such as total investment by everyone in the economy.

discount rate   (1) In banking, the rate at which the central bank is prepared to lend reserves to commercial banks. (2) More generally, the rate of interest used to discount a stream of future payments to arrive at their present value.

discouraged workers   People who would like to work but have ceased looking for a job and hence have withdrawn from the labor force, because they believe that no jobs are available for them.

discretionary fiscal policy   Fiscal policy that is a conscious response (not according to any predetermined rule) to each particular state of the economy as it arises.

disembodied technical change   Technical change that raises output without the necessity of building new capital to embody the new knowledge.

disequilibrium   The absence of equilibrium. A market is in disequilibrium when there is either excess demand or excess supply.

disequilibrium differential   A difference in the prices paid to different units of the same factor that will set up movements of the factor, which, in turn, will eliminate the differential once equilibrium is reached.

disequilibrium price   A price at which quantity demanded does not equal quantity supplied.

disposable personal income (Y_d)   GNP minus any part of it not actually paid to households minus personal income taxes paid by households plus transfer payments to households; personal income *minus* personal income taxes.

distributed profits   Profits paid out to owners of a firm. For incorporated firms the distributed profits are called *dividends*.

dividends   Profits paid out to shareholders of a corporation.

division of labor   The breaking up of a production process into a series of repetitive tasks, each done by a different worker.

dollar standard   A system under which countries hold reserves in, and settle debts with, U.S. dollars, but the dollar is not backed by gold or any other physical source of monetary value.

double counting   In national income accounting, adding up the total outputs of all the sectors in the economy so that the value of intermediate goods is counted in the sector that produces them and every time they are purchased as an input by another sector.

dumping   In international trade, the practice of selling a commodity at a lower price in the export market than in the domestic market for reasons that are not related to differences in costs of servicing the two markets.

duopoly   An industry that contains only two firms.

durable good   A good that yields its services over an extended period of time. Often divided into the subcategories *producers' durables* (e.g., machines, equipment) and *consumers' durables* (e.g., cars, appliances).

economic efficiency   The least costly method of producing any output.

economic growth   Increases in real, or constant-dollar, potential GNP.

economic profits or **losses**   The difference between the revenues received from the sale of output and the opportunity cost of the inputs used to make the output. Negative economic profits are economic losses. Also called *pure profits* or *pure losses,* or simply *profits* or *losses*.

economic rent   The surplus of total earnings over what must be paid to prevent a factor from transferring to another use.

economies of scale   Reduction of costs per unit of output resulting from an increase in output; a negatively sloped *LRAC* curve over a range of output.

economies of scope   Economies achieved by a firm that is large enough to engage efficiently in multiproduct production and associated large-scale distribution, advertising, and purchasing.

economy   A set of interrelated production and consumption activities.

effective rate of tariff   The tax charged on any imported commodity expressed as a percentage of the value added by the exporting industry.

elastic demand   The situation in which, for a given percentage change in price, there is a greater percentage change in quantity demanded; elasticity greater than unity.

elasticity of demand (η)   A measure of the responsiveness of quantity of a commodity demanded to a change in market price, defined by the formula

$$\eta = \frac{\text{percentage change in quantity demanded}}{\text{percentage change in price}}$$

With negatively sloped demand curves, elasticity is a negative number. Sometimes the above expression is multiplied by -1 to make measured elasticity positive. Also called *demand elasticity, price elasticity*.

elasticity of supply (η_S)   A measure of the responsiveness of the quantity of a commodity supplied to a change in the market price, defined by the formula

$$\eta_S = \frac{\text{percentage change in quantity supplied}}{\text{percentage change in price}}$$

embodied technical change   Technical change that is intrinsic to the particular capital goods in use, and hence that can be utilized only when new capital, embodying the new techniques, is built.

employment   The number of adult workers (16 years of age and older) who hold full-time jobs.

endogenous expenditure   See *induced expenditure*.

endogenous variable   A variable that is explained within a theory.

entry barrier   Any natural or man-made impediment to entry into an industry, such as patents, economies of scale, and established brand preferences.

envelope   Any curve that encloses, by being tangent to, a series of other curves. In particular, the *envelope cost curve* is the *LRAC* curve, which encloses the *SRATC* curves by being tangent to each without cutting any of them.

equilibrium condition   A condition that must be fulfilled if some market or sector of the economy, or the whole economy, is to be in equilibrium.

equilibrium differential   A difference in factor prices that would persist in equilibrium, without any tendency for it to be removed.

equilibrium price   The price at which quantity demanded equals quantity supplied.

equity capital   Funds provided by the owners of a firm the return on which depends on the firm's profits.

European Monetary System   an agreement among the countries of the European Community (except the United Kingdom) to fix exchange rates among their own currencies and then let their joint rate float against the dollar.

excess burden   The value to taxpayers of the changes in behavior that are induced by taxes; the amount that taxpayers would be willing to pay, over and above the direct burden of taxes, to abolish the taxes.

excess capacity   The amount by which actual output falls short of capacity output (which is the output that corresponds to the minimum short-run average total cost).

excess capacity theorem   The proposition that equilibrium in a monopolistically competitive industry will occur where each firm has excess capacity.

excess demand   A situation in which, at the given price, quantity demanded exceeds quantity supplied. Also called a *shortage*.

excess reserves   Reserves held by a commercial bank in excess of the legally required minimum.

excess supply   A situation in which, at the given price, quantity supplied exceeds quantity demanded. Also called a *surplus*.

exchange rate   The price in terms of one currency at which another currency, or claims on it, can be bought and sold.

excise tax   A tax on the sale of a particular commodity; may be a *specific tax* (fixed tax per unit of commodity) or an *ad valorem tax* (fixed percentage of the value of the commodity).

execution lag   The time that it takes to put policies in place after the decision has been made.

exhaustible resource   See *nonrenewable resource*.

exogenous expenditure   In macroeconomics, elements of expenditure that do not vary systematically with other variables, such as national income and the interest rate, but are determined by forces outside of the theory. Also called *autonomous expenditure*.

exogenous variable   A variable that influences endogenous variables but is itself determined by factors outside the theory.

expectational inflation   Inflation that occurs because decision makers raise prices (so as to keep their relative prices constant) in the expectation that the price level is going to rise.

expectations-augmented Phillips curve   The relationship between unemployment and the rate of increase of money wages or between national income and the rate of increase of money prices that arises when the demand and expectations components of inflation are combined.

expenditure-changing policies   Policies that change the level of aggregate desired expenditure.

expenditure-switching policies   Policies that maintain the level of aggregate desired expenditure but change the relative proportions of its components, domestic absorption, and net exports.

external balance   A situation in which the balance of payments accounts, or some subset of them, are at their target levels.

external economies of scale   Scale economies that cause the firm's costs to fall as *industry output* rises but that are external to the firm and so cannot be obtained by the firm's increasing its own output.

external value of the dollar   The value of the dollar expressed in terms of foreign currencies; changes in the dollar's external value are measured by changes in the exchange rate.

externalities   Effects, either good or bad, on parties not directly involved in the production or use of a commodity. Also called *third-party effects*.

factor markets   Markets in which the services of factors of production are sold.

factor mobility   The ease with which factors can be transferred between uses.

factor services   The services of factors of production that are used to produce outputs.

factors of production   Resources used to produce goods and services to satisfy wants; frequently divided into the basic categories of land, labor, and capital.

fair game   A game of chance for which the expected value of the outcome is zero.

fair trade laws   Laws providing import duties intended to eliminate unfair competition from foreign goods caused by foreign-government subsidies or predatory pricing by foreign producers. Also called *trade remedy laws*.

falling-cost industry   An industry in which the lowest costs attainable by a firm fall as the scale of the industry expands.

favorable balance of payments   A credit balance on some part of the international payments accounts (receipts exceed payments); often refers to a favorable balance on current plus capital account (that is, everything except the official settlements account).

fiat money   Paper money or coinage that is neither backed by nor convertible into anything else but is decreed by the government to be accepted as legal tender and is generally accepted in exchange for goods and services and for the discharge of debts.

final demand   Demand for the economy's final output.

final goods   Goods that are not used as inputs by other firms, but are produced to be sold for consumption, investment, government, or exports during the period under consideration.

financial capital   See *money capital*.

fine tuning   The attempt to maintain national income at or near its full-employment level by means of frequent changes in fiscal or monetary policy.

firm   The unit that employs factors of production and produces goods and services to be sold to households, other firms, or the government.

fiscal drag   The tendency for tax revenues to rise faster than government expenditure as full-employment income rises due to economic growth, thus causing a falling, cyclically adjusted budget deficit.

fiscal policy   The use of the government's tax and spending policies in an effort to influence the behavior of such macro variables as the GNP and total employment.

fixed cost   A cost that does not change with output. Also called *overhead cost, unavoidable cost.*

fixed exchange rate   An exchange rate that is maintained within a small range around its publicly stated par value by the intervention of a country's central bank in foreign market operations. Also called a *pegged rate.*

fixed factor   An input that cannot be increased beyond a given amount in the short run.

fixed investment   Investment in plant and equipment.

flexible exchange rate   An exchange rate that is left free to be determined by the forces of demand and supply on the free market, with no intervention by the monetary authorities. Also called *floating exchange rate.*

floating exchange rate   See *flexible exchange rate.*

foreign exchange   Actual foreign currencies or various claims on them, such as bank balances or promises to pay, that are traded for each other on the foreign exchange market.

foreign exchange market   The market where different national monies, or claims to these monies, are traded against each other.

45° line   In macroeconomics, the line that graphs the equilibrium condition that aggregate desired expenditure should equal national income $(AE = Y)$.

fractional reserve system   A banking system in which commercial banks are required to keep only a fraction of their deposits in cash or on deposit with the central bank.

free good   A commodity for which the quantity supplied exceeds the quantity demanded at a price of zero; therefore, a good that does not command a positive price in a market economy.

free-market economy   An economy in which the decisions of individual households and firms (as distinct from the government) exert the major influence over the allocation of resources.

free reserves   See *net unborrowed reserves.*

free trade   The absence of any form of government intervention in international trade, which implies that imports and exports must not be subject to special taxes or restrictions levied merely because of their status as "imports" or "exports."

free-trade association   An agreement among two or more countries to abolish tariffs on all, or most, of the trade among themselves, while each remains free to set its own tariffs against other countries.

frictional unemployment   Unemployment caused by the time that is taken for labor to move from one job to another.

fringe benefits   Compensation other than wages for the benefit of labor, such as company contributions to pension and welfare funds, sick leave, and paid holidays.

full-cost pricing   Setting price equal to average total cost at normal-capacity output plus a fixed markup.

full employment   See *high employment.*

function   Loosely, an expression of a relationship between two or more variables. Precisely, Y is a function of the variables $X_1, \ldots, X_n$ if, for every set of values of the variables $X_1, \ldots, X_n$, there is associated a unique value of the variable Y.

functional distribution of income   The distribution of total national income among the major factors of production.

G   See *government expenditure.*

gains from trade   The increased output due to the specialization according to comparative advantage that is made possible by trade.

Giffen good   An inferior good for which the negative income effect outweighs the substitution effect, so that the demand curve is positively sloped.

GNP deflator   See *implicit GNP deflator.*

GNP gap   See *output gap.*

gold exchange standard   A monetary system in which U.S. currency is directly convertible into gold and other countries' currencies are indirectly convertible by being convertible into the gold-backed U.S. dollar at a fixed rate.

goods   Tangible commodities, such as cars or shoes.

government   All public officials, agencies, and other organizations belonging to or under the control of state, local, or federal governments.

government expenditure   Includes all government expenditure on currently produced goods and services and does not include government transfer payments. Represented by the symbol G as one of the four components of aggregate expenditure.

Gresham's law   The theory that "bad," or debased, money drives "good," or undebased, money out of circulation, because people keep the good money for other purposes and use the bad money for transactions.

gross domestic product (GDP)   National income as measured by the output approach; equal to the sum of all values added in the economy or, what is the same thing, the values of all final goods produced in the economy.

gross investment   The total value of all investment goods produced in the economy during a stated period of time.

gross national product (GNP)   The value of total output produced, and incomes earned, by domestically based producers and factors of production. Measured from the expenditure side of the national accounts, it is the sum of consumption, investment, government expenditure on final output, and net exports; measured from the income side of the national accounts, it is the sum of factor incomes, plus depreciation, plus indirect taxes net of subsidies. It can be valued at *current prices* to get *nominal GNP*, which is also called *GNP at current, or market, prices,* or at base-year prices to get *real GNP*, which is also called *GNP at constant prices.*

gross national product at market prices See *gross national product.*

high employment Employment that is sufficient to produce the economy's potential output; at high employment, all remaining unemployment is frictional and structural.

high-employment GNP (Y^*) See *potential GNP.*

high-employment national income (Y^*) See *potential GNP.*

homogeneous product In the eyes of purchasers, every unit of the product is identical to every other unit.

horizontal merger See *merger.*

household All of the people who live under one roof and who make, or are subject to others making for them, joint financial decisions.

human capital The capitalized value of productive investments in persons; usually refers to value derived from expenditures on education, training, and health improvements.

hypothesis of diminishing returns See *law of diminishing returns.*

I See *investment expenditure.*

implicit GNP deflator An index number derived by dividing GNP, measured in current dollars, by GNP, measured in constant dollars, and multiplying by 100. In effect, a price index, with current-year quantity weights, measuring the average change in price of all the items in the GNP. Also called *gross national product deflator.*

import quota A limit set by the government on the quantity of a foreign commodity that may be shipped into that country in a given time period.

import substitution industry Domestic production for sale in the home market of goods that previously were imported; usually involves some form of protection or subsidy.

imputed costs The costs of using factors of production already owned by the firm, measured by the earnings that they could have received in their best alternative use.

income-consumption line (1) A curve showing the relationship for a commodity between quantity demanded and income, *ceteris paribus*; (2) a curve drawn on an indifference curve diagram and connecting the points of tangency between a set of indifference curves and a set of parallel budget lines, showing how the consumption bundle changes as income changes, with relative prices being held constant.

income effect The effect on quantity demanded of a change in real income.

income elasticity of demand A measure of the responsiveness of quantity demanded to a change in income, defined by the formula

$$\eta_Y = \frac{\text{percentage change in quantity demanded}}{\text{percentage change in income}}$$

income statement A financial report showing the revenues and costs that arise from the firm's use of inputs to produce outputs over a specified period of time.

incomes policy Any direct intervention by the government to influence wage and price formation.

increasing returns A situation in which output increases more than in proportion to inputs as the scale of a firm's production increases. A firm in this situation, with fixed factor prices, is a *decreasing cost* firm.

indexation The automatic change in any money payment in proportion to the change in the price level.

index number An average that measures changes over time of such variables as the price level and industrial production; conventionally expressed as a percentage relative to a base period, which is assigned the value 100.

indifference curve A curve showing all combinations of two commodities that give the household an equal amount of satisfaction and between which the household is thus indifferent.

indifference map A set of indifference curves based on a given set of household preferences.

induced expenditure In macroeconomics, elements of expenditure that are explained by variables within the theory. In the aggregate desired expenditure function, it is any component of expenditure that is related to national income. Also called *endogenous expenditure.*

industry A group of firms that produces a well-defined product or group of related products.

inelastic demand The situation in which, for a given percentage change in price, there is a smaller percentage change in quantity demanded; elasticity less than unity.

infant industry argument for tariffs The argument that new domestic industries with potential for economies of scale, or learning by doing, need to be protected from competition from established, low-cost foreign producers, so that they can grow large enough to achieve costs as low as those of foreign producers.

inferior good A good for which income elasticity is negative.

inflation A rise in the average level of all prices. Sometimes restricted to prolonged or sustained rises.

inflationary gap A negative output gap, that is, a situation in which actual national income exceeds potential income.

infrastructure The basic installations and facilities (especially transportation and communications systems) on which the commerce of a community depends.

injections Income earned by domestic firms that does not arise out of the spending of domestic households and income earned by domestic households that does not arise out of the spending of domestic firms.

innovation The introduction of an invention into methods of production.

inputs   Intermediate products and factor services that are used in the process of production.

interest   The payment for the use of borrowed money.

interest rate   The price paid per dollar borrowed per period of time, expressed either as a proportion (e.g., 0.06) or as a percentage (e.g., 6 percent). Also called the *nominal interest rate* to distinguish it from the *real interest rate*.

interest rate control   The use of the interest rate as the instrument by which the central bank attempts to influence its target variables. See *base control.*

intermediate products   All outputs that are used as inputs by other producers in a further stage of production.

intermediate targets   Variables that the government cannot control directly and does not seek to control ultimately, yet that have an important influence on policy variables.

internal balance   State of the economy when real national income is at its target level.

internal economies of scale   Scale economies that result from the firm's own actions and hence are available to it by raising its own output.

internal value of the dollar   The purchasing power of the dollar measured in terms of domestic goods and services; changes in the internal value of the dollar are measured by changes in an index of U.S. prices.

internalization   A process that results in a producer's taking account of a previously external effect.

invention   The discovery of something new, such as a new production technique or a new product.

inventories   Stocks of raw materials, goods in process, and finished goods, held by firms to mitigate the effect of short-term fluctuations in production or sales.

investment expenditure   Expenditure on the production of goods not for present consumption.

investment goods   Goods that are produced not for present consumption, i.e., capital goods, inventories, and residential housing.

invisible account   A form of balance-of-payments account that records payments and receipts arising out of trade in services and payments for the use of capital. Also called *service account.*

invisibles   All those items of foreign trade that are intangible; services as opposed to goods.

involuntary unemployment   Unemployment due to the inability of qualified persons who are seeking work to find jobs at the going wage rate.

isoquant   A curve showing all technologically efficient factor combinations for producing a specified amount of output.

isoquant map   A series of isoquants from the same production function, each isoquant relating to a specific level of output.

Keynesians   A label attached to economists who hold the view, derived from the work of John Maynard Keynes, that active use of monetary and fiscal policy can be effective in stabilizing the economy. Often the term encompasses economists who advocate active policy intervention in general.

Keynesian short-run aggregate supply curve   A horizontal aggregate supply curve, indicating that, when national income is below potential, changes in national income can occur with little or no accompanying changes in prices.

kinked demand curve   A demand curve facing an oligopolistic firm that assumes its competitors will match its price reductions but will not respond to its price increases. At the firm's current price-output combination, its demand curve is kinked and its marginal revenue curve is discontinuous.

k percent rule   The proposition that the money supply should be increased at a constant percentage rate year in and year out, irrespective of cyclical changes in national income.

labor   A factor of production consisting of all physical and mental efforts provided by people.

labor force   The total number of persons employed in both civilian and military jobs, plus the number of persons who are unemployed.

labor union   See *union.*

Laffer curve   A graph relating the revenue yield of a tax system to the marginal or average tax rate imposed.

laissez faire   Literally, "let do"; a policy advocating the minimization of government intervention in a market economy.

land   A factor of production consisting of all gifts of nature, including raw materials and "land," as understood in ordinary speech.

law of demand   The assertion that market price and quantity demanded in the market vary inversely with one another, that is, that demand curves are negatively sloped.

law of diminishing returns   The hypothesis that, if increasing quantities of a variable factor are applied to a given quantity of fixed factors, the marginal product and average product of the variable factor will eventually decrease. Also called *hypothesis of diminishing returns, law of variable proportions.*

law of variable proportions   See *law of diminishing returns.*

legal tender   Anything that by law must be accepted for the purchase of goods and services or in discharge of a debt.

less-developed countries (LDCs)   The lower-income countries of the world, most of which are in Asia, Africa, and South and Central America. Also called *underdeveloped countries, developing countries,* the *South.*

leveraged buy out (LBO)   The practice of borrowing the money that is necessary to acquire controlling stock in a firm.

life-cycle theory   A hypothesis that relates the household's actual consumption to its expected lifetime income rather than (as in early Keynesian theory) to its current income.

lifetime income   See *permanent income.*

limited liability   The limitation of the financial responsibility of an owner (shareholder) of a corporation to the amount of money that the shareholder has actually invested in the firm by purchasing its shares.

limited partnership A form of business organization in which the firm has two classes of owners: general partners, who take part in managing the firm and who are personally liable for all of the firm's actions and debts, and limited partners, who take no part in the management of the firm and who risk only the money that they have invested.

liquidity preference (*LP*) function The function that relates the demand for money to the rate of interest.

logarithmic scale A scale in which equal proportional changes are shown as equal distances (for example, 1 inch may always represent doubling of a variable, whether from 3 to 6 or 50 to 100). Also called *log scale, ratio scale.*

logrolling The political practice in which two or more voters agree to support the other's programs in exchange for support for his or her own.

long run A period of time in which all inputs may be varied, but the basic technology of production cannot be changed.

long-run aggregate supply (*LRAS*) curve A curve showing the relationship between the price level of final output and the total quantity of output supplied when all markets have fully adjusted to the existing price level; a vertical line at $Y = Y^*$.

long-run average cost (*LRAC*) curve The curve relating the least-cost method of producing any output to the level of output when all inputs can be varied.

long-run industry supply (*LRS*) curve A curve showing the relationship between the market price and the quantity supplied by a competitive industry when it is in equilibrium.

long-run Phillips curve (*LRPC*) The relationship between national income and the price level when all goods and factor markets are in long-run equilibrium.

Lorenz curve A graph showing the extent of departure from equality of income distribution.

Lucas aggregate supply curve A curve expressing the hypothesis that national output varies positively with the ratio of the actual to the expected price level.

M Imports; a country's total expenditure on imports.

M1 Currency plus demand deposits plus other checkable deposits.

M2 M1 plus money market mutual balances, money market deposit accounts, savings accounts, and small denomination time deposits.

M3 M2 plus large denomination time deposits (CDs), term repurchase agreements, and money market mutual funds held by institutions.

macroeconomics The study of the determination of economic aggregates, such as total output, total employment, the price level, and the rate of economic growth.

managed float Intervention in the foreign exchange market by a country's central bank to respond to particular circumstances in pursuit of an unofficial exchange rate target, but not to maintain an announced par value. Also called *dirty float.*

marginal cost (*MC*) The increase in total cost resulting from raising the rate of production by one unit. Mathematically, the rate of change of cost with respect to output. Also called *incremental cost.*

marginal efficiency of capital (*MEC*) The marginal rate of return on a nation's capital stock. The rate of return on one additional dollar of net investment, that is, an addition of one dollar's worth of new capital to capital stock.

marginal physical product (*MPP*) See *marginal product.*

marginal product (*MP*) The change in quantity of total output that results from using one unit more of a variable factor. Mathematically, the rate of change of output with respect to the quantity of the variable factor. Also called *incremental product* or *marginal physical product* (*MPP*).

marginal-productivity theory of distribution The theory that factors are paid the value of their marginal products so that the total earnings of each type of factor of production equals the value of the marginal product of that factor multiplied by the number of units of that factor that are employed.

marginal propensity to consume (*MPC*) The change in consumption divided by the change in disposable income that brought it about; mathematically, the rate of change of consumption with respect to disposable income ($MPC = \Delta C/\Delta Y_d$).

marginal propensity not to spend The fraction of any increment to national income that is not spent on domestic production ($1 -$ the marginal propensity to spend; that is, $1 - \Delta AE/\Delta Y$).

marginal propensity to save (*MPS*) The change in total desired saving related to the change in disposable income that brought it about ($\Delta S/\Delta Y_d$).

marginal propensity to spend The fraction of any increment to national income that is spent on domestic production; it is measured by the change in aggregate expenditure divided by the change in income ($\Delta AE/\Delta Y$).

marginal rate of substitution (*MRS*) (1) In consumption, the slope of an indifference curve, showing how much more of one commodity must be provided to compensate for the giving up of one unit of another commodity if the level of satisfaction is to be held constant. (2) In production, the slope of an isoquant, showing how much more of one factor of production must be used to compensate for the use of one less unit of another factor of production if production is to be held constant.

marginal revenue (*MR*) The change in a firm's total revenue resulting from a change in its rate of sales by one unit. Mathematically, the rate of change of revenue with respect to output. Also called *incremental revenue.*

marginal revenue product (*MRP*) The addition of revenue attributable to the last unit of a variable factor ($MRP = MP \times MR$). Mathematically, the rate of change of revenue with respect to quantity of the variable factor.

marginal tax rate The amount of tax that a taxpayer would pay on an additional dollar of income; that is, the fraction of an additional dollar of income that is paid in taxes.

marginal utility The additional satisfaction obtained by a consumer from consuming one unit more of a good; mathematically, the rate of change of utility with respect to consumption.

margin requirement The fraction of the price of a stock that must be paid in cash, while putting up the stock as security against a loan for the balance.

market An area over which buyers and sellers negotiate the exchange of a well-defined commodity or group of related commodities.

market-clearing price Price at which quantity demanded equals quantity supplied, so that there are neither unsatisfied buyers nor unsatisfied sellers, that is, the equilibrium price.

market economy A society in which people specialize in productive activities and meet most of their material wants through exchanges voluntarily agreed upon by the contracting parties.

market failure Failure of the unregulated market system to achieve optimal allocative efficiency or social goals because of externalities, market impediments, or market imperfections.

market for corporate control An interpretation of conglomerate mergers, leveraged buy outs, and hostile takeovers as mechanisms that place the firm in the hands of those who are able to generate the most value product.

market rate of interest The actual interest rate in effect at a given moment.

market sector That portion of an economy in which commodities are bought and sold and in which producers must cover their costs from sales revenue.

market structure All those features of a market that affect the behavior and performance of firms in that market, such as the number and size of sellers, the extent of knowledge about each other's actions, the degree of freedom of entry, and the degree of product differentiation.

medium of exchange Anything that is generally acceptable in return for goods and services sold.

merchandise account See *trade account*.

merger The purchase of either the physical assets or the controlling share of ownership of one firm by another. In a *horizontal* merger both firms are in the same line of business; in a *vertical* merger one firm is a supplier of the other; if the two are in unrelated industries, it is a *conglomerate* merger.

merit goods Goods such as housing and medical care that are deemed to be especially important.

microeconomic policy Activities of governments designed to alter resource allocation and/or income distribution.

microeconomics The study of the allocation of resources and the distribution of income as they are affected by the workings of the price system and by government policies.

minimum efficient scale (*MES*) The smallest output at which long-run average cost reaches its minimum because all available economies of scale in production and/or distribution have been realized. Also called *minimum optimal scale*.

minimum wages Legally specified minimum rate of pay for labor in covered occupations.

mixed economy An economy in which some decisions about the allocation of resources are made by firms and households and some by the government.

monetarists A label attached to economists who stress monetary causes of cyclical fluctuations and inflations and who believe that an active stabilization policy is not normally required. Often the term encompasses conservative economists who oppose active policy intervention in general.

monetary base The sum of currency in circulation plus reserves of the commercial banks, equal to the monetary liabilities of the central bank.

monetary equilibrium A situation in which the demand for money equals the supply of money.

monetary policy An attempt to influence the economy by operating on such monetary variables as the quantity of money and the rate of interest.

money Anything that acts as a medium of exchange, a store of value, and a unit of account.

money capital Money that a firm raises to carry on its business, including both equity capital and debt. Also called *financial capital*.

money income Income measured in monetary units per period of time.

money market mutual fund (MMMF) Liquid financial instruments that earn high yields, are checkable, but are subject to transaction restrictions.

money rate of interest See *interest rate*.

money substitute Something that serves as a temporary medium of exchange but is not a store of value.

money supply The total quantity of money in an economy at a point in time. Also called *the supply of money*.

monopolist A firm that is the only seller in some market.

monopolistic competition (1) A market structure of an industry in which there are many firms and freedom of entry and exit but in which each firm has a product somewhat differentiated from the others, giving it some control over its price; (2) more recently, any industry in which more than one firm sells differentiated products.

monopoly A market containing a single firm.

monopsony A market situation in which there is a single buyer.

moral hazard A situation in which an individual or a firm takes advantage of special knowledge while engaging in socially uneconomic behavior.

multilateral balance of payments The balance of payments between one country and the rest of the world taken as a whole.

multiplier The ratio of the change in national income to the change in autonomous expenditure that brought it about.

NAIRU (Short for *nonaccelerating inflationary rate of unemployment*.) The rate of unemployment associated with potential national income and at which a steady, nonaccelerating or nondecelerating inflation can be sustained indefinitely. Also called *the natural rate of unemployment*.

Nash equilibrium In the case of firms, an equilibrium that results when each firm in an industry is currently doing the best that it can, given the current behavior of the other firms in the industry.

national debt The current volume of outstanding federal government debt.

national income In general, the value of total output and the value of the income that is generated by the production of that output.

natural monopoly An industry characterized by economies of scale sufficiently large that one firm can most efficiently supply the entire market demand.

natural rate of unemployment See *NAIRU*.

natural scale A scale in which equal absolute amounts are represented by equal distances.

near money Liquid assets that are easily convertible into money without risk of significant loss of value and can be used as short-term stores of purchasing power, but are not themselves media of exchange.

negative income tax (NIT) A tax system in which households with incomes below taxable levels receive payments from the government that are based on a percentage of the amount by which their income is below the minimum taxable level.

negotiable order of withdrawal (NOW) A checklike device for transferring funds from one person's time deposit to another person.

net exports The value of total exports minus the value of total imports. Represented by the expression $(X - M)$ as a component of aggregate expenditure, where X is total exports and M is total imports.

net investment Gross investment minus replacement investment.

net national income (NNI) The sum of the four components of factor incomes (wages, rent, interest, and profits).

net national product (NNP) at market prices Sum of wages, rent, interest, profits, and indirect taxes minus subsidies.

net unborrowed reserves The total reserves of the commercial banking system minus required reserves minus the reserves that have been borrowed from the central bank; that is, excess reserves minus borrowed reserves. Also called *free reserves*.

neutrality of money The doctrine that the money supply affects only the absolute level of prices and has no effect on relative prices and hence no effect on the allocation of resources or the distribution of income.

newly industrialized countries (NICs) Formerly underdeveloped countries that have become major industrial exporters since World War II.

nominal national income Total national income measured in dollars; the money value of national income.

Also called *money national income* or *current-dollar national income*.

nominal rate of interest See *interest rate*.

nominal rate of tariff The tax charged on any imported commodity.

noncooperative equilibrium Any equilibrium reached when firms calculate their own best policies without cooperation—tacit or explicit—with other firms.

nonmarket sector That portion of an economy in which commodities are given away and producers must cover their costs from some source other than sales revenue.

nonrenewable resource Any productive resource that is available as a fixed stock which cannot be replaced once it is used.

nontariff barriers Restrictions, other than tariffs, designed to reduce the flow of imported goods.

normal-capacity output The level of output that a firm hopes to maintain on average over the business cycle; typically, somewhat less than full-capacity output.

normal good A good for which income elasticity is positive.

normal profits The opportunity cost of capital and risk taking just necessary to keep the owners in the industry. They are usually included in what economists, but not businesspersons, call *total costs*.

normative statement A statement or theory about what ought to be, as opposed to what is, was, or will be, true.

NOW See *negotiable order of withdrawal*.

oligopoly An industry that contains two or more firms, at least one of which produces a significant portion of the industry's total output.

open market operations The purchase and sale on the open market by the central bank of securities (usually short-term government securities).

opportunity cost The cost of using resources for a certain purpose, measured by the benefit given up by not using them in their best alternative use.

organization theory A set of hypotheses that predicts that the substance of the decisions of a firm is affected by its size and form of organization.

output gap Potential national income minus actual national income. Also called *the GNP gap*.

outputs The goods and services that result from the process of production.

Pareto-efficiency See *Pareto-optimality*.

Pareto-optimality A situation in which it is impossible by reallocation of production or consumption activities to make all consumers better off without simultaneously making others worse off (or, as it is sometimes put, to make at least one person better off while making no one worse off). Also called *Pareto-efficiency*.

partnership A form of business organization in which the firm has two or more joint owners, each of whom takes part in the management of the firm and is personally responsible for all of the firm's actions and debts.

paternalism Intervention in the free choices of individuals by others (including governments) to protect them against their own ignorance or folly.

pegged rate   See *fixed exchange rate*.

per capita GNP   GNP divided by total population.

perfect competition   A market structure in which all firms in an industry are price takers and in which there is freedom of entry into and exit from the industry.

perfectly contestable market   See *contestable market*.

permanent income   The maximum amount that a household can consume per year into the indefinite future without reducing its wealth. (A number of similar, but not identical, definitions are in common use.) Also called *lifetime income*.

permanent-income theory   A hypothesis that relates actual consumption to permanent income rather than (as in the original Keynesian theory) to current income.

personal income   Income earned by, or paid to, individuals before allowance for personal income taxes on that income.

petrodollars   Money earned by the oil-exporting countries and held by them in short-term, liquid investments.

Phillips curve   Originally, a relationship between the percentage of the labor force unemployed and the rate of change of money wages. Now often drawn as a relationship between the percentage of the labor force employed and the rate of price inflation or between actual national income and the rate of price inflation.

point elasticity   A measure of the responsiveness of quantity to price at a particular point on the demand curve. The formula for point elasticity of demand is

$$\eta = \frac{\Delta q}{\Delta p} \times \frac{p}{q}$$

With negatively sloped demand curves elasticity is a negative number. Sometimes the above expression is multiplied by -1 to make elasticity positive.

point of diminishing average productivity   The level of output at which average product reaches a maximum.

point of diminishing marginal productivity   The level of output at which marginal product reaches a maximum.

policy instruments   The variables that the government can control directly to achieve its policy objectives.

policy variables   The variables that the government seeks to control, such as real national income and the price level.

political business cycle   Cyclical swings in the economy generated by fiscal and monetary policy for the purpose of winning elections.

portfolio investment   In balance-of-payments accounting, foreign investment in bonds or a minority holding of shares that does not involve legal control. See also *direct investment*.

positive statement   A statement or theory about what is, was, or will be true, as opposed to what ought to be.

potential GNP (Y*)   The real gross national product that the economy could produce if its productive resources were fully employed at their normal levels of utilization. Also called *potential national income, national income, high-employment GNP, high-employment national income*.

potential income   See *potential GNP*.

poverty gap   The number of dollars per year required to raise everyone's income that is below the poverty level to that level.

poverty level   The official government estimate of the annual family income that is required to maintain a minimum adequate standard of living.

precautionary balances   Money balances held for protection against the uncertainty of the timing of cash flows.

present value (PV)   The value now of one or more payments to be received in the future; often referred to as the *discounted present value* of future payments.

price ceiling   A government-imposed maximum permissible price at which a commodity may be sold.

price-consumption line   A line connecting the points of tangency between a set of indifference curves and a set of budget lines where one absolute price is fixed and the other varies, money income being held constant.

price discrimination   The sale by one firm of different units of a commodity at two or more different prices for reasons not associated with differences in cost.

price elasticity of demand   See *elasticity of demand*.

price floor   A government-imposed minimum permissible price at which a commodity may be sold.

price index   A number that shows the average of some group of prices; expressed as a percentage of the average ruling in some base period; price indexes can be used to measure the price level at a given time relative to a base period.

price level   The average level of all prices in the economy, usually expressed as an index number.

price taker   A firm that can alter its rate of production and sales without significantly affecting the market price of its product.

price theory   The theory of how prices are determined; competitive price theory concerns the determination of prices in competitive markets by the interaction of demand and supply.

principal-agent problem   The problem of resource allocation that arises because contracts that will induce agents to act in their principals' best interests are generally either impossible to write or too costly to monitor.

principle of substitution   Methods of production will change if relative prices of inputs change, with relatively more of the cheaper input and relatively less of the more expensive input being used.

private cost   The value of the best alternative use of resources used in production as valued by the producer.

private sector   That portion of an economy in which the organizations that produce goods and services are owned and operated by private units, such as households and firms.

producers' durables   See *durable good*.

producers' surplus   The difference between the total amount that producers receive for all units sold of a commodity and the total variable cost of producing the commodity.

product differentiation   The existence of similar but not identical products sold by a single industry, such as the breakfast food and the automobile industries.

production   The act of making commodities—either goods or services.

production function   A functional relation showing the maximum output that can be produced by each and every combination of inputs.

production possibility boundary   A curve that shows which alternative combinations of commodities can just be attained if all available resources are used; it is thus the boundary between attainable and unattainable output combinations.

productive efficiency   Production of any output at the lowest attainable cost for that level of output.

productivity   Output produced per unit of some input; frequently used to refer to *labor productivity*, measured by total output divided by the amount of labor used.

product markets   Markets in which outputs of goods and services are sold. Also called *goods markets*.

profit   (1) In ordinary usage, the difference between the value of outputs and the value of inputs. (2) In microeconomics, the difference between revenues received from the sale of goods and the value of inputs, which includes the opportunity cost of capital, so that profits are *economic profits*. (3) In macroeconomics, profits exclude interest on borrowed capital but do not exclude the return on owner's capital.

progressive tax   A tax that takes a larger percentage of income the higher the level of income.

proportional tax   A tax that takes a constant percentage of income at all levels of income and is thus neither progressive nor regressive.

protectionism   Any government policy that interferes with free trade in order to give some protection to domestic industries against foreign competition.

public goods   See *collective consumption goods*.

public sector   That portion of an economy in which production is owned and operated by the government or bodies appointed by it, such as nationalized industries.

public utility regulation   Regulation of such things as prices and profit rates in industries that have been deemed to be natural monopolies.

purchase of goods and services   In the national income accounts, the amount of money that governments spend on real resources that the governments use.

purchasing power of money   The amount of goods and services that can be purchased with a unit of money. The purchasing power of money varies inversely with the price level. Also called *value of money*.

purchasing power parity (PPP) exchange rate   The exchange rate between two currencies that adjusts for relative inflation rates.

pure rate of interest   The rate of interest that would rule in equilibrium in a riskless economy where all lending and borrowing is for investment in productive capital.

pure return on capital   The amount that capital can earn in a riskless investment; hence, the transfer earnings of capital in a riskless investment.

quantity demanded   The amount of a commodity that households wish to purchase in some time period. An increase (decrease) in quantity demanded refers to a movement down (up) the demand curve in response to a fall (rise) in price.

quantity exchanged   The identical amount of a commodity that households actually purchase and producers actually sell in some time period.

quantity supplied   The amount of a commodity that producers wish to sell in some time period. An increase (decrease) in quantity supplied refers to a movement up (down) the supply curve in response to a rise (fall) in price.

random sample   A sample chosen from a group or population in such a way that every member of the group has an equal chance of being selected.

rate base   The total allowable investment to which the rate of return allowed by a regulatory commission is applied.

rate of inflation   The percentage rate of increase in some price index from one period to another.

rate of return   The ratio of net profits earned by a firm to total invested capital.

rational expectations   The theory that people understand how the economy works and learn quickly from their mistakes, so that, while random errors may be made, systematic and persistent errors are not made.

ratio scale   See *logarithmic scale*.

real capital   The physical assets that a firm uses to conduct its business, composed of plant, equipment, and inventories. Also called *physical capital*.

real GNP   See *constant-dollar GNP*.

real income   Income expressed in terms of the purchasing power of money income, that is, the quantity of goods and services that can be purchased with the money income; it can be calculated as money income deflated by a price index.

real national income   National income measured in constant dollars, so that it changes only when quantities change.

real product wage   The proportion of each sales dollar accounted for by labor costs (including the pretax nominal wage rate, benefits, and payroll taxes).

real rate of interest   The money rate of interest corrected for the change in the purchasing power of money by subtracting the inflation rate.

real-wage unemployment   Unemployment caused by too high a real product wage. Also called *classical unemployment*.

recession   In general, a downturn in the level of economic activity. Defined by the Department of Commerce as a fall in real GNP for two successive quarters.

recessionary gap   A positive output gap; that is, a situation in which actual national income is less than potential income. Also called a *deflationary gap*.

regression analysis A quantitative measure of the systematic relationship between two or more variables. *Simple regression* concerns the relation between Y and a single independent variable, X_1; *multiple regression* concerns the relation between Y and more than one independent variable, $X_1, \ldots, X_n$. Also called *correlation analysis*.

regression equation An equation describing the statistically determined best fit between variables, or best estimate of the *average* relationship between variables in regression analysis.

regressive tax A tax that takes a lower percentage of income the higher the level of income.

relative price The ratio of the money price of one commodity to the money price of another commodity; that is, a ratio of two absolute prices.

renewable resources Productive resources that can be replaced as they are used up, as with physical capital; it is distinguished from nonrenewable resources, which are available in a fixed stock that can be depleted but not replaced.

rental price of capital The price paid to rent the services of a unit of capital for a period of time.

replacement investment The amount of investment that is needed to maintain the existing capital stock intact.

required reserves The reserves that a bank must, by law, keep either in currency or in deposits with the central bank.

reserve currencies Currencies (such as the U.S. dollar) that are commonly held by foreign central banks as international reserves.

reserve ratio The fraction of its deposits that a commercial bank holds as reserves in the form of cash or deposits with a central bank.

resource allocation The allocation of an economy's scarce resources of land, labor, and capital among alternative uses.

retained earnings See *undistributed profits*.

return to capital The total amount available for payments to owners of capital; the sum of pure returns to capital, risk premiums, and economic profits.

revenue sharing The return of some of the revenue collected by the federal government to a state or local government for unrestricted expenditure; a noncategorical or general grant-in-aid.

rising-cost industry An industry in which the minimum cost attainable by a firm rises as the scale of the industry expands.

risk averse individuals Individuals who do not like risk and will engage in a risky activity only if the expected return is high enough to compensate them for the risk they will have to bear.

risk lovers Individuals who like risk and will engage in some risky activities that do not even have a positive expected return in order to get some of the pleasure that the risk entails.

risk neutral individuals Individuals who are indifferent about the amount of risk a given activity involves but will engage in the activity as long as the expected return is positive.

risk premium The return on capital necessary to compensate owners of capital for the risk of loss of their capital.

sample A small number of items, chosen from a larger group or population, that is intended to be representative of the larger entity.

satisficing A hypothesized objective of firms to achieve levels of performance deemed satisfactory rather than to *maximize* some objective.

saving All disposable income that is not spent on consumption.

scarce good A commodity for which the quantity demanded exceeds the quantity supplied at a price of zero; therefore, a good that commands a positive price in a market economy.

scatter diagram A graph of statistical observations of paired values of two variables, one measured on the horizontal and the other on the vertical axis. Each point on the coordinate grid represents the values of the variables for a particular unit of observation.

search unemployment Unemployment caused by people continuing to search for a good job rather than accepting the first job that they come across after they become unemployed.

sectors Parts of an economy.

securities market See *stock market*.

selective credit controls Controls on credit imposed through such means as margin requirements, restrictions on installment buying, and minimum down payments on mortgages.

sellers' preferences Allocation of commodities in excess demand by decisions of those who sell them.

service account See *invisible account*.

services Intangible commodities, such as haircuts or medical care.

shareholders See *stockholders*.

short run A period of time in which the quantity of some inputs cannot be increased beyond the fixed amount that is available.

short-run aggregate supply (SRAS) curve A curve showing the relation between the price level of final output and the quantity of output supplied on the assumption that all factor prices are held constant.

short-run equilibrium Generally, equilibrium subject to fixed factors or other things that cannot change over the time period being considered. For a competitive firm, the output at which market price equals marginal cost; for a competitive industry, the price and output at which industry demand equals short-run industry supply and all firms are in short-run equilibrium. Either profits or losses are possible.

short-run Phillips curve (SRPC) A relationship between unemployment and the rate of wage inflation or between national income and the rate of price inflation, drawn for a given state of expectations about the future rate of inflation.

short-run supply curve A curve showing the relationship between quantity supplied and market price, with one or more fixed factors; it is the horizontal sum of marginal cost curves (above the level of average variable costs) of all firms in a perfectly competitive industry.

simple multiplier The ratio of the change in equilibrium national income to the change in autonomous expenditure that brought it about, *calculated for* a constant price level.

single proprietorship A form of business organization in which the firm has one owner, who makes all the decisions and is personally responsible for all of the firm's actions and debts.

size distribution of income The distribution of income among households, without regard to source of income or social class of households.

slope The ratio of the vertical change to the horizontal change between two points on a curve.

social benefit The contribution that an activity makes to the society's welfare.

social cost The value of the best alternative use of resources available to society as valued by society. Also called *social opportunity cost.*

social regulations The regulation of economic behavior to advance social goals when competition and economic regulation will fail to achieve those goals.

special drawing rights (*SDRs*) Financial liabilities of the IMF held in a special fund generated by contributions of member countries. Members can use SDRs to maintain supplies of convertible currencies when these are needed to support foreign exchanges.

specialization of labor An organization of production in which individual workers specialize in the production of particular goods or services (and satisfy their wants by trading) rather than produce everything they consume (and satisfy their wants by being self-sufficient).

specific tariff An import duty of a specific amount per unit of the product.

specific tax See *excise tax.*

speculative balances Money balances held as a hedge against the uncertainty of the prices of other financial assets.

stabilization policy Any policy designed to reduce the economy's cyclical fluctuations and thereby to stabilize national income at, or near, a desired level.

stagflation The coexistence of high rates of unemployment with high, and sometimes rising, rates of inflation.

sterilization Operations undertaken by the central bank to offset the effects of the money supply of balance-of-payments surpluses or deficits.

stockholders The owners of a corporation who have supplied money to the firm by purchasing its shares. Also called *shareholders.*

stock market An organized market where stocks and bonds are bought and sold. Also called *securities market.*

structural unemployment Unemployment due to a mismatch between characteristics required by available jobs and characteristics possessed by the unemployed labor.

substitute Two commodities are substitutes for each other when both satisfy similar needs or desires. The degree of substitutability is measured by the magnitude of the positive cross elasticity between the two.

substitution effect A change in the quantity of a good demanded, which results from a change in its relative price, eliminating the effect on real income of the change in price.

supply The entire relationship between the quantity of some commodity that producers wish to make and sell per period of time and the price of that commodity, other things being equal.

supply curve The graphical representation of the relationship between the quantity of some commodity that producers wish to make and sell per period of time and the price of that commodity, other things being equal.

supply of effort The total number of hours of work that the population is willing to supply. Also called *total supply of labor.*

supply of money See *money supply.*

supply schedule A table showing for selected values the relationship between the quantity of some commodity that producers wish to make and sell per period of time and the price of that commodity, other things being equal.

tacit collusion The adoption, without explicit agreement, of a common policy by sellers in an industry. Also called *conscious parallel action.* See also *collusion.*

takeover bid See *tender offer.*

tariff A tax applied on imports.

tax expenditures Tax concessions, such as exemptions and deductions from taxable income and tax credits, that are designed to induce market responses considered to be desirable. They are called *expenditures* because they have the same effect as having no concessions and then spending money on subsidies and other transfers to the groups getting the concessions.

tax incidence The location of the burden of a tax; that is, the identity of the ultimate bearer of the tax.

tax-related incomes policy (TIP) Tax incentives for labor and management to encourage them to conform to wage and price guidelines.

technical change See *technological change.*

technological change Any change in the available techniques of production. Also called *technical change.*

tender offer An offer to buy directly, for a limited period of time, some or all of the outstanding common stock of a corporation from its stockholders at a specified price per share, in an attempt to gain control of the corporation. Also called *takeover bid.*

term See *term to maturity.*

terms of trade The ratio of the average price of a country's exports to the average price of its imports, both averages usually being measured by index numbers; it is the quantity of imported goods that can be obtained per unit of goods exported.

term to maturity   The period of time from the present to the redemption date of a bond. Also called simply the *term*.

time deposit   An interest-earning bank deposit, legally subject to notice before withdrawal (in practice the notice requirement is not normally enforced) and until recently not transferable by check. Also called *savings deposits*.

time series   A series of observations on the values of a variable at different points in time.

time-series data   A set of measurements or observations made repeatedly at successive periods (or moments) of time. Contrasted with *cross-sectional data*.

total cost (*TC*)   The total cost to the firm of producing any given level of output; it can be divided into total fixed costs and total variable costs.

total fixed cost (*TFC*)   All costs of production that do not vary with level of output. Also called *overhead cost* or *unavoidable cost*.

total product (*TP*)   Total amount produced by a firm during some time period.

total revenue (*TR*)   Total receipts from the sale of a product; price times quantity.

total utility   The total satisfaction resulting from the consumption of a given commodity or group of commodities by a consumer in a period of time.

total variable cost (*TVC*)   Total costs of production that vary directly with level of output. Also called *direct cost* or *avoidable cost*.

tradeable emission permits   Government-granted rights to emit specific amounts of specified pollutants that private firms may buy and sell among themselves.

trade account   A section of the balance-of-payments accounts that records payments and receipts arising from the import and export of tangible goods. Also called the *visible account* and the *merchandise account*.

trade remedy laws   See *fair trade laws*.

transactions balances   Money balances held to finance payments because payments and receipts are not perfectly synchronized.

transactions costs   Costs incurred in effecting market transactions (such as negotiation costs, billing costs, and bad debts).

transfer payment   A payment to a private person or institution that does not arise out of current productive activity; typically made by governments, as in welfare payments, but also made by businesses and private individuals in the form of charitable contributions.

transmission mechanism   The channels by which a change in the demand or supply of money leads to a shift of the aggregate demand curve.

treasury bill   The characteristic form of short-term government debt. A promise to pay a certain sum of money at a specified time in the future (usually 90 days to 1 year from date of issue). Although treasury bills carry no fixed interest payments, holders earn an interest return because they purchase them at a lower price than their redemption value. Also called *treasury note*.

two-part tariff   A method of charging for a good or a service, usually a utility such as electricity, in which the consumer pays a flat access fee and a specified amount per unit purchased.

undistributed profits   Earnings of a firm that are not distributed to shareholders as dividends but are retained by the firm. Also called *retained earnings*.

unemployment (*U*)   The number of persons 16 years of age and older who are not employed and are actively searching for a job.

unemployment rate   Unemployment expressed as a percentage of the labor force.

unfavorable balance of payments   A debit balance on some part of the international payments accounts (payments exceed receipts); often refers to the balance on current plus capital account (that is, everything except the official settlements account).

union   An association of workers authorized to represent them in bargaining with employers. Also called *trade union, labor union*.

unit costs   Costs per unit of output, equal to total variable cost divided by total output. Also called *average variable cost*.

utility   The satisfaction that a consumer receives from consuming a commodity.

value added   The value of a firm's output minus the value of the inputs that it purchases from other firms.

value of money   See *purchasing power of money*.

variable   A magnitude (such as the price of a commodity) that can take on a specific value but whose value will vary with time and place.

variable cost   A cost that varies directly with changes in output. Also called *direct cost, avoidable cost*.

variable factor   An input that can be varied by any desired amount in the short run.

velocity of circulation   National income divided by quantity of money.

vertical merger   See *merger*.

very long run   A period of time that is long enough for the technological possibilities available to a firm to change.

visible account   See *trade account*.

visibles   All those items of foreign trade that are tangible; goods as opposed to services.

voluntary export restriction (VER)   An agreement by an exporting country to limit the amount of a good exported to another country.

wage and price controls   Direct government intervention into wage and price formation with legal power to enforce the government's decisions on wages and prices.

wage-cost push inflation   An increase in the price level caused by increases in labor costs that are not themselves associated with excess aggregate demand for labor.

wealth   The sum of all the valuable assets owned minus liabilities.

windfall profit   A change in profits that arises out of an unanticipated change in market conditions, such as a sudden increase in demand. Negative windfall profits are sometimes called *windfall losses*.

withdrawals Income earned by households and not passed on to firms in return for goods and services purchased, and income earned by firms and not passed on to households in return for factor services purchased.

X Exports; the value of all domestic production sold abroad.

X-inefficiency The use of resources at a lower level of productivity than is possible, even if they are allocated efficiently, so that the economy is at a point inside its production possibility boundary.

X − M See *net exports*.

INDEX